SPURGEON
PRINCE OF PREACHERS

To Gary,

With thanks for your friendship and encouragement. What a joy to work with you in the needful ministry of long-term care! May you find much food for thought, encouragement + challenge as you read of God's unique servant, Charles Haddon Spurgeon.

In Christian love & deep respect,

Dick, Hess

12 - 93

Proverbs 27:17

C. H. Spurgeon in a characteristic pose.
—*courtesy of Dr. Craig Skinner*

SPURGEON
PRINCE OF PREACHERS

Lewis A. Drummond

Foreword by
Carl F. H. Henry

KREGEL PUBLICATIONS
Grand Rapids, MI 49501

Spurgeon: Prince of Preachers © 1992 by Kregel
Publications, a division of Kregel, Inc., P.O. Box 2607, Grand
Rapids, MI 49501. All rights reserved. All photographs,
unless otherwise noted, are courtesy of the author.

Cover Photo: Pilgrim Publications
Cover & Book Design: Alan G. Hartman

Library of Congress Cataloging-in-Publication Data

Drummond, Lewis A.
Spurgeon: prince of preachers / Lewis A. Drummond.
  p. cm.
Includes biographical references and index.
1. Spurgeon, C. H. (Charles Haddon), 1834-1892.
2. Baptists—England—Clergy—Biography. I. Title.
BX6495.S7D78   1992   286'.1'092—dc20   92-15242
[B]   CIP

ISBN 0-8254-2473-9 (paperback)
ISBN 0-8254-2472-0 (deluxe hardcover)

2 3 4 5 Printing/Year 96 95 94 93

Printed in the United States of America

This Biography Is Dedicated to:

BETTY L. DRUMMOND

Faithful, loving, helpful wife, friend, and co-laborer in the work. She first inspired me to write this biography of Charles Haddon Spurgeon after reading his fascinating life story. To her I am eternally grateful for all she has meant to me.

Blessed be the day that I began
A pilgrim for to be;
And blessed also be that man
That thereto moved me.

'Tis true, 'twas long ere I began
To seek to live forever.
But now I run fast as I can;
'Tis better late than never.

Our tears to joy, our fears to faith
Are turned, as we see.
Thus our beginning (as some saith),
Shows what our end will be.

—John Bunyan

Contents

8   *Contents*

Illustrations

Foreword

Charles Haddon Spurgeon (1834-1892) is one of evangelical Christianity's immortals. In this distinctive biography, appearing on the centennial of Spurgeon's death, Lewis Drummond accomplishes a remarkable literary feat. On one hand, he gives us what one might at first not expect from a 1,300 page manuscript, a highly readable and spiritually rewarding account of one of the great Christian pulpiteers of all time. On the other hand, he sets Spurgeon's life story in the context of Bunyan's *Pilgrim's Progress* in an intriguing way.

One may appropriately add a word about the propriety of a modern biography of Spurgeon from Dr. Drummond's pen. Dr. Drummond, now president of Southeastern Baptist Theological Seminary, Wake Forest, North Carolina and formerly Billy Graham Professor of Evangelism at Southern Baptist Theological Seminary, Louisville, Kentucky, served in England, and taught for five years in Spurgeon's Theological College, London, a citadel of Baptist scholarship where England's indebtedness to Spurgeon remains a vivid memory.

Spurgeon had in fact begun the College in 1856 as the "Pastors' College" to train men "evidently called to preach the Gospel." Despite his own rural upbringing and lack of formal college training, Spurgeon became by age 22 one of England's most popular preachers. An avid reader, he had a personal library of 30,000 volumes. Some 3,500 of his sermons have been published.

To be sure, preaching was only one of the multiple ministries that Spurgeon fostered. But his fame as a preacher led in 1860 to the building of the Metropolitan Tabernacle to accommodate the crowds that turned out to hear him. The congregation came to number 5,500 and Spurgeon added over 15,000 members during his 37-year London ministry.

Every young minister knows how easy it is to become indebted to Spurgeon, not only for his original insights but for his skill in shaping sermons. I myself, after leaning heavily on Spurgeon in a few early messages, decided that for the sake of originality it was better to read him after my sermons were prepared. Yet almost invariably some comment of Spurgeon's won its way into the content of my messages.

An evangelical Calvinist, Spurgeon treasured the Puritans. He considered Paul, Augustine, Calvin, John Owen, and the Puritans his spiritual forebears. The proliferating modern critical views of the Bible dismayed him, and equally as much any theological evasion of the full deity of Christ. He refused ordination and disliked the title "reverend."

Dr. Drummond tells this intriguing story, and much more, with historical fidelity and literary skill. His book is a highly meritorious addition to Christian biography.

DR. CARL F. H. HENRY
Evangelical
Theologian and
Author

Introduction

A young Victorian lad ran up the stairs and began rummaging through an unused second story room in his grandfather's home. The lone window had been sealed off because of an earlier illogical "window levy" that taxed home owners on the number of windows in their dwellings. The air hung musty, the room seemed forebodingly dark as little Charles stumbled onto some old leatherbound books. He blew off the dust to discover they were Puritan theological works; the grandfather boasted about being what seventeenth century Britishers called a "Reformed" pastor. The boy lived with his grandfather pastor in Stambourne, England, northeast of London. It would seem, however, that a few ancient volumes could hardly excite a little fellow under six. But this lad was different. He could already read well and he loved books, even though he was at first struck only by the beautiful leather bindings. His hands picked up a worn copy of *The Pilgrim's Progress* by the Reformed Puritan, John Bunyan. Charles thought he had found a treasure. He read it—he read it over and over again, poring over its pages more than one hundred times during his life. The characters in the famous allegory became his heroes throughout the years. The pilgrimage of another pilgrim began: Charles Haddon Spurgeon had found a new path to trod.

Less than fifteen years later, the Rev. Charles Haddon Spurgeon received a call to become pastor of a great historic Baptist chapel in London. Only nineteen years of age at the time, he quickly took the city by storm. In a few short years, hundreds of thousands were reading his weekly published Sunday sermon. It seemed the whole evangelical world sought him. He truly became the "Prince of Preachers," as many called him. But despite the fame, Spurgeon always remained something of a singular pilgrim. Bunyan's Pilgrim's "progress" became his.

Considering these facts, this new biography of Charles H. Spurgeon picks up pithy poems, places and personalities of Bunyan's classic allegory and makes them the motif of Spurgeon's life and ministry. Moreover, such an approach avoids superficiality in presenting the Spurgeon saga, as he exemplified in so many ways the progress of "Christian," Bunyan's chief character. Hopefully, the shape and form of Spurgeon's journey will come to life in this framework and we can grasp its contemporary relevance, for all true believers in Jesus Christ find themselves "pilgrims" on the same journey he traveled.

The year 1992 marks the 100th anniversary of Spurgeon's death. Thus, it seems a strategic moment to produce a new, more exhaustive, evaluative biography of the "Prince of Preachers," as he became known. Although Spurgeon's works remain a "best seller" in evangelical circles, and much of his work is constantly reproduced, a biography of this nature appears appropriate at this centenary time. Furthermore, perhaps the principles that guided Spurgeon in his pilgrimage will challenge other pilgrims to walk the paths he trod toward the "Celestial City."

Acknowledgments

I must give gratitude to my able secretaries, Mrs. Lisa Sealy, Mrs. Becky Newsome, Mrs. Debbe Hill, Mrs. Karon Hadley, and Mrs. Lori Settle, for their help and work on the original manuscript. Also, I express appreciation to Spurgeon's Theological College in London and Regent's Park College, University of Oxford, Oxford, England, for the use of their archives, as well as that of the Metropolitan Tabernacle, Spurgeon's London church. Also, I wish to thank William Jewell College of Liberty, Missouri that holds Spurgeon's personal library. I further acknowledge my debt to the fine research of Dr. Craig Skinner. He has studied the life of Spurgeon for more than ten years. I was particularly dependent on his labors for the Epilogue. He also supplied many of the priceless illustrations in the book. Above all, I am grateful for the excellent research done by three of my former graduate students: Dr. Timothy McCoy, Dr. Larry Michael, and Dr. Vasile Talpos. I leaned heavily on McCoy's work on Spurgeon's conversion and theology. Michael's research into the Down Grade Controversy and the Baptismal Regeneration Controversy was the basis for my presentations. I used Talpos' thesis for the background of Victorian England—as well as similar research by McCoy and Michael. Then, invaluable were the unpublished theses of Dr. Jerry Sutton on the Down Grade Controversy and Dr. Ronald Meredith on Spurgeon's social ministry. Patricia Stallings Kruppa has produced an excellent Ph.D. thesis (and Biography) on Spurgeon. I am grateful for her work. Also, a Th.D. thesis by Melton Mason, Jr. proved most helpful in Spurgeon's theology. I appreciate all these scholars for their able work. I give them credit for their most helpful research and the contribution they made to this biography. So many have been helpful in many ways and I express gratitude to all. May God use their labors and this biography to His Glory.

One final note: the reader may find errors in spelling, duplications of punctuation, capitalization, etc., in some of the quoted material in this book. It seemed wise not to correct these errors, but to present the quotations as they are for greater authenticity and originality.

Metropolitan Tabernacle interior.

1

"Behold . . . a Man . . . Christian, for That Was His Name"

INTRODUCING CHARLES HADDON SPURGEON: ANOTHER PILGRIM

A photograph of Spurgeon in his home study.
                                    —*courtesy of Dr. Craig Skinner*

Who would true valor see,
Let him come hither;
One here will constant be,
Come wind, come weather.
There's no discouragement
Shall make him once relent
His first avowed intent
To be a pilgrim.
                              —*John Bunyan*

The snow pelted down as the sword-like wind howled off the frigid ocean, cutting him to the bone. There are few piercing winds as bitter as those off England's North Sea in January. With head down into the veritable gale, trying to ignore the miserable weather, he trudged on. Early that Sunday morning he had struck out so as not to be late. He simply must get to his destination. What would bring a fifteen-year-old Victorian boy out on a day like this? Surely, nothing could be exciting enough in Colchester, Essex, to brave such a storm any day of the week, let alone on a Sunday, the day of rest for the English Victorians.

He stopped, shivered, and looked down the swirling white street. The snow, the cold, the trek—perhaps it was simply too much. At that moment he remembered his mother telling him about a small church on old Artillery Street just a few steps ahead. As he approached the intersection of the short lane, he reasoned, *The church where I intended to go is still some distance off, I will attend the little church my mother told me about.*

The church! He was going to a church? A fifteen-year-old normal boy plodding through snow and braving the cutting wind to go to church on a miserable January day? There must be a story behind this. There is!

Charles, for that was his name, had determined he would attend every church in his hometown, Colchester, a small community some forty miles north and east of London in the county of Essex. He had to find *the answer*. Of course, for a young Essex lad to go to church was the norm; in 1850 the Victorians were notoriously religious. Historians agree, religion permeated every segment of society. But to visit every church in town, especially if it meant going out on such a day, was more than unusual even for the Victorians. What *answer* did he seek?

It had all begun some years earlier when little Charles walked into an unused upstairs room of the manse where his Congregational grandfather/

preacher lived. In the musty old room he discovered a copy of John Bunyan's *Pilgrim's Progress*. The lad pored over the pages, and that classic book of Bunyan sparked a deep concern in the boy. It launched another pilgrim on his way. That journey eventually led the lad all the way through the many pitfalls "Christian" endured on his adventure to the "Celestial City."

An impending traumatic drama of that pilgrimage brought Charles out that Sunday morning in the pitiless weather. Like Bunyan's "Christian," he struggled to leave the "City of Destruction" and grasp salvation. *The answer* he sought centered in his conversion to Christ. He had fixed his vision on the "Celestial City" and would not be deterred. But seek salvation as he would, redemption's peace eluded him; the burden still weighed heavily on his shoulders. It had been a long, hard struggle, and he simply must find forgiveness and relief. His Puritan readings had given birth to guilt, remorse, and misery in his very soul.

Charles was determined to go to every church in Colchester until the heavy burden fell away in the "open grave," as Bunyan put it. He simply must find the liberating *answer* in the salvation of Jesus Christ.

However, it was not all despair. Charles also entertained a steadfast hope; his Puritan heritage had taught him that. He hopefully reasoned, "Surely some good preacher will tell me how to be saved and rid me of this guilt and sense of sin." Yet no church conferred a moment of comfort to his confused and distraught mind. That strange Puritan mixture of guilt and hope permeated his entire personhood. Right at that moment, in the midst of the misery of his soul and the wintry weather of the day, he recalled his mother urging him to attend the Primitive Methodist Chapel on Artillery Street. His mother had often prayed for her children's conversion. Charles knew that, and it deepened his concern as he heard his mother intercede for his salvation. Charles tells us:

> I remember, on one occasion, her praying thus: 'Now, Lord, if my children go on in their sins, it will not be from ignorance that they perish, and my soul must bear a swift witness against them at the day of judgement if they lay not hold of Christ.' That thought of a mother's bearing swift witness against me pierced my conscience, and stirred my heart.[1]

So down the street he went, thinking he might find his *answer* among the Primitive Methodists.

When young Spurgeon timidly entered the little church building, he could hardly have been impressed. It measured only about thirty by forty feet with a small balcony overhead. Moreover, not more than fifteen people had assembled. One could hardly blame the Colchesterites; turning out on a day like that demanded real dedication. Charles brushed off the snow, blew on his cold hands, and quietly slipped in and sat down about five or six pews from the rear, on the preacher's right, somewhat hidden under the small overhanging gallery. With head bowed—not because of the miserable weather now, but because of the miserable heart burden he bore—he hardly looked up as the service began.

Charles previously nursed a few misgivings about worshiping in a Primitive Methodist chapel. They had a reputation for virtually splitting one's eardrums with their vociferous singing. Most people called them the "Ranters," but Charles hardly noticed, he felt so miserable. He did note, nonetheless, that the pastor, who would normally deliver the message, had not arrived when the service began. Charles thought perhaps the pastor had been held up by the storm. So a man who looked like a lanky layman took charge of the service. The full number of hymns were sung, the prayers, offered in typical Primitive Methodist fashion, were prayed. It all proved quite different for young Spurgeon with his Congregational, Puritan background. He felt very much alone. The sermon began as the Primitive preacher took his text: "Look unto me and be ye saved, all the ends of the earth" (Isaiah 45:22). The preacher proved to be more primitive than just in name; he did not even pronounce the words correctly. He appeared to be uneducated, uncouth, and his speech almost unbearable to sophisticated ears. Charles' quick mind took note of that also. Although only fifteen years old, Charles was quite intellectually sophisticated. It all boded for a bad experience. But suddenly, right in the midst of it all, utterly unexpected, *it happened!* Light flashed all around! Heaven itself seemed to come down. The salvation of Christ shone all over the pew. Charles was elated, almost translated. What had happened?

THE DIVINE MOMENT

The young man should be permitted to tell the story in his own words; he revelled in recalling the marvelous event. He declared:

> Personally, I have to bless God for many good books; I thank Him for Dr. Doddridge's *Rise and Progress of Religion in the Soul*; for Baxter's *Call to the Unconverted*; for Alleine's *Alarm to Sinners*; and for James's *Anxious Enquirer*; but my gratitude most of all is due to God, not for books, but for the preached Word,—and that too addressed to me by a poor, uneducated man, a man who had never received any training for the ministry, and probably will never be heard of in this life, a man engaged in business, no doubt of a humble kind, during the week, but who had just enough of grace to say on the Sabbath, 'Look unto Me, and be ye saved, all the ends of the earth.' The books were good, but the man was better. The revealed Word awakened me; but it was the preached Word that saved me; and I must ever attach peculiar value to the hearing of the truth, for by it I received the joy and peace in which my soul delights. While under concern of soul, I resolved that I would attend all the places of worship in the town where I lived, in order that I might find out the

way of salvation. I was willing to do anything, and be anything, if God would only forgive my sin. I set off, determined to go round to all the chapels, and I did go to every place of worship; but for a long time I went in vain. I do not, however, blame the ministers. One man preached Divine Sovereignty; I could hear him with pleasure, but what was that sublime truth to a poor sinner who wished to know what he must do to be saved? There was another admirable man who always preached about the law; but what was the use of ploughing up ground that needed to be sown? Another was a practical preacher. I heard him, but it was very much like a commanding officer teaching the maneuvers of war to a set of men without feet. What could I do? All his exhortations were lost on me. I knew it was said, 'Believe on the Lord Jesus Christ, and thou shalt be saved;' but I did not know what it was to believe on Christ. These good men all preached truths suited to many in their congregations who were spiritually-minded people; but what I wanted to know was,—'How can I get my sins forgiven?'—and they never told me that. I desired to hear how a poor sinner, under a sense of sin, might find peace with God; and when I went, I heard a sermon on, 'Be not deceived, God is not mocked,' which cut me up still worse; but did not bring me into rest. I went again, another day, and the text was something about the glories of the righteous; nothing for poor me! I was like a dog under the table, not allowed to eat of the children's food. I went time after time, and I can honestly say that I do not know that I ever went without prayer to God, and I am sure there was not a more attentive hearer than myself in all the place, for I panted and longed to understand how I might be saved. I sometimes think I might have been in darkness and despair until now had it not been for the goodness of God in sending a snowstorm, one Sunday morning, while I was going to a certain place of worship. When I could go no further, I turned down a side street, and came to a little Primitive Methodist Chapel. In that chapel there may have been a dozen or fifteen people. I had heard of the Primitive Methodists, how they sang so loudly that they made people's heads ache; but that did not matter to me. I wanted to know how I might be saved, and if they could tell me that, I did not care how much they made my head ache. The minister did not come that morning; he was snowed up, I suppose. At last, a very thin-looking man, a shoemaker, or tailor, or something of that sort, went up into the pulpit to preach. Now, it is well that preachers should be instructed; but this man was really stupid. He was obliged to stick to his text, for the simple reason that he had little else to say. The text was,—

'LOOK UNTO ME, AND BE YE SAVED, ALL THE ENDS OF THE EARTH.'

He did not even pronounce the words rightly, but that did not matter. There was, I thought, a glimpse of hope for me in that text. The preacher began thus:—'My dear friends, this is a very simple text indeed. It says, "Look." Now lookin' don't take a deal of pains. It ain't liftin' your foot or your finger;

it is just, "Look." Well, a man needn't go to College to learn to look. You may be the biggest fool, and yet you can look. A man needn't be worth a thousand a year to be able to look. Anyone can look; even a child can look. But then the text says, "Look unto Me." 'Ay!' said he, in broad Essex, 'many of ye are lookin' to yourselves, but it's no use lookin' there. You'll never find any comfort in yourselves. Some look to God the Father. No, look to Him by-and-by. Jesus Christ says, "Look unto Me." Some of ye say, "We must wait for the Spirit's workin'." You have no business with that just now. Look to Christ. The text says, "Look unto Me."'

Then the good man followed up his text in this way: 'Look unto Me, I am sweatin' great drops of blood. Look unto Me; I am hangin' on the cross. Look unto Me; I am dead and buried. Look unto Me; I rise again. Look unto Me; I ascend to Heaven. Look unto Me; I am sittin' at the Father's right hand. O poor sinner, look unto Me! Look unto Me!'

When he had gone to about that length, and managed to spin out ten minutes or so, he was at the end of his tether. Then he looked at me under the gallery, and I daresay, with so few present, he knew me to be a stranger. Just fixing his eyes on me, as if he knew all my heart, he said, 'Young man, you look very miserable.' Well, I did; but I had not been accustomed to have remarks made from the pulpit on my personal appearance before. However, it was a good blow, struck right home. He continued, 'and you always will be miserable—miserable in life, and miserable in death,—if you don't obey my text; but if you obey now, this moment, you will be saved.' Then, lifting up his hands, he shouted, as only a Primitive Methodist could do, 'Young man, look to Jesus Christ. Look! Look! Look! You have nothin' to do but to look and live.' I saw at once the way of salvation. I know not what else he said,—I did not take much notice of it,—I was so possessed with that one thought. Like as when the brazen serpent was lifted up, the people only looked and were healed, so it was with me. I had been waiting to do fifty things. But when I heard that word, 'Look!' what a charming word it seemed to me! Oh! I looked until I could almost have looked my eyes away. There and then the cloud was gone, the darkness had rolled away, and that moment I saw the sun; and I could have risen that instant, and sung with the most enthusiastic of them, of the precious blood of Christ, and the simple faith which looks alone to Him. Oh, that somebody had told me this before, 'Trust Christ, and you shall be saved.' Yet it was, no doubt, all wisely ordered, and now I can say,—

> 'E'er since by faith I saw the stream
> Thy flowing wounds supply,
> Redeeming love has been my theme,
> And shall be till I die.'

I do from my soul confess that I never was satisfied till I came to Christ; when I was yet a child, I had far more wretchedness than ever I have now; I will even add, more weariness, more care, more heart-ache than I know at this

Spurgeon: *Prince of Preachers*

day. I may be singular in this confession, but I make it, and I know it to be truth. Since that dear hour when my soul cast itself on Jesus, I have found solid joy and peace; but before that, all those supposed gaieties of early youth, all the imagined ease and joy of boyhood, were but vanity and vexation of spirit to me. That happy day, when I found the Savior, and learned to cling to His dear feet, was a day never to be forgotten by me. An obscure child, unknown, unheard of, I listened to the Word of God; and that precious text led me to the cross of Christ. I can testify that the joy of the day was utterly indescribable. I could have leaped, I could have danced; there was no expression, however fanatical, which would have been out of keeping with the joy of my spirit at that hour. Many days of Christian experience have passed since then, but there has never been one which has had the full exhilaration, the sparkling delight which that first day had. I thought I could have sprung from the seat on which I sat, and have called out with the wildest of those Methodist brethren who were present, 'I am forgiven! I am forgiven! A monument of grace! A sinner saved by blood!' My spirit saw its chains broken to pieces, I felt that I was an emancipated soul, an heir of Heaven, a forgiven one, accepted in Christ Jesus, plucked out of the miry clay and out of the horrible pit, with my feet set upon a rock, and my goings established. I thought I could dance all the way home. I could understand what John Bunyan meant, when he declared he wanted to tell the crows on the ploughed land all about his conversion. He was too full to hold, he felt he must tell somebody.

It is not everyone who can remember the very day and hour of his deliverance; but, as Richard Knill said, 'At such a time of the day, clang went every harp in Heaven, for Richard Knill was born again,' it was e'en so with me. The clock of mercy struck in Heaven the hour and moment of my emancipation, for the time had come. Between half-past ten o'clock, when I entered that chapel, and half-past twelve o'clock, when I was back again at home, what a change had taken place in me! I had passed from darkness into marvelous light, from death to life. [2]

He found the answer; he found Jesus Christ. Christ is The Answer. Charles Haddon Spurgeon was gloriously converted. He had become a Pilgrim. From that initial experience, Spurgeon never tired of telling the simple good news of the Gospel. Throughout his life, all the way on his journey to the "Celestial City," he exalted the blood of Christ as God's only way of redemption. On his tombstone is engraved the favorite hymn he quoted in relating his conversion story:

> E'er since, by faith, I saw the stream,
> Thy flowing wounds supply.
> Redeeming love has been my theme,
> And shall be 'till I die.

In that little Primitive Methodist Chapel, under the preaching of an unlettered man, a pilgrimage of ministry began that no one there could have dreamed of, even in their wildest imagination. [3]

Four years later, at the age of nineteen, Charles Spurgeon received the call to become the pastor of the historic New Park Street Baptist Chapel in dynamic London. Notables like John Gill, Benjamin Keach and John Rippon had served as ministers of the famous congregation. For thirty-seven years, Spurgeon preached in that great English city, growing the largest evangelical congregation in the world. Through the years, the eulogies raised in honor of the young preacher almost defy belief. Davenport Northrop, a contemporary of Spurgeon, called him "the most celebrated preacher of modern times . . . the most conspicuous figure in the religious world . . . the Saul among the prophets, standing head and shoulder above the others." [4] German theologian and professor Helmut Thielicke declared, "Sell all that you have (not least of all some of your stock of current sermonic literature) and buy Spurgeon (even if you have to grub through second-hand bookstores) . . . Let him be a Socrates who helps you to find your own way." [5] Homiletician Andrew Blackwood asked, "Who since Paul has done so much to advance the Kingdom of God?" [6] Phant and Pinson stated, "Spurgeon's oral style may have been the finest ever produced by the Christian pulpit." [7] B. H. Carroll, Baptist educator, went so far as to hold that Spurgeon stands as the finest preacher in the entire history of the Christian Church. He called Spurgeon "the greatest man of modern times." [8]

It is understandable why Spurgeon attracted so much praise. The sheer mountain of work he produced through his London years was phenomenal. During the nearly four decades of ministry, he added over 14,000 new members to his church. Two thousand two hundred and forty-one of Spurgeon's sermons were published up to the time of his death in 1892. After that, a weekly publication of one of his messages was produced until 1917, which finally brought the number to over 3,800 published sermons. For a period of time, Spurgeon's Sunday sermon was even wired across the Atlantic to America and printed in the Monday edition of secular newspapers. And all that is not to mention the scores of other full volumes he penned. Many consider Spurgeon one of the ten greatest English authors with an estimate of up to 300 million copies of his sermons and books printed. During his life the whole evangelical world seemed to hang on his words; and he is still constantly republished to this day. He became a household word, and remains so to this moment in many evangelical circles. At any rate, there are more books, at least religious works, in print today by Spurgeon—a century after his death—than any living or dead English writing author.

One could rationalize this popularity away by arguing that the Victorians were religious almost to a fault. Moreover, they were known as a nation of "sermon tasters," and Spurgeon became the prince of preachers in his day. Hence, masses came to hear him and read him. It is only natural, therefore, the argument could run, that their heroes would be of the religious ilk. Be that as it may, there still existed in the Spurgeon saga something far more significant than that. The London orator became infinitely larger than a mere sociological phenomenon. What was that "something more" the "boy preacher" from Essex, as he was called in his early years, possessed that so captivated his day? The answer is simple; yet, very profound: Charles Spurgeon filled the role of a genuine Christian, a true man of God, on another pilgrimage in the context of a dynamic spiritual awakening. A real revival broke out all around Spurgeon as he began his London ministry. He himself said:

> We have felt in our souls, not that we *may* have revival, but that we *must* have it. We must draw near to the Angel of the Covenant and wrestle afresh with the determination, that we will not let him go unless he should bless us. [9]

The "Angel of the Covenant" did not disappoint the preacher, for nearly forty years revival blessings flowed and nurtured his ministry. This becomes increasingly evident as one walks with this 19th century "Pilgrim" through the pathways of his journey to the "Celestial City."

REVIVAL PREREQUISITES

A central question revolves around the revival principle that so significantly helped to produce Spurgeon's unique ministry: What type of servant of Christ does it take to be the pastor of a great and growing church that is experiencing a significant spiritual awakening? The answers are varied.

Foundationally, a *Spirit-filled* minister is God's manner of man to be a successful servant of the Gospel. Spurgeon surely exemplified what it means to be "filled with all the fullness of God" (Ephesians 3:19). Spurgeon stated:

> If there were only one prayer which I might pray before I died, it should be this: 'Lord, send thy church men filled with the Holy Ghost and with fire.' [10]

Spurgeon, in the profound sense, experienced the Spirit's fullness. Yet, like all effective spiritual men of God, he had his full count of critics. He became the recipient of a veritable barrage of barbs. Nonetheless, the detractors notwithstanding, no pastor ever preached with more spiritual power—and popularity—than did Spurgeon. The remarkable conversions that occurred in the Metropolitan Tabernacle, as his church later became known, attest to his dynamic life and ministry. All saw him as a man "mighty with God."

A free spirit, unencumbered by tradition, forms another prerequisite to usefulness. Charles certainly qualified there. He could never be bound by the rigid Victorian ethos of his day, as shall be seen many times over. He became a stellar innovator of the first magnitude. To defy deadening traditions seemed his forte. The preaching that flowed from his pulpit precipitated a revolution in itself. Castigated by London's sophisticates as "vulgar" and "crude," his pungent Anglo-Saxon style so intrigued and captivated the "common" people that they came by the tens of thousands to sit enthralled at his earthy oratory. Spurgeon genuinely reveled in his simple "vulgar" preaching. He said:

> If I was saved by a simple gospel, then I am bound to preach that same simple gospel 'till I die, so that others may be saved by it. When I cease to preach salvation by faith in Jesus, put me into a lunatic's asylum, for you may be sure that my mind is gone. [11]

Moreover, the Stockwell Orphanage, the Pastors' College, the almshouses, the Evangelist's Association, the many new churches planted, and similar social and spiritual works that he started spoke volumes to needy Londoners. They felt that at last they found a free spirit who would lead his Tabernacle to do whatever became necessary to meet their pressing human needs. Spurgeon, like a bird suddenly released from its snare, flew with a message of fascinating freedom and freshness that bore hope on its wings to London's perplexing social and spiritual problems. And "the common people heard him gladly."

Furthermore, an effective minister of Jesus Christ also must be a good, disciplined thinker—at least he should be. Could Spurgeon think? He never received a formal theological education. He gathered more than one barb from his detractors for that fact. The critics called him "dull" and "stupid." Spurgeon planned to attend theological college, but circumstances conspired against it. That fascinating story will be recorded later. However, the lack of formal theological training certainly did not spell mental mediocrity for the London preacher. He had a brilliant intellect. His earlier years demonstrated it clearly, and his succeeding years confirmed it. He studied large Puritan portfolios every week and annotated them heavily. Moreover, he read widely in contemporary literature. Having something of a photographic mind, he could classify all he read and possessed the unusual gift of instant recall. He amazed people with his ability. He had a mind like the proverbial steel trap. Through the years he amassed a library of 30,000 volumes, most of them heavy theological works. A cursory survey of his library shows how diligently he read and carefully studied virtually every single one. [12] In addition, his keen spiritual perception equaled his mental grasp. He could analyze a situation and come up with a spiritual solution with amazing speed. Spurgeon proved to be a most able thinker and scholar, lack of formal training notwithstanding.

In addition, a minister of Christ must be human. Charles surely measured up. He exhibited a warm, outgoing personality. He loved people and his sense of humor was winsomely contagious. For example, during a general parliamentary election, he arrived unaccustomedly late for a speaking engagement. Explaining his tardiness, he related he had stopped to vote. "To vote!" asked a super-pious critic, "but my dear brother, I thought you were a citizen of the New Jerusalem!"

"So I am," Spurgeon retorted, "but my 'old man' is a citizen of this world."

"Ah! But you should mortify your 'old man,'" the critic's commented.

"That is exactly what I did," Spurgeon rejoined, "for my 'old man' is a Tory and I made him vote Liberal." That ended the encounter.

Spurgeon received considerable criticism for injecting a good portion of humor in his sermons. Charles defended himself saying, "If you knew how much I held back you would not criticize." On one occasion he won a competition for the best joke. It runs as follows: a man once said to Charles, "You are out of it in joking about my *red* hair. It is not *red*, it is golden." "Ah! Yes, golden," Spurgeon replied, "*eighteen carrot*." A friend of Charles once remarked, "What a bubbling fountain of humour Mr. Spurgeon had. I have laughed more, I verily believe, when in his company than during all the rest of my life besides."[13] His humor spoke of a happy *Christian*. Helmut Thielicke said of Charles, "Spurgeon's cheerfulness is not evidence of his having the natural charisma of 'a good sense of humor,' . . . his humor rather bears witness to the grace that is at work in him."[14] Thielicke put it well again when he said, "Suddenly the kingdom of God popped up not only in men's hearts but in their diaphragms."[15]

An interesting insight into the almost playful humor of the man is found in his application form for life insurance. On the medical questionnaire, one question read: "Whether the Life proposed has ever been afflicted with any Fits or Convulsions since Infancy." (A typical question in the nineteenth century medical circles.) Spurgeon wrote: "No, unless convulsions of laughter are meant."[16] On another occasion, Spurgeon's wit saved the day. He had a remarkable memory for faces and names, and was seldom wrong in his identification of the members of his huge congregation. On one occasion, however, he was at fault. "How are you, Mr. Partridge?" he said to a gentleman who came into his vestry to greet him. "I am very well, sir," he answered, "but my name is Patridge." "Ah, well," instantly replied Mr. Spurgeon, "I promise you that I will make game of you no more."[17] Fast thinking rescued him from embarrassment.

Spurgeon had his deeply serious side, however. He often suffered depression, at times serious depression, as shall be seen as his pilgrimage unfolds. His rheumatic gout was something of the culprit in that continuous problem. Moreover, he took his preaching with deep seriousness, even to the point that often he would be so under the burden of his message, and the responsibility of standing in Christ's stead, that his deacons would come for prayer into the vestry before the service and find him literally nauseated. Spurgeon said, "Never have I to preach but I feel terribly sick—literally sick, I mean—so that I might as well be crossing the Channel."[18] No uncalled for light-heartedness intruded. He had a most sensitive spirit—almost too sensitive at times.

Not only that, if one aspires to be mighty before God, one must have a passion to point people to faith in Christ. Here Spurgeon excelled. Consequently, his evangelistic ministry proved as powerful—and as profoundly appreciated—as his pastoral, preaching, and social ministries. He preached in barns, theatres, or wherever people would gather. As biographer Nichols put it:

> Spurgeon's preaching has been evaluated, his writings analyzed, his philanthropy considered, and his political involvement summarized. However, it was the role of Pastor/Evangelist which dominated his ministry. Evangelism was at the heart of all that he sought to do. Whether preaching from the pulpit or speaking with individuals, Spurgeon was always an evangelist. The many avenues of evangelical ministry all arose from his consuming passion for souls. [19]

Nichols is correct. Spurgeon himself said, "I could scarcely content myself even for five minutes without trying to do something for Christ." [20] He reveled in conversions stemming from his ministry, stating, "I would rather be the means of saving a soul from death than be the greatest orator on earth." [21] He translated that passion into helping others become "evangelists." In 1867, the Metropolitan Tabernacle had 250 members engaged in evangelistic work.

Moreover, Spurgeon realized that if London were to be truly taken for Christ, evangelism must center in the planting of new churches. In this labor he likewise excelled. He knew a passion for souls must result in sensible practical work, like beginning new congregations. He said, "When you bewail the world's inequity . . . weeping will do nothing without action." [22] As a result, by 1878, forty-eight new churches were established under his guidance in the greater London area alone. The people won were innumerable.

Furthermore, for one to be used in revival, prayer and tribulation are essential. Tribulation always seems to play a vital role in the Holy Spirit preparing a servant of God for great service, for trials drive people to fervent prayer. Spurgeon's trials are legendary. All through life he experienced trials that drove him to despair and thus to his knees. He confessed, in Bunyan's allegorical style, "There are dungeons underneath the Castle of Despair as dreary as the abodes of the lost, and some of us have been in them." [23] But despair always inspires prayer. Fortunately, Spurgeon inherited a great praying church. He knew, as he said, "Prayer meetings are the throbbing machinery of the Church." [24] How the people of New Park Street Baptist Church did pray! They actually prayed down revival. But prayer must be personal as well as corporate. Could Spurgeon himself pray? He could; he actually seemed to walk in a spirit of continuous prayer. Though not given to long formal prayers, he prayed "without ceasing." He stated, "you cannot measure fire by the bushel, nor prayers by their length." [25] He believed that and practiced it. Actually, he only spent one or two whole nights in prayer in his entire life, but he walked with God in such depth that he could move from conversation with a friend and then into prayer in a moment.

Above all, God's man, to be significantly used by God, must be just that: *God's Man.* Spurgeon had many unusual gifts. He was a man with a brilliant mind and a captivating personality. He possessed a marvelous voice and his natural gift of oratory skills amazed the multitudes that came to hear him. He could organize work brilliantly. But primarily, he loved Jesus Christ with all his heart. He was a Christian man in the full biblical sense of the word. Spurgeon's deepest desire centered in living a life of God-honoring Christian holiness. He declared:

> I would sooner be holy than happy if the two things would be divorced. Were it possible for a man always to sorrow and yet to be pure, I would choose the sorrow if I might win the purity, for to be free from the power of sin, to be made to love holiness, is true happiness. [26]

Charles had one consuming purpose and goal: to exalt his Savior in godly living and preach the Gospel with power.

Simply put, Charles Haddon Spurgeon, lifted up by the reviving and quickening power of the Holy Spirit, began a pilgrimage that would ultimately give England, and the world, one of the greatest pastoral, evangelistic, social ministries ever seen. That opinion is shared by many, not just a few superficially enamored admirers. Spurgeon was a giant in effecting revival.

Thus, when the 19-year-old "boy preacher" from Essex took up his charge at the New Park Street Baptist Chapel, later to become the great Metropolitan Tabernacle of London, the Spirit of the Lord launched a new era of ministry. A man named "Christian" had arrived and the world would soon know it. At the time of his move to England's capital city, though few realized it, one of the most distinguished of all English-speaking preachers was about to explode on the evangelical scene. The shock waves of that explosion can still be felt over London today—and around the world. So after this brief introduction to Pastor Charles H. Spurgeon, we now turn to his fascinating life and times.

To present a mere, rigid chronological account of Charles Haddon Spurgeon's pilgrimage proves difficult, and not very profitable if one would grasp the dynamics of his ministry. Therefore, some of the chapters that follow are more topical than chronological, although a general sequence of events is sought. Moreover, to understand any personality, one must come to grips with the day and place in which that person lived. Thus we begin with a brief overview of Spurgeon's Victorian London.

2

"The City of Destruction"

SPURGEON'S VICTORIAN ENGLAND

Old Surrey Gardens Music Hall.

The dunghill-raker, spider him,
The chicken, too, to me
Hath taught a lesson; let it then
Conformed to it be.
The butcher, gardener in the field,
The robin and his bait,
Also the rotten tree doth yield
Me argument of weight.
To move me forth to watch and pray
To strive to be sincere,
To take my cross up day by day,
And serve the Lord with fear.
                                    —*John Bunyan*

Introduction

I n John Bunyan's perceptive allegory, Pilgrim left his city that he had
loved so long because he became convinced God had devoted it to
destruction. He thus started his journey seeking the indestructible
"Celestial City." But that did not end his involvement in his doomed
community. He had friends and family there. Something of his heart remained
in that city. The Kingdom of God versus "The City of Destruction" has
always been a paradoxical problem for pilgrims. Spurgeon's nineteenth
century England proved no exception. They both loved and despised their
"city." The negative side of their cherished Calvinism doomed the "city."
Conversely, a deep concern and social consciousness for the well-being of
their culture pervaded the Victorian evangelical mindset. They were firmly
committed to correcting their society for God and good; they had friends
and family there. The positive side of Calvin and his Geneva experiment
contributed to that attitude, hence the paradox. This two-sided approach to
social structures largely spawned and gave birth to the Victorian era.
Furthermore, among the Victorians, no more sterling example of this attitude
to church and culture emerged than in the ministry of Charles Haddon
Spurgeon. The great preacher said:

> Socially we are one body, and the sickly member is an injury to the whole.
> Drunkenness in one class is damage to us all; a want of thrift causes loss to the
> whole community; vice anywhere prepares contagion for all ranks; abomina-
> ble laws oppressing a few are a real injury to the many. As in a sea-dyke, every
> single rat is an enemy to every Dutchman, so every wrong in this kingdom
> wounds us all more or less. It were well that all good men felt this, and

bestirred themselves. To benefit the community we must seek the good of every individual man, woman and child; and for a nation to do well, each individual must work righteousness. [1]

These ideas characterized most nineteenth century evangelical Christians. They had a stake in "The City of Destruction." They believed in the essential oneness of human society, sinful though it be. Therefore, they constantly gave themselves to social reform and philanthropic enterprises as well as evangelism. Righteousness and benefiting the community must go hand in glove. Such endeavors in London by famous preachers and dedicated laymen like Spurgeon, Rev. Hugh Price Hughes, Rev. Archibald G. Brown, Mr. Quintin Hogg, the founder of the famous Polytechnic on Regent Street, and perhaps above all, Lord Shaftesbury, typified the great accomplishments by evangelicals in the leading cities of Europe and America. The Victorian Christians, gripped by a deep commitment, sought to bring religion and its benefits to people and to the structures of society. For them, Christianity must relate itself to the pressing social and spiritual issues of the ordinary affairs of daily life. They sincerely strove to integrate the spiritual into the secular. However, if that secular city rejected the salvation and holy influence of Christ, it would surely become a "City of Destruction."

This paradoxical grasp of culture not only became the working socio-spiritual philosophy of the nineteenth century evangelicals, it also perpetuated the Victorian era to the extent it gave stability, amid exploding cultural change, to one of the strongest, most stable societies ever built. Even considering the dramatic upheavals that rocked the era, there persisted a seemingly unchanging, almost rigid stability in Britain. Perhaps one rationale for this anomaly rests in the fact that no major wars erupted during the Victorian days. Of course, that does not exhaust the reasons for the stability of nineteenth century Britain; many features made the Victorians what they were. Although Spurgeon was a product of his times, he departed from many of the stable norms of his day. Perhaps Spurgeon's revolutionary approach to ministry can be explained because the Victorians were, in many significant respects, revolutionary people, despite their quest for stability. Horton Davies said, "It is a false stereotype that presents the Victorians' Age as a succession of mere storms in a teacup. It was rather a period of explosions of political, social, moral, scientific and religious revolution." [2] Therefore, to understand fully the Metropolitan Tabernacle pastor, we must grasp something of the social dynamics of the era.

THE DYNAMICS OF THE DAY

When Queen Victoria ascended the throne in 1837, several deep and profound cultural currents surged like a torrent throughout staid and stable Great Britain. Unprecedented change began to become the order of the day.

The Industrial Revolution, the increasing power of Parliament, the rise of the working masses, moral and spiritual upheavals, and a thousand other crosscurrents all played their part in bringing the Georgian era to an end. In this setting, the churches found themselves forced to make radical adjustments. And they did not become derelict in their duty. They entered virtually every segment of society and attempted to touch it with a relevant ministry. Some historians have minimized the influence of the Church in Victorian Britain. But, as Young, Snyder, and Rutan put it, "It is a . . . mistake to underestimate the importance of the church in the life of early nineteenth-century England."[3] Christians made their impact felt in developments such as the Oxford Movement, the evangelical thrust, the rising acceptance of Non-conformity, the Prayer Revival of 1859, and a host of other dramatic movements. In these spiritually fluid days, Spurgeon entered like a storm on the changing scene and moved multitudes of Victorians closer to God. What characterized those significant times in which Charles Haddon Spurgeon exercised his ministry?

Spurgeon's Victorian Britain can be best seen by viewing it from a threefold perspective: one, The Dynamics of Early Nineteenth Century Society; two, Victorian Social and Political Life; and three, Victorian Religious Movements. This will afford at least a bird's-eye view of the turbulent times, the *sitz-in-leben* of Victorian days, as the historians would express it.

Of course, to write so briefly, as this chapter must be, attempting to describe nineteenth century Britain is quite presumptuous. Many volumes on the Victorian era have been penned by able historians and sociologists. Therefore, one must be very selective, even subjective. Still, as stated, a grasp of the era, even if most sketchy, is necessary to understand fully the London preacher.

THE DYNAMICS OF EARLY NINETEENTH CENTURY SOCIETY

As the nineteenth century dawned on Britain's lush verdant countryside, the social demographics largely consisted of small towns and villages, even though urbanization had begun its rapid rise. The families in their quaint little cottages were somewhat isolated and kept largely to themselves. The family unit continued to be tight-knit and quite stable. Still, they did have some interaction with their neighbors and depended upon them for certain social needs. They were not pure isolationists. Nonetheless, everyday life moved on a rather static, unexciting plane. Wages remained low; widespread unemployment plagued many areas, and life proved difficult, especially in the growing metropolitan ghettos of London, Manchester, and Glasgow. To say the least, the cities left much to be desired. As has been said, "The towns were characterized by ugliness, grime, congestion, poorly built housing, lack of sanitary facilities, and pure water."[4] When the Crimean War finally ended, the discharge of large numbers of soldiers created even higher unemployment and worsening conditions. Periodic economic recessions ran through the nineteenth century.

However, the Crimean War with its Florence Nightingale, and the Duke of Marlborough's defeat of Napoleon at Waterloo in 1815, spawned a new spirit of nationalism. Britishers reveled in the news of victories on the battlefield. Britons all the way from the Court of St. James to the working man's pub boasted of their United Kingdom. The soldiers were greatly loved and honored. The navy ruled the waves and everyone shouted, "Britannia for aye."

All was not well, however. Justice suffered. The legal punishments against crime were many times extreme and brutal; for example, in 1818, more than 200 felonies carried the death penalty. Prejudices and unfair treatment toward certain classes of society remained entrenched. The law appeared unbalanced so as to protect the employer and his holdings, and the reality proved as true as the appearance. The poor, largely disenfranchised from the main flow of society, enjoyed few privileges. Human rights had to wait for the next century. Moreover, many considered any attempt to change the unfair, unbalanced system a criminal offense. The spirit, if not the actual structure, of the old feudal system prevailed, and in a limited sense continued to the end of the Victorian era. The Tories, the conservative political party, tended to foster this general ethos. Spurgeon, a staunch conservative in theology, distinctly disagreed with conservative Tory policies. He voted "liberal" on most political issues—as illustrated by the political anecdote recorded in Chapter One.

In the early nineteenth century, Britain began to dominate the world in several respects, despite many internal problems. This is particularly true in geographical extension and political-economic influence. London became the largest city and financial center of the world. The British pound sterling controlled the currency exchange centers of the West.

Another facet of nineteenth century British dominance occurred as a result of a veritable population explosion.

In 1801 the population in England registered only 8.9 million. By 1901 the number had reached 32.5 million, virtually quadrupling. Spurgeon's London grew from 1.1 million to 6.6 million in that same one hundred year period. Manchester, the first urban center of the industrial revolution grew apace. Some say the revolution began in the city of Shrewsbury in Shropshire, but most historians see Manchester as the first center of the revolution. Scotland and Wales also grew tremendously, not to mention Ireland. Furthermore, British political institutions, the Parliament and the constitutional monarchy, increasingly influenced political philosophy and thinking around the globe. Commerce, capital, and the accumulation of British manufacturing enterprises invaded a multitude of countries. Moreover, the long reign of Queen Victoria (1837-1901) provided the political stability and conditions that fostered British world leadership. As one historian put it, "In many ways the nineteenth century could be called the British century."[5]

THE NEW QUEEN

Appropriately, the Victorian era revolved around Queen Victoria. One cannot truly understand nineteenth century Britain without understanding its queen. She was a personification of the times. Historian Latourette said, "The queen both symbolized and reinforced much that characterized that period."[6] When Victoria donned the crown in Westminster Abbey on June 23, 1837, the world had become accustomed to seeing British political power wielded by old men who were either disreputable or inept, or both. King George III had died in 1820. He was followed by George IV, who died in 1830. Then William IV reigned until his death in 1837. Now a simple, young, innocent girl seemed destined to raise the crown dramatically from the casual contempt into which it had fallen. The time was ripe. The people held high hopes and expectations for their new sovereign.

Lord John Russell asked England to pray that the little princess would be filled with the purest intentions and desires, and that she might bring about the abolition of slavery, see crime diminished, and education improved. Baron Christian Stockmar took up residence in the palace as friend and advisor to Victoria to guide her in these reforms. Yet, he was barely eighteen years old himself! Would the people's expectations be realized?

Victoria, not particularly gifted with superior intelligence, was nevertheless high-spirited and determined to fulfill her duties. When her governess, Ms. Leazen, some years earlier had shown little Victoria a chart of the royal family and the ascension to the throne, the young girl suddenly realized for the first time she would one day be queen. As the realization dawned, she looked up at her governess and simply said, "I will be good." She meant it. She did become a good queen, if not a brilliant one. As one historian expressed it, "Under Queen Victoria the monarchy regained the respect it has lost under her two predecessors."[7] She had received a thorough education in languages, history, sports, music, dancing and the forms of etiquette expected of a princess; thus the expectations for the reign of Queen Victoria looked very good.

At the death of William IV in 1837 (three years after Spurgeon's birth), Victoria ascended the throne at the tender age of eighteen. She remained queen until her death in 1901. In her six decade reign, Britons saw Victoria as a very moral, religious person. Some present-day historians, however, have placed a few question marks over her morality in her later years after the death of Albert. The princess' early religious education came partly through her governess. However, the Dean of Chester, George Davies, became her primary spiritual mentor. Davies, practically the only clergyman Queen Victoria ever saw, had a spiritual simplicity that significantly molded the young girl's religious and moral mindset. Before assuming the crown, she had enjoyed the non-liturgical, short worship of her household prayers. Now, young Victoria as queen had to attend the elaborate formalism of Anglican worship. As a result, she harbored a dislike for long services, solemn music, and pedantic preaching, so sadly characteristic of much high-church Anglicanism.

Another person who shaped Victoria's religiosity was Melbourne, the Whig prime minister. His influence proved somewhat negative, however, for he bred in the Queen a certain distrust of all religious enthusiasm. He told her that Dr. Pusey and Mr. Newman of the Oxford school were actually violent people. He said William Wilberforce and the evangelicals were no more than enthusiasts. He further declared that Quakers were sly and that Luther could be seen as a very questionable man. He concluded saying all hermits were rogues. He held that commonplace sermons were better than dramatic sermons. This caused the queen to shy away from the controversies characteristic of dynamic religion. Many shared this negative attitude. Unfortunately, this developed in the young sovereign a sense of separation from the main spiritual movements within the Established Church of the day.

On February 10, 1840, Victoria married Prince Albert of Saxe-Coburg-Gotha in Germany. She made him her Prince Consort. Albert proved to be a very capable man and in some sense the most "Victorian" in all the royal court. He gave himself to domestic studies, artistic appreciation, and intellectual pursuits. He made a significant contribution not only to Victoria herself, but to all of Great Britain. Albert, being a good German, was a faithful member of the Lutheran church. Like most of his fellow Protestant countrymen, he feared clerical power, the Pope, and all claims to ecclesiastical dominance. His Germanic religious background proved far different from the quiet, rather rigid religious atmosphere of Oxford or Cambridge. Germany enjoyed considerably more freedom of thought. Biblical criticism, with its rationalistic approach, brought about a more liberal attitude in Albert's fatherland. The Prince Consort imbibed of that spirit. As a result, the Prince seemed incapable of sympathizing with the Anglican Church or most of the newer religious movements of the day. He felt the Church of England to be insufficiently reformed. The dynamic sixteenth and seventeenth centuries had failed to move the Established Church far enough to the left; thus he became critical of the whole British religious establishment. Victoria, though not quite as critical as her husband, admired the scholarly clergymen.

Many Victorians, especially the more sophisticated, focused on the new spirit of liberalism and individualism set afoot in Britain, a liberalism not necessarily endorsed by Victoria and Albert, but certainly not opposed by them either. The philosophies of David Hume's urban skepticism, Charles Darwin's hypothesis of evolution, and Hegelian rationalism were soon applied to the social, ethical, and religious structures of British society. In the latter part of the century, Herbert Spencer expanded the new spirit into a

grandiose scheme by formulating a whole developmental, evolutionary theory of society. These dynamics tended to relegate Christianity to a mere
passing phase of history. Philosophical and psychological determinism began their rise to acceptance. It paved the way for later philosophers like
Gilbert Ryle and Bertrand Russell; it opened the door for the acceptance of
behavioristic psychologists such as B. F. Skinner. Matthew Arnold, Thomas
Carlisle, Thomas Hardy, and George Eliot in their more popular writings
aired their skepticism about the Christian faith. George Bernard Shaw finally gave to the new rationalism its ultimate conclusion and laughed at Christianity and the Church. Humanism deeply entrenched itself in the psyche of
many nineteenth century urbanites. By 1884 the atmosphere had become
such that the Fabian Society emerged with its totally socialistic philosophy.

Nonetheless, this rational spirit did not dampen the queen's essential
ethical temperament. In her lifetime Victoria's moral image proved quite
impeccable. However, it is difficult to determine just what effect she exerted
on the moral standards of the nation. She did not have a philosophical bent,
and, therefore, showed little concern for the subtleties of ethical values. Her
charm, and what subsequent influence she did exert, centered in the fact that
she never lost her early childlike belief in the elementary tenets of morality.
This may well have been the reason she always personified the figure of
morality and gave her name to that brand of moral and ethical principles.

After Victoria received the sceptre, Lord Russell not only asked the
people to pray for their new queen, he implored the populace to derive their
strength, their conduct, and their loyalty from enlightened religion and moral concepts so that the reign of their sovereign might influence all the
nations of the earth for good. Because of the ensuing popularity of Victoria
and the currents set loose during her reign, there can be little doubt that
many heeded Russell's admonition. The Victorian era did influence large
segments of society for a better life. Her reign truly precipitated "a society
of remarkable order and balance,"[8] both socially and politically. What characterized this social-political "order and balance"?

VICTORIAN SOCIAL AND POLITICAL LIFE

Victoria's reign of peace and political stability permitted, even fostered,
important social and cultural change. The Industrial Revolution raced along,
as new technology continually emerged. In July of 1829, the new twelve
passenger omnibuses, pulled by two horses, appeared on the streets of London. George Shillibear, the inventor, received much praise for the innovation. At the time of Spurgeon's birth in 1834, the first railroad had been
operating four years. By 1850, there were 5,000 miles of railroads in Britain.
Energy from steam and later by electricity radically changed the lifestyle of
the whole western scene. Wealth grew rapidly; but, tragically, it was un-
equally distributed. The Industrial Revolution certainly did not improve the

lot of all people. The exploitation of the workers degraded adults. Women and children, shackled with long working hours, often labored under terrible conditions that did not change dramatically until the beginning of the twentieth century. But the depressing situation did spawn the trade union movement. Still, poverty, alcoholism, and sexual vice ran rampant. Overcrowded slums and insanitary, deplorable housing and a host of other blights plagued the poorer sections of the large cities. Parts of London could only be described as a squalor. All over Britain the working masses suffered deprivation. For example, a cotton mill laborer in Lancashire made only nine shillings, nine pence per week; farm workers earned one shilling, 2 pence a week. Approximately 1,427,187 paupers roamed the streets in the 1840s. But the move to the cities still continued in a non-ending stream. By 1851, the urban population surpassed the rural population for the first time in British history.

Despite those pressing problems, this fluid century, as already implied, witnessed dramatic development in the sciences that boded for a better future. Not only that, British social, philosophical, and political thought influenced millions. Movements such as Marxism were formulated in London. Perhaps the most significant social movement occurred when the supremacy of Parliament became firmly established in the early part of the century. The monarchy had not yet been reduced to mere figurehead status as it largely functions today; nonetheless, the power structure clearly rested in the hands of the prime minister and his cabinet. This gave the common people something of a word in the social-political structures of their country.

NEW BILLS

Politically, the Victorian era began with the passing of the Test and Corporation Act of 1828, the Catholic Emancipation Act in 1829 and the Reform Bill of 1832. These acts allowed Protestants and Catholics, not just Church of England members, to hold seats in Parliament and run for public office. Along with the Second Reform Act of 1867, which virtually doubled the electorate, these laws gave multitudes suffrage rights who had never enjoyed them before. The Reform Bill of 1884 and the Redistribution Act of 1885 produced universal male suffrage. The two major political parties in the early decades of the nineteenth century were the Whigs and Tories. The Whigs tended to represent commercial interests, while the Tories, more politically conservative, gravitated toward small rural landholders. Moreover, the Liberal Party and the Conservative Party began experiencing increasing popularity. Wider voter's rights started the transfer of political leadership from the aristocracy to the middle class.[9] Spurgeon, who never retreated from issues, be they theological or social, became a political liberal, as previously seen. His devotion to the Liberal Party was so complete, he is reported to have said he would "rather vote for the Devil than a Tory." Spurgeon modified that statement, but he was never reticent to express himself. He felt a real obligation to involve himself in all the issues of the hour.

Despite the radical changes occurring in Britain, the old established land families still exercised considerable political influence, especially in the earlier decades of the century. But with the population explosion, urbanization and various economic crises, the sentiment grew that the government should be more broadly represented. In 1846, when Prime Minister Robert Peel repealed the Corn Laws which prohibited the importation of cheap food from abroad, his move split the Tories.[10] This precipitated twenty years of political confusion. The Whigs and Tories at times formed a coalition, but these arrangements fell into demise, which in turn gave more prominence to the Liberals and Conservatives. As the Liberal and Conservative Parties thus gained strength, the brilliant Jew, Benjamin Disraeli, came to the helm of the Conservatives and William Gladstone ascended to the leadership of the Liberal Party. Gladstone, the "Grand Old Man" of Victorian politics, as he was known, ultimately became the most influential politician of the nineteenth century. A friend of Spurgeon, Gladstone regularly exchanged letters with the great preacher. He often invited Spurgeon to breakfast or dinner at 10 Downey Street, although Charles could rarely if ever attend. Nonetheless, Spurgeon supported Gladstone and very forthrightly exercised his considerable influence to support the Liberal Party in the general elections of 1880 and 1886. Paradoxically, the only time the Prime Minister heard Spurgeon preach took place on January 8, 1882. Under Gladstone, the Liberals tended to occupy an increasingly important role in the affairs of the nation, and by 1868 they had acquired a majority in the House of Commons. Except for six years, this continued until 1898.

IMPERIALISM

It must never be forgotten or minimized that the nineteenth century for Britain was an age of aggressive imperialism. After Napoleon's defeat at Waterloo in 1815 by Wellington, until the latter part of the century, Britain expanded her political and economic interests all over the world. She boasted a great army and navy and the largest merchant fleet on the seas. Although the motivation for this expansion was mostly economic, with it came political power and the opening of the door for the expansion of Christian missions. Although the colonialism of Victorian England now stands condemned by many, it did nonetheless present significant opportunities for worldwide missionary labors. At the Diamond Jubilee of Queen Victoria in 1897, the British Commonwealth controlled one quarter of the world's land surface and surely dominated the sea lanes as missionary work expanded dramatically. Spurgeon's attitude regarding imperialism shall be seen later.

The new era, no doubt, saw many dramatic changes for good. The Industrial Revolution brought its blessings as well as its blights. This movement produced more jobs and the cities grew as rapidly as their economies. By 1850, the country had become reasonably prosperous, although city slums still persisted. As the progress continued, real wages increased 45 percent between 1880 and 1896. Still, the Victorians faced urgent, perplexing problems. As pointed out, the economy with its *laissez faire* philosophy often slumped into recession. For example, the "great depression" of the early 1870s through the 1890s worked its hardships. The agrarian society began dissolving in the social revolution. Urbanization, with its increasing population in the burgeoning towns, forced to the fore the quandary of providing for the deep spiritual needs of the mobile people. Unfortunately, the lower classes of society, such as the blue collar workers, continued to suffer as the general strengthening of the social and religious life of England still left them relatively untouched.

One of the strange phenomena of British church life centers in the fact that the blue collar classes have never been reached with the Gospel in large numbers. The only exceptions of notoriety are the Wesley-Whitefield revival, the Salvation Army and similar missions, and to some extent, Spurgeon's ministry. The trade union movement, alongside the total impact of the Industrial Revolution, had created a large segment in society that became known in Britain simply as the "working class." Their ranks were made of the "serfs" from the towns and villages when the old feudal system and its remnants broke up. These new urbanites should have been ripe fields for evangelical churches. Yet, few were reached by the traditional approach to ministry. This opportunity challenged Spurgeon. He said, "In London, we are, as it were, in an ocean, and we may spread our nets as often as we please."[11] Traditional London working masses were all but disenfranchised from certain segments of society, and that mentality seemingly spilled over into the churches. Often segregated in the squalor of London's slums, they were cut off socially and economically from the upper classes who seemed to control much of church life. Thus the workers remained largely unreached by the Gospel, even though strong religious forces surged through the country. The churches in Britain to this day often remain primarily a middle-class institution. Spurgeon became in some sense an exception. A local newspaper declared:

> He received into church-membership a large number every week, but most of them were from the country, and it was quite cheering when by chance there happened to be one true Londoner.[12]

It must be granted, Spurgeon did not reach in great numbers for church membership masses of *old* Londoners. Still, the rural newcomers to the metropolis, many of whom on their arrival joined the lower ranks of society, responded positively to the ministry of the Metropolitan Tabernacle. In that sense, Spurgeon did touch lower class families for actual church membership. Moreover, in his evangelistic activities, working class people came to hear him, even if they did not join his church in large numbers. At any rate, Spurgeon saw himself as reaching such people. In a sermon entitled "Heaven or Hell," which he preached in a field beside King Edward's Road in Hackney, he said, "I have been accused of getting all the rubble of London around me." He said that proudly. He had real appeal to that segment of society, at least more so than the Established Church.

With all these religious dynamics and movements, we must come to grips with the Victorian Church to understand the tremendous impact Spurgeon made.

VICTORIAN RELIGIOUS MOVEMENTS

R. K. A. Ensor has said, "No one will ever understand Victorian England who does not appreciate that among the highly civilized, in contradistinction to more primitive countries, it was one of the most religious that the world has known." [13]

Chaduck added to that sentiment by stating, "Throughout the Mid-Victorian age the evangelical movement was the strongest force in British life." [14] Somervell even goes so far as to say, "During the nineteenth century, Evangelicalism was the moral cement of English society." [15] Prime Minister William Gladstone added to these evaluations of the significance of religion in nineteenth century British life by saying, "I have known 95 of the world's great men in my time, and 87 of these were followers of the Bible." [16] The Victorians truly were "notoriously religious." Despite the growing humanism of the era, some form of the Christian faith influenced almost every level and vestige of society, at least ostensibly. One must grasp this fact to come to real grips with the deep dynamics of the Victorian years. Charles Haddon Spurgeon stood in the midst of this religious fervor, and influenced it tremendously. Meredith considers him perhaps the most significant voice since the days of Wesley and Whitefield. [17]

Yet paradoxically, as the nineteenth century progressed, rational skepticism seemed to grow with it, at least in the more intellectual circles. This aggressive skepticism precipitated a serious challenge to the churches. With these influences on the loose, continental philosophers and even some theologians launched radical attacks upon traditional views of the Bible. The works of men like David Strauss and Julius Wellhausen soon began to "expurgate, negate, or modify," as one put it, the whole Christian revelation as understood by the average nineteenth-century believer. Their writings shook the faith of many. The Victorian era introduced a period when it seemed the vigorous forces of new thought would reduce historic Christianity to a position of very little influence in western life.

Three ascending philosophical views made their claim on the British religious mindset: utilitarianism, evolution, and idealism. Utilitarians held that any action is right if it can be proved by its own "rightness," that is, if it gives the greatest amount of pleasure to the greatest amount of people. Jeremy Benthaus (1748-1832) became something of the author of utilitarianism, although it had earlier roots in Epicurianism, Thomas Hobbes, and David Hume. The evolutionary hypothesis, of course, had its birth in Charles Darwin (1809-1882). [18] Herbert Spencer (1820-1903) developed the evolutionalogy hypothesis into an all-inclusive philosophical system. The impact of Darwinian thought was tremendous and remains so to the present hour, although modified extensively. Perhaps the most direct attack on traditional, orthodox faith arose from the new spirit fostered by scientism and rationalistic biblical criticism. This so-called "Rise of Rationalism" generated many doubts in the belief systems of ordinary Victorians. It boasted many powerful names. Philosophers like Immanuel Kant, and probably above all, Frederick von Hegel, the originator of Absolute Idealism, are some of its authors and progenitors, although its roots go back centuries. The powerful impact of epistemological rationalism forced the Church of England to fall into the futile exercise of attempting to reconcile Christianity with science and radical biblical criticism. As an example of this approach, Benjamin Jowett and Frederick Temple published *Essays and Reviews* in 1860, while in 1862 John William Colenso produced *The Pentateuch Critically Examined*. Fortunately, the evangelical bishops of the Church of England along with other evangelical leaders widely condemned these publications. Of course, the empiricism and rationalism of the nineteenth century produced many benefits in scientific advance. For this there is much to be grateful, but when a purely rational, empirical epistemology (search for truth) is applied to Scripture, serious problems always emerge. For example, no rational difficulty arises with the biblical declaration that Jesus sat by the seashore and taught. But then the Scriptures state he fed 5,000 with a few fish and loaves and went away walking on the water. That last declaration of the Bible is not purely rational, it is revelational. If one pits rationalism over against revelation and in the process makes rationalism the supreme epistemological criteria, real trouble begins. That, in essence, is what "new thought" proposed. It resulted in a reductionism that drained the supernatural elements from the Word of God. Hegel made God himself wholly rational. His dictum became: "The Real is rational, the rational is Real." That virtually destroyed God's ultimacy. Spurgeon, as can be imagined, valiantly battled this approach in the so-called "Down Grade Controversy" that shall be investigated later.

Anti-supernaturalism and secularism spread throughout the more intellectual classes of Britain—it had already captured the minds of many continentals. The final fallout of the rationalistic reductionism of these intellectuals reduced Christianity to merely the ethical teachings of the Bible. They contended, at least the extreme radicals in the movement, the only real contribution of the New Testament centered in Jesus' ethical and moral teachings. In the so-called "quest for the historical Jesus," the transcendental, historical elements of the faith: the miracles, the divinity of Christ, the substitutionary atonement, the resurrection, etc. were downplayed, if not outright rejected. Yet at the same time, the masses of Victorian working classes found such fundamentally important controversies far removed from their daily lives. They could generate little concern or interest in these arguments. For the better part, they just believed the Bible for what it says.

However, as is so often the case, when a new philosophy emerges on the scene, it tends to take the day. Toward the end of the century, the influence of the rationalistic, skeptical thinkers and theologians enjoyed a wide hearing in many circles. Thus there were pleas for revolutionary and radically liberal creeds. These, of course, Spurgeon and the evangelicals rejected. As stated, Spurgeon was very much alive to these dynamics, finally putting his life and ministry on the line in protest. Spurgeon did not oppose modern scientific thought *per se*. He believed in what he termed "real science." But anything that contradicted God's clear Word, Spurgeon unequivocally rejected.

Still, and in spite of all the rational offensives launched against orthodox Christianity, the nineteenth century became a religious epoch. As Owen Chadwick expressed it:

> Victorian England was religious. Its churches thrived and multiplied, its best minds brooded over divine metaphysics and argued about moral principle, its authors and painters and architects and poets seldom forgot that art and literature shadowed eternal truth or beauty, its allegiance to divine law, its men of empire ascribed national greatness to the providence of God and Protestant faith.[19]

During this turbulent time, tremendous spiritual movements roared through the nation like the new steam locomotives. Three primary religious movements were afoot in those dynamic days: Roman Catholicism, the Church of England, and Nonconformity.

THE ROMAN CHURCH

The Roman Catholic Church had little strength in early Victorian Britain. It suffered the brunt of many attacks from the evangelical wing of the Church of England and the Nonconformists—Spurgeon being no exception in firing broadsides against Rome. The Vatican possessed little appeal to evangelicals of any ilk. Beginning with the dissolution of the monasteries by Henry VIII, carried through by Elizabeth I and James I, the Church of England (especially the Puritan wing of the Church) fought for reformation. The Puritan movement became the real heart of the British version of the continental Reformation. Space precludes discussing that fascinating historical battle here, although something of its spiritual impact will be approached shortly. However, there remained vestiges of Romanism in so-called "high-church" Anglicanism. In that arena, the war still raged. It will be remembered that Prince Albert felt the reformation of the Church of England must go further. Spurgeon surely would agree wholeheartedly with Albert. It should be understood that Spurgeon entertained throughout life a very negative attitude toward Romanism. For example, a fellow Baptist once said to Spurgeon he had attended a Catholic Mass in Paris and had "felt very near the presence of God." Spurgeon replied that this proved the text, "If I make my bed in hell, behold thou art there."[20] But then, it must be realized that such an attitude toward Rome was typical of Nonconformity in the Victorian period.

THE ANGLICAN CHURCH

At the beginning of the Victorian years, Anglicanism found itself in some disarray. For example, over half of the clergy did not even live in their own parish. In this context, a deep-seated need for reform arose. To some extent the Oxford Movement addressed that need. This new thrust oriented a reasonably large segment of the church toward the Anglo-Catholic temperament and brought about a certain amount of renewal to the Church of England.

THE TRACTARIANS

The Oxford Movement, or Tractarian Movement as it became known because of a series of published tracts, sprang into being in 1833. It could not be called a purely religious phenomenon; rather, it emerged more or less as a political-religious reaction against the impact created by the Reform Bill of 1832. Its birth came about as an effort to reassert the spiritual and historical authority of the Anglican church. However, it soon took on a strong theological and ecclesiastical tone that raised it to the level of a significant spiritual movement.

Three major figures surfaced in the thrust: John Keble, Edward Pusey, and John Henry Newman. Each man, vitally interested in keeping the basic foundations of high-church Anglicanism, sought to stem the erosion of the Church. John Keble is usually cited as creating the new mood. His approach, being more intuitional and instinctive rather than intellectual, became an inspiring motivator in the movement. The romanticism of the period had strongly influenced Keble.

Pusey, on the other hand, gained a reputation as a very able professor and theologian. He had a great love for the ceremonial. His whole understanding of Christian service centered in an utter commitment to a life of obedience to the Anglican Church. He influenced the movement tremendously. By 1840, the term "Puseyism" connoted the views of high-church Anglicanism at Oxford University. His students at Oxford gave Pusey strong support even though Pusey's approach on episcopal authority and elaborate liturgical rites took on the flavor of Roman Catholicism. A great study center remains in Oxford University to this day, known as "Pusey House."

Newman, however, became the central figure of the new emphasis and popularized the concepts. He had a powerful personality and influenced to some extent the whole religious life of the country. Newman, along with other scholars from Oxford, published a series of tracts calling Anglican clergymen to recognize their apostolic origin. As pointed out, this is what coined the phrase "Tractarian Movement." Newman believed the Established Church provided the only security for salvation. He expressed this in his series entitled *Tracts for the Times*. He published his first tract in September of 1833. Newman's high churchmanship expanded as the movement gained momentum. His most famous *Tract Ninety* openly confessed that the doctrinal positions of the Church of England were not at all incompatible with Roman Catholicism. This incensed the officials of Oxford University. It forced Newman in 1843 to leave Oxford and live in a rural home in Littlemore. In 1847, he made the move expected by all, a conversion to Roman Catholicism, becoming an ordained priest. He received his clerical orders at the Vatican itself.

Newman returned to England in 1879 and Pope Leo XIII elevated him as a cardinal. He became one of the leading Roman Catholic scholars of the Victorian age. His *Idea of a University* (1852), advocating liberal education, proved a watershed publication. His *Apology of pro vita sua*, written in 1864, stands as one of the most important autobiographical works of the era.

As can be imagined, the Oxford Movement with its interest in intellectual and liturgical matters had no widespread impact on the working classes with their meager education. Spurgeon agreed with the tractarian emphasis on God revealing Himself in nature and creation, but the London pastor rejected virtually all the rest of the movement. Tractarian theology and high churchmanship did not suit Spurgeon's understanding of the faith. He said, "Modern Tractarianism is a bastard popery, too mean, too shift, too double-dealing to delude men of honest minds."[21] Strong words indeed! However, to its credit, tractarianism did help the Established Church see its role in society. Moreover, the movement stressed the Church's mission to all people. This fresh emphasis appealed to certain segments of society. Further, despite its innate weaknesses, it did not become a pure "ivory tower" movement. Thus it brought at least a limited measure of new life to the old institutions of high-church Anglicanism. Keble, Pusey, and Newman in their differing ways proved that the Church could be saved from the deadening effect of institutionalism.

THE BROAD CHURCH MOVEMENT

In the same spirit, another movement permeated Anglicanism. It acquired the title: "The Broad Church Movement." Like the Tractarian Movement, the thrust arose out of dissatisfaction with the cold formalism of the Established Church and utilitarianism of nineteenth century Britain. Probably the impulse of romanticism gave it impetus as well. The movement began around 1830 and has also been called "Liberal Anglicanism." It took a latitudinarian approach to the Christian faith, following something of the philosophical idealism of Immanuel Kant. Kant said, "the true religion, . . . is now here and from now on is able to maintain itself on rational grounds." Following that basic tenet, revelation was given a subservient role, as previously described, and German rationalism dominated its theological approach. It resulted in a man centered religion. The movement thus reduced itself to simple theological liberalism. The adherents rejected the unique authority and inspiration of the Scriptures and declared the Bible should be read and critically examined just "like any other book."[22] Notable personalities such as Coleridge, F.D. Moeurice, and Charles Kingsley arose on this liberal scene. They felt fostering social justice should be the prime work of the Church. Thus they precipitated liberal theology and a social gospel. Of course, Spurgeon adamantly opposed such an approach. He said, "Our grand object is not the revision of opinions, but the regeneration of natures. We would bring men to Christ."

ANGLICAN EVANGELICALISM

However, evangelicalism also formed a most significant stream in the Church of England. Historian Latourette contended that because of the dynamic revival movements of the nineteenth century, the Church of England had its real evangelical reformation in that century, not the seventeenth century as commonly held. During those dramatic days, Evangelicals in the Established Church founded several new theological colleges for preparing their ministers. For example, the London College of Divinity in 1863, Wycliffe Hall in Oxford, 1877, and Ridley Hall in Cambridge, 1881, were established. Among Anglican Evangelicals, the Keswick Convention arose in 1875. This new emphasis sought the nourishing of spiritual life. The annual Keswick gatherings also had great success among Nonconformists and continental Pietists. Keswick continues to this day, although not with the strength it once enjoyed.

The new liberalizing spirit of the Victorians profoundly affected all Evangelicals. This proved to be true especially for Nonconformist Evangelicals. The Test and Corporation Acts were finally repealed after nearly a century-and-a-half. These old, archaic laws made it virtually impossible for Nonconformists of any theological persuasion to exert much influence outside their own circle. They were barred from significant political activity. The repeal now opened Parliament to them. There remained a subtle sense of social inferiority to be sure, but things were obviously changing to the benefit of all Evangelicals.

THE NONCONFORMISTS

As a result of the new spirit of the age, Nonconformity grew among the masses and became the most vigorous religious movement in British history since the Reformation. The only possible equal was the great Wesley-White-field awakening of the previous century. Nonconforming Protestants, often called "Dissenters," and later the "free church" movement, increasingly became prominent in the religious life of the country. The large majority of Protestant Nonconformists consisted of five groups: Presbyterians, Independents or Congregationalists, Baptists, Quakers, and Methodists. Most "protestors" were urban middle-class believers. The small villages often boasted good Protestant churches as well, although their numbers were very small. Nonconformity thus grew rapidly through the growing industrialization and urbanization process. If anyone were to make inroads to the working classes, the Nonconformists had the best opportunity.

Earlier in the Victorian era, as previously made clear, Nonconformists struggled under legal restrictions and pressure. The Established Church had virtual control of the religious life of Britain, at least the legal side of religion. C. H. Spurgeon always strongly advocated disestablishment of the Church to break up that monolith of power. Considerable abuse did occur, especially earlier in the century. For example, Nonconformists were not accepted for degrees in Oxford and Cambridge. Institutions like Dr. Williams' Library in London grew up as an alternative in the training of Nonconformist ministers. Protestant clergy could not perform the marriages of their church members in their own churches. They could not even officiate at the funeral services in their churchyards. Fortunately, by the middle of the century, many restrictions were eliminated. Oxford and Cambridge began admitting Nonconformists. Most significantly, the movement experienced great strength through the spiritual awakenings that moved through Evangelicalism generally. The revival of 1859, generated through the influence of the prayer revival in the United States, swept across Ulster, Scotland, Wales, and finally England. Through this revival, one million people joined churches. Charles G. Finney and later Dwight L. Moody, along with C. H. Spurgeon, were among the moving spirits of these awakenings. As will be seen in full detail later, Charles Haddon Spurgeon did much to influence this revival setting.

Although the Established Church and Rome had their adherents, Evangelicalism provided much of the dynamic faith to Victorian Britain. As far as the vast majority of church attenders were concerned, it virtually captured the religious scene. As one historian put it, "the Evangelical Awakening formed the bed-rock of early Victorian religion."[23] It tended to be a lay movement in some respects, even at times manifesting an anticlerical character. The positive results were a general religious influence in society that moved many to church on Sundays, and many to genuine faith in Jesus Christ. This gave Evangelicalism a more acceptable image and status in society.

As the Nonconformists began acquiring a new position in society, they also began to influence the abolition of slavery, the championing of free trade, and the repeal of many restrictions of the Established Church. Church taxes were abolished in 1868. Oxford and Cambridge Universities fully opened their doors to Nonconformists and Roman Catholics by 1871. Nine years later, in 1880, the burial acts removed the last of the major grievances. Step by step the Evangelicals moved forward. The influence of men like Spurgeon played a major role in these reforms.

Evangelicalism proved to be quite different from Rome and the Tractarians in its approach to liturgy and worship. For the Evangelicals, the focus of their services centered on the sermon. Great preachers like R.W. Dale, Alexander Maclaren, Charles Haddon Spurgeon, Joseph Parker and others tremendously influenced the whole religious outlook of England and other English-speaking countries.

The influence of Evangelicalism flowed in two channels through Britain, viz, "low church" Anglicanism and especially in the Nonconforming churches such as the Baptists, Methodists, Presbyterians, Congregationalists, Brethren and other Independents. The approach of the evangelical Nonconformists can be seen in two theological perspectives. Most analysts agree that the first ingredient can be found in seventeenth-century Puritanism. The Puritans emphasized order, law, and authority. Secondly, Nonconformists were impacted by the fervor, vitality, and enthusiasm of the eighteenth-century revival. Experience rather than argument greatly influenced Evangelicalism.

In theology, Nonconformity ranged from the moderate Calvinism of the majority to the evangelical Arminianism of the Methodists. Varieties of evangelical thought abounded. However, certain broad principles were tenaciously held. Even though traditional Calvinism slowly declined, evangelicals still preached the cross, the depravity of mankind, and justification by faith alone. However, due to the erosion in Reformed thought, most rejected extreme views of the doctrines of predestination and reprobation. Yet, most evangelicals still embraced something of the Calvinistic concept of sovereign grace. A kind of modified Calvinism seemed to be developing that embraced some, but not all, of the edicts of the Synod of Dort. Puritanism still influenced Evangelicalism.

As stated earlier, Evangelicalism was certainly not restricted to Nonconformity. It thrived in "low-church" Anglicanism. The Puritan-pietistic movement of the sixteenth and seventeenth century left that legacy. The question is often raised, "Who were these people called Puritans?" Such a query is important to this study, because Spurgeon saw himself as a recipient of that Puritan legacy. Gladstone gave him the title, the "Last of the Puritans." A brief historical review of the movement makes it clear why Spurgeon so admired the Puritans and studied them avidly; and actually became one.

THE PURITAN MOVEMENT

History has not been too kind to the Puritan movement, at least in some circles. This is somewhat unjustified because the Puritans in their finest expression were simply godly people who stressed piety, evangelism and social work. This is true of the Puritan dissenters and those in the Anglican Church as well. For example, William Wilberforce, a product of the Wesley-Whitefield revival, the greatest Parliamentary orator of his day, is credited with abolishing the slave trade. The Puritan-pietistic movement left a remarkable legacy to the nineteenth century. A significant historical chain reaction occurred over most of Europe in the movement that brought dynamic days to European and American Christianity. A brief look at this development will aid in understanding the "Last of the Puritans."

To pinpoint the prime patriarch of Puritan-pietism proves rather difficult. The spiritual roots reach deep into medieval mysticism. Nonetheless, several historians start with the sixteenth-century preacher, William Perkins of Warwickshire. He is considered by many as the progenitor of the pious. Others claim John Hooper of Somerset as the "morning star" of the movement. [24] Arthur Hildersham also made an early impact on the movement. Regardless of whom we tap as the beginner, most agree that the movement had its birth in English religious circles. But it must be admitted that almost simultaneously the new spirit dawned on the Continent. Perhaps the awakening simply rose as the morning sunrise on the whole Western European religious scene among Teutonic peoples as a reaction to the so-called "Protestant Scholasticism" that had darkened the Reformation scene. Yet, a chain of influence can be demonstrated beginning in England.

The theological roots of the thrust received their sustenance primarily from the Zwingli-Bucer-Calvin axis of the Reformation. It began to show its early, essential characteristics within English Puritanism and the Dutch Reformed churches of the seventeenth century. These in turn influenced Lutheranism through spiritual giants like Arndt, Spener, Francke, Bengel and their followers. It will help our understanding of the vast influence of the movement to see this historical development in more detail.

PURITAN BEGINNINGS

Many Anglo-Saxons have been fond of linking the phenomenon of Puritanism primarily, if not exclusively, to older purely English traditions. It seems significant, however, when the earliest Puritans quoted books of devotion, they often referred to Continental mystics. Furthermore, in the openness of Edward VI of England to the Continental Reformation, many exiles from the Netherlands, Germany, and even Italy came to London. When they were later forced to leave, along with many Englishmen, under the persecution of Mary, they traveled to continental centers such as Geneva, Zurich, Basel, Strasbourg, and Frankfurt. In this setting the British-Continental pietistic mix apparently began and the piety of the reformed tradition sunk its taproot into European soil generally.

Furthermore, Calvin's *Institutes* were translated into English, profoundly influencing early Puritan thought. In this Calvinistic context William Perkins made his significant impact. Although he died young, his accomplishments were amazing. He is little known today, yet throughout the seventeenth century, England and the American colonies regarded him as but a little less than Calvin himself. After his untimely death a contemporary wrote, "The precious name of Mr. Perkins shall like an ointment poured forth, fill all quarters of this land with a fresh and fragrant sweetness."[25] Other names linked to the Perkins' tradition were Richard Rogers, John Dod, Henry Smith, and John Cotton of New England.

By the dawn of the eighteenth century, there was what has been called "a flood tide of Godliness."[26] Skyrocketing on the scene came men like John Downame, Daniel Dyke, and John Smyth. Stellar spiritual stars were Richard Baxter, the epitome of Puritan-pietism, John Bunyan of the mighty pen, Jeremy Taylor and a host of others. By the end of this dramatic century, Puritan-pietism had the corner on dynamic Christianity in Britain.

THE MOVE TO THE NETHERLANDS

Across the English Channel, the churches of pietistic persuasion were unified in spirit under the theological orbit of the Netherlands. Dutch Reformed Pietism was almost the direct result of British Puritan influence. William W. Teellinck of the Netherlands, who is usually regarded as the father of Continental Pietism, came to England several times and fell under the influence of John Dod and Arthur Hildersham. His conversion took place in a Puritan home in Britain. William Ames, the early systematic theologian of Dutch Pietism and a most influential leader, had been a student at Cambridge and a devoted disciple of William Perkins. At the same time, however, it must be recognized that long standing traditions of piety were native to the Netherlands as personified in men like Gerhard Groote, Ruysbrocek, the Brethren of the Common Life, the Anabaptists, and Pre-reformation mystics such as Coornhert. Nonetheless, Teellinck and Ames among others were deeply indebted to English Puritanism.

A short time later Lodensteyn of Delft arose on the horizon. He was an especially effective preacher and pastor. He shared the convictions of his predecessors, the Puritans and Teellinck. Others followed such as Brakel, John Teellinck (William's son), Saldenus, and deLabadie, the radical Pietist.

At this junction, Pietism moved from its early base in the Low Countries and permeated northwestern Germany. The outstanding personality among the early Pietists in Germany was Theodore Untereyck of Mulheim. Studying at Utrecht in the Netherlands, influenced by Lodensteyn and other Dutchmen, he was converted in that pietistic context. Others soon came along, such as Neander the hymnologist, Alardin, and Buchfelder. The German historian Paulus Scharpff tells us that, "because of lively communications between the Reformed of the Netherlands and those of western Germany, Dutch Reformed Pietism was the first of several piestic movements to penetrate Germany."[27] This surging new movement quickly began to influence Lutheranism.

ADVENT OF LUTHERAN PIETISM

The rapid rise of Lutheran Pietism must be viewed against the backdrop of deep-seated religious hostilities, the Thirty Years War in particular. These socio-religious upheavals opened the German mind for the advent of the awakening. Further, a growing reaction against sterile Lutheranism also set the stage along with the foundation laid in the mystical elements of Luther's own writings. Luther's indebtedness to the mystical writings of Tauler and the Friends of God is clear.

From English Puritanism, through the Dutch, and then into northwest Germany, the movement spread far and wide in the Lutheran church. John Arndt (1555-1621) became the most significant early personality of Lutheran Pietism. Although he always considered himself a true Lutheran, his pietistic orientation took a central place in his understanding of Christian experience. Sadly, some of Arndt's followers became extremists. But the influence of John Arndt himself proved most significant and widespread, especially through his great work *True Christianity*. Few devout Lutheran homes would have been without a copy.

PHILIPP SPENER

Others followed in the pietistic historical train until Philipp Jakob Spener (1635-1705) arrived on the scene. Spener grew up in surroundings in which a "mixture of Arndtian and Puritan piety set the tone for daily living."[28] Often called the "name most intimately associated with Pietism,"[29] Spener took his master's and doctor's degrees at the University of Strasbourg where he lectured until 1659. Often hearing the preaching of deLabodie the Dutch pietist, he remarkably combined Arndt's mysticism and practical Puritan attention to daily piety. He rose high in the Christian circles of his day. In 1670 he founded the famous *collegia pietatis* in Frankfurt. This was Spener's term for small Bible study groups. Five years later he published his classical *Pious Desires*. Though constantly in the center of controversy, he never permitted himself to lapse to the level of his critics. His genuine piety secured the admiration of most. The strain of the controversy, however, finally led to his acceptance of the pastorate of Saint Nicholas Church in Berlin where he lived out his last years.

Spener's promotion of the *collegia pietatis* became one of the prime factors that sparked the flames of controversy that raged around him. Granted, the idea of small groups meeting to study and deepen the spiritual life of believers—the essence of the *collegia pietatis*—was hardly revolutionary in itself. What fanned the flames centered in the fact that he offered a definite program to implement the scheme and then proceeded to promote it. He felt that the Lutheran Reformation had stopped short at the reformation of doctrine and had failed to include the reformation of the spiritual life. This approach, as could be expected, came to be viewed as a threat by the traditionalists. Yet Spener argued that even Luther recognized the principle. Spener was thus determined to carry Reformed theology to its logical and practical conclusion. This spawned the *collegia* and laid out the program for developing what he called the *eccelesialae in ecclesia*, the true church within the institutional church. His genius can be seen in that he became one of the first to grasp the full implications of the priesthood of all believers.

Spener stood as a significant figure in the entire pietistic movement. He closed one era and ushered in another. Actually, the term "Pietist" was first used in 1664 to designate his Frankfurt disciples. He became a man for the hour—and for all seasons. The speculations of the "Protestant schoolmen" no longer attracted the minds of young churchmen. Spener's widespread influence wielded a severe blow to sterile orthodoxy and brought about a new fresh wind of the Spirit throughout Lutheranism. In a very short time, however, the mantle of Pietism's Elijah fell on a young Elisha: August Hermann Francke. Through the ministry of this young prophet, the Lord God of Elijah significantly manifested himself.

HERMANN FRANCKE

Francke (1663-1727) was born twenty-eight years after Philipp Spener. As Spener stood as the preaching giant of German pietism, Francke became its educator *par excellence*. Trained in the universities of Erfurt, Kiel, and Leipzig, he was destined to become the new central figure of the movement among Lutherans.

After Francke completed his education, he moved to Erfurt to serve as an assistant pastor in a local church. There he began his teaching ministry by presenting practical lectures on the Scriptures for university students. The traditional professors took a rather negative view of such teaching. Soon he followed his mentor's footsteps in persecution. Pressure mounted until he was given only forty-eight hours to get out of town. The very day he received his eviction notice, however, he received an appointment as professor of Greek and Oriental languages at the University of Halle. In a few years the University elevated him to full professor of theology. This fortunate move to Halle came through the influence of his pietistic father, Philipp Spener.

Francke found his life's work at Halle. Very popular with the students, he combined intellectual ability with a warm, devoted Christian experience. Through his educational ministry, the University of Halle became the radiating center of pietistic influence.

Francke also gave himself to ardent social work. His creative genius produced a myriad of social ministry. He labored in deprived sections of his city and transformed whole areas.

Francke's writings, however, probably stand as his most significant contribution. His famous *Directions for Profitable Bible Study* influenced many. His works were known and appreciated in all of Europe and America. Susanna Wesley, John Wesley's mother, became a faithful reader. John himself later traveled to Halle and came to appreciate the movement. Franke carried on voluminous correspondence. The American Puritan preacher Cotton Mather became a constant recipient of his letters. Pietism took the offensive under Francke. Before the eighteenth century few attempts at world evangelization were launched, except in a colonialism context. But now a "resurgence of the unquenchable evangelistic spirit in Christianity"[30] erupted. In 1705, a small contingent of Halle and Dutch Pietists set out for India, almost one hundred years before William Carey went to that nation. This became the prime move for Protestant mission work in the Far East.

Francke's full contribution to Pietism is difficult to assess. To say the least, he certainly became a turning point in the movement. His social, educational, and missionary emphases brought profound depth and a powerful thrust to the awakening.

THE MORAVIAN REVIVAL

Francke's star pupil, destined for fame and notoriety, was Count Nikolaus Ludwig von Zinzendorf (1700-1760). Growing up in a pietistic family (his father was close to Spener), he spent several years studying at Halle. During those days he took his noon meal with Francke himself. The influence of Francke and Halle proved incalculable on the young Count.

After Halle, Zinzendorf studied law at Wittenburg. But he could not be content with a career in law. As he said, his only passion was "to live for the One who has given his life for him, and to lead others to Jesus."[31] In 1727, he received ordination as a Lutheran minister.

By 1722, displaced, persecuted Moravian Brethren (the "Hussites from old Moravia") had begun to gather at Herrnhut, the small village on Count Zinzendorf's estate. In a Herrnhut religious service one Lord's Day, the heavens opened and the great Moravian revival broke. From this outpouring of the Spirit, the whole pietistic movement spread to many distant points.

The history of Moravian missions is legendary. No doubt, Zinzendorf shone as the guiding star and inspiration of the world thrust. He traveled far and near preaching the Word. He sailed to America and met much success despite considerable opposition. Five productive years were spent ministering in England. His missionaries touched innumerable places and lives. Scharpff declares, "Zinzendorf was undoubtedly the most unique and outstanding personality of eighteenth century Pietism in Germany."[32]

Through the Moravian contribution, Pietism began to complete its circle of development and move back to Britain where it had begun under the influence of early Puritans like William Perkins.

BACK TO ENGLAND AND THE EIGHTEENTH-CENTURY AWAKENING

The role played by the Moravians in the Wesley-Whitefield drama is well known. Of course, the Wesley brothers' conversion was not wholly dependent upon Moravian influence, as some have advocated, and they influenced George Whitefield even less. Other movements such as the various religious societies that emerged in England in reaction to seventeenth-century rationalism made their contribution. Anthony Harnech of the deLabodie pietistic school significantly touched those societies, and sensitive minds like the members of Wesley's and Whitefield's Oxford Holy Club were deeply impressed. Francke's writings also influenced the parents of John and Charles Wesley. It is also clear that the Wesleys and Whitefield were strongly impressed by the Puritan tradition. Whitefield's Calvinism accounts for the eighteenth century concern for methodical holiness.

Still, the Moravian testimony directly precipitated John Wesley's famous "Aldersgate" experience. John first became open to this testimony after he saw the calmness of the Moravian Brethren on the storm-tossed ship bound for Georgia on the voyage to America. This story is often repeated. Later in America, the following interview took place between John Wesley and the Moravian bishop, Professor Spangenberg of Jena:

> Spangenberg: "Do you know Jesus Christ?"
> Wesley: "I know he is the Savior of the World."
> Spangenberg: "True, but do you know that he has saved you?"
> Wesley: "I hope he has died to save me."
> Spangenberg (later): "I fear they were vain words."

Back in England, a short time later, John Wesley wrote in his journal:

> Wednesday, May 24, 1738. In the evening I went very unwillingly to the (Moravian) Society in Aldersgate Street, where one was reading Luther's preface to the Epistle to the Romans. About a quarter before nine, while he was describing the change wrought by God in the heart through faith in Christ, I felt my heart strangely warmed. I felt I did trust Christ, Christ alone, for salvation and an assurance was given me that He had taken away my sins, even mine, and saved me from the law of sin and death.

A few months later, along with some Moravian Brethren, the great Fetter's Lane "Little Pentecost" occurred and the great Wesley-Whitefield revival fully dawned.

George Whitefield, as is well known, had his evangelical experience some two years prior to John Wesley and was preaching very effectively. Charles Wesley preceded his brother in conversion as well. But now George, John, and Charles joined hearts and arms as never before, and the movement started that historians contend saved England from a fate similar to the devastating French Revolution.

Thus, with the pietistic writings and the influence of the Moravian movement upon Britain through the Wesley-Whitefield awakening, mainstream Pietism returned to its English source. This does not mean Puritanism had died in Britain during the development of Continental Pietism. And, of course, important spin-offs impacted various places around the world. But the somewhat circular historical development of the movement from Perkins to the Low Countries, to northwest Germany, into the Lutheran stream, and then from the Moravians back to Britain is quite fascinating. What the English people sowed in germinal Puritanism it bountifully reaped a hundredfold in the great eighteenth century awakening. Moreover, the genius of Puritan-pietism makes it clear why Gladstone called Spurgeon "the last of the Puritans."

The great British eighteenth century awakening gave impetus to Evangelicalism in Britain and thus precipitated the "great century" that followed. In this entire mix, Spurgeon became a recipient of the blessings and emerged as a notable figure. Evangelicalism took on a new aggressiveness as it drank from the riches of the Puritan-pietistic legacy. Actually, it finally resulted in Evangelicalism becoming the strongest force in the Church in Britain. When a person was spoken of as "a serious Christian" or "a religious" person, it usually meant that he or she held evangelical traditions. This whole movement became Spurgeon's heritage. Moreover, the Puritan-pietistic approach set the stage and opened the heart and mind of Evangelicalism for the great Prayer Revival that proved so important in Spurgeon's early London ministry. By 1860, the evangelical prayer awakening had spread to every corner of Great Britain. Its matrix was the Puritan-pietistic thrust of two hundred years running.

One of the significant effects of the Prayer Revival centered in a renewed concern for the poor and suffering. A host of practical philanthropists arose, going straight to the heart of the slums of industrial England to alleviate suffering and injustice, always willing to foster any legislation or action that would bring about social improvement. Lord Shaftesbury worked as never before.[33] New orphanages were founded and a society was established for the Prevention of Cruelty to Children (1889). The licensing of prostitution was repealed. A host of ministries developed.

Oxford and Cambridge were profoundly affected by the 1860 prayer movement. Weekly prayer meetings at Oxford grew rapidly, finally forming the Daily Prayer Meeting, which has been held each day in term for over 100 years. Cambridge experienced a similar movement of prayer and renewed dedication to evangelical piety and service. But what role did Spurgeon's Baptists play?

THE BAPTISTS

Spurgeon proudly claimed to be a Baptist. The Baptist movement, although not the largest of the Nonconformist element in British Evangelicalism, still proved to be significant. Throughout his life, Spurgeon devoted himself to that particular denomination. The choice to become a Baptist proved to be a prophetic decision, because through the years the Baptists grew into one of the largest Protestant denominations in the world. In that growth and development Spurgeon played no small part.

As previously seen, Spurgeon's early years unfolded outside the Baptist tradition. After his conversion experience in the Primitive Methodist chapel, his Congregational parents and grandparents were startled that he should choose the Baptist way of expressing his Christian life and ministry. An interesting and rather humorous anecdote arose in this context. After he announced to his parents his determination to become a Baptist, his mother said to him, "Son, I have often prayed for your conversion, but I never thought you would become a Baptist." Charles, with his usual quick wit, replied, "Mother, that shows you that God has not only answered your prayers but has done exceeding abundantly above all you asked or thought." But a more serious story lies behind Spurgeon's commitment to being baptized by immersion—the Baptist way—and thus entering into the Baptist fold. That story must wait for a future chapter, however. Nonetheless, it will be helpful to see how Baptists came on the religious scene in Victorian Britain. Insight into Spurgeon's commitment to Baptists and their rituals can then be better understood.

The Baptist movement initially began as a particularly British sect having emerged out of the left wing of the English protestant Reformation movement. Some historians contend that the new thrust was influenced by different groups on the Continent, particularly the Anabaptists. There may be some validity in this claim, but Baptist origins and theology are basically English. In this left wing of the British Reformation movement, one particular dissenting group became convinced that baptism should be applied to believers only. As a result, they outright rejected pedo-baptism. They reached this position because of a deep and profound commitment to a very high view of the Scriptures. These dissenters discovered no case of infant baptism in the New Testament. Church tradition fell to a secondary role as the Reformed concept of *sola scriptura* dominated their thinking. They then moved on and came to the conclusion that the baptism believers should receive is total immersion. In many early Baptist documents, the term "baptism" is often supplanted by the term "dipping." As these developments solidified, and as the movement spread, churches began to be planted and they acquired the nickname "Baptists."

Two basic groups of Baptists emerged in Britain in the early days of the movement: the General Baptists, the older of the two groups, and the Particular Baptists, who came on the scene approximately thirty years later. The terms "general" and "particular" centered in their differing theological views concerning the atonement. As the names imply, the General Baptists held to a general atonement, that is, they contended that the atonement of Christ, effected by his crucifixion and resurrection, should be applied to all people who would repent and believe. The Particular Baptists, holding to a high-Calvinistic view of the atonement, believed that Christ died only for the elect; therefore, only the elect could be saved. The General Baptists date from 1609 and the first Particular Baptist church was constituted in London in 1638.

Another important distinction separated these two groups. The General Baptists were more "connectional" in their denominational attitude than were the Particular Baptists. They had a closer knit fellowship among the various congregations. Not only that, at times they were rather hostile toward the Church of England. The Particular Baptists, to the contrary, held a more fluid attitude concerning separatism and "connectionalism." The churches tended to be far more independent in their stance relative to one another.

These early Baptists were rather scattered throughout England. They did not form anything that could be properly called a denomination. Nevertheless, they eventually began to grow in numbers and thus began to share specific confessions of faith. This precipitated a more united stance, and as a result, a more cohesive denominational life began to emerge.

British Baptists, strangely enough, did not have their actual birth in Britain. A group of separatists had made an exodus from England to Amsterdam. Among them were Hughe and Anne Bromheade, prominent lay-leaders. Their ministerial leader was John Smyth. Because of persecution in Britain in 1609, they made their way across the English Channel and the small group began to meet together in the Dutch city. It can be marked as the first Baptist church in any modern sense of the word. The British believers in Amsterdam believed in the idea of a general atonement and thus gave birth to the General Baptist churches.

In the early days of the General Baptists, baptism by immersion was not strictly adhered to. It took some years before the insistence arose that all believers should be immersed. Most historians hold that the restrictive demand of immersion for all church members was not actually introduced among the Baptists until 1640-1641. For example, William Whitsitt (1841-1911), a Southern Baptist historian in America, drew this conclusion. It caused considerable controversy in his day, as there were those who felt Baptists can be traced historically back to the first century and the ministry of John the Baptist. Regardless of the historical debate on the issue, it can be concluded that immersion as a mode of baptism followed the belief in believer's baptism not too many years after the founding of the first Baptist church in Amsterdam. To this day, however, some Baptist churches in Britain do not adhere to the strict rule of insisting on immersion for church membership. These churches are called "open membership churches."

It was probably inevitable that some of the British Baptists in Amsterdam would return home and establish a church. This they did in 1611. The new congregation rose up and grew under the leadership of Thomas Helwys (1570-1615). Helwys had helped John Smyth form the Baptist church in Amsterdam in 1609. Two years later he led a remnant back to England and in that setting the Baptists first took root at Spitilsfield in London. This became the foundation of the General Baptist work in Britain.

As can be imagined, serious difficulties, even persecutions, arose for the Baptists. Being separatists, they were under pressure from the Established Church. Not only that, accepting believer's baptism exclusively, they repudiated infant baptism. This put them in double jeopardy in their relationship to the Anglicans. But they were stalwart people and stood firm in their convictions.

The reason behind much of the opposition of the Church of England revolved not just around the Baptist view of adult baptism itself, but around the theology it clearly implied. Anglican dogma stated that baptism grafted a child into Christ, thus becoming the antidote for original sin. This endowed baptism with sacramental regenerative power. The Established Church held that baptism bestowed this power even irrespective of the faith of the parents. For all practical purposes, baptism in Anglican thought became "baptismal regeneration." Against this dogma Spurgeon spoke vehemently and gave birth to the so-called "Baptismal Regeneration Controversy." That interesting story waits for a future chapter. Yet, it can be seen that the early ventures of the Baptists in Britain did not have an easy road to travel because of their views on the subject.

A few years after the beginning of the London work in 1611, another significant church was established in Bristol. This church, known as the Broadmead Baptist Church, became a leader in the early years of the movement and continues to the present day. It became a paradigm of the succeeding stages through which separatist Baptists developed. They first rejected infant baptism and favored believer's baptism. Eventually they advocated baptism by immersion. Paradoxically, the Broadmead Church became an open membership church. However, this type of development was not uncommon throughout Britain during the seventeenth century. As pointed out earlier, immersion for all members was not introduced in the British Baptist churches in any generalized sense until about 1641. This is made clear by the fortieth article of the *Confession of Faith of the Seven Congregations of Churches of Christ in London, 1644*. This early document prescribed immersion as the mode of believer's baptism with the following words:

> That the way in manner that the dispensing of this ordinance is dipping or punching under waters; it being a sign must answer the thing signified, which is that interest the saints have in the death, burial and resurrection of Christ; and that as certainly as the body is buried under the water and risen again; so

certainly shall the bodies of the saints be raised by the power of Christ in the day of the resurrection to reign with Christ.

The Confession of 1644 is the first confession where immersion was described and stands as proof positive of the change that was made in the early '40s. Not only that, the name "Baptist" first came into use shortly after 1641. The derogatory name "Anabaptists" was always resisted by the brethren. They often designated themselves as those who were "unjustly called Anabaptists." As long as they sprinkled or poured as the mode of baptism, they perhaps could be readily called Anabaptists or "Repetition of Baptism." But now another act was introduced: immersion, and that opened the possibility for a new designation. Thus, they began to call themselves "Baptized Christians." In due time, as can be imagined, the simple term "Baptist" began to typify the movement. Before 1641, the followers of Helwys and his successor Murton held close fellowship with many Mennonites. In 1626, there was a movement inaugurated to effect the organic union of the two groups. But after 1641, those relationships were entirely eradicated. The Mennonites severed themselves from the possible union when many of the Baptists introduced immersion as the only scriptural mode of baptism.

An interesting anecdote arose out of the Broadmead Church in Bristol in 1671 (probably March 4, 1671). A certain S. Spurgeon became a deaconess of the Broadmead Church in that year. Moreover, persecution ran rampant against many of the Baptists in those days. Baptists suffered especially from the Conventicle Act (1644). This particular act outlawed any unauthorized religious gathering of more than five persons beyond one's immediate family. The Broadmead Church experienced the harshness of this law, and so, no doubt, did S. Spurgeon. Actually, religious bounty hunters were paid to ferret out illegal worship gatherings. Charles Spurgeon, sensitive to his ancestry, especially if some endured persecution for their faith, would revel in any connection between this S. Spurgeon and himself. No connection can be authoritatively established, however.

It has been pointed out that the General Baptists were essentially Arminian in their theology. In their first confession of faith (1611), this becomes very clear. Arminian ingredients in that confession are as follows:

> That God before the foundation of the world hath predestined all that believe in Him shall be saved, Ephesians 1:4, 12; Mark 16:16; and all that believe not shall be damned.

> That man may fall away from the grace of God, Hebrews 12:15; and from the truth which they have received and acknowledged, Hebrews 10:26; after they have tasted of the heavenly gift are partakers of the Holy Ghost, and have tasted of the good word of God and of the powers of the world to come.

Such doctrines were quite offensive to the Calvinists, and hence to the Particular Baptists who came on the scene in the 1640s. Particular Baptists held firmly to particular redemption and to the security of the believer, closely following the edicts of Dort. The *First London Confession of 1644* sets forth the theology held by the Particular Baptists. In this *Confession* the Baptists defended themselves against the charges of pelagianism, anarchism and immorality. They reasserted their strict adherence to essential Calvinistic doctrines. It must be said that although the 1644 *Confession* in general possesses a "Reformed" ethos, it does not represent the higher Calvinism that intruded itself quite strongly into the *Second London Confession of 1689.* The importance of the 1644 *Confession* centers in the fact that it formed the first Baptist confession of faith produced by a group of Particular churches. Moreover, it prescribes the form of baptism. Aspects of the *London Confession* are most interesting. For example, concerning the Scriptures, the *Confession* holds tenaciously that the Bible is the only:

> rule of . . . knowledge, faith and obedience, concerning the worship and service of God, and all other Christian duties. It is not man's inventions, opinions, devices, laws, constitutions or traditions unwritten whatsoever, but only the Word of the God contained in the canonical scriptures. In this written word, God has plainly revealed whatsoever he hath thought beforehand for us to know, believe, and acknowledge, touching the nature and office of Christ, in whom all the promises are yea and amen to the praise of God.

As implied above, the *Confession* also adheres to a very high Christology. It states:

> Touching his office, Jesus Christ only is made the mediator of the new covenant, even the everlasting covenant of grace between God and man, to be perfectly and fully the prophet, priest and king of the church of God forevermore.

The *Confession* itself is very long and stands as a landmark in early Particular Baptist theology.

There also exists a historic paper called the "Kiffin Manuscript." Although it is very brief, it represents one of the clearest and most authoritative accounts of one of the seedbeds of the Particular Baptist Movement in England. Further, the development of the Particular Baptist thrust can be viewed through the so-called JLJ Church as it emerged and developed in the Southwark section of London. This congregation was established in 1616. Henry Jacob became its first leader. The pastors who followed in Jacob's train were John Lenthrop and Henry Jersey, hence the JLJ Church acquired its nickname. They were rather mild separatists, but through the years they grew more rigid in their rejection of the Church of England. The separatist's spirit finally grew until the church became a thoroughgoing dissenting Baptist church. This congregation, along with other contemporary emerging Particular Baptist churches, adhered strictly to the "five point" Calvinistic theological system.

It is interesting that the Kiffin Manuscript shows that the JLJ Church came to believe that baptism ought to be dipping the body into the water, resembling burial and rising again (Colossians 2:12; Romans 6:4). This conviction was in place by 1640, one year earlier than the first record found among the General Baptists. It seems significant that this early Particular Baptist church had its origin in the Southwark area of London. Spurgeon became pastor of the New Park Street Baptist Church in that very spot. Particular Baptists apparently flourished in that section of the Capital.

Particular Baptist work, as described above, grew rapidly after its developmental inception. As a case in point, Thomas Collier (d. 1691) surfaced as a leading pastor in the west of England as the movement spread. An excellent theologian and a skillful church planter, his evangelistic zeal and adeptness enabled him to organize the many scattered churches into associations. He also brought together and moderated several theological differences between the General and Particular Baptists.

It should be noted that through the years as the Particular Baptists flourished, the General Baptists slowly slipped into decline and began to deteriorate. The General Baptists moved into a liberal theological stance, many ultimately becoming Unitarians and universalistic in their doctrine. They fell into the *Socinian* heresy. As a consequence, evangelistic fervor waned and weakness set in. Conversely, the Particular Baptists, with their Calvinistic theology and evangelistic zeal, planted churches all over Britain, becoming by far the most significant Baptist movement in the country.

One bright spot developed in General Baptist life, however. Although doctrinal controversy and spiritual decline characterized the General Baptists in the first half of the eighteenth century, the conversion of a man by the name of Dan Taylor (1738-1816) signaled hope. He became responsible for the formation of the so-called "New Connection." This New Connection brought a new spark of life to the General Baptists. It was a return to basic evangelicalism. The movement under Taylor became a Baptist reflection of the Wesley-Whitefield Revival. After 1770, the date of the founding of the thrust, Taylor and his New Connection reform movement grew into the most influential segment of General Baptist life in Britain. The element of the General Baptists known as the "Old Connection," that is, those who rejected Taylor's reform movement, finally declined to virtual extinction.

Taylor, a coal miner's son, came to Christ through the Wesleyan Movement. Later, however, he left the Methodists, becoming convinced the Scriptures taught believer's baptism. Taylor founded churches, schools, and developed a Christian literature ministry. He exercised an itinerant ministry, traveling and preaching throughout England. His ministry extended as far north as Yorkshire. Taylor's fellow reformers, William Thompson and John Slager, aided him significantly. Offended by the Unitarian views of many General Baptists, they set out to reform their denomination. They began their work in Lincoln. A group of Baptist churches there followed their lead and formed the New Connection. No General Baptist leader surfaced of greater significance than Dan Taylor. His conservative reaction against the deteriorating doctrine of the General Baptists proved invaluable.

Despite the new life generated among the General Baptists, the Particular Baptists, with their strong evangelism and missionary emphasis, captivated eighteenth century Baptist life. Of course, the Particular Baptists had their highs and lows. For example, when early leaders such as William Kiffin and Benjamin Keach passed off the scene, a decline in leadership set in. Matching the decline in leadership, an exaggerated hyper-Calvinism developed. It surfaced in men such as John Brine, and especially John Gill, who was one of Spurgeon's predecessors at the New Park Street Baptist Church. Gill, a strong Calvinist, created a massive work on systematic theology. His thought became known as "Gillism." Tongue in cheek, Spurgeon described Gill's systematic theology works as a "continent of mud." More seriously, Spurgeon appreciated much of the theology of the brilliant John Gill.

Some years later, illustrious names came on the scene in the Particular Baptist movement, men such as Robert Hall, Andrew Fuller, and William Carey. Theologically, these men retained a basic Calvinistic foundation, but they believed fully in human instrumentality and responsibility in the spread of the Gospel. This modification of high-Calvinism moved them to give themselves to preaching, missions and Gospel invitation. The new approach, along with its practical application of the Gospel, became known as "Fullerism," named after Andrew Fuller. In this context the great William Carey developed the Baptist Mission Society. The new organization captured the missionary mindset and enthusiasm of English Baptists, and Carey's influence extended all over Europe and to Colonial America. The birth of modern English speaking missions ensued. William Carey himself sailed to Serampore, India as a missionary as Fuller headed the Society back in Britain. In that context, Carey wrote the book *Inquiry*, considered one of the most informational Baptist books of all times.

As notable as William Carey became, Andrew Fuller shared a similar spiritual reputation. Born in 1754, going to his reward in 1815, he grew up among the hyper-Calvinists in a small town near Cambridge. Even as a youth, he had questions about the strict Calvinism of John Gill and others. As a young pastor, he rejected its strictures for a more moderate approach to theology. This significant move, one which placed a more balanced emphasis on human responsibility, did much to foster the impact of the great awakening that was sweeping both sides of the Atlantic during those days.

Another important personality in the movement, Robert Hall (1728-1791), likewise felt that "Gillism" had moved too far from a proper, balanced understanding of the Gospel. In 1779, he preached a powerful sermon from Isaiah 57:14, "And it shall be said, 'Build up, build up, prepare the way, remove every obstacle out of the way of my people.'" The sermon was titled "Zion's Travelers," but often referred to as "Hall's Album." In his message,

Hall urged people to come to Christ and to remove any stumbling block that prevented sinners from doing so. It proved to be a monumental moment. An important milestone in the development of Particular Baptist evangelism had been reached. In the setting, aside from the hyper-Calvinism of John Gill and his predecessors, a new day dawned in Particular Baptist life. In this context and this basic theological understanding, Spurgeon found his own foundations.

As the nineteenth century dawned, it boded to be a great era for British Baptists. Casting off the old restraints and remnants of hyper-Calvinism, the future loomed bright. They extended the Baptist Missionary Society so as to reach more nations for Christ. Further, they all had a mutual commitment to congregationalism as the form of church government. This mutual spirit helped bind them together, albeit rather loosely. Consequently, as new churches came into being, the need for some form of connectionalism became increasingly apparent. Several early efforts in this area were made. They took the form of "societies" to meet specific needs in political, philanthropic, and religious arenas.

The following Particular Baptist societies came into existence:

The Baptist Missionary Society (1792)
The Baptist Home Missionary Society (1797)
The Baptist Irish Society (1814)
The Baptist Building Fund (1824)

Out of these societies and similar early attempts grew other works such as the Particular Baptist Fund, the Widows' Fund, Colleges or "Academies," etc. The work movement was clearly solidifying and growing.

Finally, the concept of a nationwide society began to gain favor among the Particular Baptists. It acquired the title of a "general" union because, as Ernest Payne put it, "its purposes were to be of a more comprehensive character than those of several already existing Baptist societies." The vision was a union of churches and ministers, banded together to support foreign and home missions, education, Sunday School, and the like. They had made some earlier attempts at connectionalism by holding general meetings from 1689-1691. No organization emerged, however. Associations of churches on a local level had also arisen, but a deep sense of the need of a general union grew. One of the most important early leaders in the movement was John Howard Hinton. He had been campaigning for a union for some time. In 1812, one year before the founding of the Union, Hinton gave a major address to an exploratory meeting concerning the forming of a Union. He made a profound impression and it proved instrumental in the forming of the British Baptist Union. One of the primary reasons, among the others previously mentioned, for the sense of the need for union was to provide for the education of ministers. Many realized that Particular Baptists needed better trained pastors. A conference was thus called to form a General Union of Calvinistic Baptists. Delegates gathered in the vestry of the Baptist chapel which met at Carter Lane, Tooley Street, Southwark, near the southern end of London Bridge. The meeting was held at 8:00 a.m. on Thursday, June 25, 1812. It proved to be an historical moment.

The Carter Lane Church had a great history. The building erected in 1757, by 1812 housed the leading Particular Baptist congregation in London. The church boasted illustrious pastors such as Dr. John Gill. John Rippon served in 1812, and under his leadership, the conference seeking a general union was held. Over sixty ministers crowded into the Carter Lane vestry. Significant men arrived, men like Andrew Fuller of the Baptist Missionary Society, John Ryland from Bristol, and John Sutcliff from Olney. Of course, the Carter Lane Church is the church Spurgeon led to its greatest heights after it moved from Carter Lane to Park Street.

The delegates decided that a meeting should be held on June 24, 1813 and that churches and associations be invited to send members seeking a formal union. Its purpose was to promote "the cause of Christ in general." [34] John Sutcliff and Robert Hall preached. Out of this significant meeting came the Baptist Union. The implications were tremendous for the growth of the entire Baptist movement.

At this stage (1813) the Union was composed exclusively of Calvinistic Baptists. But in 1832, the Union re-organized itself and re-defined its objectives. [35] This opened the door for closer ties with the New Connection General Baptist churches. Moreover, as the century progressed, the conflict between Calvinism and Arminianism subsided. Andrew Fuller became a mediator who helped span the gulf, and "Fullerism" emerged as the actual bridge between the Particular Baptists and the New Connection General Baptists. This inaugurated the amalgamation of the two groups. The growing union was formalized sixty years later in the complete merging of the two groups of Baptists.

The formation of the Union in 1813 did not solve all issues, however. For example, an episode known as the Serampore Controversy erupted. After Carey went to India and settled in Serampore, the mission grew and many other missionaries joined him on the field. At that time, they set their own priorities and policies and decided how the work should take place on the field. For years they maintained a good relationship with Andrew Fuller, the general secretary of the Baptist Missionary Society. Fuller had moved the society headquarters to London and expanded the entire work tremendously. Then a controversy arose about who had the final authority in the direction and development of the work. Moreover, the issue surfaced as to whether the property bought out of missionary earnings belonged to the missionaries or to the mission. This resulted in a missionary "Triumvirate, of Carey, Marshman and Ward," and they split off from the Baptist Missionary Society in 1827 to form their own group. The division persisted until 1837. Fortunately, they finally settled their differences, reunited, and the work progressed on the mission field as well as in the homeland.

The Baptists, though seeking union and cooperation, were still fiercely independent. Each church held tenaciously to its autonomy and decided its issues locally. This grew out of their doctrine of the church. What did they believe about the local church? Gerald Borchert tells us.

> Baptist Confessions of Faith are generally clear in their affirmation that the (local) Church is a body of self confessing baptized believers. In the First London Confession (1644), it is affirmed that the Church
>
>> . . . is a company of visible Saints, called and separated from the world . . . to the visible profession of the faith of the gospel, being baptized into that faith, and joined to the Lord, and to each other, by mutuall [sic] agreement . . .
>
> . . . To understand the Baptist view of the Church is to recognize that Baptists from the beginning have sought to restore the visible church to New Testament standards by keeping its membership as nearly identical as possible with the invisible church.
>
> Not only is such a view opposed to a state church concept but it strikes against concepts such as infant faith or what Baptists would consider to be pre-faith membership patterns. Some other Christians may be very troubled by such a proposition but it is consistent with the way Baptists view the Church. The 'invisible' Church, of course, encompasses . . . 'the body of Christ which includes all of the redeemed of all the ages.' In summary then, it can be said that for Baptists local church membership in general implies regeneration, confession of (believing) faith and believer's baptism. [36]

In this context and with this theology, the Baptists grew and their evangelizing work spread dramatically. Little did the early London Baptists realize the force released in 1813. Baptists have become one of the largest, worldwide evangelical denominations in the history of Christianity. In this historical matrix, Charles Haddon Spurgeon was baptized and joined the St. Andrew's Street Baptist Church in Cambridge, and another era began.

CONCLUSION

What can now be said by way of summary concerning the progress of Great Britain during the reign of Queen Victoria? A renewed consecration to Christ swept Evangelicalism. A new spirit of toleration emerged as institutions opened to all people. Denominations grew stronger and more effective. The Evangelicals had become accepted, and the Tractarians moved in the direction of becoming Anglo-Catholics. Liberal theologians began expressing their views far more openly with the rise of rationalism and Germanic theology. In the midst of sociological turmoil, religion progressed dramatically. The Industrial Revolution, bringing a better life for many, along with the Evangelical revival, became the greatest social forces of the day. Organization and freedom were two of the significant characteristics that marked the revolutionary epoch. Democratic institutions and parliamentary government grew in strength, largely through William Gladstone securing the passage of major legislation. Gladstone and the Liberal party fought for stricter licensing of public houses, sought to protect the poor tenant farmers who were being evicted from their land, and precipitated other important reforms. The only area of politics in which Spurgeon disagreed with Gladstone was on the controversial Irish home rule issue. Actually, the final resolution to the Irish problem awaited the administration of David Lloyd George. When death claimed Gladstone in 1898, the Victorian age probably lost its greatest statesman.

On January 22, 1901, Queen Victoria died, having reigned for 64 years. The Victorian era thus came to an official conclusion, although the demise of the age had already been in the making for some time. An increasing population kept the churches filled, but the importance and subsequent influence of the Church began to decline as the end of the era loomed on the horizon. In this dynamic and fluid setting, Charles Haddon Spurgeon did his monumental work to save his "City" from "Destruction."

3

"Yonder Wicket-gate"

SPURGEON'S PILGRIMAGE TO CONVERSION

Any nineteen-year-old swept to such pulpit fame might be just as self-conscious as young Charles Spurgeon in this rare photograph.
—*courtesy of Dr. Craig Skinner*

This hill, though high, I covet to ascend;
The difficulty will not me offend,
For I perceive the way to life lies here.
Come, pluck up, heart; let's neither faint nor fear.
Better, though difficult, the right way to go,
Than wrong, though easy, where the end is woe.

—John Bunyan

Introduction

The Spurgeon clan's historical roots are implanted deep in and around East Anglia, that beautiful section of England north and east of London, commonly called the "Fens." The county of Essex can particularly boast of being a Spurgeon stronghold. A lovelier spot in England can scarcely be found; the farms that dot the countryside paint a picture in themselves. In many ways, nature created some of its loveliest landscapes in that verdant countryside. Perhaps this accounts for Charles H. Spurgeon's deep fondness for nature. He delighted in the handiwork of God. For Spurgeon, the nineteenth Psalm communicated gladness: "The heavens declare the glory of God and the firmament showeth his handiwork" (Psalm 19:1). He particularly loved the Epping Forest, north of London. In the nineteenth century, even the trains had to make an excursion around the lovely forest so as not to mar its beauty—and lost twenty miles in the detour. The British have always cherished their countryside and were ecologists far before that term became a byword. In this setting and spirit the Spurgeon clan thrived.

SPURGEON'S ROOTAGE

As far back as 1465, legal documents in the general East Anglia area record the name of Spurgeon. In 1575, Thomas Spurgeon worked as a tenant on the stately Manor of Dynes, Great Maplestead. Stretching right into the twentieth century, a holding situated in the Fens area is known as "Spurgeons." At Much Dunmow, Felsted, Blacknotlye, Eastwood, Thundersley, and South Beanflet, Spurgeons can be found in the records as early as the seventeenth century. The East Anglia population in those days came from many varied backgrounds. In 1609 there were 1,300 folk of foreign origin in the city of Colchester alone.

As the seventeenth century dawned, an important event occurred in the Spurgeon family. A certain Job Spurgeon, a Quaker from Dedham and a

71

contemporary of John Bunyan, suffered a measure of persecution for his Christian faith. He experienced a "distress," as it was called in those days. He had a levy laid on him for attending a Nonconformist meeting. In the 1600s, to gather with a group to worship outside an Established church made one a criminal. Job was guilty—and paid the price. The records state that six years later, he was arrested again for the same offense. When he refused to pay the fine, the judge required him to give sureties for his good behavior, or go to prison. To the Chelmsford Prison he went, along with three other Nonconformists. This second arrest took place in the midst of a remarkably cold winter. The men lay for fifteen weeks on the cold stone floor of the prison covered only by a mat of straw and with no fire. Job Spurgeon finally became so weak through the ordeal he found himself unable to lie down and had to sit up in a chair most of the time. Job was Charles Haddon Spurgeon's great grandfather's great grandfather, and Charles related the event with pride. [1] C.H. Spurgeon almost gloried in the fact that one of his ancestors had endured trials for his faith. He once said, "I had far rather be descended from one who suffered for the faith than to bear the blood of all of the emperors in my veins." [2] One wonders if he had ever heard of Ms. S. Spurgeon of the Broadmead Church in Bristol and her "distress" as recorded in the previous chapter. One feels that if he had, he would have recorded it—he reveled in such stories.

The more direct line of Charles' family can be traced through the branch of the clan that lived around Halstead, Essex. Spurgeons had thrived there for some twelve generations. The family lineage proves quite fascinating.

In 1551, accounts relate that Richard Spurgeon held considerable land in the Halstead district. Few landowners graced the area in those days; Richard must have been a man of notable means. In 1718, a certain Clement Spurgeon acquired an important position in a local Independent chapel. Two years after taking his place of leadership, the church books record that he and his wife sold to the congregation the land on which the church was built. The price? Fifteen pounds! That was a tidy sum in the early eighteenth century. His will showed he had considerable properties at his death. Clement Spurgeon's brother, John Spurgeon, worked as an apothecary. He also had become a man of means, giving £100 toward the repairs of the church building in which his son, Samuel Spurgeon, served as the minister. An interesting entry is found in the church records of that particular congregation: "April 9, 1736. To cash paid the Reverend Mr. Spergin for preaching one whole Lord's day, fifteen shilling." [3] A goodly stipend for a day of preaching! But now we are getting close to Charles.

Clement Spurgeon was the grandfather of James Spurgeon, C. H. Spurgeon's grandfather. James served as pastor of the Nonconformist church in Stambourne for 54 years. Clement's nephew Samuel, a pastor, began a lineage of clergymen that carried on through to Charles Spurgeon—four generations. We shall see much of James and his influence on Charles as the life of C. H. Spurgeon unfolds.

An interesting note can be found in the ancient records of the "Parish Register of Burnham Thorpe." On March 13, 1769, a certificate of marriage between Elizabeth Spurgeon and her husband is registered. One of the witnesses at the wedding who signed the register was a young boy just ten years of age. He signed his name as "Horace Nelson." His father later changed the lad's first name to "Horatio." Thus the famous Lord Nelson of the Battle Trafalgar, a great British hero, played a small role in the Spurgeon saga. Nelson's statue stands high above Trafalgar Square in London today. As Fullerton put it, "Trafalgar Square (where a statue of Nelson rests) has something to say to Newington Butts (the part of London where C. H. Spurgeon served as pastor)."[4]

Something like nineteen variations of the Spurgeon family name can be discovered in various old records. In 1273, we find a William Spirgin in Norfolk. Robert Spurgynne served as an Anglican victor in Fouldon in the year 1576. In 1712 John Spurgeon became mayor of Yarmouth. Other forms of the name vary, from Spirgon to Spurgien. The English were notorious for spelling their names with different sets of vowels.

A case can be made that the very first Spurgeons in Great Britain were Norsemen, although some biographers differ. One over-zealous genealogist claimed he could trace the Spurgeon line clear back to Doonesday Book, an eleventh century tax assessor's book. The root of the Spurgeon name is actually a diminutive of "Sporr," which is the Norse word for "sparrow." W. Y. Fullerton, a close friend of C. H. Spurgeon, argues that the family is of Norwegian origin. He contends that the idea the Spurgeons were of Dutch extraction may have sprung from a statement by Charles when he said, "I remember speaking to a Christian brother who seemed right happy to tell me that he sprang from a family which came from Holland during the persecution of the Duke of Alba, and I felt a brotherhood with him in claiming a like descent from Protestant forefathers."[5] Spurgeon did not say he claimed a Dutch origin, only a Protestant heritage. Most other biographers, however, contend Spurgeon did have a Dutch heritage. And it must be admitted that many Dutch refugees settled in East Anglia. Moreover, Charles Spurgeon looked very Dutch in his build; and a portrait of Charles and a portrait of Paul Kruger closely resemble each other. Of course, it is possible that some Dutch blood had mingled with many Norsemen of the area. Biographers G. Holden Pike, Richard Briscoe Cook, Shindler, and several others hold that the family was surely of Dutch origin. Also, this contention found a place in the *London Graphic* for November 5, 1890, stating "the Spurgeon family is of Huguenot origin." Pike states that "the earliest known representatives of Mr. Spurgeon's family were of Dutch extraction is an interesting fact."[6] Pike argues that Spurgeon's ancestors were driven out of their ancient home in the Netherlands by the persecution that broke out during the rule of Philip II of Holland. This took place some two and a half centuries before the birth of C. H. Spurgeon. Pike contends that the Spurgeon family, with a large number of other refugees, crossed the North Sea to escape death at the hands of Ferdinando Alvarez, Duke of Alba. He tells us this hearty band was the cream of Protestant believers. It is true that the revoking of the "Edict of Nantes" drove many Dutch believers to England, some settling in Norfolk and some in Essex. As a result of the revoking of the Edict, Alvarez, a Spanish general who had at his command 20,000 mercenary troops, entered the low countries in the year 1567 and proved to be a man right after the heart of Philip II. Philip, a fervent Roman Catholic, commissioned the Spanish general to persecute the Protestants. This greatly pleased Alvarez; he delighted in carrying out the policies of the monarch—with vigor. When Alvarez died in 1589, he boasted he had sent 18,000 Protestant believers to the executioners—not counting thousands driven into exile. Pike goes on to state that Spurgeon always manifested an interest in Holland, and "it yielded him satisfaction to know that his sermons and other works were extensively circulated in the Dutch language."[7]

In 1863, Spurgeon visited several chief cities in the Netherlands. On that tour he received the honor of an interview with the Queen herself. Pike states that at such a time the "stirring memories of the sixteenth century would come to his mind: He would think of his own kinfolk, who escaped with their lives, and of those who had remained behind to lay foundations of a great country, and in many instances to pour out their blood in its behalf."[8] Pike may have overworked his imagination somewhat on that statement, but he then goes on to argue that Spurgeon's love of trees, shrubs and flowers was a typical characteristic of the middle class Hollander. That seems an even greater use of conjecture. However, Spurgeon did look Dutch and surely loved nature.

So, it remains somewhat questionable whether Pike and others who contend for Spurgeon's Dutch origin are correct. Biographer Fullerton may well have been right when he argued that C. H. Spurgeon's ancestry really stems from the Norseland. Fullerton served with Spurgeon as a fellow preacher and close friend. It seems doubtful he could be mistaken here. But then, Pike was close to Spurgeon also. Of course, as previously suggested, the possibility exists that the Spurgeon family could have mixed with Hollanders and thus generated some confusion as to the actual ancestry of the great preacher.

The Spurgeon clan, regardless of its origins, never became a family of great notoriety. But of more importance, a strong tradition of Nonconformity and piety was handed down through the generations. Spurgeon said, "There is a sweet fitness in the passing of holy loyalty from one grandsire to father, and from father to son."[9] In many respects, Spurgeon did have a noble heritage— at least from the spiritual perspective—and that pleased Charles well.

SPURGEON'S BIRTH

The great preacher was born in a quaint little cottage at Kelvedon, Essex; a small village of 1500 at the time of his birth. The beautiful River Blackwater flows by it. A large manor house once belonging to Edward the Confessor stood there for years, but had been demolished by Spurgeon's day. The Massacre of the Danes under Ethelred in November 1002 began at Kelvedon. The little village had a small measure of notoriety. The actual date of Spurgeon's birth was June 19, 1834, ten days after William Carey had died in India, and the same year the Houses of Parliament in London burned. The death of one giant occurred almost simultaneously with the birth of another, and a spiritual flame was ignited that glowed brighter than a burning Parliament building. God does not leave himself without a witness. Britain can surely attest to that spiritual reality.

James Spurgeon, the grandfather, baptized baby Charles on the 3rd of August, 1834. Those records are found in Somerset House in London. Although some biographers claim there was no ancestor in the Spurgeon family named Charles for two generations, Pike states Charles was named after his mother's brother, which is probably correct.

Spurgeon's second name, Haddon, came about in an interesting fashion and Charles always enjoyed telling the story. His grandfather, James, before becoming the pastor of the Stambourne Independent Chapel, had spent some years in business as a country shopkeeper in Halstead, the town of his birth in 1776. One of the chief commodities of James Spurgeon's store was good English cheese. As would be the normal procedure in those days, he would buy the cheese from a wholesale dealer and then sell it to the customers at a retail price. On a certain occasion, a friend of grandfather James by the name of Haddon said to him, "Mr. Spurgeon, you should go down to the cheese fairs at Derby and Leicester and buy what you want at first hand; you would get a much larger profit if you do so." "Oh!" replied grandfather, "I could not do that, for I have not sufficient money to spare for such a purpose." "You need not have any difficulty on that score," said the generous man. "If you tell me when the next fair is to be held, I will let you have the money, and you can pay me back when you have sold the cheese. I have such confidence in your Christian integrity, that I shall be glad to aid you in this way." [10] Grandfather James immediately took the gentleman up on his offer and went down to Derby and Leicester and bought cheeses. He sold them at a good profit and then went to his generous friend to repay the sum with interest. When he asked how much interest he owed on the loan, Mr. Haddon said, "Oh, Mr. Spurgeon, that is not my way of transacting business! I had that money laying idle and you have done me a great service in putting it to such good use, so I mean to give you 5% for your trouble in laying it out for me; and when the season comes round again, I want you to buy another lot of cheeses on the same terms."

It is thus quite understandable why the name Haddon became deeply appreciated by the Spurgeon family. James, when he had a son born to him, gave him the middle name of Haddon in remembrance of his friend's extreme generosity. That son was Charles' uncle Haddon, who used to announce the hymns at the Stambourne Chapel in the worship services. It was quite natural, therefore, that when John, Charles' father, had a son, he should give him the name of Charles *Haddon* Spurgeon. An interesting sequel to the story emerged when William Olney, a deacon at the New Park Street Baptist Church, London, where Charles later became pastor, built a large mission in Bermondsey. He named the premises Haddon Hall. Spurgeon said, "It always seems to me that this chain of circumstances is a fresh illustration of the inspired promise, 'The righteous shall be in everlasting remembrance.'"[11]

The year of Spurgeon's birth, 1834, proved an important year politically for Britain. Lord Melbourne had just succeeded Earl Gray as Prime Minister. He became a singularly important figure in British politics. Two years earlier, 1832, a serious cholera epidemic struck Kelvedon but had subsided by the time of Charles' birth. Charles' father, John, was engaged in business, keeping a shop in Kelvedon during these days, but apparently it did not prove to be very lucrative. Ten months after Charles' birth, John and his wife Eliza moved to Raleigh in Essex, then on to Colchester, and a few months later little Charles went to live with his grandparents in Stambourne. Spurgeon wrote his last book *Memories of Stambourne* about Stambourne, Essex where he lived with his pastor-grandfather for some five years. He rarely mentioned his birth at Kelvedon or his days in Colchester, except to share the story of his conversion. Still, the cottage in which he was born remains until this day and boasts a brass plaque as the birthplace of "The Prince of Preachers."

THE PARENTS

Spurgeon's mother's maiden name was Eliza Jarvis. She was born at Otton Belchamp on May 3, 1815, being the youngest sister of Charles Parker Jarvis, Esquire of Colchester. Everyone knew her as "a woman remarkable for piety, usefulness and humility."[12] Eliza had only turned nineteen years of age when Charles, her first born, came into the world.

Charles' father, John, the second of ten children, was born at Clair, Suffolk on July 15, 1810. Some biographers claim he was born in Stambourne in 1811. James Spurgeon did move to Stambourne in 1810, so the mystery remains. A chronological chart (see appendix A) of the whole Spurgeon family published in 1906 claims the 1810 date. At any rate, he was somewhere around twenty-four when his famous son Charles was born. John Spurgeon stood nearly six-foot tall and was rather portly—a good specimen of an English country man. As well as being a business man, he preached the Gospel fervently and served as an able Independent minister. He possessed a strong voice, and because of that was chosen to announce the hymns at open air gospel meetings in Colchester. Charles inherited that voice. For years John worked in Colchester as head-clerk in a coal, coke and shipping office during the week and served as pastor of the Tolesbury Independent Church on weekends. Tolesbury was located some nine miles from Colchester. John had attained mid-life before he entered the ministry full time.

Spurgeon, deeply devoted to his parents, especially held his mother Eliza in profound reverence. Her dedication to the children reminds one of John Wesley's mother, Susanna. Although not in the best of health, Eliza prayed with and read the Bible to her children daily. She was a short woman— Charles inherited that trait—but she stood tall in the Spirit. Her Christian devotion affected Charles tremendously, as shall be seen.

After some years in Colchester, Charles' parents moved to Braintree. They then went on to Cranbrook, in Kent, and next to London to take the pastorate of the church in Fetter Lane. Finally, John took his wife to the church at Upper Street, Islington. After a long, happy and fruitful life, he died at Croydon on June 14, 1902, outliving his son Charles by ten years. Eliza, his wife, preceded her husband in death in 1888, four years before Charles died. The Spurgeons were never wealthy, and for years struggled with a large family, as did most nineteenth century Independent Christian ministers. But the home exemplified a godly family and enjoyed the blessings of God.

From these humble beginnings and background, the greatest preacher of the Victorian era came on the scene. Later in life, Spurgeon said:

> We want again Luthers, Calvins, Bunyans, Whitefields, men fit to mark eras, whose names breathe terror in our foeman's ears. We have dire need of such. Whence will they come to us? They are the gifts of Jesus Christ to the Church, and will come in due time. He has power to give us back again a golden age of preachers, a time as fertile of great divines and mighty ministers as was the Puritan age, and when the good old truth is once more preached by men whose lips are touched as with a live coal from the altar, this shall be the instrument in the hand of the Spirit for bringing about a great and thorough revival of religion in the land. [13]

Little did the Spurgeon family realize when their firstborn came into the world, he would fill such a role and join in that noble train of pulpit giants who ushered in the golden age of preaching in the Victorian British church.

THE MOVE TO STAMBOURNE

Four months after the Spurgeon family moved to Colchester from Kelvedon, the parents sent fourteen-month-old Charles to live with his grandparents in the heart of the Essex countryside at Stambourne. Grandfather and Grandmother Spurgeon visited Charles' family in Colchester and took the baby boy home with them. The year was 1835. The Ecclesiastical Survey of 1676 recorded that the county of Essex had the greatest proportion of Protestant

Nonconformists in all of England. Stambourne actually had a clear majority of Nonconformists. That proved to be fertile soil for little Charles to grow in.

The attractive little rural village of Stambourne is nestled in farmlands a few miles west of the road between Halstead and Haverhill. It stands at the source of the winding Cale River. In Spurgeon's day it only had a blacksmith shop, a store in a house, two pubs, a cottage school and a few dwellings, along with the Independent Congregational church and the Anglican Church. The population numbered a mere 500 in Charles' day, with no post office, physician or policeman. But it was a quiet, happy, restful place—one Charles never forgot. Through life he nourished fond memories of the place where his grandfather James Spurgeon had lived and ministered to the Independent congregation since 1810.

The reason young Charles went to live with the grandparents remains somewhat obscure. It has been conjectured that his parents found themselves in a rather difficult financial situation; hence the move. This seems the most logical reason. They probably moved from Kelvedon to Colchester for that very reason. Moreover, Charles Spurgeon's uncle, his mother's brother, lived in Colchester. Yet, other children were born into the family, and they were not transplanted. John and Eliza had seventeen children in all; nine died in infancy. Charles did not return to his parents until he was six years of age. But, the Lord's providential purpose can be perceived in this circumstance. Grandfather James ministered in the spirit of the great Puritan divines. It was said of him, he was "one of the last representatives of the Old Dissent."[14] He represented the old Georgian era—Puritans in some of their best expressions. Charles had a happy childhood, and much molding of character took place in the grandparent's home. He never escaped the profound influence of his early Puritan upbringing.

SPURGEON'S CHILDHOOD IN STAMBOURNE

Spurgeon fondly remembered and vividly described the house in which he lived with his grandparents. He wrote about it years later in *The Sword and the Trowel* in 1888. Pleasant and precious memories tumbled from his pen. He described the house as a gentleman's mansion of the olden times. A quite wealthy man had formerly owned the home, a true manor-house in many ways. How it became the manse of the Nonconformist minister is lost in the dust of time. Few Nonconformist pastors had such a mansion, but a spacious home was necessary for the pastor's large family. Nine children were born to James and his wife, three girls and six boys. Still, for a dissenting pastor to have a house of such size and quality was most unusual. Such houses were normally reserved for the Established churchmen. In Spurgeon's words, it stood as a "noble parsonage." The two-hundred-year-old house boasted eight windows in front, although three or four had been plastered up, painted black and then marked out in lines to imitate glass. The reason was that illogical window tax. In those days, windows were considered an extravagance—Spurgeon quipped that light must have been considered a luxury. As a result of the tax, many people plastered up their windows to keep from paying the extra pounds to the local government. Darkness thus shrouded room after room in the manse. The only light would be the candles, and those were used sparingly. Spurgeon said, "What a queer mind must his have been who first invented taxing the light of the sun!"[15] In the front part of the house, in a certain room, one window had escaped the tax-collector, and a kneading trough rested on a shelf in the bright room. On the little shelf Charles would always find "something for the child." Perhaps it would be a piece of pastry. Grandmother did spoil him.

Through the front door one would step into a spacious hall, as Charles put it, "innocent of carpet."[16] A great fireplace dominated one wall, on which hung a painting of David and the slaying of Goliath the Philistine giant. The entire hall floor, paved with brick, was always carefully sprinkled with fresh sand. In the country homes in those days, and even into Spurgeon's later life, such was the custom. The boy Spurgeon loved to stand in the sandy hall with the door open and watch the rain run off the top of the door frame spout into a washtub. In the hall, in a corner, stood a child's rocking horse. Painted gray, it could be ridden astride or side saddle. Spurgeon said, "This was the only horse that I ever enjoyed riding."[17] Agility did not grace the young man. Charles, short from the knees to the waist, was always a bit awkward and often fell down. Sports never appealed to him, but he made up for it in his studies.

On the right side of the hall, a door opened to the parlor. Roses generally grew about the window in the lovely room and sometimes even intruded through the window casing into the room itself. In what Spurgeon called the "best parlor," portraits of the grandparents and the uncles graced the walls. On one of the pieces of furniture sat a large basin which grandfather James used for baptisms. In Spurgeon's description of the manse in his *Autobiography* he put the term "baptisms" in quotation marks. Despite his Congregational background, he became convinced, as shall be discovered, that the New Testament taught baptism by immersion as the only true baptism. Nevertheless, it was a pretty bowl, and he said, "In my heart of hearts, I believe it was originally intended for a punch bowl; but, in any case, it was a work of art, worthy of the use to which it was dedicated."[18] Around the old fireplace many happy hours were spent as Spurgeon read and revelled in the fellowship of his grandparents and especially his Aunt Ann, the unmarried daughter of the grandparents who remained at home. It was a beautiful house; it was a happy home.

GRANDFATHER JAMES

Spurgeon's grandfather James was a most interesting and influential character, especially to Charles. A mature minister of the Gospel, a true old Puritan, he believed the Bible to be literally the Word of God, verbally inspired in its entirety. Born in Halstead, Essex on September 29, 1776, even as a boy he was very seriously minded and while still in his early years became a member of the Independent Church in Halstead. Later, while serving an apprenticeship in Coggshall, he became a member of the Independent Church there and sat under the pastoral care of Rev. S. Fieland. He followed his business pursuits back in Halstead until the age of twenty-six when he felt a definite call to enter the Christian ministry. In 1802 he enrolled in Hoxton Academy. After two years of study, he became pastor in Clair, in the county of Suffolk, taking a struggling congregation in a very difficult situation. But the church prospered under his leadership.

In Stambourne, Essex the Independent Church had flourished under the protracted ministry of Mr. Beddow. In the 200-year history of the church, they had only had four ministers. In 1810, Mr. Beddow left the church, and James Spurgeon received a unanimous call to the pastorate of the Stambourne congregation. May of 1811 saw his installation as pastor. He remained in that charge over half a century and everyone regarded him very highly. They respected and loved their pastor. He said, "I have not had one hour's unhappiness with my church since I have been over it." [19] Not many ministers can say that.

Through the years, other churches sought James Spurgeon to become pastor, but his commitment to the people in Stambourne persisted throughout his life. He rarely preached in any other church but his own. He was a sturdy man and every inch a rather imposing figure. He had a large head, and as someone said, there was much good in it. He had a strong voice—it must have been a family trait. Being very earnest and practical in his preaching of the Gospel, he proved to be a perfect portrait of the old school Puritan divine. Staid, quiet, and uniform in his attire and in his lifestyle, he was very neat. In many respects he resembled John Wesley in manner and stature. He always dressed himself in a dress cravat, a frilled shirt, and a vest with deep pockets. He wore breeches, buckled shoes, and silk stockings, which were typical clothing during the reign of George III, King of England when he was born. He really looked the part of the venerable Nonconformist minister of a past generation. Invariably he would have a handful of candy to give to the children wherever he went. As can be imagined, they loved him dearly. Young people responded to James as well. His gentle manners, sincere piety and impeccable Christian conduct purchased for him not only an excellent Christian testimony but the good will of his neighbors. He had no wealth, but that of the spirit. He once said to his grandson Charles, "Charles, I have nothing to leave you but rheumatic gout; and I have left you a great deal of that." [20] But he left Charles much more. He bequeathed to him a goodly heritage of the Puritan understanding of the Christian faith that Charles thrived upon the rest of his days.

James was broad-minded in his attitude to other true believers, regardless of their denominational affiliation. He could never be accused of being a narrow Nonconformist, although he held tenaciously to his Puritanism. He enjoyed excellent fellowship with the Rector of the Parish church, an evangelical Anglican in the best sense of the term. They much agreed on doctrine and the central issues of the Christian faith. Moreover, grandfather James exhibited significant preaching gifts. A listener of James' preaching said, "To hear him once makes my wing-feathers grow a foot! I could mount as an eagle after being fed with such heavenly food!" James could preach. Further, the evangelistic fervor of the man always surfaced in his messages. Whenever he stood in the pulpit to preach, he invariably called people to faith in Jesus Christ. He declared the whole council of God in of all of its realities.

James Spurgeon had a gentle spirit. For example, on one occasion when John, Charles' father, was still a boy at home, he did something to offend his father. James Spurgeon said that if he did that once again, he would be meted out a punishment that he would remember if he lived a hundred years. The elder Spurgeon regretted that he had made such a rash threat, but when young John again got caught in the guilty act, his father James called him and told him that he must inflict the threatened punishment. He made his son follow him out into a corner of the corn field beyond the ear shot of anyone. Young James, trembling, conceived every form of punishment possible for his father to inflict. When they arrived at the chosen spot, the father made his son kneel down. Then he picked up two straws of wheat and lightly brushed his cheek. "There," said father James, "I have kept my word; you will never forget that punishment." Charles, the grandson, as he related the story, said that his father never did forget that punishment.

James also possessed great faith. A Nonconformist pastor in grandfather Spurgeon's day rarely had any wealth, to say the very least. One time, with still a very large family at home, James' cow died and he did not have money to buy another. There were ten hungry children who needed milk. His wife asked, "What will you do now?" James replied, "I cannot tell what we shall do now, but I know what God will do. God will provide for us; we must have milk for the children."[21] That reply of faith God honored, and every need was supplied.

Grandfather James believed in a literal devil, and that a person could actually be assaulted by the evil one. On one occasion, as a young man, he had a dream in which he thought he saw Satan. He had a habit of praying alone in a secluded spot in a small area called Honeywood Park, which lies near Halstead. In this "night-vision," Satan in a rage declared to James that if he ventured again along this well beaten path in a season of prayer, he would be torn to pieces. James Spurgeon took this as a genuine threat from the enemy. However, he would not depart from his spiritual exercise; he walked right up the path to the place where he had always engaged in intercession and prayer. He reached the spot in a very nervous and excited state, perspiration standing out on his face. Yet, no demon appeared, but on the ground, to his amazement, he found an enormous gold ring. No one ever came forward to claim the prize. He was not married at the time, but when he did marry, the wedding ring for his bride was fashioned from the gold that he had discovered in such a mysterious way. This speaks of the spirituality of the man.

Much like Charles, his grandfather had a keen sense of humor. Some say the grandfather, along with a farmer named Will Richardson whom Spurgeon knew in those early years, were the inspiration and prototypes of John Ploughman, the character in Spurgeon's well-known books by that name. Will Richardson became little Charles' friend, and his common sense philosophy formed something of Charles' alter ego, as did Grandfather James. James Spurgeon was asked one day how much he weighed. In rather typical John Ploughman fashion, he replied, "Well, that all depends on how you take me: if weighed in the balances, I am afraid I shall be found wanting, but in the pulpit they tell me that I am heavy enough."[22]

Grandmother Spurgeon was a lovely lady in a quiet and retiring way. As pointed out, nine children were born to the couple, and she took much care in the spiritual training of the children. She employed herself with many works of charity and benevolence, often serving as chairperson of such groups. She became very dear to Charles in his young years. He loved her very much, and she him. Being a woman of deep piety, she became a real inspiration to the boy.

But it was the daughter who remained home, Aunt Ann, who really mothered little Charles. Down through the years he cherished warm affection and memories for his Aunt Ann. The young boy spent many happy days with his doting Aunt. She was always arranging for him to indulge in a good pastry or a drink of cold milk. She no doubt spoiled the little fellow. Spurgeon said, "Aunt Ann, would spoil 'the child' again if she had a chance."[23] All knew her as a godly young woman and of pronounced influence on Charles' life.

THE PRECOCIOUS CHILD

It was in the Stambourne manse, it will be recalled, Charles discovered his greatest treasure: Bunyan's *Pilgrims Progress*. Even as a mere child, when many other children were doing their best to spell one-syllable words, he could read well. As a little boy, lying on the floor in front of the fireplace, he did much of his reading by the crackling firelight and flickering candle. Out of this came later many of his ideas for his famous lecture, *Sermons from Candles*. In those Stambourne days, some of the large Puritan portfolios he read were almost too big for him to carry. As he peered over the rather grotesque woodcuts of Pilgrim's journey, he became burdened over the heavy load on Pilgrim's back until it rolled off. Charles said, "I thought I would jump for joy, when after he had carried his load so long, he at last got rid of it."[24] During those years with the grandparents he also read with keen interest, even as a little lad, Foxes' *The Book of Martyrs*. Little wonder, therefore, that his first real literary essay at the age of sixteen was "Antichrist and her Brood." He devoured Daniel Defoe's *Robinson Crusoe*—a Puritan book which few understood. He became a typical bookworm, studying quite heavy Puritan works. He was a precocious child, especially in reading. He said, "When I was but a child, I could have discussed many a knotty problem of controversial theology."[25] He devoured books all through his youth—and not just theology books. On one later occasion he read *Spanish Bullfights*. His parents punished him for it. He said, "They were right, for I should like to forget even the half I read in the book, but I cannot, it sticks like glue. Bad books are a terrible thing."[26] Out of those early experiences, Charles said, "Out of the darkened room I fetched those old authors when I was yet a youth, and never was I happier than when in their company. Out of the present contempt, into which Puritanism has fallen, many brave hearts and true will fetch it, by the help of God, 'ere many years have passed. Those who have daubed at the windows will yet be surprised to see heaven's light beaming on the old truth, and breaking forth from it to their own confusion."[27]

Spurgeon may well have learned some things about preaching from his grandfather's preparation. The grandfather always prepared his sermons for Sunday morning by sitting in the "best parlor" of the stately manse. Young Charles was always seated in the room with him; the idea being that he might be quiet there. But how to keep him quiet? His grandfather thought he found at least a reasonable solution; he had Charles sit and read an old copy of *The Evangelical Magazine*. However, Spurgeon did not find this venture to have much of a sedative effect. Even the inevitable portrait of a missionary on some mission station failed to arrest his attention. Another means of stilling the young boy proved much more effective. His grandfather warned him that he would not be able to preach well if he were distracted by the lad's restlessness. It worked. Little Charles would wonder what would happen to the poor people who did not learn the way to heaven. He said, "This made me look at the portrait and the mission station once more."[28] Hardly did he dream that one day some other child would see his face in *The Evangelical Magazine*. But life in the manse, even though very religious for a small, active boy, never seemed dull. Spurgeon loved to be allowed to read the Bible at family prayer time. He thoroughly enjoyed those hours. On one occasion, while reading a passage of Scripture from the Book of Revelation that referred to the "bottomless pit," he turned to his grandfather and asked what this could possibly mean. The grandfather brushed aside the question with, "Pooh, pooh, child, go on." Charles was not about to be put off quite that casually. Everyday when Scripture reading time arrived, he would again read the same passage on the "bottomless pit" and ask the same question, "What does it mean?" But grandfather Spurgeon continued to dismiss the query. Charles tried to find answers in his own little mind about what would happen when people fell into a pit that did not have a bottom. What would happen when they fell out of the bottomless pit at the other end? He would continually pose the question at the family worship hour. Finally, his grandfather gave in and answered the question in a way that brought terror to Charles as the old pastor explained the true biblical meaning. Spurgeon said:

> I can remember horror in my mind when my dear grandfather told me what his idea of the 'bottomless pit' was. There is a deep pit, and the soul is falling down—oh, how fast it is falling! The last ray of light at the top has disappeared, and it falls on—on—on, and so it goes on falling—on—on—on—for a thousand years! It is not getting near the bottom yet? Won't it stop? No, no, the cry is. On—on—on. I have been falling a million years: Am I not near the bottom yet? No, you are not so near the bottom yet; it is the *'bottomless pit.'* It is on—on—on, and so the soul goes on falling perpetually into a deeper depth still, falling forever into the 'bottomless pit'—on —on—on—into the pit that has no bottom! Woe, without determination, without hope of this coming to a conclusion! [29]

There were happier, less heavy, experiences for Spurgeon while living at Stambourne, however. He delighted to see the huntsmen with their red coats as they chased the fox. When he viewed such scenes, he declared quite emphatically that he would one day be a huntsman. He talked about other happy days in his grandfather's manse—for instance the "apple in the bottle" incident. In his *Autobiography* he related the story:

> I remember well, in my early days, seeing upon my grandmother's mantelshelf an apple contained in a phial. This was a great wonder to me, and I tried to investigate it. My question was, 'How came the apple to get inside so small a bottle?' The apple was quite as big round as the phial; by what means was it placed within it? Though it was treason to touch the treasures on the mantelpiece, I took down the bottle, and convinced my youthful mind that the apple never passed through its neck; and by means of an attempt to unscrew the bottom, I became equally certain that the apple did not enter from below. I held to the notion that by some occult means the bottle had been made in two pieces, and afterwards united in so careful a manner that no trace of the joint remained. I was hardly satisfied with the theory, but as no philosopher was at hand to suggest any other hypothesis, I let the matter rest. One day, the next summer, I chanced to see upon a bough another phial, the first cousin of my old friend, within which was growing a little apple which had been passed through the neck of the bottle while it was extremely small. 'Nature well known, no prodigies remain.' The grand secret was out. I did not cry, 'Eureka! Eureka!' but I might have done so if I had then been versed in the Greek tongue. [30]

Spurgeon could always make application of these early childhood experiences in his sermons. He said he had learned from the experience of the "apple in the bottle" that the young should be brought to the house of God by every means possible in the hope that later in life they would love the place where the Gospel is preached. But he did contend that sermons should not be so long and dull as to bore the young folks. Another good lesson from an apple in a bottle! No doubt, young Spurgeon was quite advanced for his years.

Those early days at Stambourne formed the general direction of Spurgeon's life. His Puritan grandfather imparted to him a love and reverence of the Puritan approach to the Christian faith from which he never escaped. Other people influenced him as well, such as the Anglican clergyman in Stambourne. The Rev. James Hopkins was the rector of the Church of England congregation in Stambourne in those days. Although he was of the Establishment, he preached the same Gospel in the same spirit as did grandfather James Spurgeon. As learned earlier, there were Puritans in the Anglican church as well as out of it. Spurgeon found it exceedingly pleasant that the two men of God, one an Established pastor and one a Nonconformist, had such respect and esteem for each other and lived in such genuine Christian fellowship. They were great friends. Little Charles would often go to the home of the Squire of the town with Mr. Hopkins and his grandfather for tea. He loved these outings. He had no boys his own age with whom to play. He grew up in the company of adults. But he soon learned to get along very well with them. How he enjoyed the Squire. Spurgeon said that the glory of the tea party was that the four, the three old gentlemen and the little boy, all had sugared bread and butter together for a treat. He said, "Yes, Stambourne had its choice pleasures!"[31]

Rev. Hopkins, of course, had a far larger income than did James Spurgeon, and the Rector never forgot to help his friend in his needs. Once, Hopkins gave a five pound note to grandfather James for a sick daughter to go to the seaside to recover from her illness. On another occasion, he sent half a joint of beef to his friend at the Independent parsonage. Such experiences with men of other denominations probably saved Spurgeon from being a narrow denominationalist. Hopkins served his congregation in Stambourne for decades. He lived to see the beginning fame of the little boy he took to the Squire's home for sugared bread and butter. He ministered until his death in 1858 and is buried in the Stambourne parish church yard.

As can be imagined, many happy hours were spent with Aunt Ann. Being the constant center of her attention may have contributed to Charles' leadership qualities—he expected people to surround him and follow him. Spurgeon was not without spiritual discernment, either, even as a child. Spurgeon's beloved Aunt Ann was fond of telling the story of young Charles' encounter with "old Roads." It seemed one of the members of the Independent Church at Stambourne, an old man by the name of Roads, often frequented the local pub to have his "drop of beer." He not only imbibed at the local public house, he also smoked a pipe. This profoundly grieved his godly pastor. The man of God would often heave a sigh at the thought of his church member's inconsistent Christian living. Charles had taken notice of his grandfather's grief. One day young Charles blurted out, so his grandfather would hear him very distinctly, "I'll kill old Roads, that I will!" Grandfather Spurgeon replied, "Hush, Hush! My dear, you mustn't talk so; it's very wrong, you know, and you'll get taken up by the police if you do anything wrong." Young Charles replied, "I shall not do anything bad; but I'll kill him though, that I will." One can imagine something of the grandfather's consternation, but he felt sure the child would not do anything untoward, so he let the episode pass off with the remark, "that strange child."

Not long after Charles walked into the house one day saying, "I've killed old Roads; he'll never grieve my dear Grandpa anymore." "My dear child, what have you done? Where have you been?" asked the grandfather. Charles replied, "I haven't been doing any harm, Grandpa, I've seen about the Lord's work, that's all." Charles would say no more. Try as they would, he would not reveal what he had done.

Before long, the mystery unraveled. A knock came on the parsonage door and there stood old Roads. Sorrow and depression etched every line on his face. He told the story of how he had been "killed." He said, "I'm very sorry indeed, my dear pastor, to have caused you such grief and trouble. It was very wrong, I knew; but I always loved you, and wouldn't have done it if I had only thought." Grandfather Spurgeon, quite taken with the old man's words, listened intently as Roads went on with his story:

> I was a'sitting in the public just having my pipe and my mug of beer, when that child comes in,—to think an old man like me should be took to task, and reproved by a bit of a child like that! Well, he points to me, just so, and says, 'What doest thou hear Elijah? Sitting with the ungodly, and you a member of the church, and breaking your pastor's heart. I'm ashamed of you! I wouldn't break my pastor's heart, I'm sure.' And then he walks away. Well, I did feel angry; but I knew it was all true, and I was guilty; so I put down my pipe, and did not touch my beer, and hurried away to a lonely spot, and cast myself down before the Lord, confessing my sin and begging for forgiveness. And I do know and believe the Lord in mercy pardoned me; and now I come to ask you to forgive me; and I'll never grieve you anymore, my dear pastor.

As can be expected, the delighted pastor freely forgave his repentant brother. And the repentance proved genuine. Mr. Houchin, the minister at Stambourne who succeeded James Spurgeon, gave the testimony of the consistent Christian life old Roads lived thereafter. Houchin said:

> Thomas Roads was one of the old men of table-pew,—an active lively little man, but quite illiterate,—not much above a laborer, but he kept a pony and cart, and did a little buying and selling on his own account . . . I found him an

earnest and zealous Christian, striving to be useful in every way possible to Him, especially in the prayer-meetings and among the young people, opening his house for Christian conversation and prayer. He only lived about four years of my time, and was sustained with a cheerful commonness to the end. When near death, on my taking of the Bible, he said, 'I have counted the leaves, sir.' I said, 'Why! What did you do that for?' And he replied, 'I never could read a word of it, and I thought I would know how many leaves were there.' This was very pathetic, and revealed much. We have a good hope of him, and miss him greatly. [32]

THE OLD CHURCH

The old meeting house where Spurgeon's grandfather preached became the supreme delight of the young boy. The Independent congregation came into being when a pastor of the Stambourne Church of England, Henry Havers, separated himself from Anglicanism. Havers had served the Established Church until his separation from the Church of England over theological disputes. Still, he read the Book of Common Prayer in the Independent Congregation up into the reign of George II. The successive pastors after Havers were all good Puritans. Through the years it became a fine church if not a large one. Spurgeon loved the people and the old building itself. The pulpit had a huge sounding board hanging over it. Charles said it reminded him of his "Jack in the Box," and he used to speculate as to what would become of his grandfather if it were to drop on him. Seated in the front of the pulpit on a table pew were all the elders of the congregation. The old house of worship had two large exterior doors in the side near the pulpit. If a sick person were brought in a carriage, the horses could be unhitched and the carriage rolled in the building so the sick could worship. It was almost like a nineteenth century "drive-in" church.

The people who gathered for worship were typical provincial people from Essex. They talked of places in the south of England as "The Shires," and referred to them as if they were foreign lands. But they loved a good sermon and would always say, "Mr. Spurgeon, I heard you well this morning." Most of the people in Stambourne always came to worship, either to the Nonconformist Church or the Anglican Church. There were few, as Spurgeon expressed it, "rough fellows" who did not go to any place of worship. By and large, religion dominated the small community. The Independent chapel accommodated some six hundred people and on Sunday afternoon the populous normally filled it. The parishioners loved to sing, and Spurgeon's grandfather once ventured upon publishing a volume of hymns.

Concerning singing, Spurgeon confessed that he could never sing well at all. He took after his grandfather in that regard. The old gentleman said that there was only one common meter tune that he could sing. He described it as, "Hum

Ha, Hum Ha."[33] Charles admitted that he could manage that—but that was about all. In fact, only once did Charles ever attempt to sing a solo. On June 4, 1889 on the occasion of his sermon on "Old Fugal Tunes" Charles sang a solo—or at least attempted it. The congregation at the Tabernacle reveled in their beloved pastor's solo; but he was definitely not a skilled vocalist.

As a boy in Stambourne, the singing style of the congregation once got him into a bit of trouble. He related the story with a bit of relish:

> The Stambourne style of singing led me into trouble when I returned to my home. The notion had somehow entered my little head that the last line of the hymn must be repeated and Grandfather had instilled into me as a safe rule that I must never be afraid to do what I believed to be right; so, when I went to the chapel where my parents attended, I repeated the last line whether the congregation did so or not. It required a great deal of punishment to convince me that a little boy must do what his parents think to be right; and though my grandfather made a mistake in that particular instance, I have always been grateful to him for teaching me to act according to my belief whatever the consequences might be.[34]

Spurgeon delighted in childish pranks. For example, in front of the meeting house there stood a "horsing block," a wooden structure like a large empty box with steps on one side. Ladies would climb up the steps on the platform that stood the same height as their horse's back. Decorum considered it a good way for women to get on their mounts in a ladylike fashion. But for Spurgeon, the horsing block was, as he expressed it, "There for another reason." He would hide inside the box. When the family came looking for him, he would hide away until they were quite concerned about what had happened to him. He also used the box to get by himself for his studies. His dear Aunt Ann had been the one who taught him to read. He devoted himself to books. Charles' father, John, said, "It was always books and books." At other times, he would slide open the top of an above ground tombstone and hide in there. He confessed: "Still, I remembered well the place, in what the tomb had formerly been. How often have I listened to the good people calling me by my name! I heard their feet close to my den, but I was wicked enough still to be 'lost,' though the time for meals was gone. Dreaming of the days to come befell me every now and then as a child and to be quite alone was my boyish heaven. Yet, there was a seventh heaven above that: Let me hear the foxhounds, and see the red coats of their pursuers, and I had seen the climax of delight."[35] Spurgeon learned a lesson even from those cherished hunting scenes. He said:

> I once learnt a lesson, while thus fox hunting, which has been very useful to me as a preacher of the gospel. Ever since the day I was sent to the shop with a basket, and purchased a pound of tea, a quarter-of-a-pound of mustard, and three pounds of rice, and on my way home saw a pack of hounds, and felt it

necessary to follow them over hedge and ditch (as I always did when I was a boy), and found, when I reached home, that all the goods were amalgamated,—tea, mustard, and rice—into one awful mess, I have understood the necessity of packing up my subjects in good stout parcels, bound round with the thread of my discourse; and this makes me to keep to firstly, secondly, and thirdly, however unfashionable that method may now be. People will not drink mustardy tea, nor will they enjoy muddled up sermons, in which they cannot tell head from tail, because they have neither, but are like Mr. Bright's Skye terrier, whose head and tail were both alike. [36]

Young Charles started his formal education in Stambourne. He attended a school conducted by "old" Mrs. Burleigh. The classes were held in part of an ancient dwelling house. It had a rickety floor, one window, and plaster peeling off the walls. Some reports of those early school days state that the precocious child did not show outstanding scholastic ability; but that seems rather doubtful, as he had a very inquiring mind.

Still, the greatest delight of Spurgeon during his early days in Stambourne was not the school or his pranks, but, again, the chapel and his grandfather's ministry. There, as he later expressed it, "The dew of the Spirit from on high never left the ministry. Wherever my grandfather went, souls were saved under his sermons." [37] Many testified to the power of his grandfather's ministry. People would say, "I heard your grandfather, and I would run my shoes off any day to hear a Spurgeon." [38] The parishioners were a good theologically oriented folk. Charles declared, "Buildings may perish, and new shrines may succeed them; but no earthly house will accommodate a sounder more useful ministry than that of my grandfather." [39] But as a hymn writer, Grandfather Spurgeon did not ring many bells. After he published a first book of hymns, he promised he would produce another if the first found acceptance. He never published a second. Charles said, "We forgive him for the first collection because he did not inflict on us another. The meaning was good, but the dear old man paid no attention to the mere triviality of rhyme. We dare not quote even a verse." [40] Perhaps the old gentleman rang bells in heaven by his hymns, for they were very sound doctrinally. But they rang few on earth because of their poor poetry. But as Charles said, we can forgive him for that.

When the sad time came for Charles, then six years old, to leave his beloved grandfather's home and return to his parents in Colchester, it understandably became the deep sorrow of his young life. He had lived with them as long as he could remember. After much weeping, he left with the comforting thought that as he looked up at the moon at night in Colchester, he would be able to see the same moon that his grandfather looked at in Stambourne. For years, Charles said he never looked up at the moon without thinking of his grandfather.

James Spurgeon, as mentioned earlier, served the Stambourne chapel for

54 years. He ministered there until he died at the age of 88 in 1864, ten years after Charles became pastor of the great Metropolitan Tabernacle in London. Spurgeon enjoyed telling the story of one day traveling to Haverhill to preach. Because of unforeseen circumstances, he arrived late. So his grandfather, who attended the service, began the worship and preached on the text: "By grace are you saved" (Ephesians 2:8). Somewhat into the message, Charles Spurgeon, now the distinguished grandson, entered the chapel. "Here comes my grandson," James explained, "He can preach the gospel better than I can, but you cannot preach a better gospel, can you, Charles?" Briskly walking up the aisle, Charles replied, "You can preach better than I can. Pray go on." Grandfather James refused, but he told him his text and explained that he had shown the people that the source of salvation is grace. Charles took up from that point and preached on the rest of the verse: "And that not of yourselves." He set forth the total inability of people to come to Christ on their own. His grandfather interrupted right in the heart of Charles' discourse, "I know most about that." Spurgeon preached while his grandfather said quietly, "Good, good." Finally, the old man burst out, "Tell them that again, Charles." Whenever Spurgeon preached on that text he could remember the words of his grandfather, "Tell them that again."[41]

Many times Spurgeon went back to Stambourne for extended holidays. On one such visit, his grandmother promised him a penny for every hymn of Isaac Watts that he could perfectly memorize and repeat. He learned so many that his grandmother had to reduce the price to half a penny, and still she feared that he would bankrupt her. Also, his grandfather offered him a shilling a dozen for all the rats he could kill in the old manse. So, as one biographer put it, "He gave himself to learning rat catching as it seemed to pay better."[42] Of course, Spurgeon said later in life that the hymns that he learned held him in the best stead, not dead rats.

A PROPHECY

Another fascinating event occurred in the summer of 1844 on one of Charles' visits back to his grandfather's manse in Stambourne. Charles was ten years old at the time and the incident quite profoundly affected his future life.

A well-known preacher by the name of Richard Knill traveled through the Fens on deputation for the London Missionary Society. He went from town to town during the summer of 1844 and, as providence would have it, he spent a little time in the Stambourne parsonage.[43] He was an outstanding preacher with a tremendous passion to win people to faith in Christ. Spurgeon called him "a great soul-winner."[44]

Richard Knill could tell fascinating stories that captivated young Charles as well as grandfather James. Being a well traveled man, he knew much about India in the early days of the century. He had been on a preaching tour in Madras, India in 1816. He thrilled little Charles with a story of an incident that happened the first Sunday he arrived in Madras. After the Sunday morning worship service, he dined with some military officers. Their worldly habits and attitudes reflected the general condition of British-Indian society at that time. High moral standards were hard to find. Knill related:

> The wine passed around merrily; they pressed me to a drink. I politely declined. The captain said, 'When you are in Rome, you must do as Rome does.' I said, 'Captain, if you urge me to drink, I will write to your sister about it, and what will she say?' The snare was broken. 'Well,' he said, 'do as you please.' They related soldier stories and I related missionary stories, and by way of application I said: 'Gentlemen, we are going to build a girls' school in Black Town near our chapel, to correspond with the boys' school, and as this is the first visit I have made, I should like to make it memorable by your becoming the first contributors. Give me something for a foundation stone.' They cheerfully responded, and sent me home in the Captain's Palanquin with £15 toward the girls' school. From that time, the Captain became a regular attender in the chapel, and sometimes ten or twelve officers came with him. [45]

Knill could communicate the Gospel of Christ in almost any setting and circumstance. He excelled as a most effective missionary-statesman. Mr. Knill not only knew India well, but also Russia. He had spent some days in St. Petersburg at the time of the overflowing of the River Neva in November of 1824 and also during the outbreak of cholera in 1830. One can imagine how fascinated young Charles and the family were to have such a distinguished guest in their home—especially telling such captivating stories.

Knill took considerable time with young Charles. During his visit he said to the boy, "Where do you sleep? I want to call you up in the morning." Charles showed him the little room where he slept, but the preacher's enquiry puzzled the lad. At six o'clock, Knill woke up Charles. In the yard of the parsonage, there were two arbors made of yew trees, cut in sugar loaf fashion. Knill led Spurgeon to the right side of the arbor and there, as young Spurgeon expressed it, "In the sweetest way," [46] he shared with the ten-year-old boy the love of Christ and the blessedness of trusting Him as Savior and serving Him even in childhood. He shared many touching stories as he presented Christ. He told Charles how good God had been to him and how wonderful it is to serve Him. Then they kneeled down and prayed that Charles would soon come to know Jesus Christ as Savior and serve Him as Lord. As they knelt together, he fervently prayed with his arms around the boy.

The two became inseparable. For three successive days, Knill shared with Charles the great truths of the Gospel and prayed for him. Just before Knill left, all the family gathered together for morning prayers. Then, in the presence of them all, Knill took little Charles on his knee and said, "This child will one day preach the Gospel, and he will preach it to great multitudes. I'm persuaded that he will preach in the chapel of Rowland Hill where I am now the minister."[47] Spurgeon later wrote, "Knill spoke very solemnly and profoundly this prophetic word. He called all those who were there to witness to what he said."[48] Then he gave little Charles a six pence as a reward if he would learn the hymn, "God Moves in Mysterious Ways, His Wonders to Perform." Knill made Charles promise that when he preached in Rowland Hill's Chapel, that hymn would be sung. The prophecy powerfully moved Spurgeon. He said, "Think of that as a promise from a child! Would it ever be anymore than an idle dream?"[49] Some time after Charles became pastor of the New Park Street Baptist Church in London, Dr. Alexander Fletcher was engaged to deliver the sermon to the children in Surrey Chapel, Rowland Hill's church. But he was taken ill, and Spurgeon preached in his place. Spurgeon consented on one condition, "Yes, I will, if you will allow the children to sing, 'God Works in Mysterious Ways.' I have made a promise long ago, so that hymn should be sung." Thus the prophecy came to fruition. Rowland Hill's chapel rang out with the hymn and the preaching of Charles Spurgeon. Spurgeon said, "My emotions on that occasion I cannot describe, for the word of the Lord's servant was fulfilled."[50]

However, later in life Spurgeon could not convince himself that the Surrey Chapel was the exact place Mr. Knill intended in his prophecy so many years earlier. Charles reasoned Knill may have had in mind the town where Knill spent his summers. Rowland Hill had served the church there also. Then, quite unexpectedly, the minister at Wooton-under-edge, which was Mr. Knill's summer residence, invited him to preach there. He went on the condition that the congregation would sing, "God Moves in Mysterious Ways." So whatever Knill had in mind in his prophecy many years past, Spurgeon fulfilled it in both places. Spurgeon said, "To me it was a very wonderful thing, and I no more understood at that time how it came to pass than I understand today why the Lord should be so gracious to me."[51]

Quite decidedly, Knill's prophecy influenced Spurgeon. Something of a mystical strain ran in the Spurgeon family, but Charles always judged those mystical experiences by the objective Scriptures. Forty years later, in a sermon preached July 17, 1871, he made reference to the Knill prophecy incident. Moreover, in the *Autobiography*, he evaluated the experience in a rather extended but fascinating account:

> Did the words of Mr. Knill help to bring about their own fulfillment? I think so. I believed them, and looked forward to the time when I should preach the Word: I felt very powerfully that no unconverted person might dare to enter the ministry; this made me, I doubt not, all the more intent upon seeing salvation, and more hopeful of it, and when by grace enabled to cast myself upon the Saviour's love, it was not long before my mouth began to speak of His redemption . . . Would to God that we were all as wise as Richard Knill, and habitually sowed beside all waters! . . . Mr. Knill might very naturally have left the minister's little grandson on the plea that he had other duties of

more importance than praying with children, and yet who shall say that he did not effect as much by that act of humble ministry as by dozens of sermons addressed to crowded audiences: At any rate, *to me* his tenderness in considering the little one was fraught with everlasting consequences, and I must ever feel that his time was well laid out. May we do good everywhere as we have opportunity, and results will not be wanting! [52]

LAST TRIP TO STAMBOURNE

Toward the end of Spurgeon's life, he went back to Stambourne. As stated, out of that venture came his last book: *Memories of Stambourne*. He traveled to Stambourne on June 8, 1891, the morning after he preached what proved to be his last sermon in the Metropolitan Tabernacle. He returned to his childhood home to get pictures that would adorn the book. Many friends urged him not to make the journey; nevertheless, he determined to do so. There seemed to be something in his heart that turned him back to those happy days with his grandparents and his beloved Aunt Ann. He became quite ill on the trip and had to be hurried back home. This particular illness completely incapacitated him for three months. But when his memories surged back: the Richard Knill prophecy, the old manse with its hall floors of brick sprinkled with sand, the sand stored in a cupboard under the stairs, and the upstairs room where he first made his acquaintance with the Puritan writers; it all filled him with joy and a few tears fell.

HOME IN COLCHESTER

When Spurgeon left his grandparents and returned to his parents in Colchester, three children had been born to the family: two sisters and a brother. Charles, being the oldest, took immediate command of the other children. He had learned how to have his way in Stambourne. Why should Colchester be any different? He had become quite an aggressive lad—some would probably say too aggressive. However, Charles also had an apprehensive streak in his dominant character: he was genuinely afraid of cows, and even as a man he would hesitate to cross a street alone.

Charles, despite his dominating ways, also possessed a great sensitivity of spirit. An illustration of that quality occurred not long after returning to his parents in Colchester; he entitled it in his *Autobiography* "My First and Last Debt." It taught him a lesson—and a principle—he never forgot. Actually, it forged his whole approach in the building of the Metropolitan Tabernacle and all his great ministry enterprises. He related the story:

> When I was a very small boy, in pinafores, and went to a woman's school, it so happened that I wanted a stick of slate pencil, and had no money to buy it with. I was afraid of being scolded for losing my pencils so often, for I was a

real careless little fellow, and so did not dare to ask at home; what then was I to do? There was a little shop in the place, where nuts, and tops, and cakes, and balls were sold by old Mrs. Pearson, and sometimes I had seen boys and girls get trusted by the old lady. I argued with myself that Christmas was coming, and that somebody or other would be sure to give me a penny then, and perhaps even a whole silver sixpence. I would, therefore, go into debt for a stick of slate pencil, and be sure to pay at Christmas. I did not feel easy about it, but still I screwed my courage up, and went into the shop. One farthing was the amount, and as I had never owed anything before, and my credit was good, the pencil was handed over by the kind dame, and *I was in debt*. It did not please me much, and I felt as if I had done wrong, but I little knew how soon I should smart for it.

How my father came to hear of this little stroke of business, I never knew, but some little bird or other whistled it to him, and he was very soon down upon me in right earnest. God bless him for it; he was a sensible man, and none of your children-spoilers; he did not intend to bring up his children to speculate, and play at what big rogues call financing, and therefore he knocked my getting into debt on the head at once, and no mistake. He gave me a very powerful lecture upon getting into debt, and how like it was to stealing, and upon the way in which people were ruined by it; and how a boy who would owe a farthing, might one day owe a hundred pounds, and get into prison, and bring his family into disgrace. It was a lecture, indeed; I think I can hear it now, and can feel my ears tingling at the recollection of it. Then I was marched off to the shop, like a deserter marched into barracks, crying bitterly all down the street, and feeling dreadfully ashamed, because I thought everybody knew I was in debt. The farthing was paid amid many solemn warnings, and the poor debtor was set free, like a bird let out of a cage. How sweet it felt to be out of debt! How did my little heart vow and declare that nothing should ever tempt me into debt again! It was a fine lesson, and I have never forgotten it. If all the boys were inoculated with the same doctrine when they were young, it would be as good as a fortune to them, and save them wagon-loads of trouble in after life. God bless my father, say I, and send a breed of such fathers into old England to save her from being eaten up with villainy, for what with companies, and schemes, and paper-money, the nation is getting to be as rotten as touchwood! Ever since that early sickening, I have hated debt as Luther hated the Pope.

Another occurrence of those early days is rather more to my credit. Long after my own sons had grown to manhood, I recalled to my father's recollection an experience of which, until then, he had never had an explanation. My brother, as a child, suffered from weak ankles, and in consequence frequently fell down, and so got into trouble at home. At last, hoping to cure him of what father thought was only carelessness, he was threatened that he should be whipped every time he came back showing any signs of having fallen down. When I reminded my father of this regulation, he said quite triumphantly,

'Yes, it was so, and he was completely cured from that time.' 'Ah!' I answered, 'so you thought, yet it was not so, for he had many a tumble afterwards; but I always managed to wash his knees, and to brush his clothes, so as to remove all traces of his falls.'[53]

He did have a sensitive spirit, which he carried through life.

In the early years, Charles began to develop a fondness for writing poetry. Victorian boys had a propensity for such things. Many undertook the task, but Spurgeon excelled. He even edited a small magazine. In one copy that is still extant, he talked about a prayer meeting and encouraged the readers to give themselves to the blessings that come from prayer. Of course, with his background, one could expect religious subjects to occupy his mind.

SCHOOL DAYS

During those early days in Colchester, Charles attended a school kept by a certain Mrs. Cook, the wife of a sea captain. He studied and worked with Mrs. Cook until he was about 10 years of age. She soon realized that she could teach him no more than what he had already learned, so the family sent him to a more advanced school, the Stockwell House School, that boasted of Mr. Henry Lewis as the headmaster. The school's honored usher (teacher) was Mr. E. S. Leeding. Leeding impressed Spurgeon significantly. Charles said, "He was a teacher who really taught his pupils; and by his diligent skill I gained the foundation upon which I built in after years."[54] By the time he entered the Stockwell House School, he had progressed exceptionally well in writing, reading, mathematics, and spelling. There he also started his studies in Greek grammar and Latin along with some philosophy. Although he never became an advanced scholar in all the ancient languages, he did become very proficient in Latin and Euclid. Moreover, he gave himself diligently to the Koine Greek of the New Testament and to Old Testament Hebrew. Between the ages of ten and eleven, on December 11, 1844, he won the first class English prize, the award being the book entitled *Natural History of Selborne*. Spurgeon treasured it throughout his life.

Biographer Conwell contends Spurgeon did not show early signs of genius.[55] Yet one seriously questions that; he was certainly far more intelligent than many of his peers. He had already read many of the Puritan theologians and possessed a reasonable grasp of the thought of men like Richard Sibbes, John Owen, John Flavel, and Matthew Henry. During these school days, Spurgeon also learned much about life in general.

Charles' younger brother, James Archer, (nearly three years younger) and the two younger sisters, Eliza and Emily were his constant companions. Becoming their natural leader, on one occasion he and the other children were at the game of playing church under the leadership of "Pastor Spurgeon." He stood up in a hayrack pretending to preach, while the others were seated on bales of hay in front of him listening to the sermon. On another occasion, James Archer and Charles were playing with toy ships in a creek. Charles, characteristic of his strong personality, had christened his ship the "Thunderer." He said he wanted a name that sounded courageous and victorious. Such was the temperament of the young lad.

Charles returned to his grandfather's home at Stambourne virtually every summer, as mentioned. He would invariably make his way to the upstairs chamber where the cache of old theological works were shelved. He said, "Out of that darkened room I fetched these old authors . . . and never was I happier than when in their company."[56] His brother, James, said:

> Charles never did anything else but study. I kept rabbits, chickens, pigs and a horse; he kept to books. While I was busy here and there, meddling with everything and anything that a boy could touch, he kept to books and could not be kept away from study. But although he had nothing to do with other things, he could have told you all about them, because he used to read about everything, with a memory as tenacious as a vice and as copious as a barn.[57]

As a young boy he had an incredible grasp of theology. An interesting event occurred during Charles' studies in the school of Mr. Henry Lewis. Suddenly it seemed as though he began to fail in his studies. His grades steadily plummeted to the bottom of the class. At first the puzzled teacher could not grasp what had happened to his young scholar, for he knew the mental ability of Charles. Finally, the light dawned: To be at the top place of the class, the student sat in a special seat of honor, but the seat was placed away from the fire, beside a drafty door. Mr. Lewis then reversed the seating arrangement and put the honored seat next to the stove. The young scholar very quickly worked his way up to the top of the class again.

Spurgeon never received any formal theological education for the ministry. Nonetheless, he did acquire a very able general education, much to his father's sacrifice. James Archer, Charles' brother, said, "How my father ever contrived to give us the training that he did, puzzles me. I know that he burdened himself to pay for the best education Nonconformity could command. If it was not better—I do not think it could have been —it was because no better was available."[58]

Spurgeon also concurred with his brother James on how able and influential Leeding and the school proved to be in his life. Spurgeon wrote at the death of Mr. E. S. Leeding in 1890 the following note:

> Mr. Leeding was usher in the school of Mr. Henry Lewis of Colchester in 1845 and I was one of the boys under his care. He was a teacher who really taught his pupils, and by his diligent skill I gained the foundation upon which I built in the after years. I left Colchester to open a school in Cambridge, and I go, first to Maidstone and then to Newmarket for some years. Then we came together again; for I joined him at Cambridge to assist in his school, and in

return to me, he helped in my studies. He has left it on record that he did not think that there was need for me to go to any of the Dissenting colleges, since I had mastered most of the subject studies therein; and his impression that I might, while with him, have readily passed through the University, if the pulpit had not come in the way. [59]

Spurgeon's parents obviously sacrificed greatly to educate their children. John, the father, said, "As the parent of seventeen children, I have frequently worn a shabby coat, when I might have possessed a good one, had I cared less for my children's education." At about the age of fourteen, after four years in the Colchester school, Charles and James Archer were sent to the St. Augustine's Agricultural College at Maidstone, southeast of London. The Church of England sponsored the Maidstone institution and Charles' uncle, David Walker, served as tutor and headmaster. The journey to Maidstone required the boys to travel through London. On the trip, Charles first encountered the city that was to be the seat of his great ministry. Even on this first trip he learned a lesson. He related:

I recollect that, when I first came to London as a boy, to go to school at Maidstone, while I was sitting in the coach, ready to start, a man came along selling knives with a great number of blades. He put one in at the window, and stuck it right before my face. Why did he want to intrude on me like that? He had no business to poke a knife in my eye; but he had never studied that kind of modesty which some of us have. If he had kept that many-bladed knife in his pocket, and quietly said, 'If there should be a person in the coach who would like to look at a knife with ever so many blades, I have one in my pocket,' he would not have sold one in a century; but he picked me out as a likely customer, and opened the blades as if he knew that such a knife would be wonderfully fascinating to a boy going to school. That man's energy taught me a lesson which I have often turned to good account when I have been trying to induct people to 'buy the truth.' [60]

In Maidstone, Charles quickly mastered his studies. An interesting encounter with an Anglican clergyman took place at St. Augustine's concerning the subject of Christian baptism. [61] The Church of England vicar came regularly to the Anglican school to give them lessons in the Christian religion. In one of the sessions, the clergyman led the class into a discussion on baptism. Charles knew very little, if anything, about Church of England theology at that time. Nevertheless, it proved to be something of a major turning point in his life. It needs to be related in his own words:

One of the clergy was, I believe, a good man; and it is to him I owe that ray of light which sufficed to show me believers' baptism. I was usually at the head of the class, and on one occasion, when the Church of England Catechism was to be repeated, something like the following conversation took place:

Clergyman.—What is your name?

Spurgeon.—Spurgeon, sir.

C.—No, no; what is your name?

S.—Charles Spurgeon, sir.

C.—No, you should not behave so, for you know I only want your Christian name.

S.—If you please, sir, I am afraid I haven't got one.

C.—Why, how is that?

S.—Because I do not think I am a Christian.

C.—What are you, then,—a heathen?

S.—No, sir; but we may not be heathens, and yet be without the grace of God, and so not be truly Christians.

C.—Well, well, never mind; what is your first name?

S.—Charles.

C.—Who gave you that name?

S.—I am sure I don't know, sir; I know no godfathers ever did anything for me, for I never had any. Likely enough, my mother and father did.

C.—Now, you should not set these boys a-laughing. Of course, I do not wish you to say the usual answer.

He seemed always to have a respect for me, and gave me *The Christian Year*, in calf, as a reward for my great proficiency in religious knowledge. Proceeding with the Catechism, he suddenly turned to me, and said, —

Spurgeon, you were never properly baptized.

S.—Oh, yes, sir, I was; my grandfather baptized me in the little parlour, and he is a minister, so I know he did it right!

C.—Ah, but you had neither faith nor repentance, and therefore ought not to have received baptism!

S.—Why, sir, that has nothing to do with it! All infants ought to be baptized.

C.—How do you know that? Does not the Prayer Book say that faith and repentance are necessary before baptism? And this is so Scriptural a doctrine, that no one ought to deny it. (Here he went on to show that all the persons spoken of in the Bible as being baptized were believers; which, of course, was an easy task, and then said to me,—) Now, Charles, I shall give you till next week to find out whether the Bible does not declare faith and repentance to be necessary qualifications before baptism.

I felt sure enough of victory; for I thought that a ceremony my grandfather and father both practiced in their ministry must be right; but I could not find it,—I was beaten,—and made up my mind as to the course I would take.

C.—Well, Charles, what do you think now?

S.—Why, sir, I think you are right; but then it applies to you as well as to me!

C.—I wanted to show you this; for this is the reason why we appoint sponsors. It is that, without faith, I had no more right than you to holy baptism; but the promise of my sponsors was accepted by the Church as an equivalent.

You have no doubt seen your father, when he has no money, give a note-of-hand for it; and this is regarded as an earnest of payment, because, as an honest man, we have reason to expect he will honour the note he has given. Now, sponsors are generally good people, and in charity we accept their promise on behalf of the child. As the child cannot at the time have faith, we accept the bond that he will; which promise he fulfills at confirmation, when he takes the bond into his own hands.

S.—Well, sir, I think it is a very bad note-of-hand.

C.—I have no time to argue that, but I believe it to be good. I will only ask you this,—Which seems to have the greater regard to Scripture,—I, as a Churchman, or your grandfather as a Dissenter? He baptizes in the very teeth of Scripture; and I do not, in my opinion, do so, for I require a promise, which I look upon as an equivalent of repentance and faith, to be rendered in future years.

S.—Really, sir, I think you are more like right; but since it seems to be the truth that only believers should be baptized, I think you are both wrong, though you seem to treat the Bible with the greater politeness.

C.—Well, then, you confess that you were not properly baptized; and you would think it your duty, if in your power, to join with us, and have sponsors to promise on your behalf?

S.—Oh, no! I have been baptized once, before I ought; I will wait next time till I am fit for it.

C.—(Smiling.) Ah, you are wrong; but I like to see you keep the Word of God! Seek from Him a new heart and Divine direction, and you will see one truth after another, and very probably there will be a great change in those opinions which now seem so deeply rooted in you.

I resolved, from that moment, that if ever Divine grace should work a change in me, I would be baptized, since, as I afterwards told my friend the clergyman, "I never ought to be blamed for improper baptism, as I had nothing to do with it; the error, if any, rested with my parents and grandparents."[62]

Church of England theology expressed in its catechism poses the question: "What is required of a person to be baptized?" The answer to the query that Charles had been instructed to give in his catechism studies at the Maidstone school declared, "Repentance, whereby they forsake sin, and faith, whereby they steadfastly believe in the promises of God made to them in that sacrament." From his Nonconformist background with its heavy emphasis on Scripture, Charles looked up the answer in the Bible. There he found the Anglican catechism to be correct concerning the biblical concepts of repentance and faith. Therefore, it dawned on him that *after* a person had repented and believed, then and only then, was he or she to be baptized. This instilled in Charles an early conviction that baptism is reserved for knowable believers only. This obviously excluded infants, and hence infant baptism. Up to this point in his life, Spurgeon had never seriously faced the question.

He had been in a Congregationalist context since a child and had never really addressed the issue of *believer's* baptism. He himself had been baptized as an infant and simply assumed the sufficiency of the act. After all, his esteemed grandfather and father preached that doctrine. When confronted with the question: "What is required of a person to be baptized?" Charles discovered from the Scriptures that repentance and faith were required, thus precluding infants, and he concluded that he had not been biblically baptized. Therefore, infant sprinkling had to be an error; and he pledged that if ever he came to repentance and faith, thus becoming a true Christian, he would be "properly baptized."

Charles confessed that at the time he did not know if there were any other persons who had the same conviction. The Baptists, who practice believer's baptism only, were so small in number and insignificant, at least to his understanding, that he did not even know they existed. As a consequence of the encounter with the Church of England catechism, he ultimately became a Baptist. He said, "I do not know that I had any vivid gratitude for any other question in the catechism, but I am very thankful for that particular one, for it led me where it was never intended to lead me by those who wrote it. It led me, however, as I believe, to follow the Scriptural teaching that repentance and faith are required before there can be any true Baptism."[63] Obviously, the ground work had been laid in his life to become affiliated with the Baptists, despite his Congregational upbringing. He was an independent thinker, as time will clearly demonstrate.

In 1848, as Spurgeon's studies progressed in Maidstone, he received a leather bound copy of *The Christian Year*. He received it as a prize for "proficiency in religious knowledge, mathematics, languages, and the applied sciences."[64] In those early years Charles' audacity surfaced on several occasions. That audacity later held him in good stead at times—but also became the cause for much criticism. It must be granted, he had a very forthright personality. For example, at Maidstone he once went about setting straight a mathematical error made by his tutor uncle. His uncle disciplined him by making him take his books out of doors and study beneath the oak tree by the Medway River. However, the uncle did recognize the unusual mathematical ability of young Charles and allowed him to make a set of calculations that a Life Insurance Society in London used for more than half a century.

Spurgeon had many intriguing experiences at the Anglican school. He enjoyed recounting one piece of mischief he engineered. It seems there was a large jar of ammonia in a classroom cupboard. Spurgeon would lead new boys in the school to it and tell them to take a good sniff. Naively, they would obey, and of course they would be quite overpowered. One day, engaging in the prank, a boy took a good sniff and fell down into a dead faint. Charles confessed it really frightened him and he did not play that game again. He probably took more liberties than the other students because, as mentioned, headmaster Walker of the school, was his uncle. At any rate, Spurgeon became a great favorite with his aunt, Mrs. Walker, and she helped him out of many difficult situations. All his life he had a winsome smile to match his bright personality that won the affection of many.

TO NEWMARKET

After the years of study in Maidstone, Charles and his brother traveled north in August of 1849 and were enrolled in a school in Newmarket, Cambridgeshire. The principal of the school was John Swindell. Spurgeon spent two years in that institution where he became an usher as well as a student. (An usher was one who taught in a secondary role to the regular teachers.)

During his school days at Newmarket, Spurgeon began to acquire a new grasp of theology, strangely enough, from an old cook in his school. Mary King, or "Cook," as all the students called her, was a good old soul and possessed a perception into the Christian faith. A big, sturdy woman, and loved by all the students, she impressed many, especially Charles. She lived in a little cottage facing St. Margaret's Anglican Church in Ipswich, but she was a member of the Bethesda Strict Baptist Church, and that made her a staunch Calvinist. The Strict Baptists were all "five point Calvinists." Mary was not theologically trained in any formal sense, but she had a logical, clear-headed approach to theology and possessed a quite profound grasp of the Scriptures. She always called herself a "housekeeper" in the school, not just a mere cook. She read *The Gospel Standard* regularly, and received much of her theology from its pages.

Mary King had a special affection for Charles and spent hours with him, instructing him in sound Calvinistic doctrine. Later in life, when she found herself in difficult financial straits, Spurgeon supported her for years until her death. Charles wrote of the impact she made on his life:

> The first lessons I ever had in theology were from an old cook in the school at Newmarket where I was an usher. She was a good old soul, and used to read *The Gospel Standard*. She liked something very sweet indeed, good strong Calvinistic doctrine; but she lived strongly as well as fed strongly. Many a time we have gone over the covenant of grace together, and talked of the personal election of the saints, their union to Christ, their final perseverance, and what vital godliness meant; and I do believe that I learnt more from her than I should have learned from any six doctors of divinity of the sort we have nowadays. There are some Christian people who taste, and see, and enjoy religion in their own souls, and who get at a deeper knowledge of it than books can ever give them, though they should search all their days. The cook at Newmarket was a godly experienced woman, from whom I learned far more than I did from the minister of the chapel we attended. I asked her once, 'Why

do you go to such a place?' She replied, 'Well, there is no other place of worship to which I can go.' I said, 'But it must be better to stay at home than to hear such stuff.' 'Perhaps so,' she answered; 'but I like to go out to worship even if I get nothing by going. You see a hen sometimes scratching all over a heap of rubbish to try to find some corn; she does not get any, but it shows that she is looking for it, and using the means to get it, and then, too, the exercise warms her.' So the old lady said that scratching over the poor sermons she heard was a blessing to her because it exercised her spiritual faculties and warmed her spirit. On another occasion I told her that I had not found a crumb in the whole sermon, and asked how she had fared. 'Oh!' she answered, 'I got on better to-night, for to all the preacher said, I just put in a not, and that turned his talk into real gospel.' [65]

Charles had strong moral convictions in those school days, even though not yet converted. For example, he would not go to the horse races, as did some of the students. Professor Everett's diary declared, "Mr. Spurgeon did not go as he thought he should be doing wrong if he went." [66]

AT HOME FOR THE HOLIDAYS

A most significant and climactic event occurred when Spurgeon went home to his parents in Colchester for a holiday period from the Newmarket school. Biographer G. Holden Pike, Spurgeon's most prolific biographer, says it occurred while Charles was at Cambridge, but that would put it too late. Pike missed the dating. It came about as an outbreak of fever at the Newmarket school, near the Christmas recess, and shut down the institution temporarily. So Charles and James made their way home to Colchester during the months of November and December of 1849, and January of 1850.

Leading up to the climactic event that occurred, during those weeks at home, Charles wrote, as a kind of "holiday amusement," an essay entitled *Anti-Christ and Her Brood; Or, Popery Unmasked.* [67] Biographer Charles Ray says he wrote it on his knees, so his "amusement" was hardly light-hearted. The chapter headings read:

Chap. I.   Popery, the Apostate Spirit.
       II.   Popery Established by Cunning.
       III. Popery, a Spiritual Darkness.
       IV.   Popery, a Mass of Superstition.
       V.   Popery, a Ravenous Wolf.
       VI.   Examination of the Claims of Popery.
       VII. Popery, a Complicated Idolatry. The Worship of Virgin Mary.
       VIII. Popery, a Polytheism. Worship of Saints.
       IX.   Popery, the Worship of Cast Clouts and Rotten Rags.

X.   Popery, a Violation of the Second Commandment.
XI.   Popery Teaches the Adoration of a Breaden God.
XII.   Popery Perverts and Destroys the Sacred Ordinances of Christianity.
XIII. Popery Surrounds Itself with Rites and Ceremonies.
XIV.   Popery, the Inventor of a False Purgation.
XV.   Popery, a Gigantic Horseleech.
XVI.   Popery, the Religion of Fools, who made a Mock at Sin.
XVII. Popery, the Enemy of Science, and the Bane of the Human Race. [68]

Obviously, Spurgeon opposed the Roman Catholic Church. The essay became a full 290 page work—a sizable production for a fifteen-year-old. Charles submitted his work in a contest sponsored by Arthur Morley of Nottingham. Morley offered a prize for an approved essay on "Popery." Spurgeon did not win the coveted first prize; yet, for his efforts he did receive a congratulatory letter and a small sum. As a lad, he always tithed to the church any money he received. In addition, whenever he won or received some fee for writing, he gave one-fifth to the Lord's work. It set a pattern for life. He said he had never after that "been able to deny himself the pleasure of having a fifth to give."[69] After the prize money came he wrote to his father saying he now could buy more books. For Spurgeon, it really was always "books, books, books."

The significance of this particular episode, which may seem rather inconsequential today, can be grasped in that it demonstrates the general Victorian Nonconformist attitude toward Rome. Actually that attitude precipitated a strong denunciation of the Roman Catholic Church in 1850. The cause of the eruption centered on what was called "Papal Aggression." In 1850 the Pope issued an edict that created a "Catholic hierarchy in England."[70]

A coalition of anti-catholicism sentiment among all classes in society developed and produced the vehement words against Rome. Spurgeon's essay proved that even as a youth he and many others held a rigid anti-catholic perspective. Evangelicals felt the Gospel was at stake.

Spurgeon's anti-catholic sentiments would be frowned upon in many circles today—and even to some extent in his own day. But it must be remembered that this transpired before Vatican II and the evangelical thrust in Roman Catholicism that followed that historic event in 1962. Moreover, Spurgeon was a thoroughgoing evangelical and had been reared in the context of Puritanism. Therefore, it is somewhat understandable that a degree of intolerance would manifest itself in his approach to the Roman Church. But, he carried that conviction throughout life. He seemingly never mellowed on the subject. For example, years later a series of articles in *The Sword and the Trowel*, the monthly periodical of the Metropolitan Tabernacle, were published attacking Rome. The series became known as the *No Popery Litera-*

ture. Spurgeon's prejudice against the Roman Church never abated. He had been steeped in that negative attitude since childhood. Kruppa suggests that his anti-catholicism was a "vital ingredient in his intellectual and emotional outlook, coloring his attitudes to ecclesiology, politics, and the state church."[71]

The paper on Popery was far from the most important event that occurred in Charles' life over the Christmas holidays, however. Spurgeon's stay at home became the scene of his dramatic conversion to Jesus Christ. That fascinating story, typical of a classic Calvinistic Puritan conversion, must be told. Charles' actual conversion experience, however, was preceded by a long agonizing period of conviction. It proved to be a long, hard journey for the religiously minded lad. But, Charles got a glimpse of "yonder wicket gate" and began to move toward the "open grave" where the heavy burden on his back would at last fall off and he would be free from the burden and remorse of sin. And he would not be deterred.

THE PILGRIMAGE TO THE CROSS

Spurgeon embarked on his pilgrimage to the cross at a very early age. He understood early on how much he needed Christ. Christian parents watched with spiritually jealous eyes over their son. He declared that had it not been for the grace of God and his godly parents, he might have been either dead or an "earnest ringleader amongst the ungodly."[72] Many had shared with him the message of Christ and the joy of forgiven sins—recall the Richard Knill incident when Charles was only ten. His grandparents, his Aunt Ann, the many preachers he heard, but especially his mother kept the claims of Jesus Christ before the precocious young man. He said about his mother:

> I cannot tell how much I hold to the solemn words of my good mother. It was the custom on Sunday evenings, while we were yet little children for her to stay at home with us, and then we sat around the table, and read verse by verse and she explained the scriptures to us.[73]

Charles' father, John, influenced his life as well. But his mother's influence cannot be overemphasized. After his conversion, Spurgeon wrote:

> You, my Mother, have been the great means in God's hand of rendering me what I hope I am. Your kind, warning Sabbath-evening addresses were too deeply settled on my heart to be forgotten. You, by God's blessing prepared the way for the preached Word, and for that holy book, *The Rise and Progress*. If I have any courage, if I feel prepared to follow my Saviour, not only into the water, but should He call me, even into the fire, I love you as the preacher to my heart of such courage, as my praying, watching Mother.[74]

The reading of the old Puritans also helped to bring Charles under conviction of his sin. As pointed out earlier, two books in particular, Joseph Alleine's *An Alarm to Unconverted Sinners* and Richard Baxter's *Call to the*

Unconverted, not to mention Bunyan's *Pilgrim's Progress*, were instruments in the hands of the Spirit of God to create in Charles a sense of the need of salvation. His conscience continually smote his tender heart. He would cry himself to sleep at night whenever he did something wrong. He said he felt deep gratitude after he came to Christ, that the Lord had given him such a sensitive conscience. Still, for years he rejected the wooing of the Holy Spirit. In those early days of constant exposure to the Gospel, as Spurgeon expressed it, "I let the years run round,—not without twinges of conscience, not without rebukes, when I knew how much I needed a Saviour; not without the warning which came from others whom I saw happy and rejoicing in Christ, while I had no share in His salvation."[75] He lamented the days he hid his face from Christ "in wilful neglect of my dear Lord whose heart had bled for me."[76] His mother's prayers, however, were beginning to catch up with him.

Eulogizing his mother again, he said, "Never could it be possible for any man to estimate what he owes to a godly mother."[77] He declared he could never forget how she fell on her knees, and with her arms around his neck would pray, "Oh, that my son might live before thee!"[78]

Spurgeon would often accompany his father, pastor of the church at Tolesbury, and hear him preach on Sunday. This also tremendously touched his life. His tribute to his father as a means of his conversion were with these words:

> Well do I remember hearing my father speak of an incident that greatly impressed him. He used to be frequently away from home preaching, and at one time, as he was on his way to a service, he feared that he was neglecting his own family while caring for the souls of others. He therefore turned back, and went to his home. On arriving there, he was surprised to find no one in the lower rooms of the house; but, on ascending the stairs, he heard a sound as of someone engaged in prayer. On listening at the bedroom door, he discovered that it was my mother, pleading most earnestly for the salvation of all her children, and specially praying for Charles, her first-born and strong-willed son. My father felt that he might safely go about his Master's business while his dear wife was caring so well for the spiritual interests of the boys and girls at home, so he did not disturb her, but proceeded at once to fulfil his preaching engagement.[79]

Charles' spiritual awareness did not stem merely from his religious environment, however. God truly addressed the lad. Thus he became convinced that as soon as a child is capable of being lost, he is capable of being saved. He believed that as soon as a child can sin that child can, by the grace of God, receive the Word of God and come to faith in Jesus Christ as that child is moved by the Spirit. He declared children can genuinely understand the Scriptures. He testified about himself saying, "I am sure that, when but a child, I could have discussed many a knotty point of controversial theology

... in fact, children are capable of understanding some things in early life, which we hardly understand afterwards."[80] Children have that simplicity of faith that enables them to believe God and hear His Word, Spurgeon argued. He related hearing a sermon one time that spoke powerfully to his heart:

> Once, under a powerful sermon, my heart shook within me, and was dissolved in the midst of my bowels; I thought I would seek the Lord, and I bowed my knee, and wrestled, and poured out my heart before Him. Again I ventured within His sanctuary to hear His Word, hoping that in some hour He would send a precious promise to my consolation; but, ah! that wretched afternoon, I heard a sermon wherein Christ was not; I had no longer any hope. I would have sipped at that fountain, but I was driven away; I felt that I would have believed in Christ, and I longed and sighed for Him. But, ah! that dreadful sermon, and those terrible things that were uttered; my poor soul knew not what was truth, or what was error; but I thought the man was surely preaching the truth, and I was driven back. I dared not go, I could not believe, I could not lay hold on Christ; I was shut out, if no one else was.[81]

But all preaching did not necessarily touch Charles' heart or meet his need. He related:

> I used to hear a minister whose preaching was, as far as I could make it out, 'Do this, and do that, and do the other, and you will be saved.' According to his theory, to pray was a very easy thing; to make yourself a new heart, was a thing of a few instants, and could be done at almost any time; and I really thought that I could turn to Christ when I pleased, and that therefore I could put it off to the last part of our life when it might be conveniently done upon a sick bed. But when the Lord gave my soul its first shakings in conviction, I soon knew better, I went to pray; I did pray, God knoweth, but it seemed to me that I did not. What, I approach the throne? Such a wretch as I lay hold on the promise? I ventured to hope that God could look on me. It seemed impossible. A tear, a groan, and sometimes not so much as that, an 'Ah!' a 'Would that!' a "but,"—the lip could not utter more. It was prayer, but it did not seem so them. Oh, how hard is prevailing prayer to a poor God-provoking sinner! Where was the power to lay hold on God's strength, or wrestle with the angel? Certainly not in me, for I was weak as water, and sometimes hard as the nether mill-stone.[82]

The long pilgrimage obviously was agonizing. In the *Autobiography*, he entitled his journey: "Through Much Tribulation." He talks about his heart being fallow and covered with weeds, but then on a certain day:

> The Great Husbandman came, and began to plough my soul. Ten black horses were His team, and there was a tough ploughshare that He used, and the ploughers made deep furrows. The ten commandments were those ten black horses, and the justice of God, like a ploughshare, tore my spirit. I was con-

demned, undone, destroyed,—lost, helpless, hopeless,—I thought hell was before me.[83]

In this setting Spurgeon began to open up to the Gospel. Still, he found no peace. He declared that the promises of God frowned upon him. Later, he could say, "the abundant benefit which we now reap from the deep ploughing of our heart is enough of itself to reconcile us to the severity of the process."[84] But at the moment, he groveled under the miserable burden of sin he carried on his shoulder. He described himself as "dead, diseased, pained, chained, scourged, bound in fetters of iron, in darkness and the shadow of death."[85] Just like Pilgrim, he had left the City of Destruction and the journey proved agonizingly miserable.

Spurgeon began to pray earnestly. He could remember the first time that he ever prayed sincerely, and ceased his perfunctory kind of prayers. But, even then, as he saw himself standing before God, the Almighty, Holy and Sovereign, he said that he felt like Esther when she stood before the King overcome with dread.

> I was full of penitence of heart, because of his majesty and my sinfulness. I think the only words I could utter were something like these, 'Ows!—Ah!', and the only complete sentence was, 'God, be merciful to me, a sinner!'[86]

But even in the midst of all of his praying, Spurgeon found no peace. Charles related that "a deep horror rested on me at the recollection of my repeated, but unanswered cries."[87] Yet he realized:

> Neither in the church militant nor in the host triumphant is there one who received a new heart, and was reclaimed from sin without a wound from Jesus.

He felt himself a deeply wounded man under profound conviction. He could resonate with the great Puritan John Owen who said, "My soul was oppressed with horror and darkness."[88] God's Law had laid hold of him and his sins stood out in bold relief to his troubled soul. The time would come when he was able to say, "We find no sword-blades so true in metal as those which have been forged in the furnace of soul-trouble."[89] In the meantime, however, he writhed in the fire. And the books he devoured at the time, as well as the sermons, struck even deeper conviction. He cried:

> Oh, those books, those books! I read and devoured them when under a sense of guilt, but it was like sitting at the foot of Sinai. For five years, as a child, there was nothing before my eyes but my guilt, and though I do not hesitate to say that those who observed my life would not have seen any extraordinary sin, yet as I looked upon myself, there was not a day in which I did not commit such gross, such outrageous sins against God, that often and often have I wished I had never been born.[90]

Paradoxically, some bright spots broke through Charles' dark clouds of tribulation. He said, "Yet I recollect, even as a child, God hearing my prayer."[91] But, despair would soon return. He finally got to the place where he could say, "If God does not send me to hell, he ought to do it."[92] He lamented, "It was my sad lot to feel the greatness of my sin without a discovery of the greatness of God's mercy."[93] All the while, it seemed the simple gospel message just could not break through to the convicted young man. He confessed, "I had heard of the plan of salvation by the sacrifice of Jesus from my youth up; but I did not know any more about it in my innermost soul than if I had been born and bred a Hottentot."[94] He argued with himself, "It surely cannot be that, if I believe in Jesus, just as I am, I shall be saved? I must feel something; I must do something."[95] He wished a thousand times that some preacher would tell him what he might do to be saved.

Yet, in all of Charles' fervent seeking of God, an inward rebellion still persisted. He said, as he opened his heart to his readers in the *Autobiography*:

> I must confess that I never would have been saved if I could have helped it. As long as ever I could, I rebelled, and revolted, and struggled against God. When He would have me pray, I would not pray: when He would have me listen to the sound of the ministry, I would not. And when I heard, and the tear rolled down my cheek, I wiped it away, and defied Him to melt my heart. There came an election sermon; but that did not please me. There came a law sermon, showing me my powerlessness; but I did not believe it, I thought it was the whim of some old experimental Christian, some dogma of ancient times that would not suit men now. Then there came another sermon, concerning death and sin; but I did not believe I was dead, for I thought I was alive enough, and could repent and make myself right by-and-by. Then there came a strong exhortation sermon; but I felt I could set my house in order when I liked, as well as I could do it at once. So did I continually trust in my self-sufficiency. When my heart was a little touched, I tried to divert it with sinful pleasures; and would not then have been saved, until God gave me the effectual blow, and I was obliged to submit to that irresistible effort of His grace. It conquered my depraved will, and made me bow myself before His gracious sceptre. When the Lord really brought me to myself, He sent one great shot which shivered me to pieces; and, lo, I found myself utterly defenseless. I thought I was more mighty than the angels, and could accomplish all things; but I found myself less than nothing.[96]

Spurgeon realized, as did the great mystic and scientist, Blase Pascal, "To make a man a saint, grace is absolutely necessary, and whoever doubts it, does not know what a saint is or what a man is."[97] But how to get that grace?

Spurgeon's struggling pilgrimage to the cross actually moved along a typical nineteenth century Puritan path. But Charles' journey, in one sense, unfolded in a strange way. He sensed a deep conviction of sin, which was typical of Puritanism, but he did not fear judgment. He confessed he feared not hell so much, he simply feared sin. All the time he had on his mind that deep Puritan concern for the honor of God's name and the integrity of His moral government. This precipitated for Charles the fundamental question as to how God could be just and yet justify a guilty sinner. He confessed that he worried to the point of being wearied over the issue. One would have thought his Calvinistic upbringing would have taught him the principle of *grace*. But he was lost, under the blinding power of sin and Satan. He felt driven almost to the brink of despair. Yet, things were decidedly coming to a climax in the life of young Spurgeon.

A STRANGE TURN

An ironic aspect of Spurgeon's spiritual journey emerged at this stage. He did not feel at liberty to talk with his parents about the deep trauma and struggle he was enduring, as common as such a struggle was in evangelical circles of the day. This may well be the reason why neither his father nor mother became the *direct* instruments in his conversion. Charles did not even share with them one of his greatest traumas—a brush with atheism. During that period, Spurgeon's rebellion once went so deep that he talked himself into being an atheist. He made his best effort to convince himself that God did not even exist. He related the rather lengthy story in a fascinating manner:

> I have never been thoroughly an unbeliever but once, and that was not before I knew the need of a Saviour, but after it. It was just when I wanted Christ, and panted after Him, that, on a sudden, the thought crossed my mind—which I abhorred but could not conquer,—that there was no God, no Christ, no Heaven, no hell; that all my prayers were but a farce, and that I might as well have whistled to the winds or spoken to the howling waves. Ah! I remember how my ship drifted along through that sea of fire, loosened from the anchor of my faith, which I had received from my fathers. I no longer moored myself hard by the coasts of Revelation; I said to reason, "Be thou my captain;" I said to my own brain, "Be thou my rudder;" and I started on my mad voyage. Thank God, it is all over now; but I will tell you it's a brief history. It was one hurried sailing over the tempestuous ocean of free thought. I went on, and as I went, the skies began to darken; but to make up for that deficiency, the waters were gleaming with coruscations of brilliancy. I saw sparks flying upwards that pleased me, and I felt, 'If this be free thought, it is a happy thing.' My thoughts seemed gems, and I scattered stars with both my hands; but anon, instead of these coruscations of glory, I say grim fiends, fierce and horrible, start up from the waters; and as I dashed on, they gnashed their teeth, and grinned upon me; they seized the prow of my ship, and dragged me on, while I, in part, gloried at the rapidity of my motion, but yet shuddered at the terrific rate with which I passed the old landmarks of my faith. I went to the very verge of the dreary

realms of unbelief. I went to the very bottom of the sea of infidelity. As I hurried forward at an awful speed, I began to doubt if there were a world. I doubted everything, until at last the devil defeated himself by making me doubt my own existence. I thought I was an idea floating in the nothingness of vacuity, then, startled with that thought, and feeling that I was substantial flesh and blood after all, I saw that God was, and Christ was, and Heaven was, and hell was, and that all these things were absolute truths. The very extravagance of the doubt proved its absurdity, and there came a voice which said, 'And can this doubt be true?' Then I awoke from that death-dream, which, God knows, might have damned my soul, and ruined my body, if I had not awoke. When I arose, faith took the helm; from that moment, I doubted not. Faith steered me back; faith cried, 'Away, away!' I cast my anchor on Calvary; I lifted my eye to God; and here I am alive, and out of hell. Therefore, I speak what I do know. I have sailed that perilous voyage; I have come safe to land. Ask me again to be an infidel! No; I have tried it; it was sweet at first, but bitter afterwards. [98]

But now Spurgeon's conversion moment was pressing in on him—the hour when all his agony would end. It had been a long, difficult struggle. After his miserable journey finally reached its goal, Charles said, "Scarcely ever since then have I known joys which surpassed the rapture of that first hour." [99]

There cannot be too strong an emphasis laid upon the importance of Spurgeon's dramatic conversion movement. As Carlile correctly commented, "That early experience in the little chapel at Colchester decided almost everything for Spurgeon." [100] No doubt, it proved to be the most significant event in his entire life, spiritually, theologically, and practically. He became a transformed man. At least one account of Spurgeon's conversion appeared in each of the fifty-seven volumes of the *Metropolitan Tabernacle Pulpit*. He seemingly never tired of sharing his testimony. In this, he appeared much like the Apostle Paul. What a day it was when he passed through "yonder wicket gate," and the burden rolled away through Jesus Christ. The full account must be told in the next chapter.

4

"His Burden Loosed From off His Shoulders"

SPURGEON'S CONVERSION AND EARLY MINISTRY

C. H. Spurgeon preaching at Exeter Hall, February, 1855.

Thus far did I come laden with my sin
Nor could ought ease the grief that I was in
Till I came hither. What a place is this!
Must here be the beginning of my bliss?
Must here the burden fall from off my back?
Must here the strings that bound it to me crack?
Blest cross! Blest sepulchre! Blest rather be
The man that there was put to shame for me.

—*John Bunyan*

Introduction

Engraved on a marble plaque, hung on the wall by the pew in the Colchester Primitive Methodist chapel where teenage Charles Haddon Spurgeon sat when "his burden loosed from off his shoulders," these words stand out in bold relief: "I looked that moment, and the grace of faith was vouchsafed to me in that *self-same* instant; and now I think I say with truth —

'Ere since by faith
I saw the stream
Thy flowing wounds supply
Redeeming love has been my theme
And shall be 'til I die."

These are the very words Spurgeon himself used as he related his dramatic salvation story. He gloried in his conversion, now he was free to serve the Savior whom he had so long sought, and who had so graciously saved him. In typical Puritan fashion, as seen in the last chapter, Spurgeon's pilgrimage to that moment when "the grace of faith was vouchsafed" to the fifteen-year-old boy, was a long arduous journey. But at last he found that "Amazing Grace," as Puritan John Newton expressed it in his classical hymn. The entire rationale of Spurgeon's conversion could be no other than the sheer grace of God leading him to that climactic moment. Charles recognized that fact as he reached out and grasped salvation, thus becoming a thoroughly converted man. Drawing an analogy from Pilgrim's Progress, as he so often did, Charles said:

He said, 'Come,' and I flew to Him and clasped Him; and when He let me go again, I wondered where my burden was. It was gone! There, in the sepulchre, it lay, and I felt light as air; like a winged sylph, I could fly over mountains of trouble and despair; and oh! what liberty and joy I had! . . . I hear His voice,— it is full of sweetness, I am forgiven, I am forgiven, I am forgiven!

THE EVENTFUL DAY

The memorable day, as most biographers agree, fell on a Sunday in January of 1850. That morning, Charles arose early to pray and read one of his Puritan works. But he found no rest of soul in his reading and prayer. As he expressed it, God was plowing his soul with "ten black horses," that is, the Ten Commandments. He went on to say, God was also "cross plowing" it with the message of the Gospel. Still, even when he heard the good news of Christ, it seemingly afforded no comfort. So, he languished on.

Charles had visited many of the chapels in Colchester, trusting to hear a word of hope, but to no avail. No one, it seemed, could point him to Christ. So on that January morning he started off again for a church, hoping that some minister would tell him how he might be saved. As portrayed earlier, the snow began to pelt down. The storm detoured him from reaching the place of worship where he had planned to go. He had originally intended to go with his father to Tolesbury, but decided against it. So, he decided to attend some church in Colchester. Down the snowy street he trekked. He then remembered a word from his mother that he should sometime visit the Primitive Methodist chapel on Artillery Street. When he passed the memorable street, because of the heavy snow and the chilling wind, he turned down the lane and entered the little chapel. He sat down with about fifteen other people. He could not even look up at the minister; misery filled his heavy heart. But in that simple setting, redemption came. He relished to remember the happy day and loved to tell the story; he was convinced of the power in one's testimony to touch others. In his book, *The Saint and His Saviour,* he recalled the joyous event. It stands as a classic expression of conversion:

> Oh that blest day! again our memory rushes back to it, and rapture glows even at its mention. Many days have passed since then; but as the one draught of sweet water refreshes the camel over many a mile of desert, so doth that happy hour still cheer us as we remember it. Beginning of the days of heaven! Firstborn of morning! Prophet of blessing! Funeral of fears! Birthday of hope! Day of our spirit's betrothal! Day of God and day of mercy!—oh that we had power to sing the joy which kindles our passions to a flame while we review thee! or rather, of that we had grace to hymn His praise who made thee such a day! Doth the stranger inquire, What hath so distinguished that day above its fellows? the answer is already knocking at the door of our lips to obtain an egress. We were released from the thraldom of sin, we were delivered from the scourges of conscience, we were ransomed from the bondage of law, we were emancipated from the slavery of corruption; death vanished before the quickening of the Holy Ghost, poverty was made rich with infinite treasures of

grace, and hunger felt itself satisfied with good things. Naked before, we on that day put on the robes of princes; black, we washed ourselves clean in a bath of blood; sick, we received instant healing; despairing, we rejoiced with joy unspeakable. Ask her who has had the issue of her blood staunched by a touch; as yon healed demoniac, or his companion who throws away the crutch of his long halting, why on that day of recovery they were glad; and they will exhibit their own persons as reasons for their joy: so, O wondering gazer, look on us and solve the mystery of our enthusiastic song. We ourselves are our own answer to your inquiries.

Let us summon memory again to lead the choir, while all that is within us doth bless His holy name. 'He spake and it was done;' 'He said, Let there be light, and there was light.' He passed by, in the greatness of his love and in the plenitude of his power, and bade us live. O eyes of beauty, how were ye outdone by his sweet looks! He was fairer than the sons of men, and lovelier than a dream when he manifested himself unto us. Lying by the pool of mercy, we pined away with disappointment, for none would put us into the healing water; but his love stayed not for an instant, he said, 'Take up thy bed and walk.' Ah, where shall thunders be found which will lend us voices? where floods which can lend us uplifted hands? for we need these to utter half His praise. Angels, your sonnets and your golden canticles are poor, poor things for our sweet Lord Jesus. He deserveth notes which your voices cannot afford, and music which dwells not within the strings of your most melodious harps. He must be his own poet, for none but he can sing himself. He knows, and only he, that depth of love within his bleeding heart, some drops of which we drank on that auspicious morning of redemption. He can tell, and only he, the transporting sound of that sweet assurance which laid our fears to rest in his own sepulchre. He alone can testify what he hath wrought; for, as for us, we were asleep on the mount of joy; 'when God turned back the captivity of Zion, we were like men that dreamed; our mouth was filled with laughter, and our tongue with singing.' He, our Light, did light a candle around us; our 'conversation was in heaven;' our souls made us like the chariots of Amminadib;

> 'Our rapture seem'd a pleasing dream,
> The grace appear'd so great.'

We cried out in wonder, love, and praise, 'Whence is this to me? and what am I, and what is my Father's house, that the Lord hath visited me, and brought me hitherto.' Our dark and loathsome prison still made our garments to smell of its mouldiness, and this quickened our gratitude for our deliverance.

The dramatic occasion never escaped Spurgeon, as the full account in chapter one of this biography makes clear. Peace had finally come to his troubled heart and he gained the full assurance that Christ's redemption had become his own. The burden truly did "loose off his shoulders." What a day for the seeking young man; and what a day for the whole Church of the

Lord Jesus Christ because of the great ministry that unfolded from that experience.

In the years that followed Spurgeon's conversion, considerable discussion erupted about the identity of the preacher on that January day, even on which Sunday it took place. Some have even debated the year. Considerable research exists on these issues, and though the answers to these questions are not of vital importance to the life and ministry of Spurgeon, it has produced widespread debate.

Of course, the salient features of Spurgeon's conversion are well established. His long, arduous pilgrimage to the cross and the joy and peace that came as he received Christ have never been questioned. Also, no one disputes the place of his conversion: the Primitive Methodist Chapel on Artillery Street in Colchester, Essex. Moreover, the sermon text the preacher used on that day was unquestionably Isaiah 45:22; "Look unto me and be ye saved, all the ends of the earth; for I am God and there is none else." All this is generally accepted. However, there has been wide disagreement about the date of Spurgeon's conversion and especially the identity of the "illiterate preacher" who preached the famous "Look" sermon. This debate casts no doubt on the reality of Spurgeon's conversion, but it does present an interesting historical quandary.

To establish the facts incontestably surrounding Spurgeon's conversion is probably impossible, but what can be deduced should prove helpful to understand more fully the life of the great preacher. We turn first, quite naturally, to the primary source of information, Charles himself.

SPURGEON'S TESTIMONY

Concerning the preacher and date of that notable Sunday, it should be made clear that Spurgeon did not doubt his recollection of the date. Charles always contended for the first Sunday in January, 1850. However, he never identified the preacher; he seemed to be quite content with the minister remaining anonymous. One wonders if he did not wish to keep the preacher's identity unknown because of his Calvinistic emphasis on God's sovereignty in the salvation experience.

The earliest data that Spurgeon himself divulged regarding his conversion is found in his diary that covered the period of April 6, 1850 to June 20, 1850. In the early pages of the brief diary, he wrote, "Saved men and women date from the dawn of their true lives; not from their first birthday, but from the day wherein they were born again."[1] He saw his conversion as the starting point of it all. This fascinating diary account of Spurgeon's early spiritual experiences will be presented later in this chapter. In his diary, Spurgeon stated emphatically that he had found Jesus Christ on the sixth of January, 1850. He later verified that same date in a message preached at New Park Street Baptist Church on Sunday morning, the sixth of January,

1856. In that sermon, he stated that exactly six years earlier, "as near as possible at this very hour of the day," he had come to Christ.[2] Ten years later, on Sunday, the ninth of January, 1876, Spurgeon declared in his message, "twenty six-years exactly last Thursday, . . . I looked on the Lord, and found salvation."[3] Moreover, Spurgeon went back to the little Colchester chapel fourteen years after his conversion on the 11th of October 1864. He preached on that occasion, and pointing to the pew where he sat on that January Sunday in 1850, he said, "I was sitting in that pew when I was converted." Spurgeon was very clear about the details. So it seems obvious that Spurgeon himself was absolutely convinced that on the first Sunday in January, 1850, in the little Primitive Methodist Chapel, he came to new life in Christ. The pulpit where the preacher stood on that occasion now rests in Spurgeon's College, London.

Spurgeon regrettably did not identify the Primitive Methodist preacher the Spirit of God used to bring him to salvation, at least not as specifically as he did the date of his conversion. He merely described the preacher as "a tall, thin man" with a "feeble voice," "a plain, unlettered, lay preacher among the Primitive Methodists." He talked about him as "an unknown person, who certainly was no minister in the ordinary acceptation of the term."[4] It will be recalled, Spurgeon said that the regular minister of the church was presumably snowed in and, "a very thin-looking man, a shoemaker, or tailor, or something of that sort, went into the pulpit to preach."[5] Spurgeon even stated, "This man was really stupid," and "did not even pronounce the words rightly."[6] All these descriptive phrases show something of his impression of the person who preached. However, these descriptions obviously do not identify the man at all. Spurgeon adamantly contended that since that snowy Sunday he had never again seen the preacher who brought him to faith in Christ, nor did he expect to see him in this life. He stated, "I have never seen him from that day and probably shall never, till we meet in heaven."[7] Most interesting, however, three different preachers claimed to be the man who preached the "Look" sermon. In the *Autobiography*, the compilers (Spurgeon's widow and Spurgeon's secretary, Mr. Harrald), stated Charles did not recognize any one of the three when he met them.[8] Spurgeon went on to say, the preacher "probably will never be heard of in this life."[9] Thus we can conclude, as far as Spurgeon was concerned, that the identity of the man is unknown and the date is quite firmly fixed as the first Sunday in January, 1850.

OTHER OPINIONS

Of course, as could be expected, many chroniclers either just agree with Spurgeon's analysis of the events or simply generalize the issues, thus avoiding any contradiction. Several biographers, however, have differed with Spurgeon's own testimony surrounding his conversion. Those who have seriously approached the details have come up with some interesting data in conflict with Charles.

Timothy McCoy, in his excellent research on the issues, points out that Spurgeon's earliest biographer, George John Stevenson, wrote at least five different accounts of the great preacher's life. His first book, published in 1857, fixed the date of Spurgeon's conversion imprecisely only stating that he was "not quite sixteen years old." [10] Nor did Stevenson attempt to identify the preacher on that day. His succeeding two works added no further insight. The most exhaustive account of the conversion story in Stevenson's work, however, is found in his fourth biography. In this work, he relied on two or three primary sources for the conclusions he drew. He seems to have gleaned some material from Spurgeon's own words, but primarily he relied on a significant pamphlet published in 1869 by Danzy Sheen. Sheen's work, entitled *Pastor Spurgeon: His Conversion, Labor, and Success*, unfortunately no longer exists. Stevenson quotes from it extensively and agrees primarily with Sheen's contention that the preacher on that occasion was the Rev. Robert Eaglen, and that the date was the fifteenth of December, 1850. Both of these conclusions go against Spurgeon's testimony, especially the date.

Stevenson's conclusion rests on the fact that Eaglen served as a circuit rider on the Ipswich Circuit of the Primitive Methodists, Colchester being part of that circuit. The Methodists' official records show that on the fifteenth day of December, 1850, Eaglen's schedule put him at the little Primitive Methodist Chapel in Colchester. Remarkably, Stevenson did not attempt to reconcile his earlier contention in the first biography with this information. By December of 1850, Spurgeon was sixteen years of age. As seen, Stevenson stated in his first work that Charles was "not quite sixteen years old." This disparity is quite remarkable, for the difference of the dates is almost a full year. Thus, Stevenson made little contribution to fixing the date of Spurgeon's conversion. His fifth and last work on Spurgeon made no further claims. However, Stevenson became one of the very first to name someone as the preacher on the occasion: a Methodist circuit rider by the name of Robert Eaglen. Stevenson used the conclusions of Danzy Sheen quite unbendingly, even though it projected him into a contradiction of dates.

DANZY SHEEN'S CONTRIBUTION

It will prove helpful to look with more detail into what Danzy Sheen said about Spurgeon's conversion, not only because of Stevenson's works, but several others have also rather heavily relied upon Sheen. Moreover, some weight must be given to his arguments, for Danzy Sheen served as a Primitive Methodist minister himself. Not only that, he took his ministerial training at Spurgeon's Pastors' College. Perhaps the most significant aspect in Sheen's awareness of the details of the preacher at Spurgeon's conversion centers in the fact that he was the son-in-law of Robert Eaglen. Did this relationship prejudge his contention? That is questionable, but Sheen did base most of his argument on personal conversations he had with Eaglen. Sheen incontestably believed that his father-in-law preached the "Look" sermon which precipitated Spurgeon's salvation experience.

In May of 1861, an interesting event occurred. At a Primitive Methodist missionary meeting, both Sheen and Spurgeon were in attendance. A very surprised Sheen heard Spurgeon say to him:

> I was converted in one of your chapels, not under one of your regular ministers, but under a local preacher whose features I shall never look upon again until the morning of the resurrection.

It puzzled Danzy Sheen that Charles would make such a statement because Robert Eaglen was still alive at the time of the conference and had met Spurgeon. Concerning Spurgeon's encounter with Eaglen, Rev. Thomas Lowe had introduced Robert Eaglen to Charles at Lowestoft some years after Charles' conversion. But Spurgeon did not recognize him; he simply said, "This is not the man." Perhaps the rationale is, if Eaglen really were the preacher of the "Look" sermon, he had gained considerable weight and was healthier and not as pale as he was in the 1850s. Eaglen had suffered from "consumption" during his earlier years and was very pale and thin from the ravages of the disease at the time of Spurgeon's conversion. But he had regained his health and had put on considerable weight by the time Spurgeon met him at Lowestoft. Still, it seems Charles could have looked into it with more concern. One is tempted to believe Spurgeon sincerely did not want to know the identity of the preacher. Perhaps it is true, as suggested, that because of his strict Calvinism, he found some satisfaction in the fact that the human instrumentality in his conversion could not be identified and was thus very secondary in his conversion. In 1855, Spurgeon declared in a sermon:

> In *breaking* hearts, God uses man continually; repeated fiery sermons, and terrible denunciations do break men's hearts; but you will bear me witness when your hearts were *healed*, God only did it. You value the minister that broke your heart; but it is not often that we ascribe the healing to any instrumentality whatever. The act of justification is generally apart from all means: God only does it. I know not the man who uttered the words that were the means of relieving my heart: 'Look unto me and be ye saved, all the ends of the earth.' I do not recollect what he said in the sermon, and I am sure I do not care to know. I found Jesus there and then, and that was enough for me. [11]

Spurgeon was zealous and jealous for all the honor and glory to go to God in the work of conversion. To Spurgeon, the human instrument was all but incidental. God's electing grace brought him to faith in Christ, Spurgeon argued. In his mind, apparently to identify the human instrument in his conversion, could possibly take away from the praise due to God alone.

Of course, it is also possible a thin, local man started the service if Eaglen had arrived at the chapel late because of the snowstorm. Then possibly Eaglen could have entered, took over the service, and preached the sermon. Remember, Charles said he could hardly look up he felt so miserable. He could have missed the change in the leaders of the service. At any rate, Spurgeon's denial of Eaglen as the preacher of the "Look" sermon apparently motivated Sheen to research the affair and precipitated the publishing of his pamphlet in 1869. Sheen thereafter contended zealously that his father-in-law, Robert Eaglen, preached the sermon that brought Spurgeon to Christ, and that the fifteenth of December, 1850 was the conversion date.

Spurgeon reviewed Danzy Sheen's pamphlet in *The Sword and the Trowel*. In that article, Spurgeon wrote:

> This pamphlet speaks far too well of us, and owes its tone rather to grateful affection than to calm judgment. The account of the sermon which was the means of our conversion is as new to us as it will be to the readers of the memoir: it may be so, but we do not think it. When Christian friends write in our honour we feel great shame that we so little deserve their praise, and painful prostration of spirit that we should have had a word said in our favour. [12]

After Spurgeon's death, Sheen produced a larger biography entitled, *Pastor C.H. Spurgeon; His Conversion, Career, and Coronation*. He made the same arguments in that volume as he did in his earlier pamphlet, save the date. He added one important element to his case, however. He gave Eaglen's own personal testimony that he was indeed the preacher of the famous "Look" sermon. Eaglen testified to the factuality of his contention by writing a letter to Sheen on the back of his sermon notes that he used that day:

> My Dear Danzy,
>
>   I have but this brief outline upon the subject which I preached in the Colchester Chapel the morning when Mr. Spurgeon Looked and was saved— but if you drop a line to Mr. Bloomfield a local Preacher on the Colchester Station and living in Colchester all though I do not know his address—he will be able to confirm the truth of the affair he spoke of it in the Lovefiest at our District Meeting at Colchester—and was a Local Preacher and Branch Steward at that time when Mr. S[purgeon] was saved and was in the Chapel that morning.
>
>   Your affectionate Father, RE [13]

One thing thus seems certain, Eaglen himself believed he was the preacher, even arguing there were those who could verify and certify his conviction.

Sheen also contended there were three different men who claimed they were present in the Primitive Methodist Chapel on the morning of Spurgeon's conversion, each of whom identified Eaglen as the preacher on that occasion. One of the eyewitnesses in the Primitive Chapel the Sunday Spurgeon found Christ and would substantiate Sheen's contention was Robert Taylor. Taylor also served as a Primitive Methodist minister. In letters to Sheen, Taylor stated:

> Mr. Eaglen was detained by the snowstorm which passed over the town. The service was commenced by Brother Samuel Nightingale, he having failed to induce either brother John Bloomfield or me to open. Soon Mr. Eaglen, accompanied by his host, Mr. John Mann, entered and preached. This was on January 13th, 1850. [14]
>
> Mr. Eaglen came . . . to Colchester and was caught in the snowstorm . . . and came late; and took the service, and I heard him preach from that celebrated text, "Look," &c. [15] This opens the possibility, suggested earlier, that Spurgeon missed the change in the leaders of the worship service.

Another eyewitness Sheen presented in his argument was Joshua Elsden. He had been a member of the Primitive Methodist Church in Colchester for some time. Sheen investigated Elsden's credentials on the matter and wrote the following:

> I [Sheen] said to him [Elsden], 'Did you see Mr. Spurgeon in the chapel on the occasion when Mr. Eaglen preached from "Look unto Me?"' His reply was in the affirmative. [16]

The third witness was John Bloomfield. Bloomfield also lived in Colchester and was a member of the Primitive Methodist Church. He served the church as the "grand station steward." This would be comparable to the chairman of deacons in a Baptist church. He wrote two letters contending that Sheen's argument and conclusions were correct. In the first correspondence, Bloomfield said:

Colchester Nov 3rd 68

> Dear Brother, I received your note through Mr. Turner and I am sorry to say I cannot find an old plan of the date of Mr. Spurgeons Conversion, but having been with his Father in the same office for about 18 years and scarcely missed a day without being in conversation with him I knew almost as much about his Family affairs as he did himself for he used to tell me many things about his family that he did not tell any one else and his Son JA (James Archer) was with us in the office for years and the Other Children down with messages some times 2 or 3 times a day, and I well remember Charles Conversion for his father told me of the Change that had taken place and I well remember his asking me who it was that Preached and I told him Mr. Eaglon of Ipswich and I have often wished I had introduced you to the Family for I know they would have treated you kindly for his Mother is a very kind Woman, but you being so far away that I did not often see you Myself but some of the Family often dropped into our Chapel as it was near for them but if any

person doubts your being the Preacher that was preaching when his Soul was Converted I am ever ready to prove the Certainty of it being there and hearing it Myself and will defy them to prove that it was not so wishing you many more Spurgeons. I remain your Brother in the Lord JB"[17]

The second letter cited from Bloomfield to Sheen reads:

Colchester, Jan 4th / 69

Dear Bro Sheen, I beg leave to state that yours of the 29th Dec arrive to hand all right and I wish I could give you the exact particulars of Mr. Spurgeons Conversion but I will answer your questions to the best of My ability 1st I believe the date you state to be about the time but I cannot say the exact date but I know that Mr. Eaglen preached the Sermon under which Mr. S was converted being there Myself and heard it and on the following week Mr. Spurgeons father asked Me who the Preacher was and where he lived and I told him Mr. Eaglen of Ipswich so I can positively answer as to the certainty of the Preacher as I am positive two or three of Mrs. Spurgeons Children used to attend our Chapel very frequently on Sunday Morning during the Winter as it was so far to their own so that I of Course should not Notice this particular time More than another and it was on the Sunday Morning Mr. S was living with his Parents at the time when he was converted I don't know that any one else is supposed that thinks he preached it and if there is I should like to see him upon the subject I have heard that some doubt as to the Identity of the preacher but I don't know where they live nor who they are I wish I did as I am prepared to settle that Matter to the best of My remembrance Mr. Eaglen laid great stress upon the word look look but I dont know that he said Young Man I known perhaps More of Mr. Spurgeons Family affairs than any one else out of the Family as we were both together nearly every day for 17 Years under one Firm and the Head of the Firm was Mrs. Spurgeons own Brother who died and left them the property that they now have and which has to be divided when the youngest child is 21 years old I quite remember the Fathers Conversion for he was not a Spiritual Minded Man when I first knew him nor was he a preacher for some time after I was with him and after he was converted we could converse together freely and did so for years though we could not agree as to doctrinal points for only here we Used to Clash I well remember the first time that I saw Mr. Spurgeon with a Bible in his writing Desk Dear Brother my Information that I can give you I should take a pleasure in doing so had I known what Mr. S was to become I would have Noted every thing down at the time you ask if Mr. Elsden has been delegate to District Meeting he has been once or twice he went 10 or 11 years since and I think he has been once since but I am not sure I have known Mr. S from a Child and all the family his Brother was with me in the same office till he left to Preach wishing you and yours every Blessing you Need in this world and in the world to come life everlasting, John Bloomfield, 15 Barrack St Colchester Essex

Sheen's arguments seem quite strong for the identity of the preacher of the "Look" sermon.

THE APPLEBY CONTENTION

However, a more recent pamphlet takes a different view from Sheen, and presents a quite strong case. Charles Appleby, the author, wrote on the preacher of the "Look" sermon as follows:

> In February 1939, the Rev. J. Asquith Baker, Methodist Superintendent Minister at Colchester, published two articles in which he sought to show that the Rev. Robert Eaglen was the preacher of the sermon which led to the conversion of Charles Haddon Spurgeon. This was not generally accepted at the time, and I am now able to state a convincing case for Samuel Heywood Nightingale, who Mr. Baker agreed opened the service on this memorable day.
>
> We are looking then for a man who is: (1) A layman with unprepared sermon; (2) A poor man, probably either shoemaker or tailor and of slight education; (3) A native of rural Essex who had lived most of his life there.
>
> In none of these respects can the Rev. Robert Eaglen, a man of education, claim to bear any resemblance to this preacher, and as Mr. Baker relates, when in after years, Eaglen was introduced to Spurgeon as the preacher of the sermon, Spurgeon said, "This is not the man." Quite apart from his appearance, Spurgeon would have certainly remembered the preacher's voice with its countrified accent.
>
> Had the Rev. Eaglen arrived late his arrival would have been noticed by Spurgeon in that small church and congregation and without a doubt Mr. Eaglen would have apologized for being late.
>
> From the above it is apparent that the preacher was not the Rev. Eaglen and since it is known definitely that Samuel Nightingale began the service, nobody else being willing to do so, it can therefore be assumed that he preached the sermon. This is confirmed by Mr. Charles Howe, a playmate of Spurgeon's, who was present and who told the late Mr. Wilson Webb that Samuel Nightingale preached the sermon, who also heard it from other sources. Mr. Webb's Uncle Brown told him that Mr. Nightingale had preached from the text 'Look unto me and be ye saved,' on the occasion of the snowstorm.
>
> Mr. Webb informed me that Mr. Bloomfield, who was also in the chapel on the day of the snowstorm, similarly told him that Samuel Nightingale preached on that occasion, adding that Samuel had not then been long in Colchester. This fits in as his youngest child was born at Weeley in 1840 and Spurgeon was converted in 1850.
>
> A brief history of Samuel Nightingale's life will serve to show how well he fits the picture of Spurgeon's spiritual father.
>
> Baptised in Weeley Church on 25 January, 1797, he was the second son of John Nightingale, Schoolmaster of Weeley, and his wife Mary Clements. This

John Nightingale and his brother Joseph had come south from Lancashire. Joseph went to London where he became a prolific writer and received a mention in the *Dictionary of National Biography*. He was in turn Methodist Local Preacher and Unitarian Minister.

Samuel, a painter and glazier, married Rachel, daughter of Daniel Maldon, a ship-owner of Harwich, and continued to live at Weeley where all their nine children, including Robert, father of Mr. Arthur Nightingale, were born. I am indebted to the late Rector of Weeley for kindly allowing me to obtain this information from the Parish Registers.

He would appear to have moved to Colchester a comparatively short time before the conversion of Spurgeon and was assisting his son, Robert, to start his tailoring business in Wyre Street which subsequently became Leanings and expanded into the clothing factory. In his death certificate he is actually described as a clothier.

He died of typhoid at Colchester on 22 May, 1866 and is buried in Colchester Cemetery where his tombstone states that 'He was a consistent member and a useful local preacher of the Primitive Methodist Connection for upwards of 22 years.'

We see from the above that he, unlike the Rev. Eaglen, exactly fits Spurgeon's description of the man who converted him . . . a layman . . . an unprepared sermon . . . poor . . . probably a tailor . . . of slight education . . . one who had lived most of his life in rural Essex.

The Rev. Eaglen's tombstone at Manchester bears the inscription that he was the preacher who caused Charles Haddon Spurgeon to 'Look to Jesus' but although I am sure Samuel Nightingale is quite content with his own epitaph, it is of interest to Colchester and Methodism to know that the preacher of the sermon was a Colchester local preacher like his wife, son, and grandson. [18]

Some questions arise from Appleby's analysis. For example, he obviously puts Bloomfield in a contradictory stance. Nonetheless, he does present an interesting case.

It seems conclusive that the preacher of the "Look" sermon is difficult to identify with certainty. But what about the date?

THE DATE

In the first place, concerning the date of Spurgeon's conversion, Danzy Sheen is hardly convincing. It is all but inconceivable that Spurgeon himself could have been almost one year in error concerning the date of his conversion, as Sheen argues. Moreover, why would Charles have been at home, away from the school in Newmarket early in December, had there not been a fever epidemic at the school? And that epidemic occurred in December of 1849. [19] In addition, there is the existence of the diary, well dated, and Spurgeon was surely saved before he wrote it. Not only that, several letters have recently come to light. When the Baptist Church House moved from London in the 1980s, correspondence was discovered and placed in the archives of Regent's Park College, Oxford. These clearly show Spurgeon's conversion sometime in January of 1850, surely before December of 1850. In a letter to his father, dated January 20, 1850, he wrote:

Newmarket

January 20th 1850

My Dear Father,

I am most happy and comfortable, I could not be more so whilst sojourning on earth "like a pilgrim or a stranger as all my fathers were." There are but 4 boarders and about 12 day boys. I have a nice little mathematical class and have quite as much time for study as I had before—I can get good religious conversations with Mr. Swindell which is what I most need. O how unprofitable has my past life been! I that I should have been so long time blind to those celestial wonders, which now I can in a measure behold! Who can refrain to speak of the marvellous love of Jesus which I hope has opened mine eyes! Now I see him I can firmly trust to him for my eternal salvation—Yet soon I doubt again; then I am sorrowful: again faith appears and I become confident of my interest in him. I feel now as if I could do everything and give up everything for Christ. Then I know it would be nothing in comparison with his love. I am hopeless of ever making anything like a return. How sweet is prayer, I would be always engaged in it. How beautiful is the Bible, I never loved it so before. It seems to me as necessary food. I feel that I have not one particle of spiritual life in me—but what the Spirit placed there. I feel that I cannot live if he depart, I tremble and fear lest I should grieve him. I dread least sloth or pride should overcome me and I should dishonour the gospel or neglect of prayer or the scriptures or by sinning against God. Truly, that we be a happy place where we shall get rid of sin and this depraved corrupt nature. When I look at the horrible pit and the hole from which I have been digged I tremble lest I should fall into it, and yet rejoice that I am on the king's highway. I hope you will forgive me for taking up so much space about myself! but at present my thoughts are most about it. From the Scriptures is it not apparent that immediately upon receiving the Lord Jesus it is a part of duty openly to profess him? I firmly believe and consider that Baptism is the command of Christ and shall not feel quite comfortable if I do not receive it. — I am unworthy of such things, but so am I unworthy of Jesus' love, I hope I have received the blessing of the one and think I ought to take the other also—. My very best love to you and my dear mother —I seem to love you more than ever, because you love my Lord Jesus. I hope yourself, dear Mother, Archer, Eliza, Emily, Louisa and Lotte are well, love to all. I have given Mr. Swindell the bottle of wine, I know he wants it more than I do. Mrs. S. is not well. May we all after this fighting life is over Meet in

> That kingdom of immense delight,
> Where health, and peace & joy unite,
> Where undeclining pleasures rise,
> And every wish hath full supplies.

And while you are here may the blessings of the gospel abound toward you & may we as a family be all devoted to the Lord. May all blessings be upon us & may

I ever remain,
Your dutiful & affectionate Son

Chas H Spurgeon —

Charles penned a letter to his mother dated June 11, 1850. It reads:

Newmarket Academy

June 11th 1850

My Dear Mother,

Many thanks to you for your valuable letter. Your notes are so few & far between & are such a trouble to you, that one now & then is quite a treasure. Truly, indeed, I have much for which to bless the Lord. When I contemplate his Divine Sovereignty, & see that my salvation is entirely of his free elected love, he has chosen me to be one of his vessels of mercy and despite all opposition from without & from within he will surely accomplish his own work. I have more than sufficiency to induce me to give up myself entirely to him who has bought me & purchased me with an everlasting redemption.

I am now enabled to rely upon his precious promises & to feel that I am as safe though so holy as the greatest saint in heaven. I have had two opportunities of addressing the Sunday School Children, and have endeavored to do so as a dying being to dying beings. I am bound to Newmarket by holy bonds. I have 70 people whom I regularly visit on Saturday. I do not give a tract and go out but I sit down & endeavour to draw them attention to spiritual realities. I have great reason to believe that God is word the people are so kind & so pleased to see me. I cannot bear to leave them. We are so feeble here that the weakest cannot be spared. We have a pretty good attendance at Prayer Meetings, but few praying men that I am constantly called upon. Our Minister is gone after a wife and has left us helpless even for less. One of our Deacons, Mr. Brown, is constantly inviting me to his house, he is rather an Arminian, but so are the majority of Newmarket Christians. Grandfather has written me, he does not blame me for being a Baptist but hopes I shall not be one of the tight faced, strict-communion sort. In that we are agreed. I certainly think we ought to forget such things in others when we come to the Lord's Table. I can & hope I shall be charitable to unbaptized Christians, though I think they are mistaken. It is not a great matter, men will differ, we ought both to follow our own consciences & let others do the same. I think the time would be better spent in talking upon vital godliness than in disputing about forms. I trust the Lord is weaning me daily from all self dependance & teaching me to look at myself as less than nothing; I know that I am perfectly dead without him; it is his work I am confident that he will accomplish it, & that I shall see the face of my beloved in his own house in glory. My enemies are many & they hate me with cruel hatred yet with Jehovah Jesus on my side, why should I fear, I will march on in his almighty strength to certain conquest & victory. I am so glad that Sarah too is called, the two of us in one household at one time then thus openly profess the Saviour's name are brother & sister in the Lord, marvelous. Father give us each the often refreshing visits of his face. I feel as if I could say with Paul 'would that I even were called so that my brethren according to the father might be saved.' What a joy if God should prove that they are redeemed ones included in the covenant of grace. I long to see your face that my heart beat with yours whilst we talk of the glorious things pertaining to eternal life. My best love to you & Father may the angel of the covenant dwell with you & enchant you by the visions of his face. Love to Eliza, Archer, many happy returns to him, Emily Lott & Less may they become members of the Church in house. I am very glad you are so well, I am hard at work for the Examination so allow me to remain your most affectionate

Charles [20]

Again, on September 19, 1850, Spurgeon wrote his father:

No 9 Union Road

Cambridge 19 Sep 50

Rec 20 Sept 1850

My Dear Father,

I received your kind letter in due time. I joined the Church here at the Lord's Table last Ordinance day. I shall write for my dismission. I intended to have done so before. The Baptists are by far the most respectable denomination in Cambridge, there are 3 Baptist Chapels. St. Andrew's Street where we attend, Zion chapel, and Eden Chapel. There is a very fine Wesleyan Chapel and some others. I teach in the Sunday School all the afternoon. Mr. Leeding takes the morning work. Last Sabbath day we had a funeral sermon from Hebrews 6.11-12. We have a Prayer Meeting at 7 in the morning & one after the Evening Service, they are precious means of grace. I trust to my soul . . . How soon would the lamps go out did not our mighty Lord, supply fresh oil, and if it were not for his unshaken promise to supply our need out of the fulness of his grace, poor indeed should I be. Yes, where Jesus comes he comes to reign, how I wish he would reign more in my soul, then I might hope that every atom of self, self confidence & self righteousness, would be quite swept out of my soul. I am sure I long for the time when all evil affections, corrupt desires, and rebellious doubting should & shall be overcome, and completely crushed beneath the Prince's feet & my whole soul be made pure and holy. But so long as I am encased within this house of clay, I know they will lurk, about, and I must have hard fighting though the victory by grace is sure. Praying is the best fighting, nothing else will keep them down.

I have written a letter to Grandpa. I am sorry he is so poorly. He wants the promises now, and why may not young and old live upon them. They are the breadcorn of heaven, the meat of the kingdom, and who that has once so asked them, will turn to eat husks, without any sweetness or comfort in them. God's power will keep all his children while he says to them how shall ye who are dead to sin live any longer therein. I feel persuaded that I shall never fathom the depths of my own natural depravity, nor climb to the tops of the mountain of God's eternal love. I feel constrained day by day to fall flat down upon the promises, and leave my soul in Jesus' keeping. It is he that makes my feet move even in the slow obedience which marks them at present, & every attainment of grace must come from him. I would go forth by prayer like the Israelites to gather up this heavenly manna & live upon free grace. Add to all your great kindness and love to me through my life, a constant remembrance of me in your prayers. I thank you for those petitions which you and dear Mother have so often sent up to the mercy seat for me. Give my love to Eliza, Archer, Emily, Louisa and Lottie and accept the same for yourself and dear Mother.

Hoping you are all quite well.
I remain,
Your obedient, affectionate Son

Chas. H. Spurgeon

Thus to argue for a December 1850 date is very unconvincing.

The basic dating of Spurgeon's life and ministry makes it almost incontestable that he came to conversion in January of 1850. The December 1850 dating would have forced the conversion day forward by almost an entire year; thus Charles would have been sixteen years of age and not fifteen as he always contended was the case. The written evidence all seems to establish a January, 1850 date with little room for argument to the contrary.

Various writers, as pointed out, have argued for three different dates. The first, was the sixth of January 1850, as Spurgeon himself held. It has also been contended that the conversion came one week later on the thirteenth of January. Robert Taylor, in the letter presented above, stated that the thirteenth of January was the time when Spurgeon came to salvation. Also, the fifteenth of December 1850 has been proposed by Sheen, and it was cited also by Stevenson. If one is willing to place weight on the evidence of the "Preacher's Plans" of the Ipswich Circuit, the fifteenth of December 1850 is a plausible date. Moreover, Charles' own father argued for this date. But it is most difficult to understand how Spurgeon's father and Charles himself could have disagreed by almost a year, plus all the other evidence cited. On the very night of that memorable Sunday, the following incident occurred. Charles' father, John, said:

> We spent the evening as an evening should be spent, reading the Bible and so on. Then by-and-by I said, 'Come, boys, it's time to go to bed.' 'Father,' remarked Charles, 'I don't want to go to bed yet.' 'Come, come,' said I, whereupon he told me that he wanted to speak with me. We sat up long into the night, and he talked to me of his being saved, which had taken place that day, and right glad was I to hear him talk. 'In the text' . . . Charles said to me, holding up his hands, 'I found salvation this morning.' [21]

Spurgeon's father, John Spurgeon, argued until the day of his death that his son's conversion took place on the fifteenth of December, 1850. But this date causes the aforementioned problem. If John had been correct on his dating, Charles would have been sixteen and Charles emphatically stated "When I was a boy of fifteen, I believed in the Lord Jesus, was baptized, and joined the Church of Christ." [22]

A new issue arises and confuses the chronology even more. In an extant, hand-written "Primitive Methodist Preacher's Plan of the Ipswich Circuit 1849-1850," Eaglen was also scheduled to preach in Colchester on the thirteenth of January, 1850. This date has more weight to it than the fifteenth of December date, because it is just one week later than Spurgeon's own personal testimony, and Taylor confirmed this date. As a consequence, Sheen, in his last work on the conversion of Spurgeon, changed his earlier, quite dogmatic view and settled on the date of the thirteenth of January 1850, but continued to argue that the preacher was Robert Eaglen. Moreover, meteorological records in London tend to confirm the thirteenth date. On January 6, 1850, London records show a bright, sunny day. Of course, it could have snowed in Colchester, but that is doubtful as Colchester is only some fifty or sixty miles from London. And on the thirteenth of January, London recorded a heavy snowstorm. Colchester had no meteorological records, but the snow storm in London on the thirteenth of January lends support to that being the "conversion Sunday."

The strange fact about the entire Sheen investigation is that most writers have ignored Sheen's research and hence his conclusions. This is even true of one of Spurgeon's most prolific biographers, G. Holden Pike. He wrote three major works on the life of Spurgeon. Further, he served as co-laborer with the great London preacher and was a personal friend. Nonetheless, in Pike's first work, he gave very little attention to any details regarding the conversion. He merely made the statement that Spurgeon's conversion came at the age of sixteen, probably relying on John Spurgeon's statements. This contention of Pike is probably no more than an imprecise overlooking of the facts.

In Pike's second biography, he goes into considerably more detail. Pike declared, "ingenious attempts" to establish Eaglen as the preacher had been undertaken. But it will be remembered that when Spurgeon and Eaglen met, Charles did not recognize him as the preacher of the "Look" sermon, saying, "This is not the man." Pike picked up on that event and therefore rejected Eaglen as the preacher. Moreover, Spurgeon's father, John, remarked to the "Daily Chronicle" that the man who preached on that Sunday morning was "a local man—a local preacher, that also worked at digging, planting cabbages, and so on." But that statement proves hard to reconcile with other statements of John Spurgeon. So Pike seemed simply to conclude that the preacher is an unknown person. Further, in the second biography by Pike, the author stated that Spurgeon's conversion occurred some months before he went to take the usher's place at Newmarket. This would nullify the fact that Spurgeon was home during the Christmas season because of the fever at Newmarket. Pike concluded the conversion probably took place sometime around the last of 1848 or early 1849. Because of all confirmed circumstances, this seems very dubious indeed. Charles would have been only fourteen years of age.

Pike's final account of Spurgeon's conversion is found in his exhaustive six volume work on the life of Spurgeon. Yet, all he said in this work was no more than what he had repeated before. Unfortunately, in his magnum opus he brought in no new information. He seemed primarily to depend on the testimony of John Spurgeon given to the "Daily Chronicle" in 1892. Pike gave no verification of his early dating. In none of Pike's research did he evaluate Sheen's evidence regarding the preacher and the dating.

Modern biographers have taken different stances. W. Y. Fullerton, in his classic biography of Spurgeon published in 1920, Carlile in 1933, Bacon in 1967, Kruppa in 1982, and Dallimore in 1984, all more or less ignore the controversy over the date and preacher in Spurgeon's conversion. Fullerton, Bacon and Kruppa used the traditional dating of the sixth of January 1850, following Spurgeon's own testimony. Carlile and Dallimore did not fix the date at all. Concerning the preacher, Fullerton simply declared that the minister is unknown. Following this line, Bacon and Dallimore likewise apparently felt that the preacher was unknown because they expressed no opinion on the identity of the man. Only Carlile mentions Robert Eaglen or Danzy Sheen. Yet, he did not come down in any conclusive way concerning the issue.

Timothy McCoy contends that the thirteenth of January 1850, was most likely the correct date of the conversion and Robert Eaglen the preacher of the significant "Look" sermon. It is difficult to disagree with his research. All the relevant, verifiable facts seem to substantiate those conclusions. Still, other contentions and arguments have been made through the years. But, regardless of who the preacher was or what Sunday Spurgeon found Christ, the young man experienced a radical and complete transformation. Furthermore, he began immediately to serve Jesus Christ with a zeal and a vigor that is almost without parallel, and that is what matters. From the day of Spurgeon's conversion, it seemed almost inevitable that he should be a preacher. The Richard Knill prophecy, the fervency of the young man from the moment he was converted to share Christ, all conspired to lead him to the pulpit. As seen earlier, even as a little lad he would often be found in a haystack preaching. There were those in his family who remembered how often the young boy would quote the verse:

> Now will I tell dissenters around,
> what a dear Savior I have found.

He would lift up one finger, which seemed to be a favorite gesture of his, (one of the early paintings of Spurgeon preaching now hanging in Spurgeon's College in London, England shows him in that stance); then, with his finger pointed to Heaven, he would finish the stanza:

> I point to thy redeeming Blood,
> and say, behold, the way to God.

THE FOLLOWING DAYS

Biographer Charles Ray contended that Spurgeon attended a Baptist chapel the Sunday night of his conversion along with his mother. The pastor preached on "Accepted in the Beloved" (Ephesians 1:6), a message on assurance. It touched Charles and did much to confirm his faith. However, the exact date of the visit to the Baptist church is uncertain, although the new convert did attend a Baptist chapel soon after his experience of salvation. Spurgeon went back to the Primitive Methodist Church on Artillery Street where he received Christ a short time after his conversion. Which came first, a visit to the Methodist or the Baptist chapel remains something of a mystery. Regardless of the sequence, he had a rather disillusioning experience at the Methodist chapel on his second visit. The preacher, being of Arminian persuasion, declared that a person could lose his salvation after regeneration. Arminians reject the idea of eternal security in Christ. And Spurgeon rejected Arminianism. Even as a new convert, Charles firmly believed in the impossibility of a Christian losing his or her salvation. His previous commitment to Puritan-Calvinism no doubt came into play on that issue. He said, "Glory be to God, we have found a Head, in whom we abide eternally secure, a Head which we shall never lose." In a later sermon, he admonished fellow believers, quoting Arnot:

> Though there be fears within and fightings without, he who bought his people with his own blood cannot lose his inheritance, and will not permit any enemy to unrest from his hand the satisfaction of his soul. The man with a deceitful heart and darkened mind, a feeble home and a slippery way, a fainting heart

and a daring foe—the man would stumble and fall. But the member of Christ's body cannot drop off; the portions of the Redeemer cannot be wrenched from his grasp. 'You are his.' Christ is the safety of a Christian. [23]

To Charles' Calvinistic ears, the Primitive Methodist preacher advocated "strange doctrine." The man preached on Romans 7:24, "Oh wretched man that I am, who shall deliver me from this body of death?" As the sermon began, Spurgeon thought, "That is the text for me." He knew, even though saved, he could not live without sin. However, the preacher contended that Paul had not yet become a Christian when he made that statement. The Primitive Methodist preacher contended for sinless perfection; thus he argued Paul could not have made such a statement had he been saved. Spurgeon felt this entirely was wrong, and decided he would never find a spiritual home in the Primitive Methodist community. Even at that very early stage in his Christian life, he was too deeply steeped in Calvinistic thought to embrace Arminianism, even if he found it in the chapel where Christ found him. Spurgeon concluded that the Primitive Methodists "are very good for people who are unconverted to go, but of fairly little use for the children of God. That is my notion of Methodism." [24]

NEW JOY

Charles' newly discovered faith filled his days with joy. He sought to meet people's needs as he ministered in Christ's name. But not all was mirth and joy for Spurgeon. He stated, "I think that about five days after I first found Christ, when my joy had been such that I could have danced for mirth at the thought that Christ was mine, on a sudden I fell into a sad fit of despondency." Because he could not immediately grasp the level of holiness that he desired, he fell into a quite deep depression. Something of a depression problem plagued him through life. He stated, "So Satan, loathe to leave my soul, pursues at hotfoot. He will have it back if he can; often, soon after conversion, there comes a time when dreadful conflict, when the soul seems as if it could not live." [25] He even experienced temptations to blaspheme and entertain profane thought. But the cloud soon lifted and Charles discovered the important principle of his freedom in Christ. He said, "I have found, in my own spiritual life, that the more rules I lay down for myself, the more sins I commit. The habit of regular morning and evening prayer is one which is indispensable to a believer's life, but the prescribing of the length of prayer, and the constrained remembrance of so many persons and subjects, may gender unto bondage and strangle prayer rather than assist it." [26] He realized legalism does not produce holiness. Although sinless perfection, Charles realized, eludes this life, God's grace proves sufficient to keep one in fellowship with Himself. Spurgeon thus came through his early "fit of despondency," and said, "At such a time, if Jesus whispers that I'm His, then the question is answered once and for all, my soul has received a token which it waves in the face of Satan, so that he disappears, and I can go on my way rejoicing." [27] Spurgeon learned early how the Christian relates to the Lord and the means of growing in grace and fighting spiritual battles victoriously through Jesus Christ. Even when one slips into the "Miry Slough of Despond," the Lord's sufficiency is enough.

After the holidays, Spurgeon returned to his studies and responsibilities at Newmarket. But a whole new light shone on all he did in contrast to the deep darkness he experienced before he left for Colchester: he had been saved. Back at Newmarket he made an appointment with the minister of the local Independent church to talk about becoming a church member. Though he called at the pastor's home on four successive days, he was not received and was thus unable to gain an interview. So, Spurgeon wrote the pastor saying that he would go to the next church meeting and propose himself for membership. This got the pastor's attention. Charles related:

> He (the pastor) looked upon me as a strange character, but I meant what I said; for I felt that I could not be happy without fellowship with the people of God. I wanted to be wherever they were; and if anybody ridiculed them, I wished to be ridiculed with them; and if people had an ugly name for them I wanted to be called by that ugly name; for I felt that unless I suffered with Christ in His humiliation I could not expect to reign with Him in glory.

Then in a letter to his father dated March 12, 1850, Charles wrote, "At our last church-meeting, I was proposed." He came into the fellowship of the church on Thursday, April 4, 1850.

After being received into church membership, Charles again wrote to his father:

> Oh, that I may henceforth live more for the glory of Him by whom I feel assured that I shall be everlastingly saved! Owing to my scruples on account of baptism I did not sit down at the Lord's Table, and cannot in conscience do so until I am baptized. To one who does not see the necessity of baptism it is perfectly right and proper to partake of this blessed privilege; but were I to do so, I conceive it would be to tumble over the wall, since I feel persuaded it is Christ's appointed way of professing Him.

He would soon follow his conviction and be baptized by immersion on profession of faith in Christ.

FIRST SERVICE

In Newmarket, he spent his days visiting the poor and sick and talking to his classmates about their relationships to Jesus Christ. He gave many hours to witnessing and helping others to faith in Christ. He would share salvation tracts with all he could see. He also taught a Sunday School class of boys, who in Charles' words, "made wheels of themselves twisting around." Robert Brown, a fishmonger, served as superintendent of the Sunday School. Charles said he learned to tell stories in that Sunday School because he was "obliged to tell them." But he genuinely loved the service of Christ. He said, "There is no time for serving the Lord like the earliest days of youth."[28]

On the first day of February, 1850, Charles dedicated himself anew to God. He expressed it beautifully in his diary.

Reference to his diary has often been made. It will be helpful to look into it to see something of the spiritual pilgrimage that Spurgeon underwent in his early days as a Christian. This diary is important because it proved to be the only time in his entire life that he kept a journal. Although somewhat lengthy, it needs to be seen in full; it demonstrates in graphic terms the spiritual struggles this new pilgrim endured and how his early Christian experience shaped his entire life. It stands as something of a classic on the early days of a new convert, akin to journals like that of Robert Murray McCheyne, John Wesley, David Brainard, and others. In the *Autobiography*, his wife, to whom he gave the diary soon after their marriage, presents a beautiful introduction, then the text unfolds:

DIARY, APRIL TO JUNE, 1850

I have sometimes said, when I have become the prey of doubting thoughts, 'Well, now I dare not doubt whether there be a God, for I can look back in my Diary, and say, "On such a day, in the depths of trouble, I bent my knee to God, and or ever I had risen from my knees, the answer was given me."'— C.H.S.

INTRODUCTION, BY MRS. C.H. SPURGEON.

Not very long after our marriage, my husband brought to me, one day, a small clasped book, and putting it into my hand with a grave and serious air, he said, 'That book contains a record of my past spiritual experiences, wifie; take care of it, but I never want to see it again.' He never did, and to me also it was a sealed book, for I did not dare to open it; and it has lain, unrevealed, for certainly forty years since the day I first saw it. But now, with reverent hands, I take it from its hiding-place, and, as I look upon the boyish handwriting, and begin to read the thoughts of my dear one's heart in the bygone years, I wonder whether I can undertake the duty of transcription, whether my eyes will see through the tears which must come, and my fingers will hold the pen without much trembling, and my heart, which loved him so well, will be able to thank God that the past is past, and the struggles and sorrows of earth are for ever forgotten in the ecstasies of eternal glory. Lord, strengthen and help me!

The contents of the little book prove to be a continuous Diary of nearly three months' duration, commencing April 6th, 1850, and ending on June 20th in the same year. As its pages cover the season of baptism, and the young convert's first efforts in service for the Lord, it is full of deep interest and pathos to all who afterward knew and loved the great preacher. I feel that I am justified in at last revealing the long-kept secret of the book, for a perusal of its soul-confessions and holy resolutions can only redound to the glory of God, and show how He was leading His young servant by a way which he knew not. And I believe God would have me do this. The words of the dear boy of sixteen are very touching when read in the light of his subsequent marvellous career. As the trunk and branches of the future tree may, in some cases, be seen faintly outlined in the fruit it bears, so we can here discern something of the form and beauty of the fair character which the Lord was preparing for a glorious service. How marked is his humility, even though he must have felt within him the stirrings and throes of the wonderful powers which were afterwards developed. 'Forgive me, Lord,' he says, in one place, 'if I have ever had high thoughts of myself,'—so early did the Master implant the precious seeds of that rare grace of meekness, which adorned his after life. After each youthful effort at public exhortation, whether it be engaging in prayer, or addressing Sunday-school children, he seems to be surprised at his own success, and intensely anxious to be kept from pride and self-glory, again and again confessing his own utter weakness, and pleading for God-given strength. What deep foundations were laid in this chosen soul, upon what massive pillars of truth and doctrine did God construct the spiritual consciousness of the man who was to do so great a work in the world for his Master! He was truly a 'building fitly framed together,' and he grew into 'a holy temple in the Lord,' 'a habitation of God through the Spirit.' So young in years, when he wrote these thoughts, yet so old in grace, and possessing an experience in spiritual matters richer and broader than most Christians attain to at an advanced age! How plainly revealed in these pages are the workings and teachings of the Divine Spirit, and how equally clear are the docility, and earnestness, and humility of the pupil! Many of the sentences in the Diary are strangely prophetic of his future position and work,—notably these two,—'Make me Thy faithful servant, O my God; may I honour Thee in my day and generation, and be consecrated for ever to Thy service!' And again, 'Make me to be an eminent servant of Thine, and to be blessed with the power to serve Thee, like Thy great servant Paul!' In these breathings, too, we see where the secret of his great strength lay. He believed and trusted God absolutely, and his faith was honoured in a God-like fashion. Deeply realizing his own weakness, he rested with child-like and complete dependence on his Lord. And God carried him, as a father bears his little one in his arms; and God's Spirit dwelt in him, to teach him all things. His whole heart was given to God and His service, God's promises were verities to him; and as 'He abideth faithful, He cannot deny Himself,' it was with both hands that He heaped gifts and grace upon His dear servant until the time came to receive him into glory. Perhaps, of greatest price among the precious things which this little book reveals, is the beloved author's personal and intense love to the Lord Jesus. He lived in His embrace; like the apostle John, his head leaned on Jesu's bosom. The endearing terms used in the Diary, and never discontinued, were not empty words; they were the overflowings of the love of God shed abroad in his heart by the Holy Ghost. One of the last things he said to me at Mentone, before unconsciousness had sealed his dear lips, was this, 'O wifie, I have had such a blessed time with my Lord!' And it was always so, the Saviour was as real to him as if his eyes could look upon Him, and it was his delight to dwell in the very presence of God, in his daily, hourly life. Full of a sweet pain has been the task I set myself to write out these details of my dear one's life for three short months; but if anyone shall be the gainer by it through being drawn nearer to God, and having clearer views of Divine truth, I shall deem the pain a pleasure, and the sorrow will bring me joy.

* * * *

Saved men and women date from the dawn of their true life; not from their first birthday, but from the day wherein they were born again. Their calendar has been altered and amended by a deed of Divine grace.—C.H.S.

THE DIARY
1850

Born,	January 6, 1850
Admitted to Fellowship,	April 4.
Baptized,	May 3.
Communed first,	May 5.
Commenced as S.S. Teacher,	May 5.
Joined Church at Cambridge,	Oct. 2.

CONSECRATION

O great and unsearchable God, who knowest my heart, and triest all my ways; with a humble dependence upon the support of Thy Holy Spirit, I yield up myself to Thee; as Thy own reasonable sacrifice, I return to Thee Thine own. I would be for ever, unreservedly, perpetually Thine; whilst I am on earth, I would serve Thee; and may I enjoy Thee and praise Thee for ever! Amen.

Feb. 1, 1850   Charles Haddon Spurgeon

1850,—A BLESSED YEAR OF JUBILEE

April 6.—I have had a blessed day of refreshing from the Lord, and from the glory of His face. Went round my Station District, and had a talk with several people. I trust the Lord is working here. Had some serious thoughts about baptism. 'The Lord is my strength and my song; He also is become my salvation.'

April 7.—Not well; the body bears the soul down. Heard Mr. S. from Gen. xxii. 8; could not take it in to heart, headache would not let me. Arminianism does not suit me now. If I were long to be so heavy as I now am, I could scarcely live. Evening, could not attend to the sermon; was happier without it. I feasted all the time on—

> 'When I soar to world unknown,
> See Thee on Thy judgment throne,
> Rock of Ages! cleft for me,
> I shall hide myself in Thee.'

Cannot think how Mr. S. could say that Esau, he trust, was converted, when the Lord says, 'Esau have I hated.'

April 8.—Walked out after breakfast, never saw more plainly the sovereignty of God's will. He has called me; I feel sure that He will carry me to glory. Not well. O God of grace, take me home when Thou pleasest! It is, 'Mercy, mercy, mercy,' from first to last.

April 9.—Happy again to-day; if such days continue, earth and Heaven will be but one;—but what have I written? I know I have sinned this day; in Heaven, I cannot. Oh, to be holy, to be like God! I trust I shall be one day. O glorious hour, O blest abode, when I am near, and like my God. Jesus, how can I e'er forget Thee, Thou life of my delights? Hold Thou me by Thy free Spirit, and pour down upon me more love to Thee! Can hardly pray, yet, O my God, remember A———! Oh, that I could do more for God! 'By grace are ye saved.'

April 10.—Much better in health. All more than hell, is mercy. How small is my sphere, yet what a great Being condescended to fix my state before I had a being! All things are ordered by God. Blessed be His name, though He slay me, yet will I trust in Him. Sin is all cleansed by Jesu's blood. Doubts and fears will soon come. 'Desire of my soul,' prepare me to meet them. The Lord's presence has not departed yet; had I the tongue of an archangel, I could not praise Him enough for this. I hope all is well at home with my dear mother; I must expect the cross soon. 'He that taketh not his cross, and followeth after Me, is not worthy of Me.'

April 11.—Have had sweet thoughts upon, 'I am the good Shepherd, and know My sheep, and am known of Mine.' How can one of His sheep be lost if He knows all His own?

I have read to-day of the iniquities of some in high places. Father, forgive them, and grant that Thy name may not be blasphemed through them! O my Beloved, sooner may I perish everlastingly than thus dishonour Thee, Thou sole desire of my heart! Heard Mr. S. from Psalm lxviii. 19-20. I love to hear him give all the honour of our salvation to God. Shepherd of Israel, guide Thy flock into all truth! Quicken me, and make me love Thee more and more!

April 12.—Earthly things have engaged too much of my thoughts this day. I have not been able to fix my attention entirely upon my Saviour. Yet, even yet, the Lord has not hidden His face from me. Though tempted, I am not cast down; tried, but not overcome; truly it is of the Lord's sovereign mercy. I would desire again this day to make a fresh application to the sin-atoning blood of Jesus to cleanse away my sins. O God, do Thou keep me down, and then I need fear no fall! O visit Zion, and preserve Thy Church; let her yet shine forth in glory! April showers have been coming down to-day; the Lord does not forget His promises. Jesus took my heart: 'or ever I was aware, my soul made me like the chariots of Ammi-nadib.' 'Tell me, O Thou whom my soul loveth, where Thou feedest, where Thou makest Thy flock to rest at noon;' I would be ever with Thee, O my spotless, fairest Beloved! Daily meet me, for Thy embrace is Heaven; sanctify me, prepare me, help me to bring forth fruit, and to be Thine for ever!

April 13.—Did not feel so tired at the end of this week; one reason is, that every day has been Sunday with me. Blessed by the Shepherd, I walk now beside the still waters. What events are transpiring in the World! Things are quite at a crisis in the Church of England. I love my little work; Lord, be with me! 'Oh the depth of the riches both of the wisdom and knowledge of God!' Trust in Him, my soul; follow hard after Him.

April 14.—Heard Mr. S., this morning, from 3 John 4,—the great subject of justification by faith. Who could dare to hope of going to Heaven, if works are the price? I could not; it would be like offering me a possession in the sun, if I could jump up to it, and take it in my hand! Afternoon,—some of last Sunday over again. Esau does not give us a very interesting sermon. Evening subject was, Decision. I am quite encouraged. Hope I shall soon have an answer from home upon baptism.

> 'Through floods and flames, if Jesus lead,
>   I'll follow where He goes.'

I would not desert Him in any one point, but keep close to Him.

April 15.—Quite well to-day, and tolerably happy. First day of the races. O God, Thou makes me to differ! Had a nice prayer-meeting. 'Also unto Thee, O Lord, belongeth mercy.' What else have I to trust to? Mr. P. came in this evening, and talked till past eleven, so that I lost some of the time I should have spent in devotion.

> 'What various hindrances we meet
>   In coming to a mercy seat!
> Yet who that knows the worth of prayer,
>   But wishes to be often there?'

April 16.—This evening the friends at the Hythe will be assembled. Grant Thy gracious blessing! Read of the land Beulah. I have been there, and that, too, before coming to Giant Despair. Comfort we must not always have, or I am afraid I should go to sleep. I am now getting drowsy in spirit. Strong Deliverer, keep my eyes open! My soul seems to long after the flesh-pots of Egypt, and that after eating Heavenly manna; help and forgive me, O my Saviour!

April 17.—Read some of 'Fuller upon Antinomianism.' My God, what a gulf is near me! I think I can say that I hate this religion; I would desire to love God, and to be as holy as my Father-God Himself. There is a little cloud betwixt me and my Sun of righteousness, but I doubt not that He still shines upon me. He has not left me. I am a living miracle, a walking wonder of grace that I am alive at all; much more, following on. May I from this time live nearer to Him, and honour His name more!

April 18.—I trust the cloud has burst. I have seen some few gleams of sunshine to-day. I will walk on in His strength, whether it be through clouds or not. Went to chapel, very few there. I have been enabled to renew my strength; may I now run in the ways of the Lord! I begin to wonder why father has not written; he has good reason, no doubt. Lord, strengthen Thy people, and revive Thy Church by Thine enlivening grace!

April 19.—I do not live near enough to God. I have to lament my coldness and indifference in the ways of the Lord. O God of restoring grace, visit Thy servant in the midst of the days! I will trust Him, I cannot doubt His power of His love.

> 'Yet, I love Thee and adore
> O for grace to love Thee more!'

I shall yet another visit, and see again His smiling face. 'Whatsoever ye shall ask the Father in My name, He will give it you.'

April 20.—Went round with my tracts; could not feel the Spirit of the Lord upon me. I seemed to have a clog upon my feet and my tongue. I have richly deserved this, for I have not prayed, or studied my Bible as I ought. I confess mine iniquity, and my sin is ever before me. Mercy! it is all mercy! Wash me anew, O Saviour, in Thy sin-atoning blood!

> 'Firm as the earth Thy gospel stands,
> My Lord, my hope, my trust.'

I cannot perish if God protects me. I can do nothing. Weak and sinful worm am I.

April 21.—This morning, Mr. S. preached from 2 Thess. iii. 3. This is the great hope of a Christian, the main comfort of my life,—the Lord will do it. Afternoon, Matt. ix. 22. Here again it is the Saviour's working; earthly physicians could not do it. Blessed art Thou, O God, for this great salvation! Evening, 3 John 4. I am not very much interested with these twice-preached sermons. On the whole, I have enjoyed much this day;—little have I deserved it, nay, not at all. No merit in me, I am sure; vilest of the vile, for so long shutting mine eyes to this great salvation and glorious state of God's people.

April 22.—The Lord has not forsaken me. Went this evening to the prayer-meeting; engaged in prayer. Why should I fear to speak of my only Friend? I shall not be timid another time, I hope the Lord has helped me in this; He will in other things. The spirit is more brisk to-day, more soaring, and more en-chanted with that Saviour who is the life of all my joy. Faith is the precious gift of God, and love is His gift; it is all of God from first to last.

April 23.—My prayer is in some measure answered; I trust the work has again revived. No desert is there in me; 'tis all of mercy, I must acknowledge. I feel that I am dependent on the Lord for all, for growing grace, and for living grace. I have my daily supply, and sure enough, I do not have two days' portion at a time. 'Tis a mercy to feel one's own dependence, and to be able to trust the Lord for all. Sing, O my soul, sing, for the Lord has redeemed thee, thou art safe!

April 23.—Letter from Mr. Cantlow. Baptism on Thursday week. God help me to live worthy of Him, and that my open confession of Him may make me more diligent! Letter from Mr. Leeding better than I had thought. Truly, O Lord, my lot is in pleasant places, and I have a goodly heritage. I am to do as I please about baptism. Never do I lose anything by zeal for the truth, and close walk with my Saviour; rather, I gain everything. Lord, Thou are my life; guide me, and allot my portion on this earth according to Thine own wisdom and love!

April 25.—Went to Burwell. Heard the examination of the children. Education is indeed a talent from the Lord. What a weight of responsibility rests upon me! I trust I shall one day employ this more to His honour. A letter from father; in truth, he is rather hard upon me. When I followed my conscience, and do not presumptuously break through the fences of the Lord about His Church, I might have expected this. My business is to follow my Saviour, and not to pick out smooth paths for myself. If in any measure I have walked worthily, I would desire to give all the glory to the great Author of my salvation. I now feel so bold that, if the devil were to reproach me, I could answer him. Lord, I would ascribe it all to Thee, that I have not yet turned back, and that no enemies have yet made me to quail with terror! Onward may I press, with Heaven itself in view, trusting my salvation entirely in the hands of my Jesus, my life, my all in all!

April 26.—How my father's fears lest I should trust to baptism stir up my soul! My God, Thou knowest I hate such a thought! No, I know that, could I from this day be as holy as God Himself, yet I could not atone for past sin. I have had a pretty good day. Fear, Mistrust, and Timorous are yet at sword's length. May I be Valiant-for-Truth, and live and die in my Master's glorious war!

April 27.—Fear, begone! Doubts, fall back! In the name of the Lord of hosts I would set up my banner. Come on, ye demons of the pit, my Captain is more than a match for you; in His name, armed with His weapons, and in His strength, I dare defy you all. How glorious 'twould be to die by the side of such a Leader! I am a worm, and no man, a vanity, a nothing; yet hath He set His love upon me, and why should I tremble or fear? I have been round with my tracts; may the good seed prosper, and take root! I have again to lament that I do not live so near to God as I ought. Blessed be the name of the Lord for that measure of grace which He has given me; I can trust Him for the rest.

April 28.—Mr. S. addressed us both morning and evening from John i. 5. I could not fix upon the subject, so as to see the train of his thought. Afternoon, how I did rejoice when I brought a man to chapel, and a boy to the Sunday-school! It is the Lord! By this encouragement, in Thy strength, I pledge myself to live yet more for Thee, to fight more constantly, and to work harder. Hold Thou me up! Support me, for I can do nothing. The Lord has been with me to-day, though my heart has been in such transports as heretofore. I will follow thorough shade as well as sunshine. Saviour, dwell with me; Thine I am, help me to serve Thee, and adore Thee, world without end!

April 29.—Went to prayer-meeting. Thought upon Matt. viii. 20. When I have the presence of the Lord, nothing is a hardship to me. I would love to lodge with my Master, and to endure all things for Him. Let not my first love chill. I have no fire within to keep it alight. Thou alone canst do this, my Lord and my God. I would anew devote myself to Thee, and glory only in Thy cross, and in Thy shame.

April 30.—Another month has passed, time rolls away, I am nearer home. This month has brought me much holy enjoyment, much privilege; how little I have done when compared with what Jesus has done for me! What a slothful servant am I of so good a Master! Roll on, ye months; bring joy or sorrow as ye will, if God be with me, all is mine! How much like Vanity Fair is this place (Newmarket)! It is crowded with visitors; I saw two engines required to take them to London. Lord, give me strength, like the engine, to go straight on, guided by Thee, my great Conductor!

May 1.—Another month now dawns upon me. I have lived through one, I will bless the Lord for it, and trust Him for this also. Help me to live more to Thy glory, and to honour Thee in my daily walk and conversation. The time of my baptism approaches. May I die to the world, and live alone for Thee! I would serve Thee, O Lord; but I feel a weight, a law working against this law, and holding me in partial bondage; let Thy grace break every fetter that withholds my heart from Thee!

May 2.—Went to the lecture, very few there, not enough for a church-meeting. Lord, revive Thy Church in Newmarket! A far happier day than I deserve, I have been able to soar a little, and see the Canaan which I desire,—though with a feeble eye. To-morrow will be a solemn day. I have been enabled more than usual to pour out my heart in prayer. I need support now, and I feel that I shall have it. How safe are all God's people! Not one of the least of them can be lost, the oath and promise of the Lord cannot be broken. 'Tis a sin to think that God, a God of truth, will ever desert His people; it is a shame, a blasphemy. 'Fear thou not, for I am with thee; be not dismayed, for I am thy God.' 'I will never leave thee, nor forsake thee.'

May 3.—My mother's birthday. May the sun of heaven shine upon her, and revive her, even as it has done upon the natural world this day! Started with Mr. Cantlow at eleven, reached Isleham at one o'clock. In the afternoon, I was privileged to follow my Lord, and to be buried with Him in baptism. Blest pool! Sweet emblem of my death and to all the world! May I, henceforward, live alone for Jesus! Accept my body and soul as a poor sacrifice, tie me unto Thee; in Thy strength I now devote myself to Thy service for ever; never may I shrink from owning Thy name!

> 'Witness, ye men and angels now,
> If I forsake the Lord!'

I vow to glory alone in Jesus and His cross, and to spend my life in the extension of His cause, in whatsoever way He pleases. I desire to be sincere in this solemn profession, having but one object in view, and that to glorify God. Blessing upon Thy name that Thou has supported me through the day; it is Thy strength alone that could do this. Thou hast,—Thou wilt. Thou hast enabled me to profess Thee, help me now to honour Thee, and carry out my profession, and live the life of Christ on earth!

May 4.—Reached Newmarket at 9; feel high in spirit, have been round with my tracts; help me to serve Thee, O my Lord! There is a report in the church that Mr. S. and I have been on the heath. Mr. A. told me of it very gruffly. Mr. H. will not commune because so many have been to the races. My Master knows, I have no need to tell Him I am innocent. Though I be cast out and rejected of the disciples, the Lord will not cast off one of His chosen. I can, in this respect, wash my hands in innocency.

May 5.—A third, but very strong sermon, from John i. 5. How ought the people of God to be a peculiar people, zealous for good works! Lord, help me to honour Thee! This afternoon, partook of the Lord's supper; a royal feast for me, worthy of a King's son. Mr. S. Addressed me before all the people. Sunday-school for the first time, and went visiting the people with friend M. I quite like my new work. Teachers' prayer-meeting after evening service, from 8 to 9; five of us engaged in prayer. Went to Mr. B.'s to supper, talked with young C., stopped to family prayer, past 10 o'clock! I have been too excited to-day, amidst the busy whirl of constant action, to feel myself so solid as I could wish. Rock of Ages, bind me to Thyself! I can feel the bad law working yet. All is of God, He will perform His promise.

> 'His honour is engaged to save
> The meanest of His sheep.'

May 6.—Went to prayer-meeting. Missionary meeting in the afternoon, upon the glory of Christ's kingdom. 'He must reign.' Saviour, come, and extend Thy kingdom over all the world, sway Thy sceptre over all hearts! Make me Thy temple, and honour me by making me an instrument of good in Thy hands! Lord, save me from pride and from sloth, my two great enemies; keep me, oh, keep and preserve me! I am an erring sheep. It is in Thy power that I trust, upon Thy strength I rely; I am less than nothing, hold me by thy Thine own right hand!

May 7.—I have again to confess my lukewarmness; I fear I am losing my first love. Coldness and deadness seem to be natural to me; I have no inward warmth, it all comes from the Sun of righteousness, but rich, free, and sovereign grace. What a mercy that I have not been altogether frozen to death, and left to perish in my sinful distance from God! Lord, help me to follow Thee, and may Thy right hand uphold me! Strength, O Lord, I need! I would not fear, but trust in Thine omnipotence.

May 8.—Teachers' business meeting. Too much joking and levity to agree with my notions of what a Sunday-school teacher should be. Lord, keep me from the evil of the world, let me not be led away; but if these are Thy people, help me to serve Thee better than they, and be more like my Master! O my God, keep me ever near to Thee, help me to live more to Thy glory, and to honour Thee more than I have hitherto done, to live alone for Thee, and to spend and be spent in Thy service! Preserve, perfect, keep, and bless me!

> 'Keep me, oh, keep me, King of kings,
> Beneath Thine own almighty wings!'

May 9.—Prayer-meeting. Mr. S. has resigned. Well, we have a better Pastor, who cannot, who will not leave us. Truly, I have sunk very low; my lamp seems going out in obscurity. Lord, fan it, keep it burning yet! I know that I can never perish; yet be pleased my God, to visit me again, to revive and uphold me, so that I may honour Thee more; make me to be an eminent servant of Thine, and to be blessed with the power to serve Thee, like Thy great servant Paul!

May 10.—Blessed be the name of the Lord, He has not left His servant, or turned away from His chosen! Though I have often sinned, and neglected the sweet privilege of prayer, yet He hath not deserted me. Had a letter from Mr. L. I hope that the Lord will bless him, and give him many souls as seals for his hire. I wonder how they are at home. Time flies away. Seasons come and go.

Lord, grant me Thy Holy Spirit to enable me to improve each moment! I am 'bought with a price.'

May 11.—Went round my district. I trust the Lord is moving upon the face of this people. It is Thy work, O Lord; accomplish it! I feel encouraged to go on in the ways of the Lord, and still to spend my spare time in His service. Prosper Thou the work of my hands! My own soul is encouraged, my life is revived, and I hope soon to enjoy the presence of the Lord.

May 12.—One of the days of the Son of man,—happy day when Sabbath shall never end! Went to Sunday-school at 9, stayed till service at 10.30, out at 12.15; Sunday-school at 1.45, service 3 till 4, visiting till 5. The day has thus been closely occupied. The morning's discourse was upon I Corinthians iv. 7. Truly, I have nothing which I have not received; I can boast of no inherent righteousness. Had the Lord not chosen me, I should not have chosen Him. Grace! Grace! Grace! 'Tis all of grace. I can do nothing, I am less than nothing; yet what a difference,—once a slave of hell, now the son of the God of Heaven! Help me to walk worthy of my lofty and exalted vocation! Afternoon, Psalm xlviii. 14, 'This God is my God for ever and ever; He will be my Guide even unto death. I can wish for no better Guide, or more lasting Friend; He shall lead me in His own way.

Lord, permit me not to choose the road, allow me not to wander into By-path meadow; rather carry me straight to glory! Evening, Acts xvii. 11. The Word of God is my chart. Lord, give me more of Berean nobility; grant me Thy grace to search the Scriptures, and to become wise unto life eternal! Thine is the gift, I cannot do it without Thee. Again would I give myself anew to Thee; bind Thou the sacrifice with cord, even to the horns of Thine altar! Let me not go away from Thee; hold me firmly in Thy gracious arms! Let Thine omnipotence be my protection, Thy wisdom my direction, Thy grace my salvation. 'Lord, I believe; help Thou mine unbelief!'

May 13.—A day of great, unmerited mercy. Happiness cannot exist here without some cloy. How sweet the joys of religion, of communion with God! Letter from home. All well. I thank Thee, Father, for such good tidings; bless me, even me also, O my Father! I would devote myself to Thee; it is my highest privilege to be able to give myself to Thee. Thy service is the greatest pleasure, the most untiring delight; I would, more than ever, wear Thy livery, be known as Thy servant, and become one of Thy peculiar people.

May 14.—In the evening, enjoyed an ecstasy of delight. I seemed transported, and able to fly beyond the bounds of this poor atom of an earth. Spiritual realities were present to view, while the flesh, like Abraham's servant, tarried at the foot of the mountain. How much do I woe; how little good do I deserve, yea, not at all!

'Let Thy grace, Lord, like a fetter,
Bind my wandering heart to Thee.!'

Blessed by Thy name for evermore! Bless the Lord, O my soul; follow hard after Him, love and serve Him!

May 15.—How feeble I am! I am not able to keep myself near to God. I am compelled to acknowledge my own deadness. I confess how greatly I have strayed from Thee, Thou great Fountain of living waters; but,—

> 'Since I've not forgot Thy law,
> Restore Thy wandering sheep.'

Revive me in the midst of the years, and make Thy face to shine upon me! How much do I deserve eternal damnation! But salvation is not of desert, but of free grace. This is the plank whereon I hope to float to glory, when this world shall be a wreck, and perish in the vast abyss.

May 16.—Went to chapel. Sermon on Psalm xxiii. 3. How much do I need this restoration! If the Lord does not do it, I cannot. 'Turn out Thine enemy and mine.' I would be passive, submitting to Thy sovereign will; Thou wilt do what is right. Lord, keep me; I will wait Thy time of revival; teach me both to work and wait, expecting and hoping that Thou wilt soon come, and restore unto me the joy of Thy salvation! I am in a low condition, yet I am eternally safe. He will lead me.

May 17.—It is now a fortnight since my baptism. How solemnly have I devoted myself to Thee! I would now repeat my vows, and again solemnly devote myself to Thee.

> 'Witness, ye men and angel now,
> If I forsake the Lord.'

In His strength I can do all things. Thou hast sworn to save, and death and hell cannot thwart Thine everlasting purpose. Hold me! Thou hast blessed me, Thou alone canst do it. If Thou dost not save, I must perish. Thou wilt not leave me, Thou hast showed me a portion of the glory of Thy face.

May 18.—Station District. When I first set out, I was all but dumb concerning spiritual things. Soon I felt the working of the Lord in some degree. Blessed be His holy name for ever and ever, and let all the redeemed say, Amen! His is the power. Beloved, This is enduring beauty! Thou art glorious to behold. Give me more of the entrancing visions of Thy face, the looks of Thy love, and more constant communion with Thee! Lord, move Thou upon the earth, and bring in Thine elect from among the condemned sinners of the world!

May 19.—Went to the Sunday-school. Mr. S. preached, this morning, from 2 Cor. iii. 6-8. How glorious is the ministration of life, how beautiful the tables of stone, when enclosed in the blessed ark of the covenant! Afternoon, Ezek. xxxvi. 27. Evening, 'What is truth?' As to interest, the sermons to-day have been a failure. Addressed the children upon Prayer. Went visiting with Mr. M., six fresh children. Evening at Mr. B.'s. Engaged in prayer at his family altar. To-day has been a sunny day with me. The Lord has visited me from on high. Rejoice, O my soul, leap for joy, renew thy strength; run, run, in the name of the Lord! He is with me, He has been with me. Weakness He has made strength! Mighty to save, Thou shalt have all my noblest songs! Let Thy grace constrain me to love Thee, and live for Thee! I am buried with my Lord and Saviour; may I be crucified to the world, and die daily! How sure is it that Thy yoke is easy, and Thy burden is light! I can do all things through Christ Jesus.

May 21.—Glorious day, happy were all like this! Oh, the safety of a Christian, as sure, but not so blest, as a saint in Heaven! Lord, how can I leave Thee? To whom, or whither should I go? Thou centre of my love, all glorious names in one, Thou brightest, sweetest, fairest One, that eyes have seen or angels know, I trust to Thee for salvation; without Thee, I can do nothing. I am utter weakness, Thou must do it all, or I shall perish! Love of loves, all love excelling, fix my wandering heart on Thee!

May 22.—My weakness is my greatest strength, for then I trust alone on Jesus, when I feel my own dependence. I am an earthen vessel, I have been among the pots of the unregenerate; make me now a vessel for Thy use! Thy blood is my trust, I am washed; who shall now blacken me so as not to leave me spotless at the last? Joy, joy unspeakable, rapture divine, I fly beyond the bound of earth, my Husband folds me in His arms, I am His, and He is mine, my glorious Prince, Redeemer, Love!

May 23.—Went to chapel, very few there. 'He restoreth my soul.' The same subject again! How true is this, how has He revived me! Short, but glorious, are the days of my refreshing,—worthy of years of sorrow and distress. O my Beloved, did my way lie over the embers of hell all my life, didst Thou but show Thyself, I would rush through the fire to meet Thee! I have not been quite so ecstatic as for some days past. I am the Lord's forever, how much do I owe to Him! My Advocate, Brother, Husband, let not my first love chill and grow cold! Keep me and preserve in Thy hands!

May 24.—A day of undeserved joy. I am not altogether banished from the presence of the Lord. Though He slay me, I cannot but trust Him, since I have had such tokens of His love. Lord, when in darkness and distress, when my head is bowed down, then return unto Thy servant to encourage and support him! For ever, oh, for ever, lashed to the Ark, and safe from the floods, I shall get at last upon the terra firma of glory! Oh, let me not dishonour Thee! Never may I bring a disgrace upon the cause of Christ! Keep me, and I shall be infinitely safe, and rest securely.

May 25.—Free grace, sovereign love, eternal security are my safeguards; what shall keep me from consecrating all to Thee, even to the last drop of my blood? Went to my district with tracts, a woman gave me 24 new ones. I fear

Mr. T. is doing much harm by telling the people that the Lord's supper will save them. Work, Lord, work! Thou hast encouraged me, may I not be disappointed! 'Bless the Lord, O my soul,' The Covenant is my trust, the agreement signed between my Elder Brother and the Almighty standeth sure. 'None shall pluck them out of My hand.'

May 26.—Went round for the children. Sunday-school in the morning. Mr. S. preached from, 'All these things are against me.' Stayed in the chapel the dinner-time, had a sweet season of prayer and communion with God. Afternoon, Jacob's consecration of himself at Bethel. I would give myself in the same manner to Thee, my best-loved King. Evening subject, Paul's great labours. Oh, could I emulate such a man, I should be the greatest on this earth!

May 27.—Life of my soul, forgive me when I am so blind as to look upon an earthly object, and forget Thine own Divine beauties! Oh, for a love as strong as death, fierce as hell, and lasting as eternity.

May 28.—Thou hast hedged me about with thorns so that I cannot get out; this is my comfort. What name can I devise for Thee, O Beloved, equal to Thy desert? All beauties joined in one perfection, 'Thou are all fair, my Love, there is no spot in Thee.' Thou didst die for me, and shall not I live to Thee? What a love is that of Jesus to me, surpassing knowledge! I can do nothing in return, but give Thee my worthless self. What! shall I dare to doubt Thy love? Can I conceive that Thou wilt leave me? Yes, I may sin so as to distrust Thee; but Thou wilt never let me go. No thief can steal away Thy precious purchase; never, never, can I be lost. Redeemed and purchased; then, how can I be snatched away? How is my soul a battlefield between the corruptions of nature and the principle of grace! They tear up the earth of my soul with the trampling of their armies; but I cannot be destroyed.

May 29.—To the Lord belongeth strength, He has given me my portion. He putteth His treasure in earthen vessels. How happy am I to be one of His chosen, His elect, in whom His soul delighteth! But I do not live up to my Heavenly calling; I could not at all without the Lord, He has helped,—He will help,—this is my comfort. His everlasting promises are my rest, my bread, my support. Make me Thy faithful servant, O my God; may I honour Thee in my day and generation, and be consecrated for ever to Thy service!

May 30.—The stormy commotion has somewhat passed away; the sun is still shining, though a cloud may pass between. I desire more constant communion with God. Went to church-meeting, had some nice cheering conversation with old Mrs. A. Two candidates proposed; we shall have no Ordinance next Sunday. The Lord can and will feed us without it. He has kept me, and He will. The strife in my soul is now hushed, peace returns as a river upon the dry places.

May 31.—Weakness am I in every point, I cannot keep myself in the least. Forgive me that I have tried it! I would now come, naked, stripped, exhausted, dead. I would cry, 'Lash me tighter, firmer, to Thy free-grace raft of life!' Mercy is all I ask for,—continued mercy. Those whom He once loves to the end; He has once loved me, I am now secure. May the live coal within be shown to the world by the burning flames of love to Thee! May that love burn up the stubble and sin!

June 1.—A new month; time soon glides away. How much more ought I to do this month than last! Desire of my heart, keep me nearer to Thy bosom this month! Went to South District. Talked with a woman who says there are contradictions in the Bible. Some good may be doing. He that can work, will work; and who shall hinder Him? in the Lord's time it shall be accomplished; His time is best. Arise, O Sun of righteousness, why should this people lie in darkness?

June 2.—Heard Mr. J. the first part of the day., Num. xxi. 4. Interesting, but rather too weak. Afternoon, Rev. xix. 12. Many crowns indeed does my Lord deserve; crown of glory shall be around His sacred, blessed head. Evening, 1 John v. 4. Strong meat; the Lord has sent the manna down this evening. 'Overcometh the world!; Glorious victory, amazing conquest, triumph Divine; and shall I, with such a promise, dare to doubt the power of God to keep, and guide, and preserve me?

Had a large class at Sunday-school, gave an address upon Death,—the dreadful sword hanging by a single hair above the head of the ungodly. Had tea at Mr. B.'s, and combated with him for what I consider 'the form of sound words.' Prayer-meeting after the evening service. Several present, six of us engaged in prayer. Bless the Sunday-school, great King! Honour thy Master, O my soul; live for Him, live in Him! I am a prince; ought I not be a good soldier, and fight for my Lord? Give me, lend me a sword, O God, and strength to wield it; let my foes and Thine be as furious as lions, Thy sword shall destroy them!

June 3.—Prayer meeting, engaged in prayer. Lord, when shall Thy set time to favour Zion come? When shall Thine elect be gathered in? 'Who shall separate us from the love of Christ?' For ever, yes, for ever, safe. Rejoice, rejoice, O my soul, and let thy joy constrain thee to work more earnestly and more zealously for Him! Redeemed and purchased, I am not my own. Letter from grandfather. How glad I am he does not differ!

June 4.—I have had evidence this day of the changeableness of all mortal things. How little does it matter to me, so that my eternal inheritance is secure! Lord, help me now to mount my watch-tower against pride and sloth! Keep me always upon the look-out, lest an enemy should come unawares; forgive me, if I have ever had high thoughts of myself! Thou makest me to feel my weakness in every part; may I now trust and rely upon the arm of Omnipotence, the mercies of the Lord! Give Strength, Lord, strength!

'He justly claims a song from me,
His lovingkindness, O how free!'

Mercy, I breathe Another's air, I am a tenant of this earth at my Master's will;
sovereign grace has kept me hitherto, upon sovereign grace I now rely. What
sweet moments have I had in answer to prayer; blessed by the Lord for His
rich mercy thus bestowed upon me! I would now live in close communion
with my King, and feast upon the riches of His love.

June 6.—Prayer-meeting. Mr. S. spoke to us upon the Babylonian Captivity.
Teachers' meeting after the service. What a want of spirituality and vital
godliness! O Lord, give me life; increase the vital spark, fan it to a flame! I can
never perish, yet would I keep upon my watch-tower, for my enemies are
many, and they hate me with cruel hatred. Help me to hate sin, and pride, and
sloth! I live only as Thou givest me life. I have not one atom of life of my own,
I must perish if Thou desert me for one moment.

June 7.—How manifold are Thy mercies toward me, O Lord! When I think of
the great salvation which has been worked out for me, and remember that
Heaven is secure, it seems too good to be true. Yet do I now believe Thy
promise; may I now be entirely Thine, Thy glory my only aim! Could I but be
like Paul, how honoured should I be! Happy is the man whom Thou teachest,
O Lord! I am happy; how can I be otherwise, since my Beloved has looked
upon me, and I have seen His glorious face?

June 8.—Could not burn with zeal as oft I have done. When, Lord, wilt Thou
arise, and let Thy power be known and felt? How sweet to flap my wings to
Heaven, with others following me; then lay my crown beneath His feet, and
call Him Lord of all! He is deserving of all honour and praise; dominion and
power are His due, and He shall have them. Many honours on His ever-
blessed head! Worthy is the Lamb who has died for me. All glorious is my
Beloved.

June 9.—Mr. S. preached. Acts xvi. 19. Did not hear to profit. Afternoon,
'Who is this that cometh up from the wilderness, leaning upon her Beloved!'
Did not hear enough about the Beloved. Evening, 'Prepare to meet Thy God.'
Oh, what a mercy to be prepared!

'So whene'er the signal's given,
Us from earth to call away,
Borne on angels' wings to Heaven,
Glad the summons to obey,
We shall surely
Reign with Christ in endless day!'

Felt rather hurt by Mr. C., he does not act quite rightly; but I hereby forgive
him. I desire to look alone to Jesus, and regard His glory only. I am too proud,

I am weak in every point; keep me, for I have no strength! I would look up to Thee,—the Strong,—for strength. I am Thine, keep me!

June 10.—Letter from dear mother. Mr. S. made her his text at the prayer-meeting. Engaged in prayer. Have not been able to be much in private prayer to-day. The joy of my Lord, however, is not gone. I can yet trust in the God of my salvation. If I ever forget Thee, let my right hand forget her fellow. What! has He done so much for me, and shall I ever leave Him? No,—

> 'While a breath, a pulse remains,
> I will remember Thee!'

June 11.—Prayer seems like labour to me, the chariot wheels drag heavily; yet they are not taken off. I will still rely upon almighty strength; and, helpless, throw myself into the arms of my Redeemer. 'Leave, ah, leave me not alone!' 'I will never leave Thee.' I shall yet walk the golden street of the New Jerusalem, I shall yet see His beauteous face. He loved me before the foundations of the earth, before I was created or called by grace.

June 12.—The Lord is my Helper, He shall plead my cause. I would desire to record the gratitude I feel for the sparing mercies of the Lord, but especially for His great grace in electing me, by the sovereign councils of His love, to be one of His redeemed ones. What! shall I not live for Him, shall I keep back a single particle of my heart, and of myself, from my charming Redeemer, my King, Husband, Brother, Friend? No; oh, give me strength to say, 'I will never dishonour Thee'!

June 13.—Dangers are around me, Satan stands in the way; I have no hope but in the Lord, no safety but in keeping straight on in the Heavenly road. In the Lord Jehovah is everlasting strength, and inexhaustible mines of eternal love are mine; the Lord reserves them for His chosen people. Went to prayer-meeting. Tried to address my Lord in prayer. Come, my Beloved, Thou art ever mine; leave me not, O do not forsake me, My King, my Saviour! Saved everlastingly!

June 14.—Examination. Mr. M. gave me 10s. for the Missionary Society. I would thank the Lord for thus opening his hand to do good. Gave a Missionary speech. Lord, keep Thy servant low and humble at Thy feet! How prone am I to pride and vain-glory! Keep me always mindful that I have nothing which I have not received; 'tis grace, free, sovereign grace that has made me to differ. Why should I be chosen an elect vessel? Not that I deserve it, I am sure; but it is rich love.

June 15.—Went round my S. District, and divided my stock amongst the people, and now, Lord, I desire to commend them to thy keeping, look upon them with pity, let them not be as sheep without a shepherd! Let Thy work go on and prosper among this people! I can do nothing; how is it that I have lived so long in my spiritual life? It is by sovereign power I stand, by Omnipotence I shall be supported. 'My grace is sufficient for thee.' I trust in Him; He will perfect His own work.

June 16.—Old Mr. W. preached; could not hear him, he spoke so low. Was set upon by him and Mrs. S. Lord, help me to take firm hold of the truth, and never yield an inch! Addressed the Sunday-school children. Oh, may I be kept humble! Pride dwells in my heart. I am now to leave Newmarket; perhaps, for ever. What a scene of changes is this world! How blest to have a house above the skies, eternal in the Heavens!

June 17.—Left Newmarket at 6. Reached Stambourne about 12. Grandfather quite well. I have had journeying mercies to-day. This life is a journey; I know that I shall one day reach the blessed end, in bliss, unfading bliss. What can I write equal to the theme of sovereign grace? It is a miracle, a perfect miracle, that God should so love man as to die for him, and to choose him before the foundation of the world.

June 19.—My birthday. Sixteen years have I lived upon this earth, and yet I am only—scarcely six months old! I am very young in grace. Yet how much time have I wasted, dead in trespasses and sins, without life, without God, in the world! What a mercy that I did not perish in my sin! How glorious is my calling, how exalted my election, born of the Lord,—regenerate! Help me more than ever to walk worthily, as becomes a saint!

June 20.—Truly my lot is cast in pleasant places, and I have a goodly heritage. I can love religion now in the sunshine; may I love it and prize it under all circumstances!

*　*　*　*

(The continuous Diary thus abruptly closes, giving only the brief intimation that the dear writer goes immediately to Cambridge, as usher in Mr. Leeding's school. There remain but three or four fragmentary entries during the ensuing months,—or years,—but these serve to show the young soldier still busy at his drill, loyal to his Lord's colours, and already bravely fighting that 'good fight of faith,' which ceased not till his Captain called him from the battlefield, to receive the victor's reward in glory. As every word of his is precious in these days, I transcribe the four succeeding paragraphs, though unable to ascertain the dates when they were written.—S.S.)

Storms have raged around me; yet, blessed be my Father's name, I have now some peace! 'But more the treacherous calm I dread, than tempest breaking overhead.' Let me not be left even here; let Thy grace still flow into my heart! O Lord, my King, reign in me, and be glorified by me! May it please Thee to dwell in such a bramble-bush as I am, so that, though burning, I may not be consumed! Ordered in all things and sure is the everlasting covenant of redeeming love. For ever settled and eternally complete in Him is my salvation. May it be completed in myself, and may I grow up to be a man in Christ Jesus, a perfect man, prepared for the inheritance of the saints in light! Oh, that my spirituality may be revived! My matchless Immanuel, let me see once more Thy face in the temple of my heart! May I know the joy, and have the faith of God's elect; may I rejoice in free and sovereign grace, saving me from the guild and power of sin! Grace is a glorious theme, above the loftiest flights of the most soaring angel, or the most exalted conceptions of one of the joint-heirs with Jesus. All power is God's, and all is engaged to protect and preserve me. Let me have my daily grace, peace and comfort, zeal and love, give me some work and give me strength to do it to Thy glory!

Heard Mr. C., or Bumpstead. Morning, 'What doest thou here, Elijah?' After-noon, 'I am the door.' Went to the prayer-meeting before and after chapel, engaged in prayer, read the hymns, and addressed the children. What an honour it is to be but a door-keeper in the house of the Lord! Oh, to be humble, and to be always at the feet of Jesus! Then should I grow more in grace, and increase in the knowledge of the Lord. The Lord is able to keep me from falling, and He will, for He has promised never to leave one of His called children.

Fair Day.—Spoke to Mr. R. How can a child of God go there? 'Vanity of vanities, all is vanity.' Forgive him, Lord, for so forgetting his high calling! I, too, should be there, but for the grace of God. I have the seeds of all evil in my own heart; pride is yet my darling sin, I cannot shake it off. Awake, O my Lord, against the mighty, for I shall die by his hand if Thou do not help me, and lead me on to triumph! Leave me, ye vain thought! I have nothing but what I have received; it is the Lord's goodness that I even have my reason.

How could I live without prayer when troubles come? How blessed to carry them to the throne! I will now say that the Lord heareth prayer, for He hath removed from me that which I feared. But, oh! could I feel the presence of the Lord as in days gone by, how joyful! Could I enjoy His face, and feast upon His love, then would it be a sort of Heaven below the skies. Yes, Thou art mine, my Saviour and my King; I am bound to Thee by love, by Thine own dying love, not mine! Fairest of beings, best-beloved, come, let me yet see Thy smiling face![29]

The diary makes it abundantly evident that young Spurgeon had embarked on an intimate walk with Jesus Christ. Prayer, Bible study, service, and the Christian disciplines had become central in his life. He stated:

Prayer is to me what the sucking of milk was to me in my infancy. Although I do not always feel the same relish for it, yet I am sure I cannot live without it . . . Prayer sweet prayer! Be it ever so feeble, there's nothing like prayer.[30]

Charles possessed a most sensitive spirit—a real heart for God, despite his confessed temptation to pride. Because of his simple honesty and transparency, as James Douglas said, "He was often disappointed, often deceived." Guileless in himself, he believed in everyone. At the same time, however, David Lloyd George, British Prime Minister, said, "He had great common sense. He had deep insight into character."[31] In social manners and decorum he was scrupulously and even anxiously courteous. His walk with Christ made him a happy man, his bouts with depression notwithstanding. Douglas tells us, "At times he was playful as a kitten, and merry as a lark, being pleasantry itself."[32] Those sterling spiritual qualities he never lost through his life.

BAPTISM IN THE RIVER LARK

As has been seen, reference to Charles' baptism is made in both his diary and letters. After coming to the conviction he should be immersed through the study of Anglican catechisms, that conviction deepened now that he had been converted. Further, Mr. John Swindell of the Newmarket school was a Baptist. He probably strengthened that awareness of need. Charles also had fellowship with some students from the Baptist Church in Isleham, a town seven miles away. Although he had never even heard of the Baptist denomination until he was fourteen years of age, he concluded, typically of Baptist doctrine, that he should not take the Lord's Supper until he had received believer's baptism. Therefore, he set himself to his previous commitment to be immersed in the Baptist mode.

Spurgeon was not as presumptuous a young lad as some have contended. He would not think of being baptized without the consent of his parents. So he wrote his father and mother, sharing his conviction that he should submit himself to immersion at the hands of a Baptist minister. On April 6th he wrote to his father:

> As Mr. Cantlow's baptizing season will come round this month, I have humbly to beg your consent, as I will not act against your will, and should very much like to commune next month. I have no doubt of your permission. We are all one in Christ Jesus; forms and ceremonies, I trust, will not make us divided.

When he did not receive a response from his father, he penned this note to his mother:

> I have every morning looked for a letter from Father, I long for an answer; it is now a month since I have had one from him. Do, if you please, send me either permission or refusal to be baptized; I have been kept in painful suspense. This is the 20th, and Mr. Cantlow's baptizing day is to be the latter end of the month; I think, next week. I should be so sorry to lose another Ordinance Sunday; and with my present convictions, I hope I shall never so violate my conscience as to sit down unbaptized. When requested, I assured the members at the church-meeting that I would never do so.[33]

He apparently had written to his grandfather as well, because in a letter to his mother written on June 11, he said:

> Grandfather has written to me; he does not blame me for being a Baptist, but hopes I shall not be one of the tight-laced, strict-communion sort. In that, we are agreed. I certainly think we ought to forget such things in others when we come to Lord's table. I can, and hope I shall be, charitable to unbaptized Christians, though I think they are mistaken. It is not a great matter; men will differ; we ought both to follow our own consciences, and let others do the same. I think the time would be better spent in talking upon vital godliness than in disputing about forms.

Spurgeon's father had some fear that his son might rely on baptism for salvation, the error of "baptismal regeneration." But recall, Charles said in this diary, April 27, 1850, "How my father's fears that I should trust to baptism stirs up my soul. My God, thou knowest that I hate such a thought." He made his position crystal clear saying:

> I had no superstitious idea that baptism would save me, for I was saved. I did not seek to have sin washed away by water, for I believed that my sins were forgiven me by faith in Christ Jesus. Yet I regarded baptism as the token to the believer of cleansing, the emblem of his burial with his Lord, outward approval of his new birth.

Spurgeon decidedly lived out that conviction some years later in what became known as the "Baptismal Regeneration Controversy." That fascinating battle will be discussed later.

Charles received his parents' consent. He wrote back to his mother, "Conscience has convinced me that it is a duty to be buried with Christ in baptism, although I am sure it constitutes no part of salvation. I am very glad that you have no objection to my doing so." Spurgeon met with Mr. W. W. Cantlow, formerly a missionary in Jamaica, and now pastor of the Baptist church at Isleham. An interesting anecdote occurred in the light of Spurgeon's decision to be baptized. When he told his mother his intent of being immersed, she said that she had often prayed that he would become a Christian but never had she prayed that he would become a Baptist. Spurgeon, with unusual insight and wit for a young man, replied to his mother that it was a demonstration that God does abundantly above all that we ask or think. So on his mother's birthday, Friday, May 3, 1850, he presented himself for baptism, just a few weeks before turning sixteen years of age. Charles dedicated himself that day to professing Christ openly in the waters of baptism.

Obtaining permission to leave school, Charles arose early in the morning in order to have at least two hours for prayer and meditation. Dressed in a jacket and a boy's turned-down collar, he walked eight miles to Isleham Ferry on the river Lark, a beautiful little stream dividing Suffolk from

Cambridgeshire. A ferry boat carried people across the small stream that provided a good spot for anglers. "What a walk it was!" Charles said, "What thoughts and prayers thronged my soul during that morning's journey." He went first to the Rev. Cantlow's home and rejoiced to see the smiling pastor. After some counsel on the meaning of believer's baptism, the couple made their way to the River Lark, a half mile from the village of Isleham. A ferry-house stood on the spot where Charles was to be baptized, and was used by the minister and candidates during a baptism. The pastor conducted a short worship service before the baptism itself. Making his public profession of faith awed Charles.

Even though it was a Friday and a quite cold day, a good number of people had assembled. On the ferry boat, on the shores, even in rowboats, people had gathered to witness the scene. Of course, not as many people attended as probably would have been the case had the baptism been held on Sunday; still, a quite respectable number gathered to see Charles baptized, along with two women, Diana Wilkinson and Eunice Fuller. These two women were held in some honor later because they were baptized in the same service as Spurgeon. Charles' description of the baptismal experience is graphic:

> The wind blew down the river with a cutting blast as my turn came to wade into the flood; but after I had walked a few steps, and noted the people on the ferry-boat, and in boats, and on either shore, I felt as if heaven and earth and hell might all gaze upon me, for I was not ashamed, then and there, to own myself a follower of the Lamb. My timidity was washed away; it floated down the river into the sea, and must have been devoured by the fishes, for I have never felt anything of the kind since. Baptism also loosed my tongue, and from that day it has never been quiet.

Spurgeon spent the evening of his baptismal day in conversation with Pastor Cantlow in the Isleham Baptist Church vestry. He then attended a prayer meeting at which he publicly prayed, one of the earliest known public prayers since he came to faith in Christ. Fullerton says the "people wondered and wept for joy as they listened to the lad."[34] The mystery of the Spirit's anointing already seemed to be on the boy.

Charles gave much of the human credit for his conversion, which he exemplified in his baptism, to his mother. In a letter dated May 1, 1850 he wrote to her:

> Your birthday will now be doubly memorable, for on the 3rd of May, the boy for whom you have so often prayed, the boy of hopes and fears, your firstborn, will join the visible church of the Redeemer on earth and will bind himself doubly to the Lord his God, by open profession. You my mother, have been the great means in God's hand, of rendering me what I hope I am. Your kind warning Sabbath evening addresses were too deeply settled on my heart to be forgotten. You by God's blessing prepared the way for the preached word.[35]

The next morning Charles returned to Newmarket and on the following Sunday he took the Lord's Supper at the Independent chapel where he had become a member. His baptism did not automatically make him a member of the Baptist church. He stated, "I did not fulfill the outward ordinance to join a party and to become a Baptist, but to be a Christian after the apostolic fashion; for they, when they believed, were baptized." [36] Charles went on to say:

> It is not a question wherever John Bunyan was baptized; but the same question can never be raised concerning me. I, who scarcely belong to any sect, nevertheless by no means willing to have it doubted in time to come whether or no I follow the conviction of my heart.

SERVICE AT SCHOOL

Spurgeon carried on his Sunday School teacher role at Newmarket. In a Sunday School workers' meeting, each teacher would alternate with the superintendent in bringing the closing message to all the scholars. When Charles spoke, the students received him so well the superintendent asked him to speak every week. Though he at first refused, he finally consented and the hour became like a regular church worship service. Moreover, he continued distributing tracts, witnessing, and serving the Lord he had come to know.

Spurgeon's ministry of distributing tracts became one of his most delightful services at the Congregational church in Newmarket. He developed a little circuit of seventy people, and on Saturday afternoons he would visit their homes. Sitting down in house after house, he would share God's truth with them. Charles regularly visited thirty-three houses in his tract ministry to reach those seventy folk. He had taken over the circuit of houses formerly served by two women who lived in Swindell's home. As a zealous new servant of Christ, he said:

> I could scarcely content myself even for five minutes without trying to do something for Christ. If I walked along the street, I must have a few tracts with me; if I went into a railway carriage, I must drop a tract out of the window; if I had a moment's leisure, I must be upon my knees or at my Bible; if I were in company, I must turn the subject of conversation to Christ, that I might serve my master. [37]

Charles' whole life in these early days seemed consumed in helping others to faith in Jesus Christ. Moreover, the evangelistic fervor kindled in his heart on the day of his conversion never abated. Spurgeon can be best understood as a Pastor-*Evangelist*.

On Sunday afternoons, Charles always took his place in the Sunday School. But he did not always see himself as a brilliant success there. Nonetheless, he could normally hold the attention of the class he taught.

Moreover, he began to learn some of the basic principles of good communication. When the boys grew uneasy and bored, he would give them a good illustration to grab their attention. One of the lads once said, "This is very dull, teacher. Can't you pitch us a yarn?" He could, and he grasped the importance of illustrations that relate scriptural realities to practical life. When he became a preacher, he also laced his sermons with pungent illustrations and anecdotes.

After Charles began addressing the entire Sunday School each Sunday, the pastor was not especially pleased with the idea. Adults began to come to hear the young man. Charles said, "I have endeavored to speak as a dying individual to dying individuals." That comment is much like the famous statement of the great Puritan, Richard Baxter. He may well have gotten it from Baxter. Spurgeon continued his witnessing, not only to unbelievers, but to any Christian he felt needed a word from the Lord. On one occasion he saw a fellow-believer enter a dance. He accosted him and said, reminiscent of his encounter with old Roads in Stambourne, "What doest thou here, Elijah?" But Charles got no response this time. It is true, his timidity had floated down the River Lark at his baptism.

Spurgeon's first formal public speech had taken place at a missionary meeting on Monday, September 10, 1849. He presented a message on missions at the Newmarket school. At that time he had not yet been converted; nevertheless, Professor J. D. Everett of Queen's College at Belfast, who heard him, said he "spoke fluently." Then on June 14, 1850, he presented another missionary speech. By this time he had come to faith in Christ and missions were truly on his heart. Actually, some contend Charles seriously faced the question about whether he should preach the Gospel in China. Though he never traveled beyond the bounds of England and the continent of Europe, a zeal for evangelism and missions consumed him throughout his entire life.

CAMBRIDGE AND BECOMING A BAPTIST

Charles left Newmarket June 17, 1850, and once again spent some time with his grandparents in Stambourne. As always, it proved a delightful time for the youth—especially now since he had come to personally know the Lord Jesus Christ. In August of the same year, he moved to Cambridge to a school established by Mr. E. S. Leeding who had been his teacher at the Colchester school in earlier days. There he remained for some very formative years as an usher with a meager salary. He also continued his studies under senior professors. He lived at 9, Union Road in Cambridge, and soon united with the St. Andrew's Street Baptist Church, the first Baptist church he joined. The St. Andrew's Street Church received young Spurgeon into membership on October 3, 1850. The records in the church business meeting minutes read: "October 3, Received . . . Mr. Spurgin." On that day, along with Charles, two others were received by letter, one was removed, one was struck off the roll because of death, and four others were dismissed to various churches. [38] Charles had now become a "full-fledged" Baptist. At the school, Mr. Leeding's practice was to allow all students and faculty to engage in half an hour of prayer each morning at 8:00. This suited the young usher well as he grew in the Spirit.

To look ahead for a moment, an interesting incident gives one an insight into Spurgeon's character. Toward the end of his time at Cambridge, Charles found himself severely financially depressed. He never sought money for his own sake; in November of 1852 he wrote his mother, "I had rather be poor in God's service than rich in my own." Still, by mid-summer of that year, he desperately needed fifteen pounds to provide his textbooks and other necessities of life. So at the end of 1853, the following advertisement appeared in the Cambridge newspaper:

> Number 60, Park Street Cambridge. Mr. C.H. Spurgeon begs to inform his numerous friends that after Christmas he intends on taking six or seven young gentlemen as day pupils. He will endeavor to the utmost to impart a good commercial education. The ordinary routine will include arithmetic, algebra, geometry, and Mensuration; grammar and composition; ancient and modern history; geography, natural history, astronomy, scripture and drawing; Latin and the elements of Greek and French if required. Terms £5 per annum.

Spurgeon was not modest concerning his teaching and intellectual ability. He apparently saw himself competent in a vast array of subjects. But his youthful pride did not degenerate into aloofness. Throughout life he never minimized his abilities, but he never ran over people or despised those of lesser gifts. Moreover, the school never started; God intervened in a marvelous way to direct the young man's path.

When Spurgeon joined the St. Andrew's Street Baptist Church in Cambridge, Robert Hall served the church as pastor. In his day, Hall became one of England's foremost Baptist preachers. He started the Lay Preacher's Association during his ministry in St. Andrew's. The Association still functions in Britain. That organization was soon to play an important role in Charles' life. St. Andrew's Church also enjoyed some renown because of the previous pastorate of Robert Robinson, author of the hymn "Come Thou Fount of Every Blessing." [39]

An interesting anecdote occurred in Spurgeon's early days in the Baptist church in Cambridge. He related the story:

> When I joined the Baptist Church at Cambridge, one of the most respectable churches that can be found in the world, one of the most generous, one of the most intelligent—this was a great many years ago, when I was young—nobody spoke to me. On the Lord's Day I sat at the Communion table in a certain pew. There was one gentleman (Mr. Watts) in it, and when the service was

over, I said to him, 'I hope you are quite well, sir?' He said, 'You have the advantage of me.' I answered, 'I don't think I have, for you and I are brothers.' 'I don't quite know what you mean,' said he. 'Well,' I replied, 'when I took the bread and wine just now, in token of our being one in Christ, I meant it. Did not you?' We were by that time in the street; he put both his hands on my shoulders—I was about sixteen years old then—and he said, 'Oh, sweet simplicity!' Then he added, 'You are quite right, my dear brother, you are quite right; come in to tea with me. I am afraid I should not have spoken to you if you had not first addressed me.' I went to tea with him that evening; and when I left, he asked me to go again the next Lord's Day, so I went, and that Sabbath Day he said to me, 'You will come here every Sunday evening, won't you?' So old Mr. Watts and young Mr. Spurgeon became fast friends.'[40]

Spurgeon went to work in the St. Andrew's Street Sunday School in Cambridge as soon as he arrived in the university city. Mr. George Apthorpe, a fellow teacher in the Sunday School, said, "Many a time I was listening to him (Charles) while teaching my own boys."[41] Spurgeon gravitated to a place of leadership among the other teachers and would read essays on Sunday School work at the city's teacher's institute. Many recognized the latent preaching ability he possessed. Charles also continued his witnessing in Cambridge. He found a unique way to reach homes. He would set writing exercises for children in his classes, then he would call at their homes to check their progress. The parents were proud of personal visits by a teacher, and as Charles established a good relationship he would minister to them. But he had not as yet delivered a regular sermon to a congregation in formal worship. He had a deep desire to hear God's call to preach, but he would not presume into the pulpit until he sensed that call. He wrote to his father:

> How I long for the time when it may please God to make me, like you, my father, a successful preacher of the Gospel. Oh that I might see one sinner constrained to come to Jesus! I almost envy you your exalted privilege.[42]

Charles' fond wish was about to be fulfilled.

While Spurgeon worshiped at the St. Andrew's Street Baptist Church in Cambridge, Mr. James Vinter served as president of the Lay Preacher's Association. This society of laymen filled the pulpits of churches in thirteen villages when they were without a pastor. The churches of Cambridge held James Vinter, known as "Bishop Vinter," in high respect. He served as a member and leader in St. Andrew's Chapel.

One Saturday morning Vinter called Spurgeon, just as Charles' responsibilities at the school were finished, and asked if he would "go over to Teversham the next evening, for a young man was to preach there who was not much used to services, and would very likely be glad of company."[43] Vinter really intended for Charles to be that "young man," but he had insight regarding Spurgeon's personality. A definite invitation to preach probably would have so frightened Charles at that stage he would have refused. So Vinter just left the request as is. The deception was perhaps justified; and it proved successful.

THE FIRST SERMON

Sunday afternoon, Spurgeon set out for Teversham with another young man who was somewhat older than himself. They walked through Barnwell, along Newmarket Road, on their way to the little congregation that met in a cottage. As they made their way to the service, Spurgeon expressed the hope that his friend would experience God's blessings and presence when he preached to the people. Startled, the other man declared that he had never preached in his life and could not preach and would not preach. He said to Charles, "Never! I was asked to walk with you, and I hope God will bless *you* in *your* sermon." Both were utterly perplexed, but Charles' companion suggested that if he would simply give one of his Sunday School addresses, it would certainly suffice. Charles said, "My inmost being was all in a trouble." So they both trudged on. Then Spurgeon reproached himself for his fear and exclaimed to himself, "Surely, I can tell a few poor cottagers of the sweetness and love of Jesus, since I feel them in my own soul." The course was set.

The small congregation had gathered under a low, pitched roof, little thatched cottage. When the young men arrived, Charles rose to speak and "got his text on his feet." His text on that most significant first sermon was "Unto you that believe He is precious" (1 Peter 2:7). The sixteen-year-old lad preached to the praise of Christ. When he finished his sermon, much gratified because he had not actually broken down (at times in his early public speaking, Spurgeon would stutter), he took up the hymnbook to announce a closing hymn. At that moment, an old lady in the congregation cried out, "Bless your dear heart, how old are you?" Spurgeon, not wishing to divulge his actual age, said, "You must wait until the service is over before making such inquiries. Let us now sing." When they finished the hymn and the service ended, good conversation and fellowship followed. The old lady put the question to Charles again, "How old are you?" He said, "I am under sixty." "Yes, and under sixteen," said the lady. Spurgeon retorted, "Never mind my age, think of the Lord Jesus Christ and His precious Spirit." That seemed to satisfy the worshipers. They had truly warmed up to the "boy preacher." At the urging of the people to return if Vinter saw fit to send him, Charles consented to come. This event inaugurated Spurgeon's preaching both on Sundays and weekdays under the auspices of the Lay Preacher's Association. The call had come and was confirmed.

Spurgeon's notoriety began to grow. Even in these very early days, his outstanding gifts were evident, and Charles showed diligence in all his responsibilities. Early each morning he would be up praying and reading the

Bible before he took up school duties. He worked at school until about five in the evening, then he would set off, almost daily, to preach to the villagers. He confessed that he made many blunders and mistakes in his early attempts at preaching; but he expressed gratitude that there were no reporters in the audiences.

THE CALL TO WATERBEACH

On October 12, 1851, Charles received the assignment to supply the pulpit at the small Baptist chapel in Waterbeach, some six miles north of Cambridge. In this very chapel, Rowland Hill, famed Baptist minister, preached his first sermon. The building itself was a very old structure with a thatched roof, much like the little cottage where Spurgeon preached his first sermon in Teversham. Charles preached very effectively on "Salvation from Sin," his text being Matthew 1:21—the same text for his last sermon at Waterbeach. Less than twelve were present at that first service, but those few were impressed. At the request of the parishioners, Spurgeon committed himself to preach for the next two Sundays; then he remained with the people for more than two years. He became their profoundly appreciated pastor, following in the office of Ron Peters who had served the church for twenty-two years. A deacon at Waterbeach, when asked how well Charles preached, replied, "Well, like a man a hundred years old in experience." [44]

Because the small congregation could contribute very little to their new pastor's expenses, Charles continued his weekday work at the Cambridge school. Mr. E. S. Leeding was no doubt grateful for that. However, as the congregation grew, they did covenant together to give young Spurgeon a stipend of £45 a year. In Cambridge he had to pay twelve shillings a week for the two rooms he occupied plus all his other expenses; his income was far from lucrative. Had it not been for the fact that many of the parishioners in Waterbeach shared their goods, vegetables, and farm products, he would have had a difficult time continuing with them. He believed in God's supply of his every need, however, and his faith received an ample reward. Later, Spurgeon reaped some of their material blessings. A certain James Toller, a layman in the Waterbeach Church, gave regularly to the Metropolitan Tabernacle ministries.

Spurgeon continued to preach in other churches during the weekdays, as well as at Waterbeach on Sundays. He described those busy days in preaching to the churches with these words:

> I must have been a singular-looking youth on wet evenings, for I walked three, five, or even eight miles out and back again on my preaching work; and when it rained, I dressed myself in waterproof leggings and a mackintosh coat, and a hat with a waterproof covering, and I carried a dark lantern to show me the way across the fields . . .
>
> How many times I enjoyed preaching the gospel in a farmer's kitchen, or

in a cottage, or in a barn! Perhaps many people came to hear me because I was only a boy. In my young day, I fear that I said many odd things, and made many blunders; but my audience was not hypercritical, and no newspaper writers dogged my heels; so I had a happy training-school, in which, by continual practice, I attained such a degree of ready speech as I now possess. [45]

It can be questioned how Spurgeon could have worked so hard at the school and then be ready to preach evenings. He gave the answer:

My quiet meditation during the walk (to the churches) helping to digest what I had read . . . I thought my reading over again while on my legs, and thus worked into my very soul; and I can bear testimony that I never learned so much, or learned it so thoroughly, as when I used to tell out, simply and earnestly, what I had first received into my own mind and heart. [46]

So at the age of only seventeen, in January of 1852, Charles Spurgeon accepted his first pastorate at Waterbeach and God fully affirmed his call to preach. On Charles' first visit to the church, one of the deacons, Mr. Coe, said, "He sat on one side of the table-pew and I on the other side. I shall never forget it. He looked so white, and I thought to myself, *he'll* never be able to preach—what a boy he is. I despised his youth, you know and thought all this, while the congregation was singing. Then when the hymn was over, he jumped up and began to read and expound the chapter about the Scribes and Pharisees and lawyers, and as he went about their garments, their phylacteries, and long prayers, I knew then *he* could preach." [47] Pike said, "He was a marvelous example of a preacher leaping at a bound, full grown into the pulpit." [48] As soon as he began to preach, the people were so impressed by his preaching, they soon forgot his age. Deacon Coe said, "He will not be here long. God has a great work for him to do elsewhere. I don't know where, but he will not be here long." [49]

Charles served the Waterbeach church until May of 1854, some two and a half years later. [50] He wrote his Aunt in March of 1853, a little over one year after his acceptance of the pastorate in Waterbeach, and said, "One year and four months ago I accepted a call to become constant minister to the Baptist Church at Waterbeach. I have been as happy as any mortal can be on earth." That joy became another confirmation of God's call to preach the Gospel of Christ. He went on to say in the same letter, "How grand is that gospel which gives ground for solid hope to poor sinners." [51]

Charles later resigned from his work at the school. He continued to live in Cambridge and would spend evenings ministering in many of the villages around the city, but he devoted himself primarily to the pastorate at Waterbeach. In his beloved pastorate he first received from the local people the name "boy preacher."

THE WATERBEACH MINISTRY

When Charles became pastor at Waterbeach, the congregation numbered approximately forty people; but under his effective ministry the church grew and made significant strides in number. People came not only from the village of Waterbeach itself, many traveled from the surrounding countryside. The church grew until the attendance numbered nearly four hundred worshippers every Sunday, a tenfold increase in less than two years. Of course, that many people could not crowd into the little building. Therefore, the windows and doors were left open and people would stand outside listening to the eloquent teenage preacher. At times, after Spurgeon preached to those inside the building, the crowd outside would be so large he would conduct another service for them.

The chapel building itself was not one to boast of, even though the Baptists had paid £100 for it. It had originally been a barn or dovecote, walled of adobe and plastered inside and out. A brick floor formed the foundation. It had a high, steep-pitched, thatched hip roof. Rude high-back benches formed the pews, and the preacher declared the Word of God from a high pulpit. It also had a small gallery, and on the posts that supported the balcony, the worshipers hung their coats. Someone said, when empty of worshipers, "it did appear sterile and barren, but seemed like heaven with God's people in it."[52] Unfortunately, the old chapel burned in 1866. Someone carelessly threw some hot coals on a heap of rubbish near the building and it burned to the ground. When the congregation erected a new house of worship, Spurgeon traveled from London and dedicated it, much to the delight of all.

The worship services before Charles came as pastor were unusual. For example, during the pastoral prayer, the congregation would stand with their back to the pulpit. Moreover, if the sermon proved dull, a sleepy hearer would actually stand up to keep awake. It must have been a humorous sight—and no doubt sent a message to the preacher. But regardless of the primitive building and worship mannerisms, a genuine revival swept through the little community of Waterbeach. There were only 1300 citizens in Waterbeach at the time, but they all knew Spurgeon, and many were spiritually transformed. Crime had been rather rampant in the small community before Charles arrived. However, as God's Spirit deepened the work through the young preacher, crime ceased—many of the criminals actually came to church. That is real revival! Spurgeon expressed the workings of the Spirit of God in those days:

> Did you ever walk through a village notorious for its drunkenness and profanity? Did you ever see poor wretched beings, that once were men, standing, or rather leaning against the posts of the ale-house, or staggering along the street? Have you ever looked into the houses of the people, and beheld them as dens of

iniquity, at which your soul stood aghast? Have you ever seen the poverty, and degradation, and misery of the inhabitants, and sighed over it? 'Yes,' you say, 'we have.' But was it ever your privilege to walk through that village again, in after years, when the Gospel had been preached there? It has been mine. I once knew just such a village as I have pictured,—perhaps in some respects one of the worst in England,—where many an illicit still was yielding its noxious liquor to a manufacturer without payment of the duty to the government, and where, in connection with that evil, all manner of riot and iniquity was rife.

There went into that village a lad, who had no great scholarship, but who was earnest in seeking the souls of men. He began to preach there and it pleased God to turn the whole place upside down. In a short time the little thatched chapel was crammed, the biggest vagabonds in the village were weeping floods of tears, and those who had been the curse of the parish became its blessing. Where there had been robberies and villainies of every kind, all round the neighbourhood, there were none, because the men who used to do the mischief were themselves in the house of God, rejoicing to hear of Jesus crucified. I am not telling an exaggerated story, nor a thing I do not know, for it was my delight to labour for the Lord in that village. It was a pleasant thing to walk through that place, when drunkenness had almost ceased, when debauchery in the case of many was dead, when men and women went forth to labour with joyful hearts, singing the praises of the ever-living God; and when, at sunset, the humble cottager called his children together, read them some portion of the Book of Truth, and then together they bent their knees in prayer to God. I can say, with joy and happiness, that almost from one end of the village to the other, at the hour of eventide, one might have heard the voice of song coming from nearly every and echoing from almost every heart. I do testify, to the praise of God's grace, that it pleased the Lord to work wonders in our midst. He showed the power of Jesus' name and made a witness of that Gospel which can win souls, draw reluctant hearts, and mould afresh the life and conduct of sinful men and women (from the *Autobiography*, Vol. I, pp. 227-228).

The Waterbeach experience deepened Charles' personality significantly. First, he learned how to deal with certain types of people he had rarely encountered before. He described them as "perfectionists, half-hearters, hypocrites and misers." He learned to minister to all sorts. Moreover, in the early days of his preaching, he was quite bombastic if not uncouth. But the good, plain country folk soon took that out of him. One of the deacons of the church, a certain Brother King, a miller, saw the great potential in the lad and loved him dearly. King toned the lad down in the matter of his many early unguarded pulpit utterances by sticking a pin in Spurgeon's Bible at Titus 2:8—"Sound speech, that cannot be condemned; that he that is of the contrary part may be ashamed, having no evil thing to say of you." Charles got the message. Through it all, Spurgeon began to feel at ease with common laboring people, and this gift proved invaluable in the years ahead.

At Waterbeach Charles made many lasting friendships. He became very close to Pastor Cornelius Elven of Bury St. Edmunds. On Spurgeon's first anniversary at Waterbeach, Elven said to him, "Lad, study hard; keep abreast of your foremost Christians; for if they outstrip you in knowledge of Scripture or power to edify, they will be dissatisfied with your ministry."[53] As previously seen, during those busy Waterbeach days, Charles still preached far and wide around the general area. Many times each week he would be found walking someplace to preach. In his early days he walked the six miles from Cambridge out to Waterbeach even though there was a rail there and back. His finances did not permit him even to ride the train. But he would walk anywhere to preach the Gospel of Christ.

As Waterbeach did much to shape Spurgeon's early ministry, it is only fair to say that he did much to shape Waterbeach. At the beginning of his pastoral ministry, as implied, the moral conditions were at a low ebb in the small community. He described it as "drunkenness, debauchery, profanity, all mixed up with poverty." It was not long, however, actually just a matter of weeks, before the little chapel filled to hear the devoted young man. Spurgeon said, "It pleased God to turn the whole place upside down."[54] He related how many who were deep in sin came to the place of worship and, hearing the Gospel of Jesus Christ, were touched. Charles described them as, "Listening their very hearts away to a voice that told of Christ weeping over forgotten mankind, reprobates, despisers, drunkards, and old men on the brink of hell; the lonely, the weary, the defeated."[55] Spurgeon's ministry in Waterbeach continued until he reached nineteen years of age. One of the interesting anecdotes that occurred during his service in the small community tells of an old miser who would come to hear Charles preach. One day, someone told Spurgeon that the old man had never given anything to anybody. Spurgeon replied that he disagreed and knew better, because one afternoon the old "miser" had given him three half-crowns, and he had bought a new hat with the money. "Well," retorted the critic, "I am quite sure he never forgave himself such extravagance, and he must have wanted his three half-crowns back again." Contrary to the critic's words, the old man came to the chapel the next Sunday and asked his minister to pray for him that he might be saved from covetousness. He confessed the Lord had spoken to his heart that he should contribute to the church half a sovereign and he had kept back half a crown. The old man could not rest for thinking of it. Such was the impact of Spurgeon's life and ministry upon all manner of people.

The generosity of the people can be found in the example of another old gentleman known as "Father Sewell." At a certain meeting to promote home missions, the old gentleman arrived just as the service was about to close. Spurgeon said, "Our brother who has just come in will, I am sure, close the meeting by offering prayer for God's blessings on the proceedings of the evening." Father Sewell stood up, but instead of praying, he began to feel in his pockets. Spurgeon said, "I'm afraid that my brother did not understand me. Friend Sewell, I did not ask you to give, but to pray." The old saint simply replied, "Aye! Aye! Aye! But I could not pray until I had given; it would be hypocrisy to ask a blessing on that which I did not think was worth giving to." Such incidents continually occurred. It was incredible how the Spirit of God moved through Spurgeon's ministry.

Charles learned to handle interpersonal relationships, even as young as he was. An old woman in Waterbeach, who had a reputation of having an abusive sharp tongue, one day encountered Spurgeon. Charles had heard about her and had already prepared in his mind what he would say if she ever accosted him. On a certain morning, as he passed by her house, she was standing at the gate. She looked at the youth and began to scold him about many things. As she assailed him, he smilingly replied, "Yes, thank you; I'm quite well; I hope you are the same." This just brought another outburst of ugly words. Still smiling, Charles said, "Yes, it does look rather as if it's going to rain; I think I had better be getting on." Finally the woman exclaimed, "Bless the man, he's as deaf as a post; what is the use of storming at him?" Quite wise for his years!

Another old lady in Waterbeach, whom Charles described as Mrs. "Much-afraid," had professed faith in Christ for over fifty years but could never be certain that she would finally enter through heaven's gates. Always doubting and fearing her own spiritual relationship to Christ, she lived in constant turmoil. One day while talking with Charles, she told him all hope was gone, that she had no faith. In fact, she believed she was actually a hypocrite and did not know Christ at all. Charles pungently replied, "Then don't come to the chapel anymore, we don't want hypocrites there. Why do you come?" The lady, somewhat surprised, replied, "I come because I can't stop, anyway, I love the people of God; I love the house of God, and I love to worship God." Charles looked at her and said, "Well, you are an odd sort of hypocrite; you are a queer kind of unconverted woman." Then Charles did something startling; he offered to give her £5 for her hope of salvation if she would sell it to him. "Why, I would not sell it for a thousand worlds." The lady got the message and that ended the conversation—and probably much of her fear.

THE FIRST CONVERT

Despite his early activities and blessings in Waterbeach, Spurgeon longed to meet someone who had actually been won to faith in Christ through his preaching. His deep desire to win people to Jesus consumed him. He said, "Souls, souls, souls,—I hope this rings in my ears and hurries me on." His first definite convert from his preaching ministry soon surfaced. A laborer's wife had come to faith through his ministry. When he learned of the event, early on a Monday morning, he walked to her cottage to see his first spiritual child. He was so elated that he said:

If anybody had said to me 'somebody has left you twenty thousand pounds', I should not have given a snap of a finger for it compared to the joy which I felt when I was told that God had saved a soul through my ministry. I felt like a boy who had earned his first guinea, or like a diver who had been down to the depth of the sea, and brought up a rare pearl.

This proved to be just the beginning of multitudes who would be won by Charles' preaching.

The quest for souls never flagged in Spurgeon's ministry. For example, he customarily traveled out from Cambridge to Waterbeach on Saturday evening and spent the night in a parishioner's home. On one such evening, he shared a room with a young man who jumped into bed before praying. Spurgeon, seeing this as an opportunity to witness for Christ, accosted him that he might be going to sleep prayerless and might never wake up. The young man fell under conviction. Both of them rose, and after two hours of sharing the Gospel, the young man received Christ. Spurgeon wrote to his father November 15, 1882 and said, "A minister needs the love of Jesus, the strength of more than one angel, and a heart large as the world." Charles exemplified that in his love to win the lost.

On another occasion, in the very same room in Waterbeach where the young man had found Christ, Spurgeon had a tremendously disturbing dream. In the dream he saw a vision of the judgment of people who had gone into eternity without Christ. It so moved him that the next day he preached a sermon to the people at Waterbeach on the fate of the lost. Hearers reported that the people turned white with fear, and their knees trembled. For years afterwards, people recalled the impact of that powerfully disturbing sermon.

On one of Charles' preaching excursions out from Cambridge, he spoke in the town of Houghton. He was invited to preach in the Houghton church and stayed in the home of Mr. Potto Brown, a wealthy layman. Brown owned a milling business and primarily supported the entire financial life of the Houghton church. He had a philanthropic spirit; he grew hothouse grapes for poor people. Potto Brown was a Quaker but quite ecumenical. His business partner had died and the six children of his deceased partner lived in his home. Potto Brown had a rigid plan in directing his household. For example, any preacher that came his way and spent the night had to have two eggs for breakfast. Brown thought the phosphorous in the eggs would be good for them. Still, not one of the six children of his deceased partner had ever come to faith in Jesus Christ.

An interesting thing happened at this juncture. In the Autumn of 1849, Charles Finney, the great American evangelist, came to England and began a ministry in Houghton. Finney and his wife, who had accompanied him, stayed in the home of Potto Brown. While Finney labored in Houghton, the Brown home was open all day so that friends could come, eat and converse on spiritual matters with the American evangelist and his wife. They came in great numbers and filled the table day after day. Before long, the six foster children of the Browns were brought to faith in Christ, as were many friends who gathered in the Brown home for meals and fellowship. One can imagine, therefore, something of the deep appreciation that Brown felt toward Finney. But when Charles Spurgeon came to preach and stayed in the home of Potto Brown, a problem arose. It is quite common knowledge that though Finney professed to be Calvinistic in theology, in reality he was essentially Arminian. Potto Brown, no doubt impacted by the ministry and theology of Charles Finney, likewise held Arminian views. On the Saturday before Charles was to preach, he and Brown had a heated discussion on the merits of Calvinism versus Arminianism. They were both strong personalities, and even though Charles was young at the time, he could hold his own in theological discussions. Potto Brown said to young Spurgeon in the course of their conversation, "Let me give you a bit of good advice, my young friend. You'll never make a preacher; so just give it up and stick to your teaching." How wrong he was. After hearing Charles, Brown had to admit that the young man had great gifts. Actually, Charles preached so well, Brown thought perhaps he had plagiarized the sermon. After Spurgeon's experience in the home of Potto Brown, he called the occasion a "felicitous misery." A good description in the light of the theological battle they must have had! Charles said the encounter became a "battle-royal." But Spurgeon appreciated Potto Brown's commitment to Christ. When Brown died, Charles wrote an article on him in *The Sword and the Trowel*, the church's monthly periodical.

It seems after this encounter in Houghton that Charles never had a profound appreciation for the ministry of Charles Finney. Perhaps Spurgeon was a bit too prejudiced toward Arminianism, so he failed to appreciate Finney's significant ministry. The American preacher made a tremendous impact not only in Houghton but later in London, preaching at Whitefield's Tabernacle. Whitefield had become Charles' idol. Still, scant references are made to Finney in the writings of Spurgeon, and when they do occur, they tend to be rather negative. This is unfortunate, because they shared much in common.

Charles was most daring in his preaching. He held back nothing that he deeply felt. An illustration of this can be found in the biography of Spurgeon by W. Y. Fullerton. He recounts the following incident:

> As an example of his daring utterances, one day he declared that a change of nature was absolutely necessary, for if a thief went to Heaven without it, he would be a thief still, and would go round the place picking the angel's pockets. During the week the Mayor of Cambridge took him to task, and told him that the angels have no pockets. Quite gravely Mr. Spurgeon said he had not known that, but he was glad to be assured of the fact by a gentleman who did know, and that he would put the thing right on the first opportunity. On the

following Monday he walked into Mr. Brimley's shop and said, 'I set the matter right yesterday, sir.' 'What matter?' he inquired. 'Why, about the angels' pockets.' 'What did you say?' the elder man asked in despairing tones. 'Oh, sir, I just told the people that I was sorry I had made a mistake, but that the Mayor of Cambridge had assured me that the angels had no pockets, so I would say that if a thief got among the angels, without having his nature changed, he would try to steal the feathers out of their wings.' Upon which his critic, who had several times found fault with him, said, 'Then I'll never try to set you right again'—which was exactly what young Spurgeon wanted him to say.

THE GROWING MINISTRY

Spurgeon deeply appreciated his younger brother James, who studied with him in Cambridge during those days. James would often accompany Charles to different preaching engagements. Of those Waterbeach days, James said:

> When I drove my brother about the country to preach, I thought then, as I have thought ever since, what an extraordinary preacher he was. What wonderful unction and power I remember in some of those early speeches! The effect upon the people listening to him I have never known exceeded in after years. He seemed to have leaped full-grown into the pulpit. The breadth and brilliance of those early sermons, and the power that God's Holy Spirit evidently gave to him, made them perfectly marvelous. When he went to Waterbeach his letters came home, and were read as family documents, discussed, prayed over, and wondered at. We were not surprised, however, for we all believed that it was in him.

Spurgeon's fame began to extend all over the general Fens area. His usefulness for the Lord and the power of his preaching gained for him considerable notoriety. As a case in point, the deacons at Isleham invited Spurgeon to come and preach. They borrowed the largest chapel in the area. But to the dismay of the deacons, only seven people arrived for the morning service. Yet, Spurgeon preached with such power that the word spread widely in the afternoon and the congregation which gathered for the evening service became so large there was not even standing room.

In those dramatic days, Spurgeon went to speak in a village near Waterbeach. Everyone knew the village as a hotbed of infidelity, immorality, and every kind of vice. It must be remembered, the impact of the eighteenth century revival under Wesley and Whitefield had largely waned by this time. The Methodists had actually been driven away from the village where Charles was to preach. Nevertheless, Spurgeon went. The people actually turned out with stones and were going to pelt Charles and some friends who had come along with him. The villagers determined to give the Baptists what they had given the Methodists. However, the young Baptist preacher proved to be up to the occasion. He was made of sterner stuff than to retreat in fear. He began by telling them he rejoiced that they had driven the Methodists away. He said, "They would only have preached error, we have come to preach the right doctrine. I am very glad you drove them away for that shows that you are sensible people." The villagers were so astounded at the audacious young man that they dropped their stones and listened to what he had to say. He returned several times. In a few weeks or months, through Charles' preaching, the character of the village changed dramatically as morality and genuine spirituality pervaded the populace. It all proved quite amazing.

In Landbeach near Cambridge another incident occurred, perhaps not so positive as others. There an old man said, "I'm the man who taught Mr. Spurgeon to smoke. My wife doesn't want me to say it, but I am the man who taught Mr. Spurgeon to smoke. You see, he came in one day to see me, and I was smoking away, enjoying my pipe. 'I think I'd like to try a pipe,' and I gave him a pipe. He sucked away until I said, 'You'd better put it down.' He laid it down and said, 'It's very nice; I'll have another try!' And try he did until he could smoke," said the man, adding, "I'm the man who taught Mr. Spurgeon to smoke." This story may be apocryphal; Spurgeon's son doubted it. At any rate, Spurgeon did smoke cigars. In a letter to his mother on December 9, 1854, he wrote about a man saying, "I sat up with him smoking. He sent me down a box of very superior cigars." Little conviction, if any, prevailed about the habit in Spurgeon's day. That issue shall be taken up later.

During these dynamic Waterbeach days, Spurgeon composed one of his first hymns. He wrote it for a jubilee service at Waterbeach on June 26, 1853. It is a quite remarkable piece for a young man of nineteen. Charles obviously outshone his grandfather James in the enterprise. The text is as follows:

> When once I mourned a load of sin,
> When conscience felt a wound within,
> When all my works were thrown away,
> When on my knees I knelt to pray,
> > Then, blissful hour, remembered well,
> > I learnt Thy love, Immanuel!
>
> When storms of sorrow toss my soul,
> When waves of care around me roll,
> When comforts sink, when joys shall flee,
> When hopeless gulfs shall gape for me,
> > One word the tempest's rage shall quell,
> > That word, Thy name, Immanuel.

When for the truth I suffer shame,
When foes pour scandal on Thy name,
When cruel taunts and jeers abound,
When 'bulls of Bashan' gird me round,
    Secure within my tower I'll dwell,
    That tower, Thy grace, Immanuel.

When hell, enraged, lifts up her roar,
When Satan stops my path before,
When fiends rejoice and wait my end,
When legion'd hosts their arrows send,
    Fear not, my soul, but hurl at hell
    Thy battle-cry, Immanuel.

When down the hill of life I go,
When o'er my feet death's waters flow,
When in the deep'ning flood I sink,
When friends stand weeping on the brink,
    I'll mingle with my last farewell
    Thy lovely name, Immanuel.

When tears are banished from mine eyes,
When fairer worlds than these are nigh,
When heaven shall fill my ravished sight,
When I shall bathe in sweet delight,
    One joy all joys shall far excel,
    To see Thy face, Immanuel.

COLLEGE?

Of course, Spurgeon constantly wondered whether he should receive formal theological education. He admitted that he had hoped he could be useful without a theological education. He said he had "an aversion" to college. Yet, so many people and friends urged upon him the value of formal theological training, he became disposed to consider a theological college course. But as he said, "I must not consult myself but Jesus." He wrote to his father, "I am now very well off, I think as well off as anyone my age, and I am sure quite as happy. Now shall I throw myself out and trust to providence as to whether I shall ever get another place as soon as I leave college?"[56] Charles' father very definitely wanted a college education for his son, but a strange experience occurred that settled his destiny about going to college.

Dr. Joseph Angus served as principal of Stepney College, a Baptist theological school. The institution is now known as Regent's Park College, the college having transferred to Regent's Park in London and then to its present location in Oxford where it stands as a part of the Oxford University system. Angus had been pastor of the St. Andrew's Street Baptist Chapel and came back to Cambridge for a visit on February 1, 1852. It is also interesting to note that Angus had been the minister for two years of the New Park Street Baptist Church in London where Spurgeon was soon to go as pastor. After leaving New Park Street, Angus became secretary of the Baptist Missionary Society. Later he served on the committee that issued the revision of the Scriptures in 1881. But at the moment, Angus was the leader of Stepney Theological College and Spurgeon became very interested in enrolling.

A friend arranged an appointment for Dr. Angus to meet Spurgeon in the home of Mr. McMillan, the well known publisher. Spurgeon, always a punctual man, called at the appointed hour and a maid showed him into a drawing room. There, to his dismay, he waited two long hours for Angus, who seemingly never arrived. Charles felt so insignificant that he was frightened to ring the bell and make inquiries as to why Angus had been so long delayed. At length he did venture to ring the bell. To his deep amazement they told him that Dr. Angus had been there for a considerable time waiting for him in another room. After a long wait, Angus decided to leave, thinking Spurgeon would not arrive, and took the train back to London. The rather stupid servant girl had put the two men in different rooms and had forgotten to tell either one of the other's presence. Thus the meeting never materialized.

As can be imagined, Spurgeon was exceedingly disappointed. That afternoon, as he made his way to a preaching appointment, he walked over Mid-Summer Common toward a little wooden bridge on the road to Chesterton. When he got to the center of the Common, the word of the Lord came to him powerfully. It seemed as though a voice spoke to him distinctly and said, "Seekest thou great things for thyself? Seek them not." Charles stood arrested on the spot. But then and there he interpreted this dramatic event as God's definite direction in his life. He gave up forever any thought of a career in a theological college. He said:

> I remembered the poor but loving people to whom I ministered, and the souls which had been given are in my humble charge: and though I anticipated obscurity and poverty as a result, yet I did then and there renounce the offer of collegiate instruction, determining to remain preaching the Word so long as I had strength to do it.

The experience proved a monumental moment in Charles' life. It brought him into a deeper consecration to Christ than he had ever known. In truth, it set the pattern for his life. He declared:

> From that first day until now, I have acted on no other principle but that of perfect consecration to the work whereunto I am called. I surrender myself to my Saviour, I gave him my body, my soul, my spirit . . . for eternity. I gave

him my talents, my powers, my eyes, my ears . . . my whole manhood! So far from regretting what I often did, I would fain renew my vows and then over again! . . . If Christ commands me to hold up my little finger, and I do not obey him, it looks like coolness in my love to him. [57]

For Spurgeon, only one thing finally mattered the rest of his life: the will of God. That was the ultimate "secret" of his effective life and ministry.

As could be expected, Dr. Angus felt Spurgeon made a tremendous mistake. Angus wrote to a certain Mr. Watts, saying, "I should regret for your friend (Spurgeon) to settle without thorough preparation. He may be useful in either case, but his usefulness will be much greater, he will fill at all events a wider sphere, with preparation, than without it." Many shared the same opinion and Spurgeon received criticism throughout the years for never having received formal theological training. But he had determined not to enter theological college and to rely upon his personal study and background to prepare him for the ministry. It is questionable whether or not Charles should have been formally educated. Conwell said, "Spurgeon would not have been the Elijah of his age with the usual college education." [58] Perhaps he would have been a better preacher, perhaps not. At any rate, he felt he found God's will on the matter and was content with it.

A LIFE-CHANGING MOMENT

While still at Waterbeach, in November of 1853, Spurgeon spoke at an anniversary meeting of the Cambridge Sunday School Union in the Guildhall. After his address, two other ministers stood to preach. Each one of them belittled his youthfulness. One came over as particularly sarcastic, saying, "It is a pity boys do not adopt the scriptural practice of tarrying at Jericho till their beards are grown before they try to instruct their seniors." After the man had made his rather rude, derogatory remark, Spurgeon asked the convener of the meeting if he might make a reply. Charles was not one to take it lying down. Spurgeon received permission and recounted the event in these words:

> I reminded the audience, that those who were bidden to remain at Jericho were not boys, but full-grown men whose beards had been shaved off by their enemies, that is the greatest indignity they could be made to suffer, and who were, therefore, ashamed to return home until their beards had grown again. I added that the true parallel to their case could be found in a minister who, having fallen into open sin, had disgraced his calling and needed to go into seclusion . . . till his character had to some extent been restored.

Although Spurgeon did not really know the dynamics of the situation, the man who had attacked him had himself fallen into open sin, and his behavior was known by the people. One can but imagine his embarrassment that the young man had perfectly put his finger right on his case, although totally unbeknownst to Spurgeon himself.

This meeting, in the normal course of things, would seem to be insignificant. However, it proved a critical, pivotal point in Spurgeon's life. God was about to throw open a marvelous door of service. Perhaps it was the mind of the Spirit that Charles not be enrolled in theological college, for what soon took place would probably not have happened had he gone on for further training. God had in store for him in the almost immediate future a fantastic ministry. Spurgeon said:

> I am more and more glad that I never went to college. God sent such sunshine on my path, such smiles of grace, that I cannot regret if I had forfeited all my prospects for it. I am conscious that I have held back from love and his cause, and I had rather be poor in His service than rich in my own. I have all my heart can wish for; yea, God giveth more than my desires. My congregation is as great and loving as ever. During all the time I have been at Waterbeach, I have had a different house for my home every day. Fifty-two families have taken me in; and I still have six other invitations not yet accepted. Talk about the people not caring for me because they give me so little! I dare not tell anybody under heaven 'tis false. They do all they can!

So Spurgeon carried on, but he would soon leave his happy congregation at Waterbeach for his ultimate life's work. His burden had loosed from off his shoulders, and now as a new man—yea, a new preacher in Christ—and the whole world waited to hear him.

5

"One Whose Name Was *Hopeful*"

SPURGEON'S EARLY LONDON YEARS:
THE REVIVAL LONG HOPED FOR

Mrs. C. H. Spurgeon

Where am I now? Is this the loving care
Of Jesus, for the men that Pilgrims are?
Thus to provide! That I should be forgiven!
And dwell already next door to Heaven.

—*John Bunyan*

Part I:
The New Park Street Chapel

Introduction

Young Charles Haddon Spurgeon could correctly be called "Hopeful." He excitedly sensed, as did Bunyan's Pilgrim, that he dwelt "already next door to Heaven." Expectations filled the heart of the young, energetic, and enthusiastic pastor. The reason? He had just ascended to the prestigious pulpit of the historic and famous New Park Street Baptist Church of London, England. Though immature in years—he was only nineteen—for some time he had insightfully hoped for a true revival of religion; his Puritan background had woven that into the very fabric of his heart and mind. Could it be that this new move to London would prove to be the time and the place that the hoped-for revival would break on the English scene? Could he possibly be God's man in the movement? Had he made that much "progress" as a "Pilgrim"? Londoners, at least the members of the New Park Street Church, felt he could effect revival. The London newspapers radically disagreed, however. The press saw no hope for this novice pastor.

The press went to war against Spurgeon. "A coarse, stupid, irrational bigot," screamed the *Saturday Review*. Another periodical castigated him as, "A stripling from Waterbeach," a "flash in the pan." The journalists even criticized his prayers, calling them "irreverent, presumptuous, and blasphemous." When he started to publish his sermons, the *Saturday Review* attacked again and called the preacher-writer a "scavenger of the literary world." Not only that, a rash of tracts against "Hopeful" were given to the public. Read by thousands, titles such as *Who is Spurgeon?*, *Review of Spurgeon's Chamber of Horrors*, and *Why So Popular?* rolled off the presses. Little hope for a true revival of religion here, they cried.

Perhaps the papers had some justification for their caustic criticisms. The Reverend Sutton of Cottenham, a Baptist pastor and actually a Spurgeon sympathizer, said young Charles filled the role as "the sauciest dog that ever barked in a pulpit."[1] At times, Spurgeon did appear rather arrogant, espe-

177

cially in those early days. But conversely, others eulogized him. One thing became increasingly certain, no one dared ignore him. Tens of thousands heard and read him regularly. Nonetheless, through it all, Spurgeon remained "Hopeful" in the controversy crackling around him.

For a time, the merciless critics almost broke Charles' heart. He said:

> I shall never forget the circumstances when a slanderous report against my character came to my ears, and my heart was broken in agony . . . I fell on my knees and said, 'Master, I will not keep back even my reputation from thee. If I must lose that too, let it go. If to be made as the mire of the street again, if to be the laughing stock of schools and the song of the drunkard once more, will make me more serviceable to my Master, and more useful to His cause, I will prefer it to all this multitude, of all the applause men can give. [2]

However, he grew through the trials and finally achieved the maturity and humility of mind where he could say:

> I was reading sometime ago an article in a newspaper, very much to my praise. It always makes me feel sad—so sad that I could cry—if I ever see anything praising me; it breaks my heart; I feel I do not deserve it, and then I say, 'Now I must try to be better, so that I may deserve it.' If the world abuses me, I am a match for that; I begin to like it. It may fire all its big guns at me, I will not return a solitary short, but just store them, and grow rich upon the old iron. [3]

This turmoil and conflict erupted when Spurgeon had just reached his early twenties. How did these London dynamics develop around such a young soldier-preacher?

THE CALL TO LONDON

It all began when Charles, as a mere teenager, spoke at the previously recorded Cambridge meeting in the local Guild Hall. His reputation as the young, eloquent preacher of the Waterbeach Baptist Church had already permeated much of the Cambridgeshire area. The young preacher of the Fens had created quite a stir in church circles. Attending the Sunday School service, Mr. George Gould, a deacon of the Baptist Church at Loughton, Essex, heard the captivating teenage orator and got captured himself.

It will be recalled that the meeting took a strange turn right from the start. The two older preachers almost exuded contempt for the young "stripling from Waterbeach." As the service got underway, one of them asked why Charles had left his "few sheep in the wilderness"; Waterbeach actually did look like a little "wilderness" village. Such sarcasm put a cold chill in the proceedings. But the elders did not know this stripling from the wilderness very well. Courteously, but very forthrightly, he replied to his critics. That ended the encounter. The young Waterbeach pastor's ark survived the deluge of derogatory criticism.

Spurgeon's shot at the critics, though a random one, was soon forgotten, except by the visitor George Gould. For some reason it impressed him tremendously. A few days later, Gould found himself in London talking with an old friend, Thomas Olney, a man of position and wealth. Olney served as a leading deacon in the New Park Street Baptist Church. The old church building sat just south of the river Thames at the foot of Southwark Bridge. The London deacon lamented to Gould that they found themselves without a pastor and had little success in acquiring the right kind of man. One could well understand the reason; the church had been planted in a most unproductive spot, unproductive for a church, that is. The land laid so low that London's famous Thames River often flooded it. Breweries, boiler works, even a vinegar factory had invaded the area as residents fled. Worst of all, Southwark Bridge found itself shackled with a toll charge. As a consequence, one could not hail a hackney carriage in half a mile north of the Thames where the city flourished. The more affluent and educated people lived there—ones that could greatly help in the building of a great church. But who would walk over the bridge and then be compelled to walk back or pay a toll charge just to hear a preacher—especially on the low-caste "south side"? One former pastor said of the church location: "A more dingy, uninviting and repelling region than where the chapel is situated, I have seldom explored. It is a gloomy, narrow street, surrounded by small, dirty looking houses." [4] Spurgeon himself said it appeared "more suitable for a tallow-melter's business than a meeting house. . . . If they have taken thirty years to look around them with the design of burying a church alive, they could not have succeeded better." [5] Spurgeon said it reminded him of the "black hole of Calcutta." The church had bought the property because it was a cheap freehold. They had been "penny wise and pound poor." The area remains rather blighted to this day. The only contemporary attraction on Park Street is a brass plaque commemorating the spot where Shakespeare's original Globe Theatre once stood. New Park Street Baptist Church building itself is long gone—fortunately.

THE HISTORY OF THE OLD CHURCH

The south London Baptist chapel enjoyed a fascinating history. The church boasted some two hundred years of ministry when Olney lamented their plight to Gould in 1853. Actually, Baptist groups had met south of the Thames before 1652, dating back to the reign of Charles II. In April of 1645, Parliament passed an ordinance that forbade any person to preach who was not an ordained minister in the Established Church or some other officially recognized Reformed Church such as the Presbyterians. As a result, Baptist preachers were held accountable. Most Britishers considered them a maverick sect and not a true church at all. Regardless, several Baptist assemblies met in the burrow of Southwark even in the face of persecution. From one or more of these groups, the New Park Street Baptist Church had its birth. The members of the New Park Street Baptist Church were justly proud of their history; the church had its inception in the "Puritan Baptist" context—a noble heritage, to be sure.

One of the small Southwark Baptist congregations suffered a split in 1652. Several left the original body over practices with which they did not agree. They began meeting in private houses or in other buildings. The man who led the splinter group in these early days was William Rider. He suffered for his conscience and convictions, but little is known of his ministry or what he actually endured for being a Baptist. One of the issues for which he was persecuted was the laying on of hands on baptized believers.

Baptist fortunes turned somewhat for the better when Oliver Cromwell began his protectorate. The old Parliament lost some of its power and England enjoyed a greater measure of liberty of conscience. Brighter days seemed to be ahead for the Baptists.

THE MINISTRY OF BENJAMIN KEACH

How long William Rider served as minister of the little congregation remains unknown. However, the church records reveal that in 1668, the pastor being deceased for some time, the congregation unanimously elected Benjamin Keach to be the pastor. Keach received his Baptist ordination by prayer and the laying on of hands at twenty-eight years of age. He exercised a most effective ministry. Keach became one of the most notable of all the pastors of the growing congregation. Moreover, he developed a very successful itinerant ministry, especially preaching throughout Buckinghamshire. The work flourished under his labors.

Keach had his difficult days, however. All dissenters did. For example, Keach wrote a book entitled *The Child's Instructor*. In that volume he made the point that children are born in sin and thus desperately in need of salvation through Jesus Christ. For this "crime" the court publicly tried and convicted him. His sentence read, "Benjamin Keach, you are here convicted for writing, printing, and publishing a seditious and schismatic book, for which the court's judgement is this, and the court doth award: that you should go to jail for a fortnight without bail or a mainprize; and the next Saturday to stand trial upon the pillory at Aylesbury in the open market from eleven o'clock till one, with a paper upon your head with the inscription: For writing, printing, and publishing a schismatical book entitled, *The Child's Instructor; or The New and Easy Primer.* And the next Thursday, to stand in the same manner and for the same time in the Market at Winslow; and then your book shall be openly burnt before your face by the common hangman, in disgrace of you and your doctrine. And you shall forfeit to the King's majesty the sum of £20 and shall remain in jail until you find sureties for your good behavior, and for your appearance at the next assizes; then to renounce your doctrines, and make it public submission as shall be enjoined you. Take him away, keeper!" [6] Keach replied, "I hope I shall never renounce the truths which I have written in that book." [7]

All attempts to mitigate the harsh judgment came to no avail and the sheriff punctually carried out the punishment. When brought to the pillory at Aylesbury, Keach simply said, "The cross is the way to the crown." [8] As soon as his head and hands were placed in the pillory, he began to preach to them. People marveled at the testimony of a man willing to stand for his convictions and the Word of God.

Everyone knew Keach as a great preacher of the Gospel and a forthright proclaimer of the whole truth of God's Word. He was also a voluminous writer, writing forty-three different works. Some of the books proved so popular that twenty-two editions were published. During Keach's pastorate of thirty-six years, he led the church into adopting and subscribing *The Solemn Covenant of the Church.*

Benjamin Keach, not very strong physically, often endured prolonged illnesses. He went to his reward on July 16, 1704, at sixty-four years of age, and was buried at the Baptist burying ground in Suffolk. When Keach lay on his deathbed, he summoned his son-in-law, Benjamin Stinton, and gave him the charge of the responsibility of the pastoral office of the church. For some years Stinton had been the associate of Keach; thus it was quite natural for the church to extend an invitation to Stinton to become their pastor. He served as their minister for fourteen years, 1704-1718. On February 11, 1718, Stinton was suddenly taken ill, simply saying to his wife, "I am going." He laid down on the bed and died.

JOHN GILL

In the year 1719, the church, now meeting at Goat Yard Passage in Horse-lie-down, Southwark, invited young John Gill to preach with a view to the pastorate. Considerable opposition to Gill arose; about one-half of the church objected to his being called as minister. The church split, so Gill and his followers left. But the ministry carried on and prospered. Ordained as a Baptist pastor on March 22, 1720, Dr. John Gill no doubt became the most illustrious minister of south London Baptists, at least up to that time.

Cantering, Northamptonshire boasted about being John Gill's early home. On the day of his birth, someone said to Edward Gill, John's father, "He will be a scholar, and all the world cannot prevent it." It sounded much like the famous Richard Knill's prophecy concerning the boy Spurgeon whom destiny set apart as one of Gill's successors. After the church split over the call of Gill to the pastorate, they began meeting in Crosby's School Room. However, they soon came back to the old building in Goat Yard and found themselves much at home in the historic premises. Gill's pastorate extended into an extraordinarily lengthy ministry. He served the congregation for fifty-one years. As Spurgeon expressed it, "He proved himself to be a true master in Israel." [9] There is no question that his scholarship exceeded all his predecessors. Though Keach was a prolific and popular writer, Gill exceeded him by far. In 1746-1748, he published his exposition of the *New Testament* in three large folios. As the consequence of his many publications and his expertise and knowledge of the Scriptures, Oriental languages, and Jewish Antiquities, Gill received a diploma from Marischal College, Aberdeen, Scotland, creating him a Doctor of Divinity. When the honor was bestowed, and the deacons in London congratulated him, he simply said, "I had not either thought it, nor bought it, nor sought it." [10] Gill's best known work is his voluminous systematic theology. Spurgeon admired it tremendously, but it is a huge work and one must plough through hours of work. Spurgeon called it "a continent of mud"; but he plodded through it, much to his profit.

Gill's ministry extended beyond his own congregation. He presented weekday lectures. The attendees at those lectures formed themselves into a society, meeting every Wednesday evening in Great Eastcheap. This lectureship began in 1729 with a discourse on Psalm 71:16, "I will go in the strength of the Lord God: I will make mention of Thy righteousness, even of Thine only." The lecture series went on for years.

In 1757, the congregation erected a new church building in Carter Lane, St. Olive's Suffolk, near London Bridge. The building opened for worship on October 9, when John Gill preached two sermons from Exodus 20:24. As pointed out, Gill served the Baptist Chapel of Carter's Lane for fifty-one years—and noble years they were. From 1720 to 1771 he thundered out high-Calvinism from his high-box pulpit. Heavy theology, even for his day! Moreover, Gill impressed one as being as ponderous in appearance as in theology and utterance. He had a pronounced tilt to his nose. A painting of Gill hung in Spurgeon's vestry; and as Spurgeon viewed the portrait, he said Gill was turning up his nose at the Arminians. The painting of Gill and his upturned nose remains in the vestry of the Metropolitan Tabernacle to this day. Regardless of the barbs he received, Toplady considered him the greatest theologian of his time, Baptist or otherwise.

Many stories surround the unique John Gill. In the *Autobiography* Spurgeon related one of the best known:

> It is said that a garrulous dame once called upon him to find fault with the excessive length of his white bands (the white bow tie old divines wore). 'Well, well,' said the Doctor, 'What do you think is the right length? Take them and make them as long or as short as you like.' The lady expressed her delight; she was sure that her dear pastor would grant her request, and therefore she had brought her scissors with her, and would do the trimming at once. Accordingly, snip, snip, and the thing was done, and the bands were gone.

'Now', said the Doctor, 'My good sister, you must do me a good turn also.' 'Yes, that I will, Doctor. What can be done?' 'Well, you have something about you which is a deal too long, and causes me no end of trouble, and I would like to see it shorter.' 'Indeed, dear sir, I will not hesitate,' said the dame; 'What is it? Here are the scissors, use them as you please' 'Come then,' said the pastor, 'Good sister, put out your tongue!'

John Gill had a quite austere personality and manner. It has been suggested this grew out of his rather secluded lifestyle plus the rigidity and determination of his disciplined mind. On one occasion he received the warning that the publication of a certain book he was about to release would lose him many supporters and reduce his income. He immediately replied, "Do not tell me of losing. I value nothing in comparison with Gospel truth. I am not afraid to be poor!" [11]

Gill, above all, must be remembered for his theological writings. His pedantic and ponderous works still grace the shelves in libraries. The books, like the preacher, are ultra-Calvinistic to the last syllable. They do seem to be a "continent of mud." But Spurgeon deeply admired the man, and his pulpit rested in a room at the Metropolitan Tabernacle for years. Students at the Pastors' College used it to preach their trial sermons.

John Gill's works and theology became known as "Gillism," reflective of the high-Calvinism that characterized most Baptists at that particular time. Many preachers hung on his words, but unfortunately the freedom of Gospel invitation became somewhat restricted because of his theological emphasis. That hardly served the Gospel as well as one would have hoped. Spurgeon made that observation himself. Although Spurgeon embraced a basic Calvinistic theology, he did not hold a *high* Calvinistic view; he was far more fervent in pressing home the Gospel invitation, as constantly seen.

That high-Calvinistic theology is fully reflected in Gill's greatest works: *The Exposition of the Old and New Testament*, *The Body of Divinity*, and *The Cause of God and Truth*. As stated, Spurgeon esteemed Gill's writings, saying, "The system of theology with which many identify his name has chilled many churches to their very soul, for it has led them to omit the free invitations of the Gospel, and to deny that it is the duty of sinners to believe in Jesus: but for this, Dr. Gill must not be altogether held responsible, for a candid reader of his Commentary will soon perceive in it expressions altogether out of accord with such a narrow system; and it is well known that, when he was dealing with practical godliness, he was so bold in his utterances that the devotees of Hyper-Calvinism could not endure him. 'Well, sir,' said one of these, 'if I had not been told that he was the great Dr. Gill who preached, I should have said I had heard an Arminian.'" [12] Spurgeon's statement helps to balance the image of Gill.

John Rippon

When the illustrious John Gill passed off the scene, the church took its next step forward under the able leadership of John Rippon. Deacon Thomas Olney, who proved instrumental in the call of Spurgeon, had sat under the ministry of Rippon. Like young Gill, who was only twenty-three years old when called as pastor, Rippon assumed the charge at the early age of twenty; a pattern seemed to be emerging—at least the church had set a precedent in Gill and Rippon. Forty members of the church thought Rippon far too young and withdrew from membership when he accepted the invitation. Rippon said it surprised him that not more than forty had disagreed with his call to the pastorate. But the dissenters left, then paradoxically went ahead and started a new church and called a man of only nineteen years of age to serve as pastor. That's the independent Baptist spirit for you, some critics would say.

Rippon received his education at Bristol Baptist College and the "young and lively Devonian," as he was called, led the Carter Lane Church to great heights of prosperity. In Rippon's day it became known as "one of the wealthiest within the pale of Non-conformity." He took up the challenging charge in 1773. Significant contributions were made in the exciting years of Rippon's ministry. Of primary importance, the product of Rippon's pen produced a real impact. For example, Rippon is widely known for his compilation of a famous hymnbook. The hymnbook blessed the churches for over half a century. Congregationalists sang from it as well as Baptists. Moreover, Rippon published the first issue of the *Baptist Register*. The periodical established itself as the forerunner of the present day official organ of the Baptist Union, *The Baptist Times*. Further, he planted the germ seed that finally blossomed out into the contemporary world-wide fellowship known as the Baptist World Alliance. His ministry proved significant and prophetic.

Conwell records an interesting anecdote in the life of Rippon:

> The happy eccentricity of the Doctor's [he received a Doctorate's degree] character may be illustrated by a little incident in connection with royalty. He was designated to read an address from the Dissenters to George III, congratulating him upon recovering from sickness. The Doctor read on with his usual clear utterance till, coming to a passage in which there was a special reference to the goodness of God, he paused and said: 'Please, Your Majesty, we will read that again' and then proceeded with his usual cool dignity to repeat the sentence with emphasis. No other man in the deputation would have thought of doing such a thing, but it came so naturally that no one censured him, or if they did, it would have had no effect upon him. [13]

Rippon led the Carter Lane Church to great heights. They enlarged the chapel building and started various agencies and societies. Spurgeon declared that a real revival of religion broke out in the church during those days. Even though it emerged in a rather quiet manner, the movement did much for the edification of the entire congregation. Rippon was a very clever and intelligent man, perhaps more clever than profound. Spurgeon declared Rippon's talents were probably inferior to those of Gill, but he had far more tact and could use his gifts in a very profitable fashion. His preaching style was very lively, affectionate, and impressed the congregations tremendously. He became a very popular man in London and most useful in the Lord's service. A multitude of people came to faith in Jesus Christ through his ministry and a remarkable number of those became ministers of the Gospel themselves. In his later days, Rippon became quite affluent. It was said that he had a "glass coach and two horses." That is no doubt apocryphal, but the Carter Lane congregation did become one of the wealthiest in the world of Nonconformity. Moreover, the members were very generous and contributed to various causes. They especially supported the Baptist Foreign Missionary Society and the Baptist Itinerant Society, the Baptist home mission work.

The church experienced many years of peace and quiet under Rippon. A fellow pastor asked him, "How is it, Doctor, that your church is always so peaceful?" Rippon replied, "Well, friend, you see, we don't call a church meeting to consult about buying a new broom every time we want one, and we don't entreat every noisy member to make a speech about the price of the soap the floors are scrubbed with." [14] Spurgeon identified with that approach, saying, "In many of our smaller churches, a want of common sense is very manifest in the management, and trouble is invited by the foolish methods of procedure." [15] Rippon's generous, affluent church instituted the almshouses which Spurgeon carried on later.

In 1830 during the reign of William IV, with the widening of Carter Lane leading up to London Bridge, the chapel had to be demolished. Rippon led his people in building a house of worship that seated 1200 people—no mean accomplishment in those days. It became known as the New Park Street Baptist Church. It seems strange that an affluent congregation would build a new building in such an unlikely spot just to save a few pounds, but they did. It has been suggested that the people refused to go in debt and purchased the site at the foot of Southwark Bridge on Park Street because that is all they could afford at the moment. Be that as it may, it could not have been a worse location.

John Rippon, however, served the Baptists of Southwark for over six decades, from 1773 to 1836, the year of his death. His benevolence, his writings, his long service, and contribution to Baptists generally were never forgotten. He had been a giant on the south London religious scene.

A rapid succession of pastors followed Rippon. Dr. Joseph Angus came first. As pointed out, after leaving the pastorate he served as secretary of the Baptist Missionary Society. Later he became tutor and principal of Stepney

College. Angus abandoned the practice of "closed communion," inviting all true believers, Baptist or otherwise, to share in the Lord's Supper. He accomplished this significant move quietly and with no disruption of the fellowship. The church did not become an "open membership" congregation, however. Then came the Rev. James Smith, who had served a congregation in Cheltenham. He served the New Park Street Baptist Chapel for eight and a half years. Finally, William Walters of Preston took up the pastorate of New Park Street Baptist Church in July 1851. He ministered there only two years.

During the rather brief pastorates after Rippon's sixty-three years, a general decline plagued New Park Street. This set the stage for the conversation between Deacon Olney and Gould. In a building that seated 1,200, only a handful were gathering to worship in 1853, despite the fact that 300 names were on the church roll. In that context, to a rather depressed Olney, Gould said of the young Waterbeach pastor, "That is the man for you. If anyone can heal the breaches and restore the waste places, Charles Spurgeon can do it." Gould's words went unheeded. Fortunately, a second encounter between Gould and Olney occurred a short time later. Spurgeon again surfaced as the topic of conversation. This time Deacon Thomas Olney came alive to the young man and consulted with another New Park Street deacon, James Low. They took the leap and wrote the teenage pastor of Waterbeach, inviting him to preach for them in London.

BACK AT WATERBEACH

Charles arrived at the Waterbeach Chapel the last Sunday morning of November, 1853, to find a letter waiting inviting him to preach at New Park Street. He read it, passed it over to his deacon Robert Coe, and remarked that it had to be a mistake. Surely, remarked Charles, another Spurgeon must be meant, for a London church with the fame of New Park Street Baptist Church— still the largest Baptist church building in London—would never invite him to preach, a young man of nineteen. Spurgeon thought that the church, which at one time had the great John Rippon as pastor, out of whose hymnbook Charles was about to choose the hymns of the day, would never ask him to preach. New Park Street shared the prestige of being one of the six London Baptist churches with a membership of over 300, despite the rather poor attendance. Coe sorrowfully shook his head. It had been delivered to the right Spurgeon. Charles' fame had spread all over Cambridgeshire. Still, Deacon Coe was a little surprised. "Had it been Cottenham, or St. Ives, or Huntingdon," he said, "I should not have wondered at all; but going to London is rather a great step from this little place." [16]

Charles, not convinced, posted a letter on Monday to New Park Street hinting that they must have made a mistake. He told them he was only nineteen and quite unknown outside the Fens.

His letter reads as follows, and speaks of Spurgeon's humility and reticence:

No. 60, Park Street,

Cambridge,
November 28, 1853.

My Dear Sir,

I do not reside at Waterbeach, and therefore your letter did not reach me till yesterday, although the friends ought to have forwarded it at once. My people at Waterbeach are hardly to be persuaded to let me come, but I am prepared to serve you on the 11th [December]. On the 4th, I could not leave them; and the impossibility of finding a supply at all agreeable to them, prevents me from leaving home two following Sabbaths. I have been wondering very much how you could have heard of me, and I think I ought to give some account of myself, lest I should come and be out of my right place. Although I have been more than two years minister of a church, which has in that time doubled, yet my last birthday was only my nineteenth. I have hardly ever known what the fear of man means, and have all but uniformly had large congregations, and frequently crowded ones; but if you think my years would unqualify me for your pulpit, then, by all means, I entreat you, do not let me come. The Great God, my Helper, will not leave me to myself. Almost every night, for two years, I have been aided to proclaim His truth. I am therefore able to promise you for the 11th, and should you accept the offer, I will come on Saturday afternoon, and return on Monday. As I shall have to procure a supply, an early answer will oblige.

Yours most truly,
C. H. Spurgeon. [17]

A quick second letter from London dispelled his doubts; it read, "You're the one, no mistake." So arrangements were made for Spurgeon to preach in London on December 18, 1853.

OFF TO LONDON

Charles found himself rather heavy-hearted as he boarded the Eastern County's Railway train on Saturday the 17th, headed toward Shoreditch Station, London. He entertained no illusions; he knew his background. The young man was a realist and thought he might well be rejected, being a simple country boy with no formal theological education. Not only that, he had already caught more than his share of criticism for his brashness, even up in the Fens, his home country. How would Londoners react? He did not even know how to dress, let alone use the sophisticated language of a cultured London church. Moreover, he realized New Park Street had an awesome history and needed a man who could rekindle the burning bush of its glory days. To be affected by pride or shallow satisfaction over the honor of being invited to preach in such an historic place never crossed his mind. Like a true Moses facing his "burning bush," he felt quite inadequate for the task.

Yet, God had moved in the matter; Charles sensed that. The Holy Spirit deeply impressed on his heart the verse, "He must needs go through Samaria" (John 4:4). If his Lord felt such a compulsion, he too must needs walk through strange "Samaritan" places; and London definitely filled that role for the young preacher. He kept repeating the text over and over to himself as the clacking of the train wheels measured the rails to the leading city of the world. He really wanted just to stay at home, but he had to go.

When Spurgeon arrived in the capital, the city almost over-awed the country lad. The streets surged with people, bustling in preparation for Christmas. The sight of the crushing mass of humanity, the dirty smoke-filled fog, the old, dingy Georgian buildings, the impersonal air of the Londoners, and a thousand other crosscurrents of impressions boggled his mind. It truly looked like a "Vanity Fair" to Charles. Worse, no church member even offered hospitality to the bewildered boy. Probably none thought he would be worth more than one visit anyway—just a Sunday pulpit supply. So the church put him up in a boarding house in Queen's Square, Bloomsbury. Not only that, they crammed him in a tiny room over the front door. Going to bed seemed like crawling into a casket.

The other young London boarders in the house looked with blasé questioning at the young man from the Fens. No wonder, he had a great black satin stock, or cravat, around his neck. He tucked a blue (one biographer said red) handkerchief with white polka dots in his coat pocket, and he used it with a wave and flurry as he spoke. He really did look the part of a country bumpkin, as the papers of the Capital City would soon accuse him of being. He even admitted to himself later that he felt "verdant green" when he came to town.

Moreover, the young men boarding at Queen's Square house told Charles about the mighty pulpit eloquence of famous London preachers. Whether by design to show up and intimidate the Cambridgeshire lad or not, it did its work. Charles went to his casket bed to the din of London traffic below, quite depressed. He could not sleep. He described his restless, miserable night:

> Pitiless was the grind of the cabs in the street, pitiless the recollection of the young city dark, pitiless the spare room which scarcely afforded me space to kneel, pitiless even the gas lamps which seemed to wink at me as they flickered amid the December darkness. I had no friend in all that city full of human beings, and to escape safely to the serene abodes of Cambridge and Waterbeach seemed Eden itself. [18]

So Charles Spurgeon received his introduction to London! Were he not deeply conscious of God's presence, he may well have made a rapid retreat back to Waterbeach. It would have been understandable; the folks in the Fens loved their young preacher and appreciated him just as he was. Cambridgeshire being home, he understood the people and they him. Wherever he preached, they packed the building to hear the young man declare the Word. Scores of people were being saved. A remarkable ministry had unfolded in his little Waterbeach. It truly had become an Eden for Charles.

The old London church, however, was suffering hard times. They desperately needed a good man. But how could it be *him*? He wondered! Furthermore, London, as a huge nineteenth century metropolis, found itself in the grips of great social change, as has been seen. Of course, this sort of sociological situation afforded the possibility for a great ministry; Charles recognized that. But what would be the outcome of it all? To say the least, all these emotional torrents proved almost more than he could cope with as he tossed and turned in his "casket" that Saturday night.

As Sunday's morning sun glistened on a clear and cold Lord's day, young Spurgeon crossed the Thames River, with all these thoughts still surging like the Thames through his heart and mind. He walked quite timidly along Holborn Hill toward Blackfriars, and then across Southwark Bridge, making his way to New Park Street Baptist Church. When he stood for the first time in front of the imposing, large, ornate, austere building, he was quite amazed at his own audacity to even think of serving such a church. He said, he "felt all alone, and yet not alone."[19] God was with him. As Charles entered the old church building he received a warm welcome—and could not resist sitting in John Gill's chair before the service began.

Soon the congregation gathered. Charles probably felt a little relieved to see only eighty people assemble in the 1,200 available seats. Some biographers say two hundred attended the first service, but that is doubtful. That figure may stem from the fact that the church had about 200 members, others say it had 300 members, which is probably the correct figure. Regardless, if he failed, not too many would know of it. So Charles bolstered up his confidence saying, "I was not yet out of my depth, and was not likely to be with so small an attendance."[20] And after all, God's leading had thrust him into this "Samaria." God would surely see him through.

The service began and the young preacher took his text from James 1:17, "Every good gift and every perfect gift is from above, and cometh down from the Father of lights, with whom is no variableness, neither shadow of turning." He entitled the message "The Father of Lights." No special, impressive sermon had been prepared. Charles determined to preach exactly as he did at Waterbeach. He could never be accused of pretense. He wanted the Londoners to know just what they would get if they saw fit to call him to their pastorate—which he felt not at all likely to happen. No superficiality about this young man; what you saw always turned out to be the real Spurgeon. He had written a fair part of his message—fortunately for its historic value. The sermon synopsis is well worth reading. It unfolds as follows:

> Every good gift and every perfect gift is from above, and cometh down from the Father of lights, with whom is no variableness, neither shadow of turning.—James 1:17.

> Some sciences and subjects of study are to us inexhaustible. We might ever find in them fresh matter for instruction, wonder, and research. If we were to descend into the depths of the earth, with the geologist, and bring up the skeletons of extinct monsters, and note the signs of great convulsions, and study the old and new formations and strata; or if we were to soar aloft, with the astronomer, and attempt to measure the heavens, and count the stars; we should ever be lost in the new discoveries which we should make. The same may be said of all the natural sciences. Whatever the subject of his study may be, it does not seem possible that man should ever be able to say, 'I have nothing more to learn; I am master of it all.'

> But should it one day happen that our race has so progressed in knowledge, and become so well informed as to leave nothing unknown,—should nature be stript of all her mystery, and the heavens, the sea, and the earth be all perfectly understood,—there will yet remain one subject upon which the sons of men may meditate, dispute, and ponder; but it shall still be unknown. That subject is,—GOD, of whom, with humble reverence, I am now to speak. May it please the great Spirit of wisdom to enlarge our minds, and guide our hearts into an understanding of that portion of truth concerning Him which is revealed in the text! We have, here,—

> I.   A MAJESTIC FIGURE.
> II. A GLORIOUS ATTRIBUTE.
> III. A GRATEFUL ACKNOWLEDGEMENT.

> I.   A MAJESTIC FIGURE.

> God is here called "the Father of lights,"—comparing Him to the sun. It is most true that this lower world is the reflection of the upper one. In it, once, the face of God might have been seen as on some glassy lake; but sin has ruffled the surface of the waters, so that the portrait is broken, and presented only in pieces. Yet there are the pieces,—the wrecks of the picture,—and we will not throw them aside. Let us lift up our eyes on high, and behold the only object which is worthy to be called an emblem of Deity. We think we can see several ideas couched in the figure used in our text by the apostle.

> 1. Independence; or, Self-existence.

> God is the only self-existent Being. The sun is not really so; but he is far more independent than any other object we know of. All else of nature is continually borrowing; vegetables draw their nourishment from the soil, ani-

mals from them, or from one another, man from all;—he is the greatest beggar in the universe. The moon lights her nightly torch at the sun's lamp, the planets rekindle theirs in his bright storehouse. Mother Earth is greatly dependent on the sun; despite the pride of her children, what is she but a tiny globule dancing in the rays of that majestic orb? The sun gives, but takes not; bestows on all, receives from none, leans on none; but lives alone, in his own solemn grandeur and glory.

Such is God, the great I AM, who sits on no borrowed throne, and begs no leave to be. All things are of Him, and by Him. He needs them not; were they all annihilated, it would not injure Him. He could exist, as He has from eternity existed alone. He has in Himself all that is worth having. On Him all things lean, He leans on none. But we can scarcely speak of Him,—

'Who, light Himself, in uncreated light,
Invested deep, dwells awfully retired
From mortal eye, or angel's purer ken.
Whose single smile has, from the first of time,
 Fill'd overflowing all those lamps of heaven
That beam for ever through the boundless sky;
But should He hide His face, th' astonish'd sun
And all th' extinguish'd stars would loosening reel
Wide from their spheres, and chaos come again.'

2. Sublimity is another idea suggested by the figure in the text. The sun is one of the most magnificent of created things; when he shows himself, the moon and stars conceal their blushing faces. Seen in any part of his course, he is a grand object. When first he tinges the Eastern sky with his rising beams, when he sits serenely in mid-heaven at noon, or when he retires in splendour at eventide, grandeur is always one of his characteristics. He is too bright for our eyes to gaze upon, although we are at such a vast distance from him.

Far more sublime is God. Who shall describe Him? His angelic servants are glorious, the starry floor of His throne is glorious; what must He Himself be?.

'Imagination's utmost stretch
In wonder dies away.'

Well may angels veil their faces, for even their eyes could not endure His brightness. No man can see Him. His train was all that Moses saw. Borrow the eagle's eye and wing, soar on and on until the glory overcomes you, and you fall reeling back to the earth; do it again and again, and you will find that man cannot see God. Clouds and darkness are round about Him, for He may truly have it said to Him,—

'Dark with excessive bright Thy skirts appear.'

3. Power also seems a prominent idea in this expression of the apostle: 'The Father of lights.' The sun is as a giant coming out of his chamber; and,

like a strong man, he rejoices to run a race. He drags the whole immense solar system along in his majestic course, nor can they oppose him. How mightily he still moves on in his appointed course!

So is God glorious in His power. No one knows His might; it is like Himself, infinite. He speaketh, and His Word is with power. He willeth, and His will is omnipotent. Who can thwart His purposes? Shall nature? No; the hills melted like wax at the presence of the Lord. They skipped before Him like rams. By His power, the waters are divided; fire singes not His servants; wild beasts are tamed. He lifteth His finger, and the flood ariseth; He droppeth it, and the waters assuage. In vain could mountains, torrents, stars, and all the elements war against Him. Who can conquer Him in battle? Shall man? No; He counteth all men but as a drop in a bucket. He that sitteth in Heaven hath His enemies in derision. Shall the devils in hell withstand Him? No; once have they fallen from the battlements of Heaven, and in vain is their loudest roar. Satan is chained, and led as a conquer'd monarch to grace God's victory over him. He is God's slave, and unwillingly doth his Master's will. O beloved, what a God is here revealed to us! Put this thought under thy pillow; and when troubles arise, still calmly sleep on, for His power protecteth thee from all evil!

4. But Beneficence seems even more the leading idea of the text. The sun is absolutely necessary to our being; there would be no light, no heat, no rain, nothing without him. He is necessary also to our well-being; the sun is indeed the great philanthropist; he visits every land, he gives freely, and gives to all, to the peasant as well as to the prince. Curse him, or bless him, he is the same; he does not refuse his light even to the felon, but he visits the prisoner in his cell.

Such also is God, the good, the greatly-good. Should He withdraw His face, Heaven would not be Heaven. Without God, the whole universe would be a valley full of dry bones, a horrible charnel-house. Oh, how good is our God! He confines not His mercies to any one race; the Hottentots are as welcome to His love as are any of us. The sinful receive His grace, and lose their former evil nature. He gives to sinners, and to the unthankful; and if men were not by nature blind, they would see by His light; the defect is in them, and not in Him.

Yon sun has shone on my cradle, it will beam on my death-bed, and cast a gleam into my grave. So doth God, the Beneficent, gild our path with sunshine. Earth were a gloomy vault without Him; with Him, it is light and joyous, the porch of a still more blissful state.

II.   A GLORIOUS ATTRIBUTE.

The apostle, having thus introduced the sun as a figure to represent the Father of lights, finding that it did not bear the full resemblance of the invisible God, seems constrained to amend it by a remark that, unlike the sun, our Father has no turning, or variableness.

The sun has parallax; or variation; he rises at a different time each day, and he sets at various hours in the course of the year. He moves into other parts of the heavens. He is clouded, eclipsed, and even suffers a diminution of light from some mysterious decrease of the luminiferous ether which surrounds him. He also has tropic; or, turning. He turns his chariot to the South, until, at the solstice, God bids him reverse his rein, and then he visits us once more. But God is superior to all figures or emblems. He is immutable. The sun changes, mountains crumble, the ocean shall be dried up, the stars shall wither from the vault of night; but God, and God alone, remains ever the same. Were I to enter into a full discourse on the subject of immutability, my time, if multiplied by a high number, would fail me. But reminding you that there is no change in His power, justice, knowledge, oath, threatening, or decree, I will confine myself to the fact that His love to us knows no variation. How often it is called unchangeable, everlasting love! He loves me now as much as He did when first He inscribed my name in His eternal book of election. He has not repented of His choice. He has not blotted out one of His chosen; there are no erasures in that book; all whose names are written in it are safe for ever. Nor does God love me less now than when He gave that grand proof of love, His Son, Jesus Christ, to die for me. Even now, He loves me with the same intensity as when He poured out the vials of justice on His darling to save rebel worms. We have all had times which we considered times of special love, when His candle shone round about us, and we basked in the light of His smiling face; but let us not suppose that He really loved us more then than now. Oh, no! He then discovered His love in a way pleasing to flesh and blood; but trials are equally proofs of His love. In the fight with Apollyon in the Valley of Humiliation, in the Valley of the Shadow of Death, or in Vanity Fair, He will be ever the same, and will love us neither more nor less than when we sing with seraphic voices the songs of Heaven.

Death, sometimes, in the prospect, is very trying to flesh and blood; but if this truth of God's unchanging love were well remembered, death would not be such a trial to us as it has been to many. We should know that He who helped Jacob to gather up his feet, and die, - that He who enabled David to say, 'Although my house be not so with God; yet He hath made with me an everlasting covenant, ordered in all things, and sure: for this is all my salvation, and all my desire, although He make it not to grow,'—and that He who permitted Stephen to fall asleep amid a shower of stones, will be the Deliverer of all who trust Him. Throughout eternity, there shall be no jars, not a breath of strife; but the same uninterrupted, blessed unity shall prevail for ever, and God will continue to bestow upon us His unchanging love. Thanks be unto Him for loving us so!

III.   A GRATEFUL ACKNOWLEDGEMENT.

The apostle, having introduced God as the Father of lights, and qualified the figure, now proceeds to ascribe all good gifts to Him alone: 'Every good gift and every perfect gift is from above, and cometh down from the Father of lights, with whom there is no variableness, neither   shadow of turning.' If it seemed perfectly reasonable that, at the rising of the sun, nature should welcome it with song, is it not even more reasonable that, at the name of the Father of lights, we should lift up a song? What is said here, is what angels can sing in Heaven; it is what Adam could have hymned in Paradise; it is what every Christian feels heartily willing to confess.

Ever since the Fall, this verse has had an added emphasis of meaning, since in us, by nature, there dwells no good thing, and by our sin we have forfeited every right to any favour from God. So that our natural gifts, such as beauty, eloquence, health, life, and happiness, all come from Him equally with our graces. We have nothing which we have not received. Earth, one day, shall make this song thrill through infinity; Heaven shall join the chorus; the region of chaos and old night shall shout aloud, and even hell's unwilling voice shall growl out an acknowledgement of the fact that 'Every good gift and every perfect gift is from above, and cometh down from the Father of lights, with whom is no variableness, neither shadow of turning.'

I have succeeded in my object if, with me, you can from your hearts say, at the contemplation of Jehovah,—'Glory be unto the Father, and to the Son, and to the Holy Ghost, as it was in the beginning, is now, and ever shall be, world without end! AMEN.' [21]

Charles preached in a dramatically different way. Even the small manuscript he used did not deter or detract from his basically extemporaneous style. The accepted preaching style of the mid-nineteenth century English minister centered in the preparation of a full, literary manuscript, and to read each chosen word most meticulously and pedantically. Some even had a prompter with the manuscript in hand if the preacher stumbled over a word. Many of the sermons came out as superb literary works, but not very communicative or practical. The whole design seemed to be to deliver weighty, eloquent discourses that tended to draw attention to the writing skill and learning of the preacher rather than to the message itself. Ever since the eighteenth century, preaching in most British churches had an almost Gothic formality. This stiff verbosity did not limit itself to the Church of England; Nonconformist churches chafed in its grip as well. Only the Primitive Methodists provided an exception. Most traditional pastors appeared awesome, aloof, and unapproachable. Spurgeon called it the "golden-headed cane era" of preaching.

Charles Spurgeon became a breath of fresh air in this heavy, almost oppressive preaching atmosphere. Because he was extemporaneous, free, and communicative, he thrilled the people with his message, even though he had written the brief manuscript for his first London sermon. After that first Sunday, rarely did he take a manuscript to the pulpit. In the "sacred desk" he flew like a captive eagle set free. A message burned in his heart, and above all he wanted to communicate it effectively to the common people. The churches sorely needed this free spirit and fresh approach. The old stilted style had virtually stultified the churches. In 1854 the Baptists added on an average of only one and one third new members per church for the entire year.

When Charles walked up the pulpit steps of New Park Street Church that December Sunday morning in 1853, with a view to becoming the church's ninth pastor, the congregation did not quite know what to think. There stood a mere boy, with a round baby face that made him look even younger than his nineteen years. In build, he had to stand as tall as possible to measure five foot six inches. Somewhat thick set, like the Dutch, he had a large head—23 inches around. His teeth protruded and were slightly crossed. His eyes did not quite match either. No one would ever call him handsome. When he grew older, he became a little portly and, at the age of thirty-five, grew a beard.

As Charles got warmed up in his message, he would pull out the bright blue polka dot handkerchief from his coat pocket and flourish it about as he made a point, looking a bit comical. But how he did preach! With enthusiastic vigor and true spiritual power he swayed the people. Spurgeon realized he must touch the heart if any good were to be done. Back in September of 1853 he had written his uncle and said, "I want more of the Holy Spirit; I do not feel enough—no, not half enough of His divine energy."[22] However, Spurgeon never went too far in an existential manner pertaining to the inner work of the Holy Spirit. He said one need not always "feel" the Holy Spirit, for the "wind blows where it wills," and thus the feelings are secondary. God clearly honored that deep understanding of the Holy Spirit and moved through the message. The people of New Park Street scooted up to the edge of their seats with excitement before Charles had transversed halfway through his sermon. Never had they heard such powerful preaching. His pungent, colloquial Anglo-Saxon vocabulary had them enthralled. Even his prayers were "earthy" and pungent. On one occasion he prayed, "O Lord, take us and mold us as the clay, though there is so much grit in us that it must hurt thy fingers." Not everyone cared for that kind of language, but he was becoming the historical transition from the ornate, Latinized oratory style in vogue since Samuel Johnson to simple, natural Anglo-Saxon communicative style. Spurgeon would have concurred wholeheartedly with Sir Winston Churchill who said many years later, "There is nothing more noble than an Anglo-Saxon sentence."

The service ended and the elated people filed out. That afternoon the good members fanned out over south London inviting friends to the evening service. They all cried, "You must come to New Park Street tonight and hear this young man from Waterbeach!" A large congregation gathered. Mrs. Unity Olney, Thomas' wife, a deeply devout Christian, suffered as an invalid and was confined to her home most of the time. Her deacon husband managed to get her to church that night. After hearing Charles she simply said, "He will do! He will do!" She expressed what virtually all felt. Another said, "It is not so much his talent or his wit that I feel so overpowering, as his sincere goodness."[23] And his prayers were so impressive. One said, "When Spurgeon prayed, it seemed as if Jesus *stood right beside* him."[24] Another declared, "You feel instinctively when he prays that here is a man strong enough to bear up on his anointed hands the prayers of a host."[25] He could truly preach and pray.

But there was one significant exception to the general affirmation of the many worshipers that first Sunday night. That evening a sophisticated young lady named Miss Susannah Thompson attended the service. She was the "exception"; she did not think much of the sermon, or the preacher. She thought him comical. But that is another story to be delightfully told later.

Charles preached Sunday night from Revelation 14:5 "And in their mouth was found no guile; for they are without fault before the throne of God." The people, profoundly moved by the sermon, actually refused to leave the old building until the deacons assured them they would do their best to induce Spurgeon to come again. Charles consented. The New Park Street Baptist Church members were greatly gratified. How different the Lord's day ended than it began. Charles summed up the happy day, saying:

> The Lord helped me very graciously. I had a happy Sabbath in the pulpit, and spent the interval with warm-hearted friends; and when at night I trudged back to the Queens Square narrow lodging, I was not alone, and I no longer looked on Londoners as flinty-hearted barbarians. My tone was altered, and I wanted no pity of anyone; I did not care a penny for the young gentlemen lodgers and their miraculous ministers, nor for the grind of cabs, nor for anything else under the sun. The lion had been looked at all round, and His Majesty did not appear to be a tenth as majestic as when I only heard his roar miles away. [26]

On Monday, Charles spent the day seeing the sights of London. He climbed to the top of St. Paul's Cathedral and bought a copy of Thomas Scott's *Commentary*. He purchased it with the fee he had received for his first London sermon. Later, however, he saw Scott's work "nothing but Milk and Water." [27] He stated in his own work *Commentary and Commentaries*, "I neither regretted the investment, nor became exhilarated thereby." [28] Charles summed up the whole day in a letter to his father. He wrote:

My Dear Father,

> The last Sabbath I spent in London was one wherein grace abounded. I went up to London bound down and out, and miserable and I feared that perhaps I had no business to go and therefore God was hiding himself from me. I thought that if it continued so I really could not preach and I was silly enough to think I would go back and not try. But when I came to the chapel the friends gathered round me and cheered my heart—and I had such a door of utterance, such attention and such large congregations that I solemnly thought "oh thou of little faith wherefore didst though doubt." [29]

THE CALL TO THE PASTORATE

Up to this point, no preacher had been invited back a second time to New Park Street, but the deacons urged Charles to preach on the first, third, and fifth Sundays in January, 1854. He consented and did very well. Being so enthusiastically received on January 29th, the deacons presented Charles the challenge to preach for a full six months with a view to becoming their permanent pastor. The members exuded excitement, all in anticipation that he would accept. Yet Charles did not encourage the situation. First, he felt inadequate because he had never been to college. The pastor of a historic London church demanded a college man! It posed a real question in Charles' mind. He wrote his father and related the interesting reaction of the deacons of the New Park Street Baptist Church to his lack of formal training: "I told the deacons that I was not a College man, and they said, 'That is to us a special recommendation, for you would not have much savor or unction if you came from College.'"[30] Spurgeon never even accepted any honorary degrees. Once when offered a Doctor of Divinity degree, he refused and said, "To tell the truth, I wouldn't give you a twopence for a bushel of 'em."[31] Then secondly, Spurgeon almost recoiled at the thought of leaving his people at Waterbeach and the effective ministry there, his "Little Garden of Eden." He said, "to leave my own dear people makes it a painful pleasure."[32] Nor did London present itself as inviting to Charles. As seen in a previous chapter, crime ran rampant. One hundred thousand children were not in school. Cholera plagues regularly ravaged the city. Slum conditions were deplorable. Lord Shaftesbury, who later became Spurgeon's best friend, had just begun his benevolent work among the needy of London. The Shaftesbury "Ragged Schools" still remained a dream. Pitiful children roamed and robbed on every street. Charles Dickens did not exaggerate in his well-known novel *Oliver Twist*. And south London suffered as one of the poorest parts of the city. But the church's call had come to Charles with only five dissenting votes—one man and four women. That made it virtually unanimous in Victorian days. Spurgeon said, "I . . . only wonder that the number was not greater."[33] Charles stated in a letter to his father, "They were so starved, that a morsel of the Gospel was a treat to them. Lots of them said I was Rippon over again."[34] That deep spiritual hunger profoundly touched Charles and began to move his heart toward London. "God wills it," he said.[35]

Spurgeon nevertheless felt convinced a six-month probationary period too long. He wrote the church,

> My objection is not to the length of time of probation, but it ill becomes a youth to preach to a London congregation so long until he knows them and they know him. I would engage to supply for three months of that time, and then, should the congregation fail, or the church disagree, I reserve to myself the liberty, without breach of engagement, to retire; and you could on your

part, have the right to dismiss me without seeming to treat me ill. . . . Enthusiasm and popularity are often like the crackling of thorns, and soon expire. I do not wish to be a hindrance if I can be a help. [36]

But he cast the die. To London he would go, if only on probation.

It is interesting how some, even several years later, attempted to hide the facts of Spurgeon's call to the church. In *The Preacher's Annual* for 1877, an article written by Rev. G. T. Dowling reads:

> Charles Spurgeon was not even severely thought of as a prospective pastor the first time he preached in London. Months passed by before he was again invited to spend a Sabbath; and even when a call was extended, it was by no means unanimous. Some families even left the church because 'that boy' was called. [37]

Spurgeon remarked: "It was a pity to fabricate an instance. The truth is exactly the contrary. The moment after my first sermon was preached, I was invited by the principal deacon to supply for six months." [38]

Back in Waterbeach, sorrow, yet resignation to God's leadership, filled the hearts of the people. One of the church members said he knew they would never be able to hold their popular young preacher, but he did not think he would be leaving so soon. Some hoped Charles would fail in London and return to them. In the *Church Book* of Waterbeach chapel, the following entry is recorded:

> Mr. Spurgeon continued to labour amongst us with very great success till the beginning of 1854, when he was called to the more important pastorate of New Park Street, where his popularity and usefulness continue beyond all parallel in modern times, being often called to preach on public occasions in all parts of the country. [39]

Some of Spurgeon's acquaintances, however, did not see him as a fledgling giant, a second Whitefield as he soon became known. They expressed surprise at the move. For example, a Colchester man said, "Charlie Spurgeon has been invited to London, and they are actually going to pay him £150 a year." [40] Charlie had truly been invited to London, but not at £150 a year.

Several circumstances conspired to thrust Spurgeon to south London. His finances pressed him severely; if he stayed at Waterbeach, he would have to take on students to supplement his church stipend. The church, doing the best it could to care for their young pastor, simply could not pay enough to live on, as frugal as Charles tried to be. Consequently, he apparently fully intended to open a school of his own, as has been seen. Spurgeon also came to realize more and more that his ministry could be broadened dramatically in a city like London. Above all, Charles deeply sensed God's leadership in the move. This becomes obvious in reading his letters and statements. His parishioners in Cambridgeshire knew all this too, so with resigned regret they released their pastor to a larger ministry. How large at the time, they never realized, even though one man said of Charles in his early Waterbeach days, "That young man will yet shake England like a second Luther." When he got to London, a lady said, "He will be a second Whitefield." They were both right.

SETTLING IN LONDON

Not unexpectedly, the church wanted Spurgeon's short probation period cut even shorter. A petition to the deacons signed by fifty men of the congregation called for a business meeting to invite the Reverend Charles Haddon Spurgeon to become their permanent pastor. So on April 19, 1884, two months before Charles' twentieth birthday, the church gathered, considering it "prudent," in their words, "to secure as early as possible his permanent settlement among us." [41] The letter and resolution read as follows:

> 30 Gracechurch Street,
> April 20th, 1854.
>
> My Dear Young Brother,
>
> I annex a copy of a resolution passed last evening at a numerously attended special church-meeting held at New Park Street Chapel.
> If you feel it your duty to accept the invitation of the Church to become its Pastor, it will be desirable that you should obtain your dismission from the Church at Waterbeach to our Church as early as you can, in order thatyou may be in a position as a member to attend our church-meetings.
>
> > I remain,
> > My Dear Young Brother,
> > Yours affectionately,
> > James Low, Chairman.

The account of the business meeting is found in the *Autobiography*:

> At a special church-meeting, held on Wednesday evening, April 19th, 1854, at New Park Street Chapel, after prayer by two of the brethren, it was resolved unanimously, that while, as members of this Church, we desire to record with devout and fervent gratitude to God our estimation of the Rev. C.H. Spurgeon's services during the period of his labours amongst us, we regard the extraordinary increase in the attendance upon the means of grace, both on Lord's-days and week-evenings, combined with the manifest fact that his ministry has secured the general approbation of the members, as an encouraging token that our Heavenly Father has directed his way toward us, in answer to the many prayers we have offered up for a suitable Pastor,—and as there are

several enquirers desirous of joining our fellowship, we consider it prudent to secure as early as possible his permanent settlement with us;—we, therefore, beg to tender our Brother, the Rev. C.H. Spurgeon, a most cordial and affectionate invitation forthwith to become Pastor of this Church, and we pray that his services may be owned of God with an outpouring of the Holy Spirit, and a revival of religion in our midst, and that his ministry may be fruitful in the conversion of sinners, and the edification of those that believe. [42]

Spurgeon well knew the opportunity the New Park Street Church opened up for him. So on April 28th Charles responded to the invitation with the following letter. Its historic importance demands a full reading. It presents an insight to the real heart of Spurgeon:

Dearly Beloved in Christ Jesus,

I have received your unanimous invitation as contained in a resolution passed by you on the 19th instant, desiring me to accept the pastorate among you. No lengthened reply is required; there is but one answer to so loving and cordial an invitation. I ACCEPT IT. I have not been perplexed as to what my reply shall be, for many things constrain me thus to answer.

I sought not to come to you, for I was a minister of an obscure but affectionate people. I never solicited advancement. The first note of invitation from your deacons came quite unlooked-for, and I trembled at the idea of preaching in London. I could not understand how it had come about, and even now I am filled with astonishment at the wondrous Providence. I would wish to give myself into the hands of our covenant God, whose wisdom directs all things. He shall choose for me; and so far as I can judge, this *is* His choice.

I feel it to be a high honour to be the Pastor of a people who can mention glorious names as my predecessors, and I entreat of you to remember me in prayer, that I may realize the solemn responsibility of my trust. Remember my youth and inexperience, and pray that these may not hinder my usefulness. I trust also that the remembrance of these will lead you to forgive mistakes I may make, or unguarded words I may utter.

Blessed be the name of the Most High, if He has called me to this office, He will support me in it,—otherwise, how should a child, a youth, have the presumption thus to attempt the work which filled the heart and hands of Jesus?

Your kindness to me has been very great, and my heart is knit unto you. I fear not your steadfastness, I fear my own. The gospel, I believe, enables me to venture great things, and by faith I venture this.

I ask your co-operation in every good work; in visiting the sick, in bringing in enquirers, and in mutual edification.

Oh, that I may be no injury to you, but a lasting benefit! I have no more to say, saving this, that if I have expressed myself in these few words in a manner unbecoming my youth and inexperience, you will not impute it to arrogance, but forgive my mistake.

And now, commending you to our covenant God, the Triune Jehovah,

> I am,
> Yours to serve in the gospel,
> C.H. Spurgeon. [43]

Spurgeon settled down in bustling London, his first home located at 75 Dover Road in Southwark. It is now demolished. The Dover Road house was a comfortable place. An insight to Spurgeon's graciousness is expressed in a letter he sent to the Misses Blunson, the ladies he lived with in Cambridge. He wrote about his new dwelling on Dover Road: "I get on very well in my present lodgings, but not *better* than with you, for that would be impossible." [44] However, Spurgeon found little time to be at home. He became so busy he hardly could set aside even an hour to rest. First, the demand on his time as a preacher dramatically increased. In a matter of a very few months New Park Street's 1200 seats filled to overflowing. Standing room only, many being turned away, became a regular Sunday routine. In a letter dated March 2, 1854, Charles wrote to his uncle James: "You have heard that I am now a Londoner, and a little bit of a celebrity. No college could have put me in a higher situation. Our place is one of the pinnacles of this denomination. But I have a great work to do, and I have need of all the prayers the sons of God can offer for me." [45] Spurgeon's disappointing failure to be admitted to Stepney Theological College, in the final analysis, had been one of God's providential moves after all.

In Charles' early London days, the deacons of New Park Street presented him with one dozen white pocket handkerchiefs. Polka dots did not flatter him in the spotlight of the rising fame shining on the nineteen-year-old pastor. Also, the black cravat had to go. The deacons in those days wore white cravats in keeping with the dignity of their office; they expected the same of their pastor, even if he did hail from the Fens. Charles always refused to wear clerical garb. He said, "Except a duck in pattens, no creature looks more stupid than a dissenting preacher in a gown." [46] Yet, he always took care to be neat, tidy, and clean; but wearing the latest fashion did not concern him at all. Perhaps this is why his deacons made a few helpful suggestions. So, the young preacher from the Fens settled in. Few realized all that God had in store for his future ministry.

THE EARLY MONTHS IN LONDON

It will be recalled Spurgeon had a difficult time financially in Waterbeach. London boded to be the same in the early months. The stipend for the new pastor at New Park Street came from pew rentals. All the rents were designated as his; but in those days, that proved precious little. But, as the crowds grew, so did the stipend. In 1853 the income of the London church amounted to a mere £300. By 1855 it mushroomed to £2,374. Finally, the income expanded to the point that Spurgeon paid for the cost of cleaning the chapel, the lights, etc. of New Park Street. He practiced this arrangement all his life—even through the years of the Metropolitan Tabernacle.

Although Spurgeon's fame began to spread over London, the Baptists did not take early notice of the rising star of their denomination. In *The Baptist Manual* of 1854 they listed the pastor of the New Park Street Baptist Church as "J. Spurgeon." They saw him as so insignificant at that moment they even failed to print his name correctly. In one of the early London Baptist general meetings, a well-meaning brother—at least one assumes he was well-meaning—prayed for Charles and asked God to bless "our young friend who has so much to learn, and so much to unlearn."[47] Charles took it all in stride.

Yet, even in the early months, several sensed the genius of the young New Park Street preacher. Mr. James Sheridan Knowles, an Irish former playwright, actor, and medical doctor, had enjoyed great success as a man of the stage. Knowles was converted and baptized by a Dr. Brock. He left the theatre and entered the Baptist ministry, securing an appointment as a tutor in elocution at Stepney College. Dr. Kitson Clark described Knowles as "perhaps the best of the tragic dramatists"[48] of his day. At one point in his career he became the lessee of the famous Drury Lane Theater in London. One Sunday in May of 1854, Knowles visited the New Park Street Church. He returned to Stepney College and said to his class, "Boys, have you heard the Cambridgeshire lad?" None of them had heard Spurgeon up to that time. Knowles went on:

> Go and hear him at once, his name is Charles Spurgeon. He is only a boy, but he is the most wonderful preacher in the world. He is absolutely perfect in oratory; and, beside that, a master in the art of acting. He has nothing to learn from me or anyone else. He is simply perfect. He knows everything. He can do anything. I was once lessee of Drury Lane Theatre; were I still in that position, I would offer him a fortune to play for a season the boards of that place. Why boys, he can do anything he pleases with his audience; he can make them laugh and cry and laugh again in five minutes. His power was never equaled. Now, mark my word, boys, that young man will live to be the greatest preacher of this or any other age. He will bring more souls to Christ than any man who ever proclaimed the gospel, not excepting the apostle Paul. His name will be known everywhere, and his Sermons will be translated into many languages of the world.[49]

It took some years for the fulfillment of Knowles' prophecy that Spurgeon would live to be the greatest preacher of the age and that his fame would spread worldwide. In Charles' early days, even a Jewish writer said, "Spurgeon was a powerful instance of the difference between scholastic attainment and genius."[50]

All this praise could easily leave the impression that Spurgeon enthralled everyone who heard him. That is not really true. Not all shared
this enthusiasm. An American, assessing Spurgeon's early days, said Charles
was:

> unpractical in either act of oratory or of preaching . . . In personal appearance
> he was not prepossessing; in style he was plain, practical, simple; in manner
> rude, bold, egotistical, approaching to the bigoted; the theology a deep-dyed
> Calvinist; in church relations, an uncompromising Baptist. One could scarcely
> image a more unpromising list of qualifications or rather disqualifications for
> public favor. [51]

Regardless of the varying opinions, one thing became certain, London
began to take serious note of the young man. A new wind seemed to blow
across Southwark dispelling the old London fog of spiritual dismay and
doubt. "The Last of the Puritans" was holding forth, and all England soon
started casting their eyes upon him. Someone said, "There was much of the
old Hebrew prophet about him." Would he become England's new prophet?
It appeared to many that he would.

THE GROWTH OF THE WORK

As Spurgeon's popularity grew, so did the crowds. The church building
simply could not hold all who wanted to hear him. Spurgeon said that his
analyzers believed, "that my originality, or even eccentricity was the very
thing to draw a London audience." [52] But more profundity than that permeated his ministry. The services he conducted scintillated with life and the
Divine presence. A graphic description of a typical dynamic service at New
Park Street in the early, romantic years is given by Charles' Scottish friend,
John Anderson. Some of the statistics seem inflated, but one can catch
something of the excitement of a typical Sunday service:

> The church is seated for 1,500; but what with the schoolroom and the passag-
> es, which were choke-full, there could not have been fewer in it than 3,000.
> The service commenced with a hymn, which was sung by the congregation
> standing. Never did I hear such singing; it was like the 'voice of many waters,'
> or the roll of thunder. No need was there of an organ in that congregation; the
> most powerful organ would not have been heard in the loud swell of so many
> living human voices. Then came the prayer. Phrenologically speaking, I should
> say veneration is not largely developed in Mr. Spurgeon; yet that prayer was
> one of the most remarkable and impressive I ever heard. He prayed first for
> confirmed believers, then for declining ones, then for sundry other conditions.
> Then there was a pause; after which he prayed for the unconverted. 'Some', he
> said, 'were present who were in this state, who, in all likelihood, would never

be in that or any other church again—who were that night to hear their last sermon—who, ere next Lord's day, would not be in this world; and where would they be? There was but one place where they would be—in hell!' He then said, or rather cried out, 'O God, God! must they perish? Wilt Thou not save them, and make that sermon the means of their conversion?' The effect was overwhelming; many wept, and I am not ashamed to say I was one of them. The text was in Psalm cxxvi. 1, 2—'When the Lord turned again the captivity of Zion, we were like them that dream. Then was our mouth filled with laughter, and our tongue with singing.' The subject raised from the text was the 'joy of the young convert.' . . . But it would be impossible to mention all the fine touches of nature in that sermon, which made the whole of that vast congregation for the moment 'kin.' His denunciations of the Sabbath-breaker and other were as terrible as his delineations of the penitent were tender and melting. Mr. Spurgeon is equally great in the tender and the terrible. Nor is he without humor. Here many will refuse him their sympathy, and think him censurable. I scarcely think he is. Others will think, and do think, differently. His taste, according to others, is immaturity of his years. I was told he was conceited. I saw no proofs of it; and if I had, was I on that account to think less of his sermons? I do not say I will not eat good bread, because the maker of it is conceited. His conceit may be a bad thing for himself—his bread is very good for me. I am far from thinking Mr. Spurgeon perfect. In this respect he is not like Whitefield who from the first was as perfect an orator as he was at the last. In respect of his power over an audience, and a London one in particular, I should say he is not inferior to Whitefield himself. [53]

An interesting and humorous event took place in the context of the huge crowds at New Park Street Church. The building, being low-lying and hemmed in, suffered from poor ventilation. Spurgeon, a man of the country, loved fresh air. The stuffiness and heat of the old building at times seemed absolutely insufferable. On several occasions Charles had asked the deacons to open permanently some of the upper balcony windows to let in fresh air. But up to that point his appeal fell on deaf ears. The deacons would not budge. One Sunday, as the congregation rushed and pushed to get in, they felt a cool, gentle breeze coming in from above. All the windows had been smashed, broken out. The people assumed a vandal must have broken in and done the destruction, even if most agreed that it was one of the best "crimes" to have been committed in south London for some time. The disturbed deacons met to investigate the matter. Spurgeon suggested a reward be offered to anyone who could uncover the culprit. It was soon discovered, however, that it would not be prudent to unearth the perpetrator. Close forensic investigation would no doubt have revealed scratches and glass fragments on Charles' cane. Some time later, Spurgeon admitted—in writing—that:

> I proposed that a reward of five pounds should be offered for the discovery of the offender, who when found should receive the amount as a present. The

reward was not forthcoming, and therefore I have not felt it to be my duty to inform against the individual. I trust none will suspect *me*; but if they do, I shall have to confess that I have walked with the stick which let the oxygen into that stifling structure. [54]

The deacons wisely dropped the matter, and the windows remained open as a wry smile broke on the faces of the people as they enjoyed the fresh air. After all, Spurgeon said, "The next best thing to the grace of God for the preacher is oxygen."

ORDINATION

In the early months of Spurgeon's ministry the deacons planned an ordination service for their new pastor; he had never been set aside for the ministry in a formal ceremony. Spurgeon objected. He had become convinced the call of God alone would be quite enough. Such a ceremony had no precedent in Scripture, he argued. He asked, "Where is the scriptural warrant for such nonsense?"[55] He facetiously said most ordinations were merely "placing empty hands on empty heads." Charles contended:

There is good reason for asking, concerning many practices,—are these scriptural, or are they only traditions of the fathers? A little Ritualism in one generation may develop into downright popery in a few years; therefore it is well to take these things as they arise, crush them in the bud. . . . We have a stern fight before us against Ritualistic popery, and it is well to clear our decks of all lumber, and go into the controversy with clean hands. . . . Confining myself to one branch of the subject, I ask,—Whence comes the whole paraphernalia of 'ordination' as observed among some Dissenters? Since there is no special gift to bestow, why in any case the laying on of empty hands? Since we cannot pretend to that mystic succession so much vaunted by Ritualists, why are men styled 'regularly-ordained ministers'? . . . Is not the Divine call the real ordination to preach, and the call of the church the only ordination to the pastorate? The church is competent, under the guidance of the Holy Spirit, to do their work; and if she calls in her sister-churches, let her tell them what she has done, in such terms that they will never infer that they are called upon to complete the work. [56]

Spurgeon then went on to say in a letter addressed to the leading deacon of the church, Mr. James Low, Esquire:

I have a decided objection to any public ordination or recognition. I have, scores of times, most warmly expressed from the pulpit my abhorrence of such things, and have been not a little notorious as the opponent of a custom which has become a kind of iron law in the country. I am willing to retrace my steps if in error; but if I have been right, it will be no honorable thing to belie my former loud outcries by submitting to it myself.

I object to ordinances and recognitions, as such, (1) because I am a minister, and will never receive authority and commission from man; nor do I like that which has the shadow of such a thing about it. I detest the dogma of apostolic succession, and dislike the revival of the doctrine by delegating power from minister to minister.

(2) I believe in the glorious principle of Independency. Every church has a right to choose its own minister; and if so, certainly it needs no assistance from others in appointing him to the office. You, yourselves, have chosen me; and what matters it if the whole world dislikes the choice? . . .

(3) If there be no authority inferred, what is the meaning of ceremony? . . . Furthermore, I have seldom heard of an ordination service in which there was not something objectionable. There are dinners, and toasts, and things in that line. There is a foolish and needless advice, or, if wise advice, unfit for public mention. I am ready to be advised by anyone, on any subject, in private; but I do not know how I could sit in public to be told.

I trust, my dear sir, that you will not imagine that I write warmly, for I am willing to submit; but it will be submission. I shall endure it as a self-mortification, in order that you may all be pleased, I had rather please you than myself; but, still, I would have it understood by all the church that I endure it as a penance for their sake. . . . [57]

Shortly thereafter, Charles preached a sermon on the "Minister's True Ordination." To his own satisfaction, at least, he set the record straight.

Spurgeon won. The deacons desisted and called off their ordination plan. Charles never "officially" became a "reverend," although in his early ministry he adopted the title of "reverend" out of courtesy. Later he changed and all knew him as simply "Pastor" Spurgeon, or "Mr." Spurgeon. He said, "*Reverend* and *sinner* make a curious combination; and I know I am the second, I repudiate the first."[58] As previously stated, he would not accept any honorary degrees. He refused all such accolades. Others followed his example. The great evangelist D.L. Moody, a fond admirer of Spurgeon, followed his lead and refused ordination. He, too, was always known as *Mr.* Moody. Spurgeon's stance on ordination no doubt influenced some of his students in the Pastors' College as well. A Chicago, Illinois paper, *The Standard*, reported on August 25, 1887 that a Spurgeon's College man had performed a wedding ceremony in America and the authorities declared it invalid because he was not ordained.

Spurgeon lived out his conviction concerning ordination on a very practical level. On one occasion he had an encounter with an Anglican minister on the subject. As is common knowledge, Anglicanism accepts the concept of apostolic succession in their theology of ordination. Spurgeon related: "I was having an argument with a clergyman one day, who insisted that only ordained priests of the Church of England are in the true apostolic succession. 'Well, what am I?' I said; 'what do you fellows make of me? You cannot surely deny that God has set His seal upon my ministry!' 'Oh, you are quite an exception,' said the cleric; 'I look upon you as a kind of Melchizedek. You had no predecessor, and you will have no successor. God has a right to make an exception if He so pleases.' 'If I am a Melchizedek, why don't you men pay me tithes, then?' I replied. He only answered with a smile; but he subsequently sent me a leg of pork; perhaps he considered it a tenth part of a pig he had killed."

Southwark Bridge, as mentioned, was a toll bridge; hence, no hackney carriages carried travelers over the river—before Spurgeon, that is. That situation experienced a radical reversal. The crowds began coming to New Park Street Chapel from north of the Thames in huge numbers. The hackney cabbies thus had a windfall, toll or not. "Over the water to Charlie's" became a byword among the cabbies as they sought passengers crossing the Thames. The streets around the chapel on Sunday were completely blocked by people and carriages pressing to get in. Even the local pubs did a thriving business from those unable to crowd into the church, or as the periodical *Vanity Fair* expressed it, on leaving the service with an "awakened sense of sin, felt it to be a relief to quench the spirit in a mug of beer." [59] Spurgeon was obviously getting a hearing of the Gospel by those who needed it.

The Baptists now began to come alive to the young Southwark preacher. On January 10, 1855, as the new year dawned with bright hope for Charles, he preached at the annual session of the London Baptists. Thirty-three churches made up the group at that time. They met in his New Park Street Church. The Baptists were no doubt delighted in their new star when he said in his sermon "the Baptists are the elect of the elect." That is "high-Baptist Calvinism."

SPURGEON'S APPROACH

Probably one of the reasons for the young preacher's early fame grew out of his frankness and blunt appraisal of almost everything in London life. The common man liked that in the preacher. Spurgeon, never reticent or backward in fully expressing himself, came over as being quite brash, especially in his early years. His emotions were always quite near the surface. That is why, no doubt, some condemned him as being rather arrogant. For instance, on an occasion, Spurgeon, as the guest preacher at a service, selected a hymn penned by Isaac Watts. The first two lines of the hymn read, "Just like his nature is his grace, all sovereign and all free." Another minister who announced the hymns during the service, when he read the first two lines of the hymn said, "We won't sing this hymn." Spurgeon went on to relate,

I felt that, under the circumstances, the hymn ought to be sung, so I said, 'If you please, we *will* sing that hymn; or we will not have any at all if we do not have that one.' So the minister shut up the book, and I went on with the sermon. I had fixed upon quite a different subject for my discourse; but when such a challenge was given to me, I felt compelled to change my theme. So I announced as my text, 'I will have mercy on whom I will have mercy, and I will have compassion on whom I will have compassion. So then it is not of him that willeth, nor him that runneth, but of God that showeth mercy,' and I preached from these words a discourse full of good, sound doctrine,—sixteen ounces to the pound,—which filled with delight the hearts of all the brethren and sisters who love the marrow and fatness of the faith which some call Calvinism, to which we trace back to our Lord Himself and His apostles. [60]

Quite obviously, Spurgeon could be quite opinionated on some issues. Some called it outright arrogance; perhaps there was a touch of that in him.

On another occasion, Charles' audacity surfaced again. He came a little late to a meeting—an exceptional thing for Spurgeon—he believed in punctuality. A disturbed deacon met him, holding out his watch as he walked up to Charles. Spurgeon, as if unconscious of this rebuke, took the watch, examined it closely, handed it back to the pompous deacon and remarked it seemed a very fine timepiece, but needed some repair.

But Charles could hardly be charged as being egotistical in his occasional audacious reactions. Although he may have appeared arrogant at times; he simply had too much Christian grace to be a real egotist. Moreover, his brashness often served him well. One Sunday at New Park Street Chapel, being overwhelmed by the vast crowd and the hundreds, if not thousands, who were turned away every Sunday, he wheeled around in the pulpit, faced the back wall, and cried out, "By faith the walls of Jericho fell down, and by faith this wall shall come down too." New building campaigns are not normally announced to churches quite that bluntly. The deacons were aghast. More than one informed the preacher they did not want to hear of it again. "What do you mean?" asked Spurgeon, "You will hear no more about it when it is done; and therefore the sooner you set about doing it the better." [61] They set about doing it! And it opened a new door of ministry, as shall be shortly seen.

It must be granted that Spurgeon took a quite authoritative approach. He became known as the "Gov'nor." He said, "There must be only one captain in a ship." Yet, his leadership in the church was always tempered with genuine love. He won his leadership stance through real Christian love and service to his people; he did not just assume it. Moreover, Spurgeon intuitively knew God had great things in store for the church and he must give them strong leadership. The proof of the value of his approach rests in the fact that the congregation numbered only 313 members when Charles became pastor and in the previous year, 1853, not one new member had been added to the roll. The official church letter to the London Baptist group of churches recorded in 1854 states, "We regret that, during the past year, we have made no additions to our number, in consequence of our being without a Pastor." [62] But ten years later, in 1864, under Charles' ministry the church membership roll grew to 2,934. At the time of Spurgeon's death, the net membership had grown to a net of over 5,000 members, with some 14,000 being added in Spurgeon's 37 years of service. One may wonder why many others did not join the church in light of the tens of thousands that came to hear him. But, as previously pointed out, the Victorians were notorious "sermon tasters." When the requirements for membership were understood, many wanted no more than a taste of Charles' outstanding messages.

BUILDING PLANS

Spurgeon's brashness in his announced building scheme was not as startling as some biographers have implied. Earlier he had tried to present the need of more space to the deacons. He had also attempted to involve some of his members in prayer over the matter. Then, the Saturday night before Charles made his announcement, he spent much of the night in prayer. So his brash statement should not have been totally unanticipated by the church. To accuse him as being outright dictatorial in his leadership style is really unfair. Yet it is true, the idea— many of his ideas—transcended the faith of most. They apparently refused to think or pray seriously about it. But many of Spurgeon's members did not know the determination and tenacity of their pastor. Typical of some of the resistance to the idea, a good lady in the congregation urged the people to sit down and count the cost, lest they get into a debt they could not pay. She later relented and changed her mind. Before long the entire church acquiesced and voted to enlarge their building. The resolution to the church reads:

> Resolved,—That we desire, as a church, to record our devout and grateful acknowledgements to our Heavenly Father for the success that has attended the ministry of our esteemed Pastor, and we consider it important, at as early a period as possible, that increased accommodation should be provided for the numbers that flock to the chapel on Lord's-days; and we would affectionately request our respected deacons to give the subject their full and careful consideration, and to favour us with their report at the church-meeting in October. [63]

The young pastor proved to be a strong, able, visionary leader with contagious courage and farsighted faith. Moreover, a genuine humility characterized his strong, administrative style. Paxton Hood declared, "His humility kills me; I feel I am no Christian at all when I am with Spurgeon." [64] Charles well knew, as he said, "We must stoop before God that we may conquer amongst men." [65] His statement characterizes his humble authority.

The renovation project called for an enlargement of the auditorium by opening the vestry and Sunday School rooms in the rear, thus incorporating them into the sanctuary. Then, a new school room designed with sliding doors on the side would further expand the seating capacity. The enlargement would cost approximately £2,000, a fair sum in the mid-nineteenth century. Where could the money be found? That question did not unseat Charles' commitment to the plan. He said they would build by faith; furthermore, every bill must be paid on time. We saw earlier Spurgeon's attitude toward debt. God Himself will provide, Charles declared. His faith flowered into fact. For example, on the last Sunday of January, 1855, Spurgeon preached on "Thou hast made us unto our God kings and priests" (Revelation 1:6). In the challenge that climaxed his message he said, "I am king, I will give as a king giveth unto a king. . . . A priest, if he sacrificed," Charles stated, "was not to give a maimed lamb or a blemished bullock. Excuse my pressing this subject," the preacher continued, "I want to get this chapel enlarged; we are all agreed about it; we are all rowing in one boat. I have set my mind on £50, and I must and will have it today if possible. I hope you won't disappoint me." As a result of the appeal, the people at once placed £50 in the plates held at the doors. As contracts were let and work completed, contractors would be paid. On occasions, only a few pounds would be left in the treasury—one time only one shilling remained. But the work never stopped for one day. God wonderfully provided. When the wall came down and the new one was put up, the last penny had been paid. This new approach to building by faith and paying all costs as they arose would one day bring forth full fruit in the construction of the great Metropolitan Tabernacle.

THE EXETER HALL MINISTRY

A period of delay occurred before the actual work on the New Park Street Chapel could begin. A Trust, different from the group in charge of the rest of the building, controlled the Vestry and the schoolrooms. It thus became necessary to apply to the Charity Commission for permission to remodel. After proper investigation, the Commission granted permission, and the work proceeded. The work now begun, for two months, February 11 to May 27, of 1885, the walls went up. But what about a place for worship during the construction period? Where would the church meet? The church could meet for the mid-week service at the Maze Pond Chapel. The weekday services presented no problem, the Maze Pond people had met in the New Park Street Chapel when their chapel underwent enlargement. But what about the huge Sunday services? In the famous Strand Street stood Exeter Hall, a large public auditorium seating some five thousand people. Public halls were quite common in Victorian London, the largest being the fabulous Crystal Palace opened by Queen Victoria a short time earlier. Exeter Hall looked very inviting to Spurgeon. It had been built primarily to hold special evangelical meetings. Several friends suggested it could possibly be used for regular church services. The proprietors rented the Hall for specific religious conferences, but to hire it out for a regular series of religious worship services by a specific denominational church was unheard of. Yet, argued Spurgeon, that is the very place. The traditional Victorians were somewhat shocked at the idea.

Such a venture struck Londoners as very innovative if not revolutionary, at least for 1855. Spurgeon always proved to be an innovator of the first order. That was part of his genius, and the basis for considerable criticism. Conventionalities, if they stood in the way of Kingdom progress, Spurgeon saw as a sin. It is often asked would he have reached the masses today as he did in the nineteenth century? The answer is unquestionably *yes*. He would assuredly not do today what he did in the Victorian era, but like all true innovators, his genius would have found what would reach the multitudes in any century or culture. An Anglican journal recognized that quality in Spurgeon. The writer stated, "Every now and then someone takes the world by storm. . . . If we mistake not, Mr. Spurgeon belongs to this small class of persons whose career seems independent of circumstances just as their genius is independent of training."

When Spurgeon and the deacons put the proposal to the owners of Exeter Hall, they were rather reticent in renting the premises on a regular basis to one church. But they finally consented, charged the congregation £15 a service, and the venture began. The question became, however, would people come? It was no foregone conclusion they would. First, Exeter Hall being a public hall and not a church building, raised a psychological barrier. Would even the average Londoner, let alone the upper stratum of society, worship in that setting? Secondly, the Hall was situated north of the Thames River, and Spurgeon and his church were south Londoners. People would have to go "over the water to Charlie's," but now most of the regular congregation would have to go north.

But go they did. Exeter Hall filled from the very first service. Nor did traditional church attenders alone crowd into Exeter Hall. In those exciting days a vast number of young people of every stripe and hue came to hear the young preacher. As one put it, "If Exeter Hall had been twice its size, it would have been inadequate still." The Strand, like New Park Street, became clogged with people and carriages. The Exeter Hall ministry caused Spurgeon's fame to infect even more London circles. He became virtually the talk of the town. Spurgeon was once asked why so many came to hear him preach and why his ministry had been so successful. He simply replied, "My people pray for me." [66] But he also proved to be a wise communicator. On one occasion he said in his sermon, "And now for the second head of my discourse—but I fear I tire, as I already see some of my friends asleep." [67] That probably woke them up. The reason for his preaching success will be taken up in the next chapter. Suffice it to say here, in scriptural language, "the common people heard him gladly," and heard him in unprecedented numbers.

THE MEDIA CONTROVERSY

The newspapers took up the Exeter Hall story in earnest. They were quite fair and generous in the early stage. For example, *The Globe* on Thursday, March 22, 1855 wrote:

> The circumstances under which this gentleman has recently come before the public are curious, and demand a passing notice. Some months since he became minister of New Park Street Chapel, and it was soon found that the building, capacious as it was, was far too small to accommodate the crowds of persons who flocked to hear the young and eloquent Divine. In this state of affairs, there was no alternative but to enlarge the chapel; and while this process was going on, Exeter Hall was engaged for him. For some weeks past he has been preaching there every Sunday morning and evening; but he has filled the great hall just as easily as he filled New Park Street Chapel. A traveller along the Strand, about six o'clock on a Sunday evening, would wonder what could be the meaning of a crowd which literally stopped the progress of public vehicles, and sent unhappy pedestrians round the by-streets, in utter hopelessness of getting along the wide thoroughfare. Since the days of Whitefield—whose honoured name seems to be in danger of being thrown into the shade by this new candidate for pulpit honours—so thorough a religious furor has never existed. Mr. Spurgeon is likely to become a great preacher; at present his fervid and impassioned eloquence sometimes leads him astray, and mars the beauty of his singularly happy style. [68]

The *Glasgow News* of Scotland also wrote:

> To the horror of some pious rival, New Park Street Chapel has become rapidly crowded, so that the congregation has had to resort to Exeter Hall till their chapel is enlarged. Even Exeter Hall is found too small to accommodate the crowds which go to see and hear the youthful and now renowned Rev. C.H. Spurgeon. Someone, who, we suspect, could give a beggarly account of empty benches, has written to some of the newspapers, holding up this successful rival to scorn because he does not preach and pray to his satisfaction— that is, we presume, in the usual jog-trot, sleepy fashion. Young Spurgeon must, therefore, be held up to contempt in the columns of such papers as choose to lend themselves to these purposes. We have seen gentlemen who have worshipped in his crowded congregation, and who state that the services are conducted with strict propriety, and that there is nothing in the service to offend even 'ears polite.' They assure us that his discourses are replete with substantial matters, and that they are couched in language vigorous and appropriate. He pays no attention to the dogmas of schools, and chooses to express his views in language of his own, which is free from the stereotyped phraseology of the pulpit; but there is no expression used unworthy of the subject, and none which judges of theology would repudiate. A number of letters have

appeared in his vindication, and to these the names of highly respectable parties are attached. It were well for rivals to mind their own business, as a young man of such energy as Mr. Spurgeon is not to be put down by envious rivals. Like other young preachers, he has his peculiarities; but these are often the indications of a genius which ripens into a brilliant maturity. [69]

Exeter Hall marked a new era in the Spurgeon saga. In those early days, Spurgeon generally received positive press. For example, *The Times* wrote: "We are delighted to hear that there is one man in the metropolis who can get people to hear his sermons from any other motive than the fulfillment of a religious obligation." [70] Spurgeon wrote his father in those days:

> On Sabbath last more than 1000 persons were put (kept) out of the Hall from wont of room—while within it was crammed to suffocation. . . . Have had Sir de Lacy Evans and it is reported Lord John Russell at the Hall. But I am sure the Lord Jehovah was there. [71]

Such was the common reaction in Spurgeon's first year and a half at New Park Street Baptist Chapel. Then the dam that held back the waters of belittlement broke, and for the next few years a flood-tide of caustic, cruel criticism all but drowned the twenty-one-year-old New Park Street Chapel pastor.

As implied earlier, some stones had already been slung at Spurgeon before the spring of 1855. And, shortly after, he moved with his working class people across the river and invaded London's blasé "West End," as that part of London is called. The move proved too much for the sophisticated, rather snobbish press. Spurgeon did come over as a "reformer," and that probably was unacceptable to the bourgeoisie members of the press. For the newspapers, the time had come for the "stripling from Waterbeach" to be called to account. To the field against Spurgeon the journalists marched; and they knew how to battle. The "censure developed into mere vulgar . . . abuse." [72]

The *Saturday Review* through the many years of Spurgeon's London ministry castigated the preacher. The editorial board of the paper ranged from ritualists to agnostics, and they supported the Tory Party and the Anglican Church. Between 1856 and 1868 they devoted almost as much space to Spurgeon as they did to Gladstone and Disraeli. These editors, led by Fitzjames Stephen, lamented that they lived in "the age of spirit-rapping and Mr. Spurgeon," [73] calling him the "Anabaptist Caliban." When a theological controversy erupted, which will be taken up later, the *Saturday Review* termed him "a course, stupid, irrational bigot," and "an ignorant, conceited fanatic." Spurgeon's reaction to that periodical brought him to the conclusion that a true Christian is "one who fears God and is hated by the *Saturday Review*." [74] Spurgeon's associates called the periodical the "Satanic Review," or the "Saturday Reviler." But the *Saturday Review* did not stand alone in attacking Spurgeon. Other critics said his preaching reminded one of "a Punch and Judy Show." *The Illustrated Times*, October 11, 1856 asked: "Will his popularity last? We more than doubt it." Even a fellow preacher in *The Sheffield and Rotherham Independent*, April 28, 1855, said of Spurgeon, "the Exeter Hall religious demagogue" was no more than a "nine day's wonder" and has "gone up like a rocket and ere long will come down like a stick." Paradoxically, that same journal in 1898 (six years after Spurgeon's death) called him, "this noble Puritan preacher and saintly Christian." The *Ipswich Express*, February 27, 1855, called him "a clerical poltroon"; The *Daily News*, September 9, 1856, accused him of "pulpit buffoonery" and "utter ignorance of theology." In Belfast's *Northern Whig* (The Times) August 28, 1859, he was known as "a rank mountebank," and the *Essex Standard*, April 18, 1855, termed him "this ranting fellow." In Scotland the secular press were reasonably positive, but the religious press said Spurgeon disgusted a respectable audience and gave the people "buffoonery." A Glasgow writer predicted he "like an early gooseberry or overgrown cucumber will go back to the nihility from whence he sprang." [75] *The Christian News* of Scotland said, "Mr. Spurgeon, in our estimation, is just a spoiled boy, with abilities not more than mediocre." At times Spurgeon seemed to lose some of his control—he got angry, saying on one occasion after a bitter attack, "Who cares what a harlot says?" At other times it put him as a pilgrim in the "Dungeon of Despair." But Spurgeon kept it all reasonably well in perspective. He wrote his mother:

> I have had some more serious smashings in the papers but by God's grace I am not scarred by all their arrows. The Lord is on *my* side, whom shall I fear. [76]

Moreover, he saw the censures as a means of growing in Christian grace. In writing to an aunt he said, "I am content to be evil spoken of, if I can but grow in grace and serve God." [77] In the heat of the media battles, Charles wrote his father:

> Dear Father,   4 March '55
>
> Do not be grieved at the slanderous libel in this week's . . .(papers). My friends have informed the publisher that he must either apologize or send the name of his solicitor that the usual course may be pursued.
>
> Of course, it is *all a lie.* [78]

Spurgeon felt these barbs, however. He said, concerning such reports:

> A company of mean-spirited, wicked men, who are no bigger than bees, mentally and spiritually can get together, and sting a good man in a thousand places, till he is well-nigh maddened by their scorn, their ridicule, their slander, and their misrepresentations. Their very littleness gives them the power to wound with impunity. Such has been the experience of some of us. . . . [79]

Still, the crowds kept coming. On some Sundays, thousands would be turned away from Exeter Hall, unable to get in. All the publicity, despite its negative castigations, resulted in bringing even more people to hear Spurgeon. He wrote his father on September 24, 1855: "What a capital advertisement! The enemy is more of a fool everyday."[80] His popularity grew; on one occasion over thirty members of Parliament came to hear him. The rumor even circulated that Palmerston had planned to attend a service, but could not because of the gout. Moreover, Spurgeon held a great attraction for men. More men came to hear him than women, which was very exceptional in Victorian Britain. At times, in Spurgeon's own words, "nine-tenths of my hearers are men."[81] He was a man's man. Despite his bodily weakness and lack of physical agility, he came over in the pulpit as very masculine. But that does not mean he did not appeal to women, as well, for he did.

THE "PENNY PULPIT" MINISTRY

Spurgeon published a sermon each week, beginning during his first year at New Park Street. That significant move had its birth on his first day at New Park Street Baptist Church when he met Joseph Passmore, a young publisher engaged in business with a Mr. Alabaster. Passmore liked Charles immediately. He had walked back to the Bloomsbury Hotel with Charles his very first Sunday in London. Passmore became Charles' first real companion in the capital city. They founded a life-long close friendship. Passmore suggested that the new pastor print a sermon each week as a "Penny Pulpit" periodical. A "Penny Pulpit" approach to disseminating a weekly sermon was actually not innovative. Pamphlets that sold for a penny were regularly produced in Britain. Thus the public had a mindset for such an approach. Charles consented; the venture began and the published sermons became so popular that in a very short time thousands were reading them regularly. The full fascinating story will be told in the next chapter.

But the press would not leave Spurgeon alone even in his writing ministry. The *Ipswich Express*, February 27, 1855, said the sermons were "redolent of bad taste, vulgar, and theatrical." A writer in the *Sheffield and Rotherham Independent*, April 28, 1855, reported, "I have glanced at one or two of Mr. Spurgeon's published sermons, and turned away in disgust." Regardless, multitudes read them as fast as they came off the press. Recently, a London television commentator talked about "British snobbery and smugness that despises new fame and above all individuality" (TV Broadcast). If it is true of London's mindset today, the Victorians were doubly guilty. Spurgeon had a reply to that sort of mentality:

> I am, perhaps, 'vulgar,' and so on, but it is not intentional, save that I *must* and *will* make the people listen. My firm conviction is that we have quite enough *polite* preachers, and that 'the many' require a change. God has owned me to

the most degraded and offcast. Let others serve their class: these are mine, and to them I must keep. [82]

History has evaluated Spurgeon's sermons far more positively than the snobbish press. As seen earlier, Professor Helmut Thielicke, twentieth-century German theologian, preacher, and author praised his works:

> I am almost tempted to shout out to those who are serving the Eternal Word as preachers, and to those who are preparing to do so, in what I hope will be a productive hyperbole: Sell all that you have (not least of all some of your stock of current sermonic literature) and buy Spurgeon. [83]

Little did the critics know Spurgeon began to build a bridge from the Latinized style in vogue for years, to the more modern communicative approach that appealed to the masses who so needed to hear the Gospel.

It is only fair to point out that Spurgeon did not stand utterly alone in his new "vulgar" stirring style of preaching. A few other brave souls followed him in the battle. Edward White, the Congregationalist minister of the Welch House Chapel, used a fresh innovative, "common" style. Furthermore, pastors like Alexander Fletcher and Paxton courageously identified with Charles through those early turbulent days. Still, there were many who would actually scorn Spurgeon on the streets as he passed by.

Perhaps the most difficult criticism Charles had to bear came from his fellow preachers. Of course, he expected the criticism of some because of theological differences. A Universalist wrote to Charles in 1865:

> You must, indeed, be stupid to imagine for one moment that your strange sayings and doings will induce *good* people to leave their own places of worship to attend . . . although 'fools rush in where angels fear to tread.' [84]

Those comments hurt Spurgeon. One reporter in the *Essex Standard* wrote: "They very properly shrink for recognizing him among the regular ministers of the Baptist Denomination." [85] Spurgeon himself said, "Scarcely a Baptist minister of standing will own me." That changed, of course, and Spurgeon related well to the Baptists of Britain, at least until the Down Grade Controversy erupted in 1887. For example, he became one of the founders of the new London Baptist Association and spoke yearly in the annual Baptist Union meetings. But in those early days, even the high-Calvinist camp leveled their guns on him—and Spurgeon claimed to be a Calvinist, though not of the "high" variety. (His theology will be discussed in a later chapter.) For example, Rev. James Wells, pastor of the Surrey Tabernacle, devoted a portion of each Sunday service criticizing Spurgeon's message that had been published the previous week. On one occasion, Wells refused to speak at a service where Spurgeon was also to bring a message. Writing in *The Earthen Vessel*, January 1855, a strict Baptist publication, Rev. James Wells, under the pseudonym of "Job," wrote:

"Concerning Mr. Spurgeon's ministry . . . it is most . . . deceptive . . . is simply deceiving others with the deception wherewith he himself is deceived."[86] In one of his writings he even cast doubt on Spurgeon's conversion. He said, "I have—*most solemnly have*—*my doubts* as to the Divine reality of his conversion." A heated controversy ensued after that and gave rise to a number of false stories.

A rash of cartoons and caricatures broke out in the press. One depicted an Anglican bishop driving an old stagecoach with two slow horses. The title of the clerical charioteer was "Church and Stage." Racing the bishop, a young preacher with flowing hair speeded on in a locomotive engine. The title of the second cleric? "The Spurgeon," of course! The titles clearly implied to the Victorians that the slow coach and the fast train showed the utter contrast between Spurgeon and the Established churchman. Another cartoon, entitled "Brimstone and Treacle," presented two preachers in their respective pulpits, one with eyes and mouth wide open and hands extended, the other wrapped up in his robe with a rather insipid smile. Naturally, Spurgeon was the "Brimstone" with his mouth open and hands extended, and the Established Church of England pastor was "Treacle," bound up in his ecclesiastical robes. A third "piece of art" with the caption, "Catching 'em Alive-o," presented Spurgeon with a tall hat of flypaper and the people caught as flies by the winsome attractiveness of the New Park Street Church pastor. Yet another showed the Archbishop of Canterbury and Mr. Spurgeon as conductors on rival buses. Of course, Spurgeon attracted all the customers. One thing was obvious—London saw Spurgeon as very different from the ordinary run of ministers on England's religious scene.

Tracts and pamphlets also received wide distribution—some pro, some con. Titles appeared like: "Does Mr. Spurgeon Do Good or Harm?" "Who Is Spurgeon?," "Review of Spurgeon's Chamber of Horrors," "The Devil vs. Spurgeon," "Mr. Spurgeon's Critics Criticises," "The Light of Genius," etc.[87] That is to mention only a few. Anecdotes—most of them sheer fabrications—were bandied about town also. For example, they accused Charles of sliding down the banister of the stairs that led up to his pulpit, illustrating how easily people can backslide. Then he would struggle back up, as the story went, to demonstrate the difficulty of regaining lost spiritual ground. One man even vowed and declared he had seen Spurgeon do it. The arrangement of the pulpit stairs at New Park Street, however, made it physically impossible. When the Metropolitan Tabernacle was built, Charles had the pulpit stairs removed from the New Park Street Church and placed in his back yard at home to show visitors it was impossible for him to slide down the railing. Another story accused Spurgeon of preaching very directly to a dissenting, disgruntled deacon at his church from the text "And then the beggar died." It was not an easy time for Charles.

The ridiculous fact about the anecdotes making the rounds is that identical stories had also been attributed to other famous preachers, some even as far back as Whitefield. Yet it all suggested the growing popularity of Spurgeon. But a slow move to a little more positive attitude began to develop as the ministry increased. Moreover, Spurgeon learned to take it all very philosophically. He wrote: "Time brings ease, and use creates hardihood. No real harm has come to any of us who have run the gauntlet of abuse; not even a bruise remains." [88]

However, Spurgeon became quite depressed in his earlier days by the negative, critical onslaught. During those difficult times, he said in a letter, "I am down in the valley partly because of two desperate attacks upon me, but all the scars I receive are scars of honor, so faint heart, on to the battle." [89] In a sermon he declared: "Master, I will not keep back even my reputation from Thee. If I must lose that too, then let it go; it is the dearest thing I have, but it shall go, if, like my Master, they shall say I have a devil and am mad." [90] He stood in the spirit of John Wesley who said that when he gave God everything he did not make an exception of his reputation. After Charles married, Susannah, his wife, printed on a large card Matthew 5:11-12, "Blessed are ye, when men shall revile you, and persecute you, and shall say all manner of evil against you falsely, for my sake. Rejoice, and be exceeding glad: for great is your reward in heaven: for so persecuted they the prophets which were before you." She read it to her husband every morning, and as she said, it was instrumental in "fulfilling its purpose most blessedly, for it strengthened his heart, and enabled him to buckle on the invisible armour, whereby he could calmly walk among men, unruffled. . . ." [91] But later, he got to the place where he almost reveled in the criticisms. For as the gossip grew, so did the crowds. Concerning those crowds, one writer exclaimed:

> Spurgeon! Spurgeon! Spurgeon! This name is in every mouth. Have you heard Spurgeon preach? Have you even seen him? Have you read such and such about him? These and such like questions everyone is asking. [92]

Spurgeon said, "For myself I will rejoice, the devil is roused, the church is awakening and I am counted worthy to suffer for Christ's sake." [93] He said on another occasion, "The devil has barked again in *The Essex Standard*. . . . Never mind; when Satan opens his mouth he gives me an opportunity of ramming my sword down his throat." [94] He went on to say, "The stings at last caused me no more pain than if I had been made of iron." [95]

THE TIDE BEGINS TO TURN

Not all members of the press were negative, however. James Grant of the *Morning Advertiser*, a paper that had almost as large a circulation as the *Times*, reported after Spurgeon's second Exeter Hall service:

It will easily be believed how great must be the popularity of this almost boyish preacher when we mention that yesterday both morning and evening the large hall, capable of holding from four to five thousand people, was filled in every part. There can be no doubt that Mr. Spurgeon possesses superior talents, while in some of his happier flights he rises to a high order of pulpit oratory. It is in pathos that he excels, though he does not himself seem to be aware of the fact. He is quite an original preacher; has evidently made George Whitefield his model; and like that unparalleled preacher, the prince of pulpit orators, is very fond of striking apostrophes. [96]

A year later Grant wrote:

Never since the days of George Whitefield has a minister of religion acquired so great a reputation as this Baptist preacher, in so short a time. Here is a mere youth, a perfect stripling, only twenty-one years of age incomparable to the most popular preacher of the day. [97]

To be compared to Whitefield pleased Charles considerably. George Whitefield stood as his early model, and remained so throughout his life. He said:

There is no end to the interest that attaches to such a man as George Whitefield. Often as I have read his life, I am conscious of a distinct quickening whenever I turn to it. He lived, other men seemed only to be half alive: but Whitefield was all life, fire. . . . My own model, if I may have such a thing in due subordination to my Lord, is George Whitefield; but with unequal footsteps must I follow in his glorious track. [98]

Dr. John Campbell, a highly respected minister also took his stand supporting Charles. They became fast friends even though Campbell was Spurgeon's senior by forty years. Charles called him "a veritable Great Heart and the Luther of the nineteenth century." [99] Campbell, editor of the *British Banner* and the *British Standard* and considered, as one said, "an excellent judge of pulpit eloquence," wrote:

Mr. Spurgeon is in all respects original . . . a preacher of Heaven's own formation; and hence all is nature and all is life, while that life and that nature are among the millions a power. . . . Art may captivate the fancy; nature alone can subdue the heart. What, then, is the source of this unprecedented attraction? It is primarily in the *soul of the man*, a soul large, liberal, and loving. [100]

Campbell always strove to be fair and balanced in his evaluation of Spurgeon. He supported the young pastor through the years. Spurgeon always expressed gratitude for Campbell's friendship and encouragement.

One of the first Nonconformist periodicals to give extended notice to Spurgeon was *The Patriot*. Its articles were normally quite positive to his ministry. They printed a review of his life in 1855. *The Patriot* had the distinction of being the oldest London Nonconformist paper. Its review encouraged the New Park Street ministry.

Charles stated when the press began to turn more in his favor (*The Times* of London never joined in the criticisms), "The press has *kicked* me quite long enough, now they are beginning to *lick* me, but one is as good as another so long as it helps fill a place of worship. I believe I could secure a crowded audience at dead of night in deep snow." [101] Later, when attitudes had grown generally better, businesses advertised their wares using Spurgeon's name—without his consent, as copyright laws were virtually non-existent in those days. Companies all the way from cough syrup to ladies' wear made capital on the preacher's popular name. Even lockets containing his miniature were on sale in the shops for seven shillings, six pence. Stores would produce yearly calendars using Spurgeon's pictures.

As time went on, other writers began to speak more positively about the young preacher. "This Essex bumpkin, by his own unaided energy, has done more for civilization and the Christianizing of south London than all the archbishops and the bishops of the establishment," wrote one journalist. When a newspaper did say complimentary things about Spurgeon, he would write them expressing his gratitude. In April, 1855 he wrote a Chelmsford newspaper:

> I am usually careless of the notice of papers concerning myself—referring all honor to my Master, and believing that dishonorable articles are but advertisements for me, and bring more under the sound of the Gospel. But you, my dear sir (I know not why), have been pleased to speak so favorably of my labors that I think it only right that I should thank you. . . . Amid a constant din of abuse, it is pleasant to poor flesh and blood to hear *one* favorable voice. I am far from deserving much that you have said in my praise, but as I am equally undeserving of the coarse censure poured on me by *The Essex Standard*, &c., &c., I will set the one against the other. I am neither eloquent nor learned, but the Head of the Church has given me sympathy with the masses, love to the poor, and the means of winning the attention of the ignorant and unenlightened. [102]

As the days moved on, some London pastors began to confirm their friendship and support of Charles. His greatest preacher friend, the highly respected Dr. John Anderson of Scotland, always had a positive word. Still, it took some time for the basic tide of criticism to turn. When praise did come Spurgeon's way, he found that as much, or more, difficult to handle than the harsh criticisms. He stated:

> I was reading some time ago an article in a newspaper, very much in my praise. It always makes me feel sad—so sad that I could cry—if ever I see anything praising me; it breaks my heart; I feel I do not deserve it, and then I say, 'Now I must try harder, so that I may deserve it.' If the world abuses me, I

am a match for that; I begin to like it. It may fire all its big guns at me, I will not return a solitary shot, but just store them up, and grow rich upon the old iron. [103]

To charge Spurgeon as being a confirmed egotist, as many did, is rather difficult to substantiate considering Charles' attitude.

THE CHOLERA PLAGUE

Exeter Hall, the crowds, the criticism and praise, the rapidly increasing responsibility, and abundant labors began to tell on the physical strength of Charles, even though he served in the vigor of youth. Not only that, just about a year after settling in London, in the midst of demanding work, an Asiatic cholera epidemic scourged London. Many people died daily. In the first week alone, 2050 people died in London. As a dedicated pastor, young Spurgeon drove all over south London to visit and minister to the sick. Several of his own members fell stricken. In a letter to his father he wrote, "Lost three (church members) on Sunday last . . . I do not know how to keep from constant weeping—when I see others die." [104] Charles' close friend, Charles W. Banks, described those dark days: "The scenes around us have been of the most solemn character. We could not walk the streets but we saw the doctors driving hither and thither—hearses, mourning coaches, and funeral processions, at almost every turn. . . these are indeed heart-aching days for the fallen sons of men; our faces have turned pale; our spirits have trembles." [105]

The young pastor labored so long and arduously that he bordered on the verge of utter exhaustion. Fatigue, constant encounter with the sick and dying, and little sleep plunged him into depression. He became seriously fearful that he too would succumb to the plague. His days were degenerating into a drudgery, filled with apprehension. He wrote his father: "The doctor is physicking me again, it is no light work." [106] One day, sick in heart, walking dejectedly down Great Dover Road on his way home from another funeral, he stopped and looked in an apothecary shop window. The shopkeeper, being a believer, had placed a placard in his window with a Scripture verse that read: "Because thou hast made the Lord, which is my refuge, even the Most High, thy habitation; there shall no evil befall thee neither shall any plague come nigh thy dwelling" (Psalm 91:9). Immediately, the Spirit of God impressed the truth on Charles' heart. He claimed the promise as his own. Dramatically he came out of his depression and went about his work completely confident God would care for him and keep him safe from the plague. The lines of an old hymn spoke to him: "Not a single shaft can hit, till the God of love sees fit." He remembered Cromwell's word, "Man is immortal till his work is done."

Still, Charles taxed himself to the limit. How he held up to it all is astounding. God surely became his strength. Moreover, his people at New Park Street deeply appreciated his devotion. He proved a true pastor as well as a great preacher.

In the heat of all the excitement and labors, it seemed that even the exhilarating services at Exeter Hall were at times almost too much for the young man. One Sunday, he preached from the text, "His Name Shall Endure Forever." One worshiper described that particular Sunday:

> I really thought he would have died there, in the face of all those people! At the end he made a mighty effort to recover his voice; but utterance well-nigh failed, and only in broken accents could the pathetic peroration be heard—'Let my name perish, but let Christ's name last forever! Jesus! Jesus! Jesus! Crown Him Lord of all! . . . Crown Him Lord of all!' and then he fell back almost fainting in the chair behind him. [107]

The renovation of New Park Street Baptist Church, when finally finished on May 31, 1855, thrilled the congregation as they moved back south of the Thames and saw the improvement on their old building. But then, to their disappointment, they found that the £2,000 expenditure was virtually a waste of money. The enlarged chapel still proved totally inadequate to accommodate the crowds. Charles said, "Our harvest is too rich for the barn." He stated that trying to get all the people into the renovated building was like trying "to put the sea into a teapot."

On Sunday, June 19, 1855, a few days after his birthday, Spurgeon preached on "Pictures of Life, and Birthday Reflections." A lithograph of Charles appeared along with the sermon. This became the first of many, and the large sale gratified the youthful pastor. In October of 1855, Spurgeon published his edition of the old *Baptist Confession of Faith of 1689*. In the Preface of the new edition, he wrote:

> This ancient document is a most excellent epitome of the things most surely believed among us . . . This little volume is not issued as an authoritative rule or code of faith, whereby ye are to be fettered, but as an assistance to you in controversy, a confirmation of faith, and a means of edification in righteousness . . . Cleave fast to the Word of God, which is here mapped out to you.

No questions arose about where Spurgeon stood theologically, especially on the Bible—he always took a typically Particular Baptist stance. The *Confession* states the Scriptures are the "only sufficient certain, and infallible rule."

With Charles' popularity continually rising, something of the Whitefield spirit gripped him and he took to the fields to preach as did his mentor a hundred years earlier. If New Park Street could not accommodate all who wanted to hear him, the fields could. On June 22, 1855 he preached in Hackney, North London. At least ten thousand people gathered to hear him. He spoke on the text Colossians 3:11, "Christ is all." To preach on Jesus, the glorious Savior, was always Spurgeon's greatest love. He said of his pulpit work, "I take my text and make a bee-line to the cross." With great power he preached and people responded with great enthusiasm. The service proved a tremendous success, unusually blessed by the Spirit of God. An elated Spurgeon wrote to his future wife, Susannah Thompson:

> Yesterday I climbed to the summit of a minister's glory. . . . the Lord was with me, and the profoundest silence was observed; but oh, the close—never did mortal man receive a more enthusiastic ovation! I wonder I am alive! After the service, five or six gentlemen endeavored to clear a passage, but I was borne along amidst cheers, and prayers, and shouts, for about a quarter of an hour—it really seemed more like a week! I was hurried round and round the field without hope of escape until, suddenly seeing a nice open carriage with two occupants, standing near, I sprang in, and begged them to drive away. This they most kindly did, and I stood up, waving my hat, and crying, 'The blessing of God be with you!' while from thousands of heads hats were lifted and cheer after cheer was given. Surely amid these plaudits I can hear the low rumbling of an advancing storm of reproaches; but even this I can bear for the Master's sake. [108]

THE ITINERANT MINISTRY

London could not exclusively hold Spurgeon. He engaged in an extremely strenuous itinerant, evangelistic ministry all over Britain, and received many accolades. Once while he was preaching in the open air in Cambridgeshire, a local farmer remarked, "Oh, it was lovely, I wish he had kept on all night." When Spurgeon traveled, the railway workers knew he was coming and treated the affair like a famous celebrity was coming to town; sort of a "holiday excitement" surrounded his arrival. In December of 1855 he preached to three thousand in the Continental Goods Depot of the North Europe Steam Navigation Company. In south Wales he preached three times until almost midnight. At Trowbridge, England, he declared the Gospel in the morning and evening, but so many had come to hear him that could not get in, a third service was held after 10:00 p.m. He traveled to Stambourne on May 27, 1856 to preach his grandfather's Jubilee Service. That was a thrill for Charles. He also reveled in the fact that he was asked to preach one of the centenary sermons commemorating George Whitefield, held in the famous Whitefield Tabernacle in Mooresfield, London; and he preached superbly. He undertook an effective mission in Scotland, his first of several. A London correspondent told an interesting story relating to what happened in Hertfordshire while Spurgeon ministered there. The people wished him to address them, but no building was available:

> A Nonconformist minister was first applied to for the loan of his chapel, but returned an indignant refusal. An application to the vicar for the use of the parish church met with a similar response. An open-air meeting in the existing

state of the weather was out of the question; and, there being no room in the village sufficiently large to accommodate a quarter of the expected audience, it began to be feared that the whole affair would rip through, more especially as Mr. Spurgeon had to leave for town by an early train on the following morning. In this dilemma a small farmer in the neighborhood offered the use of a large barn, which was gladly accepted. An extemporaneous pulpit was hastily constructed, and long before the hour appointed every corner of the place was crowded with expectant listeners. On entering the pulpit Mr. Spurgeon informed his congregation that, although he had been only asked to give one sermon, it was his intention to deliver two. After a long and brilliant discourse in his own peculiarly forcible and impressive style, he paused for a few minutes, and then proceeded:—'And now for sermon number two—a plain practical sermon. Our friend who gave us the use of this building is a poor man. When I saw him this morning he wore a coat all in tatters; his shirt absolutely grinned at me through the holes. Let us show our appreciation of his kindness by buying him a new suit of clothes.' The suggestion was immediately adopted, and in the course of a few minutes some £10 or £12 were collected. On his return to London Mr. Spurgeon related the circumstance to some of his congregation, who testified their appreciation of the respect paid to their pastor by subscribing a further sum of £20 for the benefit of the Hertfordshire farmer. [109]

The days were strenuous, yet the exciting itinerant evangelistic ministry grew and reached many for Christ. Before long all Britain seemed open to the Gospel. Spurgeon's travels during this period are an epic in themselves. They will be examined in their evangelistic effectiveness in a later chapter.

Moreover, speaking to great crowds with their adulations did not consume all Spurgeon's interest or time. His deep concern for people could be extended individually as well as to the masses. Charles seemed compelled to speak upon spiritual matters to everyone with whom he came in personal contact. He felt all Christians should engage in personal witnessing. As he saw it, to neglect sharing one's faith made it more difficult for the church to win people. He observed:

Sometimes, I have found it less easy than it might otherwise have been to influence certain persons for good because of the neglect of those who ought to have done the work before me. As an instance, he shared the following experience: 'I was trying to say a word for my Master to a coachman, one day, when he said, to me, "Do you know the Rev. Mr. So-and-so?" 'Yes,' I replied; 'I know him very well; what have you to say about?' "Well," said the man, "he's the sort of minister I like and I like his religion very much." 'What sort of a religion is it?' I asked. "Why," he answered, "he has ridden on this box-seat every day for six months and he has never said anything about religion all the while; that's the kind of minister I like." It seemed to me a very doubtful compliment for a man who professed to be a servant of the Lord Jesus Christ. [110]

The young preacher always accommodated himself to the needs of any with whom he might speak. He seemed to know just how to deal with almost any type of individual. He once met a man who superficially agreed with all he said. When Charles spoke of the way of salvation the man readily agreed, although it became quite evident his heart had not been touched. So at last, feeling that it would be hopeless to continue the conversation, Spurgeon bluntly said, "The fact is, one of these days you will die and be damned."

During the days of Spurgeon's growing notoriety, he could not drive down the street without being recognized and hailed by the populace—rather heady notoriety for a young man! The tide really was turning in his favor. His itinerant ministry was making him a byword throughout Britain. Still, the outstanding aspect of this strenuous period of labor were the regular services at New Park Street Church. Policemen had to be there every Sunday to control crowds. People ran to get standing room, with at times a thousand turned away. With this dynamic ministry going on, the decision was wisely made in June of 1856 to return to Exeter Hall for at least evening services, while morning worship would still be held at the New Park Street Chapel. But, something very significant for Spurgeon happened before the return to Exeter Hall. That story must be told.

LOVE AND MARRIAGE

When Miss Susannah Thompson heard Charles on his first Sunday at New Park Street, as previously described, she was not particularly attracted to him or his preaching. Being a highly cultured, lovely London lady, Susannah looked at Charles in those early days as a "country bumpkin." She remarked:

> I was not at all fascinated by the young orator's eloquence, while his countrified manner and speech excited more regret than reverence . . . but the huge black satin stock, the long badly trimmed hair, and the blue pocket handkerchief with white spots . . . these attracted most of my attention and I fear awakened some feelings of amusement. [111]

Susannah said, "So this is his so-called eloquence! It does not impress me. What a painful countrified manner! Will he ever quit making flourishes with that terrible blue silk handkerchief! And his hair—why, he looks like a barber's assistant!"[112] The polka dot handkerchief and wild hair were just too much.

Susie, as affectionately called, lived with her parents who were members of New Park Street Baptist Church. At the time of Charles' call to London, they were not very active, having lost interest because of the declining attendance in the church. Susie's father had become a prosperous merchant, a ribbon manufacturer. She, being the only daughter, lived in quite cultured circumstances. Her background and Charles' differed, one would surmise, to the point of incompatibility. Susannah consented to hear Charles on that first Sunday night for only one reason; she said, "It would be a shame to have a man come so far and find the church so poorly attended." She apparently had little personal spiritual concern at the time, and surely no interest at all in Charles himself. Nonetheless, she had a quiet, sweet disposition. Though she found Charles not in the least attractive, that soon changed.

The Olneys first pointed out the qualities of Susannah to Charles. The Olneys and the Thompsons shared a close friendship. Susannah was an attractive young lady of 21, two years the senior of Charles. Of slight build, as one put it: "Had she weighed a pound more, she might have been a bit heavy; had she weighed a pound less, some might have thought her too slender." Beautiful long chestnut curls framed her oval face. Her fingers were slender and tapering, almost symbolic of her Victorian grace. A genuine smile lit up her bright hazel eyes. Early pictures show Susie to be a quite lovely young lady. Charles must have noticed; yet, at the beginning of their relationship, his only interest was to minister spiritually to the winsome young woman.

Susannah did not hold membership in the London church when Charles became pastor. The Olneys, concerned for her spiritual welfare, had communicated their concern to Charles. William Olney, old Thomas Olney's son, became a counselor to Susie before the marriage. He aided her significantly in her spiritual life. During the Spring of 1854, Charles and Susannah met several times in the Olney home. As Charles' ministry gained momentum, so did Susannah's spiritual development. She began regularly to hear Spurgeon preach. Soon she became deeply concerned about her relationship to Jesus Christ. She said, "Gradually I became alarmed at my back-sliding state and then, by a great effort, I sought spiritual help and guidance." [113] At that moment, Charles sent her a copy of his favored book *Pilgrim's Progress*—his first gift. On the fly leaf he inscribed: "Miss Thompson, with desires for the progress in the blessed pilgrimage. From C. H. Spurgeon, April 20, 1854." A little later she gave Charles her first gift to him, a complete set of John Calvin. That surely pleased him well. Spiritual concern dominated their interest at that stage. Susannah later said, "I don't think my beloved had at that time any other thought concerning me than to help a struggling soul heavenward . . . by degrees, though with much trembling, I told him of my state before God; and he gently led me, by his preaching, and by his conversations, through the power of the Holy Spirit to the cross of Christ for the peace and pardon my weary soul was longing for." [114]

But the friendship soon deepened. They began to see each other on a more social level. On June 10 of '54 they attended the opening of the gigantic Crystal Palace exhibition building at Sydenham—the Palace had been moved from its original site in Hyde Park. They sat side-by-side in the grandstand, chaperoned, of course. The Victorians would have expected that. As usual, Charles was reading a book. How Susie liked that is unrecorded, but one can imagine. Still, it took a most pleasant turn. The volume, not one of Charles' heavy Puritan works, was surprisingly a book of poetry on love and marriage, Martin Tupper's *Proverbial Philosophy*. He leaned over to Susie and had her read one or two lines: "Seek a good wife from thy God, for she is the best gift of His providence . . . Therefore think of her, and pray for her weal." Charles then looked at her affectionately and asked in a low, soft voice, "Do you pray for him who is to be *your* husband?" Susie blushed, dropped her eyes as her heart beat faster—probably Charles' pulse quickened somewhat too. He asked again softly, "Will you come and walk around the Palace with me?" They slipped away alone to stroll through the palms and flowers and exhibits of the beautiful Crystal Palace. Love began to blossom. Susie said, "During that walk on that memorable day in June, I believe God Himself united our hearts in indissoluble bonds of true affection, and, though we knew it not, gave us to each other forever." [115]

They found many occasions to be together. Both purchased season tickets to the Crystal Palace and romantically strolled there often. The Crystal Palace became a trysting place for many courtships. The magnificent building had a lovely "Fountain of Glass," a four ton cut crystal fountain. Someone described it as "like a splinter from an iceberg; it pours down an increasing stream of water with a delicious murmuring sound." One wonders how Charles and Susannah felt as they gazed at the sight, and then into each other's eyes. Susannah said in August, "loving looks, and tender tones and clasping hands, gave way to verbal confession!" Very Victorian! Two months later, on August 2, 1854, in the garden of her grandfather's house, Charles asked Susannah to be his wife. Her answer? Yes! The bride-to-be wrote of the beautiful moment:

> To me, it was a time as solemn as it was sweet; and with great awe in my heart I left my beloved, and hastening to the house and to an upper room I knelt before God and praised and thanked Him with happy tears for His great mercy in giving me the love of so good a man. [116]

Susie wrote again of that day in her diary, "It is impossible to write down all that occurred this morning. I can only adore in silence the wonder of my God, and praise Him for all his benefits." [117]

Charles, as his letters show, proved as eloquent in love as in preaching. They are charming epistles, as were Susie's to him. He once wrote her from Pompeii and said, "I send tons of love to you, hot as fresh lava." The Victorians had a way of writing such things.

Shortly thereafter Susie applied for church membership at New Park Street. She wrote out her testimony of faith to Charles, and he wrote back: "Oh! I could weep for joy (as I certainly am doing now) to think that my beloved can so well testify to a work of grace in her soul . . . Whatever befall us, trouble and adversity, sickness or death, we need not fear a final separation, either from each other or our God . . . I feel so deeply that I could only throw my arms around you and weep." [118] Charles baptized Miss Thompson, his "beloved," on February 1, 1855.

Not everything went perfectly smooth in the courtship, however. Charles preached up to twelve times every week, leaving little time for courtship. One particular week he preached fourteen times in six days. Charles wrote to Susannah in July of 1855 and declared, "Unless I go to the North Pole I never can get away from holy labours." On one occasion Charles took Susie to a large preaching service where he was to deliver the sermon. As soon as they arrived, Charles, totally preoccupied with his message and the service, forgot Susie. She had to fend for herself. She just left and went home alone. She flew into her house not a little upset. She confessed, "I *was* angry." Her mother tried to reassure her of Charles' love. When the young preacher came to himself after the service and realized he had forgotten his fiancée, he hurried to her Brixton home very apologetic. Charles came running into the house calling, "Where's Susie? I have been searching for her everywhere and cannot find her." Susie's mother told him the story; they reconciled and the romance flourished. But Susannah learned that her future husband, as God's servant, put Christ's service first and was becoming a famous man. Their life together would be very different from most nineteenth-century families. Even before they married, Charles would visit Susie every Monday and edit his Sunday sermon while she sat there in silence. A different courtship! Miss Thompson proved to be a remarkable young lady. In April of 1855, Susie accompanied Charles to Colchester to meet his parents. During the happy holiday, the parents "welcomed and petted" their future daughter-in-law.

Susannah now began to spend much time in the activities of New Park Street Chapel, and not only because of her interest in Charles. She had truly come into a real relationship with Jesus Christ. She learned to love the service of the Lord. As the "wall of Jericho"—the back wall of New Park Street—continued coming down, she alone collected £500 for the project, one-fourth of the total cost. And her love deepened in like proportion for the famous young preacher. Susannah quite naturally thrilled at Charles' popularity. Her heart went out to him as he labored under the strain of the Exeter Hall services. Often she wanted to reach out to him. She said:

> A glass of Chili vinegar always stood on a shelf under the desk before him, and I knew what to expect when he had recourse to that remedy. Oh, how my heart ached for him! What self-control I had to exercise to appear calm and collected and keep quietly in my seat up in that little side gallery! How I longed to have the *right* to go and comfort and cheer him when the service was over! But I had to walk away, as other people did,—I who belonged to him and was closer to his heart than anyone there! It was a severe discipline for a young and loving spirit. [119]

Charles faithfully corresponded with Susie when he traveled away from London. Spurgeon undertook a preaching mission to Scotland in July of 1855, his first long journey by train. In that sort of setting, he penned many beautiful letters.

In loving terms, he wrote to Susie:

> I have had daydreams of you while driving along. I thought you were very near me. It is not long, dearest, before I shall again enjoy your sweet society, if the providence of God permits. I knew I loved you very much before, but now I feel how necessary you are to me; and you will not lose much by my absence, if you find me, on my return, more attentive to your feelings, as well as equally affectionate. . . . My darling, accept love of the deepest and purest kind from one who is not prone to exaggerate, but who feels that there is no room for hyperbole. [120]

The courtship progressed happily along for nearly another year. The Thompson family moved from Brixton to Falcon Square in the city of London, thus the young couple were able to see each other more. On December 22, 1855, Charles sent Susannah a copy of his first full volume of published sermons, *The Pulpit Library*. He inscribed it saying, "In a few days it will be out of my power to present anything to *Miss* Thompson. Let this be a remembrance of our happy meetings and sweet conversations." In a few days they married.

THE WEDDING

Everyone agreed, the wedding was beautiful—a deep spiritual experience for all. Dr. Alexander Fletcher of Finsbury Chapel solemnized the ceremony on Tuesday, January 8, 1856, at the New Park Street Chapel. The day was dark, damp, and cold, but by 8:00 a.m. people started streaming in the chapel. The streets clogged up as happy guests made their way to Park Street. Special police from M-Division had to be sent to control the flow of the crowds. Within half an hour the chapel filled, with two thousand turned away who remained on the street to see the newlyweds depart. During the joyous service, the attenders sang the hymn "Salvation, O the Joyful Sound." The hundredth Psalm was read and followed by a short sermon. The vows were repeated and the pronouncement made; Charles and Susie became husband and wife. As they left the chapel, the crowds outside cheered loudly as the smiling couple drove away. In that day, God established one of the happiest homes in Victorian England. As Mrs. Charles Haddon Spurgeon expressed it, "God Himself united our hearts in indissoluble bonds of true affection and gave us to each other forever." She said she was "happy beyond words." [121]

The young couple made their way across the English Channel for twelve delightful honeymoon days in Paris, staying in the Hotel Meurue. They visited historic palaces, churches and museums. Susie spoke French very well, so no language problem hindered. Susie coined a term of endearment for Charles: "Tirshatha." The term is an ancient Persian word meaning "Your Reverence." She loved Charles deeply and always cherished a spiritual reverence for her preacher husband. Likewise, Susie was always to Charles: "Our angel and delight." He often addressed her as "Wifey," his term of endearment. Susie and her Tirshatha enjoyed a most happy honeymoon. The short days were soon over, but never forgotten. On the channel crossing back home, she whispered to Charles, "O Tirshatha, often before have I been in Paris, but this time it has been ten times as charming in my eyes, because you were with me." Their romance resembled the traditional Victorian tale of lavender and old lace, reminiscent of the Brownings of Wimpole Street.

When the happy couple returned to London from their honeymoon—the call of duty had to be answered—they enjoyed a public welcome by their church members. They moved into 217 New Kent Road, their new home. Charles was back in the pulpit on January 20th. A few years later they moved into their second home on Nightingale Lane near Clapham Common, southwest of New Park Street Chapel. A year and a half later, on September 20, 1857, their twin boys were born. Charles and Susie christened their boys Thomas and Charles. Some biographers have stated that Charles was preaching at New Park Street when the announcement of his sons' birth came to him. However, that is not true; September the 20th fell on Saturday and Spurgeon never preached on a Saturday in his entire life. He stayed home all day when the twins were born. When Charles sent out the birth announcement, he wrote a large 2 on the envelopes. Both boys became Baptist ministers; Thomas followed in his father's footsteps and became pastor of the Metropolitan Tabernacle at Charles' death—but more of that later.

An interesting anecdote is given by Susie when her twin boys were born:

> I make a passing reference to the birth of our twin-boys, in order to contradict emphatically a story, supposed to be very witty, which was circulated extensively, and believed in universally, not only at the time it was told, but through all the following years. It was said that my dear husband received the news of the addition to his household while he was preaching, and that he immediately communicated the fact to his congregation, adding in a serio-comic way,—
>
> > 'Not more than others I deserve,
> > But God has given me more.'
>
> I am sorry to say there are persons, still living, who declare that they were present at the service, and heard him say it!
>
> Now the truth is, that the boys were born on *Saturday* morning, September 20, 1856, and my dear husband never left the house that day; nor, so far as I know, did he ever preach on the seventh day at any time, so the statement at

once falls to the ground disproved. But I think I have discovered how the legend was manufactured. Looking through the sermons preached near to this date, I find that, on Thursday evening, September 25,—five days after the event referred to,—Mr. Spurgeon delivered a discourse on behalf of the Aged Pilgrims' Friend Society, and in the course of it made the following remarks:— 'When we take our walks abroad, and see the poor, he must be a very thankless Christian who does not lift up his eyes to Heaven, and praise his God thus,—

> 'Not more than others I deserve,
> But God has given me more.'

If we were all made rich alike, if God had given us all abundance, we should never know the value of His mercies; but He puts the poor side by side with us, to make their trials, like a dark shadow, set forth the brightness which He is pleased to give to others in temporal matters.'

I have no doubt that some facetious individual, present at this Thursday evening service, and being aware of the babies' advent, on hearing these lines repeated, pounced upon them as the nucleus of an attractive story, liked the two facts in his own mind, and then proclaimed them to the world as an undivided verity! Most of the stories told of my dear husband's jocoseness *in the pulpit* were "stories" in the severe sense of the word; or possessed just so small a modicum of truth internally that the narrators were able, by weaving a network of exaggeration and romance around them, to make a very presentable and alluring fiction. It was one of the penalties of his unique position and gifts that, all through his life, he had to bear the cross of cruel misrepresentation and injustice. Thank God, that is all left behind for ever!

Though I am quite certain that the lines in question were not quoted by my beloved in public in reference to the double blessing God gave to us, I should scarcely be surprised if he made use of them when speaking to friends in private. If his heart were full of joy and gratitude, it would be sure to bubble over in some child-like and natural fashion. I have quite recently received a letter from a lady in the country, telling me of her visit to an old man,—an ex-policeman, named Coleman,—who, though bedridden, never tires of relating his memories of Mr. Spurgeon in those early days. He was stationed at New Park Street Chapel, on special duty, when the crowds came to hear 'the boy-preacher,' and he delights to tell how, after a short while, the street became so blocked that the chapel-gates had to be closed, and the people admitted a hundred at a time. 'Ah!' said he, 'he was a dear, good young man, he did not make *himself* anything; he would shake hands with anyone, he would give me such a grip, and leave half-a-crown in my hand; he knew that we policemen had a rub to get along on our pay. I know there were many he helped with their rent. He did look pleased, that Sunday morning, when he said, 'Coleman, what do you think? God has blessed me with two sons!' I used to go in and sit just inside the door, and get a feast for my soul from his discourses. I shall see him again soon, I hope.

Of course, this little story lacks the piquancy and sparkle of the former one; but it has the advantage of being *true*. [122]

HOME LIFE FOR THE SPURGEONS

Susie missed her husband as he carried on his itinerant ministries. Spurgeon's constant absences from the home proved something of a trial to his young wife. Many times, as she would be sitting up late at night waiting for Charles, she would pace up and down the hallway, praying that he might soon come home safely. A thrill of joy always shot through her heart when she heard him coming up to the door.

Only once did she really break down when Charles left for a distant preaching engagement. She just could not keep back the tears. Charles said, "Wifey, do you think that when any of the children of Israel brought a lamb to the Lord's altar as an offering to Him, they stood and wept over it when they had seen it laid there?" Susie replied, "Of course not." Charles went on tenderly, "Well, don't you see, you are giving me to God in letting me go to preach the Gospel to poor sinners, and do you think he likes to see you cry over your sacrifice?" Susie commented later, "Could ever a rebuke have been more sweetly given? It sank deep into my heart, carrying comfort; and thence-forward when I part with him, the tears were scarcely ever allowed to show themselves, or if a stray one or two dared to run over the boundaries, he would say, 'What! Crying over your lamb, Wifey!' And this reminder would quickly dry them up and put a smile in their place." [123]

Finances proved a problem at times because Charles gave so much to various needs. His generosity at times exceeded his resources. He once needed to pay some taxes and had no funds. But they were a couple with great faith. They prayed and right at the moment an anonymous letter arrived containing £20. Their faith was honored and their needs were met.

Mrs. Spurgeon tells an interesting event that occurred later in their life. Spurgeon did much of his sermon preparation for Sunday morning on Saturday evening. One particular Saturday night he just could not seemingly put his text and his thoughts together. He read the commentaries, but things simply did not come together. Susie told the rest of the story:

> He sat up very late and was utterly worn out and dispirited, for all his efforts to get at the heart of the text were unavailing. I advised him to retire to rest and soothed him by suggesting that if he would try to sleep then he would probably in the morning feel quite refreshed and be able to study to better purpose. 'If I go to sleep now, Wifey, will you wake me very early so that I may have plenty of time to prepare?' With my loving assurance that I would watch the time for him and call him soon enough he was satisfied; and like a trusting, tired child, he laid his head upon the pillow and slept silently and sweetly at once.

By-and-by a wonderful thing happened. During the first opening hours of the Sabbath, I heard him talking in his sleep, and aroused myself to listen attentively. Soon I realized that he was going over the subject of the verse which had been so obscure to him, and was giving a clear and distinct exposition of its meaning with much force and freshness. I set myself with almost trembling joy to understand and follow all that he was saying, for I knew that if I could but seize and remember the salient points of the discourse he would have no difficulty in developing and enlarging upon them. Never a preacher had a more eager and anxious hearer! But what if I should let the precious word slip? I had no means at hand of 'taking notes' so, like Nehemiah, 'I prayed to the God of heaven,' and asked that I might receive and retain the thoughts which he had given to his servant in his sleep, and which were so singularly entrusted into my keeping. As I lay repeating over and over again the chief points I wished to remember, my happiness was very great in an anticipation of his surprise and delight on awakening; but I had kept vigil so long, cherishing my joy, that I must have been overcome with slumber just when the usual time for rising came, for he awoke with a frightened start, and seeing the telltale clock, set, 'Oh, Wifey, you said you would wake me very early, and now see the time! Oh, why did you let me sleep? What shall I do? What shall I do?' 'Listen, beloved,' I answered; and I told him all I had heard. 'Why! That's just what I wanted,' he exclaimed; 'that is the true explanation of the whole verse! And you say I preached it in my sleep?' 'It is wonderful,' he repeated again and again, and we both praised the Lord for so remarkable a manifestation of His power and love. [124]

Many such happy anecdotes occurred in the marriage of Charles and Susie.

The Spurgeons' first home on Nightingale Lane in Clapham was a modest home. It was pulled down in 1869 to make way for a larger home on the same spot, which can still be seen today. [125] The contented couple named both their Nightingale Lane houses "Helensburgh House." As mentioned, in July of 1855, Charles had engaged in a very successful preaching tour through Scotland, being invited there by his friend, the Rev. John Anderson of Helensburgh (a town twenty-four miles northwest of Glasgow). The town became Spurgeon's base during the tour. Biographers differ as to whether or not Charles and Susie named their London house after the Scottish town. He may have done so, for Spurgeon, as often seen, loved God's natural world, and Helensburgh was a lovely spot. At Aberfeldy, on his 1855 Scottish trip, Charles became so overwhelmed with the beauty of the land that he clapped his hands for joy at the glory of God in creation.

The happy couple delighted in their Helensburgh House. Mrs. Spurgeon described it:

The house was a very old one; and, in its first estate, I should judge it had been an eight-roomed cottage, with underground cellars afterwards turned into kitchens. Some bygone owner had built another story, and thrown the eight small rooms into four better-sized ones; but, even with this improvement, they were narrow and incommodious. To us, however, they were then all that we could desire, and the large garden made up for all the inconveniences indoors. Oh, what a delightsome place we thought it, though it was a very wilderness through long neglect,—the blackberry bushes impertinently asserting themselves to be trees, and the fruit trees running wild for want of the pruning-knife! It was all the more interesting to us in this sweet confusion and artlessness because we had the happy task of bringing it gradually into accord with our ideas of what a garden should be. I must admit that we made many absurd mistakes both in house and garden management, in those young days of ours; but what did that matter? No two birds ever felt more exquisite joy in building their nest in the fork of a tree-branch, than did we in planning and placing, altering and rearranging our pretty country home.

What a boon such a retreat was to my beloved, can be well understood by all zealous workers who know the penalties exacted by weary brains and jaded powers. At this time, Mr. Spurgeon's sermons were having a phenomenal sale both at home and abroad, and the generous arrangements of the publishers, together with the increased income from the church, made possible the purchase of the freehold of this house and grounds; and the fact of the place being old and long untenanted, enabled him to obtain it on very easy terms. It had some queer corners in it, which we peopled with mysterious shadows for the mere gratification of afterwards dispersing them. A large brewhouse sort of erection at the side was a great puzzle to us, with its flagged floor, its great boiler in one corner, and its curious little rooms, like cells, which we converted into apple-chambers.

But the sensation of the place was the well, which altogether fascinated us, and did not withdraw its spell till the demolition of the old house broke the charm by covering it up entirely, and leaving only a common pump-handle 'en evidence.' It was a wonderful well; the water came up pure, sparkling, and cold as ice. The story of it was, as far as I can recollect, as follows:—A former occupant of the house had resolved, at any cost, to have water at that particular spot. So he hired well-diggers, and they began to dig. At one hundred feet depth, they stopped. There was no sign of water. 'Go on,' said the master; 'you must go deeper.' They dug another two hundred feet, and came to the solid rock! 'Now,' said he, 'you must bore, for I am going to have water here if I bore to the centre of the earth for it.' So they bored, and bored, and got quite disheartened, for they had now gone 460 feet into the bowels of the earth! But the master insisted that they should continue their efforts; and, one day, they came up as usual to have their dinner, but they never went down to the rock again, for the water had burst through, and covered up their tools, and risen high in the well! Was not the man right glad that he had not relinquished his object, and was he not well rewarded for his perseverance? He was a benefactor to succeeding generations, too, for the delicious water had quite a fame round about the place, and residents in our time used to send and beg the favour of a large jugful of 'water from the well.' [126]

The couple loved animals, as do most Britishers. Charles had a huge cat named "Dick" which weighed twenty-one pounds. Their faithful dog was called "Punch." Later, the Spurgeons moved to a lovely, large home in Norwood, south London. They named it "Westwood." It was a beautiful structure. It is demolished now, but the street on which it sat is called Spurgeon Street.

An interesting event occurred at Helensburgh House in the early years of their marriage. Toward the end of the year 1858, Spurgeon was at home with a quite serious illness, the first long confinement of ill health that he endured. John Ruskin, the famous author, visited them. In those days, Ruskin often worshiped at the Surrey Gardens Music Hall where Spurgeon preached and had become a very close friend of the great preacher. When he came into Spurgeon's home and saw how ill his friend actually was, Ruskin cried out with tears, "My dear brother, my dear brother, how grieved I am to see you thus!" [127]

On one occasion, Ruskin related to Spurgeon a very unusual and remarkable story. Ruskin himself vowed to the validity of the event. They had been talking together about God's providence and His care for His people and the miraculous deliverances that He sometimes grants in times of danger. Ruskin told of a certain Christian man, a widower, with several children, who had purchased or rented an old farmhouse in the country. He desired that the children should have a better place for their growth and development. Before moving in, he took the children out to see the new home. While talking to the real estate agent, the children ran off on a self-conducted inspection tour of the new place. They ran here and there and everywhere, all over the house and the grounds. Full of fun and frolic, they inspected their future home. When they had completely gone through all the rooms of the home and much of the grounds, they decided they must see under the structure. So they went helter skelter in search of finding the basement. They soon found a door at the head of some dark stairs, and were rushing down at great speed when they suddenly were arrested in startled amazement. Standing at the bottom of the steps they saw their mother with outstretched arms waving them back and silently forbidding their further passage. One can imagine, with fear and yet joy, they turned and fled upstairs to their father telling him that they had seen mother. They cried that she had been smiling lovingly at them but had eagerly motioned them to go back. In absolute astonishment the father listened to the children's account and of course realized that something most unusual had happened. He immediately went to investigate. At the far end of the narrow, gloomy stairs, he found a deep, open well. Unquestionably the children in their mad dash down the stairs would have fallen into the well and no doubt perished. The Lord and His mercy had interposed. Spurgeon, not given to unscriptural mystical experiences, placed little worth on supernatural accounts that had no basis in the Bible. In this particular case, however, both Spurgeon and Ruskin were convinced that

God had permitted the appearance of their mother in order to save the children from certain catastrophe. Perhaps nothing less than such a vision could have prevented the calamity.

The Spurgeons had some incredible visits in their home. They are stories in themselves. The couple, always most hospitable, often entertained exciting guests. The sum of it is, the delightfully happy family maintained a happy, open home.

THE SCOTTISH TOUR

On Spurgeon's July 1855 preaching tour of Scotland, when he preached in Glasgow, before the stated hour of the services, the churches in which he preached filled while thousands of anxious worshipers found it impossible to be seated. In a lengthy article, the *Glasgow Examiner* reported:

> He has appeared amongst us, and the London verdict has been fully confirmed by immense audiences, that have been eagerly spellbound by his oratory. According to reports, he indulged somewhat freely in the out of the way expressions on the first Sabbath of his sojourn in the city; but such was not the case last Sabbath, and the last Sabbath's discourse was still more fascinating and attractive. . . . There is the ready, acute perception which never fails to bring out fresh and striking illustrations from any text on which the attention is directed. Again, there is an extensive acquaintance with literature, which, by the aid of a retentive memory, can at a moment's notice furnish the speaker with choice and appropriate material. And lastly, there is the power of voice, the volubility of utterance, which enabled him to get on with great ease, and at the same time to give powerful effect to his sentiments. [128]

The impact Spurgeon made in Scotland stands as something of a parallel to the tremendous ministry of George Whitefield in Cambuslang, a suburb of Glasgow, when the great eighteenth century revival spread all over the north country. As the writer in another paper, *The Glasgow Daily Bulletin*, said, "Spurgeon owes his celebrity to the possession of first class oratorical gifts, which seem to have attained maturity and development at a very early age, so that he has established a reputation at a period of life early from that which ordinary men enter upon a profession." [129] Moreover, it must be remembered that Spurgeon had only been a Christian five years at the time. High praise for a twenty-one-year-old man! God blessed the ministry more and more as Spurgeon traveled and preached.

Part II:
The Later New Park Street Ministry

Introduction

Spurgeon's first year and a half in London had passed. He had married, had become the veritable talk of the town, and had seen hundreds come to faith in Jesus Christ. Now the course was set as he moved into his expanding ministry.

THE SECOND EXETER HALL MINISTRY

On June 8th, 1856, Spurgeon launched the second series of services of Exeter Hall. The multitudes wanting to hear him demanded the move, although they still held the morning services at the New Park Street Chapel. The crowds at Exeter were even greater on the second venture than at the first invasion of the large auditorium. Spurgeon marvelled at the people's hunger to hear the Word. He said:

> Dear me, how little satisfied the crowd! What are other preachers up to, when, with ten times the talent they are snoring along with prosy sermons and sending the world away? The reason is, I believe, they do not know what the Gospel is. [130]

It became evident that a more commodious building was absolutely necessary for Charles' ministry. Not only that, the owners of Exeter Hall let it be known that they could not rent the Hall on any long-term continuous basis to only one denomination. The days at Exeter Hall were thus numbered. Meanwhile, Charles had received a gift from a friend on his 21st birthday with this note: "I would much enjoy the thought of being the first contributor toward the purchase of a hall, or the building of a tabernacle which would accommodate as many hundred as our chapel now holds scores." This note planted a seed of faith; the dream of the Metropolitan Tabernacle began to take shape.

However, the building of such a tabernacle remained some years away. What to do at the moment? New Park Street Chapel proved grossly inadequate, and Exeter Hall would soon close its doors. The solution the church leaders came up with seemed incredible to the Victorian mind-set.

THE SURREY GARDENS MUSIC HALL MINISTRY

A new concert hall had just been built in the Royal Surrey Gardens, a public park south of the Thames River that boasted spacious lawns, a zoo, picnic areas, a lake, and similar amenities. Large fireworks displays delighted the visitors; even a huge sea turtle that children could ride lumbered about the grounds. The new Hall, the Surrey Gardens Music Hall, could accommodate more than ten thousand people. It was the most commodious and beautiful building for public amusement in the city, save the Crystal Palace. Mr. M. Jullian, the musical conductor of the Hall, on one occasion attracted as many as thirteen thousand for a concert. Someone conceived the idea that Spurgeon could use it for preaching. Objections by the traditional Victorians were, of course, raised from every corner. That would be "worldly," some criticized. Others cautioned it might be dangerous for such a large crowd to gather for a religious service. One of Charles' own deacons pleaded with him not to preach in "that devil's house." But Spurgeon replied, "We did not go to the music-hall because we thought it was a good thing to worship in a building usually devoted to amusement, but because we had no other place to go to." [131] Some even thought Spurgeon could not fill it. Being a place of secular amusement, many said it would never be suited for divine worship. "Preposterous," cried some people.

By this time Spurgeon had grown immune to cruel criticism, attacks and outmoded traditionalism. He well realized, as he said, "The tears of affliction are often needed to keep the eye of faith bright." [132] Along with the Deacon Olney, he surveyed the building and his eye of faith beamed brightly—he thought it ideal for his purposes. The deacons agreed and the decision came down: to the Music Hall they would go. The news immediately spread all over London. Surrey Gardens Music Hall would become host to Spurgeon and his New Park Street Baptist Church! That was as rash a move as London could grapple with. As one put it, "In the squares, the streets, the lanes, the alleys, as well as in the workshops and country houses, and all the chief places of concourse, it has been, through each successive day, the one great object of thought and converse." [133] The evening of Sunday, October 19, 1856 would see the first service. To sense how revolutionary this idea was for Victorian London, Spurgeon's friend Dr. Campbell remarked:

> Ecclesiastically viewed, Sunday last was one of the most eventful nights that have descended on the metropolis for generations. On that occasion the largest most commodious and most beautiful building erected for public amusement in this mighty city was taken possession of for the purpose of proclaiming the gospel of salvation. There, where for a long period wild beasts had been exhibited, and wilder men had been accustomed to congregate, in countless

multitudes, for idle pastime, was gathered together the largest audience that ever met in any edifice in these Isles to listen to the voice of a Nonconformist minister. [134]

Unfortunately, it became a day of infamy.

THE TRAGEDY

Before the opening day at the Music Hall, Spurgeon had a strange, subtle uneasiness. He said, "I felt over-weighted with a sense of responsibility, and filled with a mysterious premonition of some great trial shortly to befall me." [135] When Sunday afternoon came, the streets near the Surrey Gardens Music Hall soon filled with people. Ten to twelve thousand eager worshipers squeezed into the Hall when the doors opened at 6:00 p.m. Another ten thousand milled about outside unable to get in. The entire area looked like a surging sea of faces. When Spurgeon arrived, the sight of the mass of humanity at first unnerved him. Campbell was right, the largest crowd ever gathered under a roof to hear a Nonconformist preacher had assembled. Spurgeon took the pulpit ten minutes before the stated hour, composed himself, and began the service.

After a few words of greeting came a prayer and a hymn. Then, in his usual style, Spurgeon read the Scriptures with a running commentary. He always did this in his New Park Street services; it was a common procedure in many Nonconformist churches. The congregation sang another hymn and Spurgeon began his long prayer. After the "Amen" *it happened.* "Fire! Fire! Fire! The galleries are giving way! The place is falling! The place is falling!" came shouts from several areas in the vast crowd. Pandemonium broke loose. A terrible panic ensued as people fled from all over the building. They trod upon each other, crushed one another, jumped over the rail of the galleries, while the banisters of one of the stairs gave way and many were trampled over. An eye witness described the mad scene:

> The cries and shrieks at this period were truly terrific, to which was added the already pent-up excitement of those who had not been able to make their exit. They pressed on, treading furiously over the dead and dying, tearing frantically at each other. Hundreds had their clothes torn from their backs in their endeavors to escape; masses of men and women were driven down and trodden over heedless of their cries and lamentations. [136]

As people in panic exploded from the Hall, the thousands outside struggled to get in. A wild scene erupted.

Spurgeon sprang to his feet attempting to quell the crowds. There was no fire, no collapsing galleries, or any real problem at all. "Please be seated," he cried. "There is no cause for alarm! Please be seated!" His resonant voice boomed over the din and almost miraculously the people composed themselves and began to settle down as they sang a hymn. Spurgeon wanted to dismiss the service immediately, even though he did not know that a real tragedy had occurred. The remaining people shouted, "Preach! Preach!" Charles attempted to do so; he did not realize anyone had been seriously injured in the pandemonium. Then a second series of cries went up. This time order was restored quickly and Charles took his text from Proverbs 3:33, "The curse of the Lord is in the house of the wicked: but he blesseth the habitation of the just." He probably thought the new text would help the general situation and speak directly to it. But it proved to be a blunder, for now some panicked anew at the thought of judgment and joined the mob at the rear still fighting to get out, or in. He spoke a few words, the hymn "His Sovereign Power Without Our Aid" was sung, and he dismissed the crowd. There were shouts until the service concluded. Charles said to the crowd, "My brain is in a whirl, and I scarcely know where I am, so great are my apprehensions that many persons must have been injured by rushing out. I would rather that you retired gradually and may God Almighty dismiss you with His blessings and carry you in safety to your home!" Sensing now that something serious must have happened, although he knew nothing of the extent of the tragedy, Charles was hurried out by friends almost in a faint.

Something truly terrible *had* happened. Seven people were dead and twenty-eight had been taken to a local hospital seriously injured. With care, friends led Charles out through a back passage so he would not see the seven corpses laid out on the ground. He did not realize anyone had died. He was graciously ushered to a friend's house in Croydon, south London, that he might escape the volcanic furor bound to erupt over him. The papers had already virtually crucified him—what would they say now? Later the grisly facts were revealed to Charles and upon hearing the devastating news, he virtually collapsed. It looked like a permanent collapse. Emotionally prostrated, he pined away in deep depression.

The next day, a man saw Spurgeon being helped from a carriage at Croydon and said, "It's Mr. Spurgeon, isn't it? It must be his ghost, for last night I saw him carried out dead from The Surrey Gardens Music Hall." [137] Rumors of that nature spread all over London.

Charles became so seriously depressed over the tragedy that he almost wished himself dead. The thought that he had in some sense occasioned the death and injury of several people absolutely devastated him. In Spurgeon's first book, *The Saint and His Saviour*, he described his agony:

> Strong amid danger, I battled against the storm; nor did my spirit yield to the overwhelming pressure while my courage could reassure the wavering, or confirm the bold; but when, like a whirlwind, the destruction was overpast, when the whole of its devastation was visible to my eye, who can conceive the anguish of my sad spirit? I refused to be comforted; tears were my meat by day, and dreams my terror by night. I felt as I had never felt before. 'My

thoughts were all a case of knives,' cutting my heart in pieces, until a kind of stupor of grief ministered a mournful medicine to me. I could have truly said, 'I am not mad, but surely I have had enough to madden me, if I should indulge in meditation on it.' I sought and found a solitude which seemed congenial to me. I could tell my griefs to the flowers, and the dews could weep with me. Here my mind lay, like a wreck upon the sand, incapable of its usual motion. I was in a strange land, and a stranger in it. My Bible, once my daily food, was but a hand to lift the sluices of my woe. Prayer yielded no balm to me; in fact, my soul was like an infant's soul, and I could not rise to the dignity of supplication. 'Broke in pieces all asunder,' my thoughts which had been to me a cup of delights, were like pieces of broken glass, the piercing and cutting miseries of my pilgrimage. . . . There came the 'slander of many'—bare faced fabrications, libellous slanders, and barbarous accusations. These alone might have scooped out the last drop of consolation from my cup of happiness, but the worst had come to the worst, and the utmost knowledge of the enemy could do no more. [138]

Yet he was alive, but what the tragedy itself did not do to prostrate him emotionally, as he himself said, the press finished. The newspapers went after him unmercifully. And his new twin boys were only one month old.

The next morning, October 20, 1856, *Daily Telegraph*, perhaps the bitterest of all, reported:

Mr. Spurgeon is a preacher who hurls damnation at the heads of his sinful hearers. Some men there are who, taking their precepts from Holy Writ, would beckon erring souls to a rightful path with fair words and gentle admonition; Mr. Spurgeon would take them by the nose, and bully them into religion. Let us set up a barrier to the encroachments and blasphemies of men like Spurgeon, saying to them, 'Thus far shalt thou come, but no further;' let us devise some powerful means which shall tell to the thousands who now stand in need of enlightenment,—This man, in his own opinion, is a righteous Christian; but in ours, nothing more that a ranting charlatan. We are neither strait-laced nor Sabbatarian in our sentiments; but we would keep apart, widely apart, the theatre and the church;—above all, we would place in the hand of every right-thinking man, a whip to scourge from society the authors of such vile blasphemies as, on Sunday night, above the cries of the dead and the dying, and louder than the wails of misery from the maimed and suffering, resounded from the mouth of Spurgeon in the music-hall of the Surrey Gardens. And lastly, when the mangled corpses had been carried away from the unhallowed and disgraceful scene—when husbands were seeking their wives, and children their mothers in extreme agony and despair—the chink of the money as it fell into the collection-boxes grated harshly, miserably on the ears of those who, we sincerely hope, have by this time conceived for Mr. Spurgeon and his rantings the profoundest contempt.

The *Daily News*, every bit as critical as the *Daily Telegraph*, reported:

> The crowd had been assembled to collect a subscription toward the erection of such a mammoth chapel (the proposed Tabernacle), and Mr. Spurgeon and his friends were unwilling that the opportunity should be lost. Therefore his intumesce reminder; therefore Mr. Spurgeon's exclamation to the panic-stricken fugitives that they were more afraid of temporal than eternal death; therefore the indecent rattling of money-boxes in their ears. We might go further and remark on the callous manner in which Mr. Spurgeon and his friends left the meeting, without one attempt to aid or soothe the sufferers; but we are willing to make allowance for the bewilderment which such a spectacle was calculated to produce.

At the end of the week (Saturday the 25th), as might be expected, the *Saturday Review* printed a long article. The writer compared Spurgeon with Joseph Smith, the Mormon prophet. It said Charles' preaching could be compared to spirit-rapping. His success, said the writer, "is simply of the vulgarest and most commonplace type. Given a person of some natural talents with matchless powers of acquired impudence, and a daring defiance of good taste and often of common decency—and he will always produce an effect. Anybody who will give himself out as some great one, will find followers enough to accept his leadership. A charlatan will never be without dupes. The crowds who flock to the various Spurgeon conventicles are only of the class who would follow the bottle conjuror, or anyone who chose to advertise that he would fly from the Monument to the dome of St. Paul's." The article then called Spurgeon "a very ordinary impostor," and suggested Sunday bands should be set playing so that there might be "a chance of thinning the crowds." The innovation, the writer argued, would "only be the substitution of one set of amusements for another." Exaggerations, blame, and all the criticism that could be conjured up was laid on Charles. Not all the papers were so demeaning, however. In a Monday evening paper, *The Sun*, the journalist wrote:

> We have inquired of respectable persons who were present, and they inform us, up to the moment, during the prayer, when the bell was heard to tinkle, and the cry of 'Fire!' was raised, no worship they ever attended was conducted with more solemnity and decorum; that the singing of a hymn by so many thousands of persons, in so vast a building, was peculiarly impressive; and that but for the intentional disturbance, the effect of the whole must have been all that could be desired. We hardly think anyone can be held responsible for not conjecturing that any even of the lowest roughs and rowdies could be found wicked enough to hazard the lives of so many persons, however willing they might have been to annoy one whom they, of course, judged a fanatical preacher. [139]

After a period of time, fortunately, most of the papers took a more objective stance and stated Spurgeon could not be held responsible for the tragedy.

Spurgeon's friends, of course, shielded him from full knowledge of the poisoned pens. The deacons and church were very sympathetic and understood Spurgeon's innocence. On Monday evening at a meeting at New Park Street Chapel, Mr. Moore, one of the deacons, reported:

> With reference to the origin of the alarm, there is no doubt that it originated from wicked designing men. Oh, that dreadful scene! You are anxious to hear about our poor pastor—he is very bad. Very bad I say, not from any injuries or bruises he has received, but from the extreme tension on his nerves, and his great anxiety. So bad is he that we were fearful for his mind this morning. Under these circumstances, only one thing could be done—that is, to send him into the country away from the scene. As we knew that a great number of persons would call at his house during the day, we sent him early this morning, so that none of his engagements can be entered into this week. From information I have just received I am enabled to tell you that to-night he is a little better, but still very prostrate. Mr. Olney (another deacon) is still in bed. Let us be more merciful to our enemies of last night than they were to us. That wicked wretch—that man whom we are justified in calling a miscreant—who first gave the dreadful signal by which so much life was lost—let us even pray for him. Who knows but that he may one day stand in this room and own his great crime, and seek for repentance? [140]

Charles and Susie went to stay at the home of church members in Croydon, hoping the isolation would help. He nevertheless spent many days in serious depression until even his wife felt that he would lose his grip on reality and never recover. There seemed no light at the end of his dark tunnel.

Nonetheless, God stood in final control, the press and the cruel critics notwithstanding. One day, strolling very forlornly in his friend's garden with Susannah, weeping with the dew, suddenly God's gracious Spirit flashed a Bible passage into Charles' sad, depressed heart, "Wherefore God also hath highly exalted Him, and given Him a name which is above every name: that at the name of Jesus every knee should bow, of things in Heaven, and things in earth, and things under the earth; and that every tongue should confess that Jesus Christ is Lord, to the glory of God the Father" (Philippians 2:9-11). Charles then reasoned within himself, "If Christ be exalted, let Him do as He pleases with me; my one prayer shall be that I may die to self and live wholly for Him and for His honor." [141]

The Word of God thundered into his depressed soul. He suddenly stopped and turning to his wife with the old light once again in his eyes, he exclaimed: "Dearest, how foolish I have been! Why! What does it matter what becomes of me if the Lord shall but be glorified?" This sudden realization burst like light and joy into his anguished spirit. It was almost like a second experience of conversion. He said:

Like a flash of lightning from the sky, my soul returned unto me. The burning lava of my brain cooled in an instant. The throbbings of my brow were still; the cool wind of comfort fanned my cheek, which had been scorched in the furnace. I was free, the iron fetter was broken in pieces, my prison door was open, and I leaped for joy of heart. On wings of a dove, my spirit mounted to the stars—yea, beyond them. Whither did it wing its flight, and where did it sing its song of gratitude? It was at the feet of Jesus, whose Name had charmed its fears, and placed an end to its mourning. The Name—the precious Name of Jesus, was like Ithuriel's spear, bringing back my soul to its own right and happy state. I was a man again, and what is more, a believer. The garden in which I stood became an Eden to me, and the spot was then most solemnly consecrated in my restored consciousness. Happy Hour! Thrice-blessed Lord, who thus in an instant delivered me from the rock of my despair, and slew the vulture of my grief! Before I told to others the glad news of my recovery, my heart was melodious with song, and my tongue tardily to express the music. Then did I give to my Well-beloved a song touching my Well-beloved; and, oh! with what rapture did my soul flash forth its praises! But all—all were to the honor of Him, the First and the Last, the Brother born for adversity, the Deliverer of the captive, the Breaker of my fetters, the Restorer of my soul. Then did I cast my burden upon the Lord; I left my ashes, and arrayed myself in the garments of praise, while He anointed me with fresh oil. I could have riven the very firmament to get at Him, to cast myself at His feet, and lie there bathed in the tears of joy and love. Never since the day of my conversion had I known so much of His infinite excellence, never had my spirit leaped with such unutterable delight. Scorn, tumult, and woe seemed less than nether for His sake. I girded up my loins to run before His Chariot, I began to shout forth His glory, for my soul was absorbed in the one idea of His glorious exaltation and Divine compassion.[142]

The mist had cleared; the sunshine of God's grace shone into the very depth of his heart and mind. He saw, as never before, it mattered not what happened to Charles Haddon Spurgeon so long as Jesus Christ was exalted.

So, with an interval of only one Sunday out of his pulpit, Dr. Alexander Fletcher supplying the Park Street Church that Lord's Day, Charles went back to his preaching. On November 2nd he again declared the glorious Gospel of Christ. He preached on Philippians 2:9, "Wherefore God also hath highly exalted him, and given him a name which is above every name." In the sermon Spurgeon said:

Now, my dear friends, I almost regret this morning that I occupy this pulpit. I regret it because I feel utterly unable to preach to you to your profit. I have thought during the period of relaxation I have had since that terrible catastrophe which has befallen us, that I had thoroughly recovered; but on coming back to this spot again I feel somewhat of the same feelings which prostrated me before. You will therefore excuse me this morning if I make no allusion, or scarcely any at all, to recent circumstances; for were I to enter into the subject, and to bring to your remembrance that solemn scene, I should speedily be forced to be silent. . . I may say, however, dear brethren, that we shall not be daunted at what has taken place; and I shall preach again in that place yet! God shall give us souls there, and Satan's empire shall tremble more yet; for I believe that God is with us, and who is he that can be against us? [143]

Two Sundays later, on November 23, 1856, Spurgeon went back to the Hall. The Surrey Gardens Music Hall heard his melodious voice again. He said, "It shall not stay us. . . Satan's empire shall tremble more than ever. God is with us; who is he that shall be against us." [144]

Spurgeon held services in the Hall for three years, until December 11, 1859 when he preached on Paul's farewell address to the Ephesian elders from Acts 20. Thousands were converted in the Music Hall ministry.

Some most interesting—and humorous—events took place at the Music Hall. Ellis relates one such event:

One day, three young men entered the Surrey Gardens Music Hall when Mr. Spurgeon was preaching there, and seated themselves in a conspicuous position, with their hats on. The officials requested them to take off their hats, but they refused to do so. Presently, Mr. Spurgeon caught sight of them, and led his discourse round to show the respect which all are bound to show to the feelings and usages of others. 'The other day,' said he, 'I went into a Jewish synagogue, and I naturally uncovered my head, but on looking round I perceived that all the rest wore their hats, and so, not wishing to offend against what I supposed to be their reverent practice, though contrary to my own, I conformed to the Jewish use, and put on my hat. I will now ask those three young Jews up in the gallery to show the same deference to our Christian practice in the House of God as I was prepared to show them when I visited their synagogue, and take off their hats.' Of course, after this kind and sensible appeal, they could do no other than comply. [145]

The tragedy, however, did something to Spurgeon he never quite overcame. He called it "the most memorable crisis of my life." Up to that time he enjoyed reasonably robust health, but after 1856, illness seemed to plague him regularly. His first protracted, serious confinement befell him in 1858 when he could not preach from October 10th to November 7th. He struggled with his health the rest of his days. In it all, especially during the terribly depressing time immediately following the Surrey Gardens Music Hall tragedy, his wife stood by his side as his great comforter. Charles said of his Susie, "My own most dear and tender wife has often been as an angel of God to me. Blessed may she be among women. She has been to me God's best earthly gift." From the human perspective, she probably kept his sanity. Spurgeon possessed an extremely sensitive spirit, and the Surrey Gardens tragedy could never be erased from his mind. Through the years, whenever a large crowd assembled to hear him, the infamous day would seemingly come forth with fresh vigor to plague his spirit. Even the verse of Scripture from which he preached on that occasion (Proverbs 3:33) revived the depressing memory. He would turn pale on hearing it. Eighteen months after the tragic day at Surrey Gardens, he preached in Halifax. A large wooden building, hastily constructed for his preaching, collapsed under a weight of snow the morning after he conducted the service. Another tragedy had been narrowly averted. Charles, deeply shaken, vowed that if lives again had been lost, he would preach no more. Twenty-five years later, Rev. R. Shindler tells of an event when Spurgeon was to preach to a very large group in Portsmouth. Some confusion in the crowd arose and immediately the Surrey Gardens Music Hall tragedy flashed in his mind like a bolt of lightning. He stood leaning his head on his hand. He could never escape the scene at the Music Hall. Yet, being a truly committed man of God, he carried on as a valiant soldier of the cross and his ministry continued to impact Britain with increasing force.

What had actually happened that fateful Sunday at Surrey Gardens? Who were the perpetrators of the awful crime? Several explanations were forthcoming. Some said thieves had hoped to create enough confusion to play their pickpocket game. Spurgeon himself had cried out when the panic started, "Take care of your pockets." Many were robbed, but no one arrested. So many clothes littered the floor of the Hall after the panic that the nearby Lock's Field police station had insufficient storage room. Others suggested that Spurgeon's enemies precipitated the pandemonium hoping to destroy his reputation and success. Police superintendent Lund was convinced that this constituted the real reason. He had witnessed the entire event and argued that thieves were not the perpetrators of the crime. Still, some took advantage of the circumstances. Perhaps it could be attributed to mere devilment. Nonetheless, whoever did it, the scene was well orchestrated. But it utterly failed, whatever its purpose. Concerning those who died, an inquest handed down the verdict of accidental death. The deacons of New Park Street offered a fifty pound reward to anyone who could lead to the discovery of who instigated the crime, but to no avail. The criminals were never discovered. Also, the church established a fund to aid the families of the victims.

As a result of the disaster, strangely enough, Spurgeon was projected into public awareness as never before. The fame of the man exploded. As one said:

> It was the accident of a serious nature that first drew the attention of the world in general to the rising influence of Mr. Spurgeon. The young preacher—he was then very young—had already secured an immense following on the south side of London. But the world on the other side, the world north of the Thames, the world of society and of the clubs of the West End, the world of Bloomsbury and Fitzroy Square, the world of Madia Bale and Highgate, and all the various microcosms knew little or nothing of the powerful young preacher

whose congregations had already far outgrown the capacity of New Park Street Chapel in Southwark. [146]

Because of the tragedy, as another expressed it:

> Mr. Spurgeon became famous at once. Society went out of its way, to put itself to trouble, to hear the young preacher whose admirers could not be contained in the building of less size than the great Music Hall . . . He found himself famous the morning after the accident, and he kept his fame. [147]

The reason for the measure of positive outcome centered in the fact that the general populace, with few exceptions, really did not blame Spurgeon. As seen, papers like the *Evening Star* wrote helpful articles to exonerate the preacher. Some journalists defended Spurgeon by answering the specific issues the public raised. The critics said he should never have preached at the Music Hall in the first place. However, the reporters pointed out that it was Deacon Moore Cone who pushed for the venue. Other detractors argued that the service should not have continued after the panic. Again the press came to the defense by stating that Spurgeon did not know of the tragedy—which was true. Charles received many barbs for taking an offering while the dead were lying about. However, wrote the reporters, no one would have done such a thing had they known of the extent of the tragedy. To say Spurgeon would have done so is ludicrous. Thus the press aided in the public relations over the dreadful event. Not only that, several of those touched by the tragedy later joined Spurgeon's church. God's grace prevailed and even made much good come out of the terrible event.

THE SERVICES CARRY ON

When Spurgeon went back to the Surrey Gardens Music Hall, the proprietors refused payment for the tragic Sunday. The Hall had been originally booked for four Sunday evenings. However, it seemed wise that the services should be held in the morning rather than the evening. There would be less chance of such a crush of people at that time. After four weeks of moving services, the success of the venture demanded that the contract be extended. Thus, Mr. Spurgeon's preaching at the Surrey Gardens Music Hall became a regular part of the London Sunday scene for three years. All classes came to hear him, breaking British tradition. *The Nonconformist*, a religious periodical, stated, "Mr. Spurgeon's popularity does not seem to be at all on the wane. Lord Mayors and Lord Chief Justices jostling journeyman carpenters in the same religious assembly are constantly being seen at Surrey Gardens." [148] Friend John Campbell wrote, "Since the days of Whitefield, no man has extracted so much attention in the metropolis." [149]

At the Surrey Gardens, attenders needed tickets and ushers strictly enforced the rule to keep out thieves. At 10:30 a.m. the doors opened and the general public soon filled any remaining seats that ticket holders had left. The Hall seated eight thousand with standing room for five thousand more. Charles packed it to capacity every time he rose to declare the Gospel. This approach to evangelism touched and reached people whom the Established Church probably would never influence. For example, a man who had not been to any church for thirty years attended and found Christ. Another, an avowed secularist, was gloriously converted and publicly burned his books. Everyone hearing Spurgeon, as one expressed it, sat "in a state of breathless attention." John Anderson's statement proved correct. Not since the days of George Whitefield did the multitudes of London, and all of Britain for that matter, take to a gospel preacher as they did to Spurgeon. Only the Spirit of God could produce such a phenomenon.

Not only did Spurgeon reach many of the artisan and working masses of London, he equally aroused the interest of the highest levels of society. Statesmen, members of the royal family, the wealthy, even Prime Minister Gladstone came to hear the young pulpit orator on one occasion later. Missionary David Livingstone once sat on the platform of the Surrey Gardens Music Hall with Dr. Armitage of New York. In the congregation that day the Princess Royal and the Duchess of Sutherland also attended. Lord John Russell, Lady Peel, Lord Shaftesbury, and Lord Campbell were some of his occasional hearers. Someone even reported that Queen Victoria herself came in disguise and heard Charles preach Christ. That may be apocryphal, but it is not beyond reason. He had become the talk of Britain; and his fame, through his printed sermons, spread all over America. By 1857 it looked as though the world would soon be at his feet.

Despite all of this fame, Spurgeon remained quite humble. For example, on the occasion when Livingstone and Armitage visited the Surrey Gardens Music Hall, Charles preached with unusual power, full of earnest appeals and heart-searching utterances. The message produced tears in many eyes. When the service concluded, Dr. Livingstone approached Spurgeon as did Dr. Armitage to offer their congratulations and to shake hands with the preacher. Mr. Spurgeon withdrew his own hand, remarking pleasantly to the American divine, "No, shake hands first with Dr. Livingstone; he is the worthier man." Still, one gets the impression that Spurgeon had to work on staying humble—but he did it very well.

The services in the Music Hall carried on unabated week after week. On January 2, 1857, Spurgeon's dear friend Richard Knill died at Chester, being seventy years of age. He had labored in Chester since 1848. In his pastorate the church mushroomed fourfold. He was a great preacher and a great tract writer. It has been stated, "No man ever had so many of his tracts circulated as Mr. Knill. Between six and seven million of them have been printed in England; translated into ten different languages, they have been scattered over the whole world. In America more than seven million have been printed, so that between the two countries, more than fourteen million have been put into circulation." [150] One wonders how many conversions resulted from that effort alone. Yet, he will always be remembered for his famous prophecy over little Charles Spurgeon at Stambourne when he envisioned the great preaching ministry Charles would exercise.

POSITIVE DAYS

Through the next years the negative public sentiment dramatically changed, with few exceptions. For example, on Tuesday November 11, 1856, Spurgeon received the deeply appreciated honor of preaching in Whitefield's Tabernacle on Tottenham Court Road. Few preachers were invited to fill the pulpit of the great Whitefield. Spurgeon was thrilled. He preached on Habakkuk 3:2, "O, Lord, revive Thy work." He poured out his heart for a spiritual awakening for all England. *The Baptist Messenger* published the message in full. The move from abuse to virtual praise was quite remarkable. The entire general reaction to Spurgeon turned positive. The newspaper reports in those transitional days were startling. Even the critical *National Review* gave him a good press. The old Latinized, hazy preaching of his predecessors began to fall into disrepute; the more pungent colloquial preaching of Spurgeon gained in acceptance. As one put it, "If we must choose between the two, we do not know whether it is not less bad to handle spiritual truths as you would handle a bullet, than to handle them as you would handle a mist." [151] On February 8th, 1857 the *Greville Memoirs* stated:

> I have just come from hearing the celebrated Mr. Spurgeon. He is certainly very remarkable, and undeniably a fine character; nor remarkable in person; in fact resembling a smaller Macauly, a very clear and powerful voice which was heard throughout the hall, a manner natural, in passion, without affection or extravagance; wonderful fluency and command of language, abounding in illustration, and very often of a familiar kind, without anything ridiculous or irreverent. He preached for about three quarters of an hour, and, to judge by the use of handkerchiefs and audible sobs, with great effect. [152]

Other papers followed in championing the young preacher. *The Western Times* (Exeter) declared that he bid fair to rival, if not to eclipse, such men as Carey, Gill, Rippon and Robert Hall. *The Christian Weekly News*, after acknowledging that many who had listened to him had gone away to speak ill of his name, declared that "others and by far the larger number have been stimulated by his earnestness, instructed by his arguments and melted by his appeals."

This reversal in the press to a more positive attitude toward Spurgeon came largely out of a letter and article published in the *Times* on April 13th, 1857. That basically revolutionized the scene. No published paper in Britain enjoyed more influence than the *Times*. Extracts from the significant letter and article penned by one who called himself "Habitans in Secco," make quite fascinating reading in light of the negative press reports Spurgeon had received for years. The *Times* journalist wrote:

> A friend of mine, a Scotch Presbyterian, comes up to town and says, 'I want to hear Spurgeon; let us go.' Oh, I am supposed to be a High Churchman, so I answered, 'What, go and hear a Calvinist—a Baptist—a man who ought to be ashamed of himself for being so near the church and yet not within its pale?' 'Never mind, come and hear him.' Well, we went yesterday morning to the Music Hall in the Surrey Gardens. At first I felt a strange sensation of wrong-doing. It was something like going to a morning theatrical performance on Sunday . . . Fancy a congregation consisting of 10,000 souls streaming into the hall, mounting the galleries, mumming, buzzing, and swarming—a mighty hive of bees, eager to secure at first the best places, and at last any place at all. After waiting more than half an hour— for, if you wish to have a seat, you must be there at least that space of time in advance—Mr. Spurgeon ascended the tribune. To the hum and rush and trampling of men succeeded a low, concentrated thrill and murmur of devotion, which seemed to run at once like an electric current through the breath of every one present, and by this magnetic chain the preacher held us fast bound for about two hours. It is not my purpose to give a summary of his discourse. It is enough to say of his voice that its power and volume are sufficient to reach every one in that vast assembly; of his language, that it is neither high-flown nor homely; of his style, that it is at times familiar, at times declamatory, but always happy and often eloquent; of his doctrine, that neither the Calvinist nor the Baptist appear in the forefront of the battle which is waged by Mr. Spurgeon with relentless animosity, and with Gospel weapons, against irreligion, cant, hypocrisy, pride, and those secret bosom sins which so easily beset a man in daily life; and, to sum up all in a word, it is enough to say of the man himself that he impresses you with a perfect conviction of his sincerity . . . Here is a man not more Calvinistic than many an incumbent of the Established Church, who 'mumbles and mumbles,' as old Latimer says, over his liturgy and text. Here is a man who says the complete immersion, or something of the kind, of adults is necessary to baptism. These are his faults of doctrine, but if I were the examining chaplain of the Archbishop of ———, I would say, 'May it please your Grace, here is a man able to preach eloquently, able to fill the largest church in England with his voice; and what is more to the purpose, with people. . .'[153]

That did it; the *Times* of London came out virtually in full support of Spurgeon. The press had so changed that even a paper that had once called Spurgeon "the Exeter Hall demagogue" later spoke of him as "this noble Puritan preacher and saintly Christian." The whole press seemed to be going Charles' way, except of course, the notorious *Saturday Review*. They were *always* critical of *all* Nonconformists. Spurgeon and the *Review* never made peace.

THE CRYSTAL PALACE

In this general time frame, a stellar honor came to Charles. A day of National Humiliation, with many activities, concerning the Indian Mutiny affair was scheduled on Wednesday, October 7, 1857. All felt the main attraction would no doubt be the worship service in the famous Crystal Palace. The huge Hall, constructed completely of glass panes opened its doors in 1851 in Hyde Park. It housed the world exposition of that year, but the city fathers moved to south London in 1854, when Queen Victoria officially dedicated it in its new location. The unusual building and its birth was the brainchild of Prince Albert, Queen Victoria's husband and Prince Consort. People came from far and wide just to see it. The crystal walls spread over a vast plot in the south London suburb of Sydenham. [154] Remember, Charles made his feelings for Susie first known as they strolled in its vast crystal rooms. That was the venue for the Service of Humiliation. The preacher for the occasion? Twenty-three-year-old Charles Haddon Spurgeon.

An interesting incident occurred a few days before the service in the Crystal Palace. Mr. Spurgeon went to the Hall to test the acoustics. Charles wanted to be sure he could adequately fill the farthest recesses of the structure with his resonant voice. He did it by standing in the spot where the pulpit would be placed. Lifting up his beautiful voice, he quoted from the Bible, "Behold the Lamb of God that taketh away the sin of the world" (1 John 1:29). A workman, busy in one of the galleries, heard him. The words seemed to come from heaven itself. Deeply smitten by the Holy Spirit and convicted of his sins, he laid aside his tools and made his way home. That night he did not rest until he had received Christ as his Savior.

The Crystal Palace service itself proved to be a great success. Trains began to run toward Sydenham at 7:30 in the morning. By noon, 23,654 had passed through the turnstiles and assembled under the glass dome, even though the day itself had turned wet and cold. One of the largest assemblies in history gathered to hear God's Word.

The pulpit used in the Surrey Gardens Hall had been set up in the northeast corner of the structure. The throng sang a hymn, then a prayer for those who suffered in the mutiny touched all the assembly. A collection was taken to aid the families of those who had endured loss in the Indian conflict. They received £675, plus £200 from the Crystal Palace Company. It almost equaled the amount collected all over London in the entire day of various activities. Another hymn was sung and the highlight, of course, came when Spurgeon preached. He took his text from Micah 6:9, "Heed ye the rod, and who hath appointed it." Inspired by the large crowd, Spurgeon preached with great eloquence and effect. He was frank, yet fair, about English involvement in India. He spoke his mind about the Hinduism of the Indians. He said the British government "should never for a moment have tolerated the vile religion of the Hindoos [*sic*] which was nothing more or less than a mass of the vilest filth that the imagination could conceive." [155] That reflected much of the mind-set of the day. Most of the newspapers claimed the message and entire event a marvelous experience. Although some reporters could not help criticizing, they were generally out of step with the positive feeling now surrounding Spurgeon.

An interesting anecdote emerged out of the Crystal Palace service. When Spurgeon took his place on the rostrum, he could see his wife seated in front of the platform. Susie was filled with emotion at the awesome responsibility her husband bore and at the expectation of the over 25,000 eager people. Her face showed the tension. Right then Spurgeon beckoned one of his deacons, whispered something in his ear, and sent him to Mrs. Spurgeon. He was overheard to say to Susannah, "Mr. Spurgeon says, please will you change your seat, so that he will not be able to see you; it ('it' was doubtless Mrs. Spurgeon's obvious emotion) makes him nervous." [156] Though she immediately moved, still one wonders how she felt about it. But the day proved very trying for Spurgeon himself—more stress than he probably realized. When the day ended, he went to bed—a Wednesday night—and did not awake until Friday morning.

ABUNDANT LABORS

The years from 1854 to 1859 were romantic indeed in the Spurgeon ministry. He seemed to grow from strength to strength regardless of criticism, tragedy, opposition, praise, fame, and everything London could hurl across his path. During that turbulent period, as responsibilities increased, he could hardly find time to sleep save from midnight to dawn. His work as an evangelist and preacher took him all over the country and on the Continent as well. This work was done in addition to the Herculean task of leading and preaching to the people of New Park Street Baptist Church itself. During the same period, he also laid the foundation plans for the Metropolitan Tabernacle. As the *Baptist Messenger* stated, "his greatness was in his usefulness."

As briefly recounted earlier, during these dramatic days of Spurgeon's ministry at the New Park Street Baptist Chapel, he published weekly sermons. They influenced many in those early years. In fact, a friendly critic once said that the sermons preached and published after 1860 were not on the high level of the earlier ones. Spurgeon replied, "Yes that may be so." [157] The reason seems to be that during these early romantic years, addressing the great crowds, the emphasis was essentially evangelistic. Later, he shifted some of his emphasis toward those already converted so as to root and ground them in the faith. Thus, something of the early exuberance and dramatic eloquence gave place to a more mellow and placid style. However, his effectiveness was as great as ever.

During these hectic, yet romantic years, all London and people farther afield demanded his presence. As described, he made his first visit to Scotland in 1855. This visit to Scotland introduced Spurgeon to the North and became something of a foundation for the impact that he had upon that country through his life. In 1858, he made a second visit to Scotland and saw that his ministry and reputation, primarily through writing, had increased tremendously. A local newspaper expressed the general Scottish sentiment through the years:

> Like his great model, Whitefield, he seemed blessed with 'no constitution.' He is endowed with a voice, strong, clear, bell-like, which could be heard by many thousands, and with a physical frame equal to a vast amount of hard work. In contour of face, he reminds us something of John Caird, and his eye has the lustrous light of genius in it. [158]

Once in Edinburgh, he felt that he had failed God. He languished under the inner agony that the Spirit of God had deserted him. He told people that the chariot wheels had been taken off. It must be granted he suffered as the victim of such mood swings to the end of his life.

Earlier, on March 27, 1856, Spurgeon made one of his most personally interesting visits to Stambourne. He also went back to his first pastorate at Waterbeach. When Spurgeon returned to the happy haunts where he had preached in his earlier years, he remarked, "I cannot remember visiting a single village or town that I have visited a second time, without meeting with some who praise the Lord that they had heard the Word of truth there from my lips." [159]

On April 28, 1858, while preaching in the Surrey Gardens Music Hall, he preached a message for the Baptist Missionary Society. On Wednesday morning, the beautiful building overflowed with the crowd. Spurgeon tenaciously held to the principle of missions, and preached many times for the missionary society.

In the summer of 1858 Spurgeon visited Ireland. He preached four times in Belfast and Dr. James Morgan of Fisherwick Place observed:

> I was not disappointed, although the mass of people were, when he preached in the Botanic Gardens. He was well heard of seven thousand persons. He was well received and deserved to be so for his plain, honest and good preaching and deportment. I much question if his influence was as good as that of Mr. Grattan Guinness, who preceded him by a few months. There was a great contrast between them. Mr. Spurgeon was gay, lively, and humorous; Mr. Guinness was solemn and earnest and very reserved. Mr. Spurgeon is by far the abler man. Yet were there a poll in Belfast tomorrow for the two, it would be in favor of Mr. Guinness. [160]

Ireland did not always view Mr. Spurgeon as the most popular preacher. Nevertheless, in 1859, when the great prayer revival (born in America one year earlier) began to sweep over Ireland, the two names most repeated by the evangelical believers of Ireland were C. H. Spurgeon and H. Grattan Guinness. More of that revival story later.

Charles conducted a great service on Clapham Common, July 10, 1859. Even though two weeks prior, lightning had struck and killed a man on the Commons, 10,000 people gathered around that same stricken spot to hear Spurgeon preach. A collection was taken for the widow of the victim of the storm. The criticism always came up that Spurgeon's peculiarity is what drew the "superficial" masses. There may be an element of truth in that. Outstanding personalities do attract. Nevertheless, such positive and lasting spiritual good took place in people's lives, and so many were genuinely converted, as one said of him, "Spurgeon! Ah, there was no humbug about him!"[161] But he had his critics until the day of his death.

Strangely, Spurgeon never visited America. In 1859 he received an offer of £10,000, $50,000 at that time, for a series of sermons in New York City. Through the years he was urged to travel to the United States. Huge sums were offered. However, he would not go on the mere basis of any amount of money. He did intend to go to America, but before the trip could be effected, the anti-slavery controversy broke, precluding the visit. That issue shall be discussed later.

February of 1860 saw the construction of the great Metropolitan Tabernacle continuing as Spurgeon went back to Ireland and spent time in Dublin. In the same year, he also traveled to Paris. While in historic Paris he preached three times in the American Chapel and twice in the Oratoire. Fullerton tells us that each evening, after he preached, Charles would be invited with others to the home of some prominent Parisian. In those gatherings, remarkable things happened, as much as in the public services. He also visited the College of Passy and addressed the missionary students there. He received a tremendous reception in Paris, even exceeding that of Scotland. Dr. Frederic Monod wrote, "Mr. Spurgeon is a new proof that God does nothing by halves. If he calls one of his servants to do special work, then he gives him the special endowments necessary for it."[162] Another Parisian said, "One would be willing to hear him during two hours at a time, among the requisites to Oratoire which he possesses, three particularly struck us. A prodigious memory, a full, harmonious voice, and a most fruitful imagination. Mr. Spurgeon is in reality a poet."[163] Mr. M. Prevost-Paradol, a Roman Catholic, declared that Spurgeon was "the most natural, and, we would be willing to say the most inspired orator we have ever had the pleasure of hearing."[164]

During these abundant years countless people considered Spurgeon "the most popular in Christendom."[165] That may be high praise and a bit exaggerated, but this indicates the escalating popularity of the young man. Of course, not everyone held the same opinion. Bishop Wilberforce, an Anglican, was asked one day if he were not jealous of the fact that the Nonconformists had Spurgeon rather than the Anglicans. He replied in a rather sarcastic manner, "Thou shalt not covet thy neighbor's ass."[166]

In June and July, 1860, Spurgeon went on a continental tour. It was his first real vacation in seven years. It may seem strange, but Charles took many of his vacations without his wife. Because of health after the birth of the children she could rarely leave the house and Charles had to get away at times. He traveled through Belgium, Germany, and Switzerland. His delight of the entire trip took place in Geneva, however. He preached twice in Calvin's pulpit. Being a strong and committed Calvinist, when he saw the medal of John Calvin, he exclaimed, "The first time I saw the medal of John Calvin, I kissed it." He went on to say:

> I preached in the Cathedral of Saint Peter. I did not feel very comfortable when I came out in full canonicals, but the crest was put to me in such a beautiful way that I could have worn the Pope's tiara if they had asked me. They said 'our dear brother comes to us from another country, now when an ambassador comes from another country, he has the right to wear his own costume in court, but, as the mark of a very great esteem, he sometime condescends to the weakness of the country which he visits, and he will wear court dress!' 'Well,' I said, 'yes, that I will, certainly! But I shall feel like running in a sack.' It was John Calvin's cloak and that reconciled me to it very much. [167]

It was a high hour for Spurgeon because of his deep and profound admiration for John Calvin's reformed theology. The appreciation that Spurgeon felt for the theology of John Calvin can best be expressed in his own words:

> I can recall the day when I first received those truths in my soul, when they were, as John Bunyan says, burned into my heart as with a hot iron; and I can recollect how I felt that I had grown on a sudden from a babe into a man, that I had found, once for all, the glue to the truth of God. One week night, when I was sitting in the house of God—I was not thinking much about the preacher's sermon, for I did not believe it—the thought struck me, *'How did you come to be a Christian?'* I sought the Lord. *'But how did you come to seek the Lord?'* The truth flashed across my mind in a moment. I should not have sought him unless there had been some previous influence in my mind to make me seek him. I pray, thought I; but then I asked myself, *'How did I come to pray?'* I was induced to pray by reading the Scriptures. *'How came I to read the Scriptures?'* Then in a moment I saw that God was at the bottom of it all, and that he was the author of my faith; and so the whole doctrine of grace opened up to me, and from that doctrine I have not departed. [168]

That is pure Calvinism. Spurgeon became convinced that one could take a simple step from Paul to Augustine and then from Augustine to Calvin. He said, "You may keep your foot up a good while before you will find such another." [169]

Near the end of April, 1863, Charles traveled to Holland. He received a tremendous reception. Fulfilling the wish of some, he preached for two hours at a time. During this trip to Holland he had an interview with the Queen of Holland and talked with her about her personal relationship to Jesus Christ. Spurgeon confessed that he did not always find it easy to witness to persons on a one-on-one basis, but he did share Christ as opportunity presented itself, even to a queen. He influenced many people in Holland. In the city of Utrecht, a peasant woman came up to Spurgeon and cried out, "Oh, Mr. Spurgeon, God bless you! If you had only lived for my soul's sake you would not have lived in vain!" [170]

May 27, 1864, saw the celebration of the tercentenary of Calvin's death. No one displayed more exuberance in celebrating that date than Charles Spurgeon. He always agreed completely with statements like that of John Knox who said that Geneva, in Calvin's day, was "the most perfect school of Christ that was ever on earth since the days of the apostles." [171]

In those busy years Spurgeon traveled to Cambridge and preached at Parker's Piece. So many people desired to speak with him after the service that friends had to clasp hands and form a tight circle around him to make it possible for him to walk to the house where he was staying. At another spot, thousands gathered from all parts of the area to hear him preach. At Risca, in south Wales, he preached three times end to end. Later in the open air, he preached again to thousands. Also, at Abercarne, 20,000 people gathered to hear his oratory. Many people attempted to get closer to the speaker in their carriages and horses. Spurgeon cried out, "Four horses and a carriage would occupy the ground of 50 people, so the horses and the carriages must remain where they are." [172] A similar experience took place at Melbourne, near Cambridge, when he preached in the open air. One could not help being reminded of the days of Whitefield.

Spurgeon continued his open air ministry at Castleton, in south Wales. At Nounton, near Cheltenham, again thousands gathered to hear him. The same circumstance was repeated at Dunnington, Peppard, Ogbourne St. George, Lymington, Swansea, and Carlton in Bedfordshire. In every service, thousands of people gathered.

At the opening of the City Road Chapel in Bristol, the multitude of people outside who could not get in the chapel became so unruly that after a short sermon the service had to be concluded. At Gradford, the largest building in town proved far too small, and in Birmingham 6,000 people gathered to hear him preach. The same scene repeated itself at Dubley, Wolverhampton, and Liverpool.

Spurgeon enjoyed travel, but he would take a holiday trip only occasionally. Rarely did he travel just for the sake of travel. Deacon Thomas Cook of tourist fame once offered to take Charles up the Nile like a prince of Egypt, but he declined the generous offer. He never visited his son Thomas during the years he served a church in Auckland, New Zealand.

SPURGEON THE LECTURER

During these hectic times, Spurgeon began to give lectures as well as preach. The Young Men's Christian Association sought him to present a series of "Exeter Hall Lectures." He consented and entitled the lectures "De Propaganda Fide." The series began on January 4, 1859 and the crowds were overwhelming. At times the audience's applause seemed endless. Spurgeon gave his series of lectures on Friday evenings. He began with the subject, "Shrews and How to Tame Them." Other interesting lectures centered on natural history, in which he used prepared diagrams. Someone said, "He seems always to do best what he is doing last." [173] The lectures lasted an hour and three quarters, and he spoke with all of the force and strength of his preaching. One of his most famous lectures was "Sermons in Candles." He had said to his students at the College that sermons could be seen in even a tallow candle. He said there were enough illustrations in a simple candle to last six months. The students questioned that seriously, so he promised to prove his words. That inspired the famous lecture, "Sermons in Candles." Later, on November 6, 1866, he repeated a lecture that he had given on George Fox to the Society of Friends in Bishopsgate. Twelve hundred people came to hear him.

By the time the early London years were coming to a close, Spurgeon had received such praise that a boy in America, on being asked on a school examination, "Who was the prime minister of England?" replied, "C. H. Spurgeon." In Mentone, France where Charles often spent time recuperating from illness, he one day went out in his carriage on a tour. Another coach passed them and the passenger asked the coachman who Spurgeon was. The coachman replied, "That is the Pope of England." Some contend his popularity soared so high that even the royalty could be envious. The cry "over the water to Charlie's," had become so common that multitudes of Londoners were doing just that. It was a romantic time of abundant labor to be sure.

Spurgeon developed many social works along with his significant preaching ministry. New Park Street Baptist Church moved out in many exciting and needy avenues of service. The church inaugurated a day school and a mission work in Guildford Street. The mission ministered to 150 children who had never been to school. The work finally reached 600 children. Spurgeon loved this type of work; he saw no dichotomy between "spiritual" and "social" ministries. He started many works of this sort in the deprived areas of London. Before long an orphanage, a college, almshouses, and a host of other ministries would be launched. He seemed a tireless, innovative worker. That significant story shall unfold later.

Despite Spurgeon's increasing bouts with bad health, he kept on preaching many times a week. As shall be seen, much of his effort during these romantic years was undertaken to raise funds for the new Metropolitan Tabernacle. Perhaps those significant early days can be summed up best from across the Atlantic by the *New York Evangelist*, a paper strongly influenced by Charles G. Finney. [174] The editor visited the capitol city and wrote that Spurgeon was "one of the lions of London—a rather young lion to be sure; but one who, since his appearance in the field, has roared so loudly to make all the nation hear."

Concerning the constant charge of conceit during the busy, popular years, Spurgeon smilingly said in answer to a friend who raised the issue:

> Do you see those bookshelves? They contain hundreds, nay, thousands of my sermons translated into every language under heaven. Well, now, add to this that ever since I was twenty years old there never has been built a place large enough to hold the numbers of people who wished to hear me preach, and, upon my honour, when I think of it, I wonder I am not more conceited than I am. [175]

Actually, Spurgeon could not really be accused of being vain. He did not think too highly or too lowly of himself. He was just honest. That, no doubt, grew out of his essential theology about the sovereignty of God. God alone, Spurgeon realized, provided the only answer to his ministry. And Spurgeon truly walked with that sovereign God. When the "dry seasons" came, as they do for all, he felt them smartly. He once wrote to Susannah:

> I fear I am not so full of love to God as I used to be. I lament my sad decline in spiritual things. You and others may not have observed it, but I am now conscious of it, and a sense thereof has put bitterness in my cup of joy. Oh! What is it to be popular, to be successful, to have abundance, even to have love so sweet as yours—if I should be left of God to fall, and to depart from His ways? [176]

That is real humility—to realize one's walk with God is all that truly matters. The man was actually quite childlike, especially in the things of the Spirit. Although criticized as a proud, young, superficial "rascal," he simply strove to be God's growing servant. Of course, his rash statements were one of the prime reasons he drew criticism. Yet, he was only in his twenties in those days and can perhaps be excused. Even if at times he did not temper his language, he learned to do so in his more mature years. At any rate, he did ascribe his expanding ministry entirely to the praise of God.

SPURGEON'S SECRET: THE HOPED-FOR REVIVAL

All of these matters raise a very basic question: What is the final secret of such a successful ministry? When Spurgeon preached, as someone said, "the spellbound audiences must have thought that John Bunyan II was speaking to them." Many other great preachers were about, men like Joseph Parker, R. W. Dale and Alexander Maclaren. People came in large numbers to hear them. Moreover, church-going was the vogue. Yet, Spurgeon seemed to have an indefinable something that superseded all those factors. What was really going on? Spurgeon himself well knew; a few others sensed it. But, it is virtually overlooked today, even by his most ardent admirers. The answer is quite simple: REVIVAL. Spurgeon came to New Park Street Baptist Church just as a deep and profound spiritual awakening burst on the scene in south London. He understood it, because a real touch of revival had attended his ministry at Waterbeach. That little Cambridgeshire crowd prepared him for the advent of a great and profound movement of the Holy Spirit.

Few biographers, it seems, have realized this revival principle in the early ministry of Charles Haddon Spurgeon. So often his success is explained merely on the grounds of his great preaching. However, good preaching alone simply cannot explain such a phenomenal ministry. Others, with a better perception, acknowledge the sovereign God as the source of his effectiveness. Still, just to let that great truth dangle with no explanation does not answer the basic query concerning Spurgeon's success. Charles himself, however, recognized the answer when he said, "The times of refreshing from the presence of the Lord have at last dawned upon our land. Everywhere there are signs of aroused activity and increased earnestness. A spirit of prayer is visiting our churches, and its paths are dropping fatness. The first breath of the rushing mighty wind is already discerned, while on rising evangelists the tongues of fire have evidently descended." Revival stemming from the sovereignty of God had dawned and deeply touched Spurgeon's ministry. That explains it all.

Spurgeon knew well the revival principles. For example, the great Wesley-Whitefield awakening had occurred in the previous century, and, as often seen, Charles deeply admired Whitefield, no doubt patterning aspects of his ministry after him. He also became conversant with the American phase of the revival called the First Great Awakening. Spurgeon held Jonathan Edwards in high esteem. Moreover, out of the eighteenth century awakening, the British Baptists were significantly touched. As historian E. A. Payne put it:

> The English Baptists are generally accorded the distinction of being the first in modern times to found a society deliberately and exclusively aimed at the evangelization of the non-Christian world, and there is no doubt at all about the important repercussions which their action had in other branches of the Church. The founders of the London Missionary Society and the Church Missionary Society, and those who sought to awaken the conscience of the Church of Scotland in regard to world-evangelization, confessed that they had been challenged and inspired by what the Baptists had done. When, in October, 1792, a little group of Midland Baptist ministers formed the Baptist Missionary Society, they did a new thing, and one of tremendous consequence. Theirs is a remarkable story. [177]

Out of that spirit rose the missionary giants William Carey and Andrew

Fuller. Fuller's book, *The Gospel Worthy of All Acceptation* (written in 1781 and published in 1784) became a classic. The great Thomas Chalmers also emerged in that context.

Strangely, some of the more strict British Baptists expressed displeasure with the Wesleyan Movement. As late as 1809 a Baptist essayist wrote of Methodism as "that odious and ill-defined mischief." [178] But the Wesley-Whitefield Awakening did much to break the supralapsarianism of high-Calvinism, thus paving the way for the evangelistic thrust to enter the Baptist movement. Supralapsarians held that God's election came irrespective of the "fall of man" and the elect alone are eternally justified; the rest are literally and specifically chosen for eternal damnation. They seemed quite satisfied merely to declare that people were either on the high road to salvation or the low road to perdition. They refused to call people to "repent and believe the gospel." Thus the churches did not engage in any significant effort for the conversion of souls. [179] The revival that broke out in Spurgeon's ministry rejected that supralapsarian spirit and theology.

When Spurgeon spoke of the "times of refreshing," he referred to the Prayer Revival that moved over the British scene in 1859-1860. That significant work conceived in prayer and gestated in intercession had its birth in America during the winter of 1857-1858. America's spiritual need in the middle of the nineteenth century cried for a solution. The Second Evangelical Awakening that swept America beginning in 1792 had all but spent its force. Social and spiritual decay had set in and was eroding the foundations of society. Civil unrest over the slavery issue brewed. The churches languished for new life and vitality, seemingly inept to impact the needy nation. The country found itself on a slippery slope.

In that sterile setting, in the autumn of 1857, Jeremiah Lamphier, a lay-missionary of the Dutch Reformed Church on Fulton Street in New York City, called for noonday prayer services. He invited any who would attend to gather in the Consistory Building of the Church to give themselves to prayer during their lunch hour. A burden weighed heavily on his heart for a fresh movement of God. A beginning touch of revival had also come to Canada a few months earlier. Also, the quest for revival had begun at Amherst, Yale, and Williams Colleges in the United States. Could New York also be touched? To that end, Lamphier called for earnest prayer. No one arrived at 12:00 on the stated day, September 23, 1857. No one had even come by 12:25, and the depressed missionary was about to write it off as a lost project. However, around 12:30 six men straggled in. Those who prayed manifested a genuine spirit of concern, so Lamphier scheduled another meeting for the next week. The following week saw the attendance doubled at the prayer service. Then at the next meeting there were even more on their knees. They decided to meet every day for prayer. On October the 7th the stock market crashed. Unemployment skyrocketed. This no doubt caused many to begin to look to God in prayer. By mid-winter, the Dutch

Reformed Church overflowed with praying people. It soon spread to the Methodist Church on John Street and then to the Trinity Episcopal Church on Broadway and Wall Streets. In February and March, 1858, every church and public hall in central New York filled to absolute capacity just to pray during the noon hour. The famous New York editor, Horace Greeley, sent a reporter on horse and buggy to the various prayer meetings to see how many were actually praying. He raced around from meeting to meeting and in one hour (he could only get to twelve meetings in that stated prayer time), he counted 6,100 men in fervent intercession for revival. In February, reporter James Bennet of *The Herald* started a series of articles on the revival. Then the landslide came. Churches everywhere began overflowing with praying people. Not only that, many conversions started taking place in these prayer services and various evangelistic meetings. In one week, New York alone saw ten thousand converted. Throughout New England church bells rang regularly at 8:00 every morning, at noon, and at 6:00 in the evening, calling people to prayer. Soon all the Hudson and Mohawk Valley were brought to prayer.

The revival set America ablaze. In Chicago, 2000 gathered daily in the Metropolitan Theater. Revivals broke out in secular schools. In a Cleveland, Ohio high school, all but two boys were converted. New social programs were launched. Charles Finney of Oberlin received a fresh thrust to his ministry. Lay people, men and women, were the spearheads of the movement. God in His sovereignty had been pleased to visit the nation with His glory. What days they were! For two years, fifty thousand people a month joined the churches. There were only thirty million people in the United States at the time.

REVIVAL SPREADS TO BRITAIN

A revival of such magnitude always encompasses vast areas. The Spirit of prayer moved across the Atlantic and initially touched Ireland. In 1856, two or three years prior to the Irish movement, a Baptist lady named Mrs. Colville had exercised an effective witness for Christ in her community. She profoundly influenced a young man, James McQuilkin of Ballymena. He was converted and with a friend began to pray for revival in Ireland. God heard their prayers, and in 1858, the Presbyterian Church of Ireland dispatched observers to the United States to investigate the Prayer Revival that had now gripped that country. They returned home thrilled. One of them wrote a book that God used in a significant way to put the Irish Christians to prayer for a similar movement in their land. Soon Belfast, Dublin, Cork, and all the countryside fell under the impact of the prayer revival. The nation bent on its knees.

As the continuing news and thrilling stories of the American awakening spread through the British Isles, in a short time Scotland became aroused.

Prayer meetings sprang up in Glasgow, Edinburgh, and virtually all the cities and towns of the country. By 1859 the United Presbyterian Church reported that one fourth of its members regularly attended a prayer meeting for spiritual awakening. A general revival then broke out, first in Aberdeen, next in Glasgow, then across the few miles of water to the Isle of Butte, and finally throughout the countryside. The loyal Scots experienced God's reviving power. An evangelist named Brownlow North was especially useful in those significant days. Furthermore, the news of the Irish awakening deepened the Scottish work even more.

Wales also came under the power of God—almost simultaneously with Ireland. A young Welshman, Humphrey Rowland Jones, had been studying for the ministry in America. Being caught up in the beginnings of the revival in 1857, he returned home in 1858 and began preaching the necessity of revival for Wales. Together with a more seasoned minister, David Morgan, hands were joined as the awakening began in Wales. Morgan and Jones worked together effectively, then Jones grew rather extreme and faded out of the picture. Morgan, however, moved from strength to strength as the revival gained momentum. Before long all Wales caught on fire with renewing power.

Finally, England began to be warmed by the conflagration. A united prayer meeting was held in the Throne Room of the Cosby Hall, London in 1859. Soon attendance reached one hundred at the noon hour service. By the end of the year, twenty-four daily and sixty weekly prayer meetings were being held in the London area. In a matter of days, the number grew to one hundred twenty; then it exploded all over the land. From London, the revival spirit spread to the counties of Surrey and Kent, then to Sussex and Hampshire on to the Isle of Wight. Berkshire, Bristol, Gloucester and Wiltshire experienced the touch of God.

As 1860 was ushered in, the Fortune, the Garrick, and Sadler and Wells theatres opened their doors for Sunday evangelistic services. Even the staid Saint Paul's Cathedral and Westminster Abbey conducted special revival services. Of course, the ministry of Spurgeon sprang into full bloom as the Metropolitan Tabernacle was soon to be entered. People also flocked to hear Evan Hopkins of later Kexwick Convention notoriety in Dorset. Charles Finney, the great American revivalist, preached with great effect in Bolton as the revival spread and deepened over England. William and Catherine Booth of Salvation Army fame were ministering with fresh power. Oxford and Cambridge Universities commenced special prayer meetings. All England, it seemed, began looking up in prayer.

As can be imagined, the awakening had its critics. The same negativism that surrounded Spurgeon in his early days was unleashed against the revival spirit. The secular press raised their voices in chorus to protest such things, thus attempting to negate the positive impact of the movement. But it soon became clear to those with spiritual perception that God ultimately had control of the matter. Historians now realize the awakening left a legacy of blessing extending even to this day. During the revival, one million new members entered the churches of Britain. Not only that, the Salvation Army, the Children's Special Service Mission, the China Inland Mission, and a host of new institutions were founded that still carry on. As Spurgeon put it:

> It were well . . . that the Divine life would break forth everywhere—in the parlor, the workshop, counting house, the market and streets. We are far too ready to confine it to the channel of Sunday services and religious meetings; it deserves a broader floodway and must have it if we are to see gladder times. It must burst out upon men who do not care for it, and invade chambers where it will be regarded as an intrusion; it must be seen by wayfaring men streaming down the places of traffic and concourse, *hindering the progress of sinful trades*, and surrounding all, whether they will or no. Would to God that religion were more vital and forceful among us, so as to create *a powerful public opinion on behalf of truth, justice and holiness* . . . A lie which would *purify the age*. It is much to be desired that the Christian church may yet have *more power and influence* all over the world for *righteousness . . . social reform and moral progress.* [180]

That was revival for Spurgeon, and all Britain experienced it in 1860, especially Charles' ministry. The Prayer Revival became the last great spiritual awakening experienced by all of the British Isles. It is true that significant blessings came to Britain in the Welsh Revival of 1904-1906. But that movement did not impact all of the United Kingdom to the same degree as did the Prayer Revival of 1860.

In an old classic, *Revivals, Their Laws and Leaders*, James Burns sets out several "laws" or principles of great awakenings. The affinity between these so-called laws and Spurgeon's ministry makes it clear he ministered in the midst of a classical revival, and that explains much of his effectiveness. What are these "laws"?

"LAWS" OF REVIVAL

Burns tells us initially that a revival always becomes a time of spiritual regeneration. God acts in a progressive way in our world. That is axiomatic. But this progressive work of God is not a steady, stabilized move upward. The Church often languishes in a protracted period of little movement, then suddenly a fresh surge of the Spirit lifts the Church and society to higher levels. Although the general trend of God's work is always upward, the progress is characterized by these ups and downs. The "ups" are the revival times. How vital these revival seasons are! Burns states:

> Revivals are necessary for the spurring of man to high endeavor, and for the vitalizing of life. Were progress to be uniform—no part of man's nature moves

until the other parts move also—advance would be so slow that life would stagnate. There could then be no high hopes, no springtide of exulting life, no eager and impetuous rush forward. Progress would be so slow as to be imperceptible, and man, robbed of high inspiration, would cease to hope, and cease to struggle. By the breath of revival life, however, God keeps the world in eager activity, and keeps the human heart ever fresh with hope. [181]

The consequences: progress and growth!

Revivals thus become a major instrument of God for revitalizing spiritual life. When awakenings occur, Christians, caught up in the movement, never remain quite the same. Whoever and wherever it touches, profound change occurs. It can be described as follows:

> We found ourselves walking in a sense of reverent awe, our minds racing with questions, our wills painfully adjusting to the demands of what God had wrought, our hearts reaching out in eager desire to tell others, and our souls lifted in glorious joy, praise, and new dimensions of loving adoration of the Lord. [182]

These movements deepen all. People are transformed as the Holy Spirit extends the work.

At times, the Spirit engulfs large, extensive areas. The great fifteenth-century Florentine revival under Savonarola remade Florence, Italy into a veritable city of God on earth. The Welsh revival of 1902-1904 so radically altered the entire Rhondda Valley of Wales that the animals employed to bring up coal from the mines had to be taken out of the collieries and retrained. Before the awakening, they responded only to the commands of their drivers punctuated with cursing. However, so many miners were converted, and with their language cleaned up, the colliery animals did not know how to work; hence, the necessity of re-training. The whole Church of Wales came alive as never before. For months many churches stayed open twenty-four hours a day. Tens of thousands were converted.

Still, revival results remain the same: profound spiritual growth. This is true whether limited or extensive in geographical impact. For, "the law which moves the mighty tides of the ocean is the same which ruffles the surface of the little pool made by the rain of a summer afternoon." [183]

Law implies an orderly sequence of movements. Do revivals exhibit this kind of movement? Do awakenings occur at definite intervals? Can any sequences be discerned? If that were possible, we could forecast their appearance with some precision. However, this is obviously not the case. History abounds with instances where churches have felt a desperate need for revival only to experience little blessing. Then when least expected, the heavens opened. Spurgeon's move to New Park Street presents a classic case in point. The term "law" in this context must not be interpreted legalistically. The Spirit moves as He wills. Yet we may believe that these periodic movements operate on what we could call "Divine law," based on the inscrutable hidden purposes of God.

This law of periodicity reveals several important facts. First, God finally controls His Church and will give His people what they need when they need it as He sees fit. Second, God's wisdom far supersedes ours, and we must always place the timing of these awakenings in the divine economy of things. Third, revivals do not come by caprice or just because the Church does certain things in a formal, structured fashion. Although the people of God have their part, the sovereignty of God is central. The law is not mechanical. Perhaps it can be best summarized by saying the needs and activity of the Church and the sovereignty of God form the warp and woof of genuine revival.

Moreover, as implied, there is always an ebbing tide before the awakening flood comes. A general defection from "the faith once delivered to the saints" (Jude 3) often infects the Church just before awakenings dawn. Dullness and lethargy pervade God's people. Dark days settle in. These periods are also characterized by straying from the central task of evangelism. Churches and pastors begin to substitute secondary ministries for this primary responsibility. Priorities get reversed.

Along with these problems, deviations from apostolic theology can subtly creep in. Compromise on ethical and moral principles tends to follow hard on the heels of doctrinal errors. A critical and blasé attitude envelops many as people grow cynical about those whom they label as "puritanical" and "pious." This no doubt accounts for much of the criticism Spurgeon received in the early days. Some actually defect and fall into open sin. In a word, plain "worldliness" takes over, and the Church sinks into a Laodicean syndrome. Yes, church programs go on, often with greater fervor. There is a form of godliness but a denying of real spiritual power (2 Timothy 3:5). With spiritual power missing, and the Church neither hot nor cold, it stands in dire danger of the Lord's Laodicean rejection (Revelation 3:16).

Although ebb times seem inevitable, the Church and the people who make up the Church are not thereby exonerated and blameless for their defections. In the final analysis, believers become what they want to become, and bear the consequences of their own actions. Christians also reap what they sow, individually and collectively.

Another important revival principle is "the fullness of time." The ebbing spiritual tide has its limits as surely as the ebb tide of great oceans. Apathy and coldness has its end. The further the tide ebbs, the greater power and force it gains to return and overflow the arid land. The ebb tide seems to create among God's true people a deep sense of dissatisfaction. A period of gloom settles in—even to the point of weariness and exhaustion. Sick in soul and heart, Christians turn to God with a deep sigh. People pray and pray.

But can these burdened believers be found? It must be recognized that even in the darkest hours, the Church always contains those who have not bowed the knee to Baal during the ebb tide. In these precious few the burden and aching grows. Finally, the longing for better things becomes intense pain, and the burdened determine with Jacob of old, "I will not let thee go, except thou bless me" (Genesis 32:26). And though God may well "touch their thigh" as He did Jacob and they limp through the rest of their days, they prevail. Revival is always born in prevailing prayer. Prayer constitutes the one, basic, unalterable, central principle and law of awakenings. Intercession opens the door to the fullness of time, and Spurgeon decidedly had a praying people. The prayer meetings in his church were tremendous. The people prayed and fasted with a tenacity that brought the blessings.

The emergence of the prophet comes next. Revivals have leaders, sometimes one, sometimes many. These leaders tend to be the incarnation of the movement; they personify the awakening in its most intense form. History is replete with this principle. It starts in the Bible with Shem, goes through giants like Noah, Abraham, Deborah (women are in this galaxy), Samuel, David, the prophets, John, the Apostles, and Paul. It continues through historical figures such as the church fathers, Francis of Assisi, Bernard of Clairvaux, Savonarola, right up to the Reformation and the Puritan-pietistic revival—and Spurgeon.

The leader of revival holds a critically important place. He or she gathers up all those intangible longings and ideas dimly felt and grasped by the masses, then personifies them, epitomizes them, sharpens them, expresses them, and gives them startling visibility. The leader's authority becomes evident and gives substance to many aspects of the movement.

Revival leadership is a double-sided event; the prophet effects the movement and vice versa. They tend to bring their own individuality to the awakening and to some extent shape and mold it. At times the leader so epitomizes the thrust that a casual look might draw one to the conclusion that the leader was the creator. However, he or she is also a product of the movement. That is to say, the revival makes the leader.

The leader is normally called upon to pay a high price. The drain and strain can be tremendous. In John Wesley's journal we read, "March 17, 1752. At the Foundry. How pleasing it would be to flesh and blood to remain at this little quiet place, where at length to weather the storm! Nay, I am not to consult my own ease but the advancing of the kingdom of God."

Although every leader, and hence every awakening, is unique and may differ radically in temperament and emphasis, the leaders still possess common denominators. Burns puts his finger on this principle when he says:

> Each of these great leaders has in common with all the others an unshakable faith in God, an overwhelming sense of a call to great service, a mysterious equipment of spiritual power which moves mountains, and a determination to do the work he is called of God to do even at the expense of life itself. In the Picture Gallery of the good and great, such men occupy the noblest place. [184]

Moreover, it must be stressed that each revival has a uniqueness of its own. As society changes from one generation to the next, as people differ in temperament and culture, so the revival must vary if it is to be relevant to its time and place. There seemingly cannot be a single movement that reaches all peoples and all cultures. For example, the Wesley ministry revolution-ized the English but left the Scots cold. But Whitefield influenced Scotland tremendously. The Reformation primarily touched the Teutonic people and left the Latins relatively unmoved.

This phenomenon reveals the wisdom of God. If all revivals were cast-iron in their manifestations, large masses would obviously go unreached. The movement must express itself in the cultural context of particular peo-ple. This is the only way it can be relevant to real life and thus change it. Consequently, a vast variety of appeals emerge in awakenings. At times the emotional impact predominates, as in the frontier revival of nineteenth-century America. At other times theological aspects dominate, as in the Reformers. Then again, volitional decision making becomes paramount. Each movement wins its way because of the particular needs of particular people at particular times.

In addition, each movement usually stands in contrast to the previous one. If the watchword of a revival is freedom in Christ, the next may well be the authority of Christ. One emphasis usually demands the balance of the next. An illustration of this principle is the Oxford movement of the early nineteenth century, with its stress on spiritual authority as a conservative reaction to the extremes of the evangelical revival in the Church of England. Yet, in it all, God works and effects a balance. Through the law of variety, the Spirit of God builds up the Church.

But, every revival has its day and then ends. Luther said that thirty years was the outer limit of an awakening. Luther may be correct about most cases, but some revivals have lasted considerably longer. Still, they end. The first check of the awakening often comes when the initial emotional tidal wave has run its course. Many who were swept along on the merely emotional level soon fall away. Of course, the more stable effects linger on long after the first emotional excitement dies. The Church and society normally remain on a higher plane.

Even when an awakening is long-lasting, however, the long-term effects eventually evaporate and decay begins. The Franciscan revival illustrates the point perfectly. In the midst of a corrupt religious scene, "never since the birth of Christianity has anything appeared on earth more pure or fair than that movement as first conceived by its originator [St. Francis], or practiced by his followers." [185] Yet, within a hundred years the vow of poverty had turned to riches, humility to tyranny, monasteries to palaces, and confession into manipulation. The deterioration so eroded the positive influence of the revival it finally turned it sour.

Theology also changes during revival times. There always seems to be a return to conservative evangelical thought. It takes this course:

1.   A return to simplicity. Believers break through complex, abstract, obscure theology and get to the basic practical truth of the Scriptures. In a word, they become evangelical in thought and theology.

2.   A return to New Testament spirit and methods. A quest for the apostolic faith and way of doing things predominates. The spirit of the first century Church is sought. The Bible becomes the pattern for service.

3.   The message of the cross. The Gospel, the *kerygma*, truth that centers in the cross of Christ becomes the focal point of preaching.

4.   The salvation of Christ as man's greatest need. In awakenings evangelism thrusts itself to the fore. Secondary ministries—as important as they are—find their proper secondary place and the winning of people to personal faith in Christ becomes central. Awakenings restore proper priorities. Redeeming love becomes the theme. Spurgeon saw this clearly.

5.   Liberal, rationalistic, speculative theology dies in many circles as the revival touches minds and lives. That man-centered thought system never brings about awakenings. This does not mean revivals spawn anti-intellectualism. That too is a perversion of the Spirit's work. This has surely been made clear in the Puritan-pietistic movement. But an empirical, purely rationalistic theology that downgrades the transcendental elements of Christianity are laid to rest in awakenings. People became vividly alive to the fact that the sovereign miracle-working God is among them, breaking in on the causal continuity of history.

6.   Cold orthodoxy reawakens to the Spirit. Conservative theological systems can soon cool and stagnate. Nothing is much "deader" than a dead, cold, rationalistic fundamentalism. When revival comes, though the actual theological position of conservative evangelicalism may not substantially change, it suddenly comes alive and glows. That change is as needed as an overhauling of so-called radical, non-biblical theology.

Certain spiritual experiences are always found in revival also. First, when an awakening breaks, a deep sense of sin pervades people. In the intense awareness of God's presence, individual guilt overwhelms the sensitized hearts of the participants, and not just conviction over heinous sins of the flesh alone. Secret and seemingly insignificant sins become a deep burden. Then, as far as possible, sins are put right through confession and restoration. Paul said, "I exercise myself to have a conscience void of offense toward God and toward men" (Acts 24:16).

Secondly, the fullness of the Spirit, that revival jewel, always glistens brightly in the experience of revival. After cleansing comes fullness. The Bible abounds with this concept. "And they were all filled with the Holy Spirit and began to speak in other tongues, as the Spirit gave them utterance" (Acts 2:4). "And when they had prayed, the place in which they were gathered together was shaken; and they were all filled with the Holy Spirit and spoke the word of God with boldness" (Acts 4:31). "And to know the love of Christ, which surpasses knowledge, that you may be filled with all the fullness of God" (Ephesians 3:19). "And do not get drunk with wine, for that is debauchery; but be filled with the Spirit" (Ephesians 5:18). An objective view of the Scriptures forces the conclusion that God wants his people filled with his Holy Spirit.

God always does this "filling work" in an awakening. Christians often need such a crisis to bring them to consecration. People need power for service. The faithful need fullness to bear fruit. All need a profound touch of God in their lives. That which the Holy Spirit does in guidance (Romans 8:14), prayer help (Romans 8:26), sealing (Ephesians 1:13), enlightenment (John 16:13), conviction (John 16:7-11), and the exalting of Christ (John 16:14) becomes an experiential reality in revival. God effects it all by filling His people with the Holy Spirit. An awakening invariably quickens this infilling of the Spirit. And the Spirit exalts Jesus Christ, infusing vitality into everything He touches. Few would refute that blessing.

Then, the flood tide of joy fills the revived believers. After cleansing and fullness, God pours out His Spirit of love, joy, and peace (Galatians 5:22). The happiest people who have ever lived are the revived. Burns states, "There is a joyousness and elasticity of spirit, and a hopefulness . . . This is the effect of a revival wherever it appears. It irradiates the atmosphere; it leaves in its tracks numberless happy men and women whose faces are aglow with a new light, and whose hearts throb with an intense and pure joy." [186] This explains why the awakened Christian Church has always been a singing people; "Where the Spirit of the Lord is, there is liberty" (2 Corinthians 3:17).

The effulgence of joy leads to the fourth spiritual characteristic of awakenings, evangelism. Joy must be shared. With the Church now aflame to bring others to Christ, the unbelieving community is so attracted by God's blessing on His people that they come by the multitudes to discover what is happening, just like the events on the day of Pentecost (Acts 2). When the Spirit falls on the Church, multitudes come and are "bewildered" (v. 6), "amazed and wondered" (v. 7), "amazed and perplexed" (v. 12), and finally throw up their hands in intellectual despair and cry out, "What does this mean?" (v. 12). This creates the context of great outreach. When unbelievers begin to ask questions, instead of criticizing, then the Gospel can be effectively communicated. Again, this was typical of Spurgeon's early days in London. In a word, when God breaks in on the Church and truly revives His people, the Spirit can reach the lost in unprecedented numbers. Acts 2 ends with about three thousand converts (v. 41), and even more marvelous, "the Lord added to their number day by day who were being saved" (v. 47).

Furthermore, those converted in the awakenings are normally growing, maturing believers. Those who were saved on the Day of Pentecost "devoted themselves to the apostles' teaching and fellowship, to the breaking of bread and the prayers . . . They sold their possessions and goods and distributed them to all, as any had need . . . praising God and having favor with all people" (vv. 42, 45, 47).

In the fifth place, lay people get prepared for ministry. The laity are often merely passive spectators. When an awakening arrives, however, the whole company of Christians are so revived that service for Christ abounds everywhere. Every revival is testimony to this principle.

The sixth principle states that great moral and ethical advances take place. Charles Finney in America saw entire towns converted and civic righteousness established. All real revivals possess an ethical and moral element. It happened in Spurgeon's ministry in little Waterbeach. Furthermore, ethics that do not grow out of a theological and spiritual base are at best dignified humanism, built on a foundation of sand that cannot finally stand the storm.

Finally, revivals spread. When a real spiritual awakening comes, it will normally spread far and wide. History abounds with that principle, as has been made amply evident.

Considering all that has been said, it would be well to cry out with the psalmist as he prayed, "Wilt thou not revive us again: that thy people may rejoice in thee? Show us thy mercy, O Lord, and grant us thy salvation" (Psalm 85:6-7). That is how the New Park Street Chapel people prayed on the arrival of their new, young pastor from the Fens. And God wonderfully responded.

Spurgeon and Revival

Spurgeon had actually been in the grip of a real revival at the New Park Street Church for several years before the British Prayer Revival of 1860. Indicative of this fact is the brief history of the church, which was placed in the cornerstone of Metropolitan Tabernacle at its dedication. A passage from that document reads:

> From the day he (Spurgeon) commenced his labours in our midst, it pleased the Lord our God to grant us a revival *which has steadily progressed ever since* . . . So did the Holy Ghost accompany the preaching of the Gospel with divine power that almost every sermon proved the means of awakening and regeneration to some who were hitherto 'dead in trespasses and sins.' [187]

The New Park Street Chapel was built in 1833, but the numbers had become relatively small in the years preceding C. H. Spurgeon's arrival in 1854. Yet, said Spurgeon, there were those "who never ceased to pray for a gracious revival . . . they hoped on, and hoped ever," as did hopeful Spurgeon. [188] Spurgeon described those early days when God's people interceded in a most unusual fashion:

> When I came to New Park Street Chapel, it was but a mere handful of people to whom I first preached, yet I could never forget how earnestly they prayed.

> Sometimes they seemed to plead as though they could really see the Angel of the Covenant present with them, and as if they must have a blessing from him. More than once we were all so awe-struck with the solemnity of the meeting that we sat silent for some moments while the Lord's Power appeared to overshadow us; and all I could do on such occasions was to pronounce the benediction, and say 'Dear friends, we have had the Spirit of God here very manifestly tonight; let us go home and take care not to lose His gracious influence.' Then down came the blessing; the house was filled with hearers, and many souls were saved. [189]

God answered almost immediately after Charles arrived in early 1854 and continued on. He himself said, "For six years the dew has never ceased to fall, and the rain has never been held. At this time the converts are more numerous than hither-to-fore, and the zeal of the church groweth exceedingly." The full revival then came in 1860.

In some sense, the beginning of the Prayer Revival in Britain can be partially traced to Spurgeon's early itinerant ministry. As pointed out, in 1858 Spurgeon traveled to Belfast, Ireland and preached four times very powerfully. One year later (1859) the revival began in that very place. Also, Spurgeon's ministry in Scotland probably helped to lay a good foundation for the spread of the movement there, not to mention his influence in London. Moreover, Spurgeon pioneered the use of secular buildings that contributed so much to the impact of the revival. Spurgeon well knew that revival helped explain his early outstanding ministry, and he deeply desired it for all of Britain. In some sense, his ministry was the forerunner of the great Prayer Revival that pervaded the general evangelical life of the United Kingdom.

The awakening work surrounding Spurgeon so profoundly deepened that for three years up to one thousand people every Sunday were turned away from the Surrey Gardens Music Hall because there was no room left for the worshipers. To know how many were converted is impossible.

Some quite amazing occurrences took place in those early revival days. For example, one Sunday in the Music Hall a man sat listening intently to Spurgeon preach. In his sermon Charles said, "There is a man sitting here, who is a shoemaker; he keeps his shop open on Sundays, and it was open last Sunday morning; he took in nine pence and there was a four pence profit; he sold his soul to Satan for four pence." The man so intently listening felt cut to the heart. He *was* a shoemaker and he *had* kept his shop open the previous Sunday and *had* taken in nine pence and he *did* make a profit of four pence. He immediately came to Christ. Dozens were saved in similar dramatic circumstances and joined the great Baptist church. The simple statistics of those years were phenomenal.

Of course, in all awakenings the religious *status quo* falls by the wayside. At times, even excesses may occur; that must be admitted. Yet, as Spurgeon said:

> We see this life and force breaking out in many places in new works for the Lord Jesus Christ, and frequently it takes very irregular forms, greatly to the distress of Spiritual Tories, who must have all things cut and dried after the most ancient fashion. We confess that we, also, are somewhat perplexed at certain of the more outrageous forms of religious energy, but even if there should be occasional irregularity it is better than the monotony of mere mechanism. [190]

Something of the breadth of Spurgeon's grasp of spiritual realities can be seen in this evaluation. He could endure some excess for the larger gain. However, that was not the forté of all Victorians. But God's Spirit was creating through Charles the largest evangelical congregation in the world. And that is not to mention the multitudes who were converted and then joined other churches, nor the social ministries that Spurgeon created. Simply put, Spurgeon reveled in revival, regardless of its weaknesses. He considered the outcome well worth the small price of some aberrations.

One question immediately thrusts itself to the fore: What lies back of this profound spiritual awakening under Spurgeon? What did he possess that precipitated revival even before the emergence of the general awakening of 1860? If revival is a primary answer to Spurgeon's staggering success, why did it happen to him at that time? Eric Hayden, one time pastor of the Metropolitan Tabernacle, saw three dominant factors. [191] The primary foundation stone, as already implied, rested on the sacrificial, fervent prayers of the New Park Street people. They were a faithful group of interceding Christians. Young Spurgeon inherited that blessed legacy. Moreover, that Spirit of prayer continued through the years of the Metropolitan Tabernacle ministry. The anecdote of Charles Haddon Spurgeon taking visitors through the Metropolitan Tabernacle and showing them the prayer room in the basement and remarking, "Here is our power house," has often been repeated. But that is apocryphal; the real story is that the prayer meetings were held upstairs on Monday night, with some 3,000 people attending.

Another central feature in the Spurgeonian revival is expressed in Charles' words: "Sound doctrine and loving invitation make a good basis of material, which, when modeled by the hand of prayer and faith, will form sermons of far more value in the saving of souls than the most philosophic essays prepared elaborately, and delivered with eloquence and propriety." [192] The revival had its birth and development in the "sound doctrine" presented with "loving invitation." Biblical doctrine presented in love cannot be divorced from revival. As discussed earlier, the great Puritan-pietistic movement that engulfed Britain and the continent has spawned many awakenings. No doubt one of the prime reasons for the spiritual impact of that powerful thrust centered in its insistence that orthodox, biblical teaching and preaching must be at the core of one's ministry. That significant movement, as we have seen, became Charles' spiritual matrix and background. Charles always considered himself a product of that tradition. Concerning the influence of his Puritan grandfather on his life, he said, "I sometimes feel the shadow of his broad brim (Puritan hat) come over my spirit. I like to feel that I serve God from my fathers." That sort of preaching Spurgeon grew up on, and did himself.

That approach made the "Last of the Puritans" very leery of any sort of humanistic ingenuity in religion that downplayed the absolute sovereignty of God and did not emerge out of biblical exegesis. Spurgeon would have been appalled at what goes on under the name of revivalistic evangelism in some circles today. There seems little doctrine and theology in it. Human persuasion, if not manipulation, appears to be the central motif. It can often be correctly defined as no more than "evangelical humanism." Thus, its continuing results can be seriously questioned. Spurgeon believed a lasting revival comes only through the power and sovereignty of God, using prayer and the plain declaration of the essential truths of a solid, orthodox, biblical theology, and that done with loving appeal. God will move in His set time and on the wings of biblical truth. Thus, Spurgeon waited on God and filled his sermons with Scripture and theology that many modern evangelists consider too "heavy" for the lighthearted crowd in today's world. Spurgeon knew, as did Paul, he would never get lasting results if people's faith rested in "the wisdom of man" rather than in "the power of God." That kind of power comes by the Holy Spirit using the profound truths of the Gospel presented with a "loving invitation" by the evangelist, all permeated with prayer. God's sovereign election does not preclude a "loving appeal" by the proclaimer of the Gospel. To the contrary; the Word of God demands it. Spurgeon knew that, and it saved him from hyper-Calvinism.

But there is a third dimension Charles Haddon Spurgeon himself may not have fully realized. Simply stated, he was God's man of the hour, and rarely does one recognize how profoundly the Holy Spirit is using one, at least at the moment. Spurgeon knew, as he said, "We must stoop before God that we may conquer amongst men," but he probably did not realize how effective his ministry truly was. God, in sovereign grace, raises up His choice prophet at the right moment to be the prophet of a great movement, whether they know it or not. Spurgeon was certainly the man the Spirit had been preparing for years. Spurgeon had already received his "accolade of fire" before coming to London. He knew experientially the power of the Holy Spirit coming upon a man. One of the basic reasons New Park Street Chapel had a revival is because they had in their new pastor from Essex a truly anointed revivalist. Spurgeon was God's chosen man for that crucial moment in history.

So through prayer, sound doctrine with loving invitation, and a genuine man of God at the New Park Street Baptist Church, the long hoped-for revival flamed to life. A new Pilgrim whose name was "Hopeful" had arrived on the scene in Southwark and the "progress" was phenomenal. The hoped-for awakening had come. The spiritual atmosphere of London crackled with excitement as hundreds of thousands thronged to hear the young man of God.

But now a Metropolitan Tabernacle had to be built to house the multitude that pressed in to hear him. To that fascinating venture and the maturing ministry of Charles Haddon Spurgeon we turn. But first, an in-depth look at Spurgeon's preaching and writing ministry will be helpful.

6

"A Very Great and Honorable Person; His Name . . . Is Evangelist"

SPURGEON'S PREACHING AND WRITING MINISTRIES

Editorial cartoons depicted the ride to heaven in the Church of England as directed by the "Old Conductor" (above) and contrasted it with Spurgeon's congregation as progressively led by the "New Conductor" (right).

—*courtesy of Dr. Craig Skinner*

Let Ignorance a little while now muse
On what is said, and let him not refuse
Good counsel to embrace, lest he remain
Still ignorant of what's the chiefest gain.
God saith those that no understanding have
(Although he made them), them he will not save.
—*John Bunyan*

Introduction

The eulogies that surround the preaching ministry of Charles Haddon Spurgeon are legendary. Never in the history of the Christian church, at least in the English-speaking Christian world, have there been more praises lauded on a preacher of the Gospel than that given Spurgeon, save perhaps George Whitefield. It may well be that some of the plaudits were exaggerations. The praises Spurgeon received on his preaching seem almost outlandish at times. Regardless, it must be granted that he stands as one of the most gifted preachers the Christian world has ever seen.

SPURGEON THE PREACHER

There is little wonder why contemporaries and succeeding generations called Spurgeon the "Prince of Preachers." As has been said, "Great preachers are rarer than great poets, painters or philosophers," and Spurgeon was one of them. He did fill the role of the great preacher Bunyan called "Evangelist." Brastow said Spurgeon was "the most impressive and permanently successful evangelistic preacher of the age."[1] In the *Baptist Magazine*, December 1887, the author called Spurgeon "the most prominent preacher of the age." Colin Chadwick described Spurgeon's preaching ministry, "a preaching career without parallel in modern history."[2] The famous preacher of London's City Temple, Dr. Joseph Parker, termed Spurgeon "a prophet, yea, more than a prophet."[3] Prime Minister David Lloyd George said, "Spurgeon was the greatest preacher of his age. It was an age of great preachers, but he was the greatest in a great age. He was a great orator. I never heard anything like it."[4] High acclaim! Spurgeon's friend, fellow evangelist and biographer, W. Y. Fullerton, declared, "He leaped full-grown upon the stage."[5] Edwin Paxton Hood in *The Lamps of the Temple* claimed, "Amongst all of the popularities, there is no popularity like his."[6] These words of praise never ceased throughout the years of his ministry, and continue to the present hour. Lorimer brought it all together, in almost hyperbolic praise, quoting

The Christian Commonwealth, of London. The writer said:

> The voice was that of Chrysostom, the ardor was that of Wesley, the unction was that of Savonarola, the doctrine was that of Bunyan, the wit was that of Thomas Adams, the originality was that of Christmas Evans, the fervor was that of John Howe, the boldness was that of Calvin, the simplicity was that of Whitefield, the pathos was that of Toplady. Yes, it was the composite character of Spurgeon's preaching which really accounted for its infinite charm. Herein he differed from every other preacher. [7]

As has often been seen, Spurgeon was continually compared to his only probable peer in English-speaking preaching history: the great George Whitefield. Grant said, "Never since the days of George Whitefield has any minister ever lived and acquired so great a reputation as this Baptist preacher." [8] Biographer G. Holden Pike stated, "In respect of his power over an audience, and the London one in particular, I should say he is not inferior to Whitefield himself." [9] Spurgeon's champion, Dr. Campbell, stated, "Spurgeon . . . a master of dialogue, he is not less master of powerful declamations—the two great things for which Whitefield himself was so remarkable." Spurgeon reveled in these comparisons; Whitefield modeled for Spurgeon what a preacher should be.

Spurgeon's effective preaching ministry will always be seen as unparalleled in the nineteenth century. He served his church as a great pastor/preacher, his city as an ardent social reformer, and perhaps above all, the larger world as an effective evangelist. He can rightly be called in Bunyan's term "A very great and honorable person, his name. . . is Evangelist." Thus to analyze Spurgeon as a preacher it seems mandatory to see him essentially as a proclaimer of the Gospel. So, with another look at his actual preaching ministry, we begin our investigation.

SPURGEON'S ITINERANT EVANGELISTIC PREACHING MINISTRY

Spurgeon's developing Metropolitan Tabernacle ministry, as it relates to his preaching, will be addressed in the next chapter. A sketch of the earlier chronology of Spurgeon's itinerant ministry has been set forth in previous chapters. But it will prove helpful here to see some of the anecdotes that occurred in his preaching itself, especially in his traveling ministry. This should help set the stage for an in-depth look at his actual preaching. Although many think of Spurgeon as the dynamic pastor of the Metropolitan Tabernacle, and such is true, his itinerant evangelistic ministry stands out as extraordinary.

Most ministers would no doubt have found the responsibilities that Spurgeon shouldered in his London ministry more than enough to consume all their time and energies. But not Spurgeon. In a letter he penned to a friend in

Cambridge he outlined a typical example of the preaching engagements for just one week:

Sabbath	Morning and evening, New Park Street; Afternoon to address the Schools.
Monday	Morning at Howard Hinton's Chapel. Afternoon, New Park Street. Evening, New Park Street.
Tuesday	Afternoon, Leighton. Evening, Leighton.
Wednesday	Morning, Zion Chapel, Whitechapel Evening, Zion Chapel, Whitechapel
Thursday	Morning, Dalston Evening, New Park Street
Friday	Morning, Dr. Fletcher's Chapel. Evening, Mr. Rogers' Chapel, Brixton. [10]

Why such a schedule? The answer is simple: he had a true burden for those lost without Christ. He engaged in a constant quest to win others to Jesus Christ. A writer said, "We have heard his voice break into sobs, and have seen the tears stream down his cheeks, as he pleaded with the unconverted and implored them to be reconciled to God."[11] He gave of himself tirelessly to touch the lost.

In one especially busy week, Charles preached over a dozen sermons in six days at places that were a considerable distance from each other; and traveling in those days had its problems and stress. It often took its toll on the rather fragile health of the preacher. On his first long journey in his earliest days, the already mentioned preaching tour of Scotland in July of 1855, Spurgeon traveled by rail, but sleep eluded him over the hours of the entire trip. When he finally arrived at Glasgow, he felt utterly exhausted and quite unwell. Biographer Ray described him as he disembarked at the train station:

> . . . tired, begrimed with dust, sleepy, not over high in spirits, and with a dreadful cold. . . . A sleep of twelve hours in a comfortable bed left him as tired as when he stepped from the train, and no wonder he declared he would not travel so far again in one day. The trip was primarily intended as a holiday and rest, but almost every day he had to fulfil preaching engagements, and in a letter to his fiancée from Aberfeldy, describing crowded services there, he writes, 'Unless I go to the North Pole I never can get away from my holy labour.'[12]

But he must reach the unconverted at any cost.

On a later occasion, Spurgeon stood on the platform of the train station waiting for his train to arrive. When it pulled into the station, the conductor announced the boarding instructions. Spurgeon had been in conversation with a fellow minister. The reverend gentleman said to Charles, "Well, I am going to the third class section of the train to save the Lord's money." Spurgeon retorted, "Well, I am going to the first class section of the train to save the Lord's servant." This simple anecdote shows that Spurgeon did take care of himself as best he could in the light of his schedule.

At times in the ardent labors, Spurgeon felt he had been forsaken of the Spirit of God and had failed. Concerning a service in Scotland, he said:

> I could not speak as usually I have done. . . . It humbled me bitterly; and if I could I would have hidden myself in any obscure corner of the earth. I felt as if I should speak no more in the Name of the Lord; and then the thought came, 'Oh, thou art an ungrateful creature! Hath not God spoken by thee hundreds of times? And this one, when He would not do so, wilt thou upbraid Him for it? Nay, rather thank Him that He hath so long stood by thee; and if once He hath forsaken thee, admire His goodness, that thus He would keep thee humble.'

It is quite fascinating to see Spurgeon's reasoning for a lack of spiritual power upon this particular occasion. It also presents another facet of the man himself. In his rationale for the "failure" of the day, he stated:

> Some may imagine that want of study brought me into that condition, but I can honestly affirm that it was not so. I think that I am bound to give myself unto reading and not to tempt the Spirit by unthought of effusions. I always deem it a duty to seek my sermons from my Master, and implore Him to impress them on my mind; but on that occasion I think I had prepared even more carefully than I ordinarily do, so that unpreparedness was not the reason for the lack of force I then mourned. The simple fact is this, 'The wind bloweth where it listeth'; and sometimes the winds themselves are still. Therefore if I rest on the Spirit I cannot expect that I should always feel His power alike. What could I do without His celestial influence? To that I owe everything. Other servants of the Lord have had experiences similar to mine. In the 'Life of Whitefield' we read that sometimes under one of his sermons two thousand persons would profess to be saved, and many of them were really so; at other times, he preached just as powerfully and no conversions were recorded. Why was that? Simply because in the one case the Holy Spirit went with the Word; and in the other case He did not. All the Heavenly result of preaching is owing to the Divine Spirit sent from above. [13]

Of course, the papers stood ready to attack. *The Christian News* described Spurgeon's oratory as "unequal and clumsy in the extreme." They went on to say:

> Mr. S., in our estimation, is just a spoiled boy, with abilities not more than

mediocre, and will for certain, if he does not retrace his steps, share the fate of 'the early gooseberry' or the 'monster cucumber' that appear almost annually in the columns of the newspapers—sinking to obscurity, leaving only a memorial of his career, that he was, and that he has descended to that nihility from which by puffing and blustering he originally and unworthily sprang.[14]

But Charles took the taunts in stride. He wrote his father, sharing his attitude to whatever fell across his path:

I am treading (this) path. Elect by grace, not for my sake, but because of God's sovereign pleasure, I rejoice in the full assurance of faith, trust in Jesus the substitute for his people.[15]

Why all this strident criticism of the man? Thielicke was probably right when he said of Spurgeon, "He spoke in clear terms. For this reason, and this reason alone, did it create disturbance and offence."[16] Spurgeon preached the simple truth and it simply offended some. It brought conviction, therein laid the rub.

Still, Spurgeon's popularity never waned through the years. Late in life, in 1889, he preached for three days on the Channel Isle, Guernsey. More than 9,000 people applied for tickets to hear him. Yet he said he would not go across the street to hear himself preach. But he would constantly go to preach, especially to address special groups. As late as 1890, with his health in a very precarious state, he spoke to the Christian Policemen's Association. And often, the Spirit of God so manifested Himself that men and women were "swayed to and fro under the heavenly message as the corn is moved in waves by the summer winds."[17] Spurgeon preached with true power despite the fact that he at times felt a failure.

NEW APPROACHES IN PREACHING

Several anecdotes have already been related regarding Spurgeon's innovative approach to the pulpit. His rejection of conventionalities made him very effective in keeping a sleepy or distracted congregation alert to his message. On one particular occasion, for example, as he preached the people were continually looking around as newcomers entered the chapel. This disturbed Charles, so he said, "Now, friends, as it is so very interesting to you to know who comes in, and it disturbs me so very much for you to look around, I will, if you like, describe each one as he comes in, so that you may sit and look at me and keep up at least a show of decency." At that moment, a gentleman, a friend of Spurgeon, entered the chapel. Spurgeon went on, "A very respectable gentleman who has just taken off his hat has arrived." Evidently, he did not need to continue the description of those who came in later. That may seem somewhat arrogant, but it certainly got the attention of the congregation.

Spurgeon also sought to communicate to the masses by using catchy, at times even trite, sermon titles. Preaching on Psalm 7:12 at the Surrey Gardens Music Hall on December 7, 1856, he titled his message, "Turn or Burn." He said in the sermon, "I feel that in too many places the decline of future punishment is rejected and laughed at as a fancy . . . but the day will come when it shall be known as a reality." Nonetheless, one cannot but feel that Spurgeon got on the communicative wavelength of the common people with such sermons. Moreover, it proves his very early theological concern for any deviation from the Gospel. All that came to fruition in the later theological battles he waged. However, he always possessed a warm zeal to win people to Christ; hence, the sensational sermon themes and the quest for gospel accuracy.

Spurgeon would go anywhere to share Christ. He preached in small churches as well as large ones. At Tring, Spurgeon ministered to the little chapel. The minister of the small congregation received only fifteen shillings a week as his stipend. Though he lived as frugally as possible, he could hardly survive. The poor pastor stood very much in need of a new suit of clothes. After Spurgeon preached to the congregation that had crammed themselves into the small chapel building, he said:

> 'Now, dear friends, I have preached to you as well as I could, and you know that our Saviour said to His disciples, "Freely ye have received, freely give." I don't want anything from you for myself, but the minister of this chapel looks to me as though he would not object to a new suit of clothes.' He then pointed to old Mr. Thomas Olney, his deacon, at whose suggestion the visit to Tring had been paid, and said, 'Father Olney, down there, I am sure, will start the collection with half-a-sovereign; I will gladly give the same amount; and if you will all help as much as you can our brother will soon have a new suit, and a good one too.'

The collection was taken, and as can be expected, it proved large enough to provide a new suit for the needy pastor. When the service concluded, Spurgeon apologized to the pastor for drawing attention to his worn clothes. The good pastor, not offended, thanked Charles for his thoughtfulness. He said, "Ever since I have been in the service of the Lord Jesus Christ, my Master has always found me my livery." The story of Spurgeon's sensitivity to need got into the newspapers and, as can be expected, was printed with many embellishments.

Another interesting anecdote occurred on a train as Spurgeon traveled out of London on his way to Bishop's Gate on the Eastern County's Railway. He suddenly discovered he had lost his ticket; moreover, he had left home without any money at all. A fellow passenger expressed some concern for his plight, but Spurgeon simply declared, "I have been in my Master's business and I am quite sure all will be well. I have had so many interpositions of Divine Providence in small matters just as well as in great ones that

I feel as if whatever happens to me, I am bound to fall on my feet again like a man on the Manx penny." When the train finally pulled into Bishop's Gate station, the conductor entered the compartment to collect the tickets. When the conductor looked at Spurgeon's companion, apparently they knew one another, and Spurgeon's fellow traveler simply said, "All right." The conductor immediately turned around and left the compartment without asking for tickets. In the providence of God, Spurgeon's traveling companion happened to be the general manager of the railway. Both he and Spurgeon considered the incident as Divine proof of God's provision and care for those who trust Him in the small matters as well as in the great affairs of life.

As can be imagined, fulfilling constant outside engagements, not to mention the regular responsibilities of the London congregation, Spurgeon had very little time for rest or even sleep. Spurgeon's writing ministry, which shall be taken up later in this chapter, also made tremendous demands. But he labored on. Actually, quite early in his life the incessant labors began to take its toll on his health. At a young age he developed chronic kidney problems, that merged into Bright's disease. This, plus his rheumatic gout, often made life difficult. Still, he worked like a Trojan.

SPURGEON THE INNOVATOR

Spurgeon quite often used highly unorthodox means of getting a hearing for the Gospel, at least unorthodox for nineteenth century Britishers. He began to advertise publicly his sermons and meetings. In Victorian England, the populace associated posters with the circus and the theater. Thus the preachers who borrowed these techniques were open to the charge of sensationalism. Charles' promotional activities precipitated that charge in the *Sunday Times.* The paper accused him of "the starring of his name in every chapel bill . . . on every available nook about the dead walls."[18] Eye-catching multicolored posters appeared all over London. The popular periodical, *Punch,* said, "Mr. Spurgeon is becoming as familiar to the readers of posting bills on the Surrey side of the Thames as 'Tom Bary' the ex-clown of Astley."[19] The writer even said that if such things continued it would not be long until a race horse would be named for Spurgeon. But before Spurgeon took this tack, the Salvation Army under the ministry of William Booth violated Victorian reserve. The Army used banjos, drums, and "hallelujah lassies." But Spurgeon incontestably proved that advertising can gather an audience; the multitudes came to hear him preach Christ. Moreover, he willingly preached anywhere, at any time, in any manner to reach people. Spurgeon said to a group of Scottish hearers, "I am not very scrupulous about the means I use for doing good . . . I would preach standing on my head, if I thought I could convert your souls."[20] Years before General Booth had made a similar statement. Spurgeon would use any legitimate means of attracting a congregation.

The negative reaction to Spurgeon's unconventional methods was such that when the Church of England's "Young Men's Society" handed out twenty thousand handbills to promote a sermon by Bishop Carlyle in Exeter Hall, the critics accused the Church of trying to "out-Spurgeon Spurgeon." Nevertheless, the detractors had to admit that Spurgeon's advertisements were most effective. Some even said that Spurgeon stood as England's master of "pamphleteer, preacher, and puffist." He was called the "Barnum of the pulpit." [21] These facts cause one to wonder why Spurgeon remained rather negative to the American evangelist Charles Finney. He too had the reputation of a radical innovator in preaching the Gospel. But, as previously pointed out, Finney's Arminianism seemed just too much for Spurgeon.

Reference has already been made several times to Spurgeon's significant ministries on the Continent. The account has already been given of Spurgeon's ministry through Belgium, Germany, France, and Switzerland. The same large crowds massed to hear him in Europe as they did in Britain. But, needless to say, Spurgeon's greatest preaching ministry centered in the New Park Street Baptist Church and later the Metropolitan Tabernacle. Spurgeon's church always stood as the primary locus of his evangelistic and pastoral outreach. In this context, his preaching made its most significant impact, as effective as his itinerant ministry proved to be. To sense something of the power of the London services, one Sunday Spurgeon stated in a sermon: "There may be a young man sitting here who is in a draper's shop, and who is wearing on his hands at the present moment a pair of gloves which he has pilfered from his employers." There was! The young man came to Charles in his vestry after this message and confessed it all. Charles preached with such communicative power that not only would incidents like the above occur, his audience would punctuate his sermons with cheers, laughter, and applause. People came from far and wide to hear him. For example, when the World-Wide Sunday School Conventions met in London (July, 1889) they went as a body to the Tabernacle on Sunday for worship. For years *The Baptist* printed weekly details of Spurgeon's Sunday services. His success can be clearly seen in the membership and baptismal statistics for the Metropolitan Tabernacle. Regrettably, baptisms rarely got reported before 1876. Still, general membership figures were regularly kept since his call to the New Park Street Church in 1854.

CHURCH GROWTH

At the end of 1854, as previously pointed out, New Park Street membership numbered only 313. By the end of 1860, the membership had more than quadrupled to reach just one half dozen under 1500 (1494). The net increase in membership during the New Park Street days grew at the average rate of 197 persons per year. Although baptisms were not recorded, it is reasonable to assume that the bulk of the additions to church membership came through baptism.

The next ten years saw outstanding growth. Between 1861 and 1870, the average church additions increased some 448 persons per year. That netted 267 persons for each year of the decade. By 1861, the membership stood at 1,875. At the end of that particular decade, 1870, the membership had more than doubled again and had risen to 4,165. For Victorian England, such development could only be described as explosive growth. The most notable feature is that first time conversions comprised the largest part of this dramatic membership increase. As a case in point, of the 1,858 total additions recorded between 1863 and 1866, 1,489, or 80.2 percent, were additions by conversion and baptism. Over the next ten years, 1871-1880, the additions to the church reflected something of the same rate. On the average, 446 persons per year joined the Tabernacle congregation. Over this period of time, however, the church only netted 111 persons per year. This came about largely because substantial numbers of the church members were sent out to establish other churches. (The story of Spurgeon's church planting activities will be recorded later.) The growth was obviously phenomenal for the day. British Baptists still reap the benefits of Spurgeon's effective evangelistic and pastoral ministry.

The largest number of people to come into the Metropolitan Tabernacle in any given year occurred in 1872 when 571 persons were added to the church. In 1871, the membership numbered 4,165; in the next ten years, the church reached 5,284 to become the largest evangelical church in the world.

The last eleven years of Spurgeon's ministry at the Metropolitan Tabernacle proved quite similar to the years that preceded it, at least as far as additions to the church were concerned. The membership reached an all time high in 1882 of 5,427. Still, it did seem that the years of dramatic net increase had peaked out. The first net loss in membership at the Tabernacle occurred in 1883, and net losses were recorded after that year also. The total additions for the entire decade of 1881 to 1891 averaged in the hundreds per year, but the losses were such that the aggregate membership figures remained essentially static. But, even in the dynamics of the Down Grade Controversy in Spurgeon's last five years (see chapter 13), baptisms at the Tabernacle remained outstanding. There was an average of 269 persons baptized every year in the Metropolitan Tabernacle during the last decade of Spurgeon's ministry. The chart on the next page gives these statistics.

End of Year	Baptisms	Total Additions	Net Gain/Loss	Total Membership
1873		359	30	4,503
1874		09	178	4,681
1875		510	132	4,813
1876	317	474	146	4,938
1877	296	437	100	5,045
1878		394	36	5,066
1879	305	445	123	5,290
1880	314	453	54	5,284
1881	279	382	67	5,310
1882	267	444	117	5,427
1883	310	449	(70)	5,341
1884	310	426	58	5,399
1885	267	353	(79)	5,314
1886	284	418	37	5,351
1887	240	357	(38)	5,315
1888	218	307	(37)	5,275
1889	310	433	79	5,354
1890	288	379	(24)	5,328
1891	182	261	(17)	5,311

Sources: C. H. Spurgeon, *The Metropolitan Tabernacle: Its History and Work*, (London: Passmore and Alabaster, 1876), p. 82; and The Sword and the Trowel.

The most significant aspect of the growth of the Metropolitan Tabernacle can be found in the membership/baptism ratio. These statistics stand out as remarkable. A chart that presents the picture is as follows:

Year	Membership	Baptisms	Ratio
1863	2,555	311	8.2/1
1864	2,937	381	7.7/1
1865	3,293	438	7.5/1
1866	3,458	359	9.6/1
1876	4,938	317	15.6/1
1877	5,045	296	17.0/1
1879	5,290	305	17.3/1
1880	5,284	314	16.8/1
1881	5,310	279	19.0/1
1882	5.427	267	20.3/1

1883	5,341	310	17.2/1
1884	5,399	310	17.4/1
1885	5,314	267	19.9/1
1886	5,351	284	18.8/1
1887	5,315	240	22.1/1
1888	5,275	218	24.2/1
1889	5,354	310	17.3/1
1890	5,328	288	18.5/1
1891	5,311	182	29.2/1

Source: Based on figures in table above.

As is obvious, as the church grew larger, the baptismal ratio deteriorated. As can be seen from the above chart, in 1865 it took only 7.5 members of the Tabernacle to win one person to Christ per year. By 1876, it took 15.6 Tabernacle members to win one to Christ. That trend continued during the dramatic days of the Down Grade Controversy of 1887 and following. The membership/baptism ratio dramatically increased to 22.1/1 in 1887 and 24.2/1 in 1888. However, this sort of phenomenon tends to occur in churches, even to the present day.

It thus seems that Spurgeon's early ministry was in some sense more evangelistically effective than were his later days. As he matured, as suggested, the shift of his emphasis tended to turn more to pastoral preaching. It is even probably correct to say that the eloquence and dramatic flair of his early preaching exceeded that of his later years. One listener complained on an occasion in the mature years that Charles' sermon did not have one "Spurgeonism" in it. But it is true, as one stated, the sermons of Spurgeon's later years may not have been as dramatic as the early ones, but they were deeper. As Spurgeon himself grew older and his responsibilities increased, his entire ministry took on more of a pastoral tone. Thus the sensationalism and excitement of his earlier days diminished, at least to some extent. Moreover, he did not make news as he had done earlier on. He had become part of the acceptable London scene. Yet, if one were to examine his entire evangelistic influence throughout his life, especially in what he did for his own students at the Pastors' College in inspiring them to win people to Christ and plant new churches, few pastors ever exercised such an effective ministry. Furthermore, though he did more pastoral preaching as he grew older, he never lost his zeal to win people to Christ. He was probably responsible for more conversions in his later years through his students and the Evangelists Association than in his earlier days, even though it took on the motif of a "second-handed" sort of ministry.

All this raises a very significant question. What was it about Spurgeon's preaching that made it so captivating? Regardless of where he preached or to whom he addressed the Gospel of Christ, he had unbelievable appeal.

People from all backgrounds, differing walks of life, and cultural divergences heard him gladly. Of course, there are several answers to the basic question concerning Spurgeon's magnetism. One could mention his style of preaching, his biblical based messages, his innovative approach to the preaching ministry; it all proved fresh and arresting.

Furthermore, as great preaching always emerges from a solid theological base, Spurgeon proved no exception. He really was a theologian, even if not in a pure technical sense. From what theological base did Spurgeon's preaching emerge that gave his messages the impact they had? That question demands some investigation.

SPURGEON'S THEOLOGICAL BASE FOR PREACHING

A presentation of the full systematic theology of Charles Spurgeon is reserved for the chapter on the most important theological controversy he faced, the Down Grade Controversy. Yet, it can be said here that the theological core that permeated Spurgeon's preaching from beginning to end centered in the Christocentric nature of his theology. The preaching of Christ stood at the very heart of his preaching ministry. This can be clearly seen in his first sermon and the last message preached at the Metropolitan Tabernacle. In both he presented Jesus Christ as the essence of all truth. In the first Tabernacle sermon he said:

> I would propose . . . that the subject of the ministry of this house, as long as this platform shall stand, and as long as this house shall be frequented by worshippers, shall be the person of Jesus Christ. I am never ashamed to avow myself a Calvinist. . . . I do not hesitate to take the name of Baptist. . . . but if I am asked to say what is my creed, I think I must reply—'It is Jesus Christ.' My venerable predecessor, Dr. Gill, has left a body of divinity, admirable and excellent in its way; but the body of divinity to which I would pin and bind myself for ever, God helping me, is not his system of divinity or any other human treatise, but Christ Jesus, who is the sum and substance of the gospel; who is in himself all theology, the incarnation of every precious truth, the all-glorious personal embodiment of the way, the truth, and the life.

In the last sermon Charles preached at the Tabernacle in June of 1891, he declared:

> It is heaven to serve Jesus. . . . He is the most magnanimous of captains. There never was his like among the choicest of princes. He is always to be found in the thickest part of the battle. When the wind blows cold he always takes the bleak side of the hill. The heaviest end of the cross lies ever on his shoulders. If he bids us carry a burden, he carries it also. If there is anything gracious, generous, kind, and tender, yea lavish and superabundant in love, you always find it in him. These forty years and more have I served him, blessed be his name! and I have had nothing but love from him. I would be glad to continue

yet another forty years in the same dear service here below if so it pleased him. His service is life, peace, joy. Oh, that you would enter it at once! God help you to enlist under the banner of Jesus even this day! Amen.

Spurgeon said to his students, "Make Christ the diamond setting of every proclamation of sermon."[22]

Quite decidedly, Jesus Christ and Him crucified formed the essence of Spurgeon's preaching. He declared:

> I received, some years ago, orders from my Master to stand at the foot of the Cross until He came. He has not come yet; but I mean to stand there till He does. If I should disobey His orders, and leave those simple truths which have been the means of the conversion of souls, I know not how I could expect His blessing. Here, then, I stand at the foot of the Cross, and tell out the old, old story, stale though it may sound to itching ears, and worn threadbare as critics may deem it. It is of Christ I love to speak—of Christ, who loved, and lived, and died; the substitute for sinners; the Just for the unjust, that He might bring us to God.

As Douglas correctly put it, "From this standpoint Mr. Spurgeon never swerved. He dropped anchor here. The Cross enchained him. Hence the life-force in his ministry."[23]

Moreover, it must be realized that for Spurgeon, nothing could replace the preaching event itself. In some oblique sense, he pre-dated Karl Barth in his emphasis on the encounter one can have with God Himself in the preaching of Christ. Of course, Spurgeon would never adhere to aspects of Barth's basic theological approach. He would not equate preaching the Word of God with the written Scriptures; yet, he saw the preaching event as a powerful instrument in the hands of the Holy Spirit to bring people face to face with Jesus Christ. It will be remembered that he said, "the written Word convicted me, but the preached Word converted me." In an open air service in 1887, near the end of his life, he asked the throng a central question: "You are not getting distrustful of the use of preaching, are you?" Then he went on to state forcefully:

> Go on with your preaching. Cobbler, stick to your last; preacher, stick to your preaching. In the great day, when the muster-roll shall be read, of all those who are converted through fine music, and church decoration, and religious exhibitions and entertainments, they will amount to the tenth part of nothing; but it will always please God by the foolishness of preaching to save them that believe. Keep to your preaching; and if you do anything beside, do not let it throw your preaching into the background. In the first place preach, and in the second place preach, and in the third place preach.

Spurgeon used many evangelistic means and methods of addressing people with the Gospel, but nothing replaced the actual preaching of Christ. He said to his students at the College Conference in 1877:

> There are the evils, brethren . . . But we have only one remedy for them; preach Jesus Christ, and let us do it more and more. By the roadside, in the little room, in the theatre, anywhere, everywhere, let us preach Christ. Write books if you like, and do anything else within your power; but whatever else you cannot do, *preach Christ*. If you do not always visit your people (though I pray God you may not be blameworthy there), yet be sure to preach the gospel . . . Preaching is our great weapon, so use it perpetually. Preaching is the Lord's battering-ram, wherewith the walls of old Babylon are being shaken to their foundations. Work on with it, brothers, work on. Preach, preach, preach, preach, preach, preach, till you can preach no more, and then go above to sing the praises of God in Heaven, and to make known the wonders of redeeming love.

Spurgeon constantly expressed concern that his students at the Pastors' College exalt Christ in their preaching. And he obviously exemplified it in his own life. From the very beginning of his preaching ministry, he declared first and foremost what he considered the *full* Gospel of God. In his initial volume of sermons published in 1855, he stated:

> Jesus is *the Truth*. We believe *in him*,—not merely in his words. *He* himself is Doctor and Doctrine, Revealer and Revelation, the Illuminator and Light of Men. He is exalted in every word of truth, because he is its sum and substance . . . Sermons are valuable in proportion as they speak *of* him and point *to* him. A Christless gospel is no gospel and a Christless discourse is the cause of merriment to devils. . . . Jesus, Jesus, Jesus, only have we laboured to extol. [24]

Spurgeon loved to preach and urge people to accept Christ. He said, "I often wish I were in China, India, or Africa so that I might preach, preach, preach all day long. It would be sweet to die preaching." He must have been telling the truth, he practically did die preaching.

Spurgeon not only preached Christocentrically, his writings were filled with the person of Christ, as shall be shortly seen. Spurgeon always considered Christ to be his "theme, and mark to aim at." No doubt homiletician J. B. Weatherspoon had it right when he said about Spurgeon:

> All who have spoken or written about him have laid hold of some deep fact in his personality or experience, but significantly, none has been dogmatic enough to say with finality, 'Here it is, this explains the power of Spurgeon.' There were in him, as in all men, certain intangibles and indefinables that refuse to be charted. The pattern of greatness cannot be purchased for the price of a book or magazine.

Yet, if one principle explains the greatness of Spurgeon's entire communicative life, it would have to be its Christocentric content. All this becomes doubly clear and significant in passages from Spurgeon's *Lectures to My Students*. In the lecture that he entitled, "Servants—Their Matter," Spurgeon emphatically stated:

Of all I would wish to say this is the sum; my brethren, preach *CHRIST*, always and evermore. He is the whole gospel. His person, offices, and work must be our one great all-comprehending theme. [25]

Moreover, and of signal importance, Spurgeon strongly emphasized to his students that "the Christian ministry should preach *all* the truths which cluster around the person and work of the Lord Jesus," [26] and that they should not just parrot clichés about Christ and salvation. When Spurgeon preached Jesus Christ, he filled his messages with deep and rich doctrinal content about the person and work of the Lord Jesus. He said:

If I preach Christ I must preach him as the covenant head of his people, and how far am I then from the doctrine of election? If I preach Christ I must preach the efficacy of his blood, and how far am I removed then from the great doctrine of an effectual atonement? If I preach Christ I must preach the love of his heart, and how can I deny the final perseverance of the saints? If I preach the Lord Jesus as the great Head and King, how far am I removed from divine Sovereignty? Must I not, if I preach Christ personally, preach his doctrines? I believe they are nothing but the natural outgrowth of that great root thought, or root substance rather, the person of the Lord Jesus Christ. He who will preach Christ fully will never be lax in doctrine. [27]

THE PERSON OF CHRIST

What did Spurgeon mean by preaching Christ with good doctrinal, Calvinistic content? As stated, Spurgeon has never been seen as a systematic theologian in the strict sense; yet, something of a systematic Christology can be derived from his many sermons and writings. At the same time, it must be held in mind that shot through it all a very practical and experiential element predominated. He did not preach doctrine merely for doctrine's sake. He did not declare his views on the person of Jesus Christ as a simple display of orthodoxy. He always lifted up who Jesus Christ was and what He did so that people might be attracted to Him as Lord and Savior. He said to his students, "We must preach most prominently those truths which are most likely to lead to this end."

Thus Spurgeon always held high the role of Jesus Christ as prophet, priest and king. Christ, in the fullest sense of the word, stands as the Lord and Savior. All the fullness of the Godhead dwelt in him bodily. Spurgeon entertained a very high view of the Incarnation. He would revel in passages of Scripture such as Philippians 2, the great *Kenosis* passage, concerning the person of Jesus Christ. Other passages in which he delighted were Acts 2:22-28; 1 Timothy 3:16; Hebrews 13:8; etc. Spurgeon clung to a historic, orthodox view of the Incarnation. He based his beliefs solely on the Bible. It must also be granted he found help in the historic Baptist confessions of faith concerning the person and work of the incarnate Christ. For example,

Spurgeon would be very comfortable with the Chalcedonian Formulation of 450 A.D. That famous and historic document declares that Jesus Christ of Nazareth was wholly and fully God, wholly and fully man, yet in one hypostatic union.

THE ATONEMENT OF CHRIST

Spurgeon also held tenaciously to Reformed doctrines on the work of Jesus Christ. We shall be looking in more depth at Spurgeon's view of the atonement in a later chapter, but here it must be made clear that his view of the Atonement centered on the traditional substitutionary view. Spurgeon preached that Christ died vicariously in the sinner's place as God's great Substitute, bearing the iniquity of the world. By this he meant that Jesus Christ on the cross became the sin bearer for all His people. Emerging out of Old Testament texts like Isaiah, Chapter 53, and New Testament passages such as 2 Corinthians 5:21, Galatians 3:13, and 1 Peter 2:24, he constantly declared emphatically and dogmatically that Jesus Christ actually took the sins of the people upon Himself and bore God's judgment for them. His sermons abound in this truth. In one of Spurgeon's messages, he declared:

> Christ did really, literally, and truly, take the sins that belonged to all who do believe on him, and those sins did actually and in very deed become his sins; (not that he had committed them, nor that he had any part or lot in them, except through the imputation to which he had consented, and for which he came into the world,) and there lay the sins of all his people upon Christ's shoulders. [28]

Spurgeon saw the atoning work of Christ as God laying the sins of the elect on His Son and transferring by imputation all the evil they ever committed. He emphasized this time and again. [29] Yet, it must be acknowledged that Spurgeon understood that Divine mystery rests there. How one's sins could be transferred upon another, even upon the Lord Jesus Christ, can never be fully fathomed in this life. But, in the divine economy, Christ's suffering effected redemption.

But Spurgeon, never a strict legalist, expressed dissatisfaction with some formulations of the theological concept of imputation. He declared on one occasion:

> Jesus Christ . . . did stand in such a position as to take upon himself the iniquity of all his people, remaining still himself innocent; having no personal sin, being incapable of any, but yet taking the sin of others upon himself—it has been the custom of theologians to say—*by imputation*; but I question whether the use of that word, although correct enough as it is understood by us, may not have lent some colour to the misrepresentations of those who oppose the doctrine of substitution. I will not say that the sins of God's people

were imputed to Christ, though I believe they were; but it seems to me that in a way more mysterious than that which imputation would express, the sins of God's people were actually laid upon Jesus Christ . . . Our sin is laid on Jesus in even a deeper and truer sense than is expressed by the term imputation.[30]

What concerned Spurgeon was giving proper emphasis to the personal aspects of the atonement, thus emphasizing the spiritual union between Christ and the believer.

Spurgeon's approach to substitution implies that the consequence of Christ bearing the sins of His people means that the Lord suffered the exact and full penalty righteously due for those sins. In a sermon preached in 1858, he stated, "It was as a substitute for sin that He did *actually and literally* suffer punishment for all of His elect."[31] This approach, sometimes known as the penal view of the atonement, presents another aspect of the substitutionary idea. Spurgeon was convinced that Christ, as the great Substitute, had on the cross vindicated the whole law of God. Therefore, sinners could be legally and fully forgiven as the penalty for their sins had been fully and legally paid; thus the righteousness of God becoming unequivocally *satisfied.*

This view of the atonement raises the question of how Christ actually paid the penalty for sin. Spurgeon held that His physical suffering paid a part, but on a deeper level, the penalty involved the agony of the spirit and soul of Jesus. On the cross, Jesus was cut off from God as He bore sins. Spurgeon declared, "Jesus was stripped naked to the last rag, and hung up on the cross, as though earth rejected him and heaven would not receive him." The culmination of the penalty that Jesus endured in His death on the cross centered in the forsaking of the Father. Spurgeon said much concerning the "cry of dereliction." He believed that Christ experienced the severing of the perfect fellowship with the Father which is tantamount to spiritual death. Put in the crudest manner, Jesus suffered the torments of eternal death and hell as He bore the sins of the world in His body. He truly did suffer divine judgment. However, Spurgeon would also affirm that though the severing of the divine fellowship became real for Jesus, "the Lord God, in the broadest and most unreserved sense, could never, in very deed, have forsaken His most obedient Son. He was ever with him in the grand design of salvation. Toward the Lord Jesus, God Himself, personally must ever have stood in terms of infinite love . . . but we must look upon God here as the judge of all the earth, and we must look upon the Lord Jesus also in His official capacity as the Surety of the covenant, and the Sacrifice for sin."[32] In simplest terms, as Spurgeon himself expressed it, "It was not until Christ died that the debt, which was due from His people to the justice of God, was fully discharged."[33] Thus God's justice was satisfied. That view is pure Reformed Calvinism.

Now, it is only fair to say that Spurgeon, with his Reformed views, did not eliminate other aspects of the atonement. He realized substitution did not completely exhaust the power of the death of Christ. He fully recognized that there were other theories that possessed a genuine element of truth. For example, he well knew Satanic forces were defeated at Calvary and the justice of God's Moral Government established. He saw the atoning work of Jesus Christ like a multifaceted jewel; every aspect of the atonement reflecting something of the light of God's redeeming love. But for Spurgeon, the heart and essence of the work of Jesus Christ on the cross effected *substitution* and *satisfaction*. He believed this approach to be biblical, Augustinian, Calvinistic, traditional Baptistic, and the truth to be unequivocally declared. He said in one of his sermons during the Down Grade Controversy:

> We understand *our Lord's death as a substitutionary sacrifice*. Let us be very clear here . . . The blood of Jesus Christ, shed because of his courage for the truth, or out of pure philanthropy, or out of self-denial, conveys no special gospel to men, and has no peculiar power about it. Truly it is an example worthy to beget martyrs; but it is not the way of salvation for guilty men. If you proclaim the death of the Son of God, but do not show that he died the just for the unjust to bring us to God, you have not preached the blood of the Lamb. You must make it known that 'the chastisement of our peace was upon him,' and that 'the Lord hath laid on him the iniquity of us all,' or you have not declared the meaning of the blood of the Lamb. There is no overcoming sin without a substitutionary sacrifice. The lamb under the old law was brought by the offender to make atonement for his offence, and in his place it was slain: this was the type of Christ taking the sinner's place, bearing the sinner's sin, and suffering in the sinner's stead, and thus vindicating the justice of God, and making it possible for him to be just and the justifier of him that believeth. I understand this to be the conquering weapon—the death of the Son of God set forth as the propitiation for sin. Sin must be punished: it is punished in Christ's death. Here is the hope of men.

Thus Spurgeon preached Christ crucified for the sins of the world.

With this very orthodox and traditional view of the person and work of Jesus Christ, all of Spurgeon's sermons unfolded in that Christocentric matrix. And, as pointed out, he did not preach these doctrines in a detached, theological manner. "Mr. Spurgeon's spiritual potency was not derived from Calvinism, but rather from his uncompromising belief that men and women are to be really saved by the Gospel . . . He always planned for immediate result." Little doubt, that explains something of the perennial appeal in the preaching of Charles Haddon Spurgeon. He lifted up Jesus Christ in a fully Orthodox, biblical fashion, but yet in a very personal, experiential, and dynamic fashion. One can see why he thoroughly enjoyed preaching the Gospel.

A "NATURAL" PREACHER

This leads to the next major facet of Spurgeon's effectiveness as a preacher. As often stressed, he preached experientially, practically, personally, and persuasively. In developing his preaching style he received much from Charles Simeon, the devoted preacher of Cambridge University. Spurgeon said, "I have no desire to become the rival of Mr. Charles Simeon; and yet if I should copy any man's outlines, I should prefer him for a model." And Spurgeon's practical, simple, natural style was never trite. As someone said, "Spurgeon is never commonplace; his heartiness and power made the most familiar expressions seem original and fresh."[34] Spurgeon had a natural freshness about his preaching that proved most captivating. Someone said, "It is as natural for him to speak as for a lamb to play, a duck to swim, or a lark to sing."[35] His human genius rested in his "naturalness" in the pulpit. He urged his students, "to preach it (the Gospel) in a *natural*, simple, interesting, earnest way."[36] He stressed, be natural and be interesting. He had no sympathy for dull pedantic preaching. In fact, he said on one occasion, "Dull preachers make good martyrs. They are so dry they burn well."[37] How did those natural, practical, interesting, methodological aspects of his preaching style have such power in bringing lost people to faith in Christ and did the building up and edifying of the saints? Several suggestions can be proffered.

AUTHORITATIVE PREACHING

One of the salient features of Spurgeon's preaching style centered in the fact that he preached with an intense amount of authority. This grew out of his basic philosophy of the Christian ministry. He said, "The grand object of the Christian ministry is to glorify God." That approach got Spurgeon out of himself and motivated him to bring glory to his Lord alone. That in itself precipitates authority. People sensed something of the authoritarian message that he declared, for it did not stem from the preacher, but from God Himself. Much in the spirit of Jesus, the people thus heard him and hung on his words.

Furthermore, several factors in Spurgeon's own person added to his authoritative ring. First, he had a deep and profound awareness of being called by God to preach. He said, "I am as much called to preach the Gospel as Paul was." On the surface, that may appear presumptuous; but he felt convinced the Holy Spirit directed his proclamation of Christ, and he ministered in the Spirit. Brastow wrote:

> In presenting the claims of the gospel, in appealing to men to accept the service of Christ, it is surely of unspeakable value to the preacher to feel that he has been called and sent to do that work, to feel that a message has been committed to him, and that in proclaiming it he is indeed an ambassa-

dor of God. It must increase a man's power tenfold. All great evangelists have felt this.

A worshiper at Spurgeon's church once said, "When I first heard him, and it has been so even since, his petitions impressed me more than his sermons . . . It appeared to me that he preached well, because he had prayed well."[38] This gave Spurgeon such moral authority that people were gripped with the compelling nature of his message. Once a critic said Spurgeon's sermons were not striking. Charles replied he thought preachers were to *feed* the sheep, not *strike* them. He fed them through prayer as well as preaching.

Moreover, Spurgeon felt authority emerges when the preacher is thoroughly convinced that the message being declared is the truth, and hence authoritative. He said:

> Believe what you do believe, or else you will never persuade anybody else to believe it. . . . You may depend upon it that souls are not saved by a minister who doubts; and the preaching of your doubts and your questions can never possibly decide a soul for Christ. You must have great faith in the Word of God if you are to be winners of souls to those who hear it.

And how can one gain the assurance that the declaration is the truth? By recognizing that the message is the truth of God. Spurgeon declared: "You must also believe that the message you have to deliver is God's Word. I had sooner that you believed half-a-dozen truths intensely than a hundred only feebly." Thus he preached with unction and authority.

PREACHING TO THE PEOPLE

Spurgeon's whole pulpit mannerism and style made him a people's preacher in the purest sense of the word. One of his contemporaries observed:

> Mr. Spurgeon is pre-eminently the preacher of the people. The scholarly will drop in to hear Dr. Vaughn or Dr. Dykes; the intellectual gather about the pulpits of Liddon or Stanley; the lovers of oratory follow Punshon; but the crowd goes to the Tabernacle.

As stressed earlier, Spurgeon preached in simple Anglo-Saxon. He tells the story of a preacher who once said in his message, "the son of Amram stood unmarred." Hearing such a phrase, Spurgeon pointed out, people would naturally ask, "Who is that?" Spurgeon then said, "the preacher would answer 'Moses, of course.'" Charles then retorted: "Then why didn't you say so." The point? Be forthright and simple! Spurgeon's preaching came over to people as "idiomatic, colloquial, simple and lucid, strong and zestful, earnest and sincere."[39] He had a homely style, he spoke the people's language. He spoke very concretely. Actually, by Spurgeon's day, the mass of Victorian people were weary of "culture" and "respectability" in the pulpit.

They wanted one of their own. Spurgeon filled that role. Spurgeon confessed, "I hate oratory, I come down as low as I can. High-flying language seems to me wicked when souls are perishing."[40] *The Daily Press* had it right when a reporter wrote, "Mr. Spurgeon is 'extraordinary' because he is one of the people and preaches to the people. The people follow him—the people love him—and he is made useful in the salvation of the souls of the people." He even had things said about him in the light-hearted periodical, *Funny Folks.* The common people truly did appreciate him. As Ritchie said, "He preaches to the people in a homely style—and they like it, for he is always plain, and never dull." Charles said, "We must preach the truths which are likely to lead to conversion, but we must also *use the modes* of handling those truths which are likely to be conducive thereto."[41] He would use no stilted phrases in French, Latin, Hebrew. He even used very little Greek. Yet, in all that simplicity, he had a wonderfully poetic style. *The Freeman* reported on March 14, 1860:

> Spurgeon is truly a poet, and without having heard him one cannot even form an idea of the richness and power of his conceptions, and thus, too, without even swerving from the simplicity which beseems the Christian pulpit, or the dignity which becomes a minister of Jesus Christ.

Spurgeon certainly was correct when he said, "The Holy Ghost did not care an atom for . . . composition . . . or rhetoric." The need is, "love of truth, conscientiousness, and gut."

PASTORAL PREACHING

It cannot be overlooked that Spurgeon's preaching centered in a pastoral context. He knew he had to be interesting to people, so he spoke to where they were living out their lives. Unapologetically, Spurgeon geared most of his sermons to the real people who sat before him. He could speak to their life situation beautifully. As Adcock said, "He lived among men and sympathized with them. Moreover, he studied them." By illustration, anecdote and plain speech, he got right down where they lived and wrestled with them in their problems. For those who were Christians, he preached to build them up in the faith. To those without Christ, he preached the simple Gospel. In the first sermon preached on a Sunday evening in the Tabernacle, Spurgeon declared:

> I beseech you never to cease to pray that here God's Word may be a quickening, a convincing, a converting word. The fact is, brethren, we *must* have conversion work here. We cannot go on as some Churches do without converts. We cannot, we will not, we must not, we dare not. Souls must be converted here, and if there be not many born to Christ, may the Lord grant to me that I may sleep in the tomb of my fathers and be heard of no more. Better indeed for us to die than to live, if souls be not saved.[42]

Perhaps the primary reason for Spurgeon's practical appeal and pulpit power centered in the unquestioned biblical content of his sermons, and in the practical application of God's Word to life. Every message he delivered he filled with Scriptural truth. His sermons always reflected invariable faithfulness to the text. As the cliché has it, he did not "take his text, depart from it, never to return again." When he took his text, he explained the text in every possible way. This became increasingly true as his ministry matured and he preached less topically and more textually. He also chose his texts carefully. He said he would not preach from a text if it would not "bite." But strictly speaking, his sermons were not expository in nature. That is to say, he did not take a lengthy passage and elucidate several verses in traditional expository style. His text normally consisted of one or two, possibly three verses at the most. The more expository type of communication Spurgeon engaged in came through his regular reading of the Scriptures during the worship when he would do a running commentary on a more lengthy passage. That actually took the form of a homily. But it must be granted that in his textual approach to preaching, the people got the text expounded from every conceivable vantage point. Thus, in a sense of the word, the people heard the Word of God from two different communicative perspectives; a homily and then a textual sermon. In that way, the Scripture came to the people in such a fashion that they heard the Bible from virtually every perspective.

Spurgeon's subjects and texts often came to him in a very natural fashion. For instance, one day he was sitting in Oberwood churchyard when he noticed five or six different paths leading to the church door. This suggested Mark 1:45: "But he went out, and began to publish it much, and to blaze abroad the matter, insomuch that Jesus could no more openly enter into the city, but was without in desert places: and they came to him from every quarter." He seemed to come up with a fresh verse every week. He did not encourage his students to announce a series of sermons. He felt that may hinder the free moving of the Spirit. He did occasionally preach series, but he would never announce them.

It must be admitted that at times Spurgeon took a measure of license or liberties with his text. His exegesis on occasion could be questioned by the more strict biblical exegetes. *The Birmingham Daily Press* once criticized severely his use of the Bible, saying:

> The London lion neither has the mane attributed to him, nor is his roar half what we expected. . . . We expected to hear striking comments on the Bible . . . (but) we had a sublime Psalm of David pulled about until it looked like a beautiful book that had been in the hands of an uncleanly boy, the book still beautiful, but big thumbmarks obscuring it by their greasiness, and defiling it by the dirt.

Fortunately, that did not occur too often and the fact that he did his best to adhere to the truth of the Scriptures became one of his important means of power in the pulpit.

PRACTICAL PREACHING

Finally, as has been stressed, Spurgeon's preaching had great effect because of his constant practical application of the Bible to the everyday lives of common people, his hearers. His appeal to the hearts of the people as he urged them to respond to the truth of God's Word always dominated his preaching. On one occasion he said:

> Go not forth from this place to talk with idle gossip on thy way home. Go not forth to forget what manner of man thou art. But hasten to thy home; seek thy chamber; shut the door; fall on thy face by thy bedside; confess thy sin; cry unto Jesus; tell him thou art a wretch undone without his sovereign grace; tell him thou had heard this morning that he came to save sinners, and that the thought of such a love as that hath made thee lay down the weapons of thy rebellion, and that thou art desirous to be his. There on thy face plead with him, and say unto him 'Lord, save me, or I perish.' [43]

In a message preached in 1888, he made the following appeal:

> Join with me in prayer at this moment, I entreat you. Join with me while I put words into your mouths, and speak them on your behalf—'Lord, I am guilty. I deserve thy wrath, Lord I cannot save myself. Lord, I would have a new heart and a right spirit, but what can I do? Lord, I can do nothing, come and work in me to will and to do of thy good pleasure . . . But I now do from my very soul call upon thy name. Trembling, yet believing, I cast myself wholly upon thee, O Lord. I trust the blood and righteousness of thy dear Son; I trust thy mercy, and thy love, and thy power, and they are revealed in him. I dare to lay hold upon this word of thine, that whosoever shall call upon the name of the Lord shall be saved. Lord, save me tonight, for Jesus' sake Amen.'

And it cannot be overlooked that Spurgeon had great confidence in the spiritual discernment that his "common" hearer possessed. He declared, "I have far more confidence in the mob than in the rich and idle few . . . The instinct of the masses can always be more safely relied upon than the caprices of the wealthy and learned few." [44] All these factors gave real authority to Spurgeon's pulpit work.

OTHER QUALITIES

Of course, there are other aspects of Spurgeon's pulpit appeal. For example, concerning natural gifts, he had "everything." His voice came close to equalling that of George Whitefield. As has already been amply illustrated, he could be heard by the tens of thousands, even in the open air. With his powerful voice, he could fill the great halls of England such as the Surrey Gardens Music Hall, the Agricultural Hall in Islington, and even the Crystal Palace. His deep, rich, resonant tones could permeate the very crevices of any building in which he preached. Not only that, he never appeared to be shouting at the people when he did preach. He would illustrate to his students that he could even whisper and yet be heard in the great Metropolitan Tabernacle. Someone said he could "Coo like a dove." As one admirer said, "What a voice! Without any lifting up, its trumpet tones ring over the Chapel, filling it with a pleasant stream of sound which must be heard or distinguished in the remotest corner as near the pulpit." He had one of those rare voices that comes along only once or twice in a generation. Not only that, people found Charles' dramatic style contagious and captivating. It will be recalled that Mr. Knowles, former director of the Drury Lane Theater, said that he would give a large sum of money to get Spurgeon on the stage. Yet, his dramatic flair was described as "never theatrical, his critics to the contrary notwithstanding . . . but . . . he was eminently dramatic. Mr. Spurgeon preached all over, not violently but naturally."[45] As implied earlier, Spurgeon did not have a striking personal appearance. Still, as a pulpit dramatist he had few, if any, peers. And in it, he was natural and never did anything for mere effect. The inflection of his beautiful voice, his appropriate yet flair-filled gestures, and the very body language that he employed in his sermons were quite remarkable for a man with no formal training, and he had these gifts from his early years.

Further, as already seen, he had a keen mind with instant recall, a measure of what today we would call a "photographic mind." The *Western Morning News* of February 1, 1892 said:

> He had mental faculty far in excess of the average. He did with ease, and spontaneously, mental feats which men of name struggle in vain to accomplish. Besides, he had what every large brain has not, large method and power of concentration. He could grasp the bearings of a subject, hold his theme well in hand, and display his thought like troops in a tactical movement.

He himself said, "I have a shelf in my head for everything, and whatever I read or hear, I know where to store it away for use at the proper time."

Spurgeon took no personal credit for his unusual mental abilities. He declared his ability was a consequence of his conversion experience. He said the "heterogeneous knowledge" he had acquired as a young man, which before his encounter with Christ seemed a jumble in his brain, as he expressed it "in glorious confusion," after coming to Christ arranged itself systematically on shelves that enabled him to call up exactly what he wanted when he needed it. Moreover, this power apparently continued throughout his life. In the same article of the *Western Morning News* of February 1, 1892 the writer went on to say:

Further, historic memory was about as perfect with him as it could well be, and no tale that he ever had to tell suffered in the telling of it. While he elaborated with ease his ideas, he made them portable and easy to bear away by a happy epigrammatic finish. It is marvelous how, when he had expounded a thought, he could thus make it live for ever in a few terse, pithy words. The same faculty shines forth in his correspondence. He had the power—a power in daily exercise, a power of impromptu, of loading language to a degree we have never seen approached.

It must be remembered that Spurgeon was an extemporaneous preacher. He took to the pulpit no more than a very simple outline of his message. Yet, his sermons possessed all the drama and pungency one would have thought came from a manuscript that had been labored over for days. But the preacher was an earnest student. *The Christian Leader* of February 2, 1888 pointed out, "Mr. Spurgeon does not write his sermons, but lays up material for them and draws upon a full barrel." Charles himself said, "I am always preparing sermons—reading and thinking."

This implies that Spurgeon had a basic, native eloquence. That is true. Even though he employed simple Anglo-Saxon language, his eloquence stood out in bold relief. Some of the passages in his sermons read almost like Shakespeare. He commanded an amazing grasp of the English language. As it has been expressed:

> With Mr. Spurgeon there was always a transparency, a crystalline beauty of expression so that it was impossible for mediocre hearers to miss his meaning, and at the same time impossible for educated people not to be stimulated and benefited.

The people would often sit spellbound. He could move them from tears to laughter and back to tears in a matter of minutes. His use of simile, metaphor and poetic analogies captivated the listeners. Yet, he did it all with amazing simplicity. For example:

> A little boy who died in Baltimore, when he was eight years old, while in London, was taken by his father to hear Mr. Spurgeon. The little fellow had heard it said that Mr. Spurgeon was the greatest preacher in the world. On being seated in the great Tabernacle for the first time he was all interest; and when the preacher began the service he leaned forward with open mouth, and listened through the entire time with most intense earnestness, scarcely moving his eye from the speaker. When the service was over, and they got into the street, his father said, 'Willie, what do you think of that man?' He stood still and looked up into his face, and asked, 'Papa, is that the greatest preacher in the world?' 'Yes, I think he is.' 'Well, then,' said the boy, with a glow of enthusiasm in his face, 'I know how to be the greatest preacher in the world.' 'How?' asked his father. 'Why, just pick out a nice chapter in the Bible, and tell just what is in it so that everybody can understand you, and nothing more.'

As often seen, Spurgeon had a master's grasp of the art of illustration. He always carried a notebook with him wherever he went. He would jot down interesting incidents and ideas that occurred during his everyday ministry. These provided valuable sources of illustrations and anecdotes. In this context, he received the expected accusation of being egotistical because many of his illustrations and references were about himself. Much of his preaching and lectures had an autobiographical motif, as did his writing. As someone said, his preaching and writings were "dominated by his own experience, his advice, his testimony, his character. When his own experience is not cited, then the reader must endure the testimony of his wife, his sons, his father, his grandfather . . . He missed no opportunity to promote his family or himself." The Archbishop of Canterbury once said, "The antiquate's *Ego* was ever before his eyes, but he made us all like him very much, and respect the *Ego* which he represented." [46] As is true with many successful men, in the pulpit and out of the pulpit, Spurgeon did not underestimate his own abilities. Be that as it may, his illustrations were always alive, relevant and practical. Thus the people did not seem to be put off by his constant references to his own experiences. Though he spoke often of himself, he can be rightly termed a master illustrator because he used illustrations from living a life in Christ to the full. But then, the Apostle Paul himself gloried in sharing his own personal testimony of conversion on the Damascus road. Furthermore, Paul's Epistles contain his own opinions of his spiritual pilgrimage and experiences. So in one sense of the word, Spurgeon preached in the Pauline apostolic tradition, though he would never claim to be inspired by the Holy Spirit in the same way as Paul when the New Testament came into being.

Important is the fact that Spurgeon was flexible in the pulpit. He gives an interesting account of that flexibility:

> Once . . . I intended to preach on a certain text, but during the hymn felt I *must* take another. So I began, not seeing how to go beyond my first topic, hoping 'secondly' would come when called for. Just when I got into difficulty, the lights went out and I had to stop. When the place was relighted I said I would take another text relating to light after darkness. One person was converted by each discourse. [47]

That approach is helpful to effective preaching.

Further, like Paul, Spurgeon rarely used allegories—and that to his credit. His use of poetry in his sermons enhanced his communication, and he used it often, especially the quoting of a favorite hymn, but he avoided allegorizing the Scriptures. Although Spurgeon illustrated his messages in a most skillful way, he did not always find illustrations easy to come by. At times even his notebook failed him to come up with a good anecdote. For example, in a letter to a Mr. Page dated June 23, 1884 he requested help on a new book of sermon outlines he was writing. He wrote:

I want your aid with anecdotes. I cannot always hit on good ones, fresh, uncommon. You may possibly suggest some exciting story, verse or other illustration when I run by.

Noteworthy is the fact that Victorians apparently made a fine distinction between sermons and speeches, although one could clearly blend into the other. And in pure speeches, as in pure preaching, Spurgeon excelled. An article in *The Freeman*, December 12, 1878, makes that clear:

Mr. Spurgeon as a Public Speaker

During the recent meetings of the Baptist Union at Leeds we heard of a discussion in relation to Mr. Spurgeon's power in the pulpit and on the platform. Several of those who took part in it contended that he was most thoroughly at home in the pulpit, and that his sermons were, by a long way, his best and most powerful efforts. Others held that, indisputable as was his pre-eminence as a preacher, his sermons were surpassed in value by his speeches. We do not know which of these opposing opinions had the majority of votes, but there was, as it seems to us, great wisdom in the remark made by a gentleman who had not previously heard Mr. Spurgeon: 'When I listened to his sermon on "Preaching Christ," I thought nothing could excel that; when I heard his speech urging us to "Drive On," I thought nothing could excel that; both were inimitable, and each was in its own way perfect.' The fact is Mr. Spurgeon is as much at home in one sphere as he is in the other. The finest elements of his power are as conspicuous in his speeches as in his sermons. Whatever he does, he does with his might, and under whatever circumstances we listen to him, we never wish him to be other than he is. . . . Mr. Spurgeon always speaks in a lively, graphic, and impressive style. His homely Saxon is full of pith and vigour. He cannot, we should think, be misunderstood, and very rarely can there be in his audience a sleepy hearer.

Many things can be said about Spurgeon's natural gifts and abilities. These have been reiterated time and again, not only in this biography but in a host of other writings. In summary, let it simply be said that his gifts far exceeded most people of his day, probably much more than the people of any era.

SPURGEON'S HOMILETICS

Concerning the formal elements of the sermons, Spurgeon did not break any revolutionary ground. He used a simple introduction. He taught his students not to make them so long that interest wanes. Although some of his introductions appear long in writing, he never really fell into that homiletical trap. He said, "Don't make the introduction too long as a rule. One preacher took so long spreading the cloth a woman lost her appetite." Spurgeon drew from various sources in the construction of his introductions. At times he used the occasion for which he preached. Then he would often talk about the text he intended to explain. In other sermons, he would employ a "contextual" approach, or he might use the subject of his sermon. To his credit, he used a variety of approaches and he knew the introduction must introduce the sermon and ellicit interest.

Spurgeon's sermons were always outlined with basic "major points" and under them "sub-points." He used a rather typical Aristotelian rhetorical style. Each point stood out distinctly and elucidated the theme. He did not slavishly follow the "3-point" sermon construction style, however. Often he would have four or more major points, and at other times only two points. He did whatever would elucidate the text well. Therefore, the outline always came over as simple and made the point. Although Spurgeon used great variety in the body of the message, he always attempted—as pointed out—to be faithful in his use of the text. For example, below is an outline of a message from John 12:26.

Introduction: Service is essential. Service of a sort may not be accepted.

    I. The Rule *of Service*
        1. By believing my doctrine.
        2. By obeying my commands.
        3. By imitating my example.
        4. By clinging to my cause.

   II. The Fellowship *of Service*
        1. In the place of consecration.
        2. In the place of communion.
        3. In the place of confidence.
        4. In the place of calm.
        5. In the place of conquest.

  III. The Reward *of Service*
        1. He shall know his Sonship.
        2. He shall have approval.
        3. He shall have honour among saints.
        4. He shall have honour in heaven.

As Baggett put it, the "development of Spurgeon's sermons are distinct, simple, and varied."[48]

The conclusions of Spurgeon's sermons are power packed. He knew how to "draw in the net." Every conclusion came over as very personal in its aim. He often, it must be acknowledged, appealed to fear. In a sermon on "Songs in the Night" (Job 35:10), he warned the man of foul mouth, the swearer, "Your mouth is black with oaths now, and if you die, you must go on blaspheming throughout eternity. But list to me, blasphemer! Dost thou repent tonight." The conclusion for Spurgeon became the time to lead people to a decision for Christ.

Sermon Preparation

How did Spurgeon prepare his sermons? What methodology did he develop that gave the messages, even in printed form, a worldwide acceptance? That is a story in itself.

Fullerton expressed a word of general caution about Spurgeon's sermon preparation: "Mr. Spurgeon's method of preparing his sermons is not to be recommended to others who are without his gifts." How true! Normally, on a Saturday afternoon, Spurgeon would invite several friends for tea. He would often conduct a small worship time with them along with his family. They all understood, however, they were to leave by six or seven o'clock. Charles would say it was time for him to get some food for his sheep. The Sunday morning sermon had to be prepared—on Saturday night.

Charles often had some difficulty in selecting the text he felt God would have him use the next morning. In his early days, this disturbed him tremendously. He had read a book on homiletics where the author said if one had a struggle finding the proper text, he was not called of God to preach. But Charles soon matured out of that false assumption. Then, after he got his text in mind, he would begin to jot down outlines elucidating that particular text. Sometimes he would write several, only to throw them away until he found one arrangement of the thoughts that satisfied him. It was not unusual for the simple sermon outline to be sketched out on the back of a piece of scrap paper or even on an old envelope. No elaborate outline came forth, as demonstrated above. In Spurgeon's early days of preaching, however, his outlines were larger and more complex than later. As a case in point, on the 9th of February 1851, preaching for the Lay Preachers Association, he prepared a message on Ephesians 1:5. The outline had four major points and 28 sub-divisions.

After Spurgeon settled on his outline, he would often have his wife Susie read several commentaries on that particular verse. Susannah gave a beautiful description of those happy hours spent together in reading the commentaries:

> For some time past it has been the dear Pastor's custom, as soon as the texts for the Lord's-day's services have been given by the 'Master,' to call me into the study, and permit me to read the various commentaries on the subject-matter in hand. Never was occupation more delightful, instructive, and spiritually helpful. My heart has often burned within me as the meaning of some passage of God's Word has been opened up, and the hidden stores of wisdom and knowledge have been revealed; or when the marrow and fatness of a precious promise or doctrine has been spread like a dainty banquet before my admiring eyes. Shall I ever forget those solemn evenings, when the sufferings of the Lord Jesus were the theme of tearful meditation, when, with love and grief our heart dividing, we followed Him through the night on which He was

betrayed, weeping like the daughters of Jerusalem, and saying, 'There never was sorrow like unto this sorrow,' or the more rapturous time when the exceeding riches of His grace was to be the topic for the morrow, and we were fairly bewildered by the inexhaustible treasures of love and grace to be found in that fair 'land of Havilah, where there is gold!'

Gracious hours are those thus spent, and unspeakably precious to my soul; for while the Lord's dear servant is reaping the corn of the kingdom for the longing multitude who expect to be fed by His hand, I can glean between the sheaves, and gather the 'handfuls of purpose' which are let fall so lovingly.

Then come delightful pauses in my reading, when the book is laid down, and I listen to the dear voice of my beloved as he explains what I cannot understand, or unfolds meanings which I should fail to see, often condensing into a few clear, choice sentences whole pages of those discursive old divines in whom he delights, and pressing from the gathered thoughts all the richest nectar of their hidden sweetness. Thus a *poor prisoner* has the first sip of the *wines on the less* well refined, the first morsel from the loves with which the thousands are to be fed and refreshed on the morrow. How can I sufficiently thank God for this drink of the brook by the way, this holy place within my home, where I find the Lord deigns to meet with me, and draw out my heart in adoration and worship? Lord, I bless and praise Thee, that thus Thou hast most blessedly fulfilled Thine own words, 'I will not leave you comfortless. I will come unto you.' [49]

After an hour or two of such preparation, Charles felt ready to preach. He believed more in preparing himself than in delivering the sermon. He strove to get his heart into the message. His wife Susannah said, "His whole heart was absorbed in it, all his spiritual force was engaged in it, all the intellectual power with which God so richly endowed him was pressed into this glorious service." As theologian Thielicke pointed out, "Spurgeon works fast upon the souls of . . . prospective preachers and repeatedly challenges them to work upon their own souls." [50] Spurgeon said, "You must have a great heart to be a great soul winner."

Spurgeon generally prepared the Sunday evening sermon on Sunday afternoon in the same manner. Always a very rapid worker, his thoughts came to him tumbling one after another in a very systematic and analytical fashion. It appears as if Spurgeon spent little time in preparation. However, Craig Skinner argues that the time-honored idea that Spurgeon prepared his Sunday morning sermon on Saturday night and his Sunday night message that afternoon really misses the mark concerning his preparation.

Skinner states:

This half-truth is repeated in almost every biography. . . . In reality he studied his topic all week. Then, from all that knowledge he chose one text on the Saturday evening. Then he either divided it up into segments, or chose a variety of perspectives from which he could discuss that text using the material he had previously gathered. Each of these elements then became a facet of his topic which enabled him to use all that pre-studied material. The most that could be said is that Spurgeon finally outlined the form of the sermon on Saturday night (and often complained that he made dozens of such outlines before he settled on the final one).

Skinner also contends Spurgeon would commission his secretaries early in the week to research subjects that he would preach on the next Lord's day. Skinner may well be correct, although it appears difficult to verify his contention. Some of the biographers who repeat the traditional view knew Spurgeon personally. Also, there were those who visited Spurgeon's home on Saturday afternoons for tea and were requested to leave around sunset so Spurgeon could prepare his message. Of course, that may be how the traditional idea grew up; they would hardly have known what he was thinking about all through the week and just assumed he did *all* his preparation on Saturday night. Be that as it may, Spurgeon was a fast thinker and could do amazing things in a matter of minutes.

He said that his thoughts came to him at a rate of twenty for every five minutes. Somehow, he had the wonderful gift of getting a text, writing a brief outline on it, hearing the commentaries on that particular verse, and being able to preach on the text with a systematic eloquence that dramatically compelled all to listen.

So along with good, lively illustration, faithfulness to the text, preaching to people's needs, and dramatic flair, it can be understood why Spurgeon received all the accolades. He knew how to communicate.

INNOVATIVE METHODS IN WORSHIP AND EVANGELISM

It is also helpful to note that Spurgeon used innovative methodologies in the worship services. It has already been stated that he would advertise, preach any place, and even be willing to "preach on his head" if that would help people to grasp the message of salvation. Of course, he never did preach upside down, but he surely employed some very practical methodological means of making his preaching ministry effective. In his early days, he often announced that those who were recently converted, or those concerned about their relationship to Christ, should meet him at a certain place and time. He said, "Whenever I was able to appoint a time for seeing converts and inquirers, it was seldom, if ever, that I waited in vain, and, so many came, that I was quite overwhelmed with gratitude and thanksgiving to God." Little wonder A. Cunningham Burley called him, "One of the greatest soul winners the world has ever known."[51] At times Charles actually felt overwhelmed by the response. Nevertheless, he always insisted on a personal and separate interview with each inquirer regardless of the number. When the Metropolitan Tabernacle was completed, he adopted the procedure of being in his vestry every Tuesday afternoon at 3:00 for conversations with those concerned for their salvation. An elder would see them first, find out the exact nature of their spiritual condition and then send them in to the pastor. This weeded out the cranks and sent only true seekers to see Spurgeon.

Charles also trained his own people to be on the alert in each service for anyone who might seemingly be concerned about his spiritual welfare. Members would be on the outlook to spot those who were touched by the sermon. They would attempt to speak with them and pray with them privately before they left the Tabernacle. Spurgeon was very warm to this method and encouraged all his members to be active in it. In an early sermon he stated:

> I should like to have all over the Tabernacle a little lot of you Christian people like sentries, watching that young man who is here for the first time to-night; watching that young woman who has been here for the last six weeks— watching your opportunity; as soon as ever you see the first wave of the Spirit's manifestation—the face is often the tell-tale sign of what is going on within—to speak to them.

Many were led to Christ by this method. An earnest word from a concerned lay person touched many lives.

Spurgeon also employed the use of special meetings organized and arranged specifically for helping those who needed Christ as Savior. Although he did not use this method extensively, he saw its effectiveness if used properly. He said, "Of enquirers' meetings en masse we have had two, of which we can speak with great confidence, for we know that they were owned of God."[52] However, Spurgeon went on to say:

> We have suspended them [the enquirers' meetings *en masse*] for a while, lest they should become a matter of routine, and in the meantime hold similar meetings at the close of other gatherings; as, for instance, after the Thursday lecture.[53]

Spurgeon, although obviously not opposed to enquirers' meetings, moved with caution, realizing the method could be dangerous and used to manipulate people. But seeing their value if used in a sensible manner, he often called for after-meetings in enquiry-rooms. He employed this method as early as 1865 in the Metropolitan Tabernacle. On the second of January of that year some six thousand people attended a mass prayer service at the Metropolitan Tabernacle. When it was concluded, "A number of Christians retired to a room below with many anxious ones, several of whom received peace with God through faith in the precious Savior."[54] Spurgeon used the method rather infrequently in his earlier ministry, but it seemingly gained more favor in his thinking as the years progressed. This may be because of the influence of the Moody-Sankey meetings in England of 1873-1875. As a case in point, in the January 1875 issue of *The Sword and the Trowel*, the writer stated, "On Monday evening, December 7, many hearts were touched, and an after-meeting was held in the vestry, at which several testified that they had found peace with God."[55] Spurgeon held a series of evangelistic meetings in the Tabernacle in February of 1878, and he gave the following report:

> One prominent feature of these February services was the successful manner in which the enquiry meetings were conducted. Workers were distributed over the building, and at the close of the service they moved toward the enquiry room, bringing the anxious with them. The interior walls were also posted with slips, pointing the way for enquirers. It was, therefore, impossible for anyone under conviction to feel that he was uncared for. Every evening the enquiry rooms were filled, and many who had been awakened under the preaching lingered to a late hour, until they 'found peace in believing.'[56]

It thus seems quite conclusive that by the latter half of the 1870s, Spurgeon employed the use of the enquiry-room with some regularity.

Spurgeon himself did not attend the enquiry-rooms and after-meetings. Others performed this duty, but always with instructions and words of warning from their pastor. For example, in a sermon preached in 1884, anticipating that someone would like to go to the enquiry-room, Spurgeon observed:

> I dare say you would, but we are not willing to pander to popular superstition. We fear that in those rooms men are warmed into a fictitious confidence. Very few of the supposed converts of enquiry-rooms turn out well. Go to your God at once, even where you are now. Cast yourself on Christ, now, at once; ere you stir an inch![57]

In a similar fashion, at a College Conference of 1890, Spurgeon stated:

> In our revival services, it might be as well to vary our procedure. Sometimes shut up that enquiry-room. I have my fears about that institution if it be used in permanence, and as an inevitable part of the services. . . . If we make men think that conversation with ourselves or with our helpers is essential to their faith in Christ, we are taking the direct line for priestcraft. In the gospel, the sinner and the Saviour are to come together, with none between.

Spurgeon saw the negative side of the enquiry-room.

Spurgeon abhorred simple "decision making." Regardless of the method used to bring people to Christ, stress on church membership and discipleship always surfaced. His interest centered in making true disciples, which meant among other things becoming church members. His preaching and use of methods constantly moved in that direction—and that to his credit also.

A WALK WITH GOD AND PREACHING

It should never be overlooked that Spurgeon realized great preaching emerged from a life in touch with God. Spurgeon constantly emphasized that reality. In an address on open air preaching he stressed the principle, but it clearly applies to all types of preaching. *The Daily News* (October 28, 1879), reported:

> The Rev. C. H. Spurgeon delivered an address on open-air preaching. After observing that his words must be brief, for he was in great pain of body, he said there was one thing which they who were engaged in preaching the Gospel must always take care of—namely, that they kept themselves by God's grace right with God. If they were to touch the hearts of their fellow-men, if they were to be used by God as his instruments they must be right with God. To be right with God they must be holy men. Unless they were holy men, they might be great speakers, but they would never have the blessing of God on their work. He did not believe that a man could go and preach to his neighbours in a street, and have the blessing of God on his preaching if he had a shop and did not keep good weights. . . . If God did not make them holy they had better shut up and keep quiet till he did.

Spurgeon also recognized the vital part prayer played in effective preaching. When asked why he had such success he would simply say, "My people pray for me." Perhaps this spiritual element presents the most foundational insight to his greatness as a preacher.

In the context of being in fellowship with the Christ one preaches, the preacher must be very earnest. Spurgeon said:

> He must feel, 'I shall die if I do not succeed. I must bring these souls to Christ. I want the blessing for them; I *must* have it.' That is the true spirit in which to go about the work. We dare not preach as if it were a matter of indifference whether souls are saved or not. We *must* have them saved. When God writes *must* across *our* hearts, He will write *must* across *their* hearts. When He teaches us to declare that they must be born again, He teaches them to see it, and he works the change. Christ will say to them, 'I must abide in thy house to-day,' and they must receive Him. So, by God's grace, our 'must' and God's 'must' will come together, and souls shall be saved. I hope in such an earnest spirit you will preach the everlasting gospel. [58]

A Summary

Much more could, and probably should, be said about Spurgeon's preaching. Perhaps his preaching success can best be summed up as follows:

> One reads Spurgeon's sermons with the result that such things as theological controversy, faulty exegesis, and unconventional methods that greatly bothered many of his contemporaries, fall into the shadows as the wonder of his great spirit and the power of his ministry emerge. One is left in no mood to be *coolly* critical, but rather shares the feeling of the theological student who, when called upon to criticize a Spurgeon sermon, said to the professor, 'Doc-

tor, I have no criticism. This is the loveliest sermon I ever read. It just did my soul good.' And the understanding professor replied, 'Bless your heart, brother, that is the best criticism you could have made. It did my soul good, too.' The story of the abundant life as well as the great sermons tends to disarm the analyst and critic. [59]

Thus, it can be concluded that Spurgeon will always stand as one of the great pulpit masters of the Christian church. He set the pattern for multitudes of preachers. He follows in the tradition of preachers like Chrysostom of Constantinople of whom it was said, "better for the sun never to shine on Constantinople than for Chrysostom to stop preaching," or men like Bernard of Clairvaux who preached so effectively that mothers would lock up their sons in their homes prohibiting them from hearing Bernard preach lest they follow him to the monastery. Spurgeon preached like the great Pre-Reformation reformer, Savonarola of Florence, who preached over three hundred sermons on the book of Revelation and spawned the great Florentine revival, or John Huss of Prague who influenced the Moravians in such a manner that during the great Moravian Revival under the leadership of Count Ludwig von Zinzendorf, they spread the Gospel worldwide. In preaching he can be numbered with the Reformers themselves: Luther, Calvin, Zwingli, and a host of others down through the great Puritan preachers like William Perkins of Cambridge, and all the giants of the Puritan-pietistic awakening. He need not even take a lesser place than the great George Whitefield. Spurgeon will always be classified historically as one of the outstanding preachers of all time.

But Spurgeon's preaching fame did not come about by his pulpit work alone. His published sermons and various writings proved of equal force, and probably extended his ministry in a fashion that he could never have accomplished any other way. Years before the days of mass communication through radio, television, and the electronic media, Spurgeon's ministry through his writings extended worldwide. As a consequence, he became a household word all over the globe as people hung on his every written word just as people in Britain hung on his preached word. This interesting saga demands an examination.

SPURGEON'S WRITING MINISTRY

Introduction

Charles Spurgeon proved as useful in writing as in preaching. Evangelist D. L. Moody said:

It is a sight in Colorado on Sunday to see the miners come out of the bowels of the hills and gather in schoolhouses or under the trees while some old English miner stands up and reads one of Charles Spurgeon's sermons. They have conversions right along.

As effective as Spurgeon's writing ministry ultimately became, his early efforts began in a quite inconspicuous manner. In 1853, he did a short series of tracts entitled "Waterbeach Tracts." In the same year, the *Baptist Reporter* published an account of a conversation between Spurgeon and a Baptist pastor from Maidstone. The Baptist minister had led Charles when still a boy to search the Scriptures regarding the Baptist concept of baptism. Even before that, as a lad of eleven, he tried his hand at writing. He composed a small magazine of fourteen pages, called *The Home Juvenile Society*. Some of these early efforts have already been recorded.

THE PUBLISHED SERMONS

After Charles came to New Park Street in 1854 as a young minister, he contributed a few expository articles to various Baptist magazines. Then, several of his sermons were published in James Paul's "Penny Pulpit." The sermons sold very well. This began to draw attention to the young, eloquent preacher as a writer. Then came the weekly publishing of his sermons and the "Penny Pulpit" ministry. Spurgeon gave his own interesting account of how his weekly published sermons came about. He wrote:

> On August 20. 1854, I preached at New Park Street Chapel from the words in I Samuel xii. 17: 'Is it not wheat harvest to-day?' The sermon was published by Mr. James Paul, as No. 2234 in his Penny Pulpit, under the title, 'Harvest Time,' and was, I believe, the first of my discourses to appear in print. Before I ever entered a pulpit, the thought had occurred to me that I should one day preach sermons which would be printed. While reading the penny sermons of Joseph Irons, which were great favourites with me, I conceived in my heart the idea that, some time or other, I should have a 'Penny Pulpit' of my own. In due course, the dream became an accomplished fact. There was so good a demand for the discourses as they appeared in the *Penny Pulpit* and *Baptist Messenger*, that the notion of occasional publication was indulged, but with no idea of continuance week by week for a lengthened period; that came to pass as a development and a growth. With much fear and trembling, my consent was given to the proposal of my present worthy publishers to commence the regular weekly publication of a sermon. We began with the one preached at New Park Street Chapel, on Lord's-day morning, January 7, 1855, upon the text, 'I am the Lord, I change not; therefore ye sons of Jacob are not consumed' (Malachi iii. 6); and now, after all these years, it is a glad thing to be able to say, 'Having therefore obtained help of God, I continue unto this day, witnessing both to small and great.' How many 'Penny Pulpits' have been set up and pulled down in the course of these years, it would be hard to tell; certainly, very many attempts have been made to publish weekly the sermons of most eminent men, and they have all run to their end with more or less rapidity, in some cases through the preacher's ill-health or death, but in several others, to

my knowledge, from an insufficient sale. Perhaps the discourses were too good: the public evidently did not think them too interesting. Those who know what dull reading sermons are usually supposed to be, will count that man happy who has for over thirty years been favoured with a circle of willing supporters, who not only purchase but actually read his discourses. I am more astonished at the fact than any other man can possibly be, and I see no other reason for it but this,—the sermons contain the gospel, preached in plain language, and this is precisely what multitudes need beyond anything else. The gospel, ever fresh and ever new, has held my vast congregation together these many long years, and the same power has kept around me a host of readers. A French farmer, when accused of witchcraft by his neighbors, because his crops were so large, exhibited his industrious sons, his laborious ox, his spade, and his plough, as the only witchcraft which he had used; and, under the Divine blessing, I can only ascribe the continued acceptableness of the sermons to the gospel which they contain, and the plainness of the speech in which that gospel is uttered.

When the time arrived for issuing Vol. I. of *The New Park Street Pulpit*, I wrote in the Preface:—'Little can be said in praise of these sermons, and nothing can be said against them more bitter than has been already spoken. Happily, the author has heard abuse exhaust itself; he has seen its vocabulary used up, and its utmost venom entirely spent; and yet, the printed discourses have for that very reason found a readier sale, and more have been led to peruse them with deep attention.

'One thing alone places this book above contempt,—and that accomplishes the deed so triumphantly, that the preacher defies the opinion of man,—it is the fact that, to his certain knowledge, there is scarcely a sermon here which has not been stamped by the hand of the Almighty, but the conversion of a soul. Some single sermons, here brought into the society of their brethren, have been, under God, the means of the salvation of not less than twenty souls; at least, that number has come under the preacher's notice from one sermon only; and, doubtless, more shall be discovered at the last day. This, together with the fact that hundreds of the children of God have been made to leap for joy by their message, makes their author invulnerable either to criticism or abuse.

'The reader will, perhaps, remark considerable progress in some of the sentiments here made public, particularly in the case of the doctrine of the Second Coming of our Lord; but he will remember that he who is learning truth will learn it by degrees, and if he teaches as he learns, it is to be expected that his lessons will become fuller every day.

'There are also many expressions which may provoke a smile; but let it be remembered that every man has his moments when his lighter feelings indulge themselves, and the preacher must be allowed to have the same passions as his fellow-men; and since he lives in the pulpit more than anywhere else, it is but natural that his whole man should be there developed; besides, he is not quite sure about a smile being a sin, and, at any rate, he thinks it is less a crime to cause a momentary laughter than a half-hour's profound slumber.

'With all faults, the purchase has bought this book; and, as it was not warranted to be perfect, if he thinks ill of it, he must make the best of his bargain,—which can be done, either by asking a blessing on its reading to himself, or entreating greater light for his friend the preacher.'

The publishing of much of Spurgeon's works through the years flourished through the friendship between Spurgeon and his publisher, the faithful deacon at new Park Street Chapel, Mr. Joseph Passmore. Both in personal and business affairs, they became the closest of friends and colleagues. For forty years the friendship continued with never a single problem arising to mar their esteem and appreciation of each other. Passmore's second son was blind, but he attended the Pastors' College and became the Baptist pastor in Whitstable.

A short time after Spurgeon's acceptance of the London church, Passmore suggested Spurgeon start his own weekly "Penny Pulpit" series. The series came to be called the "New Park Street Pulpit." When Passmore made the proposal to Charles, the young preacher gave his consent, as seen, "with much fear and trembling." But they pressed forward and on January 7, 1855, the first of the long series commenced. Spurgeon titled the first sermon, "The Immutability of God." Passmore produced a weekly sermon from that date until 1917. They ceased because of the paper and metal shortage of World War I, the "Great War" as it is known in Britain. Even after Spurgeon had laid down his mantle some twenty-three years before, the sermons were published and widely read week by week. More shall be seen about the impact of the sermons in a moment.

OTHER EARLY WRITINGS

Spurgeon not only produced a weekly sermon, he began early on to write books as well. One of his first works Spurgeon titled, *Smooth Stones Taken from Ancient Brooks*. His fiancée, Susie, helped him in compiling the material for this small volume. Another early venture, partly intended as an answer to the slanders under which he constantly suffered, was the publication of a new edition of the *Baptist Confession of Faith*. He produced the *Confession* with personal notes; it received a reasonable circulation. Spurgeon had a deep conviction that he should do this work, as is shown by the following letter:

TO ALL THE HOUSEHOLD OF FAITH, WHO REJOICE IN THE GLORIOUS DOCTRINES OF FREE GRACE,—

Dearly-beloved,
I have thought it meet to reprint in a cheap form this most excellent list of doctrines, which was subscribed unto by the Baptist ministers in the year 1689.

We need a banner, because of the truth; it may be that this small volume may aid the cause of the glorious gospel, by testifying plainly what are its leading doctrines. Known unto many of you by face in the flesh, I trust we are also kindred in spirit, and are striving together for the glory of our Three-in-one God. May the Lord soon restore unto His Zion a pure language, and may the watchmen see eye to eye!

He who has preserved this faith among us, will doubtless bless our gospel evermore.

So prays your brother in the gospel of Jesus,

C. H. Spurgeon.

Another early, larger volume, *The Saint and His Saviour*, contained some 140 pages. Spurgeon sold this work to a publisher for fifty pounds, a quite high price in those days. But it enjoyed an unusually large sale and put hundreds of pounds into the publisher's purse. Regardless, they never gave the young author more royalties. Passmore did not publish this volume. After that experience, Passmore and Alabaster became Spurgeon's regular publisher. Joseph Passmore was not only a personal friend of Spurgeon, he was also a nephew of Dr. Rippon.

Still, Spurgeon found writing, in his own words, "a drudgery." The words did not flow as easily from his pen as they did from his pulpit. When he wrote his early book *The Saint and His Saviour*, he said, "Never was a book written amid more incessant toil." [60]

Moreover, as Charles received constant criticisms for his preaching, he likewise endured the same negativism over his writing. Several friends even advised him to give up the venture on the ground that he would probably never gain any success as an author. Nevertheless, he carried on despite all the discouragement, "drudgery," and "slavery." And his perseverance paid off. He produced one hundred thirty-five books and edited another twenty-eight. Furthermore, he has been constantly republished through the years until the present moment. As mentioned earlier, there are more books in print by Spurgeon one hundred years after his death than any English author.

Spurgeon's success as a writer proves to be quite paradoxical when one realizes what a real drudgery writing was to him. He once said:

It is a delight, a joy, a rapture, to talk out my thoughts in words that flash upon the mind at the instant they are required; but it is pure drudgery to sit still and groan for words without succeeding in obtaining them. Well may a man's books be called his 'works,' for if every man's mind were constituted as mine, it would be work indeed to produce a quarto volume. Nothing but a sense of duty has impelled me to finish this little book, which has been more than two years on hand. Yet have I at times so enjoyed the meditation which my writing has induced, that I would not discontinue the labor were it ten times more irksome; and, moreover, I have some hopes that it may yet be a pleasure to me to serve God with the pen as well as with the lip.

At times, Spurgeon got credit for work he did not do, often work for which he did not want any credit. For example, a C. *M.* Spurgeon of Cambridge Heath, London, wrote a pamphlet entitled, "Where Are the Dead." C. *H.* Spurgeon received many letters over it and had to disassociate himself from it.

SPURGEON'S CLASSICAL BOOKS

Many of Spurgeon's works became classics. Space precludes outlining all the volumes that flowed from his fruitful pen. But a few merit mention. His *Lectures to My Students* still speaks to ministers, young and old alike. The volume came about as a compiling of Spurgeon's weekly lectures on the ministry to the students at the Pastors' College. Compiled and published, they remain in print to the present moment.

Another significant volume is Spurgeon's *An All-Round Ministry*. This also remains in print. It presents the principles of the balanced ministry that Spurgeon himself exercised. Perhaps the most popular of Spurgeon's works, at least in his day, is his well-known *John Ploughman's Talks; or Plain Advice for Plain People*. After the success of this small volume, he published in the same vein *John Ploughman's Pictures; or More of His Plain Talk for Plain People*. These books contained simple, homely Christian advice that touched a multitude of subjects. They are similar to the Book of Proverbs. A sample of Spurgeon's approach in those popular works reads:

John Ploughman's Pictures

IF THE CAP FITS, WEAR IT

FRIENDLY READERS: Last time I made a book I trod on some people's corns and bunions, and they wrote me angry letters asking, 'Did you mean me!' This time, to save them the expense of a halfpenny card, I will begin my book by saying,

> Whether I please or whether I tease,
> I'll give you my honest mind;
> If the cap should fit, pray wear it a bit;
> If not you can leave it behind.

No offence is meant; but if anything in these pages should come home to a man, let him not send it next door but get a coop for his own chickens. What is the use of reading or hearing for other people? We do not eat and drink for them; why should we lend them our ears and not our mouths? Please then, good friend, if you find a hoe on these premises, weed your own garden with it.

These two works have been reprinted often. In the fall of '83 the "Conditional Immortality Association" of Britain published a pamphlet entitled *John Ploughman's Wife*—a plagiarism on Spurgeon's character. Charles reacted quite strongly because the "wife" disagreed with Spurgeon's "John." Perhaps Charles' reaction was due in part because there were allusions to smoking in the pamphlet.

Mention has already been made of Spurgeon's well-known work, *The Saint and His Savior*. It became very popular. One of his most read works, *The Soul Winner: How to Lead Sinners to the Saviour* remains in print. This work has been responsible for many persons coming to faith in Christ. Reprinted by Fleming Revell with a foreword by Helmut Thielicke, it blesses people to this hour.

Another fine volume that came from Spurgeon's earlier pen, calling on Bunyan's *Pilgrim's Progress*, was titled *Around the Wicket Gate*. Charles wrote this to help people to faith in Christ. The opening paragraph begins, "Great numbers of persons have no concern about eternal things. They care more about their cats and dogs than about their souls. It is a great mercy to be made to think about ourselves, and how we stand toward God in the eternal world . . . It would be an awful thing to go dreaming down to hell, and there to lift up our eyes with a great gulf between us and heaven."[61] Spurgeon said in the preface to this book, "I am in terrible earnest to get my hesitating friends over the threshold. Come in! Come in! is my pressing entreaty. 'Wherefore standest thou?' is my solemn inquiry."[62] This book is one of Spurgeon's most fervent attempts to lead people to faith in Christ through the pen.

Of course, many are familiar with Spurgeon's last work, *Memories of Stambourne*. This book was penned a short time before his death. It paints a beautiful picture of his childhood memories. Today, Stambourne boasts only 299 citizens. The old Independent Church and beloved manse where Charles spent his early years have disappeared. Only the Parish Church and the Red Lion Pub remain.

All agree that Spurgeon's *magnus opus, The Treasury of David*, gets highest marks for a devotional commentary. Published originally in six volumes, Spurgeon virtually exhausts the Book of Psalms. It took him 21 years to complete the work. He finally published the last volume in 1883. With the able help of one of his secretaries, Mr. J. L. Keys, he produced one of the most monumental works on the Psalms ever accomplished. Spurgeon himself was exceedingly proud of the work. It stands today as a monument to his insight, thoroughness, tenacity, and above all, his practical grasp of what the Word of God is saying. It also remains in print and is an invaluable reference set. Gracey and George Rogers aided Spurgeon in that work as well. But Spurgeon relied most heavily on the research of his secretary, J. L. Keys, Actually, Keys helped the pastor in many of his works. He once wrote his secretary: "Look out, and summarize the explanations given by some four or five leading commentators to the expression 'Grace for grace': John 1:16." Keys' son became a pastor and entered the College. At his admittance Spurgeon wrote the young man the following letter:

> April 26, 1884
>
> Dear Mr. Keys,
>
> It will give me peculiar pleasure to welcome you into the college next August. It is gladdening to me to see so many of the sons of my students following their father's course. We expect each generation to excel its predecessor. May our Lord keep you and preserve you in his service here. Thus reward (you) hereafter.
>
> Yours heartily,
>
> C. H. Spurgeon

Then there always stands the so-called *Autobiography*. This large, four-volume work came after the death of Spurgeon. Although it first appeared in four volumes, it has recently been condensed and published as a two-volume set. It contains personal reminiscences, considerable correspondence, excerpts from sermons, various writings, anecdotes, and a host of other fascinating material that came largely from the pen of Spurgeon. He had intended to write an autobiography, but never accomplished the task. After the death of the master preacher and writer, all the material was put in its present form by his widow and his secretary. It still stands as probably the most comprehensive and perceptive look into the life of Spurgeon. Along with the *Treasury of David*, it became one of the two greatest works of the preacher. Spurgeon also had planned to write extensively on the Book of Isaiah as he had done on the Psalms, but his life ended before he could attempt that herculean task. Many other fascinating works flowed from his pen. The above mentioned works comprise just a very small sampling of over 100 books he wrote.

VARIOUS WRITINGS

The sermons and volumes that Spurgeon penned do not comprise the entire writing ministry of the preacher. A great number of smaller articles appeared in a variety of forms. The largest number of articles written by Spurgeon appeared in the well-known *The Sword and the Trowel* publication. This monthly periodical, produced by Spurgeon's church, addressed current issues, spiritual problems, religious news, etc. In *The Sword and the Trowel* Spurgeon expressed his opinion on a multitude of matters. For example, in *The Sword and the Trowel* Spurgeon threw out the first challenge that precipitated the Down Grade Controversy. The periodical enjoyed wide circulation and the sheer volume of work Spurgeon produced in it is astounding. In the first issue, Spurgeon outlined the purpose and content of the periodical. It reads:

THE

SWORD AND THE TROWEL

JANUARY, 1865

Our Aims and Intentions.

When Israel sojourned in the wilderness, all the people pitched their tents about the ark of the Lord, and made the holy place their common centre; yet each tribe was distinguished by its own banner, and marched under the conduct of its own chiefs. Even so in the Church of God, our Lord Jesus and the common salvation are the central point about which believers gather, but the standards of peculiar associations of Christians cannot well be dispensed with. We feel that we need to uplift a banner because of the truth, and with hopeful heart we do so this day.

Our Magazine is intended to report the efforts of those Churches and Associations, which are more or less intimately connected with the Lord's work at the Metropolitan Tabernacle, and to advocate those views of doctrine and Church order which are most certainly received among us. It will address itself to those faithful friends scattered everywhere, who are our well-wishers and supporters in our work of faith and labour of love. We feel the want of some organ of communication in which our many plans for God's glory may be brought before believers, and commended to their aid. Our friends are so numerous as to be able to maintain a Magazine, and so earnest as to require one. Our monthly message will be a supplement to our weekly sermon and will enable us to say many things which would be out of place in a discourse.

The Sword and the Trowel has been re-established under the auspices of the present Metropolitan Tabernacle.

Spurgeon also produced a host of pamphlets, articles, and other works. He had a most fruitful pen. Thus the "scavenger of the literary world," as Spurgeon's critics called him, carved his niche on the religious literary scene, thereby becoming an evangelist to the world.

When Spurgeon began his weekly published sermons, at the young age of twenty-one, little did he realize that he had launched a global ministry. Although he preached face to face to the masses in London each Sunday, the congregation at the Metropolitan Tabernacle shrunk infinitely small in comparison to the multitudes who never saw his face or heard his voice, yet felt the profound impact of his printed sermons. An Englishman dying in Brazil said, "I shall never see Mr. Spurgeon on earth, but I shall tell the Lord Jesus about him when I get to heaven." But we move now to see more detail about the influence of the published sermons.

THE "PENNY PULPIT" AND ITS INFLUENCE

Every year the "Penny Pulpit," each weekly sermon filling about eight pages of small type, was compiled and printed as a full volume. This continued for the years the church met on Park Street. The sermons were published under the title, *The New Park Street Pulpit*. Later, when the congregation moved to the Metropolitan Tabernacle in Newington Butts, the yearly publications received the title, *The Metropolitan Tabernacle Pulpit*. This latter series began in 1861 when Spurgeon was twenty-seven years old. In the year the Metropolitan Tabernacle series began, Parliament abolished the duty on paper. Spurgeon's publishers therefore extended the eight pages of small type to twelve pages of larger, more readable type. Of the sixty-three volumes finally produced, each one contained from 52 to 60 sermons, except for the last edition which failed to be completed because of the conditions of the First World War.

Of course, the question surfaces: how is it possible to print so many of Spurgeon's sermons after his death? It must be remembered that he preached at his Church three times every week and only one of the three messages reached the press each week during his life. Thus a great backlog of his sermons sat ready for publication. Even today there have been reports of other sermon manuscripts being unearthed. Furthermore, along with the sixty-three volumes that comprise the *New Park Street* and the *Metropolitan Tabernacle Pulpit*, approximately a dozen more volumes of sermons on specific themes have been produced. An insightful appraisal of Spurgeon's mammoth amount of sermonic material was given by the *British and Foreign Evangelical Review* of April 1877. The article reads:

> The chief desire amongst Christians is to gain an assurance of God's Love, and to the subject Mr. Spurgeon constantly recurs, not discussing it with a wave of the hand, but taking it up fully and elaborately. Many excellent sermons act merely as a mental stimulus: they instruct, and even to some extent excite, but they do not meet the deep needs of the soul. It is, we believe, one of Mr. Spurgeon's chief sources of power that he devotes himself almost entirely to the great concern. It is this that has made his writings so dearly prized by the dying. There is no more enviable popularity than the popularity this eminent minister has amongst those who are in the presence of the profoundest realities. When cleverness and eloquence have lost their charms, the dying often listen hungrily to Mr. Spurgeon's writings, when nothing else, save the Word of God, has any charm or power.

Dr. Pusey once said:

> Multitudes of educated Christian men loved Charles Spurgeon, in spite of intellectual differences, for that reason. From the days when Samuel Rutherford so preached his Master as to compel the Duke of Argyll once to cry out,

'Oh, man keep on in that strain!' no one, we may safely say, has set forth the claims of Christ to men's love and service with such winning sweetness, and such melting pathos, with such eloquence of the inmost soul, as Charles Spurgeon. It may be that the dark background of his theology, to which the mind of this age could not by any effort accommodate itself, threw into greater relief this side of his teaching. The outside darkness of unbelief and irreligiousness was, indeed, made very terrible. But the inner world of spiritual experience was wondrous fair. And no human computation will be able to reckon the number of weary toilers in the working and lower middle classes whose narrow surroundings have been brightened and idealised by the glow from the realm of faith to which this man achieved, to convince multitudes of struggling people, in the midst of a life which everything tended to belittle, that their character and career were a matter of infinite concern to the Power who made them, that they could not afford to treat sin lightly, or to throw themselves away as though they were of no account.

Spurgeon constantly received the accusation of being simple if not superficial in his writings. He tried to be simple. But as Fullerton says, "Let not the reader be deceived by their apparent simplicity—it is the ease of genius, there is a depth as well as clearness; Spurgeon was, in fact, one of the great Doctors of Divinity, he had an intuitive knowledge of the ways of God, and of the needs of the human heart, and in all his preaching his one object was to commend God to men. Robert Louis Stevenson, in writing to a friend in London, says: 'I wish you to get *Pioneering in New Guinea*. It is a missionary book, and it has less pretensions to be literature than Spurgeon's sermons.' But even if Spurgeon's sermons had no claim to be considered as literature, it would be wise advice, 'I wish you to get them.' A distinguished professor in one of our theological colleges was accustomed at times after his divinity lecture to read one of the sermons to his students, and he generally introduced it by saying, 'Now let us have some of Spurgeon's heart-warming mixture.'"[63] The *Times* gave its evaluation of Spurgeon's published sermons:

> Mr. Spurgeon laid his foundation in the Bible. His utterances abound with Scriptural text, figure, metaphor and allusion. Whatever he says sends his hearers to the sacred record. But starting from this basis, he has added to it a stock of reading such as few men can show in their talk or in their writing. He cannot be accused of not being a man of the world, or of not knowing the ways of the world, for he reads the Book and the book of nature, too. His style is illustrated with almost pictorial brightness. What remains? The very tail of the matter. He occasionally drops a phrase to provoke a smile from the soft cheeks of ladies and gentlemen, and to make them think for the moment that they could say the thing better. We are not sure that Latimer and Ridley's sermons would not jar on modern refinement quite as much, but they never would have reformed the Church of England with smooth words and a pure classic style.

The Bishop of Ripon, went even further. Speaking in his cathedral after Spurgeon's death, he eulogized the great sermons of Spurgeon with these words: "The power of Mr. Spurgeon lay in this, that though from a critical standpoint, he did not understand the Old Testament, yet being so much imbued with a spiritual conception he had drawn from patient and careful study of the Bible, he often escaped the very mistake which from a critical standpoint he might have fallen into." Proper praise for powerful "simple" preaching.

Spurgeon preached and published from every book of the Bible, and he used some texts many times. Occasionally, he would repeat a sermon. Often, when on his itinerant ministry, he would preach the message he had delivered the previous Sunday in London. Yet, he was never repetitive to the point of becoming commonplace. Above all, as previously discussed, the power of his sermons rested in their biblical content. He once said at a meeting of the Bible Society:

> What a storehouse the Bible is, since a man may continue to preach from it for years, and still find that there is more to preach from than when he began to discourse upon it. What pyramids of books have been written upon the Bible, and yet we who are students find no portion over-expounded, but large parts which have been scarcely touched. If you take Darling's *Cyclopædia* and look at a text which one divine has preached upon, you will see that dozens of others have done the same; but there are hundreds of texts which remain like virgin summits, whereon the foot of the preacher has never trod. I might almost say that the major part of the Word of God is still in that condition: it is still an Eldorado unexplored, a land whose dust is gold. For twelve years most of my sermons have been reported and printed, and yet in my search for something new I pace up and down my study, embarrassed with the abundance of topics, not knowing which to choose. [64]

After the elimination of the duty on paper and the sermon enlargement from the eight to the twelve page format, another three volumes of Spurgeon's messages were produced. The sermons came largely from Spurgeon's Sunday and Tuesday evening services, and were entitled *The Pulpit Library*. The first sermon in the first volume was "Is It Not Wheat Harvest Today?" Spurgeon titled the first sermon of volume two of *The Pulpit Library*, "Prove Me Now" (Malachi 3:10). Spurgeon preached this message at New Park Street on the morning of the day when the disaster occurred at the Surrey Garden Music Hall. It had something of a prophetic ring. Spurgeon said, "See what God can do, just when a cloud is falling on the head of him who God has raised up to preach to you." [65] This was typical of the type of preaching he did.

WORLDWIDE SERMONS

By the end of the publication of Spurgeon's sermons in 1917, one hundred million copies of his weekly sermons had been sold. Since that day they have been reprinted and republished in a myriad of formats so that the number is almost incalculable. On one particular occasion, a publisher received an order for a million copies of one sermon. Once a quarter of a million copies of his sermons were bought to be distributed to students in the universities, members of Parliament, the crowned heads of Europe, and the householders of Ireland.

The worldwide distribution of Spurgeon's sermons defy imagination. For example, a businessman in Australia paid for their insertion in several weekly papers "Down Under." Because space in the paper had been purchased, they were put in the format of an advertisement. However, the ad projected the Gospel before the people in a mode that commanded their attention. For a period of time, an enterprising American newspaper syndicate had the Sunday morning sermon cabled across the Atlantic for publication in American newspapers. The first American paper to publish the cabled messages was the *Cincinnati Commercial Gazette*. Then dailies in Boston, Philadelphia, and St. Louis picked them up until they were syndicated in many papers. This continued until the syndicate discovered that a rival had managed to tap the wires. This killed it. Spurgeon wrote a very characteristic paragraph on the enterprise and its early demise: ". . . the sermons were not long telegraphed to America, so that our friends who feared that the Sabbath would be desecrated may feel minds relieved. . . They (the sermons) had been ours, but they were so battered and disfigured that we would not have owned them. In the process of transmission the eggs were broken and the very life of them was crushed. We must prefer to revise and publish ourselves."[66]

Spurgeon's messages were also translated into several other languages. For example, a special German edition was produced for the Leipzig Book Fair of 1861. All major language groups could read Spurgeon in their native tongue. They found translation into Arabic, Chinese, Telegue—in all, twenty-three different tongues. *The Echo* reported on January 10, 1888, that some of Spurgeon's sermons translated into Russian received a stamp of the Seal of the Russian Orthodox Church. A description of the impact of the sermons in Russia reads:

> Writing in 1881 to Mr. Spurgeon, a minister stationed at St. Petersburg says: 'By your sermons, etc., you are having a part in the great work of spreading Christ's kingdom both in St. Petersburg and in the interior. You are well known among the priests, who seem to get hold of your translated sermons, and, strange to say, I know cases in which the Censor has readily given consent for your works to be translated when he has been reluctant respecting many.' Another friend in the Russian capital made it his business to circulate as many of the translated copies as he could procure, the priests apparently being the most eager recipients.
>
>   Another friend in Russia, who wrote in 1880, says: 'I came to this country about twenty-four years ago, and have been about in various parts of the

interior ever since . . . I have a wife and eight children. A few weeks ago I explained to them the meaning of the Orphanage, and appealed to their feelings; the result was that I was authorised to go to their savings-bank and take out three roubles four kopecks as the children's contribution. We have now made up the sum to fifty-five roubles, which will be forwarded to you from St. Petersburg by a cheque.'

In the more remote parts of the Czar's vast empire Mr. Spurgeon's works are not only known, but are promoting the spiritual enlightenment of the people in a way no less striking than gratifying. Writing to the Pastor from Warschaw in 1882, Mr. F. H. Newton, of the German Baptist Mission, thus refers to his adventures: 'I have during the last few weeks been visiting a number of our Baptist Churches in Silesia and Russian Poland; and I think you will be interested to hear of their activity and Christian faith. In almost every town and village one of the first enquiries put to me is, And how is Brother Spurgeon? In many of the outlying stations, where no stated missionary can be sustained, your printed sermons are regularly made use of: and I am sure you will be thankful to our one Master to learn that here in Poland, and elsewhere, many of the Church members attribute their first religious awakening to hearing some of those sermons read.'

That sort of scenario was repeated in many parts of the world.

McCoy pointed out that Spurgeon's production of sermons may be roughly divided into three periods. The first period emerged during the exuberant, evangelistic days when Spurgeon, as a very young man, employed all the eloquence and dramatic qualities he owned. The second period surfaced in the more pastoral period wherein the mellowed man preached more to build up and edify the saints. The third period, characterized by Spurgeon's later years, displays the depth, maturity and spirituality he had accumulated through his over thirty years in London. Also, during this later period, Spurgeon saw the influx of Germanic rationalistic theology invading his beloved country. Therefore, more of a polemical element intrudes in the sermons throughout that later period.

For many years Spurgeon's weekly "Penny Pulpit" sermons had an average circulation of approximately 25,000. At times, many more thousands were sold, especially when Spurgeon preached on special occasions or on certain topics. For example, Spurgeon's message on "Baptismal Regeneration" sold 350,000 copies when printed as a pamphlet. In 1863 the five hundredth weekly message was published. At that time, the sermons had already sold more than eight million copies. At Spurgeon's death in 1892, tens of millions of copies had been produced. At the cessation of the series on May 10, 1917, the last sermon, number 3,653, brought the number to the aforementioned one hundred million copies.

Through the years the earlier criticism of Spurgeon's written works began to subside. The charges of sensationalism and superficiality abated and his writings became generally respected. When Passmore and Alabaster moved their publishing offices to Paternoster Row, the prestigious street of British publishers, it became symbolic of the new acceptability of Spurgeon's publications.

To grasp something of the breadth of acceptance of Spurgeon's sermons, when Dr. David Livingston traveled through Africa, he carried with him a copy of Spurgeon's sermons. Some years later, after Livingston's death, his daughter discovered the book of sermons in one of her father's old trunks. She found it well thumbed, with the pencilled comment, "Very good. D.L."

THE INFLUENCE OF SPURGEON'S WRITTEN MESSAGES

The influence of Spurgeon's published sermons at times seems almost unbelievable. On one occasion, Spurgeon counseled with a woman whose husband had left home, and fled the country. The Metropolitan pastor dared her to believe that her husband would be converted, and even become a member of the Tabernacle Church. At that very time, on board a ship, her husband stumbled upon one of Spurgeon's sermons. He read the story of the Gospel and accepted Christ immediately. He returned to home and wife, and a few months later, his wife introduced him to Spurgeon. The couple were happily reunited in Christ and the church. Once, during a voyage to Oregon, someone found a copy of a Spurgeon sermon and pressured one of the passengers to read it aloud. Practically the entire contingent of passengers plus some of the crew gathered around the reader. Sometime afterwards, in San Francisco, the reader of the sermon met a man who declared that he had heard him "preach." "Of course," the reader replied, "I am not the preacher, my friend." The man related that he had heard him read the sermon by Spurgeon that day. He was one of the sailors and he said, "I never forgot that service; it made me feel that I was a sinner, and I had found Christ and I was so glad to see you again."

One of the most fascinating events surrounding the reading of a Spurgeon sermon occurred in a South American city. There, an Englishman had been confined to prison for life, apparently for murder. An English friend visited him and left behind two English novels. But as the providence of God would have it, between the leaves of one of the novels, a Spurgeon sermon had been wedged. The message influenced the prisoner tremendously, for in the sermon Spurgeon referred to the murder of Palmer. The Gospel presented in the message gave the prisoner such hope in Christ that, though he never expected to be released from prison, he had come to know Jesus Christ as Savior and would one day experience the great liberation of heaven.

Once at a missionary assembly in Chicago, the plea went forth for a missionary volunteer to go to the far west. In a certain area of the western part of the United States, no less than two hundred people had come to faith in Christ through reading Spurgeon's sermons, and they desperately needed a missionary.

The power of Spurgeon's sermons affected a Scottish woman. Under conviction of her sin, she tried to burn her Bible and a copy of one of Spurgeon's sermons. Twice the sermon fell out of the fire, the second time half consumed. This so aroused her curiosity that she read the fragment and was converted on the spot.

A man, keeping sheep in the bush near Ballerat, Australia, picked up a sheet of newspaper. One of the sermons that the Australian gentleman had paid for spread across the page, looking like an advertisement. The man confessed that if he had realized the article was a sermon he would never have read it. But seeing it in the newspaper in the form of an advertisement, he became interested, read it, and found Christ. Another instance is told of a young man who worked in a printing office. One day he picked up a crumpled piece of paper out of the wastepaper basket. It turned out to be one of Spurgeon's sermons, in this case, a message on the atonement. He opened it out and it revealed to him the way of life; he became a dedicated Christian.

One of the most unusual occurrences concerning Spurgeon's sermons took place in England:

> A dying publican's wife, in England, recently gave the following encouraging testimony, as narrated by the evangelist who visited her. He says: 'I was asked to go to a public house in Nottingham and see the landlord's wife, who was dying. I found her rejoicing in Christ as her Saviour. I asked her how she had found the Lord. "Reading that," she replied, handing me a torn piece of paper. I looked at it and found that it was part of an American newspaper containing an extract from one of Spurgeon's sermons, which extract had been the means of her conversion. 'Where did you get this newspaper from?' I asked. She answered: "It was wrapped round a parcel which was sent me from Australia." Talk about the hidden life of a good seed! Think of that, a sermon—preached in London, conveyed to America, an extract reprinted in a newspaper there, that paper sent to Australia, part torn off (as we should say, accidentally) for the parcel despatched to England, and, after all its wanderings, conveying the message of salvation to that woman's soul. God's Word shall not return unto Him void.

Accounts of this nature go on almost interminably. The influence of Spurgeon's sermons and the thousands converted through the reading of his published messages really becomes all but incredible.

Spurgeon's sermons found particular acceptance in the United States. Tens of thousands awaited his weekly publications. This went on for several years until Spurgeon preached a sermon on slavery. As pointed out earlier, he took a very firm stand against the despicable system. The sales of his sermons in the America, especially in the South, drastically diminished. In fact, Spurgeon was hung and burned in effigy because of his stand. But, being a man of moral integrity, he gladly endured the decrease in sermons-sales for his conviction. Spurgeon never cut corners in any area of his spiritual convictions, regardless of the costs.

Nonetheless, all over the United States, stories of Spurgeon's far reaching influence constantly surfaced. Spurgeon regularly received letters from people telling him how the sermons had touched their lives. Spurgeon talked about letters from people who were "rough dwellers in the wild," living "far away in the bush," or "far away in the backwoods." He once received a letter from Minnesota telling him that in their community of some five or six hundred people, several families subscribed to his sermons. In Corpus Christi, Texas, a semi-literate, eighty-two-year-old man once wrote Spurgeon recounting how much the sermons had done to the local Christians in faraway Texas. Spurgeon reveled in the evidence of the blessings that attended his printed works. He once said that a message from an American backwoodsman proved "more precious to me than a big banknote."[67] Spurgeon heard that one single sermon, "Compelled Them To Come In," had led almost three hundred people to faith in Jesus Christ. This pleased the Metropolitan pastor exceedingly. He reveled in stories like that of an American cowboy who wrote that, after reading one of Spurgeon's sermons, he had "given up Bowie knives and revolvers, to become a child in the Spirit."[68] A preacher in Tennessee one time testified that "nine years ago I was a wild young man; but I was converted through the reading of one of Spurgeon's sermons and I am now pastor of a large and influential church."[69]

Spurgeon may have been a little naive, but he accepted these testimonies uncritically. He said, he stood "more astonished at the fact than any other man can be, and I feel no other reason for it than this—the sermons contained the Gospel, preached in plain language, and this is precisely what multitudes need beyond anything else." He gave all glory to the Lord and the power of the Gospel.

As can well be imagined, pulpit plagiarism of the sermons became common. Many hearers would write to him and report that his sermons were being regularly preached by others. Spurgeon enjoyed this. In 1879, he said rather wryly, "So many have copied my style, and so considerable a number have borrowed my discourses, I submit that I am the orthodox example rather than the glittering exception . . . an old fashioned kind of body, who was treated as an established part of the ecclesiastical life of this great city."

Spurgeon's sermons could be found—and often used—almost anywhere. In the railroad stations in Scotland, Spurgeon's sermons sold side by side with the newspapers. It is said that two-thirds of the homes in Ulster, Northern Ireland, would have one or more copies of Spurgeon's sermons.

One of the most beautiful and positive incidents of the plagiarism of Spurgeon occurred in Charles' own experience. As has been noted, Spurgeon at times fell into despondency and depression. His depression would even run so deep on occasion that he would begin to question his own relationship to God, and if he truly had been saved. Once, in such a state, he walked into a small chapel to spend an hour in worship with the people, unknown to the congregation and to the preacher as well. In the grace of God, the pastor preached one of Spurgeon's sermons on the assurance of faith. Spurgeon, deeply and profoundly touched, said that he "made my handkerchief wet with my tears" as God spoke to him through the message and gave him the full assurance of faith. When the service concluded, Charles went to the pastor and expressed how profoundly grateful he was for the message and how it had touched his life. The pastor asked who he might be. One can imagine the embarrassment when he found out that Charles Haddon Spurgeon was the visitor. As Charles expressed it, the pastor "turned all manner of colors." The good preacher said, very sheepishly, "Oh, Mr. Spurgeon, that was your sermon." Spurgeon in his typical gracious and Christlike demeanor replied, "Yes, I know, but wasn't it gracious of the Lord to feed me with the food that I had prepared for others." This incident provides insight to the graciousness of the man and the power of the sermons.

Another fascinating story comes from Alexander Maclaren, the well known biblical expositor and Baptist pastor from Manchester. Maclaren, while still a youth in Scotland, told of how his employer would go each week from the little Scottish village where he lived into a large nearby town to buy supplies. The employer's wife always had a parting admonition: "And, John, dinna forget Spurgeon." The reading of Spurgeon had become a regular weekly ritual for the family. They would gather around the small fire in their little cottage, and they would all listen as one of the family members read aloud from the weekly sermon. Maclaren said:

> Perhaps the glamour of the past is upon me, perhaps a lad was but a poor judge, but it seemed to me good reading—slow, well-pronounced, reverent, charged with tenderness and pathos. No one slept or moved, and the firelight falling on the serious faces of the stalwart men, and the shining of the lamps on the good grey heads, as the gospel came, sentence by sentence, to every heart, is a sacred memory, and I count that Mr. Spurgeon would have been mightily pleased to have been in such meetings of homely folk. . . . Who of all preachers you can mention would have held such companies but Spurgeon? What is to take their place, when the last of these well-known sermons disappears from village shops and cottage shelves? Is there any other gospel which will ever be so understanded of the people, or move human hearts as that which Spurgeon preached in the best words of our tongue? The good man and his wife have entered into their rest long ago, and of all that company, I know not one now; but I see them as I write, against the setting of gold, and I hear the angel's voice, 'Manasseh is saved,' and for that evening and others very sacred to my heart I cannot forget Spurgeon.

There were actually remote parts of the British Isles and around the world, where one of the few links they had with the outside world was

Spurgeon's sermons. Some even reported there were places where people did not know the names of Gladstone or Disraeli, but they knew at once the name of Spurgeon.[70] An old Scot one time said that before he died he wished that he would have the opportunity to travel to London, "to see Madam Tussaud's (wax museum), and hear Mr. Spurgeon."[71]

Because of the wide dissemination of Spurgeon's written messages, when he traveled throughout the countryside, he had a ready-made audience to hear him. In the *Freeman*, the following observation was made:

> The coming of Mr. Spurgeon to any city, town or village, either in England, Wales, or Scotland, is an event which moves the entire population, Church and Nonconforming, rich and poor, church-going and non church-going. In a city such as Manchester, the 'upper ten' talk of it on the 'Change,' while down to the cabmen and bootblacks it is the theme of conversation. . . . No other preacher in this age wields such power, and it may be questioned whether anyone else has ever done it in these Islands save John Knox in Scotland and Christmas Evans in Wales.

In America, similar testimonies emerged. Dr. Joseph Cook of Boston recalled how much Spurgeon's sermons had touched his life:

> I recollect vividly myself going into the empty upper rooms of those classic Latin commons at Phillips Exeter Academy, Andover, and reading aloud for an hour, nearly every Sunday morning from the sermons of this young and until recently unknown preacher of London. His light was beginning to fall upon this land as early as 1854, and it has been growing . . . ever since.

By 1879, hundreds of thousands of copies of Spurgeon's sermons were sold in the United States. *The Christian Herald* declared, "It is safe to say that no other preacher has ever had such extenses of hearing in the U.S. as Charles Spurgeon."[72] A reporter from the *Richmond Herald* on his return from a European tour said, "Of course I went to see Spurgeon, I would as soon think of leaving London without seeing Westminster Abbey or the Tower . . . as to leave England's metropolis without hearing Spurgeon."[73] To help American tourists determined to hear Spurgeon, London bus drivers would make the announcement that they were getting close to Spurgeon's Tabernacle three miles in advance of Elephant and Castle where the Tabernacle was situated. As W.T. Stead said, "The Tabernacle was one of the pilgrim's shrines of the nineteenth century, one of the unifying nerve centers of our race."[74]

D. L. Moody declared, "Everything that I could get a hold of in print he ever said, I read." When Moody crossed the Atlantic in 1867 and saw Spurgeon for the first time, he related, "My eyes just feasted on him, and my heart's desire for years was accomplished." President Garfield of the United States was one of the few presidents who died in the White House. When his wife Lucretia performed her sad task of gathering her husband's possessions and vacating the presidential mansion, she discovered a program of a Metropolitan Tabernacle service. She wrote to Spurgeon that the discovery assuaged her grief and she found strength in the memory that she and her husband had felt the comfort in attending one of Spurgeon's services.[75] Of course, preachers all over the world of all denominations read—and used—Spurgeon. *The Church Review* (March 11, 1887) related: "We know more than one priest of the Church of England who habitually buys and studies Mr. Spurgeon's sermons and devotional writings." On one occasion, in a little chapel in Chardiganshire, the pastor of the tiny congregation was preaching a sermon of Spurgeon's verbatim. He became so engrossed in reading word for word that he blurted out before he caught himself, "And now I turn to you, the hundreds in the gallery."

THE PRODUCTION METHOD

The method by which the sermons were printed after the verbalization of them in the services constitutes an interesting story. It began by someone in the congregation taking down the sermon in longhand—this was during the days before any electronic devices were available. The sermon then would be delivered to Spurgeon on Monday morning in longhand, manuscript fashion. He would edit it quite extensively. It would then go in that form to his publisher. The type would be set and the galleyproof sent back to Spurgeon. Once again, he would extensively edit it and return it to the publisher for the final typesetting and printing. In that simple fashion, from the actual preaching of the sermons to the editing of the longhand manuscript (the person must have been a very rapid writer), to the galleyproof and its corrections, finally into the hands of the public, comprised the sequence. Of course, something inevitably gets lost in the publication of any sermon. Spurgeon's own personality, his dramatic style, his resonant voice, etc. could not be experienced. Yet, Spurgeon edited the sermons so well that all the impact of his personality did not fall on the printer's floor. As *The Country Quarterly* (April 28, 1887) reported, "Mr. Spurgeon's sermons lose less of power in the process of change from the word *spoken* to the word *written* than those of any other preacher." Moreover, the writing discipline sharpened Spurgeon's communicative skills. For example, he always preached just long enough to fill the twelve necessary pages for publication. That normally meant forty to forty five minutes. Whether it be the spoken word or the written word, his acumen in communication excelled.

The sermon for which Spurgeon received the greatest testimony concerning its influence to bring people to Christ was preached in the revival year of 1859. He titled the message, "Compel Them To Come In" (Luke 14:23). Hundreds of people joined various churches as a result of its influence. From all over the world, letters came from those who declared that the sermon had been the means of salvation. Two other sermons preached in the Surrey

Garden Music Hall were especially honored by the Holy Spirit. One was entitled, "Looking Unto Jesus" (Hebrews 12:2). Spurgeon himself admitted it was "one of the most simple of the series, and likely to be overlooked by those who are seeking anything original and striking." Yet, God used it, bringing many people to faith in Christ. The other sermon Spurgeon called, "The Shameful Sufferer." It also had a strong influence upon its readers.

In 1861, an unusual sermon entitled "Simon" went to twenty-four pages in length and was printed in gold. It sold for a full shilling, the proceeds going for the aid of the building of the Metropolitan Tabernacle. The sermon, "Things That Accompany Salvation," is considered the most eloquent of all Spurgeon's sermons, and exhibits the greatest mental powers that the preacher had.

On rare occasions, Spurgeon tried his hand at poetry. One cannot but conclude they were not of the highest literary value. For example, he wrote:

> Some go to church to take a walk;
> Some go there to laugh and talk;
> Some go there to meet a friend;
> Some go there their time to spend;
> Some go there to meet a lover;
> Some go there a fault to cover;
> Some go there for speculation;
> Some go there for observation;
> Some go there to dose and nod;
> The wise go there to worship God.

Still, the poem has a bit of down-to-earth appeal, and that would satisfy Spurgeon—and probably most of the congregation.

What more can be said about the preaching and writing ministry of Spurgeon? Probably never in the history of Christendom, at least up to Spurgeon's point in time, has one man's messages touched more people. And all that happened before the days of mass communication where a preacher can now preach to millions of people through the electronic media. The sheer magnitude of Spurgeon's ministry in his writing and preaching was unparalleled in his day, and in many respects, in ours. As Helmut Thielicke said, "Here was the miracle of a bush that burned with fire and yet was not consumed. This bush from old London still burns and shows no signs of being consumed." The sermons, "Even for us . . . are still a bubbling spring whose water needs no filtering or treatment." In all this, God used Charles Spurgeon mightily as a messenger of the Gospel of Jesus Christ. He truly filled the role of "a very great and honorable person, his name . . . is Evangelist."

Newspaper cartoonists saw the
State Church as "The Slow
Coach" (above) and Spurgeon's
evangelical enthusiasm as
exciting as a ride on the newly
invented steam engine—the
"Fast Train" (right).
 —*courtesy of Dr. Craig Skinner*

7

"His Name . . . Was . . . *Faithful*"

SPURGEON'S EARLY YEARS AT THE METROPOLITAN TABERNACLE

Metropolitan Tabernacle.

The trials that those men do meet withal
That are obedient to the heavenly call
Are manifold and suited to the flesh,
And come, and come, and come again afresh;
That now, or sometime else, we by them may
Be taken, overcome, and cast away.
O let the pilgrims, let the pilgrims, then,
Be vigilant, and quit themselves like men.
                                        —*John Bunyan*

"We will not go into debt for this house of God. I decline to preach in the place until it is paid for."[1] With these words Spurgeon set the pattern for the building of the expansive Metropolitan Tabernacle. He said he would never open the new tabernacle if any debt remained; he declared to do so would make him "a guilty sneaking sinner."[2] He intended to be faithful to his convictions and to his ministry. "Faithful" does describe the man.

THE NEW TABERNACLE

Early in the ministry of the great London preacher—he had been pastor of the New Park Street Baptist Church for only two years—it became evident to most that a large church building must be built to hold the vast crowds coming to hear him. As could be expected, many Londoners convinced themselves that to think of building a chapel of any great size would be sheer folly. Some years before the Presbyterian pastor Edward Irving, who died the same year Spurgeon was born, had captured the imagination of London by his dramatic oratory and preaching. A magnificent church was built to house the crowds that came to hear Irving's oratory, but he soon faded from the scene. He left little more than a beautiful church building and a huge debt. The critics said the same would be true of Spurgeon; he too would be left with an empty building and a large debt. But Spurgeon determined he would never preach in the building until the last penny had been paid. At least there would be no debt left as a legacy of his ministry, perhaps a big building, but no debt. He declared, "The Bible never tells us to get out of debt; it tells us we are not to have any."[3] Still, the London critics were not dilatory in condemning the concept. Even some in Spurgeon's own congregation were skeptical. Spurgeon's reaction? "Build or I resign; either erect the tabernacle or I become an evangelist." Spurgeon threw down the gauntlet. As one put it, "He himself was always in advance of his people."[4]

Such examples of Charles' firm and very decisive leadership manifested themselves throughout his ministry. For example, when Spurgeon found a member of the congregation who differed from the church's basic doctrinal stance and practice, he would simply say to that person, "Please withdraw from the church." He did not mind rebuking others when the occasion called for it. Once he told a man his conscience must be new for he never seemed to use it. He settled matters in a word. He once declared publicly, "I am the captain of this vessel. If there should be a Jonah in this ship, I shall in as efficient a spirit as possible pitch him out. I shall not think that because Jonah is there I ought to leave, but I will stand by the ship in all weather as well as in sunshine."[5] In that spirit Spurgeon not only built the spiritual and doctrinal structure of the Metropolitan Tabernacle, but the building itself. For all practical purposes, he made the final decisions. "Faithful" was also forthright.

Because of Spurgeon's determination, in June of 1856 the church appointed a building committee. Biographer Lorimer stated that "at their first private meeting Spurgeon exclaimed, 'I hear some of you are doubtful; if so go through that door and stay there.' At a later meeting he repeated the statement. Twelve went out. Said he, 'Any more?' Three more departed, and with seven he marched to victory." That account may be apocryphal, yet he once said, "Lead me not into temptation means to me, bring me not into a committee."[6] All this speaks of the determination, if not the often accused brashness, of the twenty-one-year-old preacher.

But could such an undertaking be realized? Charles said, "It is the glory of Omnipotence to work by improbabilities."[7] He declared, "I like to see a man trying to do the impossible. Any fool can do what he *can* do."[8] His gardener one day said to son Thomas, "SPURGEON! Ah, there was no humbug about him!"[9] His commitment to be faithful to God's Word and principles received divine approval—and of those who knew him. It was no idle boast when Spurgeon said, "You may write my life across the sky, I have nothing to conceal."[10] However, Spurgeon did have his moments of doubt. He wrote to his mother during the construction of the Tabernacle, "Pray that I am not so foolish as to doubt my Lord, for He will give me the desires of my heart."[11] He had his struggles.

TWO ISSUES TO FACE

Two important issues came before the New Park Street Church pertaining to building the new edifice. What would the venture cost, and where would the new church building be erected? The answer to the latter issue found its resolution in the Puritan heritage of Spurgeon. In Newington Butts, south London, some Puritan preachers had suffered martyrdom. An ancient record shows that a number of early dissenting Puritans, holding something like Baptist doctrine, were burned at "the Butts at Newington." Another old record dated 1564 relates how "three men were condemned as Anabaptists and brente (burned) in the highway beyond Southwark toward Newington." [12] That deeply appealed to Spurgeon's Puritan mindset. Of course, many suggested other places rather than Newington Butts. Some wished to build in Kensington, others in Holloway, some even wanted to go to the Clapham area of London. Spurgeon persisted and said it *must* be Newington Butts. He declared, "I have made up my mind not to go elsewhere." [13] The "Last of the Puritans" had spoken, and that settled that.

The male members of the committee, British real estate law required men, met again on September 7th to address the issue of location. But it was settled even before the meeting began. It is reported that every man who had a wife, daughter, or sister had the injunction given to them that no matter what anyone else said, they should vote with the pastor. When the meeting came to order, Spurgeon declared, "Baptists were burned right there. The blood of the martyrs is the seed of the church. Besides, right beside there many great London highways converge." [14] They voted overwhelmingly with Spurgeon. All opposition died.

The answer to the second issue, the cost, as is so often the case, started rather conservatively, but grew in proportion as the vision and the needs of the new building grew. On Michaelmas Day 1856, in the New Park Street Baptist Chapel, the congregation crowded in to discuss the matter. The sum of £12,000, or at the most £15,000, seemed quite adequate to provide the structure necessary for the ministry of their young pastor. The building finally cost £31,322. Had the deacons realized that the price would escalate to such proportions, they may well have completely rebelled. But God led them along step by step. *The Times, The Daily News,* and *The Saturday Review,* wrote news articles declaring that Spurgeon wanted to build a chapel to hold 15,000 people. At the first public meeting to launch the fundraising program, Spurgeon denied that such a thought had ever entered his mind:

> It has, however, been judged that a place of worship capable of accommodating about 5,000 persons is necessary. For my own part, I have no wish for such a large sanctuary; only I cannot bear to see Sabbath after Sabbath, as many people go away as are able to enter the chapel where we have been accustomed to assemble for worship. It is the will of the people to come in great multitudes to listen to my proclamation of the truths of the gospel; I have not asked them to come, it is of their own free will that they meet with us; and if it is a sin for me to have so many hearers, it is at least an uncommon sin, which many others would like to commit if they could. It has been said, 'Let those who wish to hear Mr. Spurgeon pay for their seats;' but that method would defeat what I have in view. I want to preach to those who cannot afford to pay

for seats in the chapel, and it is my wish to admit as many of the general public as possible. [15]

In this spirit, the plans for the new tabernacle were laid.

Securing the location in Newington Butts did not prove to be an easy task, however. They found a good site, but it required long and tedious negotiations with the owner, a fishmonger company. On the land sat St. Peter's Hospital, an old almshouse of the fishmonger's company. But on that spot Spurgeon had set his heart—it must be the new venue for his expanding ministry. The particular site had been occupied since 1615 by St. Peter's Hospital. New almshouses of the fishmonger company had recently been built in Wandsworth, thus clearing the old site and its ancient buildings. The erection of the Tabernacle on that particular place would benefit not only the congregation of Spurgeon's church, but also enhance the entire district of Newington Butts. Finally, after much work, on December 13, 1858, it could be announced to the church that negotiations were complete and the land available for purchase. Mr. W. Joynson, of St. Mary Cray, a great admirer and friend of young Spurgeon, immediately gave £400 toward the expense of obtaining an Act of Parliament that would be necessary to legalize the sale of the land. Thus all barriers were cleared. So it was done.

THE NEW DESIGN

Now with the site secured by the New Park Street Baptist Church, the building committee offered premiums of £50, £30, and £20 for the three best designs for the new structure. The church presented to the designers the architectural style desired. The committee let the architects know that Gothic architecture would not be acceptable. They preferred something on the general plan of the Surrey Gardens Music Hall, for two reasons. First, it had proved to be acoustically well designed. Second, Spurgeon himself insisted that the design be built in the Greek style. He had no desire for the old Gothic traditional building as it smacked too much of medieval Catholicism. Spurgeon said, "I look at a building from a theological point of view, not from an architectural. There are two sacred languages in the world . . . Hebrew of old . . . the other is not Rome's mongrel tongue, Latin; . . . it is Greek! I care not how many an idle temple has been built after this fashion . . . the standard of our faith is Greek, and this place is to be Grecian. We owe nothing to the Goths as religionists. Every Baptist place should be Grecian, not Gothic." [16] As the New Testament was written in Greek, Spurgeon declared that would be well suited to the preaching of the Gospel.

Surprisingly, more than 250 architects applied for the circular that laid out the particulars on construction of the tabernacle building. By January 31, 1859, the last day for receiving plans, 62 sets of designs and one model had been submitted to the building committee. The committee, wanting the designs to have a wide exposure, arranged an exhibit at the Newington Horse and Carriage Repository. A large number of the general public viewed them. The awarding of the first and the third prize came by vote by the competitors themselves. Forty of the designers selected the plans of E. Cookworthy Robins for the first prize of £50. Spurgeon and the building committee had also chosen Robin's design as among the top three. However, the design of Mr. W. W. Pecock, who received the second premium, was considered more suitable and was therefore adapted with some modifications. The primary design modification related to the large towers to be built on each of the structure's four corners. Each tower would cost £1,000. Being frugal and practical, Spurgeon rejected the towers, considering the money could be spent more usefully. He said, "Mere show, take them off. I will have no ornament that has no practical value." He encountered opposition with the rejoinder, "You can't leave them off; the roof looks too high without them." Spurgeon countered, "Those who look at the tabernacle from the outside have not subscribed; they cannot judge its beauty." [17] The towers came off.

With the preparations for the new tabernacle now well underway, it is interesting how "Metropolitan Tabernacle" became the official name of the building. Spurgeon had used the word "tabernacle" in his original proposal to his New Park Street Baptist people. Moreover, his goal from the beginning had been to have a large tabernacle type structure that could reach multitudes for Christ. Spurgeon was thus committed to the word "tabernacle." He thought it a more appropriate term for their church building than "temple," because the people of God had not yet come to the eternal temple, but like the Israelites of old, they were passing through the wilderness; therefore, their place of worship could only be at best temporary. So the term "tabernacle" seemed most apropos. Spurgeon said, "We have not here the King in person—the divine Solomon, till he come, call it a tabernacle still." The word "metropolitan" actually came through a suggestion by the architect himself. Thus, the title "Metropolitan Tabernacle" became the official name of the new church building.

CONSTRUCTION BEGINS

As the preliminary construction preparations for the new church structure reached an advanced stage, the time came for the laying of the cornerstone. On Monday evening, August 15, 1859, Spurgeon conducted a prayer meeting for the ceremony. The next day, a crowd of 3,000 gathered as Sir Samuel Morton Peto, member of Parliament, presided in the laying of the foundation stone. In the foundation stone a large ceramic jar containing a Bible, the Baptist Confession of Faith, a hymnbook of Dr. Rippon, and a program of the day's activities were laid. Spurgeon said, rather facetiously, "They put in no coins because they did not have any to spare." But it proved to be an inspiring moment. A banner with the inscription "Christ is the Cornerstone" graced the scene.

The service began with the singing of the 100th Psalm, followed by a fervent prayer offered by the Pastor. Then a declaration on behalf of the deacons was read, presenting a brief history of the church. After that, Spurgeon stated:

> In the bottle which is to be placed under the stone, we have put no money,—for one good reason, that we have none to spare. We have not put newspapers, because, albeit we admire and love the liberty of the press, yet that is not so immediately concerned in this edifice. The articles placed under the stone are simply these: —The Bible, the Word of God; we put that as the foundation of our church. Upon this rock doth Christ build the ministration of His truth. We know of nothing else as our standard. Together with this, we have put 'The Baptist Confession of Faith,' which was signed in the olden times by Benjamin Keach, one of my eminent predecessors. We put also the declaration of the deacons, which you have just heard read, parchment. There is also an edition of Dr. Rippon's Hymn Book, published just before he died; and then, in the last place, there is a programme of this day's proceedings. I do not suppose that the New Zealander who, one day, is to sit on the broken arch of London Bridge, will make much out of it. If we had put gold and silver there, it is possible he might have taken it back to New Zealand with him; but I should not wonder, if ever England is destroyed, these relics will find their way into some museum in Australia or America, where people will spell over some of our old-fashioned names, and wonder whoever those good men could be who are inscribed here, as Samuel Gale, James Low, Thomas Olney, Thomas Cook, George Winsor, William P. Olney, George Moore, and C. H. Spurgeon. And I think they will say, 'Oh! depend upon it, they were some good men, so they put time in stone there.' These deacons are living stones, indeed; they have served this church well and long. Honour to whom honour is due. I am glad to put their names with mine here; and I hope we shall live together for ever in eternity.

After Spurgeon's remarks, Sir Samuel Morton Peto congratulated the pastor and all the members of the church, remarking that he trusted that the building would be opened free of debt. He need not have said that, Spurgeon had already determined it would. His convictions about being in debt began many years earlier when as a lad he got in trouble over purchasing a slate pencil, as seen in chapter three. After Peto's remarks, Spurgeon again picked up the mantle and spoke for a considerable time. He declared again that the building should be Grecian because God had spoken in the New Testament through the Greek language. He then outlined the basic doctrines of the church that would meet on that spot. He concluded his remarks with these words:

I look on the Tabernacle as only the beginning; within the last six months we have started two churches,—one in Wandsworth and the other Greenwich,—and the Lord has prospered them; the pool of baptism has often been stirred with converts. And what we have done in two places, I am about to do in a third, and we will do it, not for the third or the fourth, but for the hundredth time, God being our Helper. I am sure I may make my strongest appeal to my brethren, because we do not mean to build this Tabernacle as our nest, and then to be idle. We must go from strength to strength, and be a missionary church, and never rest until, not only this neighbourhood, but our country, of which it is said that some parts are as dark as India, shall have been enlightened with the Gospel.

When Spurgeon finished his message, he presented a challenge and gave the opportunity for any who desired to make a contribution toward the building fund. To the delight of all, a Mr. Inskip of Bristol stood up and stated he represented a very wealthy gentleman who could not attend because of illness. This anonymous gentleman had a deep devotion to the service of Christ and had sent Mr. Inskip there to say that he would contribute £3,000 toward the erection of the great tabernacle. Inskip went on to state that if twenty people would come forward with £100 each, he would contribute another £2,000 to meet theirs. This challenged the entire gathering and many responded with donations that afternoon. Also, before many days passed, 20 men had come forward with £100 and Mr. Inskip's anonymous friend was delighted to give the additional £2,000. In an evening meeting on the same day, the Lord Mayor of London, Alderman Wire, presided and the total contributions of that day amounted to nearly £5,000.

By April 2, 1860, the building fund had grown to £18,904. It became evident that the early estimate of £12,000 would cover only about one-half of what was needed to complete the building. This did not deter Spurgeon, however, although some members of the committee all but shrank away from the responsibility of raising so much more money. But Spurgeon had no qualms. From the very beginning he secretly believed that the original estimate would be quite insufficient to construct the kind of building he felt God would have them to build. He said:

'It may as well be twenty thousand as ten, for we shall get one amount as readily as the other. . . . Brethren, we must pray that God will be pleased to give us the money, and we shall surely have it. If we had possessed more faith, we should have had it before now; and when this Tabernacle is built, we shall find money enough to build a dozen. Look at what Mr. Muller, of Bristol, has done by faith and prayer. When this land was threatened with famine, people said, "What will you do now, Mr. Muller?" "Pray to God," was the good man's answer. He did pray, and the result was, that he had an overwhelming increase.' Charles Haddon Spurgeon, too, prayed earnestly and in full faith, so that he received equally remarkable answers to his petitions. [18]

In those days Spurgeon unreservedly gave himself to the building of the tabernacle. He contributed £5,000 of his own money. More significantly, he traveled all over the country collecting large sums for the completion of the building. Wherever he went he preached and took an offering. In those days of exhaustive itinerant ministry, he not only raised large sums, he saw many people come to Christ.

RAISING FUNDS—AND SOULS

Aspects of Spurgeon's early itinerant preaching have been presented earlier. However, it helps to see how he used this method to help secure funds for the new tabernacle. On one of Spurgeon's itinerant visits of preaching and fund-raising, he made a trip to Scotland. It lasted only a few days, but the collection for the building fund amounted to £391. Yet, when the needs of the church where he preached were pressing, he gladly gave his services without any honorarium; and the entire collection would be donated to the local needs. For example, he preached in the pavilion of Grand Stand Epsom on Friday, June 11, 1858, received an offering of £60, and it all went to the local chapel. Briefly alluded to earlier, on Sunday, July 10, 1859 Spurgeon did a most kind thing. Some little time before, a storm had coursed through London, lightning had struck a tree in Clapham Common killing a man who stood beneath it. Spurgeon preached on that particular spot and took a collection for the widow of the dead man. Ten thousand people had come to hear Spurgeon preach. He delivered his message using a wagon as his pulpit. He took his text from Luke 12:40, "Be ye therefore ready also," and the congregation contributed more than £27 toward the support of the grateful widow.

In August of 1858, Spurgeon made his first visit to Ireland. There he preached to vast congregations in Belfast. The Irish contributed generously toward the construction of the Metropolitan Tabernacle. Spurgeon made several trips to the Emerald Isle. On one of these trips, he learned with satisfaction that many of the ship's crew were earnest Christians who held regular prayer meetings and read his published sermons. Spurgeon traveled to the village of Castleton near Cadiff to preach on July 20, 1859. He preached twice in a field and again a congregation of over 10,000 people assembled. In May of the following year, he preached in the fields near Abercarne to a vast throng of some 20,000 people. It must be remembered the population of Britain and its cities did not number near what they do today. For 20,000 to gather in a field to hear a Baptist preacher was phenomenal.

Spurgeon also went abroad during these years. He conducted very effective services in Paris during February of 1860. He preached five sermons in three days in the French capital and collected a total sum of £64 by using donation boxes left at the door where people could make a contribution as they exited. He preached in the American Church in Paris and the Reformed Church of the Oratory. There he collected £40 for the poor of Paris.

As usual, some of the London press used the Paris trip for an occasion to criticize the young pastor. But, as one biographer put it, "He very early in life acquired strength to stand by himself and live without and above praise." [19] Conversely, the French newspapers, even those of the Roman Catholic Church, gave him a good press and spoke kindly of the preacher. The *Journal des Depots* wrote:

> One listens with pleasure to his powerful and sympathetic voice, which never rises or falls beyond proper limits, and yet fills the whole church with its sweet cadences. The man who possesses these gifts and uses them so generously is not yet twenty-six years of age. It is impossible to look upon his energetic and loyal face without reading there conviction, courage and earnest desire to do the right. This orator, who is the most popular preacher in a country where liberty of speech and conscience exercises such potent influence, is not only the most modest, but also the most simple of men. It is true that he has the happiness to address a nation which does not think it necessary to be unjust in its public criticism; but after all, Mr. Spurgeon owes to himself alone the great and salutary influence that he has acquired, and yet no one could ever rightly accuse him of egotism. It is without affectation that he, unreservedly, ascribes all the glory to God. It seems to us that all disputes concerning religion ought to vanish before such an apostle; and to recognise his power is but just. As for us who have seen in this youthful and eloquent preacher one of the most happy examples of what modern Christianity and liberty can produce, we feel that it is an honour to come into contact with such a man as Mr. Spurgeon, and to exchange with him the grasp of friendship.

In the same year, a few months later, Spurgeon again traveled to the Continent, this time with his wife Susannah. They first went to Belgium, spending time in Antwerp and Brussels. Quite surprisingly, he said:

> In Brussels I heard a good sermon in a Romish Church. The place was crowded with people, many of them standing, though they might have had a seat for a halfpenny or a farthing; and I stood, too; and the good priest—for I believe he is a good man—preached the Lord Jesus with all his might. He spoke of the love of Christ, so that I, a very poor hand at the French language, could fully understand him, and my heart kept beating within me as he told of the beauties of Christ and the preciousness of His blood, and of His power to save the chief of sinners. He did not say 'justification by faith,' but he did say 'efficacy of the blood,' which comes to very much the same thing. He did not tell us that we were saved by grace and not by our works; but he did say that all the works of men were less than nothing when brought into competition with the blood of Christ, and that the blood of Jesus alone could save. True, there were objectionable sentences, as naturally there must be in a discourse delivered under

such circumstances; but I could have gone to the preacher and have said to him, 'Brother, you have spoken the truth;' and if I had been handling his text I must have treated it in the same way as he did, if I could have done it as well. [20]

This is rather startling considering Spurgeon's attitude toward the Roman Catholic Church. But wherever Spurgeon heard the truths of the Gospel, he appreciated it. It shows something of the growing and maturing breadth of the man.

Traveling from Brussels, Spurgeon and Susannah visited many cities on the Continent: Cologne, Frankfurt, Heidelberg, Baden, Freiburg; they then went on to Zurich and Lucerne in Switzerland and, at last, to Geneva. After leaving Geneva the happy couple crossed the Alps by Simplon Pass. As they made their way over the mountain pass, they accepted the hospitality of the Monks at a Hospice on the very top of the mountain. Spurgeon said:

> It pleased me to find that there were Augustinian Monks, because next to Calvin I love Augustine. I feel that Augustine's works were the great mind out of which Calvin dug his mental wealth; and the Augustinian Monks, in the acts of charity seem to say, 'Our master was a teacher of grace, and we will practice it, and give to all comers whatsoever they shall need, without money and without price.' Those Monks are worthy of great honor; they are spending the best and noblest part of their lives on the top of a bleak and barren mountain that they may minister to the necessities of the poor. They go out in the cold nights and bring in those who are frostbitten; they dig them out from under the snow, simply that they may serve God by helping their fellow men. I pray God to bless the good works of those Monks of the Augustinian order. [21]

Again, Spurgeon's words of appreciation for a Roman Catholic Order show his broadening perspective. He appreciated good doctrine and preaching wherever he heard it, also acts of Christian charity and love touched him deeply. Charles Ray contends that this continental trip was "perhaps the most enjoyable holiday that Charles Haddon Spurgeon ever spent." [22] He and Susie spent eight weeks on the Continent. Each day remained a vivid memory in the mind of the young Puritan. Also, he brought back a sizable donation for the Tabernacle construction.

FUNDS FROM UNUSUAL SOURCES

The different ways in which money came in for the building of the Tabernacle often surprised everyone, even Charles. One day, when he was in financial straits, an old, poorly dressed woman came into the pastor's vestry. No one knew her, but she said, "Thus saith the Lord, Behold I have commanded a widow woman there to sustain thee." She laid £50 on the table and left never to be seen again. How could Spurgeon doubt God's providential provision?

On another occasion in 1859 Spurgeon drove with a friend into the country to preach. A carriage in hot pursuit overtook them, and the man in the carriage asked Spurgeon if he would get out of his vehicle and ride in his gig, because he wanted to speak to him. When they were together, the complete stranger related that as a businessman he wanted to assure Spurgeon of success in the building of the great Tabernacle. He said God's work could never fail. Then he went on, "You will have many friends that will feel anxious about it. I want you never to feel anxious or downcast. What do you think will be required at the outside to finish it off altogether?" Spurgeon replied, "£20,000." (About £10,000 had been collected at that time). "Then," said he, "I will let you have £20,000 on condition that you keep only so much of it as you need to finish the building. I only expect to give £50, but you shall have bonds and leases to the full value of £20,000 to fall back upon." [23] The securities were sent to Spurgeon immediately. In the two years that followed until the building was completed, when many people were criticizing the preacher for the extravagance of the project and even declaring the hopelessness of carrying it through, Spurgeon had the means in hand to finish it completely if everyone else forsook the project. "They little knew how much reason I had for my assurance, nor how my faith had been strengthened by this token of God's favour." [24] God met not only the faith of Spurgeon but the generous benefactor as well. He did need to give but £50; the rest of the funding came in, often in miraculous ways. It can truly be said that Spurgeon built on faith.

On a similar occasion, suffering a protracted illness, Spurgeon began to doubt whether he could meet all the obligations that were pressing in upon him. His depression did assail his faith at times. Right at that juncture one of his deacons came to him and poured out on his bed papers that represented all his investments. The good man of God said to his pastor, "There! I owe everything that I have in the world to you, and you are welcome to all that I possess. Take whatever you need, and do not have another moment's anxiety." It was the very medicine that Spurgeon needed. He said, "It seemed to me, very much as the water from the well of Bethlehem must appeared to David." [25] As could be expected, however, Spurgeon used none of it.

INCESSANT LABORS

Spurgeon's itinerant ministry continued during those days. He had a vast capacity for work—and he redeemed the time, making each hour count. There were those who raised the question about whether he was working himself to death. He traveled, preached, and wrote continually. But he had his eye on what mattered. He said to himself as he said to others, "I beseech you to love not only for this age, but for the next also. I would fling my shadow through eternal ages if I could." [26] Often, when invited to preach, he would give the stipulation that a collection would be taken and it should be divided, half for the church in which he preached and the other half for the tabernacle building fund. During these days he would undertake many different tasks and engagements. For instance, on May 21, 1801 the tomb of John Bunyan was restored. Charles took part in the ceremony. Actually, as much as he loved Bunyan's *Pilgrim's Progress*, he felt for the mature Christian Bunyan's *The Holy War* proved more helpful. He contended the former was best for a babe in Christ, but the latter best after growing in grace. So he labored on tirelessly.

As always, wherever Charles went to preach, whether in church buildings, barns, meeting halls, or even in the open air, people thronged. Often he could hardly get to the pulpit because of the crowds waiting for him. He often had to fight his way to the front of the congregation. However, in his kind and cheerful way, he always had a pleasant word for the people. Once he preached to a large congregation in a little village in Kent. The chapel overflowed. The deacons, aware that the people were mostly farmers and accustomed to ample fresh air, had opened the windows of the little chapel building. During Spurgeon's message, a considerable breeze sprang up. Blowing through the open windows, it rustled the leaves of Spurgeon's Bible, and blew his hair into his eyes and over his forehead. He wore his thick head of hair parted neatly, not quite in the middle. He stopped in the middle of his sermon and said, "Will someone kindly close the window?" A deacon who was sitting in the back of the chapel immediately got up to meet the preacher's request. He felt that it would be impossible to move through the people so he went to the outside and attempted to close the window from there. But the only way he could get the window closed was with a broom to push the window up, as it had been opened from the top down. While attempting to get the window closed, the wind became stronger and Spurgeon again said, "Please shut the window." Outside the deacon, being a short man, labored his best to get the window shut, but he could not reach it even with the broom handle. He needed a chair or a stool to stand on. He could find none, so he ran to the nearest cottage to borrow one. But the second appeal of Spurgeon motivated two other deacons to try to get the window closed. They were also unsuccessful. Again, Spurgeon stopped in his sermon and in his own whimsical way, pushed back the lock of hair out of his eyes and said, "Really, I am not like Burton Beer, best on draught." This brought a resounding round of laughter from the people and in a matter of seconds the window went up. But Spurgeon, being such a moving preacher, soon turned the laughter into tears of deep feeling as his sermon progressed. When the service ended, a good collection was received. It has been said that he taught many people how to give.

Another time Spurgeon declined to preach in a stuffy little chapel. He said, "It is cruelty to animals, and very unnecessary cruelty too, when there is a beautiful apple orchard with soft green grass and plenty of shade tree close."[27] The orchard belonged to a fine Anglican churchman and he gladly let Spurgeon know that he would be most happy for the Baptists to use it for the day. So Spurgeon preached in the open air and did a memorable job.

Spurgeon's itinerant ministry took him in all directions as he continued to preach, win people to faith in Jesus Christ, and raise funds for the Tabernacle. In all of Spurgeon's itinerant ministry during those days, he raised £11,253 for the Metropolitan Tabernacle. Then on August 21, 1860, a large gathering was held in the unfinished Tabernacle. The people assembled to give thanks to God for the success with which they had thus far been blessed. Of course, they used the occasion to raise more funds for the Tabernacle. In the setting of the service, Spurgeon presented a full account of the entire enterprise from its inception until the immediate moment, and for its future. He also reiterated the voluntary principle upon which the building was being built. He said:

> We earnestly desire to open this place without a farthing of debt upon it. You have heard that sentence again and again. Let me repeat it; and I pray that our brethren here, who have the command of the public Press, will repeat it again and again for me. It is not because a small debt would weigh upon this Church too much; we are not afraid of that; it is just this, we think it will tell well for the whole body of believers who rely upon the voluntary principle, if this Tabernacle is completed without a loan or a debt. Our place of worship has been spoken of in the House of Commons, it has been mentioned in the House of Lords; and as everybody happens to know of it since it stands so conspicuously, we want to do our utmost, and we ask our brethren to give us their help, that this forefront of Nonconformity for the time being, they have about it no failure, no defect to which anyone can point and say, 'Your voluntaryism failed to carry the project through.' I believe in the might of the voluntary principle. I believe it to be perfectly irresistible in proportion to the power of God's Spirit in the hearts of those who exercise it. [28]

Clearly, Spurgeon not only had deep convictions about debt; he also wanted the Metropolitan Tabernacle to prove that Nonconformity can exist without state support and, therefore, so could the Established Church. More than one underlying conviction rested behind the voluntary principle Spurgeon employed in the building of the Metropolitan Tabernacle.

The newspapers continually struck a critical note. One reporter wrote that to call the building the "Metropolitan Tabernacle" savored of arrogance. One paper had even suggested that the pastor might star himself as "the Metropolitan." The term "Metropolitan" designated a very high official in the Greek Orthodox Church. Whether the reporter had that in mind is questionable, but Spurgeon could hardly fill the role of "Metropolitan." Still, they were certainly building a metropolitan edifice considering the fact that more than a million people had already contributed to its erection. One significant thing about the entire fund raising program was that many of the contributions had come in small amounts from average people.

Within the next six or seven months, after the critical newspaper report of Spurgeon as a "Metropolitan," the entire cost of the building, £31,132 had been raised. Money was contributed by practically every denomination. Not only that, money had come in from many parts of the world: Europe, Asia, Africa, America, and Australia. Beyond question, the building of the Metropolitan Tabernacle by voluntary contributions marked an epic in English Nonconformity. Everyone became convinced it was accomplished by the sovereign grace of God. At the very first church meeting held in the new Metropolitan Tabernacle, the pastor wrote in the church book:

> I, Charles Haddon Spurgeon, the least of all saints, hereby set to my seal that God is true, since He has this day fulfilled my hopes, and given according to our faith. O Lord, be Thou praised world without end, and do Thou make me more faithful and more mighty than ever!   —C. H. Spurgeon [29]

Also found in the church book, in Spurgeon's own handwriting, is a statement signed by himself, the deacons, the elders, and many church members, led by Mrs. Spurgeon:

> We, the undersigned members of the church lately worshipping in New Park Street Chapel, but now assembling in the Metropolitan Tabernacle, Newington, desire with overflowing hearts to make known and record the lovingkindness of our faithful God. We asked in faith, but our Lord has exceeded our desires, for not only was the whole sum given us, but far sooner than we had looked for it. Truly the Lord is good and worthy to be praised. We are ashamed of ourselves that we have ever doubted Him; and we pray that, as a Church, and as individuals, we may be enabled to trust in the Lord at all times with confidence, so that in quietness we may possess our souls. In the name of our God we set up our banner. Oh, that Jehovah-Jireh may also be unto us Jehovah-shammah and Jehovah-shalom! To Father, Son, and Holy Ghost we offer praise and thanksgiving, and we set to our seal that God is true. [30]

In March of 1861, the Metropolitan Tabernacle saw completion. By the end of the month, the third and last service of the New Park Street congregation was held at Exeter Hall. As a tribute to the providence and care of the Lord, not a single workman on the new building had been injured. Spurgeon and Mr. Cook, the Secretary of the Building Committee, had prayed earnestly upon their knees, right in the midst of all the scaffolding and bricks and mortar soon after the structure was begun, that God would protect every workman. Their prayers had been answered.

OPENING CEREMONIES

The opening services and celebrations lasted almost a month. It all began with a great prayer meeting on the morning of Monday, March 18, 1861.

The service was held at seven o'clock. By the appointed hour, over a thousand people had gathered in a thanksgiving service of prayer for God's astounding provision and care. A week later, at that same early morning hour, another large prayer meeting was held.

In the afternoon of the 20th, Spurgeon delivered his first sermon in the Metropolitan Tabernacle. He preached from Acts 5:42, "And daily in the temple, and in every house, they ceased not to teach and preach Jesus Christ." The same evening Rev. W. Brock of Bloomsbury Chapel spoke from Philippians 1:18, "Christ is preached; and I therein do rejoice, yea, and will rejoice." The next night more than 3,000 who had contributed to the building fund gathered. Sir Henry Havelock presided. On the following evening, the ministers and members of the neighboring churches along with 4,000 others gathered to offer their congratulations to the congregation upon the completion of their fine building.

The first Sunday the church met in the new Tabernacle became a memorable event. Spurgeon preached from 2 Chronicles 5:13-14.

He made a most important point in that message. He preached with great fervor and said:

> Let God send the fire of His Spirit here, and the minister will be more and more lost in his Master. You will come to think less of the speaker and more of the truth spoken; the individual will be swamped, the words uttered will rise above everything. When you have the cloud, the man is forgotten; when you have the fire, the man is lost, and you only see his Master. Suppose the fire should come here, and the Master be seen more than the minister, what then? Why, this church will become two or three or four thousand strong! It is easy enough for God to double our numbers, vast though they are even now. We shall have the lecture and we shall see in this place young men devoting themselves to God; we shall find ministers raised up and trained and sent forth to carry the sacred fire to other parts of the globe. Japan, China, and Hindustani shall have heralds of the Cross who have here had their tongues touched with the divine flame. Through us, the whole earth shall receive benedictions; if God shall bless us, He will make us a blessing to multitudes of others. Let God but send down the fire and the biggest sinners in the neighbourhood will be converted; those who live in dens of infamy will be changed; the drunkard will forsake his cups, the swearer will repent of his blasphemy, the debauched will leave their lusts—
>
> Dry Bones be raised and clothed afresh
> And hearts of stone be turned to flesh.' [31]

For several nights, important services and gatherings were held. On Sunday, April 7, the first communion took place, while on the following Tuesday Spurgeon led the first baptism. Twenty candidates presented themselves. On Wednesday, April 10, a very large communion service was held. Someone described it as probably the largest communion service since the day of Pentecost. Members joined the church in rapid succession.

THE NEW BUILDING

When passersby saw the new building, it struck them as an imposing structure. It had a simple beauty and grandeur about it. Some felt that it looked small, but Spurgeon found satisfaction in that it did not look too large and ostentatious. The building, with its auxiliary rooms measured 174 feet long on the outside. The inner auditorium proper had 25,225 square feet of floor space and was 146 feet long and 81 feet wide. It had an elliptical ceiling 62 feet above the main floor. The auditorium floor level was some ten feet above the ground level, which required a large set of steps. Besides many pews on the main floor, there were two large galleries or balconies. They wrapped completely around the building, even around the back of the pulpit. The seating capacity in the pews themselves came to approximately 3,600. At the ends of the pews were flat folded seats that could be let down, held by iron rods. They could seat another thousand. Not only that, there was standing room for well over a thousand more. Often 6,000 people packed into the building. On the evening of Spurgeon's jubilee, Lord Shaftesbury presiding, one deacon said, "We counted eight thousand out of her; I don't know where she put 'em, but we did." [32]

Behind the auditorium, on level with the first balcony, were three vestries. The center one was for Spurgeon and the others for the deacons and elders. On a level with the second gallery, ladies' parlors and rooms for storing Bibles and books were located.

The auditorium itself had no pulpit, at least in the traditional sense. A curving platform projected out from the wrap-around first balcony. An open railing surrounded the platform, which held only a table and a settee for the pastor. Behind the settee sat a row of chairs for the deacons. The chairs were padded in red velvet with arm rests, much like the seats in the first class sections of the trains. On the first gallery rail, over the pulpit, a large round clock was hung. Below this preaching platform on the ground floor level, another curving platform contained a marble baptistry. It had been constructed high enough that the baptisms were fully visible by all people. A temporary floor covered the baptistry on which they placed the communion table and chairs when the church observed the Lord's Supper.

The church had a full basement with a large lecture hall that could accommodate 900 for the study of God's Word. Also, the basement contained a Sunday School room for 1,000 children. There were six classrooms, kitchen, lavatory, and several other rooms as well. There was a ladies' room for weekday meetings, young men's classrooms and secretaries' rooms on the ground floor. Yet, the accommodations proved insufficient for all the work and ministry that went on; adjoining buildings had to be used.

The Tabernacle was a well-built structure and very sturdy. Spurgeon could never forget the tragedy at the Surrey Gardens Music Hall. He had constructed the building in such a fashion that, should the need ever arise that the people needed to leave the building quickly and safely, each gallery had its own set of stairways. They were of large size and ran all the way down to the individual exit doors.

The building had no organ or choir loft. A so-called "Precentor" set the pitch of each hymn with a tuning fork and then led the singing with his own voice. Spurgeon said, "Services of religion will be conducted without any peculiarity of innovation. No musical or aesthetic accompaniment will ever be used." [33] Spurgeon's views on music probably would be questioned in many circles today. But he had strong views. He said:

> What a degradation to supplement the intelligent song of the whole congregation by the theatrical prettiness of a quartet, the refined niceties of a choir, or the blowing off of wind from inanimate bellows and pipes. We might as well pray by machinery and praise by it. [34]

Moreover, the Puritans did not use musical instruments, so why should Spurgeon?

Some accounts of the Metropolitan Tabernacle tell us that all the pews were free, defying the custom of pew rentals. They argue Spurgeon wanted seats free for those who needed to hear the Gospel. He insisted no one should have to pay to hear the Good News. Others contend that regular admittance by church members came through buying "tickets." But it seems quite conclusive that at least some pews were rented. The actual church minutes at the Tabernacle reflect this. They were called "seat subscriptions." Still, a portion of seats were kept "free."

The completion of the Metropolitan Tabernacle gave Spurgeon a marvelous venue in which to preach and minister. It also became a testimony to the strength and solidity of his work. Thus, Spurgeon settled into his service at the Tabernacle. The building was destined to be the scene of many outstanding blessings. A month after the Tabernacle opened, 77 persons were received for baptism and church membership. The following month another 72 were received. God blessed his work from its very outset. At this time, the great prayer revival surged in full force through Britain. In many senses of the word, Spurgeon's ministry epitomized that significant movement of the Holy Spirit.

After the building of the Metropolitan Tabernacle, some of the people attempted to continue services at New Park Street Chapel as well. However, it soon became apparent that no need for such a large building in that district existed. According to the church business minutes, a resolution was passed March 26, 1866 to sell the property, with the provision that the money be used to meet the needs of the Metropolitan Tabernacle and its charities. This was done in conformity with the government Charity Act, 62 section. Therefore, the congregation sold the property by auction, along with the alms-houses. They received £5,000. The money acquired for the sale of the almshouses was used to build new ones. The church minutes of September 3, 1866 read: "The property would certainly have been sold for considerably less had not our Brother Higgs continued to bid until a fair price was obtained."[35] They knew how to do things!

Although pew rentals, in the strict sense of the term, had been abolished and "seat subscribers" instituted, there were 3,000 such seat holders in the new Tabernacle. Those who wanted to be assured of a seat paid a certain amount and were always admitted first before the service began. Then five minutes before the service commenced, others were admitted. It was always a struggle to get in. This "seat subscriber" principle became the primary source of income for the ministry of the Metropolitan Tabernacle. No collections were taken during the regular worship services. The upkeep of the church and the pastor's stipend came from that source of revenue. In 1868, Charles' stipend was £1250. Some years later, he declined any salary after his sermons began to sell so well. This basic financial structure kept the entire ministry of the church solvent.

The great Tabernacle became the scene of Spurgeon's ministry for some thirty years. It burned to the ground on April 20, 1898 during the ministry of Spurgeon's son, Thomas. The congregation completed a new tabernacle in 1900, although considerably smaller in capacity. Still, the facade was able to be retained, and so the frontage view appeared identical to what it had been in Charles Spurgeon's day. Moreover, the new structure did have an organ. Then, during the days of the Second World War, the building received severe damage by bombing attacks. After the war it was again rebuilt, but once more considerably smaller, seating only about 1,500 people. Still the same facade was intact and from the front it looks as it did in 1861. In recent years, the present auditorium (that upon its completion after the war seated about 1,500 people) has again been divided into a seating capacity of approximately 600 people. Offices and other accommodations make up the remainder of the present building. That full story will unfold in the Epilogue.

MEMORABLE SERVICES

There were many memorable services at the Metropolitan Tabernacle. One of the most unforgettable services at the Tabernacle was held on the Lord's Day, December 15, 1861, soon after the Tabernacle had been opened. Late on the previous night, the Prince Consort, Albert, died. Spurgeon read a few comments he had written concerning the rather untimely death of Queen Victoria's husband. However, because he had prepared another sermon, he postponed a sermon on the subject until the following Sunday. On the next Lord's Day, he preached from Amos 3:6, "Shall there be evil in the city, and the Lord hath not done it?" He entitled the message "The Royal Deathbed." In his introduction he paid tribute to the character and influence of Prince Albert:

> The evil mentioned in the text is that of calamity, and we might read the verse,—'Shall there be a calamity in the city, and the Lord hath not done it?'—a question exceedingly appropriate at the present time. There has been evil in this city; a calamity of an unusual and disastrous nature has fallen upon this nation. We have lost one who will to-day find a thousand tongues to eulogize him; a Prince whose praise is in the mouth of all, and who is in such repute among you that is needless for me to commend his memory to your hearts. We have lost a man whom it was the habit of some to suspect so long as he lived; he could do little without arousing their mistrust; they were always alarmed by phantoms of intrusion and unconstitutional influence; but now that he has departed, they may sincerely regret that they could not trust where confidence was so well deserved. Not of lack of homage to his rank, his talents, or his house, could he complain; but from his tomb there might well come the still small voice of memory, reminding us of many causeless suspicions, a few harsh judgments, and one or two heartless calumnies. I was pleased by a remark made by the leading journal of the age, to the effect that the Prince Consort's removal might suggest deep regrets for our thrifty homage and the measured respect. He has deserved nothing but good at our hands. Standing in the most perilous position, his foot has not slipped; dwelling where the slightest interference might have brought down a storm of animosity upon his head, he has prudently withheld himself, and let public affairs alone as much as possible. Looking upon the nature of our government, and the position of the throne in our constitution, I can but say, 'Verily it is a heavy calamity for such a Queen to lose such a husband.' [36]

The message was deeply appreciated throughout the Commonwealth.

The following year, a tragedy occurred in the coal mines in Upperton. The Hartly Colliery exploded. On the Thursday night service, Spurgeon preached from Job 14:14, "If a man die, shall he live again?" In that sermon, he declared:

> Once more the Lord has spoken; again the voice of Providence has proclaimed, 'All flesh is grass, and all the goodliness thereof is as the flower of the field.' O sword of the Lord, when wilt thou rest and be quiet? Wherefore these repeated warnings? Why doth the Lord so frequently and so terribly sound an alarm? Is it not because our drowsy spirits will not awaken to the realities of death? We fondly persuade ourselves that we are immortal; that, though a thousand may fall at our side, and ten thousand at our right hand, yet death shall not come nigh unto us. We flatter ourselves that, if we must die, yet the evil day is far hence, If we be sixty, we presumptuously reckon upon another twenty years of life; and a man of eighty, tottering upon his staff,

remembering that some few have survived to the close of a century, sees no reason why he should not do the same. If man cannot kill death, he tries at least to bury him alive; and since death will intrude himself in our pathway, we endeavour to shut our eyes to the ghastly object. God in Providence is continually filling our path with tombs. With kings and princes, there is too much forgetfulness of the world to come; God has therefore spoken to them. They are but few in number; so one death might be sufficient in their case, that one death of a beloved and illustrious Prince will leave its mark on courts and palaces. As for the workers, they also are wishful to put far from them the thought of the coffin and the shroud: God has spoken to them also. They were many, so one death would not be sufficient; it was absolutely necessary that there should be many victims, or we should have disregarded the warning. Two hundred witnesses cry to us from the pit's mouth,—a solemn fellowship of preachers all using the same text, 'Prepare to meet thy God, O Israel!' If God had not thus spoken by the destruction of many, we should have said, 'Ah! it is a common occurrence; there are frequently such accidents as these.' The rod would have failed in its effect had it smitten less severely. The awful calamity at the Hartley Colliery has at least had this effect, that men are talking of death in all our streets. O Father of Thy people, send forth Thy Holy Spirit in richer abundance, that by this solemn chastisement higher ends may be answered than merely attracting our thoughts to our latter end! Oh, may hearts be broken, may eyes be made to weep for sin, may follies be renounced, may Christ be accepted, and may spiritual life be given to many survivors was the result of the physical death of those who now sleep in their untimely graves in Earsdon churchyard! [37]

Of course, one could question Spurgeon's theodicy, that is, his theological explanation of the tragedy; yet, after Spurgeon preached, he made an appeal for the widows and orphans who suffered from the calamity. Although it was a very inclement night, and many had already contributed to a relief fund for the widows and orphans of those killed, the congregation still generously subscribed £120.

A most memorable service was held in the Metropolitan Tabernacle in March of the following year when Spurgeon preached on 1 Samuel 7:12, "Then Samuel took a stone, and set it between Mizpah and Shem, and called the name of it Ebenezer, saying, 'Hitherto hath the Lord helped us.'" He titled his sermon, appropriately, "Ebenezer." It had both an autobiographical and a historical content as he made most interesting allusions to the Lord's gracious help to both pastor and the great congregation of the Tabernacle. In his introduction, Spurgeon said:

Looking at God's hand in my own life, and acknowledging that hand with some record of thankfulness, I, your minister, brought by Divine grace to preach this morning the five hundredth of my printed sermons, consecutively published week by week, set up my stone of Ebenezer to God. I thank Him, thank Him humbly, but yet most joyfully, for all the help and assistance given in studying and preaching the Word to these mighty congregations by the voice, and afterwards to so many nations through the press. I set up my pillar in the form of this sermon. My motto this day shall be the same as Samuel's, 'Hitherto hath the Lord helped me;' and as the stone of my praise is much too heavy for me to set it upright alone, I ask you, my comrades in the day of battle, my fellow-labourers in the vineyard of Christ, to join with me in expressing gratitude to God, while together we set up the stone of memorial, and say, 'Hitherto hath the Lord helped us.' [38]

SPURGEON THE PASTOR

Spurgeon kept his relationship to the people of the church always on a high level. Indicative of that fact is the esteem in which they held him—and he them. He also had the happy faculty of gathering around him great leaders. He could inspire them to wholehearted devotion to the causes that he felt should characterize the Metropolitan Tabernacle. All had absolute faith in the pastor's sincerity, piety, and ability. Rarely did anything loom on the horizon that would bode of unpleasantness in church relations. All knew him, especially the students at the College, as the "Gov'nor." He did take a quite authoritarian stance in the life of the church; yet, he did it in a spirit of graciousness and Christian decorum that elicited the deep respect of all who worked with him. He always looked upon his church members, especially the officials of the church, as brethren in Christ and fellow workers in the Gospel. He would invariably consult with them on matters of importance. He wrote on one occasion:

My present staff of deacons consists of particularly lovable, active, energetic, warm-hearted, generous men, everyone of whom seems especially adapted for his own particular department of service. I am very thankful that I have never been the pastor of a dead church controlled by dead deacons. I have seen such a thing as that with my own eyes, and the sight is truly awful. I recollect very well preaching in a chapel where the church had become exceedingly low, and somehow the very building looked like a sepulchre, though crowded that one night by those who came to hear the preacher. The singers drawled out a dirge while the members sat like mutes. I found it hard preaching; there was no 'go' in the sermon, I seemed to be driving dead horses. After the service I saw two men who, I supposed, were the deacons,—the pillars of the church,—leaning against the posts of the vestry door in a listless attitude, and I said, 'Are you the deacons of this church?' They informed me that they were the only deacons, and I remarked that I thought so. To myself I added that I would have been a riddle. Here was a dead church, comparable to the ship of the ancient mariner which was manned by the dead. Deacons, teachers, minister, people—all dead, and yet wearing the semblance of life. . . . All my church-officers are in a very real sense my brethren in Christ. In talking to or about one another, we have no stately modes of address. I am called 'the Governor.' I suppose because I do not attempt to govern; and the deacons are known among us as, 'Brother William,' 'Uncle Tom,' 'Dear Old Joe,' 'Prince Charlie,' Son of Ali,' and so on. These brethren— are some of them esquires, who ought also to be M.P.'s; but we love them too well to dignify them. One day I spoke rather sharply to one of them, and I think he deserved the rebuke I gave him; but he said to me, 'Well, that may be so; but I tell you what, sir, I would die for you any day.' 'Oh! ' I replied, 'bless your heart, I am sorry I was so sharp; but still, you did deserve it, did you not?' He smiled, and said he thought he did, and there the matter ended. [39]

Spurgeon's frequent illnesses always elicited the understanding and sym-pathy of his deacons. Spurgeon once said that he feared they would be tired of having a poor crippled pastor. One deacon replied, "Why, my dear sir, we would sooner have you for one month in the year that anyone else in the world for the whole twelve months." That sentiment was embraced by all. Spurgeon looked with pride on his deacons. And he was so practical in it all. For example:

On one occasion, Mr. Spurgeon, in the midst of his sermon, turned to the deacons, who occupied seats immediately behind him, and without apprecia-bly interrupting the course of his sermon, said in a low voice, 'Pickpocket, Mrs. So-and-So's pew,' and resumed the thread of his discourse. Two deacons left their seats, and, passing out by the stairs behind, re-entered the Tabernacle on the area floor from opposite, one of them bringing with him the policeman stationed at the doors. They met in the aisle by the pew indicated, and the pickpocket was taken out, most people supposing it was merely a case of fainting. [40]

Many of the deacons in Spurgeon's ministry became his intimate friends, like travel director Thomas Cook, aforementioned. Thomas Olney and his son, William, were very close to their pastor. Thomas died in November of 1869. He was called "Father" Olney. Especially close to Spurgeon was Deacon Passmore, his publisher, as pointed out previously. Spurgeon had high requirements for his deacons. He demanded that deacons meet the scriptural qualifications. Rare did the occasion occur when a deacon went astray. One such incident did take place, however. The following entry is recorded in the church business minutes of May 3, 1866:

Our pastor, having taken his place in the meeting, stated that it was with great sorrow he had to announce that the elders, deacons, and himself had been obliged to investigate certain matters affecting the character and position of Brother George Moore. The result was that Mr. Moore had requested to have his name removed from the church book and to retire his office of deacon. Our pastor read the letter from Mr. Moore and recommended the church to accept his resignation without any further investigation. It is agreed that George Moore's name be removed from our church books. [41]

Spurgeon ended this citation in the church minutes in his own hand with these words: "Alas! Oh, solemnly confirmed May 3, C. H. Spurgeon." It is to be noted that George Moore was called Mister, switched from "Brother Moore." Church discipline was strict, but it is obvious that this situation broke the pastor's heart. Spurgeon believed in structuring the life and leadership of the church on biblical grounds and principles regardless of personal grief.

CHURCH OFFICERS AND STRUCTURES

The deacons who served the Metropolitan Tabernacle were appointed for life or until they retired or were disciplined as was Mr. Moore. Spurgeon held the conviction that this office should be filled by the same people throughout their years of Christian service in the church. Their help in the general ministry of the Metropolitan Tabernacle proved invaluable.

Spurgeon also believed that certain men should be set aside for the office of elder. Their responsibility revolved around watching over the spiritual affairs of the church. After examination and consideration, the church selected several elders on a yearly basis, not for life as were the deacons. The pastor strongly emphasized that the elders' duties related primarily to the spiritual affairs of the church, and not to the temporal matters, as that was given to the deacons. The city of London was divided into areas over which Spurgeon commissioned an elder to care for the spiritual needs of that section of the church field. Some called the plan "Baptist Presbyterianism." Like the deacons, Spurgeon could rightly boast of his elders. He said:

> My elders have been a great blessing to me; they are invaluable in looking after the spiritual interests of the church. The deacons have charge of the finance, but if the elders meet with cases of poverty needing relief, we tell them to give some small sum, and then bring the case before the deacons. I was once the unseen witness of a little incident that greatly pleased me. I heard one of our elders say to a deacon, 'I gave old Mrs. So-and-so ten shillings the other night.' 'That was very generous on your part,' said the deacon. 'Oh! but,' exclaimed the elder, 'I want the money from the deacons.' So the deacon asked, 'What office do you hold, brother?' 'Oh!' he replied, 'I see; I have gone beyond my duty as an elder, so I'll pay the ten shillings myself; I should not like "the Governor" to hear that I had overstepped the mark.' 'No, no, my brother,' said the deacon; 'I'll give you the money, but don't make such a mistake another time.'

> Some of the elders have rendered great service to our own church by conducting Bible classes and taking the oversight of several of our home-mission stations, while one or two have made it their special work to 'watch for souls' in our great congregation, and to seek to bring to immediate decision those who appeared to be impressed under the preaching of the Word. One brother has earned for himself the title of my hunting dog, for he is always

ready to pick up the wounded birds. One Monday night at the prayer-meeting, he was sitting near me on the platform; all at once I missed him, and presently I saw him right at the other end of the building. After the meeting I asked him why he went off so suddenly, and he said that the gas just shone on the face of a woman in the congregation, and she looked so sad that he walked round and sat near her in readiness to speak to her about the Saviour after the service.[42]

A most interesting but tragic incident occurred concerning one of Spurgeon's proposed elders. A man had been suggested for the office of elder; others, however, felt him unsuitable for the office. Consequently, he did not receive the appointment. The man proved to be a negative influence in the life of the church. He often did his best to annoy and offend the pastor. He was unsuccessful, but nevertheless the problem persisted. One Sunday, when he had been particularly troublesome, Spurgeon said to him, "Brother . . . will you come and see me tomorrow morning?" The man replied in an angry way, "I have got my living to earn, and I can't see you after 5:00 in the morning." Spurgeon replied, "Oh! That will suit me very well, and I will be at your service and have a cup of coffee ready for you tomorrow morning at 5:00." When the hour arrived, Spurgeon received the man. As usual, the disgruntled brother had a complaint to lodge. He complained he had lost £25, a fair sum of money, serving the church. But everyone said that it had been his own private speculation and the church had no involvement in it at all. He indignantly grumbled that he could not afford to lose such a large sum. Immediately Spurgeon counted out five £5 notes and gave them to the man. He wanted to know, of course, if they had come out of church funds. Charles replied, "No, I feel that you cannot afford such a loss and though it is no concern of mine I willingly give you the money." The pastor related, "I saw a strange look come over his face, but he said very little more, and I prayed with him and he went away. At 5:00 in the afternoon he sent around for my brother to go to see him. When he returned, he said to me, 'Brother, you have killed that man by your kindness, he cannot live much longer. He confessed to me that he had broken up two churches before and that he had come to the Tabernacle Church on purpose to act in the same way and he had especially sought to put you out of temper with him,—which he never could do,—and he told me he was a devil and not a Christian.' I said to him, 'My brother once proposed to have you as an elder of the church.' He seemed very surprised and asked me, 'Did he really think so much of me?' I answered, 'Yes; but the other elders said that you had such a dreadful temper that there would be no peace in their midst if you were brought in to them.'"[43]

The story ended when the man committed suicide by cutting his throat. Spurgeon said, "I felt his death terribly and the effect of it upon the people generally was much the same as when Ananias and Sapphira were slain because of their lying unto the Holy Ghost: 'Great fear came upon all the church and upon as many as heard these things.' I had often spoken of 'killing people by kindness' but I never wish to have another incident of it in my own experience." [44] The incidents of the miraculous work of the Holy Spirit in the days of the Tabernacle ministry were astounding.

The deacons normally served as elders as well as on the diaconate. However, the elders never served as deacons. Theoretically, the deacons were less important than were the elders. Because of the scriptural presentation of the two offices, the elders had superior duties because they were the spiritual leaders of the church and were responsible for the spiritual life of the congregation. However, from the pragmatic perspective, the deacons became superior for several reasons. First, United Kingdom law made individual persons stand behind the ministry of the church from a financial perspective. The Metropolitan Tabernacle deacons were legally responsible for the financial viability and solvency of the Tabernacle's sister institutions like the almshouses, the orphanage, the Pastors' College, etc. That is to say, individual deacons were responsible by law to see that the financial needs of all the institutions were met. The church as a congregation was not responsible. This gave the deacons a very important position. It is thus understandable why they were elected for life; although the church by-laws did not state a given period for the tenure of the deacons. Of course, had a financial exigency ever arisen in the various institutions, it probably would have been the case that the whole church would have stood financially behind the deacons. Nevertheless, they were the responsible party by law, and this made their position in the church most important. Secondly, the elders' office was seen as a lesser office from the practical perspective because they were only elected for one year. But they did do the spiritual ministries, which shall be discussed in a moment. This "inversion" of the practical significance of the two offices came about largely as the various social ministries of the Tabernacle developed.

The Tabernacle also had the office of trustee. They were officially called "Trustees of the Tabernacle property." They were elected for life. Thomas Cook and Thomas Olney were trustees, as was Spurgeon himself.

Not long after the inauguration of the ministry in the Metropolitan Tabernacle, the church revived another New Testament office, that of teacher. Spurgeon contended this was a scriptural office, set up by the Holy Spirit "for the edification of the saints in the matter of Word and lecture." The history of the Baptist Church in Southwark, from which the Metropolitan Tabernacle had emerged, had been the scene of several godly men holding such a post. For example, Benjamin Keach became a teacher under William Rider's pastorate. C. H. Spurgeon pointed out that to appoint a teacher of the church avoided the danger of dividing the unity of the pastorate. He was convinced a teacher would be a valuable aid for the edification of the saints in the Word of God. Consequently, John Collins, who had actually been doing the work of a teacher for years, at the pastor's suggestion officially became recognized as the teacher of the Metropolitan Tabernacle. But in less than a year, Collins received a call to the pastorate of a Baptist church in Southampton. Shortly after that Thomas Ness became teacher at the Tabernacle. But, as the Spirit of God led, he also received a call to a pastorate in less than a year. Therefore, the church finally decided that instead of appointing another teacher *per se*, that the Rev. James Archer Spurgeon, Charles' next younger brother, should become assistant pastor. In business session the congregation called James Archer on October 16, 1867. The church business minutes dated January 6, 1868 record James A. Spurgeon's letter of acceptance of the post of assistant to his older brother Charles:

> I feel that it is my privilege to be the first in love to him, so that it is rather a joy than a fetter to be thus associated. It is with trembling as well as rejoicing that I look forward to my future work with you. [45]

James Spurgeon was formally inducted on January 6, 1868. This proved a most significant move. James proved to be a very able man and administrator. He had a keen business sense and became a tremendous help to his brother. This shall become increasingly evident as the life of Spurgeon's ministry continues to unfold. James Archer Spurgeon had been pastor of the Baptist Church in Southampton for some years. After a very successful pastorate in Southampton, he became the minister of the Notting Hill Baptist Church, London. While he served with his brother Charles at the Metropolitan Tabernacle as assistant, he established and became pastor of the Baptist Church in West Croydon. It became one of the most flourishing churches in the greater London area. Thus James wore two hats: assistant pastor to his brother and full pastor in West Croydon. The Croydon church exists to this day and is known as "Spurgeon's Tabernacle." That, of course, should not be confused with the Metropolitan Tabernacle where Charles was pastor. For two years after the death of Charles, James Archer remained as acting pastor at the Tabernacle, later to give up the position to his nephew, Thomas Spurgeon. That story shall come later.

Certain conditions were expected of James in his ministry at the Tabernacle. It was clearly understood that although he had been called as assistant minister, he should not consider himself as "having any claim to occupy the pulpit or any rights of possession such as was supposed to belong to ministers in the ordinary case." Further, he should give "aid mainly in pastoral work, in visiting the sick, and seeing inquirers, in attending at church meetings, and as such other works as naturally fall the lot of a pastor." [46] Charles always spoke with greatest appreciation of his brother's help and cooperation. He said that it relieved him of much anxiety and hence left him free to give more time to those aspects of the Metropolitan ministry that depended so largely on his personal leadership and direction.

Spurgeon enjoyed the services of another associate for a period, Rev. W. Stott. It was said of him, "A more spiritual, lowly, or earnest man does not exist." [47] He proved a true help to the pastor, though little mention is made of him.

PROCEDURES FOR CHURCH MEMBERSHIP

As previously pointed out, the elders filled the very important function of preparing people for church membership. When anyone indicated that he or she wished to receive Christ and follow the Lord in baptism and church membership, elders were immediately dispatched to that person. The elders that were sent to the prospective church members were called "messengers." They interrogated each prospective member about the reality and vitality of their spiritual experience. A formal report on their visit and interview was then presented to the church by the messengers during a business session. If the reports were favorable, the church accepted the person as a viable candidate for baptism and church membership, then he or she would be baptized and received into church membership. Some reports in the church minutes concerning the elders' investigation of various candidates are most interesting. Several examples follow:

November 1, 1865
George Bantick
16 Holeand Street
Blackfuais

Has been in London about 3 years and attended the Tabernacle ever since. He always led a moral life but not until he heard our pastor did he know himself to be a sinner in the true sense, and this has been a gradual work, likewise his knowledge of Christ as an all sufficient Saviour his doctrinal knowledge is very limited but I think him sincere and gave him a card.

T. Cooke

December 13, 1865
Robert S. Sparrow
66 London Road
Southward

About five years ago was seriously impressed by a Christian brother talking to him about his soul. Has been attending the ministry here about 2 years, was in Mr. Hank's class but moving to a distance could not attend and although having been with the Wesleyans, I found him to be perfectly sound in doctrine and though he has been a Christian for some time and never joined a church, the sermon last Sunday quite decided him to come and cast in his lot with us as he says to make a public profession and to show his colours. Sees baptism to be an ordinance for believers only. I can confidently recommend him. Gave him a card.

G. Croker

March 6, 1867
   Obadiah Simkin
   Gurney St.

This young man has been a seeker of the best things for 3 or 4 years, but could not see plainly the great work of Christ at the atonement for sin until lately our dear pastor's preaching in the Hand of the Spirit has been made a blessing to the enlightenment of his mind upon that important subject. The recent meetings has brought him out so that he wishes to be baptized and join the Lord's people. He appears to be a sincere Christian and has attended the Tabernacle (with his wife who is a member with us 3 or 4 years). I have confidence in him as one who loves Christ and gave him a card.

                                                        George Coust

   Susanah McCrombie
   No 6 York St.
   London Rd.
   March 6, 1867

The case of this poor young woman is somewhat interesting. It appears that up until very lately, she has lived altogether without any religious impression on her mind, both her and her husband. But latterly her mind has become greatly impressed about the reality of spiritual things so much so that her distress of soul has been very great—more especially by attending the meetings held in the Tabernacle. Particular the 2 held by the friends for the unconverted. Her distress was great until the Lord revealed himself to her mind as he who could save to the uttermost. The blood that can wash away all her sins is most precious to her. She has found great peace in praying to the Lord in secret, who has answered her bitter crying and given her peace to look to Jesus. It appears she has lived with a quarry man as her husband but was never legally married. But they lived together as man and wife. But when the Lord met her, she saw it was not right and is anxious to be married and is sorry . . . She made a full statement of her case without any compulsion. I gave her a card.

                                                        George Coust

June 5, 1867
   Elizabeth Layzell
   4 Bessdon St.
   Lockfields

This giving person is only 12 years of age, but after a good deal of conversation with her, I found she had knowledge and experience beyond her years. Her mother is a member with us and 4 or 5 branches of the family. Brother Dunn was with me during my conversation with her. She attends his place of worship at East Street and he thinks with me that she is one of the lambs of the flock. Six months ago she was convinced of sin from hearing the chapter read on the sufferings of Christ in the Garden Gethsemane. She earnestly sought the Lord for pardon and has found the burden removed. She loves the Saviour and wishes to give herself up entirely to his service. She says she knows she is saved. When asked 'How do you know that?' she replied, 'because I believe in Jesus Christ.' 'How does Jesus Christ save you?' she replied, 'His precious blood atones for my precious salvation.' Brother Dunn and I felt satisfied.

I gave her a card
W. Dransfield

Baker George
   16 Martin St.
   November 21, 1866

This good friend thinks he has known the Lord 40 years—but was puzzled concerning election until he heard our pastor. Has attended his ministry these last 10 or 11 years. Has never united himself to any Christian church—relies wholly on Christ. His wife and daughter are both members. Gave a card.

R. Hellier

Lewis Vincient Sale
   15 Park Place
   Kennington Cross
   December 23, 1866

This young man is the son of a godly mother residing at Bagshot in Surrey. He has been in London some little time but was giddy and knew not the Lord. He often tried to be religious but as often he did fail. A good young man persuaded him one Sunday afternoon to accompany him to the Stafford Room, Wedgeward Road where a great number of young men got hold of him and began to talk to him about religion and in the course of conversation brought forth that all important Scripture, 'The blood of Jesus Christ, God's Son, cleanseth from all sin.' This he says took right hold of him and he was led to hate and forsake sin and to believe in Jesus. He has been about to several chapels to hear, but has heard our pastor at the Tabernacle and wished to be baptized and join the church. I believe the Lord has begin the good work in him and encouraged him to come among us and gave him a card.

George Coust

When a candidate received a positive response from visiting elders, the expression "gave satisfactory statement of a work of grace in his soul and the messenger reporting favorably . . ." is always found in the church minutes. This meant the messengers considered the person genuinely saved and thus ready for baptism and church membership. Then the candidate would be voted on by the church in official session. When the messengers gave their report, the candidates for baptism and church membership were at times asked to come before the church in business session and give their own personal testimonies before the entire congregation. Perhaps this was occasionally done because the messengers were not completely satisfied with their interview and would then ask the candidates to present themselves before the church for testimonies. Then usually, if the candidate's testimony sounded satisfactory, the messengers would move that the candidate be received for baptism and subsequent church membership. At other times candidates for church membership could be brought to the church for consideration before the messengers had visited with them. For example, it will be remembered that Spurgeon set aside a day each week, and at times other days, to counsel with people concerned about their spiritual welfare. These persons could be brought before the church upon recommendation by the pastor. The work of the messengers may then have been bypassed by people who saw the pastor and obtained his approval. But even then, after the person was named, messengers would be sent to them for any further help the candidate might need. In the church minutes of January 15, 1866, the following note can be found: "The following persons were proposed as candidates for church membership and the messengers appointed: Hannah White, 15 Burton Street, Eaton Square; William Smith, 18 Cross Street, Newington; etc."

Often the question is raised, when and how did the "interested people" surface? Several avenues were used to single out those that were concerned that they might make an indication of their interest and then be visited by one of the elder messengers. First, many were brought to the Metropolitan Tabernacle by church members. Many of the congregation were great witnesses for Christ. They would witness to friends and family and then bring them to the Metropolitan Tabernacle. When interest was aroused and they were ready for an interview by the messengers, it was carried out.

Also, there were instruction classes for concerned people. This was practiced regularly. Obviously, if a person showed enough interest to go to an instruction class on the Gospel, he or she would certainly be open to being led to Christ and a subsequent visit by an elder and then be presented as a candidate for baptism and church membership. And there were also the enquiry meetings.

Furthermore, people would just come into the Metropolitan Tabernacle because of the reputation of Spurgeon himself and the great ministry of the church. In that setting, as previously pointed out, members would be on the alert for those who seemed to be under conviction. After the service, contact would be made with them by the church members. Spurgeon constantly trained his lay people in personal evangelism.

Then, many potential converts would be contacted and influenced in the total ministry of the church. There was such a multiplicity of Tabernacle ministries going on through agencies like the Sunday School, the almshouses, and various enterprises that concerned people were constantly surfacing in that setting. It is not to be minimized how many came to Spurgeon on his counseling days. Not a few came to Christ in that context. As stated, they would normally be approved for membership on Spurgeon's recommendation. As a case in point, the church minutes of February 22, 1886 read: "The following persons having been seen by the Pastor were this evening proposed for Church fellowship and the messengers appointed." Then 41 names and the appointed messengers were listed. Noteworthy is the fact that this took place in 1886 when Spurgeon's health had become quite precarious. He was a diligent, sacrificing laborer.

Spurgeon employed every legitimate way to touch people with the Gospel. However, one basic emphasis always remained paramount in all the evangelistic methods employed at the Tabernacle: the principle that people should never be led to a mere subjective experience. Such an experience, Spurgeon believed, boded for superficiality if not a false decision, that would bear no fruit in true salvation. There was even a measure of emphasis upon the idea that in evangelism, people should not be urged to trust Christ immediately, but be "pointed to yonder wicket gate," that the unconverted might fall under true conviction by the Holy Spirit. Then, constantly being pointed to Jesus Christ, they would come through a struggle to a genuine experience of repentance and faith. Spurgeon felt deeply that people must earnestly seek Christ and not just be run through a quick succession of verses of scripture and then led to some decision that might prove false and superficial. For example:

> A man once came all the way from Holland to ask Mr. Spurgeon a very important question. He was sitting in his vestry seeing inquirers, when the young Dutchman came in and spoke in broken English.
>
> 'Where have you come from?' asked Mr. Spurgeon.
>
> 'From Flushing, sir, by boat. I want to know, sir, what I must do to be saved.'
>
> 'Well, it is a long way to come to ask that question. You know what the Word says: "Believe on the Lord Jesus Christ, and thou shalt be saved."'
>
> 'But I cannot believe in Jesus Christ,' said the man.
>
> 'Well,' said Mr. Spurgeon, 'now look here. I have believed in Him a good many years, and I do trust Him; but if you know something or other against Him, I should like to know it, for I do not like to be deceived.'
>
> 'No, sir,' said he, 'I do not know anything against Him.'
>
> 'Why don't you trust Him, then? Could you trust me?'
>
> 'Yes, I would trust you with anything,' said the Dutchman.
>
> 'But you do not know much about me,' said Mr. Spurgeon.
>
> 'No, not much; only I know you are a preacher of the Word, and I believe you are honest, and I could trust you.'

'Do you mean to say,' said Mr. Spurgeon, 'you could trust me, and that you could not trust the Lord Jesus Christ? You must have found out something bad about Him. Let me know it.'

The man stood thoughtfully for a moment, and then said, 'Dear sir, I can see it now. Why, of course I can trust Him; I cannot help trusting Him. He is such a blessed One that I must trust Him. Good-bye, sir; I will go back to Flushing; it is all right now.'

With this sort of emphasis, many were reached for Christ and the fall away was remarkably minimal. It proved to be the kind of evangelism in depth that grew the greatest church of its day. That pattern is well worth pondering in the rather superficial evangelism that is so often promoted at the contemporary moment. It is interesting that A. C. Dixon, a well-known name in evangelical circles in the nineteenth century, did not do well at all at the Metropolitan Tabernacle when he first preached there. He came over as somewhat superficial in his urging of people to receive Christ. The whole evangelistic thrust and context of the church was not very receptive to his approach and methodologies. They did believe in people coming to faith in Christ by the typical Puritan route which allowed time for the Holy Spirit to bring the person under deep conviction and to a genuine conversion. Only then would one be ready for baptism and church membership.

Baptism became the "door" to actual church membership in the Tabernacle. After all were convinced a person had truly come to Christ, he or she would then be baptized and admitted to membership. Citations like the following in the church minutes are seen: "Lord's Day, February 4, 1866. The following persons having been previously baptized were this evening received as members in full communion with this church. Joseph Dent, William Stuart, etc., 54 in all."

DISCIPLINE AT THE TABERNACLE

At times there would be lapses of faith in the Tabernacle congregation. When that occurred, the church was quick to administer discipline. But it is important to understand that the discipline always took on a redemptive motif. The person who stood in need of reproof was never simply excommunicated out of hand. Restoration was always sought. Elders would be sent to the person in the attempt to reclaim them. All discipline found its base in 1 Corinthians 5. For Spurgeon, the glory of Christ and His Kingdom must come first. The restoration of the offenders was important, but it took a secondary role to securing the glory of Christ. If the offending person refused to be reconciled to God and the church he was dropped from membership. This was in line with Calvin's interpretation of the Corinthian letter. The church followed the biblical rules of discipline meticulously. The Scriptures state the Apostles directed officers to investigate discipline cases, judge the matter, and bring the matter before the church. Then the church, with sadness, would ratify the report if restoration could not be effected. This method was strictly followed in all cases by the Metropolitan Tabernacle. Moreover, no "court trial" before the church ever occurred; therefore, no disgrace would be blazoned before the world. Yet, the church could question the investigation if it were deemed necessary. At times the case may have been so scandalous that only a report would be given without details. Then, the church would ratify it. All felt that the ridicule that would come from the world was not worth divulging sordid details. At other times, members would be disciplined for no more than "non-attendance." That may seem strange today in our contemporary lack of standards.

In the church minutes of the Metropolitan Tabernacle, some interesting incidents of discipline are found. The church minutes always reflected full church action on any member who needed to be disciplined. Some of the accounts are as follows:

January 22, 1866
The following persons not having filled up their places for a considerable time, it is agreed that their names be removed from our church books—Ann Mannings, William B. Avery, Sarah Avery, Mary Ann Cross, and Troby Cameron (Note: agreed to excommunicate.)

February 12, 1866
Thomas Culleson and Sarah Homer having absented themselves for a considerable time and there being every reason to believe they do not intend to fill up their places, it is agreed that their names be removed from our church books.

Sannderson Jeffreys, not having filled up his place for a considerable time—Brother Songbotham is appointed messenger to visit him.

March 26, 1866
Our pastor stated that rumours affecting the moral character of Fred Inglis reached him. It is therefore agreed that Brethren Jones and Hackett be appointed to investigate the case.

July 9, 1868
William Pavey having been guilty of highly inconsistent conduct—the elders have investigated the case and recommend that his name be removed from our Church books. The Church unanimously confirms their decision.

Our Pastor being not present, reported the case of Thomas Mayo who had been guilty of gross misconduct and whose case had been fully investigated by the elders. It is agreed that he be excommunicated from the fellowship of this church.

Restorations were also recorded in the church minutes. For instance, on January 16, 1888, the following note is found: "Upon the recommendation of the Pastor and Elders it was agreed that the name of Joseph Denwick be restored to the church roll."[48]

Of course, members were dismissed for reasons other than disciplinary matters. An interesting note in the church minutes of February 19, 1866 reads as follows: "In most of the cases our friends have removed out, it is believed have united themselves with other churches." This reflects the fact that people must have united with other churches and did not necessarily inform the Metropolitan Tabernacle. How often this took place is difficult to ascertain, but it was apparently a quite common practice. Another interesting case arose when one was dismissed on his own request. He wrote:

Dear Sir,

I have joined the Wesleyan body because I agree with them in their doctrine in preference to yours. I am very sorry I have not informed you before this.

I am
Yours in Christ,
John Olliner

Letters from the Tabernacle actually recommending members to other churches were seemingly not normally sent. When a person had united with another church, their names were simply dropped from the roll and the church where the person joined was informed of the dismissal. For example, in the minutes of January 15, 1866, the following citation is found: "A letter was read from the church at Unicorn Yard regarding the dismission of James B. Warren and Mary Warren to their fellowship. Agreed that the usual dismissary letter be sent in each case." Apparently, when someone joined another church, letters were sent to the church just saying that they were dismissed from membership in the Metropolitan Tabernacle. A letter of "recommendation" did not enter the picture, as is the practice of most Baptist Churches today. This approach of the Tabernacle must have been the custom of all the British Baptist churches in the nineteenth century, for in the same minutes, this citation is found: "A letter was read from the Church at Eccleston Square dismissing Mrs. Givilim to our fellowship. Agreed that she be received into communion after baptism." It must have been that in this particular case, the woman was a member of a non-Baptist church due to the fact of the expression in the citation "after baptism." Another citation from the minutes of January 22, 1866 reads: "A letter was read from Simerick dismissing Mary Ann White to our fellowship and it is agreed that she be received into communion with this church." Note here that the expression "with baptism" is not listed. One must surmise that she came into the fellowship from another Baptist church. It is also interesting to note that people coming into the church on transfer of membership were apparently not fully received until a letter of dismissal from their previous church was received. As an example, on September 17, 1868, the church minutes record that Miriam Davis was received from the Lewes Church when they received a letter from the church in Lewes.

CHURCH BUSINESS

The Metropolitan Tabernacle engaged in business sessions frequently. Much business needed to be done, and having a congregational type church government, business sessions abounded. As a case in point, there were eight church meetings in March of 1866. Eight were held in April, seven in May, nine in June, and this is typical of any given year. In the church minutes, some interesting citations can be found that give an insight to the overall life of the church. For example:

March 3, 1867
The Particular and Strict Communion Baptist Church at Zion, Chadwell St. Clerkenwell writes to Metropolitan Tabernacle:

We cannot dismiss any of our members to a church that holds the doctrine of 'Duty Faith,' and opens the Lord's table to all that profess to love God irrespective of their baptism and membership with the Church of Christ; and therefore we cannot dismiss James Porter to your communion. If therefore you receive Mr. Porter into your communion, you must receive him in the ordinary manner as if he were not a member of a church and we shall consider that he is no longer in our communion.

Reaction:

Agreed that James Porter be received into communion with this church.

In a letter found in the church minutes of July 23, 1866, signed by C.H. Spurgeon in behalf of Metropolitan Tabernacle, it is recorded:

We affectionately urge that while you hold fast those peculiarities, in which you in common with ourselves are distinguished from other sections of the church, you will cherish through large heartedness toward all the disciples of Christ and ever be prepared to say with the Apostle, 'God's mercy and peace be unto *all* them that love our Lord Jesus Christ in sincerity.'

CHS (largeness of heart to all evangelicals)

Other interesting notes are found in the church records:

July 26, 1866
We desire as a church to express our hearty congratulations with our beloved pastor on the baptism of his sister this evening . . . and we join our earnest

prayers with his that the two little ones who yet remain of its family may be early brought to a knowledge of our Lord and Saviour Jesus Christ. (Referring to the Spurgeon twins, no doubt.)

May 16, 1867
A certain Bro. W. Jones requested his name to be removed because of bankruptcy—had been investigated earlier.

February 18, 1868
A large number of the members were present at this meeting and it was a season of great spiritual enjoyment. (Not all business meetings are dull.)

The Annual Church Meeting—January 24, 1866
Our Pastor Presided

The meeting commenced with singing and prayer. The business accounts for the year 1865 having been audited and a summary thereof having been prepared, was read and is as follows. Dr. Thomas Olney, Treasurer, in account with the Metropolitan Tabernacle.

Then:

Our Pastor stated that our Brother William Knight had united himself with a church in America. It is therefore agreed that his name be removed from our church books.

February 8, 1866
The deaths of Brother Baldock, Brother Banks and Sister McDonald were reported.

The Tabernacle would grant full standing as a church to its missions. For example, the church record states:

On July 16, 1866, New Baptist Chapel, Stockwell, requested permission to become a church—granted.

At a church Meeting held on February 15, 1866 the following letter, requesting a new church be formed at Claremont rooms. It was read and ordered to be entered in the minutes:

We the undersigned being members of the church at the Tabernacle who are working in the cause of the Lord at Claremont Chapel Crown Street, Wyndham Road, Damberwell desire to make known to you that the Lord hath manifestly blessed our labours in the conversion of souls and we believe that it would be for the furtherance of the Gospel, and to the glory of our Lord, if we were formed into a church upon the same principle and having the same privileges as those churches which have sprang from your loins.

> Signed
> Samuel Henry Richards
> Alfred Babington
> Officers pro tem
> John Spansworth
> Minutes
> and 18 others

Agreed that the brethren and sisters whose names appear at the foot of the letter be dismissed to form a church at Claremont rooms.

The church minutes always started with the phrase "The minutes of the last church meeting were read and confirmed." The minutes also reflected, as could well be expected, the statistical analysis of the church at the current moment. The finances, overall church membership, etc. were always brought before the people to keep them well informed. After the minutes were duly recorded, they would be "certified," usually by C. H. Spurgeon. An interesting anecdote occurred in that context. In the March 5, 1866, minutes, the signature of C. H. Spurgeon was smudged with ink. He must have done it himself, because he wrote underneath it, "Certified, C. H. Spurgeon, shocking pens, it being a custom to use the worst possible pens in our vestry." It showed something of Spurgeon's humor, and also, a mild rebuke. There were times when the minutes were certified by W. Olney, deacon, or sometimes by James Spurgeon. Later in Spurgeon's ministry church business meetings were held on Monday evenings at 6:00 p.m. and just termed "Church Meeting." Moreover, at times an elder would preside over the meeting.

Such constituted the essential makeup of the structured life of the great Tabernacle and its ministry. In this setting the work flourished under the blessings of God.

The Services at the Metropolitan Tabernacle

The services at the Metropolitan Tabernacle were dramatic and dynamic. Every Sunday, with few exceptions, the great building overflowed for both the morning and evening services. Though the Tabernacle seated between five and six thousand people, the building was never, except on unusual occasions, unfilled. Even the Thursday evening services reached a multitude. Often there was an overflow into the top gallery during the mid-week service. Spurgeon once said:

> Somebody asked me how I got my congregation; I never got it at all. I did not think it was my duty to do so. I only had to preach the Gospel. Why, my

congregation got my congregation. I had eighty, or scarcely a hundred when I preached first. The next time I had two hundred: every one who heard me was saying to his neighbour, 'You must go and hear this young man!' Next meeting we had four hundred, and in six weeks eight hundred. That was the way in which my people got my congregation. Now the people are admitted by tickets. That does very well; a member can give his ticket to another person and say, 'I will stand in the aisle,' or 'I will get in with the crowd.' Some persons, you know, will not go if they can get in easily, but they will go if you tell them they cannot get in without a ticket. That is the way congregations ought to bring a congregation about a minister. A minister preaches all the better if he has a large congregation. It was once said by a gentleman that the forming of a congregation was like the beating up of game, the minister being the sportsman. But there are some of our ministers that can't shoot! I really think, however, that I could shoot a partridge if I fired into the midst of a covey, though I might not do so if there were only one or two. [49]

Spurgeon always arrived one-half hour before the service began to select the hymns and have prayer. Then five minutes before the stated hour a bell would ring, and that opened the door for those without "pew subscriptions." Spurgeon and deacons would then enter and the worship began. By Charles' side sat deacon Thomas Olney. The services were very simple in makeup. The "order of service" normally ran as follows:

> Silent Meditation
> Pastoral Prayer
> Hymn
> Bible Reading with Comments
> Long Prayer
> Hymn
> Sermon
> Benediction

However, the spirit and vitality of the services were deeply impressive regardless of the lack of liturgy.

Descriptions of the services that took place in the Metropolitan Tabernacle in those days are quite captivating, especially from outsiders who could give a more objective view than some of the regular attenders. One lengthy but fascinating account stated:

> It was high time to go and hear Spurgeon. We had procrastinated long enough about the matter, and now it must be put off no longer. What if the Tabernacle were a Sabbath-day's journey distant? We ought to be able to manage that exertion for once in a way; and anything was better than the grave reproach under which we lay as long as it could be said of us that we lived in London and yet had never been to hear the foremost, if not the most remarkable, of London preachers. So we made the effort and went.

We had heard so much about the magnitude of the congregations at the Metropolitan Tabernacle that we were determined at any rate, that it should not be our fault if we missed an eligible seat. Accordingly we found ourselves in the enclosure rather more than half an hour before the stated time of service. A few people were passing the gates with us, but as yet there was no indication of 'the crush.' Congratulating ourselves on being thus beforehand, we pushed boldly forward, with a view to enter the building by one of its fifteen doors, when there confronted us no less than three scandalized individuals, whose faces wore every expression of horror and indignation. 'You cannot get in without a ticket,' was the hopeless announcement. 'Tickets,' we exclaimed, 'we have none.' 'Then take your place on the steps,' was the chilling rejoinder; 'the general public is admitted at five minutes to eleven.' It was bad enough to have our zeal thus damped at the outset, but to be reminded that we were nothing better than a portion of 'the general public' was a hard blow. We did not, however, like to forego the advantage due to our punctuality without an effort. If this had been a concert now, or a theatre, we had about us a silver key which would doubtless have gained us admission; but the janitors of a place of worship, we considered, were not 'tippable' subjects. While we were rather in a dilemma, a fourth individual came up with a packet of small envelopes in his hand. 'I can give you a ticket,' said he, 'if you wish to go in.' We were ready to fling our arms round his neck as we gasped 'How much?' 'We make no charge,' replied he with the envelopes, loftily, handing us one; but you can put what you like in this toward the support of the Tabernacle, and drop it in yonder box!' This, then, was the incantation, the 'open sesame' we had been seeking. Seizing the welcome envelope, we retired to a corner, and followed the direction given us; after which, with a proud sense of being rather better than one of the general public, we marched triumphantly forward, inwardly reflecting that whatever the fervour of the spirit animating the authorities of the Metropolitan Tabernacle, their diligence in business was exemplary.

The great clock on the platform points to ten minutes to eleven, and then suddenly we hear three smart claps from the other end of the building. The effect of the signal is magical. We rise from our seats, and next moment find ourselves in the longed-for pew. There is a buzz on conversation, which is at first quite alarming. Is this a place of worship or a concert hall? one mentally inquires. People talk in unabated voices and even laugh; and one of the old ladies in one pew waves her umbrella affectionately to her crony in another. It doesn't seem very reverential, but we put it down to the disturbing effect of a great number of people. But all are not here yet. The clock crawls on to five minutes to eleven, and we think of 'the general public' outside. A glance shows that there are still a fair number of empty places for them; and at the thought, lo! here they come. The aisles resemble for the moment the platform of a railway station on an excursion day—at least as far as the eagerness of the candidates for the seats goes. The noise, happily for our reputation as a body of worshippers, is not quite so great. And now every seat is full. The flaps along the aisles are let down and occupied, the gangways in the galleries are packed, the back pews up in the ceiling are tenanted, and we know that at last we are here assembled. But how can any one voice make itself heard here, above this hubbub of shuffling and talking and laughing? We are within twenty yards of the platform, and even yet have our misgivings about hearing; and what of those poor 'general publicans' away there as far as one can hurl a ball?

It is eleven o'clock. The door at the back of the platform opens, and a stout, plain man, with a familiar face, advances haltingly to the table, followed by some dozen deacons, who proceed to occupy the stalls immediately behind the pastor's seat. Mr. Spurgeon is not a young man now, and to us he looked feeble in body and not in health. We rather envied his feelings as, having spent a moment in prayer, he looked round the vast assembly, and were by no means disposed to grudge him an iota of the pride which, mingled with thankfulness, must assuredly have filled his breast at the sight. 'Now let us pray,' he said, and in an instant there fell a hush over that entire company which, had we not witnessed it, we could scarcely have imagined possible. The first sentence of Mr. Spurgeon's prayer was delivered in absolute silence; and we had no difficulty in setting at peace, once for all, our misgivings as to the possibility of hearing. Dropping coughs presently broke the stillness of the congregation, which sometimes conspired to make an absolute tumult; but from first to last Mr. Spurgeon's voice rose superior to all, nay, even seemed to gain power from these very oppositions.

He read through the opening hymn while a tardy batch of the general public was thronging the aisles and bustling into seats, without strain or effort, and in a voice which must have penetrated to every corner of the building. Mr. Spurgeon, we understand, has on more than one occasion said that he can whisper so as to be heard in every part of the Tabernacle, and that he can shout so as to be heard nowhere. In that art lies the secret of his mechanical power as a speaker. It is not by stentorian exertion, but by well-regulated modulation and studied articulation, that he succeeds as he does in bringing all within the compass of his voice. The process is exhausting neither to his audience nor (it would seem) to the speaker—the former are talked to rather than shouted at, and the latter, instead of waging a hopeless struggle with space, is mainly concerned to keep his voice at a sufficiently subdued pitch during the service.

To any one who has not been in a similar scene, a hymn sung by a full congregation at the Metropolitan Tabernacle has a thrilling effect. It is no ordinary thing to see four and a half thousand people rise simultaneously to their feet, still less to hear them sing. For a moment during the giving out of the hymn it occurred to us to look wildly round for the organ, which surely must be the only instrument which could lead all those voices. There is none: and we are sensible of a pang of hurried misgivings as we nerve ourselves to the endurance of all the excruciating torments of an ill-regulated psalmody. A gentleman steps forward to Mr. Spurgeon's side as the last verse is being read, and at once raises a familiar tune. What is our delight when not only is the tune taken up in all its harmonies, but perfect time and expression! The slight waving of the precentor's book regulates that huge chorus, as a tap will regulate an engine. The thing is simply wonderful. We feel that tight sensation of the scalp and that quiver down the spine which nothing but the combination of emotion and excitement can produce. We are scarcely able for a while to add our voices to that huge sea of melody which rises and falls and surges and floods the place. If Mr. Spurgeon's powers of voice are remarkable, those of his precentor are, to our thinking, marvellous. His voice can be heard above all the others, he holds his own, and is not to be run away with, and in the closing hymn, he is as unflagging as in the first. 'Now, quicker,' cries Mr. Spurgeon, as we reach the last verse; and it is wonderful to notice the access of spirit which this produced. We sit down, deeply impressed. After all, what instrument or orchestra of instruments can equal in effect the concert of the human voice, especially in psalmody?

The reading of Scripture followed, accompanied by a shrewd, earnest running commentary, which, though sometimes lengthy, never became wearisome. Mr. Spurgeon is not one of those who believe that Holy Scripture is its own expounder, and certainly in carrying out this view he manages to present the lesson selected in a good deal less disconnected manner than many who, with less ability, attempt a similar experiment. Another hymn, chanted, followed, and then a prayer. Mr. Spurgeon's prayers are peculiar, their chief characteristic being, to judge by the specimen we heard, boldness. We do not mean to insinuate that he rants, or becomes vulgarly familiar in his address to the Deity. But he wastes no words in studied ornament, his petitions are as downright as fervent, and his language is unconventional. 'This is Thy promise, O Lord,' he exclaims toward the close of this prayer,' 'and Thou mayst not run back from it.' We have rarely heard this style of address adopted more freely than by Mr. Spurgeon, and we must confess that it does not exactly accord with our prejudices. Still we may safely say the earnestness of his prayer went far to atone for what struck us as the minor defects of language, which, after all, may have been the reverse of defects to the uncritical portion of our fellow-worshippers.

The most remarkable part of the whole service, however, was the sermon. And here we may as well observe at once, that any one who goes to the Metropolitan Tabernacle expecting to be entertained by the eccentricities of the preacher is doomed to absolute disappointment. . . . We could not help admiring his choice of words. It is pleasant to hear once more half an hour of wholesome Saxon all aglow with earnestness and sparkling with homely wit. You yield yourself irresistibly to its fascination, and cannot help feeling that after all this is better stuff than most of the fine talking and Latin quotations and elaborate periods heard elsewhere. Mr. Spurgeon told a story in the course of his sermon. It was an extremely simple one about a simple subject, but the effect was remarkable. The coughing gradually died away, or became very deeply smothered, and a complete silence fell on the audience. With masterly skill the speaker worked up the narrative, omitting nothing that could give it power, and admitting nothing that would weaken it. You saw the whole scene before you; you heard the voice of those who spoke; you shuddered at the catastrophe; you sighed when all was over. 'And so it is with us,' said the preacher, and not another word was necessary to apply the moral.

While the sermon was going on, we could not resist the impulse to look round and see how our old ladies were enjoying it. It did one good to see one nodding her approval of each sentence, and sometimes lifting her hand to her tell-tale eyes. Other two sat close together, and we are certain that their ribs must have ached by the time it was all over from the amount of nudging that went on. Indeed as we looked round galleries and basement, and saw that sea of attentive faces, we felt reproved for our own inattention, and gave over taking observation, to listen.

Punctually to the time (and nothing can exceed the punctuality of everything connected with the Tabernacle) Mr. Spurgeon closed his Bible, and with it his address. As if relieved from a spell, the congregation coughed and fidgeted and stretched itself to such an extent that, for the first time that morning, the preacher's voice seemed at fault. But the concluding hymn gave ample opportunity for throwing off the pent-up energies of his listeners, and the final prayer was, like the first, pronounced amid a tense silence.

The regular congregation would commonly give their places for those who did not know Christ so they could have an opportunity of hearing Spurgeon. A writer gave this dramatic and most descriptive account of how the services began:

At 6:15 we find ourselves in Newington, opposite the most stolid and matter-of-fact-looking place of worship. Nothing can be more practical-looking than this vast edifice. Not an inch of space is devoted to idle ornament, not a ton of stone is sacrificed to effect. There is a Greek portico, no doubt; but the portico of the Greeks was useful to keep the sun from the philosophers who taught, and the portico of the Tabernacle is useful to keep the rain off those who come to learn.

People are crowding in at about the rate of two hundred a minute, quite as fast as the business-like doors can swallow them up. Tram-cars and omnibuses come up the gates, set down their swarm of serious-looking folk and pass away empty. Now and then a hansom cab rattles up, drops a commonplace bride and bridegroom, or a commonplace elderly couple, and departs. But the vast majority of those who come arrive on foot, and toil up the steps with laggard feet, as though they had walked from a great distance. We do not observe any of the very poor. The waifs and strays of many shires remote from London, and the usual visitors from the two cities, twelve towns, and the one hundred and forty-seven villages that go to make up the metropolis, appear all to be in the social zone between the mechanic and the successful but not fashionable tradesman. We find no one as low as a working man, no one who follows any liberal or learned profession. (Here the narrator is wrong, but not so wrong as if it had been a morning service.) There is a steady persistence in the way these people come up these steps, as though they were quite sure of finding within exactly what they seek. There is no hesitancy or loitering. Each one has come to hear Spurgeon preach, and each one is resolved to get as good a seat as possible. The congregation does not look super-spiritualised or super-depraved. It is Sunday, and its worldly work for the week is over, and this day has been laid aside for rest and business of the other world, and this congregation has come to look after its work for the other world or to rest.

At twenty minutes past six we enter. All places on the floor have been occupied for some time; all seats on the first tier are full, so we climb up the steep, high stone steps throughout the square, desolate-looking stair-well. Everything here, as outside, is practical, except the steps, which are so high as almost to be impracticable. In a moment we are in the spacious body of the church. Beyond all doubt, this is one of the most novel sights in London. The vast lozenge-shaped space is paved with human heads and packed 'from garret to basement' with human forms. 'Over the clock' there is a little room to spare, but in less than five minutes the seats there are appropriated, and for fully five minutes before the hour at which the service is announced to begin there is not a vacant seat in the church.

Inside, too, all is practical and business-like in the arrangements. The light is capital, the colour is cheerful, the seats are comfortable and commodious. There is no attempt to produce a dim religious light, no subduing or dulling of spent tertiary colours, no chance of any one posing as a martyr because of occupying one of the seats. When the acoustical properties of the building are tested they are found to be most admirable. The place was evidently designed and built that the congregation might sit in comfort, and hear and see without strain to the senses.

Fortune favoured me, and we got a place in the first row, about half-way down the left-hand side of the platform. Upon the seat to be occupied by each person is a half-sheet of paper, printed on one side, and bearing the heading 'Hymns to be sung at the Metropolitan Tabernacle on Lord's Day evening, August 11, 1878.' Under the heading comes the following paragraph preceding the hymns: 'It is earnestly requested that every sincere worshipper will endeavor to join in the song, carefully attending to time and tune; and, above all, being concerned to worship the Lord in spirit and in truth. The hymns are selected from "Our own Hymn Book," compiled by Mr. Spurgeon. It is a special request that no one will attempt to leave the Tabernacle until the service is quite concluded, as it creates much disturbance, and renders it difficult to hear the preacher.' For the present, each person has the half-sheet of paper folded up, or is studying it, or using it as a fan.

On a level with the first tier of seats is Mr. Spurgeon's platform. It protrudes into the well of the amphitheatre, so that it is visible from all parts of the church. Upon it are a table, chair and sofa. On the table rests a Bible. From the

platform to the floor runs down each side a semi-spiral flight of stairs leading
to a lower platform, situated immediately under and in front of the higher. The
carpet of the platform and the cover of the sofa are of the same hue—deep red,
approaching plum colour.

Precisely at thirty minutes past six several men come down the passage
directly behind the platform. First of these is a stout, square-built, square-
jawed man of between forty and fifty. Although most of those present this
evening are strangers, there is no commotion upon the entry of the famous
preacher. There are two reasons for the apparent insensibility, one physical,
one mental. The physical reason is that the building is so admirably constructed, so successfully focussed upon the small patch of platform, that every man,
woman and child in the house can see the preacher from the moment he
reaches the parapet of his balcony. The mental reason is that at the root of the
attendance of this vast concourse here this evening lies the business idea.
There is no personal enthusiasm toward the preacher. The people have come
on business, and are too good business people to jeopardize their business-like
calm by a disturbing interest in anything whatever but the subject-matter of the
evening's service. It is rarely that a preacher of such wide and lasting popularity exercises so little personal magic over a congregation.

The service opens with a prayer. Looking down from the height at which
we sit, the great number of bright-coloured hats and bonnets of the women on
the floor of the house look like a parterre of flowers, and, higher up, the first
tier, sloping from the back to the front, presents the appearance of flowers on a
vast stand. At the beginning of the prayer the whole multitude bend forward
with one impulse, the bright hats and bonnets and bald and grey heads are lost
to view, and in their stead appears a dark grey surface, made up of broadcloth-
clad backs of the men and dark shoulder articles of the women.

When the prayer is concluded there is a faint rustling sound, and looking
down again we see the heads are now uplifted, and close to each head a half-
sheet of paper held at a convenient distance for reading. We glance carefully
round, and as far as we are able to see no one is without a paper and every one
seems studying his own. There are four hymns in all, and one is about to be
sung. Mr. Spurgeon gives it out slowly and with enormous distinctness. The
effect of his voice in giving out the hymn is very peculiar. The words come
separately and individually, and take their place, as it were, with intervals
between them, like men who are to assist at a pageant, arriving one by one and
marching to their posts. The first stanza having been read over and the first
line repeated, all rise to their feet by one act of accord. The choir start the
hymn (a special band of singers for this particular evening), and between five
and six thousand voices take it up with great precision as to time and great
accuracy as to tune. The vast volume of sound does not deafen or disgust. It is
mild and suppressed. You know it has the strength of a giant, but you feel it is
not using it tyrannously. At our back is a poor, slender-looking man with a
red-brown beard. He is like a shoemaker out of work. His voice comes in with

clear, sharp edge, a counter-tenor. By our side is a woman, a maid-of-all-work we guess her to be. She strikes in only now and then with a few low contralto notes she is sure of; she never risks a catastrophe up high. She has only about three and a half notes, but she never loses a chance of contributing them when the occasion offers. On our other side is a fresh-coloured schoolgirl home for the holidays. Her voice is a thin soprano, and seems to roughen the edges of the counter-tenor's. But when this happens there floats in upon our exercised ears the dull, low boom of a rolling bass. Who the owner of the bass is we cannot find out. We look around vainly endeavouring to discover. Now we fix on one, now on another, but this *ignis fatuus* of a voice eludes our most exhaustive efforts to run it to—flesh. Meanwhile abroad in the hollow roof of the building the confluent concord of five thousand voices swells the hymn to an imperial paean. [50]

THE PREACHING

A vivid description of the preaching in the Metropolitan Tabernacle is worth recording:

> Mr. Spurgeon's text was, 'I will give you rest,' and he got a number of headings out of and by means of an ingenious device well known to grammarians, by a changing of the emphasis in this way—
>
> > I will give you *rest*.
> > I will give *you* rest.
> > I will *give* you rest.
> > I *will* give you rest.
>
> Besides that, he got a fresh effect in the course of his sermon by reading it very staccato, in the manner of Uncle Tom, who had to spell painfully through his Bible, thus: 'I—will—give—you—rest.' Indeed, from what he said, he appears to think, that if we could unlearn our spelling lessons we should get a better idea of what we read by being forced to go more slowly. That idea is not to be ridiculed. I know that on the same principle I often seem to get a clearer view of the inner meaning of a passage in a foreign author, which I have had a difficulty in translating. What seemed to hold the interest of his audience most was Mr. Spurgeon's frequent *ad captandum* little touches of pathos, such as, 'If your mother—ah! you have no mother now—were to give you a little book with her name in it you would not part with it for its weight in silver.' Then there were little personal touches, as when he told of the sleepless nights he had spent through headaches, and how he got rid of worries—'God knows,' he added 'I have more than most.' And there was a touch of romantic sadness, the sadness of age that looks back on youth, as he told how merry he used to be in the early days of his Christian life, and how a grave comforter had said, 'The black ox has not gored you yet,' and truly, I thought to myself, *atra cura*, the

grim, haunting figure behind the horseman, grows more constant in his attendance as we grow older, be we Christians or not. And again, when relating a
touching little incident about an old friend who had 'gone home,' he said that
among that huge congregation there were some who would be gone before
they met again, and he added, with a sadness that drove home his previous
reflection, 'I could wish it were my lot to go first among you.' But I cannot say
that his personal appearance gave the impression that these gloomy thoughts
came from bad health; on the contrary, except that he is a little stiff in the legs,
the preacher looks as strong and energetic as ever he did, and made, as he
spoke, all the usual marchings and countermarchings between the rails of the
platform, the Bible stand and the chair, which he now and then balanced on his
hand. [51]

OTHER ASPECTS OF WORSHIP

The congregation also practiced "open communion," that is to say, any true
Christian, member of Metropolitan Tabernacle or not, could participate with
the congregation in the celebration. When they did observe the Lord's Supper,
they used non-fermented wine. Spurgeon boasted about that in an article in
The Bible Temperance Education, March, 1887. By 1887, Spurgeon had
become a total abstainer, but not so in his early ministry. In a sermon at New
Park Street Chapel on September 6, 1857 he said, "I am no total abstainer. I do
not think the cure of England's drunkenness will come from that quarter." He
was taken to task for that statement in a pamphlet dated October 29, 1857.
Later in life, Spurgeon also became a vegetarian. Once when asked to say
grace over a sumptuous meal, he prayed, "Lord, we thank thee that we do not
often get such a meal as this, else we should be ill." [52]

In those days it became as common for visitors in London to hear Spurgeon as to go to see St. Paul's Cathedral or Westminster Abbey. Commenting on American visitors, a writer penned: "By far the larger number of
Americans who cross the Atlantic there were two desires; one to visit
Shakespeare's tomb in the lovely church by the river at Stratford on Avon;
and the other to listen to Spurgeon at the Metropolitan Tabernacle." [53] Often
Americans who were prejudiced against the pastor of the Metropolitan Tabernacle would be completely won over by the tremendous impact of his
preaching and the services. The British people themselves were of the same
mind. A fellow Britisher once wrote:

> For a generation no country trip to town has been complete without a visit
> to the great religious theater—we use the word in no invidious sense—where
> Mr. Spurgeon so completely filled the stage. And yet the man who wielded
> and maintained this tremendous influence was at no pains to accommodate his
> teaching to new light, to soften its inexorable conclusion, to shade off its
> pitiless dilemmas. The web of his speech was as simple as that of John Bright's,
> and the effect he produced on his hearers strikingly similar. The mere mental

refreshment of such a method to men and women must have been enormous, apart from the moral stimulus. The sight of the strong face, and the homely figure moving easily about the platform, the flow of simple Saxon speech, the rich, deep voice, that penetrated to every spot of the vast oval of the Tabernacle, one can recall, but never completely realise the attraction they had for thousands and tens of thousands of Englishmen. [54]

Of course, there were the critics too. Some of the younger—one is tempted to say, jealous—Baptist preachers called the Metropolitan Tabernacle "the modern Vatican in Newington Butts."

To sense something of the influence of Spurgeon in his early Tabernacle years, at the Crystal Palace on August 2, 1877, a great fireworks display took place. One of the set pieces included a "fire portrait" of C. H. Spurgeon. A discerning visitor once said, "He was one of two most delicate elocutionists I have ever heard, the other is Lord Cooleridge. What made the elocution of both so extraordinary is that they both spoke without the slightest apparent defect. There was no motion of the body, scarcely even a visible movement of the lips; yet the voice penetrated to the remotest fringe of the audience; not a cadence, not a half-tone, lost." [55] Perhaps the greatest compliment of the preaching and power of Spurgeon was given by the renowned preacher R. W. Dale. He said:

> While they were worshipping with him, the glory of the Lord shone round about them, and this has never been to the same extent their experience in listening to any other man. Never again will they listen to a preacher at whose word God will become so near, so great, so terrible, so gracious; Christ so tender and so strong; the Divine Spirit so mighty and so merciful; the Gospel so free; the promises of God so firm; the troubles of the Christian man so light; his inheritance in Christ so glorious and so real. Never again. It is wonderful that such large numbers of Christian men should, in the Divine order, be made so dependent on one man. [56]

SPURGEON THE MAN

As implied earlier, Spurgeon's appeal certainly did not rest in his appearance. In the Tabernacle days, although he always dressed well, he never took any particular pleasure to be seen in the latest fashion. Even in his early days, as one of his school day pupils said, "The prevailing fashion in dress never troubled young Spurgeon; whether people were reminded by the cut of his coat or the shape of his stock of a former generation or of the present was a matter of no concern." [57] He generally dressed in a frock coat, but never went to a really fashionable London tailor. Spurgeon just wanted to be comfortable, but neat. Fullerton relates that he remembered with humor Spurgeon's concern about being comfortable. In traveling in cold weather, he had a good rug with two cuts cross-wise at the center through which he thrust his head and thus kept warm. The rug would spread over his knees and warm the rest of his body. He would travel about London in that get up.[58] On one of Spurgeon's visits to the Continent, he entered a hotel in Paris with several very well dressed friends. As usual, he carried his wide brimmed, soft hat in one hand, very commonly dressed. The porter of the hotel, remembering that he had seen him before, mistakenly thought him to be the courier of the party. He beckoned Spurgeon to one side and asked in a whisper, "Who are these gentlemen you have brought with you this time?"[59]

Spurgeon would never be mistaken for an athlete. One of his great admirers wrote in 1859, "His figure is awkward, his manners plain, and his face, except when illumined by a smile, admittedly heavy."[60] Another said:

> He was rather small and delicate, with pale but plump face, dark brown eyes and hair, and a bright, lively manner, with a never-failing flow of conversation. He was deficient in muscle, did not care for cricket or other athletic games and was timid at meeting cattle on the road.[61]

Fullerton describes him:

> He was, as has been indicated, under medium height, short from loin to knee, so that he never sat far back in a chair, but with body well developed, chest deep and wide (forty-one inches over the waistcoat), head massive (twenty-three inches round) and covered with thick dark hair, which afterwards turned iron grey; the ear being remarkable, its orifice opening to the front, instead of to the side, like most other ears. From his youth he was stout in build. When he first went to Waterbeach they thought him too pale and too young to be much of a preacher, and, later on, an observer, describing him in the Surrey Gardens Music Hall, said: 'He was pallid, without whiskers, with his hair parted down the middle.' But one of the earliest ballads about him when he came to London had a refrain which embodied the popular estimate: 'O my plump, my rosy Spurgeon.'
>
> The very build of this man, as in the case of John Bright, marks him out as a man of the people. Physically he has no angles. Note men of this make. Notwithstanding their diversity, they have this in common—they require no introduction anywhere. Whatever the company, they are at their ease. There is no putting them out. This applies whether there be education or not. Where there is education and intelligence, as in the case with which we are now concerned, we see perfect naturalness and facility or movement; the power to rise or stoop to the occasion without the least suspicion of stiffness; the ability to give out and take in, whatever the circumstances or situation might be!

Spurgeon was so multi-faceted in his personality that it made it extremely difficult to paint his portrait adequately. During one of his sojourns to Mentone in the south of France, a well-known portrait painter called at his hotel, the Beau Revage, asking Spurgeon if he might sit for a portrait. Charles replied, "You cannot paint me. I sat several times . . . on the fourth or fifth occasion he threw down his brush with the remark, 'I cannot paint your portrait, Mr. Spurgeon, you have sat to me all these times and you have never looked twice alike. Your face seems quite altered on each occasion.'" After hearing this the painter exclaimed, "Well, if he could not paint your portrait, I'm sure I cannot."[62] All of this is not to say that Spurgeon cared not at all how he looked. He one time sat for a photographer. Four proof copies of four poses were produced and sent to Spurgeon that he might choose the one that should be used for a permanent photographic portrait. Spurgeon wrote:

> Nightingale Lane
>   Clapham
>   May 29
>
> Gentlemen,
>   I do not like the four enclosed, and will sit again if you will destroy them.
>   1 & 2 give more prominence than is absolutely needful to my unwieldy *corpus* & 3 & 4 are so stiff that one would imagine a rod of iron to be run through the center.
>   I will let you know the first hour at which I can be with you.
>   Yours truly
>   C. H. Spurgeon

Perhaps a bit of vanity did intrude after all.

Paxton Hood painted a good verbal portrait of how Spurgeon looked. He described the scene:

> We were greatly amazed, as we stood at his chapel doors waiting to enter, to see him as he came and passed along to the vestry respectfully lift his hat and bow again and again to his waiting auditors; there was so much audacious, good-natured simplicity, both in the act itself and on the face of the actor, that we could not help smiling right heartily. It was evident he was not indisposed to appropriate to himself a certain amount of personal homage. His face is not coarse, but there is no refinement in it; it is a square face; his forehead is square; we were wishing, although we are not phrenologists, that it had indicated a little more benevolence of character.[63]

One time Spurgeon submitted himself to an examination by a Phrenologist—a popular thing in Victorian England. A phrenologist would examine a person's head and then give his opinion concerning what he thought the real character of the individual might be. Spurgeon's phrenologist, after examining him, said, "I infer that he is not pugnacious, but desires distinction. Mr. Spurgeon's success is attributable in no small measure to laudable ambition." A small book was published with the title, *The Phrenological Characteristics of Rev. C. H. Spurgeon and the Basis of His Success as a Preacher.*

Dr. Joseph Parker, famous preacher, wrote:

> He had a remarkable face and head. The head was the very image of
> stubbornness: massive, broad, low, hard; the face was large, rugged, social,
> brightened by eyes overflowing with humour and softened by a most gracious
> and sympathetic smile.' Dr. Cuyler, in comparing him with Henry Ward Beech-
> er, said there were only two things they had in common, both were fat, and
> both were humorous.

James Douglas said:

> Could any face more fully suggest geniality, friendliness, warmth of affec-
> tion and overflowing hospitality? His greeting was as warm as sunshine. It
> mattered not what might be the shadow on the spirit, or the trouble of the
> heart—it vanished away at the voice of his welcome. There was a light on his
> countenance that instantly dissipated all gloom.
>
> Lavater has placed language in the eye, but what may we not place there?
> The whole soul looks out of her windows. Mr. Spurgeon's eye denoted repose,
> and at the same time intense observation. His is not the dreamy or contempla-
> tive eye in the least degree. He is wide-awake, he sees everything there is to be
> seen. He can tell at a glance who are present and who are absent in his great
> congregation. His is an eye that in conscious hours never slumbers. He is as
> quick in perception as he is ready in speech!
>
> Another thing strongly marked in his eye is his mirth; but no photograph
> can bring this out, for it appears in the twinkle. His is the laughing, gleeful eye.
> His love of fun stood him to the end, and no saddening of experience could
> tone it down one jot.

These many descriptive passages from friends and observers present something of a portrait of the man that people saw when Spurgeon stood in the
great Metropolitan Tabernacle and preached. Despite his rather common
appearance, his whole demeanor proved captivating to the thousands that
came to hear him declare the Gospel of Jesus Christ.

THE METROPOLITAN LECTURER

During these productive years Spurgeon began to present lectures and
addresses as well as preach, as pointed out in the previous chapter. His first
lecture was delivered at the Surrey Gardens Music Hall. He spoke on "A
Christian's Pleasures." In that address, he touched upon every amusement
prevalent in the day. He talked about such games as chess, giving his judgment upon the various pleasures and pastimes of the British people. And he
did not spare any form of pleasure with which he disagreed. He said, for
example:

> It used to be a comparatively harmless thing for ladies and gentlemen to
> spend all evening over a pack of cards or a box of dice, without any money

being at stake; but we have had such practical proof that the worst crimes have sprung from this apparently inoffensive practice, that every Christian mind must revolt from it. Besides, I have always felt that the rattle of the dice in the box would remind me of that game which was played by the soldiers at the foot of Christ's cross, when they cast lots for His vesture and parted His garments among them. He who sees His Saviour's blood splashed on the dice will never wish to meddle with them. Some persons ask, 'What do you think about dancing?' Well, I never hear the subject mentioned without having an uncomfortable feeling in my throat, for I remember that the first Baptist minister had his head danced off! I am sure I should have to be off my head before I should indulge in that pastime. The usual associations of the ball-room and dancing parties are of such a character that it is marvellous to me how Christians can ever be found taking pleasure in them. A safe rule to apply to all occupations is, 'Can I take the Lord Jesus Christ with me if I go there? If not, it is no place for me as one of His followers.'

In Spurgeon's lecture *De Propaganda Fide* he made a quite significant pronouncement concerning war. He said:

There is one thing I must say, I often hear Christian men blessing God for that which I cannot but reckon as a curse. They will say, if there is a war with China, 'The bars of iron will be cut in sunder, and the gates of brass shall be opened to the Gospel.' I cannot understand how the devil is to make a way for Christ; and what is war but an incarnate fiend, the impersonation of all that is hellish in fallen humanity? How then shall we rouse the devilry of man's nature:—'Cry Havoc, and let slip the dogs of war,'—and then declare it is to make straight in the desert, a highway for our God—a highway knee-deep in gore? Do you believe it? You cannot. God does overrule evil for good; but I have never seen yet—though I look with the cautious eye of one who has no party to serve—I have never seen the rare fruit which is said to grow upon this vine of Gomorrah. Let any other nation go to war; and it is all well and good for the English to send missionaries to the poor inhabitants of the ravaged countries. In such a case, our people did not create the devastation, so they may go there to preach; but for English cannon to make a way in Canton for an English missionary is a lie too glaring for me to believe for a moment. I cannot comprehend the Christianity which talks thus of murder and robbery. If other nations thus choose to fight, and if God lets them open the door for the Gospel, I will bless Him; but I must still weep for the slain, and exclaim against the murderers. I blush for my country when I see it committing such terrible crimes in China, for what is the opium traffic but an enormous crime? War arises out of it, and then men say that the Gospel is furthered by it. Can you see how the result is produced? then your eye must be singularly fashioned. For my part I am in the habit of looking straight at a thing—I endeavour to judge it by the Word of God—and in this case it requires but little deliberation in order to arrive at a verdict. It seems to me that if I were a Chinaman and I saw an Englishman preaching in the street in China, I should say to him, 'What have you got there?' 'I am sent to preach the Gospel to you.' 'The Gospel! what is that? Is it anything like opium? Does it intoxicate and blast and curse and kill?' 'Oh, no,' he would say—but I do not know how he would continue his discourse; he would be staggered and confounded; he could say nothing. There is a very good story told of the Chinese that is quite to the point. 'A missionary lately went to them with some tracts containing the ten commandments; a Mandarin read them, and then sent back a very polite message to the effect that those were very good; indeed, he had never read any laws so good as those, but there was not so much need of them in China as among the English and the French. Would the missionary have the goodness to distribute them where they were most wanted?'

Spurgeon stood as an avowed pacifist all of his life. This fact is not too well known about the great preacher, but speaks of something of his approach to the political dynamics of the nineteenth century when to conquer and colonize nations had become the vogue.

Spurgeon gave many lectures on semi-religious subjects. He presented a very well researched lecture on "Southwark," in the lecture hall of the Tabernacle three months before its actual completion. It centered on that area of London and the religious history south of the Thames. Later published as a small booklet, it demonstrated his research abilities.

One of Spurgeon's most fascinating and popular lectures he entitled "The Gorilla and the Land He Inhabits." On the platform, when he delivered the lecture, he placed a stuffed gorilla. He also illustrated this lecture with colored lantern slides. He dealt with the recently published works of M. Paul Du Chaillu, *Explorations and Adventures in Equatorial Africa.* The religious thrust of the lecture centered in his attempt to inspire the Christian church to send missionaries to the newly explored lands of Equatorial Africa.

When Spurgeon first gave his "gorilla" lecture, the convener of the evening made the remark, "We are now to be entertained by Mr. Spurgeon's lecture on the gorilla; but after ages,—according to the development theory,—we shall doubtless have a gorilla lecturing on Mr. Spurgeon."[64] Again, as could be expected, a cartoon was produced of a gorilla lecturing with a bust of Mr. Spurgeon on the lecture table and a host of gorillas listening to the lecture, elated by the fiery oration of the gorilla lecturing on Mr. Spurgeon.

During those days (1873) Spurgeon received an offer from America to come and lecture. Mr. William Summer of Brooklyn made him a fabulous offer, but he refused. Yale University invited him to give the Lyman Beacher Lectures on preaching. R. W. Dale had engineered that invitation, but he never went. Also, the Williams Lectures of Boston offered $500.00 a lecture that he refused.

In typical style, the press took the offensive and again attacked Spurgeon for his lecture efforts. He was described as "the ass of the conventicle," "a broken down Boanerges," "a Mary-Andrew." The press likened his lectures to comic journals. In a somewhat unusual reaction, Spurgeon sent a long letter to the press, answering their objections and criticisms. A friend had written Spurgeon urging him to give some reply. So Spurgeon sent a defense to his critics. The full text is well worth reading. It reads:

> I have been dumb . . . under the cruel rebukes of my enemies, and the ungenerous reproofs of pretended friends. I have proved hitherto the power of silence, and although most bitterly tempted, I shall not change my custom, or venture a syllable in order to stay these mad ravings. But your brotherly note deserves one or two words of answer.

1. Have I well weighed what I have done in the matter of these lectures? Aye,—and so weighed it that neither earth nor hell can now move me from my course. I have a life-work to perform, and toward its completion, through evil report and good report, I speed my way.
2. You imagine that my aim is merely to amuse, and you then speak very properly of 'stooping.' Indeed, if it were so, if I had no higher or nobler aim in view, it would be stooping with sorrowful emphasis; but, then, think you that the devil would care to roar at me? Why, surely, it would be his best policy to encourage me in forsaking my calling, and degrading my ministry!
3. 'Is the Master's eye regarding His servant with pleasure?' Yes, I solemnly feel that it is; nor am I conscious of any act, or motive,—the common infirmity of man excepted,—which could cause me to incur Divine displeasure in connection with that which is, to me, the work of my life.
4. With regard to laughter,—you and I may differ upon this matter, and neither of us be quite infallible in our judgment. To me, a smile is no sin, and a laugh no crime. The Saviour, the Man of sorrows, is our example of morality, but not of misery, for He bore our griefs that we might not bear them; and I am not John the Baptist, nor a monk, nor hermit, nor an ascetic, either in theory or practice. Unhallowed mirth I hate, but I can and do enjoy my Father's works, and the wonders of Creation, none the less, but all the more, because I am a Christian. At any rate, I hold my own views upon this point; and during eleven years of ministry, I have seen no ill effect, but very much good from my preaching, although the charge has always been laid at my door that I sometimes provoke the visible faculties.
5. Concerning 'sowing to the flesh,' I have not done so in these lectures, but have rendered honest and hearty service to my Lord, and believe that spiritual fruit has already been reaped.
6. As to the grief of friends, let them, as well myself, be ready to bear the cross; and let them not attempt to evade reproach by weeping where no tears are needed. I have given no cause to the enemy to blaspheme, or

only such blessed cause as shall be renewed with greater vigour than ever.

P.S. Get the 'Gorilla' lecture; read it, and see if there be any evil in it; yet it is the least religious of them all.'

As in the earlier days, the abuse and ridicule heaped upon Spurgeon the lecturer had no effect whatsoever in diminishing his popularity. If anything it increased his notoriety. For example, on March 7, 1863, Princess Alexandria of Denmark, in line to become the Queen of Great Britain and Ireland, made a public entry into London. The streets teemed with throngs who wished to see her. At that very moment, Spurgeon drove into town in his closed Brougham carriage, hoping to escape notice. He wore a very tall hat to disguise his appearance. As he moved along, however, his carriage was forced to a standstill on London Bridge by a nineteenth century traffic jam. Suddenly, a working man who had often attended services at the Tabernacle recognized him. Like a flash, the news spread among the crowds who had come to see Princess Alexandria that Spurgeon was there. They literally thronged the carriage giving the preacher such an ovation that even the Princess herself would have envied. They cheered him as men and women struggled to get just a glimpse of his face. As one expressed it, his hand was nearly wrung off, and his arm almost drawn out of it socket by the enthusiasm of the delighted bystanders.

Other notable lectures that Spurgeon gave at the Metropolitan Tabernacle were "Two Wesleys," "Sermons in Candles," and "Eccentric Preachers." All of these have been published and are available in the Archives at Spurgeon's College in London. Spurgeon also gave lectures away from home in those earlier Metropolitan Tabernacle years. An interesting incident occurred in the City Hall of Glasgow. As Spurgeon entered the large hall in the company of the Lord Provost, a policeman stopped him in the entrance of the building informing him that no one without tickets could be admitted. Neither Spurgeon nor the Lord Provost had tickets, so Spurgeon explained to the constable that his companion happened to be the Lord Provost. The policeman replied that he did not know the gentleman nor did he care, but if he actually were the Lord Provost he certainly would not wish him to disobey his orders. He had his directions and instructions from the inspector himself to let nobody in without a ticket and he fully intended to obey his orders. The Lord Provost retorted, "But this is Mr. Spurgeon, and he has to deliver the lecture." "I cannot help that," rejoined the constable, "I have my orders and he shall not come in without a ticket."[65] Finally, however, after much argumentation, Spurgeon and the Lord Provost got tickets and the inspector himself came and escorted them into the hall. Spurgeon told of this event often in his sermons to demonstrate the success of persistence, especially the persistence people should exercise to come to faith in Christ.

GREAT PREACHING

Spurgeon preached many great sermons in those early days of the Metropolitan Tabernacle. Of course, to give an account of them all is impossible; every message made its own specific contribution.

In these early days, the most renowned sermon Spurgeon preached at the Metropolitan Tabernacle was on "Baptismal Regeneration." He delivered that message on Sunday Morning, June 5, 1864. It sparked a controversy of tremendous magnitude. During these years the battle between biblical orthodoxy and continental "new theology" was heating up. In that context, Spurgeon realized he must defend the Gospel as well as preach it. Of course, in a real sense that spirit always characterized the man. It all became more vivid and explicit to him in the early 1860s, as shall be seen in the Baptismal Regeneration Controversy. But that story must be reserved for a later chapter. Moreover, even in those Metropolitan Tabernacle days, he began to sense that all in his own denomination were not firm in orthodox theology. He hinted in a letter to Mr. Medhurst that he had toyed with the idea of starting a new group or union.

In the fascinating and powerful ministry of the preacher, he always kept his marvelous sense of humor. On one occasion Spurgeon introduced a very short, fat man as "this terrestrial ball." One Sunday Spurgeon went into his pulpit (a mere table) to discover someone had stolen the clock that sat on the table. In his inimitable style he remarked that the thief must have been more concerned about time than eternity.

A FACE LIFT

By 1867, due to the tremendous crowds that constantly thronged the Tabernacle, repairing and redecorating the interior of the building became necessary. They closed the Tabernacle and for five Sunday mornings (March 24-April 21, 1867), Spurgeon preached in the Agricultural Hall in Islington. The large hall could hold up to 20,000 people, and Spurgeon filled it to overflowing every Sunday. Actually, the services drew the largest congregations to which Spurgeon ever consistently preached inside a building. The only exception of a larger gathering inside a building was the great fast day service in the Crystal Palace some years earlier. But that occurred only once. An interesting note can be found in the church business minutes concerning the ministry in Islington. It reads as follows:

> May 20, 1867
> We desire to record in our church book our devout thanks to God for sustaining our Pastor during the time in which he preached to the vast congregation assembling in the Agricultural Hall . . . several cases of conversation have come under the notice of our elders.

The demanding service of these years began to take its toll on Spurgeon. In September of 1873 he wrote to a friend, "I am only staggering along under my load."[66] He had more frequent bouts with gout as well. The church was aware of the toll the service exacted on their pastor.

The Tabernacle received a second redecorating in August of 1883. In that context, Spurgeon invaded Exeter Hall for the third and last time while repairs were going on. It was said when he got back to Exeter Hall the old dramatic flair returned and Spurgeon did great evangelistic preaching. Spurgeon never used polemics in his evangelism. He felt the pure, simple declaration of the Gospel always proved best and most effective to produce conversions. He said that Butler's *Analogy*, a philosophical approach, had probably not converted anyone. But a simple little Gospel book entitled *Dairyman's Daughter* had brought thousands to the Savior because it was a book on the *experience* of Christ.

A New Helensburgh House

During these days the Spurgeon home on Nightingale Lane was pulled down and a new Helensburgh house was built, Mr. William Higgs, the builder of the Tabernacle, serving as the architect. Being a more commodious and imposing home than the old Helensburgh house, the garden also was re-sculptured under the direction of Mr. Shirley Hibberd. He laid out the lawn in such a way that the preacher could play "the old Puritan game of bowls" with his sons and friends. It was a fine, comfortable home.

Later, Spurgeon moved farther south into a very beautiful house called Westwood. He loved his Westwood home and did much of his work and study there. Often pressed with so many responsibilities, he guarded each moment at home. One day a man called on Spurgeon and announced to the person who met him at the door, "Say, if you please, a servant of Christ asks for a few moments of Spurgeon's precious time." The doorkeeper left to tell Charles, then returned and said to the man, "Mr. Spurgeon requests me to say that he is occupied with your Master." More of the Westwood story will be told later.

Although Charles and Susannah lived in very fine homes, they never amassed any significant wealth. Right at the time the new Helensburgh house was being built, he received another offer to go to America and to bring a series of lectures and sermons with an offer of £10,000 and all expenses paid. Spurgeon declined because he felt it his responsibility to stay at home and care for the ministry there. This so impressed some of his friends and helpers that they gave liberally to defray the principal part of the cost of his new home. Spurgeon met with the generous donors, thanked them and gave a marvelous and eloquent speech. The address bears repeating as it shows something of the generous and grateful heart the man of God possessed. He said to his donor friends:

It was a law of Abdul the Merciful that no man should be compelled to speak when overwhelmed by kindness. Doth a man sing when his mouth is full of the sherbet of Shiraz, or a prince dance when he wears on his head the crown of Ali, with its hundredweight of jewels? Or, as Job saith, 'Doth the wild ass bray when he hath grass? Or loweth the ox over his fodder?' As he that marrieth a virgin is excused from war, so he that receiveth a great gift is exempted from a public speech. My heart is as full of thanks as Paradise was full of peace. As the banks of Lugano ring with the songs of nightingales, so my whole being reverberates with gratitude; and there is another, for whom I may also speak, who echoes all I utter, as the cliffs of Meringen prolong with manifold sweetness the music of the horn.

From you,—it comes with double pleasure like the nuts and the almonds that were carried to Joseph fresh from his father's tents. From my brethren,—it is a flower dripping with the dew of Hermon, and perfumed with the fragrance of affection. From my fellow-soldiers,—it comes as a cup of generous wine in which we pledge each other for future battles. From my children in the faith,— as a love-token such as a tender father treasures. From the church,—it is offered as a sacrifice of sweet smell acceptable unto God.

A house,—founded in love, walled with sincerity, roofed in with generosity. Its windows are agates, its gates carbuncles. The beam out of the wall shall talk with me, and the stones shall give me sermons. I shall see your names engraven on every room; and I shall read, in a mystic handwriting, the record that your love was weighed in the balances, and was not found wanting.

The time of your love. During my life;—not like the poor philosopher, who was starved to death, but who afterwards had a pillar erected in his honour. This house will be a monument of your generosity, and so it will be a double memorial.

There is no intent on my part to rest now that I have a new house. If possible, I shall work harder than before, and preach better than ever.

Mrs. Spurgeon, who by this time had become a virtual semi-invalid, had been staying in Brighton, attempting to regain strength while the house construction went on. As soon as the new home was ready to be occupied, she returned to London. To show something of the devotion of her husband, he had busied himself long hours with the purchasing of new furniture and fixtures so nothing would worry his wife. He even chose all the draperies, wallpaper, and fittings. Charles had everything in order and fully complete when Susie returned to London somewhat restored in her health.

SUSANNAH'S HEALTH

Susannah had surgery performed by Sir James Simpson of Edinburgh, who had traveled from Scotland to Brighton twice for the purpose. No biographer seems to mention the nature of Susannah's illness, even though they talk of it and her continual health burden. But it is a well-known fact that Dr. James Simpson specialized in gynecology. After the birth of the twins, it seems that Mrs. Spurgeon had continual problems, and no doubt the cause of her semi-invalid state was the result of gynecological problems. The Victorians, of course, would never mention that. After the distinguished surgeon had performed his services, Spurgeon asked the amount of his fee. The good doctor, who deeply admired Spurgeon, replied, "Well, I suppose it should be a thousand guineas, and when you are Archbishop of Canterbury I shall expect you to pay it; until then let us consider it settled by love."[67]

Susannah's illness constituted a constant heartache to Charles. As he sought to be of help and to comfort her in her problems, he would often ask the question, "What can I bring you, Wifie?" One day she replied playfully, without any serious intent, "I should like an opal ring with a piping bull-finch." Spurgeon looked quite surprised, "Ah, you know I cannot get those for you!" Spurgeon and his wife joked about her request several times in the next few days. But one Thursday evening not long afterwards, Charles came home from the Tabernacle and showed his wife a tiny box. She opened it eagerly and therein she found a beautiful opal ring, which he placed on her finger. Quite naturally, Susannah wanted to know where Charles had gotten the ring. He told her that an old lady, whom he had one time visited when she was ill, had sent a note to the Tabernacle asking if someone would call upon her to receive a small present that she wished to give to the pastor. Spurgeon's private secretary visited the old lady and received from her the opal ring. Surely the goodness of God shone upon them even in their difficulties. Little tokens of His grace abounded in the Spurgeon home. But there is more. Not long thereafter, Susannah again traveled to Brighton. A few days later Charles went to visit her. As he entered her room he had with him a large parcel. As she quite eagerly tore open the covering, she found a bird cage containing a beautiful, piping bullfinch. One can imagine the astonishment and joy when she saw that her second wish had been granted. After Susie traveled to Brighton, Charles went to see a dying friend. After praying with the sorrowful couple, the lady of the home said, "I want you to take my pet bird to Mrs. Spurgeon, I would give him to none but her, his songs are too much for my poor husband in his weak state, and I know that 'Buloyn' will interest and amuse Mrs. Spurgeon in her loneliness while you are so much away from her." Charles, of course, shared with his friends how God in His providence had fulfilled the wishes of his wife. Even in comparatively trifling situations, God certainly blessed the marriage in a marvelous way. Both of them recognized that the gifts were really gifts from a loving Heavenly Father.

The Spurgeons were proud of their twin boys. Thomas served in Auckland. Charles called him "Son Tom," and Susannah called him "my Seagull." Charles, Jr. was a pastor and he had the reputation of sounding just like his father. They truly were fine boys.

In these productive years, Charles suffered his first long-term illness that laid him up for a protracted time. After attending his first—and only— Lord Mayor's annual banquet in 1869, he came down with a mild case of the small-pox. He remarked, "I have only once been in such high society, and then I caught the small-pox, so I have determined never again to form one of that company."[68] And he kept his word. Two years later, he was out of his pulpit again for twelve weeks due to illness. A pattern began to be set. But as it was said of Spurgeon, "He made no parade of his afflictions. What he had to bear, he bore uncomplainingly, and as far as possible, silently, and in the retirement of his home."[69] That is quite remarkable, for, as one put it, "His griefs were as deep as his joys were high."[70]

During these difficult days, many of the great benevolences of the Metropolitan Tabernacle developed, such as the Stockwell Orphanage, the alms-houses, and many other significant social works. The already established Pastors' College grew apace as did other earlier benevolent works. Charles' social ministry comprises one of the most important aspects of his ministry. As one said, "He was not a pious puddle-paddle . . . Bountifully endowed with common sense, he saw that unless his vocation was made serviceable in benefitting the lives of multitudes about him, his success in life would be meager indeed."[71] Thus we turn to the development of the social ministry of the Metropolitan Tabernacle orator. As he was "Faithful" in preaching and evangelism, so was he in social concern.

Spurgeon's last home: "Westwood."

8

"A Man . . . Whose Name Was *Help*"

SPURGEON'S SOCIAL, EDUCATIONAL, AND OUTREACH MINISTRIES

Stockwell Orphanage.

Behold ye how these crystal streams do glide
To Comfort pilgrims by the highway side;
The meadows green, besides their fragrant smell,
Yield dainties for them, and he that can tell
What pleasant fruit, yea, leaves, these trees do yield,
Will soon sell all that he may buy this field.

—*John Bunyan*

Introduction

The Bible says, "Jesus went about doing good" (Acts 10:38). No passage of Scripture describing the earthly ministry of our Lord is more all-inclusive, powerful and pointed than this word from Luke. Wherever our Lord met a need, He stepped into that hurting life and with His touch of grace and love alleviated the want. Down through the years, true Christians have exemplified this spirit of Jesus. God's people are called to address the needs of the world. Christ taught that everyone shall be judged on how well they feed the hungry, clothe the naked, visit those in prison, and give a simple cup of cold water to the thirsty. Those deeds prove the genuineness of one's spiritual experience. Therefore, a social consciousness and commensurate work, exercised in the name of Jesus Christ, rests right at the core of Christianity.

Luke also tells us that our Lord "came to seek and to save that which was lost" (Luke 19:10). If anything spoke of Jesus' attitude toward people, it was His deep concern for their spiritual well-being. He introduced the straying to the Father, forgave the sins of the wayward, and being lifted up, drew all people to Himself. The Lord well recognized that the greatest need of any person is the salvation He came to provide. Thus to neglect sharing the Gospel of salvation is tantamount to treason to Christ Himself. Everything pales in Christian service and ministry when compared to the evangelization of the world.

One recurring tragedy of the Christian church, however, has been the separation of social ministries and spiritual, evangelistic ministries. Often, a rigid dichotomy has been struck between these two allied services for Christ. This dilemma can be seen vividly in the twentieth century, particularly in North America, in the polarization of the so-called "social gospel" and "saving gospel." Such a situation inevitably brings the Church to a low estate. This kind of dichotomy never has our Lord's stamp on it. The New Testament Church, the Church down through the centuries of its history in its greatest hours, always combined in a harmonious unity these two merging ministries.

397

Such a separation of services was unknown in the dynamic eighteenth century during the great revival of those days. For example, John Wesley, a fervent evangelist, started prison reform, credit unions for poor people, and a host of other social concerns. Whitefield, Wesley's partner in revival, shared the same spirit. Few people realize that one of the primary purposes of George Whitefield (who was an evangelist of the highest order) in coming to America during the days of the First Great Awakening was to found and fund an orphanage in Savannah, Georgia. The same approach characterized continental Christians. The great pietistic leader, Hermann August Francke, in Halle, Germany had many different social ministries in which he and his pietistic students engaged. The Halle Church reached something of its highest hour because of this approach to ministry in the dynamic eighteenth century.

The nineteenth century proved no exception. Evangelical Christians engaged in extensive social ministries as well as in fervent and effective evangelism. The names of significant Christian leaders like Lord Shaftesbury and William Wilberforce will always shine as brilliant stars in the constellation of Christian concern for needy people. The Church fulfills its mission in that setting and context.

Almost unparalleled in church history, the ministry of Charles Haddon Spurgeon epitomized the perfect blending of evangelistic fervency and deep social concern. We have already investigated in some depth his utter commitment to leading people to faith in Christ. Perhaps the world shall never see a more effective pastor-evangelist than C. H. Spurgeon. But right beside that concern for people's souls stood his commitment to fulfill people's needs. He devoted much of his time and energy to that end. He will always stand as a symbol of a minister who developed his life of service in the beautiful balance of social ministries and evangelistic commitment. And the world knew it. *The Examiner,* a New York paper, on July 10, 1884, called Spurgeon "an evangelizing philanthropist." In this he appeared very much like his Lord. He truly could be called "A man . . . whose name was 'Help.'"

LONDON'S NEED

Spurgeon could always be moved by the desperate needs of Londoners. Spurgeon's London in the mid-nineteenth century was every bit as tragic as Dickens' description of the city in his novel, *Oliver Twist.* The London slums really did have its share of Fagins and Artful Dodgers and poor little Olivers. The beautiful monuments and historic places of London like Trafalgar Square, Piccadilly, and the noble spires of Westminster Abbey, were a far cry from the ramshackled houses on the waterfront and the pubs and squalor. The average professional thief had hardly reached his teenage years. Young girls were drawn into prostitution at an alarming rate and at an unbelievable age. Poverty and disease and overpopulation were an integral part of everyday living for many Londoners in Spurgeon's day.

In 1850, Henry Mayhew did a careful study of the lower classes of London society in relationship to their living standards, average income, and other social aspects of life. He estimated that in 1850 over 10,000 costermongers roamed the streets selling their simple little wares. Yet of these, Mayhew said, "They don't find a living, it's only another way of starving." [1] Less than ten percent of these London poor were literate. Most of the costermongers were faithful to their spouses, but they had never gone through the marriage ceremony simply because they could not afford the fee for the license. Tragically, less than three percent had ever been inside a church. These poor, bedraggled, street sellers worked from dawn to dark peddling their wares, but seldom making enough money to eat a decent balanced meal. Their normal diet consisted primarily of tea and bread or occasionally bread with some grease, which passed for gravy.

The spiritual condition blared out as deplorable as the social condition. One young lad, discussing religion, said:

> As for going to church, why, I can't afford it—besides, to tell you the truth I don't like it well enough . . . I never heard about Christianity . . . I have never heard a little about our Saviour—they seem to say he were a goodish kind of a man; but if he says as to how a cove's to forgive a fellow who has hit you, I should say he know'd nothing about it. [2]

Mayhew declared that over 50,000 people made their living in some fashion in the dregs of London. The term "mud larks" applied to them typified their squalid lives. These poor people would wade up to their waists in the slime of the Thames River at low tide searching for nails, bones, pieces of metal, or an old coin, hoping that they could somehow sell them. They generally earned less than four pence a day. Mayhew said that he once counted over 200 sewer searchers in London. These people would actually wade through the sewers of London looking for various objects that might be sold. Laws were passed that would restrict such activities because many had drowned or had been attacked and killed by hoards of rats. Still, these pitiful people carried on. Some collected dog dung to sell to tanneries for curing leather. There were bone grubbers and rag pickers, pathetic wretches who would rummage through dung piles, back alleys, and the garbage heaps of the city hoping to find perhaps rags, bones, or metal that might be sold. None ever earned over three shillings a week. Mayhew tells how he had "often seen the bone grubbers eat the black and sodden crust that they had picked out of the gutter." [3] Of course, these were among the worst of London's poor. In the working class districts, where the common laborers worked, the situation was some better. Yet even these people's lives in many senses of the word were miserable and their education even worse. In a Parliamentary study of 1863, a matchbox maker related that she:

> Never was at school in her life. Never went to church or chapel. Never heard of England or London, or the sea or ships. Never heard of God. Does not know what he does. Does not know whether it is better to be good or bad.[4]

Those who worked on the docks fared no better. Unemployment ran rampant, thus, the employer could do just as he willed. Men were hired as jobs arose and fired when the jobs were complete. Mayhew said:

> The scenes witnessed at the London Dock were of so painful a description—the struggle for one day's work, the scramble for twenty-four hours extra sustenance and extra life were so tragic a character. . . . I have said that at one of the docks alone I found that 1,823 stomachs would be deprived of food by the mere chopping of the breeze.[5]

It is understandable why many of these desperate wretches of London life turned to crime. Mayhew said that in 1860 London had 3,000 known thieves. On top of those known thieves, Mayhew estimated another twelve to fifteen thousand roamed at large, many of whom were pickpockets and were often active among the crowds that assembled at Spurgeon's Metropolitan Tabernacle. Crime in London increased at an average annual rate of 11.7% between 1805-1851. Prostitution was rife. The London Female Preventative and Reformery Institution estimated that the number of prostitutes in London alone ran as high as 80,000. Girls that worked in the factories during the day would often engage in prostitution at night to help feed themselves. Spurgeon spoke out strongly on these sad issues. He compared London to Sodom "in its most putrid days." *The Pall Mall Gazette* (January 7, 1885) printed some stark revelations on London's poor, the open vice, and leaders' debauched lives by patronizing prostitutes. Spurgeon cried out, "O God, have mercy upon the land whose judgment seats and palaces are defiled with vice . . . Woe unto thee, O land, when thy great ones love the harlot's home . . . Deep is our shame when we know that our judges are not clear in this matter . . . What is coming over us? "[6] Obviously, life in Spurgeon's London was not completely characterized by the Barretts of Wimpole Street.

Outcries arose against these deplorable conditions. W. C. Preston wrote a popular pamphlet entitled, "The Bitter Cry of Outcast London." In this small tract, he voiced his outrage about the middle class religious establishment and its unconcern for the lower classes of London. He said:

> Whilst we have been building our churches in solacing ourselves with our religion and dreaming that the millennium was coming, the poor had been growing poorer, and the wretched more miserable, and the immoral more corrupt. The gulf has been daily widening which separates the lowest classes of the community from our churches and chapels, and from all decency and civilization. It is easy to bring an array of facts which seem to point to the opposite conclusion to speak of the noble army of men and women who penetrate the vilest haunts, carrying with them the blessings of the Gospel; of

the encouraging reports published by missions, reformatories, refuges, temperate societies; of theatre services, midnight meetings and special missions. But what does it all amount to? We are simply living in a fools paradise if we suppose that all our agencies combined are doing a thousandth part of what needs to be done, or a hundredth part of what could be done by the church of Christ. We must face the facts, and these compel the conviction that this terrible flood of sin and misery is gaining on us.[7]

SPURGEON'S CONCERN

Into this situation Spurgeon made his mark. G. M. Trevelyan, noted historian, said that for the poor and destitute of the Victorian society, "No one but the Nonconformist minister was their friend."[8] Lord Shaftesbury would have agreed with Trevelyan. He maintained that most of the philanthropic movements of the century emerged from the evangelicals. And among these, Spurgeon stood tall. He had a humble background himself, and could thus empathize with the humbler classes of the city. He would walk through the slums of the back streets of London to acquaint himself with the misery of those poor and destitute members of society. Moreover, Spurgeon decided not to minister just to those who would come to him in need, he would reach out to touch the outcasts as well. In *The Sword and the Trowel* he wrote:

> It is no use waiting until one universal Charity Organization scheme shall be carried out. We might as well tarry until an organized provident drops quartern loaves and pats of butter at every householders door. Schemes and plans and all very well, but he who waits till a scheme has put a chicken into his pot will go without a pullet for a lifetime . . . . We cannot be content to be pampered while our brethren pine in want. Down with the barriers and let the rich and poor meet together, for the Lord is the Maker of them all.[9]

For this very reason, Spurgeon chose the site of the Metropolitan Tabernacle near the "Elephant and Castle," a very busy pub, right in the heart of the working class district of London's south side. He said, "Religion must be intended for this life; the duties of it cannot be practiced, unless they are practiced here."[10] For Spurgeon, Christianity must be a practical, down-to-earth religion that brought the teachings and ministry of Jesus right home to where people lived. He was considered "vulgar" by the sophisticates of the day. However, he reveled in the criticism because it was to these "vulgar" people that he wanted to speak and to reach out and meet their needs. Furthermore, Spurgeon saw society as an organic whole—we saw that earlier in chapter two of this biography. He recognized that if one part of society suffered, the rest of the body of people suffered also. He told the readers of *The Christian Commonwealth*:

> The true welfare of a country is not that of a class but of the whole body corporate. The rich cannot prosper without the poor, nor the poor apart from

the rich. The workman suffers if the master is impoverished, the employer is a loser if the artisan declines. Socially we are one body, and a sickly member is an injury to the whole . . . To benefit the community we must seek the good of every individual man, woman, and child; and for a nation to do well, each individual must work righteousness. [11]

This, of course, does not mean Spurgeon was oblivious to the existence of various strata in society. He was a realist about those things. Yet, he realized that society still did have an organic unity about it, and thus one person's plight affects another. Therefore, when he felt he helped one individual, he aided society as a whole.

SPURGEON'S SOCIAL PHILOSOPHY

Spurgeon advocated the breaking down of barriers between the classes, but not the eradication of the classes themselves, thus merging all people into a classless society. He contended that each rank or stratum of society ought to know and keep its divinely appointed place, yet be open to one another. He said:

> Everyone of you (Englishmen) seek to cultivate a generous spirit toward his neighbor. Let not the rich oppress the poor; let not the poor envy the rich, let us all pull together heart and soul, as being brothers of one race. . . . My dear friends, let us not think that our national prosperity must always endure through the intrinsic excellence of our constitution. No, our confidence must be in our God, and, under God, in ourselves; in our honesty, in our integrity; in our generous sympathy with one another; in the keeping of each rank in its own place; in the non-intrusion of any man into another man's rights; in respect to property and respect to labor, in respect to learning and respect to manhood . . . capitals in reform, but not in revolution; in radicalism, so far as to destroy everything that is radically wrong; and in conservatism so far as to conserve every particle of right. [12]

Spurgeon believed that the social classes formed an essential part of society, but this gave no excuse for any sort of class antagonism. He plainly declared the upper class should never feel superior to the so-called lower classes, nor should the lower class despise the upper class. Regarding the lower classes he said, "The world calls them inferiors, in what way are they inferior? They are thine equals, really, though not so in station." [13] Spurgeon may have been naive concerning the human heart if he thought the poor would not envy the rich or that the rich would not look down upon the poor. Yet, this simplicity of the man was admirable.

Spurgeon's conviction concerning the structures of society removed any fear of socialism. In *John Ploughman's Talks* he laid down his ideas about the class struggle in England:

As for lazy fellows who will eat till they sweat and work till they freeze, I don't mind what short commons they get, but a real hard working man ought to be able to get for a day's work enough to keep himself and his family from hunger. If this cannot be done, something is wrong somewhere, as the man said when he sat down on a setting of eggs. I am not going to blame the farmers, or the landlords, or the Parliament men or anybody; but the land is good and yields plenty for man and beast, and neither horse nor man should be starved. [14]

Spurgeon believed that if the working class people would put in an honest day's work and if their employers were willing to pay them a fair wage, there would be no animosity between the classes at all. This again showed something of the almost simplistic approach Spurgeon manifested at times.

But Spurgeon would allow no one to avoid the responsibility to help people in need. He believed that genuine charity demanded that people get right down into the heart of the situation, put their hands on the plow, and cut a furrow for Christ. He demanded active involvement on a one-to-one basis if people really wanted to do something about society's ills. He said:

This is an age of proxy. People are not charitable, but they beg a guinea from somebody to be charitable with. It is said that charity nowadays means that A finds B to be in distress, and therefore, asks C to help him. Let us not in this fashion shirk our work. Go and do your own work, each man bearing his own burden, and not trying to pile a double load on other men's shoulders. [15]

Spurgeon put this into practice in his own life. He was always known as a "soft touch" for anyone in real need. Throughout his life, hundreds of thousands of pounds passed through his hands. At his death, he left his family with relatively little. His generosity was legendary.

SPURGEON'S INDIVIDUALISM

It must be understood that Spurgeon's approach to social problems essentially expressed itself as a personal one-on-one endeavor. This individualistic approach for the solving of society's ills did much good. Moreover, as implied, Spurgeon also appreciated the approach to meeting needs by changing the actual structures of society. For example, when William Booth of the Salvation Army proposed a vast and complex scheme by which English society should be totally reorganized to counteract all of the problems of industrialization, Spurgeon actually came out in favor of the scheme and urged all Christians to "carry out these plans with such modifications as they see fit." [16] He was *not* adverse to sweeping social changes. Nonetheless, he still believed that seeing an individual come to faith in Christ and become a converted person still presented the best and basic means of revolutionizing society. He thoroughly committed himself to the principle that "no social plans will make our earth a paradise while sin still curses it, and Satan is abroad." [17] He believed that people's natures must be changed if society is to have any lasting change. Thus, the problems of people were to be met essentially by individuals touching other individual lives in a charitable way and ultimately leading them to Jesus Christ. In this respect, therefore, Spurgeon was primarily a Christian philanthropist and not a social reformer. He must be understood in this light.

THE CHURCH AND ITS MAKEUP

Spurgeon carried out this individualistic principle in the entire life of the Tabernacle. He did have poor people in his congregation, especially in the first half of his London ministry. As late as 1883 he wrote:

> The number of the poor of the church is very great and quite out of proportion to the usual condition of churches; hence the poor fund needs strengthening. . . . It is our joy and honor to be a church in which the working class and the poor abound; but this fact tries our finances sternly. [18]

Although the leadership of the church came primarily from the artisans and the middle class members of the congregation, many poorer members made up the bulk of the congregation. An observer in Spurgeon's church in these years commented:

> While waiting for the preacher you glance at your neighbors. In the pews are many who are thoughtful, Christian people; there are scholarly and clerical men—some of distinguished appearance—scattered throughout the crowd, yet the first feeling of a well-bred New Englander is a certain disgust. These blear-eyed men, these loudly dressed, coarse-faced women, these poverty stricken, unwashed street denizens thronging around you—some in your very pew. . . . Spurgeon has his Master's credentials. 'The common people heard him gladly, the poor have the gospel preached to them.' [19]

In the latter part of Spurgeon's ministry, however, the congregation did become increasingly middle class. This gave him a financial base to do more to reach the needy of London. However, Spurgeon's increasing popularity, especially with the middle classes, diminished some of his lower class appeal. Still, as he looked around at the folk who lived and worked near the "Elephant and Castle," he longed to reach these people just as he had done in the vigor of his youth. In some sense, he had become a captive of his own popularity with the middle classes; nevertheless, he did all within his power to reach out to poor, needy people.

Spurgeon exemplified an ecumenical spirit in all his social concerns. In June, 1889, the Prince of Wales asked Charles to serve on a committee to perpetuate the work of Father Damien among lepers. He accepted. Father Damien was Roman Catholic. In the light of Spurgeon's attitude toward

Romanism, his acceptance demonstrated his broad approach in meeting social needs. Spurgeon was the only Nonconformist minister on the committee. Some leading persons with whom Spurgeon served were Lord Randolph S. Churchill, the Archbishop of Canterbury, Baron Rothschild, William E. Gladstone and others. All the papers reported it. Then, quite strangely, Spurgeon denied in *The Sword and the Trowel* that he served on the committee. However, the daily papers declared he did. The mystery of the riddle remains unsolved. But the expanse of his several ministries leaves no doubt where his heart was. A volume could be written on each social ministry Spurgeon inaugurated through the pastorates of the New Park Street Church and the Metropolitan Tabernacle. Space forbids such an exercise, of course, but at least a serious look at each is necessary to understand who this man was that preached to thousands. Each aspect of his social concern reads like a romance. He will always be known as a great preacher, but he was a Christian philanthropist of the first order as well. We must move to view these ministries.

THE PASTORS' COLLEGE

We must go back a few years to the earlier London days of C. H. Spurgeon to catch the picture of the founding of what he consistently called "his first-born and best beloved," the "Pastors' College Evangelical Association of Ministries," its official name. Actually, one must go back to the early revival days of New Park Street. Spurgeon said the Pastors' College owed its birth directly to a revival of religion.[20] And how Spurgeon loved that work! He said, "This is my life's work, to which I believe God has called me and therefore I must do it. To preach the Gospel myself and to train others to do it is my life's object and aim."[21]

It all began when a young man, Thomas William Medhurst, who had been much concerned about his relationship to Christ wrote to Spurgeon for help. A protracted correspondence and friendship developed between Spurgeon and Medhurst until finally the young man received the full assurance of salvation and became a thoroughly committed Christian. The first letter that Spurgeon wrote to Medhurst that led him to Christ reads:

You ask me a very important question: 'Are you one of God's elect?' This is a question neither you nor I can answer at present. I will ask you an easier one: 'Are you a sinner?' Can you say 'Yes?' All say yes; but then they do not know what the word sinner means. A sinner is one who has broken all his Maker's commands, despised His name, and run into rebellion against the Most High. A sinner deserves hell, yea, the hottest place in hell; and if he be saved, it must be entirely by unmerited mercy. Now, if you are such a sinner, I am glad to be able to tell you the only way of salvation, 'Believe on the Lord Jesus.'

I think you have not yet really understood what believing means. You are, I trust, really awakened, but you do not see the door yet. I advise you seriously to be much alone, I mean as much as you can; let your groans go up to heaven if you cannot pray; attend as many services as possible, and if you go with an earnest desire for a blessing it will come very soon. But why not believe now? You have only to believe that Jesus is able and willing to save, and then trust yourself to Him. [22]

The climactic moment for Medhurst came in one of the Thursday evening sermons at the New Park Street Chapel when Spurgeon preached the simple Gospel of Christ. When Charles learned of Medhurst's newfound faith, he rejoiced. The youth expressed his desire to be baptized and join the church, and of course, Spurgeon promptly responded. In the pastor's notebook the following entry is found:

Thomas William Medhurst—a very promising young man—his letters to me evince various degrees of progress in the pilgrim's road. He has been very anxious, but has now I trust, found refuge in the Rock of Ages. [23]

Almost immediately after Medhurst's conversion, only two months later, he began preaching in the open air. His simple ministry was attended with marked success. At the same time, several members of the New Park Street Chapel complained to Spurgeon about the young man's preaching. It was painfully obvious, they declared, that the "want of education" in his preaching ministry stood out in bold relief. Some even went so far as to suggest that his preaching should be stopped for fear it might bring disgrace to the Gospel.

Spurgeon, sensitive to the situation, interviewed young Medhurst. The fledgling preacher readily admitted to what had been said. "But," he declared, "I must preach, sir; I shall preach unless you cut my head off." [24] As humorous as it may seem today, some critics of young Medhurst took his words seriously and exclaimed to Spurgeon, "Oh, you can't cut off Mr. Medhurst's head, so you must let him go on preaching."

This incident, though it may seem of little significance, led to the foundation of what became known simply as the Pastors' College. Although Medhurst's preaching left much to be desired, two people had become members of the New Park Street Baptist Chapel because of his ministry. Spurgeon took serious note of that and suggested to the young preacher that he should prepare himself educationally for the ministry. The pastor recognized the hand of God upon him. Charles even promised to bear the expense of his tuition and support during his period of training. Medhurst was deeply grateful. It proved most significant for the young preacher and also showed something of the generosity of Spurgeon, he had little money. He had only been pastor of the New Park Street Baptist Church one year, and his wedding to Susannah was fast approaching. Charles said, "With a limited income, it was no easy thing for a young minister to guarantee £50 a year." [25]

However, he gladly made the sacrifice, and when he did marry, Susannah gladly entered the spirit of the work. She said that they "planned and pinched" at home to help support young Medhurst.

Being a young man of twenty years of age and just out of his apprenticeship, Medhurst gladly responded to Spurgeon's proposal and in July of 1855 went to live with the C. H. Hoskens of Beckesleyheath. Hoskens served as pastor of the Crayford Baptist Church. He became Medhurst's tutor. The young preacher progressed quite well in his studies. Moreover, once a week he would spend several hours with Spurgeon absorbing every word as Spurgeon lectured to him on the various aspects of Christian ministry. Even at this time Spurgeon had the germinal idea of training students. He wrote to Medhurst and said, "I have been thinking that when you are gone out into the vineyard, I must find another to be my dearly beloved Timothy just as you are." [26] Consequently, Spurgeon gathered a set of textbooks and various theological works to help train others as opportunity arose. This small beginning ultimately became the nucleus of the library of the Pastors' College.

Medhurst progressed well in his studies. He continued his open-air preaching at Beckesleyheath, and once Spurgeon went with him to preach along his side. After the service, he heard two old ladies discussing the sermon. "How did you like Mr. Spurgeon?" asked the first, to which her companion replied, "Oh! very well, but I'd sure have enjoyed the service more if he hadn't imitated our dear Mr. Medhurst so much." Many gave testimony to the blessings they had received from the preaching of the young student. This impressed Spurgeon to the point that he felt that he must continue in his desire to train young men for the ministry. Spurgeon, always aware of his own lack of formal theological education, spent many hours overcoming that handicap. He said:

> I had no college education. I do not say this by way of boasting, far from it, I would have learned more if I had had the opportunity, but, that not being the case, I made the very best of the opportunities I had. [27]

Thus, he wanted the best opportunity for others in their preparation for the Gospel ministry, and that meant the founding of a theological college.

Near the end of 1856, Medhurst preached at Kingston-on-Thames and settled into the pastorate of the Baptist church there. He continued his studies, however. Again, to show the magnanimous spirit of Spurgeon, the church at Kingston-on-Thames repaid Spurgeon the amount of money that he was regularly expending on the young student's tuition. But, at the end of a few months of this arrangement, Spurgeon gave the whole amount to Medhurst saying, "That is yours." Medhurst refused to accept the money, so Spurgeon took on a second student by the name of E. J. Silverton and began to train him.

On March 21, 1857, as these early educational ventures were maturing, Medhurst went to live with the Rev. George Rogers of Albany Road, Camberwell, a very effective Congregational minister. This brought Spurgeon's dream to a climax. He became convinced he must launch out and begin to train young pastors on a more formal and extensive basis. The concept of the Pastors' College came to fruition. Spurgeon asked the Rev. George Rogers to become the principal of what he would call the Pastors' College. Rogers accepted this position. Spurgeon said, "The work did not begin out of any scheme, it grew out of necessity." [28] Indicative of the breadth of Spurgeon (only in his early twenties himself) was his grasp of the importance of education for the ministry. He well understood that those who would faithfully preach the Word of God must be prepared to do so. Although Spurgeon received no formal theological education himself, it was often said of him, "He is not by any means the foe of learning." He studied long and hard. Moreover, his secular education was quite good for his day, even if he did not attend a theological college. Spurgeon would say to his students, "You are preparing for the ministry, but do not wait till you have entered it—you may never live to do that . . . secure your best diploma now. Begin with speed, with fire, with learning, and live to save men now". [29]

An interesting facet of Spurgeon's evangelical ecumenical spirit centers in the fact that he engaged a Congregationalist as the first principal of the College rather than a Baptist. Rogers was a thorough-going evangelical, although he and Spurgeon disagreed on the doctrine of baptism. Fullerton tells us, "Many a friendly triad those two have had on the subject of baptism." [30] One can well imagine. George Rogers would joke about it; he said he felt like a black sheep amongst a washed flock. But they stood in full agreement on the essentials of theological Calvinism. Actually, the crest chosen to be the college symbol was the hand grasping a cross with the motto, "et Teneo, et Teneor," best translated, "I hold and I am held." That was good Calvinism; Spurgeon and Rogers could shake hands on that.

Spurgeon started the Pastors' College on the foundational premise that God alone calls His servants to the Gospel ministry. They do not take it upon themselves; nor do others choose for them. They respond only because of the call of God. Moreover, Spurgeon did not accept the testimony of superficial, emotional individuals who came to him as proof positive that God had laid his hand upon them and called them to the ministry. He would only accept those who possessed a deep inward conviction that they were fit for the Lord's work and had been genuinely called, and absolutely must, therefore, preach the Gospel. Moreover, Spurgeon wanted students who had already preached some. Not only that, he required that all the students exhibit sincere piety. Spurgeon always said that piety had a priority over Greek or Latin. Further, Spurgeon made it clear that the college did not exist to make ministers, but to train them. Only God could make a minister, Spurgeon argued. That became the pervading philosophy of the entire enterprise. Students had to give good evidence that they had been called, were committed to be trained, were able to fulfill that calling, and had a genuine walk with Jesus Christ. Each student underwent careful scrutiny. Spurgeon personally wrote every prospective student seeking evidence that their calling emanated from a distinct call of the Holy Spirit. Nor did he hesitate to refuse admission when he felt it unwise. He once wrote to a student:

> I fear you are not likely to make a thoroughly efficient minister. . . . I could not have you become, as many are, a charge upon a people who have to put up with you. . . . I would not increase the army of the in-efficients. . . . I must decline your application. . . . I counsel you to go on as you are, and do all you can for our Lord. [31]

When students did give genuine evidence of a true call from God, and a willingness and adeptness to declare the Gospel, Spurgeon would allow no barrier to arise prohibiting their education. This meant that some would have to learn the very rudiments of English. On rare occasions, Spurgeon even admitted students who were illiterate. Others were often deficient in various areas of learning. So the College did its best to bring them up to at least a minimal standard in general education: English, mathematics, science, history, and allied fields were taught. Friends came to Spurgeon's aid in those early days and offered their assistance to the College. Their help proved invaluable.

In a lengthy passage, Spurgeon explained clearly his reasons for the founding of the institution. He said:

> We had before us but one object, and that was, the glory of God, by the preaching of the Gospel. To preach with acceptance, men, lacking in education, need to be instructed; and therefore our institution set itself further to instruct those whom God had evidently called to preach the Gospel, but who laboured under early disadvantages. We never dreamed of making men preachers, but we desired to help those whom God had already called to be such. Hence, we laid down, as a basis, the condition that a man must, during about two years, have been engaged in preaching, and must have had some seals to his ministry, before we could entertain his application. No matter how talented or promising he might appear to be, the College could not act upon mere hopes, but must have evident marks of a Divine call, so far as human judgment can discover them. This became a main point with us, for we wanted, not men whom our tutors could make into scholars, but men whom the Lord had ordained to be preachers.
>
> Firmly fixing this landmark, we proceeded to sweep away every hindrance to the admission of fit men. We determined never to refuse a man on account of absolute poverty, but rather to provide him with needful lodging, board, and raiment, that he might not be hindered on that account. We also placed the literary qualifications for admission so low that even brethren who could not read have been able to enter, and have been among the most useful of our students in after days. A man of real ability as a speaker, of deep piety, and

genuine faith, may be, by force of birth and circumstances, deprived of educational advantages, and yet, when helped a little, he may develop into a mighty worker for Christ; it would be a serious loss to the Church to deny such a man instruction because it was his misfortune to miss it in his youth. Our College began by inviting men of God to her bosom, whether they were poor and illiterate, or wealthy and educated. We sought for earnest preachers, not for readers of sermons, or makers of philosophical essays. 'Have you won souls for Jesus?' was and is our leading enquiry of all applicants. 'If so, come thou with us, and we will do thee good.' If the brother has any pecuniary means, we feel that he should bear his own charges, and many have done so; but if he cannot contribute a sixpence, he is equally welcome, and is received upon the same footing in all respects. If we can but find men who love Jesus, and love the people, and will seek to bring Jesus and the people together, the College will receive two hundred of such as readily as one, and trust in God for their food; but if men of learning and wealth should come, the College will not accept them unless they prove their calling by power to deliver the truth, and by the blessing of God upon their labours. Our men seek no Collegiate degrees, or classical honours,—though many of them could readily attain them, but to preach efficiently, to get at the heart of the masses, to evangelize the poor,—this is the College ambition, this and nothing else.

We endeavor to teach the Scriptures, but, as everybody else claims to do the same, and we wish to be known and read of all men, we say distinctly that the theology of the Pastors' College is Puritanic. We know nothing of the new ologies; we stand by the old ways. The improvements brought forth by what is called 'modern thought' we regard with suspicion, and believe them to be, at best, dilutions of the truth, and most of them old, rusted heresies, tinkered up again, and sent abroad with a new face put upon them, to repeat the mischief which they wrought in ages past. We are old-fashioned enough to prefer Manton to Maurice, Charnock to Robertson, and Owen to Voysey. Both our experience and our reading of the Scriptures confirm us in the belief of the unfashionable doctrines of grace; and among us, upon those grand fundamentals, there is no uncertain sound. Young minds are not to be cast into one rigid mould, neither can maturity of doctrine be expected of beginners in the ministry; but, as a rule, our men have not only gone out from us clear and sound in the faith, but with very few exceptions they have continued so.

No one, if they qualified spiritually, received a rejection letter. For example, the first black student from Africa was admitted in 1878. The question of women in the ordained ministry did not arise in Spurgeon's day. Presently, however, women are admitted to the College.

Before long, more than a dozen students had been enrolled. Six or seven had already accepted pastorates while they studied and were exercising an effective ministry. The classes were held at first in George Rogers' home in Camberwell. This arrangement continued until the Metropolitan Tabernacle was completed in 1861; then the students were given a classroom of their own in the basement of the new church building. During this period the Pastors' College began to take real shape.

In the earlier days, the students boarded out in the homes of people in twos or threes. This arrangement kept them from being cut off from the ordinary affairs of family life, as sometimes happened in other boarding colleges. This practice continued for some time.

The work prospered well. So successful was the growth of the College that at a church meeting in the Metropolitan Tabernacle, the following resolution was passed:

> That this church rejoices very greatly in the labours of our pastor in training young men for the ministry, and desires that a record of his successful and laborious efforts should be entered in our church-books. Hitherto, this good work has been rather a private service for the Lord than one in which the members have had a share, but the church hereby adopts it as part of its own system of Evangelical labours, promises its pecuniary aid, and its constant and earnest prayers. [32]

A weekly offering was taken for the support of the Pastors' College and generous gifts were often contributed privately. Further, Spurgeon gave untold thousands of pounds to "his first-born and best beloved."

The ministry of the Pastors' College did not end with those called to full-time pastoral ministry. Members of the Metropolitan Tabernacle, though they may have had no call or interest in entering the pastorate themselves, but still wanted to get a well-rounded education, attended classes that were held in the evening. Moreover, a weekly lecture to the students given by the pastor was open to the public.

As the number of students increased, it finally became obvious that a separate building for the College would be necessary. Thus, they built a large structure at the rear of the Tabernacle on freehold land purchased from the Ecclesiastical Commissioners of the Church of England. At one time, the land had been a rectory vegetable garden; Spurgeon facetiously declared that he intended to grow dissenters in it instead of cabbages. C. H. Spurgeon laid the foundation stone on October 14, 1873, and the new College building opened with a series of special meetings during September of the next year. The building and its furnishings cost something over £15,000. The new structure also served for part of the Sunday School work in the Tabernacle.

Spurgeon reflected his own approach to the ministry in that he always held that the ultimate object of the College and its activities should culminate in the conversion of people. His first student, Mr. Medhurst, once complained to the "Gov'nor," as all his students affectionately called him, that he had been preaching for three months without a single convert. "Why," said Spurgeon, "you don't expect conversions every time you open your mouth, do you?" "Of course not," Medhurst answered. "Then that is just the reason you haven't had them," Spurgeon replied. [33] However, on one occasion Spurgeon himself had to eat those words. He had preached in a large warehouse at Bedford. A tea followed the affair, and an old gentleman said to him, "There was one thing I did not like this afternoon. You prayed that the Lord might be pleased to bring, here and there, one or two men out of the throng. I could not pray that. I wanted all of them." "You are quite right, sir," replied Spurgeon. [34]

Spurgeon had a great way with the students. He got right down to their level and spiritual needs. Biographer Ray tells that one time "just before the students went away for their vacation, the president said, if he had been able to afford it, he would have given every man a present. 'To you,' he said to one, 'I would give a corkscrew, because although you have a good deal in you, you cannot get it out.' 'As to you, my brother,' turning to another student, 'I should give you a sausage stuffer, for you need to have something put into you.' A third student was to have a canister of gunpowder to be set alight exactly at the second head of his discourse to stir him up." [35]

As can well be imagined, the single most exciting event of each week in College was the Friday afternoon lecture given by the President, Charles Haddon Spurgeon. (Spurgeon took that honorary title.) In the early days, he would have the students in his home for the lectures. Later, as the student body grew, he lectured in the College hall. Those lectures produced the well-known book *Lectures to My Students*. It has been published repeatedly through the years. The lectures are virtually as valuable today as they were when they were first delivered. *The Lectures* center on the time-honored biblical truths that make for an effective ministry. Spurgeon, however, did not always give formal theological lectures on Friday afternoons. At times he would give readings from the poets. Spurgeon was especially fond of Milton, Cowper, Wordsworth, Coleridge, and Dr. Hamilton's *Christian Classics*. Often he would read from the great Puritan works. But, whatever Spurgeon would present in his lectures, it always proved to be a lesson in elocution. Because of Spurgeon's involvement with his own students, he also produced the volume, *The Art of Illustration*. His famous book *Commenting and Commentaries* also emerged in that context. At times, the Friday afternoon hour would be given to purely extemporaneous unprepared preaching, not by Spurgeon but by the students. On one such occasion a student was given the word "Zaccheus" and he was to stand up and preach upon it. He rose immediately and said, "Mr. President and brethren, my subject is Zaccheus, and it is therefore most appropriate to me; for first, Zaccheus was of little stature, as I am; secondly, Zaccheus was up a tree; so am I; thirdly, Zaccheus made haste to come down; and so will I," and immediately he resumed his seat. All the students wanted him to go on, but Spurgeon said, "No, he could not add anything to a perfect little speech without spoiling it." [36]

Spurgeon, as always, took the practical, workable approach in ministerial training. Someone said critically that he had set up a "clerical factory." No, said Charles, he had instituted a "parson killer." He intended to kill the old "parson" image and manner of ministry in his students. Some wit called the institution "The Royal College of Spurgeon's" (not Spurgeons). But the College did turn out good practitioners who could prescribe the remedy for many an ill.

As can be imagined, many cranks applied for admission to the Pastors' College. But Spurgeon always dealt with them very abruptly:

> I have more than once felt myself in the position of the Delphic oracle, not wishing to give wrong advice, and therefore not able to give any. I had an inquiry from a brother whose minister told him he ought not to preach, and yet he felt that he must do so. I thought I would be safe in the reply I gave him, so I simply said, 'My brother, if God has opened your mouth, the devil cannot shut it; but if the devil has opened your mouth, I pray the Lord to shut it directly.' Some time afterwards, I was preaching in the country, and after the sermon a young man came up to me and thanked me for encouraging him in preaching. For the moment I did not recall the circumstances, so he reminded me of the first part of my reply to his inquiry. 'But,' I said, 'I also told you that if the devil had opened your mouth I prayed the Lord to shut it.' 'Ah,' he exclaimed, 'but that part of the message did not apply to me.' [37]

Spurgeon's great sense of humor constantly bubbled forth in the context of the College. He really felt in his element with the students. On one occasion, the deacons of a certain church asked the President if he would send a student who could "fill the chapel." Spurgeon replied that he did not have one big enough for that, but he thought he could send a student who might fill the pulpit. On the more serious side, however, Spurgeon was responsible for sending men to Australia, New Zealand, Canada, Haiti, the Falkland Islands, North and South America, South Africa, Amsterdam; the ministry of the Pastors' College began to extend itself worldwide. A certain Brother Patrick became the first man to go to the foreign field—to Africa. Spurgeon wrote him:

> I am sure from your personal character and from your course in College that I may place unlimited confidence in you, and far more is my confidence in the Lord whom you and I unitedly serve with our whole hearts, He will help you play the man. . . . You believe that the gospel will meet the need of any creature in the form of man. . . . You will keep wholly and only to the cross. There hangs our hope as well as the hope of these to whom we go. Hammer away with the old gospel. . . . Take special care to be much with HIM. . . . Carry your daily worries to your Master and they will not be worries. . . . On your head may the Holy Spirit pour out the anointing oil. [38]

The great Metropolitan Tabernacle people prided themselves in their support of the College. On one occasion, the College had a need. Someone suggested to Spurgeon that they pray. Charles replied, "Yes, we will pray, but first we will take up an offering." He had a very practical spirituality. It became an honor to contribute as many pounds as possible to the work.

The Tabernacle folk always entertained the men who met each year for the College Conference. One member, Mr. T. R. Phillips, always gave an annual sumptuous dinner for the Pastors' College during the Conference at his estate, Quarry Farm in Surrey county. These conferences were normally conducted the week before the Baptist Union met in the spring. All the former students would gather for fellowship, preaching, lectures, and re-membering old times. The College Conference program began in 1865 and has continued up to the present moment. By the 1870s, the attendance had grown into the 800s. As again can be imagined, the President's address, which Spurgeon gave 27 years in succession, always proved to be the high-light of the Conference. The last address Spurgeon gave in this setting he entitled, "The Greatest Fight in the World." Passmore published it, and it had a tremendous circulation. One man sent a copy to every minister and clergyman in Great Britain. It was also translated into several other languag-es. It stands as a classic to this day.

In the early years, the College founded "The Pastors' College Society of Evangelists." Two outstanding students, who became great evangelists, were W. Y. Fullerton, Spurgeon's biographer from Ireland and a young man by the name of Smith. Spurgeon teamed them up, and in their evangelistic work they saw many come to Christ. The Society greatly furthered evange-listic work in England. Especially significant, as mentioned before, was the work of planting new churches. The first church the students instituted was East Hill Chapel in Wandsworth. Also, "The Pastors' College Missionary Association," was raised to help support missionaries in North Africa, France, and South America. Reaching the people for Christ worldwide always stood at the heart and core of the Pastors' College.

As the College continued to grow in numbers, so did the needs. But God wonderfully provided the necessary funds. The method of fund raising was basically a resort to prayer, and the funds never failed to come in. Spurgeon greatly admired George Müller of Bristol in his orphanage work. The story of Müller's ministry of faith is well known. Spurgeon felt the same chal-lenge of faith as did Müller. Spurgeon reasoned, if Müller can sustain an orphanage of 1,000 children by faith, God can surely care for a college of those He has called to preach.

It is true, Spurgeon's faith often went through severe trials. But the trials always brought blessings. As a case in point, the sales of Spurgeon's ser-mons in America brought in 600 to £800 a month. All of it went to the Pastors' College. When the sermon sales in America dramatically decreased because of his stand on slavery, Spurgeon's faith got a real test, but he prevailed. From his own income he devoted every penny he could, he then saw God supply the need in marvelous ways. On another occasion, needs at the College arose to the point that he decided to sell his horse and carriage to raise funds. But Rogers pointed out that such an action would, in the long term, not be wise as the carriage was absolutely necessary for Spurgeon to get about. Then unexpectedly, reduced to his last sovereign, Spurgeon received a letter from a banker stating that a lady had just deposited £200 to be used for the education of young men for the ministry. Not many weeks later, another unknown friend deposited £100 in the same bank. Right then, at a dinner given by Passmore and Alabaster to celebrate the publication of Spurgeon's 500th sermon, the attenders raised the sum of £500 for the College. One day a full £1,000 was received from an unknown donor for the College. Other large sums regularly came in; God honored the commitment of faith and supplied every need.

As the Pastors' College developed in students and curriculum, so did the faculty. David Gracey, a gifted scholar, received his education at Glasgow University. He left the Presbyterian Church to become a Baptist and entered the Pastors' College as a student. He shortly became the first tutor in classics. After the death of George Rogers, he became principal. W. R. Salway became a science lecturer and Professor A. Ferguson English became a tutor in elocution. Also, the President's brother, James Archer Spurgeon, rendered great help to the College.

Spurgeon would regularly have the students at his home for a field day. One can imagine the good times such gatherings afforded. It became a much anticipated event for all the young ministers.

As implied earlier, Spurgeon was exceedingly selective in whom he admitted to the College. The story is told of a young man who applied that had a strange twitch of his jaw. His pastor highly commended him, but Spurgeon refused his admittance. The "Gov'nor" said, "I could not have looked at him while he was preaching without laughter, if all the gold of Tarsus had been my reward, and in all probability nine out of ten of his hearers would have been more sensitive than myself."[39] At times there would be those who would come to him who had failed in other callings. They almost invariably testified that they had turned to the ministry because they regarded their lack of success in other areas as "the Lord shutting up all other doors." Spurgeon had no sympathy. He would always say, "The ministry needs the very best men, not those who cannot do anything else. A man who will succeed as a preacher would probably do right well either as a grocer or a lawyer or anything else."[40] Biographer Ray tells the following story about a student applying to the Pastors' College:

> Perhaps the most remarkable young man who ever sought admission to the College was one who sent word into the vestry one Sunday morning that he must see the distinguished preacher at once. 'His audacity admitted him,' says C. H. Spurgeon, 'and when he was before me, he said, "Sir I want to enter your College, and should like to enter it at once." 'Well, sir,' I said, 'I fear we

shall have no room for you at present but your case shall be considered.' 'But mine is a very remarkable case, sir; you have probably never received such an application as mine before.' 'Very good, we'll see about it; the secretary will give you one of the application papers, and you can see me on Monday,' He came on the Monday, bringing with him the questions, answered in a most extraordinary manner. As to books, he claimed to have read all ancient and modern literature, and after giving an immense list, he added, 'This is merely a selection; I have read most extensively in all departments.' As to his preaching, he could produce the highest testimonials, but hardly thought they would be needed, as a personal interview would convince me of his ability at once. His surprise was great when I said, 'Sir, I am obliged to tell you that I cannot receive you.' 'Why not, sir?' 'I will tell you plainly. You are so dreadfully clever that I could not insult you by receiving you into our College, where we have none but rather ordinary men; the President, tutors, and students, are all men of moderate attainments, and you would have to condescend too much in coming among us.' He looked at me very severely, and said with dignity. 'Do you mean to say that, because I have an unusual genius, and have produced in myself a gigantic mind such as is rarely seen, I am refused admittance into your College?' 'Yes,' I replied, as calmly as I could, considering the overpowering awe which his genius inspired, 'for that very reason,' 'Then, sir, you ought to allow me a trial of my preaching abilities; select me any text you like, or suggest any subject you please, and here, in this very room, I will speak upon it, or preach upon it without deliberation, and you will be surprised.' 'No, thank you, I would rather not have the trouble of listening to you.' 'Trouble, sir! I assure you it would be the greatest possible pleasure you could have.' I said it might be, but I felt myself unworthy of the privilege, and so bade him a long farewell. The gentleman was unknown to me at the time, but he has since figured in the police court as too clever by half. [41]

Moreover, Spurgeon had a very practical approach to the ministry of his students. When churches would ask for recommendations, he would get right down to the heart of the matter. For example, a small country church once applied to him for a pastor, but offered a salary ridiculously small. Spurgeon wrote, "The only individual I know, who could exist on such a stipend, is the angel Gabriel. He would need neither cash nor clothes. He could come down from heaven every Sunday morning and go back at night, so I advise you to invite him." [42]

Charles showed the same pragmatic approach with his students. He once said to a student who was about to leave for his first pastorate:

I want you to go under an operation before you leave. I am going to put out one of your eyes, to stop up one of your ears, and to put a muzzle on your mouth. Then you had better have a new suit of clothes before you go, and you must tell the tailor to make in the coat a pocket without a bottom. You understand my parable? 'I think so, sir,' replied the student, 'but should like your interpretation.' Well, there will be many things in your people that you must look at with the blind eye, and you must listen to much with the deaf ear, while you will often be tempted to say things which had better be left unsaid, then, remember the muzzle. Then all the gossip you may hear, when doing pastoral work, must be put into the bottomless pocket.[43]

In Spurgeon's own words he well summarized the entire enterprise:

The College was the first important institution commenced by the pastor, and it remains his first born and best beloved. To train ministers of the Gospel is the most excellent work, and when the Holy Spirit blesses the effort, the result is of utmost importance both to the Church and to the world.[44]

In 1881, Spurgeon gave an encouraging resumé of the work. He said, "The Pastors' College as of late maintained the even tenor of its way, knowing little of external attack and nothing of internal strife. Regular in its work and fixed in its purpose, its movement has been calm and strong. 'Bless the Lord, Oh my soul!' is my one song, and I feel as if I could repeat it a thousand times."[45]

As can be well understood, the College took a definite stand on the basics of Christian theology. Spurgeon declared very forthrightly:

The College started with a definite doctrinal basis. I never affected to leave great questions as moot points to be discussed in the hall, and believed or not believed, as might be the fashion of the hour. The creed to the College is well known, and we invite none to enter who do not accept it. The doctrines of grace, coupled with the firm belief in human responsibility, are held with intense convictions, and those who do not receive them would not find themselves at home within our walls. The Lord has sent us tutors who are lovers of sound doctrine and zealous for the truth. No uncertain sound has been given forth at any time and we would sooner lose the house than have it sold.

Heresy in colleges means false doctrine throughout the churches; to defile the fountain is to pollute the streams. Hesitancy which might be tolerated in an ordinary minister would utterly disqualify a teacher of teachers. The experiment of Doddridge ought to satisfy all godly men that colleges without dogmatic evangelical teaching are more likely to be seminaries of Socinianism than schools of the prophets. Old Puritanic theology has been . . . received by those in our college, and on leaving it they have almost with one consent remained faithful to that which they have received. The men are before the public in every part of the country and their testimony is well known.

Moreover, Spurgeon's practicality reflected his philosophy of theological education. He said:

Scholarship for its own sake was never sought and never will be within the Pastors' College; but to help men to become efficient preachers has been and ever will be the sole aim of all those concerned in its management. I shall not, in order to increase our prestige, refuse poor men or zealous young Christians whose early education has been neglected. Pride would suggest that we take 'a better class of men;' but experience shows that they are not better, that imminently useful men spring from all ranks, that diamonds may be found in the rough, and that some who need most pains in their polishing, reward our labor a thousand fold. [46]

When Spurgeon was ill and could not carry on the work, it particularly grieved him. His brother James came to his aid during those periods. Spurgeon stated on one occasion:

> I have been very ill through the greater part of the past year and have therefore been unable to give much personal service to the college as I usually have done.
>
> This has been a sore trial for me, but it has been much alleviated by my beloved brother J. A. Spurgeon, the Vice-President, who has looked after everything with great care; and I have also been greatly comforted by the knowledge that the tutors are as deeply concerned about the holy service as ever I can be.

The College, as surmised, became a significant source of evangelism and missionary work. The purpose of the mission work through the Missionary Association of the College centered on placing men and women where no Gospel witness had entered. Not only that, the College had a "temperance society." Spurgeon said that this good work "tends to keep alive among the men a burning hatred of England's direst curse." [47] At this time Spurgeon had become a teetotaler. As is common knowledge, this was not true in his earlier days. That interesting pilgrimage shall be discussed later. The College also had a Home and Foreign Bible Society.

Spurgeon developed a very important subsidiary to the College. In 1862 he founded the Evening School, briefly mentioned earlier. This venture provided adult education for those who were either illiterate or lacking in some particular aspect of their basic education. Designed to reach those who could neither afford the time nor the money to attend a regular day school, it became something of a forerunner for such work. Spurgeon became the prime innovator in this area and developed the model that the British government took up many years later. In this respect, Spurgeon was nearly fifty years ahead of his time. Not until the earlier part of the twentieth century did the government begin to organize evening schools for working classes. It gleaned from the experience of Spurgeon, along with several others, who also saw the need to provide a basic education for those who had the motivation to avail themselves of it.

The Evening School curriculum included a Bible class, advanced English, elementary and advanced Greek and Latin, French, and lectures on science, as well as the traditional disciplines. The response of many south

Londoners truly encouraged Spurgeon. Classes ran from 150 to 200 in attendance, and required using the basement of the Metropolitan Tabernacle as well as the buildings of the Pastors' College. A close connection existed between the Pastors' College and the Evening School. Many of those who graduated from the Evening School went on to enroll in the College to study for the ministry. It became something of a "feeder school." Consistent with the principle of the Pastors' College, no fees were charged lest some laborer trying to get an education while supporting his family would be eliminated. Consequently, hundreds advanced from the ranks of illiterate unskilled laborers to a higher level—not only in education but in employment as well. And many entered the ministry. This became one of Spurgeon's most significant and helpful works.

Perhaps the most significant auxiliary work of the Pastors' College, and that which made the greatest long lasting contribution, was the work done in church planting. Scores of churches were planted in London and throughout the country because of the College students' efforts. Obviously, the College involved itself in many practical ministries. And so the work went on.

Spurgeon himself served as President of the College until his death in 1892. Then James A. Spurgeon became President until 1896 when Charles' son Thomas held the post. He continued in that role until 1907 when the office of President was eliminated. George Rogers continued as Principal until 1881. Rogers became affectionately known as "Father Rogers." After retiring in 1881, he lived in South Norwood. He died at the age of 91, just four months before Spurgeon's death. David Gracey took over as principal. He continued until 1893, one year after Spurgeon's death, and was succeeded by Percy Evans, who served until 1925. Since then, there have been several principals and many tutors. The term "tutor," designated the teaching faculty, and is still used today. "Professor" is a title never used at the College.

Something of the same spirit, ethos, and methodology that surrounded the work of the College in the days of Spurgeon continues to the present moment. Anyone called of God to the Gospel ministry is still admitted, regardless of their ability to pay. The Pastors' College is now known as Spurgeon's College; its name was changed in the 1950s. The College moved from the confines of the Metropolitan Tabernacle in 1923 and acquired a large estate in South Norwood, called Falkland Park, where it is now housed. It continues to teach many young people and prepare them for the Christian ministry. One of the largest pastor training colleges in Britain, and by far the largest in the Baptist denomination, it stands as a continuing monument to Spurgeon's insight in grasping the importance of ministerial training. Through the many years of its existence, thousands have gone out to serve Christ all over the world. Charles, along with Bunyan's character, can truly be called "Help."

Spurgeon not only concerned himself about ministerial training, he had a great heart for the plight of orphans. That concern also forms a fascinating story.

THE STOCKWELL ORPHANAGE

If the Pastors' College was Spurgeon's "first born and most beloved," the Stockwell Orphanage came a very close second in the devotion of the London pastor. The story of its birth, growth and ministry bears a striking resemblance to the history of the Müller Orphanage in Bristol. Much like Müller's work, Spurgeon's orphanage work became a romance of faith.

Spurgeon had a great love for children, and they for him. Children idolized him. Spurgeon's own childlike simplicity, a prominent feature throughout the entirety of his life, gave him an air of positive sincerity that stirred deep admiration in children, and in older folk, too, for that matter. He is "innocent as a child," said Prime Minister Gladstone. Evil thoughts found little or no place in his disposition and deceit formed no part of his Christian character. His näivité in relationship to others at times proved a detriment; he took people at face value and they could very easily deceive him. Yet, when it came to spiritual realities, Spurgeon had great discernment. He could easily detect a false, superficial piety; and when people had a genuine relationship with Jesus Christ and were Spirit-filled believers, he immediately could detect the depth of their spirituality.

Like George Müller, C. H. Spurgeon had for some time entertained the dream of an institution to provide for orphan children and for those whose parents were unable or unwilling to provide for them. The first time Spurgeon met Müller in November, 1854, he was so awed, he said, "I could not speak a word for the life of me."[48] He spoke of him as "that heavenly man." Charles once visited Müller's Orphanage and said, "I never *heard* such a sermon in my life as I *saw* there." Charles went on to say, "I think sometimes, that I would not mind changing places with George Müller for Time and Eternity, but I do not know anybody else of whom I would say so much."[49] Müller received his inspiration from the German pietist Herman Franke. Yet, Charles never seemed to find the way in which to launch an undertaking like Müller's until something unexpectedly happened.

In August, 1866, while writing an article for *The Sword and the Trowel*, he incidentally mentioned the need for some institution to care for neglected orphans. As seen earlier, London's streets were filled with them. The result of that simple mention of need, almost an off-handed remark, God greatly used. Mrs. Hillyard, the widow of a wealthy clergyman of the Church of England, read the article. She recently had been received into the membership of the Metropolitan Tabernacle, having left the Established Church. Spurgeon's reference to the needs of the orphans touched her deeply. She felt impressed to be of some use in this needy work. She prayed over the matter, and the Holy Spirit deepened her conviction. She wrote Spurgeon and offered him a sum of money for an orphanage if he would establish and superintend it himself. Spurgeon could hardly believe what he read. The widow pledged the unbelievable sum of £20,000. At the same time Spurgeon had written his small article in *The Sword and the Trowel*, at the Monday evening prayer meeting, he said, "We are a large church, and should be doing more for the Lord in this great city. I want us to ask Him to send us some new work; and if we need money to carry it on, let us pray that the means may be sent." They prayed and it all came together when Mrs. Hillyard came forward with her sizable pledge of money.

When Spurgeon received the promise of such a sum, he took it as a direct answer to prayer, thus the will of God. So he and William Higgs made an appointment and called upon Mrs. Hillyard at her modest home. They honestly feared there had been some mistake. They began the interview by saying they had called about the £200 she had mentioned in a letter. "Did I write £200?" exclaimed the lady, "I meant 20,000." "Oh yes," said Mr. Spurgeon, "You did put down 20,000, but I thought that perhaps there was a naught or two too many."[50] No, she meant 20,000, not 200. Spurgeon, always a man of integrity, asked first whether some relative should receive the money. Mrs. Hillyard settled that point; no relative stood in line for the legacy. Spurgeon suggested that perhaps the money should be sent to George Müller at Bristol. Nothing would satisfy her but that Mr. Spurgeon should inaugurate the work. Of course, this found a ready reception in his own heart and that settled the matter then and there. In a few days, Spurgeon received the money by mail and the Stockwell Orphanage, as it became known, had its birth. In the board room of the orphanage, they placed a stained glass window, depicting the interview. The first building to be constructed was called "The Silver Wedding House." The money she gave for the new orphanage had been a gift to her from her husband on their silver wedding anniversary. Mrs. Hillyard lived for some years to revel in what she had initiated. Her last words as she died on January 13, 1880 were, "My boys! My boys!"

Throughout the years, Spurgeon took the same approach to the orphanage work as he did to the Tabernacle. He would not build a building unless all the funds had already been provided. He said:

> Mark you, it will be so in the erection of this orphan's home. We shall see greater things than these if only our faith will precede our sight. But if we go upon the old custom of our general societies, and look first out for regular income, and get our subscribers and send round our collectors and pay our percentages—that is, do not trust God but trust our subscribers—if we go by that rule we shall see very little, and have no room for believing. But if we shall just trust God and believe that he never did leave a work that he put upon us, and never sets us to do a thing without meaning to help us with it, we shall soon see that the God of Israel still lives and that his arm is not short.[51]

Not only in the building of the buildings, but even in the daily maintenance of the work, there was to be no reliance on mere lists of pledges, not even on "regular" contributors. Charles felt such methods were not only unreliable but did not honor the principle of faith. This work was to be a work of pure faith. And God met Spurgeon's needs in a marvelous way. Spurgeon himself set the example; when funds ran short, he became the first to give everything he could spare. He challenged his trustees to do the same.

Not only in the initial stages of the founding of the Stockwell Orphanage, but through the years examples and illustrations abound on how God met Spurgeon's faith by providential provision. Once, while dining with some friends in London, the subject of the Orphanage and some necessary new construction being undertaken came up in the conversation. Charles mentioned that he did not have the money in hand for all their needs, and in a day or two the building contractors would require payment. However, he quickly declared his confidence that God would provide. Just as the meal ended, a servant entered with a telegram. Spurgeon eagerly tore it open and found that an unknown donor had just handed in £1,000 for the Orphanage. Again, at another time when the funds were completely exhausted, the concerned leaders of the work met for prayer. They earnestly poured out their hearts that God would send the needed help. Gifts began to pour in that very day. Sums amounting to nearly £400 were received. Spurgeon gathered the kind of people around him who could pray and claim God's promises, and hence, the results followed.

Mrs. Hillyard's first large donation, of course, is what started the entire project. She had been earlier advised by a friend, a Congregational minister of Brixton, to give her legacy to Spurgeon. Mrs. Hillyard had expressed the desire to do something significant for the Lord, thus the Congregational pastor suggested that no one could guide and direct her in this better than Spurgeon. Almost at that very moment, a copy of *The Sword and the Trowel*, with Spurgeon's article on an orphanage, came into her hands. So the Lord brought the two circumstances together and the orphanage was launched. In a second letter to Spurgeon she wrote, "That which the Lord had laid upon my heart at present is the great need there is of an orphan house . . . especially one conducted upon simple Gospel principles."[52] The dedication of this lovely Christian woman and her devotion to God radiates through lives of thousands of orphans as a beautiful lasting token of God's grace.

The early conversations between Spurgeon and Mrs. Hillyard had taken place in August and September, 1866. After the initial matter was settled, Spurgeon immediately wrote a preliminary notice in *The Sword and the Trowel* outlining the plan. In January of the following year a good plot of land was found and purchased. Spurgeon wanted a site in easy reach of the Tabernacle. They fortunately were able to acquire a site of two and one-half acres just off the well traveled Clapham Road. Negotiations for the property almost broke down, however, when the owner, sensing the search committee's eagerness to establish an orphanage on that particular site, tried to raise the price scandalously high. The committee was inclined to seek another site. But Spurgeon went himself to see the owner. He pointed out the unsuitability of the property for any other purpose and even finally threatened the owner with a fine of £1,000 because of his obstinacy. Upon this stern word from the pastor, the original terms were confirmed.

Spurgeon appointed a group of trustees to administer the entire work, and a Festival of Praise was held on the grounds on September 9. Spurgeon had planned for the first building to be commenced at once, but a panic in the financial market depressed the securities of Mrs. Hillyard's gift. Thus, it seemed wise to wait for a season. This setback, in the providence of God, proved in the end to be a blessing in disguise. The Stockwell Orphanage retained considerably more endowment than probably would have been the case if the money for the construction had been spent immediately. Not only that, when Spurgeon announced the project, it excited the imagination of many and funds began to come in from various sources.

Before the actual construction began, Spurgeon hit upon a very innovative scheme in the structure of the Orphanage. He had determined that the children should not be massed together in large rooms like the old workhouses. He said he wanted to "form the orphans into large families instead of massing them together in the workhouse system."[53] So he organized the orphans into smaller single family groups with a "house mother" over each unit. Sensitive to the fact that institutional life could be very impersonal, he wanted the children to grow up in these smaller family units, although it would be more expensive. He said:

> Children need something more than a roof and four walls to shelter them; they want a home where the virtues of a Christian character shall be fostered and developed. To ignore social instincts in filial reverence by massing hundreds of children together in one huge building is to incur a grave responsibility, if not to provoke a failure, fought with most lamentable consequences. On the other hand, when an institution is adapted as far as possible to compensate the loss of parental influence and control, one essential element of success is secured.[54]

Thus, each "home," although large, nevertheless became something of a self-contained "family" with a Christian "mother" at its head. The meals, however, were always taken in a common hall for the sake of convenience and economy. Moreover, family prayers were conducted each morning before the duties of the day began. Spurgeon designed the entire orphanage buildings to effect an atmosphere like a family home. This approach, in many senses inaugurated by Spurgeon, has become the accepted structure for orphan work today.

By August, 1867, Spurgeon had in hand a large sum toward the erection of the orphans' buildings. Mr. George Moore of Bow Churchyard had become a large donor. A Mrs. Tyson left in her will £25,000. Gifts continually came in to meet the many needs. The following March, the same anonymous contributor who had sent Spurgeon the encouraging telegram during the dinner engagement, as described earlier, wrote a letter to Charles in which he said:

> I have this day dropped into your letter box an envelope containing two bank notes (£2,000), one which is for the college and the remaining £1,000 to help complete the orphanage. The latter led me to contribute to the former, I am a stranger to you, but not to your sermons. [55]

Spurgeon took the letter as a gentle rebuke of the Holy Spirit. He had feared that the Orphanage might cut into the College needs. In reality, the antithesis occurred; the College had substantially benefited by the Orphanage.

In June, 1868, the Baptist churches of Great Britain presented £1,200 as a testimonial to Spurgeon for the erection of two houses at the Stockwell Orphanage. These were called the "Testimonial Houses." A "Sunday School House" was given by the Tabernacle Sunday School and the ministers trained in the Pastors' College donated a "Student's House." The "Merchant's House" came as a gift of a business man. The "Workman's House" was built through the combined gift of the contractors and the laborers who worked on the buildings. All these small houses cared for the family units that comprised the Orphanage. All the buildings had been completed by the end of 1869. God had met Spurgeon's faith.

Spurgeon did not wait until the completion of the buildings to seek out the needy children of London. In July, 1867 he engaged a lady to receive the first four orphans into her own home until the first buildings could be completed. Again Mrs. Hillyard stepped in and sold a silver plate to pay the cost of the maintenance for the boys.

Concern arose about who would lead the newly constituted Stockwell Orphanage. A very able man had presented himself and was elected to the post. However, at the last minute he declined to fulfill the engagement. Right then, the Rev. Vernon J. Charlesworth called on Spurgeon. He impressed Spurgeon and Charles asked him if he would become the headmaster. He had been assistant pastor to Newman Hall at the Surrey Chapel and had proved himself a tremendously able man. He agreed to take the post and was duly installed. His influence on the boys at the orphanage became beneficial for the lads throughout their lives. He guided the orphanage until his death in 1914. Never was there a man more suited for his task than Charlesworth. His love for the children affected their lives tremendously. Spurgeon constantly expressed his satisfaction with Charlesworth's services, and through the years, their relationship remained most cordial. They supplemented each other in the work of the Orphanage beautifully.

Once Spurgeon addressed the trustees of the Orphanage. He said that he wished to call their attention to the fact that the headmaster, Vernon Charlesworth, had introduced a child into the institution without the permission of the managers. He furthermore added that this was not the first time such a thing had happened. The trustees, somewhat disturbed, proposed that Mr. Charlesworth should be called in and asked for an explanation. That would not be necessary, Charles laughingly said. The recent addition happened to be a new son born into his own family. After Charlesworth's death, Spurgeon's son Thomas became director. Upon Thomas' resignation, his brother Charles, Jr. took up the work as President-Director.

Spurgeon had often been asked why he did not start an orphanage for girls, as there were just as many poor girls without homes as there were boys. It was not until 1879 that he saw his way clear to establish such a work. The needs of little orphan girls touched Spurgeon's heart so he again took the leap of faith. In 1879 the board of managers negotiated to build and fund a girl's wing to the Stockwell institution. Mrs. Hillyard, again the first to contribute, gave £50. Spurgeon gave the next fifty. Once more, God's provision proved ample and funds came in. When the girl's wing of the Orphanage was opened, Mrs. Spurgeon wrote a lovely note on June 22, 1880. It reads:

> The 'Girls' Orphanage' has been inaugurated amidst great rejoicing, the Lord inclining His people's hearts to give liberally to the work, so that its 'stones were laid in fair colors' of faith and hope, and my beloved sees this new 'labor of love' abundantly prospering in his hands. Blessed be the Lord who thus giveth to His servant the 'desire of his heart,' fulfilling 'all his petition.' The people gathered round with glad hearts and beaming faces, and many a prayer ascended from loving lips that the dear children, who should be housed, and taught, and cared for in the new homes, might all grow up there in the fear and love of God, and be a blessing in their day and generation.
>
> The band of thirty little girls marching along in front of the boys ('place aux dames!') attracted much attention, and touched all hearts; some of them are such wee mites, and they look very pretty and tender, when compared with the hosts of sturdy boys, who come tramping by in such overwhelming numbers that one wonders if there be any end to them! Few can look unmoved on such masses of orphan children; for in spite of their merry faces, their bright ways, and their happy laughter, the painful fact will force itself upon the mind of the observer that every one of these little ones is taken from a desolate home, where the saddest of all earth's bereavements has been suffered; for the children are 'fatherless,' and the wife is a 'widow.' There was 'April weather' on many a face to-day; I saw the tears stealing down cheeks on which approving smiles were struggling for the mastery; but the sunshine gained the victory, and the pitying drops were quickly wiped away, for the happy condition and appearance of the children led all to forget the sorrow which brought them there, in intense thankfulness for their present joy and future prospects.
>
> If ever the strange title of 'Godfather' were permissible, I think it would be in the case of Mr. Spurgeon toward his boys and girls at Stockwell; for God has made him, as it were, in His stead, a 'father of the fatherless, and a judge

of the widow!' The Lord bless him on his birthday, and on every other day, and give him many more years in which to be a blessing to the Church, the College, the Orphanage, and the world!

This presents an insight into the spirit of the Spurgeon family and the orphans.

Soon the Stockwell Orphanage completed the entire pre-planned quadrangle. With an infirmary, gymnasium, and dining hall, it stood as a monument not only to Christian love and philanthropy, but above all to faith.

Throughout the many years at the Orphanage—it still thrives today in a new location—the principle of faith always prevailed. In December, 1873, Spurgeon wrote:

> To our surprise the report of the secretary was 'All bills paid but only £3 in hand.' Prayer went to work at once and results followed. Will the reader, however, picture himself with more than two hundred and twenty boys to feed and only £3 in hand. He may say, 'The Lord will provide,' but he would feel the force of this if he were in our straits.

But God did provide and the needs were continually met, often right at the last moment. God remained faithful.

Spurgeon himself would visit the Orphanage regularly. He served as the president and the children always received his visits with uproarious joy. In *The Daily Telegraph*, May 6, 1880, the reporter wrote:

> As to the happiness of the orphans, there is no doubt about it. When Mr. Spurgeon opened the door there was a shout of delight at the appearance of their friend. It was like a welcome to an old school fellow, and was repeated in every house we entered. Not the kind of cheer that requires a lead, but one that sprang up on the instant when it was known that Mr. Spurgeon was at the orphanage.

There was no distinctive dress for either the girls or boys. They dressed like other young people. Spurgeon did not want the children to look like recipients of charity by wearing uniforms. They could express their own individuality. He wrote:

> Orphanhood is a child's misfortune, and he should not be treated as though it were his fault. In a garb with a symbol of dependence it is difficult, if not impossible, for an orphan to preserve a feeling of self respect; and we wish the older institutions were free to break through the traditions which have so little to be said in their favor.[56]

Concerning the education of the children, they received what would be known in the nineteenth century as a good English education. This would fit them for commercial positions. Many came to occupy places of trust and importance in the larger business world of Britain. The government inspectors did a very thorough investigation of the institution in 1837 and described it in their report as "an admirable institution; good in design, and, if possible better at execution." Dr. Henry Gervis, of St. Thomas Hospital also wrote, "I cannot speak too highly of all the arrangement and of the admirable manner in which the institution is conducted." The Orphanage committee, numbering fourteen, admitted boys ages six to ten and girls ages seven to ten. The entire London community regarded Spurgeon's Stockwell Orphanage as admirable in every sense of the word. Dr. Barnardo, who instituted an excellent orphanage work, spoke at the Metropolitan Tabernacle giving his warm approval of Spurgeon's work. Barnardo and Spurgeon became friends and regularly corresponded.

Above all, Spurgeon decided that the Stockwell Orphanage should be a Christian institution, not sectarian, but thoroughly Christian. Over every bed there hung a Bible text and a motto for each individual child. Charlesworth was a Congregational minister; the orphanage never became a strictly Baptist institution, although Baptist principles guided the work. The Orphanage opened its doors to all denominations. The children of Anglican parents numbered more than any other denomination, even more than Baptists. In the last report on the work that Spurgeon gave during his lifetime (1891), the statistics concerning the religious background of the children read as follows:

Church of England	609
Baptists	415
Congregational	168
Wesleyan	143
Presbyterian	28
Brethren	12
Roman Catholic	3
Moravian	2
Bible Christian	3
Society of Friends	2
Salvation Army	1
Not Specified	200

Moreover, the children came from all parts of the United Kingdom. But, as could be expected, the larger portion hailed from the greater London area.

The spiritual life of the children had top priority in the entire program of the institution. On Sunday morning the children attended the Metropolitan Tabernacle and neighboring chapels. On Sunday afternoon, under the direction of Mr. W. J. Evans, a superintendent in the Orphanage for over thirty years, a band of Sunday School teachers came in from the local churches to teach the children. Every Wednesday a week night service was held. Many, if not all, of the children came to faith in Christ. Several entered the ministry. The first orphanage lad to go to the foreign mission field was John

Ingles Mayard. As a little boy he entered Stockwell in 1869. He went to the Congo at the age of 25. Tragically he died a few weeks after his arrival in Africa. His last words were, "As He will; all is well."

Spurgeon exhibited a very personal interest in the children, often on a one-to-one basis. John B. Gough tells a touching tale in that regard:

> Mr. Spurgeon invited Mr. Gough to go with him to the infirmary. 'We have a boy,' said he, 'very ill with consumption; he cannot live, and I wish to see him, for he would be disappointed if he knew I had been here and not seen him.'
>
> They went into the cool and sweet chamber, and there lay the boy. He was very much excited when he saw Mr. Spurgeon. The great preacher sat by his side. Holding the boy's hand in his, he said, 'Well, my dear, you have some precious promises in sight all around the room. Now, dear, you are going to die, and you are very tired lying here, and soon you will be free from all pain, and you will rest. Nurse, did he rest last night?'
>
> 'He coughed very much.'
>
> 'Ah, my dear boy, it seems very hard for you to lie here all day in pain, and cough all night. Do you love Jesus?'
>
> 'Yes, sir.'
>
> 'Jesus loves you. He bought you with His precious blood, and He knows what is best for you. It seems hard for you to lie here, and listen to the shouts of the healthy boys at play. But soon Jesus will take you home, and then He will tell you the reason, and you will be so glad.'
>
> Then, laying his hand on the boy, without the formality of kneeling, he said: 'O Jesus, Master, this dear child is reaching out his thin hand to find Thine. Touch him, dear Saviour, with Thy loving, warm clasp. Lift him as he passes the cold river, that his feet be not chilled by the water of death; take him home in Thine own good time. Comfort and cherish him till that good time comes. Show him Thyself as he lies here, and let him see Thee and know Thee more and more as his loving Saviour.'
>
> After a moment's pause he said: 'Now, dear, is there anything you would like? Would you like a little canary in a cage, to hear him sing in the morning? Nurse, see that he has a canary to-morrow morning. Good-bye, my dear; you will see the Saviour perhaps before I shall.'
>
> Mr. Gough adds: 'I have seen Mr. Spurgeon holding by his power sixty-five hundred persons in a breathless interest. I knew him as a great man universally esteemed and beloved, but as he sat by the bedside of a dying pauper child, whom his beneficence had rescued, he was to me a greater and a grander man than when swaying the mighty multitude at his will.'

Such was Spurgeon's spiritual concern.

A Young Christian's Band with monthly meetings, a Band of Hope, and a branch of the International Bible Reading Association were all part of student activities. Spurgeon always advised the children with good practical principles. He would urge them, as one might expect, to read the Puritans. He said to the boys and girls, "Go at them like mice at a rich cheese; eat your way through, and fatten as you go."[57] Every year a substantial part of the funding was secured by the boys themselves. Under the direction of Mr. Charlesworth, a boys' choir and bell ringers would visit various towns and give concerts. Collections among the congregation at the concert were given to the Stockwell Orphanage. In 1884, for example, after traveling expenses had been paid, they netted £1,132.

Spurgeon himself hit upon a fund-raising scheme. Through the years, as a hobby, he had collected engravings, woodcuts, etchings, etc. on the Reformation—one of his keen interests. He had 240 such articles. He put them on display and charged six pence for admittance. This program initially came about as a celebration of his 49th birthday in August of 1883 at the Orphanage. Spurgeon spent seven of his birthdays at the institution. His birthdays were always noted in the papers. Three generations of Spurgeons spoke at the Orphanage on May 1, 1875. Those speaking were, John, Charles and his two sons, Charles, Jr., and Thomas. It was the first time the two boys spoke at a public gathering. The birthday celebration on June 20, 1876 at the Orphanage witnessed five Spurgeons speaking: James, John, Charles, Sr. Thomas, and Charles, Jr.

Christmas always proved a delightful time for the children, because Charles would spend Christmas Day with them. It was a wonderful gesture by their pastor and president that he would give Christmas Day to the children. And they loved him dearly for it. On one Christmas the boys gave Charles a present inscribed, "From the boys of the Stockwell Orphanage to their best earthly friend, C. H. Spurgeon." It no doubt touched their pastor; he truly was their best friend on earth. Spurgeon said, "They compassed me about like bees." Whenever Spurgeon visited the Orphanage, he left sufficient money with the headmaster to provide a penny apiece for each orphan. On some occasions Spurgeon would conduct a spelling bee between the Sunday School students of the Orphanage and the Sunday School students of the Metropolitan Tabernacle. That always brought joy and excitement. Even into the latter years of Spurgeon's life, when he would be away in the south of France because of illness, he would always write to the children. A beautiful example of this is found in a letter written on January 24, 1874 when a little boy had died at the Orphanage. Charles wrote:

> Dear Boys, I have been much impressed by hearing that death has been to the Orphanage. Are you all prepared if he should shoot another arrow into one of the houses and lay another low? I wonder who will be the next! Dear boys, would you go to Heaven if you were now at once to die? Wait a bit and let each one answer for himself. You know you must be born again; you must repent of sin; you must believe in Jesus. How is it with you? If you are not saved you are in great danger, in fearful peril! Be warned, I pray you! I cannot

bear to think of one boy going from the Orphanage to hell; that would be terrible indeed. But to rise to Heaven, to be with Jesus for ever; why, this makes it worth while even to die a hundred deaths.

I hope my dear friend, Mr. Charlesworth, and all the teachers and matrons and nurses are well; I send them all my kindest regards. I often think about you all. I want to see you all happy here and hereafter. May you grow up to be honourable Christian men; and if God should take any of you away, may we all meet in Heaven! Will you pray a special prayer, just now, that the death of one boy may bring all of you to Jesus to find eternal life? Be diligent in school, be very kind in the houses. Do not cause us pain, but give us all joy, for we all love you, and desire your good.

Mr. Charlesworth will, on my behalf, give you a couple of oranges all round, and I will pay him when I come home. Your loving friend, C. H. Spurgeon.

Charles stayed so close to the children that it could be said that every one of the 500 children residents in the orphanage had once shaken his hand. Through the years, thousands of children have been touched and ministered to by this great benevolent work. The work found acceptance in all of London. On the twentieth anniversary of the orphanage, all the papers reported the event.

When the orphans grew up and left the institution, they often contributed directly, or through their friends, large sums toward the maintenance of those who followed them. Some of the ways that funding came in is quite fascinating. At one time a friend of the orphanage gave six dozen bunches of turnips and then added, "I hope someone will send you the mutton." Within an hour a farmer had sent a whole sheep. Spurgeon once got to the heart of the matter with an individual. He said, "Somebody has written to me that he will put the orphanage in the corner of his will, I said, 'Do not do that on any account, because if you put it in the corner you will tear it off someday. Kindly put it in the centre and see that it is done in the right way.'"[58]

In a word, Spurgeon moved into a very needy area in London with its massive problem of street urchins. In the name of Christ he raised a great work. Through the years God provided in marvelous and unusual ways and many lives were rescued from a life of deprivation, poverty and degradation.

THE OLD LADIES HOME

Another significant contribution to the needs of hurting Londoners centered in Spurgeon's work in the almshouses, called the Old Ladies Home. Spurgeon inherited the work when he came to the New Park Street Church. As mentioned earlier, this ministry dated back to the work of Dr. John Rippon. During his ministry, Rippon had developed six such institutions. Its purpose, by its very name, was to meet the needs of elderly women who had no family upon which they could rely. In those days no social programs of any consequence came from governmental sources. The churches met these kinds of needs, along with the work of philanthropists like Lord Shaftesbury and others. The almshouses were designed to provide all the comforts of a Christian home without any expense to the women.

Spurgeon gave a very detailed and interesting account of the beginning of the Old Ladies Home, along with the history of the Tabernacle, as he made his appeal for assistance in the work. He wrote:

> Dr. Rippon once said that some of the best people in His Majesty's dominion were in his church, and he used to add with a nod, 'and some of the worst.' Some of the latter class seem to have got into office at one time, for they were evidently a hindrance rather than a help to the good man, though from his independent way of doing things the hindrance did not much affect him.
>
> As well as we can remember, the story of his founding the almshouses and schools in 1803, it runs as follows: The doctor urged upon the deacons the necessity of such institutions; they do not see the urgency thereof; he pleads again, but like the deaf adder, they are not to be charmed, charm he ever so wisely. 'The expense will be enormous, and the money cannot be raised,' this was the unnecessary croak of the prudent officers. At length the pastor says, 'The money can be raised, and shall be. Why, if I don't go out next Monday, and collect £500 before the evening meeting, I'll drop the proposal; but while I am sure the people will take up the matter heartily, I will not be held back by you.' Disputes in this case were urged in very plain language, but with no degree of bitterness, for the parties knew each other, and had too much mutual respect to make their relationship in the church depend upon a point of difference. All were agreed to put the Doctor to a test, and challenged him to produce the £500 next Monday, or cease to importune about almshouse. The worthy slow-coaches were up to time on the appointed evening, and the Doctor soon arrived. 'Well, brethren,' said he, 'I have succeeded in collecting £300, that is most encouraging, is it not?' 'But,' said two or three of them at once, in a hurry, 'You said you would get £500 or drop the matter, and we mean for you to keep your word.' 'By all means,' said he, 'and I mean to keep my word, too, there is £800 which the friends gave me almost without asking, and the rest is nearly all promised.' The prudent officials were taken aback, but recovering themselves, they expressed their great pleasure, and would be ready to meet the pastor at any time and arrange for the expending of funds. 'No, no, my brethren,' said the Doctor, 'I shall not need your services. You have opposed me all along, and now I have done the work without you, you want to have your say in it to hinder me still, but neither you nor any other deacons shall plague a minister about this business. So, brethren, you can attend to something else.' Accordingly, the old trust deed of the almshouses had a clause to the effect that the pastor shall elect the pensioners, 'no deacon interfering.' The present pastor had great pleasure in inducing the Charity Commis-

sioners to expunge this clause, and give the pastor and deacons, unitedly, the power to select the objects of charity.

The original endowments, after payment of repairs, do not suffice wholly to provide for six inmates, and there are now seventeen; the support of the remaining eleven involves a heavy draught upon the communion fund of our church, which is already fully weighed down with poor members. We greatly need at least £5,000 to endow the almshouses, and place the institution upon a proper footing. Already C. H. Spurgeon, Thomas Olney and Thomas Greenwood have contributed £200 each toward the fund, and we earnestly trust that either by donations or legacies, the rest of the 5,000 will be forthcoming. This would only provide five shillings per week for each poor woman, which is little enough. If more could be raised it would be so much the better for the pensioners. The pastors are anxious to see this matter put into proper order; they confess that the responsibility of having increased the number of rooms and alms-women rests mainly on them, and therefore they feel that their work is not done till at least five shillings per week shall have been provided for their poor sisters; if it could be double that amount they would be glad. We wish to leave the Tabernacle in good working order when our work is done; but the present burden might prove far too heavy for our successors; indeed, they ought not to be saddled with it. In future years the church may find itself barely able to support its own expenses, and we do not think that we are justified in leaving it the legacy of so heavy a charge. Our present anxiety is to get the ship tight and trim, and this is one of the matters which is not in a satisfactory condition. Brethren, let us set it straight. Our aged sisters are worthy of all that we can do for them, and their grateful faces often make our hearts glad. We should like to see more alms-rooms, and we hope some one will build and endow a row for aged men. We have had a hint that this project is taking shape in the mind of a generous friend; we hope he will carry it out in his own lifetime, rather than wait and have it done by a legacy. [59]

Spurgeon, profoundly committed to the almshouses work, gave himself to it as he did to the Pastors' College and the Stockwell Orphanage. He frequently contributed large sums of his own money for its support. No one ever knew how many bills Spurgeon himself paid for the Home, but he continually settled small accounts for heating, groceries, clothing, and small comforts. On one occasion, at his silver wedding anniversary when he received a gift of £5,000, he presented the whole of it as an endowment for the Home. Strange as it may seem, some newspapers accused Spurgeon of hoarding large sums of money. Although he loathed answering criticisms, he would at times be compelled to deny such accusations to let people know that he was not a rich man. He became the largest contributor to all the Metropolitan Tabernacle enterprises as he systematically gave away his income. At times, the bills of the Old Ladies Home were paid twice. The officers of the church would pay a bill only to discover that Spurgeon had personally and quietly paid it himself.

When the New Park Street Church moved to the "Elephant and Castle" and the Tabernacle had been built, it became clear that the almshouses needed to be moved also so that they might be nearer the new sanctuary. That way the women could attend chapel at the Metropolitan Tabernacle. They found a good site in Station Road, Walworth, in sight of the railway station at the "Elephant and Castle." As pointed out, the "Elephant and Castle" was an important intersection of several roads in Spurgeon's day. Today it is a large round-about, with thousands of cars and buses constantly going by. At the time the Metropolitan Tabernacle was built there, only a few commercial buildings graced the area, a pub, a railway station, and one or two other sites. Today a large shopping center covers the area.

In 1867, with the money obtained from the sale of the old almshouses near New Park Street Chapel, along with £1,750 that had been contributed by friends, the new block of buildings was constructed. The almshouse complex building consisted of seventeen different units or rooms occupied by the women. The ladies admitted had to be members of the Metropolitan Tabernacle and over sixty years of age and destitute. Also, the home included a headmaster's house and two schoolrooms that were used every weekday by about 400 children. They were under the tutelage of a headmaster. The homes met the need well and Spurgeon generously gave of himself to that benevolent work.

THE COLPORTAGE MINISTRY

In August, 1866, Spurgeon wrote an article in *The Sword and the Trowel* on the necessity of combatting the theological error filtering throughout the Christian community in the mid-nineteenth century. The article suggested that one of the best means of combatting heresy would be the distribution of wholesome Christian literature. Almost immediately a member of the Tabernacle congregation, Mr. E. Boustead, offered a substantial amount of money for the establishment of a society of colporteurs. As can well be imagined, Spurgeon rejoiced in this rapid response to his suggestion. On September 3 of the same year, at a meeting of friends whom he had called together to consider such a ministry, they formed an association "to extend the circulation of the scriptures, and to create the diffusion of sound religious literature, in order to counteract the evils arising from the perusal of works of a decided Romish tendency." [60] This gave birth to the Metropolitan Tabernacle Colporteurs Association.

At its inception, it had been designed to operate primarily along Baptist lines. However, as the work grew it became obvious that it must be broadened and the ranks of the colporteurs should include members from various denominations. The only basic requirement was that they should be men of sterling Christian character, holding firmly to the evangelical doctrines of Orthodox Christianity. Most of the colporteurs, as could be expected, were preachers. Spurgeon described their work as "one of the cheapest and most effective means of scattering Gospel light in the darkest places."[61] The profits they made from their sales, they used to support themselves. Often, however, the profits of the sales did not give them a decent living, so Christian friends would often guarantee their work with a subscription of £45 a year. This relieved the central office of much financial responsibility and care. As always, Spurgeon supported the association with his own gifts and promoted the work by his writing. He said:

> I believe it to be one of the most efficient and economical agencies in existence and as education increases, it will be more and more so. The sale of vicious literature can only be met by the distribution of good books; these can best be scattered in rural districts by carrying them to the houses of the people; and even in towns, the book-hawkers' work greatly stimulates their sale. The colporteur not only endeavors to sell the books, but he visits from door to door; and, in so doing, converses with the inmates about their souls, prays with the sick, and leaves a tract at each cottage. He is frequently able to hold prayer-meetings, open-air services and Bible readings. He gets a room, if possible, and preaches; found Bands of Hope, and makes himself generally useful in the cause of religion and temperance. He is, in fact, at first a missionary, then a preacher, and by-and-by, in the truest sense, a pastor. We have some noble men in the work.[62]

One room of the Pastors' College housed the headquarters of the Association. For many years Mr. Steven Wigney served as the general secretary of the movement. They held an annual conference of the colporteurs and Spurgeon normally spoke, giving his support and blessing.

How many people were brought to faith in Christ and how many Christians were built up in the faith by the faithful work of the colporteurs defies imagination. They went throughout the entirety of the country from house to house knocking on doors sharing the Gospel; God blessed the work tremendously.

THE PASTOR'S AID SOCIETY

Another venture undertaken by the Tabernacle was the Pastor's Aid Society, founded in 1879. This work emerged in connection with the book fund of Mrs. Spurgeon. That interesting work will be detailed momentarily. This aspect of the ministry came through the generosity of friends who gave grants of money and clothing to help poor ministers, hard pressed financially through illness or other circumstances of life. The society benefited many pastors. Pastors in Spurgeon's day were normally grossly underpaid. Many lived on the very verge of poverty. But rarely was a complaint heard. When Mrs. Spurgeon would hear of a needy pastor and his family, as funds were available, she immediately attempted to meet those needs. Many words of gratitude were expressed to her for this work. This leads to Mrs. Spurgeon's significant work in the so-called Book Fund.

THE BOOK FUND MINISTRY

Spurgeon always outwardly appeared to the casual observer to be a healthy and robust man. His very demeanor spoke of vitality. However, as so often seen, he frequently endured long and painful illnesses. His wife Susannah was a great comfort and strength to him during those times. But, as discussed earlier, she was far from well herself. Actually, Susannah's illness and confinement proved a greater trial to Charles than his own frequent bouts with sickness. For a few years Susannah became a virtual invalid, and, of course, the subject of Charles' affectionate care. Her imprisonment made her that much dearer to him. He could find no words to express his admiration for her beautiful, patient Christian character in the midst of many months and years of confinement. For weeks on end she would have to sit in an easy chair, hoping that the day might come when she could again engage in some activities of the church, or at least care for the domestic duties of the home. However, as the years came and went, she remained a semi-invalid. She longed to be of more use in the Lord's service and to be of help in the many labors of her husband. Fervently praying for some opportunity to serve Christ, she was directed by the Lord to the establishment of what became a very central and important aspect of the Metropolitan Tabernacle ministry: the Book Fund.

The Book Fund had a providential beginning, as did most of Spurgeon's benevolent enterprises. In the summer of 1875, Spurgeon completed his first volume of *Lectures to my Students*. He handed a proof copy to his wife and asked her what she thought of the book. After reading it carefully, Mrs. Spurgeon declared that she wished she could place a copy in the hands of every minister in England. Quite casually Spurgeon said, "Then why not do so?" Without a moment's hesitation she replied, "How much will you give?" It sparked an idea, and she prayed much about it to see if God might lead in the matter. Suddenly it dawned upon her that the money needed to launch such a project was already at hand. Susannah had a little habit of putting away in a drawer every crown piece that came into her hands. She counted the coins and found the amount would exactly cover the cost of sending out 100 copies of the *Lectures*. "In that moment," she tells us, "though I knew it not, the Book Fund was inaugurated."[63]

In July, 1875, Spurgeon published a note in *The Sword and the Trowel* stating that a copy of the recently issued *Lectures to My Students* would be sent free to 100 Baptist ministers. The demand was so great that Mrs. Spurgeon felt obligated to send out an additional 100 copies. But they had no funds. So, in the next edition of *The Sword and the Trowel*, Charles set forth the need, and asked if something could be done to provide poor ministers with much needed books for their study and preparation of sermons. Spurgeon wrote, "Some of the applicants say they have not been able to buy a new book for the last ten years! Does anyone wonder if preachers are sometimes dull?"[64] Immediately, contributions began to roll in, the first being a gift of 5 shillings in stamps sent anonymously. Within two months, Mrs. Spurgeon was sending out parcels of books, not only the *Lectures* but other and more expensive theological and biblical works. After that initial beginning, Mrs. Spurgeon said she never needed to ask for a shilling. The entire undertaking was quite simple. She secured gifts of books and money from Christian donors with which she then would supply the scant libraries of poor preachers.

These grants of books extended not only to Baptist ministers but to pastors of all denominations. Moreover, Susannah distributed books other than those authored by her husband; although as could be expected, a large portion came from his pen. A myriad of letters began to flood in from the poor ministers who had benefited from the Book Fund. The letters revealed the poverty of the pastors of the smaller congregations. Spurgeon little dreamed of the dire circumstances in many pastors' homes. Even in the Church of England, particularly among the curates, the need was great. They all benefited tremendously from the Book Fund. Spurgeon called the fund "a fountain in the desert."

Also growing out of the Book Fund, as mentioned earlier, the Pastor's Aid Fund touched poor pastors. Gifts of money, wearing apparel, etc. helped many. The Pastor's Aid distributed about £300 annually while the expenditures for the Book Fund reached approximately £1,200 per year. At the end of Spurgeon's life, close to 150,000 volumes had been distributed among pastors. The work received wide acclaim.

Articles about the Book Fund ministry constantly appeared. For example, *The National Baptist*, March 1, 1883 wrote, "Again, Mrs. Spurgeon has made the Christian world her debtor." Even one or two poems were written about the work. Susannah wrote two books herself: *Ten Years of My Life* and *Ten Years After*. Much in the spirit of Bunyan's *Pilgrim's Progress*, and, of course, her husband, in her last book she wrote:

I can see two pilgrims treading this highway of life together, hand in hand,—heart linked to heart. True, they have had rivers to ford, and mountains to cross and fierce enemies to fight, and many dangers to go through; but their Guide was watchful, their Deliverer unfailing, and of them it might truly be said, 'In all their affliction He was afflicted, and the Angel of His preserve saved them; in His love and in His pity He redeemed them; and He bare them, and carried them all the days of old.' . . . But, at last, they came to a place on the road where two ways met; and here, amidst the terms of a storm such as they had never before encountered, they parted company,—the one being caught up to the invisible glory,—the other, battered, and bruised by the awful tempest, henceforth toiling along the road,—alone. But the 'goodness and mercy' which, for so many years, had followed the two travelers, did not leave the solitary one; rather did the tenderness of the Lord, 'lead on softly,' and those green pastures for the tired feet, and still waters for the solace and refreshment of His trembling child. [65]

Spurgeon's personal library consisted of up to 30,000 volumes. When William Jewell College of Liberty, Missouri acquired Spurgeon's personal books at the turn of the twentieth century, only five to six thousand volumes remained. Although it cannot be verified, it can probably be assumed that after the death of the pastor, his widow sent many of his own books to poor pastors through the agency of the Book Fund. Moreover, Spurgeon himself gave away some 5,000 volumes to students of the Pastor's College. The ministry tremendously aided the spread and the preaching of the Gospel throughout Britain.

The Book Fund work seemed to help restore Susannah's health. At any rate, she became well enough in 1882 to become president of the Tabernacle Auxiliary for Zenana Mission Work. Spurgeon said:

> I gratefully adore the goodness of our heavenly Father in directing my beloved wife to a work which has been to her fruitful in unutterable happiness. That it has cost her more pain than it would be fitting to reveal is most true; but that it has brought her a boundless joy is equally certain. [66]

A very considerable number, some say over 20, other benevolent works emerged out of the Metropolitan Tabernacle; not to mention the Sunday School, Bible teaching classes for women which grew to some five or six hundred young ladies attending to the study of God's Word each week, and similar works. All these benevolent ministries met real needs. A few such ministries deserve at least a short word.

THE ROCK LOAN TRACT SOCIETY

This organization loaned copies of Spurgeon's sermons to those who lived in the isolated country villages in Britain. Many homes were reached and many lives transformed through this significant work.

THE ORDINANCE POOR FUND

This work of the Tabernacle centered on ministering to its own members. It distributed food and goods to the poor members of the church. In the 1870s, this particular society dispersed about £800 worth of aid each year. The work grew and God blessed the effort until it was dispensing approximately £4,000 worth of food and goods to needy people annually.

THE LADIES BENEVOLENT SOCIETY

This work was formed in the spirit of Dorcas. A group of ladies dedicated themselves to the making and supplying of clothes for the poor.

The Ladies Maternal Society

This work came into being to aid pregnant women among the London poor. Workers made with their own hands linen clothing and distributed them to poor women, thus aiding those expectant mothers in whatever way they could.

The Metropolitan Tabernacle Poor Minister's Clothing Society

This facet of Spurgeon's ministry, as the name indicates, provided clothing for poor pastors. Charles served as president of the Society, as he did in nearly all of the various social works. One can imagine how appreciated this work became.

Other Works

Other works were the "Flower Mission," started in 1877. Flowers would be sent in from the country, young ladies would arrange them and take them to people in the hospital. "The Baptist Country Mission" sent young men to preach and evangelize in country towns with a view to starting new churches. For blind people, Spurgeon inaugurated "Mr. Hampton's Blind Mission." This was a Sunday School work for blind children, with a tea conducted every Sunday afternoon for all the blind who would come. Normally, 200 blind people and their friends would come for tea. "Mrs. Thomas' Mother's Mission" reached out to poor women. A work known as "Mrs. Evan's Home and Foreign Missionary Working Society" made up boxes of clothing for missionaries as well as for poor pastors. Spurgeon served as a member of the "Particular Baptist Fund" that had been inaugurated in 1717 by Benjamin Stinton. He took up a yearly offering for the work.

There seemed no end to the variety of social ministries the Metropolitan Tabernacle undertook. It was a working church. And Spurgeon would give himself, not only to his own organizations, but to others as well. For example, in 1876 he addressed the 39th Annual Meeting of the "Female Servants Home Society." He gave them good Christian counsel on how to live. He told them they should not read fiction, but memorize Bible verses. For that he got some criticism.

The Alcohol Issue

Another area in which Spurgeon demonstrated a growing awareness, and a deepening conviction of social concern, was in the area of alcohol abuse. Alcoholism, with its debilitating effects, posed a devastating problem in nineteenth-century British working class people. The English have always been known to appreciate a mug of ale, but for the lower classes this became a serious problem. M. Dorothy George, in her book *London Life in the Eighteenth Century*, contended that the dramatic rise in the life expectancy of Britishers after 1850 came about due to the passage of stricter laws regarding the production of cheap corn whiskey.[67] Many Victorian reformers wished to see total prohibition woven into the fabric of British law and society. Thus, organizations like the Blue Ribbon Society and the Band of Hope Association arose. These were only a few of the prohibitionists' organizations.

The problem of drinking in nineteenth-century England was much more serious than just a typical British working man having his daily pint of beer at the local pub after work. Drunkenness had become a serious social problem. The working man, out of boredom or despair, often threw away on drink what little money he did make while his family lacked for the daily necessities of life. For example, Mayhew contends that the alcohol problem played a central role in the misery of the dock workers and their families. During the 1850s, the publicans acted as the hiring agents of the various dock-loading firms. Thus, the publicans had considerable control over the dock workers and forced them to spend a good deal of their wages on the cheap beer sold in their pubs. However, the problem went far beyond the dock workers; drinking became one primary factor contributing to Britain's general social ills. That is when evangelicals threw down the gauntlet and went to war with the alcohol industry.

In the early years, Spurgeon was never totally convinced of the value of total abstinence, as pointed out. It must be admitted that he enjoyed a pint of ale or a glass of wine in the evening. Once, as a young preacher, he wrote to his mother how gratified he felt that a friend had given him a bottle of very fine wine. *The Christian Reader* even reported on July 5, 1883, that Spurgeon stood against "temperance wine" (non-alcoholic) for church communion, preferring the real thing. That report is unverifiable.

This is not to say Spurgeon was not in sympathy with the social and humanitarian motives that lay behind the temperance societies. In fact, temperance societies often met for lectures and rallies in the Tabernacle auditorium. Spurgeon, well aware of the devastating effects of drunkenness and alcoholism upon many families, regarded alcoholism as a disease people must rid themselves of. It may well have been that after seeing the devastating effects of alcohol, Spurgeon had a dramatic change of attitude. He became a total abstainer and "donned the blue ribbon" of the temperance movement. Teetotallers would sport a blue ribbon as a testimony to their convictions. This took place in 1887, the year of the Down Grade Controversy, just five years before his death. When he took this stand, it was not because he believed that alcohol was inherently evil—he realized that the

Lord Himself had turned water into wine. But he did take his position in the hope that his example would encourage alcoholics, or potential alcoholics, to do the same. He said to a large rally at the Metropolitan Tabernacle, "I don't need it for myself, but if it will strengthen and encourage a single soul among the 5,000 that are here, I will put it on."[68] He would don the blue ribbon and hence take his stand as a total abstainer.

In Spurgeon's own inimitable way, once he joined the temperance movement, he became one of its strongest and most vocal advocates. He even went so far on one occasion as to say, "Next to the preaching of the Gospel, the most necessary thing to be done in England is to induce our people to become abstainers."[69] This was actually before he wore the blue ribbon. When he published his famous *John Ploughman's Talks and Pictures*, he wrote in the preface that "the chief purpose of the book, was to smite evil—and especially the monster evil of drink."[70] Obviously, he had become a strong advocate for temperance.

SPURGEON'S WEAKNESS IN SOCIAL ISSUES?

Perhaps Spurgeon can be faulted to some extent for seeing the basic approach to social problems on the aforementioned individualistic, philanthropical basis. It can be asked, would Spurgeon have changed his basic approach to social need and social change had he lived longer? It is true, as stressed, that in many senses he was a child of his day with its individualistic approach to all social dynamics. Would he, like his contemporaries, John Clifford and Price Hughes, well-known Baptist ministers, have come out strongly for the actual revamping of the structures of society itself had he lived longer? Perhaps he would, but perhaps not. One is almost forced to conclude that Spurgeon's social views probably would have changed little had he lived out his three score and ten years. Spurgeon changed very little in his theology or approach to any situation. One would have wished that he would have seen more of the importance of changing the structures of society that fostered problems as well as touching individual lives. And it may well be true, as he said, until sin and Satan are dealt with, little change will occur in society. And that calls for an individual approach. Yet, his great heart did reach out to the huddled masses of society; and, though his approach did not afford the final answer for everyone, he made a tremendous contribution to the social needs of his day. For that he is truly called, in Bunyan's pictorial way, a man named "Help." Although he probably never would have joined the Fabian Society, he still wanted to see society changed and in his own unique way did much to see it take place in his sphere of influence.

An interesting comparison can be made between John Clifford and Spurgeon. Clifford became a very central figure in the Baptist denomination in the later years of the century. Clifford was only two years younger than

Spurgeon, but outlived him by many years. As someone said, "Where Spurgeon might be considered the 'last of the Victorians' in his individualist philanthropic approach to social problems, so Clifford might well be described as the first of the new breed."[71] Clifford was highly educated and earned a doctorate from the University of London. Clifford's sympathy for the lower classes of society projected him into active involvement in social reform. Contrary to what Spurgeon would have done, he joined the Fabian Society and did his best to influence Parliament on behalf of social legislation. Clifford said:

> Politics are one of the organs and instruments by which two Christians hasten the coming of God. I hate the selfishness which leads the world to the devil and loses the soul in uncertain and blind efforts to save it.[72]

Clifford did have a point to make. It seems that Spurgeon might have done well to have heard.

We shall see Clifford again in the Down Grade Controversy. Not only did Spurgeon and Clifford disagree in the matter of how to approach social ills, they also disagreed in the problem of the "new theology" that was sweeping Britain and precipitated the Down Grade Controversy.

Much that has been said may imply that Spurgeon did not involve himself in the political life of the country. That is not true. In certain areas of social concern, he deeply involved himself. But that story must wait for another chapter. Let it simply be said, Spurgeon was a man of God who reached out to people in need in the way that he saw best. He gave himself to win people to faith in Christ and also did his best to feed the poor and meet their needs.

Of course, there are always the skeptics who write off philanthropic endeavors as the meddling of pious do-gooders. In the nineteenth century, no governmental bureaucracies existed to which one could appeal for their physical and social needs. It had to be carried out by conscientious Christians. As one has put it, "If it had not been for the concern of those earnest Victorians, the suffering which resulted from the worst effects of industrialism would have been without relief." Thus Spurgeon's ministry reached out in a multitude of significant and important ways, not only to share the Gospel of Christ, but to alleviate the pressing needs of people in many difficult walks of life. The pastor-evangelist became a great philanthropist and Christian social worker. Lord Shaftesbury summed it up well when he said, "Few men have preached so much and so well, and few men have combined so practically their words by their actions."[73]

The Metropolitan Tabernacle Almshouses and School. *—courtesy of Dr. Craig Skinner*

9

"The Interpreter"

SPURGEON'S MID-METROPOLITAN TABERNACLE YEARS

Metropolitan Tabernacle baptistry.

Well, Ignorance, wilt thou yet foolish be,
To slight good counsel ten times given thee?
And if thou yet refuse it, thou shalt know
Ere long the evil of thy doing so.
Remember, man, in time, stoop, do not fear,
Good counsel taken well saves; therefore hear.
But if thou yet shalt slight it, thou wilt be
The loser (Ignorance) I'll warrant thee.

—John Bunyan

Introduction

T he matrix of Spurgeon's phenomenal ministry was the Holy
Scriptures. Everything Spurgeon said and did essentially emerged
out of his understanding of the Bible. In the best sense, Bunyan's
"Interpreter" exemplified C. H. Spurgeon. The largest single
volume Spurgeon wrote bears that actual title. His continuing ministry at the
Metropolitan Tabernacle demonstrated that basic biblical principle; he was
an interpreter of the Word. It has been said that he "knew only two subjects
really well—the text of the English Bible and the writings of the Puritan
divines." [1] That may well be true, but in Spurgeon's thinking, that comprised
everything one needed to know for Christian service. That approach led the
mid-years of the Tabernacle ministry into great growth and effectiveness,
and ultimately precipitated Spurgeon's first serious theological battle, the
Baptismal Regeneration Controversy. Both the expanding ministry and the
controversy came as Spurgeon began reaching the pinnacle of his worldwide
popularity. Both aspects demonstrate a fascinating development of the man.
He actually became a legend in his own day. But before examining those
mid-years of the man, we must go back to pick up the threads that led to
those dynamic days. A rigid year-by-year account is not followed so that the
sense of Spurgeon's developing ministry can be more clearly seen.

THE DEVELOPING MINISTRY

As Spurgeon's ministry developed throughout Britain and on the Continent, it had become his custom to preach on the first Sunday morning of
each year from a text selected by an esteemed clergyman of the Church of
England. One New Year's morning, Spurgeon preached on "True Unity
Promoted" from Ephesians 4:3, "Endeavoring to keep the unity of the Spirit
in the bond of peace." Further, as each new year dawned, all London ob-

445

served an annual week of prayer. Spurgeon joined in the prayer ministry. The new year's weekly prayer meetings at the Tabernacle were always crowded, as fervent intercession pervaded the entire atmosphere. It proved a high hour for the Tabernacle congregation. This ministry of prayer became an important spiritual experience for all London. On successive evenings, meetings would be held in chapels and churches in the various parts of the city. These meetings would be visited by Spurgeon and he would often give an address at each place. Great blessings flowed. As Edward Leach stated:

> A blessing was expected. First it came as a little cloud. An earnest spirit of revival then manifested itself in the simple church. The flame spread. The new year approached. It was decided to open it with a special week of prayer. The first day six thousand souls filled the Tabernacle. Earnest addresses were delivered, sobbed out petitions presented to the throne of Grace, and the Holy Ghost descended, making saints feel intensely their miserable insignificance, and sinners their wretched condition, as unsaved and undone. . . . [2]

More and more, Spurgeon's ministry was being accepted as a regular part of the London scene. One would have thought that this sort of ministry and general acceptance would have moderated Spurgeon's reaction to the Established Church and forestalled the baptism controversy. But as shall be seen, it did not.

The year 1865 saw another significant step in the developing ministry of Spurgeon. In January of that year, the first issue of *The Sword and the Trowel* came off the press. The monthly magazine became significant as it gave Spurgeon a regular organ to express his views on a variety of subjects. Articles that related to the general spiritual life, news from various mission fields, theological issues, etc. made up its content. Objection arose to the magazine in its early days. Some feared it might injure the sale of the *Baptist Magazine*, the recognized monthly organ of the Baptist denomination. That periodical had been in existence for more than fifty years. Once, before the inauguration of *The Sword and the Trowel*, Spurgeon had been a joint editor of the *Baptist Magazine*. When he left that work, he felt at liberty to publish a periodical of his own. His experience with the *Baptist Magazine* apparently had not been too positive, so he launched into his own periodical adventure. The influence of the magazine, especially in relation to the multiple ministries of the Tabernacle, proved most helpful. For example, in an early edition of the publication, a section was devoted one month to the Stockwell Orphanage. The article depicted an orphan sitting down telling his troubles to Charles. The little lad told the pastor how friendless he sometimes felt. In response, Spurgeon wrote:

> Sitting down upon one of the seats in the Orphanage grounds, we were talking with one of our brother-Trustees, when a little fellow, we should think about eight years of age, left the other boys who were playing around us, and came

deliberately up to us. He opened fire upon us thus, 'Please, Mister Spurgeon, I want to come and sit down on that seat between you two gentlemen.' 'Come along, Bob, and tell us what you want.' 'Please, Mr. Spurgeon, suppose there was a little boy who had no father, who lived in a Orphanage with a lot of other little boys who had no fathers; and suppose those little boys had mothers and aunts who comed once a month, and brought them apples and oranges, and gave them pennies; and suppose this little boy had no mother, and no aunt, and so nobody never came to bring him nice things, don't you think somebody ought to give him a penny? 'Cause, Mr. Spurgeon, that's me.' 'Somebody' felt something wet in his eye, and Bob got a sixpence, and went off in a great state of delight. Poor little soul, he had seized the opportunity to pour out a bitterness which had rankled in his little heart, and made him miserable when the monthly visiting day came round, and as he said, 'Nobody never came to bring him nice things.' [3]

As can well be imagined, the article brought "little Bob" a plentiful supply of pocket money. Not only that, the article became the means of helping other orphans. It further served Spurgeon as an illustration of the way in which personal appeals might be made for the support of the various Tabernacle institutions. During the lifetime of Spurgeon, the circulation of *The Sword and the Trowel* ranged from ten to fifteen thousand..

A circulation of that number may not seem to be an extremely large circulation, but Spurgeon did not seek numerical success for his periodical. Spurgeon aimed the magazine at a specialized target group. First, he determined that the magazine would not be interdenominational. He wanted a Baptist thrust. That, quite naturally, limited its circulation. Further, he refused to develop a large staff for its publication; he himself became the primary editor. Of course, he knew that his own name would attract subscribers just as readily as a list of brilliant editors and contributors. So with limited staff, which necessitated a limited production size, he launched out. And he achieved the "success" he sought.

In the first issue, Spurgeon commenced a series of expositions on the Book of Psalms. This finally resulted in the *Treasury of David* in seven volumes, no doubt his greatest literary achievement. In the production of *The Sword and the Trowel*, several competent friends, some of whom had graduated from the Pastors' College, helped their editor-pastor. George Rogers, the principal of the College, assisted Spurgeon in the editorship. Edward Leach became one of the early contributors to the periodical. Leach later became a sub-editor in 1871 when he accepted the editorship of *The Freeman*.

The Pastors' College also went on making strides. The newly founded College Association drew up a doctrinal base for the organization at its first meeting. The organization became known as the College Conference. The new doctrinal confession was relatively simple: they proposed and adopted the principles that all of the members of the brotherhood should believe in the Calvinistic "doctrines of grace," in believer's baptism by immersion, and that they should be committed to the Kingdom of God and the fulfilling of its mission. All the conferees agreed to the statement and enjoyed times of fellowship, preaching, and sharing. Spurgeon was in his element. He related to the attenders the story of how he had commenced the College with just one student and how the funding from America, upon which he had so heavily depended, suddenly dried up because of the slavery issue. Spurgeon described these difficult days:

> The funds of the College got very low, and when they were at the lowest, some lady unknown sent a cheque for £200, and afterwards another for £100 was sent. The number of students is now ninety-three, and means has never yet been wanting for their support. The weekly offerings of the church began at £3, and now they are £50 or £60 per week. Money, in fact, is sent from all parts of the world. The number of students settled over churches during the past year is about thirty. A fund has been established, which now amounts to £5,000, to assist in the enlargement and rebuilding of chapels, on the principle of advances without interest, repayable by instalments extending over a series of years. The expenditure of the College is now about £3,500 a year. About sixty-two of the students of the College are now settled as pastors of churches in various parts of the country. [4]

Spurgeon constantly called the Conference men to prayer. He well knew how foundational prayer was to a vital ministry. He said:

> It was agreed upon at the Conference that we should all try to set apart Monday, June 21 as a day of special prayer that the Holy Spirit may cause the springs of supplication to flow very freely. Let us meet with one accord and cry mightily for a baptism of the Holy Spirit. We need personal renewal; our churches want quickening, the whole Church of God requires refreshing. . . . The clouds are waiting for our prayers and then they will burst in blessings upon us. [5]

The work grew and continued, and the College began to reach new heights of effectiveness in the education of men for ministry.

In the same month of the same year (1865), Spurgeon presented for the first time his famous *Sermons in Candles* lecture. The lecture, previously mentioned, was given in behalf of The Band of Hope Union, an organization that advocated total abstinence from alcoholic beverages. W. R. Salway, a lecturer in science at the Pastors' College, was an ardent total abstainer. On this occasion, he had the satisfaction of inaugurating a Band of Hope group in connection with the Metropolitan Tabernacle, and the first members to be received were the twin sons of the pastor. They were then only eight and a half years old. As the two boys dedicated themselves to abstain from alcohol all of their days, loud applause broke out in the congregation. Mr. Salway placed around the neck of each boy a "Band of Hope" medal.

The Freeman describes the reaction in these words: "Master Charles, in a clear voice that was distinctly heard by nearly, if not quite, all present, thanked the audience for the kind way in which they had welcomed him into the Band of Hope, and said he hoped he should always be a teetotaler. Master Thomas said: 'My dear friends, I thank you for your kindness and hope I shall grow up to be an honorable man and to keep my promise.'" [6] In reply to the vote of thanks that Spurgeon received for having this meeting, he said, "I am not a teetotaler myself, and it is not likely that I shall ever be. I believe, however, that if children are brought up to abstain from alcoholic liquors, they will never need them; and therefore I think it right that they should have no instruction on the use of them from their parents . . . knowing that the society does a great deal of good, I am glad to help it as much as I possibly can." One can well imagine how the *Saturday Review*, Spurgeon's constant nemesis, reacted to his rather contradictory stance. In the March 18, 1865 edition, the *Saturday Review* declared:

> There were those present who looked on this pretty ceremonial with different eyes. . . . But the crowning absurdity of the whole business was wisely reserved for the end. After Mr. Spurgeon had done with his candles and the rest of his apparatus, a veteran teetotaller got up, and, after some remarks on the glories of water, summoned two little boys with knickerbockers and red stockings to the front of the stage. The more flippant of the spectators might have anticipated a light gymnastic performance, either as a testimony to the unimpaired strength of the aged abstainer, or the emblematic of something in the Bible. However, the teetotaller announced that they bore a name that would be honoured in history; so the audience, who had been in a manner guessing riddles all night about the candles, conjectured, and rightly, that they beheld the sons of their 'pastor.' Then solemnly each was admitted a member of the Band of Hope Union, and ceremoniously invested with the medal of the order. The enthusiasm of the multitude knew no bounds. They cheered and waved hats and handkerchiefs, and the little boys made two tiny speeches, and then the several hundreds of people cheered and waved hats and handkerchiefs again till they were all hoarse and dizzy. This is the kind of thing for which the multitude are to be got at! [7]

Remember, however, later in life Spurgeon did "take the pledge" and became a teetotaler. Spurgeon finally seemed to realize his testimony was at stake on the issue. R. T. Booth penned the "blue ribbon" on Charles and that pledge must have communicated to the country, for at Spurgeon's death, *The Pall Mall Gazette* (February 18, 1892) printed, "Under *no* circumstances did he touch alcohol in any form whatever." Of course, they forgot all the early years. Perhaps they recalled that once, earlier in his ministry, Spurgeon got into a conflict with the brewers and some clergymen. It seems the breweries had become stock companies, and some clergymen bought stock. Against this alliance, Spurgeon raised his voice in unmistakable terms.

During this mid-life time, Spurgeon regularly presided over the meetings of the Evangelists who were working in connection with the Metropolitan Tabernacle. Many of the evangelists, as pointed out earlier, were students trained in the Pastors' College, but there were also some fifty other young men who voluntarily gave their time for the evangelistic ministries of the Tabernacle. They could be found around the countryside, preaching in cottages and halls, or even in the open air as opportunity presented itself. Not only that, approximately eighty other men and women would go out on Sunday, taking Spurgeon's sermons bound up as tracts, and distribute them in the homes of the poor or working people. Some of the laborers became very effective evangelists, such as the aforementioned W. Y. Fullerton, Spurgeon's best known biographer. This work became one of Spurgeon's most effective evangelistic outreach ministries. They ranged far and wide over Britain, and in various ways presented the Gospel of Christ to multitudes of people who might not have heard it any other way.

Special evangelistic services were often held at the Metropolitan Tabernacle, hosted by Spurgeon. In February of 1879, Fullerton and Chamberlen preached in the Tabernacle for an entire month. D. L. Moody spoke at the Metropolitan Tabernacle to start the series of services in his London crusade. Spurgeon always highly commended and appreciated their contribution. Such was the evangelistic fervor of the church. The Tabernacle also had an "Evangelistic Choir" that would be used on such occasions—quite different from the regular service.

Often a "Free Sunday" evening would be held at the Metropolitan Tabernacle. Members who held seats would be asked to stay home so the unconverted could get in to hear the Gospel. One weakness in the evangelistic ministry of the Tabernacle revolved around the fact that the regular members filled up the seats and left little room for the unconverted. These special "Free Sunday" services helped the situation to some extent.

SIGNIFICANT SERVICES

Spurgeon preached a great sermon August 4, 1867, on Job 14:14, "All the days of my appointed time will I wait, till my change come." On Thursday evening, April 16, 1868, Spurgeon preached at the Tabernacle the annual sermon for the "Young Men's Association in Aid of the Baptist Missionary Society." In this memorable sermon, he took his text from Acts 2:17, "Your young men shall see visions." Of course, he was still reasonably young himself and speaking to young men, so he challenged them in a very practical way. He declared:

> Suppose that there should be a number of young men here who know each other very well, young men who have been trained in the same sanctuary, nurtured in the same church, who should meet together to-morrow, or at such

other time as shall be convenient, and say to one another, 'Now, we are in business, we have just commenced in life, and God is prospering us, more or less; we are taking to ourselves wives; our children are coming around us; but, still, we trust we are never going to permit ourselves to be swallowed up in a mere worldly way of living; now, what ought we to do for missions?' And suppose the enquiry should be put, 'Is there one amongst us who could go and teach the heathen for us?' As we, most of us, may not have the ability, or do not feel called to the work, is there one out of twelve of us young men, who have grown side by side in the Sunday-school, who has the ability, and who feels called to go? Let us make it a matter of prayer, and when the Holy Ghost saith, 'Separate So-and-so to the work,' then we, the other eleven who remain, will do this,—we will say to him, 'Now brother, you cannot stop at home to make your fortune or to earn a competence; you are now giving yourself up to a very arduous and difficult enterprise, and we will support you; we know you, and we have confidence in you; you go down into the pit, we will hold the rope; go forth in connection with our own denominational Society, but we will bear the expense year by year among ourselves! Have you faith enough to go trusting that the Lord will provide? Then, we will have faith enough, and generosity enough, to say that your wants shall be our care; you preach for Christ, we will make money for Christ; when you open the Bible for Christ, we will be taking down the ship shutters for Christ; and while you are unfolding the banner of Christ's love, we will be unfolding the calicoes, or selling the groceries; and we pledge ourselves always to set aside your portion, because, as our brother, you are doing our work.' I wish he had such godly clubs as these,—holy confederacies of earnest young men who thus would love their missionary, feel for him, hear from him continually, and undertake to supply the means for his support. Why, on such a plan as that, I should think they would give fifty times, or a hundred times, as much as ever they are likely to give to an impersonal Society, or to a man whose name they only know, but whose face they never saw. I wonder whether I shall ever live to see a club of that kind; I wonder whether such an association will ever be formed by members of this church; or of any of the churches in London. If it shall be so, I shall be glad to have seen a vision of it. [8]

Spurgeon rejoiced to see something of the realization of his vision. In 1875, one of the leaders of a Tabernacle Bible class, a certain Stephen Wheatney, took up the challenge of raising £50 a year toward the support of G. F. Easton, a missionary with the China Inland Mission. Through the years, the teacher and his class continued to raise that amount for the support of this able missionary. A system of "Missionary Circles" and "Carey's Penny" supported a number of Tabernacle missionaries as Spurgeon kept the challenge of missions constantly before the people.

Something of the versatility of the maturing Spurgeon can be seen on March 2, 1869 when he preached in the Tabernacle to several thousand children. The young people of the congregation and all the Sunday Schools were brought together for a special service designed exclusively for them. Spurgeon's text on that occasion was Psalm 71:17, "Oh God, Thou hast taught me from my youth." Spurgeon always said he was proud of the fact that no one needed to bring a dictionary to the Tabernacle whenever he preached. He always strove to communicate, especially to the children. On this particular occasion, he put several questions to the young worshipers. They answered promptly and accurately. Something of the style of Spurgeon in cases like this can be seen in the following account. Spurgeon asked:

> Why should we go to God's school early? I think we ought to do so, first, because it is such a happy school. Schools used to be very miserable places; but, nowadays, I really wish I could go to school again. I went into the Borough Road School, the other day, into the Repository, where they sell slates, and pencils, and books, and all such things. The person who was there opened a box, and said to me, 'Do you want to buy any of these things?' I said, 'What are they? Why, they are toys, are they not?' He answered, 'No, they are not toys: they are used for the lessons that are taught in the kindergarten school.' I said, 'Why, if I were to take them home, my boys would have a game with them, for they are only toys.' 'Just so,' he replied, 'but they are what are used in the kindergarten school to make learning the same as playing, so that little children should play while they are learning.' Why, I thought, if that were so, I should like to go at once! Now, those who go to God's school are made much more happy than any toy can make children. He gives them real pleasure. There is a verse,—I don't know how many of you can repeat it,—I will say the first line; you say the second, if you can.

> Mr. Spurgeon:—''Tis religion that can give'—
> The Children:—'Sweetest pleasures while we live;'—
> Mr. Spurgeon:—''Tis religion must supply'—
> The Children:—'Solid comfort when we die,'
> Mr. Spurgeon:—Yes, we made that out very well between us. Then let us be off to God's school early, because it is such a happy school.

The narrative from the *Autobiography* goes on to state:

> Mr. Spurgeon delivered a similar discourse to a congregation of children on Lord's-day afternoon, February 26, 1871, only on that occasion his subject consisted of Dr. Horatius Bonar's hymn, beginning,—

> > "I lay my sins on Jesus,
> > The spotless Lamb of God."

> During the course of his remarks, the Pastor made the following reference to an object-lesson that he had given to the children many years before:—'It is a long while ago since I gave an address on a Sunday afternoon; but I daresay

some of you, who are growing into young men and young women, recollect that I brought a large piece of scarlet cloth to show to you. I had asked my dear wife to have it tested, and it had been boiled ever so many times; and it had been soaked in water ever so long before I brought it here. I could hardly tell you how much it had been rinsed, and rubbed, and scrubbed, and boiled. It was red when it went into the copper, and it was quite as red when it came out; the colour could not be taken out of it. I have heard that red rags cannot be made into any sort of paper except that red blotting-paper that we use, for this reason, that men cannot get the colour out. That is just like our sins; they are upon us like bright red stains, we cannot get them out, do what we may, apart from the Lord Jesus Christ; but if we are washed in His precious blood, we become as white as snow. Not only does the crimson colour go, but not so much as a spot remains.'

Toward the close of the sermon, Mr. Spurgeon related to the children this interesting reminiscence of his boyhood:—'Now the last wish is,—

'I long to be with Jesus.'

That is the best of all. But, dear boys and girls, you cannot sing that in your hearts unless you carry out the first part of the hymn, for we cannot be with Jesus till first He has taken upon Himself our sins, and made us like Himself. I do not think many of you go to a boarding-school, but I know what I used to do when I was at a school of that kind. I wanted to get home for the holidays; and six weeks before breaking-up time came, I made a little almanack. There was one square for every day; and, as the days passed, I used to mark them over with my pen, and make them black. Didn't I like to see them getting blotted! First I said, 'There are only five weeks and six days before the holidays come,' then it was, 'five weeks five days,' and then, 'five weeks and four days,' and so on, till it was within a fortnight of the vacation, and then I began to feel that it was almost time to go home. You see, I was longing to go home; and that is how you and I will feel when we become like Jesus, we shall long to be with Jesus, where saints and angels sing His praises for ever. But, in order to be able to look at death in that light, we must first lay our sins on Jesus.' [9]

On the Sunday before Spurgeon's fortieth birthday, June 14, 1874, he preached on Deuteronomy 2:7, "For the Lord thy God hath blessed thee in all the works of thy hand; he knoweth by walking through the great wilderness: these forty years the Lord thy God hath been with thee, thou hast lacked nothing." This sermon was largely autobiographical. In one of the most interesting and characteristic passages, Spurgeon said:

The work of some of us has been to preach the gospel; and if the Lord had given us a few scores of conversions, we would have loved Him for ever; but inasmuch as He has given us thousands upon thousands of converts, how shall we find language with which to praise Him? He has blessed the work of our hands, so that a vast church has been gathered, and many smaller ones have sprang from it; one enterprise has been taken up, and then another; one labour which seemed beyond our power has been achieved, and then another, and yet another; and at His feet we lay the crown. I must confess my Lord's special favour toward me, the very stones in the street would cry out against me if I did not. Brethren, you have had a share in the blessing,—have a share also in the praising. Enemies have arisen, and they have been exceedingly violent, only to fulfil some special purpose of God, and increase our blessing against their will. Sickness has come, only to yield discipline; we have been made weak that we might become strong, and brought to death's door that we might know more of the Divine life. Glory be to God, our life has been all blessing from beginning to end; ever since we knew Him, He has dealt out blessing, and blessing, and blessing, and never a syllable of cursing. He has fulfilled to us the word, 'Surely blessing I will bless thee and multiplying I will multiply thee.' [10]

On the twenty-fifth anniversary of Spurgeon's London ministry, the Metropolitan Tabernacle conducted a large bazaar. In the 25 years of his service, the membership had grown from 313 to 5,346. They raised £6,352—and Spurgeon, in his typical generous style, gave it all to his almshouses. Spurgeon never forgot that Bunyan wrote, "There was a man, some thought him mad, the more he gave away, the more he had." The London papers warmly commended Spurgeon for this spirit of Bunyan. All knew him and respected him for his generosity. He said, "Nobody will know until I'm dead how little C. H. Spurgeon cared for money." [11] Most all the papers had turned basically positive to Spurgeon by this time. *The Daily Telegraph*, *The Echo*, and *The Times* wrote articles eulogizing Spurgeon's personal fidelity and valuable work. "He is one of the most tremendous workers of the day," said *The Daily News*, (January 18, 1879). And Spurgeon would use the papers; he believed in advertising the Word. He said, "Advertise, for the life of business is printer's ink." Of course, religious news was current news to the Victorians.

Charles' popularity continually grew. Lithographs of Spurgeon were advertised and sold: "In best finished gold frames, 19 x 23 inches—25 shillings." Even his wife endorsed a new cooking stove called the "Patent American Kitchener." Many products advertised their wares by reference to Spurgeon. He truly had become a household name.

When the USS Trenton was at anchor in Gravesend on the Thames near London, Monday, August 11, 1879, Spurgeon came aboard and preached to a very receptive crew of American sailors. The Lord Mayor of London presided at the annual Metropolitan Tabernacle tea, May 4, 1881.

In many respects, the most explosive Sunday service in those days was June 5, 1864 when Spurgeon preached his sermon on "Baptismal Regeneration." In printed form, it sold hundreds of thousands of copies and precipitated Spurgeon's first major theological controversy. Spurgeon, as constantly seen, tenaciously clung to conservative theological views. He would allow no deviation. As seen, if a member differed theologically or morally, Spurgeon would say, "Please withdraw from the church"—and that was that. The Baptismal Regeneration conflict shall be taken up shortly.

Such were the typical services, preaching and events of Spurgeon during the dramatic middle years of his ministry in London. Services and sermons of this sort were regular fare at the Metropolitan Tabernacle. His fame went from one height to the next.

TRAVEL AND MINISTRY

During these years, travel also became a real part of the life and ministry of Spurgeon and his wife. Mrs. C.H. Spurgeon, in the *Autobiography*, devoted an entire chapter to "Some Reminiscences of Foreign Travel." It always proved a delightful time for her. She said:

> One ten minutes of time, on the St. Gothard Pass, will never be forgotten. I had walked alone, in the advance of the carriage—my beloved and Mr. Passmore being too comfortably idle to leave their seats, and, at a turn of the road, I came in sight of the grandest part of the route, the Devil's Bridge. Not a living creature was visible; the mighty masses of granite rock towered on each side of me, with the deep and savage gorge between, where the Reuss foamed and boiled, and there in the near distance were the old and the new bridges spanning the awful chasm. I had so often seen pictures of the spot, that I recognized it at once; but the reality overcame me with awe. I leaned against the side of the rocky pathway, and gave way for a moment to a feeling of utter terror and loneliness. What if the carriage should never appear round that bend of the road? What if I were really alone in that sublime but desolate place? Then a sudden reaction took place, and I felt so safe, so near to the very heart of God in the midst of His marvellous works, that, to this day, I cherish the realization I there had of the certainty of His presence, and the glory of His power. [12]

Susannah remembered the "dreamy delights" of their two visits in Venice. She said, "The 'bright of the sea' is enshrined in my memory as a creation of exceeding lovingness, glowing with all the prismatic hues of a gorgeous sunset, and enwrapped in a veil of golden mist, just as I last saw her when returning from a trip to the Island of Lido, on whose shores we had spent a most enjoyable day."

The happy couple took an interesting voyage to Hamburg and Heligoland. Susannah eulogized the day, earlier described, when Spurgeon preached in Calvin's pulpit, robed in the black Geneva gown. She said, "Oh, there was at least one wife who was proud of her husband that day!" [13] Apparently Susannah never forgot the happy days of travel with her husband. She related:

In after years, during the long, lonely months occasioned by my ill-health, memories of our tours were always fresh and fragrant, and one of the compensations of my sickness was to go over again in thought all the difficulties, and dangers, and delights we had met with on our travels; and this pleasure would be doubled when my husband could spend a little time by my couch, and the talk turned to those sunny days, and we together recalled our most amusing adventures, and laughed heartily at the blunders and mistakes we either made or mastered. Ah! There were some strange tales to tell; I think I could fill a volume with the memories of those delightful journeys. [14]

Many were the delightful times that the Spurgeons and their friends traveled through Europe, taking in the beautiful scenery of the Alps and the lovely cities of the Continent.

INCREASING ILL HEALTH

During these mid-years, Spurgeon had been increasingly absent from the Tabernacle due to ill health. In a letter to his father, October 16, 1875, he wrote, "These pains are very depressing, besides taking me away from active service." [15] Frequently, he found himself in the grips of "Great Despair," the character in *Pilgrim's Progress*. After he reached his mid-forties, his illness and seasons of depression increasingly plagued him. His inherited rheumatic gout played havoc as Bright's disease began taking its toll. In another letter he stated, "I have never lost my calm faith in God, but at times I have been so depressed that the cable has been strained to the utmost." [16] His malady cut more and more into his ministry as the years progressed. He began to take quite regular winter retreats for recuperation in Mentone on the French Riviera. These trips greatly helped, and probably prolonged his life. One can sense his virtual jubilation when feeling better after one of his bouts with illness. He wrote to his mother February 2, 1877:

I have greatly improved in this place and from tottering on my staff. I have become able to climb the mountains. Best of all my timorous mind is gathering comfort and I am much more at rest. [17]

Whenever it became necessary to be absent from his people, he constantly kept in touch with them. Charles always manifested great care for his flock. As Susannah said, "He still bore them upon his heart as much as when he was laboring in their midst. Some of the choicest letters he ever wrote to the church and congregation under his charge were sent home from foreign lands, once his thoughts flew back to the much loved house of prayer where he was wont to keep holy day with the great assembly." [18] On one journey with his wife in June, 1865, he wrote back to a member of the Tabernacle:

Bel Alp,
Canton Valais

My Dear Mrs. Bartlett,

With constant thanksgiving, I remember your work of faith and labour of love; and I pray the Lord to sustain you, and make you still a joyful 'mother in Israel.' Your heart yearns most for the souls under your care; and, therefore, when I have just thanked you with my whole heart for all you do for me and my Master's cause, and have asked your continual prayers on my behalf, I will rather write to the class than to you.

To those of them who are saved, will you present their Pastor's kindest remembrances, and say, —I beseech you to walk worthy of your high calling? Watchfulness is to be our daily spirit; we must not sleep in an enemy's land. Those who go near the brink of precipices may one day fall over them, and familiarity with sin may sooner or later lead to the commission of it; and our God alone knows the misery which a fall may cause to you and to those who love your souls. Our sisters form a numerous and influential part of the church; and when their hearts are in a thoroughly spiritual condition, they have a wonderful power for good. We want no better band of missionaries than the godly daughters, sisters, wives, and mothers in our midst. When it is well with you, pray for me, and let this be your prayer,—that I may return to you 'in the fulness of the blessing of the gospel of Christ.' I am now writing far up in the mountains; the air is cold and bracing, the view is wide and lovely; the high hills, with their snowy heads, seem just on a level with me; all is still and calm, and my body and soul are both growing well and strong. Now, in spiritual matters, I want you who belong to dear Mrs. Bartlett's class to live on the mountain, high up, near to God, far from the world, where your view of Divine truth will be clear and wide; and I want you there to grow strong and healthy in Heavenly things, that you may do wonders in Christ's Name.

To those who are unsaved, how shall I write? I must first pray,—O God, deliver them from their sins, and from Thy wrath! Last night, the lightning seemed to set the mountains on a blaze; it flashed from peak to peak, and made the clouds appear like great thrones or furnaces of fire; the terrible God was abroad, and we were awed with His presence. I could look on cheerfully, and say, 'My Father does it all'; but what must it be to have this God for your enemy? Young friends, I beseech you to consider your condition as having an omnipotent God full of anger against you for your sins. May you realize your danger, and seek His face before you feel the terror of His hand! What a sweet short sentence is that, 'God is love'! Think it over. If Satan tempts you to despair, hold it up before his face. If sins or doubts prevail, remember that 'God is love.' But do not forget that He is a consuming fire. He will either consume you or your sins,—you or your self-righteousness. Jesus felt His Father to be a consuming fire in the day when the Divine wrath fell on Him to the uttermost; if He had to endure it, what will those feel who live and die in sin? May you be led to trust Jesus with your souls now! May you all be saved! May we all meet in glory to part no more! Till then, I am,—

Your earnest minister,
C. H. Spurgeon. [19]

PRAYER MEETINGS

Spurgeon had inaugurated a young people's prayer meeting in the Tabernacle lecture hall on Monday evenings. It proved a tremendous success. The young people came in large numbers, the attendance always reached between six and seven hundred. This work received special attention by the London pastor while he was away. He would always write his beloved praying young people. One such letter was written from Paris:

Paris,
Jan. 16.

Dear Young Friends,

I have your welfare continually upon my heart, and therefore thought I would pen a few sentences to you. I was much encouraged by the prayerful attention and deep feeling which I saw last Monday in many of you. It filled me with great hope concerning you. I see that you desire to have your sins forgiven, and to escape from the wrath of God, and I am therefore rejoiced; but I pray God that the signs of grace may not end with these mere beginnings and desires. Buds are beautiful, but we cannot be satisfied with them; they are only good because blossoms often become fruit. Mere blooms on the trees, and no fruit, would be a mockery of expectation. May it not be so with you!

I am writing in my chamber in Paris at midnight. I could not sleep till I had said to you,—Put your whole trust in Jesus at once. All that you want of merit, He will give you; all that you need of help in the Heavenly life, He will bestow. Only believe Him. You who are saved, be sure to wrestle with God for the salvation of other young people, and try to make our new meeting a great means for good. You who are unawakened, we pray continually for you, for you are sleeping over hell's mouth; I can see your danger, though you do not. It is therefore time for you to awake out of sleep. I send my earnest love to you all, praying that we may meet on earth in much happiness, and then at last in Heaven for ever.

Your anxious friend,
C. H. Spurgeon [20]

From Mentone, he wrote his young people these words:

Mentone
Jan. 23.

My Dear Young Friends,

I am delighted to hear that you came together in such large numbers last Monday in my absence, for I hope it shows a real and deep anxiety among the seekers to find the Saviour, and among the saved ones to plead for others. You do not need the voice of any one man to secure your attention; the Word of the Lord Jesus, by whomsoever spoken, is life and power. It is to Him that you must turn all your thoughts. Sin has separated between you and your God, and Christ alone can bring you back to your Heavenly Father. Be sure that you remember what it cost Him to prepare the way of reconciliation; nothing but His blood could have done it, and He gave it freely, bowing His head to death upon the tree. It must have been no light matter which cost the Redeemer such a sacrifice; I beseech you, do not make light of it. Hate the sin which caused Him so much agony, and yield to the love which sustained Him under it.

I hear that in London you have had fogs and rain, here it is all flowers and summer, and the difference reminds me of the change which faith makes in the soul. While we are unbelievers, we dread the wrath of God, and walk in gloom; but when we believe, we have peace with God, and enjoy His favour, and the spring of an eternal summer has commenced. May the Spirit of God, like the soft South wind, breathe upon you, and make your hearts bloom with desires, blossom with hopes and bring forth fruits of repentance! From Jesus He proceeds, and to Jesus He leads the soul. Look to Him. Oh, look to Him; to Him alone; to Him simply; to Him at once!

Your anxious friend,
C. H. Spurgeon [21]

Spurgeon loved young people. He delighted in performing wedding ceremonies for happy Christian couples. He would counsel them on how to remain happy. He would say the husband is the head, but the wife is the neck that turns the head as she likes.

Quite naturally, Spurgeon's "first-born and most beloved," the College, received many choice letters. Again writing from Mentone, he said:

Mentone,
Saturday evening.

Beloved Brethren,

In my absence, I never cease to remember you, because I have all in my heart, as the hope of the church, and the future benefactors of the world. I trust every man is conscientiously labouring at his studies, never wasting an hour. Your time for study is so short, and so much will be required and expected of you, that I beseech you to quit yourselves like men. Every moment with you is worth a Jew's eye, and its profiting will be a hundred-fold in the future. We have to cope with no mean adversaries. Our antagonists are well equipped and well trained. Our trust is in the Lord alone, and we go forth armed only with a sling and a stone; but we must practise slinging till we can throw to a hair's-breadth, and not miss. It was no unpractised hand which smote so small a target as Goliath's brow. Do not let the devil make fools of you by suggesting that, because the Lord works, you may be idle. I do not believe it of the least among you.

Brethren, for our Lord's sake, maintain a high degree of spirituality; may the Holy Spirit enable you so to do! Live in God that you may live for God. Let the church see that her students are her picked men. I rely upon you, in my absence, to help in all meetings for prayer or revival to the utmost of your ability. Nothing would give me greater joy than to hear that, while I am away, the Lord was moving some of you to make up for my lack of service.

I am much better. Here, 'everlasting spring abides;' and though flowers wither, there are always fresh ones to fill their places. The balmy summer air is as oil to my bones.

I sent my sincere love to you all, and especially to your honored tutors, and the venerable Principal, to whom be long life, and the same to you all! My dear brother will be to you all that I could have been, and you will pray for him and also for—

Your loving friend,
C. H. Spurgeon. [22]

Of course, Charles wrote many letters to the church as a whole. On February 12, 1874, from Mentone where he had been recuperating, he wrote the following letter:

Mentone,
Feb. 12.

Beloved Friends,

By the time this letter is read to you, I shall, if the Lord will, be on my way back to you; and my prayer is that I may return 'in the fulness of the blessing of the gospel of Christ.' Very greatly have I been cheered by hearing of your prayers for me, and still more by the news of the good and great work which the Lord is doing in your midst. It is glad tidings indeed. How grateful I am that dear brethren among you at home have been so highly honoured that God has worked by them so abundantly! I rejoice in their joy. The report of conversions in the families of the members is peculiarly refreshing. God grant that not one family may be unblest!

I am myself greatly better, and very thankful that it is so, for I long to be an eye-witness and a partaker in the revival work. Oh, that it may go on till not one hearer shall remain unsaved!

Beloved friends, join all of you heartily in the work, and let none in any way damp it by unloving, unholy, or careless walking. The clouds of blessing will blow away from us if worldliness be allowed to prevail. Sin in the church will be the death of revival, or else the revival will be the death of sin. Let no one among us besmear himself with the blood of souls by a careless conversation in such solemn times as these. May the Holy Ghost quicken us all into newness and fulness of life! God bless you all! So prays—

Yours in Jesus,
C. H. Spurgeon. [23]

Spurgeon not only remembered the people at the Tabernacle on his journeys, but when his wife was home ill, and he had to travel, they wrote each other very loving letters. A classic example follows:

In 1868, my travelling days were done. Henceforth, for many years, I was a prisoner in a sick-chamber, and my beloved had to leave me when the strain of his many labours and responsibilities compelled him to seek rest far away from home. These separations were very painful to hearts so tenderly united as were ours, but we each bore our share of the sorrow as heroically as we could, and softened it as far as possible by constant correspondence. 'God bless you,' he wrote once, 'and help you to bear my absence. Better that I should be away well, than at home suffering,—better to your loving heart, I know. Do not fancy, even for a moment, that absence could make our hearts colder to each other; our attachment is now a perfect union, indissoluble for ever. My sense of your value, and experience or your goodness, are now united to the deep passion of love which was there at the first alone. Every year casts out another anchor to hold me even more firmly to you, though none was needed even from the first. May my own Lord, whose chastening hand has necessitated this absence, give you a secret inward recompense in soul, and also another recompense in the healing of the body! All my heart remains in your keeping.' [24]

Susannah never accompanied Charles on his trips to Mentone, except on the last visit at the time of his death. From Mentone, on one occasion, he wrote the following letter to Susannah back in London:

To-day while I was lying on the beach, and Mark Tapley was slyly filling our pockets with stones, and rolling Mr. Passmore over, who should walk up but Mr. McLaren, of Manchester, with whom I had a long and pleasant chat. We are to go to Monaco to-morrow together. He has three months' holiday. I am glad I have not; but I should wish I had, if I had my dear wife with me to enjoy it. Poor little soul! she must suffer while I ramble. Two clergymen have had a long talk with me this evening. It began by one saying aloud to the other, 'I hear Mr. Spurgeon has been here.' This caused a titter round the table, for I was sitting opposite to him. Mentone is charming, but not very warm. It is as I like it, and is calculated to make a sick man leap with health. How I wish you could be here! [25]

Though he seemed to enjoy himself in Mentone, he quite obviously missed his dear "Wifey."

Spurgeon was obviously also an ardent correspondent. He wrote thousands of letters, and this was before the days of dictation machines and word processors. On rare occasions Spurgeon would dictate a letter to his secretary, but that was not the usual pattern. He wrote all of his letters by hand himself, and they are valued treasures yet today. Many of his letters are still extant and make fascinating reading. In his early correspondence, his handwriting was superb and the letters long. As pressures mounted, however, his handwriting deteriorated, and the letters became shorter and shorter. During the trips abroad Spurgeon would always be accompanied by friends, his secretary, who would normally be with him, and especially his dear friend Joseph Passmore. As one views his life, it seems as though Spurgeon was rarely alone. He loved people and always surrounded himself by admirers. This does not mean that he did not have his own solitude and quiet times, but he enjoyed the company of people and rarely went anywhere by himself. If his wife or children could not be with him, he always found someone to keep him company. He had a veritable army of friends. But especially did he love to be at home with his wife and children.

HOME LIFE

During this period the new "Helensburgh House" on Nightingale Lane was completed. As previously mentioned, in 1869 the old house was pulled down and the new one built in its place. Charles always provided a happy home for his wife and their twin sons. Although the days were often marred by Susannah's illness, many happy hours were spent on Nightingale Lane. At times, Susannah, like Charles, had to leave due to ill health. Spurgeon once wrote to his father, "My poor wife is wasting to a shade." [26] But in a more positive vein, in a letter to his mother concerning Susannah's poor health, he wrote, "This hounding trouble has its bright side, and it abundantly sanctifies so that all is well." [27] Charles always cherished a very loving relationship with his sons. Family devotionals were a regular part of the Spurgeon household. Son Thomas said, "Family worship was a delightful item of each day's doings." [28] During those devotional times, others would often be invited. Once, Thomas related, "We had two fresh arrivals to morning prayers. Strangers to father, they had requested, through the waiter, admission to our worship, so a stately mother and a tall daughter from Belgrade Square were made right welcome." [29] Charles, Sr. normally took charge of the worship and conducted their seeking of the Lord in family devotions. Thomas said, "his unstudied comments, and his marvelous prayers, were an inspiration indeed. I did not wonder that requests were received for a share in this privilege." [30]

Spurgeon would often take the boys on an outing when the weather and his own health permitted. They would drive up one of the beautiful English valleys and then stroll back. They generally took their lunch, and "Old George," who was Spurgeon's personal servant in later days, would always be there to help. Spurgeon rejoiced in the good times he shared with his twin boys. Thomas said of one of these occasions, "We lunched beneath the fir trees, where meanwhile the birds were singing to us. No wonder, then, that the poetic fire burst forth, and C.H.S. gave vent to his delight in extempore rhyme. It should be perhaps explained that we had been reading Cooper together before the meal." [31]

On some of the continental travels, Spurgeon would at times get an excursion party organized and, with his boys personally host and conduct the tour. Wherever they were, the party had a joyous time. When they were off on a trip and staying in a hotel, as Thomas described it, "After dinner, there was generally an adjournment to the smoking room, where father chatted freely with the other visitors at the hotel, who were by no means loathe to exchange sentiments with the distinguished preacher. And he could discourse on almost anything. How pleased he was to meet an aged Mennonite Baptist there, an Alsatian Baron who had translated some sermons, and had come all the way from Cannes to see him and was received, one evening with due ceremony, in the private sitting room."

Thomas tells of once spending a whole day with his father and George Müller. Concerning the relationship of Spurgeon and Müller, Thomas said, "Dear father declares himself to be far better able to 'trust and be not afraid' through intercourse with Mr. Müller." [32] These small insights into the relationship Spurgeon enjoyed with his children indicate the deep affection and love he had for them and his willingness to share his very life with them. He was not only a loving husband, he was a devoted father. Mrs. Spurgeon described the family with these words, "The loving relationship existing between the dear father and his twin sons." [33] When Spurgeon died, and his son Thomas became pastor of the Tabernacle, Charles had so poured his life into his son that it was quite natural for Thomas to follow in his father's footsteps.

Many interesting experiences took place at Helensburgh House. On one occasion, a very unwelcome visitor came to the Spurgeon home. Spurgeon's hospitality was renowned, but this man was far from welcome. Actually, serious consequences could have ensued had not Spurgeon, the master of the house, handled the situation well. A man came up to the door. Charles happened to be passing the entrance hall just as the man rapped loudly at the door. Without considering who the visitor might be, Spurgeon opened the door. A wild looking man, armed with a huge stick, sprang in, slammed the door, and stood with his back against it. He blurted out in most menacing tones that he had come to kill Mr. Spurgeon. Spurgeon seemed trapped; there was no way out or no opportunity to summon any assistance. But Spurgeon, always up to the hour, said "You must mean my brother, his name is Spurgeon." Charles realized that if he would go to Croydon to find Charles' brother James, there would be opportunity for warning. "Ah," said the insane fellow, "it is the man that makes jokes that I mean to kill." Charles replied, "Oh, then you must go to my brother, for he makes jokes!" "No, no," replied the man, "I believe you are the man. Do you know the asylum at ————? That's where I live, and it takes ten men to hold me." Right then Spurgeon saw his opportunity. He drew himself up to his full height, all five feet six inches of it, but still a rather imposing figure, and shouted with his most impressive, deep, rich voice, "Ten men! That is nothing; you don't know how strong I am. *Give me that stick.*" The poor man, thoroughly cowed, handed over his weapon. Spurgeon seized it, opened the door, and almost shouted, "If you're not out of the house this very moment, I'll break every bone in your body." The man fled in fear. Of course, Spurgeon at once gave the information to the police and he was apprehended and taken back to the mental hospital. Needless to say, a near tragedy had been averted. [34]

Spurgeon enjoyed describing a further encounter that he once had with one of his neighbors on Nightingale Lane. He had been laid up for some time with a protracted and painful bout of the gout. After feeling some better, he went for a short drive hoping he would thereby gain a little strength. A neighbor came up to the carriage and pointing to Spurgeon's bandaged hand and foot, said, with scorn and contempt, "'Whom the Lord loveth, he chasteneth.' I would not have such a God as that." [35] Spurgeon said he felt his blood boil with indignation. He then answered, "I rejoice that I have such a God as that; and if He were to chasten me a thousand times worse than this, I would still love Him; yea, though he slay me, yet will I trust him." Such was Spurgeon's victorious attitude toward his deteriorating health. On another occasion, the same neighbor, in something of a better frame of mind, said to Spurgeon, "I don't believe in shutting myself up with a lot of people in a stuffy building; I like plenty of fresh air and I worship the God of nature." "Yes," replied Spurgeon, "your god is made of wood, is he not: and his worship is carried on with a great deal of noise, isn't it? I hear you at your little game before I start for the Tabernacle on a Sunday morning." The man was addicted to playing in the skittle alley, a nineteenth century game that used wooden pins. Spurgeon went on to describe this kind of attitude as, "Those men who talk about natural religion, as far as I know them, have no religion at all. I have noticed that the people who say, 'we can worship God without attending any religious service,' or believing in Jesus, do not really do so." [36]

SPURGEON'S FELLOW-LABORERS

Spurgeon produced some of his greatest works during these productive days. But no single person, by himself, could do all the research necessary and produce the mammoth amount of material that Spurgeon did. He had a valuable co-worker and personal secretary, Mr. John Lewis Keys. He worked with Spurgeon for a quarter of a century as his literary assistant. Keys was especially helpful to Spurgeon in the production of the *Treasury of David*. In the preface of Volume One, Spurgeon wrote, "The research expended on this volume would have occupied far too much of my time, had not my friend and amanuensis, Mr. John L. Keys, most diligently aided me in investigations at the British Museum, Dr. William's Library, and other treasuries of theological lore. With his help, I have ransacked books by the hundreds; often, without finding a memorable line as reward; but, at other times, with a most satisfactory result." [37] In the volumes that followed, Spurgeon constantly mentioned the value of Mr. Keys' help. All of Spurgeon's publications from 1867–1891 passed through the hand of Keys. He read all the proofs of the sermons, *The Sword and the Trowel*, almanacs, and the many books that were issued during that productive period. He was also a writer himself and contributed many articles to *The Sword and the Trowel*. Not only that, Keys spent much time in evangelistic and pastoral work at Wimbledon, Whitstable, and Streatham. Keys outlived Spurgeon by some seven years and served the preacher as a very close friend.

Spurgeon had another very able secretary, Mr. J. W. Harrald. He also worked long and hard with Spurgeon in much of his labors. Spurgeon made constant reference to him in various ways and expressed his gratitude for the invaluable service that he rendered. Harrald worked with Mrs. Spurgeon to produce the four volume classical *Autobiography* after Charles' death.

Reference has also been made to "Old George." He was Spurgeon's faithful servant for many years. He had worked for Mr. Thorne, a friend of the Spurgeon family. At Thorne's death, the butler said to Charles, "Ah, sir! I closed my old master's eyes, and now . . . (my) occupation is gone." Spurgeon replied, "Well, George, what do you say to coming to take care of me?" "Do you really mean it, sir?" asked George. "Yes, of course I do." Charles replied. "Oh! Then I'll dance for joy," exclaimed George, "for nothing would please me more, and I'll serve you faithfully as long as you will let me stay with you." [38] Spurgeon would often say that "Old George" made him think of Mr. Pickwick's Sam Weller. If anyone were to ask George what was his name, he would always answer, "George Lovejoy. Don't you know what the apostle says, 'the fruit of the spirit is love, joy'?" Every morning Spurgeon would ask, "Well, George, how are you this morning?" George's inevitable answer was, "first rate, sir, as fresh as a salt fish." Spurgeon stood as "Old George's" hero. When Spurgeon died in January, 1892, no one mourned more sincerely than "Old George." He followed Spurgeon in death in January, 1898. He was always a faithful servant. Quite clearly, Spurgeon was fortunate to be surrounded by such friends and helpers. Spurgeon lived in the setting of a loving home with a devoted wife, children who loved and cared for their father, and servants and secretaries that made his life blessed indeed. The goodness of God certainly attended the man in his entire life.

THE DULL TIME

In the midst of these extremely busy years, Spurgeon seemingly began to grow a bit stale. As Pike put it, "The ominous symptoms which are produced by overwork had begun to show themselves. Preaching had become a task and a drag rather than a pleasure; the work seemed to have lost some of its freshness, although the observers in the pews there did not appear to be any falling off of power, or of good effects following." [39] Wisely, Spurgeon took an eight week holiday. It may seem an inordinate time, but it proved to be a very refreshing experience for Charles. He came back ready to meet the work with new vigor and vitality. He was human, and had simply needed the rest.

One can well imagine how difficult it would be to fill Spurgeon's pulpit in his absence. But the work went on well, despite Charles being gone. As Pike declared, "As regard to those who would occupy the pulpit in his absence, he (Spurgeon) said: 'I had been hoping that I should receive some intimation as that given by an old lady to Dr. Leifchild. She said 'There, now, you are a good man; you are not like some preachers, who, when they go away, get dull sticks to fill their pulpit; whenever you go away, you always get a better preacher than yourself.' On the whole, all things had gone on well, however, and one who had preached most acceptably was a young man from the College, that fact yielding particular satisfaction all around." [40] Spurgeon's satisfaction abounded to discover that one of the College students had done so well during his absence. Charles apparently chose the pulpit supplies himself, as indicated by many extant letters from Spurgeon on that subject. Although he always used caution to have good pulpit supplies when he was gone, no one, of course, could really fill his preaching shoes. Still, Spurgeon felt at ease when he was away. He had his brother James at the helm in his absence. Charles once wrote James, "I know it is all right so long as you are there." It is true that whenever Spurgeon was absent for any protracted period, the funding of the various institutions would invariably fall off. But then, almost immediately after his return, the funds would flow in again and the work would flourish. Quite remarkable is the fact that, with Spurgeon's frequent travels to preach and his often being laid aside because of illness, the congregation never tired of his leadership. No one ever suggested that he should not continue as pastor, regardless of how much he had to be away. They expressed their feelings to Spurgeon when he chafed under the burden of being out of his pulpit far more often than he desired. Such was the love of the congregation for their minister.

SPURGEON AND THE BAPTISTS

During these productive years, Spurgeon constantly undertook new work, especially through the Pastors' College. For example, a new chapel was planted on Drummond Road in Bermondsey. Spurgeon laid the memorial stone August 4, 1865. The building could accommodate 600 people and was constructed at a cost of £1,500. Spurgeon himself subscribed two-thirds of this along with his people at the Tabernacle. A preaching station and a Sunday School had existed for some time in the Bermondsey area. The population growth in that general part of London began skyrocketing, thus a permanent place of worship seemed an absolute necessity. So they built. Spurgeon said:

> My object in having the chapel built in this neighborhood is a purely disinterested one. I and my congregation would be as happy in our Tabernacle, so far as we personally are concerned, if this chapel had never been completed; but when I look around and consider the spiritual destitution, I feel constrained to strive to supply the need by every means in my power. It has been said that working men would not listen to the Gospel, but I believe that is a libel on them, and I hope to see this chapel full of them, for I am sure they are attached to the Bible, and value their souls just as much as any other class. [41]

Later in the day, after the stone-laying ceremony, they set a tea at the Metropolitan Tabernacle where the pastor congratulated the people on the commencement of this significant work. Spurgeon conducted this type of church planting ministry all over the London area. As previously pointed out, many of the Baptist churches that are in London to this day are a consequence of Spurgeon's planting ministry:

> Our plan in London has been to do little where we could not do much; to open many rooms, and to start many small communities in the hope that some of them would live to become self-supporting churches . . . our building fund is of the greatest possible assistance in our good work. We have been much cheered by our success in London, and hope to sow yet more largely in the fruitful fields. [42]

By this time the College had already supplied nineteen pastors to the established London district churches alone. Moreover, eight new churches had been formed as the work grew. Not only that, ten other congregations had been planted which needed new chapels built, while preaching was carried on in seven other stations in the hopes that churches would soon be formed. Moreover, several old dying churches had been revived by the work of the students.

It must always be understood, as so often stressed, in all these multiplied activities, Spurgeon relied essentially on the prayers of his people. He well realized, as he put it, "There is a distinct connection between importunate, agonizing prayer and success."[43] He went on to emphasize:

> A minister must be upheld by his people's prayers, or what can he do . . . I beg a special interest in your prayers . . . When a diver is on the sea-bottom, he depends upon the pumps above, which sends him down air . . . I feel the fresh air coming in at every stroke of your prayer-pump.[44]

But as seen earlier, Spurgeon did not believe in long, drawn out prayers. He said, "Long prayers injure prayer meetings. Fancy a man praying for twenty minutes, and then asking God to forgive his shortcomings."[45]

On one occasion during these mid-years, the Baptist Union opened its annual session in Upton Chapel, Lambeth Road, London. Spurgeon took a leading role. At the same time, the Baptist Home Mission and the Baptist Irish Society, which for more than 50 years had been separate entities, were united. This greatly furthered the work. On the occasion of the first anniversary at Bloomesbury Chapel, Spurgeon attended and presented a message on "Home Evangelization, The Work of All the Churches." Spurgeon declared there were many towns in the country in which no Baptist witness could be found. Consequently, people of Baptist persuasion had joined other congregations. This should change. He said:

> If the Churches did more in the work of home evangelisation it would be a cure for many ills. Fuller said that his Church was in a very sad state, and that there was a deal of quarrelling till someone proposed that they should send a missionary to the heathen, and then they had no time to quarrel. If the Churches have objects before them to work for, there is not much likelihood that the mighty energy which the Baptists possess will spend itself in internal conflicts, but in the service of God. This work also will be a means of spiritual edification. There is no making a thorough soldier unless he sees some real service, and there is no hope of making advanced Christians without setting them to some earnest Christian work. The growth which comes only from meditation will be the growth of the conservatory, but if we work hard as well as pray, we shall grow so that the wintry frost will not be able to bite our root, nor touch our leaf.[46]

Spurgeon went on to say that if he were a man of wealth, he would hire someone to go out and preach the Gospel wherever he would have opportunity. Also at this same time, the aforementioned Colportage ministry at the Tabernacle began.

LEARNING FROM THE SCOTS

About this time, Spurgeon made another visit to Scotland. As always, the Scots received him well. He attended the sessions of the Free Church Assembly of Scotland. Charles learned many good things during this visit in

Scotland, things he found he could put to use at the Metropolitan Tabernacle. He was particularly struck with the systematic way in which the Free
Church organized its various enterprises. He also liked the mode in which
the printed reports were presented to the Presbyters. As a consequence, he
recommended to the Metropolitan Tabernacle that committees should be
formed to promote the circulation of literature, to see after the Sunday
School, to arrange for the establishment of a Day School, and to organize
the benevolent services. He also organized committees for foreign missions,
and another to present petitions to Parliament as occasion called for it.
Clearly, Spurgeon saw the importance of administration as he learned it
from his Scottish brethren.

As has been regularly seen, Spurgeon had a deep commitment and concern for foreign missions. In 1866 (July 30), he held a meeting at the
Metropolitan Tabernacle as a farewell service for missionaries who were
about to take up their service in India. Spurgeon said that he wanted to see
the great heroic age of missions once again return. Everyone desired to see
great examples of self-sacrifice that would stir the hearts of the people.
Spurgeon said:

> Some have spoken of the astonishing labours of such men as Francis Xavier,
> and of the Jesuits of China, whose zeal was truly apostolic. I think that if
> something rare were done—something so rash as to astonish people, as in the
> case of poor rash Carey—that a greater blessing might accompany our mis-
> sionary work. There is a feeling growing up in many churches—I only say
> what others have stated—that there is less preaching by missionaries than in
> former times. Translations, writing tracts, and teaching knowledge are, I con-
> sider, subordinate things to preaching the Gospel. The pulpit is, I consider, the
> great Thermopylae of Christendom, and, so I am accustomed to say to the
> students of the College, 'If you cannot preach, you can do nothing.' I venture
> to say that because missionaries are apt to forget it. [47]

Spurgeon loved to see the work thrive over Europe. In August, 1867,
Charles sailed to Hamburg and opened a new chapel for John Oncken, the
great German church planter. Oncken became known as "The Apostle of the
Continent." The event even drew visitors from America and several European countries. A conference was held in connection with the new chapel
opening and the entire affair received wide acclaim. A commemorative cup
was produced, and one can still be found in the archives of Spurgeon's
College in London.

About that time, another cholera epidemic broke out in London similar to that which took place in Spurgeon's early days. The unsanitary
conditions and the crowded squalor of London spread the plague and
ravished the city. One Sunday, during the height of the epidemic, Spurgeon preached on Amos 3:3-6. He stated that not every affliction should
be seen as a judgment sent by God. He said that he did not believe in

judgments coming upon particular persons except in extraordinary cases. He felt that individuals were rewarded or punished in the next life. But, as there would be no nations *per se* in the future life, countries were punished in this age.

Toward the end of the summer of the same year, the congregation which had been left and were still meeting at the New Park Street Chapel, closed down the building. There had been those who so loved the old building they would not move to the new Metropolitan Tabernacle. They had found Mr. George Kew to conduct their service, but he left for another field of ministry, so the old chapel finally closed its doors. As seen earlier, it was such an unsavory part of London that it proved very difficult to maintain the work unless they had another Spurgeon. The congregation that had filled the building during Spurgeon's early days had again dwindled to a very small group of people. The sale of the property provided funds for the establishment of a Day School and the almshouses, as previously seen.

Unusual Events

Unusual things would happen to Spurgeon as his notoriety spread. One day as he was walking down the street, he tells us, "I remember, in the streets of London, a man took off his hat and bowed to me—'the Reverend Mr. Spurgeon; a great humbug.' I took off my hat, too, and said, 'I am obliged to you, sir, that I am great at anything.'" [48]

Spurgeon felt he had much in common with the Society of Friends, or the Quakers. He never forgot that his ancestor, Job Spurgeon, a member of the Society, suffered for conscience's sake in Chelmsford Jail during one of the severe winters of the seventeenth century. That account can be seen in Chapter Three. Nonetheless, Spurgeon became somewhat disturbed that the Society of Friends had not maintained all of the early zeal of their Puritan forefathers and the spiritual principles which George Fox had so ably exemplified. Spurgeon had an opportunity of doing something about it when asked to speak at the Quaker Institute at Bishop's Gate Street. At the time of the service, the crowds overflowed the building. Mr. Charles Gilpin, a member of Parliament, presided at the meeting. Lord Houghton and W. E. Foster, another member of Parliament, attended. Many of the leading members of the Quaker denomination had also assembled.

In typical Quaker fashion, a time for silent prayer was given, and then the chairman said that he hoped Mr. Spurgeon fully realized what dedicated men of God George Fox and his followers were. Spurgeon, feeling very much at home, confessed to them he had held Fox in great admiration and had long desired to speak to them. He said he did not wish to deliver an ordinary lecture, but to speak informally. They all expected Spurgeon to give a lecture on George Fox, a lecture he had given in various places before. But he gave a stirring appeal to the Friends to bear a stronger testimony for Christ in the world. The Friends received him well and a heart's desire of Spurgeon had been fulfilled.

MORE BAPTIST WORK

The Baptists of Great Britain during these productive years had about 2,400 churches and a quarter of a million members. Still, the general condition concerning the Baptist work and leadership was "preeminently unsatisfactory." [49] The problem centered on a serious lack of able leaders. Few apparently cared to take a leadership role in the developing Union. The general situation even precipitated the curtailing of some operations of the Baptist Missionary Society in India. The age-old problem of lack of funds raised its head. *The Freeman* said, "There are voices in our midst which would ring through the land, but which are silent except to their own congregations. There are men whom we should all gladly follow, but they carry no standard, and utter no call. Almost the only exception to this statement is Mr. Spurgeon." [50] This raises the question, could Spurgeon take the lead and make a contribution to the development of the denomination at large? *The Freeman*, very positive to the idea, wrote:

> By his wondrous popularity and wondrous power—aided, as we believe, by much of the Divine Grace—Mr. Spurgeon has obtained a following not only in London, but throughout the land. His voice is heard by thousands every Sunday; his written words are read by hundreds of thousands every week. But, through the peculiarity of his position, Mr. Spurgeon has hitherto stood much alone. He is the head of a denomination within a denomination. He takes little part in the concerns of the Baptist body as such. We believe this is not Mr. Spurgeon's own desire. If we are not mistaken, he has expressed, again and again, the desire to unite more heartily with his brethren. Why should he not do so? Is there anything that keeps him apart from the Baptist body in spite of himself? Truly, he has much to do already; but there is no man who could do more to rouse the body as a whole to action, no man who would be welcomed more cordially by the denomination generally as a counsellor and a brother beloved. If *The Freeman* could do anything to bring Mr. Spurgeon and the Baptist body generally in cordial and loving union and co-operation, the day on which such union was effected would be to its conductors one of the proudest of their lives. [51]

In the Autumn meeting of the Baptist Union in 1863, held at Bradford, a general consensus prevailed among the pastors and people that the most pressing need was for more unity; in this way alone could concerted action be undertaken to develop the cause of Christ through Baptist work. At the same time, all expressed sympathy for the Baptists on the Continent who in certain places suffered persecution. In Saxony, for example, many of the Baptists had been exposed to a series of bitter and unrelenting persecutions and hostilities from the Lutheran clergy. Often their assemblies had actually been dispersed and the pastor arrested, treated like a felon, and had personal property confiscated. Delegates raised the question how Baptist brothers under pressure might be helped. Some wanted to leave the situation primarily in the hands of the Evangelical Alliance, but Spurgeon came to the fore and strongly advocated the drawing up of a petition to be sent directly from the Baptist Union to the King of Saxony. Charles urged the Baptists to implore the king to stop the Lutheran pastors from their designs. Spurgeon increasingly took a leading role in Baptist affairs.

In the Bradford meeting, Spurgeon preached at St. George's Hall, on the Thursday evening session, October 12, on Psalm 52:16, "When the Lord shall build up Zion, he shall appear in His Glory." The building was filled and "the crush for admittance was tremendous." [52] Everyone was deeply impressed and began to recognize the importance of a stronger union among the Baptists. *The Freeman* proved right, Spurgeon could do the job.

THE LONDON BAPTIST ASSOCIATION

In the fall of the same year, London Baptists put in motion a plan for the reorganization of the London Baptist Association. In this, Spurgeon took a high profile. Spurgeon's commitment to the new Association brought a great amount of satisfaction to many people. It was said:

> There are but few amongst us who will not remember the old Association of Baptist churches in the Metropolis, an Association which for many years did some good, until at last, through sheer inanition, it died out; killed, because at length it ceased to find anything else to do. During the years which have intervened since then, the process of isolation has been working steadily and disastrously among us, until at length the Baptists in London had seemed to become utterly powerless for any concerted action, and, what is worse still, for any mutual sympathy. [53]

To end the dismal scene, Spurgeon sent a circular letter, inviting the cooperation of all willing Baptists to come together and form a totally new Association. Three meetings were scheduled at the Metropolitan Tabernacle for this purpose. The first meeting was designed for pastors only. They would discuss the articles of the Association. The second meeting would include both pastors and deacons, who together would further discuss the decisions made by the pastors in the first meeting. This was to be followed by a general meeting of all concerned Baptists for prayer. Eighty pastors attended the primary meeting and Spurgeon presided at the devotional service that preceded the business. An excellent spirit prevailed. *The Freeman* said:

> The brethren assembled represented well nigh every shade of opinion amongst us, although, if any party predominated, we should say that it was that of our

strict communion brethren. Still, it was most apparent that the ruling which of all present was to give as little place as possible to differences of opinion, and rather to find out the common basis on which they could practically agree. [54]

The pastors at the first meeting agreed that the London Baptists had been characterized essentially by disunion, and that the time had come to end it and replace it all with something far better. Mr. Lewis, pastor of Westbourne Grove Chapel, presented a basic program for a new Association. The primary philosophy of the new organization, according to Lewis, must be the cultivation of brotherly love, and to advance the cause of Christ in the general London area, one new chapel should be built each year. Lewis further proposed that ministers, members, and delegates assemble quarterly, and the first gathering each year would be designated as the annual meeting. If a church had less than 250 members, they could send one delegate. After that, two delegates could be sent, and the large churches were allowed one representative for every 250 members. The president was to be elected annually, and the expenses handled through subscriptions. *The Freeman* wrote, in a very positive vein, "We are thankful, too, that the basis of this new Association is so broad. It does not rest on the technicalities of the creed, but simply on the wide basis of evangelical sentiment." [55]

No one worked harder for the new Association than Spurgeon. His addresses at the meetings, speaking in favor of the new Association, were received with enthusiasm. Spurgeon became president of the Association in 1869. Thus the London Baptist Association was organized and has flourished until the present time. Spurgeon was a Baptist and he threw himself into the development of the denomination. The contribution of Spurgeon and his significant work is incalculable.

CONTINUING INNOVATIVE EVENTS

During these productive years Spurgeon continued his travels. In November, he journeyed to Newcastle and preached in a large assembly in the Town Hall. The pastor of the sponsoring chapel was the Rev. Carr. The congregation was in the process of building a new church building, the second congregation that Carr had been instrumental in organizing in Newcastle in a four-year period. When Spurgeon preached to the people in the Town Hall, he challenged them to give to the building fund. He gave £400 himself; such was the magnanimous spirit of the London pastor. Some years later Carr became identified with the work of the Metropolitan Tabernacle.

The same year, on two successive Friday evenings, the famous preacher, Dr. Joseph Parker, gave two lectures at the Metropolitan Tabernacle. Spurgeon occupied the chair on each occasion. Parker first lectured on "Nonconformity in Relation to the Book of Common Prayer." His second lecture struck the theme, "Reasons for a Nonconformist Aggressive Policy." Parker had given these lectures before and had caused a stir in different parts of the country and in Scotland. The Metropolitan Tabernacle folks received him well.

The same year saw a stir among those turned to eschatological ideas. Somehow or other, the word spread that the end of the world was coming and would occur in that very year. Tracts had been produced and many opinions expressed. A rumor made the rounds that the tracts had been written by Spurgeon. Someone sent the tracts to the Metropolitan Tabernacle pastor and asked whether he had been the responsible author. At a meeting in the Tabernacle, he gave his answer:

> You will hear of me in Bedlam when you ever hear such rubbish as that from me. The Lord may come in 1866, and I shall be glad to see Him; but I do not believe He will, and the reason why I do not believe He will is, because all these twopenny-half-penny false prophets say He will. If they said that He would not come, I should begin to think He would; but, inasmuch as they are all crying out as one man that He will come in 1866 or 1867, I am inclined to think He will not arrive at any such time. It seems to me that there are a great many prophecies which must be fulfilled before the coming of Christ, which will not be fulfilled within the next twelve months; and I prefer to stand in the position of a man who knows neither the day nor the hour in which the Son of man cometh, looking always for His appearing, but never interfering with those dates and figures which seem to me to be only proper amusement for young ladies who have nothing else to do, and who take to that instead of reading novels, and for certain divines who have exhausted their stock of knowledge about sound doctrine, and therefore try to gain a little ephemeral popularity by shuffling texts of Scripture, as the Norwood gipsies shuffled cards in days gone by. [56]

Money-raising schemes for various causes took innovative turns. For example, to reflect back a few years, during three days of the Christmas week (1865), a large bazaar was held at the Metropolitan Tabernacle for the purpose of building new chapels in and around London. The very first day of the bazaar, seventeen hundred persons visited the various rooms and displays. The receipts of the first two days amounted to over £800, which was a large amount of money in those days.

An annual meeting was always held at the Tabernacle and all looked forward to it as a great occasion. During these years, up to 1,500 people would come in the afternoon to the teas. The current expenses and budget matters would be shared with the congregation by "Father" Olney.

From time to time, a series of revival meetings would be held at the Tabernacle. This proved to be especially effective among the younger people of the Tabernacle.

The newly formed London Baptist Association meeting was held in Bloomsbury Chapel following its inauguration. At this particular time, sixty-four churches were represented. Spurgeon preached and the people heard him gladly. The very positive attitude concerning the new Association continued to grow as Spurgeon took a leading role.

Reports would be given regularly concerning the work of the College in these years. For example, during the second Conference of the College, the members of the College and interested people assembled at Upton Chapel on Lambeth Road. President Spurgeon gave the annual address, and in the evening about 400 friends, who were subscribers to the Pastors' College, were invited to tea and supper at the Tabernacle. The accounts for the year were presented and it was discovered that about £4400 had been expended in the twelve months, of which £1600 had been contributed through the weekly offerings at the Tabernacle. Spurgeon reported that all the funds had come in purely spontaneously as he had never intended to have a roll of subscribers upon whom he could depend. The *Christian World*, March 16, 1866 gave the following report:

> Believing it to be God's work, they looked prayerfully and with confidence to Him to send the means necessary for its maintenance and prosecution, assured that when these failed the time would have come for giving it up. The funds had at times been very low, but never wholly exhausted. The amounts received had been spent in the most economical manner possible: chiefly upon the students' board, and in the purchase of books for their use. Mr. Spurgeon reminded the meeting that there were charges in connection with this College not incurred by any other. It sometimes happened, for example, that students had to be clothed as well as fed and educated; while, beyond the limits of the College proper, large evening classes were conducted, into which any Christian young man in business might enter and receive a good education free of all cost, except, perhaps, in the matter of elementary books. From these classes many of the College students had been obtained. Proceeding to specify the settlements of students during the year, Mr. Spurgeon mentioned the names of no less than a score of young men who had gone forth, either to gather new congregations or to revive old and almost defunct Churches, and who had met with success that in several cases seemed perfectly marvellous, and in nearly all exceedingly gratifying. It was pointed out, moreover, that the most rigid discipline is exercised in respect of the students, and that men who discover unfitness for the ministry, in respect either of their talents or characters, are dismissed. Mr. Spurgeon deeply regretted to say that some who had turned out badly were sent to him with the strongest recommendations, and that others whose aspirations for the ministry were discouraged and repressed by their pastors and the Churches to which they belonged, had proved themselves to be divinely called to the work. He begged that ministers and gentlemen would never recommend to him any young man about whose character and qualifications they had the least doubt, or unless they knew him thoroughly. To do otherwise was to commit a grievous wrong, and that in many ways. Testimoni-

als ought to be sacred things, and not signed, as they often were, on mere hearsay evidence. Regarding the Chapel-Building Fund started two years ago, to which £5,000 was to be paid in during five years, to be lent out without interest, £2,500 had been received, and the whole of it lent; and this was not more than half the sum that could be so employed with excellent effect, if it could be obtained. [57]

Mrs. Bondit's Sunday School class continued to grow at a good rate. She had started with only three and it had grown to over seven hundred. It had been in service for several years, and was increasingly valued by the pastor. He said it exemplified "one of the most remarkable classes of modern growth." [58] The members regularly contributed funds to the College and once presented the pastor with a personal gift of £100. Of course, Spurgeon gave it to the College.

As the years progressed, so did the work at the Tabernacle; all the various ministries flourished. The London Baptist Association continued to grow. In the second year of its life, the annual meeting was held at the Tabernacle and all the representatives were entertained by Spurgeon and his people. Spurgeon lamented the fact that in the year 1867, only 1,700 had been added to the churches of London. The number of members belonging to all the churches of the Association was approximately 23,000. Spurgeon said, "I earnestly hope that our increase will be much greater next year, and that the Holy Spirit's influence will be manifestly felt, both by ministers and deacons, and churches and congregations." [59]

The same year saw an exceptionally heavy gale sweep across the south of England. The Stockwell Orphanage received severe damage when one large wooden building, a playroom for the boys, collapsed. The structure had cost about £600 to erect, and a larger amount would be needed to rebuild. *The Morning Star*, a local paper stated, "We desire that this heavy blow upon a most excellent institution will awaken public sympathy, and that Mr. Spurgeon's good work may not be hindered." The paper's wish was realized by the faith and generosity of God's people. They soon met the loss that came as a result of the storm.

These types of ministries and services continued throughout the years and probably comprised the most productive period of Spurgeon's life. It seems almost incredible that a man, whose health began to fail and whose wife had become a semi-invalid, could accomplish all that he did. The hand of the Spirit of God rested powerfully upon Charles Haddon Spurgeon.

During this time, as mentioned, Spurgeon preached his famous Baptismal Regeneration sermon. It sparked his first major controversy. He had gone through a very controversial time with the media in his early days in London. But the Baptismal Regeneration Controversy ballooned into major proportions. That story must be told in some detail.

SPURGEON THE CONTROVERSIALIST

In many senses of the word, Spurgeon had become very accustomed to controversy; he encountered opposition at virtually every turn of the road. As a novice preacher, when he came to the New Park Street Baptist Church, he immediately found himself thrust into a major conflict with the media. The conflict and controversy with the press, secular and sacred, has been well documented in an earlier chapter. But the trying time put a bit of steel in his back and probably prepared him for more major conflicts. Not only that, a running theological debate constantly dogged his heels. The hyper-Calvinists on the one hand would not receive him because of his fervent preaching of the Gospel, especially as he gave emphasis to the plea for decisions for Christ. But the Arminians, and even the more moderate Calvinists, rejected him because he did give theological assent to the traditional five points of Calvinism. Misunderstanding abounded. The Belfast *Daily Mercury*, January 13, 1857, declared Spurgeon guilty of "enforcing the sternest and most repulsive form of an ultra-Calvinism . . . his doctrines limit the benefit of the Gospel to the favored few." [60] The *Daily News* reported, in September 1856, "His doctrine is not new, on the contrary, it is nothing more than old Calvinism revived." [61] Spurgeon evaluated his own beliefs in the following words:

> There is no soul living who holds more firmly to the doctrines of grace than I do, and if any man asks me whether I am ashamed to be called a Calvinist, I answer—I wish to be called nothing but a Christian—but if you ask me, do I hold the doctrinal views which were held by John Calvin, I reply, I do in the main hold them, and rejoice to avow it. [62]

Yet, at the same time, he pleaded with people to come to Christ like a fervent Arminian. He came to Christ himself in that context. Consequently, the high-Calvinists would not have him nor would the freewill Arminians. So the theological battle raged on. The only place in which Spurgeon found no controversy seemed to be among his own people. After the first few skirmishes with his deacons and leaders over enlarging the New Park Street Chapel and the launching of the Tabernacle, he had several wonderful decades of peace and harmony with his congregation. But outside those circles, conflict plagued him. Some of the battles, it must be granted, were of his own doing. After all, he said, "Men who conquer go in for attack." [63] Attack he did. Yet, he went through those early encounters relatively unscathed.

SMALL SKIRMISHES

As Spurgeon's ministry continued to develop in London, he found himself embroiled in another conflict, the Rivulet Controversy. In November

1855, a small volume of hymns was published entitled, *Hymns for Heart and Voice, The Rivulet,* by Thomas Toke Lynch, pastor of a small chapel on Grafton Street, London. Lynch was 37 at the time, and he had been a regular contributor to *The Christian Spectator* magazine. He had domestic problems and found much solace in composing his poems in *The Rivulet.*

Few paid much attention to the new hymnal until James Grant reviewed it in *The Morning Advertiser.* Grant wrote, "It is with regret and pain we are compelled to say . . . there is not from beginning to end, one particle of vital religion or evangelical piety in it."[64] Then a rash of articles raised by Grant's review hit the press.

Campbell of *The British Banner* said, "*The Rivulet* (is) . . . the most unspiritual publication of the kind in the English language." Campbell wrote "Seven Letters," addressing them to "Principals and Professors of Independent and Baptist Colleges in England," saying there was less evangelical truth in *The Rivulet* than in the hymns used by the Unitarians.

Charles Spurgeon made few, if any, verbal remarks, but he entered the fray by writing in *The Christian Cabinet.* Strangely, *The Christian Cabinet* had previously reviewed *The Rivulet* in a favorable light before Spurgeon's articles. Of these hymns Spurgeon said, "Perhaps the hymns are not the fair things that they seem." He said they were like mermaids with glistening eyes, but a fishy body and a snaky tail. The heart of the Gospel actually became the issue in the controversy as far as Spurgeon was concerned. But that always became the core of the issue for the Metropolitan pastor.

People forgot about *The Rivulet* hymnbook in itself; it got lost in the battle to show what the true elements of the Gospel were. Thus one said, "the agitation has proved a mighty impetus to the ministry, the cardinal elements of the Gospel have had more prominence than for many years."[65] One pastor said, "Never did I feel so concerned clearly and unmistakably to set forth the atoning sacrifice of Christ in all its fulness as now."[66] So perhaps truth did gain in it after all. At any rate, the controversy faded away and evangelicalism had its say.

Four years after the Rivulet Controversy, Spurgeon took on an opponent who served a nearby church in London, J. Baldwin Brown, pastor of the Clayland Chapel and later the Brixton Independent Church. In 1859, Brown published a book of sermons under the title *The Divine Life in Man.* It caused a mini-uproar in British Nonconformity. After its publication, evangelical pastors, leaders, and knowledgeable laymen came to the conclusion that Brown was a disciple of Maurice and "unsound upon the doctrine of the atonement."[67] J. Howard Hinton, editor of the *Baptist Magazine,* stated:

> To my own conviction, I am pleading for vital Evangelical truth—for the truth of God, and for the souls of men. I speak because I would feign contribute somewhat, however little, to withstand what I take to be the first open inroad,

into English evangelical Nonconformist churches, and of a theology fatally deficient in the truth and power of the Gospel. [68]

The widely read journal of the Baptists in England, *The Freeman*, put a somewhat more favorable turn to Baldwin Brown's writings. This threw *The Freeman* in opposition to Hinton's article in the *Baptist Magazine*. A swift reaction to *The Freeman* arose and written protests came from several leading ministers of the Baptist Union. Seven different men, Spurgeon being one of them, signed their names to the following letter addressed to *The Freeman*:

> Mr. Hinton has rendered a timely and valuable service to Evangelical Christianity by his animadversions on those portions of Mr. Brown's book and, for our part, we thank God that our brother's pen has been so well and so ably employed. We are no more lovers of controversy in the Church than is your reviewer, but if errors subversive to the Gospel are advocated by some of her ministers, it is the duty of others to withstand them; and we honor Mr. Hinton, that at a period of life when he might be naturally disastrous of repose, he has stepped forward in the vindication and defense of some of the vital doctrines of the faith. [69]

Spurgeon, now well into his London ministry, preached a sermon on April 15, 1860, which dealt with the issue of the hour:

> I have often thought, that the best answer to the new theology is, that the true Gospel was always preached to the poor . . . I am sure that the poor will never learn the Gospel of these new divines, for they cannot make head or tail of it; nor will the rich either. After you have read one of their volumes . . . it sours your temper, it makes you feel angry, to see the precious things of God trodden underfoot . . . we can allow a thousand opinions in the world, but that which infringes upon the doctrines of a covenant salvation, through the impudent righteousness of our Lord Jesus Christ—against that we must, and will, enter our hearty and solemn protest, as long as God spares us. [70]

On May 21, 1860, Spurgeon shot his final barb in the controversy in a lengthy letter addressed to two major newspapers. In it he chided *The Freeman* for its self-professed role as the "organ" or representative of the Baptist denomination. Spurgeon wanted the record straight that the Baptist journal did not speak for him, and hopefully not for the majority of the Baptist Union on the Brown issue. What upset Spurgeon the most rested in the fact that the editors of *The Freeman* seemed to regard as trivial a serious concern expressed by the six other ministers and himself. Moreover, those signing the statement were leaders in the denomination. Of the seven men who signed the letter, four became presidents of the Baptist Union and two were future executive secretaries of the denomination. Spurgeon also expressed concern that those outside his own Baptist circles might be damaged. He was deadly fearful of the "new school theology," which Brown seemed to espouse.

About the same time, another book of significance was published entitled *Essays and Reviews*. It too advocated the "new theology," that is, theological liberalism. Although the evangelical establishment by and large rejected the book, it did prophetically point to the fact that this new approach had begun to gain ground. By the end of the century, many evangelicals had been influenced by the "new theology." Spurgeon began to grow suspicious that the Baptist Union itself may not be completely free of this new thought. In many senses of the word, the "Divine Life in Man" Controversy foreshadowed Spurgeon's most devastating encounter with the Baptist Union, the famous Down Grade Controversy.

Another controversy that should be briefly surveyed is the so-called "Slavery Question Controversy," alluded to earlier. This did not occur in Spurgeon's own country, but rather in America. It has already been pointed out that Spurgeon's sermons sold very well in the United States. In 1860, the same year as the Divine Life in Man Controversy, an interesting event took place at the New Park Street Church during a midweek prayer service. A fugitive slave from South Carolina, John Andrew Jackson, shared his testimony concerning his sufferings and subsequent escape from slavery. The congregation sat enthralled for over an hour. When Jackson finished his testimony, as one put it, "the excitement was white-hot." [71] Spurgeon jumped on his feet and passionately declared:

> Slavery is the foulest blot that ever stained a national escutcheon, and may have to be washed out with blood. America is in many respects a glorious country, but it may be necessary to teach her some wholesome lessons at the point of the bayonet—to carve freedom into her with the Bowie knife or send it home to heart with revolvers. Better far should it come to this issue, that north and south should be rent asunder, and the states of the union shivered into a thousand fragments, than that slavery should be permitted to continue. [72]

Spurgeon went on to say:

> Some American divines seemed to regard it, indeed, with wonderful complacency. They have so accustomed themselves to wrap it up in soft phrases that they lose sight of its real character. They call it a "peculiar institution," until they forget in what its particularity consists. It is, indeed, a peculiar institution, just as the devil is a peculiar angel, and as hell is a peculiarly hot place. For my part, I hold such miserable tampering with sin in abhorrence, and can hold no communion of any sort with those who are guilty of it. [73]

As could be imagined, many tried to get Spurgeon to tone down his rhetoric. They realized that income on sermon sales from the States would be greatly hindered. But Spurgeon, tenacious to the end, would not retract any of his statements. As previously seen, American publishers began to edit his sermons, removing all references to slavery. Not only that, they also removed passages relating to open communion, as many evangelical

Americans, especially Landmark Southern Baptists, practiced "closed communion," that is, in the church's observance of the Lord's Supper, only those who belonged to the local congregation could participate. Rumors began to circulate in the United States that Spurgeon had perhaps changed his thinking from what they had read earlier. Henry Ward Beecher, famous pastor in New York, knowing what was actually happening, wrote Spurgeon demanding that the truth be known. Spurgeon had no idea that such editing had been taking place without his permission. When thus asked to clarify himself on the issue, he wrote specifically to papers in America to let his convictions be fully known and understood. He was further urged by his good friend, Dr. Campbell of the *Baptist Banner*, to write "a thunderbolt" on the subject. He responded by composing a "redhot letter." [74] Spurgeon addressed the letter to the *Watchman and Reflector*. In it he said:

> I do from my inmost soul detest slavery anywhere and everywhere, and although I commune at the Lord's Table with men of all creeds, yet with a slaveholder I have no fellowship of any kind or sort. Whenever one has called upon me, I have considered it my duty to express my detestation of his wickedness, and would as soon think of receiving a murderer into the church or into any sort of fellowship as a man stealer. Nevertheless, as I have preached in London and not in New York, I have seldom made any allusion to slavery in my sermons. [75]

Spurgeon's letter was printed in many American journals, and the prophecies that American sales would be drastically reduced came to pass. The American press began to abuse him with the same vehemence the London press had heaped upon him in his early years. The old South, especially embittered, either deleted or totally boycotted anything referring to Spurgeon. Scathing letters and even threats of violence were sent to him. Effigies of Spurgeon were burned in public and his books set ablaze in many Southern bonfires. A report from Boston declared:

> Our Baptist papers are overflowing with indignation, and call on all publishers and booksellers to banish the books of your worthy young friend from their countries. . . . The poor slave-holders are at their wits' end, and know not what to do to save their doomed system. The Montgomery Mail says the Vigilante Committee at that place is engaged in burning dangerous books, and that two volumes of Spurgeon's Sermons have been contributed to their bonfires.[76]

Spurgeon's financial loss was quite considerable, but he did not change his attitude or rhetoric one iota. After the Civil War, Spurgeon's sermon sales began to rise again in America. Of course, Spurgeon's stand on the slavery issue was typical of British evangelicals. But it is correct to say that none proved to be more outspoken than he.

THE BAPTIST MISSIONARY SOCIETY DISAGREEMENT

During these days he even fell into conflict with his own Baptist Union. Spurgeon got into an ongoing debate with the Baptist Missionary Society. The controversy centered around differing views on how to raise funds. In 1863, the Baptist Missionary Society slipped into a financial bog. The Society had to curtail some of its operations in India through lack of sufficient funds. Consequently, they turned to Spurgeon to seek his support. But they soon discovered that Spurgeon was dissatisfied with the organization. The Society sent a deputation to the Tabernacle in an attempt to discover Spurgeon's complaints. In a lengthy response to the inquiry of the Baptist Missionary Society, Charles cited four reasons for his disagreement with their approach to foreign missions. First, he believed that funds should only be raised through faith, thus he opposed the Society's voluntary subscription plans. Secondly, he held that the churches, rather than the Society, should be directly responsible for the actual sending out of missionaries. Thirdly, he argued that disunity among the Baptist Missionary Society's leadership seriously hindered the work; and fourthly, he criticized the basis of membership in the Society. Membership rested purely on a financial basis and had no relationship to the spiritual vitality of the members.

The Baptist Missionary Society invited Spurgeon to a meeting of the Society where he could present his objections in person. He spoke in detail on the four points he had raised. A long deliberation followed and the committee of the Baptist Missionary Society finally agreed to consider one of Spurgeon's complaints, the one dealing with qualifications for membership. Prior to Spurgeon's issuance of disagreement, all persons who would subscribe ten shillings and six pence a year were considered members of the Society. Spurgeon said, "The devil himself might be a member on such terms."[77] The committee recommended that a change be made and the qualifications for membership should read, "all persons professing themselves as Christians subscribing ten shillings and six pence a year . . . are considered as members thereof."[78] When the resolution from the committee was put before the membership they amended it further by adding the words, "concurring in evangelical principles and objects of the Society."[79] The general committee met the following day, on April 9, 1864, and someone proposed a third formula for adoption. They suggested the word "evangelical" be dropped from the qualification of membership and a more nebulous phrase injected, stating only "all persons concurring in the religious principles and objects of the Society."[80] The final fallout? The expression "Christian profession" became only "concurrence in religious principles." Spurgeon hardly won that particular battle.

Spurgeon made a public appeal when he addressed the Baptist Missionary Society's Annual meeting April 28 of that year. He stood up and attempted to resurrect something of the vision of William Carey. He declared, "We are to depend for our success on him who has bidden us go and teach all nations, baptizing them in the name of the Father and of the Son and of the Holy Ghost."[81] He attempted to challenge Baptist church members concerning their individual responsibility for supporting missionaries. He said to the gathering:

> If you could see my heart, you would see nothing in it but the purest love of this Society, even when I say everything about its faults. It is because I love the Society that I want to see a more thorough revival of individual sense of responsibility. To whom did Christ give his commission? Not to a Society, but to individuals. [82]

Spurgeon's message received tumultuous applause.

Nothing of much importance happened for a year or more, but in the general meeting of the Society in April of 1866, a motion was made by William Landels, and was seconded by C. H. Spurgeon. It read:

> The following persons shall be considered members, namely the pastors of churches making an annual contribution, ministers who collect annually, and all Christian persons concurring in the objects of the Society who are donors of ten pounds and upwards, or subscribers of ten shillings and six pence annually to its funds. [83]

So out of the four things that Spurgeon wanted to see changed in the work of the Baptist Missionary Society only one really got any direct consideration or attention. Nonetheless, Spurgeon seemed to be reasonably satisfied and in 1867 became a member of the Baptist Missionary Society general committee. Spurgeon's primary concern "that the BMS should be seen to be the missionary agency of the churches of the Baptist denomination, and not a mere voluntary society ruled by its subscribers,"[84] saw some realization.

Needless to say, Spurgeon had become accustomed to conflict before the first really major controversy erupted, the Baptismal Regeneration Controversy.

THE BAPTISMAL REGENERATION CONTROVERSY

In 1864, one of the supreme conflicts of Spurgeon's life erupted. He confronted the Church of England over basic Anglican dogma concerning baptism and regeneration. The general scenario is well depicted in these words:

> In 1864, the Rev. C.H. Spurgeon threw down the gauntlet in defiance to the Church of England upon the point of infant baptism and regeneration; when Presto! such a theological battle ensued as was never before seen or heard of. The whole religious world of London flung itself into it; the press groaned under the infliction; the pamphlets which followed, pro and con, in prose and verse, serious and burlesque, being almost innumerable. [85]

It all began Sunday morning June 5, 1864 at the Metropolitan Tabernacle. On that Lord's day Spurgeon preached his "best-selling" sermon entitled "Baptismal Regeneration." In his message he aimed pointedly at two
Anglican issues which he considered threats to the essential truth of the
Gospel. One: he reacted to the official Church of England contention that
the spiritual regeneration of infants came about through "the sacrament of
baptism"; the Established Church's confessional statement in the Book of
Common Prayer actually did declare such a view. Two: he spoke against
what he considered the hypocrisy of evangelical Anglicans who actually
rejected this doctrine, but continued to utilize the Book of Common Prayer.
To understand the full dynamics of the conflagration Spurgeon sparked, it
will be wise to explore some contributing elements which led to his controversial and explosive sermon.

THE BACKGROUND

Actually, the debate over baptismal regeneration was not something that
the Anglican church had ever addressed before Spurgeon's vehement outburst. Some fifteen or twenty years before Spurgeon precipitated the Baptism Controversy, Rev. George Gorham, an Anglican pastor, asked to be
moved from his parish in Cornwall to another locale. He felt that his present
parish did not afford adequate educational opportunities for his children. In
August, 1847, an official offered him the parish of Brampford Speake, a
small farming community of approximately 400 people near Exeter. This
arrangement had been engineered by the Lord Chancellor, Lord Cottingham.
He served as the governmental authority responsible for certain relocations in
the Established Church.

Henry Phillpotts, the Bishop of Exeter, however, resisted the move and
refused to countersign the proposal as the ecclesiastical authority in that
particular area. Phillpotts had the reputation of being a high-Anglican, and
Gorham was reputed to hold solid evangelical views. Therefore, Phillpotts
refused to institute Gorham until he had been "properly examined." Consequently, Gorham endured fifty-two hours of written and oral examinations
on the Prayer Book; a most unusual procedure, especially in light of the fact
that all the questions centered on the doctrine of baptismal regeneration.

When the exhaustive examination was completed, Phillpotts refused once
more to install Gorham, arguing his views on baptismal regeneration had
proved heretical. Gorham had rejected the idea that the baptism of infants
became a means of regeneration for infants. Gorham contended the Bible
never presented baptism as a channel of grace, it simply symbolized faith.
Regeneration, he argued, only comes through genuine faith and repentance.
The Bishop decreed Gorham's symbolic view of baptism to be incorrect and
thus Gorham must be refused his new parish. As can be imagined, a furor
arose in Anglican circles. Bishop Phillpotts'decision finally came before the

Archiepiscopal Court of Canterbury—and was upheld. Gorham, in turn, appealed to the highest Ecclesiastical Appeals Court, the Judicial Committee of the Privy Counsel.

The hearings and appeals and delays dragged on for two and a half years. Finally, the Judicial Committee reached its decision March 9, 1850. The Judicial Committee did its best to avoid any declaration concerning doctrine and only affirmed "that Gorham had not taught so clearly and undoubtedly against the articles in formularies as to warrant the Bishop's refusal." [86] Therefore, regardless of Phillpotts' refusal to endorse Gorham, he should be installed in the new parish by the Fiat Decision of the Archbishop of Canterbury.

The controversy had clearly created a situation with much at stake on both sides of the issue. If regeneration came by the baptism of infants only, that would be the end of the Evangelical party, and no doubt there would be another exodus from the Established Church as had happened numerous times in previous centuries. But then, the Tractarians or high-Churchmen put themselves in a difficult stance. It placed them in the precarious situation that any ruling by the Privy council, comprised largely of laymen, would jeopardize the authority of the Church to rule in ecclesiastical matters. Consequently, there would be danger that they, too, would withdraw from the Church of England if the Judicial Committee upheld Gorham's case.

But the issue died down, Gorham got his position and the unity of the Church of England held. Still, the Evangelical party made some points, and a broader view of baptismal regeneration had been effected than the high-Churchmen had desired. Of course, this broader interpretation had ramifications for the entire Established Church. It meant that Anglican clergymen from both ends of the theological spectrum were left to their own doctrines and consciences concerning the efficacy of the rite of baptism. This boded for possible conflict between the Evangelicals and the high-Churchmen as both had very little respect for the other's views. All this set the stage for Spurgeon's attack on the doctrine of baptismal regeneration. The situation was very fragile in the Anglican Church and Spurgeon's move would obviously open old festering wounds that persisted from the Phillpotts-Gorham encounter.

Spurgeon clearly held the same basic views on baptismal regeneration as did his evangelical Anglican friends. Their doctrine of conversion and regeneration coalesced. Thus, they had good rapport and esteemed one another quite highly. But Spurgeon felt very strongly about infant baptism. Once Spurgeon was looking through some books in a secondhand book shop. He met a Pedo-baptist, who, pointing to a book on infant baptism said, "Here, Mr. Spurgeon, here is your thorn in the flesh." "Finish the quotation, brother," said Charles, "the messenger of Satan to buffet me." Still, Spurgeon and conservative Anglicans shared good fellowship in the Evangelical Alliance organization.

SPURGEON'S CONTENTION

Spurgeon felt his evangelical brethren of the Established Church had impaled themselves on the horns of a dilemma. The dilemma in which they placed themselves was quite simple: they did not hold to baptismal regeneration as the Book of Common Prayer definitely advocated; yet, at the same time, every Anglican clergyman at his ordination took an oath declaring "the Book of Common Prayer containeth in it nothing contrary to the Word of God." [87] Spurgeon argued this smacked of duplicity, even outright hypocrisy. Although Anglican clergymen may not have believed that the Prayer Book taught baptismal regeneration, Spurgeon argued that it did. Moreover, he strongly contended that the doctrine of salvation by faith can in no way be reconciled to salvation by works, and as baptism is a human work, it therefore has no part in regeneration. His entire soteriology demanded repentance and faith as the only means of grace, and that, he argued, is impossible for an infant to do. Baptism for Spurgeon always stood as a *symbol* of salvation; therefore, only repentant believers should experience it. Pedo-baptism is heresy, Spurgeon argued.

Spurgeon argued that *infant* regeneration was an outright contradiction in terms. So he addressed the issue head on. He preached and sent letters to newspapers. Spurgeon took a very strong stand, feeling compromise is "treason to God," [88] because the essence of the Gospel stood on trial. Spurgeon made no apology for his stand. He would never remain silent for any reason if he were gripped by the deep conviction that truth sat on the judgement seat. Kruppa stated, "Throughout his ministry he was embroiled in controversies large and small which led him to sacrifice friendship, monetary gain, party unity, and denominational solidarity on the altar of 'the truth.'" [89] For Spurgeon, he felt he had no choice. His deep convictions on salvation forced him to conclude that the doctrine of baptismal regeneration "sent millions to hell." [90] On this basis he sounded the trumpet. He even had an old baptismal font placed in his garden as a bird bath. He called it the "spoils of war."

Of course, the question can be raised, why did Spurgeon as a Baptist interfere into the affairs of the Church of England at all? It could be argued he should have left the Anglicans alone. But he felt compelled to take his stand because of the fact that the doctrine of baptismal regeneration misled people regarding their salvation. That comprised a primary and central issue to the whole Kingdom of God. As stressed before, anything that attenuated or perverted the essential Gospel, Spurgeon felt constrained to address. Even though such a stance, he well knew, would do much to bring division into Anglican circles, he truly felt God's leadership in the matter. He once said in a letter to his Aunt, "If I can but feel in my soul the influence of the Holy Ghost causing a war, a strife, a struggle, I can afford to be careless about what the mere moralist or formalist may say." [91] He carried those convictions through life. Thus, the Baptismal Regeneration Controversy may have been inevitable for Spurgeon.

So, in June, 1864, Charles came to his people in the Tabernacle and preached his famous and unforgettable sermon on Mark 16:15-16: "And he said unto them, go ye into all the world and preach the Gospel to every creature. He that believeth and is baptized shall be saved; he that believeth not shall be damned." Interestingly, at least from today's vantage point, modern critical scholarship views this passage in the last chapter of Mark's Gospel as a spurious passage. Neither the Codex Vaticanus or Codex Siniaticus contains it. Those who adhere to the Majority Text, the Byzantine Text, do feel it to be authentic, but the overwhelming majority of modern scholarship rejects everything in Mark 16 from verse 9 and following, feeling the passage was not in Mark's original Gospel. Spurgeon, as an uncritical scholar of the New Testament, did not even address that issue. He simply took his text and preached his sermon which became a bombshell as it fell and exploded on the Anglican Church.

THE SERMON

In the sermon itself, Spurgeon began his message with a few introductory words, reminding everyone that the Apostles often used the sword of the Spirit, the Word of God, to "put to flight all their foes." He went on to say that the New Testament Church would never adapt the Gospel to the whims of the people or the culture or philosophies of the day. They would always take a hard and firm stand against any deviation from the truth. Spurgeon said:

> This morning in the name of the Lord of hosts, as my helper and defense, I shall attempt to do the same; and if I should provoke hostility—if I, through speaking what I believe to be the truth, lose the friendship of some, and stir up the enmity of more, I cannot help it. The burden of the Lord is upon me, and I must deliver my soul. I have been loathe enough to undertake the work, but I am forced to it by an awful and overwhelming sense of solemn duty. [92]

The people soon began to realize they were about to hear something of significance and importance from their pastor. They were absolutely right. Spurgeon went on to declare that a significant error was held by some and verbalized by all throughout the entire Anglican Church; moreover, it stood in direct contradiction to the Word of God. He explained the heretical doctrine of baptismal regeneration could be plainly seen in the Anglican Prayer Book. He then declared to his people, "We will confront this dogma with the assertion, that baptism without faith saves no one."[93] He went on to argue that the preaching of baptismal regeneration as found in the Prayer Book not only stood condemned biblically, but it influenced people to the point that it was damning their eternal souls. He said that regardless of whether a person was "baptized, re-baptized, circumcised, confirmed, fed upon sacraments, and buried in consecrated ground,"[94] the person's eternal destiny rested on the basis of his faith alone.

The people were on the edge of their seats by this time. Spurgeon then raised the second question: How could one defend any clergymen in the Church of England who did not believe in baptismal regeneration, yet repeated the words of the Prayer Book when they baptized infants? Spurgeon, in his inevitable style, quickly answered, "Why, then, do they belong to a church which teaches that doctrine in the plainest of terms?"[95] The answer seemed clear to Spurgeon; evangelicals who stayed in the Anglican communion and glossed over this plain teaching of the Prayer Book, or in some sense condoned it, were guilty of outright hypocrisy. These clergymen, he argued, accepted their living from a Church holding a position which they could not honestly affirm, a deviation that strikes right at the very heart and core of the Christian faith. This situation Spurgeon could not abide without the charge of duplicity. Why do they not come out from the Church if this be the situation, Spurgeon reasoned. To stay within the bonds of Anglicanism, and yet say that they did not fully believe in the Prayer Book, but had taken the pledge that nothing in the prayer book contained anything contrary to sound doctrine, comprised "one of the grossest pieces of immorality perpetrated in England."[96] The inconsistency of the situation, "immorality" in Spurgeon's terms, centered in the fact that Anglican clergymen ministered in a church context where babies were thought to be regenerate because of their baptism; yet, because the clergymen held evangelical views, when that child grew up they said it had to become regenerated and converted by repentance and faith. How could this be? How could they do this? Spurgeon spared not. His words were direct, forceful, inflammatory and quite judgmental.

In the earlier part of Spurgeon's sermon, he came over as more congenial to the Tractarians who honestly and fully believed in baptismal regeneration. He argued that at least they were consistent and thus honest and moral in their stand. He said:

> If Baptism does regenerate, let the fact be preached like a trumpet tongue, and let no man be ashamed of his belief in it. . . . My brethren, these are honest churchmen, who, subscribing to the Prayer Book, believe in baptismal regeneration, and preach it plainly . . . let us oppose their teaching by all scripture and intelligent means, but let us respect their courage in plainly giving us their views. [97]

Of course, Spurgeon did not in any sense condone the high-Churchmen's theology. He respected their uncompromising proclamation of their views; at least they were not hypocritical. Still, he seized the opportunity to censure severely their doctrine of baptism and the practice of high-Anglicanism. Spurgeon stood vehemently opposed to the entire concept of baptismal regeneration. He condemned it as potpourri and a form of Puseyism and contrary to the Holy Scriptures. He said with all the fervor he could muster:

> We want John Knox again. Do not talk to us of mild and gentle men, of soft manners and squeamish words. We want the fiery Knox and even though his preaching should kick'ding our pulpits into blades' yet were well if he did rouse our hearts into action. [98]

Spurgeon then reached the climax of his sermon, and in his dramatic and fervent style, he said:

> If I am not mistaken, the day will come when we shall have to fight for a simple spiritual religion far more than we do now. We have been cultivating friendship with those who either believe baptismal regeneration, or profess that they do, and swear before God that they do when they do not. . . . A great winnowing time is coming to God's saints, and we shall be clearer one of these days than we are now from the union with those who are upholding potpourri, under the pretense of preaching protestantism. We shall be clear, I say, of those who teach salvation by baptism, instead of salvation by the blood of our blessed Master, Jesus Christ. Oh may the Lord gird up your loins. Believe me, it is no trifle. It may be that on this ground Armageddon shall be fought. [99]

Spurgeon's sermon powerfully moved the people. (The whole sermon text can be found in Appendix B.) The furor that resulted, almost incalculable to the young Metropolitan Tabernacle preacher, spread like wildfire throughout religious circles. Later, in the aftermath to his sermon, Spurgeon commented, "May God grant that the controversy which this sermon commenced may lead to the advancement of His truth, and the enlightenment of many." [100]

To say that Spurgeon reveled in controversy really overstates the case. To say that he did not avoid it is surely true. Pike tells us, "Spurgeon was (once) accused of being a coward. It was given out that the Established Church in England was 'so cowing that even Spurgeon is afraid to baptise on the Sabbath, and skulks into the clandestineness of a week-day service!' That was what one writer said; but another replied: 'Mr. Spurgeon may do many things which we condemn, but he does not "skulk" in anything.'" [101] One thing is certain, the controversy that resulted from his Baptismal Regeneration sermon brought about the largest, furthest reaching controversy he had ever faced up to this time. The sermon itself probably lasted about an hour in delivery, but that hour rocked the whole religious scene in England.

Again, as in Spurgeon's slavery sermon and the rapid decline of sales of his sermons in America, Spurgeon was convinced this would all but end his sermon publications in Britain. He said:

I was delivered with the full expectation that the sale of the sermons would receive very serious injuries; in fact, I mentioned to one publisher that I was about to destroy it with a single blow, but . . . I deliberately counted the cost.[102]

But Spurgeon was proved wrong. His sermons received a reception as never before. The Baptismal Regeneration sermon alone, by the end of the year, had sold 350,000 copies. By the turn of the century, a few years after Spurgeon's death, over a half a million copies of it had been printed and sold. It became by far the most popular sermon he ever preached, at least popular from the standpoint of interest, if not acceptance.

THE FALL-OUT

Spurgeon's message set off a veritable flood of sermons and pamphlets from Evangelicals in the Church of England, the high-Churchmen, and the Evangelicals generally. Many prominent churchmen, as expected, vehemently opposed Spurgeon. Rev. W. Goode, the Dean of Ripon, Rev. Hughes Stowell of Manchester, Rev. Joseph Bardsley, and a host of others took a strong stand against Spurgeon. Even in the United States, Henry Ward Beecher got drawn into the affair and preached a critical sermon against Spurgeon. Poems were written to address the issue. A humorous poem written by W. Line hit the point well. It reads:

The Controversy

And what's it all about
Old Mother Church cries out;
What's all this Botheration
About Regeneration!
They say that we tell lies
Whenever we baptize—
That surely must be wrong,
We have practised it so long,
The sprinkling of the babies,
We have done so for ages;
Then there's my precious sons,
They are the learned ones!
They have been brought up at college,
They have the key of knowledge,
They know Latin and Greek—
They surely ought to speak;
And spoke they have, and vex on,
In not answering the question.
It really is too bad
That a simple country lad

Should be accounted famous
And yet an ignoramous;
The people must be fools
To be made such easy tools
As to build a Tabernacle,
From which the shots do rattle
With pestilential fire,
Upon our great Goliath.
It's really not agreeable
That one so weak and feeble
Should talk so loud, and prate
About the Church and State;
Time was he should be gagged
This simple country lad,
Or shut him up in prison
Or else have cut his weasand;
But we cannot do so now,
Or else I would, I vow;
It had been better if my sons
Had been wise and held their tongues,

And had not let the people seen
How unscriptural we have been—
But in vain is all this bother
They will stick close to their mother,
For none else would e'er be giving
Them such a tidy living.
But what has Spurgeon said
That has to this conflict led—
That the Established Church a trade is
To manufacture babies
Of every sort and size
By having them baptized;

To make them into saints—
High time for loud complaints;
But the Lord Himself proclaims
That Believers in His name
Should be baptized, and then
Make manifest to me
In whom they have believed
And what they have received;
But not a word is said
About the sprinkling of a babe;
'Tis ridiculous, alas!
'Tis a mockery! a farce. [103]

Quite naturally, the strongest reaction came from the high-Church Anglicans. A host of pamphlets were written with such titles as "Infant Baptism Vindicated," "Exposure of the Fallacies in Mr. Spurgeon's Sermons," "The Evil Speaking and Ignorance of Mr. C.H. Spurgeon," "What Is To Be Done with This Spurgeon?" One interesting pamphlet from the high-Church perspective, reflecting the high-Calvinism in some high-Church circles, stated:

> The Church of England regards the new birth as the work of the Spirit of God. As the infant has nothing to do with bringing about his first birth, neither has he the second. He is passive in both cases. [104]

Another interesting pamphlet received the title, *Mr. Spurgeon's Catechism.* The author raised a series of questions. It reads:

THE QUESTION WHICH NO BAPTIST CAN ANSWER.

Q.— What is the Kingdom of God?

A.— The Kingdom of God is the Church of God which begins on earth and will be cleansed and perfected in Glory. It is the net which gathers "of every kind," (Matt. xiii. 47,) and therefore cannot be the Church above in glory. All things which offend shall be gathered out of it, therefore they must have been in it; therefore, while they are in it, the Kingdom of God is the visible Church of God on earth.

Q.— Can Infants be Members of the Church of God on earth?

A.— Infants may be members of the Church of God on earth, for Christ said "Suffer little children to come unto me, and forbid them not: for of such is the Kingdom of God."—Mark x. 14.

Q.— How may Infants enter the Church of God as Members?

A.— Infants should enter the Church of God by being born of Water as well as of the Spirit, for Christ said "Except a man be born of Water and of the Spirit, he cannot enter the Kingdom of God."— John iii. 5.

Q.—   Why do Baptists forbid children to enter the Church by being born
of Water?

A.—   "We cannot tell." (Matt. xxi. 27.)
This is the question which no Baptist can answer. [105]

Of course, Spurgeon had his answers for that query.

Other clergymen raised other questions. In a pamphlet *Weighed in the Balances* by Rev. Joseph Bardsley, this writer asked:

1.   How could Mr. Spurgeon speak in 1861 of the Evangelical Clergy as 'our honored Evangelical brethren,' and denounce them in 1864 as men who 'equivocate and shuffle'?

2.   How could he hold 'sweet communion' with them up to about May last, and stigmatize them on the first Sunday of the following month as 'time-servers,' with whom 'God's servants' were to hold 'no more truce or parley'? When and how did he get the fresh light which produced so great a change in his views?

3.   How does he reconcile, with fairness and candour, when discussing the teaching of the Church on Baptism, his withholding the dogmatic statements of the Articles, which 'contain the true Doctrine of the Church of England'?

4.   On what principle does he claim the privilege of rejecting the literal meaning of some texts of the Bible, and of interpreting them by other texts, and yet of denying to the Clergy the right to apply the same canon of interpretation to the Prayer Book, when its very Preface shows that it was intended to be so explained?

5.   Will he tell us where the Church requires the Clergy to 'swear that Baptism saves the soul'? or where she 'teaches salvation by Baptism instead of salvation by the blood of our blessed Master, Jesus Christ'? As Mr. Spurgeon has addressed a few questions to Churchmen, we submit the above for the consideration of him and his friends.

Spurgeon's attack against high-churchmanship was nothing new. As early as 1855, he stated that their views were "a lie so palatable that I can scarcely imagine the preachers of it have any brains in their heads at all." [106] Spurgeon displayed little reticence to use strong language against high-Anglicanism. Perhaps his vehemence against Rome spilled over into the Romanist implications that the high-Church, and especially the Puseyites, held. He said once in a sermon:

I think I have none here so profoundly stupid as to be Puseyites. I can scarcely believe that I have been the means of attracting one person here so utterly devoid of every remnant of brain as to believe the doctrine of Baptismal regeneration. [107]

Spurgeon never held back, but one wonders if such harsh language was really necessary to get the point over. Nevertheless, as a man of deep, strong convictions, he preached from the heart, and defending the Gospel was his forte.

The Evangelicals of the Church of England were likewise very upset by the Baptismal Regeneration sermon. Many of the Evangelicals considered Spurgeon as a friend and fellow-worker in the Gospel. Not only that, they had been some of his earliest defenders during the media controversy when Spurgeon first came to London. Beyond that, they had actually supported him monetarily in several of his projects, even the building of the Tabernacle itself. One can imagine their shock when suddenly they became the target of Spurgeon's maligned attack on their integrity and branded them as blatant hypocrites. Spurgeon had put their whole ministerial integrity on the line. They felt deep disappointment, if not resentment, toward their evangelical counterpart in the Baptist denomination for accusing them so harshly. The Evangelicals did not object to Spurgeon's doctrines, for they held the same views on baptismal regeneration. But they objected to the manner of his approach to the issue. An evangelical Anglican wrote:

> I commend him and would heartily join with him in his earnest and dogmatic condemnation of the corrupt and popish dogma of baptismal regeneration. But what I repudiate and throw back with all the righteous indignation which such a false and reckless accusation can call forth is, the daring assumption and most abominable imputation that the whole evangelical body of the Church of England are untrue and false in their use of that service. [108]

Other evangelical Anglicans spoke out far more pointedly in their criticisms of Spurgeon. The Rev. W. Goode, Dean of Ripon, said that Spurgeon's sermon confirmed their earlier suspicion that he was an "ignorant ranter." Goode went on to say:

> As to that young minister who is now raving against the Evangelical clergy at this point, it is to be regretted that so much notice has been taken of his railings. He is to be pitied, because his entire wont of acquaintance with theological literature leaves him utterly unfit for the determination of such a question, which is a question not of mere doctrine, but of what may be called historical theology . . . to hold a controversy with him upon a subject would be to as little purpose as to attempt to hold a logically constructed argument with a child unacquainted with logical terms. [109]

A host of pamphlets written by the evangelical clergymen emerged alongside the others. They took titles such as "An Honest Evangelical Reading of Prayer Book Doctrine on the Subject," "An Exposure of the Fallacies and Misrepresentations in Mr. Spurgeon's Sermons," "False Regeneration and its Counterfeits," plus a myriad of other writings.

Spurgeon's sermon not only aroused the interest of the Church of England, it also grabbed the attention of Evangelicals of other denominations. But their reaction, as could be expected, took a more moderate tone than the Church of England clergymen.

Of course, the basic question remains: What did the evangelical clergy of the Established Church actually believe about their baptizing of infants? It seems Spurgeon was essentially right in saying they did not believe in baptismal regeneration as such. The Evangelicals did not believe that any baptismal service could convey the saving grace of Christ. They did not believe that the Holy Spirit was necessarily conveying grace at the moment an infant received baptism. They believed, rather, that the baptismal rite only became a means of grace to those who rightly received it, and that not necessarily at the moment it was actually administered. A contemporary theologian, speaking on behalf of the Evangelicals stated:

> The warrant to baptize infants was through the covenant standing of a *believing* parent and it was concerning such children, according to the Evangelicals in the church, that the charitable supposition was made that they would be receivers of the grace of regeneration. [110]

The Reformed emphasis on "covenant theology" lies at the heart of the issue. It can thus be seen why the Evangelicals believed that Spurgeon had mistakenly maligned their motives, and therefore stood unjustified in his sharp criticisms.

Spurgeon truly had been very harsh and judgmental. He stated in his sermon that evangelical Anglicans were exemplifying to all people how to "lie to get a living." [111] He further charged that the doctrine had also precipitated an exodus from the Church by many clergymen and their finding their way into the Roman Catholic Church. He pointed out that Roman Catholicism had been rather weak numerically in England up to this point, but their ranks were dramatically increasing due to the number of Anglicans who were increasingly defecting to Rome. This situation alarmed the Metropolitan Tabernacle preacher.

FURTHER REACTIONS

As is well known, for many years, there have been three "streams" in the Church of England: One, the high-Church Anglicans that would be epitomized in Spurgeon's day by the Tractarian movement; two, the Evangelicals who comprised a large part of the Evangelical Alliance organization in Spurgeon's day; three, for years there has also been a stream that rested somewhere between the high-Church and the Evangelical wings of the Establishment. We have seen the high-Church and Evangelical reaction to Spurgeon's serving, what about this middle stream? They also had a definite view of baptismal regeneration. They believed that regeneration was a two-step process. For them, infant baptism was a very important first step. Rev. J. H. Titcomb said:

> Every child is ingrafted into the invisible membership with Christ's body, and receives therein an altered relationship with God; which, although it gives him no necessary regeneration, yet places him in a regenerated state or condition. [112]

This statement is rather ambiguous, but one would suppose that they felt the necessity of a personal regeneration experience after baptism, when a person came of age to understand moral right and wrong. Still, their position remains somewhat unclear. A middle road, probably of necessity, becomes a muddled road on an issue like baptismal regeneration. This middle road, Spurgeon did not really address in any direct way.

As the controversy heated up across Britain and began to make front page news in Ecclesiastical circles, Spurgeon preached a number of supplementary sermons. Expressing his typical approach, he said, "When the gauntlet of battle is thrown down, I am not the man to refuse to take it up. No, indeed!" [113] Three weeks after the first famous sermon, he preached from Hebrews 13 a message entitled "Let Us Go Forth." Immediately after preaching that sermon, he preached two more on the subject, "Children Brought to Christ and Not to the Font," and "Thus saith the Lord, or The Book of Common Prayer Weighed in the Balances of the Sanctuary."

In preaching on "Children Brought to Christ," Spurgeon attempted to refute the Anglican clergyman's view who quoted Jesus' blessing of the little children as a proof text for their views on baptism. His sermon on "Thus Saith the Lord" replied to the personal attacks made upon him. Concerning the Dean of Ripon, Spurgeon stated:

> He speaks with all the positiveness of a personal acquaintance covering my reputed ignorance, and for my own part, I am not so very anxious to question so very reverent an authority.

Spurgeon would repay sarcasm with sarcasm. But the essence of the sermon attacked the Book of Common Prayer and the heresy that he felt it contained.

In some respects, Spurgeon almost seemed to enjoy the controversy. He felt in his element defending Gospel truth and the authority of the Scriptures. For him the Word of God stood unique as the only authority in religious matters. He said, "It is not for us to sit in judgment upon the Word, but to let the Word judge us." [114] We shall see more of Spurgeon's views on the authority and nature of the Scriptures in the chapter on his theology.

Whether Spurgeon enjoyed the conflict or not—he probably did not enjoy some of the personal aspects of it—he definitely took the offensive in controversy. The defensive stance thrust upon him in the media controversy got completely reversed in this situation. He himself created this conflict and therefore became something of the master of it. In the midst of it all, a friend once said to him, "I hear you are in hot water." "Oh, no," Spurgeon answered, "It is the other fellows who are in the hot water, I am the stoker, the man who makes the water boil."[115]

For Spurgeon, to be on the battlefield for God's truth assured him of victory. He said:

> The good work grows in my hands; the battle thickens; the victory is all the nearer. My sermon on Baptismal Regeneration has stirred up the rattlesnake's dens; but as the venomous fangs cannot reach me, they may rattle as they please. Of course, I can lose the friendship of the Evangelicals, but I can bear that sooner than an ill conscience.[116]

Spurgeon's prophetic word came to pass; he did lose friendships. Even Lord Shaftesbury had a difficult time with Spurgeon on this issue. Shaftesbury said, "You are a very saucy fellow."[117] Spurgeon really was a saucy fellow. While preaching in Bury St. Edmunds during the time of the controversy, he made a joking reference to a baptismal font as a spittoon. Saucy, if not arrogant!

Even Spurgeon's very close friend, Dr. Campbell, editor of the *British Banner*, remained silent during the height of the controversy. Some time later, however, he did do a series of articles on the subject. He stated that Spurgeon's arguments came over "clear, cogent, and unanswerable." But Campbell did admit that Spurgeon's appeals were "occasionally marked by an acritude of spirit, fitted to startle, to scandalize, and exasperate."[118] In all, Campbell published seventeen articles on the subject, trying to effect a balance on both sides of the dispute. To show something of Campbell's appreciation for Spurgeon's powerful ministry, he said that deference should be given to Spurgeon by the Anglican clergy. He almost eulogized Spurgeon when he wrote:

> The case of such a man is extraordinary, unparalleled, and when placed in the balances of critical judgment . . . it is . . . just and fair to make a very large allowance for strong language—language stronger than I could have used; but, with his talents, temperament, views, and convictions, and placed in his circumstances, I might have spoken as he spake, without at all feeling that I had violated the strict rules of verity, justice, and Christian propriety.[119]

For Campbell, the real issue centered around the fact of whether or not the evangelical clergy actually accepted the doctrine of baptismal regeneration in their adherence to, and statements about, the Anglican Prayer Book. He was well aware of the fact that all Evangelicals rejected the idea of baptismal regeneration, those inside and outside the Established Church.

Spurgeon obviously had put Anglican Evangelicals in a very embarrassing situation. He presented to the watching world a serious discrepancy in their ministries, if not in their integrity. All did not appreciate what Spurgeon had done, especially the harsh language he used. For example, B.W. Noel, who had been a clergyman at the Church of England and later became pastor of a Baptist Church in London said in a letter to Rev. C.H. Spurgeon, "Someday, perhaps, you will see that you have been rash and uncharitable, when you only intended to be faithful."[120] The Evangelical Alliance generally reflected something of the spirit of Noel's approach to Spurgeon.

REACTION IN THE EVANGELICAL ALLIANCE

The Evangelical Alliance stood as a most significant confederation of ministers in England during Spurgeon's day. They included Baptists as well as Anglicans and other Evangelicals. The fellowship had always been strong. Nonetheless, at times there had been some doctrinal difficulties over baptism in the Alliance before Spurgeon's attack. For example, in 1862, R.W. Dale, the well-known Congregationalist minister, delivered a lecture in which he pointed out the contradiction in the teachings of the Prayer Book and the doctrine of Evangelicals on the subject of Baptism. This and other events tended to put some strain on the Evangelicals, but nothing like Spurgeon's attack.

Spurgeon, an active member of the Alliance, perhaps did not realize the difficulty he precipitated in that loosely federated group. The ex-Anglican, and now Baptist, B.W. Noel felt that Spurgeon had violated the spirit of the Evangelical Alliance. The fourth resolution of the British Evangelical Alliance charter reads:

> Then when required by conscience to assert or defend any views or principles wherein they differ from a Christian brethren who agree with them in vital truths, the members of this Alliance will aim earnestly, by the help of the Holy Spirit, to avoid all rash and groundless insinuations, personal imputations, or irritating allusions; and to maintain the meekness and gentleness of Christ by speaking the truth in love.

Obviously there were those, especially Noel, who felt that Spurgeon had violated this resolution.

LEAVING THE ALLIANCE

As all of these dynamics began to converge, Spurgeon made the decision to resign his membership in the Evangelical Alliance. Perhaps conscience did prick him, as he realized that he had violated the spirit of the Alliance resolution. His sermons were certainly not "meek, gentle, or loving." Spurgeon stated that he could no longer be linked with those with whom he differed. The strained relationship obviously proved uncomfortable to Spurgeon and hence he withdrew.

Another significant factor emerged that helped precipitate Spurgeon's resignation from the Alliance. James Davis, the secretary of the Evangelical Alliance, sent a letter to Spurgeon in which he demanded that Spurgeon should either retract his harsh words or withdraw from the Alliance. Spurgeon mistakenly believed that letter had been written with authority of the entire committee. He withdrew his membership immediately. Charles said:

> Not being able to retract a syllable of our utterance, and being unwilling to embroil the Alliance in our conflict, we withdrew from it. We have since learned that the letter was unauthorized, and several members of the Alliance committee have expressed regret that we have acted upon it . . . only that is clear . . . (nothing) would allow us to attend Alliance gatherings while we are practically under its ban. [121]

Unfortunately, Spurgeon did not know that Davis had personally written to him and did not speak for the official committee of the Alliance.

When Spurgeon resigned from the Alliance, he wrote two letters. One, naturally, he addressed to the Evangelical Alliance in which he simply stated his withdrawal. In his letter, he wrote:

> I have waited long and patiently for signs of reform in the ecclesiastical conduct of these brethren, and I have not spoken until my hopes of their spontaneous repentance has expired . . . I . . . do thereby withdraw myself from your Alliance. [122]

The other letter Spurgeon addressed to "the Christian public." In that open letter he attempted to prove that his stand against the evangelical clergy in the Church of England was "neither novel nor singular." [123] Spurgeon attempted to show that others had taken the same stance he had. In that letter he stated:

> I confidently appeal to the great heart of the British people against the charge of inventing a rash or groundless accusation. To the most high God I leave my work in this matter. He knoweth that zeal for this truth alone urges me to pursue my present path involving me as it does in all the pains which contumely and hatred can inflict. [124]

So Spurgeon severed his relationship with the Evangelical Alliance, even if it meant standing alone. Spurgeon, absolutely content to do so, felt it "not dishonorable to be right even in the minority of one." [125]

RESULTS OF THE CONTROVERSY

In the context and dynamics of the controversy Spurgeon made the decision, mentioned earlier, to drop the title of Reverend. He had actually not liked the designation for many years, as seen in his attitude toward ordination. From this time on, he wanted to be known simply as Mr. Spurgeon or Pastor. This position he held the rest of his life.

Of course, Spurgeon enlisted many supporters and fellow soldiers in the battle. Scores of Baptists gave their wholehearted affirmation to Spurgeon's stance. Pastors like William Landels, Leonard Strong, R. A. Belman, and Spurgeon's first theological student, T. W. Medhurst, all entered into the fray by writing pamphlets supporting Spurgeon. Actually, one document contained the signatures of 33 Baptist ministers giving Spurgeon strong support. The pamphlet contained these words:

> We heartily tend to Mr. Spurgeon our sincere sympathy amid the obloquy which is faithful protest against error as provoked and would assure him that he has by the courageous utterance of the truth greatly served the kingdom of our Lord and Saviour Jesus Christ. [126]

And this is not to mention Evangelicals of all denominations who stood with Spurgeon.

A further consequence of Spurgeon's stand, and his withdrawal from the Evangelical Alliance, helped him to bring about the founding of the London Baptist Association. This move became significant and perhaps one of the most positive things, at least for the Baptists, that came out of the Baptismal Regeneration Controversy. The London Baptist Association continues to this day. The original 59 churches that joined the group at its inception now number 279 churches.

In the setting of the controversy, the question began to be asked if Spurgeon would withdraw from the Baptist denomination, as well as the Evangelical Alliance, and form a sect after the manner of Wesley. Spurgeon did have something of an independent spirit, but such a step was far from his mind. Even the Down Grade Controversy, which struck out far more severely at the Baptists than did the Baptismal Regeneration Controversy, did not precipitate Spurgeon starting a new denomination. Spurgeon remained a member of the Baptist denomination, at least in some sense, until the day of his death.

FINAL ANALYSIS

One wonders if Spurgeon really accomplished a great deal through this period of strife. Pike contended, "In point of fact, Spurgeon was not formed for controversy; he was most effective in opposing error when he simply proclaimed the truth." [127] But as could be expected, Spurgeon's friends said, "The blast had a happy effect. It purified the Theological atmosphere." [128] That may be true to some extent. However, Spurgeon's biographer, Fullerton, said it may have been futile because "the self-same church continued in the self-same way." [129] Yet, at the same time, Spurgeon did stand for what he believed to be true, and that is important. The same judgment can be made relative to the Down Grade Controversy that came in the last years of Spurgeon's life. He once again stood firm and if nothing else was accomplished, that strong position will always be a classic illustration of standing for the truth.

One thing does seem quite clear, the pastor and his church did not appear to suffer from the controversy, at least from the standpoint of numerical growth. The Metropolitan Tabernacle not only remained as strong as ever, it continued its growth. The church received 486 new members into its fellowship during 1864, the greatest number to date in the ministry of Spurgeon. Although Spurgeon quite obviously alienated a number of his evangelical friends, it did not seem to impact the masses in any appreciable way. Most people care little for theological battles and remain largely on the sidelines. The Metropolitan Tabernacle continued to be filled to capacity every Sunday and the work went forward in a very positive fashion. Not only that, in the end many of Spurgeon's critics finally affirmed admiration for him, including Lord Shaftesbury. Further, Spurgeon himself seemed to mellow a bit at least later in life. He actually rejoined the Evangelical Alliance, seemingly laying aside the vociferous attack during the controversy itself. He said:

> I can never forget the many gracious and faithful men who remain in this church (the Church of England), nor can I cease to pray for them. Toward these brethren, as earnest adherent and promulgators of evangelical truth, I sincerely cherish the warmest love . . . may the providence of God and the power of the Spirit render the way to the visible fellowship of believers more plain. [130]

It does seem to be true that Spurgeon's primary concern centered in a defense of the Gospel and the elimination of error that would prevent people from hearing the simple message of salvation and thus be barred from the gates of heaven. Remember, Spurgeon always stood first and foremost as an evangelist. Moreover, he believed in the infallibility the Bible and would attack anything that lifted up a standard against it, at least as he interpreted it. He would never shrink from any situation that would hinder people from hearing what he felt to be essential truth.

These mid-years for Spurgeon at the Tabernacle, the 1860s and 1870s, were filled with many exciting and interesting events; some of them very positive, some of them, such as the Baptismal Regeneration Controversy, quite negative. However, they were certainly exciting days. Spurgeon worked as never before. It seemed, despite his increasing problem with illnesses, he was a man who could labor without ceasing. His friend, Dr. Campbell, said, "Mr. Spurgeon was seen to be superior to all the frailties of humanity. . . . his Sabbath efforts are such as might well exhaust and lay up for a day or two the strongest men [but he rose above it]." Spurgeon had become known as the greatest preacher and evangelist of the country. He also became known as a great controversialist as well. In many respects, he was all that.

SOME SUMMARY EVENTS

The middle years of Spurgeon's Tabernacle ministry, despite the many victories, had their down times. One month only seven people joined the church. A deacon said to Spurgeon, "This won't pay, Gov'nor, running all this big place for seven new members a month." But the crowds and additions soon came back. Moreover, Spurgeon's popularity had so grown that stores would print his picture on their yearly calendars. He had become so respected that when (October, 1880) a thief broke into Spurgeon's study and stole his gold-headed cane, the thief battering the head and selling it to a pawn shop, the owner of the shop realized whose it was and returned it to Charles. *Punch* took up the story and made much of it—including the thief. *The Christian Chronicle* called Charles, "The other prime minister of England." *The Chart and Compass* termed him "Archbishop Spurgeon." Moreover, *The Canadian Baptist* wrote, "A limit should be put to eulogism. Mr. Spurgeon is a man; during the last few weeks he has been as nearly deified as a man can well be." Probably true! The general attitude of the press was expressed in *The Echo*, "Of Mr. Spurgeon himself, it need only be said that he was Mr. Spurgeon." In it all, Spurgeon could never be accused of "social climbing." He refused many notable invitations. All of his popularity had its negative side, of course. For example, a man by the name of Arthur Barker falsified letters as if from Spurgeon commending him as he prepared to go to America on a preaching tour. But the ministry went forward with the versatility and innovation that Spurgeon alone could bring to it. Services at the Metropolitan Tabernacle were met with tremendous acceptance and power. A vivid description of a service during those mid-years reads:

> Such a sight, I believe, can be witnessed nowhere else than in England. I had been in my seat in front of the platform about two minutes when Mr. Spurgeon entered. The photographs of the shop windows had prepared me to expect to see a man of heavy, not to say coarse, countenance, but the photographs do the original great injustice. Precisely at a quarter to eleven Mr. Spurgeon advanced to the railing of the platform and said, in a clear, soft voice, which filled the building without effort, 'Let us worship God in prayer.' Accustomed to the habit of worship in the Church of England, it was with regret I found that there was no provision for kneeling, and that that appropriate attitude had not been renounced because the congregation preferred to stand. The sight of six thousand people sitting during the worship of prayer is not pleasing. Mr. Spurgeon, however, stood. He does not pray so well as he preaches—his prayer was good so far as it went. It was very high and mystical, abounding with figurative expressions from the Hebrew poetry; but it was defective in the element which we all prize so much in the Litany—a tender, lowly, human sympathy. Mr. Spurgeon once referred to those present as a 'chosen people,' and there was too much of this exclusive feeling throughout the service. The confession of

sin struck with me as meagre and general. In one of the 'Tracts for the Times' it is said that the prayers of the Church of England are pitched in too low and plaintive a key, and it is hinted that there is a penal judgment on that Church. For the first of these opinions I think there is some foundation. The prayers of the Tabernacle, on the other hand, seemed to me over-confident. The singing is accomplished without instrumental aid, being conducted by a precentor, who stands beside Mr. Spurgeon. Of course, under such disadvantages only slow tunes can be sung; but the voices were kept together much better than might have been expected. No psalm was read, and only one lesson, a portion of the Second Epistle to the Corinthians. Mr. Spurgeon is a good reader, and it was satisfactory to hear him give the hymns out himself. . . .

Having read his text, he advanced from the side table, where his Bible lay, to the rails, on which he leaned with both hands while uttering his first few sentences. He at once fixed the attention of the vast audience by connecting his text with common human experience, then set forth its original, heroic sense in the life of the Apostle, and afterwards announced that he should treat it as of general application. I did not think the sermon well organised. For instance, having announced that his subject would be the art of dying daily, he made certain preliminary requisites of that art the first division of this sermon before he explained what he understood by this daily dying. Probably, however, there were few in the building to whom this would be a serious objection. At all events, the people listened with breathless attention from first to last, a fact which I commend to the attention of those who are telling us that sermons and preaching are out of date. [131]

It must have been an exhilarating experience to sit in the Tabernacle and engage in a worship service like that.

On one occasion an American evangelist held a series of meetings for children in the Tabernacle. The teachers in the Sunday School were quite captivated by the evangelist's methods and expressed the desire that something like this should become a regular part of Tabernacle life. Accordingly, arrangements were made for a large gathering of young people in the chapel. The program proved very successful. That same month Charles preached a sermon on Genesis 42:22, "Do not sin against the child." It was a sermon on the conversion of children. In his message he said that often sermons were too obscure for children, the words being too long, the sentences too involved and the matters too mysterious. As always, he held forth the simplicity of the Gospel and warned parents, teachers, and especially preachers, that they should present the Gospel in its simplicity so that children may come to faith in Christ. However, Spurgeon continued to be cautious in child evangelism methods. He remained dubious of the inquiry room unless run very well.

Spurgeon continued his involvement in the Baptist Union and was a regular attender at its annual meetings. The Pastors' College flourished.

Spurgeon gave this report one year on the progress of the College:

> The work of training young ministers has, through our College, been carried
> on during another year beneath the wings of Providence and under the smile of
> grace. Young men have offered themselves in abundance, and many of them
> of a superior order of grace and talent. All our needs have been supplied by the
> Lord, who is our bountiful treasurer, as constantly as faith has made drafts
> upon His bank. The gold and the silver have been received more largely than
> in any previous year, and peace and spiritual energy have been very abundant-
> ly enjoyed. Our experience leads us to cling more closely than ever to the
> principle of faith and prayer, as far better than paid collectors and machinery.
> The number of the men has been, during the latter half of the year, greatly
> decreased, and we abstained from receiving fresh brethren, because it seemed
> to us preferable to introduce new blood by bringing in a considerable band of
> new men at one time. We are not looking forward to a large accession in the
> first week of April. For some months during the year there were no applica-
> tions for preachers made by the churches, and our men turned their attention to
> founding new churches, with the result that the Kingdom of the Lord was
> increased. The applications of churches are now coming in, the cessation being
> temporary; and there can be no doubt that the College, at its fullest number is
> needed to supply the demands of our denomination. It will be remembered that
> a very large proportion of our brethren have created their own spheres, and
> others have accepted pastorates where the prospects were such as to repel all
> others, and, by God's grace, in many instances they have made the wilderness
> to blossom as the rose. The need of Gospel preachers increases every day. The
> field is boundless, and still the labourers are few. This College is our life-work,
> and we therefore feel as if we owed to every donor a weight of personal
> obligation, which we now acknowledge with many a prayer to God for each
> one. Since the College commenced, two hundred and eighty men have been
> received for training in its regular classes, and at least five hundred have had
> instruction in the evening classes. One hundred and eighty-six students have
> gone from us to settle in the ministry, of whom one hundred and seventy-seven
> still remain in the work, the rest having either died, been laid aside by illness,
> or relinquished the work from other causes. Forty-four distinct new churches
> have been formed by the agency of our College. Thirty new chapels have been
> erected as the result of our agency. In London, at the present moment, we are
> making efforts to establish churches in eleven destitute districts. There are
> sixty-four students in the College at this moment and one hundred and fifty
> under tuition in the evening classes. [132]

In those same dramatic years, the various ministries made steady progress.
The Tabernacle remained financially strong. Approximately £20,000 a year
was being raised for the various programs of the church. Collections at the
Lord's Supper for poor members reached close to a thousand pounds every
time the church observed communion. The Ragged School work went on

well. Minor skirmishes came up in Spurgeon's mid-years worth a brief word because of their human interest appeal. For example, a Mr. Linscott, a member of the Bible Defense Association, got into a discussion with a certain Mr. Antill. Antill had made a statement to the effect that the pastor of the Metropolitan Tabernacle had said, "There are entrances in hell a span long." Linscott did not believe Spurgeon had said that. He wrote Spurgeon concerning the issue. Spurgeon answered with the following letter:

> Newington, S.E., June 12, 1869.
>
> Dear Sir,—I have never at any time in my life said, believed, or imagined that any infant, under any circumstances, would be cast into hell. I have always believed in the salvation of all infants, and I intensely detest the opinions which your opponent dared to attribute to me. I do not believe that on this earth there is a professing Christian holding the damnation of infants, or if there be, he must be insane, or utterly ignorant of Christianity. I am obliged by this opportunity of denying the calumny, although the author of it will probably find no difficulty in inventing some other fiction, to be affirmed as unblushingly as the present one. He who doubts God's Word is naturally much at home in slandering the Lord's servants.—Yours truly,
>
> C. H. Spurgeon. [133]

Such matters, as it was always true in church life, Spurgeon took in stride.

On Monday, September 21, 1874, Spurgeon baptized his twin boys at the age of eighteen. That high hour for Charles and Susannah thrilled the entire congregation. The press made much of it. *The South London Press*, September 26, 1874, printed a large article on the happy event. They also published an article on the contrast between Spurgeon's baptizing and his father baptizing three infants at Islington Congregational Chapel. That in turn evoked an article in the *Christian World* on September 25, 1887. The Spurgeon boys were received into the church October 4th. At the Metropolitan Tabernacle, baptism in itself did not automatically bring one into the church membership. They had to be officially received after baptism. Charles, when baptized as a boy of fifteen, it will be recalled, did not even become a member of a Baptist church until he moved to Cambridge. Soon thereafter, both Thomas and Charles, Jr. entered the Pastors' College. They had intended to go into business, Thomas in a wood-engraving establishment. But both felt the call to ministry and Charles, Jr. became pastor of South Street Baptist Church in Greenwich. His father preached his installation service. In the message he looked his son right in the eye, leaning over the pulpit, and gave him the charge: "Preach up Christ, my boy, preach Him up." Charles, Sr. baptized the first converts of Charles, Jr. and Thomas, June 26, 1876. Charles appreciated God's hand on his boys. He said, "When I have you (Thomas) and Charles at my side to preach the same great truths, we shall by God's grace make England know more of the Gospel's power." [134] Thomas later went to New Zealand and became a pastor in Auckland. The evening classes at the Tabernacle continued to grow. Spurgeon's writings also kept up along with all the feverish activity of the Tabernacle. He was making good progress on the *Treasury of David* and *John Ploughman's Talks* were doing well. It was said:

> His 'John Ploughman's Talk' confirms our views of what goes to make up a popular preacher. As is the book so is the man. Mr. Spurgeon, we believe, exaggerates and intensifies the popular style. He deals in broad sayings, in plain speaking, in strong, vigorous, unqualified expressions. That is what an effective sermon should be, and is the essence of a proverb. A preacher cannot waste—if it is wasting—his time in looking out for counter-views, in making allowance for qualifications. He scorns limitations and distinctions. The proverb and the preacher are here at one. Hence it is that people preach best in their youth, and that many a good preacher gets afraid of the pulpit, and in mature age suspects his old telling talk, and the confident, decisive, and therefore attractive matter and manner of his earlier years, as a larger experience of men and things makes him reflective, cautious, and, as his hearers say, timid, and uncertain, and hesitating. A man with ripe views, or rather whose views are getting constantly modified and checked as he sees more of life, cannot preach well. It requires a certain narrow-mindedness to preach what is called effectively. Youth is the season for vigorous language and earnest convictions, and for confidence and decision. And as it is with intellectual, so it is with aesthetical, qualities. A formed judgment revolts at the crudities and unarguing assumptions, and, in all senses of the word, the presumptions of the earlier stages of intellectual growth, and revolts also at an over-confident and blustering manner. A man must have something, perhaps much, of the feminine nature to preach well. A woman of good feelings and intentions feels it to be a moral duty to express exactly what is in her mind—what are her convictions—only because they are her sincere and honest convictions. So must the preacher, if he is to preach well—that is, to preach sermons that will tell. His concern, he thinks, is not so much with what may be said on the other side, but, because a thing is in him, to out with it, as he would say. This is Mr. Spurgeon's manner. It is in his book as in his sermons. It is simply unfaithful to suppose that there are two sides to any question, and to be in earnest is only to be quite certain of your own line, and immeasurably scornful of everything else. A preacher, to be very popular with congregations, such as most congregations are, must be dictatorial, magisterial, contemptuous, violent, and addicted to strong language. Whether these qualities are faults or excellence, far be it from us to say; but they are Mr. Spurgeon's, and he is a popular preacher; and he has published a book full of abrupt, unproved, and unargumentative assertions. And proverbial philosophy, as it is oddly called, exactly because there is no philosophy in it, consists of assumptions of this coarse and impetuous, but telling, character. [135]

The sermons continued to be read by the tens of thousands and the number of conversions from all over the world that resulted from their reading was tremendous.

Spurgeon invited Dr. Pentecost to preach in the Metropolitan Tabernacle in 1874. An interesting encounter ensued. Charles had preached at Pentecost's church in Clapham, so he reciprocated by having Pentecost at the Tabernacle. In the service, Spurgeon laid down the doctrinal aspects of the truth discussed, and Dr. Pentecost then made the practical application. But here trouble began. Pentecost related the struggle he had to give up cigars. Of course, Spurgeon enjoyed his cigars. He had said on one occasion after being chided for smoking, if anyone could show him in the Bible where it said, "Thou shalt not smoke," he would give it up. He went on to say there were Ten Commandments, he did not wish to make an eleventh against cigars. When Pentecost sat down, Spurgeon sprang to his feet and defended his smoking. He said he "smoked to the glory of God." That raised more than a few eyebrows. He received considerable criticism for his comment. Later, in a letter to *The Daily Telegraph* (September 23, 1874), Spurgeon wrote:

> I demur altogether and most positively to the statement that to smoke tobacco is in itself a sin. It may become so, as any other indifferent action may, but as an action it is no sin. Together with hundreds of thousands of my fellow-Christians I have smoked, and with them I am under the condemnation of living in habitual sin, if certain accusers are to be believed. As I would not knowingly live even in the smallest violation of God's law, I will not own to sin, when I am not conscious of it. There is growing up in Society a Pharisaic system which adds to the commands of God the precepts of me; to that system I will not yield for an hour. The preservation of my liberty may bring upon me the upbraidings of many of the good and the sneers of the self-righteous; but I shall endure both with serenity, so long as I feel clear in my conscience before God.
>
> The expression 'smoking to the glory of God' standing alone has an ill sound, and I do not justify it; but in the sense in which I employed it I still stand to it. No Christian should do anything in which he cannot glorify God—and this may be done, according to Scripture, in eating and drinking and the common actions of life. When I have found intense pain relieved, a weary brain soothed, and calm, refreshing sleep obtained by a cigar, I have felt grateful to God and have blessed His name; this is what I meant, and by no means did I use sacred words triflingly. If through smoking I had wasted an hour of my time, if I had stinted my gifts to the poor, if I had rendered my mind less vigorous, I trust I should see my fault and turn from it; but he who charges me with these things shall have no answer but my forgiveness.
>
> I am told that my open avowal will lessen my influence, and my reply is that if I have gained any influence through being thought different from what I

am, I have no wish to retain it. I will do nothing upon the sly and nothing about which I have a doubt.[136]

Spurgeon had a time living that experience down. It really was a blunder, and his explanation of it all fell rather short of the mark. Someone once wrote to Spurgeon and asked if he smoked. Charles replied, "I cultivate my flowers and bury my weeds." That reply, though clever, was not much of an answer. Actually, it is regrettable, he did not know what smoking actually does to one's health.

Charles also had a "bone to pick" with funeral directors. He felt funerals were expensive and pompous. He said, "Reform away the absurdities connected with the burial of the dead." It seemed, however, his words changed little.

Spurgeon had now been pastor of his great congregation for some fifteen years. He celebrated his 35th birthday as he often did, with the children at the Stockwell orphanage. A happy day for all! But now the mid-years had been met and there remained a continuing significant ministry before him. Deteriorating health began to take its toll, but the work went on regardless. The mid-years, despite all of the controversies and problems, were perhaps the happiest and most fruitful in all of his ministry. They were surely his busiest. In a letter written to his mother on June 20, 1881, he said:

> I am pretty well, for last week I preached four times, spoke at four public meetings, held four prayer meetings, one communion and one long committee meeting, and gave a lecture. I only hope it will last.[137]

But his wife's illness still remained a burden. Writing to his Aunt, he said:

> Today my dear wife is very, very ill. Her pains are most distressing to witness. Few suffer as she does and for patience she surpasses all I ever heard of. She lives so near to God that I do not wonder she is sustained. I am both saddened and charmed every time I see her.[138]

On another occasion he wrote about Susannah's health; one can sense his grief: "My dear wife has been as bad as ever for the last ten days. All wrong in the interior of the poor body."[139] She once even broke a rib from hard coughing. Charles, in a letter to his father, wrote, "Coughing can be a serious thing."[140] On another occasion, he wrote to a patent medicine company giving a testimony to George Thomas Congreve's cure for consumption and chronic bronchitis. He may have been speaking for his wife. At any rate, Congreve published the letter.

In it all, Spurgeon took his stand on every issue and bore up under every burden. A trip to America was again raised; the slavery issue had died down and his sermons were again popular. America wanted to hear him. *The Watchman and Reflector* in the spring of 1870 wrote:

If Charles H. Spurgeon were to visit America, as multitudes hope he will, he would receive a welcome from the denomination to which he especially belongs that would gratify even his warmest admirers. With Mr. Spurgeon actually present among us, we should like to see the man or the paper that would then denounce his church as a 'nondescript organisation,' a 'hybrid concern,' uttering in theory hypocritical words of delusion, etc. Further, it may not be doubted as to who would then exhibit toward the distinguished London preacher the most consideration, who would be foremost among his 'personal friends,' or who would evince the most pride in him as a bright ornament of the great Baptist denomination. By the way, the fact of Mr. Spurgeon's being open communion—in which *The Watchman* differs from him as widely as any— does not, we infer, damage his sermons in papers which rely largely on these to build themselves up, and which take particular pains (even at the expense of a perpetually false witness against others) to make it appear that they alone are 'sound' on the communion question. [141]

But Spurgeon was deeply engrossed in everything going on in the life of his native country, so the trip did not materialize. Spurgeon involved himself not only from the religious and spiritual perspective of Britain, but from the political as well. That strange mix of secular society being the "City of Destruction," but also one that needed to be ministered to and redeemed, constantly motivated him. That is how he understood the Bible, and as the "Interpreter" of the Word that is how he shaped his ministry. Thus he gave himself to evangelism and political issues. The political dynamics of Spurgeon's ministry is a story within itself. To those issues we turn.

10

"There Came Forth a Summons to Mr. Standfast"

SPURGEON THE POLITICIAN

Spurgeon's study at home in "Westwood."

O world of wonders! (I can say no less.)
That I should be preserved in that distress
That I have met with here! O blessed be
That hand that from it hath delivered me!
Dangers in darkness, devils, hell, and sin,
Did compass me, while I this vale was in.
Yea, snares, and pits, and traps, and nets did lie
My path about, that worthless silly I
Might have been catched, entangled, and cast down.
But since I live, let Jesus wear the crown.
—*John Bunyan*

Introduction

Charles H. Spurgeon had learned how to fill the role of "Mr. Standfast." Nor did he simply "play" the role; he authentically filled it with his life and influence. He set his compass toward what he felt should be the direction and ministry of the Metropolitan Tabernacle, and steadfastly held to the course. In his theological position, as has been made evident in the Baptismal Regeneration Controversy, he remained steadfast. But not just in his theology did Spurgeon stand fast; he also held very tenaciously to his political convictions. Whenever issues arose of morality, ethics, religion, or what he simply felt were the best politics for the country, he remained unswerving. Moreover, he wielded real political power, even swaying one entire election. These factors are another interesting facet in the intriguing life of the Metropolitan Tabernacle pastor.

SPURGEON'S POLITICAL PHILOSOPHY

In many respects, Spurgeon echoed the political philosophy, even the life philosophy, of William E. Gladstone, the "grand old man" of British Victorian politics. Gladstone honestly believed "that the whole of human life is the service of God." Philip Magnus, Gladstone's biographer, contends that Gladstone's entire political career revolved around an effort to apply Christian principles to the whole spectrum of political life.[1] Needless to say, Gladstone's approach made him a popular political personality with the evangelical Nonconformists of Britain, not the least of which was Charles Haddon Spurgeon.

Thus, Spurgeon and Gladstone established real rapport; they became true friends. In a letter to his father dated July 20, 1882, Spurgeon wrote, "Mr.

511

Gladstone invites me to breakfast at Downing Street on the 27th, but I shall be in Scotland. I am sorry to miss the opportunity." [2]

Gladstone and his son, W. H. Gladstone, visited the Metropolitan Tabernacle on Sunday evening January 8, 1882, and walked all the way back to #10 Downing Street. It was an important occasion needless to say. Spurgeon did not know that Gladstone intended to be there, although Charles did receive a call in the afternoon to inquire whether or not he would preach because the Prime Minister planned to come. The deacons therefore quickly arranged to receive their national leader.

Gladstone and his son arrived at 6:15 and were conducted to the minister's vestry. They sat with Spurgeon until the service time. A contemporary account says:

> The rumour that the Prime Minister had arrived rapidly spread throughout the congregation, and as half-past six approached, every eye was turned toward the small door at the rear of the platform, from which the pastor and his officers emerge. With customary punctuality, Mr. Spurgeon opened the door and descended the stairs, followed by his deacons; behind them was seen the calm and pallid countenance of the Premier, accompanied by his son. The elders of the church brought up the rear. [3]

Spurgeon had no time to prepare a special message, so he preached what he had planned. He delivered a message on the healing of the woman who had the issue of blood, found in Mark 5:30. Spurgeon preached as though no imminent personality was there. He emphasized the importance of faith in his message. After the service, the preacher and Gladstone retired to the vestry. The deacons and elders shook hands with Mr. Gladstone who congratulated the pastor on having such a great group of fellow laborers. The newspapers took up the story with zest. An article in *The Standard* the next day read:

> The announcement that the Prime Minister was among Mr. Spurgeon's audience at the Tabernacle on Sunday night is in many ways a suggestive item of news. Fifty years ago the 'stern and unbending hope' of the Conservatives might have been inclined to scoff at the seer who would have risked the prophecy which has now come true. But in the course of half a century Mr. Gladstone has changed, and the Church, if in its main features the same as that in whose defence the young Member for Newark wrote his maiden work, has so widened its sympathies and moderated its asperities as to leave room for an honest appreciation of even the energetic Baptist preacher who, for thirty years, has exercised so marked an influence on a certain section of the community. When Mr. Spurgeon first began his ministrations in New Park Street Chapel, London did not know well what to make of 'the new light.' He was young, fiery—unfriendly critics said illiterate—and, it was agreed by most men, a little vulgar. The canons of pulpit oratory seem not to have been framed

for him. His similes were drawn from sources hitherto untapped, and his endless anecdotes, apt though they were to the point to be illustrated, not infrequently savoured of irreverence. Yet the preacher drew; and the more he offended the smooth commonplaces of the polite world the fuller his chapel became and the wider grew his fame. Park Street became too small for him, and the Tabernacle in Newington Butts had not been well finished before it was clear that a hall even double its size would prove too limited for the crowds which gathered from far and near to listen to the popular pastor. Mr. Spurgeon has so long been a recognised institution of the metropolis that it is hard to believe that at a period still easily remembered he was the subject of harsh criticism and what almost amounted to vituperation. . . . Mr. Spurgeon is today as eagerly run after as ever. Any ill-feeling which he once provoked has entirely disappeared, and few strangers now pass through London without visiting his Tabernacle. Accordingly, when the Premier and his son, and at an earlier date Mr. Bright, paid him a visit, they were only following a custom which has grown very general amongst all classes in this country—Churchmen as well as Dissenters. . . . The world is wide, and requires many men to make it what it is. There may be differences of opinion regarding the advantages to be derived from sermons such as those which have so long been a specialty of the Tabernacle. But it requires no great stretch of liberality even in the most devout of Churchmen to allow that, take him all in all, the world would be the poorer by the loss of the Baptist minister who has been honoured by preaching before so eminent a theologian as the present Premier.

The Freeman wrote, "The pastor had too many visitors of similar quality to allow of his making any difference on their account."[4] Because the event made all the papers, considerable correspondence followed. In one letter to Spurgeon from an Anglican, the writer said, "You nonconformists are bidding fair to be the ruin of this country." This criticism came about because the Church of England saw Spurgeon as an enemy over his stand against an established church. Gladstone's visit to the Tabernacle was virtually tantamount to putting Spurgeon on par with Anglican clergy. This did not set well with many Anglicans. Cartoons appeared in the papers. Poems were even written. One read:

> For when the place was filling
> Commencing time at hand
> Came Holy Willy and his son
> to join the pious band.

> The deacons ran to meet them
> The pastor from his den,
> Rushed forth, discourse forgotten
> To greet these noble men.

An acrostic also received wide circulation. It read:

G—reat in evasion and equivocation
L—eader of all the ritualists in the nation
A—nd yet to the rationalists an inclination
D—isregarding fear, his party to uphold
S—o that be done, his country may be sole
T—ruckels to Rome, the Romish vote to win
O—r to the House, held atheist Bradlaugh in
N—ot long since Enraght's ritual he approves
E—ven as now—Spurgeon's Dissent he loves.

Gladstone's strength as a Christian politician rested in the fact that he could translate political issues into moral matters. He had a genius for such an approach. Thus Gladstone exemplified for Spurgeon what the politician should be, and what Spurgeon, in most instances, fully supported.

Spurgeon was also held in great esteem by David Lloyd George, a later Prime Minister. *The British Weekly* published a letter October 9, 1892 from George to Spurgeon's publisher, Passmore. It reads as follows:

> Dear Mr. Passmore,—You have sent me one of Mr. Spurgeon's best efforts. There is no gift anyone could send me which I could value more highly. The corrections make it infinitely more interesting, and they give me a wider insight than I ever had into his great sense of style. From the point of view of enriching one's command of Anglo-Saxon words which are best adapted for effective use in speech, I know of no study which is more profitable than the reading of Mr. Spurgeon's sermons. For the variety, for the vigour, for the music of words he is pre-eminent, and this is one of the best samples of his style. It quivers with the vitality of his robust inspiration.
>
> I was brought up to admire and honour that great man sincerely, and I still revere his memory.
>
> I remain, yours sincerely,
>
> (Signed) D. Lloyd George.

God and the Nation

As true in most ages, the Victorian age being no exception, some clergymen and church members believed that politics were just too dirty a business in which to be involved. Spurgeon proved to be the antithesis of that attitude. He fully committed himself to the principle that the governance of England should be conducted along moral, godly guidelines, thus he should speak out on issues. He had become convinced that the ascendancy of the British Empire in economic and political matters resulted from the providential blessings of God upon the nation due to its commitment to Christian principles, so he must help maintain those principles. In many respects,

Spurgeon believed that God touched Britain as a "chosen nation" in something of the same manner that Israel had been the recipient of God's special blessings. He said:

> I believe we are a more highly favored nation than even Israel of Old. God hath done more for Britain, or certainly as much, as He did for Abraham's race, and even if we have not rebelled and revolted as often as did Israel in the wilderness, yet our little rebellions, if they were so, would be great because of the greatness of God's goodness. [5]

Later, a sect known as "British Israelites" grew up and claimed they, the British, were the "lost tribe of Israel," hence the recipients of His special blessings. Of course, Spurgeon would have no part in anything like that.

In Spurgeon's resounding sermon at the Crystal Palace on the national fast day over the Indian Mutiny, he expressed his convictions on God and the nation, preaching that God alone had bestowed the blessings on Britain that the nation enjoyed. He even contended that God had led to the discovery of the Guy Fawkes treachery, and that God had conquered Canada and defeated Napoleon through the armies of Britain. These convictions of Spurgeon harked back to the Reformation days. The Reformation movement in Great Britain lay at the very roots of the Puritan movement; therefore, quite naturally, the "last of the Puritans" came to the conclusion that Britain achieved its greatness because of its commitment to the Puritan Reformation. In a sermon preached at the New Park Street Baptist Church in his early days, he said:

> This land is the home of liberty. But why is it so? I take it, it is not so much because of our institutions as because the Spirit of the Lord is here—the spirit of true and hearty religion. There was a time, remember, when England was no more free than any other country . . . Who won our liberties for us? Who have loosed our change? Under the hand of God, I say, the men of religion—men like the great and glorious Cromwell, who would have liberty of conscience or die . . . We owe our liberty to men of religion, to men of the stern Puritanical school . . . And if we are ever to maintain our liberty (as God grant we may), it shall be kept in England by religious liberty—by religion. The Bible is the Magna Carta of Old Britain.

It may be true that Spurgeon forgot that "the grand and glorious Cromwell" had little concern for religious liberty, at least regarding his Catholic foes. Still, Charles argued strongly that Britain as a Christian commonwealth had attained its leadership, and would retain that leadership in the world scene, because of its Christian stand. Therefore, he believed politicians should be Christians. He stood as the antagonist of Bradlaugh, a politician who confessed to being an outright unbeliever. Spurgeon said there ought to be a "theistic" test for public servants. When a certain Lord Justice Williams died in a brothel, Spurgeon spoke out loud and clear against politicians and leaders living immoral lives and flaunting non-Christian principles of morality.

SPURGEON'S PARTY POLITICS

Spurgeon thus concluded that Christian citizens should vote for the right sort of candidate and involve themselves in national affairs, especially when the issues before the commonwealth had a religious and spiritual tone. Spurgeon held these strong views, not only because of the practicality of them, but also because of his conviction that this was a biblical principle. He argued that God expected even the Jews of the exile to seek the peace of those countries in which they had been held captive. "Should Christians be less generous?" he asked. He believed that Christians should apply the golden rule to every aspect of life, and that certainly meant the political arena as well as the "more spiritual." He said, "If we could not pray over politics we should doubt their rightness." [6] He even contended that one might just as well argue that a Christian should never be a surgeon or a telegraph clerk than to say that believers should not be involved in the political realm. [7]

As could well be expected, however, Spurgeon did not believe that Christians should be embroiled in the "smoke-filled rooms" seeking political plums or participating in shady deals of party politics. He would never himself sit on a political platform, nor would he allow the Tabernacle to be used for party politics. He said no one has a right as a clergyman to use his position to promote mere party ends. For Spurgeon, issues of a moral and religious nature were what mattered, not party politics. Yet he received considerable criticism for "playing politics." *The Baptist* and *The South London Press*, along with *The Daily Telegraph*, wrote negative articles on Spurgeon and his political activities. *The Echo* on April 21, 1877 took another view, however, and justified Spurgeon's statement that he spoke as a person, not as a pastor. It grew into quite a flap. *The Christian Commonwealth*, *The Southwark Recorder*, *The Irish Baptist Magazine*, and *The Christian Reader* all wrote articles. Some commended Spurgeon and some condemned him.

Joseph Parker of London's City Temple, however, spoke out even more vehemently and involved himself more deeply in issues than Spurgeon, and he received more criticism for it. *The Baptist*, in an article written April 29, 1887, said, "He is constantly looking for a new (political) subject." Negative reaction by many Nonconformists toward those who spoke out on political issues characterized the day.

As Spurgeon grew older and more sophisticated, and became more aware of the real nature of hard core politics; he wanted no part of it. He spoke out forthrightly against this sort of political chicanery:

The Right Honorable Member for the town of Corruption (who) view with the equal Right Honorable Representatives for the country of Bribery; and the most noble Conservative place hunter will not be outdone by the Liberal office lover. [8]

This raises the question, did Spurgeon affiliate with any particular political party and throw his weight there? Or did he remain independent and vote on specific issues and politicians as he saw them exemplifying Christian principles? The answer to the latter question is a resounding, *NO*, although he once said, "I belong to the party which knows no party." [9] All of his life he strongly advocated the Liberal Party. Yet at the same time, he always urged Christians to be moved by religious principles, not just party loyalty. The reason for Spurgeon's lifelong support of the Liberal Party grew out of his conviction that the Liberals, more than any other party, stood for the Christian ideals that he himself espoused. Thus, he greatly admired Gladstone and took a firm stand against Disraeli, whom he considered rather self-seeking. For Spurgeon, the Liberal Party stood for political liberty, while he viewed the Conservatives as representing the Established Church and the aristocratic elite. Being a preacher of the "crude masses," he would naturally be adverse to the Conservatives. He said once, it was reported, "I'd rather vote for the devil than a Tory!" [10] But Spurgeon denied he made such a statement. He explained, "I certainly should not vote for the devil under any circumstances, nor am I able to conceive of him as so restored as to become a Liberal. I think he has had a considerable hand in the invention of many a story which has of late been published concerning me." [11]

It is therefore quite understandable why Spurgeon became a supporter of Gladstone and the Liberal Party, as well as a leader in the Liberation Society, whose purpose was the separation of the Anglican Church from the state. Spurgeon felt convinced that the disestablishment of the Established Church stood as one of the most vital needs of Britain. He considered the union of state and church, in his own words, "spiritual fornication." Thus when political issues came to the surface that had these moral, religious connotations, Spurgeon always urged his people to vote, and to vote Liberal. He had little patience with those who would say Christians should not soil their hands in politics, not even to vote. (Recall the anecdote recorded earlier when Spurgeon was accosted by a super pious brother who criticized him for voting.) In simple terms, Spurgeon believed that politics, just like every aspect of the Christian life, ought to be governed by the leadership of God. He preached to his congregation:

> I long for the day when the precepts of the Christian religion shall be the rule among all classes of men and all transactions. I often hear it said, 'do not bring religion into politics.' This is precisely where it ought to be brought and set there in the face of all men as on a candlestick. I would have the cabinet and members of Parliament do the work of the nation as before the Lord, and I would have the nation, either in making war and peace, consider the matter, by

the light of righteousness. We are to deal with other nations about this or that upon the principles of the New Testament. [12]

Spurgeon finally became so committed in the necessity of bringing Christian principles into the political arena that he published a detailed political philosophy for the Christian. He framed it in the form of a series of logical queries. It strikes right at the heart of Spurgeon's whole philosophy; it needs to be seen in full. He wrote:

1. Are not all mankind under law to God, and where, and when did the King of all the earth announce that nations were to be free from his control, and free from all recognition of his existence and authority?

2. Ought not a nation in all questions which necessarily involve religion, to decide for God, and according to his Word, rather than for infidelity; and when a question is decided by numbers, is not every citizen burdened with a share of responsibility, and should he not give his vote on the Lord's side?

3. If the case of a government appointed for secular rule be exactly parallel with that of a company for the management of a railway, so that neither may go beyond their special business, are not both government and the company still bound by the laws of God; as, for instance, that which allots for one day in seven for rest? And can either of them break such laws without sin? If it be true, that both are free from the allegiance to the law of God, where is this affirmed or implied in Scripture?

4. If a government has nothing to do with religion, by what right are public houses closed on Sundays at certain hours? Why are theatres closed on the Lord's day? Why are chaplains provided for the army and navy? Why is religion taught in reformatories? Why is divine service held in gaols? Why are public works closed on the Lord's day? Why does not Parliament sit on Sundays? We venture to challenge the believers in the non-religious principle to endeavor to carry out the logical inferences of their own assertion; most devoutly hoping that they will never succeed.

5. If a government should cease to acknowledge God at all, or in any sense, would it not at once become religious in the very lowest and worst sense, and be to all intents and purposes atheistic, and would it not necessarily by disregarding the Sabbath, and in other ways, become a persecuting government toward the Christian faith, at least in the case of its servants and employees? And would it not thereby involve all its Christian subjects in a share of its sin?

6. As the non-respect of God's word is as much a religion as the respect of it, and as the avowed believers in this religion are a small minority of the nation, is it consistent with justice that the governing power should

be controlled by the negative faith or nonfaith of the minority, in a word, by their irreligion? If not, then in questions which necessarily involve religion, must not the government decide for respect to God and his Word?

7. How can religion be eliminated from education, unless it be eliminated from the teacher himself? If books of history and science, and all reading lessons be expurgated of every religious idea, and the Bible be excluded, will not the work still be incomplete till we raise teachers of a colourless character, or so utterly destitute of all zeal, that they will never intrude their faith in God, his providence, his Word, or his Son?

8. Supposing this last fact to be accomplished, what results beneficial and desirable are likely to follow from the teaching? What results which Nonconformist Christians could look upon with pleasure when on their knees in intercession before God?

9. If it be said that Sabbath schools will make up the deficiency, is it remembered that in large towns the government schools will mainly gather those who never have gone to such schools and never will? Is it also remembered that many of the lowest class of parents who now send their children to the Sunday-schools as their only chance of learning to read, will probably withdraw them when they are forced to acquire that accomplishment or at least can do so for nothing elsewhere? Is it really believed by Christian men that mere reading, writing, and arithmetic, without religious instruction will elevate our street Arabs, and train the waifs and strays of London to be honest men and good citizens?

10. Is this the freedom which our fathers fought and bled for, and this the liberty for which Nonconformists have suffered and laboured—the liberty to deny to those who ask for it, permission for their children to read the Bible in the government schools? If it be so, was the object worthy of the effort? Is it not tantamount to gaining authority to withhold from our degraded juvenile population the fairest chance of moral elevation which was ever placed within their reach?

11. As we have now with considerable clearness taught the world that the State has no power within the sphere of the Church, would it not be as well to teach the further lesson, which is needed to balance the first, namely—that God is King of kings and Lord of lords? Is it not true that parliaments, and kings, and nations, may say, 'Let us break his bands asunder, and cast his cords from us,' such language ill becomes Christian men?

The controversy that erupted over the Education Bill of 1870 is what precipitated Spurgeon's writing the above guidelines. Quite clearly, however, he went beyond that particular issue and outlined his entire political philosophy. That philosophy grew out of his basic theology, namely, that God is sovereign over all of life, and that includes politics, business, the home and every other aspect of one's being. Therefore, every Christian shares the responsibility to see to it that godly ideals are infused into the very fabric of society, and that forces one into the political arena.

SPURGEON'S INFLUENCE

But the pragmatic question is, did Spurgeon exercise any significant influence in the political life of Britain? Did he contribute anything positive and Christian toward the destiny of Victorian England? To this a resounding *YES* can be given. For one so popular, and a man of such deep convictions and views, and never reticent to speak clearly on any political issue, he influenced his many followers significantly. His destiny forced on him political influence, at least on London's south side, if not over the whole country. Again, it should be understood that he adamantly refused to be involved in the unsavory maneuvering of party politics; but when he spoke on a pressing moral issue, people listened and the media took note. Thus, his forthright declarations influenced quite profoundly several elections, especially the general elections of 1880 and 1886. In those years, Spurgeon had hit his peak of popularity and acceptance; thus he made his influence felt.

SPECIFIC AREAS OF INFLUENCE

The very fact that Spurgeon urged his Metropolitan Tabernacle people, and all Britons for that matter, to exercise their suffrage rights made a significant contribution in itself. He wrote a general letter during the 1886 election urging people in Lambeth to vote Liberal. It demonstrates how strongly he felt about exercising one's voting rights—and how he felt about the Tories. It reads:

Nightingale Lane
   Balham, Surrey.
   March 18th, 1880

   To the LIBERAL ELECTORS of LAMBETH

Friends,
   I am informed by persons of judgment that if the Liberal cause should not succeed in Lambeth at this election, it can only be through the apathy of its professed supporters. I trust that no such apathy now exists, and that every Liberal elector will present himself at the poll. The crisis involves such weighty matters that every man should record his vote for that which he conscientiously believes to be the side of right. Indifference will be a crime against the best interests of the commonwealth.

I can understand that quiet people are anxious to avoid the noise and worry of mere party strife: I do not look upon the present contest in that light. We have something else to consider besides our own ease or personal advantage. Great interests are at stake, and he who does not vote for the right will, by his silence, give consent to the wrong, and become a sharer in it.

Do you sorrow over the warlike policy which has thrust might into the place of right, and invaded weak nations with but scant excuse? Then return the two candidates who are opposed to the Beaconsfield Ministry.

Do you believe that constant bluster creates political uneasiness, disturbs our peaceful relations with other nations, and thus hinders trade and commerce? Then send to Parliament the Liberal candidates to strengthen the hands of Mr. Gladstone.

Do you believe that great questions of progress at home should no longer be pushed into a corner? Then increase the number of the men who are the advance guard of liberty.

Lovers of religious equality, your course is plain, and you will not leave your duty undone. With hand and heart support the men who would rid religion of State patronage and control.

You who would ease the national burdens by economy and retrenchment, vote for Messrs. McARTHUR and LAWRENCE.

You who would promote temperance cannot support the party whose most eager partizans belong to the opposite camp.

Imagine another six years of Tory rule, devoid alike of peace and progress, and you will rouse yourselves to do your duty, and all hazard of a repetition of the Southwark disaster will be far away.

Your friend and neighbor,

C. H. SPURGEON

Whenever the Prime Minister or local leaders called an election, no matter how small a circumstance it may have seemed, Spurgeon would urge the people to vote. He argued:

> God has made us our own governors in these British Isles, for, loyal as we are to our Queen, we practically are Caesars to ourselves. We are now called upon to exercise one of the privileges and duties which go with liberty, let no man be neglectful in it. Every God fearing man should give his vote with as much devotion as he prays. [13]

In Spurgeon's day, universal suffrage had not yet arrived on the British scene. Spurgeon, however, constantly advocated extending the franchise to all people. He believed that farmers, laborers, merchants and people in all walks of life ought to have the right to vote. He thoroughly believed it to be better to risk giving voting privileges to those who were not highly educated than to leave the reigns of government in the hands of the elite aristocrats. He committed himself to the democratic process in the fullest sense of the word. In an interview in the *Pall Mall Gazette,* he said:

But I have no fears about the future nor any terrors of the growing power of the democracy. I do not think that the great body of Englishmen ever go very far wrong in matters of political justice when a case is fairly put before them. . . . I have far more confidence in the mob than in the rich and idle few who sneer so superciliously at those who are doing good for God and man. . . . The instincts of the masses can be much more safely relied upon than the caprices of the wealthy and leisured few. [14]

This approach was quite revolutionary to the Victorians. Many in the higher echelons of society feared that a mass rebellion always lurked in the background and could arise from the ranks of those whom they considered "irresponsible." Many felt that to give everyone the vote courted real danger to an otherwise stable society. Even the word "democracy" to many of these people spelled caution if not fear. In some strata of society, especially the sophisticates of the day, it carried the idea of riots, revolution and political chaos. They argued that the masses of the common people with their lack of education and mere emotional reaction to most issues were just too volatile to allow democracy in its fullest form. Conservatives feared people could be easily swayed and whipped up into a frenzy that would shake the very foundations of a stable Britain. To many superficially sophisticated Victorians, everyone "ought to know his place and keep it."

With this basic ethos permeating large segments of British society, it becomes understandable why Spurgeon stood against such an attitude and took his stand as a staunch Liberal. The Liberal Party stood for everything the aristocratic Conservative party did not. And Spurgeon, the preacher of the "uneducated masses," felt he should watch over their political rights as well as their spiritual health. Thus he steadfastly fought the elitism of the political Conservatives of the day. How did it work out in the rough and tumble affairs of life?

SPURGEON'S PRACTICAL APPROACH

In British politics, representatives to the House of Commons are elected according to various areas or burroughs in the country. The political party that sends a majority of members to Parliament chooses the Prime Minister. In the previous elections before 1880, in the borough of Lambeth, near the Metropolitan Tabernacle, a Conservative representative had regularly been elected. The Conservatives, dominating the House, selected Disraeli as the Conservative Prime Minister. Spurgeon adamantly opposed Disraeli's aggressive foreign policy in the Balkans, South Africa and Afghanistan. Spurgeon took up the gauntlet in the 1880 general election and assumed as his own responsibility to see to it that the borough of Southwark, his own borough, (and Lambeth if possible) would never see a Conservative elected. Thus he spoke out against the Conservatives in his sermons and in *The*

Sword and the Trowel, even printing various leaflets against the Conservative candidates. He distributed them in the burroughs of Southwark and Lambeth. Spurgeon's absolute commitment to his convictions is shown in one leaflet he distributed. He wrote:

Friends,

Your defeat, upon a late occasion, has furnished a temporary cause of triumph to the Conservative party, and it must be your unanimous resolve to wipe out the stain by returning the two Liberal Candidates who now seek your votes. This can be done, but not without a vigorous effort, and the polling of many who, on the last occasion, neglected their duty.

No Liberal should, on this occasion, imagine that his help is unnecessary; each man should act as if all depended upon his vote. Our opponents are not to be despised, and their supporters are in real earnest; therefore, Liberals of Southwark, quit yourselves like men, and bestir yourselves for the grand old cause!

I have received from many trusty friends the best commendations of your two Candidates, Messrs. COHEN and THOROLD ROGERS, and I am glad that they have the hearty confidence of the leaders of the Liberal opinion in the Borough. Disunion no longer weakens you, and I hope that apathy has been stung out of you; what remains but to go in and win?

Great questions are involved in the struggle; never were weightier issues before the nation. A responsibility of the most serious kind is thrust upon us all, and we must face it. Every man must this day exercise his franchise without fail.

Are we to have another six years of Tory rule? This is just now the question.

Are we to go on slaughtering and invading in order to obtain a scientific frontier and feeble neighbors? How many wars may we reckon upon between now and 1886? What quantity of killings will be done in that time, and how many of our weaker neighbors will have their houses burned and their fields ravaged by this Christian(?) nation? Let those who rejoice in war vote for the Tories; but we hope they will not find a majority in Southwark.

Are we, for years to come, to bully and bluster all around the world, and frighten away trade and commerce? If you dread the thought—poll for ROGERS and COHEN. Shall all great questions of reform and progress be utterly neglected for years? They will be, unless true Liberals come to the front.

Shall the struggle for religious equality be protracted and embittered? It will be so if the New Parliament is made of the same material as the old.

Shall our National Debt be increased? Our imperial expenditure be swollen, and the very word 'retrenchment' become a jest? It must be so, if the present Government be kept in power.

You know the great principles which are at stake, and you have now a fair field for fighting them out. There need be no personalities, and there should be none, for the Candidates on both sides are worthy of their prominence.

This is as it should be, and it will make the Southwark contest the more notable.

A Liberal success, for which you look with brightest hope, will inspire all your comrades.

In the name of Peace, Justice, Reform, and Progress, muster your forces.

Southwark once led the van in advanced Liberalism, and it has now come down to be represented by two Conservatives!

Will you not alter this state of things? Have you not had enough of it already? The remedy is in your own hands.

Your Friend and neighbor,
C. H. Spurgeon

Did Spurgeon taste success? The answer again is a resounding *Yes*. The Liberals took the general election and Gladstone became Prime Minister. The Southwark borough put two Liberal representatives whom Spurgeon endorsed in the House of Commons. Spurgeon received the credit for this reversal in south London. One observer called him "the greatest single influence in South London in favor of Liberalism, upon whose every word thousands and thousands hang, as if it were the very bread of life." [15] In the same publication, the author wrote:

> At elections, School Board and Parliamentary, his followers display an energy and discipline which leave nothing to be desired. They are men of faith who do not lose heart in times of adversity and reaction. Their human sympathies as well as their spiritual have been warmed by the flame which burns in the bosom of the devout and fearless and Great Heart of the Metropolitan Tabernacle. [16]

It is interesting that the above article was not penned by a political Liberal, but by a rigid opponent of Spurgeon's political views. He had called Spurgeon one of the "unfittest—a painful anachronism," but he recognized Spurgeon's ability to make his political views felt.

IRISH HOME RULE

The general election of 1886 saw a repeat of the 1880 election. Spurgeon deeply influenced that political event, only with a twist. Spurgeon had always been a loyal supporter of Prime Minister Gladstone. However, on the issue of home rule for Ireland, he vociferously disagreed with Gladstone. During the nineteenth century, Ireland had been a very volatile political arena for several years. Violence, political assassinations, bombings, and general upheaval characterized Ulster. In the light of these dynamics, Gladstone propounded the idea in 1886 that Ireland should have a measure of home rule with a Parliament of her own. In this way, he reasoned, Ireland might be able to deal more effectively with her problems. One can imagine how this came over to many Victorian Englishmen in their pride for the great British Empire. To them, the British Isles stood as the emanating center of the worldwide Empire; to think of giving home rule to one of the islands sent a severe shock wave throughout the land. It struck right at the heart of their imperialist mentality. Not only that, many Nonconformists felt very uneasy over the well-being of the Protestants of the northern counties in Ireland. They feared there would be Catholic discrimination against the minority Protestants of the north, if not outright persecution. Spurgeon therefore broke with Gladstone on this very divisive political issue. Spurgeon never doubted the sincerity or motivation of the Prime Minister, but he believed him to be essentially wrong. In the *Times* of June 3, 1886, a special article put forth Spurgeon's position. In that article Spurgeon was quoted as saying:

> We feel bound to express our great regret that the great Liberal leader should have introduced his Irish Bills. We cannot see what our Ulster brethren have done that they should be cast off. They are in great dismay at the prospect of legislative separation from England, and we do not wonder. They have been ever our loyal friends, and ought not to be sacrificed. Surely something can be done for Ireland less ruinous than that which is proposed? The method of pacification now put forward seems to us to be full of difficulties, uncertainties, and unworkable proposals. It is well meant: but even the best and greatest may err. Is it not possible for those who desire the welfare of Ireland and the unity of the Empire to devise a more acceptable scheme? We cannot look forward with any complacency to Ulster Loyalists abandoned and an Established Irish Catholic Church; and yet these are by no means the greatest evils which we foresee in the near future should the suggested policy ever become fact.[17]

In the general election of 1886, Irish home rule became the central issue. This placed Spurgeon in a dilemma. He certainly did not wish to campaign for the Conservative party; yet, the leader of his Liberal Party advocated a policy he could not in any way endorse. He took the middle road, refusing to endorse the Conservative Party, but throwing his weight behind the candidates of the Liberal persuasion who themselves opposed Gladstone's Irish policy. Again south London heard Spurgeon's admonitions to vote the "Christian way." The Tories capitalized on Spurgeon's statements that seemed to condemn the Liberal party, while the Liberals published Spurgeon's denunciations of the Conservative party. For example, Spurgeon said that "the Tories are not to be trusted."[18] That particular statement delighted the Liberals and they used it. The Conservatives had their quotes, too. So the paradoxical situation persisted.

Thus Spurgeon exercised his influence. How widespread that influence became and the nature of the final outcome of his stance is a matter of debate. One historian has questioned whether the working classes of London were influenced by any Nonconformist leader. Henry Pelling, in *Social Geography of British Elections, 1885-1910*, argued that the working classes remained quite unaffected by the influence of any Nonconformist preacher. He noted that in many south London boroughs such as Hackney, Lambeth and Peckham, the vote was not consistently Liberal. Thus he concluded:

> In general, therefore, we must conclude that if Nonconformity exerted any distinctive force in those constituencies where it was supposed to be relatively strong, it was not enough to be statistically noticeable. It is a reasonable assumption that both churches and chapels . . . (were) a very minor factor in London politics. [19]

One can question Pelling's conclusions from several perspectives, however. First, Pelling discussed a time outside of Spurgeon's particular day of power. Moreover, in the 1886 elections the working class district of Southwark did vote as Spurgeon encouraged them to do. Not only that, the Irish problem had actually split the Liberal Party. That muddled the issue. Then on a national scale, the Nonconformists themselves disagreed over the issue of Irish home rule; consequently, a considerable amount of their influence waned. Thus one wonders if Pelling's conclusions are not somewhat dubious. The fact that Spurgeon influenced people to vote and to vote Liberal seems reasonably incontestable, at least as far as areas of south London are concerned. The fact that he influenced the borough of Southwark and perhaps several others in the general south London area seems a safe assumption.

One thing can at least be concluded, Spurgeon's life and ministry influenced more than just purely religious affairs. As the spiritual leader of many common people, he did influence profoundly two major national elections. He influenced many, arguing that Christians have an ethical and religious responsibility to see that government moves along moral and religious lines and thus ought to be concerned about how the government is run.

Of course, Spurgeon encountered strong opposition from the Conservatives, one has put it, to "almost chronic" dimensions. That bothered the south London pastor very little. For Spurgeon, the Conservatives represented the wealthy few, the landed gentry and aristocracy, whom he felt held the masses down in an attempt to quell the rising tide of democracy. Spurgeon saw this spirit epitomized in the House of Lords. To him the House of Lords had become no more than a tool of upper class "political parasites" to stifle good policies. Spurgeon would point to the occasion when the House of Lords delayed the passage of a bill on Irish disestablishment that would bring the state church out from under the control and support of the state. In the light of that which he felt was a gross injustice, Spurgeon commented:

> The delay in doing justice to Ireland occasioned by the tyrannical action of the Lords is precisely what we expected and desired. The country will be led to ask how long these titled defenders of injustice are to rule a free people and

forbid the nation to fulfil its will. The bishops ought to be removed from the Upper House forthwith; let them look after their flocks and they will have more than enough to do. With one or two exceptions, they are always the friends of everything oppressive.[20]

So he spoke as he always did, right to the point and unapologetically. His commitment to Irish disestablishment ran deep. In a letter to Gladstone he wrote:

The Tabernacle
  Newington
  April 16

To the Rt. Honorable
W. E. Gladstone, Esq.

Sir,
  As one among thousands I have watched your career with an almost affectionate admiration; not only because for the most part I have agreed with your politics, but because I have seen in you a man actuated by a sense of right, in contradistinction to the pitiful shifts of policy.
  I have been made bold to write to you this one word to say that in your present struggle to do justice to Ireland by the disestablishment of the Church of the few, you have not only the zealous cooperation of Dissenters interested in politics, but the devout prayers of those to whom it is a matter of solemn conscience that our Lord's kingdom is not of the world. We see in you an answer to many a fervent petition that the day may come when the Church of Jesus may believe in her Lord's power and not in human alliances. Whether you would personally go with us in that view is not the point, but going as far as you do, so purely, so conscientiously we invoke the aid of the God of Providence to help you.
  I felt ready to weep when you were threatened with so much contumely by your opponents in your former struggle, and yet I rejoice that you were educating the nation to believe in conscience and truth. It is nothing to you that I sympathize with you, and yet in moments of vexation a child's word may cheer a strong man; and it is for this that I felt that I must say to you that I trust you will be sustained under the yet more virulent which will certainly come upon you. The sense of right will be to you as a sword and buckler, and if again deserted by recreants as you may be, you will stay yourself upon the Eternal God in whose custody the jewels of right and justice are ever safe.
  I do not expect even a line from your Secretary to acknowledge this. It will content me once in my life to have said 'Thank you' and 'God-speed' to such a man.

Yours very respectively,
C. H. Spurgeon

Thus it can be fully and confidently concluded, Spurgeon, as a loyal supporter of the Liberal party and an opponent of the Conservatives, influenced society significantly. But how did Spurgeon come down on the political issues central in his day? These interesting facets of Spurgeon's political involvement demand investigation.

DISESTABLISHMENT

The question of a state church, especially in the Victorian era, was as hot a political issue as it was a religious concern. Should the Church of England be supported by the state, its basic decisions controlled by Parliament, thus becoming the only "legitimate" church in the land? That was the question. Nonconformity saw the disestablishment of the Church as one of its chief goals. Spurgeon, of course, held very strong, opinionated views on the issue.

Spurgeon came to London the very year the Liberation Society took on its new name and became active in disestablishment. Spurgeon thrust himself vigorously into the movement. He seemed to chafe under the innuendo that being a Nonconformist automatically cast one into the status of being a second class citizen. Although as the nineteenth century progressed, most of the discriminatory laws against Nonconformity had been removed, still the general attitude of society implied that the Anglican ministers were the true ministers of the nation. Nonconforming churches were commonly called "chapels," the term "church" being reserved for the Established congregations. Most Nonconformists found it all rather galling. One offensive aspect of Establishment centered in the fact that every Anglican bishop automatically became a member of the House of Lords, thus controlling to some extent issues in Parliament. Often these bishops felt Nonconformists should be merely "tolerated." That hardly set well with the Nonconformists, especially free-thinking Charles Haddon Spurgeon. In this setting, the Liberation Society was established with one purpose and goal: To see the obliteration of the Establishment and the total separation of church and state. Spurgeon involved himself in this battle with all the fervor of his faith. Often he lashed out against the whole idea of an Established Church. In May, 1880, in *The Monthly Record of the Protestant Evangelical Mission*, he addressed the populace urging them to vote for the politicians who would work for disestablishment. He wrote, "Lovers of Religious Equality, your course is plain, and you will not leave your duty undone. With hand and heart support the men who would rid Religion of State Patronage and Control." He would often chide people for not getting involved in politics, especially in political-religious issues like disestablishment. Actually, the issue of state support for the Church of England became a theological doctrine to the Metropolitan Tabernacle preacher. He said:

We are told that we enjoy *toleration*, the very word is an insult. What would the members of the dominant sect think if we talked of tolerating them? We shall never be satisfied until all of religious communities stand upon an equal footing before the law. . . . An Established Church is a spiritual tyranny. . . . That which our fathers died to overthrow we are compelled to support. We cannot help being indignant; we should be less than men if our blood did not boil within us at such injustice.[21]

Spurgeon received considerable criticism for his position, but also some praise for his stand. For example, *The American Churchman* said, in 1885, "Of course, it goes without saying that the distinguished Baptist preacher is only logical in holding this position."

As the nineteenth century wore on, the Established Church gradually lost its unique and exclusive privileges and Nonconformity was granted more "toleration." The Liberation Society played no small role in this reform. They constantly agitated for change, and Spurgeon, being one of the key members of the Society, spoke at many of their rallies and literally raged against ideas such as Nonconformists having to undergo Established Church rites before being buried in church graveyards. He deplored the fact that an Anglican Church registrar had to be present at a Nonconformist wedding to legalize the union. The fact that ecclesiastical courts had the exclusive right to preside over disputes in wills and bequests incensed him.

One thing that galled Spurgeon most was that Nonconformists had to help pay the actual bill for the meagerly attended Anglican churches. Spurgeon found that absolutely outrageous. In an interview with W. T. Stead, he said:

It is a great and crying injustice to all those who do not belong to it; a great obstacle in the way of Christian unity, and an institution that seems to me entirely indefensible. That the church of the aristocracy cannot support itself, while the churches of the poor are able to do so is to me utterly incredible.[22]

Even though Nonconformity began to enjoy more concessions, Spurgeon did not soften his attitude toward the Establishment. Every time the Established Church received something of a setback and the Nonconformists moved a step forward, it motivated him even more to advocate the complete separation of church and state. His almost vehement attitude can be found expressed regularly in his sermons and writings. In *The Sword and the Trowel*, he wrote:

We can never rest until the Episcopacy is established and perfect religious equality is found everywhere. Leave to bury our dead in the graveyards which belong to every Englishman will be a liberty for which we will not even say 'thank you,' for it is no more than our right. As for the idea that this is the end of our demands, it is preposterous. There must be no patronage or oppression of any faith by the State, and all men must stand equal before the law whatever their creed may be; and until this is the case our demands will not cease.

He said the problem with the Established Church fighting disestablishment was that it was "blinded by gold dust."

Spurgeon always puzzled over the fact that the Established Church of England, which mostly catered to the upper, wealthier echelons of society, could never fully finance itself. He would point out, at least by innuendo, that the churches of Nonconformity could meet their needs without enforced tithe taking. Why could not the wealthy Established Church do the same? The Established Church did not stop taking taxes until the last third of the nineteenth century. But it must also be admitted that some Nonconformist chapels were not as financially strong as one would have hoped, perhaps not even as strong as Spurgeon implied. Spurgeon himself raised funds for poor ministers constantly and his wife conducted "The Book Fund" that sent religious books to poor ministers. One Anglican bishop once pointed out Spurgeon's inconsistency in his denunciations. Spurgeon had little to say in reply. Spurgeon at times did give himself to hyperboles; that must be admitted.

Later in life, Spurgeon renounced his commitment to the Liberation Society. In April, 1891 he resigned his membership. No one, not even his contemporaries, seemed to have an explanation for this. The only rationale seems to be, as Spurgeon declared, the Society had become infected with liberal theological convictions. But that should not have affected the political issue of disestablishment. Yet, Spurgeon could never tolerate liberal theology, no matter where he found it. Then it must be remembered that in 1891 Spurgeon was a very sick man. Perhaps he did not see things with the clear objectivity that he had in his younger days. Moreover, he had become exceedingly sensitive to liberal theology because of the Down Grade Controversy that had precipitated his withdrawal from the Baptist Union. That mindset seemed to force him to separate himself from anything that even appeared to move in a theologically liberal direction. Perhaps Spurgeon saw himself as inconsistent if he did not withdraw from the Liberation Society with its theologically liberal trend if he had broken from the Baptist Union for the same reason. At any rate, he said:

> We wish success to those who advocate justice in religious liberty, be they who they may; but the important matter to us is the spiritual question, which must be kept apart . . . the spiritual and political will not mix; in these days, at any rate. . . . We will not by this question be brought into a parent union with those from whom we differ in the very core of our souls upon matters vital to Christianity. [23]

But the Liberation Society had embraced more liberal trends for years. As stated by Meredith, "that Spurgeon could work hand in glove with members of the Liberation Society of over 30 years and not notice these theological differences until late in life" is rather strange. He had been willing to work with many of these same men for many years, then suddenly he could no longer cooperate. Meredith may be correct when he says, "It was as though, once he began to look for points on which he disagreed with the mainstream of theological thought, a chip appeared on his shoulder and the slighted deviation from orthodox Calvinism would now serve to knock it off."[24]

However, Spurgeon constantly maintained his concern for disestablishment. He still claimed a vital interest in the issue, but after the Down Grade Controversy and his separation from the Liberation Society, he took little actual part in the movement.

IMPERIALISM

Spurgeon has been written on from virtually every perspective. Monographs, biographies, and his own writings have flooded the bookshelves for more than 100 years. Yet, one area of Spurgeon's life has been almost universally neglected, namely, his position on war and imperialism. This seems rather strange, because everyone understands the nineteenth century as the "age of imperialism." All the countries of Europe were vitally involved in imperial affairs. After the Berlin Conference of 1884, a "scramble" for empire building burst on the scene. For example, European powers partitioned off Africa and divided the Far East into "spheres of influence." A caustic parody on this was done in the 1970s, approximately 100 years later, in a film entitled, "Oh, What a Lovely War." In that film, the leaders of the world gathered in symbolic fashion and before a map of the world each took their part. It was a graphic portrayal of the spirit of the late nineteenth century. How did Spurgeon react to this? Did he react at all? Of course! He was as outspoken on this issue as on every other problem of the day. Why biographers have refused, or at least neglected, this area is something of a puzzle. It should be approached.

A disturbing question arises in the context of Victorian imperialism: how could British foreign policy be justified among a people who were quite altruistic and believed in the love of one's fellow man? With this the politicians had to wrestle. They normally took a very simplistic, questionable line; they argued that the "barbarians" of the Orient and Africa should be very thankful and grateful that Western civilization had come to them and they had become recipients of all the benefits of "Christian" nations. Even if these benefits came in the form of guns, troops, and armies, it was a benefit still. And the propaganda worked. The people of Europe bought it. The political leadership wielded a masterful stroke. Even the Liberal Party got on the imperialistic bandwagon in the guise of the "white man's burden." As a case in point, Gladstone ordered the invasion of Egypt to "protect" the natives and the Britishers that were there. He also justified the "Jameson Raid" in South Africa, insisting that the rights of the British miners in Transvaal should be protected. But history has plainly shown that though some benefits did accrue to the native population when the European imperialists invaded their lands, the primary motive was national interest at best and personal greed at the worst. Yet, it must be granted that the Liberals did not take nearly as hard a line on the "necessity" of imperialism as did the Conservatives.

How did Spurgeon react to this? The situation did not dupe him for one moment. He constantly complained that such imperialistic policies and the mistreatment of the native populations were totally unchristian. He never accepted the propaganda that Britain's own national interests provided any justification for such actions. Spurgeon deplored the kind of nationalism that bred pride in imperialism. He sarcastically said, "Britannia rules the waves. Does she? Put Britannia on the waves, and see."[25] He did not make the subtle mistake of making Great Britain the Kingdom of God. He saved himself, for the better part, from mixing nationalism and his personal religion, although at times his nationalism rose high in his thinking and rhetoric.

That which particularly disturbed Spurgeon was the oriental opium trade the British government supported and defended. Spurgeon found it inconceivable that the governmental policies of a nation supposedly founded on Puritan Christianity could actually traffic in narcotics, and that against the will of the Chinese people themselves. "Utterly indefensible," Spurgeon argued. In denouncing it he said:

> The opium trade, by almost universal consent, is one of the most iniquitous, most deadly, and most accursed evils of the nineteenth century. If war is slaying its thousands, the opium trade is slaying its tens of thousands. The mournful tale of its immoral and destructive effects is faithfully and fearlessly told. . . . The responsibility for its origin, its extension, and its enforcement, in spite of remonstrances and prohibitions, is clearly shown to sit with the British government of India and consequently with England and the British crown.

Spurgeon rightly complained, "We send out missionaries to the heathen Chinese while acting more heathenly than he does! Was ever inconsistency more glaring?"[26] Of course, he needed to remember the opium traders were hardly missionaries, nor were missionaries representatives primarily of Britain; they spoke for the Kingdom of God, not Whitehall.

Whether Spurgeon saw Britain and Anglo-Saxon people as a superior race can be debated. Some have found a slight racist sentiment in one of his earlier sermons. In a message he pictured someone from a "heathen" land begging for a British believer to bring the blessings of the Gospel to his uncivilized people. Spurgeon said:

> What though our skin be of a colour less fair than yours? . . . It is true, our kings and princes are only fit to rank with your beggars. . . . We are men—we are your brothers—younger brothers, it is true—we have not had a double portion of the inheritance; brothers too whose fathers spent their past in riotous living; but why should the children's teeth be set on edge because the fathers

have eaten sour grapes? Why must the son of Ham forever bear the curse of Canaan?

One wonders if there really were not a slight sense of racial superiority in his attitude, at least at that time. After all, he did live in the Victorian era and would but reflect something of that culture, right or wrong from our vantage point today. And even though some of Spurgeon's statements like, "The curse of Ham," certainly did have racial overtones, it must be remembered that Spurgeon vehemently opposed slavery, even at the cost of his sermon sales dramatically falling off in America. Nevertheless, this does not justify the fact that Spurgeon in his early years may have had a tinge of prejudice. Hopefully, that attitude fell into oblivion as he matured.

It does seem that Spurgeon's attitude did change through the years. He became not only more knowledgeable of the world, but also more mature in his Christian faith. In his later years he never hinted of any inherent racial superiority. Actually, in his last years he denounced racism. He said:

> Next, notice, that we ought never to be moved by the supposed superiority of a race. I have heard it said that it would be far better to try and convert the superior races than to consider the more degraded. . . . Let us feel that the degraded Africans, the dwarfs of the woods, the cannibals of New Guinea and all such are to be sought quite as much as the more advanced races. They are men; that is enough. [27]

Such an attitude is outstanding for Victorian England.

Thus one can conclude that Spurgeon fiercely opposed political imperialism all of his life. Even on the relationship of Britain to India, he held his ground. Referring again to the 25,000 people gathered in the Crystal Palace on the National Day of Mourning after the Indian mutiny, young Spurgeon, with all the audacity of youth but also the conviction of a genuine Christian, brought into question Britain's whole role in India. In the nineteenth century, India shone as the bright star in the imperialism spectrum. Queen Victoria had herself crowned, not only as Queen of the Britons, but also of the Indians. That large subcontinent became the grand prize of the British Empire. In his sermon at the Crystal Palace, Spurgeon claimed that if the Indian nation, even as a whole, had revolted, he would not have launched a crusade against them. That shocked the average Englishman. Yet, Spurgeon held his ground and remained "Mr. Standfast." He stayed consistent with his political conviction that every nation on earth should be free from foreign intervention and domination. Every country, Spurgeon argued, regardless of its size, political power, wealth, or how undeveloped it may be, had the inalienable right to govern itself as it saw fit. He declared:

> Whatever great powers have interfered with smaller inoffensive nationalities, for the sake of increasing their territory, or their influence, they are verily

guilty; . . . wherein our civilized races have oppressed and degraded aboriginal tribes, the sin cries out before the high heaven.

It is most commendable that Spurgeon made this anti-imperialistic declaration at the very height of British aggression. All the European countries were on the move to gobble up their share of the world. They considered it their right. Even Spurgeon's own Liberal party on occasion slipped into that general mindset. Spurgeon stood solidly in opposition, feeling it to be a national sin, especially as it came at the expense of the poor native people who had no power of their own to resist.

Although Gladstone was a friend and a political ally in many respects, Spurgeon forthrightly criticized Gladstone's policy on the invasion of Egypt. He cried out:

What have we to do in the Sudan? Being there, what is to be done? Might not a withdrawal from it involve a sea of bloodshed greater than that which seems imminent if we remain? Who knows what is best in so perplexing a case? The evil lay in our first interference and the sooner we quit the place the better if honorable engagements permit. Peace is our duty.

This certainly does not mean that Spurgeon opposed bringing Christianity to the nations of the world. He had firmly committed himself to the mission enterprise. Ever since his conversion in 1850, world evangelization beat in his breast. He even believed that England had a responsibility to bring something of a higher culture, along with the blessings of the Gospel, to those who lived in ignorance and paganism. But he firmly held that the Gospel and the Gospel alone could bring civilization to these underprivileged nations. He continually argued that the message of Jesus Christ had always proved far more potent than economics or any political maneuvering or even education itself to raise the standards of the undeveloped nations of the world. He said:

Preaching the Gospel will effectively civilize, while introducing the arts of civilization will sometimes fail. Preaching the Gospel will lift up the barbarian while attempts to do it by philosophy will be found ineffectual.

Spurgeon chafed under the insensitivity of the British approach to all these matters. To think that those who preached the Gospel of peace and love should be seen in the context of imperialism that sought to bring civilization in by military action, he found totally unacceptable. Spurgeon fervently believed that the missionary enterprise would prosper far better if the governments and armies of the countries from which the missionaries had come forth had stayed at home. He asserted:

There would have been greater probability of the Gospel spreading in India if it had been let alone, than there has ever been since the domination of Great Britain (in India) . . . I had rather go to preach to the greatest savages than live, than I would go to preach in a place that is under British rule.[28]

One can well imagine how this was heard by fervent British patriots. But Spurgeon took his stand with no apologies. He exposed the Victorian hypocrisy for what it was. The excuses and justification of British imperialism for subjugating people around the world did not convince him in any way whatsoever. He saw through the lame excuses to the reality of the situation, and in typical style exposed it for what it was.

To Spurgeon's credit, and others like him, they had some effect in moderating the imperialism of the late nineteenth century. Had they not raised a call of alarm, it may well have resulted in far more people suffering under the cruel hand of their imperialistic masters. Time after time Spurgeon blasted Disraeli for his actions. Regardless of what it might mean to Britain as an individual nation, and the Conservative Party as a political entity, and even to the economy of the country, Spurgeon found no justification for subjugating the nations that were not strong enough to resist Britain's army. For Spurgeon, Disraeli and the Conservatives' foreign policy was unholy and totally unacceptable.

Disraeli's Machiavellian approach that the end justifies the means simply did not wash with Spurgeon. Gladstone and many of the Liberal Party did not totally accept that approach either. What the outcome would have been had not the altruistic attitude of men like Spurgeon and, to some extent, Gladstone come to the fore, only history could tell. They made their contribution in the denunciation of a blatant and totally unfeeling imperialism. Spurgeon was appalled that England would "bully Russia, invade Afghanistan, pour out our wrath on the Zulus, and stand sword in hand over against Burma." Of course, one paradox of the issue is, as pointed out, that two years after the general election, Gladstone shelled Alexandria and invaded Egypt. Many of those who had lifted their voices against the imperialism of Disraeli gave their blessings to Gladstone. But such shifts in the political climate are common, despite how totally inconsistent they may seem. Nonetheless, Disraeli may well have suffered his defeat in the election of 1880 because he did not take into account the Nonconformists approach to the imperialism of the day. The Nonconformists did have a conscience; and they expressed it. In these dynamics, Spurgeon made a significant contribution. This leads to his attitude on war.

WAR

Another facet of Spurgeon's understanding of Christian politics moved him into a contradictory stance with many of his fellow Britons. He adamantly and consistently opposed war. Throughout his life, he never modified his views nor did he ever soften his language concerning what he considered the "horror of war." In Spurgeon's denunciation of war he described it as "a great crime—murder on a huge scale—and a little less than hell let loose among men." He referred to war as "an unutterable evil, a curse to humanity, a pestilence to nations, and frequently an atrocity." [29] This may seem quite startling, because Spurgeon held a very conservative Calvinistic theology, and the fact of history is that conservative Christianity has never been noted for its opposition to war. Often there has been almost an amalgamation of the Christian faith and national patriotism in the support of war when it has broken out. Of course, Britain had never been engaged in any major war during Spurgeon's lifetime. Yet, there were several minor incidents, for example, the Crimean War and other skirmishes. But Spurgeon never faced a Hitler or a Stalin, not even a Kaiser. Perhaps his attitude would have been different had such been the case. But he stood against war throughout his life. This is not to say that Spurgeon, in principle, took a pure pacifist position. He did not. Still, in every situation that arose concerning war and imperialism, he never failed to condemn it. There cannot be found a single instance in his entire life and ministry when he supported violence or warfare in any sense. But he did not take a passive stand on protecting oneself, nor did he support the nineteenth century efforts to abolish capital punishment. He absolutely committed himself to the philosophy that the well-being and protection of the general populace must be protected at all costs. That saved him from an unbending pacifism. But this raises the question: what to do if a real despot attacks a peace-loving nation and thus threatens millions of lives? Spurgeon answered, "When we see war threatened on behalf of a detestable tyranny, contrary to all the dictates of humanity and religion, we cannot do otherwise than implore the Judge of all the earth to save us from such an astounding wickedness, and to remove from office the man whose rash bravados give rise to our fears." [30] Still, Spurgeon could never find any justification for the outbreak of war and the massive loss of lives that always seemed inevitable. Nor did he have any positive word to say about the idea that wars can open up the road for the spread of the Gospel. He declared:

> Whenever England goes to war, many shout, 'It will open the way for the gospel.' I cannot understand how the devil is to make way for Christ; and what is war but an incarnate fiend, the impersonation of all that is hellish in fallen humanity. . . . For an English cannon to make way in Canton for an English missionary, is a lie too glaring for me to believe for a moment. I cannot comprehend the Christianity which talks thus of murder and robbery. [31]

His preachings and his writings are punctuated regularly with comments regarding his utter abhorrence of warfare. Yet, paradoxically, at the mass rally at the Crystal Palace over the Indian Mutiny, he prayed, regarding the soldiers, "To bid them remember that they are not warriors merely, but executioners, and bid them go with steady tramp to battle, believing that God wills that they shall utterly destroy the enemy that has defied Britain and defiled themselves among men." [32] Still, he would always argue that arbitration and counsel not only solved disputes, it is much preferred. He wrote in *The European Correspondent,* November, 1887, concerning the Treaty of Arbitration between the United States and the United Kingdom:

> Concerning the substitution of arbitration for war there can surely be no question among Christian men. I rejoice that the two great Protestant nations (the United States and the United Kingdom) should lead the way in making permanent arrangements for the settlement of differences in a reasonable manner. May they succeed so admirably as to lead others to follow their excellent example. It is surely time that we reasoned like men instead of killing like tigers.

Spurgeon's attitude to war, obviously, played an important part in his life and approach to politics. Yet, it seems none of his biographers, except Patricia Stallings Kruppa, have commented upon it. But Spurgeon was clearly committed to the fact that war must be addressed as a vital issue. He certainly preached and wrote enough about it. Spurgeon expressed outrage at the outbreak of the Crimean War. All of his sympathies went out to those who had suffered. And that sympathy extended not just to the Britons. He said, "The death of an enemy is to me a cause of regret as well as the death of a friend. Are not all my brethren?" Spurgeon made that statement in his second year at the New Park Street Baptist Church. This was not a mature, liberalizing view of an established clergyman, but the fervent conviction of a young, very conservative, Calvinistic, outspoken young minister. His heart was always toward those who suffered.

Again, in 1870, war broke out between France and Prussia. Spurgeon denounced it severely, condemning the attitude of Napoleon III and Wilhelm I. He published an open letter in *The Sword and the Trowel* concerning the affair and asked Napoleon and Wilhelm:

> Whatever do you see in fighting that you should be so fierce for it? One would think you were a couple of gamecocks, and did not know any better . . . Do you fancy that your drums and fifes, and feathers and fineries, and pomp, make your wholesale murder one whit the less abominable in the sight of God? Do not deceive yourselves, you are no better that the cut-throats whom your laws condemn, better, why you are worse, for your murders are so many.[33]

In 1876 he earnestly prayed in public concerning the current Turkish barbarianism, asking that God would preserve peace in the world, and if rulers did not learn wisdom, that God would remove them. He again became the recipient of severe criticism, but the prayer made such an impression that it was published and translated into German and Serbian. Spurgeon received a letter from Austria thanking him that at least one Englishman really understood the Turks.

All Britons knew General Gordon as a professing Christian and a thoroughgoing Bible believer. He had become a hero to the pious Victorians.

Joshua?
King David?

But he came under Spurgeon's condemnation for trying to amalgamate his warfare with his Christianity. Spurgeon condemned "the combination of soldier and Christian which leads to shooting or hanging of men in cold blood." Spurgeon went on to say, "It is almost treason to whisper that the hero spirit is at certain junctures more firm than gracious; but it is so . . . War is a horrible business. Look at it how you may; and nonetheless so because an earnest believer finds himself able to figure in it." [34] Spurgeon idealized the situation; he believed that the Gospel would eventually bring about a cessation of war. He said, "Only let the Gospel be preached, and there shall be the end of war." He argued that if the Gospel ever reached all of the world and nations became fully Christian, that would be the end of war. Spurgeon seemingly got caught up in something of the utopianism of nineteenth century post-millennial dreams. Again, paradoxically, he himself stood theologically as a pre-millennialist. Nonetheless, he preached:

> And do we not believe that when the Gospel is fully preached, and has its day, wars *must* cease to the end of the earth!
> . . . I have a fond belief that the day is coming, when Nelson, on the top of his monument shall be upset, and Mr. Whitefield set there, or the apostle Paul. I believe that Napier, who stands in the square there, will lose his station. He shall say about these men, 'They were very respectable men in the days of our forefathers, who did not know better than to kill one another, but we do not care for them now!' Up goes John Wesley where stood Napier! [35]

Spurgeon obviously had deep and profound convictions against war. In a lengthy editorial in *The Sword and the Trowel*, he gives his full reasons why he so adamantly opposed war. In the April, 1878 edition of the periodical, these words are found:

> At intervals the world goes mad, and mad in the very same direction in which it had confessed its former insanity, and resolved never to rage again. England, at set seasons, runs wild with the war lunacy, foams at the mouth, bellows out, 'Rule Britannia,' shows her teeth, and in general shows herself like a mad creature: then her doctors bleed her, and put her through a course of depletion until she comes to her senses, settles her down to cotton-spinning and shop-keeping, and wonders what could have ailed her. A very few months ago it would have been difficult to discover an apologist for the Crimean War, and yet in this year of grace 1878 we find ourselves surrounded by a furious crowd whose intemperate language renders it almost a miracle that peace yet continues. If they do not desire war, they are mere bullies; but if they do desire it, they certainly go the right way to bring it about.
> The mistakes of former days should minister to the wisdom of the present generation, for history is a nation's education; it is, therefore, to the last degree unfortunate when the people relapse into their acknowledged errors, and repeat the blunders of their sires. If our country has been fairly depicted by the

advocates of war, its condition is disappointing to the believer in progress, and alarming to the patriot who gazes into the future. We are still pugnacious, still believers in brute force, still ready to shed blood, still able to contemplate ravaged lands and murdered thousands without horror, still eager to test our ability to kill our fellowmen. We are persuaded that a large portion of our fellow citizens are clear of this charge, but the noisier, if not more numerous party, clamour for a warlike policy as loudly as if it involved no slaughter, and were rather a boon to mankind than an unmitigated curse. A mysterious argument, founded upon the protection of certain mythical "British interests" is set up as an excuse, but the fact is that the national bull-dog wants to fix his teeth into somebody's leg. . . .

What is the cause of these periodical outbreaks of passion? Why does a peaceful nation bluster and threaten for a few months, and even commence fighting when in a short time it sighs for peace? The immediate causes may differ, but the abiding reason is the same—man is fallen, and belongs to a race of which infallible revelation declares 'their feet are swift to shed blood; destruction and misery are in their ways, and the way of peace have they not known.' . . . Civilized man is the same creature as the savage; he is washed and clothed, but intrinsically he is the same being. As beneath the Russian's skin you find the Tartar, so the Englishman is the savage Briton, or plundering Saxon, wearing broadcloth from the wool of sheep, but with a wild, fierce heart within his breast. . . . Doubtless some good runs side by side with this characteristic of our countryman, and we are far from wishing to deprecate bravery and valour, but at the same time this is one of the difficulties which the peace advocate must not fail to recognize. . . . Observe the bold dash of the Irish, the stern valour of the Scotch, the fierce fire of the Welsh, and the dogged resolution of the English, and you see before you stormy elements ready at any time to brew a tempest.

What then is to be done? . . . We would persuade all lovers of peace to labour perseveringly to spread the spirit of love and gentleness, which is indeed the spirit of Christ . . . the truth as to war must be more and more insisted upon: the loss of time, labour, treasure and life must be shown, and the satanic crimes to which it leads must be laid bare. It is the sum of all villainies, and ought to be stripped of its flaunting colours, and to have its bloody horrors revealed. . . . War brings out the demon in man, wakes up the hellish demon within his fallen nature. . . . Its natural tendency is to haul nations back into barbarism, and retard the growth of everything good and holy. When undertaken from a dire necessity, as the last resort of an oppressed people, it may become heroic, and its after results may compensate for its immediate evils, but war wantonly undertaken, for self-interest, ambition, or wounded pride is evil, only evil, and that continually.

Spurgeon did not stand alone in his practical—if not philosophical—pacifism. England had experienced a long period of relative peace, and the enjoyment of peaceful years permeated much of society. Thus many found the thought of war a hateful thing. Moreover, Spurgeon, along with many of his Nonconformist friends, argued that political ends are never to take ascendancy over spiritual realities. What mattered most to Spurgeon was the extension of the Kingdom of God. He wanted to see a Christ-like spirit permeate all of society. No political move, especially war, should violate that basic ideal. This attitude precipitated his adamant stand against imperialism and war. For Spurgeon, it greatly hindered the spread of the Gospel. In like manner, he opposed war because he saw it as unconscionable for a Christian who wanted to see the Gospel of peace spread to people while they slaughtered one another on the battlefield. Even his view against disestablishment grew out of his basic conviction that extending the Kingdom of God must come first. He believed that the union of church and state actually hindered the growth and furtherance of Christ's Kingdom. Thus he advocated that Christians ought to involve themselves in politics and promote policies that the Kingdom of God may be furthered, and oppose all actions that hindered it.

To Spurgeon's credit, in all these matters, he never let the temporal concerns outweigh the spiritual. He kept them in good biblical balance. There is always the tendency for one to gain the ascendancy over the other; but Spurgeon strove to keep the balance and in that respect was quite successful.

PUBLIC EDUCATION

Few people who really knew Spurgeon ever questioned his personal intellectual ability, despite his limited formal education. The annotated volumes that comprise his personal library still stand as a monument to his grasp of some of the finest academic books of the day. In the book review section of *The Sword and the Trowel*, Spurgeon makes constant reference not only to the great theologians but contemporary writers like Dickens and Darwin. In many senses, he became a true intellectual, though self-taught. Moreover, Spurgeon's concern for mental development extended beyond his personal interests. He was thoroughly convinced that education stood as essential to the progress of society. Through the years Spurgeon's writings make it evident he fully believed that a healthy society must have a healthy education. He voiced his commitment to a well-rounded education for all people with these words:

> By order of Government the roads in Prussia are lined on each side with fruit trees. Riding once, early in September, from Berlin to Halle, an American traveller noticed that some trees had a wisp of straw attached to them. He enquired of the coachman what it meant. He replied that those trees bore choice fruits, and the straw was a notice to the public not to take fruit from

those trees without special permission. 'I fear,' said the traveller, 'that in my country such a notice would be but an invitation to roguish boys to attack those very trees.' 'Haben Sie keine Schules?' (Have you no schools?) was his significant rejoinder. Rest assured, dear reader, that next to godliness, education is the mainstay of order. [36]

He thus committed himself to the principle that every person had the right to receive a well-rounded education. Therefore, it is not surprising that he displayed a vital interest in the Education Act of 1870 and let his influence be felt in the quest for public education. That is not to mention his commitment to his "first-born and best beloved," the Pastors' College. As already seen, he founded the evening school in the basement of the Metropolitan Tabernacle so that illiterate working class people of London might learn to read. Spurgeon wanted people to be as educated as circumstances allowed.

As could be expected, Spurgeon wanted the educational enterprise of the nation to be as Christian as possible. Commensurate with his views on politics, education also must be permeated with the principles of the Christian religion. He said, "Ever since I have known Christ, I have put Him in the center as my sun. Each science revolves around it as a planet with the minor science as satellites to their planets." [37] In line with this, he wanted to see the entire educational system of Great Britain enhanced both academically and religiously as these two disciplines worked hand in glove. He deplored the fact that in even the elite schools of the day, "many of the sons of the gentry in that establishment were more ignorant of scripture than the boys in some of our ragged (religious) schools." [38]

Victorian Britain did have a tremendous need; the general educational system left much to be desired. Actually, no system of national education came on the scene until 1870. Many advanced nations of the Western world had already developed reasonably efficient and inclusive educational systems. But Britain remained far behind. Only the middle and upper classes of society had the privilege of a reasonable, advanced education. It seems incredible when one realizes the Industrial Revolution had already revolutionized the country, producing technology the world little dreamed of. Yet Britain languished for a general educational system. Spurgeon came to the forefront to see it developed. He well realized that general education boded to be a political issue; and thus with his involvement and commitment to Christian principles in politics, he threw himself into the fray. Spurgeon's concern regarding education is understandable; the general ignorance of the working class peoples of nineteenth century Britain was appalling. Estimates are that among the working classes of London, no more than ten percent could even read and write. The educational level advanced little among the street cleaners and rag pickers. Menial task people hardly exceeded the bush people of Africa in their education. In those days, as unbelievable as it may seem, young people in Britain did not even know who, or

even what, the Queen was. The most alarming aspect of the general ignorance of the people, at least to Spurgeon, revolved around the unbelievable
number who had never even heard of God. Multitudes could not even tell
where on the map or even what England as a country meant—and they lived
right in it. The whole situation for the working class people, especially the
street urchins, was degrading and humiliating. Henry Mayhew, sociologist,
argued that the lack of education produced the deplorable conditions, especially in the larger cities. He said:

> The cause of the vagrants wandering through the country—and indeed through
> life—purposeless, and *unprincipled*, in the literal and strict meaning of the
> term, lies mainly in the defective state of our educational institution; for the
> vagrants, as a class, it should be remembered, are not educated. [39]

Surely, one would have thought, the nation would have risen to such an
unbelievable challenge. But few heard, and less heeded, the challenge.

In those days, England boasted about what a fine education one could
receive in the so-called "public" schools, calling them public schools being
a gross misnomer. These institutions had been established primarily for the
children of the higher echelons of society and nobility, save a few scholar-
ships for the underadvantaged. Famous schools like Eton, Harrow, and Rug-
by, schools in existence to this day, typified that approach to education. But
they were in reality private, exclusive schools that charged heavy tuition and
had high entrance requirements. The average common young person could
not even dream of entering such an institution.

The best education in England in those days could be found in the schools
operated by the Established Church. They had originally been brought into
existence for the education of the clergy. Still, few were privileged enough
to enter their portals.

The Puritan Reformation had earlier made its impact felt on the education
of a broader spectrum of society. This movement gave rise to the "grammar" schools. These proved to be good schools. By and large, the clergy ran
these schools, or perhaps in some instances resident scholars were the directors. Although they did not have the academic level of the public schools,
they did at least provide some reasonably good education. Men like
Shakespeare, Bunyan, Wesley, and others were educated on this level. Some
made it to the universities after that, but those numbers were relatively few.

When the Industrial Revolution swept over Britain with all its force, the
working masses were submerged in the urban crush and thus unreached
with any educational program. Children, at an unbelievably early age, went
into the factories, if not into the workhouses. They labored long hours; an
education was simply out of the question. From time to time, some concerned people made an effort to alleviate the illiteracy and irreligion of these
masses of children. For example, in 1833, Parliament gave a grant of £20,000
to the Church of England for the education of the poor. Tragically, however,

the Church squandered it trying to teach sectarian dogma. In 1839 J. A. Roebuck, a very innovative politician, proposed to Parliament that the education of the poor should not be merely a Church concern, but should be taken up by the government itself. They heard him, surprisingly enough, and the House of Commons established a "Committee of the Privy Counsel" to monitor funds spent for public education. However, the House of Lords, led by the Bishops, defeated the plan, fearful that the Church of England might lose its controlling hand on the education in the country. Such was the educational milieu in Spurgeon's early days.

To the credit of Parliament, in the 1840s, several bills came before the House relating to public education. Further, bills were passed that addressed the plight of children in the workhouses of the country. For example, in 1843 the Commons proposed the Factory and Education Bill. This bill set out a program to abolish children working in factories who were under eight years of age. Further, children from the ages of eight to thirteen were only permitted to work six and one half hours a day, and then they must attend school three hours. Those over thirteen were not allowed to work more than twelve hours a day. Again, religious differences defeated the bill. The Tories wanted to turn all the schools over to the Anglican Church. This boded for still more confusion and the deprivation of education to the working masses of children. Nonconformity raised its voice against this situation, circulating a petition that had four million signatures. It caused such a stir that the Factory Act of 1844 was brought before the House of Commons. It created half days in school for children that they might have at least some benefits of public education. But as can well be imagined, after working so many hours, the small children were too exhausted, if not too dirty, to even go to school. So the practical outcome benefited the working mass children very little.

As has been implied, the intrusion of the churches, Anglican and Non-conformist, muddled the situation in nineteenth century education. Most of the education took place under the leadership of the various denominations and, as a result, public education in general languished. Yet, it is only fair to say that the only real general concern for the education of children centered in the churches. Furthermore, church involvement did not necessarily prove to be all bad; many denominations genuinely tried to raise the educational level, and good religious training often accompanied the effort as well. But as the 1860s were ushered in, those of insight, both in the established and dissenting churches, began to realize that a general system of public education, controlled by the state, had become an absolute necessity. One leader in this movement was the famous preacher of Birmingham, Dr. R. W. Dale. He headed an organization known as the National Education League. This movement precipitated the Education Act of 1870. Although the bill had many shortcomings, it sparked a series of acts that finally put education into the hands of the government. That, clearly, proved to be a tremendously significant move. The 1870 measure itself required education for all British children under thirteen. Fees were charged to those who could afford them, otherwise children could attend school free. But a problem arose as to what should be done with the existing schools that were largely church owned and operated. Parliament solved the issue by funding the existing schools as long as they served the public in the area in which they were located. This, of course, brought about the religious problem that most children would be educated from an Anglican perspective. Spurgeon objected to Anglican religious instruction for three reasons. First, he did not agree with Church of England dogma. Second, he feared such doctrinal teaching would help maintain the states quo. Third, he did not think such religious instruction would win souls to Christ. Thus, he opposed the approach. Fortunately, Nonconformists were permitted to withdraw their children, but only upon written request. And then, what about areas where no church school could be found? Several problems were seemingly left dangling in the bill.

As can be imagined, Nonconformity spoke out loudly against the religious aspect of the Education Bill. The Liberal party itself split over the issue. All were of the conviction that a system of public education had to be instituted, but general disagreement arose as to how it could be effected. It forced to the surface the question about the existing Nonconformist schools; would they receive state subsidies as well as the Anglican schools? Some even asked if any religious schools should receive public support. This, of course, brought about the issue as to whether or not religion should be part of the curriculum. And if the answer were in the affirmative, what would be the approach? Would Presbyterian, Baptist, or Methodist, dogma be taught? One can imagine something of the confusion and heated arguments that resulted. Spurgeon thrust himself right into the thick of the public debate. Meredith points out that this issue of public education was unique for Spurgeon. He states:

> It was one of the few pressing problems that seemed to have him genuinely puzzled. He was convinced that public schools were necessary if Britain were to retain her power in the modern world. He was also convinced that public instruction of some sort was imperative if the country were to maintain its moral principles. Beyond that, however, he was unsure just what the course of action should be. He explained to his readers, 'We have not spoken upon the Education Bill, because we see no course proposed, and have none of our own to suggest. The matter can only appear easy to those who have not carefully considered it.' [40]

Despite Spurgeon's lack of a clear point, the above quotation makes it obvious that Spurgeon did strongly favor public education. Moreover, he felt convinced that the teaching of the Christian religion must be a vital part of education, as much as any other academic discipline, perhaps even more so. For Spurgeon, Christianity was the integrating principle of all intellectual pursuits. He also recognized that the church schools had failed to reach the masses for education. Thus he came to the conclusion that some form of state-operated program of education was mandatory, even if it had many perplexing facets. In *The Sword and the Trowel* he wrote:

> Are we to regard Sabbath-schools as the climax of all Christian effort for the young? . . . The laudable efforts of our tens of thousands of the debt which is due from the church of Christ to the little ones around us. . . . Taking it at its best, and rating it at its highest supposable value, we are Radical enough to assert that it is not all that the children of this age require, nay, nor one half of what might be, and must be done for them if England is to become a Christian country. Education of a secular sort has been too long withheld by the bickering of rival sects; the nation is now in such a humor that it will have no more of such unenlightened bigotry, but will insist upon it, that every child shall be taught to read and write. Since the Sectarian system has in England most evidently failed to reach the needs of millions, a purely secular system will be established, and will be thrust upon us whether we will or no. There will be a great outcry about the divorcing of religion from education, but we shall not join in it, partly because it is useless to cry over spilt milk—the thing must be, and there is no preventing it; and yet more, because we see our way to a great real gain out of a small apparent loss. . . . The present teachings of our weekday schools is as we believe as nearly as possible a sham, and a most mischievous sham too, since it satisfies the Christian conscience, and lulls to sleep energies which need to be aroused to the performance of a much-neglected Christian duty.

Spurgeon's earlier approaches to public education centered around the principle of non-sectarian education. This, of course, implies that religion should not be an academic pursuit in one's educational career. But through the years he changed. He lent his voice to the general outcry developing in England over the divorcing of the Christian religion from education. As a case in point, in June, 1870, Spurgeon chaired a public rally in Exeter Hall to discuss the Education Bill. The body that gathered were by and large of the Christian persuasion and they overwhelmingly adopted Spurgeon's proposal that Bible reading should be allowed in public schools, if the parents requested it for their children. This put him in conflict with R. W. Dale of Birmingham and the National Education League, which called for a secular educational program. Spurgeon agreed that certain creeds, especially the catechism of the Anglican Church or restrictive denominational teachings, should be barred from education; but surely children should have the right to hear the Word of God read, he argued. In addressing the group, Spurgeon said, "Our cry is undenominational education, but the Bible read in the school by all children whose parents which desire them to read it; and these we trust will be the great majority of the nation."[41] But in this quest, Spurgeon suffered disappointment. His "nondenominational" approach was defeated and the government supported the Anglican schools. Even in the schools where the Anglicans did not have their influence, religious instruction became a general practice, and not just for those who requested it. All had to hear Anglican dogma with its many weaknesses, but at least a national system of public education did get launched. True, it precipitated problems down through the years; nevertheless, it did open the opportunity for children to be educated. Unfortunately, it began to sow the seeds of distrust between Gladstone and the Nonconformists. It probably drove in a wedge of disagreement between Spurgeon and Gladstone that reached the breaking point in the split over Irish home rule. Concerning that issue, discussed earlier, Spurgeon wrote to a Mr. Morgan on June 24, 1886 and said, "I have been able to follow Mr. Gladstone hitherto, but in his Irish policy I am unable to agree with him. Like Mr. Bright, I am much grieved to differ from our great leader, but I do so most thoroughly."[42] Spurgeon also disagreed with Gladstone when the Prime Minister appointed Lord Rippon, a Roman Catholic, as Viceroy of India. A cartoon appeared July 3, 1880 depicting Spurgeon as Brutus stabbing Gladstone as Caesar in the back with a Rippon dagger. Still, Spurgeon never left the Liberal party, nor wrote off Gladstone *per se*.

OTHER ISSUES

Many other aspects of British political life felt the impact of the dissenters' movement generally, and Spurgeon in particular. For example, the dissenters made their influence felt in the debates over the Anti-corn Law League, the Ten Hours Bill, and Chartism. Actually, the Liberal party relied heavily for support on the Nonconformists of Britain in these issues. Many policies of nineteenth century liberalism were deeply influenced by the Evangelicals. Lord John Russell himself said, "I know the dissenters, they carried the Reform Bill."[43] In all these affairs, Spurgeon played his role of a philanthropic politician in the best sense of the word. He not only stood in the vanguard of reforms like the establishment of general education for the poor, he served on a plethora of committees and societies for the betterment of society. Whenever he could, he lent his influence to see society elevated, especially the working masses. A significant part of Spurgeon's success as a pastor emanated from his genuine concern for the lower class people. In *The Evening Star*, October 1856, the writer said:

> But where are the artisan classes,—that keen-eyed, strong-minded race, who crowd the floor at political meetings or cheap concerts, fill the minor theatres and struggle into the shilling gallery at the Lyceum or Princess? So very scanty is there attendance upon the most noted preachers, that it is their adhesion to Mr. Spurgeon which has made that gentleman a prodigy and a phenomenon.

The common people loved a man who would not only speak their language, but would go to political war for their rights and for their betterment.

All this social consciousness and political involvement grew out of Spurgeon's understanding of the Christian faith. A gutty, down-to-earth, day-by-day application of all that Jesus taught in the Sermon on the Mount motivated the Metropolitan Tabernacle pastor. For Spurgeon, Christian experience, to have the ring of reality about it, needed to be applied to every aspect of daily life. For him, no facet of life lay outside the boundaries of Christian involvement. Therefore, he saw no problem of society below the dignity of a Christian to attack. He would involve himself wherever a need arose. He would even battle for prisoners who had not been conclusively shown to be guilty of a crime. No issue escaped his notice. A rally was held on December 10, 1890 concerning the persecution of Jews in Russia. Over that issue he wrote in *The Times*, December 11, 1890: "I am indignant that the Seed of Israel should be oppressed by those who bear the name of Christian, but are utter strangers to the mind and Spirit of Christ." He even involved himself in the economic world by addressing the London Stock Exchange in 1875.

For all these endeavors Spurgeon should be highly commended. Concerning the superficially pious who would not involve themselves in the practical problems of society, Spurgeon said, "Those excessively heavenly people who cannot condescend to such worldly work, ought not to eat their dinners for that is a very fleshy operation."[44]

Spurgeon's deep spiritual conviction that our Lord always showed concern for the social needs of the people, as well as their spiritual plights, constantly spurred him on. He saw his involvement in politics as the direct application of Jesus' words that we are to love our neighbor as ourselves. He argued that the saintliest of believers are concerned about their own physical needs as well as their spiritual. Everyone cared for his body, as well as his soul, regardless of how dedicated a Christian he or she may be. Therefore, if we care for others as we care for ourselves, we must be concerned about their lives. Thus he concluded:

> The Christian man should always be the helper of everything which promotes the health and welfare of the people. Christ was not only the bread from Heaven, but the Giver of the bread of life to the poor and needy. He fed thousands of the fainting with the loaves and fishes. If all other hands be fast closed, the hand of the Christian man should be always open to relieve human necessity. Being a man, the believer is brother to all men—rich and poor, sick and healthy—and he should seek their good in every possible way, aiming still at the highest good—namely, the saving of their souls.

Consequently, Spurgeon involved himself to the extent that he really became a politician for the downtrodden. Concerning these lower classes, whom he loved, he said, "The world calls them inferiors, in what way are they inferior? They are thine equals."[45] He admonished his hearers, "Everyone of you (Englishmen) seek to cultivate a generous spirit toward his neighbor. Let not the rich oppress the poor; let not the poor envy the rich, let us all pull together, heart and soul, as being brothers of one race."[46]

At the same time, it must not be forgotten, that Spurgeon did not see the *ultimate* solving of society's problems on a purely political, sociological basis. Real change for Spurgeon came primarily through individual conversions. That, he argued, stood as everyone's utmost need. For Spurgeon, Christian experience alone could finally revolutionize society. He certainly did not avoid advocating sweeping social changes. But, as stated earlier, he was absolutely convinced that "no social plans will make our earth a paradise while sin still curses it, and Satan is abroad."[47] He saw England's social ills through spiritual lenses. Hence, he preached the Gospel to lead people to conversion, and then threw his weight into the political arena to stop the onslaughts of the devil in the dehumanizing of people. Therefore, Spurgeon saw his primary task as evangelism, not purely political reformation. And to evangelism, converting the individual, he gave of his best, not neglecting the other. From this perspective he must be judged.

Of course, the most substantial criticism leveled at Spurgeon by modern sociologists centers in their judgment that he approached the various problems of society on too much of an individualistic basis. And it is true, as emphasized, Spurgeon's humanitarian philanthropy was essentially aimed at individual conversion rather than seeking out the root cause of society's ills and attempting to resolve the problem before it gained such a foothold in society. Spurgeon rarely, if ever, came up with a concrete plan to change the system itself, even though he forthrightly spoke out against the system's ills and lent what support he could toward reform. But as seen, he always argued that the root cause of society's problems is sin and the cure for sin is salvation. Nevertheless, he did thrust himself in the political arena, and that in a positive fashion. We can be grateful that the evangelist saw the need, even in his own day, of political involvement as a part of Christian experience. In this regard, "Mr. Standfast" stood head and shoulders above many of his fellow countrymen.

11

"Mr. Great-heart . . . Was Their Guide"

SPURGEON'S MATURING MINISTRY

C. H. Spurgeon's twin sons photographed at twenty-one years of age. Charles (Jr.) at left, became Pastor of Greenwich, while Thomas ministered in Australia and New Zealand, succeeding his father in the London pulpit in 1894.   —*courtesy of Dr. Craig Skinner*

Brave Faithful, bravely done in word and deed
Judge, Witness, and Jury have, instead
Of overcoming thee, but shown their rage:
When they are Dead, thou'lt Live from age to age.
—*John Bunyan*

Introduction

As Spurgeon matured as a man and as his ministry gained stature, depth, and acceptance, Bunyan's unique character "Mr. Great-heart" certainly represented the London pastor. His magnificent social ministries as epitomized in the Stockwell Orphanage, the almshouses, The Pastors' College, the evangelistic work, and the host of other ministries previously presented, all flourished as Spurgeon continually threw himself into these Christian enterprises. The Metropolitan Tabernacle continued its growth cycle and his work increasingly influenced the world. He had a great heart, and he exemplified it in the entirety of his ministry. As the years passed, his spiritual grasp deepened as did his awareness of human need and his effectiveness in meeting those needs. To meet Spurgeon in the developing years was to meet Mr. Great-heart.

THE MATURING YEARS AND SEVERAL EVENTS

Here we see Spurgeon at his best. He had come through many struggles, and was a better man for it. In recounting these latter days, we range over several years on a more topical than chronological basis to gain an insight into the maturing Spurgeon, a complex, enigmatic preacher.

As the maturing years unfolded for Spurgeon, a most important event occurred, an event over which Spurgeon rejoiced: Gladstone sought to seek the disestablishment of the Irish church. The ecclesiastical excitement ran high, especially for the Nonconformists. Throughout London and the provinces, a multitude of meetings for and against Gladstone's resolution to disestablish the Irish church sprang up. Some meetings took on the aura that this move of Gladstone heralded the decline of the Establishment in the entirety of the British Isles, not just for the Irish. Spurgeon threw himself into the fray full tilt. He enthusiastically joined hands with Lord Earl Russell, John Bright and Prime Minister Gladstone. They went to war for disestablishment. On April 19, 1868 Spurgeon preached in the Tabernacle from 1 Corinthians 11:25: "After the same manner also he took the cup, when he had supped, saying, 'This cup is the new testament in my blood: this do ye, as oft as ye drink it, in remembrance of me.'" His sermon title was "He Must Reign." His theme centered on Jesus Christ as the ultimate ruler. The sermon took an enigmatic twist in that Spurgeon said some favorable things concerning the reign of Napoleon, a man of war and imperialism which Spurgeon abhorred. He said Napoleon had attempted to build an empire on justice and had given a fine code of laws. Yet, he failed, Spurgeon said. He then quoted Napoleon's well-known statement made during his exile on St. Helena Island: "My empire is passed away. I founded an empire on the sword, and it has failed; Jesus Christ has founded his empire on the law of love, and it will stand forever and ever!" [1] Said Spurgeon, "So it should be." Christ alone is the true liberator of captive nations. And the church must be free from the state. Spurgeon declared, "Christ must reign." All felt the impact of the high hour. Spurgeon was in his element.

As disestablishment enthusiasm grew, "one of the most remarkable meetings ever held within any building in this country" [2] came about. The Metropolitan Tabernacle sponsored a large rally and demonstration for the National Reform Union. An hour before the rally, the Tabernacle filled to overflowing, even the aisles being crowded with people, while thousands waited outside unable to gain admission. On the preacher's platform sat several members of Parliament. John Bright took the chair. The meeting centered on a lecture given by Mr. Mason Jones on the subject of the Irish church. It was a night to be remembered for Spurgeon's Tabernacle. One described the scene in these words: "It would be impossible to describe in words the enthusiasm of the meeting, while the sight of 7,000 persons waving their hats and handkerchieves was not one soon to be forgotten." [3] The traditional image of the Englishman as a person of reserve certainly disintegrated on that occasion. The enthusiastic people virtually went wild. Spurgeon could bring that out in an audience.

The Irish disestablishment question soon resolved itself. Although there were those who felt some uneasiness that Protestantism might suffer under the disestablishment principle, Parliament passed the law, the Irish church was "free," and it all brought much joy to Spurgeon.

Charles still remained something of a controversialist, even in the mature years. After all these years the media still leveled severe criticism against the preacher. It might not be far from the truth what Sir Henry Woonton, a Tory journalist, said about the media, "An ambassador is a man of virtue who lies abroad for the benefit of his country; and a news writer is a man without virtue, who lies at home for his own profit." [4] Normally, Spurgeon refused to answer the critics. However, he did take up his pen to defend himself at times, especially when misrepresented. Reflecting back a few years in *The Record*, May 8, 1868 he wrote a long letter to the editor in which he said:

SIR,—I have no complaints to make of your criticisms upon my language and conduct, both are doubtless more or less faulty; you have a right to criticise them, and I have pleasure in enduring your censures. Even when your remarks are most severe I do not feel aggrieved, for I am severe also. In the present conflict you conceive yourself to have great principles to defend, and you are bound to cut right and left at those who assail them. I also am conscientious in pushing forward principles which are dear to me, and I cheerfully accept the consequences of my advocacy. But I write you to-day because I cannot suppose that you would willfully misrepresent any man, and because I would give you an opportunity to abstain in future from unfounded reflections upon me. I have spoken so severely about what I consider to be the anomalous position of the Evangelical party, and have so little guarded my expressions, that you have many *fair* points of attack and need not fight unfairly, which will be more to your discredit than to my injury, and, worse still, will lead the public to think that religious controversialists will condescend to mean things in order to overthrow an opponent—an impression which will be greatly injurious to our common evangelism.

I allude to your scarcely dignified mention of the aid afforded by Churchmen in the erection of the Tabernacle. Now it may be, and I trust was, the fact that many Episcopalians gave small sums at collections toward that object, and to such I am still indebted; but, so far as our accounts show, there were no donations of any mentionable amount from any persons known to us as Episcopalians, with but one, or perhaps two exceptions, and those happen to be persons whose views upon the Irish Church are quite as much in harmony with ours as with yours. I am not ungrateful for the very minute aid which was thus accorded, but it is made to figure so largely in your journal and other kindred papers that I thought you must be labouring under some misapprehension. I should scarcely imagine that any man out of Hanwell would assert that I accepted the donations referred to with an implied contract that I was henceforth bound to the expression of opinions favourable to the Establishment. No sort of condition was appended to or implied in these kind but comparatively trifling gifts, or they would have been indignantly refused. I do not believe that any gentleman in the whole Episcopal body would be so little-minded as to offer a voluntary contribution to a member of another church and then twit him upon the reception of it. We Nonconformists, who have so few amongst us of the great and noble, and may not, perhaps, presume to claim any great refinement of manners, would hardly like so greatly to demean ourselves, and therefore I suspect that this view of the subject has escaped you, and that upon second thoughts you will withdraw the allusion which you may have been led to make in a moment of natural irritation. A great question deserves to be handled a little more magnanimously by the organ of a great party.

I must further trouble you for another moment. It has been insinuated, more or less plainly, that I had sinister motives in deprecating an attack upon the State Church in connection with the Bicentenary Celebration. Those who choose to think so after the following explanation may enjoy the pleasures of malignity undisturbed by me. I held, and still do hold, that the main body of the expelled Nonconformist divines were State Churchmen in their opinions, and would have remained perfectly content in the national Establishment if it had been moulded in their will. I did not, therefore, see how their expulsion could bear upon our views as anti-State Churchmen; and as I thought the public would believe that we were claiming these divines as on our side, I did not think it a fair mode of warfare. Happily those good men were driven out of the Establishment, as I heartily pray that all our Evangelical clergy may be if they will not secede voluntarily; but the expelled Puritans were not ecclesiastically dissenters of the modern school, nor does the weight of their testimony tell for the principles of the Liberation Society. I wish it did. This it was which held me back; and, I may add, there did not seem to me to be so much need at that time as there is now for the discussion of the position of the Evangelicals. Pardon me for observing that every year appears to some of us to add to the culpability of those who remain in fellowship with undisguised Romanists, and calls us more and more loudly to bear testimony against what seems to us an unhallowed union.

One word more. The letter of Lord Shaftesbury is more calculated to soften asperities than your indulgences in them. If it be a great stretch of charity for Evangelical clergymen to appear with me on a platform where we meet on the common ground of service to philanthropy, the Gospel, and the Redeemer's cause, how much more charity, with my view of their position, must I require to be found in such a connection? After all that has been said severely, and perhaps angrily, on either side, Evangelical Christians may well co-operate in holy service, since with all our conflicting views we alike love the Gospel and hate Popery, and hope to meet in the same heaven.

I cannot expect you to insert this; but if you will oblige me by so doing, I shall—though determinately opposed to your views in many respects—remain, yours respectfully,

C. H. SPURGEON.
Clapham, May 4, 1868.[5]

Spurgeon could ably defend himself—he had a very quick wit, and when he wetted his pen he could clearly hold his own in the arena. Perhaps it should be made clear that *The Record* was not a secular newspaper but an evangelical organ. That many misunderstood Spurgeon is patent. As has been said, some reporters "understood Spurgeon about as perfectly as Spurgeon himself would have understood a prima donna at the opera."[6] But of course, the 19th century was a volatile age and things heated up fast. It also must be said that *The Record* did respond to Spurgeon's defense by reminding the great preacher that in his early days, when others severely criticized him, they had spoken well of him.

Spurgeon's extensive ministry during these years exerted an increasing influence on the people. Even as early as 1870, the Stockwell Orphanage flourished tremendously. The trustees had 1,000 applications for admission in hand. Spurgeon felt a pressing need for an infirmary at Stockwell, so the Tabernacle held a bazaar in June of that year to raise funds. In the evening Spurgeon gave a scintillating lecture. The following day the Earl of Shaftesbury presided at the annual meeting. He described Stockwell Orphanage as representing "a blessed and holy work, reflecting great honor upon all concerned in it."[7] In the provision of God, the attenders to the bazaar contributed large sums, one lady giving a donation of £400 to be divided between the College and the Orphanage. Such events were typical of Spurgeon's continuing ministry.

During these effective days, Charles' illnesses increasingly took greater hold of him. One evening on leaving Exeter Hall after a very effective service, he developed a painful attack of his rheumatic gout. He was only absent from his pulpit for one Sunday in this battle, but his illnesses continued to develop until at times he would be out for even months at a time.

One refreshing aspect of worship at the Metropolitan Tabernacle was Spurgeon's honesty and practicality. His piety had a guttiness to it that appealed to his "common people." During one service, as the people prepared for a season of prayer, he said:

> Now, it is a very cold night, and if anybody prays very long somebody will be frozen to death. . . . I am not like Paul, and cannot restore him to life, so please don't render a miracle necessary since I cannot perform one.[8]

The services were alive. The singing and praising of God by the Metropolitan Tabernacle people inspired many a visitor. Spurgeon loved singing the great old Puritan hymns. He said, "Triumphs of joy and avalanches of praise were never more perfect in the Tabernacle than when we sang these grand old fugal tunes."[9]

Spurgeon involved himself on a wide scale, and not just in his own ministries; he let his influence be felt in other Christian enterprises during these productive years. For example, he dedicated new buildings at the centenary of the College at Cheshunt, a theological institution for the training of young ministers. The Earl of Shaftesbury laid the memorial stone and Spurgeon preached. The ceremony was in memory of the founder, Lady Huntington. This great woman of God had established the College at Trebecca in Wales about the year 1767. The Countess had died in June of 1791 and Cheshunt College was then transferred to Cheshunt. Lady Huntington, as is well known, had been the benefactress of the ministry of George Whitefield and others during the eighteenth century awakening. She made a tremendous contribution to evangelical Christianity through many years of the dramatic Wesley-Whitefield Revival. Spurgeon spoke at the dedication on the theme of the importance of a theological college as the example of Christ gathering men around him to further the Gospel. He referred to the

Apostles having been students. In his message he also paid tribute to Lord Shaftesbury. Spurgeon said concerning the great Christian philanthropist:

> The more I know of that good man, the more I feel that his coming into association with various Christians is not a mere formal act, but that his heart is really with all them that love the Lord Jesus Christ. Those of us who often come into contact with him admire the depth and earnestness of his piety. No doubt he is thoroughly a member of the Church of England; but he is much more a member of the Church of Christ. For myself, I am glad to come here, though, of course, I never worship God with a liturgy, and certainly never shall. Yet if you have grace enough to do it—and I should say it takes a good deal—I am glad that you are able. [10]

As the years unfolded, it became increasingly the vogue to speak of Spurgeon as the modern Whitefield, even more than in his earlier days. People visualized the Tabernacle at Newington Butts much like, at least in principle, the eighteenth century tabernacle at Mooresfield where Whitefield preached and ministered so effectively. Charles had become so popular and esteemed that busts were made of him. A bust in Parisian Marble sold for twenty shillings, or one in terra-cotta for fifteen shillings. Spurgeon continually gave of himself all around the country. Later in that same year Spurgeon attended the quarterly meeting of the London Baptist Association. Their meetings were special occasions for Spurgeon, because he had played such an important role in the founding of the Association. The associational gatherings were social affairs as well as carrying on the business of the Association and hearing spiritual challenges. At a large rally in Exeter Hall, he took the chair. The meeting promoted Bible reading in schools.

Spurgeon as a Lecturer

By this time Spurgeon had totally given up the idea of ever visiting the United States. In replying to one invitation to lecture in America he said:

> Gentlemen, I am very much obliged by your very courteous letter, but you are under mistake. I am not a lecturer. I now and then give a lecture for some good object; but I do not do it well, and, moreover, have no ambition in that line. I am very glad to preach, but not if there is any charge at the door. Moreover, I have no kind of idea of visiting the States. [11]

He said concerning this invitation, "Here I am and here I must be until I go to another and yet more glorious land than yours." [12] Mr. Great-heart would give his heart to Britain alone.

Spurgeon was, of course, being too modest concerning his lecturing. He gave excellent lectures, though he despised the work, and found it difficult. He said that the Great Commission was not go and *lecture* all nations. He viewed lecturing as the "severest of all toil." He never looked forward to a lecture without some inward pain, never began it without hesitation, and never finished it without thinking he was a fool to attempt it and should be a greater fool to attempt it again. That was his own evaluation of his lecturing. Still, his lectures received wide acclaim and people flocked to hear him.

What made Spurgeon a good lecturer centered on the fact that his convictions were strong. He did not hesitate to dig in and go to battle for issues he felt important. In one sense, he was a peace-loving man, but he would fight for Christian truth. That always makes for good lectures, if not good debates.

It must be admitted, Spurgeon had a difficult time accepting subtleties; he thought in blacks and whites. He said, "As regards intellectual opposition to the Gospel, truth will ultimately triumph; for in the end 'God has said' will surely stand against 'man has thought.'"[13] At times his dogmatic approach put some people off. It tended to stifle debate. Perhaps it would have been well for Charles to have remembered the Baptismal Regeneration Controversy. Yet, being utterly committed to all that he believed, he therefore left little room for debate. That attitude at times put him out on a limb.

All this is not to imply that Spurgeon was a narrow-minded bigot. It is true, that along with his firm convictions and occasional associations with narrow-minded people, he appeared at times to be rather short-sighted. Once in the early '70s, he precipitated a bit of a flourish of controversy in a sermon entitled, "The Signs of the Times." In his message he attacked pedo-baptism as Romanish. This not only got some Anglicans upset with him (they no doubt remembered the Baptismal Regeneration sermon) but the Presbyterians, Congregationalists, and Methodists were also unhappy with the sermon. However, it did not generate nearly the heat that the Baptismal Regeneration Controversy did, and it soon settled down. Again it was symbolic of Spurgeon's thinking always in proverbial blacks and whites, leaving little room for debate. Still, he really had a more open mind than his rhetoric seemed to indicate. This was especially true as he matured.

Spurgeon never overcame his mood shifts. At one time he would be extremely optimistic, at another time he seemed a depressed pessimist. On occasion he manifested feelings of utter inadequacy, at other times he would exude such confidence that observers perceived him as proud and arrogant.

But Spurgeon labored incessantly, despite his personal, inner struggles. He never backed off his goals because of circumstances or criticisms. Actually, he had learned to take what life threw across his path with a good sense of humor. As seen, he received criticism for too much humor, especially in the pulpit. He retorted, it is "less a crime to cause a momentary laugh than a half hour's profound slumber." For example, in one of his earlier excursions across the English Channel, he went through France and on to the beautiful city of Nice. On this trip he encountered an unusual plague of mosquitos. Spurgeon seemed very vulnerable to the insects, and having fought them incessantly he finally said that the mosquitos were saying to one another,

"Fee, fie, fo, fum, I smell the blood of an Englishman." Still, it must be acknowledged that the work at times did press in upon Spurgeon so much that he felt fragmented and forgetful. He said on one such occasion, "No one living knows the toil and care I have to bear. I ask for no sympathy, but ask indulgence if I sometimes forget something. I have to look after the orphanage, have charge of a church with 4000 members; sometimes there are marriages and burials to be undertaken; there is the weekly sermon to be revised, *The Sword and Trowel* to be edited; and besides all that, the weekly average of 500 letters to be answered. This, however, is only half my duties; for there are innumerable churches established by friends with the affairs of which I am closely connected, to say nothing of those cases of difficulty which are constantly being referred to me." [14] He was a busy man.

In the maturing years, James Wells, the strict Baptist preacher of the Surrey Tabernacle, passed away. It will be remembered that he regularly took time every Sunday to criticize Spurgeon's previous Sunday sermon. The Metropolitan Tabernacle preacher was never Calvinistic enough for Wells. However, Wells exercised a good ministry of over forty years at the Surrey Tabernacle. He was born of humble parents and received little or no education. He began to preach in a very obscure corner of Southwark, but his devotion and genius soon won for him a favored place in Calvinistic evangelicalism. Although Spurgeon and Wells had much in common, their differences in finer theological points precluded them from being very cordial friends. Nevertheless, when Wells suffered his last illness, Spurgeon sent him the following letter:

Clapham, March 11, 1871.

My Dear Friend,—I must apologise for intruding upon your sick chamber, and must beg you not to be troubled by it; but I am very anxious to know how you are, and shall be very grateful if some friend will inform me. I had hoped that your sickness was but a temporary affliction and would soon pass away, but now I hear conflicting rumours.

I assure you of my deep sympathy in your protracted confinement from the labour which is so dear to your heart. Only to be kept out of the pulpit is a bitter sorrow, even could the bed be one of entire rest. I fear, however, that you are enduring days and nights of languishing; and I pray the Lord, the tender lover of our souls, to lay under you His supporting arms. He comforts omnipotently, and no griefs linger when He bids them fly. He breaks us down, and while we lie prostrate He makes us glad to have it so, because His will is done.

You, who have so long been a father in the Gospel, are no novice in the endurance of trial, and I trust that you will be enabled to play the man as thoroughly in lonely suffering as in public service. Immutable purposes and infinite love have been themes of your constant ministry to others. May the Holy Ghost make these mighty floods of consolation to roll in upon your own soul, till all things else are swallowed up in your heart's holy joy! Personally I own my great obligations to the furnace and the hammer; and I am sure that you also rejoice in the assurance that tribulation worketh patience, and brings, through the supply of the Spirit, a long train of blessings with it. May you be delivered from all excessive care as to your church and your work—the Lord's work is safe in the Lord's hands. Happy is it for us when we can feel it to be so. May your sick chamber be the very gate of heaven to your soul, the presence of the Lord filling the house with glory.

Do not think of acknowledging this; but if you are able to have it read to you I hope someone will be so good as briefly to tell me how you are.—With most sincere respects, yours truly,

C. H. Spurgeon. [15]

Spurgeon never bore a grudge; he would always go out of his way to be kind to others.

THE CONSCIOUSNESS OF CALL

Many asked why Spurgeon worked so hard, especially in the light of his health problems. The answer is simple; his "workaholic" lifestyle no doubt grew out of his deep sense of call. He always seemed to be on the road preaching, because he knew God had called him to the work.

Spurgeon's immense productivity and popularity won admiration, even by many less orthodox men. In the first week of August, 1880, a Unitarian journal presented an article on Spurgeon and his works. They complimented Spurgeon very highly with these words:

A special interest seems at all times to attach to the name of the great South London preacher. When it is mentioned, or when it is seen in print, the attention, not to say curiosity, of almost all classes seems to be attracted and drawn. . . . Without the imposition of the hand of a bishop, Mr. Spurgeon seems to have had the hand of God resting upon him. In the early days of Mr. Spurgeon's popularity it was commonly supposed that his success would be merely meteoric, and, like the shooting-star, would fade away as quickly as it came; but all such suppositions were beside the mark. With some it might, and doubtless would, have been so, but not with a man like him. In addition to the most laborious earnestness, zeal, and enthusiasm he has ever betrayed the greatest self-sacrifice, sincerity, and singleness of purpose; and these qualities combined, and withal guided and toned by consummate common-sense, have made him, in addition to being a notorious man, a man—even where not agreed with—to be trusted and admired. It is impossible to speak of his labours and those of his devoted friends without to many minds seeming to border, and that even when nearest to the truth, upon the apparently fabulous and fanciful. . . . We have only attempted a statement of some of the more important of this deservedly popular man's herculean doings, the very personal charity of whom is immense, as witness the devotion to his Christian work of the noble pecuniary testimonial which was raised for him on the completion of the twenty-fifth year of his pastorate. In religion he is a Baptist and a Calvinist, in politics a strong Liberal, in practice a broad, genial, thorough, and catholic man, and we wish him success in his noble and self-denying efforts. He is an example, not only to every Unitarian minister, but also to every other minister as well. He has succeeded, as in the long run others may, if they like, succeed, because he has deserved success. Theologically we are not in sympathy with him, nor will he expect us to be; but we can distinguish between theology and practical religion, and we wish both him and his good and noble-hearted wife renewed health and long life, not only to pursue their good works, but also to be a blessing and a comfort to each other in the doing of them.[16]

In 1881 the Spurgeons celebrated their silver wedding anniversary. Had it not been a season of illness for Charles, it would have been a much larger affair than it was. At that particular time he could not with any regularity take his place at the Tabernacle; he could scarcely get the editing work done on his weekly sermons from the printers. So the celebration was kept small for the Spurgeons. But by April, Spurgeon began to see considerable improvement in his health and he found himself able to preach the annual sermon at the Baptist Missionary Society at Exeter Hall. He took as his text Isaiah 51: 2-3, "Look unto Abraham, your father." He got so caught up in his message, it seemed to the people that he was again a young man in the vigor of his youth during the days at the Surrey Gardens Music Hall. It proved a most delightful evening for all.

In the spring of 1881 the annual Conference of the Pastors' College was held at the church of Charles Spurgeon, Jr. in Greenwich. Unfortunately, Charles, Sr. had become ill with another onslaught of gout and was unable to attend. This was most disappointing to all. So, Sir George Williams presided, and the principal of the College preached on the subject "When I Am Weak, Then I Am Strong." Spurgeon was much missed.

About this time Spurgeon began to view the Baptist Union with a bit of suspicion and distrust concerning recent theological trends. One incident that precipitated this early distrust centered around a well-known Unitarian who had been welcomed at one of the Baptist Union annual meetings and allowed to speak a few words. He had come as a guest of the mayor rather than of the Union itself, but no one objected. Spurgeon made some rather caustic remarks about it in *The Sword and the Trowel*. Perhaps he did not understand the full circumstance, nonetheless, Charles was somewhat taken to task by two leading ministers for his remarks. His critics wrote in *The Baptist*:

> The article in *The Sword and the Trowel* (referring to the Leicester meetings) has filled us with surprise and grief. We have, acting on our own responsibility, sought an interview with Mr. Spurgeon in order to put before him certain

facts which might have led him to modify his harsh judgment. He has thought it well, however, to decline to receive us, on the ground that he had 'said his say, and had no wish to discuss the matter further.'. . . The distressing paragraph in Mr. Spurgeon's article which refers to 'loose thinkers' and their 'loudness' is to us quite incomprehensible. The epithet itself is a shameful one, and when combined with the insinuation that the persons so contemptuously referred to have no 'fixed principles' is simply cruel. . . . We think that if Mr. Spurgeon had spent as much time in acquainting himself with these simple facts as he has in 'careful thought and earnest prayer,' both the tone and substance of his article would have been different, and that he would not have used his great name and influence to wound the feelings of those who are as faithful to the Master, and as anxious to know and teach the truth, as himself. [17]

But Spurgeon did not stand alone in his criticism of the Union. Another person contended that the denomination had become "attached and affected by the dry rot of false liberalism." The stage was being set for the prelude to the Down Grade Controversy, to be discussed later. Spurgeon became disturbed enough about the growing tendencies in the Baptist Union that he attended his last annual meeting in 1882, two years before the celebration of his jubilee in 1884. Spurgeon preached at the Baptist Union meeting in '82, but it was his last. Yet, as late as 1882 the Baptist Missionary Society made him an honorary member. Also, in that same year, he entertained the London Baptist Association Committee in his home, Westwood.

INTERESTING CORRESPONDENCE

Spurgeon continually received many intriguing and interesting letters from a variety of personalities. For example, he received a very warm letter from Florence Nightingale. It reads:

Dear Sir,

Nurse Masters, of our training school at St. Thomas's Hospital, and who is one of a reinforcement of nurses whom we are sending out to join our nursing staff at the Montreal Hospital, was recently admitted by you to baptism and communion. She spoke of it to me with deep earnestness.

It occurred to me that you might, among the young women of your flock, know some, sound in body and mind, who would like to be trained for a hospital nursing life, which has now sufficient reward, both in the good to be done and in the maintenance to be earned, to be attractive to suitable candidates. The harvest is ready, but the labourers still are few.

I write under the severe pressure of business, and ever-increasing illness, which has kept me a prisoner to my room for years, so you will excuse a brief letter. I have heard that you are yourself frequently afflicted. May I express my deep regret at your suffering, and my earnest hope that your life may long be spared?

May God be with us all!

FLORENCE NIGHTINGALE [18]

Of course, he received considerable correspondence from Lord Shaftesbury. One touching letter from Shaftesbury, the philanthropist, reads:

My Dear Friend,

God be with you to Mentone, at Mentone, and back again, and may He give you all the health you seek for His service!

Well may you be 'weary, and worn, and sad.' The open, avowed, boasted, modern infidelity is terrible, but the almost universality of the Laodicean spirit is still worse. You will come back and find that socialism, contemptuous unbelief, and an utter disregard of anything but that which tends to make this world the 'be-all' and the 'end-all' of our existence, have attained vastly increased proportions during your absence.

There is nothing for it but to preach 'Jesus Christ and Him crucified,' with perpetual exhortation to His people to pray for His speedy return. Such a preaching of Christ has been your main strength. May God keep you in that frame of mind!

Put, I request you, the little book I now send you, in your pocket.

Yours very truly,
SHAFTESBURY.

P.S.—I shall distribute largely your volume, *Flowers from a Puritan's Garden.* [19]

He received a warm, humble letter from D. L. Moody:

Newcastle, Oct. 11, '81

Dear Mr. Spurgeon,

Yours of the 9th is to hand, and in reply let me say that I am thankful for your very kind note. It quite touched my heart. I have for years thought more of you than of any other man preaching the gospel on this earth; and, to tell you the truth, I shrink from standing in your place. I do not know of a church in all the land that I shrink from as I do from yours;—not but what your people are in sympathy with the gospel that I try to preach, but you can do it so much better than I can.

I thank you for inviting me, and (D.V.) I will be with your good people Nov. 20. Will you want Mr. Sankey, or will your own precentor have charge? Either will suit me.

Remember me to your good wife, and accept of my thanks for your letter of cheer.

Yours truly,
D. L. Moody. [20]

Another interesting letter is written by Prime Minister W. E. Gladstone. He wrote:

Hawarden Castle,
Chester,
Jan. 16, '82.

Dear Mr. Spurgeon,
I was not at all surprised at what happened, and had not the smallest disposition or cause to suspect you. My life is passed in a glass bee-hive: with this particularity, that I fear many see in it what is not there, by which I am unjustly a gainer.
I thank you very much for the interesting book of photographs which you have been so good as to send, with an inscription I am very far from deserving. I wish I had a better return to make than the enclosed; but these are the best I can lay my hands on.
When you were so good as to see me before and after your service, I felt ashamed of speaking to you lest I should increase your fatigue, but before very long I hope to find a better opportunity. In the meantime, I remain,

With sincere respect,
Faithfully yours,
W. E. GLADSTONE. [21]

He also received a letter from Lord Radstock who had made a tremendous Christian impact in Russia. His letter reads:

St. Petersburg,
11/4/'82.

Dear Mr. Spurgeon,
The Baptists in South Russia, who are, I believe, nearly all close-communionists, are to have a great Conference in May as to whether they should not open their doors to the Lord's children in general. It is deeply important that they should decide aright. There are many thousands of Christians in South Russia among the Molokans and Stundists, and it is most desirable, on all accounts, that they should be as united as possible. Will you write a letter to them, addressed to Pastor Liebig, Odessa, encouraging them to take the true ground of union in the Lord's Name, at any rate as regards receiving Christians at the Lord's table?
Here, we are going on quietly, in spite of difficulties. You would be rejoiced at the faith and love shown by some in the highest class here. Continue in prayer for this land, with thanksgiving. The fields are white unto the harvest, but the labourers are so few and shackled; —yet 'He must reign.'

Ever yours in the Lord,
RADSTOCK. [22]

He received a letter from George Williams, the founder of the Young Men's Christian Association:

71, St. Paul's Church Yard,
London,
May 23rd, 1889.

My Dear Mr. Spurgeon,
Thank you very much for so kindly sending for my acceptance the *Outlines of the Lord's Work in Connection with the Pastors' College.* It is not necessary for me to repeat my assurances of prayerful sympathy and interest, for you know you have these;—but if my hopes for your usefulness, and the spiritual success of your manifold labours, are fulfilled, your joy will indeed be full.

We are anticipating, with supreme pleasure, seeing you to-morrow evening, and are praying that the Master Himself may give you some special word, that may be productive of abundant spiritual fruitfulness.

                                        Believe me,
                                        Yours ever truly,
                                        GEORGE WILLIAMS.[23]

Moreover, many interesting personalities visited the Metropolitan Tabernacle. In June of '84 the King of Maore worshiped in Spurgeon's church.

SPURGEON'S APPROACH

Spurgeon always strove to keep a basic positive spirit, despite his bouts with depression and of his constant conflicts, many of which he bore alone. It seems as though he had no real confidant outside the family. Therefore, he never had anyone really to share the burdens that depressed him, except, of course, his wife. Perhaps he was just "a little bigger than life" in the minds of the multitudes and hence, kept at arms' length.

Spurgeon loved truth, plain truth, and was transparently honest. This, of course, at times made him blunt. But he led his people well—and they followed him. For example, in his early days at the New Park Street Baptist Church, one newly elected deacon always complained about everything. Many of his complaints were directed against the pastor. Once he was complaining to Spurgeon, and another deacon who was there said to the complainer, "Look here, my friend, we have but one captain on board this ship, and that's Mr. Spurgeon; and if you don't agree with what he wishes done we shall see that you are cast overboard like Jonah was." Spurgeon smiled and added, "Yes and I will ask God to send a respectable whale out to swallow you up."[24] Good common sense, plain truth, and honesty, although rather blunt!

Yet, even in spite of Spurgeon's indomitable spirit and strong leadership, he often had feelings of inadequacy. As a case in point, he hated to preach in "the City," the square mile that comprises the heart of London. His anxiety ran so deep when he had to preach in the City to the sophisticates of London's elite that he could not sleep the night before, or even the night after. Illustrated earlier, this anxiety often ran so deep that he would be nauseated before preaching even to his own people in his own church, those who loved him, revered him, and to whom he had declared the Gospel hundreds if not thousands of times. The City frightened him. To many, he appeared utterly self-confident and in command of everything that he touched, yet he suffered from fits of anxiety. Such was the paradoxical and complex nature of Spurgeon.

Although he loved his home and London dearly, Spurgeon also loved to travel. In his many journeys about the country he made plans for a special visit to Bristol. The trip began with a stop at the opening of a bazaar at London's Westbourne Park Chapel, a beautiful building newly built by Dr. John Clifford and his congregation. Charles delivered the sermon and spoke on the decadence of the "old connection" of General Baptists and the spread of negative theology among the Independents. Clifford was a General Baptist in background, but of the "new connection" persuasion. He planned to bring the same message the following morning at Bristol. At Paddington Station he boarded the 1:50 p.m. train to Bristol with his good friend, G. Holden Pike. Spurgeon was very animated and cheerful on the journey and shared with those who were traveling with him a lengthy passage from his second series of *Lectures to My Students*. He also related the good times he had experienced on his excursion on the Thames and his adventures in Scotland. On arriving in Bristol, Mr. Gange met the party and they made their way to the pastor's home. On the way, they stopped for a few moments at Broadmeade Chapel, the historic Baptist church of Bristol mentioned in Chapter 2. They dined with Mr. Gange in the evening, along with four Bristol ministers who had been educated at the Pastors' College. Spurgeon was a cheerful and brilliant conversationalist. In the setting of the evening's entertainment, Mr. Spurgeon's luggage was brought in and he turned one of his bags upside down. Out spilled a collection of all his works bound in morocco and gold, numbering 44 volumes. These were a gift to the Bristol Baptist College Library. They cost £31, 3 shillings. Charles supplemented the gift with £68, 17 shillings in cash, making a total of £100, which he handed over for the Bristol College for the purchase of other books. The Pastors' College could have used the funds, but Mr. Great-heart had a heart for God's work wherever he found it. The next day Spurgeon gave an address to the College students that lasted three quarters of an hour. The young men from the local Congregational Institute joined the Baptists and the lecture was appreciated by all. Later, Spurgeon preached his sermon at Coleston Hall to the greatest crowd that perhaps had ever been congregated in that building. People came from miles around to hear the great preacher. The report circulated that £10 had been offered for a seat. But Spurgeon never countenanced such things. He returned to London on the following day. He constantly kept this kind of itinerary. In the next few days he broke down with his old archenemy, rheumatoid gout, and was unable to keep his engagement at the Norwood Association chapel.

Spurgeon had to deal with a multitude of problems. Being pastor of a large congregation, he regularly faced death among his people—and often they were his friends. One friend who had been very instrumental in the building of the Tabernacle, Deacon Thomas Cook, the famous travel company founder and director, passed away. Spurgeon took all these difficult times in the Spirit of Christ. Something of the graciousness of Spurgeon is shown by an incident that occurred in the earlier years with his literary helper G. Holden Pike. One Saturday afternoon Pike called on Spurgeon at the manse. He was not known to the servants who answered the door, and the servant told Pike that Spurgeon was in bed and could not be disturbed. Pike immediately retired with some disappointment. On the same evening he received the following note:

> My Dear Friend,—I am annoyed beyond measure that you have been here and gone and have been denied me. The fact is I had a heavy headache, and told my people not to wake me; but I expected to be up to see you. I wrote you a card early on Friday. Our general rule is to reserve Saturday from callers, and hence you were refused; but it was owing to your modesty and goodness in great part. As soon as I came down I asked for you, and was mortified to find you had departed. Please write me, and accept my apologies and say what it is you would see me upon.
>
> Yours truly,
> C. H. SPURGEON

When the National Education Act was passed (discussed in the previous chapter), Spurgeon saw this as an opportunity for extending the work of the Colportage Association. In *The Freeman*, he wrote the following article:

> We have at the Tabernacle fourteen men now, and they are supported, some of them, by brethren who are present, and friends of this society too. About £30 a year raised by a district gives to it a man who will be ready to preach if the pastor is ill, going from house to house, praying with the sick and talking with the dying. He is kept busy with the fact that he must sell his books to raise the other half of his income, and so he carries the Word of God with him in two respects, often where a pastor could not be maintained. . . . Our agricultural districts are sadly in want of help. Who can go and take a walk and talk to a ploughman without discovering the need of the Gospel? And, on the other hand, there is coming this education which is to be given to all, and there must go with it on the part of the Church of God an increased effort to give religious education side by side with it, or else the possibilities may be that you shall only do what has been done in Hindustan—convert men from idolatry into

Atheism, and bring people from the stupidity of a dormant intellect into the vicious activity of an intellect that seeks for anything but God. [25]

It seems a tendency for young men in the ministry to be very zealous for conversions; but as the mature years come upon them, they lose something of that early evangelistic zeal. Spurgeon refused to fit that mold. For example, in the '70s at a stone-laying ceremony for a new church in Faversham, Spurgeon preached while the mayor, Mr. C. Bryant, presided. A great group of people assembled and Spurgeon preached on the principles of a successful working church. He said:

> I would say to the members of this church, 'Do not be satisfied unless you have conversions.' Ministers may preach earnestly and prayerfully, but I consider there is little good done if there are not conversions. I regret that there are churches in which there have been no conversions for months and years, and yet if they are spoken to on the subject they will say they are 'very comfortable.' That is the worst part of it. Imagine a large fire breaking out in Faversham, and the engines being sent for, and on arriving somewhere near the fire the men stopping, taking seats on the engines, and lighting up their pipes, and on their being asked how they were getting on with the fire, the reply being, 'Oh, we are not doing anything toward putting out the fire, but we are uncommonly comfortable.' All I can say is that if a man can be comfortable when good is not being done he is no use to any church, and the sooner he is packed off to attend some other than the Lord's business the better. [26]

In a similar vein, at another memorial stone-laying of the new Baptist college, Brighton Grove in Rusholome, Spurgeon told the ministerial students how to go about their work. In his address he declared:

> Preach all the Gospel; do not preach one end of it. Some do so; they can never preach the whole of the balances, they are so occupied with one scale—they are small moons; they never get into the full moon; they never see a full-orbed Gospel. I saw a man in Rome roasting chestnuts; he put them in a cylinder which revolved over a fire, and thus all the chestnuts were roasted. I like to see in the ministry all the chestnuts roasted. I have known men who have bought a barrel organ with five tunes in it, and whenever they have played it has always been one of the five tunes. There is an infinite variety in the truth; give the whole of the truth, and God will bless one part of the truth to one, part of it to another. [27]

He never deviated from these principles himself. He kept his evangelistic fervor and balance to the end. He was always the people's preacher and he realized that above all, the people needed the full Gospel.

One of the best descriptions of Spurgeon was written by John De Kewer Williams. He said:

> What was it, then, that made him the greatest of his age—incomparable—that

gave him a breadth and depth of influence unparalleled? Had he been asked the secret of his success, he would certainly have said, 'By the grace of God I am what I am;' and he might have said, 'I did fear God, and I never did fear any man.'

But as God works by means, we may consider the circumstances which made him the power that he was. As a man he was not commanding, he was not at all imposing, he was not fascinating. He had none of the fine frenzy of the poet; and could not produce it in others. And he acquired no artistic, no dramatic, no sacerdotal graces. His elocution was perfect, but he was not eloquent. He had no taste for art, and knew little of science, except agricultural chemistry, which enabled him to tell the farmers, You may use your phosphates and superphosphates as you please, but you will never have a harvest without 'The Dew.' Artistically he was nowhere as compared with Whitefield, or the great French preachers, or Cardinal Wiseman; and so he was never a drawing-room preacher; and though the noble and the mighty went to hear him out of curiosity, none of them ever joined his flock. He has been called 'The People's Preacher.' When he was young they brought out a caricature of him and the most popular preacher of that day, and called the two Brimstone and Treacle, and most would have concluded that the other would be far more attractive. It was not at all so; and now the very name of the sweet preacher is forgotten, but the name of the stern preacher liveth evermore.

So I conclude that nature had done little for him beyond a noble voice, not touching and not thrilling, but very telling, and a tenacious memory, and an uncommon quantity of common-sense. . . . Then how came this to pass? how came it that he did what no other preacher, lecturer, or entertainer ever did before—kept together a congregation of five thousand week after week, and year after year? Well, two centuries ago, when finished preachers were common, La Bruyère said, 'Until there appear a man who, with a style learned from the Holy Scripture, shall explain to the people the Divine Word familiarly and with singleness of heart, the orators and declaimers will be followed.' Spurgeon was just that man—'mighty in the Scriptures;' and full of Psalms and hymns and spiritual songs; everything about him was scriptural, and his one business was ever to explain the Word of God, and never to explain it away. 'The higher criticism,' imported from Germany, was his scorn; but he loved simplicity and godly sincerity. No great linguist, he knew full well his full and forcible mother tongue, and how to use it. A very English preacher, most at home in London. So his English speech went straight into the English heart; the feather that winged the arrow of the Gospel. This well fitted his mother-wit, which he was not careful to restrain, which appears to perfection in his volumes of proverbs which he wittily called 'The Salt-Cellars.'[28]

This was the kind of man he always was.

Notwithstanding all of Spurgeon's greatness and gifts, he had his imperfections, and there were always those more than ready to point them out.

Some, for example, thought him lacking in the warmth of affection so that he appealed to "every faculty of the mind but seldom, if ever, to the heart. Neither in the tones of his voice nor in the strain of his address is there even an attempt at the tender or the pathetic."[29] Moreover, as has been often recorded, he was constantly accused of egotism and arrogance. Although these criticisms have been exaggerated, Spurgeon did perhaps leave himself open to some of those charges. Yet at the same time, others said the exact opposite of his critics. Many saw him as humble and a heart-warming man. And one thing is certain, the grace of God rested upon him, and he so sought the glory of Christ in it all that God used him in a significant way. All had to acknowledge that. He was genuinely committed to God. This can be clearly seen in his Sunday morning prayers in the Tabernacle. The richness and the variety of his striking prayers is telling of the depth of his spirituality. In the preface of a book printed after Spurgeon's death in which are chronicled several Sunday morning prayers, the editor wrote these words. "Mr. D. L. Moody . . . had come 4000 miles to hear Spurgeon. What impressed him most was not the praise, though he thought he had never heard such grand congregational singing; it was not Mr. Spurgeon's expositions, fine though it was, nor even his sermon; it was his prayer. He seemed to have access to God that could bring down the power from heaven. That was the great secret of his influence and his success."[30] He was a spiritual man in every sense of the word. His spirituality profoundly touched lives. As a single case in point, *The Christian Chronicle*, February 22, 1882, reported:

> Cannon Wilberforce, it is said, manifested increased spiritual earnestness since the Rev. C. H. Spurgeon stayed with him as guest during the sittings of the Baptist Union in Southampton a year or two ago.

What constituted Spurgeon's spiritual makeup?

SPURGEON'S SPIRITUALITY

As emphasized so often, Spurgeon's entire life, his spirituality no exception, found its essential roots in the Bible. For the Tabernacle preacher, life in the Spirit found its foundation in the Holy Scriptures. As Raymond Brown expressed it, "His spirituality was essentially a Biblical spirituality."[31] This immediately implies that Spurgeon could not in the strict sense of the word be identified with the mystics, although he did admire the medieval mystic, Bernard of Clairvaux. Actually, he himself would not want to be numbered among them. Spurgeon would be much more in harmony with the great second century thinker and spiritual leader, Irenaeus. Spurgeon never sought to be an innovator theologically or spiritually. He believed that all Christians receive the unique gift of the Holy Spirit, and the Holy Spirit uses the Holy Scriptures to lead believers into a biblical understanding of who Jesus Christ was and is and the way to develop an intimate walk with Him.

Spurgeon saw in Jesus Christ spirituality exemplified. The Lord, as revealed in the Scriptures, became Spurgeon's model and the pattern for true spirituality. This had a very pragmatic effect on his pulpit ministry. Spurgeon never really ran dry in his preaching because he was never able to exhaust the Scriptures. The same can be said for his spiritual experience of Christ. The Lord Jesus Christ is infinite and ultimate; therefore, there was a constant flow of spiritual life into his own experience. Nor did Spurgeon ever try to live spiritually beyond his means; his entire spiritual experience was predicated upon a personal experience of Christ as grasped in the Scriptures.

SPIRITUALITY AND THE BIBLE

Spurgeon's approach to spirituality as rooted in the Bible implies several things. First, the Bible demands study. Spurgeon was living in a Bible-loving age; therefore, his admonitions to immerse oneself in the Scriptures received a warm reception. At that same time, however, Spurgeon exercised care in his use of the Bible. He had an experience in his early life that taught him an unforgettable lesson. He said, "I have a very lively, or rather deadly, recollection of a series of discourses in Hebrews, which made a deep impression on my mind of the most unbelievable kind. I wished frequently that the Hebrews had kept the Epistle to themselves, for it completely bored one poor Gentile lad. By the time the seventh or eighth discourse had been read, only the very good people could stand it. These, of course, declared that they had never heard more valuable expositions. But those of a more carnal judgment, it appeared to us that each sermon increased in dullness. That Epistle exalts its readers to suffer the word of exhortation, and we did so." Dull exposition, even based upon the Scriptures, does not necessarily bring people into grips with the Word of God and hence into spirituality, according to Spurgeon.

The Scriptures always played a central role in Spurgeon's life. Even as a small boy he knew the language of the Bible and many of the stories contained in the Scriptures. This was because of the good rootage he received in Stambourne from his grandfather James. Remember the story of Spurgeon challenging old Roads at the pub in Stambourne and confronting him with the Scriptures. As a teenager, that dramatic verse of Scripture, "Look unto me and be saved," influenced Spurgeon so profoundly that it brought him to faith in Christ. Immediately after his conversion he began to weigh every sermon in the light of the Word of God. He acquired an amazing grasp of the Bible even as a teenager. Of course, the rest of his life continued as a testimony to those foundations that were deeply rooted in his earlier days. It was Spurgeon's deep conviction that the Bible imparts life, and that constitutes the essential secret of his spirituality.

Moreover, for Spurgeon it was not just a question of knowing the words and stories or memorizing the Bible; rather, it centered in being so affected by the message of the Scriptures that spirituality would automatically result. He could repeat Jeremiah's words, "Thy words were found and I did eat them, and they became unto me the joy and rejoicing of my heart" (Jeremiah 15:16). Spurgeon could honestly say, "There is a style of majesty about God's Word, and with this majesty a vividness never found elsewhere. No other writing has within it a heavenly life whereby works miracles and even imparts life to its reader. It is a living and incorruptible seed. It moves, it stirs itself, it lives, it communes with living men as the living Word. Solomon says concerning it, 'It shall talk with thee.' Have you ever known what that means? Why, the book has wrestled with me, the book has smitten me, the book has comforted me, the book has smiled on me . . . the book has frowned upon me. The book has crossed my hand, the book has warmed my heart. The book weeps with me and sings with me, it whispers to me and it preaches to me. It maps my way and it holds my goings. . . . It is a live book, all over alive from its first chapter to its last word is filled with mystic vitality, which makes it the preeminence over every other writing to every other living child of God. . . . The grass withers and the flower falls away but the Word of the Lord endures forever." [32]

Spurgeon clearly recognized and believed the Word of God imparts life, and that in very personal terms. Spurgeon constantly illustrated this principle from his own personal experiences. He said, "You need not bring life to the Scripture. You should draw life from Scripture. Ofttimes a single verse starts up as Lazarus came forth from the call of the Lord Jesus. When our soul has been faint and ready to die, a single word applied to the heart by the Spirit of God has aroused us, for it is a quickening as well as a living word in Scripture. I am so glad of this, because at times I feel altogether dead but the Word of God is not dead in coming to it, we are like the dead man when he was put into the grave of the prophet, rose again as soon as he touched his bones, even these bones of the prophets these words of theirs spoken and written thousands of years ago would impart life to those who will come into contact with them. The Word of God is thus overflowingly alive." [33] Spurgeon believed in the inexhaustibility of the Scriptures to impart life and to develop spirituality. Never did the Scriptures fail Spurgeon in his entire ministry nor in his spiritual quest to know Christ better. It became the source and the giver of life.

All this implies that the Bible not only demands study, but it demands meditation. One is not merely to read the Scriptures or simply to learn its truths, but to meditate upon it that the Holy Spirit might use the truth to speak personally to the heart. Often the Bible cuts deeply. Augustine said, "He is not an effective teacher of hearts who is not first a listener within." [34] This is especially applicable to the preacher. He must not only have a message for others, but the message must speak to his own heart and life as well. He preaches to people, but he also preaches to himself. The story will be remembered of Spurgeon once hearing his own sermon preached where he was worshiping. His reaction was, "Wasn't it good of the Lord to feed me with the food I had prepared for others?" Spurgeon always listened to his own messages. That also became an essential mark of his spirituality.

At the same time, real spirituality, as it emerges from the Bible, is not just for one's own personal consumption, it must be shared with others. Real spirituality moves in a fashion that flows out in service to others. All of that emerges from a simple openness to the Bible. Spurgeon said, "A few minutes silent openness of soul before the Lord, has brought us more treasures of truth than hours of learned research." [35]

OTHER SOURCES OF SPIRITUALITY

This does not mean that Spurgeon would not find spiritual truth from other writings. He was an avid reader of the Puritans and a host of other authors as well. He found great challenge and inspiration and strength from them. One of Spurgeon's favorite Puritan writers was Richard Sibbes. Puritan theology played a significant role in his spirituality. It is also important to see the catholicity of Spurgeon's spirituality. Spurgeon may not have been happy with the word "catholicity," but it is used in the sense of a mature reaching out into many areas to find spiritual truth and reality. He drew widely from a broad range of Christian experience and truth, which down through the centuries of Christian history have strengthened God's people. The Bishop of Ripon once said about Spurgeon, "He was a soul who sits in an observatory to view the heavens but had his telescope so adjusted that he can only follow the course of the star through one portion of the sky." [36] That is untrue and unfair; the Bishop apparently had not read Spurgeon. True, Spurgeon would have identified himself with the Apostle Paul, the Puritans, and found everything of ultimate truth emerging from the Word of God, but Spurgeon was quite broad in his approach. He probably gleaned that approach from the Puritans who were themselves broad-based in their approach to spirituality. The English Puritans were always eager to grasp what God was saying in all the centuries. They continually harked back to the things that God had revealed to his people through the years. And it has been said Spurgeon lit his torch at the Puritan fire.

Spurgeon vividly recognized that Christians who truly want to walk with God must look back to the past and all that God has done in the lives of those who have preceded them. Therefore he immersed himself in their writings. Spurgeon constantly raised his own horizons by gleaning from others. He did not point his spiritual telescope to just one portion of the sky at all, as the Bishop of Ripon charged. In some ten or twelve lectures he quotes the following people: In the Patristic period he refers to Justin Martyr, Tertullian, Origen, Gregory of Nazianzus, Basil of Caesaera, Jerome, and of course the great Augustine. He also would quote from the school of Alexandria and Gregory the Great. Coming into the Medieval era one of his favorites, as mentioned, was Bernard of Clairvaux. And, of course, one can well imagine how often he quoted John Bunyan. It was once said that to hear Spurgeon was like hearing a second Bunyan. But his catholicity of appreciation extended to George Fox of the Quakers, the saintly Richard Baxter, and the encyclopedic writer John Owen. He also quoted Isaac Ambrose and John Howe along with Joseph Alleine and Benjamin Keach, one of his predecessors at the New Park Street Baptist Church. He was also fond of Jeremy Taylor. Coming closer to his own era his favorite preacher was George Whitefield. But he also gleaned from Rowland Hill, Jonathan Edwards, David Grainer, John Gill, Andrew Fuller, John Newton, John and Charles Wesley, Adam Clarke, Samuel Drew, Henry Martyn, Robert Murray McCheyne, John Angel James, not to mention in his own day Lord Shaftesbury and Henry Ward Beecher along with Andrew Dukes, F. W. Faber, and even some Tractarians. That is not to mention half of those with whom he was conversant. Little wonder, therefore, that he said, "He who dares to prescribe one uniform standard of experience for the children of God, is either grievously ignorant or hopelessly full of self esteem."[37] For Spurgeon, spiritual uniformity was not God's rule. In grace, as well as in providence, he believed in variety.

Spurgeon also recognized a rich variety in conversion experience. For example, his wife said, "I went to church in my mother's womb. And from my earliest days, if you'd ask me as a little child, I would have told you I loved Jesus." For Susannah, her initial experience of Christ was not dramatic. Spurgeon, as we have seen, had a very climactic conversion moment in the little primitive Methodist chapel in Colchester. But he did not feel his experience superior to his wife's at all. He said, "I can't really honestly remember the day I was born, but I know that I am alive."[38] He was saying that one need not be vividly aware of the moment of conversion, just so long as one knows that they are genuinely alive in Christ. He contended there is a rich variety in conversion experiences. Spurgeon possessed an ecumenical spirit in his spirituality that came over as refreshing.

SPIRITUALITY AND DISCIPLINE

Spurgeon believed in a disciplined spirituality. This meant diligent, meditative study of the Scriptures, as seen above. It also meant a breadth of study and openness to all that God has done and said to His people through the ages. Of course, it meant a life of disciplined prayer. He also believed in fasting. Much has already been said about Spurgeon's prayer life, but it must be remembered that though he did not spend long hours in prayer, he lived in a constant attitude of prayer, and that takes diligence and discipline as well. Prayer became such a vital part of Spurgeon's life that he simply breathed the atmosphere of God's presence. Therefore, Spurgeon saw discipline in all these areas as vital if one aspires to be spiritual.

A disciplined spirituality also means diligence in service. One is to share Christ, to serve Christ, to reach out and speak to the needs of people. Spurgeon's spirituality had a very pragmatic ring to it. He would say that if one's Bible study and prayer life does not culminate in reaching out to touch other lives in sharing Christ and meeting needs, it is a false, superficial spirituality. This, of course, explains the constant diligent giving of himself, even in the face of sickness, adversity, and criticism, to serve his Lord. To walk with Christ in spirituality means serving Christ in a fervent commitment of oneself to others.

Therefore, it can be correctly concluded that spirituality for Spurgeon was real, practical, workable, and Christ honoring. He did his best to live up to all the precepts of what the Bible says the Christian should be in relationship to his Lord. And that is spirituality on the highest plane.

THE NEGATIVE SIDE OF SPIRITUALITY

Spurgeon's spirituality had its negative side. He said, "Dirt in the heart throws dust in the eyes." He was adamantly opposed to theatre going, as a case in point. He declared if it became a habit among believers it would be the death of piety. Once, a drama played in London's Shaftesbury Theatre by the title, "Judah." In a special performance for ministers the place was filled. Spurgeon reacted strongly. He said the church has "played the harlot beyond any church in any age." [39] But he did not oppose alcohol until late in life. This conviction he no doubt gleaned from the Puritans. For them, beer was "the Puritan drink."

It has also been pointed out that Spurgeon had a strong position on dancing. He said it was a healthy exercise, but dancing by mixed sex he opposed. The next week *Punch* had a cartoon of aged deacons dancing in the vestry. Spurgeon's views were obviously not always respected. But Spurgeon's negative side came over in a very practical, almost earthy way. He once said, "A man full of pudding is not likely to be full of power. The process of digestion won't help your sanctification." Still, Spurgeon's spirituality took on an essentially positive tone. He said, "Beseech Christ to chisel His likeness into your features." [40] Similarly, he declared, "When you come to the end of self, then, and not before, do you reach the beginning of God." [41] That is basically positive.

Spurgeon's spirituality, as implied, was clearly never separated from assertive action. He was fully convinced that one's personal walk with God had to be accompanied with a sufficient amount of earnestness, faith and work. Spirituality without aggressive action would never do for Spurgeon. He said:

> It seems to me if a man is a Christian, Christianity ought to eat him right up. It ought to go right through him, and he should be known to be first and foremost a Christian man. Let him be all the rest on an equality with his fellow-men,

and I think he may even be superior to them in business tact and capacity. I believe that religion will even sharpen his intellect, and that often communion with God in prayer will give him that calm frame of mind which will enable him to do his business all the better. Where is the self-sacrifice of the early days? Here is a great army of us, interesting one another, amusing one another, pleasing one another, perhaps edifying one another, and there is the great world outside, with only here and there a struggling missionary preaching the Gospel. [42]

In Spurgeon's thinking, David Livingston epitomized these spiritual principles. When the great Scottish missionary died in Africa, and the news was received in London, there was probably as much sorrow at the Metropolitan Tabernacle as anywhere in the country. Spurgeon always treasured that worn copy of Charles' own sermons that the great missionary and traveler had carried with him until his death. Spurgeon's spirituality was biblical, historical, catholic, and very practical. Lorimer sums it up well by saying:

> To him the spiritual was not the phenomenal but the true and abiding. Hence, he walked with God as with an actual presence, he talked with God as with a veritable personality, and he trusted Him, not with that trust that leaves the Almighty, because He is Almighty to do everything, as though impotence and idleness could be in any sense to His glory, but with the faith that works, endures, suffers, leaving the results to Him who in every instance must give the increase.

INTERESTING EVENTS

During these maturing times, Spurgeon encountered considerable interest in prophecy from fellow believers. Spurgeon, though a confessed premillennialist, never took a dogmatic stand in his views of prophecy. In a letter written to the editor of *Messiah's Herald*, the pastor of the Tabernacle made the following remarks:

> The more I read of the Scriptures as to the future, the less I am able to dogmatize. I see the conversion of the world, and the personal pre-millennial reign, and the sudden coming, and the judgment, and several other grand points; but I cannot put them into order, nor has anyone else done so yet. I believe every prophetical work I have ever seen (and I have read very many) to be wrong in some points. I feel more at home in preaching Christ crucified than upon any other theme, and I do believe he will draw all men unto him. [43]

During these productive years, the Tabernacle Church had 125 lay preachers among its members. Graduates from the College continued going all over the world. A good number had already settled in churches in the United States. Still, the need in London itself remained great. During this period, four million people populated the London area for whom scarcely any spiritual provision was made. Out of this need came Spurgeon's zeal to plant churches.

SPURGEON'S ABILITIES

As Spurgeon matured, he seemed able to rise to any situation. As a case in point, a group of young lawyers once dined with him at a friend's house. Previously, they had ridiculed Spurgeon for his lack of formal education. So they planned to confront him with some esoteric and detailed questions to embarrass him and show up his lack of college training. But Charles knew a little about almost everything and in some respects a lot about many subjects. Before the evening was over, the lawyers sat in amazement at his grasp of a wide range of subjects. Their skepticism turned to admiration. His unbelievable grasp of so many subjects was quite profound.

An interesting and very satisfying event took place in the life of C. H. Spurgeon on March 12, 1873. His brother James had built a fine new church building in Croydon where he had pastoral responsibility along with his ministry with Charles at the Tabernacle. On that particular date, Charles preached at the opening of what became known as the Croydon "Spurgeon's Tabernacle." As stated earlier, the name of the church was not named after Charles but after his brother James. It bears that sub-title to this day and is still active in north Croydon.

A happy time for Spurgeon took place when the director of the Stockwell Orphanage, Mr. Charlesworth, was baptized. This pleased Charles very much.

At times the orphanage would fall on difficulties and badly need funding. Spurgeon, being a man of fervent prayer, would pour out his heart to God. He would pray, "These are thy children, and this is thy work; send us this day a considerable sum of money, if that will be well." On one such occasion, immediately after his prayer, he went home and composed a letter to appeal for funds. In 24 hours £800 came in. This was before the letter could be sent out, so Spurgeon cancelled the letter at the printer's and never sent it out.

As the Metropolitan Tabernacle had now grown to the largest Protestant congregation in the world, it surpassed the first African congregation in Richmond, Virginia in the United States that had formerly claimed that honor.

SPURGEON'S ILLNESSES

Charles continued to suffer more and more from the gout. It was quite amazing, if not amusing, the different things that were said about Spurgeon and his problem with the recurring rheumatic gout. Once a clergyman wrote to Spurgeon to inform him that his gout was sent as divine judgment for opposing the Established Church. *The Sussex Daily News* took a different view than the critic on the matter, however. In the article the author said:

We say nothing of the anti-Christian character of this clergyman's communication, and merely content ourselves with remarking that he seems to have forgotten all about the Tower of Siloam and the lesson which the Great Teacher, whom he ought to reverence, drew from it. What we would more particularly point out is, how strange it is that the clergyman, who is, no doubt, a fine old Tory of the ancient school, should have considered Mr. Spurgeon's gout a judgment upon him. Why, the gout is simply the most aristocratic and most Conservative institution in the country. It was a companion of Pitt, it was the intimate associate of the late Lord Derby. No church dignitary lower than a dean, or a canon at the very lowest, would presume to say that he had the gout. Instead of taunting Mr. Spurgeon with being tormented with it, we feel much more inclined to chide him for his impertinence in venturing to claim acquaintance with it. What levelling, radical, democratic times these are! We shall be having Mr. Arch laid up with a swollen foot next and Mr. Odger taking to crutches and colchicum!

Others accused Spurgeon of suffering because God's heavy hand rested upon him as a result of his intolerance. But it was far from humorous. He had written about his painful gout in these words, "Lucian says, 'I thought a cobra had bitten me and filled my veins with poison; but it was worse, it was gout.' That was written from experience, I know." Spurgeon said on another occasion, "I pity the dog that has felt as much pain in his four legs as I have felt in one." [44] Rheumatic gout leads to depression, as often seen. That Spurgeon met on his road to the Celestial City "Giant Despair" there is no doubt. On November 7, 1881 he wrote to his mother saying, "I hope to be at Mentone by Saturday . . . My brains are nearly addled and the very idea of rest charms me." [45] *The Conduct Record Visitor* expressed it well when they wrote, "He is no dry land sailor, but has done business in great waters." At times the "great waters" were very deep. Once he wrote to his father (September 8, 1883) congratulating him on not suffering what he called "the family foe," [46] rheumatic gout. It did run in the Spurgeon clan, but Charles' father had escaped. In many letters to the family, Charles complained of his illnesses. He knew there he would gain a sympathetic ear. Many have glossed over the fact that gout induced depression; but, to understand Spurgeon, one must understand his depressions. He often found himself in the grip of deep depressive moods. Spurgeon went through his times of tribulation as the Spirit of God honed his spiritual maturity to a fine point that he might hit the mark with his ministry. He himself said, "Why this depression, why this chicken-hearted melancholy? If I cannot keep a public Sabbath, yet wherefore do I deny my soul her inner Sabbath? The causes are not enough to justify yielding to despondency. Up my heart! Play the man, and thy casting down shall turn to lifting up. 'Hope thou in God.' Hope carries stars in her eyes. Her light is fed by secret visitation from God . . . Let us fly to our God! Blessed downcastings that drive us to thee, O Lord." [47] Though

Spurgeon was often cast down he could lift himself up through faith in God's faithfulness. In times of treading the deep waters, he found strength by looking to Jesus Christ. In writing to his Aunt on June 30, 1881 he said, "I find nothing bears me up but a simple trust in the blood which cleanses from all sin. There is our sure and abiding hope."[48] Charles said in an interview recorded in *The Quiver*, November 1881, "It's a great thing to learn to trust in God. At first it is wonderfully like walking on a tight-rope, but afterwards it is the simplest thing." As has been said by one of his biographers, he would pull "the key of promise out of his bosom and begin to try the dungeon door, in whose 'nasty and stinking cell' he had so long lain. Lo, the bolts came back, one after another, though 'some went damnably hard,' until he was safe again on the King's highway."[49]

MENTONE TRIPS

Spurgeon's trips to Mentone to flee the dreadful, miserable London winters helped him tremendously. Spurgeon actually made twenty annual visits to the French Riviera. He loved Mentone, saying, "I think we will hasten on to Mentone." When he would arrive and go to his favorite hotel, The Beau Revage, he would say, "Ah, now I feel at home." He did feel at home. Mentone seemed to exhilarate him. Once an organ grinder outside his hotel was not doing very well in making any money as he played away. So Spurgeon took over for awhile, then passed his hat and got sixteen shillings for the man. Such was the outgoing personality of Charles.

In his earlier visits he stayed at the Hotel de la Paix or the Hotel des Anglais. Later the Beau Revage became his cherished hideaway. A group of friends always accompanied him on his ventures to Mentone. Often his very close friend, deacon and publisher, Joseph Passmore, and almost without exception Mr. Harrald, his secretary, were always there. Usually a few other deacons would accompany him as well. On one of his trips to the continent on his way to Mentone to recuperate and rest, Charles stopped at a hotel in Marseilles. He called for a porter to come and light a fire in the fireplace that he might be able to bear the pain in his limbs a bit more. When the porter came to light the fire he had brought with him some vine branches to get the fire started. When Spurgeon saw the vines about to be burned, he literally cried in agony as he thought of the eternal destiny of fruitless branches of the vine that were producing no fruit and were only fit to be burned.

Spurgeon loved much about Mentone. He tremendously enjoyed visiting Dr. Bennett's garden behind his hotel. It became a favorite retreat for Charles. There was a saracenic tower in Dr. Bennett's garden, a lovely spot where Spurgeon would study and do some of his writing and work. Also, a lovely spot with a line of cypress trees ran through a dense mass of olive trees at the back of the Chalet des Rosiers, the Swiss villa where Queen Victoria strolled when at Mentone. Many notable Britishers spent time on the Mediterranean in Mentone. Spurgeon and his secretary spent many enjoyable hours in the quiet nooks of the area.

There were also many lovely valleys surrounding Mentone. Spurgeon never forgot one experience that he had in the Gorbio Valley. He wrote:

> In this valley I have spent many a happy day, just climbing to any terrace I preferred, and sitting down to read. I once left *Manton on Psalm CXIX*, by the roadside, and before the next morning it was returned to me. Here, too, on Christmas day, 1879, I learned what it is to 'Walk in the Light.' I had been ill with gout; and, on recovering, arranged to drive up this valley as far as the road would serve, and then send away the carriage, walk further on, have our lunch, and, in the afternoon, walk gently back to the spot where we left the conveyance, the man having orders to be there again by three. Alas! I had forgotten that, as far as the upper portion of the valley is concerned, the sun was gone soon after twelve! I found myself in the shade before lunch was over, and shade meant sharp frost; for, wherever the sun had not shone, the earth was frozen hard as a rock. To be caught in this cold, would mean a long illness for me; so, leaning on the shoulder of my faithful secretary, I set forth to hobble down the valley. The sun shone on me, and I could just move fast enough to keep his bright disc above the top of the hill. He seemed to be rolling downward along the gradually descending ridge, like a great wheel of fire; and I, painfully and laboriously stumbling along, still remained in his light. Of course, it was not the time for our Jehu to be at the appointed spot; so, with many a groan, I had to stagger on until a stray conveyance came in our direction. Out of the sunshine, all is winter: in the sunlight alone is summer. Oh, that spiritually I could always walk in the light of God's countenance as that day I managed to keep in the sun's rays!

> Like Enoch, let me walk with God,
> And thus walk out my day;
> Attended still with heavenly light,
> Upon the King's highway.

Spurgeon also would often walk out to the sea and watch the waves. He did enjoy it when a storm arose and he could see the storm toss the ocean about.

Spurgeon had gone to Mentone for so many years that he witnessed what once had been a small village grow into a town of considerable size. He had explored every nook and cranny and hardly a walk or a drive in the entire neighborhood escaped his investigation.

PICNICS

When the weather permitted, Spurgeon loved to go out on a picnic. The lady who prepared the picnics that Spurgeon and his party enjoyed once remarked, "I can't make out you English people at all; you have nice hotels and houses where you can have your meals in comfort, and yet you go and eat your dinner in a ditch!"[50] But Charles loved it. He would often start out for a day with a light lunch and a waterproof rug to spread on the ground to ward off his recurrent rheumatism. With either a volume of Brooks or Manton or another Puritan divine, or with a biography of some great Christian, Charles and his secretary would have a great day in reading. Spurgeon's books *The Clue with the Maze, Illustrations and Meditations*, and *Flowers from a Puritan's Garden* were largely composed in a pleasant spot on the cypress walk of Mentone. One favorite place for the picnic parties was Beaulieu, translated "beautiful place." The route to it led directly through Monte Carlo, with its famous gambling casinos. Spurgeon was always glad to see that part of the journey behind him. He said that the whole region seemed to smell of brimstone. He heard of the many suicides that were the result of gambling at Monte Carlo. On one of his early visits to the Riviera he went to see the gamblers in the casino. After that he avoided the place like the plague, at least as best he could. He saw the ruin that a place like the gambling casino brought.

SPIRITUAL LIFE AT MENTONE

Of all the people who visited Mentone, none enjoyed it more than Spurgeon. As he generally had several traveling companions or friends who wished to be near him, his party usually occupied a considerable portion of the hotel. The Beau Revage had a homelike atmosphere and the proprietors would even ring a bell at the time for family prayers. There were other guests who wished to be present, and people would even come from other hotels and villas in the neighborhood and take part in the daily prayer time led by Spurgeon. He would give a brief exposition of Scripture and then prayer would follow. Those who would worship with the Spurgeon party at prayer time came from many denominations. On the Lord's Day afternoon all shared in a communion service, which Spurgeon also led. Recall, Spurgeon was not a believer in closed communion; he invited all believers to the Lord's table. Many people were touched and blessed by the Mentone ministry of Spurgeon. He also preached and worshiped on occasions at the French Protestant Church of Mentone. God used him powerfully in that setting.

Spurgeon related an interesting story when back in London at the Tabernacle in June of 1883. In a sermon he said,

> Some years ago, I was away in the South of France; I had been very ill there, and was sitting in my room alone, for all my friends had all gone down to the mid-day meal. All at once it struck me that I had something to do out of doors; I did not know what it was, but I walked out, and sat down on a seat. There came and sat next to me on the seat a poor, pale, emaciated woman in the last

stage of consumption; and looking at me, she said, 'O Mr. Spurgeon, I have read your sermons for years, and I have learned to trust the Saviour! I know I cannot live long, but I am very sad as I think of it, for I am so afraid to die.' Then I knew why I had gone out there, and I began to try to cheer her. I found that it was very hard work. After a little conversation, I said to her, 'Then you would like to go to Heaven, but not to die?' 'Yes, just so,' she answered. 'Well, how do you wish to go there? Would you like to ascend in a chariot of fire?' That method had not occurred to her, but she answered, 'Yes, oh, yes!' 'Well,' I said, 'suppose there should be, just round this corner, horses all on fire, and a blazing chariot waiting there to take you up to Heaven; do you feel ready to step into such a chariot?' She looked up at me, and she said, 'No, I should be afraid to do that.' 'Ah!' I said, 'and so should I; I should tremble a great deal more at getting into a chariot of fire than I should at dying. I am not fond of being behind fiery horses, I would rather be excused from taking such a ride as that.' Then I said to her, 'Let me tell you what will probably happen to you; you will most likely go to bed some night, and you will wake up in Heaven.' That is just what did occur not long after; her husband wrote to tell me that, after our conversation, she had never had any more trouble about dying; she felt that it was the easiest way into Heaven, after all, and far better than going there in a whirlwind with horses of fire and chariots of fire, and she gave herself up for her Heavenly Father to take her home in His own way; and so she passed away, as I expected, in her sleep.[51]

Such were the remarkable incidents that occurred in Spurgeon's Mentone visits.

Spurgeon called Mentone the "sunny south." The sunshine and the clean air of Mentone helped to increase not only his spirits, but it seemed restorative to his health. Walking by the seashore, he would always revel in nature and would make applications to biblical truths.

Once in Mentone he fell down a marble staircase, but did not realize at first how seriously he had been hurt. He knocked out two front teeth as he turned a double somersault. The money fell out of his pocket into his Wellington boots. He humorously described the whole transaction as "painless dentistry, with money to boot!" But it did lay him up for a few days. Spurgeon had a great sense of humor in all circumstances.

Charles would constantly write back to his church in London from Mentone. Typical of the many letters that he wrote, one reads:

Mentone,
Feb. 7.

My Beloved Friends,

After enjoying a few restful nights and quiet days, I feel myself coming round again, and my heart is full of praise and thanksgiving to our gracious God. Your prayers have been incessant, and have prevailed; and I am very grateful to you all. As long as I am able, it will be my joy to be of service to you; and my only grief has been that sickness has weakened my powers, and rendered me less able to discharge my happy duties among you. The post I occupy needs a man at his best, and I have of late been very much the reverse. However, we know who it is that giveth power to the faint, and so we trust that feeble efforts have not been ineffectual.

I shall be doubly indebted to the goodness of our Lord if the remainder of my rest shall confirm the beneficial work which has commenced. The further repose will, I hope, make me stronger for the future.

I have not yet heard tidings of the special services, but I hope that every member is at work to make them a success. Pray about them, speak about them, attend them, assist in them, bring others to them. Our two evangelists are the right instruments, but the *hand of the Lord* is needed to work by them. Call upon Him whose hand it is, and He will work according to His own good pleasure. The times are such that churches holding the old truths must be active and energetic, that the power of the gospel may be manifest to all. We need to uplift a banner because of the truth. So numerous a church as ours may accomplish great things, by the power of the Holy Ghost, if only we are once in downright earnest. Playing at religion is wretched; it must be everything to us, or it will be nothing.

Peace be with you all, and abounding love!

Your hearty friend,
C. H. SPURGEON. [52]

Once from Mentone he wrote these words:

I am altogether stranded. I am not able to leave my bed, or to find much rest upon it. The pains of rheumatism, lumbago and sciatica, mingled together, are exceedingly sharp. I am aware I am dwelling in a body capable of the most acute suffering.

An excerpt from another letter, to Susannah, reads:

After the deadly chill of Thursday night at Nice, I feel gout coming on . . . My left foot is badly swollen, and the knee joint is following suit. I have had very little sleep, and am very low.

Needless to say, the church in London and Susannah rejoiced to hear from their beloved pastor.

BACK HOME

Whenever Spurgeon returned from his excursions to Mentone, the people at the Tabernacle were delighted to have him back. Spurgeon also always rejoiced to return home. He loved his native land. He said, "the sight of the eyes makes glad the heart." In March of one year he had been away for a protracted period. On the Sunday he was once again to fill the pulpit, one could sense a spirit of expectation permeating the entire building. As Spurgeon began to make his way toward the vestry, all saw he could walk with comparative ease. The rest in Mentone had done him good. Beyond question, these excursions to the south of France prolonged Spurgeon's life. They provided times of recuperation from illness and rest from the pressures of the London pastorate, but they also became productive in that much writing was accomplished. Without these "vacations," Spurgeon may have passed on much earlier than he did and produced considerably fewer works. A group of deacons and others surrounded Charles before he could enter his vestry. They all remarked about how glad they were to see him back. He replied, "Glad to see you again; there are no faces like yours!"[53] When he was seated in the vestry, he told one of his friends that he felt like a new man and all rejoiced to see how really good he looked. The attendance at the service itself was simply overwhelming. A great number had to be shut out to avoid undue pressure. He preached that morning on Job 36:2, "Suffer me a little, and I will show thee that I have yet to speak on God's behalf." He preached in his best style. The following evening a thanksgiving service was held for his safe return. Again the chapel filled. The same week the Butchers' Festival was celebrated at the church at Newington Butts. On Friday Spurgeon lectured at the College resuming his weekly lectures for the students. When he entered the lecture hall the young men burst out into singing the doxology. He lectured for about an hour and a quarter on "Experimental Preaching." The students drank in every word. He would always throw himself into his work unreservedly whenever he returned home.

When Spurgeon returned from another of his excursions to Mentone in January of 1880, after an absence of three months, he preached on Psalm 68: 20 and 21, "He that is our God." As he spoke to his people he thanked everyone for carrying on the work so well during his long absence. He went on to say, "I feel sure that I have returned greatly refreshed, I hope to have a long spell of happy, loving and useful service among you. It is a great mercy that everything at the tabernacle does not depend on the presence of the pastor, but that in his absence all manifest so much earnestness."[54]

DIFFICULT BUT PRODUCTIVE DAYS

As the years unfolded, even when Charles returned from restful Mentone, his malady seemed to increase. Although he suffered times of ill health as a young man, after his 43rd year in 1877, his condition steadily worsened. He was far from a well man and his condition slowly deteriorated through the years. He could not always count on being able to fulfill his obligations. He once wrote his friend Mr. Tolar of Waterbeach: "Dear Friend, I shall be occupied til the last moment, therefore meet me at Paddington on Monday evening at 6:30. I shall be delighted with your company. Be ready with a sermon for a Tuesday in case I should break down." At the Metropolitan Tabernacle itself, there were times when a substitute was held in attendance should Spurgeon be unable to preach at the last moment. The price that Spurgeon had to pay for his hard labors began coming down on him. It cost him more than people ever realized. He suffered such pain at times that he had to preach with one knee upon a chair and could not move from the spot. But if he had enough physical strength just to stand, hang onto the railing and preach, he would do it. He proved to be a true soldier of the cross. Spurgeon sharply felt the burden of his condition, especially when it took him out of the pulpit, often for two or three of the most valuable months of the year. He said, "We *could* do more, we *would* do more, if we were not laid prostrate at this very moment, our work requires our presence. Therefore, while we live, every interval of relief shall be laid out in His service. The time is short, the work is great, the Lord must be trusted more simply." [55] In one of his more seriously depressed states, he actually intimated that he might resign the Metropolitan Tabernacle. The immediate reply from his church was, "We would rather have you one month in the year than any other twelve." [56]

Other things took its toll on Charles' health. The constant financial burden of all the ministries burdened him. Spurgeon once confessed the burden of this. He said, "During a long serious illness, I had an unaccountable fit of anxiety about money matters." [57] Money matters did depress him, but he could normally drag himself up out of those anxious moments by his faith in God. Moreover, he never seemed to escape the continuing memory of the Surrey Garden Music Hall tragedy. Whenever he was in the extremity of pain from his gout, or something would trigger the vividness of the whole ghastly scene, he would get extremely agitated. Once he was crossing the Alps at Col Di Bal Dobbia, an eight thousand foot pass over the beautiful mountains. As they were making their way along the trail a baggage mule slipped and started sliding down the slope. Fortunately, it did not go over the edge but stopped short of the rim and was rescued. But the scene so upset Spurgeon that he immediately sat down in the snow, even at that 8,000 foot level, and would not, could not, for a long time be persuaded to move. His wife Susannah, who was with him, said:

> We coaxed and pleaded to no purpose; so we sat down with him in the snow ... that awful night at Surrey Hall was responsible ... the delicate organism of his wonderful brain had then sustained so much pressure, in some part of it, that any sudden fright would have power for a moment or two to disturb its balance. [58]

In Spurgeon's last years, the trauma of the Down Grade Controversy put him in depression for months at a time. Spurgeon would cry out, "The chariot wheels drag heavily, even prayer seems like labor." [59] Like Pilgrim in Bunyan's allegory, he knew what it was to be in the "Delectable Mountains" and at the next stop be in the "Castle of Giant Despair." But, even when depression rolled over his soul he could say, "Depression comes over me whenever the Lord is preparing me for a larger blessing for my ministry. It has now become to me a prophet in rough clothing, a John the Baptist, heralding the nearer coming of my Lord's richer benison."[60] One cannot but admire the tremendous faith of the man—and insight; the struggle with depression did prepare him for something better that God had in store.

Spurgeon's sensitivity to people always surfaced in these hours of depression. He said, "I would go into the depths a hundred times to cheer a downcast spirit. It is good for me to have been afflicted, that I might know how to speak a word in season to one that is weary."[61] He knew what the Apostle Paul meant when he said in 2 Corinthians 1:3-4, 6:

> Blessed be God, even the Father of our Lord Jesus Christ, the Father of mercies, and the God of all comfort; Who comforteth us in all our tribulation, that we may be able to comfort them which are in any trouble, by the comfort wherewith we ourselves are comforted of God. And whether we be afflicted, it is for your consolation and salvation, which is effectual in the enduring of the same sufferings which we also suffer: or whether we be comforted, it is for your consolation and salvation.

A beautiful letter came from Montreal, Canada to Spurgeon that aptly illustrates this principle:

> Oh, Mr. Spurgeon, that little word of yours, 'I am feeling low,' struck a chord which still vibrates in my spirit. It was to me like reading the Forty-second Psalm. I imagine there is nothing in your ministry to the saints that comes home more tenderly to tried and stricken souls than just what you there express, 'I am feeling low.' The great preacher, the author of *The Treasury of David*, this man sometimes, aye, often 'feels low' just as they do. In all their affliction he was afflicted—this is what draws hearts to Jesus; and the principle is just the same when the friends and intimates of Jesus 'feel low.' The fellow feeling, thus begotten, makes many wondrous kind.
>
> Your friend in Jesus,
JOHN LOUSON.

Spurgeon well learned, as Lacordaire wrote, "It is like with the orator as with Mt. Horeb, before God strikes him, he is but a barren rock, but as soon as the divine hand has touched him, as it were with the finger, there bursts forth streams that water the desert." In one sense, therefore, Spurgeon revelled in his depression. That is faith.

One of the delights of Spurgeon throughout the mature years was the annual meeting of the Evangelists' Association. At the height of their activities, they would report up to 1100 evangelistic services per year. Mr. Spurgeon was always eager to show that the work of this group of able proclaimers of the Gospel presented a favorable contrast to the sensational revivalism of the more superficial evangelists. He remarked:

> A woman said to one of our brethren a little while ago, 'If what you preach is true, I am a lost woman.' He said, 'I am sure it is;' and she replied, 'I have been to the Revivalists and have been saved ten times, and it has never been any good; it has been of no use whatever.' [62]

Spurgeon still had his problems with the press. An Anglican newspaper once reported that according to Spurgeon's own words, "he would prefer to be a member of the established church than the congregational union." This startled many and a friend asked him for an explanation. Spurgeon replied:

> Nightingale Lane, Clapham,
> October 26, 1878.
>
> Dear Sir,—I should be glad to know when and where I said anything of the kind. Under no conceivable circumstances could I be in the English Church. To the best of my knowledge and belief I never said anything which could be construed into the extract quoted. I have tried to remember, but the very thought is so new to my mind that I can recall nothing approximating to it. If such an expression were ever used by me, there was some connection to explain it. Please see into it. You may print this note.
>
> Yours truly,
> C. H. SPURGEON.

Some sensations caused by the press were really quite ludicrous. One such incident occurred through an article that appeared in an American newspaper in which Spurgeon was charged with intemperance. The offending writer sent the following letter to an English newspaper to explain the situation:

> SIR,—In your issue of the 31st January you say, 'Neal Dow has charged the Rev. Mr. Spurgeon with intemperance, saying that he goes to the South of France every year because of the gout, which is due to his intemperate habits.' You have been led into an error. It is not true that I have charged Mr. Spurgeon with intemperance or with any other habit.
> In the *New York Daily Witness* of December 4, 1878, was a long article of mine on Christian charity, in which I said, 'Here is a case calling loudly not to be judged uncharitably.' Then I spoke of a famous London preacher who freely drank beer, brandy, and sherry. And I said that one morning at a gentleman's house, where he led the family devotions, after the prayer was over, before rising from his knees he struck a match and lighted his cigar. I mentioned no name.
> The American press caught it up, and sent it flying all over the country, headed, 'Neal Dow on Spurgeon.' It was an impertinence to do so. Why not

say, 'Neal Dow on Dean Stanley, or Canon Farrar, or Newman Hall?' No one has any warrant from me to say that I had Mr. Spurgeon in mind when I wrote that article.

Respectfully,
NEAL DOW.
Portland, Maine, U.S.A. 17th February

Spurgeon continued to bear the brunt of continual criticism. Once someone took him to task for riding in his carriage on Sunday thus making his horse work. Charles replied he was free from sin because his horse being a Jew had been resting on Saturday, the Jewish sabbath.

CONTINUED SERVICE

Spurgeon carried on his labors in many fields and with great fervency. He continued to be deeply involved in the home mission movement of British Baptists, often speaking to the mission. One of the burdens he addressed related to the fact that the villages had often been neglected by evangelicals and this had opened the door for theological perversions either to prevail or new ones to creep in. There were places in Scotland, he would remind the Baptists, which were still fiercely Catholic, although the Reformation had been going on there for over two hundred years. He talked about parishes in England where Swedenborgism, the Mormons, and other cults flourished, but where there had been complete neglect by Baptists. Those are places where churches should be planted, Spurgeon argued.

Spurgeon often spoke at public meetings in London's Guild Hall. Christians in all walks of life would attend and he would present addresses on relevant issues. For instance, in speaking to young ministers, he would always urge them to work hard. Spurgeon, very sensitive to the role of pastors, once said, "A church, when it goes wrong, goes bad first among its ministers." [63] He went on:

I recommend every young minister to make his pulpit his first business. The pulpit is the Thermopylae of Christendom. Your people may grumble that you don't go about and drink as many cups of tea at their houses as they would like. If you give them good food on the Sabbath they will put up with a great deal. If the Sabbath joint is only a grim scrap of mutton with plenty of divisions and nothing to divide, you will soon discover, whatever else you may do, that your people will not be satisfied. In the next place, do not neglect visitation. It is true that I cannot visit my four thousand three hundred and fifty members. If I were endowed with as many heads as a hydra, and bodies also multiplied, I could not do it. But my visitation is done by the elders. One young pastor lately said to me, 'I have no time to visit.' 'Goodness gracious!' said I, 'what have you got to do?' 'I have got my sermons to get up!' 'Your sermons? Well, I suppose you are never in bed after six in the morning? From six to nine you have three hours—six times three are eighteen—that is, two clear days in the week of nine hours each. That ought to be enough for your sermons—all before breakfast.' Now I do not say that everybody must get up so early in the morning, but I say that we must make long days. A Puritan once got up at five o'clock and went into his study, and, hearing a blacksmith's hammer going, fell upon his knees and said, 'O God, have mercy upon me! Does this man get up to serve his master before I rise to serve mine?' Our days are so few that we must make them long ones and take time by the forelock. [64]

Spurgeon would always have a word for the deacons, and never did he fail to give some truth to the entire congregation of lay people. Actually, he saw no real difference between the clergy and the laity in service; all were to be servants of Christ. In speaking to the deacons once at the Guild Hall he stated, "It has been reported that I once said that a deacon is worse than the Devil, because if you resist the Devil he will flee from you, but if you resist a deacon he will fly at you." He went on to explain, "Now I never said that—not because it is not true of some deacons, but because it never happened to be true in my case. I have always been blessed with the best of deacons. I believe they are the strength of our churches, and I don't know what we should do without them."

Charles always exalted his Baptist heritage. *The English Independent* once urged him to "put the curb a little on his denominational zeal." That did not deter Spurgeon. The Baptist churches that he started, especially in the London area, remain a tribute to his commitment to Christ and his denomination. Moreover, he continued his open air preaching with zest. Once at Parker's Piece he preached to ten thousand people. Mr. Cuff described the event:

> I heard Mr. Spurgeon in the open air at Cambridge at the meeting of the Baptist Union in 1870. The place of the service was Parker's Piece. The pulpit was a wagon. The crowd was enormous, and stretched out in all directions from the wagon, which was the centre. The text was 'Preaching peace by Jesus Christ.' The crowd wept and laughed by turns as the marvellous pathos and eloquence of the preacher poured itself out on us all. I remember helping to guard him through the throng to the house of his host. The people were so mad to shake hands with him, and get a word from him, that we joined hands and made a circle, while the dear man walked in it. Every now and then some old friend of early days got near. He was at once recognised by Mr. Spurgeon, and, of course, he must be shaken by the hand. This went on till we had more trouble with the preacher than the crowd. At length he was safe inside the door of the garden of his friend. That visit to Cambridge by the great preacher will never be forgotten. He was the best open-air preacher I ever heard; but then he was out of sight the best anywhere and everywhere. [65]

He would often preach up to an hour to the masses that would assemble out in the fields. He preached with such effect that it was "worthy of Whitefield in his best days." Furthermore, he would continually give himself to any movement for the betterment of society. He continued his interest and contribution to the Ragged School Union, a society devoted to the educating of the "ragged children" in the very poor sections of London. Mr. John Kirk, secretary of the Ragged School Union, said about Spurgeon:

> From the earliest days of Mr. Spurgeon's coming to London he recognized the value and importance of ragged schools; hence he was ever ready to lend a service to the cause, and in his death the Ragged School Union and every ragged school worker lost a true and sympathetic friend. His undoubted fondness for children and deep pity for the poor and suffering led him to see in this service on behalf of neglected children the most effective and kindly means of reaching the lapsed masses. . . . It was for many years his custom to call together annually—generally in the week of prayer for ragged and Sunday schools, the Sunday School Teachers' Association of the Tabernacle who were privileged to listen to wise and helpful words. On several occasions the workers of ragged schools were also specially invited, and representatives were asked to take part in the proceedings and get some information to the movement. . . . I shall never forget Mr. Spurgeon's hearty and brotherly kindness on all occasions when I had to ask his aid in any matter. [66]

Charles would speak at the Female Servants' Home Society, a work designed to give encouragement and help to servant girls. Some say he was responsible for this society.

As Charles went about speaking wherever any doors of invitation opened, he would also open the doors of the Tabernacle to others. Newman Hall of Christ Church Lambeth spoke at the Metropolitan Tabernacle. John Clifford, later to become in some measure Spurgeon's opponent in the Down Grade Controversy, first preached at the Metropolitan Tabernacle at Spurgeon's invitation in the '70s while Charles was off in France for rest. Spurgeon also preached at Clifford's church on Praed Street, London. Once, in conversation with Clifford in the vestry before the service began, Spurgeon said, "I cannot imagine, Clifford, why you do not come to my way of thinking"–referring to his Calvinist theology. John Clifford answered, "Well, you see, Mr. Spurgeon, I only see you about once a month, but I read my Bible every day." At times Spurgeon met his match. But the days were filled with variety and excitement. His popularity continued as he matured. Even some years before, at the Surrey Gardens days, a bazaar displayed two portraits, one of Lord Palmerston and one of C. H. Spurgeon. Over the portraits hung the heading "The Two Prime Ministers."

The previous chapter related Spurgeon's deep commitment and involvement in the political arena regarding public education. When officials announced the first election for the London School Board, it aroused great public interest. Many people were undecided how they should vote. Spurgeon, seizing on the occasion, allowed no time to pass; he made his own convictions known and urged people to vote the "right way" on the issue. He wrote to the editor of *The Daily News* on Wednesday, November 16, 1870. His letter reads:

> SIR,—Having been asked to give my opinion as to the forthcoming election for the School Board for Lambeth, and being unable to attend public meetings, I venture to address a few remarks to the public through the medium of the Press. It is very undesirable that this election should become a contest between Church and Dissent. Surely we can give the present measure a fair trial without importing religious disputes into a matter in which we are all equally concerned for the general good. It is most pleasant to observe that all the candidates, with, perhaps, one exception, agree that the liberty for Bible reading given by the Bill should be carefully maintained; beyond that none have expressed a desire to go, nor could they if they would. The qualifications for the Board as to character and position it is not needful to discuss, but we will for the moment assume that all the candidates are in this respect equal—a supposition which each elector will readily be able to substantiate or reject. One very important requisite is not, however, found at all—viz., acquaintance with the subject in hand. If we had to select a national astronomer, we should rightly consider a man's character and standing as collateral matters, but the main thing would be his knowledge of astronomy; so in the present case, one very important element is the candidate's acquaintance with education, educators, educational processes, and educational literature. Some members of the Board should very fitly represent the financial element, and keep the expenditure in check; others should represent the working classes, who are on the receiving side of the question, and see that the economy does not degenerate into meanness; but first and foremost we need educationists—practical teachers—men who understand the work which the Board will be called upon to do. . . . [67]

SPURGEON, THE GRACIOUS HOST

Despite the many responsibilities and demands on his time, Spurgeon always reserved Saturday afternoon for the reception of friends at Helensborough House, his happy home in Clapham. In winter they gathered in Spurgeon's spacious study, and in the summer they would fellowship on the garden lawn. He always kept an open door to the Tabernacle deacons and others involved in ministry. Missionaries, preachers, and other leading Christians from America and the colonies could often be found at the Saturday gatherings. The most welcome people would be those who were co-workers with Spurgeon in the various aspects of his ministry. Spurgeon said no one was ever surrounded by "a more noble band of helpers." The Saturday afternoon fellowships were always a time of enriching encounters and simply good times. Spurgeon never flaunted the airs of a "great man." He would share things with his friends right out of his heart, often things that he could never have told in public. He would express his opinions about people, books, public movements, anything of current interest. His friends were fascinated at his breadth of interests, and, as one put it, "even his dog, Punch, seemed an interested auditor."[68] Spurgeon, a lover of nature, loved animals. He invariably had his dog Punch by his side and his large cat named Dick.

Spurgeon said at one Saturday gathering, "You know, I am not the reverend gentleman."[69] He wanted people to be relaxed and feel at home. He was a great conversationalist. One of his biographers states that he equalled Samuel Johnson, the literary monarch of the 18th century. He had an astounding command of subjects and would fascinate people with the extent of his knowledge. To have been with him on a Saturday afternoon, and not known him intimately, one would assume that a man of this breadth and personality would find writing and preaching very easy. But as has already been shown, he harbored a dread of crowds, and found writing the work of a slave. Spurgeon never wrote his sermons; that was too much for him. When questioned on the point he would declare that he would prefer being hanged rather than go through the ordeal of writing his sermons. But on the Saturday afternoons at Helensborough House, everyone found themselves in a happy atmosphere, with Spurgeon the center of enthusiastic attention. It was simply a joyous time for all. Robert Taylor of Norwood described one of the happy events with these words:

> Mr. Spurgeon greatly enjoyed his beautiful garden and grounds, and had almost equal pleasure in showing to visitors on his Saturday afternoon receptions his rare flowers and rare books. A few years ago a good minister from America who had visited him gave him some pain by an overdrawn description in the public Press of his residence and its surroundings. Referring to it, he said one does not like an exaggerated picture like that, as if one were a self-indulgent Sybarite lapped in luxury. And then he added, in a tone of chastened seriousness, 'My Master, I am sure, does not grudge me the enjoyment of my garden. I owe it to Him. It is about the only luxury in which I indulge. I am very hard worked. I have no time for social intercourse. I have neither time nor strength to move about and find refreshment in variety and change as others do; but I have my garden with its flowers and its fine prospects, and I praise Him for it.'[70]

THE HOME

A beautiful description of Spurgeon's Helensburgh House was penned in *The World*, October 4, 1876. It bears a reading as it gives insight, not only to the writer's attitude and admiration for Spurgeon, but who Spurgeon really was as a man at home. It reads:

It is difficult to say where Mr. Spurgeon may be considered most at home; for his time is spent in moving quickly to and from the Tabernacle, the Pastors' College, the schools, almshouses, and orphanages, of which he is the guiding spirit. Perhaps the most hard-working man on the Surrey side of the Thames, he finds but little leisure for taking his ease in his house in Nightingale Lane—a quiet nook hard by Wandsworth Common. He passes his life, when not actually preaching or working, in a pony chaise, varied by occasional hansom cabs. Wrapped in a rough blue overcoat, with a species of soft deerstalking hat on his head, a loose black necktie round his massive throat, and a cigar burning merrily in his mouth, he is surely the most unclerical of all preachers of the Gospel. . . . Bowls—not the noisy American tenpins, but the discreet old Puritan game—is the favourite sport of the great preacher, who plays 'whenever he can find time,' which is not very often. He confesses that in choosing bowls and tobacco as his amusements he is following good old Roundhead traditions, and loves to refer to the Lord Protector's enjoyment of a game of bowls with grave college dons. While savouring with keen gusto his hard-earned amusements, he escapes utterly from the hair-splitting of theologians, the bias of the bowl being the matter to which he bends his faculties. But there are other relaxations for Mr. Spurgeon—amusements in themselves, it is true, but yet indulged in with method." [71]

Spurgeon had a great sense of humor, as often seen. Those who would gather with him at Helensburgh House would be assured of a good laugh. Once he talked about some workers who cared for his garden that were believers in sinless perfectionism. But under their work the garden and lawns had deteriorated rather badly. Spurgeon said to a visiting friend one day, "You see, these men were so holy that they did not get here til eight in the morning when they should have been here at six; and then I discharged them and took sinners in their place." [72] Once he told a story to the Tabernacle congregation about a dog in his garden. The tale goes:

There was a dog which was in the habit of coming through the fence and scratching in his flower-beds, to the manifest spoiling of the gardener's toil and temper. Walking in the garden, one Saturday afternoon, and preparing his sermon for the following day, he saw the four-footed creature—rather a scurvy specimen, by-the-by—and having a walking stick in his hand, he threw it at him with all his might, giving him some good advice about going home.

Now, what should my canine friend do but turn round, pick up the stick in his mouth, and bring it and lay it down at my feet, wagging his tail all the while in expectation of my thanks and kind words? Of course, you do not suppose that I kicked him . . . no. [73]

Spurgeon's gatherings on Saturday were not restricted to Baptists. Often Mr. Rogers, principal of the Pastors' College, came as a guest. Mr. Alabaster, an ardent Church of England member and Spurgeon's printer and pub-

lisher, often came. Charles was broad-minded concerning denominationalism; as long as people were solid in the evangelical faith, they got along
very well. The only evangelical group that Spurgeon seemed to have an
aversion for was the Salvation Army. Although he said positive things at
times about William Booth and his work, he did not enthusiastically embrace their methods. In a letter to a friend marked private, who apparently
very much admired the Army, Spurgeon wrote on March 8, 1883:

> I have bourne silently with much that has grieved my heart. . . . I have even
> now said but little. But to you privately I would say that my view of the
> Salvation Army and its works is now the very reverse of yours. If I thought it
> right to say all that I think and know, you would indeed judge me too severe.
> Time will show. I am disappointed and saddened, and fear the worse conse-
> quences from this system.

Of course, if a group deviated from the Gospel, Spurgeon had harsh words,
such as his denunciation of Roman Catholicism and Campbellism. Concerning this later movement, he wrote a Mr. Curham on September 3, 1855:

> I should always be glad to see you, except upon the matter of "The Common-
> wealth and Campbellism, and its covert apostles." Upon this I wish to have no
> discussion, for if you are resolved to espouse that cause it would be idle to talk
> it over. I certainly shall have nothing to do with it. Toward yourself I have ever
> the warmest feelings of love and regard.

In these afternoon get-togethers Spurgeon always enjoyed his cigar. Moreover, he had friends who kept him supplied with boxes of the very best
brands. As Spurgeon would puff away he would enjoy a game of bowls,
known in America as "bowling on the green." Being a very sedate kind of
exercise, this suited Spurgeon to a tee. But he did not get too excited, even
about bowls. One biographer said that one would only seldom see him
indulge in the pastime, even if it was a favorite game of the Puritans. More
often he would take his seat, engage in conversation, until everyone around
him sat with rapt attention. The Spurgeon home proved a delight to all. As
the afternoon began to wane, tea would be served for any who wished to
stay. Then there would always be those who would continue on for family
prayers that came immediately after tea time. When all had finally left,
Spurgeon would go to work on his sermons for the following day. He fondly
compared his Tabernacle congregation to a flock of chickens, and his work
in the study to prepare sermons the work of gathering food for them. As
seen, his final sermon preparation was of quite short duration. He once said
to a brother minister, "If I cannot 'break' my text to my use in an hour, it is
all over with me." "Breaking the text" meant for Spurgeon to look well at all
the words, setting them and arranging them in divisions in a good outline
form. Spurgeon prayed earnestly over his messages. He always advised his
students to do so. He felt it indispensable for preaching. After he got his

basic outline, everything then went straightforward. He would read the commentaries on his text, or have his wife read them to him. His favorite commentary was the time-honored Puritan work by Matthew Henry. He could then fill in the outline in his mind from the wide range of reading that he had at his fingertips. He possessed an unbelievable gift of recalling all that he needed to preach. Such was a typical Saturday for the preacher.

SPURGEON THE MATURE SOUL WINNER

Spurgeon's soul-winning efforts always formed a vital part of his labors. As his ministry grew, he spent more time with individuals in personal counseling and witnessing, as did his Puritan forbearers. Moreover, his devotion to winning just one started a beautiful chain reaction on an occasion. It was Spurgeon's example that first inflamed the imagination of D. L. Moody. Moody decided that he would speak to one person about his soul every day of his life. Spurgeon had no small part in that dedication. Henry Drummond then felt the impact of Moody's approach, especially in the inquiry room. In 1873 this contagious spirit precipitated Drummond writing his well known essay on "Spiritual Diagnosis." H. A. Walters says that this essay "marked the beginning of the modern movement of scientific evangelism, if not the psychology of religion as well."[74] As biographer Richard Ellsworth Day expressed it, "It is an unbroken glow through Drummond to Moody, Moody to Spurgeon, Spurgeon to the Puritans, and from the Puritans to Pentecost."[75] But Spurgeon had mastered the New Testament principle of personal evangelism long before he became a great preacher. He began his personal work, as we have seen, immediately after his conversion. Everyone eulogizes Spurgeon's preaching, but John B. Gough saw another side that he admired even more. He said, "I have seen Mr. Spurgeon holding by his power 6500 people in breathless interest; but as he sat by the bedside of a dying child whom his beneficence had rescued he was to me a greater and grander man then he was swaying the mighty multitude at his will."[76]

The number of hours that Spurgeon spent in his personal ministry is really quite amazing. He said:

> From the very early days of my ministry in London, the Lord gave me such an abundant blessing upon the proclamation of his truth that, whenever I was able to appoint a time for seeing converts and inquirers, it was seldom that I waited in vain. On one occasion I had a very singular experience, which enabled me to realize the meaning of our Lord's answer to his disciples' question. . . . 'Jesus saith, my meat is to do the will of him that sent me.' Leaving home early one morning, I went to the Chapel and sat there all day long. . . . I may have seen some thirty or more persons during the day, one after another; I was so delighted that I did not know anything about how the time passed. A little before ten o'clock (p.m.) I felt faint; and I began to think at what hour I had

my dinner . . . I had not had any! I never thought of it, I never even felt hungry, because God had made me . . . so satisfied with Divine manna, the heavenly food of success in winning souls. [77]

His wife, Susannah, gave testimony that Charles' personal work went on year after year. She said:

> Tuesday afternoons with rare exceptions, he gave himself to the truly pastoral and important work of seeing inquirers at the Tabernacle; and in no part of his service was Mr. Spurgeon more happy.

Charles, Jr., wrote after his father's death:

> Father liked me to go out driving with him; he would tell of recent instances. In this way I learned much of the holy art of dealing with anxious inquirers, an art of which he was indeed a master.

The legacy of Spurgeon's mature personal ministry went on, even after his death. Some time after Spurgeon had gone, an ex-policeman, an old bedridden man named Coleman, never tired of telling about the early days when he would walk to church to hear "the boy preacher." Old Coleman said, "Oh, he was a dear, good young man, he did not make himself anything! He would shake hands with anyone, he would give me such a grip, he did look pleased, that Sunday morning, when he said, 'Coleman, what do you think? God has blessed me with two little sons!' I used to go in and just sit inside the door, and get a feast for my own soul from his discourses. I shall see him again soon, I hope!" Spurgeon had a personal touch that was never lost on people. He said he knew all 5,000 members of the Metropolitan Tabernacle personally. Simply put, he loved people and gave himself to them. Furthermore, the evangelistic impact of the ministry continued unabated through the years. For example:

> A few years ago, a large-meeting of the working-classes was held in London, at which the Rev. Joseph Burns gave an address. At the close of his remarks, a person present rose in the midst of the audience, and asked if he might be allowed to say a few words. Permission being given, he thus spoke:—
> Friends, said he, holding up his clenched hands, look at me. These fists once struck the devil's blow; these feet trod the devil's steps: this body was the devil's home: this soul was the devil's victim. But a change was wrought in me. One day a religious tract was put into my hands, and I read it, and then Jesus Christ was too strong for the prize-fighter. The tract led me to see my evil ways, and my soul was in such a state that I groaned and wept, and could neither eat nor sleep; so what do you think I did? I thought I would go and hear Mr. Spurgeon preach; and on the Lord's-day morning I went. And he did preach a sermon too! just the sermon that suited me. He lifted up Jesus as the Refuge for a poor sinner's soul; and I said to myself, That is just what I want: Jesus shall be the Refuge for my soul:' and when I said that, there and then my

soul got liberty. And now look at me. What a difference! These hands now work for Jesus: these feet walk with Jesus: this body is a temple of the Holy Ghost: this soul is the purchase of Jesus' blood. [78]

THE COLLEGE CONFERENCES

Some of the happiest times the maturing Spurgeon spent were at the yearly College Conferences. On one such occasion, Dr. Usher prayed very earnestly for the children of all the pastors and ministers who were attending the Conference. Spurgeon immediately picked up on that and thought that he might write to the sons and daughters of all the conferees. He had two letters lithographed, one adaptable for younger children and one for those who were older. These were sent to the children of the members of the Conference. Many boys and girls who read the letters were led to faith in Christ. At another College Conference, several ministers attending walked through Lincoln's Inn Fields on their way to the meeting. As they were walking along someone asked, "Is this the Royal College of Surgeons?" "No," one of the companions answered, "it is the royal college of Spurgeon's." Actually, the Royal College of Surgeons is in Lincoln's Inn Field, but they were on their way, as they saw it, to something far more important; Spurgeon's annual College Conference.

TWENTY-FIVE YEARS OF SERVICE

As the seventh decade of the 19th century began to phase out, one of the greatest of all celebrations at the Metropolitan Tabernacle took place, the previously mentioned "silver anniversary" of Spurgeon's ministry—the completion of 25 years in London. All of his friends and fellow workers were determined that this event should not pass without proper recognition. When they put the proposal to Spurgeon, with his natural reticence, he declined any personal benefit for himself. He stated that if his friends wished to make some sort of a gift to express their gratitude and appreciation, they might raise a £5000 testimonial fund as an endowment for the almshouses. That particular work at the time had become the heaviest burden to Spurgeon. His friends wanted him to receive some personal benefit from their gifts, but he adamantly refused. So the church agreed, and in January, 1879, a large bazaar in aid of the almshouses was held at the Tabernacle. That day alone saw £3463 raised, and, along with what friends had already given, the total came to £6,476 and 9 shillings for the testimonial fund—a very remarkable sum. These bazaars should not be associated with the more questionable and worldly methods of raising funds which Spurgeon condemned. Spurgeon later had to admit that the bazaar method for fund-raising had deteriorated in worldly hands and was probably best left alone entirely.

Unfortunately, Spurgeon had experienced a long and painful illness during the time his friends were preparing to celebrate his pastoral "anniversary." He had spent several months at Mentone with his son Thomas, and recovery was very slow. Not until April of 1879 was he able to return to London, and that against the advice of his medical consultants. The church set May 20, a Tuesday, as the date for the presentation of the testimonial. At the significant service, Spurgeon reviewed the events of the past 25 years. In his sermon Charles said:

> Brethren . . . there is about 'the midst of years' a certain special danger, and this led the prophet as it shall lead us at this time to pray in the words which I have selected for my text: 'O Lord, revive Thy work in the midst of the years, in the midst of the years make known.' Youth has its perils, but these are past; age has its infirmities, but these we have not yet reached; it is ours then to pray against the dangers which are present with us 'in the midst of the years.' The middle passage of life with us as individuals and with us as a church is crowded with peculiar perils. There is a certain spur and stimulus of novelty about religious movements which in a few years is worn out. I well recollect when we were called 'a nine days' wonder,' and our critics prophesied that our work would speedily collapse. Such excitement had been seen before and had passed away; and this would be one among other bubbles of the hour. The nine days have lasted considerably long;—may nine such days follow them in God's infinite mercy! Now, whatever detractors may say, we know that there was then a life, an energy, a freshness about everything which was done by us as a church which we could hardly expect to continue with us for all these years. From an admirable fervour many cool down to a dangerous chill. This is to be bemoaned where it has occurred, and it is to be feared where as yet it has not happened, for such is the natural tendency of things. Beloved brethren, I have prayed to God, that when what is called the *esprit de corps* is gone from us, the *Esprit de Dieu* may still abide with us; that when the spirit which grows out of our association with each other declines, we may be sustained by the Spirit which unites us all to the Lord Jesus. [79]

In recounting the goodness of God through the years, Spurgeon gave all praise to the Lord. He said, "It was not I, but the grace of God which was with me." On the Monday after the moving sermon of Sunday, the church gathered to celebrate in a praise service, then on Tuesday the great meeting for the presentation of the testimonial was held. The event lasted for several hours and everyone rejoiced in all that God had done. It seemed all wanted to express in some way their appreciation and deep love for their pastor. A deputation from the London Baptist Association presented a letter of congratulations to Spurgeon. Deacon William Olney made the presentation. His speech was short, but he spoke for the entire congregation when he conveyed the love and esteem in which they held their pastor.

Spurgeon rose to thank the people for the gifts to the almshouses, but when he rose such an outburst of cheering erupted that considerable time elapsed before he could make himself heard. When the deacons learned that the sum collected had exceeded the £5000 Spurgeon had requested for the almshouses, they pressed their pastor to accept the balance for his personal use. But as could be expected, he resolutely refused to do so. In his acceptance speech for the testimonial gift he said:

> It is a testimonial of gratitude to God for twenty-five years of happy communion and prosperity, and unto God let the testimonial go—all of it, with the exception of a bronze clock for my study, which I will accept as a memorial of the fond affection of my dear people toward me. . . . Oh, that I could do more for Christ and more for the poor. For these I have turned beggar before now, and shall not be ashamed to beg again. The outside world cannot understand that a man should be moved by any motive except that of personal gain; but if they knew the power of love to Jesus they would understand that greed of wealth is vile as the dust beneath his feet to the lover of the Saviour.[80]

Spurgeon continued:

> I daresay you have all heard that 'Spurgeon makes a good thing out of the Tabernacle.' Well, whenever anybody hints that to you, you may, on my authority, assure them that I do. I should not like anybody to think that my Master does not pay His servants well. He loadeth us with benefits, and I am perfectly satisfied with His wages; but if any persons assert that, by my preaching in this place, I have made a purse for myself, I can refer them to those who know me and my way of life among you. 'Ah, but,' they say, 'he has had a testimonial of £6,000 presented to him.' Yes, he has had it, and he thanks everybody for it. Perhaps there are some other persons who would like a similar testimonial, and I wish they may get it and do the same with it as I have done. Legacies left to me, and sums subscribed for the Orphanage and College, and so on, are spoken of as if I had some private interest in them, whereas I have neither a direct nor indirect pecuniary interest in any of these works to the amount of a penny a year. With regard to all things else, from the first day until now, I have acted on no other principle but that of perfect consecration to the work whereunto I am called. I have no riches. I sometimes wish that I had, for I could use money in an abundance of profitable ways. What have I gained of late years in my ministry here? I have received all that I wished by way of salary, but I have for years expended almost all of it in the cause of God, and in some years even more than all. As far as my pastoral office is concerned, the net income for myself, after giving my share to all holy service, is not so much that any man could envy me. Yet this is not your fault, or anyone's fault; it is my joy and delight to have it so. The Lord is a good and gracious paymaster; and inasmuch as men say, 'Doth Spurgeon serve God for nought?' Spurgeon replies, 'No, he is paid a thousand times over, and finds it a splendid thing to be in the service of the Lord Jesus.' If anyone will serve the Lord Jesus Christ after the same or better fashion, he too will make the same

splendid thing of it; he shall have splendid opportunities for working from morning till night, and far into the night on many an occasion; splendid openings for giving away as much as he can earn; splendid opportunities of finding happiness in making other people happy and easing the sorrows of others by entering into hearty sympathy with them.

FIFTY YEARS OLD

Five years after the pastoral silver anniversary on June 19, 1884, another large celebration was held at the Tabernacle. Charles Haddon Spurgeon became 50 years of age. Once again, the deacons of the church were charged with the responsibility to make arrangements for the formation of a testimonial fund which would be presented to the pastor. On this occasion they insisted it must be accepted for his own personal use. But when the matter was broached, Charles let them understand that he would accept no money for himself but would be glad if the amount should be devoted to the Lord's work. Consequently, a fund was opened which soon reached £4500. But he did accept the gift of a new carriage from his publisher and friend Joseph Passmore.

The happy event lasted over two evenings, June 18 and 19. Many distinguished people attended. D. L. Moody addressed the Wednesday evening meeting. He told about his first trip to London in 1867 and his visit to the Metropolitan Tabernacle. Moody related he had always harbored in his heart a deep desire to hear Spurgeon. He confessed that after his arrival in England he followed Spurgeon wherever he preached. He heard Charles preach in the great Agricultural Hall in Islington, little realizing that he himself would preach there one day. Moody said:

> I want to say to you, Mr. Spurgeon, 'God bless you.' I know that you love me, but I assure you that I love you a thousand times more than you can ever love me, because you have been such a blessing to me, while I have been a very little blessing to you. When I think of a man or woman who has been in this Tabernacle time after time, and heard the Gospel, I pity them, deep down in my heart, if they are found among the lost. I have read your sermons for twenty-five years, and what has cheered my heart has been that in them was no uncertain sound. In closing, let me give you a poem that one of our American Indians wrote: 'The first line began with, 'go on,' the second line was, 'go on,' and the third line was 'go on,' and this was all he could write. I say, 'Go on, brother, and God bless you!' [81]

Three generations of Spurgeons were present for the celebration. The pastor, his father, and his son, Charles, Jr. On the 19th, Thursday, Lord Shaftesbury presided over the meeting. Other notables present were Joseph Parker, Newman Hall, and Sir William McArthur, MP, and the archdeacon of Westminster Cathedral. Spurgeon told how he would disperse the money.

He pledged some of the gifts to the Jubilee House, St. Thomas' Hospital, some to the almshouses and to the Baptist Fund for the Relief of Poor Ministers, some to the Colporteurs Association, the book fund, and many other agencies. Finally, Spurgeon declared that he wanted to give £250 toward the cost of the new tabernacle building in Auckland, New Zealand for his son, Thomas. He concluded his remarks with these words:

> Now I thank everybody who has given a hundred pounds, and everybody who has given a penny. God bless you and return it to you in every way. One of our brethren told you the other night what once happened to me. I had been preaching in a country place, and a good woman gave me five shillings. I said to her, 'Well, my dear friend, I do not want your money.' She said, 'But you must take it; I give it to you because I get good from you.' I said, 'Shall I give it to the College?' She answered, 'I don't care about the College, I care about you.' 'Then I will give it to the Orphanage.' 'No,' she said, 'you take it yourself.' I said, 'You want it more than I do.' She replied, 'Now do you think that your Lord and Master would have talked like that to the woman who came and broke the alabaster box over Him? I do not think He would.' She added, 'I know you do not mean to be unkind. I worked extra to earn it and give it to you.' I told her that she owed me nothing, and that woman owed the Lord everything. 'What am I to do with it?' She said, 'Buy anything you like with it. I do not care. Only mind, you must have it for yourself.' I mention the incident because it is much in the spirit that the friends have given now. The Lord bless you! The Lord bless you! The Lord bless you yet more and more, you and your children!

Some biographies of Spurgeon came out on his fiftieth birthday. But as expected, the event, and the biographies, precipitated the inevitable criticism. One cynic wrote: "Everybody with plenty of leisure and taste for gush is now writing the life of Mr. Spurgeon. Are good clergymen so scarce? Why, there are more lives of Spurgeon about than lives of Jesus Christ."

An unsettling incident surrounded this notable meeting. A certain terrorist group called the Fenians had threatened to blow up the Tabernacle while it was crowded with people celebrating the event. The public knew nothing of the threat, but the police surrounded the Tabernacle and the officials naturally felt the strain. When the celebration passed with no problem, they thanked God for a safe and happy time.

After the presentation of the generous testimonial funds that Spurgeon received on his silver and golden anniversaries, he had a barrage of letters begging for assistance. All his life he endured this sort of thing, particularly when the newspapers published reports of the fortunes that supposedly had been left the preacher, all of which were never true. And Spurgeon, always of a kind mind, would help people time and again. Even street beggars who would call at his house were generously treated. Actually, the street urchins all called the preacher a "soft tommy." But Spurgeon said, "I'd rather be remembered as a soft tommy than as a hard jack." Of course, his generosity to his family abounded. In writing to his parents, December 22, 1891, near his death, he said:

> I could not think of lessening your amount by one farthing. It is a pure undiluted joy to be able to help one so immeasurably dear to me. Long may you live to receive it, even if I am no longer among the living upon the earth. It gives one great peace to think that in this matter I have put you beyond risk. [82]

His letters often contained such passages. He must have helped them regularly. Later, Charles found the widow of Christmas Evans. She lived a very deprived life, unable to work, nearly starving. He supported her financially the rest of her life. As one said, "He was as princely in his giving as he was in his preaching."

THE FRUITFUL DIFFICULT YEARS

These were great years. As Dallimore expressed it, "Between 1875 and 1885 Spurgeon's ministry reached heights it had never attained before. Although the seeds sown in London had already brought a great harvest, during these years the fruit proved still more abundant, and it came with the richness and a steadiness that was new even to a work so blessed of God as his had been." [83] As Charles began to grow older, the signs of the strain on his strength and vitality became increasingly visible, even to himself. He wrote his mother May 3, 1882, "I am a creaking door and the hinges don't hold oil long." [84] Charles' preaching also began to experience the noticeable change mentioned previously. As earlier described, in Spurgeon's early years in London, his preaching was full of drama and possessed an outstanding vitality. In all the vigor of his youth he moved about the platform and preached in a very dramatic style. As the years moved along, however, his basic style changed considerably. The papers recognized it. *The Globe*, March 23, 1887, wrote, "Of late years Mr. Spurgeon has so agreeably toned down his utterances on most subjects." He was mellowing. As he matured personally, he became more determined, as Dallimore put it, "To be able to say with Paul, 'We preach not ourselves, but Christ Jesus the Lord.'" [85] He had become very sensitive to the possibility of drawing attention to himself by some oratorical gesture or particularly striking statement which would cause his hearers to fail to see Christ. By 1875 he had developed a far more conversational style of preaching. He moved about very little and did not use many gestures in his sermons. He avoided anything that would look like mere oratory. He strove to stay behind the cross that the people might see Christ. But this change in style in no way diminished the earnestness and the power of his messages. A writer in *The Indian Witness*, July 24, 1886 reported: "I first heard Spurgeon preach in 1865, in 1876, the third time in 1880, and now again in 1886. The impression made on the first occasion has never been in the slightest degree changed."

Although some say his early preaching was better than his later, the actual fruit of his later preaching brings that statement into question. Perhaps Spurgeon preached with more drama and oratory earlier, but that does not necessarily produce better preaching.

As Spurgeon's physical problems progressed, Mrs. Spurgeon seemed a little better. Her undertaking the work of the Book Fund seemed to increase her vigor. Yet, there were many times when for days or weeks she could not perform her tasks. One of the longest protracted illnesses of Charles occurred in 1879 when he was absent from the Tabernacle pulpit for five full months. He stayed under the medical supervision of Dr. R. M. Meller of Norwood in his later years. But as has been said, Charles always ministered at the Tabernacle too long and always returned from his recuperation period too soon to get really well.

Along with his trips to Mentone in the winter, each summer he went to Scotland for two weeks where he became the guest of Mr. James Duncan of Benmore Castle, a very wealthy and earnest Christian brother. Scotland refreshed the preacher.

When Moody made his second visit to Britain, accompanied by his song leader Ira D. Sankey, Spurgeon wrote requesting Moody to preach in the Tabernacle when he came to London. Moody, of course, replied in the affirmative. He closed his letter to Spurgeon with these words:

> In regard to coming to your tabernacle, I consider it a great honor to be invited; and, in fact, I should consider it an honor to black your boots; but to preach to your people would be out of the question. If they will not turn to God under your preaching, 'neither will they be persuaded, though one rose from the dead.'
>
> Yours with much love,
> D.L. Moody

When Moody arrived in London and preached an extended crusade, like Spurgeon, he and Sankey faced an onslaught of criticism from the media. They were charged with fanaticism and every other criticism that could be conjured up. Spurgeon, who had sailed through those waters, came to their defense. He addressed a meeting of the Bible Society at which the Archbishop of Canterbury was present. Charles strongly denied anything fanatical had ever occurred in Moody and Sankey's work. In another meeting, defending the Americans, he said, "We are happy to have our friends here (in London) because somehow or another they manage to get the popular ear. Our brethren have got a grip on the masses, and they preach the Gospel. We do not have it very distinct from a great many voices. But I know what Mr. Moody means when he speaks and what Mr. Sankey means when he sings. I have never seen men carry their meaning more fully on their lips."[86] On Moody's third trip to London in 1881, Spurgeon was ill and resting at Mentone. He again wrote Moody asking him to preach at the Tabernacle. Spurgeon said Moody was the only man who could say "Mesopotamia" in two syllables. Moody visited Britain in 1867, 1873-75, 1881-84, and 1891.

In the midst of all of his labors and illness, Spurgeon still produced a host of writings. Besides the writings he did for *The Sword and the Trowel* and the editing of his weekly sermons, he averaged approximately 500 letters per week with his own hand. One can almost be thankful that the telephone had not been invented in his day; it saved him for the labor of writing which continues to bless us yet today.

During all this time, Spurgeon continued to travel. One time in Leeds, the place was so packed that hundreds were unable to obtain admission. When Spurgeon would be in Scotland for his summer holiday, he would usually preach in the open air on a Scottish hillside. In those settings he would preach to ten to fifteen thousand people. Spurgeon received invitations from a multitude of places and sources. On one occasion the Methodist Free Churches invited him to attend their annual general assembly. Despite his Calvinism, he was appreciated by the Methodists for his commitment to the Gospel and the winning of souls to faith in Christ. He received an invitation to Australia during these hectic days, but, of course, he had to refuse as he had refused the American and Canadian visits. His brother James spent ten weeks in Canada. In reply to the gracious Australian invitation he said, "How I wish I could glide over and return in a month."[87] It is a pity air travel had not come about in Spurgeon's day.

During those busy days, by November of each year Spurgeon would be so physically exhausted and vulnerable to his struggle with gout and developing Bright's disease, he would have to leave London. One year, just before the time of his leaving for the south of France, he became so weak in the middle of his sermon that he actually had to stop and ask the congregation to sing a hymn while he attempted to recover his strength. The next day, as he set out on his trip for the south, rumors had it that he was dying. The rumors were not true; yet, he was very ill. But his productivity despite it all was fantastic. In the twelve-year period before 1880 the number of persons baptized at the Metropolitan Tabernacle amounted to thousands. Many churches were built throughout the land. On the 50th anniversary of Spurgeon's birth, portrayed above, Lord Shaftesbury heard the list of the 66 organizations that Spurgeon conducted and remarked:

> I will begin by saying he stands as a marvel before you; fifty years old, and thirty-one years out of that fifty have seen him in the ministry! He began his ministry when only nineteen, and see him now going on as he began. He has not been puffed up by success, but humbled and animated the more to go on in his noble career of good which God in His merciful providence had marked out for him, and for the benefit of mankind. I cannot but call your attention to this; but your attention is not required to it. I want to tell you what we outsiders think.

What a tale of his agencies read to you just now! How it showed what a powerful administrative mind our friend has! That list of associations, instituted by his genius, and superintended by his care, were more than enough to occupy the minds and hearts of fifty ordinary men. It seems to me to be the whole world in a nutshell. He carries on his Orphanage and various other institutions, and I would impress upon you that in which I think he shines the brightest—in the foundation and government of the Pastors' College. My worthy friend has produced a large number of men, useful in their generation, to preach the Word of God in all its simplicity and force, adapted to all classes, more especially to the large masses around us, to bring forward the principles of elementary truth—no single man has produced such a body capable and willing to carry on the noble work as our friend whose jubilee we celebrate to-day.[88]

One Friday at the Pastors' College, Spurgeon looked over the sea of eager faces and spotted a stranger. After the lecture, the stranger accosted Spurgeon and said, "Are you in need of money, Mr. Spurgeon?" Charles replied, "Always in need of money here, sir." Spurgeon told the stranger of the College needs and the colportage work, and the visitor gave £100 for each, and then he said, "Ah, but there is something for which you have a greater need than these." He was referring to the Orphanage. "Yes," Spurgeon replied. For that institution he gave a very large donation. When he completed his errand of graciousness, the stranger said, "You must sit here in your chair for five minutes after I am gone; you must not try to find out who I am. I promised God to do this some years ago, and I have never done it till now, and now my conscience is relieved."[89] To this day, no one knows who the stranger was. But such stories were not really unusual; God provided in marvelous ways for the work.

Charles was forever giving people something. In the many happy hours that were spent by visitors in Spurgeon's home he would often pluck an "everlasting flower" that he had taken from his garden to give to the visitor as a memento. A smoker might get a "very particular cigar" or another might get a memento such as a olive wood box from Mentone. On one occasion George Goldston of Hastings received a table from the preacher. In those days, furniture would have a certificate of quality attached. Spurgeon, with his usual humor wrote the following: "This is to certify that the table this day sent to Mr. Goldston has never been known to turn, twist, dance, fly up into the air, or otherwise misbehave. It has not been addicted to convivial habits, and has never been known to be on a roar. As a most studious piece of furniture it is sent to a studious man, with the kind regards of C. H. Spurgeon."[90]

THE MOVE TO WESTWOOD

As the years passed along, Spurgeon moved from his happy home, Helensburgh House, to Beulah Hill in Norwood, some miles south. His physicians advised him to relocate in an area out of the immediate damp and fog of London. Beulah Hill seemed the exact spot. He went out one day to investigate what could be found in Norwood. There he saw a beautiful house for sale. When a friend suggested that it would be ideal, Charles immediately replied that it was too expensive and too grand a place for him even to consider. Almost at that very moment a developer came along wanting to buy Spurgeon's place on Nightingale Lane. He offered him an excellent price, an amount almost sufficient to cover the cost of the Beulah Hill property. Spurgeon took this as a token from the Lord that he should acquire the new home in its much more desirable locale. Spurgeon purchased the property. It was higher ground and because of his rheumatic condition and his wife's ill health, they considered it a blessing of God that the place became available.

The beautiful home, named Westwood, was located on a nine-acre plot. The house looked much like a typical Victorian gentleman's residence. Soon Spurgeon began redecorating the place. He changed the drawing room into a library and the billiard room into his study. Beautiful trees dotted the nine-acre plot and the whole surrounding area spoke of quiet and peace. It afforded a beautiful vista to the south over the fields of Thornton Heath. A full description of life at Westwood was sketched in an evening journal at the time of Spurgeon's Jubilee Celebration in 1884. It was written by John B. Gough and reads:

> Westwood, where he at present lives, is a house on the extreme western edge of Beulah Hill, the southern ridge of the wooded heights of Sydenham. A more charming spot it would be difficult to find in the loveliest suburbs of London. The house, which is a large one, stands in the midst of well-wooded and spacious grounds, commanding from its windows an extended view of a wide expanse of Surrey. All is so peaceful and still that the house and the grounds might be fifty miles from town instead of being but three-quarters of an hour's drive from the Tabernacle—that swarming hive of ceaseless activity in the heart of busy London. The house is approached by a carriage-drive entered by the lodge gates. The miniature lake, in which a somewhat water-logged boat was floating at the time of our visit, lies immediately below the house. The grounds are tastefully laid out, the lawns well-kept, the shrubberies in good order. Mr. Spurgeon loves to bask in the sunshine, and regrets nothing so much at Menton as the delight of bathing in the southern sunlight all day long. A friend recently gave him a waterproof mattress, on which he can be in the grounds at Beulah Hill without fear of rheumatics; but the blazing effulgence of the southern skies no mattress can supply. The stables and coach-house lie out of sight down the hill. They are protected against witches, warlocks, and all the uncanny tribe by a monstrous horseshoe, weighing a couple of hundredweight, the gift of a friend who evidently deemed quantity an invaluable specific against evil spirits. There is a fountain with gold-fish in another part of the garden, and any number of beehives; for Mr. Spurgeon is a great

apiarian, and loves to hear the murmur of the bees as he strolls through his small domain. The borders of the kitchen-garden are all aglow with pinks and other homely English flowers, the beds of which yield every week a heavy crop of floral fragrance for the slums of Southwark. The flower-mission in connection with the Tabernacle—there is almost everything in connection with the Tabernacle except a theatre and public-house—sends its gleaners regularly to Westwood, and their baskets of flowers gladden many a home in the dark and dreary alleys of London. Rustic arbours and convenient seats offer pleasant resting-places; nor is the sense of restful seclusion and tranquility much disturbed even by the presence of one or two fat pigs, ugly with the beauty of their breed, which run about the garden as if it belonged to them. . . .

Within, the house is very bright and airy. The first thing that strikes a visitor is the peculiar arrangement by which Westwood in summer-time stands all day long with all its doors open to the air and sunlight without any insecurity. Within the hall, entrance to the house is barred by a wire-lattice fastened with a small brass lock, allowing free egress to the air, but excluding all more unwelcome intruders. Mr. Spurgeon rather prides himself upon this contrivance, and in the hot and stuffy London summer it would be a benefit to be able to leave the door open without any sense of danger. Passing the lattice door, recalling reminiscences of the wicket-gate, the visitor finds himself in a small entrance-hall, from which the dining-room opens to the right, and Mrs. Spurgeon's book-fund room, Mrs. Spurgeon's own room, and Mr. Spurgeon's library. Mrs. Spurgeon's room, from whence she directs the distribution of the books provided by a book fund, adjoins the small room, where innumerable volumes accumulate until the fortnightly wagon arrives from the Globe Parcel Express and carries them off from Westwood to all parts of the world. Mr. Spurgeon received me in his study just as he came in from the garden, upon which the study windows open directly. From the windows the eye wanders over the kitchen-garden, murmurous with bees, to Thornton Heath, with Croydon in the distance. In this study Mr. Spurgeon keeps two private secretaries constantly going. He has two or more at the Tabernacle, one or two at the College, and others elsewhere. One of them at Westwood is a shorthand writer, and, together with his colleague, he is kept busy till six. All moneys sent for the College, Orphanage, etc., are sent direct to Mr. Spurgeon, who is the paymaster-general of all his institutions. 'It is my constant labour,' said Mr. Spurgeon, 'to thrust off some portion of my work on other shoulders, but it all comes back on me. The more I do, the more there is to do.' The study is a work-a-day room, the walls lined with books, and the spacious table in the centre bearing abundant traces of work and wear. Mr. Spurgeon himself, in a white felt wide-awake and a light alpaca garden coat, chatted pleasantly of men and things. A genial, hearty man, full of shrewdness and humour, whose character has broadened and deepened as he has made his way through life, and who, having lived down the calumnies with which he was almost overwhelmed at first, now marvels most of all at the all-encompassing atmosphere of reverence and love in which he spends his life. Mr. Spurgeon has mellowed much with time; like a generous wine, he has improved with age.[91]

A barrage of criticism came over Spurgeon's move. Some descriptions of the houses and the grounds that were circulated exaggerated the truth beyond recognition. Some said Spurgeon had moved into a home fit only for a prince. An American minister visiting London and seeing the estate said it seemed like Buckingham Palace. Spurgeon ran into criticism no matter what he did or did not do.

Spurgeon's home was not only a lovely place to live, it became a place of business and worship; the family gathered each evening at 6:00 p.m. for prayers. Spurgeon's two secretaries, Mr. J. L. Keys and Mr. J. W. Harrald were there every day working through the mail, helping Spurgeon in his writing and research, and performing a number of duties, thus relieving Spurgeon of untold tedious hours. Here G. Holden Pike spent many days in the Westwood study helping his friend. The Book Fund also had its headquarters in Westwood. Mrs. Spurgeon had a room that literally overflowed with books to be sent to poor pastors.

Westwood was a very fine place and served a great purpose. There Spurgeon lived through the rest of his days. Helensburgh House in Clapham still exists although it is now a part of a series of row houses. Westwood on Beulah Hill was demolished many years ago, but the street that ran in front of Westwood has been named Spurgeon's Lane.

In the earlier part of Spurgeon's maturing ministry, his old friend, James Grant, retired from the editorship of *The Morning Advertiser*. Grant received a testimonial gift from his friends amounting to £1100. No doubt Spurgeon was one of the heavy contributors.

When Spurgeon produced the thousandth sermon in the *Penny Pulpit* series, as an evangelist, he appropriately preached on "The Prodigal Son," from Luke 15:17, "And when he came to himself, he said, 'How many hired servants of my father's have bread enough and to spare, I perish with hunger!'" When Passmore and Alabaster published the sermon the following Thursday, it was received as a unique token in the history of preaching. Expressing the gratitude felt worldwide for Spurgeon's writing ministry, *The Freeman*, the denominational organ of the Baptists at that time, stated:

> In his sufferings and the retirement, total or partial, which they enforce it is something to know that he has the thanks, the sympathy, and the prayers of thousands whom his living voice has never reached, and who would regard the loss of their weekly printed sermons as a serious spiritual privation. They have been weekly 'letters, weighty and powerful,' in thousands of Christian homes; and thousands of invalid Christians, unable to repair to the House of God, have found their own houses made Bethels by these welcome preachers.
>
> But the fact itself of one Christian teacher being endowed with the gift implied in all this is in itself a marvel. Possibly there have been a few Christian

preachers who might with similar press facilities have done the same. Probably a Chrysostom whose generally extemporised discourses were, like Mr. Spurgeon's, taken down by shorthand writers, might have done it—a truly noble predecessor. But, as a fact, our brother is the first Christian teacher whose sermons through so many years have sustained the ordeal of weekly publication. . . . Let us thank God, and take courage; 'the good old Gospel' has its thousands who rejoice in it yet. [92]

Spurgeon's published sermons were so popular that The Religious Tract Society would take excerpts from them and publish them as tracts.

It is interesting to see the development of Baptist periodicals during the protracted ministry of the Baptist Union. The first official organ was known simply as *The Baptist*. This emerged into the periodical current in much of Spurgeon's ministry, *The Freeman*. This gave place to *The Baptist Weekly* which later in turn became the contemporary official organ of the Baptist Union, entitled *The Baptist Times*. These papers of the Baptist Union have chronicled through the years the history of British Baptists and hence have made a significant contribution to the understanding of what has been accomplished among British Baptists.

But Spurgeon was now growing old. Even the work he so loved at times began to become a burden. He wrote to his father on January 23, 1882:

> The work is getting to be too great for me. I need more grace and more nerve. I may get to heaven before you even now. . . . I look up and the Lord knows my needs. He is all-sufficient, as for me I am no better than a dead dog in my own sight, though, dear to the Lord. [93]

On top of all of that, he was about to face the greatest trial in his life: the Down Grade Controversy. That dramatic moment deserves a searching enquiry. "Mr. Great-heart" was about to become a man "Valiant-for-Truth."

12

"I Am One Whose Name Is Valiant-for-Truth"

SPURGEON'S THEOLOGY AND
THE DOWN GRADE CONTROVERSY

The last photograph of gout-ridden Charles Spurgeon taken prior to his death at Mentone, France, in 1892.

—*courtesy of Dr. Craig Skinner*

Who so beset him round
With dismal stories,
Do but themselves confound;
His strength the more is.
No lion can him fright,
He'll with a giant fight,
But he will have a right
To be a pilgrim.
                              —*John Bunyan*

Part I:
Spurgeon's Theology

Introduction

In the struggles of Bunyan's "Pilgrim," no one he met on his journey to the Celestial City more typified Charles Haddon Spurgeon, especially in his later years, than "Mr. Valiant-for-Truth." Spurgeon knew what he believed as truth and stood willing to defend his position valiantly and at all costs. Moreover, he left no one in doubt concerning the basis and foundation of his systematic theology—it was dynamic Calvinism. Typical of Spurgeon's Calvinistic approach are the many words he uttered eulogizing Calvin. Typical of such statements, Spurgeon said:

> Calvin is a tree whose 'leaf shall not wither;' whatever he has written lives on, and is never out of date, because he expounded the word without bias or partiality.

Spurgeon never hesitated to put himself in the framework of the traditional five points of historic Calvinism as originally expressed by the Synod of Dort. Of course, he was convinced Calvinism had all its roots in the Bible. Nonetheless, he had bronze busts of Luther and Calvin in his vestry, indicative of his love of the Reformers and their theology. The Reformed doctrine of grace became the *summum bonum* for the Metropolitan Tabernacle pastor.

As we discovered in an earlier chapter, Spurgeon said he learned his basic theology, while still a young man, from Mary King, a simple servant woman. Spurgeon, in his zeal, probably exaggerated his dependence upon the simple woman for his Calvinistic grasp. He surely gleaned a large portion of his theology from his grandfather and father and from the Puritan works he constantly read. Mary King entertained a very rigid Calvinism, but Spurgeon modified those early views. He no doubt mellowed from the unbending rigidity of Mary King because of the influence of his father, and especially his grandfather. Also, being a committed Biblicist, his own study of the Scriptures greatly influenced his essential theology. Further, his zeal to evangelize put balance in his Calvinism. Still, Spurgeon breathed a Puritan, therefore a basic Calvinistic atmosphere from his birth, and he never really changed throughout life; nor did he want to. Someone said, "Here is a man who has not moved an inch forward in all his ministry, and at the close of the nineteenth century is teaching the theology of the first century."[1] Those words, meant as a criticism of Spurgeon, he took as a compliment. He stood as the bulwark of conservative, evangelical theology for his day. His defense of his understanding of the Christian faith, especially as seen in the various theological controversies in which he engaged, became something of the evangelical, conservative rebuttal to Germanic higher criticism. At any rate, at his death in 1892, no single conservative theologian in Britain became as outspoken for the evangelical defense of the faith as did Spurgeon.

Spurgeon's intransigent attitude does not mean he did not expose himself to the academic world. To the contrary, he gave himself to master every week at least a half dozen of the hardest books he could find. He said, "I am bound to give myself unto reading, and study and prayer, and not to grieve the Spirit by unthought-of effusion."[2] He would point to his huge personal library and say, "I have read them all."

Regardless of the source of Spurgeon's convictions, he committed himself to a Calvinistic system because he saw that system rooted and grounded in the Scriptures. He was convinced that Calvinism reflected pure Pauline theology and hence the proper understanding of Christian realities. He said:

> We only use the term 'Calvinism' for shortness. That doctrine that is called 'Calvinist' did not spring from Calvin; we believe that it sprang from the great founder of all truth. Perhaps Calvin himself derived it mainly from the writings of Augustine. Augustine obtained his views, without doubt, through the Spirit of God, from the diligent study of the writings of Paul, and Paul received them of the Holy Ghost, from Jesus Christ, the great founder of the Christian dispensation. We use the term then, not because we impute any extraordinary importance to Calvin's having taught these doctrines.
>
> The old truth that Calvin preached, that which Augustine preached, is the truth that I must preach today, or else be false to my conscience and my God. I cannot shape the truth; I know of no such thing as paring off the rough edges of a doctrine.[3]

One of Spurgeon's annotations written on the margin of his copy of Calvin's *Commentaries on the Epistle of Paul the Apostle to the Romans* reads: "who rejoices greatly to consult this greatest of expositors."[4] He did rely heavily on Calvin. On several other margins of Calvin's works, Spurgeon wrote, "uncomparable Calvin."[5] In the light of this essential philosophical and theological approach, Spurgeon developed a reasonably systematic theological base for his biblical preaching and exposition. And he would unhesitatingly battle for it.

WHY THE BATTLE?

The fact that Spurgeon was a controversialist also must be grasped to understand this nineteenth century pilgrim. The Rivulet Controversy, The Baptismal Regeneration Controversy, and above all, the Down Grade Controversy, not to mention his encounters with the press and even the segment of the Evangelical Church that opposed him, make it clear that he stood firm on his convictional grounds and did not mind going to battle to defend them. His commitment to what became known as "old-fashioned theology" cost him dearly. But it was because of the nature of his basic convictions that he fought as he did. He was convinced the Gospel itself was at stake; and, if the Gospel is lost, souls will be lost. His utter commitment to evangelization stood at the root of his defense of the faith. He said of himself, "He was a man with a mission."[6] But more of that in a moment.

Moreover, Spurgeon held so firmly to his basic early beliefs that he would not admit into his system anything that was "new," that is, "new" in any sense that would contradict the time-honored truths of Reformed thought. In speaking to the students at New College, London, he said:

> You and I believe in the doctrines of the Gospel. We have received the certainties of revealed truth. There are things which are verily believed among us. We do not bow down before men's theories of truth nor do we admit that theology consists of 'views' and 'opinions.' We declare that there are certain verities, essential, abiding, eternal, from which it is ruinous to swerve. I am deeply grieved to hear so many ministers talk as if the truth of God were a variable quantity, a matter of daily formation, a nose of wax to be consistently reshaped, a cloud driven by the wind. . . . I have been charged with being a mere echo of the Puritans, but I had rather be the echo of truth than the voice of falsehood . . . rest assured that there is nothing new in theology except that which is false; and that the facts of theology are today what they were eighteen hundred years ago.[7]

Spurgeon's approach may be seen by many today as very narrow, perhaps even bigoted and unenlightened. He certainly received that sort of criticism during his life, and perhaps with a small measure of justification. For example, in the margin of his copy of Adam Clarke's *Commentary*, he annotated a page with the following remark: "Take heed reader. This is dangerous ground for those who are not grounded and settled."[8] He wrote concerning Day's *Exposition of the Book of the Prophet Isaiah*, "This day sheds small light on the subject. Probably the writer had all the day in his name. The more oftener consulted the less will it be esteemed. It was written for children according to the preface and we pity the children who have to read it."[9] He even went so far as to annotate Clarke's work with these words: "adapted to blind the eye and prevent the truth in Jesus from shining upon the soul."[10]

It has been suggested that if Spurgeon had received a proper theological education, he would not have been so unbending and "narrow" in his doctrinal approach. Yet one wonders! Remember, he read widely in many fields. His grasp of literature, biography, science, history, poetry, and many other intellectual disciplines was remarkable. Nor was he always caustic in his annotations of books he had read. One example of a positive comment is his word in the margin of Winslow's, *No Condemnation in Christ Jesus*: "Dr. Winslow is always sound and sweet but his works are better adapted for general readers than for students. He is extremely diffuse."[11] He would often write on the front page of a book "highly value," or "CHS values this book."[12] But Spurgeon was not the kind of man to be deterred once he had set his hand to the plow, and he set his hand to the Calvinistic handle of truth and never looked back. He may have done better to have been broader, yet Reformed truth is where he stood, even to the point of putting his reputation and ministry at stake. For Spurgeon, theology must center on the doctrines of grace and nothing else. He truly became "the heir of the Puritans."

Further, as suggested, it should not be minimized that Spurgeon the theologian and controversialist must be seen as primarily an evangelist. He realized "if the church would effectively evangelize today, it must do so from a strong theological base."[13] C. E. Autrey has properly declared, "There can be no effective and permanent evangelism without theology . . . theology is to evangelism, what the skeleton is to the body."[14] Evangelist Billy Graham also put it correctly when he stated, "If there is one thing that the history of the church should teach us, it is the importance of the theology of evangelism as derived from the Scriptures."[15] Spurgeon himself said,

> Be well instructed in theology, and do not regard. . .those who rail at it because they are ignorant of it. Many preachers are not theologians, and hence the mistakes which they make. It cannot do any hurt to the most lively evangelist to be also a sound theologian, and it may often be the means of saving him from gross blunders.[16]

Spurgeon grew increasingly critical of the evangelist and his preaching "which lies mainly in shouting 'Believe! Believe! Believe!'"[17] Thus the Metropolitan Tabernacle evangelist developed a solid soteriology. Spurgeon's soteriology actually formed the foundation of his entire theology. That is probably why Spurgeon was not reticent to preach the full Calvinistic system in an evangelistic context. He had no time for superficial preaching that attenuated the full Gospel. He said in his well-known book, *The Soul Winner*:

Do not believe, dear friends, that when you go into revival meetings, or special evangelistic services, you are to leave out the doctrines of the gospel; for you ought then to proclaim the doctrines of grace rather more than less. [18]

It would appear incontestable that Spurgeon's great evangelistic fervor did much to mellow, systematize and perhaps even crystallize his theology.

Above all, it must be said that Spurgeon's theology and his defense of it essentially grew out of the Bible, at least as he saw it. For Spurgeon, the Scriptures alone stood as the final authority in Christian truth and realities. If some theological declaration did not emerge from the Scriptures and lacked a solid base in the Bible, Spurgeon had very little, if any, time for it. He would never preach anything that he did not feel was rooted and grounded in the Word of God. And for the truth of Scripture he would battle. Therefore, to understand Spurgeon's theology one must understand his basic approach to the Scriptures. This becomes the first major building block in Spurgeon's system of thought.

BIBLICAL AUTHORITY IN SPURGEON'S THOUGHT

In the pure sense of the word, Spurgeon never wrote any theological works. At any rate, he certainly never systematized his thought in writing. Therefore, to discover his theology of the Bible one must glean it through his sermons and other writings. However, in reading Spurgeon, his Biblicism stands out in bold relief.

It became clear Spurgeon realized the ultimate question in all theology has to be the question of authority. Where does one find the source of reliable truth concerning the Christian faith? This constitutes the ultimate query and forms the foundation stone upon which to build. What one sees as the basis or source of authoritative truth determines all the rest. But differing concepts concerning the nature of authority has also been a rock of controversy. It has divided the Church, often confused important doctrinal issues, and been the source of much conflict.

Perhaps it may oversimplify the issue somewhat, but it seems correct to say that through the course of the history of theology, three sources of truth have formed the bedrock upon which various thinkers have built their faith. First, there are those whose entire theological superstructure has been founded upon, and solely upon, the Scriptures. A perfect case in point are the Reformers. The principle of *sola scriptura* became the working theological principle of the Reformation, and those brave men gave their lives for the principle. It has been the heart of Evangelical Christianity through the years. All committed Evangelicals hold that the only source of final religious authority rests in the Holy Bible. This is the traditional Baptist, and Spurgeon's, position.

Secondly, tradition has played a very major role for some in their attempt to discern spiritual realities. The Roman Catholic Church stands as the primary example of this approach. When the Pope or Church Councils speak on matters of religion, morals and faith, they speak with authority. Of course, Rome has attempted to amalgamate the Bible and the tradition of the Church as the basis of authority, but this has often thrust them into peculiar if not contradictory stances. When a conflict arises between tradition and the Bible, Rome has tended to let tradition predominate, although a rationalization of the conflict is often given.

Thirdly, some see authority resting in human experience. The rational mind is given by God and thus some see it as the basis of authority. Consequently, rationalism becomes the final presupposition against which all other claims for truth are judged. In a similar fashion, the inner experience of believers is often given an authoritative role. The existential experience of religion some see as the final authority. The rationalization of experience with the Scriptures may be sought; still, one's personal inner experience becomes judged as to the final word. One of the strange paradoxes of the day centers in the fact that often this humanistic approach will bring some sort of amalgamation of rationalism and existentialism to bear upon traditional Christian truths and attempt to derive the final answer in that context.

Thus, the basis of religious authority becomes the key issue in developing one's theology. What is seen as the source of authoritative truth has to be where one finally rests and develops a system of doctrine.

For Spurgeon, as has been made amply clear, authority on all matters of religion rests in the Bible. He had no appreciation for the rationalistic "new theology" beginning to permeate British theological and ecclesiastical circles that found much of its source in German rationalism. This "modern thought" had no appeal to Spurgeon at all. He stated:

> Our 'modern thought' gentry are doing incalculable mischief to the souls of men. Immortal souls are being damned, yet these men are spinning theories. Hell gapes wide, and with her open mouth swallows up myriads, yet those who should spread the tidings of salvation are 'pursuing fresh lines of thought.' Highly cultured soul-murderers will find their boasted 'culture' to be no excuse in the day of judgment. For God's sake, let us know how men are to be saved, and get to the work; to be for ever deliberating as to the proper mode of making bread while a nation dies of famine is detestable trifling. It is time we knew what to teach, or else renounce our office. . . . Men who have no personal rest in the truth, if they are not themselves unsaved, are, at least, very unlikely to be the means of saving others. He who has no assured truth to tell must not wonder if his hearers set small store by what he says. We must know the truth, understand it, and hold it with firm grip, or we cannot be of service to the sons of men. [19]

As was said of Spurgeon, "By Divine grace he stood at the farthest remove from the rationalist." [20] Actually, this "new thought" became the enemy Spurgeon fought in the Down Grade Controversy.

This is not to say Spurgeon remained totally unaffected by other religious ideas. From time to time, he would appeal to tradition. He made references to the various creeds of the church and would cite what traditional Evangelicals generally accepted. But all these creeds, traditions and ideas of the Church, even the Evangelical Church, had to be reduced to a secondary role compared to the Scriptures. He said:

> As for all these human authorities, I care not one rush for all three of them. I care not for what they say, pro or con, as to this doctrine. I have only used them as a kind of confirmation of your faith to show that whilst I may be railed upon as a heretic and a hyper-Calvinist, after all I am backed up by antiquity . . . the great truth is always the Bible, and the Bible alone. [21]

For Spurgeon, no tradition had any final authority, although he would use it occasionally to support his views.

Spurgeon also appealed to experience. He was especially fond of relating personal spiritual experiences, often sharing his own personal experience of conversion. He said once in a sermon, "I hope I do not trouble you too often with personal experiences but . . . it seems to me that every Christian should add his own personal testimony to the heap of evidence which proves the truth of our God." [22] He even went as far as to say, "I believe that the doctrine which a man's innermost experience confirms to him in the day of trial, and in the day when he is nearest to God, is to him, at any rate, the very truth itself, and worthy of his credence." [23] Yet even here, Spurgeon did not place personal experience above, not even alongside, the Scriptures. He was clear and explicit about that fact when he said, "Brethren, how careful should we be that we do not set up . . . anything in opposition to his Word, that we do not permit the teachings of a preacher to usurp the honor due to the Lord alone . . . 'Thus saith experience;' these be but idle gods which defile the temple of God . . . seeing that they usurp the place of the Word of God." [24] Though Spurgeon had a vital personal existential experience of Jesus Christ, he would never exalt religious experience to usurp the place of the Bible as an authoritative source of truth. He well knew the weakness of one's humanity.

It has already been intimated what Spurgeon thought about reason. A purely reasoning approach to truth, to test everything by sheer human capabilities, he considered folly. Human reason can be at fault as well as existential experiences. The age-old battle between revelation and reason was really not a battle for Spurgeon. For the Metropolitan Tabernacle preacher, reason must take a secondary role to the revelation of God, first in the person of the Lord Jesus Christ, and secondly, in the written revelation of the Lord called the Holy Bible. He said, "We give glory to God in reference to revelation when we receive it, every jot and tittle of it, and bow our minds before it." [25] He obviously saw the Scriptures as revelational as well as the person of Christ.

One of the clearest evidences of Spurgeon's exaltation of revelation over reason took on a paradoxical tone, if not a contradictory stance. It centered in his use of the so-called doctrines of grace. It has already been stated that many high-Calvinist churches closed their doors to him because he could not fill their expectations of hyper-Calvinism. The Arminians also had very little time for him and few pulpits would open because of the Calvinistic stance he did take. In simplest terms, he held a quite rigid Calvinistic theology but preached and gave Gospel appeals like a fervent Arminian Methodist. This put him in a paradoxical stance and precipitated the accusation that he would pray that God would call out His elect and then elect others as well. This certainly failed as a purely reasoned approach, so the question can quite correctly be raised, why was he not systematic in keeping to one line of theology and hence save himself from this troubling stance? The answer is very simple, Spurgeon steadfastly refused to bring any sort of a resolution to what he considered to be the revealed truth of God in the Scriptures, regardless of how rational or irrational they may appear on the surface. He said, "I would sooner a hundred times over appear to be inconsistent with myself than to be inconsistent with the Word of God." [26] Spurgeon was definitely not a rationalist. The primary point Spurgeon made concerning the inadequacy of human reason centered in his view of human depravity. He said, "No man's eyes are opened by syllogisms . . . Reason alone gives no man the power to see the light of heaven." [27]

This is not to say, however, that Spurgeon thought reason played no role whatsoever in formulating doctrine. He said, "of carnal reasoning, we would have none, but of fair, honest pondering, considering, judging, and arguing, the more, the better." [28] A careful reading of his sermons shows that he had a good analytical mind and his sermon outlining showed the use of acute reasoning and logical sequence. As discovered earlier, Spurgeon did not particularly admire Charles G. Finney. But he did compliment Finney's use of argument. He said Finney's "power rests in his use of clear arguments." [29] Actually, Spurgeon may have been more rational, at least in methodology, than he willingly admitted. He strove to be clear with the Word of God, for that mattered most in religious authority. That at times made him appear rational. So Spurgeon actually did affirm rationalism as far as it could be used to understand the Bible and formulate good scriptural arguments.

If Spurgeon held a view of the Scriptures that placed tradition, reason, personal experience, or any other human factor in a secondary authoritative role, what did he actually believe about the Bible itself?

SPURGEON'S VIEW OF THE SCRIPTURES

Spurgeon gave his view of the nature of the Bible in a few words: "To me, a sentence of Scripture is the essence of logic, the proof-positive, the word which may not be questioned." [30] For Spurgeon, the Bible presents unequivocal, logical truth. Thus it possesses complete authority concerning the truth of God. He made this crystal clear when he said, "'Thus saith the Lord' is the only authority in God's church." [31] Spurgeon readily acknowledged that God revealed himself in the works of creation. Yet, this natural revelation falls far short of bringing any redemptive knowledge of God. He would argue that it does not reveal God's ultimate purpose for creation, nor does it even show how God's purpose for humanity will be fulfilled. Spurgeon reveled in nature and would agree that "the heavens declare the glory of God and the firmament showeth His handiwork" (Psalm 19:1). But natural revelation can give no more than a vision of the glory of God. God reveals Himself *redemptively* in Christ through the Holy Scriptures. Spurgeon viewed the Bible as a "wonderful" library about God. The Book contains enough propositional truth to last anyone throughout the entirety of their life. Therein the whole purpose of God can be discovered. At the same time, Spurgeon could not be charged with ignorance about the makeup of the Bible. He did not have a naive approach to the authoritative Word. He recognized it came from the pen of men inspired by the Holy Spirit. He well knew that the Bible consisted of different types of literature: history, narrative, poetry, theology, etc. He recognized the Old Testament had been written in the more classical language of the Hebrew people he actually had a reasonable, workable grasp of biblical Hebrew. However, he did feel more at home in the *koiné* Greek language of the New Testament. He saw the importance of hermeneutics, principles of interpretation. Moreover, he fully realized that hermeneutically the New Testament depended upon the Old Testament, and that the Old Testament has no final interpretation apart from the New. Thus he kept an overall balance in his approach to Scripture. He warned, "do not drop into the semi-blasphemy of some, who think the New Testament vastly superior to the Old, they are of equal authority." [32] Further, just because the Bible is composed of many types of literature, and that many voices spoke from its pages, Spurgeon would never consent to the idea that the words of some, Jesus for example, stood as more reliable or more authoritative than those of the Apostle Paul. Some theological thinkers in his day held that the words of Christ carried more weight in spiritual matters than those of Paul. Spurgeon admitted that if one were to compare the Lord Jesus and Paul from a purely human perspective, the concept has credence. But that does not apply to the Scriptures. When Paul wrote, he wrote as much under the inspiration of the Spirit as did those who communicated the words of the Lord in the Gospels. Spurgeon argued, "whether the Holy Ghost speaketh by Isaiah, or Jeremiah, or John, or James, or Paul, the authority is still the same." [33] This statement came in 1889 when the Down Grade Controversy had already taken place. That basic premise of Spurgeon had carried him through those difficult days. Spurgeon would readily grant the Scriptures were penned by human authors, but they were so "God breathed" that what they said, their very words, became the very Word of

God, just as if God had written it Himself. The whole Bible stands as totally inspired.

Spurgeon did not have a naive or "magical" view as to how the Bible came down through the ages. He knew its history. Furthermore, he was well aware of the fact that the authors of the Bible were human and spoke in a human way. The question can then be raised, how can the Word of God be distinguished from other human books, and how does one know that the Bible does speak God's words? Spurgeon squarely faced that issue and said the Scriptures have a self-attesting reality because God reveals Himself through its truths. In the Bible God has shown His nature, His character, His purpose and will, His plans, and even His method of operation. In the Scriptures God tells us of Himself. The Bible also stands as a propositional revelation from God concerning humanity; his creation, fall, ruin, salvation, duty and God's ultimate and eternal fulfillment in every human life.

By inspiration, Spurgeon did not mean natural inspiration as great writers and artists would experience. Biblical inspiration far exceeded that experience. In the Scriptures the Holy Spirit inspired the writers, right down to the very words. Spurgeon held firmly to the view commonly known as "verbal inspiration." He said:

> I do not know of any other inspiration. We need a plain revelation upon which we can exercise faith. If the Lord had spoken to us by a method in which his meaning was infallible, but his words were questionable, we should have been rather confused than edified.
>
> We believe that holy men of old, though using their own language, were led by the Spirit of God to use words which were also the words of God. The divine Spirit so operated upon the spirit of the divine writer, that he wrote the words of the Lord . . . to us, every word of God is pure . . . we believe that we have the words of God preserved for us in the Scriptures. [34]

Spurgeon never actually produced a full systematic view of inspiration. He just made the sort of generalized statements as presented above and left it there. Actually, he said, "We care little for any *theory* of inspiration: in fact we have none. To us the plenary verbal inspiration of the Holy Scriptures is a fact and not a hypothesis." [35] However, Spurgeon certainly did say enough concerning the Scriptures to glean his views. Moreover, in 1888, he reissued for his students at the Pastors' College, the book by Dr. L. Gaussen, professor of Systematic Theology at Geneva: *Theopneustis: The Plenary Inspiration of the Holy Scriptures.* In the preface of this theological classic, Gaussen wrote:

> The turning point in the battle between those who hold the 'faith once delivered to the saints' and their opponents lies in the truth and real inspiration of the Holy Scriptures. This is the Thermopylae of Christendom. If we have in the word of God, no infallible truth, we are at sea without a compass. 'If the foundations be removed, what can the righteous do?' And this is the founda-

tion loss of the worst kind . . . we can have a measure of fellowship with a
mistaken friend who is willing to bow before the teaching of scripture if he can
be made to understand it; but we must part company altogether with the
errorist who overrides prophets and apostles and practically regards his own
inspiration as superior to theirs. We fear that such a man will before long
prove himself to be an enemy of the cross of Christ, all the more dangerous
because he will profess loyalty to the Lord whom he dishonors. . . . It is a
delight to turn from the dreamings of the new school to the certainties of the
Word of God. [36]

Spurgeon affirmed Gaussen's position. Simply put, Spurgeon clearly held
that the Scriptures, though written by men, were totally inspired by God and
thus ultimately not of human origin. The Bible stems from divine initiative
and not of human and that meant the entire Bible, Old Testament and New.
Spurgeon obviously held to the plenary inspiration of the entire Bible. Spurgeon said concerning the Word of God, "I am the Book of God: Read me. I
am God's writing: Open my pages, for I was penned by God; read it, for He
is my Author." [37] Therefore, the Bible has absolute authority in all of its
many utterances.

Spurgeon went on to argue that if the Bible is the Word of God, then the
human authors should certainly give God "credit" for that fact. And Spurgeon felt this was certainly the case. He pointed out that expressions like,
"Thus saith the Lord" can be found over two thousand times in the Scriptures. For example, Jeremiah proclaimed, "Here ye, and give ears; be not
proud: for the Lord hath spoken" (Jeremiah 13:15).

Spurgeon contended for the authority of the Scriptures from other perspectives as well as its divine origin. Spurgeon held that the Bible possessed
absolute authority and truth because of its immutability. He saw God's
Word as settled once and for all. It came from heaven because it was settled
in heaven, the very seat of God's enthronement. Thus it can never be altered
on earth. As Jesus said, "Heaven and Earth shall pass away but my words
shall never pass away" (Matthew 24:35).

Spurgeon went on to say that the Bible is authoritative because of its
faithfulness, and that faithfulness is based on God's faithfulness. What God
has said has always been true and invariably comes to pass. Thus, His
promises can be relied upon and everything that He has said can be trusted
because God has shown Himself as trustworthy.

Spurgeon then pointed out that Jesus affirmed the authority of the Scriptures. Our Lord said, "It is written, man shall not live by bread alone, but by
every word that proceeds out of the mouth of God" (Matthew 4:4). In this
passage Jesus clearly shows His reverence for the authoritative Word of
God as found in the Bible of his day, the Old Testament. Spurgeon once
preached on this passage and said that in one's search for truth, it is not
found in an infallible Church or infallible Apostles or any infallible man, for

that is not where infallibility rests. Rather, "we have a more sure word of testimony, a rock of truth upon which we rest, for our infallible standard lies in 'It is written'." [38] Thus the Bible stands as authoritative because Jesus Himself saw it that way. The Lord said that not one "jot or tittle" will pass away until all has been fulfilled. The fact that Jesus believed in the total authority, total inerrancy, of the Scriptures is patent. No one, even the most liberal theologian of any age, denies that fact.

Spurgeon further argued for the validity of the Scriptures as the Word of God because of fulfilled prophecy. For example, he pointed to Isaiah 7:14, which he felt speaks of the birth of Jesus, and said, "This expression is unparalleled even in Sacred Writ; for of no other woman could it be said beside the Virgin Mary, and of no other man could it be written that His mother was a virgin." [39] He pointed out that Micah 5:2 prophesies the exact place of the birth of our Lord. This too came to pass. These sorts of arguments, Spurgeon continually made to undergird his conviction that the Bible was the inspired Word of God. Thus he concluded, "This volume (the Bible) is the writing of the living God: each letter was penned with an almighty finger; each word in it dropped from the everlasting lips, each sentence was dictated by the Holy Spirit . . . everywhere I find God speaking: it is God's voice not man's; the words are God's words, the words of the Eternal, the Invisible, the Almighty, the Jehovah of the Earth." [40]

In a sermon in 1883, Spurgeon declared, "The sacred Scriptures are the record of what God hath spoken." [41] He did not in any sense of the word mean that in the Barthian, or neo-orthodox sense, which declares the Bible to be just a record of God's revelation, not revelation in itself. To the contrary, Spurgeon meant by his statement that God not only reveals Himself in an existential, living manner to people, the biblical account of those revelations becomes a propositional revelation in itself. In a word, Spurgeon believed that there can be a written revelation of God as well as a personal existential revelation of God. He would never say, as some neo-orthodox thinkers do, that the Bible contains but is not the Word of God in total. Spurgeon said, "The Bible does not merely contain the Word of God, but it is the Word of God." [42] Those views become very significant because of their encroachment into British theological circles that ultimately resulted in the Down Grade Controversy.

Thus, Spurgeon's view of inspiration and the nature of Scripture led him to the logical step that the Bible is the unique, infallible, inerrant Word of God. He unequivocally took that position, stating:

> It (the Bible) is also a book pure in the sense of truth, being without admixture of error. I do not hesitate to say that I believe that there is no mistake whatever in the original holy scriptures from beginning to end . . . there is not an error of any sort in the whole compass of them. [43]

Although Spurgeon readily acknowledged that the Bible primarily concerns itself in the work of God relative to the redemption of humanity, and that the primary thrust of the Bible dealt with spiritual and religious realities, he contended that "the Holy Spirit has made no mistake, either in history, physics, theology, or anything else." [44] He further said, "if I did not believe in the infallibility of the Book, I would rather be without it." [45]

Simply put, Spurgeon took his stand as an "inerrantist," but not a blind, unintelligent inerrantist. Spurgeon's view on inerrancy and infallibility applied only to the original autographs (manuscripts). He understood the extant manuscripts were not original autographs and that there had been errors in translations and thus textual problems existed. Consequently, he urged his students to study the original languages and find the best possible text. Not only that, Spurgeon was always open to new translations and appreciated the scholarly contribution of those who would wrestle with manuscripts to find what language would best reflect the original autographs.

THE BASIS OF INFALLIBILITY

The question can be raised as to the basic underlying reason Spurgeon held such a high view of the Scriptures and argued for its authority. The answer again is quite simple, yet not simplistic. For Spurgeon, it was a matter of faith and the entire experience of God in one's life. The only source of authority that vindicated his own spiritual experience was found in the pages of the Bible. Tradition, existential experience, human reason, and every other epistemological (truth-seeking) principle that would claim its role as the sole and final source of truth and reality, Spurgeon laid aside and clung instead to the Bible. His religious understanding and grasp of the whole Christian faith rested solely upon that one foundation. Though it must be granted that this constituted a pure "leap of faith," it also must be recognized that every other claim for authority is a "leap of faith." This rests upon the fact that human reason, existential experience, empirical apprehension, etc., are all basically epistemological presuppositions and demand "faith." Therefore, Spurgeon found his leap of faith into the Scriptures as the most coherent, satisfying foundation upon which to build his view of religious authority. It coincided with his own experience of God. Faith became the starting point of his whole view of Scripture. Thus, all theology, according to Spurgeon, must be built upon a faith commitment to the Bible because it stands as the sole authority. He laid his essential foundation on the Word of God alone.

But Spurgeon did not have a mere abstract theological view of an infallible Bible. Although he held tenaciously to a very high view of the Scriptures, for him it was a very practical book; a book to be believed, acted upon, and preached. Spurgeon well realized that a primary intent of the Bible is to bring people to salvation in Jesus Christ as Lord and Savior. He said:

We may begin with Genesis and go on to the book of Revelation, and say of all the holy histories, 'these are written that ye might believe that Jesus is the Christ, the son of God' though this Bible is a wonderful library of many books, yet there is such a unity about it that the mass of people regard it as one book, and they are not in error when they do so: this one book has but one design, and every portion of it works to that end. Of the whole canon of inspiration we may say, as we read every detail, 'These are written that ye may believe that Jesus is the Christ, the son of God.'"[46]

For Spurgeon the Bible becomes in God's hand "the sword of the Spirit." Thus he saw it as a Sword to be yielded in ministry and service. He said, "The word of God is said to be quick . . . horrible . . . cutting . . . piercing . . . discriminating . . . revealing of the inner self . . . It is an instrument to cut to the hearer's heart . . . a book to criticize and show us our need."[47] Spurgeon constantly exhorted his students to "rightly divide the word of truth" (II Timothy 2:15). In this way alone can Christian ministers make full proof of their ministries. A preacher's chief aim must be to communicate clearly and forcefully the Word of God. He said, "The Word of God is not committed to God's ministers to amuse men with its glitter, nor to charm them with the jewels in its hilt, but to conquer their souls for Jesus."[48] For Spurgeon, the Bible was just that, the very Word of God to break the heart and bring the soul before the throne of God, thus bringing them to a redemptive knowledge of the Lord Jesus Christ. Upon this foundation Spurgeon built his entire theology and ministry.

Spurgeon's Doctrine of God: Theology Proper

Spurgeon expressed his basic understanding of the reality and character of God in these words:

> We believe, that there is but one holy living and true God; that there are three persons in the Godhead, the Father, the Son, and the Holy Ghost, who are equal in nature, power and glory; and that the Son and the Holy Ghost are as truly and properly God as the Father.[49]

For Spurgeon, theology proper revolved around these essential truths about the Godhead. In his own inevitable style, he put a practical ring to this basic theological statement. He totally agreed with Hebrews 11:6, "He that cometh to God must believe that he is, and that he is a rewarder of them that diligently seek him." For Spurgeon, God existed in a full trinitarian nature and must be believed in and sought after. What did all this mean for Spurgeon?

It meant for the Tabernacle preacher that God is eternal. God existed when there were no heavens or earth or any other created thing. The eternal God spoke creation into being. He is the One who created that marvelous relativism that exists between time and space. The finite, limited creation came into being because the Eternal so decreed it. What is this eternal, creating God like, that all people everywhere are to seek? Spurgeon would have been in complete agreement with the *Westminster Larger Catechism* which states:

> God is a Spirit, in and of himself infinite in being, glory, blessedness, and perfection; all sufficient, eternal, unchangeable, incomprehensible, everywhere present, almighty, knowing all things, most wise, most holy, most just, most merciful and gracious, long suffering, and abundant in goodness and truth.[50]

Such a God certainly has a "personality." Spurgeon saw God as a *personal* Being. Moreover, although God manifests Himself as a Trinity, there is an essential unity or oneness in the Godhead that makes the Divine Three Persons, One. The great schema of Israel resonated in Charles' heart: "The Lord our God is one Lord, and there is no God beside him" (Deuteronomy 4:35). Spurgeon said, "We believe that there is one God and although we rejoice to recognize the Trinity, yet it is ever most distinctly a Trinity in unity."[51] Spurgeon readily agreed this truth defies mere human rationalism. How three can be one will always remain something of a mystery. Nevertheless, "truth is revealed in the holy Scriptures and we accept it as a matter of faith."[52] When the Bible speaks, and it certainly speaks of the Trinity, that settled the matter for Spurgeon. Spurgeon well recognized the fact that the one God who manifests Himself in a personal trinitarian fashion, implies that each person of the Trinity has a specific office or duty. This brings at least something of a rationale to the idea of the Trinity.

Spurgeon further saw God revealing His divine personal nature and character in the various names that the Bible uses to describe the Most High, for example, in names such as Elohim, Yahweh, El-Shaddi, etc. Spurgeon held that the triune God attributed these names to Himself to express different aspects of His nature and being, as well as His different inter-relationships with His creation. In a message from Jeremiah 30:17, "I will restore health unto thee, and will heal thee of thy wounds, saith the Lord," Spurgeon said, "The promise of this verse will be exceedingly sweet to those who feel their personal need of them . . . oh, you that are sick at heart, here is a word for you from the God of all grace: Jehovah-raphi himself says, 'I will restore health unto thee, and I will heal thee of thy wounds.'"[53]

Spurgeon further saw the magnitude and majesty of God's personhood in the various "activities" that are ascribed to him. God is seen as living, loving, active, self-motivated, and all-knowing intelligence. Spurgeon said, "We believe in a great God to whom all things are known and by whom the least matters are observed. Our God is neither unobservant nor indifferent."[54] Above all, God is seen in his active existence as exercising will. It was always something of a mystery to Spurgeon, yet something that he firmly believed, that God "doeth according to his will" (Daniel 4:34, 35). Out of His all-knowing nature, He does all things well.

Yet, the majesty of God is seen supremely in the unique character of His personhood. God is seen as holy, true, loving, righteous, faithful, etc. Spurgeon rejoiced in each of these marvelous attributes of God. When Spurgeon preached on the various characteristics of God, he reveled in the very person of the Lord. Preaching once from John 17:25-26, which makes reference to the *righteous* Father, Spurgeon said:

> He is 'righteous,' having the attributes of a Judge and Ruler: just, impartial, by no means sparing the guilty. He is 'father' . . . loving, tender, forgiving. In His character and in His dealings with His people He blends the two as they were never combined before. [55]

Spurgeon also exalted in the mercy of God. He preached many sermons on this subject. He once said, "The mercy of the heart of God is, of course, the mercy of great tenderness, the mercy of his infinite gentleness and consideration." [56] In some senses, Spurgeon summarized the greatness of God's personal characteristics by ascribing to Him perfection, infinity, and unchangeable self existence. He said:

> My brethren, you need not that I marshall in array a host of confirmative passages, for the eternal self existence of God is taught throughout the scriptures, and is implied in the name which belongs only to the true God, Jehovah, 'I am that I am' . . . the only Being, the root of existence, the immutable, and Eternal One . . . He is the one only underived self existent, self sustained being . . . there is no moments of beginning with the Eternal, no starting point from which to calculate age. [57]

All of this implies that God is perfect in power and authority. As the Reformed theologians expressed it, and as Spurgeon loved to preach it, God is absolutely *Sovereign* in all of His being and doings; He is absolute and infinite. In His sovereign power He governs all that is. He has made it all for His glory, and He rules over it as Lord. God is omnipotent. He can do all things. Nothing is too hard for the Lord. God is also transcendent and omnipresent. He is everywhere at all times in all places and transcends it all. He is not limited by the time space framework in which creation finds itself. He fills heaven and earth. Spurgeon said, "Let us remember, then, that in the three kingdoms God is everywhere, in the kingdom of nature, of providence, and of grace, we may say of each spot, 'surely God is in this place.'" [58] Furthermore, God's infinite, ultimate nature means that He is omniscient— He knows all things. There is nothing beyond the pale of God's knowledge. Our Lord told us that the very hairs of our head are numbered. God is all seeing and all knowing, cognizant of everything. He utterly transcends the time-space framework in which we as limited creatures live out our lives. Simply put, God is Ultimate Reality.

All of this, however, does not mean that God simply exists and there is no purpose for creation. To the contrary, Spurgeon believed that purpose permeates everything God is and everything God does. His actual attributes speak of purpose, and above all, His purpose is seen in His outflowing love for those for whom Christ died. Spurgeon said concerning the great love of God:

> God has such love in his nature that he must needs let it flow forth to a world perishing by its own willful sin; and when it flowed forth it was so deep, so wide, so strong, that even inspiration could not commute its measure.[59]

Moreover, Spurgeon contended that the ultimate purpose of God will be fulfilled without fail. Nothing can thwart the final plan of God for His creation. This will be seen in more detail in a moment when Spurgeon's soteriology, which centered on the doctrines of grace, will be discussed.

With this background in theism, one can well imagine the path that Spurgeon took concerning the person of the Lord Jesus Christ. Spurgeon's Christology was traditionally orthodox and Reformed in its entire approach.

THE PERSON OF CHRIST

For Spurgeon, the Lord Jesus Christ stands as the epitome of God's revelation of Himself. Yet, this man of Galilee is called a Child, a Son; and at the same time the Everlasting Father. The mystery of the Trinity prevails. This can only be grasped by understanding the redemptive role of Christ in history. Spurgeon had no question in his mind that Jesus Christ, sharing all the attributes of God, was preexistent with the Father. In preaching from John 17:24, he declared, "There was a day before all days, when there was no day but the Ancient of Days. There was a time before all time, when God only was: the uncreated, the only existent One, the Divine Three, Father, Son, and Spirit lived in blessed consort with each other."[60] All of this implies that Jesus Christ is deity in Himself. Spurgeon argued the Scriptures make this patent. He is called God, the Son of God, the Lord, the Holy One, and many other attributive names which clearly declare His deity. In the person of Jesus Christ, the eternal Son, the attributes of God are manifest. Christ the eternal Son, and the self-existent, immutable God are synonymous. Jesus said, "Verily, verily, I say unto you, before Abraham was, I am." As the New Testament scholar Joachim Jeremias declares, these great "I am" statements of Jesus are to be equated with the "I am" revelation of God in the burning bush of Moses. The Lord Himself constantly declared His oneness with the Father, and hence His ultimate and final deity. Jesus went so far as to say, "Believe in me even as you believe in God" (John 14:1) Spurgeon, as stated previously, stood in complete agreement with the Calcedonian formulation (A.D. 450) wherein Jesus Christ is declared to be "very God of very God" and yet "very man of very man." That God should be in human flesh and come to us in the form of a God/man is mystery indeed, but the Scriptures declare it and for Spurgeon that settled the matter once and for all. That basic doctrinal position became the essence of the issue in the Down Grade Controversy, at least as Spurgeon saw it. The deity of Christ is the heart of Christianity and must be defended at all costs.

Thus the Incarnation, in many senses of the word the ultimate mystery, formed the bedrock of Spurgeon's Christology. He said, "I wish that I had the power to bring out this precious doctrine of the incarnation."[61] But it goes beyond human reason and human capability to explain fully. Although Mary was Jesus' mother, God was his Father. Though he received a human nature from Mary, His divine nature came from God. When Jesus Christ was born of the Virgin Mary in the miraculous conception of the Holy Spirit, He was truly born a man. He was totally human. He walked the dusty pathways of Galilee; He got hungry and tired, even at times exasperated. He suffered physical pain and heartbreak; He even wept. He was a man. He was tempted with the specter of unbelief, presumption, false worship, and everything Satan could hurl across his path; yet, all without sin (Hebrews 4:15) He was a human being in every sense of the word. Spurgeon pointed out that our Lord even had a very human name. Jesus is his own personal, human name given by God. Spurgeon always avoided the Docetic heresy that so exalted the deity of Jesus Christ that His humanity got lost in the process. He said:

> We shall be wise never to disassociate the deity of Christ from his humanity, for they make up one person . . . the two natures are so thoroughly united in the person of Christ that the Holy Ghost does not speak of the Lord Jesus with theological exactness, like one who writes a creed, but he speaks as to men of understanding, who know and rejoice in the truth of the one indivisible person of the Mediator. [62]

These truths are to be joyfully experienced and thus preached.

Important to the preaching of Jesus Christ, as already implied, Spurgeon refused to preach mere doctrine about Christ. He made this clear in his first volume of sermons at the New Park Street Church. He declared:

> Jesus is *the truth*. We believe in *Him,—not merely* in his words. *He* himself is Doctor and Doctrine, Revealer and Revelation, the Illuminator and Light of Men. He is exalted in every word of truth, because he is its sum and substance . . . Sermons are valuable in proportion as they speak *of* Him and point *to him*. A Christless gospel is no gospel and a Christless discourse is the cause of merriment to devils. . .[63]

This approach of Spurgeon characterized his preaching of Christ throughout the entirety of his ministry. He preached Christ very practically. One is hard put to it to find any sermon where Jesus Christ was not presented and extolled and practical applications made. This is also true of his writing and his lecturing. In his *Lectures to My Students*, in one discourse entitled "Sermons—Their Matter," Spurgeon declared:

Of all I would wish to say this is the sum; my brethren, preach *Christ*, always and evermore. He is the whole gospel. His person, offices, and work must be our one great all encompassing theme. [64]

This is not meant to say that in Spurgeon's preaching of Christ he felt it unimportant to preach specific Christological doctrines. He held that if one "preaches Christ's person he must preach doctrine." [65] Still, he never preached doctrine merely for doctrine's sake *alone*. The pragmatic element was always present.

THE COVENANTS

All this exaltation of Christ means one must declare the covenantal relationship into which Christ brings those who exercise repentance and faith. Spurgeon earnestly contended that "all God's dealings with man have had a covenant character." [66] He went so far as to say that the nature and implication of the covenant idea stands central to *all* theology. For Spurgeon there were two covenants, viz. the covenant of works and the covenant of grace. To understand these, Spurgeon said, enables one to understand "the key to all theology." [67] He argued that to be ignorant of the concept of the covenants was to "know next to nothing about the gospel of Christ." [68] The two covenants became the organizing principle for Spurgeon's understanding of theology. He gave his summary of the covenant of works in the following manner:

> There is my law, O man; if thou on thy side wilt engage to keep it, I, on my side will engage that thou shalt live by keeping it. If thou wilt promise to obey my commands perfectly, wholly, fully, without a single flaw, I will carry thee to heaven. But mark me, if thou violatest one command, if thou dost rebel against a single ordinance, I will destroy thee for ever. [69]

He summarized the covenant of grace as follows:

> Christ Jesus on his part engages to bear the penalty of all his people's sins, to die, to pay their debts, to take their iniquities upon his shoulders; and the Father promises on his part that all for whom the Son doth die shall most assuredly be saved. [70]

To put it in simplest terms, for Spurgeon "the covenants of works was, 'do this and live, old man,!' But the covenant of grace is, 'do this, O Christ, and thou shalt live, old man.'" [71]

Spurgeon would often highlight the radical differences between the two covenants. He argued that the primary difference centered in the contracting parties. That is to say, the covenant of works was ratified between God and all humanity with Adam as the representative federal head of the entire race. But the covenant of grace was an agreement between God the Father and God the Son. And Jesus Christ became the covenant head of all God's elect people. Furthermore, Spurgeon held that the two covenants were not compatible, that is, the covenant of works included everyone while the covenant of grace applied only to the elect. He further held that the covenant of works was "conditional on Adam's standing," while the covenant of grace was "perfectly unconditional with us."[72] Because of the work of the Lord Jesus Christ in his life, death and resurrection, the covenant of grace gives the elect faith, repentance, good works, and salvation. It is all a purely unconditional act of the grace of God in the lives of His people, chosen by grace. The covenant of works, which was broken by Adam, brought sin into the world. As a consequence of the Fall, it can no longer be a means of salvation for anyone, for all have sinned (Romans 3:23). But the covenant of grace, designed and accomplished in the mind of the sovereign God before the foundation of the world, is the immutable means for the salvation of God's elect. This obviously leads to the core of Spurgeon's soteriology, known in Reformed theology as the "doctrines of grace." But before delving into this scheme, we must see Spurgeon's theology on the Holy Spirit to complete the trinitarian approach of the great preacher.

SPURGEON'S DOCTRINE OF THE HOLY SPIRIT

Spurgeon had a definite pneumatology. Again, basing his theological structure on the Scriptures, he constructed a full doctrine of the Holy Spirit. He was cognizant of the fact that not only did the Bible speak much of the Holy Spirit, but one could not really understand the Trinity apart from the honoring of the third person of the divine Triad. He said:

> To believe and love the Trinity is to possess the key to theology. We spoke of the father, we spoke of the son; let us now speak of the Holy Spirit. We do him all too little honor, for the Holy Spirit condescends to come to earth and dwell in our heart; and not withstanding all our provocations he still abides within his people.[73]

Spurgeon declared the Bible reveals the Holy Spirit as possessing all the attributes of a person. Never should He be known as an "it" but as a "He." The Holy Spirit is constantly introduced as a person, not merely an influence or motivation to good.

Moreover, Spurgeon constantly contended the Holy Spirit is a *divine* Person. He possesses all the perfections and attributes of God. That means The Holy Spirit can be characterized as eternal, omniscient, omnipresent, and omnipotent. Spurgeon further reminded his hearers that He is called the *Holy* Spirit:

> The personal name of the Third Person of the Blessed Trinity is the 'Holy Spirit,' which words describe his nature as being pure, spiritual, immaterial existence, and His character as being in Himself and in His workings preeminently holy.[74]

For Spurgeon, the Holy Spirit always represents the divine presence of the living Christ within. Spurgeon found great satisfaction in the indwelling work of the Spirit. He stated:

> God gives his Holy Spirit, as it were, to be a part of the reward which he intends to give to his people . . . so God gives us his Holy Spirit to be in our hearts as earnest of Heaven . . . When you have Him, you have a plain indication to your soul of what heaven will be.

Spurgeon urged his people to rest in that glorious reality, this "earnest" of the Holy Spirit. The Holy Spirit enters the repentant believing heart and regenerates. The Bible calls it being "born again" (John 3:7).

Furthermore, Spurgeon was convinced the Holy Spirit lives within regenerate believers to fill them to overflowing with His presence, thus empowering them for service. In a sermon, he said:

> What cannot the Spirit of God do? He sent tongues of fire at Pentecost . . . and men of every nation heard the Gospel at once. He turned three thousand hearts by one sermon to know the crucified Savior to be the Messiah. He sent the apostles like flames of fire through the whole earth, till every nation felt their power. [75]

Spurgeon also saw the work of the Holy Spirit as the One who creates and sustains revivals. He realized great results always accrue when the Spirit falls in awakening power. He said in a letter dated June 13, 1887, during the dynamics of the Down Grade Controversy: "If the Holy Spirit will visit our churches with a revival what great results will follow." Spurgeon apparently realized that the final answer to the Down Grade Controversy would be realized only as the Spirit revived the work.

Not only does the Holy Spirit regenerate, revive and indwell Christians and empower them for service, the Holy Spirit, as His name implies, creates holiness in the life of the believer. The biblical concept of sanctification stood as a most important theme for Spurgeon, not just doctrinally, but practically. Spurgeon saw sanctification as a vital experience. He constantly proclaimed it. One of his biographers, Ernest W. Bacon, states:

> Sanctification to him was a three-fold work of Father, Son, and Holy Spirit, which began in regeneration and went on as a continuing and ever-deepening process throughout life, making a believer more godly and Christlike until his entrance into Heaven. [76]

Spurgeon was well aware of the fact that human effort accomplishes nothing, only the Holy Spirit can effect sanctification in the believer. By His constant and renewing work alone does the believer become Christlike.

Spurgeon also saw the Holy Spirit's inner work as vital and essential for all facets of Christian service. He said:

> Miracles of grace must be the seal of our ministries; who can bestow them but the Spirit of God? Convert a soul without the Spirit of God! Why, you cannot even make a fly, much less create a new heart and a right spirit . . . our ends can never be gained if we miss the cooperation of the Spirit of the Lord.[77]

If one ever aspires to win people to Christ, Spurgeon argued, it will come about only because of the work of the Holy Spirit. The Holy Spirit, guiding, directing and empowering the Christian, uses the believer as the divine instrument to fulfill the commission of Christ. Empowering the believer for winning souls, He leads them to lost people and then gives them wisdom to communicate the truth of Christ. Simply put, no one can preach, testify, witness, or engage in any aspect of Christian ministry until he becomes empowered and directed by the Holy Spirit of God. Spurgeon's pneumatology had all its doctrinal roots in the Bible and took on the cast of a very pragmatic and existentially oriented truth. The doctrine of the personal involvement of the believer with the Holy Spirit leads to the biblical teaching on angels.

THE ANGELOLOGY OF SPURGEON

Most nineteenth century Christians had not succumbed to pure rationalistic reasoning, as have some contemporary believers. Thus to believe in the reality and ministry of angels was common. The idea of angels boggles the minds of many today. Even the contemporaries who do believe in the reality and ministry of angels, lay little stress or importance on the theme. This was not true of Victorian Evangelical believers, especially Spurgeon. He said:

> I have more angelology in me than most people. I know my imagination sometimes has been so powerful that I could almost, when I have been alone at night, fancy I saw an angel fly by me, and hear the horse hoofs of the cherubim as they dashed along the stony road when I have been out preaching the word.[78]

Spurgeon held to a traditional evangelical view of angels. He saw them as heavenly messengers who had the privilege of serving and worshiping the God of all creation in His very presence. They abide in an intimate and holy relationship with God. They are His direct creation and fulfill the divine purpose perfectly. They are certainly not people. Hebrews 2:22, 23 clearly states that in the eternal realm, "there is an innumerable host of angels" who are distinct from the "spirits of just man made perfect." They are different from human beings in that they are not corporal but individually created spiritual beings. Therefore, they do not fall under the general category of "race." They neither marry nor are given in marriage. They possess superhuman intelligence, are not limited by time or space, although as creations they are limited by God. Yet, their power and might far transcends that of mankind. Moreover, there seem to be ranks among the angels. The cherubim and the seraphim, for example, appear to be more exalted than other angels. Also, Gabriel and Michael are presented in the Bible as "Archangels." Michael means "the mighty one." Gabriel is particularly seen as a special messenger, a carrier of God's great messages. They have a very exalted position. But all heavenly beings serve God and worship Him in perfect holiness. Spurgeon said, "The seraphim may furnish us with a pattern for Christian service; as the throne of God becomes the impulse of the service." [79]

Spurgeon seemed most interested in the "commission" of angels. The Bible says God commissions His angels to guard His people, those who believe in Jesus. Spurgeon definitely believed in guardian angels. In a sermon, he stated:

> We have each of us a guardian angel to attend us; and if there be any meaning in the passage, 'in heaven there are angels who always behold the face of my father which is in heaven,' it means that every person has a guardian spirit, and every Christian has some angel who flies about him, and holds the shield of God over his brow; keeps his feet, lest he should dash it against the stones; guards him, controls him, manages him; injects thoughts, restrains evil desires, and is the minister and servant of the Holy Ghost to keep us from sin, and lead us to righteousness. [80]

Not only do God's angels bring messages and watch over God's people, they minister in the moment of death and convey the spirits of the redeemed into the presence of Christ. For Spurgeon, the biblical concept of angels and their ministry for the people of God should be grasped for one's consolation and strength. He declared:

> Perhaps in mid-air at this moment there may be battles between the bright spirits of God and the spirits of evil. Perhaps full often, when Satan might tempt, there comes against him a mighty squadron of cherubim and seraphim to drive him back . . . If God has charged his angels to protect and save his people from all harm, depend upon that they are secure. [81]

Thus, for Spurgeon, angels formed a vital part of the Christian experience. And though few sermons are preached on this theme today, the Bible has much to say, and that moved Spurgeon to declare those truths.

SATANOLOGY AND DEMONOLOGY

Spurgeon believed the Scriptures also clearly teach that a host of angels fell into sin and were cast from heaven. This precipitates the doctrine of demonology. The Bible abounds in this concept also. Again, Spurgeon held traditionally orthodox views. Satan, a created being, had a personality and a very exalted position in God's hierarchy. Although he was originally an angel of light and served in the presence of God, he fell from that lofty state.

When he did, he took a host of angels with him. Spurgeon said, "We doubt not, from certain hints in scripture, that he (Satan) occupied a high place in the hierarchy of angels before he fell; and we know that these mighty beings are endowed with vast intellectual power, far surpassing any that have ever been given to beings of human mold." [82] The Scriptures declare that Satan's fall came about because of his attempt to exalt himself above God. Simply put, he fell through pride.

It is unknown when Satan fell, but when he did, many fell with him. He organized a kingdom and hierarchy of his own that has set itself up opposing the Kingdom of God. As the "Adversary," he works as "the accuser of the brethren" (Revelation 12:10), "man's adversary" (1 Peter 5:8), and as a "roaring lion walking about seeking whom he may devour" (1 Peter 5:8). Spurgeon well knew how the spiritual battle goes on. He said concerning Satan:

> From the day on which he was expelled from heaven, and dragged with him a third part of the stars of glory, he has been God's bitterest foe; and . . . man, from the hour in which it was said, 'the seed of the woman shall bruise the serpent's head.' [83]

Satan, the father of all lies and the sower of discord among the brethren, is the "wicked one" who would bring God's people to ruination.

Not only is Satan the foe of all that God attempts to do in and through His people, but he blinds the minds of those who believe not lest the light of the Gospel of Christ should shine unto them (1 Corinthians 4:4). Satan attempts to keep people in the bondage of sin and blindness that they might not come to faith in Jesus Christ. In this regard, Spurgeon preached:

> Is it not a shocking thought that if I am living in sin, then I am the bondslave of Satan, and I am doing his work for him? If the devil be in the heart the whole life will be more or less tainted by the presence of that archenemy of God and man. Do not laugh at sin, then; do not dare to trifle with it, for it is dangerous and deadly, because it is of the devil. [84]

The primary work of Satan is to keep the unsaved deceived that they cannot or will not come to Christ as Savior.

Furthermore, Satan, though he knows the truth of God, constantly attempts to pervert God's divine revelation and by the use of that means, keep people from a grasp of spiritual realities. In this respect, Spurgeon said:

> The devil is very sound in the divinity . . . I believe him to be one of the most orthodox individuals in creation. Other people may disbelieve the doctrines of revelation, but the devil cannot, for he knows the truth, and though his will belies it often, he is so crafty that he understands that with the soul convinced of sin, his best method is not to contradict the truth but to pervert it. [85]

(1) The devil continually wars against the truth; hence, against the people of God as they attempt to disseminate the truth.

① Perhaps via the "core sin" in each of us: getting us to believe that GOD is not WHO HE says HE is.

Though Spurgeon said much about Satan, he seemingly said little about the work of demons and their possession of people's minds and bodies. About all he said was, "We never see anything of satanic possession now-adays . . . but . . . still amazing is the power of sin over man." Perhaps Spurgeon was a victim of the nineteenth century where demonology had not yet taken on that particular flavor, though the Bible is full of it. Unfortunately, Spurgeon was rather weak on this issue.

THE CORE

But now we must address the basic theological proposition raised earlier, namely, the five distinctive doctrines of grace. This Calvinistic perspective, as we have so often seen, became something of the core of Spurgeon's theology. As a case in point, when the new Metropolitan Tabernacle opened on Thursday the eleventh of April, 1861, five different ministers preached on the five great themes of the doctrines of grace: human depravity, election, particular redemption, effectual calling, and final perseverance. Spurgeon's purpose in opening the Tabernacle with this series, according to his own words, was to set forth:

> Those things which are verily received among us, and especially those great points which have been so often attacked, but which are still upheld and maintained, truths which we have proved in our own experience to be full of grace and truth. [86]

Spurgeon stood fully committed to these doctrines. But it should be noted he did not demand that everyone assent to all points as a necessary prerequisite for the experience of redemption itself. He certainly believed that Arminians could embrace their essential, contrary views and still have a genuine experience of Christ; yet, he did believe that his cherished Calvinism was true and that "with all courage and fervency of spirit, believing that we are doing God's work and hold up a most important truth." [87] He declared that the doctrines of grace contained the heart and essence of the proclamation of the Gospel. Spurgeon held these views throughout the entirety of his life and ministry. In a letter to *The Freeman*, along with six other ministers, he wrote:

> Those doctrines are dear to us as epitomizing and concentrating the theology of the Bible, as constituting, through the presence and power of the Christian Comforter, the spiritual life of our churches. [88]

But, as often stated, Spurgeon saw no conflict between these doctrines and the plea of salvation. Actually, when he declared the plan of salvation, he often did it in the terms of these doctrines of grace. He had become convinced that "if people begin to study their Bibles, . . . they must invariably, if believers, rise up to rejoice in the doctrines of grace." [89] Quite obviously, here lay the foundation of this basic theology. The five points of the Synod of Dort is where Spurgeon hung much of his thought.

Yet, one must not charge Spurgeon with being so committed to the Calvinistic system that he became a rote repeater of the doctrines. To the contrary; he actually said, "Many make theology into a kind of treadwheel, consisting of five doctrines, which are everlasting repeated, for they never go to anything else."[90] He declared, "We care far more for the central evangelical truths than we do for Calvinism as a system."[91] He went on to say, "Truth is no more to be contained in one rigid system than the ocean in a shell."[92] Yet, paradoxically—if not in contradiction—he said earlier, "Calvinism *is* the gospel."[93] He did seem to mature from his earlier statements, for although the five-point system of Calvinism formed a major part of Spurgeon's theology, he became far too broad and flexible for that system to hem him in. Yet, it does present an outline upon which we can pin a large measure of his basic doctrinal positions.

THE DOCTRINES OF GRACE

The doctrines of grace center essentially in the covenant idea. These doctrines also imply the Christian view of humanity, anthropology, and Christology. The system is best approached in the traditional fashion, beginning with the doctrine of human depravity and sin.

Total Depravity

As has been previously seen, Spurgeon stood adamantly opposed to the Darwinian view of natural evolution. He lectured against it and his sermons reflected the same. For Spurgeon, man and woman was the crown of God's *creation*, thus he could never embrace any naturalistic approach in his anthropology. Spurgeon believed that the Holy Spirit had clearly revealed "that God created the first man, Adam, after his image and in His likeness, an upright, holy, and innocent creature."[94] Adam was thus a direct creative act of God, not evolved by nature, chance, or some impersonal power. God created, it did not "just happen." Spurgeon's anthropology emerged out of his Reformed presuppositions.

Spurgeon's emphasis that humanity has been created in the image of God means that God imparted to the human family, however limited, reason, will, dominion, emotions, and above all, the ability to live in fellowship with God. For Spurgeon, all these time-honored truths were central.

But Adam and Eve fell into sin. Though they lived in perfect fellowship with God in the garden of Eden, they disobeyed God. Spurgeon saw Adam and Eve as distinct, individual, historical personalities. He accepted the full historicity of the Genesis account of creation and the fall; he believed in the historicity of all of Genesis. He adamantly refused to "demythologize" the account. Theories such as the Wellhausen concept and the advent of "new thought" that denied the historicity, especially of Genesis 1-11, did not impress Spurgeon in the least. To the contrary, he scorned it. For Spurgeon, there was a genuine, historic Adam and Eve, a genuine temptation by a real Satan that took place in a literal garden of Eden. From the happy state, God's crowning creation fell into sin, and God expelled them from the garden as a judgment for their rebellion. He forthrightly preached:

> Think of the havoc which the tyrant, sin, has made of our natural estate and heritage. Eden is withered; its very sight is forgotten. Our restfulness among the trees of the field, freely yielding their fruit and God hath said, 'In the sweat of thy face shalt thou eat bread.' The field we till has lost its spontaneous yield of corn: 'thorns also and thistles shalt it bring forth to thee.' Our life has lost its glory and immortality; for, 'dust thou art, and unto dust shalt thou return.' Every woman in her pangs of travail, every man in his weariness of labor, and all of us together in the grief of death, see what sin has done for us as to our mortal bodies. Alas, it has gone deeper; it has ruined our souls, sin has unmanned man. The crown and glory of his manhood has been thrown to the ground. All our faculties are out of gear. All our tendencies are perverted. [95]

The tragic fall of Adam and Eve brought upon their entire posterity a bent to sin and evil, expressed as a "total depravity." The whole race is now corrupt, totally depraved. Spurgeon believed people must be brought to see the truth of sin and corruption, for, as he said, "Ignorance of self is ignorance of God." [96] Sin manifests itself in several ways in human life. The actual words that are used in the Scriptures typify that fact. The word "transgression" is often used in the Bible. For Spurgeon, transgression meant to break the law of God. He said, "transgression of the law of God" is sin. [97] Sin is simply disobedience to the clearly revealed will of God, the willful deliberate resistance of a person to the authority and lordship of Christ in one's life. This not only happened in Adam and Eve's experience in the garden of Eden, because of the depravity of the human heart since that moment in time, it becomes the experience of all. Further, Spurgeon knew that the word often used in the New Testament to typify sin simply means "missing the mark." Humanity in its depravity can never measure up to the moral standards God demands. Only one man ever accomplished that, the Lord Jesus Christ. Sin is iniquity that prefers the fulfilling of one's desires in one's own way rather than in God's way. This "misses the mark."

But from where did sin arise? This throws one back upon the "fall" and the resultant depravity. Spurgeon said:

> Until I know how much all my powers are debased and depraved, how thoroughly my will is perverted, and my judgment turned from its right channel, how really and essentially vicious my nature has become, it cannot be possible for me to know the whole extent of my guilt. . . . The fact is, that man is a

reeking mass of corruption. His whole soul is by nature so debased and so depraved that no description which can be given of him even by inspired tongues can fully tell how base and vile a thing he is. [98]

This may seem strange language to the contemporary ear, but to Spurgeon, of the Puritan ilk, sin becomes exceedingly sinful. Yet at the same time, it must be granted that the Bible addresses the subject on that basis. Spurgeon, when criticized for his theology, would point to the *Baptist Confession of Faith of 1689*. He wrote a preface to a new edition of the confession. On the depravity issue, the *Confession* reads:

> Although God created man upright and perfect, and gave him a righteous law, which had been unto life had he kept it, and threatened death upon the breach of it, yet he did not long abide in this honor; Satan used the subtlety of the serpent to subdue Eve, then by her seducing Adam, who, without any compulsion did willfully transgress the law of their Creation and the command given unto them, in eating the forbidden fruit, which God was pleased, according to his wise and holy communion, having purposed to order it to his own glory.
>
> Our first parents, by this end, fell from their original righteousness and communion with God, and we in them, whereby death came upon all: All becoming dead in sin, and wholly defiled in the faculties and parts of body and soul.

With all this, Spurgeon fully agreed. Furthermore, sin and depravity are universal. Spurgeon said, "All men have evil hearts; albeit their hearts may not be equal inclined to the coarser vices in which some indulge, yet there is in every sinner, the black spot of alienation from God, forgetfulness of God, love of sin and dislike to God when he is thoroughly known." [99] He believed that all humankind, none excepted, had fallen, although "men did not fall separately and individually;" [100] rather, "all of us fell without our own consent, without having, in fact, any finger in it. Actually we fell federally in our covenant head, that head being Adam." [101]

There were, of course, those who objected to Spurgeon's view of the federal headship of Adam. Their argument stated that this could not be just. Spurgeon's reply, as could well be expected, centered on his typical approach, "If God sees the justice of it, you ought to be content with it." [102]

Spurgeon said several things about human depravity. First, he declared that human depravity is natural depravity. People are lost from the beginning. Moreover, he declared that human depravity is total in every aspect. He said, "there is no good thing in an unconverted man." [103] All this does not imply that people were not responsible or accountable for their sin. Everyone stood accountable for every sin they ever committed. He said:

> In Adam's sin, you did not sin personally, for you were not then in existence; yet you fell; neither can you now complain thereof, for you have willingly endorsed and adopted Adam's sin by committing personal transgressions. You

have laid down your hand, as it were, upon Adam's sin, and made it your own, by committing personal and actual sin. Thus you perished by the sin of another, which you adopted and endorsed. [104]

Obviously, Spurgeon held to both original sin and to actual sins committed by real sinners. Sin formed the basis for God's judgment and damnation; human depravity extends that far.

Let it be stressed again that this does not mean that human will is totally dead and plays no part in salvation. Spurgeon fully acknowledged, on the basis of Scripture, that people genuinely have a free will. He fully believed in the free agency of the human experience. He said, "The work of the Spirit, which is the effect of the will of God, is to change the human will, and so to make men willing in the day of God's power." [105] Spurgeon believed that human will plays a vital role in salvation; therefore, people are fully responsible to come to Christ as the Spirit of God speaks to them. He held that human responsibility in the light of the sovereignty of God was actually a moral matter. He once stated, "every time when a sinner cannot, the real reason is that he will not. All the cannots in the Bible about spiritual inability are tantamount to will nots." [106] But he always balanced this off by explicitly stating human ability to come to Christ by one's own power without divine aid is impossible. He said, "There is spiritual powerlessness to come to Christ." [107]

Yet, it must be granted that in Spurgeon's preaching, he gave far more emphasis to moral inability than to natural inability. Hence he called people to faith in Christ with all the fervency of a Wesleyan. With the hyper-Calvinists after him on one side and the Arminians on the other, he walked down the middle, and when accosted with the issue, simply replied that he did not try to reconcile friends. He said, "They are two truths of holy Scripture, and we leave them to reconcile themselves, they are friends, and friends do not need any reconciliation." [108] And he fearlessly preached it. Murray stated, "Spurgeon took these two truths, man's duty to believe, and his sinful inability to do so, and used them like the two jaws of a vice to grip the sinner's conscience." [109] Although he was a committed Calvinist, he could say, "I am a thorough Calvinist but I am not one of a school. I am free to preach all God's Word and am bound to no set form of man's invention." [110]

Now what is the result of this dire, depraved human situation? In answer Spurgeon declared, "In the blacklist of the unregenerate there is no exception to their condemnation." [111] What is this condemnation? Separation from God, which is the epitome of judgment. That is the essence of hell, that is the core of God's judgment, that is the ruination of all humanity. "The wages of sin is death" (Romans 6:23). What is the answer to this dire situation? God elects to save and forgive His own. The sacrificial sufferings of Jesus Christ comprise the heart of the truth to be proclaimed.

Divine Election

Divine Election served as a prominent part in preaching the Gospel for Charles Haddon Spurgeon. He saw it as God's way to redeem fallen, depraved people. He believed God reached down to certain people in their sin and chose them for redemption. This is their only hope for forgiveness and eternal life. Moreover, he contended that the doctrine of election should not only be proclaimed, but should be proclaimed fearlessly and unapologetically because it stands as the truth of God. He saw it as emerging from the Scriptures; therefore, it had a very practical positive value for evangelism and Christian living. There were several elements that made up Spurgeon's understanding of the doctrine of predestination and election.

In the first place, Spurgeon believed, as did all Reformed thinkers, that election was unconditional and absolute. He stated, "Whatever may be God's reason for choosing a man, certainly it is not because of any good thing in that man." [112] Persons did not become a recipient of God's electing grace to eternal life because they had exercised good works or any other human activity. They were elected because God chose to elect them to salvation. When Spurgeon was asked the question, why did God choose just certain ones, he simply replied, "the only answer that can possibly be given is this: God wills to do it." [113] Moreover, Spurgeon clearly taught and held that election was eternal. Election came before the foundations of the world. He put it this way: "Before sun and moon had been created, or any of the visible things were formed, God had set his heart upon his people in Christ and ordained them to eternal life in Him." [114] Spurgeon not only believed that God's election preceded all time, it would stand everlastingly to the end of time. He said, "If we be chosen of God and precious, then we are chosen forever." [115] Another important point in Spurgeon's doctrine of election centered in his contention that God's sovereign choice is personal. A doctrine circulating in the nineteenth century, not to mention succeeding generations, held that election really meant that God chose nations, not individuals. This Spurgeon completely and thoroughly rejected as nothing more than subterfuge attempting to take the sting out of the doctrine. He held that God determined who and the exact number of individuals that would be saved. He declared, "They shall be a number certain and fixed, which shall neither be diminished nor increased, but shall abide the same according to his purpose and will." [116]

In the fourth place, Spurgeon's view of election did not move him to believe in reprobation. That is to say, he did not believe that God elected and predestined people for eternal hell. He was accused of this, but he always vehemently denied it. He called it "the wicked and horrible doctrine of sovereign and unmerited reprobation." [117] He did not believe the idea had any scriptural basis. He saw it as impugning the character of God. He forthrightly declared:

Salvation is of God . . . damnation is of man. If any of you are damned, you will have no one to blame but yourself; if any of you perish, the blame will not lie at God's door; if you are lost and cast away, you will have to bear all the blame and all the tortures of conscience yourself . . . remember, if you are saved, you must be saved by God alone, though if lost, you have lost yourselves.[118]

This stance put Spurgeon in a paradox if not a dilemma. He was castigated as being self-contradictory and his position totally irreconcilable. Spurgeon's answer, however, was stated very clearly. He said:

That God predestines, and that man is responsible, are two things that few can see. They are believed to be inconsistent and contradictory; but they are not. It is just the fault of our weak judgment. Two truths cannot be contradictory to each other. If, then, I find taught in one place that everything is fore-ordained, *that is true*; and if I find in another place that man is responsible for all his actions, *that is true*; and it is my folly that leads me to imagine that two truths can ever contradict each other. These two truths, I do not believe, can ever be welded into one upon any human anvil, but one they shall be in eternity: they are two lines that are so nearly parallel, that the mind that shall pursue them farthest, will never discover that they converge; but they do converge, and they will meet somewhere in eternity, close to the throne of God, whence all truth doth spring.[119]

That settled the issue for Spurgeon. He refused to attempt to reconcile the issue that if some are elected to salvation and cannot be saved unless they are elected, the rest are by innuendo "automatically" doomed to perdition. Spurgeon never attempted a rationalistic scheme to reconcile all paradoxes or anomalies. He would not give in to the hyper-Calvinists who believed in reprobation nor to the Arminians who refused to accept the concept of divine election.

It has been made clear and should be emphasized again that Spurgeon certainly did not believe that the concept of election should ever preclude one from extending a genuine and universal invitation to Christ. Spurgeon fully believed in the doctrine of election but also that Gospel invitations should be urged upon people. His whole ministry spoke of that approach. He said, they are "equally precious portions of one harmonious whole."[120] He said so often, "I believe both free agency and predestination to be facts, how they may be made to agree I do not know or care to know; I am satisfied with anything God chooses to reveal to me, and equally content not to know what He does not reveal."[121] So, he stayed in the tension of his theological determinism and his loving appeal of the Gospel, just like his Puritan idols. Was he justified in so doing? The only human rationale to be brought to Spurgeon's stance centers in the basic fact that, as seen, he was essentially a biblical preacher, and he believed the Bible taught both truths, so he preached it unapologetically and did not attempt to rationalize the quandary. To deny one side of the equation was to deny a portion of the Scriptures. This he would never do. So, he just preached the Word as he found it. As previously stated, he is reported to pray for the salvation of the elect, and then ask God to elect more. [122] A man who would pray like that could hardly be charged with hyper-Calvinism.

In the sixth place, Spurgeon believed that the doctrine of election provided real hope for people. Of course, he knew the doctrine of election, when declared incorrectly, could become an impediment to people coming to Christ. But on the other hand, he believed that the doctrine could be presented in such a way, in a positive manner, that would actually bring people to faith in Christ. He preached:

> But I say, take courage, take hope, O thou sinner, that there is election. So far from dispiriting and discouraging thee, it is a very hopeful and joyous thing that there is an election. What if I told thee perhaps none can be saved, none are ordained to eternal life; wouldst thou not tremble and fold thy hands in hopelessness, and say, 'Then how can I be saved, since none are elect?' But, I say, there is a multitude elect, beyond all counting—a host that no mortal can number. Therefore, take heart, thou poor sinner! Cast away thy despondency—mayest thou not be elect as well as any other? for there is a host innumerable chosen. There is joy and comfort for thee. [123]

He would urge unbelievers not to ask, "Am I one of the elect?" He would simply say that if anyone felt concern about their relationship to Christ, they should repent and believe in the Lord Jesus Christ and they would be saved. That would obviously occur if they were one of the elect. In Spurgeon's approach to the preaching of the Gospel, election should never be "a barrier against any sincere seeker of the Savior." [124] If a person were sincerely seeking Christ, and were willing to repent and believe, and would do so, they need not fear of failing to be one of the elect.

Spurgeon's last salient point in the doctrine of election declared that it gives confidence to the proclaimers of the Gospel. He argued that when one preached the Gospel, he could be confident that God would call the elect to salvation. He said, "so we cannot labor in vain, we must have some; the covenant renders that secure." [125] Spurgeon obviously believed wholeheartedly in the doctrine of election, yet in a wholesome, positive fashion that made him a most effective evangelist.

Particular Redemption

Here Spurgeon gets to the real core of his Christological preaching. Particular Redemption centers on the atonement effected by the Lord Jesus Christ. The work of Christ in His life, death and resurrection Spurgeon declared as "of past decrees and of future glories, this is the pivot." [126] He was thoroughly convinced that "the doctrine of the precious blood, when it gets into the heart, drives error out of it and sets up the throne of truth." [127] Thus the doctrine of atonement became the very heart of his preaching.

Spurgeon's doctrine of the atonement rested upon several presuppositions. In the first place, Spurgeon firmly believed that the atonement was absolutely necessary because of the nature and character of God. God is sovereign and He does exactly as he pleases, and He was pleased to redeem depraved humanity. Furthermore, God is infinite and inflexible in justice. He said, "When his subjects rebel, God (marks) their crime and never forgets them until he has punished it, either upon them, or by their substitute." [128] Thirdly, though God is just and must punish sin, He is infinite in love and mercy. God should never be thought of as merely being severe in justice and no more; He also must be understood as loving. Moreover, these divine attributes of sovereignty, justice, and love, are perfectly harmonized in the God whom Christians worship. Also, however, Spurgeon saw clearly the divine dilemma in the human situation. When a person who has sinned against God is brought before the bar of God's eternal judgment, "God is gracious, and he desires to save him. God is just, and he must punish him . . . how will the two conflicting attributes work in God's mind?" [129] Spurgeon knew the answer. He grasped fully the wonderful mystery of the atonement. Jesus Christ would be the *Substitute*. He would die, suffer judgment, in the place of sinners, and the justice of God would thus be satisfied. Spurgeon pictured Jesus Christ, the divine Substitute as praying to the Father:

> My Father, on my part, I covenant that in the fullness of time I will become man. I will take upon myself form and nature of the fallen race . . . in due time I will bear the sins of all my people. Thou shalt exact their debts on me; the chastisement of their peace will I endure, and by my stripes they shall be healed. [130]

In God's great grace, infinite wisdom, and sovereign power, He devised the scheme of letting the punishment of human sin fall upon His own Son. Sin had to be punished. Spurgeon said, "That sin intrinsically and in itself demands and deserves the just anger of God, and that anger should be displayed in the form of punishment." [131] Timothy McCoy in his excellent analysis of the soteriology of Spurgeon put it this way:

> Spurgeon argued for its validity on at least three grounds. First, he contended that virtually every conscience, certainly awakened ones, would endorse the assertion that 'virtue deserves reward, and sin deserves punishment.' Second, he believed that the biblical witness was unambiguous: 'The soul that sinneth, it shall die' (Ezek. 18:4, 20). Third, he maintained that 'the necessities of moral government require that sin must be punished.' Supported by these arguments, therefore, Spurgeon's 'basic postulate' was 'that punishment is the pure reaction of a holy God toward sin, that is neither capricious, arbitrary nor unjust.' [132]

Finally, Spurgeon argued that the cross represented more than just a mere display of the justice of God. This "display" approach to the atonement was something of Charles Finney's view, and perhaps accounts for some of the reasons why Spurgeon was always rather resistant toward Finney's theological position. Spurgeon declared, "Jesus Christ did not die to make God loving, but he died because God was loving. The cross was not just a display of the justice of God. It was God actually punishing Christ for the sins of others, and that was a manifestation of infinite grace and love." One further aspect of the sacrificial atonement of Christ must be noted: Spurgeon's view of the covenant concept. This will be discussed shortly.

Thus for Spurgeon the two key words in the atonement are "substitution" and "satisfaction." Christ, who knew no sin, took upon himself the sin of fallen humanity and as their great Substitute endured the judgment and justice of God. Spurgeon said:

> I believe in an atonement in which Christ literally took the sin of his people, and for those endured the wrath of God, giving to justice *quid pro quo* for all that was due to it, or an equivalent for it: bearing, that we might not bear, the wrath that was due to us. [133]

Here the key idea is imputation. God actually transferred the sins of the elect to Christ as he died for their sins. The cross became far more than just a physical death, as terrible as that was. As pointed out in the chapter on Spurgeon's preaching, he saw Jesus suffering the actual judgment of God. The cry of dereliction, "My God, My God, Why hast thou forsaken me?" (Matthew 27:46) was a cry of spiritual agony as God heaped the judgment of hell upon His Son. And in the judgment of God for sin that Christ endured for the sins of the world, the justice of God was met and was totally *satisfied*. The atonement was effected. God's justice was satisfied. That became the core of the atonement; and that became the core of Spurgeon's theology. He said, "I have always considered, with Luther and Calvin, that the sum and substance of the gospel lies in that word substitution—Christ standing in instead of man." [134] He said:

> Christ did really, literally and truly, take the sins that belonged to all who do believe on him, and those sins did actually and in very deed become his sins; (not that he had committed them, except through the imputation to which he had consented, and for which he came into the world,) and there lay the sins of all his people upon Christ's shoulders. [135]

Christ has thus become God's answer to sin and human depravity. This God-man, this incarnate deity, this One altogether lovely, has become in Himself the redemption so desperately needed. Spurgeon said that humanity can only be "restored by another representative; so, in the infinite wisdom and mercy of God there came into the world the second Adam, man, really man, though much more than man, for He was also God, and He offered the atonement for the offense committed against the law, such an atonement that whosoever believeth in Him hath His sins forever put away. Thus we rise in the same manner as we fell, only in a very different Person. We fell in the first Adam; we rise in the second Adam; we fell, in the first Adam, through no fault of our own; we rise, in the second Adam, through no merit of our own; it is of the free grace of God that we are received back into his favor." [136] Jesus, as Spurgeon said, "seemed to be the sun that never had a setting, always shining, always progressing in His mighty course." [137] He lived the perfect life, but he came primarily not to live, but to die for the Adamic race. As the Messiah, Jesus said, "The Spirit of the Lord is upon me, because He anointed me to preach the gospel to the poor. He has sent me to proclaim release to the captives, and recovery of sight to the blind, to set free those who are downtrodden, to proclaim the favorable year of the Lord" (Luke 4:18-19). He essentially came into the world to die for Adam's fallen posterity and thus become the head of the new race. This is what affects the covenant relationship between God and sinners. This is imputed righteousness. There Spurgeon stood unswervingly. He said:

> It was necessary that we should not merely be washed from sin—for that would leave us naked—but that we should be clothed in righteousness. . . . His (Christ's) resurrection has brought to light our righteousness and clothed us with it; so that at this moment every man that believeth in a risen Saviour is robed in the regal robes of the righteousness of God. [138]

Because of the substitutionary work of Christ in the atonement, God was "satisfied" and now the believer has the righteousness of Jesus Christ Himself imputed to the believing heart.

To this basic substitutionary view of the atonement, Spurgeon tenaciously clung. He said, "I do not conceive 'substitution' to be an exploration of the Atonement, but to be of the very essence of it." [139] Creeping into the evangelical scene at that time were other theories of atonement, known as the governmental theory, the moral influence theory, etc. But Spurgeon would not move from the penal substitution view of the atonement. For that view he vociferously fought, especially in the Down Grade Controversy. He said he believed that substitution must be proclaimed as the central truth of Christ's atonement.

One final question needs to be raised concerning Spurgeon's view of the atonement, namely, for whom did Christ die? Did he die for the whole world, or for the elect alone? Spurgeon, again, held very emphatic ideas about this doctrine, once more taking the traditional Reformed view. He asserted, "As for the work of our Lord Jesus, you and I believe in the special substitution of Christ for his elect; what we call 'particular redemption' is held most firmly by us." [140] He stated, "Jesus paid the dreadful debt of all his elect." [141] Throughout his ministry Spurgeon consistently maintained that Jesus did not die for the sins of the whole world to secure the salvation of all, but He died to secure the salvation only of the elect.

At the same time, again rather paradoxically, it should be recognized that Spurgeon, at least in some sense, did affirm a general or universal dimension to the atonement. He did believe that the merits of Christ's sacrifice were infinite. He contended that if God had willed it, Christ's death would be sufficient "to have saved not only all this world, but ten thousand worlds." [142]

Not only that, Spurgeon held that because of the life, death and resurrection of the incarnate Christ, He has authority over all creation. Due to Christ's universal mediatorial power, everyone is in the position to come to Him if they will but believe. This further meant for Spurgeon that everyone should hear the Gospel, that it should be fully proclaimed to all people by the Church and that everyone should heed. In Spurgeon's view, the universal command to repent and believe is grounded in the work of Christ on the cross.

Finally, the atonement in some sense affected the entire created order. As Paul put it, "The whole creation groans and travails waiting . . . " (Romans 8:22). This does not mean that every person will be redeemed. But it does mean that Christ shall one day reign supreme on earth. Therefore, in some generalized sense, the atonement brings blessings upon all peoples. For Spurgeon, what Christ wrought defies description.

Effectual Calling

Spurgeon, once more following the edicts of the Synod of Dort, believed that a general call should be extended to all, but it would prove effectual only for the elect. A universal invitation must be extended to every person through the preaching of the Gospel; however, it will only be effectual for those whom God has chosen. He believed that the call of Christ to every person comes with such power that if a person chooses not to obey, "He shall be without excuse in the day of judgment." [143] But when the call comes to those who are the elect and chosen of God, it comes so effectually they will hear, they will heed, they will respond, and they will be saved. The Holy Spirit changes their wills, and though they with their own volition repent and believe, they do so because they are the elect of God and have been moved upon by the Holy Spirit by the effectual call of the Gospel.

This, of course, raises the question why one should give a general call at all? Spurgeon presented a twofold reply. In the first place, he said, the general call is the only call which the preacher can give. He does not know who the elect are. The inner effective call is solely the work of the Holy Spirit. In the second place, the effectual call comes in the context of the general call. God calls His elect in that setting, thus the preacher stands responsible for giving the general call to all. Though the general call is not efficacious in itself, in the declaration of the Gospel, the Holy Spirit will take the truth and bring the elect to faith in Christ.

For Spurgeon, the effectual call actually becomes a process. He said:

Whereby God secretly, in the uses of means, by the irresistible power of his Holy Spirit, calls out of mankind a certain number, whom he himself hath before elected, calling them from their sins to become righteous, from their death in trespasses and sins to become living spiritual men, and from their worldly pursuits to become the lovers of Jesus Christ. [144]

There are several implications to this effectual call. First, the effectual call is vitally related to God's eternal purpose in election. Those who are elect shall be effectually called, all of them. God shall not lose one. Furthermore, Spurgeon firmly believed that without any calling, there would simply be no salvation, and without election there is no calling. Thus the two were intrinsically connected. This is God's way of bringing to faith in Christ those whom He has chosen. He contended that, "This call is sent to the predestinated, and to them only; they by grace hear the call, obey it, and receive it." [145] This further implies that those who respond to the call may be assured that their response is the stamp of authenticity concerning their election.

Then, the effectual calling is intrinsically united to the redeeming work of Christ. These called ones are the ones for whom Christ died, and He did not die in vain. They shall surely be effectually called. God would never let the death of His Son be of no effect in people's lives.

Fourthly, as implied above, the effectual calling of God's chosen ones shall be accomplished by the grace and power of God. Spurgeon maintained that:

Every man that is saved, is always saved by an overcoming call which he cannot withstand; he may resist it for a time, but he cannot resist so as to overcome it, he *must* give way, he *must* yield when God speaks. If he says, 'Let there be light,' the impenetrable darkness gives way to light; if he says, 'Let there be grace,' unutterable sin gives way, and the hardest-hearted sinner melts before the fire of effectual calling. [146]

Of course, it was this divine sovereignty, human responsibility anomaly, referred to so often, that brought such criticism on Spurgeon. For example, C. Irving Shaw wrote in a pamphlet:

The preacher's (Spurgeon's) theology is a spiritual tyranny that wars against nature and Scripture, and usually it only allows those who believe it to speak the truth by accident and to be satisfied with a creed that has been correctly summed up by an old divine thus—
  You can, and you can't,
  You shall, and you shan't
  You will, and you won't
  You will be damned if you don't. [147]

The Christian Commonwealth, July 24, 1884, spoke of "the constancy of Calvinism and the inconsistency of Mr. Spurgeon's use of it." *The Chart and Compass* (June 1885) wrote: "Mr. Spurgeon is a perfect paradox. A preacher of Calvinism, yet the greatest Arminian of this age." One wonders if they really understood Spurgeon and his biblicism.

Spurgeon also emphasized that the doctrine of effectual calling possesses a very practical application to one's life in Christ. It was his conviction that the effectual call is essentially a holy calling. God calls people to righteousness, holiness, love and to bear the "fruit of the Spirit." Although Spurgeon stood adamant that good works do not bring salvation, they are certainly the evidence of one's effectual call and subsequent redemptive experience.

Finally, Spurgeon was convinced that the effectual call had definite implications to the doctrine of the final perseverance of the saints. He said:

> If he hath called thee, nothing can divide thee from his love. The wolf of famine cannot gnaw the bond; the fire of persecution cannot burn the link, the hammer of hell cannot break the chain; old time cannot devour it with rust, nor eternity dissolve it, with all its ages. Oh! believe that thou art secure. [148]

When one is effectually called by the grace and power of God, they will surely be kept by that same power. This leads to the last point of Spurgeon's doctrine of soteriology, final perseverance. This, of course, constituted one of the areas of real disagreement with the Arminians.

Final Perseverance

Arminian doctrine held that a person who willed to come to Christ could also will to reject Christ after coming to Him in faith. This concept Spurgeon utterly repudiated. People who have received saving faith will persevere in their faith until the end. Moreover, he did not see perseverance as a mere appendix to the Gospel, for Spurgeon it stood at the center of it. He said:

> That doctrine of the final perseverance of the saints is, I believe, as thoroughly bound up with the standing or falling of the gospel, as is the article of justification by faith. Give that up and I see no gospel left. [149]

Spurgeon gave a very prominent place to preaching on final perseverance, probably because of his own conversion experience. It will be remembered that immediately after his conversion he went back to the Primitive Methodist church where he had been converted, and when he heard the preacher declare that a person could be lost after they had been saved, everything within him rejected the doctrine. He felt in his own heart, and from his study of the Scriptures, that the perseverance of the saints could be fully justified from the Bible, as well as from experience.

What did Spurgeon actually believe about this doctrine? The first clue can be found in the fact that, in 1855, as previously seen, he reissued the *Baptist Confession of Faith*. That document reads as follows concerning the issue:

> Those whom God hath accepted in the beloved, effectually called and sanctified by his Spirit, and given the precious faith of his elect, can neither totally nor finally fall from the state of grace, but shall certainly persevere therein to the end, and be eternally saved. [150]

In simplest terms, Spurgeon believed that no one could possibly finally fall away from a *state of grace*. Spurgeon stressed it was a state of *grace*, not works. As he expressed it, "No sheep of Christ shall ever be lost. None that he has purchased with his blood, and made to be his own, shall ever wander away so as to perish at last." [151]

Spurgeon had no superficial view of the doctrine. He would have revolted against the contemporary expression: "once saved always saved," implying that one could make something of a "profession of faith" and then live any way one wished. To the contrary, Spurgeon said:

> The Scripture does not teach that a man will reach his journey's end without continuing to travel along the road; it is not true that one act of faith is all, and that nothing is needed of daily faith, prayer, and watchfulness. Our doctrine is the very opposite, namely, that the righteous shall hold on his way; or, in other words, shall continue in faith, in repentance, in prayer and under the influence of the grace of God. [152]

Spurgeon emphasized that the doctrine was the doctrine of the *perseverance* of the saints. The redeemed have the responsibility to persevere to the end. But all God's true people will do that very thing. Moreover, God's persevering people are not coerced to persevere against their will. True believing people have a will to persevere and want to serve the Christ whom they have come to know and love.

Thus Spurgeon strove to maintain the divine and the human elements that are both ingredients to perseverance. Again, an inherent tension in Spurgeon's position surfaces, but again he found this no problem. He said, "I would seek to live as if my salvation depended on myself, and then go back to my Lord, knowing that it does not depend on me in any sense at all." [153]

Spurgeon argued for this final point in the doctrines of grace from both a theological and a biblical perspective. Theologically, it stood as the logical conclusion of the doctrine of particular election. The entire Calvinistic five-point system hung together in this rationalistic manner, one implying the other and each being dependent upon the other. In that sense, Spurgeon did become a systematic theologian and relied upon his rational reasoning. But he also argued biblically for the doctrines. There are many passages of Scripture that Spurgeon felt clearly taught the perseverance of the saints. Thus he was perfectly content to preach it, and preach it with all his might. Furthermore, the doctrine of perseverance implied Christian living and a holy lifestyle. That made it vital and important.

Thus Spurgeon formulated his basic soteriology around Christology, the atonement, and the doctrines of grace. What was the purpose of God's redeeming act in Jesus Christ? The answer for Spurgeon: "the chief end of man is to glorify God and enjoy Him forever," the great Calvinistic Westminster Confession. That is where Spurgeon rested his theological case.

SPURGEON'S ESCHATOLOGY

Spurgeon confessed to be a pre-millennialist. That statement within itself perhaps speaks volumes to some. Nineteenth century premillennialists loved to get Spurgeon in their camp. *The Episcopal Recorder*, November 1, 1888, wrote: "C. H. Spurgeon (is a) . . . pronounced premillennialist." There has been a decided tendency to equate Spurgeon with the whole premillennial, dispensational system of Darby, Scofield, and others. But that cannot be sustained. He opposed Darbyism. This can be seen when he requested someone to compile fifty hymns on the return of Christ for prayer meeting. He wrote, "I do not want them very millenarian, I want *Second Advent* hymns."[154] Actually, he revolted against any rigid system. He said:

> the slave of systems I will never be; for the Lord has loosed this iron bondage from my neck, and now I am the joyful servant of the truth which maketh free. . . . offend or please . . . I will preach every truth as I learn it from the Word. . . . It is better to be silent before the Lord than to dream of supplementing what he has spoken.[155]

There are, therefore, several qualifications that need to be made concerning C. H. Spurgeon's premillennialism. As stated, he did not take a traditional dispensational approach to eschatology. He refused to spend an inordinate amount of time discussing, for example, the relationship of the rapture to the tribulation period, or like points of eschatological nuance. An elaborate dispensational chart would have little or no appeal to Spurgeon. Any dispensational framework that has a tendency to divide the Scriptures into segments, some applicable to contemporary life and some not, did not get his attention at all. He probably would have rejected any such scheme. He kept to the basics of future things.

Spurgeon also sternly opposed those who tried to predict the end of the age. He said it was "another form of fortune telling." Of course, thoughtful eschatologists of all persuasions never do this. Still, he was absolutely committed to the visible, bodily premillennial return of Christ, a literal millennial reign of Christ on earth, and the bodily resurrection of the just and unjust. Though he believed in a literal thousand-year reign of Christ on earth, he believed the lost and saved both would be resurrected *before* Christ's millennial reign. Therefore, only the regenerate will live on earth during the millennium. The millennium will then just merge into eternity. He came to this position after he was 25 years old, although earlier he did hold a more traditional pre-millennial view. As firm as he was in many areas, he did not try to dogmatize his eschatology where he felt uncertain. He said:

> The more I read the Scriptures as to the future, the less I am able to dogmatise. I see the conversion of the world, and the personal pre-millennial reign, and the sudden coming, and the judgment, and several other grand points; but I cannot put them into order, nor has anyone else done so yet. I believe every prophetical work I have ever seen (and I have read very many) to be wrong in some points. I feel more at home in preaching Christ crucified than upon any other theme, and I do believe He will draw all men unto Him. [156]

Actually, Spurgeon had a quite balanced view of the entire eschatological scene. He said:

> As often as we come across it (the second coming) in our expositions, we do not turn aside from the point, but if guilty at all on this point, it is rather in being too silent than saying too much. . . I scarcely think it would be justifiable for me to spend my time upon prophetic studies for which I have not the necessary talent, nor is it the vocation to which my Master has ordained me. [157]

In surveying Spurgeon's sermons concerning future things, five themes surface time and again: the resurrection, the second coming of Christ, judgment, hell and heaven. This formed a balanced basic eschatological approach for the London pastor.

The resurrection of the dead is the great hope of the Christian experience, Spurgeon declared. As Job asked, "If a man die, shall he live again?" (Job 14:14). To this basic query Spurgeon gave a hearty, positive *amen*. He believed absolutely in the resurrection of the dead, both of the just and the unjust. That is to say, he believed in the resurrection of the saints, and secondly in a resurrection of sinners. He stated:

> Many of you believe you will have a body in heaven, but you think it will be an airy fantastic body, instead of believing that it will be a body like this— flesh and blood (although not the same kind of flesh, for all flesh is not the same flesh,) a solid, substantial body, even such as we have here . . . but if ye were Christians as ye profess to be, ye would believe that every mortal man who has ever existed shall not only live by the immortality of his soul, but his body shall live again, that the very flesh in which he now walks the earth is as eternal as the soul, and shall exist forever. [158]

In preaching, Spurgeon would use the expression "the immortality of the soul." Whether he meant this in a Greek philosophical sense or just employed the current cliché, is difficult to discern with any precision. One thing is evident, the Bible certainly does not teach the immortality of the soul; rather it declares the resurrection of the body. Only God has immortality and dwells in the light (1 Timothy 6:16). And it appears fair to say that Spurgeon seems to make that clear in his statements about the nature of the eternal body. He probably cannot be charged with Platonism. And his view on the resurrection was predicated on the literal bodily resurrection of Jesus Christ. He had no equivocation on Christ's bodily resurrection.

This leads to the second major element of Spurgeon's eschatology, namely, the nature of the second return of Jesus Christ. He believed in the visible, bodily return of the Lord. He said:

> That same Jesus who went up from Olivet into heaven is coming again to earth in like manner as his disciples saw him go into heaven. We have his own word for it, and this makes assurance doubly sure, moreover, the great scheme of redemption requires Christ's return . . . He comes to gather his people together. He comes to glorify them with himself on the same earth where once he and they were despised and rejected of men. [159]

After the return of Christ, Spurgeon saw a general judgment of the saved and the lost. Preaching from Romans 14:10-11, he stated:

> Saints and sinners too, only on what a different footing, are all to be judged out of the books, and out of the Book of Life . . . to the saints the judgment of the things done which shall be according to righteousness, for these things shall be taken into evidence that they were indeed reconciled to God . . . so bright will be the righteousness of a saint through faith that no accuser will appear. [160]

Spurgeon argued there will be great rewards for the saints, the greatest of which is heaven itself. Although salvation is a gift and can never be merited, he believed that heaven has rewards for those who have trusted Christ. Saints will be judged in accord with their commitment to the Savior. In his sermons Spurgeon often spoke of heaven as a very definite place. He meant by this that it had a particular location and will be a literal, eternal place of blessing for the redeemed. Through the work of the glorified Christ, all the elect have a place prepared in His Father's house. Spurgeon said, "The main thought which we now have of heaven, and certainly the main fullness of it when we shall come there, is just this; we shall see Jesus." [161] Heaven awaits the saved.

The antithesis of heaven is hell. This is the place, according to Spurgeon, where the lost sinner will spend eternity. It is an eternal place, a literal abode of everlasting punishment and torment to all those who have rejected Jesus Christ. Satan and his demons will ultimately be there as well. Spurgeon often addressed the question: would a loving God send his created children to hell? As previously stated, he simply answered, God does not send them, they send themselves by their rejection of Jesus Christ.

Spurgeon preached on hell, though he took no delight in it. He considered it a dreary task, but he always laid out hope in his preaching of it. He said:

> You know . . . that while I believe in eternal punishment, and must do, or throw away my Bible, I also believe that God will give to the lost every

consideration consistent with His justice and love. There is nothing vindictive in Him, nor can there be in His punishment of the ungodly. [162]

Still, he really did not try to justify God's actions, he simply preached God's Word. The fact that some preachers of his day had seemingly forgotten the doctrine of eternal punishment concerned him. He contended that the Bible was clear on the subject and therefore it should be taught.

Simply put, Spurgeon's eschatology centered in the literal return of Christ, the resurrection of the just and the unjust, heaven for the elect, hell for those who did not know Christ, and the reign of our Lord on earth.

SPURGEON'S ECCLESIOLOGY

Spurgeon obviously had a varied ecumenical background and spirit. Being brought up in the Independent church, converted in a Primitive Methodist fellowship, then finding himself in the Baptist denomination and taking a leading role therein for the better part of his life, all precipitated a broad approach to ecclesiology. Yet, the views he did hold, he held firmly. Spurgeon visualized the Church as the culmination of the prototype found in Israel. He said:

> At first the church was indeed a little flock, a few chosen out of . . . Abram, the Syrian, ready to perish, and a few godly ones in his household. Then the stream widened a little, and they became the twelve tribes; and soon the dispensation became more clear; Moses was raised up, and Aaron, and whom God had chosen. Then the angels decided to look into the typical rights and ceremonies of that ancient dispensation. [163]

The first dispensation, the Covenant of the Law, formed the prototype of the Church. That Covenant finds its ultimate fulfillment in the New Covenant, made up of the body of all believers whose faith has been placed in Christ's saving grace. This implies Spurgeon believed in the so-called "invisible" or "universal" Church. He did, but this does not mean that Spurgeon had such a broad view of the Church that he did not have very definite doctrinal views concerning the "visible" congregations. First of all, Spurgeon did not equate the visible Church with everyone whose names appeared on a local church roll. He said concerning the visible church:

> I refer to the really elect, called and justified, which are a spiritual Church. There are to be found in the visible church in all of its sections, a people truly saved in the Lord, not a field of mingled weed and tares, but all plants of the Lord's right hand planting. [164]

Thus the Church in its fullest sense is made up of the saved of all times.

Moreover, the Church is the Church triumphant, because it has a triumphal Lord. Spurgeon clearly contended that Christ is the head of the Body and has all authority in the Church, just as He has full authority over heaven and in earth. The *Baptist Confession of Faith* states:

> The Lord Jesus Christ is the head of the church, in whom, by the appointment of the Father, all power for the calling, institution, order, or government of the church is invested in a supreme and sovereign manner. . . . In the execution of this power wherewith he has been so entrusted, the Lord Jesus calleth out of the world unto himself, through the ministry of the word, by his spirit, those that are given unto him by his father, that they may walk before him in all of the ways of obedience, which he prescribeth to them in his Word. Those thus called, he commandeth to walk together in peculiar societies, or churches, for their mutual edification, and the due performance of that public worship, which he require of them in the world. [165]

With this confession Spurgeon fully agreed, being committed to a Baptist understanding of the nature of the Body of Christ.

Who then should join a visible local church? Spurgeon spoke very clearly. He said:

> The proper persons to be added to the visible church of Christ are those who believe to the salvation of their souls who are from day to day experiencing the saving power of the name of Jesus by being delivered from sin, by being saved from the customs of the world, by being saved in the sense of sanctified from the various corruptions and lusts which rule among the sons of men . . . the Church has no right to exclude any of the saved because their knowledge or experience is not that of advanced believers. [166]

For Spurgeon, these "proper persons" have several characteristics. First, they are called and regenerated by the power of the Holy Spirit. Secondly, they have been cleansed from sin by claiming the promises of Christ for forgiveness. Thirdly, they consecrate themselves to God by being a people that belong totally to Him. They stay in communion with God and with each other. They profess Christ openly. These virtues characterize a true Christian, and only true Christians make up the true Church.

LOCAL CHURCH ORGANIZATION

Spurgeon often spoke about the organization of the local church as well as the spiritual dynamics of the local congregation. He believed that the ministry of a church was predicated upon the principle of gifted members, called out by the Holy Spirit to fulfill the ministry. He understood the biblical structure of the apostles, prophets, evangelists, pastors/teachers, as recorded in Ephesians 4:11. He was convinced that no one should ascend to the preacher/teacher role who had not definitely been set apart by God as an undershepherd of the Lord Jesus Christ. He said to his students:

We believe that the Holy Ghost appoints in the church of God some to act as overseers, while others are made willing to be watched over for their own good. All are not called to labor in word and doctrine, or to be elders, or to exercise the office of the bishop; nor should all aspire to such works, since the gifts necessary are nowhere promised to all; but those should addict themselves to such important engagements who feel, like the apostles, they have received this ministry. [167]

Spurgeon spoke interchangeably about pastors, bishops, and elders. He saw these, at least in some sense, as the same essential position. Yet, as seen, Spurgeon did have a definite office of elder in his church. He also held that the office of deacon filled a vital role in the life of a local congregation. He had many very able deacons in his church. As previously pointed out, the elders held their office for just a limited time while the deacons were elevated to that office for life. He thus fell into the rather traditional Baptist view of how churches should be structured.

Finally, Spurgeon was absolutely convinced and committed to the fact that the Church had a great mission from God. And what might that mission be? Spurgeon found the answer in Matthew 28:19-20: "Go therefore and make disciples of all the nations, baptizing them in the name of the Father and the Son and the Holy Spirit, teaching them to observe all that I commanded you; and lo, I am with you always, even to the end of the age." The mission of the Church is to extend the Kingdom of God by leading people to faith in Jesus Christ through the preaching of the Gospel and the edifying of the elect as they carry out their place in the Kingdom to fulfill God's mission worldwide.

In this Kingdom context, the ordinances of the Church were believer's baptism and the Lord's Supper. In Spurgeon's catechism he defined these ordinances. He held a traditional Baptist Theology on the subject. Spurgeon firmly taught that there were only two such ordinances for the corporate life of the church: Baptism and the Lord's Supper. As made amply clear, baptism, as Spurgeon saw it, was total immersion in water as a symbol of the death and resurrection of Jesus Christ and the believer's identification with Christ in death and resurrection. It conveys no sacramental value; it is symbolic. The Lord's Supper, or communion, is also symbolic of the Lord's passion. It has no sacramental power. Moreover, it is open to all true believers, not just one's own denomination or local church members. Spurgeon was broader in his view of the Lord's Supper than some fellow Baptists. For this he received criticism, but he held tenaciously to his convictions.

An interesting anecdote came out of Tennessee in America. In *The Tennessee Baptist*, September, 1888, someone raised the question whether Spurgeon could baptize people and serve communion in light of the fact he was not ordained. The answer came down that he could baptize new converts because the church had authorized him to do so, but it was questioned whether he could legitimately serve the Lord's Supper. Of course, those answers arose out of the Southern Baptist Landmark Movement. Further, when the Down Grade Controversy erupted and Spurgeon broke with the Baptist Union, some said he should have gone all the way and instituted "closed-communion" in the Metropolitan Tabernacle. They accused him of having a "half-way attitude." [168]

This comprised Spurgeon's essential view of the Church. It can be simply summarized by saying that he believed in the universal, invisible Church. That is, he held to the church being the body of all believers of all the saints of all ages, and in the visible church, those who truly were regenerate, the elect of God, and gathered in specific places for worship, praise, and the carrying out of the great commission. Only truly regenerate people are to be members of a local congregation and they are to be followers of the Lord in believer's baptism and observing the ordinances of baptism and the Lord's Supper. They extend the Kingdom of Christ around the world until the end of the age. And in the midst of it all the living Christ dwells. Spurgeon was an historic Baptist. But he said, "If I thought it wrong to be a Baptist, I should give it up, and become what I believe to be right." [169] He was, above all, a biblicist.

Thus we have something of the essence of the theology of Spurgeon. What can be said about it?

AN EVALUATION OF SPURGEON'S THEOLOGY

Spurgeon obviously held conservative theological views. Was he justified in his stance? Kruppa tells us he offered four reasons for the position he defended. First, he argued from his own experience of Christ. He felt that the manner in which God honored his ministry attested to the truthfulness of his theology. Secondly, Spurgeon constantly appealed to the Puritans. He saw it as the best of British thought and practical Christianity; thus to believe as they believed he considered most wise. Thirdly, Spurgeon was convinced that "modern thought" presented such a watered-down Gospel that it had no real power or appeal. Finally, he believed that the biblical faith demanded simply taking God at His word. Thus, he dogmatically preached what he felt the Bible taught. In Spurgeon's justification for his conservative views, he does seem justified. [170]

Moreover, it may also be helpful in an evaluation of Spurgeon's theology to lay aside some misconceptions concerning the man and his thought. First, Spurgeon was a Calvinist. However, there have been those who have made unjustifiable claims upon Spurgeon. Contemporary hyper-Calvinists, for example, often wish to claim him as one of their own, although in Spurgeon's own day they uniformly rejected him. For example, Spurgeon has been classified in the more high-Calvinist camp in Ian Murray's book, *The Forgotten Spurgeon*, although Murray does make some concessions to Spurgeon's rejection of hyper-Calvinism. Spurgeon held to the edicts of the Synod of Dort, as has been made obvious, but Spurgeon's Calvinism was a balanced kind. Although he stood far from the Arminian position, especially concerning particular redemption, election, and the perseverance of the saints, he did express words of appreciation for their clear preaching of Christ. Spurgeon himself confessed, "We care far more for the central evangelical truths than we do for Calvinism as a system . . . our warfare is with men who are giving up the atoning sacrifice, denying the inspiration of the holy scriptures, and casting slurs upon justification by faith. The present struggle is not a debate upon the question of Calvinism or Arminianism, but the truth of God versus the inventions of men. All who believe the gospel should unite against that 'modern thought' which is its deadly enemy."[171] The problem with writers like Ian Murray seems to be that they tend to relate Spurgeon's Calvinism to the Down Grade Controversy (to be discussed momentarily) despite Spurgeon's plain denial that this was the issue in that significant debate. Spurgeon did not think the preaching of Calvinism stood synonymous with the preaching of the Gospel. He said, "I believe most firmly in the doctrines commonly called Calvinist, and I hold them to be very fraught with comfort to God's people; but if any man shall say that the preaching of these is the whole preaching of Gospel, I am at issue with him. Brethren, you may preach these doctrines as long as you like, and yet fail to preach the Gospel; and I will go further, and affirm that some who have even denied those truths, to our own grief, have nevertheless been Gospel preachers for all that, and God has saved souls by their ministry . . . preach Christ, young men, if you want to win souls."[172] Spurgeon had an evangelistic zeal that would never allow him to fall into a diverting trap.

Moreover, there have been those who contend, from their high-Calvinistic perspective, that Spurgeon never gave an open Gospel invitation for the lost to come to Christ right then and there. Eric Hayden, perhaps one of the most knowledgeable people concerning Spurgeon's life and ministry, rejects this idea. Hayden has pointed out:

> I am more fortunate than these mere academic students of Spurgeon, for my own grandfather and grandmother were members of Spurgeon's tabernacle and used to regale me with stories of the great preacher when I was a boy. My grandfather told me that Spurgeon would often request an enquirer to go below to one of the basement lecture halls to be counseled by his elders. Naturally, the very architecture of the Metropolitan Tabernacle with its rostrum and baptistry, and all available floor space taken by pews, did not lend itself to hundreds coming forward to an invitation to receive Christ, so he did the next best thing. In *The Sword and the Trowel* for 1865 Spurgeon published a paper by a former student of his Pastors' College. It was entitled 'How to Get At Enquirers.' One method suggested was: 'Request the anxious to remain in their seats while the rest leave . . . as there is often a reluctance to be seen

walking up the aisle.' This Spurgeon frequently did, urging his 200 or so elders to be 'on the watch for souls.' There is also an account of Spurgeon himself kneeling and praying with an enquirer in the front of the lecture hall. [173]

On one occasion Spurgeon gave an invitation in a service to come forward publicly. In *The Sword and the Trowel* of 1865, page 70, it is stated: "C. H. Spurgeon earnestly exhorted those who had accepted Christ as their Savior to come forward amongst his people and avow their attachment to his person and name. Words of kindly encouragement and of loving persuasion, were addressed to the timid and retiring ones, who feared to avow themselves to be the Lord's, lest they should fall back into sin and dishonor his name. This was followed by an appeal to those who had confessed the name of Jesus." Simply put, Spurgeon did give invitations at times much like the Wesleyan Arminians did.

Although Spurgeon was called, granted facetiously, a "Bishop," he stood as far removed from the idea of any sort of "apostolic succession theology" as he could. Recall, he refused to be ordained. But this has been made amply clear.

Furthermore, as seen in this brief survey of his theology, he certainly believed in the Church universal. He was anything but what Americans call a "Landmark" Baptist. He was far too ecumenical for that. Those of this persuasion who wish to claim him do not understand his ecclesiology at all.

As strange as it may seem, there have been those who claimed Spurgeon was not a Puritan. Of course, in one sense, there may be a note of truth in that claim if one wishes to restrict Puritanism to Church of England Reformers. Anglican Puritans had no desire to leave the Church; they sought its reformation. If one defines Puritanism in that restrictive sense, and thus eliminate the Dissenters, Spurgeon did not qualify as a Puritan. Yet, at the same time, in the theological and spiritual traditions of Puritanism, Spurgeon fully qualified. To say that Puritanism must be restricted to the Anglican Church alone takes too narrow a view of the movement. Spurgeon himself claimed to be in the spirit of the Puritans and probably did not object at all to Gladstone's designation of him as "the last of the Puritans," except in the sense he did not see himself as the *last* of the Puritans; he felt there were many more, and many would follow on. It will be recalled concerning Spurgeon's Puritan-spirited grandfather, that Spurgeon said, "I often feel the shadow of his broad brim come over my spirit." Spurgeon was a Puritan in the best sense of the word, as were many other Independents and Dissenters as well.

The mistake of some who claim Spurgeon in their own camp is probably due to the fact they have taken isolated statements of the great preacher and made them the sum and substance of his complex personality and theology. He was such a man of fame in his own day, with that fame continuing, that one can easily fall into the trap of claiming him as one's own. But such is unfair to the man and his theology. But now we must turn to more positive aspects of Spurgeon's thought for a cursory evaluation.

POSITIVE RESULTS

There are several things that need to be understood at the outset. First, Spurgeon clearly recognized the vital relationship between theology and Christian ministry. He firmly believed that practical ministry should emerge out of basic theology. For Spurgeon, absolute commitment to and understanding of foundational, biblical, evangelical truths stood as essential in any effective life of service to Christ. Secondly, Spurgeon openly confessed his utter commitment to the Bible. This made his theology seem paradoxical at times. But in this sense, he ministered much in the tradition of Calvin himself. Calvin preached the Bible as he found it. For Spurgeon, authority rested in *sola scriptura*, although from time to time he would attempt to corroborate his position by tradition, experience, reason, even the creeds. Still, primarily, as an absolute believer in the infallible Word of God, he built his theology on the Bible as he understood it.

Finally, Spurgeon's theology completely revolved around Jesus Christ, the Lord he loved. He constantly cried to his students and to all preachers, "preach Christ." This became the core of his Christian understanding. His entire theological framework rested upon the foundation of the life, death, and resurrection of Jesus Christ. This meant, of course, that the atonement of Christ sunk deep roots in his theological approach. Furthermore, this naturally resulted in his emphasis on a God-centered theology, rather than a human-centered approach to Christian truth. He said:

> The great system known as 'the doctrines of grace,' brings before the mind of the man who truly receives it God and not man. The whole scheme of that doctrine looks Godward, and regards God as the first, and the plan of salvation is chiefly arranged for the glory of the most high.[174]

The point has been labored, but it is most important to emphasize in any evaluation of Spurgeon's theology that he formulated his thought in the context of theological tension. Practically every major point of his theology had that inherent tension because of his purely biblical approach. He never tried to resolve major conflicts such as divine sovereignty and human responsibility, as we have seen. Some see this as a weakness; yet, Spurgeon argued to the contrary. When reason attempts to lay aside, or to rationalize, that which the Bible does not attempt to do, Spurgeon saw that as an error. Although he was criticized for his approach, he unswervingly kept to his principles to that end. He always appealed to the Scriptures, and for himself, that was enough. He explained:

> There are some who read the Bible, and try to systematize it according to rigid logical creeds; but I dare not follow their method, and I feel content to let people say, 'How inconsistent he is with himself!' The only thing that would grieve me would be inconsistency with the Word of God. As far as I know this

> Book, I have endeavoured, in my ministry, to preach to you, not a part of the truth, but the whole counsel of God; but I cannot harmonize it, nor am I anxious to do so. I am sure all truth is harmonious, and *to my ear* the harmony is clear enough; but I cannot give you a complete score of the music, or mark the harmonies on the gamut. I must leave the Chief Musician to do that. [175]

Of course, there were those who would not criticize Spurgeon for his paradoxical stance. To the contrary, they commended him. Fullerton said, "Spurgeon's great contribution lay in his ability to cling to two concurrent truths without diminishing the significance of either." [176]

Moreover, Spurgeon had a very practical reason for holding truth in tension. He felt this to be the best way to evangelize people. As an evangelist, he would unhesitatingly employ any approach he felt had its roots in the Scriptures that he could use to bring others to faith in Jesus Christ.

As Spurgeon grew older, he shifted some of his emphasis in theology. In his early days at New Park Street, he declared very forcefully his essential orthodox Calvinism. But later in life, as his doctrinal position became widely known, he preached less vociferously on these issues. His doctrinal emphasis moved more to the fundamentals of the faith concerning the person and work of Christ, the substitutionary atonement, and similar central doctrines. This speaks highly of the man. He matured as a Christian; he matured as a theologian. He must be evaluated in that light.

Although as Spurgeon grew older and mellowed in his theological approach, he never really changed theologically, he just approached the issues more maturely and in a more balanced fashion.

However, some of Spurgeon's contemporaries seemed to loose their basic theological moorings. He said, "We used to debate on particular and general redemption, but now men question whether there is any redemption at all worthy of the name." [177] This shift that had crept into the British religious scene culminated in the famous Down Grade Controversy that broke Spurgeon's heart. In some sense, it cost him his life. To that disturbing, yet fascinating, event in Spurgeon's life we must turn.

PART II
The Down Grade Controversy

Introduction

I n 1887 Spurgeon printed a series of articles denouncing liberal theology in *The Sword and the Trowel*. The articles declared that the "new theology" had put the Church on the "Down Grade." They became the spark that ignited the fire storm that swept through the Baptist Church. But the roots of the Down Grade Controversy go back some years before its actual ignition in 1887. Actually, several cultural, philosophical, and scientific events that took place in Victorian Britain played a preliminary role. They created a general ethos that proved conducive to the reception of the "new theology."

DARWINISM

One significant factor in setting the stage for the Down Grade Controversy was Darwin's publication of *The Origin of the Species*. This epoch-making work made its revolutionary impact felt in philosophical as well as anthropological and biological circles. Yet, philosopher Alfred North Whitehead said the last two decades of the nineteenth century "closed with one of the dullest stages of thought since the time of the First Crusade."[178] That seems a strange statement in light of all that was going on. A whole developmental, evolutionary theory began to take such a hold on the mindset of many Victorians that it resulted in a humanistic approach to all reality. Whitehead's statement is difficult to justify. Moreover, as is so often the case, that general humanistic atmosphere soon infiltrated theological circles. It began to manifest itself as an emphasis on human development and far less upon a God-centered approach to the realities of life as had prevailed for centuries. This lent itself to the exultation of reason and appealed very much to the typical philosophical empiricism that has characterized the intellectual circles of Britain for many years. Coupled with continental rationalism as typified in thinkers like Kant and Hegel, the stage began to be set for a serious liberalizing of traditional theology.

THE THEOLOGICAL DEVELOPMENT

The rise of rationalism began to get its grip on the British mentality more profoundly as the Victorian era moved into its last decades. As suggested earlier, theological rationalism had already permeated continental religious circles. This laid the foundation for the spawning of so-called "higher criticism" and all that it implied in the development of biblical theology. Higher critical rationalistic presuppositions began to precipitate the placing of question marks over certain traditional orthodox doctrines such as eternal punishment. As one put it, "The weakest link of the religious consensus was the doctrine of hell."[179] But some rationalistic questions even extended into such vital areas as the unique deity of Christ and the miraculous, supernatural elements of the Scriptures. Central to this whole approach was the "quest for the historic Jesus." J. R. Seeley's *Ecce Homo* (1865) mirrored the work of others who had pioneered in the field like David F. Strauss and J. E. Renan. Ironically, Strauss finished his *Life of Jesus* the year Spurgeon was born. The quest attempted to find who Jesus "*really*" was." They sought to "get behind" the stories recorded about Jesus in the New Testament. They felt the Gospel accounts could not be seen as real history, at least in many of their details. Moreover, they believed the supernatural aspects of the four Gospels could not possibly be true. Their rationalistic-empiricism precluded it. To them, the world operated on a pure humanistic cause/effect principle. The whole point of Seeley's approach, along with Strauss and Renan, was simply "they tried to eliminate the supernatural, and reduce Jesus merely to a magnetic teacher."[180] Out of the school of thought called the Tubingen School there came a thrust, built on philosophical rationalistic presuppositions, that finally discredited the authenticity of an alarming portion of the Scriptures. For example, only four of Paul's letters were held by the Tubingen School as authentic. The others were seen as later works of the "Pauline school." Against this weak view of inspiration and the subsequent ideas about the nature of the Bible, Spurgeon vehemently reacted. As seen, for Spurgeon the Scriptures were the infallible Word of God. He fully subscribed to the "all-or-nothing fallacy." That is to say, if the Bible is untrue in any one part, it cannot be relied upon anywhere; either it is *all* inspired and inerrant or none of it is. He declared, "We will never attempt to save half the truth by casting any part of it away. . . . We will stand by all of it or none of it. We will have a whole Bible or no Bible."[181] It had to be all or nothing at all for Spurgeon. He argued that humanistic rationalism cannot decide what is true or untrue when it comes to the Word of God. Spurgeon added, "Unless we have infallibility somewhere, faith is impossible."[182] Revelation supersedes reason when conflicts arise.

The continental rationalistic approach which Spurgeon reacted against actually spawned classical 19th century liberalism. As it permeated Germany and the continental Church, it soon crossed the English Channel and began to break across the shores of Victorian England. Of course, there were challenges to the onslaught. Scholars such as Westcott, Hort, Ramsay, and Lightfoot challenged the new wave. Spurgeon, from a less technical perspective than these scholars, nevertheless joined them and said, "Germany has been made unbelieving by her preachers, and England is following in her tracks."[183] He went as far as to say, "Avowed atheists are not one-tenth as dangerous as those who scatter doubt and stab at faith." [184] But the continental philosophical atmosphere, aided by the theory of evolution, spawned pure rationalism, growing scientism, humanism and higher biblical criticism. And this atmosphere began to make strong footholds in the British scene, throwing the Church on the defensive.

Spurgeon reacted strongly against this liberal trend. When he read a book he felt truly heretical, he would tear it into small pieces lest anyone read it and be led astray. Perhaps there was some justification in this, for when orthodox theology and evangelical fervency begin to be eroded, spiritual decline invariably sets in. Some of the earliest indications of this decline in Victorian Britain were in the "Broad Church" wing of the Established Church of England. As the erosion ate away at the vitals, especially in the Established Church, the Bishop of Rochester sensed that the churches were on an ebb tide. [185] R. F. Horton expressed the same idea when he wrote, "the great majority of the English people were drifting toward a state of 'non religion.'" [186] Against this decided trend, Spurgeon felt compelled to raise his voice; for him it was simply the old, traditional heresies exerting themselves once again, this time in a new form. He declared, "the improvements brought forth by 'modern thought' we regard with suspicion, and believe them at best to be dilutions of the truth, and most of them old, rusted heresies, tinkered up again, and sent abroad with a new face put upon them, to repeat the mischief of which they wrought in ages past." [187]

Spurgeon was clever enough not to get sidetracked or embroiled in the purely scientific aspects of the new rationalism. He had no quarrel with biology or physics *per se*. Even when the scientists let their rational-empirical epistemology dogmatically deny Scriptural truths, Spurgeon would simply point out their own epistemological weakness by declaring their "truths" were subject to debate and questioning also. He said, "All that we are certain of today is this, that what the learned were sure of a few years ago is now thrown into the limbo of discarded truth." [188] For Spurgeon, only the truth of God, as discovered in the Bible, remains eternally true. Thus he could argue as convincingly from his presuppositional perspective as the rationalistic scientists could from theirs.

INROADS TO EVANGELICALISM

In the early years of this erosion and the subsequent secularization of society, the conservative evangelical churches, those of the Anglican persuasion and dissenting churches like the Baptist, remained somewhat isolated. Before long, however, the erosion began to be subtly sensed even in these circles. In the quest for "intellectual freedom," an attitude developed against those who held tenaciously to orthodox doctrine. To cling to traditional ideas began to be viewed as a dogmatism that infringed upon freedom and thus stultified intellectual pursuit. Against this criticism Spurgeon said, "If the pulpit is declining in power (which he believed was the case), it is due in a great measure to the men who mistake error for freshness, self-conceit for culture, and a determination to go astray for nobility of mind."[189] That rationalism of the Enlightenment was catching up with the theological strides made in Puritan Britain—the British Baptists not being excepted. Spurgeon's denomination began to feel the shock wave of the earthquake that had already shaken the Continent. As early as 1860, cause for attention arose. A book written by J. B. Brown, *The Divine Life in Man* disturbed many. Brown's doctrine of the atonement came over as weak and he fell under suspicion. Spurgeon said:

> I have often thought, the best answer to the new theology is, that the Gospel was always preached to the poor. . . . I am sure that the poor will never learn *the Gospel* of these new divines. . . . It sours your temper, and makes you feel angry, to see the previous things of God trodden under foot. Some of us must stand out against these attacks on truth, although we love not controversy.[190]

Other early effects of the new movement surfaced in 1871 at the meeting of the Baptist Union. At that general convention, T. Vincent Tymns suggested that the Baptist Union constitution be revised. The matter was thrown into committee and after two years the committee made a suggested alteration to the document. They moved that the phrase "evangelical sentiments" be deleted and in its place a declaration of principles be adopted which read, "In this Union it is fully recognized that every separate church has liberty to interpret and administer the laws of Christ, and that the immersion of believers is the only Christian baptism." Although this approach brought some unity to the Union with its already diverse views, the deletion of the phrase "evangelical sentiments" should have been seen as an omen that everything was not well in Spurgeon's own Baptist family.

In the mid '70s an upbeat note could be heard in the religious life of Britain. The work of Moody and Sankey brought a measure of new life to the evangelical world of Victoriana. An outstanding Baptist leader in this general period, Samuel Harris Booth, became the general secretary of the Baptist Union. All knew him as a committed Evangelical. He figured very prominently in the Down Grade Controversy that would soon come. But in the 1870s his election did make things look somewhat better. Yet, the optimism was short lived.

Biblical criticism of the more negative, destructive type continued to receive a growing acceptance. In 1877 Samuel Cox wrote *Salvator Mundi*. In that particular theological work he rejected the traditional biblical doctrine of eternal punishment and put in its place the "larger hope." This universalistic approach became one of the central issues in the Down Grade Controversy. Still, the Baptist Union, largely dominated by particular Baptists, rejected such a doctrine. That same year, 1877, the Counsel and Assembly of the Baptist Union voted for the amalgamation of the Baptist Union, which was essentially

Calvinistic, and the New Connection Association of the old General Baptists. Although this seemed in many respects a strengthening move, it did bring into the Union some people of varying views. In the evolution of the Baptist Union, a pattern crystallized that connectionalism and practical concerns were more important than doctrinal issues. This clearly contributed significantly to the Down Grade Controversy.

OTHER FACTORS

Other important factors figured in setting the scene for the Down Grade. As briefly discussed earlier, between 1863 and 1866, something of an ongoing debate erupted between Spurgeon and the Baptist Missionary Society. In a sense this foreshadowed the coming controversy, although it occurred some twenty years earlier. It will be recalled that Spurgeon had strong convictions about how funds should be raised for Christian causes. Spurgeon disagreed with the approach of raising subscriptions for the Baptist Missionary Society. It seemed a minor matter, but it must be seen as a factor, at least psychologically. It helped harden Spurgeon's convictions that when theology deals with the essentials of the faith, it becomes more important than denominational fellowship. That attitude helped set the stage for the theological battle.

Many incidents then occurred in the 1880s in the Baptist Union that boded to be harbingers for the coming battle. As early as 1880 Spurgeon began to feel unrest. The cry had been continually raised that Baptists do not accept creeds; their only creed is the Bible. Spurgeon remarked in *The Canadian Baptist*, December 2, 1880:

> Away with creeds and bodes of divinity! This is the cry of today. Ostensibly it is reverence for the Bible, and attachment to charity which dictate the clamorous denunciation, but at the bottom it is hatred of definite truth.

Against these types of inroads that struck at evangelical orthodoxy, Spurgeon felt compelled to speak out. To understand why Spurgeon always seemed to spark controversies and was so outspoken, one must realize he felt that silence on such issues constituted complicity with evil. He said, "Trimming and temporizing amiable silence, and unfaithful compromises are treason to God."[191] So speak out he did. Mr. "Valiant-for-Truth" could never be accused of being "Mr. Pliable."

Spurgeon's doubts concerning the Baptist Union arose again sometime late in 1881, or at least at the beginning of the following year. A denominational paper ran an article on the Baptist Union and its critics. The article seemed to be directed mainly toward Spurgeon who had apparently made some remarks at the Pastors' College Conference that the Baptist Union meetings were rather cold. At any rate, Spurgeon declined to speak at the next autumn meeting which in turn began to spark rumors that he intended to withdraw from the Union. Spurgeon made a reply to the rumors in the following letter:

> From a remark as to the spiritual chill of the Union meetings, you infer a looseness of attachment to the Baptist Union, if not an intention to break away from it. This is, indeed, a monstrous leap of logic. . . . Personally, I have shown my goodwill to the Union gatherings by very frequently speaking and preaching at them; and . . . I have declined to do this at the next autumn gathering . . . my sole and only motive (being) that I wish others to have their turn. . . .[192]

Nevertheless, later in the year, Spurgeon did agree, after much persuasion, to speak at the Baptist Union Assembly in Portsmouth. In his address he said, "I am afraid as to matters of doctrine I would not like to bring a loose charge against any, but I would say that there are some churches that have gone aside from Christ." [193] Yet, he did not find himself ready to take a "monstrous leap" out of the denomination.

Spurgeon again intended to absent himself from the Baptist Union Assembly in the spring of 1882 in Liverpool. He finally yielded to repeated invitations of eminent persons and attended and spoke. Hugh Stowell Brown, a leading pastor from the host city, pleaded with him to go, so he consented. But the following year, 1883, Spurgeon reached a turning point as far as his involvement in the annual meetings was concerned. He would attend no more. In some senses, this may have been providential, because that year John Page-Hopps, a local Unitarian minister, gave an address.

In 1877 Spurgeon had written, "The Baptists are coming together. . . . never were the signs more hopeful . . . we see everywhere the true evangelic spirit, in happy contrast with other quarters where intellect is idolized and novelty of doctrine sought after." [194] Even as late as May of 1881 Spurgeon had written in *The Baptist*, "No one more heartily desires the prosperity of the Union than I do; no one is more satisfied with its desires and plans." [195] That statement occurred in the more hopeful 1870s. But as the 1880s progressed, so did his doubts about the orthodoxy of some of his Baptist brethren. Spurgeon worried first that some were departing from traditional Calvinism. He had witnessed such a defection earlier among the Congregationalists. But he saw deeper issues looming on the horizon. Ernest Payne, Baptist historian, puts his finger on Spurgeon's more serious concern when he points out that in the quest for Christian unity, the Baptists slipped into "a lack of serious theological and ecclesiological interest." [196] This, as expressed earlier, precipitated the situation where union and cooperation among many Baptists became more important than doctrinal issues. Spurgeon saw this as a very unhealthy shift for the Baptists, even for the evangelical thrust in general. As seen, Spurgeon always reacted very negatively to any and all inroads of the "modernists." He described them in contemptuous terms such as "jelly," "souffles," "whipped cream," "slobbering kisses," and the like. It has been suggested that perhaps because Spurgeon did not fill the role of the athlete or storming soldier, "for the very reason that Spurgeon was so 'unmanly' in the ordinary situations of life, that made it mandatory for him to take a stand in the one area where he could 'play the man,' and play the man better than anyone—in defense of his beliefs." [197] That seems a rather superficial rationale for Spurgeon "going to war" over the "new theology." He had much deeper convictions and motives than that.

SPURGEON'S SUSPICIONS

At this stage, Spurgeon began to look hard at the doctrinal integrity of the Baptist Union. The views of younger men particularly disturbed him. The first incident that occurred was the acceptance by some of Samuel Cox's *Salvador Mundi*, as mentioned previously. Cox served as the pastor of the Mansfield Road Baptist Church in Nottingham. His view of "the larger hope" moved him toward universalism. Cox could propagate his views among Evangelicals because he also served as editor of the monthly theological magazine, *The Expositor*. Spurgeon declined to review Cox's book or even mention it in *The Sword and the Trowel*. By 1889 (two years into the Down Grade Controversy), a number of Baptists, who had largely rejected the book when Cox first published it in 1877, considered it a "remarkable book." There seemed to be something of dramatic reversal among Baptists concerning Mundi's approach to the idea of retribution. All these trends and dynamics disturbed Spurgeon.

The next event occurred in 1883 when, as pointed out, a Unitarian minister, John Page-Hopps, spoke briefly at the annual Baptist Union meeting in Leicester. In his message, Page-Hopps made some "semi-jocular remarks." Many took offense. The affair deepened when the word spread that Page-Hopps had actually been trained at the New Connection General Baptist College at Leicester. Archibald Brown, a Baptist Union Council member, pastor of the second largest church in London and a graduate of the Pastors' College, wrote Spurgeon about the meeting outlining all the heresies he heard at the Leicester meeting. He wrote, "'The spirit of the age' seems to have found a welcome in our midst . . . it is the spirit of anti-Christ." [198] Historian Payne recorded, "When Spurgeon learned of what had occurred, he told Samuel Harris Booth, who that year resumed the secretariatship of the Union, after a break of two years, that he thought of 'withdrawing quietly . . . a seceder from the talk but not from the work of the union.'" [199] Interestingly, John Clifford, who became something of Spurgeon's antagonist in the Down Grade and later president of the Baptist Union, was a contemporary of Page-Hopp's at the New Connection College at Leicester.

Spurgeon took the Page-Hopp's incident most seriously. He wrote to his brother-in-law, William Jackson, in a letter dated November 8, 1883, "I have fired the first shot, and the battle is beginning . . . we shall see who loves truth and who is a traitor. . . . I think I must personally withdraw from the Baptist Union." The word began to spread. Charles Davis wrote to Spurgeon and said, "It would be a terrible grief to multitudes of us if you were to cease from the Union. An irreparable blow would be inflicted on the denomination." [200]

Richard Glover attempted to present a response to the Unitarian's remarks at the Leicester Assembly. Glover said:

> I am glad to believe that Christ will smile upon many who cannot call him God, but who will perhaps at last be glad to wake up and find that he was divine, though they did not know that he was more than just their best teacher and truest friend. [201]

Spurgeon had written about the incident in *The Sword and the Trowel*. James Thew and J. G. Greenhou wrote a joint letter to *The Baptist* chiding Spurgeon for his article in *The Sword and the Trowel*. In the same year, Spurgeon said in *The Morning Light*, (February 3, 1883), "If a man got a firm grip of biblical truth now-a-days, they were termed bigots." At a College Conference he said:

> We believe in the inspiration of God's Word, and that it is on the whole, in all its essentials, so clear and so distinct that its meaning is knowable and more, that its meaning is known to us; and when we bow to that *we are condemned at once for dogmatism.*

He wrote another article in *The Sword and the Trowel* that year against attempts to obliterate the distinction between good and evil. In 1885 Spurgeon said at the College Conference in March, "The times are dark, the churches dull." It may seem incidental, but later in 1889 he spoke out against the Revised Bible. He said the Authorized King James Version was good Saxon English. He did like to cling to certain traditions.

Spurgeon's concern for doctrinal integrity, especially the doctrine of the person of Christ, deepened. He said the Church of England was "eaten through and through with overt Unitarianism." In his typical preaching style, he declared in *The Episcopal Recorder*, September 30, 1886, "The swine are trampling in the pearls at this time, and nothing restrains them. Nevertheless, the pearls are pearls still." He went as far as to declare:

> Nothing remains upon which a certain school of preachers have not spit their skepticism . . . many who preach not faith but doubt . . . frequently are the fundamental doctrines of the Gospel assailed. [202]

If this were true of the Established Church, what about the Baptists? This increasingly became Spurgeon's question.

Spurgeon's words, however, should not be interpreted in a manner to make him a narrow, closed-minded, ultra-conservative, obscurantist thinker. He was considerably broader than that. After all, he profoundly admired Augustine who said:

The truth is neither mine nor his nor another's; but belongs to us all whom Thou calmest to partake of it, warning us terribly, not to account it private to ourselves, lest we be deprived of it.[203]

The Metropolitan Tabernacle pastor had a breadth few seem to appreciate. For example, he reviewed in *The Sword and the Trowel* a recently published book on textual criticism by Professor Briggs, a "new theology" thinker. In the review, he expressed "unqualified approval and . . . lively admiration of the entire work."[204] Spurgeon expressed appreciation for the benefits of scholarly discipline. He would endorse what he considered to be good and helpful wherever he found it. What primarily concerned him was the essential Gospel, especially the person and work of Christ, not theological secondary issues, conservative as he was in his entire theology. At the same time, however, he did revolt against the liberal, blasé attitude of the pseudo-sophisticated preachers who seemed to be saying, at least as Spurgeon understood them, "All who hold orthodox views are dolts, dunces, persons deprived of culture, and utterly unacquainted with science."[205] Liberal thinking can degenerate into that attitude, as can ultra-fundamentalism. As Spurgeon rightly said, latitudinarianism does not bring brotherly love, but rancor.

Spurgeon again refused to attend the Baptist annual assembly in 1886. *The Christian Commonwealth* commented, "It is an open secret that Mr. Spurgeon's absence was largely owing to a want of sympathy with the Union." These early to mid-1880s, however, were very positive years for Spurgeon in many respects. In 1884 he celebrated his jubilee birthday. In 1885, he completed *The Treasury of David*, his magnum opus. Several very positive things happened before the outbreak of the controversy.

THE ELM ROAD INCIDENT

Quite clearly, Spurgeon had already moved toward a confrontation, at least psychologically. At that point, another incident occurred. It began in 1884 at the Elm Road Baptist Church in Beckenham, southeast London. Samuel Harris Booth served as pastor and had also resumed his responsibilities as secretary of the Baptist Union upon the death of William Samson. Booth had served as secretary before Samson's appointment, but upon the death of Samson, Booth again became general secretary, thus fulfilling two roles: pastor and secretary. As pastor, Booth secured an assistant minister from Regent's Park College for the Elm Road Church. A young man by the name of W. E. Bloomfield became associate pastor to relieve Booth of his heavy, dual load. This seemingly innocuous move precipitated a very sensitive situation. Historian Payne wrote, "I am now convinced that what occurred played a larger part than I thought in precipitating subsequent events."[206]

While Bloomfield was serving as Associate Pastor with Booth at the Elm Road Church, a serious situation arose. Ernest Payne explained:

> Booth soon became dissatisfied with Bloomfield's sermons. He alleged that they contained 'not infrequent statements which pointed . . . to Universalism' and that there was 'a constant appeal by name to such writers as Maurice, Robertson, George Eliot, Kingsley and other prominent opponents of Evangelical doctrine.' Booth was supported in his protests by the Rev. James Smith, a retired missionary, who had served for many years in Delhi. Smith thought that Bloomfield did not sufficiently 'warn men of the dangers of refusing Christ.' Without consulting the church Booth dismissed Bloomfield. The church showed its support of the young man, whereupon Booth resigned the pastorate and withdrew his membership. [207]

In his resignation letter as pastor to Elm Road Baptist Church, Booth wrote:

> The gospel I have preached is this: that as guilty and helpless, a sinner needing the Mercy of God, I cannot become one of His redeemed children except through the converting grace of the Holy Spirit; that I have no hope with God my Father but in Him who in His death became my substitute and who wrought the miracle of the incarnation, that he might suffer in my place. . . . By teaching these truths, we stand against the attempt to bring into our churches what is known as the 'New Theology' which teaches that such phrases as the Atonement, the Church or The Fall are only mental conceptions and not actual facts. As opposed to such nebulous theology, I have preached not about Christ, but Christ himself. I have pointed perishing sinners to the Lamb of God who beareth away the sin of the world. In that Old Faith I have lived and in that Old Faith, God helping me, I will die. [208]

The charge against Bloomfield, as seen above, essentially centered on comments he had made from the pulpit and precipitated Booth's resignation. Spurgeon responded to Booth's resignation in the following letter:

> October 20, 1885
> *Personally* I know nothing, for I have not seen the young man's MSS (manuscripts), and the Council by refusing a motion to let them come before all ministers on Committee virtually shelved me from having anything to do with the investigation. . . . I am deeply grieved about the whole affair: it is only part of a whole. I don't think you went to work in the right way, but you did the right thing. I only say this to be frank. But I am altogether with you on the main issue, and whoever said that I thought Bd. (Bloomfield) to be sound invented a falsehood. What are we to do next? Anyhow *we* shall hold together. Yours very heartily, C. H. Spurgeon. [209]

One of the most salient features that brought about the confusion in the whole Down Grade affair seems to be that Booth not only informed Spurgeon of the Elm Road situation with Bloomfield, but told him of other serious theological problems throughout the entire Union. Booth apparently pleaded with Spurgeon to take a stand. It appears Booth believed that only Spurgeon could really raise a voice against the tide of the "new theology" invading the Baptist Union; hence, he should be the one in the vanguard to throw up a bulwark against the onslaught of rationalistic critical theology. It seems to be the case that Booth gave Spurgeon facts and names concerning what he considered as heretical doctrine preached by those who were deviating from orthodox Christianity. However, Booth apparently got a pledge from Spurgeon that he would not reveal the source of his information, or, above all, the names and places that were the core of the developing heresy. This boded to put Spurgeon in a difficult stance. If he were to heed Booth's admonition and go on the attack, he would be in a difficult spot if he were asked to give names and places and actual heretical doctrines, for he had pledged to Booth that he would not reveal the facts. This would leave Spurgeon open to the charge that he really had no substance for his accusations and was therefore just creating a "tempest in the teapot." We shall see later this is exactly what transpired.

Back at Elm Road Church, as can be surmised, the situation threw the church into a real quandary. They requested the London Baptist Association to help settle the dispute. The Association stepped in to examine the evidence for the allegations. Members of the investigating Associational committee were E. B. Underhill, J. W. Todd, and J. R. Wood. They examined forty-one of Bloomfield's sermons. They produced their official report in November of 1885 and exonerated Bloomfield from all of the charges laid against him. However, the atmosphere was still so charged that four months later Bloomfield resigned from Elm Road and assumed the pastorate at Turret Green Church in Ipswich. Following that move, in September of 1886, largely through the efforts of Charles Williams, president of the Baptist Union at that time, Booth and his wife returned to Elm Road church, but only as members. It is interesting that Bloomfield, despite being the center of controversy in the two-year period from 1884 to 1886, became principal of Rawdon Baptist College and later president of the Baptist Union.

CORRESPONDENCE TO OPEN THE CASE

In the heated Elm Road debate, three letters were written that prove central to one's understanding of the Down Grade Controversy. The first letter was the October 20th letter written by Spurgeon to Booth, presented above. In that correspondence it is clear Booth did consult with Spurgeon on the affair, and probably about other problems in the Union besides the Elm Road situation. Sometime later, Dr. H. G. Wood wrote to Payne and put his finger on the real issue. As touched upon above, Booth had sworn Spurgeon to confidentiality on the matter, not about Elm Road alone, but especially in the Baptist Union as a whole. He wrote:

> I have always understood that Booth took the initiative in consulting Spurgeon about his, Booth's, misgivings as to the orthodoxy of some members of the Council and that Spurgeon was precluded from mentioning names and giving details because Booth insisted that the information he had given must be treated as confidential . . . I have very little doubt that Booth did consult Spurgeon, and in view of the Bloomfield episode, it is most likely that he did.[210]

We shall see shortly how serious this became for Spurgeon's credibility in the Down Grade. A third letter was written from Pearce Carey to Seymour Price in 1887. In that correspondence, he mentioned his days at Regent's Park College. Carey wrote in his letter, "I had my own problems due to (the) challenge to Dr. Angus' lectures in Eternal Punishment: a challenge which cost me four years of denominational exile."[211] Consequently, Carey left Regent's Park in 1884 being totally dissatisfied with Angus' approach. This demonstrated, as Spurgeon had suspected, that there were young men coming out of Baptist Colleges who did not believe in eternal punishment.

But it was not just these letters alone that verify theological problems in the Baptist Union. George Howelles wrote an article concerning his days at Regent's Park College. He declared there were basic theological problems that he encountered during his studies at the College. He stated that during his matriculation at Regent's Park in 1888, "Certain ministers in the denomination, not to mention many others outside, had dared to question the eternity of hell-flames for sinners, on the ground that the everlasting torment for lost souls was inconsistent with the Fatherhood of God."[212] Not only that, but on one occasion, when an older minister led the devotional time at Regent's Park, he prayed, "Oh, God . . . when we hear the shrieks of the damned ascending from the everlasting flames from the bottomless pit, give us grace to shout 'Hallelujah, hallelujah.'" A response to the prayer from someone in the College was, "I would rather risk sharing the agonies of the damned, than joining in the hallelujah's of the saints." Such was the reaction of the College to the traditional doctrine of eternal punishment.

Another situation developed in October of 1885 that further moved Spurgeon toward precipitating the Down Grade Controversy. At Swansea, at a Baptist Missionary Society conference, James Thew addressed the delegates. A contemporary described Thew as, "the quiet and cultured preacher who drew large chapel congregations at the Belford Street Chapel, Leicester." In his address, Thew "depreciated references to the eternal punishment of the heathen." The sermon, when Spurgeon became aware of it, drew sharp criticisms from the Metropolitan Tabernacle preacher. In replying to Spurgeon's denunciation, Alfred H. Baynes, then secretary of the Baptist Missionary Society, assured Charles that "so long as he (Baynes) was secretary, Thew would not again be asked to speak or preach for the BMS."[213] Yet, at the same time, the gauntlet had again gone down.

DEVELOPING TRENDS

Ernest Payne, Baptist historian, who later became general secretary of the Baptist Union, in analyzing the general situation at this time, contended that "it was the views of some of the younger men that more seriously troubled Spurgeon, including those of two or three who were members of the Baptist Union Council." [214] Not only Spurgeon, but Samuel Booth as well, were both concerned about these developing trends and issues. Booth's orthodoxy was as unquestioned as Spurgeon's. But, Payne said, "There were other prominent ministers, whose sermons were widely reported in the press and whose views were likely to disturb both Booth and Spurgeon."

Payne had keen insight to the entire affair. Besides his widely accepted *The Baptist Union: A Short History*, Payne wrote another unpublished document on the events leading up to and surrounding the Down Grade Controversy. It was kept in the vault of the Baptist church house on Southampton Row in London for many years. Few were given the privilege of even reading it. This author had such a privilege and read the document carefully. After a careful reading of Payne's "secret" evaluation of the Down Grade, it remained a bit of a puzzle why it was kept under lock and key. Very little could be found in it that had not already been published in Payne's *Short History*. Only one or two references to specific colleges and individuals were mentioned in the document besides what had already been written in Payne's classic history. A strange set of circumstances took place during the move of the Baptist Union from its central London location on Southampton Row to its present location at Didcot, near Oxford. The document was lost for a time in the move, but now has been recovered and is found in the Archives at Regent's Park College in Oxford.

DEEPENING CONCERN

As the concern deepened, Thew's sermon is probably what precipitated Spurgeon writing a strong letter to Booth on October 22, 1885. In that correspondence Spurgeon went so far as to say, "the Baptist Union, means, I suppose, to drive out the orthodox. What is to be done, I know not. I would enter my earnest protest against the dubious notes which are continually put forth at its gatherings." [215] Spurgeon again wrote Booth in February of 1886 and said:

> I must beg you and Mr. Williams to consider me as out of the running in the matter of the Union. You know my intense love and respect for you and Mr. Williams, but the past meetings of the Union have convinced me that it is not for my good to be present at them, nor can I do any good by linking myself with them. I am anxious *not to be* asked, that I may not be obliged to decline. [216]

Quite evidently, Spurgeon's disillusionment with the Baptist Union had deepened considerably by 1886. The crisis drew near.

JOHN CLIFFORD EVENS THE SCORE

John Clifford, mentioned previously, played a significant role in the Down Grade. As Clifford's work prospered at his pastorate, the Westbourne Park Baptist Church, he came to prominence more and more. Late in the year of 1866, he wrote a book entitled *The Dawn of Manhood*, a compilation of twelve of his sermons. Clifford received a critical review of his book from Spurgeon's *The Sword and the Trowel*. Clifford wrote in December of 1866 to reassure Spurgeon:

> . . . The censure of the *Baptist Weekly* on my doctrinal position I did not reply to . . . but you are my friend, a friend of many years and a friend beloved; and I therefore feel I may appeal to your justice for a fair hearing.[217]

It may seem a little strange that Clifford would appeal to Spurgeon as he came from a General Baptist background and thus held to a general atonement. That issue contributed to the controversy that was beginning to develop between Spurgeon and Clifford. Spurgeon had charged Clifford with giving way too much to "modern thought." Clifford rejected Spurgeon's criticism saying:

> I have been fighting against compromise for at least twenty years. At this present hour I am suffering in manifold ways for my courage; and if I know my heart at all, it has but one fear, and that is lest I should so present God's Gospel to men that it should hurt and hinder rather than help and save.[218]

But Spurgeon and Clifford were friends. Spurgeon understood Clifford's position as a General Baptist and did not consider him one of the more serious heretics; hence, the basis of Clifford's appeal to Spurgeon. Yet, obviously, they did not see matters eye to eye, especially in the controversy of fellowship vs. doctrine.

It would have seemed that Clifford's letter to Spurgeon would have been sufficient to clear Clifford from any connection with the "new theology." However, William Bloomfield is quoted by Margent in his biography of Clifford as commending Clifford's "broad interpretation of Evangelicalism, his appreciation of the work of Biblical Scholarship, his resolute opposition to blind conservatism, his repudiation of the antagonism between Religion and Science . . . and his steadfast adherence to the New Testament idea of the Church."[219]

There must have been a measure of general unrest about Clifford, however, and not just on Spurgeon's part. When Clifford received the nomination for the vice-presidency of the Union in 1887, James Douglas of Kenyon Chapel in Brixton opposed the nomination stating, "I must . . . place in the foreground the faith once delivered to the Saints. I do not look upon Dr.

Clifford as a sufficient exponent of that faith for the office of vice-president." [220] The contention against Clifford seemed to be that he rejected the doctrine of the inerrancy of the Scriptures. Clifford had come to the place where he said, "The question of inspiration is in no way . . . fundamental to Christianity . . . The Christian does not depend for assurance of joy upon any external document or authority whatever." [221] With this, of course, Spurgeon wholeheartedly disagreed. It obviously helped draw the line between Clifford and Spurgeon more sharply and further set the stage for the Down Grade Controversy. Clifford shall be seen again later in the battle.

THE FATAL YEAR

The religious atmosphere was obviously becoming quite charged as 1887 dawned. Spurgeon being ill and still recuperating in Mentone in January of that year, seemed to improve in health very little. Unfortunately, he had to remain in France an inordinate amount of time that year. This placed him out of direct contact with the leadership of the Baptist Union. This may well have accounted for some misunderstandings that took place. But other factors helped create the increasing negative ethos that closed in around Spurgeon.

In 1887, Spurgeon had a serious disagreement with Joseph Parker of the City Temple. Parker wrote an "Open Letter" to Spurgeon on various matters, primarily theological issues, of disagreement. The full text will be seen in the next chapter. One of the problems over which Spurgeon and Parker disagreed was theater attendance, not to mention theological disagreements. Parker attended the theater regularly. Spurgeon vigorously condemned both the theater and social dancing. Recall, he reminded his people that the first Baptist (John) "had his head danced off." Concerning his own members at the Tabernacle, any theater attender "would cease to be a part of my fellowship." [222] Yet, he never condemned smoking, nor gave it up. The relationship between Spurgeon and Parker deteriorated quickly after Spurgeon's rebuke.

Not only that, the political scene in Britain boiled in turmoil. The Liberal Party divided over the issue of home rule for Ireland. It will be remembered that Spurgeon broke with Gladstone over this issue and supported Joseph Chamberlain. This again put Spurgeon in a lonely stance, as most of the Nonconformist leaders supported Gladstone. The illness, the rupture of fellowship between Parker and Spurgeon, the political issue, all seemed to conspire to isolate Spurgeon. The stage was set for a blowup. Spurgeon was still at Mentone when the real explosion occurred. What ignited the fuse was the so-called "Down Grade Articles."

THE "DOWN GRADE ARTICLES"

The first widespread public awareness of the oncoming controversy centered in the publishing of the "Down Grade Articles." In the March, April,

and June 1887 editions of *The Sword and the Trowel*, three articles appeared
stating that "apostasy from evangelical truth would lead to rationalism and
disaster." The articles were unsigned, but it is common knowledge that they
were written by Robert Shindler, who later wrote a biography of Spurgeon
entitled *From the Usher's Desk to the Tabernacle Pulpit*. It may seem rather
strange that Spurgeon did not author these early Down Grade Articles, thus
becoming the one who fired the first broadside against heterodoxy, but he
no doubt approved them. The author, Robert Shindler, claims Spurgeon
actually supervised the writing of the articles while in Mentone.

Shindler's articles struck the theme that any moving away from Calvinis-
tic, evangelical doctrine would eventually lead to theological and spiritual
disaster. Shindler, a committed Particular Baptist, served as pastor of the
Baptist church in Addleston. He stood as a completely committed Calvinist.
In Shindler's first article (See Appendix C for the full text), published in
March of 1887, he wrote:

> By some means or other, first the ministers, and then the Churches, got on 'the
> down grade,' and in some cases the descent was rapid, and in all, very disas-
> trous. In proportion as the ministers seceded from the old Puritan godliness of
> life, and the old Calvinistic form of doctrine, they commonly became less
> earnest and less simple in their preaching, more speculative and less spiritual
> in the matter of their discourses, and dwelt more on the moral teachings of the
> New Testament, than on the great central truths of revelation. Natural theology
> frequently took the place which the great truths of the gospel ought to have
> held, and the sermons became more and more Christless. Corresponding re-
> sults in the character and life, first of the preachers and then of the people,
> were only too plainly apparent. [223]

That is how the conflict got its name: "The Down Grade Controversy."
Shindler saw the church on a slippery slope, sliding on the down grade. And
with this as his starting point, Shindler attempted to show historically that
many mainline denominations had already started down that slippery slope:
the Presbyterians, Independents and General Baptists. Moreover, entering
the "down grade" had proved disastrous for them. He said that through the
years the "deadening doctrines . . . had made little inroad upon the Particular
Baptists," [224] and he certainly did not want what had happened to others to
happen to them. Thus he issued his stern word of caution and warning!
What he meant by the expression "deadenings doctrines" was Arminianism,
Baxterism (something of a middle road between Calvinism and Arminianism), Antinomianism, Arianism, and Socinianism. For Shindler, to leave
Calvin was to enter on a slippery down grade that would eventually propel
one downward into the pits of the Socinianists. He argued that those who
entered on the down grade seldom stayed where they had originally intended and would slip down the slope until they were in a position that finally
spelled disaster. He went on:

Those who turned from Calvinism may not have dreamed of denying the proper deity of the Son of God, renouncing faith in his atoning death and justifying righteousness, and denouncing the doctrine of human depravity, the need of Divine renewal, and the necessity for the Holy Spirit's gracious work, in order that men might become new creatures, but, dreaming or not dreaming, this result became a reality.[225]

Shindler ended his article by stating, "Commonly it is found in theology that which is true is not new, and that which is new is not true."[226] This statement was very much reminiscent of a similar statement of Spurgeon's. Although Spurgeon did not personally write the article, the first article was footnoted by Spurgeon. He stated, "earnest attention is requested for this paper. There is need of such warning as history affords. We are going downhill at breakneck speed."[227] So Spurgeon, through Shindler, threw down the gauntlet and entered the public arena with the battle.

Of note is the fact that Shindler did not accuse the Particular Baptists of having widely strayed from the Calvinistic, evangelical path. He simply threw out a warning that to tolerate and embrace the "new theology" had been disastrous for other denominations.

THE SECOND ARTICLE

The second article by Shindler (See Appendix D) appeared the following month under the title, "The Down Grade: Second Article." In this article the writer became more pointed; he surveyed the Anglicans, Independents, and General Baptists. He argued that the Arminian influence had become such a degrading influence among them, that it landed some of them in outright Socinianism. In this article, Shindler virtually equated Calvinism with evangelical theology. He made it clear that "a want of adequate faith in the divine inspiration of the sacred scriptures"[228] was the root cause for people slipping into heterodoxy. He presented the time-honored argument that when anyone sets reason over against revelation and reason alone becomes the essential principle in discovering truth and reality, "all kinds of error and mischiefs, are the results."[229] He wrote:

All the while a man bows to the authority of God's Word, he will not entertain any sentiment contrary to its teaching. 'To the law and the testimony,' is his appeal concerning every doctrine. He esteems that holy Book, concerning all things, to be right, and therefore he hates every false way. But let a man question, or entertain low views of the inspiration and authority of the Bible, and he is without chart to guide him, and without anchor to hold him.[230]

He also stated:

. . . where ministers and Christian churches have held fast to the truth that the Holy Scriptures have been given by God as an authoritative and infallible rule of faith and practice, they have never wandered very seriously out of the right way. But when, on the other hand, reason has been exalted above revelation, and made the exponent of revelation, all kinds of errors and mischiefs have been the result. [231]

Spurgeon would have agreed wholeheartedly with Shindler's approach to the necessity of bedrock truth as rooted in the Scriptures. But with the fact that Shindler more or less equated Calvinism with evangelical truth, Spurgeon did not quite agree. For example, the following month, April 1887, Spurgeon wrote, "we are asked whether Methodists are upon 'the down grade' and we are happy to reply that we do not think so." Spurgeon went on to say:

> In our fellowship with Methodists of all grades we have found them firmly adhering to those great evangelical doctrines for which we contend. . . . We care far more for the central evangelical truths than we do for Calvinism as a system. . . . Those who hold the eternal verities of salvation, and yet do not see all that we believe and embrace, are by no means the objects of our opposition: our warfare is with men who are giving up the atoning sacrifice, denying the inspiration of Holy Scriptures, and casting slurs upon justification by faith. The present struggle is not a debate upon the question of Calvinism or Arminianism, but of the truth of God versus the inventions of men. [232]

Obviously, Spurgeon's concern did not center on defending Calvinism per se. He felt that he was defending the essential Gospel, not any theological system.

The Christian Commonwealth (Sep. 14, 1887), however, saw the widening controversy as a battle between Arminianism and Calvinism. They declared: "neither Calvinism nor Arminianism is either fit to live or likely long to do so." Actually, there were many who saw the battle as essentially between Calvinism and Arminianism, but Spurgeon was clearly above that. Yet, at the same time, in an article in *The Sword and the Trowel*, March 1887, Spurgeon did admit that Arminians stood more in danger of entering the "down grade" than Calvinists. Of course, he was taken to task for that.

It must be granted that Shindler hit home in his second article when he surveyed the General Baptists. But in so doing, he was fair and did draw a firm distinction between the "old connection" and the "new connection" of General Baptists. He wrote that "the latter was formed in 1770, and was the result of the heterodoxy of the former." [233] He firmly believed that the old connection had virtually become Arian and thus had tragically entered the down grade. Of course, in this context the Particular Baptists had their birth, and as they rejected the heresy, they clung close to orthodox Calvinism. As could be expected, the General Baptists were quite incensed. In *The General Baptist Magazine* (May '87) they wrote:

We felt ourselves so stirred by what seemed to us the unwarranted assumptions and fallacious reasonings of the writer, that we could not wait until the month had come round, when we might have replied in our own pages.

THE THIRD ARTICLE

In Shindler's third article, he brought his historical survey up to the contemporary moment. In this article he first attacked Andover Seminary in the United States that had been founded in 1808 by Jedidiah Morse in reaction to the liberalism at Harvard University. Shindler went on to point out that some 75-80 years later, Andover too had experienced the "down grade" syndrome. Sydney Ahlstrom, in his *A Religious History of the American People*, wrote:

> As the century's turn approached, a kind of religious peace became manifest in New England. With the new historical, philosophical and religious attitudes as common ground, Andover Seminary even returned to Harvard, where for over two decades the joint faculty achieved great distinction and influence.[234]

Shindler used the American Baptist seminary as an example of how classical liberal theology can quickly engulf a theological institution. Shindler pointed out that Andover's "founders were sound Calvinists of the Cotton Mather type, and the College was instituted for the special purpose of training men in that faith." But, as professors began to get on the down grade and depart from the faith of the founders, "they attempted to show us a more excellent way, . . . the new theology . . . produced by some kind of evolution from the old; and hence . . . called 'Progressive Orthodoxy.'"[235] And what caused the general defection? Shindler was very emphatic; it was a deviation from a commitment to the infallibility and inspiration of the Holy Scriptures. He was convinced that even Arminians, when they kept sound on the Scriptures, could keep themselves from slipping down the slope. He said, "The Wesleyan Methodists of all parties are sound on that question. . . . Whatever 'down grade' tendency there may be in Arminian theology, faith in the inspiration of the Word of God and in the atoning work of the Lamb checks all downward progress."[236] Thus the first three articles were written. (For full text of Article number 3, see Appendix E.)

REACTIONS

When the three articles first appeared, they did not attract an inordinate amount of attention, no more than Spurgeon always attracted. Although the ferment had been brewing for some time, it did not seem at first that the articles would cause the furor they did. Ernest Payne related:

> [Most people] generally regarded them as an attack on the General Baptists with the theme—then not uncommon in certain circles—that Arminianism

tends toward Arianism and Socinianism, but there is little evidence that they caused serious concern . . . E. B. Underhill (Secretary of the Baptist Missionary Society) later confessed that he had rejoiced when he read the articles, never thinking that they would soon be turned on the Baptist Union.[237]

However, some articles did appear. For example, in the *Word and Work*, April 7, 1887, they commented:

The writer sees clearly the present danger in the light of the historic past. . . . Surely every right minded man, who is not prepared to surrender the faith, will concur with him in this opinion.

A few others reacted as well. Some writers almost had mild disdain for the articles. *The Christian World* (May 5, 1887) called Spurgeon's concern merely a case of the "Spiritual Fidgets." They wrote:

. . . if Mr. Spurgeon or other leaders of evangelical thought are nervous and apprehensive lest the younger generation should lose their hold of the regenerative power enshrined in the Gospels and Epistles of the New Testament, we are persuaded that their fears are not only exaggerated, but utterly unfounded.

T. R. Stevenson echoed that sentiment in a letter to *The Christian World* (May 5, 1887): "Surely, Mr. Editor, the cry of 'Wolf' is getting stale." Stevenson went on: "We want details. Do tell us *who* the heretics are, and *why* they are such. *Out with it*. . . Otherwise, . . . he (Spurgeon) runs a risk of bearing false witness against his neighbors." In *Word and Work* (May 12, 1887) T. R. Stevenson was taken to task: "Mr. Stevenson must be a very careless reader of *The Sword and the Trowel*." *The Inquirer*, a Unitarian periodical no less, wrote, "We are not quite so sure as Mr. Stevenson that Mr. Spurgeon is bearing false witness against his neighbors." However, the real conflagration was just about to heat up to white hot temperature.

SPURGEON'S ARTICLES

In August, September and October, Spurgeon followed Shindler's articles with three articles from his own pen. He wrote further articles, but the initial three articles set the full tone of Spurgeon's writing on the issues. In these articles he broadened the scope of the growing conflict considerably. Shindler had restricted his criticisms primarily against those who had slipped away from Calvinism. Spurgeon began to wage war on a much wider front. He titled his first article in August of 1887, "Another Word Concerning the Down Grade." (See Appendix F.) In this article he described the decline of evangelical doctrine generally among Dissenters. As true of his preaching style, in his writing Spurgeon used pungent Anglo-Saxon to get his message across. He declared:

The Atonement is scouted, the inspiration of Scripture is derided, the Holy Spirit is degraded into an influence, the punishment of sin is turned into a fiction, and the resurrection into a myth, and yet these enemies of our faith expect us to call them brethren and maintain a confederacy with them.[238]

He further stated:

No lover of the Gospel can conceal from himself the fact that the days are evil . . . yet our solemn conviction is that things are much worse in many churches than they seem to be, and are rapidly tending downward. . . . It now becomes a serious question how far those who abide by the faith once delivered to the saints should fraternize with those who have turned aside to another gospel. Christian love has its claims, and divisions are to be shunned as grievous evils; but how far are we justified in being in confederacy with those who are departing from the truth?[239]

Spurgeon then concluded his argument declaring he would never subordinate truth for denominational unity. He said he would stand regardless of the cost. He concluded his article by admonishing all Evangelicals:

If for a while the evangelicals are doomed to go down, let them die fighting, and in the full assurance that their gospel will have a resurrection when the inventions of 'modern thought' shall be burned up with fire unquenchable.[240]

A VITAL CONCERN

This first article of Spurgeon revealed another side to the Down Grade coin that for Spurgeon was a serious concern, namely the spiritual life of those who were on the down grade. He said, "at the back of doctrinal falsehood comes a natural decline of spiritual life, evidenced by the taste for questionable amusements, and weariness of the devotional meetings. . . . The fact is, that many would like to unite church and stage, cards and prayer, dancing and sacraments. . . . When the old faith is gone, and enthusiasm for the gospel is extinct, it is no wonder that people seek something else in the way of delight."[241] Spurgeon was as vitally concerned about the erosion of spiritual Christianity as he was about doctrinal orthodoxy. He listed a few incidents of this extreme danger. He said:

A plain man told us the other day that two ministers had derided him because he thought we should pray for rain. A gracious woman bemoaned in my presence that a precious promise in Isaiah which had comforted her had been declared by her minister to be uninspired. It is common to hear working-men excuse their wickedness by the statement that there is no hell, 'the parson says so.'[242]

In discussing the Down Grade, many writers have focused primarily if not exclusively upon the theological, doctrinal aspects of the battle. Of course, theology held a very central place in the controversy. Nevertheless, Spurgeon was just as involved in speaking against the spiritual deterioration that resulted from a loss of doctrinal integrity as he was in the loss of doctrinal integrity itself. He warned, "The coals of orthodoxy are necessary to the fire of piety."[243] This aspect of the Down Grade, so often overlooked, must not be forgotten. Spurgeon was not only a Calvinist, he was a spiritual minded man devoted to a life of godliness and holiness, a Puritan in every sense of the word. His Puritanism extended beyond theology into spirituality as well. Spurgeon wrote in *The Freeman*, June 3, 1887:

> The growing desire for a deepened spiritual life in our churches is concurrent with some remarkable instances of evangelistic success in various parts of the country. May they be the earnest of greater things?

Others saw this side of the issue too. A moral issue arose in May (10th) of 1889 centering around the "Forest of Dean Liberal Association." *The Baptist* on the same date called it the "Down Grade with a vengeance." This aspect of the controversy must be put in its proper perspective, which so often writers have seemingly failed to do.

THE ISSUE

The question can be raised, was Spurgeon right in his accusations, even though they were based upon Booth's criticisms of Bloomfield and others? Could it possibly be that he simply loved controversy? Or did perhaps the fact of his progressing illness of Bright's Disease affect his judgment? Some said it did. There are others who have intimated that he had such an ego he thought he could marshal forces behind him and strike down any theological foe.

History has proved Spurgeon did have a real case. And he was quite aware of the epicenter of the earthquake that sent reverberations all over Europe. Remember, he contended that "Germany was made unbelieving because of her preachers, and England is following in her track. Attendance at places of worship is declining, and reverence for holy things is vanishing; and we solemnly believe this is to be largely attributable to the skepticism which has flashed from the pulpit and spread among the people." Speaking to ministers, he said, "Let him be a converted man, and let him be one who believes what he preaches; for there are those around us who give us the idea that they have neither part nor lot in the matter."[244]

THE CONTROVERSY GROWS

By August of 1887, the controversy was beginning to heat up considerably. In September Spurgeon wrote another article entitled, "Our Reply to Sundry Critics and Enquiries." (See Appendix G.) He began this article by setting out four problems which he considered "matters vital to religion." The basic issues were 1) prayer-meetings were being devalued, 2) ministers were frequenting theaters, 3) "Broad School" newspapers were not respecting the truths of revelation, and 4) sound doctrine is lacking in the ministers. This article demonstrates Spurgeon's concern for the spiritual as well as the doctrinal.

In the article Spurgeon also replied to his critics who had suggested that he was sick and needed a long rest. He said, "With pretended compassion, but with real insolence, they would detract from the truth by pointing to the lameness of its witness . . . if we are to debate with Christians we should feel sure that, however short they may run of arguments, they would not resort to personalities." He went on to say further:

> Incidentally this breach of Christian courtesy goes to show that the new theology is introducing, not only a new code of morals, but a new tone and spirit. It would seem to be taken for granted, that if men are such fools as to adhere to an old-fashioned faith, of course they must be idiots, and they deserve to be treated with that contemptuous pity which is the quintessence of hate. [245]

Others suggested that Spurgeon had just written in haste and thus had not thought through the entire issue. To this criticism, Spurgeon replied, "We have waited long, perhaps too long, and have been slow to speak. . . . Had there been a right spirit in those who resent our warning, they would either have disproved our charge, or else they would have lamented its truthfulness, and have set to work to correct the evil which we lamented." [246]

Spurgeon expressed particular concern about the colleges. He no doubt had Rawdon College and Regent's Park College, as a Baptist example, in mind. He agreed with a Congregational minister who had also expressed concern about the trends in the theological schools. The Congregational pastor wrote, "I am disposed to think that your (Spurgeon's) conviction is faint compared to what the reality would warrant." Spurgeon then went on to contend that the situation was really rather deplorable. And he launched some of his criticisms at his fellow Baptists. He said, in his own unique, almost caustic, way:

> Many preachers resembled the man who put his watch in the saucepan to boil while he stood with the egg in his hand watching; they boiled the Bible and watched the congregation to see the effect. [247]

He further said concerning the weak theology of some preachers, "Some would bring their candles to show the sun." [248]

Even Oscar Wilde said:

> Many a worthy minister who passes his life in good works and kindly charity, lives and dies unnoticed and unknown; but it is sufficient for some shallow, uneducated parsman out of either University (Oxbridge) to get up in his pulpit

and express his doubt about Noah's ark, or Balaam's ass or Jonah and the whale, for half of London to flock to his church and to sit open mouthed in rapt admiration at his superb intellect.[249]

Spurgeon then concluded his article by suggesting that the churches were being divided and a polarization emerging between the orthodox and the heterodox. Obviously, if such were the true situation, Spurgeon had a right to be alarmed.

In October of 1887, Spurgeon completed his third article under the title "The Case Proved." (See Appendix H.) This article was essentially an elaboration and a bolstering up of his previous charges against heresy invading the Baptist Union. He first addressed those who denied there were problems among the Baptists. He wrote, "In many quarters the main question has been not 'How can we remove the evil?' but, 'Is there any evil to remove?'" Many were saying, particularly the writers, that they saw little or nothing of a departure from a faith among Baptist and Congregational ministers. Spurgeon suggested that the trouble with those who take this line was that they "view matters from a standpoint which makes them regard as mere changes of expression, novelties which we judge to be fatal errors from the truth."[250] Spurgeon felt that those who refused to see any deviation from "the old paths" were really expressing a denominational bias. He said, "Brethren who have been officials of a denomination have a paternal partiality about them which is so natural and so sacred, that we have not the heart to censure it. Above all things, these prudent brethren feel bound to preserve the prestige of 'the body,' and the peace of the committee . . . our Unions, Boards and Associations are so justly dear to the fathers, that quite unconsciously and innocently, they grow oblivious of evils which, to the unofficial mind, are as manifest as the sun in the heavens."[251]

In the context of this article, Spurgeon made a very interesting observation. He wrote, "to break the seal of confidential correspondence, or to reveal private conversations, would not occur to us."[252] This was probably a reference to the pledge of silence that Spurgeon had made to Booth. That pledge, mentioned earlier, thrust Spurgeon in a quandary that lost him much support. It proved a real blow to Spurgeon's credibility. Thus his critics dismissed him as a sick old man who was exaggerating the entire affair and really had no concrete evidence to substantiate his charges. And Spurgeon just had to bear it. Spurgeon's refusal to reveal names put him in an untenable stance. Craig Skinner points out:

> In the 'Down Grade' controversy he (Spurgeon) refused to share information about individuals publicly which had been given to him privately by the Baptist Union, although this would have cleared his own name. When advised, very late in the situation, that the information given was to be considered confidential, he (refused) without revealing the materials which would have cleared him of unjust criticism.[253]

With this assessment modern historians agree.

Why Samuel Booth would not come forward remains a mystery, but does not speak very well of him. He just let Spurgeon take the brunt of it all. Could it be Booth preferred a Baptist Union with doctrinal deviations to no Union at all? Perhaps that is at least part of the answer.

Another intriguing aspect of Spurgeon's last article surfaced in an extensive quote from the *Christian World*. Spurgeon stated that it was "the most conclusive evidence that we are correct in our statement that 'the new theology' is rampant among us." [254] His quotation from the *Christian World* reads:

> We are now at the parting of the ways, and the younger ministers especially must decide whether or not they will embrace and undisguisedly proclaim that 'modern thought' which in Mr. Spurgeon's eyes is a 'deadly cobra,' while in ours it is the glory of the century. It discards many of the doctrines dear to Mr. Spurgeon and his school, not only as untrue and unscriptural, but as in the strictest sense immoral; for it cannot recognize the moral possibility of imputing guilt or goodness, or the justice of inflicting everlasting punishment for temporary sin. It is not so irrational as to pin its faith to verbal inspiration or so idolatrous as to make its acceptance of a true Trinity of divine manifestation cover polytheism. [255]

Spurgeon argued this should speak for itself and thus completely make his case. Thus the trilogy of Shindler and the second trilogy by Spurgeon himself laid out before thousands of readers the issues at stake in the Down Grade.

THE BEGINNING OF THE FALLOUT

With the six articles, Spurgeon had convinced himself that the Baptist Union meeting in Sheffield that year (1887) would give serious and heartfelt attention to his accusations. However, Spurgeon was bitterly disappointed. The Union meeting in Sheffield kept strictly to the agenda and no formal discussion of Spurgeon's charges took place at all. Spurgeon had not sent any communication to the council or officials of the Union. If he wanted the Union to address the matter he probably should have, but he thought it would surely come to the floor. Douglas points out:

> Mr. Spurgeon kept hoping, hoping on, that . . . some declaration would be given in sympathy with the stand he had taken. But no. No word was spoken of the kind he passionately longed for—everything was cast the other way. The shock of the disappointment that this occasioned is not to be told. Mr. Spurgeon reeled from the blow. [256]

Of course, it became a topic of conversation over a cup of tea. Many of Spurgeon's opponents attempted to slander him by making illusions to his sickness. According to Kruppa, he "was dismayed to discover that what he considered a stirring manifesto for reform was dismissed as an old man's

senile joke by many younger members of the Baptist Union."[257] When he
spoke out, it seems incredible how few followed him. Later he would discover that even those who had written him about the deviations in the
denomination would accuse him of sounding an alarm without any real
substance or evidence. Spurgeon had no doubt grossly overestimated his
influence and the power of his articles. He apparently did not really understand the new generation of pastors. He had received such acclaim for all he
did up to that point that he had simply missed the new attitudes growing up
around him.

At the time of the Annual Sheffield meeting, some had gone so far as to
say they considered that the flap over the Down Grade had considerably
subsided. In reality, it had not yet broken in full force. The stage for the final
explosion took place when Spurgeon refused to fellowship with the "heretics" in the Baptist Union. He said in his last article "with deep regret we
abstain from assembling with those whom we dearly love and heartily respect, since it would involve us in a confederacy with those with whom we
can have no communion in the Lord."[258] Then, just before the assembly in
Sheffield, the London correspondent of *The Scotsman* printed the rumor that
Spurgeon would actually resign from the Union if the heretical ministers
were not expelled. Spurgeon's secretary outright denied that rumor. Later
the well-known evangelical paper, *The Freeman*, thought it a joke. But it did
all point up the fact that many thought Spurgeon's articles were rather
foolish and hence to be summarily dismissed. That attitude no doubt precipitated the fact that the Sheffield Assembly completely ignored the issue.
During one session at Sheffield, a brief reference was made to Mr. Spurgeon. When a certain Mr. Hughes mentioned Spurgeon's name, applause
broke out. And when Hughes then proceeded to criticize the Down Grade,
there was an outcry, but from a very marked minority.

Needless to say, Spurgeon was offended by the entire affair, but even
more so by a speech given by one of his former students, E. G. Gang of
Bristol. Gang delivered an address in Sheffield that Spurgeon considered an
attack on Calvinism. It looked as if even some of his own men were contributing to the problem. That deeply hurt Spurgeon. He really did not understand the convictions and approach of some of the younger men. He said, "I
am suffering enough just now to drive a man out of his mind, but abuse and
scorn have not the sting in them which is found in the hesitancy of friends."[259]

THE WITHDRAWAL

The fact that the Baptists did not hear Spurgeon's clear trumpet sound
and prepare for battle, and that even some of his own men made light of the
problem, led Spurgeon to make the fatal decision. He would resign the
Baptist Union, the Union of which he had been a member for decades and to
which he had contributed so much. On October 28, 1887, Charles Haddon

Spurgeon formally withdrew from the Baptist Union. He wrote a brief letter of resignation to Samuel Booth, the General Secretary of the Union:

Westwood, Beulah Hill, Upper Norwood,
October 28, 1887

Dear Friend,—I beg to intimate to you, as the secretary of the Baptist Union, that I must withdraw from that society. I do this with the utmost regret; but I have no choice. The reasons are set forth in *The Sword and the Trowel* for November, and I trust you will excuse my repeating them here. I beg you not to send anyone to me to ask for reconsideration. I fear I have considered too long already; certainly every hour of the day impresses upon me the conviction that I am moving none too soon.

I wish also to add that no personal pique or ill-will has in the least degree operated upon me. I have personally received more respect than I desired. It is on the highest ground alone that I take this step, and you know that I have long delayed it because I hoped for better things.—Yours always heartily,

C. H. Spurgeon [260]

Booth must surely have expected Spurgeon's resignation, because they had corresponded frequently on the issue. Yet, Booth appeared as though he had been completely oblivious of such an eventuality. He left the impression that Spurgeon's resignation had caught him totally off guard. He answered Spurgeon:

Beckenham, October 31, 1887

I cannot express adequately the sense of pain such a step has caused me, nor can I at present calmly think of the future. I can only leave it as it is for awhile, merely adding that I think that you have wounded the hearts of some— of many—who honour and love you more than you have any idea of, and whose counsel would have led to a far different result.

S. H. Booth [261]

So the die was cast. In reality, Spurgeon's withdrawal from the Baptist Union in some sense of the word became what might be termed "the official" beginning of the Down Grade Controversy. It became the talk of Evangelicals everywhere.

The Metropolitan Tabernacle responded with sympathy. The church minutes of October 31, 1887 read:

Resolved

That we the Deacons and Elders of the church worshipping in the Metropolitan Tabernacle hereby tender to our beloved Pastor our deep sympathy with him in the circumstances that have led to his withdrawal from the Baptist Union and we heartily concur in our sincere appreciation of the steadfast zeal with which he maintains the doctrines of the Gospel of our Lord Jesus Christ in their inspired and apostolic simplicity.

> James A. Spurgeon, Co-Pastor
> William Olney
> W. Passmore
> Thomas H. Olney
> 37 Others

Then in January of 1888, the church minutes read:

> Annual Church Meeting 1888
> January 31st
> CHS presiding
>
> The following resolution was proposed by Pastor J. A. Spurgeon and seconded by Brother B. W. Carr: That the church worshipping at the Metropolitan Tabernacle in annual meeting assembled, desires to express its hearty sympathy with its beloved pastor, C. H. Spurgeon in the testimony for truth he has recently borne by his articles upon 'The Down Grade,' endorses his action in withdrawing from the Baptist Union (follows him in the course he has taken) and pledges itself to support him by believing prayer and devoted service in his earnest contention for the faith once for all declined to the saints.
>
> Enthusiastically carried unanimously.
>
> An address of sympathy was read by Bro. Fairman.

One operating principle of the British Baptist Union centered on the fact that individuals as well as churches could become a member of the Union. Spurgeon withdrew his personal membership, but this did not necessarily mean the Metropolitan Tabernacle would also withdraw membership. But, as could be expected, the Metropolitan Tabernacle voted to follow suit a short time later. The official minutes of the Baptist Union state that the Tabernacle withdrew membership in October of 1888. Spurgeon's resignation caused a furor and a sensation throughout the Baptist world; actually, throughout the whole religious world. The explosion was heard everywhere. Spurgeon's critics immediately said he "sometimes strikes out in the dark." He actually did precipitate a situation for the critics to assail him; he put himself in something of a contradictory stance. He had said, "we may all unite around the cross." But he broke with many who were right there with him. To some it seemed illogical. Yet, it is also only fair to say, he did not break with them personally, he broke with the Union that harbored and accepted those who did deny the essence of the cross.

THE PRESS REACTION

The press came to the fore, as could be expected, and gave much attention to the entire issue. Spurgeon's own evangelical friends of the media gave him little support. *The Pall Mall Gazette*, October 29, 1887. wrote, "An appeal to Mr. Spurgeon." *The Spectator* (Oct. 29, 1887) wrote:

Mr. S. and the Baptist Union

We have always entertained a very sincere respect for Mr. Spurgeon and regard him, indeed, as one of the most earnest, honest, and high-minded of the religious teachers of the day, though not one of the most discriminating.

The secular press had a field day. *The Birmingham Post* called it "the breakup of dissent." The Birmingham paper said Spurgeon had "seceded from the Baptist denomination," which was really not true; he only resigned from the Union, not the Associational connection. On November 25, 1887, *John Bull* printed an article entitled "The Decomposition of Dissent." Articles also appeared in *The Suffolk Chronicle* and *The Auckland Chronicle, The Star,* and others. Many pamphlets were published under such titles as "The 'Down Grade' Controversy: An Appeal to Preserve the Union" by G. D. Evans, "The Down Grade . . . Before the Ark of the Lord," "The Down-Grade Controversy: The Sadducees Warned to Flee from the Ark of the Lord, The Wrath to Come" by Vincent Hall, and "What Saith the Scripture: A Word to Those Who Think of Leaving the Baptist Union" by W. P. Lockhart. Spurgeon's reaction to the press was, "Let the dogs bark; it was their nature."[262]

One interesting fact in the media blitz that followed Spurgeon's withdrawal from the Baptist Union is that three Anglican publications supported Spurgeon in his decision to withdraw. *The Rock, The Record,* and *Church Bells* all sided with Spurgeon on the issue. And, as unbelievable as it may sound, Spurgeon's old media enemy, *The Saturday Review,* actually supported him, declaring him to be "a competent witness." Articles were written in *The Freeman, The Baptist, The Christian Leader,* and other religious periodicals.

Spurgeon's withdrawal from the Union caused a stir in America. As a single case in point, in November of 1887, Spurgeon wrote a letter to the *Western Recorder,* a Baptist periodical out of Louisville, Kentucky. This publication in 1887 had a wide circulation in the south and southwest. Thomas T. Eaton had just become editor and was a confirmed Evangelical. He had championed a campaign to eliminate "new theology" from Southern Baptist Theological Seminary of Louisville. It became known as the Whitsitt Controversy. Later the *Western Recorder* became the official periodical of Kentucky Baptists alone, but in Spurgeon's day it enjoyed a very broad reading and had the reputation of defending evangelical truth. In his letter Spurgeon gave his reasons for departing from the Baptist Union, he wanted his American friends to understand his reasoning. This periodical would get the word out to many. It reads:

Mentone
Nov. 25. 87

Dear Friend,

I do not wish friends in America to judge the matter hastily: they cannot know
the ins & outs of the case. But I would have them believe that I would not have
quitted our Baptist Union if I had not felt driven to do so.

It has never comprehended the more strongly Calvinistic brethren; but that
is not by complaint. It has in it a few very pronounced 'modern thought' men.
These are by no means to be charge with reticence, & they have had sufficient
opportunities to inflict their novelties upon us. I have protested, & protested;
but in vain.

Many do not believe that this 'new theology' exists to any degree worthy of
notice. I know that it does, & cannot but wonder that any should question it.
Of course those who think all is well think me a needless alarmist. Another
section is first of all for peace & unity, & hopes that the erring ones will come
right; & therefore they are grieved to see the matter ventilated.

Others hope to purge & save the Union. All my best desires go with these;
but I have no hope of it. Essentially there is no doctrinal basis to begin with, &
many believe this to be a great beauty. 'Down with all creeds' seems to be
their watchword.

Protests failing, I left; & this has caused more enquiry than a thousand
papers would have done. I do not see that *I* could have done else. Others might
not lie under such a compulsion till they have tried to mend matters & have
failed as I have done. With no confession of faith, or avowal of principle, there
is nothing to work upon; & I do not see the use of repairing a house which is
built on the air.

Thank you much for your clippings. Send more, please, when you read
them.

Yours ever heartily,
C. H. Spurgeon [263]

Would America understand Spurgeon's withdrawal from the Union? Denominational life in America, generally speaking, took a more rigid and
connectional tone than in British Baptist life. But Spurgeon's American
Baptist friends not only understood, they fully supported Spurgeon in his
stand. The reply from the *Western Recorder*, which probably spoke for the
vast majority of American Evangelicals, reads as follows:

December 24, 1887

Rev. Charles H. Spurgeon.
Dear Sir & Bro.

I send a copy of the *Western Recorder*, with your letter to Bro. Van Denlip
of New York, who is on our staff.

We heartily thank you for the firm stand you have taken in behalf of God's truth, and for the noble testimony you have borne to time honored Baptist principles. So far as we can learn, this is the sentiment of the Baptists of the Southern States, and for the most part, of the Northern States as well.

We are not much troubled with the New Theology, outside of New England. I know but two New Theology Baptist preachers in all the 15 Southern States, & they keep quiet about it, and I hope they will come straight. If they were blatant I would have little hope.

I wish to heartily endorse all you have said and done in regard to withdrawing from the Baptist Union, and to bid you Godspeed in the good work of our Master.

I would like to have you write some for our paper, and am willing to do about it whatever is the proper thing. Our Southern Baptist Theological Seminary is here-with 144 students, and it is the largest in the circulation of the Recorder vigorously in every direction. We took charge Oct. 1st and have averaged 80 new subscribers a week. We have now 8000 subscribers and intend to have 20,000. We are spending on improving and pushing the paper every cent received from both subscribers and advertisers. It is not necessary for any of us to get any part of our support by an increase in our circulation. I mention this in the hope of convincing you that in the columns of the *Recorder*, is a good place for you to reach the Baptists of this country. If I could publish that you would write for us, that would greatly help us. Can you not let us have something from your pen during 1888? Of course we are willing to remunerate you, at whatever rate you think is right.

If you are willing to favor us with an article or two during the year; please say so that I may tell my reasons, and you can send on at your convenience what you write.

> Very respectfully and truly
> Your bro. in Christ.
> T. T. Eaton [264]

The press stirred up the evangelical spirit of the day. Public meetings were held in various places to discuss the breach in fellowship between Spurgeon and the Union. Three outstanding leaders, John Aldis, Joseph Angus, and Alexander Maclaren, all appealed for restraint among the Baptists. But the controversy now became the talk of the day, and it raged on.

Upon Spurgeon's withdrawal from the Union, some of his associates, including his son Charles, immediately resigned from the Union. As the controversy began to gain momentum and heat up, in the November issue of *The Sword and the Trowel*, Spurgeon gave his rationale for withdrawing from the Union. This was the allusion which Spurgeon made to Booth in his resignation letter. He presented his reasoning in the following words:

> Believers in Christ's atonement are now in declared union with those who make light of it; believers in Holy Scripture are in confederacy with those who

deny plenary inspiration; those who hold evangelical doctrine are in open alliance with those who call the fall a fable, who deny the personality of the Holy Ghost, who call justification by faith immoral, and hold that there is another probation after death, and a future restitution for the lost. Yes, we have before us the wretched spectacle of professedly orthodox Christians publicly avowing their union with those who deny the faith, and scarcely concealing their contempt for those who cannot be guilty of such gross disloyalty to Christ. To be very plain, we are unable to call these things Christian Unions, they begin to look like Confederacies in Evil. [265]

For Spurgeon, the issue became fellowship or truth. He wrote:

It now becomes a serious question how far those who abide by the faith once delivered to the saints should fraternize with those who have turned aside to another Gospel. Christian love has its claims, and divisions are to be shunned as grievous ends; but how far are we justified in being in confederacy with those who are departing from this truth. It is a difficult question to answer so as to be in the balance of the duties. [266]

Spurgeon further said:

We must at all costs be true. Unity is most desirable, Charity is chief among the graces; but even these must not be obtained with the blood of slaughtered truth. [267]

It is exceedingly difficult in these times to preserve one's fidelity before God and one's fraternity among men. Should not the former be preferred to the latter if both cannot be maintained? We think so. [268]

There is another matter which needs to be thought of as well as union, and that is TRUTH. To part with truth to show charity is to betray our Lord with a kiss. [269]

Spurgeon concluded it all by saying, "To pursue Union at the expense of truth is treason to the Lord Jesus." [270] And that settled it for the great preacher.

Before Spurgeon's November article in *The Sword and the Trowel*, the October 7, 1888 issue of *The Freeman* wrote a derogatory article, briefly referred to earlier. It reads:

Of course, the great joke was the Down-Grade question. It did not seem to be treated very seriously. It was about thus: Most thought it was but the 'big gooseberry' of the dull season. The successful men had little sympathy with the outcry. The unsuccessful thought, 'Say what you will, there is something in it.' [271]

But it certainly was not a joke. Weymouth deplored the fact that "such a subject was treated only as a joke by such men." [272] This deeply and profoundly grieved Spurgeon and his friends, even though later *The Freeman* issued an apology for the statement. But, later the periodical became more pointed in its reaction. *The Freeman* wrote on January 6, 1888:

> If this charge (of heresies) can be substantiated, the Union should without delay take every possible step to rid itself of the accused thing. If it cannot, Mr. Spurgeon has done a grievous injury to the ministers and churches of the Baptist denomination, for which, if faithfully dealt with, he will not be slow to make amends.

A week later *The Freeman* wrote, taking something of a self-contradictory stand:

> It is hoped Mr. Spurgeon will not become the formal accuser in a case of heresy, and that the Council of the Baptist Union will not request him to prosecute those.

The reaction to Spurgeon's withdrawal by the Council was recorded in *The Freeman*, January 20, 1888:

> Resolution by J. T. Brown:

> That the council deeply regrets the resignation of membership in the Union by the Rev. C. H. Spurgeon, whose great gifts and usefulness are matters of joy and thankfulness to them and to the whole Church of God. But inasmuch as the conciliatory efforts of the deputation have been unavailing, the council have no alternative but to accept his resignation.

> It passed, 75 being present.

The Council also resolved:

> Mr. Spurgeon should not have made charges: as Mr. Spurgeon declines to give the names of those whom he intended them to apply, and the evidence supporting them, these charges, in the judgment of the council, ought not to have been made.

As the controversy continued, the articles multiplied. Spurgeon said, "I am in seas of trouble, but the Lord High Admiral is on board."[273] *The Baptist Magazine*, the official organ of the Baptist Union, spoke on Spurgeon's resignation in these words:

> The hope we ventured to express in our last number has not been fulfilled. Mr. Spurgeon has withdrawn from the Baptist Union. No one can say that he has acted hastily, or believe for a moment that it has not been 'on the highest ground alone' that he has taken this step. Even those who are disposed to question the wisdom and utility of his act must nevertheless respect his motive, and honour him for doing—in obedience to a sense of right and from loyalty, as he conceives it, to the truth—what we trust he has done without pain. As the announcement of actual withdrawal was so long delayed, we were hoping that

it would not come at all. In that hope we have been disappointed. It is some satisfaction, however, to know that Mr. Spurgeon has no intention of placing himself at the head of a secession from the Baptist Union, and forming another denomination. We have, as it is, not only denominations enough, but rather too many. That the Union has lost the benefit of Mr. Spurgeon's membership, and his great influence for good, we most sincerely regret.

To Mentone: The Battle Continues

Early in November, Spurgeon left London to go to Mentone again for recuperation. In his absence, the Pastors' College ministers met at Dahlston Junction Chapel on November 18 to discuss the Down Grade problem. Principal Gracy presided over the meeting. In that meeting three resolutions were passed. The first resolution expressed sympathy with Spurgeon and his decision to leave the Baptist Union. The second resolution made reference to an attempt to devise some means of enticing Spurgeon to return. The third resolution, however, postponed any united action until the Union Council had issued a report. Spurgeon reacted to these resolutions with these words, "I think the three resolutions most wise, as well as most loyal to the truth. I never desire my friends to follow me slavishly in every action, but to be influenced by that grand motive which I hope inspires me."[274] To those with whom Spurgeon felt close, he gave his own more intimate reasons from withdrawing from the Union. He said:

> It was incumbent upon me to leave the Union, as my private remonstrances to officials, and my repeated pointed appeals to the whole body, had been of no avail. My standpoint had become one from which, as an earnest man, I could see no other course but to withdraw.[275]

Spurgeon went on further urging his students:

> Let us daily pray for each other, in reference to the work which lies before us, that we may be faithful unto death—faithful not only to the doctrine of truth, but to the spirit of love—warring our warfare without trace of personal bitterness, but with stern resolve to spare none of the errors which insult the sacrifice of our Lord, destroy the way of salvation in this life, and then seek to delude men with the dream of salvation after death.[276]

Then, concerning the Baptist Union, Spurgeon stated:

> It is a great grief to me that hitherto many of our most honored friends in the Baptist Union have, with strong determination, closed their eyes to the serious divergences from truth. I doubt not that their motive has been in a measure laudable, for they desired to preserve peace, and hoped that errors, which they were forced to see, would be removed as their friends advanced in years and knowledge. . . . But at last even these will, I trust, discover that the new views

are not the old truth in a better dress, but deadly errors with which we can have no fellowship. [277]

While in Mentone, Spurgeon received a conciliatory letter from James Culross of Bristol College, the current President of the Union and a very devoted man of God. Spurgeon responded in a letter dated November 26, 1887: "Do I need to say that, with you, and such brethren as Dr. Maclaren, Mr. Aldis, and Dr. Angus, I have no sort of disagreement, except that you stay in the Union and I am out of it? . . . You feel union of heart with men who publicly preach Universal Restitution: I do not. I mean, you feel enough fellowship to remain in the Union with them: I do not. It is the same with other errors. Still, I am in fellowship with you,—Union or no Union." [278]

NO CREED

In Spurgeon's letter to Culross, he raised that which he saw as one of the central issues regarding the Down Grade, namely, the absence of a creed. He wrote:

> So long as an Association without a creed has not aliens in it, nobody can wish for a creed formally, for the spirit is there; but at a time when 'strange children' have entered, what is to be done? Whatever may theoretically be in your power, you practically have no power whatever. You will go on as you are: and unless God's grace calls back the wanderers, their numbers will increase, and their courage will cause them to speak out more plainly, to the sorrow of the faithful one who shielded them in patient hope of better things. [279]

Spurgeon further said:

> Your very clear declaration, that the Union could not have a creed, or as I read it, could not declare its doctrinal views otherwise than by practicing baptism and the Lord's supper, closes the door finally against me . . . The good men who formed the Union, I fancy, had no idea that it would become what it now is, or they would have fashioned it otherwise. [280]

Spurgeon also defended himself to Culross against those who contended he had made no attempts to work within the system. He declared he had written "Presidents and Secretary on former occasions, and I have written my remonstrances again and again without avail." [281]

Several attempts were made to effect reconciliation. First, there was the resolution of the College students that means should be sought to reconcile the situation. Then on December 13, 1887, a special convened meeting of the Baptist Union Council met at the Mission House of Furnival Street in London. At that meeting of some 80 representatives (100 were on the Council roster), Angus submitted a Declaration that he and several others had drafted. The Declaration was essentially of an historical nature. It reiterated the various changes that had occurred in the Union since 1832. It affirmed the loyalty of the whole denomination to evangelical thought and set out certain doctrinal fundamentals that all believed. At this meeting James Archer Spurgeon, Charles' brother, urged that the Union adopt a fuller, more comprehensive doctrinal statement of faith that would be virtually identical with that of the Evangelical Alliance. One of the paradoxes of the situation is that James Spurgeon did not resign from the Union with his brother Charles. More shall be seen about that strange turn of events later. But the meeting came virtually to naught. The draft that Angus had drawn up was tabled along with the motion of James Spurgeon to adopt a statement of faith. Perhaps one of the primary reasons for this tabling rested in the fact that many at the Union felt that the charges that Spurgeon had brought were inaccurate.

NEW DISCOVERIES

An interesting historical note seems appropriate here. All the minutes of the Union Council meetings concerning the Down Grade Controversy were thought to be lost. When the Baptist Church House was moved from London to Didcot, the contents of the archives vault were cleaned out and all the documents sent to Regent's Park College. The Down Grade minutes were discovered in the vast amount of material. They apparently have not been seen for one hundred years, but now are available at Regent's Park. In that December 13th meeting some most interesting discussion took place. For example, a certain Mr. W. P. Lockhart said, "He (Spurgeon) thinks that he has done things which he has never done and that is what we have to face, brethren, and the ground of the thing that he thinks he has done he has been influencing large numbers of people. . . ." [282] The caustic words refer to Spurgeon's contention he had consulted with Baptist leaders on the theological problems in the Union. Lockhart simply did not believe Spurgeon. One thing that probably stirred up the Council was that Spurgeon had called the Union a "conspiracy of evil." That was rather harsh language, it must be admitted. But the ungracious words by Lockhart precipitated James Spurgeon's departure. The minutes read: "Mr. (James) Spurgeon here retired after saying that he could not long remain in the meeting after what had been said about his brother." [283]

The question was again raised, by Dr. Culross, President of the Union, why does not Spurgeon give concrete evidence of his charges? The minutes record Culross saying:

> Now I think we (have the right) to ask of (Spurgeon) who charge(s) us with the dereliction of duty to our Reedeemer [sic] where are the proofs? In our documents? Are the proofs to be found in our Constitution? Where are the proofs to be found? In the history of the past? Surely brethren if we be to blame a history of 70 years would afford ample ground for the proof required.

When you remember that during that period you have had 50 or 60 presidents occupying this Chair, men who have honorable positions in our denomination, stainless lives, all purity and all holiness. Surely had these men gone wrong, you might have found a proof of it. . . . The great work has yet to be accomplished of proving that we make void the Gospel of Jesus Christ. [284]

Booth made his reply to Culross. Samuel Booth again sidestepped the issue in a very questionable fashion. The minutes record his words:

Again I say that whatever conversations I have had with Mr. Spurgeon were not of a kind to formulate charges against brethren in order that I might submit them to this council. It never entered into my mind that Mr. Spurgeon intended the things which may have passed in conversation to be brought here and formulated as charges. [285]

The members of the Union Council also justified their rejection of Spurgeon's accusations by arguing that when members of the Baptist Union moved into a Unitarian stance, they had ceased to be associates.

What also incensed James A. Spurgeon in the Council meeting before he withdrew was that he knew Booth had not related the facts of the case. When Spurgeon learned of the situation in Mentone, he wrote back to his wife: "For Dr. Booth to say I never complained, is amazing, God knows all about it, and He will see me write it." [286] Spurgeon, quite naturally, wanted to tell the whole situation concerning the conversations between Booth and himself and what Booth had actually related to him. On one occasion he wrote:

They keep on clamouring for *names*. . . . I don't want any one to be drawn in to personalities, but if they cry 'names,' we shall have enough to give them. [287]

But right at that juncture Booth wrote, "My letters to you were not official but in confidence. As a matter of honor you cannot use them." [288] Spurgeon maintained that confidence and it put him in the position (previously pointed out) of being unable to reply to those who demanded concrete cases of defection from the faith. Thus he appeared to be the one who had fabricated in his vivid imagination the whole scenario. So the Baptist Union Council argued on over the situation.

At the December 13th meeting the Union Council voted to send a delegation to Mentone to talk with Spurgeon. After Booth read Spurgeon's letter of resignation from the Baptist Union, the minutes record:

Mr. Vincent moved and H. M. Bumpus seconded: 'that the Council receive with the deepest regret the letter of their beloved friend Mr. Spurgeon, announcing his withdrawal from membership in the Baptist Union, and request the Revs. J. Culross DD, A. Maclaren, DD, J. Clifford, DD and S.H. Booth DD, to visit him at Mentone without delay, that they deliberate with him as to how this unity of our denomination in truth, love, and good works may best be attained, and that after their return they with the President of the Union formulate such resolutions as this council may consider at its meeting in January. This resolution was carried with no dissident.

The deputation of Culross, Clifford, Samuel Harris Booth, and Alexander Maclaren contacted Spurgeon, telling of their desire to come to Mentone. But Spurgeon declined to see them, saying he would see them on his return to London the first of the year.

THE CHARGE

Actually, the Council had raised a quite serious charge against Spurgeon. Had he or had he not been in correspondence with leaders of the Baptist Union over these doctrinal deviations that precipitated his articles in *The Sword and the Trowel*, and finally culminated in his withdrawal from the Union? After the council met, Spurgeon wrote a letter to the editor of *The Baptist* dated December 19, 1887. In his correspondence he affirmed his "private remonstrance to officials and repeated pointed appeals to the whole body" was absolutely true. He declared he had complained to the President of the Union back in 1883 after the Leicester meeting. Not only that, he contended "since then I have repeatedly spoken to the secretary (Booth) on the subject, as he will willingly admit,"[289] Spurgeon went on to argue that he had considerable correspondence with Mr. Williams and Dr. Maclaren. Spurgeon brought his argument to a close by writing, "I will not venture to say definitely how many of the Council knew my views and feelings by hearing me utter them at various times, but more than enough to justify my statement to Mr. Mackey."[290] Yet, in the dynamics of it all, Spurgeon kept a quite amicable, Christian spirit and acquiesced to the Council's request for a meeting with its representatives on his return from Mentone. His health did not permit a meeting in France.

On January 13, 1888, Spurgeon was back in London and met with the Union's representatives, Culross, John Clifford, and Samuel Booth at the Metropolitan Tabernacle. Unfortunately, Alexander Maclaren could not attend. The meeting itself proved to be quite tense and Spurgeon adamantly refused to withdraw his resignation. He wanted the Union to formulate a statement of faith. Baptists had traditionally done that through the years. Spurgeon was committed to the principle of a statement of faith as a bulwark against heresy. He declared:

> I am unable to sympathize with a man who says he has no creed; because I believe him to be in the wrong. . . . He ought to have a creed—he must have one, even though he repudiates the notion. . . . The objection to a creed is a very pleasant way of concealing objection to discipline, and (reveals) a desire for latitudinarianism. What is wished for is a Union, which will, like Noah's

Ark, afford shelter for the clean and unclean, for creeping things and winged fowls. [291]

Thus he urged them to adopt a statement similar to that of the Evangelical Alliance. Spurgeon contended that Angus' declaration simply did not go far enough. Spurgeon said that even if an evangelical statement of doctrine were drawn and accepted, he would still not immediately rejoin the Union. He would want to see how it would be implemented and enforced in the life of the Union.

Spurgeon's resistance to rejoin the Union as it then stood centered around two issues. First, he did not believe that the Union had any authority over those who got on the theological down grade. Secondly, he contended that even the Union's constitution contained no provision for dealing with the divergences of doctrinal opinion. Illustrative of the point, in a Union Council meeting in March of 1888, Spurgeon was present, and when asked about any defections from traditional orthodoxy, Spurgeon replied, "To put the matter briefly, this brother is preaching that there are two deities, a good and a bad . . . but *there is nothing in our Union to put him out.*"[292] Spurgeon's attitude and opinions caused some resentment and bolstered up the contention that Spurgeon's accusations were "a charge against anonymity."[293]

Perhaps the greatest mystery of the meeting centers in the fact that, even in the dynamic of a private interview seeking reconciliation, Samuel Booth would not confess he had fed Spurgeon names and issues, and thus the doubts cast upon Charles' integrity were groundless. The question has been raised, why did Spurgeon not challenge Booth at that meeting? The answer again seems to be that Spurgeon simply kept his word to Booth and would not reveal what he had pledged to keep secret. As a consequence of his gentlemanly and Christian adherence to his word, he received the slander of others. Simply put, the meeting was a dismal failure. Nothing was accomplished. The accusations remained, the representatives of the Union were helpless.

THE IMPASSE

A perfect impasse had been created. At the meeting of the Union representatives and Spurgeon, they had demanded that he either recant of his accusations or give concrete evidence for them. John Clifford was to write, "What is wanted is not wild rumor, but evidence . . . not the gossip of careless and malevolent tongues, but fact . . . tested evidence on which the accused himself has been fully heard."[294] When Spurgeon refused to do both, the dilemma was crystallized. Something had to be done. The Union was, in many senses of the word, on the line for its own integrity because of the powerful personality and wide-spread reputation of Spurgeon. R. F. Horton stated, "Such was the fame and deserved authority of the great preacher, that to lie under his censure was to forfeit the favor of by far the larger portion of evangelical Christians."[295] What to do?

The answer to the situation came about at the January 18, 1888 meeting of the Union Council. In that gathering two resolutions with respect to Spurgeon were passed. The first resolution accepted Spurgeon's resignation with deep and profound regret. The second resolution that embittered so many and was so controversial became known as the "Vote of Censure." The resolution read:

> That the Council recognized the gravity of the charges which Mr. Spurgeon has brought against the Union previous to and since his withdrawal. It considers that the public and general manner in which they have been made reflects on the whole body, and exposes to suspicion brethren who love the truth as dearly as he does. And, as Mr. Spurgeon declined to give names of those to whom he intended them to apply, and the evidence supporting them, those charges in the judgment of the council, ought not to have been made.[296]

Both motions passed by an overwhelming majority. As inconceivable as it may seem, only five members voted in opposition to the resolution, one being James Spurgeon. William Landalls moved the motion. He had been a very close associate of Spurgeon for many years and a strong supporter of Spurgeon during the Baptismal Regeneration Controversy. As can be understood, Spurgeon felt deeply hurt by the insinuations implied in the resolution, and, of course, by the fact that William Landalls had made the motion. He received it as a vote of censure for his stand in the controversy. It may be that Spurgeon was too sensitive at this point. John Clifford maintained throughout his life that the so-called "censure" was never meant to be that. Marchant, in his biography of Clifford, said:

> He agreed with it, but to the end of his life he stoutly denied that it was intended as a censure, or that its terms (regardless of intention) made it so. During the last two years of his life this was one of the main things that he wanted to make clear to his fellow Baptists. He claimed that all the survivors from 1888, including the seconder of the resolution (Rev. Edward Medley), agreed with him.[297]

More and more it seemed as though the confrontation was between Spurgeon and Clifford, but that really is not true. It was a Union matter. Glover, in the *Evangelical Nonconformist*, stated that the Union Council really could not face the charge there were those in their midst who had actually got on the "down grade" and thus lost at least a measure of their evangelical faith. Moreover, Glover contended they were afraid that any admission of Spurgeon's specific charges would lead to fruitless controversy in the Union. As a result:

> The policy which they adopted was to attempt to put the responsibility for disturbing the peace of the Union back on Spurgeon. They took the position

that his charges were too vague to merit serious investigations, that he had failed to substantiate them by naming any ministers who were guilty. However useful this policy might have been politically, it can only be described as dishonest trifling with the subject.

Glover went on to argue there was a measure of dishonesty in the Council's pronouncements. He contended that several members of the Council were in basic theological disagreement with Spurgeon on at least one or more of the issues involved. Glover stated that John Clifford and his chief supporters, Alexander Maclaren and Charles Williams, had themselves rejected the doctrine of the inerrancy of the Scriptures. And all knew that Samuel Cox, a distinguished Baptist minister had embraced universalism. Glover held that the situation really was such that the Council's demand that Spurgeon prove his charges by naming the guilty persons constituted no more than a political maneuver. Glover observed that:

> If Spurgeon had named the popular Clifford or Maclaren as a heretic, he would have greatly prejudiced his case . . . (On the other hand) to have named only extremists like Cox would not have served Spurgeon's purpose, which was to stop the slow drift of less extreme men away from the old evangelicalism.[298]

But a final resolution did come before the body to "decide to hold another meeting of the Council in February to consider Mr. Spurgeon's proposals in regard to a declaration of faith."[299]

The Baptist Magazine quite naturally came to the defense of the Union's actions. It argued that "even if Mr. Spurgeon's charges had been capable of substantiating (and we cannot for a moment admit that they are), the manner in which they have been made seems to us utterly at variance with the mind of Christ."[300] The magazine further contended that Spurgeon should have privately addressed those with whom he had disagreed. They concluded that had Spurgeon done this, he would have never needed to withdraw from the Union and he would not have "made what we cannot but regard as the greatest mistake of his life."[301]

SPURGEON'S DEFENSE

Spurgeon could hardly take all the accusations lying down. In *The Sword and the Trowel* of February of 1888, he gave his response. He presented his reasons for not making specific charges and also his proposed solution for correcting the basic problem. He wrote:

> I brought no charges before the members of the Council, because they could only judge by their constitution, and that document lays down no doctrinal basis except the belief that 'the immersion of believers is the only Christian baptism.' Even the mention of evangelical sentiments has been cut from their printed programme. No one can be heterodox under this constitution, unless he

should foreswear his baptism. I offered to pay the fee for Counsel's opinion upon this matter, but my offer was not accepted by the deputation. There was, therefore, nothing for me to work upon, whatever evidence I might bring. [302]

Spurgeon's whole argument, as repeatedly seen, rested on his conviction that no binding authority existed in the Union to which any appeal of heresy could be made. He then once again stated the Union's doctrinal position was indefinable. He very forthrightly declared:

> I would like all Christians to know that all I asked of the Union is that it be formed on a Scriptural basis; and that I never sought to intrude upon it any Calvinistic or other personal creed, but only that form of belief which has been accepted for many years by the Evangelical Alliance, which includes members of well-nigh all Christian communities. [303]

Spurgeon argued no charges could be alleged if there were no standards of judgment. Spurgeon also gave as a reason for his refusal to supply names that he would be liable to lawsuits for slander. His brother James had warned him of that possibility. Such possible problems existed in Spurgeon's day as in ours. One wonders, however, how much of a factor in Spurgeon's thinking these arguments really were. It has already been made amply clear that he had given his word to Booth that he would not reveal names. That seems to be the primary reason, although perhaps the threat of a lawsuit and the other rationale did cause him some pause. A. C. Underwood, in his *History of the English Baptists*, drew a similar conclusion. He said:

> More than once (Booth) had written to Spurgeon complaining of the theological views of certain Baptist ministers. . . . When Spurgeon was asked to substantiate his charges . . . he reminded Booth of these letters, but the latter pleaded with him not to divulge them, but to treat them as private and confidential. Spurgeon was placed in a difficult position by his honourable compliance with his friend's request. [304]

This seems to be the real heart of the issue concerning Spurgeon's silence. Why this was not recognized by the Council—and appreciated—remains a mystery. If these facts are so clear today, surely they were known in Spurgeon's day. There were even writings to vindicate Spurgeon's charges. Perhaps it is true, as the accusation had been made, there were those on the Council itself who disagreed theologically with Spurgeon and perhaps had at least one foot on the down grade themselves and thus looked for an easy way out. The Council may have used a measure of political maneuvering. The tragedy is, Spurgeon lived with the censure the rest of his days. As biographer Carlile pointed out:

> Spurgeon never was righted. The impression in many quarters remains that he made charges that he could not substantiate, and when properly called upon to produce the evidence he resigned and ran away. Nothing is further from the

truth. Spurgeon might have produced Dr. Booth's letters; I think he should have done so.

The position was more than difficult. Mr. Spurgeon and Dr. Booth had been friends for many years. Both acted in good faith. Spurgeon had plenty of evidence; there were the utterances of well-known men which had been published in the pages of the *Christian World*, and the *Independent*, the *Freeman*, the *British Weekly* and the *Baptist*. Reference to the files of these journals for 1887 and 1888 can still be made, and will provide ample proof of the truth of Spurgeon's general charge. [305]

The battle of words and writing went on.

THE DECLARATION

Another meeting of the Council took place on February 21, 1888 in which the Angus' Declaration, which had been tabled previously, again became the issue. A proposal was made to present it to the general assembly in April. James Spurgeon supported the proposal, and the vote carried 35 to 5 to present the statement of faith to the Union. Perhaps this would save the situation. But then John Clifford wrote a preamble to the Statement of Faith which reads:

> . . . that the doctrinal beliefs of the Union . . . must be determined by the doctrinal beliefs of the churches and Associations of which the Union was composed. Secondly, that the Council of the Union therefore disclaims altogether any authority to formulate a new and additional standard of theological belief as a bond of union to which assent shall be required. [306]

At first, James Spurgeon felt Clifford's preamble would be acceptable. But in consultation with his brother Charles, he agreed that the preamble changed the entire character of the Declaration. James, therefore, informed the group that he had a stronger Statement of Faith than Angus' Declaration that he wished to present, and would present it by amending Angus' statement at the April meeting. But Angus' position, along with Clifford's preamble, prevailed and James lost the battle. As a result, Thomas Greenwood, along with James, withdrew from the London Baptist Association.

Obviously, one of the problems that caused the Down Grade to be such a knotty problem centered in the fact that Baptists have tended to consider themselves a non-creedal people. They have a natural suspicion of any creedal statement. But Angus' simple Declaration could hardly be called creedal. After the preamble, penned by John Clifford, all it consisted of was first a brief statement on the nature of the ordinances of baptism and the Lord's Supper. Then a declaration setting out the nature of the Baptist Union was outlined. Following that, a simple doctrinal statement affirmed the inspiration of the Scriptures, the sinfulness of man, the person and work of

Christ, justification by faith, the work of the Holy Spirit, the reality of the resurrection, and final judgment. Despite some of the weaknesses of the declaratory statement, it nevertheless read in many ways quite similar to the doctrinal basis of the Evangelical Alliance. What weakened it so severely in Spurgeon's thinking was Clifford's preface. The Council met again on April 20, three days before the assembly meeting at the London City Temple. James Spurgeon said he would not press for an amendment if Clifford's preamble would be withdrawn. The Council met and agreed upon this course. The vote passed with only 17 dissenting.

THE ASSEMBLY MEETING

On April 23, the Assembly met in Dr. Parker's City Temple. The body listened to an address by the new President, John Clifford. He entitled his sermon "The Great Forty Years." In his message, Clifford outlined and recounted the spiritual fervor of the New Testament Church during its first four decades. He compared the Union's evangelical approach with the early church, thus defending it against Spurgeon's charges. Practically everyone felt it to be a very stirring and impassioned sermon. In the spirit of the hour, the excited crowd accepted the Council's preliminary resolutions without any serious debate. Then the declaratory statement of Angus was presented. It began by disavowing and disallowing any power to control any individual. It further went on to disclaim any role that it might have to enforce legislation, despite the deletion of Clifford's preamble. This was serious. Moreover, a footnote was added to the last clause which stated that some "brethren in the Union . . . have not held the common interpretation of these words of our Lord." [307] The clause referred primarily to the resurrection and the judgment of the last day. Charles Williams delivered a speech in strong support of the footnote. This in reality gave acceptance to those who held an annihilationist or universalistic theological position. James Spurgeon seconded the motion for the Declaration, but not for the speech of Williams. C. H. Spurgeon said later, "In the declaration I rejoice, and still more in the kindly spirit which found joy in conciliating opponents; but the speech of Mr. Williams launches us upon a shoreless sea." [308] It does seem incontestable that there were avowed universalists in the Baptist Union.

There were many who felt that the passing of the Declaration would surely open the door for Spurgeon to rejoin the Baptist Union. The Union accepted Angus' Declaration almost unanimously: 2,000 in favor and only 7 declining votes. The London Baptist Association also accepted it overwhelmingly. When the convener announced the vote there was actually cheering on the floor. They thought surely this would settle the controversy. But, to Spurgeon it had a devastating effect. He interpreted it as another censure, this time from the Assembly itself and not just from the Union Council that had previously taken their rather censorious stand. He wrote to a friend on April 26:

My brother thinks he has gained a great victory, but I believe we are hopelessly sold. I feel heartbroken. Certainly he has done the very opposite of what I
should have done. Yet he is not to be blamed, for he followed his best judgment. Pray for me, that my faith fail not. [309]

Spurgeon's brother James disturbed him; he had actually seconded the
motion for the Angus Declaration, even including the footnote. Charles
lamented what he considered the misjudgment of his brother. Spurgeon felt
that the Union truly had been launched on a "shoreless sea." After the April
1888 General Assembly, Spurgeon made no more moves or overtures toward the Baptist Union nor they toward him.

At the end of April, Spurgeon also withdrew from the London Baptist
Association which he had helped to found in 1865. But the personal fellowship did not die. For example, in February of 1889, the London Baptist
Association sent Charles a telegram expressing good wishes for his health.
He responded in a very brotherly fashion. He was commended for his
gracious response by T. Vincent Tymns in *The Baptist*, even though Tymns
said he "depreciated Mr. Spurgeon's action in respect to the Association."
Even though Charles had withdrawn from the London Baptist Association,
he obviously still had fellowship with some persons in the group. Remember, he once said to James Culross, "I am in fellowship with you, Union or
no Union."

It had been suggested in *The Daily Telegraph* in April (8th) 1889, that
Spurgeon subtly desired to join the Church of England. He responded,
saying he "never dreamed of entering the Church of England." [310]

THE NEW DECLARATION

About two months before the Assembly meeting, Spurgeon had presented a new Declaration of Faith to the organization of the College men, and
eighty former students defected. Spurgeon was all but devastated at the
rebellion of his own men. He wrote to a friend on Feb. 21, 1888, "I have
been sorely wounded and thought I would quite break down, but the Lord
has revived me and I shall yet see his truth victorious. I cannot tell you by
letter what I have endured in the desertion of my own men. Ah me! Yet the
Lord liveth, and blessed be my rock!" [311] But Spurgeon left the door open for
his "straying sheep." In writing to Mr. Near, Feb. 10, 1890 he said:

Any brother who will sign the basis can return to our College Association, but
I would not entertain any proposal to make the signature optional. [312]

And again in a letter to Near dated Feb. 22, 1890 he wrote:

Those who hold the fundamental truths can return to us on the terms laid
down, and on no others. . . . I have suffered enough for one life time from

those whom I had lived to serve . . . Those who wish to return can come and welcome, and no one more pleased to see them than I; but not to doubtful disputations and cavillings.[313]

The new creed was penned by Spurgeon and thirty other ministers. It proved to be a strong affirmation of evangelical theology. It reads:

We, as a body of men, believe in the 'doctrine of grace,' what are popularly styled Calvinistic views (though we by no means bind ourselves to the teaching of Calvin, or any other uninspired man), but we do not regard as vital to our fellowship any exact agreement upon all the disputed points of any system, yet we feel that we could not receive into this our union any who do not unfeignedly believe that salvation is all of the free grace of God from first to last, and is not according to human merit, but by the undeserved favour of God. We believe in the eternal purpose of the Father, the finished redemption of the Son, and the effectual work of the Holy Ghost.

1. The Divine inspiration, authority, and sufficiency of the Holy Scriptures.
2. The right and duty of private judgment in the interpretation of the Holy Scriptures, and the need of the teaching of the Holy Spirit, to a true and spiritual understanding of them.
3. The unity of the Godhead and the Trinity of the persons therein, namely, the Father, the Son, and the Holy Ghost.
4. The true and proper Godhead of our Lord Jesus, and his real and perfect manhood.
5. The utter depravity of human nature in consequence of the Fall, which Fall is no fable nor metaphor, but a literal and sadly practical fact.
6. The substitutionary sacrifice of the Lord Jesus Christ, by which alone sin is taken away, and sinners are saved.
7. The offices of our Lord as Prophet, Priest and King, and as the one Mediator between God and man.
8. The justification of the sinner by faith alone, through the blood and righteousness of the Lord, Jesus Christ.
9. The work of the Holy Spirit in the regeneration, conversion, sanctification, and preservation of the saved.
10. The immortality of the soul, the resurrection of the body, and the judgment of the world by our Lord Jesus, which judgment will be final, according to the words of the Great Judge: 'These shall go away into eternal punishment, but the righteous into eternal life.'
11. The Divine institution of the Christian ministry, and the obligation and perpetuity of the ordinances of Believers' Baptism and the Lord's Supper.

We utterly abhor the idea of a new Gospel or an additional revelation, or a shifting rule of faith to be adapted to the ever-changing spirit of the age. In particular we assert that the notion of probation after death, and the ultimate restitution of condemned spirits, is so unscriptural and un-protestant and so unknown to all Baptist Confessions of Faith, and draws with it such consequences, that we are bound to condemn it, and to regard it as one with which we can hold no fellowship.

The refusal to endorse the declaration and the subsequent defections of the Pastors' College men are difficult to understand. Surely, one would have thought they could embrace the above declaration. Perhaps George Rogers was correct when in April of 1887 he said young ministers went astray theologically because they wanted to be known as intellectuals.

A NEW COLLEGE ASSOCIATION

In May, due to the defection of Spurgeon's former students, the Pastors' College Conference was re-formed as the Pastors' College Evangelical Association. They adopted the Confession of Faith presented above which Spurgeon had written along with other ministers. This same statement Spurgeon had suggested to the Baptist Union, but they rejected it. In contrast to the declaratory statement accepted by the Baptist Union and the London Baptist Association, Spurgeon's Confession of Faith differed from the declaratory statement of the Union in its emphasis on the inspiration of the Scriptures, the substitutionary sacrifice of Christ, and the hopeless perdition of all who rejected Jesus Christ as Lord and Savior. For Spurgeon, these three essential doctrines had to be maintained especially in the light of those who had started on the down grade. Spurgeon centered his concern on the plenary, verbal inspiration of the Scriptures, the vicarious, sacrificial atonement of Jesus Christ, and the future punishment of unbelievers. In these areas the inroads of biblical criticism had made themselves felt. To Spurgeon, these doctrines were not secondary matters, they stood right at the heart of the Christian faith. He wrote in *The Sword and the Trowel*:

> There can be no compromise: We cannot hold the inspiration of the Word and yet reject it; we cannot believe in the atonement and deny it; we cannot hold the doctrine of the fall and yet talk of the evolution of spiritual life from human nature; we cannot recognize the punishment of the impenitent and yet indulge the 'larger hope.' One way or the other we must go. Decision is the virtue of the hour. [314]

These were the issues, and clearly they truly are issues to defend at all costs.

A little over a year before his death, in 1890, as pointed out, Spurgeon withdrew from the Liberation Society. As seen, this group fought for the disestablishment of the Church of England. Although Spurgeon had labored for disestablishment all of his ministry, he felt that the battle for the essentials of the Evangelical faith took on far more importance than disestablishment.

SPURGEON'S SUPPORTERS

In many senses of the word, Spurgeon did not stand alone in his decisions over the Down Grade Controversy. There were many in Britain who supported him, although he received censure by his own Baptist friends. As implied earlier, his greatest support actually came from evangelical Anglicans, the very group he had once so severely criticized in the Baptismal Regeneration Controversy. A classic example is the case of Canon Francis Cruse. He had written a very denunciatory pamphlet against Spurgeon in 1864, but then he published a very positive pamphlet defending Charles in 1888. When Spurgeon withdrew from the London Baptist Association, Charles expressed his appreciation for the hearty support he had received from the Evangelical Alliance. When he spoke to the Alliance, they "greeted him with such a reception so tumultuous that tears streamed down from the preacher's face." [315]

As paradoxical as it seems, many of Charles' closest Baptist friends deserted him, as he conversely gained friends and allies in the Established Church. Almost miraculously, former adversarial papers like *The Rock* and, as mentioned, *The Saturday Review,* actually defended him. It all proved a strange turn of events. Canon Basil Wilberforce entertained him, bishops and archbishops befriended him, and he found himself in the good graces of much of Anglicanism. Moreover, as the previous letters have demonstrated, he was widely supported among all evangelical circles in America, including the Baptists, particularly Southern Baptists.

It must be admitted that in some sense of the word, Spurgeon assumed a martyr's role. Having withdrawn from the Baptist Union, the London Baptist Association, the Liberation Society, he felt quite alone, even somewhat ostracized. He tried to rise above the crisis and say that his denominational isolation did not really affect him or his ministry. In the heat of the controversy itself, he wrote to a friend, "I shall live if I am quite alone; in fact, I shall live all the better, for the more associations, the more care and trouble." [316] His wife Susannah became a tower of strength to him. Charles said to her, "You are an angel of God to me . . . Bravest of women strong in the faith, you have ministered unto me . . . God bless thee out of the Seventh Heaven."

SPURGEON'S AFFILIATIONS

It has been said that Spurgeon really cared little for denominationalism. His ecumenical background and approach, some declared, had put him in a frame of mind where association with those of like faith did not concern him. It can be understood why some would think this of Spurgeon. He had said in a letter to a Mr. Wright, "I have no wish to join any Association, for I fear they will all sooner or later go wrong." [317] But he had a change of heart and mind. On June 16, 1888, Spurgeon wrote to Mr. Near the following letter:

The Surrey, Middlesex, and Suburban (Association) is quitting the Union, and I shall probably unite with it. This will be an Association outside of the Union, sound in doctrine and thus the nucleus of a fresh Union.

He went on to condemn the Baptist Union saying:

But there are many more rotten men in the Union than I dreamed of. The whole head is sick, the whole heart faint. [318]

He had made it clear he would not join any association affiliated with the Baptist Union. For example, apparently some association sent him papers to fill in if he wanted to join them. He replied:

Having no connection with the Baptist Union, and no wish to be thought to have any, I must decline to fill up the papers you have sent. You have only fulfilled your official duty; but I have no wish to appear in the Handbook at all while it is the organ of a Confederacy against which I sorrowfully protest. [319]

Spurgeon was even more deeply convinced the Baptist Union had become a "confederacy of evil." In June of 1888 he wrote to a friend: "The more you have to deal with that evil confederacy the worse you will like it." [320] Such rhetoric caused deep resentment by many in the Union.

But the Surrey and Middlesex Association did leave the Baptist Union—perhaps to include Spurgeon in their ranks. At any rate, he joined them. In his letter of intent, October 30, 1888, he wrote the following:

I feel that I can endorse your principles . . . I apply for personal membership with you on the belief that you are not a part of the Baptist Union. [321]

Spurgeon could well endorse the doctrinal position of the Association. They had a Declaration of Faith that set forth evangelical Calvinism. It reads:

Surrey and Middlesex Statement of Faith

Declaration

That among the truths believed and held by the Churches comprising this Association, the following are entitled to special enumeration:—

1. The Divine inspiration of the Scriptures of the Old and New Testaments and their absolute sufficiency as the only authorized guide in matters of religion.
2. The existence of three equal persons in the Godhead—the Father, the Son, and the Holy Spirit.
3. Eternal and personal election to holiness here, and eternal life hereafter.
4. The depraved and lost state of mankind.
5. The atoning efficacy and vicarious nature of the death of Christ.
6. Free justification by his imputed righteousness. The necessity and efficacy of the work of the Holy Spirit in conversion and sanctification.

7. The final preservation of the saints.
8. The duty of all men to whom the Gospel is made known to believe and receive it.
9. The spirituality of the Kingdom of Christ, and His supreme authority as sole Head of the Church.
10. The resurrection of the dead, both the just and the unjust.
11. The general judgment.
12. The eternal happiness of the righteous, and the eternal misery of such as die impenitent. [322]

So Spurgeon once again affiliated himself with a Baptist body. The Metropolitan Tabernacle concurred with their pastor's decision. The church minutes record:

> May 5, 1890:
> Special Church Meeting: after service
> Pastor CHS presiding
>
> Deacon Buswell offered prayer, the Pastor then stated that he had for some time been a personal member of the Surrey and Middlesex Baptist Association, but he thought that in the interest of the Church as source of strength to the Association, this Church should be affiliated. Resolved: that this Church do apply for admission to the Surrey and Middlesex Association. [323]

It seems Spurgeon's joining of the Association brought criticism to the group. Charles wrote them:

> I am afraid I have caused you a deal of trouble and reproach. I don't think I should have professed to join you had I known that there has been so much contention. [324]

But Spurgeon maintained his desire to join the Association and spoke at the Associational meeting on May 21, 1889. He was elected a member on that date. He spoke again in 1890 and multitudes came—he was still very popular. Spurgeon's only lingering concern about the Surrey and Middlesex Association was that it might establish too strong ties with the Baptist Union. He wrote to them in the following manner:

> I apply for personal membership with you on the belief that you are not a part of the Baptist Union. Of course, consistency requires that if you declare yourself to have quitted a tree you cannot hold on to one of the branches. [325]

James Spurgeon, who had also joined the Association, was elected Moderator of the Association. After the Surrey and Middlesex Association accepted Charles, he became as active as he could. He was also instrumental in having the name of the Association changed to the Home Counties Association. So Spurgeon and his Metropolitan Tabernacle were not Independent Baptists, as some would like to emphasize. He had a denominational loyalty, even if not quite as strong as his brother James. But that he had an independent spirit also there can be no doubt. Yet, he saw the tremendous value of the fellowship of like-minded believers; hence, he joined the Home Counties Association and remained in that group until his death.

EVALUATIONS OF THE DOWN GRADE

Many evaluations have been made concerning Spurgeon during this most traumatic event. As late as May (29) 1891, *The Baptist* reported, "No living man has done so much for the Baptist denomination as he." Others called him the Athanasius of the day. His creed, they said, was "equivalent for the Athanasian Creed." [326] Such words surface the question often raised, did Spurgeon then win the battle? But surely the issue is not did he win or lose; the issue is he stood unswervingly for what he believed to be the essentials of the faith. To his credit, he did not battle over theological minutia such as eschatology or even ecclesiology. Actually, his emphases did not even center on his cherished Calvinism as a system. His concern for his Calvinistic position only related to those aspects of Calvinism that touched on the fundamentals of the faith. For these he stood, and that is what matters.

In June (26th) 1891, Spurgeon and twenty-nine others published in the *Word and Work* what they called their "A Timely Manifesto." It reads as follows:

> Recent serious departures from the doctrines of grace have been viewed by many with alarm and anxiety. As it became daily more apparent that the surrender of vital truth is more common and widespread than at first supposed, it was laid on the hearts of a few friends to meet together for prayer and consultation. After weeks of waiting and counsel it seemed good to them to form a Fraternal Union of all like-minded men who were still content to walk in the old paths. Having issued invitations to those whom they believed to be in full sympathy with them, the ready response they received proved the time to be ripe for a protest against abounding errors, and a manifesto of the doctrines still dear to not a few. The following statement, in printed form, has, we believe, been widely circulated:—
>
> We, the undersigned, banded together in Fraternal Union, observing with growing pain and sorrow the loosening hold of many upon the Truths of Revelation, are constrained to avow our firmest belief in the Verbal Inspiration of all Holy Scripture as originally given. To us, the Bible does not merely *contain* the Word of God, but *is* the Word of God. From beginning to end; we accept it, believe it, and continue to preach it. To us, the Old Testament is not less inspired than the New. The Book is an organic whole. Reverence for the New Testament accompanied by skepticism as to the OLD appears to us absurd. The two must stand or fall together. We accept Christ's own verdict

concerning 'Moses and all the prophets' in preference to any of the supposed discoveries of so-called higher criticism.

We hold and maintain the truths generally known as 'the doctrines of grace.' The Electing Love of God the Father, the Propitiatory and Substitutionary Sacrifice of His Son Jesus Christ, Regeneration by the Holy Ghost, the Imputation of Christ's Righteousness, the Justification of the sinner (once for all) by faith, his walk in newness of life and growth in grace by the active indwelling of the Holy Ghost, and the Priestly Intercession of our Lord Jesus, as also the hopeless perdition of all who reject the Saviour, according to the words of the Lord in Matt. XXV. 46, 'These shall go away into eternal punishment,'—are, in our judgment, revealed and fundamental truths.

Our hope is the Personal Pre-millennial Return of the Lord Jesus in glory.

It was signed by thirty men, including Spurgeon and his son, Charles, Jr. Then, a word of interpretation followed:

Perhaps the use of the phrase 'verbal inspiration' may give rise to misrepresentation. It is not intended thereby to assert the dictation, word by word, to the writers of the various books, of the language they employed; nor is it meant to convey the impression that the words of wicked men or of Satan recorded in the Book are inspired of God; but only that the human authors were guided by the Holy Ghost to choose the best and most fitting words for the conveyance to man of the Divine revelation. In such a Volume thoughts can only be expressed in words, and unless these have Divine authority there is no sufficient guarantee against error. It is to be hoped that an oft-explored objection will not again be raised.

Such a manifesto as this is at least timely, and the men who sign it make no secret of their creed.

Let it again be said, for it is the heart of the matter, Spurgeon defended the bulwarks of the faith, not the implied nuances. The atonement of Christ, the inspiration and total authority and truthfulness of the Scriptures, the reality of eternity, etc.; for these he stood, and they are not peripheral matters. If these doctrines are laid aside by human rationalization, what is left of the Christian faith? So Spurgeon stood and stood tall and brave. Lorimer is probably right when he says:

It must be remembered that during the last years of his life, whether he confessed it or not, he felt deep down in his soul that he was the Elijah of his age, and that practically he was the lonely prophet of Horeb standing out against the priests of Baal in behalf of the precious teachings of Heaven.

Whether he won or not is secondary. God calls His servants to stand, not to be victorious in the eyes of the world, or even in the eyes of a non-discerning Church.

Moreover, history has shown Spurgeon to have taken basically the right course. First of all, he was a man of integrity and would not betray his own word in the encounter with Booth. History has fully vindicated him on that point. Furthermore, he saw essential Christian truth as more important than mere superficial unity. History always proves that to be correct. Unity is important and Spurgeon recognized it; thus he joined the Surrey and Middlesex Baptist Association, and, moreover kept himself in fellowship with Evangelicals. But basic truth must come first! Also to his credit he adamantly refused to start a new Baptist group. He received much pressure to do so. A word actually began to make its way around evangelical centers: "Spurgeonism." *The New York Independent* in 1866, after extolling Spurgeon's virtues, wrote:

> If this goes on for another twenty years, Spurgeonism will be a vast organic and wondrously vitalized body; and, should circumstances warrant, this body may, as many intelligent Baptist ministers think, probably assume the name of its founder, and Spurgeon follow the example of Wesley, by founding a sect.

Spurgeon's reaction was, "There is no word in the world so hateful to our heart as that word Spurgeonism, and no thought further from our soul than that of forming a new sect."[327] As far back as 1866 in *The Sword and Trowel* (March 1866), he wrote: "It is true that it has long been in our power to commence a new denomination, but it is not true that it has ever been contemplated by us or our friends."

POSITIVE CONTRIBUTIONS

The Down Grade Controversy made three positive contributions. First, it helped clear up the hazy theology some entertained. In that context, the evangelistic fervor of many was ignited. The statistics of the Baptist Union in the next few years showed good growth. Secondly, it interested lay people in theology. That is always positive. Thirdly, it helped Spurgeon and the Baptist Union to understand one another as to who they truly were. These were all contributions. The affair also helped the Pastors' College in that it forced the College Conference to adopt a constitution and statement of faith that eliminated some, but probably strengthened the work in the long run. Spurgeon had founded some 200 churches and they moved on in good fashion, charged by the affair. Finally, he willingly sacrificed his reputation for the truth as he understood it. John Wesley once said, "When I gave my life to God, I did not make an exception of my reputation." History smiles on that. One thus can conclude Spurgeon's basic vindication in the Down Grade Controversy, even if he did not always make the right choice or battle wisely.

The entire Down Grade Controversy demonstrated an important truth: at times the majority opinion is not always right. The Baptist Union Council should have been far more sensitive to the situation when they passed the vote that for all practical purposes censured Spurgeon. It made reconciliation difficult if not impossible for the great preacher. They should have taken Spurgeon's fears and warnings far more seriously, especially at the time of the Sheffield Assembly in 1887. The situation Spurgeon revealed was a reality, not a joke as some alleged. By the time the real issues surfaced, it was too late. Too many dynamics had set themselves up. History clearly reveals that reality.

Also, the Down Grade demonstrated that leaders can make tragic mistakes. Some say Spurgeon was too much influenced by Samuel Booth. Others say Spurgeon's entire approach was the biggest mistake he ever made. But if any mistake was made in the entire episode, Samuel Booth, the general secretary, stood guilty. Why he would not admit that he had given information to Spurgeon, and then manipulated Spurgeon into keeping quiet over the situation, remains something of a historical mystery. One would have thought that the man would have had integrity enough to confess to the reality of the situation. But he refused to get down to the real heart of the matter. Had Booth done what is right, it probably could have diffused the entire affair, as far as Spurgeon was personally concerned, although it would still have caused controversy. But the controversy would have been over those who were guilty of actually being on the down grade, not over Spurgeon personally. That muddled the whole affair. It has been suggested that if another man, such as the Baptist statesman, J. H. Shakespeare, who succeeded Booth as secretary, had been the secretary of the Union at that time, things might have been quite different. It seems that the stakes were just too high for Booth. Consensus votes and opinions of leaders do not always have the final right answer.

Furthermore, when truth is defeated, error will continue to grow with its deadening effect. Immediately after the death of Spurgeon, another incident occurred known as the "Aked Incident." In July of 1892, just a few months after the demise of the Metropolitan Tabernacle preacher, C. F. Aked, Baptist minister of Liverpool, exchanged pulpits with R. A. Armstrong, a Unitarian minister. The well-known and highly respected F. B. Meyer intended to bring a resolution before the Baptist Union to do something about the case. But the editor of *The Baptist Magazine* wrote, "Some will doubt the wisdom of raising the question in the Union in any form, and will claim for each church liberty of action, but there is no doubt that, as a denomination, we view with great disfavors as tending to impair our testimony to the gospel, the exchange of our associated churches with ministers who do not hold to the deity of Jesus Christ." [328] The quest for the liberty of churches and for the unity of the denomination had grown to the proportion after Spurgeon's "censure" in the Down Grade Controversy, that even this was tolerated. The Union began to pay the price.

Furthermore, the situation certainly made one thing apparent: there were

genuine aberrations that infected the Baptist Union. The advent of rationalistic theology that precipitated the Down Grade went through many circles in
Britain. Moreover, that infection soon crossed the Atlantic and raged through
the American scene. Virtually every mainline denomination in the United
States has felt something of its impact. It precipitated the so-called "modern-
ist-fundamentalist" controversy in the early decades of the twentieth century. And it continues to the very moment. In the 1970s, almost 100 years
after Spurgeon's Down Grade Controversy erupted, a Christological controversy again arose in the Baptist Union. Michael Taylor, principal of the
Northern (Baptist) College in Manchester at the time, addressed the Baptist
Union annual meeting at Westminster Chapel in 1970 on the subject, "How
much of a man was Jesus." He presented a quite clear Unitarian view.
Again, a serious eruption took place in the Baptist Union. Baptist laymen
like Sir Cyril Black, M. P., known as the conscience of Parliament, took a
very forthright stand against the Unitarian views of the principle. Dr. George
Beasley-Murray, principal of Spurgeon's Theological College and moderator of the Baptist Union Council that year, took a similar stand. Beasley-
Murray insisted that Taylor be struck from the "approved list" of Baptist
ministers. Beasley-Murray had argued that Taylor denied the unique deity of
Jesus Christ, which violated the Baptist Statement of Faith that had been
passed in the aftermath of the Down Grade Controversy. The Baptist Council refused to do so and Beasley-Murray, much to his credit and the admiration of Evangelicals around the world, resigned in protest from his position
on the Union Council. Even the Roman Catholic Church of England applauded Beasley-Murray for his stand on the deity of Christ. Some thirty
churches left the Baptist Union at that time. The next year the Union passed,
virtually unanimously, a resolution affirming the deity of Christ. The resolution before the Assembly read: "We affirm the humanity and deity of Christ
and repudiate any tendency to deny either." But damage was done, and it
seemed like a small repeat of the Down Grade Controversy.

The same "new theology," with its historical critical method, coupled with
rationalistic presuppositions, touched Southern Baptist life in the 1980s. The
similarities between the Down Grade Controversy of Spurgeon and what
became known as the "inerrancy debate" in Southern Baptist life has striking
parallels. If Southern Baptists survive the onslaught, it will be something of an
aberration of history. So often rationalistic theology finally takes the day.

Lessons to be learned from the Down Grade Controversy can be invaluable to Evangelicals. For the battle rages on and probably shall until the
second advent of our Lord Jesus Christ. In the Down Grade Controversy
itself, the battle was not between Charles Spurgeon and John Clifford personally, as some have tried to make it. Nor in more contemporary times was
it between Michael Taylor and Sir Cyril Black. In the final analysis, such
controversies are spiritual. It is the age-old battle of truth versus error. The
Bible speaks in clear tones as to the real issues that are at stake, the true

nature of the warfare, and the outcome. The results of failing to stand for truth are obvious. In Europe, since the arrival of the "new thought," the Church has dramatically declined. For example, The Baptist Union in Britain, which once boasted over 500,000 members, is now reduced to less than 200,000. Of course, many factors, sociological, cultural, and otherwise, feed into that situation, but the fallout from the Down Grade Controversy certainly played its part as well. When basic theology goes, basic ministry diminishes and that always proves devastating to the ongoing institutionalized church.

CONCLUSION

The writing of the new Declaration of Faith by Spurgeon, the forming of a new organization for the Pastors' College, and the apathetic attitude of the Baptist Union in general finally closed the Down Grade Controversy. Spurgeon had become an isolated figure. The Baptist Union emerged from the Down Grade Controversy scathed and bruised, yet not shattered. Only five churches and thirteen personal members had actually withdrawn from the Union. In the short term, it looked as though all that Spurgeon had done had fallen to the ground and he was left alone. He carried on for another five years of ministry. In many respects, though devastated in health, and much misunderstood, his last years of ministry at the Tabernacle were significant and honored by God. The Puritans before him had stood; therefore, Mr. Valiant-for-Truth had stood. "The Last of the Puritans," along with predecessors in the faith, ultimately conquered. God's blessings still abode on his ministry. To that final chapter in the great preacher's life we turn.

13

"The Celestial City"

SPURGEON'S LAST DAYS OF SERVICE

Hobgoblin, nor foul fiend
Can daunt his spirit;
He knows, he at the end
Shall life inherit.
Then fancies fly away,
He'll fear not what men say;
He'll labour night and day
To be a pilgrim.

—John Bunyan

Introduction

The Down Grade Controversy proved devastating to Spurgeon. Not only did it become a trauma from the perspective of his relationship to the Baptist Union, it also affected his relationship to many of his brethren. The fact that some graduates of the Pastors' College did not support him in his stand deeply disappointed and hurt him. By the time of the Down Grade, his health had deteriorated seriously; the Controversy then struck an even more severe blow upon his fragile body. In many senses of the word, Spurgeon never really recovered from the Down Grade. Once, after Charles' death, Thomas Spurgeon said to Archibald Brown, "The Baptist Union almost killed my father." Brown replied, "Yes, and your father almost killed the Baptist Union." It was an exceedingly difficult time for everyone. The "Celestial City" began to glow brightly for Mr. Valiant-for-Truth; Spurgeon's last years could never be quite the same. Yet, he had always been a resilient personality and after the heat of the Down Grade Controversy abated somewhat he snapped back reasonably well. Even in the midst of all the opposition and ill health, he continued to make a significant contribution to the cause of the Gospel through his ministry at the Metropolitan Tabernacle. He had fought a long, hard battle and, as seen, even in the warfare had kept his sense of humor. As the end drew near, which he seemed to sense, what strength, energy and influence he had left he enthusiastically threw into the arena as he battled for truth and souls for Christ. In reality, a sense of victory characterized his last days. He wrote:

> Autumn begins to lay its hands upon all things. The vigor of the year is past, and the sabbath season of the woods has come. . . . Every falling leaf is a sermon. 'Far from the city's dust and din' we wander till our feet are arrested by the tiny tarn which give drink to bird and beast; and by its brink we sit us down and muse upon a fading world, and the generations of its life which rise

like the waves of the sea only to die upon the shore. Yet life abides and death cannot drive it from its throne. The leaves fall, but the forest lives on: men perish, but the race survives. Better still, the Lord of all things lives; and as his watchful eye watches over the floweret which blooms in the innermost wood, so does he care for me. Lost as I might well be amid these pathless forests, yet he broods around me, and I am at home in him. When, like a faded leaf, I hang upon the tree awaiting my end, I will not fear; for when the time shall come for me to flutter to the ground, he will be with me, and direct my way, as surely as though I were the only creature he ever made. [1]

Such words are remarkable for a man in Spurgeon's situation with all its conflicts, deteriorating health and multiple problems. He had a resilient faith.

FROM THE DOWN GRADE FORWARD

In the spring of 1888, one year after the outburst of the Down Grade Controversy, Spurgeon received another blow. While unwell himself, Charles lost his mother. She had been ill for a considerable time, but in the spring apparently seemed to be feeling better. Although she had become an invalid, she deeply wanted to go to Hastings. So on May 18 of that year, her family took her to the beautiful, historic, south-coast city. But there she suffered a chill from the miserable weather. Bronchitis set in, and in a few short days, on May 23, she died. Her husband, Rev. John Spurgeon, and two of his daughters sat by her side as she passed away. The internment took place in Croydon Cemetery on May 26. Charles gave the funeral address. The following day, James, Charles' brother, preached on the influence of Timothy's mother, Eunice and his grandmother, Lois. The application to Mrs. John Spurgeon was beautiful. Everyone knew the tremendous impact that Charles' mother had made on him in leading him and the other children to faith in Christ.

A short time later, the Stockwell Orphanage celebrated Spurgeon's 54th birthday. Unfortunately, he could only stay a short time for the festivities; his frailty would not permit him to be out for very long in those days. The cold and cheerless weather made it worse, and though the hours spent at the Orphanage always delighted Spurgeon, he soon had to leave and face another dreary day of pain at home.

Still, despite Spurgeon's absences from public life due to illness and his controversial stands, his popularity never waned. Although, as Fullerton said, Spurgeon was not a good controversialist but a better witness, the controversy did not diminish his acceptance by the masses. Even his negativism toward the Baptist Union did not cause the crowds at the Metropolitan Tabernacle to fall away. In July 1887, *The Chart and Compass; Sailor's Magazine* called him "Archbishop Spurgeon." It was a mistake, but in some sense, that is how people saw him. He still made news. Practically everything he said made news. *Funny Folks* (July 31, 1887) published the following article:

> Mr. Spurgeon told an audience this week that his method of destroying hornets was to drop a red-hot poker in their nest and leave it there. This treatment seems rather barbarous, and we wish the eloquent divine had recommended baptism instead but no doubt it is in accordance with his practice of dealing with sinners—give it them hot.

One can surmise this amazed Spurgeon and perhaps relaxed some of the tension created by the Down Grade. Some hinted Charles' illnesses affected the tone of his ministry, for example, *The Freeman* (September 2, 1887) implied that. Yet, it is doubtful, for his sense of humor never seemed to leave him. In 1887 *Great Thoughts* conducted a poll of the greatest preachers of the land—Spurgeon came in number one.

Indicative of Spurgeon's continuing popularity, on September 21, 1888, *The British Weekly* wrote, "Mr. Spurgeon has been preaching incessantly since his boyhood and is, if anything, more popular than ever." *Church Bells* wrote in their December 9, 1887 issue, "Mr. Spurgeon has survived the ridicule of *Punch* and the scorn of the *Saturday Review*." Perhaps the best word that could be said was presented in *The National Baptist*, Philadelphia, July 31, 1889: "There is a man who has probably been more assailed and lied about than any other man in England, and, perhaps, in modern times . . . amid it all, he has not, so far as we know, once replied or denied the charges. He has just gone right on, doing God's work in God's own way. As a result, the lies have stopped." [2]

In August of the same year, Charles attended the jubilee of Wellington Square Chapel in Hastings where W. Barker had served very ably as pastor. Spurgeon preached in the morning and then in the afternoon gave an address. In his message, he remarked:

> What a company before the Throne look down on this place—not gaudy in architecture, especially the schoolroom. I believe that grand buildings ruin good fellowship in the church itself. People used to meet in the plain old building and not to one another; but now in the handsome building people did not speak to one another; it would be unbecoming. They walked up the aisles on stilts with a new pair of gloves on, and entered the stately catacomb places. [3]

Near the end of August, 1888, the Baptist Union again faced a critical episode. A speaker at the annual meeting had published views on the inspiration of the Scriptures that seemed to deny outright the unique inspiration of the Bible. This began to turn the evangelicals toward vindicating Spurgeon in the stand he had taken during the Down Grade. *The Rock*, a popular publication, wrote: "We have no desire to have fellowship with those who would practically rob us of our Bibles. Far better the intolerant priest, who would by persecution endeavor to prevent us from reading that book, than the so-called preacher of the Gospel who will present us with a book called the Bible, but will at the same time deprive us of our faith in that sacred volume as *the* Word of God."[4]

The possible controversy this could have stirred up in the wake of the Down Grade never materialized, however. A minimum of fanfare was raised. Spurgeon had not the heart for another encounter, being so feeble in health; he said little about it. He had been so decimated by the Down Grade Controversy, that he had to get away as soon as possible. Yet, before his trip south, while still in London, he showed amazing energy. For example, early in September he was the life of the party when Mr. and Mrs. C. F. Allison entertained the tutors and the students of the Pastors' College at their country house, Town Court, Orpington. Later in the month, at the annual College meeting held at the Tabernacle, Spurgeon again lectured, and did it in his very best style. By this time he had become a member of the Surrey and Middlesex Baptist Association, as pointed out in the last chapter. This important move dispelled the doubts of his contemporaries, and later historians, concerning his commitment to the Baptist faith. He was not an anti-denominationalist.

Spurgeon would still travel about in those difficult days and preach and lecture as opportunity and strength permitted. During the last of September in 1888, he gave a very moving address to the Southwark branch of the YMCA meeting at the Tabernacle. He reflected back on his own young days as a Christian and how much those early experiences of service to Christ had influenced and molded his entire life. In speaking to the young men, he said:

> As far as I myself am concerned, I cannot imagine what I should have done at the present time if I had not been a servant of the Lord Jesus Christ when I was 15 and pastor of a church when I was 16. Those first years molded all the rest of my life. If I had not then preached, I should not now have preached, and I think it is so with you.[5]

The next day after his address to the YMCA, he preached at the opening of the new Surrey Chapel building. Unbeknown to himself, he used the same text that Rowland Hill had used at the opening of the old sanctuary in 1783. The pastor of the famous Surrey Chapel, Mr. Benjamin, Sr., after Spurgeon's death gave a beautiful remembrance speech of Charles and his relationship to the Surrey Chapel. He said:

> The first time I heard my late dear friend preach was on a Thursday night at the Tabernacle. I said to a gentleman sitting next to me. 'What is the secret of this man's success?' He said, 'Why, the man is real. I will illustrate what I mean. A conversation took place the other day in the house of business where I am employed about the most popular preachers in London. Everyone said that Spurgeon stood the first. One man said, "I used to think that Spurgeon was a humbug until I went to hear him. He preached from the text, Am I my

brother's keeper?'" Among other things he said that he regarded every man as his brother. I said I will test the fellow to-morrow. The next morning I went to his home in Nightingale Lane; I rang the bell. When the servant answered the door I said, 'Will you tell Mr. Spurgeon that his brother wants to see him?' She seemed to hesitate. I said, 'Will you kindly carry my message?' She took the message and at once returned, asking me into the study, 'Well, my friend, what is the object of your visit?' I said, 'Well, sir, I heard you preach yesterday, and you said that you regarded every man as your brother. I am a man and I am out of work, and I thought I would come and see if you would regard me as your brother.' He laughed right heartily and said, 'Well, I have had a good many visitors, but I think you are the strangest I ever had; but keep your seat and you shall have some refreshment.' He rang the bell, and when the girl came he said, 'Bring this good gentleman something to eat. Never mind, cold beef, pickled onions, anything you have got.' I enjoyed the refreshment immensely; he chatted with me all the time; gave me a note to take to one of the deacons, and then prayed with me. I can never forget that visit. Now," said the man, "I was not out of work nor did I want anything, but I thought I would test the fellow and see if he would practise what he preached.'" So my friend said to me in the pew, 'That is the best illustration I can give you that the man is REAL.'

"Yes, he was real, and that was the main secret of his great success. He was real in all that he said and did; in his love, sympathy and benevolence. How often I have had proof of this in my thirteen years' ministry at Surrey Chapel! How his great heart was struck when old Surrey Chapel was lost to the Christian Church![6]

THE DOWN GRADE FALLOUT

Still, the Down Grade Controversy refused to be laid to rest, especially in the Baptist Union. As late as April 24, 1891 *The Baptist* wrote, "Mr. Spurgeon is utterly out of touch with minds . . . plagued with doubts and problems." They apparently printed the criticism because of Spurgeon's dogmatic, Calvinistic theology. In evangelical circles in Britain and around the world, the Down Grade had become a continuing item of discussion. And of note, most of the evangelical world sided with Spurgeon. For example, the Baptist Convention of the Maritime provinces of Canada passed a resolution of sympathy and communicated it to Spurgeon. Deeply appreciative, in October of 1888 Spurgeon sent his Canadian friends the following reply:

Upper Norwood, London,
October 5, 1888.

To the Ministers and Delegates forming the Baptist Convention of the Maritime Provinces of Canada.
DEAR BRETHREN IN CHRIST,—I heartily thank you all for the words of

cheer which you have sent me. Such a resolution, from such brethren, at such a time, gladdened me greatly. From the depths of my soul I thank all the brethren, and I pray the Lord richly to recompense them. I am grateful that you have not misjudged my action in reference to the English Baptist Union, from which I have felt bound to separate myself. I have not acted from sudden impulse, much less from any personal grievance; but I have been long protesting quietly, and have been at last compelled to make a stand in public. I saw the testimony of the churches becoming obscure, and I observed that in some instances the testimony from the pulpit was very wide of the Word of God, and I grieved over the state of things which is sure to follow upon defection from the Gospel. I hoped that the many faithful brethren would be aroused to the peril of the situation, and would earnestly endeavour to cleanse their Union of the most flagrant offenders. Instead of this, I am regarded as a troubler in Israel by many, and others feel that, important as truth may be, the preservation of the Union must be the first object of consideration. Nothing could have more fully proved to me that my protest is rather too late than too early.

On surveying the position, I perceive that the basis of our Baptist Union afforded nothing to work upon if a reform were attempted, for any person who has been immersed is eligible for membership. So far as anything found in the printed basis is concerned, every immersed person has a right to join it. Within its bounds there is neither orthodoxy nor heterodoxy, for all have an equal right of place. This does not appear to me to be the right condition of matters, and therefore I quitted the confederacy. Altogether apart from the soundness or unsoundness of individuals, the compact itself is on wrong grounds, and can never produce real unity. There are numbers of faithful, honoured, and beloved brethren in the Union; but these, by their presence and countenance, are bolstering up a confederacy which is upon a false foundation. It is not for me to censure them, any more than it was for them to censure me; but I cannot but feel that a more decided course of action on their part would have secured for our country a testimony to the truth which is greatly needed in these evil times; whereas their shielding of the false and erroneous has given a sanction to evil teachers which they are not slow to perceive.

The pain I have felt in this conflict I would not wish any other man to share; but I would bear ten thousand times as much with eagerness if I could see the faith once for all delivered to the saints placed in honour among the Baptist churches of Great Britain. I resolved to avoid personalities from the very beginning; and, though sorely tempted to publish all that I know, I have held my peace as to individuals, and thus have weakened my own hands in the conflict. Yet this also I had rather bear than allow contention for the faith to degenerate into a complication of personal quarrels. I am no man's enemy, but I am the enemy of all teaching which is contrary to the Word of the Lord, and I will be in no fellowship with it.

Nothing has occurred to cause my mind the least alienation from Baptist brethren who hold the doctrines taught in Holy Scripture. Far otherwise, I have never had a doubt as to the Scriptural correctness of our view of baptism; and I rejoice that with the mass of those who obey the Lord in this matter I am still in hearty union. Assuredly I am *one with you*, and all the more consciously so because you have not hesitated to stand by me in the hour of trouble, when many shun my company and condemn my conduct.

God bless you, my beloved brethren, and keep you in His faith as at this day! May the Lord increase and strengthen you more and more, and bless all the 'Maritime Provinces' through your works of faith and labours of love. You are not ashamed to state your beliefs. You do not wish to cover up error by a cloudy, indefinite state of things, which, like darkness, encourages evil. You love the truth, and therefore do not shun the light. May the Holy Ghost be with all your ministers, and dwell in your members! Peace be to you and grace!

Unable to write all that I feel, I turn to prayer, and beseech our God in Christ Jesus to bless you exceeding abundantly above all that we ask or even think.—Yours most gratefully and lovingly,

C. H. SPURGEON. [7]

All of this feverish activity took its toll. The pressure of the Metropolitan Tabernacle itself was tremendous. By 1888 the average attendance at the Sunday School for children had reached 1,541, with 105 teachers and 97 classes. And that was a small part of the work. Charles broke down again and had to take to his bed on October 20. A month later, he regained some strength and started for the south of France to recuperate. This forced him from his pulpit in the Tabernacle for more than four months.

OFF TO MENTONE

In November Spurgeon left England and traveled to Mentone. On the journey south he stopped in Paris and watched the construction of the Eiffel Tower. It became known as the "Eighth Wonder of the World." Charles said it was "consistent with the genius of the age." He wrote an article about it in *The Sword and the Trowel.* He may have been a little too enthusiastic, but the Tower still attracts tourists. One of his notes to the Metropolitan Tabernacle reads rather sadly. He loved his people dearly, and said, "Your old and feeble minister" sends his greeting from the south of France.

But he gained strength. He wrote back home on November 13, 1888, saying "I have had sufficient rest from pain to enjoy the revision of this sermon." Nor did he lose his sense of humor. He wrote, December 8, 1888, "I am still somewhat like Mephibosheth who did eat continually at the king's table, and was lame in both his feet." On the last Sunday of that year he met with the accident described earlier when he fell down the marble steps and knocked out two teeth and his money spilled into his boot. He had injured himself more than he at first thought with his humorous description of it. He wrote:

KIND FRIENDS,—My injuries are far greater than I supposed. It will take some time before foot, mouth, head, and nerves can be right again. What a mercy that I was not smashed quite up! The angels did their work well, for another stone would have brought me to mine end.

Through what a stupor I have passed! Yet in a day or two I shall be none the worse. I am overcome with gratitude. May I be spared to keep my own footing to the end, and let the down-graders know how terrible is a fall from the high places of the Lord's truth.—Yours very truly,

C. H. SPURGEON [8]

When the news was received back in London that he had taken the fall, a telegram of sympathy was sent by Mr. T. V. Tymns in behalf of the London Baptist Association.

CONTINUING ABUNDANT LABORS

Spurgeon stayed in Mentone until February 18 of the next year (1889). On his way home, he arrived in Paris on a Tuesday and spent the night. The following day he got back to his beloved London. On February 24, the Tabernacle overflowed as the members welcomed their pastor home. The deacons urged him to pace himself to keep his strength for the duties that lay ahead. He really was a very sick man and wearing out fast; yet, he had a flow of humor as bright as it had been when he was a youth at the New Park Street Baptist Church. In May 1889, the College Conference met at Dalston Junction Chapel. Spurgeon, quite up to the hour, addressed the students and those who had gathered on "Our Power, and the Conditions of Obtaining It." A supper meeting followed and a collection brought in £2,800 for the College. A short time after the Conference, he planned a trip to Waterbeach. Mr. Toller, a close friend, wanted him to spend the night in the little village of his first pastorate. But Spurgeon wrote:

DEAR FRIEND,—I am very grateful for your kind help. Working on from day to day with the College, it is a great mercy to be preserved from all anxiety as to money matters. I praise God for moving His servants to supply the needs of the Institution, and I thank you for being one of them. The sum of two guineas has been safely received by me. The Lord have you ever in His holy keeping!—Yours, with hearty thanks,

C. H. SPURGEON

P.S.—I wonder you can give as much as you do, for farming seems very bad. Success to you! [9]

Although Spurgeon did not have near the strength of body that he had in his earlier days, his enthusiasm never waned. He threw himself as much as possible into every task before him. In May he addressed the Colporteurs, in

June he preached to a party of sailors at a special service at the Tabernacle. In the same month he gave an address to a large group who had met to hear some old fugal hymns of the past. He officiated at the marriage of Rev. David Davies, minister at West Brighton, and Miss Ellen Higgs, of Brixton. The next month he traveled all the way to Guernsey and held a number of services celebrating the work of F. T. Snell. An all-day missionary convention was held at the Tabernacle in the fall of the year. In three meetings, Spurgeon, Alexander Maclaren and John McNeal, a young Scottish preacher in those days, preached on missions. They challenged people concerning the worldwide propagation of the Gospel. As seen so often, Spurgeon always cherished a deep commitment to foreign missions. He had been a close friend of Hudson Taylor, the founder of the China Inland Mission, and he had led the Tabernacle to give toward that outstanding faith work. Several young men from the College were leaving for the foreign field under Taylor's sponsorship, and they also spoke at the missionary meetings. One can imagine the excitement of the people in hearing these young men of God share their testimonies. Later that year, Spurgeon received an invitation to Sheffield to attend a lavish banquet given by the Sheffield Master Cutler Organization. Spurgeon replied, "You are most kind, and so is the Master Cutler; but I am so taken up with work that I must not leave home." He attended the autumn meeting of the Surrey and Middlesex Association at Wimbledon, October 28, 1889. He preached in the afternoon on "Mary and the Sepulcher" from John 20:11-16. And all these activities were in addition to the regular services and responsibilities of the Tabernacle and the multiple ministries that Spurgeon was responsible for overseeing. In the light of his illness and weakness and the controversial atmosphere of London at that time, it is incredible that the man could carry on as he did. And he still had his share of criticisms and negative reactions to contend with. For example, in 1889 a position of nurse was sought by a Nonconformist with a letter of recommendation from Charles Haddon Spurgeon. She was the best qualified, though not a member of the Established Church. One board member said, "Well, we will not have that one who is recommended by Mr. Spurgeon." This caused a flap, probably the issue being Spurgeon's continuing battle for disestablishment.

That same year a report in the *Woman's Penny Paper* (October 12, 1889) said that Mrs. Armistan Chant preached at the Metropolitan Tabernacle on a Sunday evening in October. If that be true (it was disputed) that would have been the first time a woman preached in Spurgeon's church. But Charles, always the innovative one, may well have permitted it. Yet, it cannot be verified.

About this time an American lady sent him a package of "a remedy for rheumatism." Spurgeon acknowledged the gift and wrote:

> The medicine has just now arrived, and as I happen to be suffering from an attack, it comes at the right time. I have already taken so many drugs that I am

like the woman who suffered many things of many physicians, and was nothing bettered. Yet I will try again. May God bless the means! The newspapers represent me as soon to be done for; but I shall outlive many of them, and be heard when some of their thunder is hushed in the eternal silence.[10]

BACK TO MENTONE

Despite his illness and the constant pronouncements of his soon demise, he showed a remarkable resilience. Still, in November 1989, he made his way again to the south of France. He was in such pain that "it was apparent to any observer that his shoulder was drawn up as if by sharp hitches of pain."[11] It really did begin to look ominous. In Mentone he began to feel some better. On December 19 he sent his Christmas greetings to the congregation at the Metropolitan Tabernacle. In his gracious style he wrote:

> BELOVED FRIENDS,—I wish you a joyful Christmas and Happy New Year. I am informed of all that is going on at home by the coming to me of Mr. Allison. My own Lord continues His shepherd care of all the flock, and feeds you by the hands of the beloved brethren who fill my place. To them who are newly converted be lovingly attentive, and endeavour to lead them to know the Lord more fully. To the meetings for prayer I entreat you to pay special heed, that there be no flagging in this the central channel of power. This is a season for thanksgiving. Let us be specially mindful of the needs of the Lord's work and the necessities of the poor. Set aside also a portion for the Surrey Gardens Memorial, which is to be the work of the coming year, a token of gratitude to the Lord our God. I am well in all but the voice. The doctor says that I have the gout in my throat, and I have no doubt that it is so. It will soon be gone. I rejoice that this loss of voice only comes when there is no need for me to speak aloud. I hope to return to you restored in body, refreshed in mind, and revived in spirit. Then, too, I trust the voice will again be the force needed for making all hear in our great sanctuary. Grace, mercy, and peace be with you all for evermore. Please pray for me always, for I always need it, and the Lord is always ready to bless. With the New Year may all enter upon an era of fuller consecration, greater holiness, and larger usefulness.—Your loving minister,
> C. H. SPURGEON.[12]

At Mentone, the daily family prayer congregation that normally numbered about 30 had risen to nearly 60. They took their place every day at half past nine in the morning, though some had to walk several miles to be present. Spurgeon remarked, "They said they would have walked for three hours rather than not attend. It needed not that the speaker should say anything fresh. If I had had to give a poem or a tale I should have broke down, but the Holy Spirit made truth ever new. . . . There was wonderful power in the Word."[13] Every morning Spurgeon expounded a passage from the book of Genesis.

Whenever Spurgeon visited the south of France he worked as well as rested. In 1890, at Mentone, he threw himself into the preparation of a commentary on the Gospel of Matthew. He would take parts of his work from the manuscript and read them to those who assembled in the Beau Revage Hotel. On this excursion to the coast, he recovered rather quickly from his bout of ill health and on February 2 he was back in the Metropolitan Tabernacle. Again, he entered enthusiastically into the work. By 1890 he earnestly advocated and worked for the Blue Ribbon Movement at the Tabernacle, the movement for total abstinence. He had come full swing on that issue. After his return to London from France, he made a trip to the Westbourne Grove Chapel and spoke, helping them to raise funds for the renovation of their building.

At the College Conference of 1890, Spurgeon again heard a plea for prayer for the children of the Conference members. He said the prayers "soon brought tears to my eyes." So, as he had done before, he lithographed an open letter to be sent to the children to tell them of Jesus. He penned on the top of the letters, "God bless this letter." In the text of the letter he wrote:

Dear ————,

You are highly privileged in having parents who pray for you . . . *Do you not pray for yourself, lad?* You do not intend to cause grief to dear mother and father, but you do. So long as you are not saved . . . think of this. Remember how much you have already sinned, and none can wash you but Jesus . . . You need it NOW . . . You cannot save yourself, but the great Lord Jesus can save you. Ask him to do it . . . Come and tell Jesus you have sinned; seek forgiveness, trust him for it. *Meet me in heaven.* [14]

In the same year, Talbot Tabernacle, Nottinghill, held their annual Conference. Spurgeon attended and was in excellent spirits. They raised £2,706 at the supper meeting—a very good sum.

Engaging in every aspect of Tabernacle life, Charles met with the Colporteurs and spoke at the Stockwell Orphanage birthday celebration. Despite weakness, he rejoiced in his work. He had a wonderful experience at the Stockwell Orphanage. A full account is given in the *Autobiography*. Spurgeon must have thoroughly enjoyed the day as he wrote a fairly long description of it. It reads as follows:

I went to the Stockwell Orphanage, on Tuesday, September 23, to walk round with an artist, and select bits for his pencil, to be inserted in a Christmas book for the Institution. We had not gone many yards before it began to rain. Umbrellas were forthcoming, and we tried to continue our perambulation of the whole square of the boys' and girls' houses; but the rain persisted in descending, and speedily increased into a downpour. Nothing short of being amphibious would have enabled us to face the torrent. There was no other course but to turn into the play-hall, where the boys gave tremendous cheers at our advent,—cheers almost so deafening as the thunder which responded to them. Go out we could not, for the shower was swollen into a deluge, so I resolved to turn the season to account. A chair was forthcoming, and there I sat, the centre of a dense throng of juvenile humanity, which could scarcely be kept off from a nearness which showed the warmth of their reception of their friend. Our artist, who, standing in the throng, made a hurried sketch, could not be afforded space enough to put in the hundreds of boys.

It was certainly a melting moment as to heat, and fresh air was not abundant; but anything was better than the storm outside. Flash after flash made everybody feel sober, and prompted me to talk with the boys about that freedom from fear which comes through faith in the Lord Jesus. The story was told of a very young believer, who was in his uncle's house, one night, during a tremendous tempest. [This, of course, was Mr. Spurgeon himself when he was a lad.] The older folk were all afraid; but he had really trusted himself with the Lord Jesus, and he did not dare to fear. The baby was upstairs, and nobody was brave enough to fetch it down because of a big window on the stairs. This lad went up to the bedroom, brought the baby to its mother, and then read a Psalm, and prayed with his relatives, who were trembling with fear. There was real danger, for a stack was set on fire a short distance away; but the youth was as calm as on a summer's day of sunshine, not because he was naturally brave, but because he truly trusted in the Lord.

While I was thus speaking, the darkness increased, and the storm overhead seemed brooding over us with black wings. It was growing dark before its hour. Most appropriately, one of the boys suggested a verse, which all sang sweetly and reverently,—

> Abide with me! fast falls the eventide;
> The darkness deepens; Lord, with me abide!
> When other helpers fail, and comforts flee,
> Help of the helpless, O abide with me!

This ended, there followed a word about the ground of the believer's trust: he was forgiven, and therefore dreaded no condemnation; he was in his Heavenly Father's hand, and therefore feared no evil. If we were at enmity against God, and had all our sins resting upon our guilty heads, we might be afraid to die; yes, and even afraid to live; but, when reconciled to Him by the death of His Son, we said farewell to fear. With God against us, we are in a state of war; but with God for us, we dwell in perfect peace. Here came flashes of lightning and peals of thunder which might well make us start; but no one was afraid. It is true we all felt awed, but we were restful, and somehow there was a quiet but general cry for '*perfect peace*.' On enquiring what this meant, I was answered by all the boys singing right joyfully,—

> Like a river glorious is God's perfect peace,
> Over all victorious in its bright increase,

> Perfect, yet it floweth fuller every day;
> Perfect, yet it groweth deeper all the way.

> Stayed upon Jehovah, hearts are fully blest,
> Finding, as He promised, perfect peace and rest.

> Hidden in the hollow of His blessed hand,
> Never foe can follow, never traitor stand,
> Not a surge of worry, not a shade of care,
> Not a blast of hurry touch the spirit there.

> Stayed upon Jehovah, hearts are fully blest,
> Finding, as He promised, perfect peace and rest.

This sung, we covered our faces reverently, and the boys were very silent, while I lifted up my voice in prayer. Then we opened our eyes again, and it was very dark, as if night had come before its time. While the flames of fire leaped in through the windows and skylights, the noise of the rain upon the roof and the tremendous thunder scarcely permitted me to say much upon Jesus as being our peace, through His bearing our sins in His own body on the tree. Yet, as well as I could, I set forth the cross of Christ as the place of peace-making, peace-speaking, and peace-finding, both for boys and men; and then we all sang, to the accompaniment of the storm-music; —

> How sweet the Name of Jesus sounds
> In a believer's ear!
> It soothes his sorrows, heals his wounds,
> And drives away his fear.

Never did the power of that Name to drive away fear appear more sweetly. To me, the words came with a soothing, cheering force, which filled me with intense delight; so we very joyfully and peacefully sang the third verse,—

> Dear Name! the rock on which I build,
> My shield and hiding-place;
> My never-failing treasury, fill'd
> With boundless stores of grace.

Just as we came to 'my shield and hiding-place,' there was a peculiarly blue flash, with a sort of rifle-crack, as if something very close to us had been struck. The boys looked at one another, but went on, in subdued tones, singing of the 'boundless stores of grace.' Teachers and others were mixed with the little army of boys, but we were all welded together in common emotion. I then reminded them that, to such a Protector, we must give our heart's love. It was a duty to love one so good as the Lord Jesus, but even more a delight to do so, since He gave Himself for us, and, by bearing our punishment, delivered us from all harm. As if by instinct, someone led off—

> My Jesus, I love Thee, I know Thou art mine,
> For Thee all the follies of sin I resign;
> My gracious Redeemer, my Saviour art Thou,
> If ever I loved Thee, my Jesus, 'tis now.

Here was a good opening to press home the question,—'Is this true of each one of you? The great desire of all who conduct the Orphanage is to lead you to take Jesus for your gracious Redeemer, that so you may love Him. Oh, that you loved Him *now*! It may be that, if you leave us unsaved, the Lord will yet bring you in; but it would be far better that you should go out from us ready for the battle of life, and covered with a holy armour, so that you might not be wounded by the arrows of sin.' Then I picked out Mr. May, who is employed at the Orphanage, and bade him tell the boys about himself. May was a boy with us at the Orphanage,—a restless spirit, so he went to sea; and, after many hardships and adventures, he was converted to God at Malta, and then came back to us, and we found him a post at his own school. As the lads knew the most of his story, May did not say very much; and what he did say was rather overborne by the rain on the roof, which sounded like ten thousand drums. The thunder added its trumpet voice, and only allowed us pauses of silence. I went on with the talk till there came a burst of thunder loud and long. I stopped, and bade the children listen to the voice of the Lord. We all hearkened to it with awe and wonder. Then I reminded them of Psalm XXIX: 'The voice of the Lord is powerful; the voice of the Lord is full of majesty. The voice of the Lord breaketh the cedars; yea, the Lord breaketh the cedars of Lebanon. The Lord sitteth upon the flood; yea, the Lord sitteth King for ever.' I told them how often I had sung to myself Dr. Watts's verses,—

> The God that rules on high,
>   And thunders when He please,
> That rides upon the stormy sky,
>   And manages the seas:
>
> This awful God is ours,
>   Our Father and our love,
> He shall send down His heavenly powers
>   To carry us above.
>
> There shall we see His face,
>   And never, never sin;
> There from the rivers of His grace,
>   Drink endless pleasures in.

As they did not know the old-fashioned tune 'Falcon Street,' to which I had been wont to sing the words, we kept quiet till, suddenly, there came another roll of drums in the march of the God of armies; and then, as an act of worship, we adoringly sang together, with full force, the words of the Doxology,—

Praise God, from whom all blessings flow,
Praise Him all creatures here below,
Praise Him above, ye heavenly host,
Praise Father, Son, and Holy Ghost.

This was a grand climax. The heavens themselves seemed to think so, for there were no more thunder-claps of such tremendous force. I need not write more. The storm abated. I hurried off to see enquirers at the Tabernacle, but not till one and another had said to me, 'The boys will never forget this. It will abide with them throughout eternity.' So be it, for Christ's sake! Amen. [15]

THE PARKER LETTER

In the spring of that year Dr. Joseph Parker of the City Temple wrote an "Open Letter to Spurgeon." Parker and Spurgeon were friends and had exchanged pulpits in February of '83, but this letter caused quite a stir, and much comment ensued. The letter from Parker reads:

The British Weekly, April 25, 1890, Parker to Spurgeon.

An Open Letter.

My Dear Spurgeon,—I want to talk to you upon a matter which has been brought under my notice as a public teacher, and which concerns you mainly in your public capacity. I know I may speak frankly, because I am speaking to a man whose heart is big and warm, a heart that has an immense advantage over his head. When people ask me what I think of Spurgeon, I always ask which Spurgeon—the head or the heart—the Spurgeon of the Tabernacle or the Spurgeon of the Orphanage? The kind of Calvinism which the one occasionally represents I simply hate, as I hate selfishness and blasphemy. It is that leering, slavering, sly-winking Calvinism that says, Bless the Lord we are all right, booked straight through to heaven first-class, and insured against both collision and explosion; as for those who have missed the train or been crushed to death, it is not for us to find fault with discriminating grace or arrest the action of Divine decrees—brother, pass the salt, and shout hallelujah till you are black in the face. That kind of Calvinism I will not condescend to hate, it is too far down in its native perdition to allow a boot to kick it and yet retain a boot's proper respectability. But when I turn to the Orphanage all is changed. All is beauty. All is love. God bless you, Spurgeon, and all the little ones you have adopted in the name of Christ. That Orphanage on earth means a grand welcome into heaven.

Now, for the matter I have in charge. It relates to the cruelty of your theological judgments—judgments which you do not mean to be cruel, yet they have all the effect of deliberate savagery. A young man rose to reply to me at a working men's meeting, and said that Spurgeon had driven him into infidelity. The young man's mother had not made any profession of religion, but was wise, affectionate, and most unselfish in her devotion to her family. She died. The young man (then a member of a Baptist church) went to you, hoping that you might be able to comfort him. He stated his case. He waited for your reply. You simply said, "He that believeth shall be saved, he that believeth not shall be damned." The young man understood (as he could hardly help doing) that his mother was in the latter condition in your opinion. He then and there, knowing what she had been in disposition and in service, determined to cast in his lot with his mother, so he left the Baptist church and united himself with a so-called unbeliever or heretic, who told him, as I should have done in the name of Christ, that the last judgment is with God, who alone knows the heart, and in God's hands we must leave the issues which we cannot explain. Your answer was not so Biblical as it looks. It is the letter, not the spirit. God only knows who "believes." I would say this to broken-hearted men: Belief is larger than profession. Christianity is infinitely larger than church membership. Your quotation was literal, yet it may have been disastrously misapplied. Quotation is not enough. You explain your texts as well as recite them. This you should have done in the case before us. There are secret disciples. We must make room for timid souls unable to balance their faith by blatancy, or to sanctify it before men with that evil-smelling unction so agreeable to the nostrils of hypocrisy. You roughly divide the world into believers and unbelievers, and you shelter yourself behind the words you have quoted. But herein you misrepresent Christ, or you turn Christ into a defendant in His own court. Christ recognised more classes than believers and unbelievers. Of one man he said, "Thou art not far from the kingdom of God;" of other men he said, "They that are not against Me are for Me." This, I think, is the tone we should adopt in reference to those who, having lived pure and gentle lives, rich in sacred influence, have passed away without making any public profession of religion.

The second case is that of a young man who came to me with the statement that Spurgeon had driven him to distraction and despair. I quote the substance of his statement:—"I cannot see my way clear to believe in all the miracles. I do not want to reject them; I want to believe them, but I cannot. I went to hear Spurgeon preach, and he simply denounced everybody like myself, and damned us for our unbelief." The young man quite writhed in pain, and cried bitterly, giving every evidence of the deepest earnestness and feeling. I ventured to tell him that damnation did not turn upon our belief of miracles, but upon our rejection of Christ Himself. Christ never made much of His own miracles, as mere signs and wonders, but He made everything of Himself. I then proceeded thus to the young man: "You are not an unbeliever; you are not a candidate for damnation. The New Testament has in it a little prayer for your especial use. Go to Christ, and say to Him, 'Lord, I believe; help Thou mine unbelief,' and He will give you peace. The bruised reed He will not break; the smoking flax He will not quench. Hold to what little you have, and the rest will come."

Plainly, my dear Spurgeon, I tell you that in all such cases you are unconsciously doing infinite harm. Nothing can be farther from your intention, yet the fact of the awful mischief remains. You bring sweeping charges against your brethren for want of orthodoxy, but I will not join you in what may be anonymous defamation. I take another course. I say to you, "Thou art the man." I accuse you of the heterodoxy of one-sidedness; I accuse you of want of spiritual discrimination; I accuse you of a bluntness which can only be accounted for by the worst kind of spiritual ignorance. The universe is not divided into plain black and white, as you suppose. It is not your function to set some people on your right hand, and the rest on your left. What if at the last the publicans and harlot should enter the kingdom of heaven, and we ourselves should be shut out? What if some who are first should be last, and some who are last should be first? I know that you are acting according to your nature, and that you are doing so honestly. But it is your nature to see one aspect of a case so strongly as to exclude every other. For example, since I began this letter I picked up a paper which contains an extract from one of your sermons, in which you say: "Every funeral is God's repetition of His anathema against sin." Who taught you such nonsense? Besides the fact that dust must die, you ought to state that since funerals were introduced something has occurred which has changed the whole aspect of death. Men may now die in the Lord! Angels may follow us to the grave. Besides, the Christian does not die—he is liberated, he is perfected, he is crowned; angels say concerning him, "He is not here, he is risen." Why do you not take in the whole case? Why do you moan over so-called death, when you might declare the glorious gospel that Christ hath abolished death?

May I add what I think it would be useful for you to do? If I cared nothing for you I should let this task alone. You know that I do care for you, and that I honour you in all your broader work, and that I would gladly serve you if I had the chance to do so. I pray for the lengthening and the comforting of your life, and for your ever-multiplying joy. In this spirit alone I write, and it is this very spirit that leads me to withstand you to the face when I think you are to be blamed. What I say about you I say openly and over my own signature. Never in my life did I make an anonymous attack upon any man. I will not begin that meanness now. You and I have not so learned Christ. I will speak frankly as to a brother beloved. Let me advise you to widen the circle of which you are the centre. You are surrounded by offerers of incense. They flatter your weakness, they laugh at your jokes, they feed you with compliments. My dear Spurgeon, you are too big a man for this. Renounce it. Take in more fresh air. Open your windows even when the wind is in the east. Scatter your ecclesiastical harem. This enlargement of your social relations will do you good, and build your character and action on a larger scale. I do not say destroy your circle; I simply say enlarge it. As with your circle, so with your reading. You are inexcusably contemptuous in your reviews of authors who have forgotten more than you and I put together ever knew. You are much too off-handed with your brother Baptist ministers. You are also much too free in your excommunications. Believe me, you are really not infallible. Pardon me if I venture upon the suggestion, that even you are at least presumably human. I almost tremble at my own temerity, for I cannot but think that any man who expels the whole Baptist Union must occupy a sovereign place in some pantheon of his own invention. I honestly believe that if you will follow out these hints in all their best meaning you will not be angry with me for offering such suggestions. Other men will write to you in a vein of condolent flattery, and will hold up their riddled gingham to save you from this fertilising shower, but you know as well as I do that their "good offices" are meant for themselves rather than for you.

Good-bye, you sturdy, honest old soul. You have been wondrously useful and wondrously honoured. I would double all your honours if I could. Am I become your enemy because I tell you the truth? In your inmost soul you know I am not your enemy, but your friend.

The City Temple. JOSEPH PARKER.

The Baptist severely criticized Parker: "His sketch (of Spurgeon) is a caricature of the man whom he professes to portray. . . . Does Dr. Parker know that he is writing sheer nonsense?" The night service at the Metropolitan Tabernacle that followed the publishing was filled to overflowing. They expected a response from Spurgeon. But all he did was walk up to the pulpit rail quite briskly, looked at the ground floor people, then the first gallery, then the second, and simply said, "Thank God there are still a faithful *few* who stand by the teaching of the Old Book." That ended it. Theologically, Parker and Spurgeon drifted apart. Moreover, Henry Ward Beecher had traveled to London and spoken at the City Temple in 1886, but Spurgeon did not invite the well-known American preacher to the Metropolitan Tabernacle. Perhaps they were too far apart theologically by this time. Some reported Spurgeon had prayed that Beecher would be converted, but that is probably apocryphal. Charles did say that Beecher had more genius than himself, but he preached more Gospel.

Spurgeon kept his concern for others' needs alive. He did not get preoccupied with his own problems. As a case in point on May 23, 1890 he wrote a Mr. Rankine about the need of painting Rankine's chapel. Charles wrote:

> Pardon me, but your chapel is very dirty. If you will have it coloured and touched up within, I think it to be done for £10,—and I will send the 10 pounds to pay for it, myself. Get specifications as to which can be done for the amount, tell the deacons to send the proposal to me, and I will give the £10. [16]

Rankine must have responded positively to Spurgeon's suggestion, because Charles wrote again on June 17, 1890: "With great pleasure I send you £10 for the renovation of the Chapel. Now may the Lord by his Spirit fill the place with his glory." [17] Spurgeon showed concern for even these small matters.

Throughout the year, Spurgeon kept as busy as his strength allowed. He addressed the Bible Society's Anniversary at Exeter Hall and left a profound impression upon everyone who attended. In July Charles spoke at the Metropolitan Music Hall, Edgeware Road, on behalf of the Hyde Park Open Air Mission, commending Charles Cook, one of his close friends. Charles Cook had labored taking extended tours to foreign prisons sharing the Gospel. In September Spurgeon preached for another friend, David Davies, at Holland Road Chapel, West Brighton. Later, he spoke to the students at Hackney College. In that address he attempted to show that all preachers, as men of faith, should look for large results.

THE PASSING OF FRIENDS

Two old friends, Dr. Trestrail and Dr. Hannawy passed away that year. Of particular sorrow to Spurgeon, that autumn William Olney went to his reward. He had been a long-time deacon, co-worker, and in many senses of the word, the pastor's closest friend, save perhaps Joseph Passmore. Spurgeon saw his work as "well nigh as effective as that of a successful co-pastor."[18] At the funeral, Spurgeon injected a high note of praise for Olney's Puritanism. He said:

> It always makes me laugh when I am called a sour Puritan, because you know there is nobody with a quicker eye for fun or with a deeper vein of mirth than I have.[19]

On October 20 Spurgeon gave a loving tribute to the man of God at the laying of the memorial stones of the Surrey Gardens Memorial Hall. Deacon Olney had been instrumental in building the Hall. The Surrey Gardens Memorial Hall was built for evangelical meetings and named after the Surrey Garden Music Hall where Spurgeon had so faithfully and effectively preached the Gospel many years before. It stood as a tribute to the good deacon's memory. Deacon William Olney was never forgotten. Again, in the autumn, Spurgeon attended the meeting of the Surrey and Middlesex Baptist Association at Malden, Surrey. At that meeting Spurgeon made the proposal that the name should be changed to the Home Counties Association. It was carried out.

About this time Spurgeon gave a strong affirmation to a newly established magazine designed for the defense of the evangelical faith. He still chafed under the onslaught of the "new theology." Such a magazine, he said, should be produced. He wrote to the editor at Weston-super-Mare:

> November 13, 1890.
>
> Dear Mr. Urquhart,—I like No. 1 'King's Own' very much. It is of a high class, and ought to secure a high-class position. I am glad that you will now have a gun-boat of your own, and will not ask leave to fire your shots at error. Another rallying-point for the good and true is now found. The importance of such an organ of orthodoxy it would be hard to estimate. May you prosper even beyond your most sanguine hope!   —Yours heartily, C. H. Spurgeon.

Almost immediately after that, Spurgeon left again for his retreat in Mentone. On December 14 he wrote his people the following note as his Christmas remembrance:

> BELOVED FRIENDS,—Although not quite well, I am now free from pain. I am grateful in the belief that I shall soon receive physical and mental power, and that I shall soon return to the ministry. I pray that I may also have spiritual power given to me. Have been able to work a little. 'The name of that city is, The Lord is there.' May that be the name of our church. Then holiness will be plenteous, vitality will be strengthened, power will be increased, usefulness will be ensured, and happiness will abound. If He be with us, He will supply us with grace, and raise for us men to fill up gaps which death has caused. His Spirit will abide and His precious Word will remain. God bless you all. Bear with me if I shall be a long time away. Send true Christian love to every member of the church, to my most attached people. Stand firm in the faith, and you will cheer the heart of your loving pastor,
>
> C. H. S. [20]

While Spurgeon recuperated in the south of France, the Tabernacle was cleaned, repaired, and painted. The renovation cost well over £1,000. It had been some time since the Tabernacle had received a face-lift. It was money well spent.

The deacons passed the following resolution at a special church business meeting while Spurgeon rested in Mentone:

> Jan. 12, 1891.   A resolution was proposed by Deacon Baswell and seconded by Deacon Hall and supported by Pastor J. A. Spurgeon that Pastor Charles H. Spurgeon should stay longer away (in Mentone) and Brother Cockrell and Brother Thompson seconded. Pastor J. A. Spurgeon be asked to write to that effect—carried unanimously. [21]

They wanted their pastor not to rush his recovery, and to come back in robust condition. It was most thoughtful.

SPURGEON'S LAST YEAR

Thus time ushered out 1890 and 1891 came in. It would become a year of sadness and remorse for all who knew and loved Charles Haddon Spurgeon, and for the whole evangelical world. It would be his last.

An unusual flap occurred that year. Many plagiarized Spurgeon. But when the Lord Mayor Savory of London in 1891 preached the January 31, 1869 sermon of Charles, it made all the papers. The message was given at Regent-Street Polytechnic. The Lord Mayor denied it. Spurgeon wrote about the affair:

> It is no business of mine to propose an explanation for the Lord Mayor, although I cannot think he is without one; but as you press the question . . .

the sermon . . . is my own . . . I delivered it extemporaneously and it is my own.[22]

The *Pall Mall Gazette* caustically called it a "brain wave," a "literary phenomenon of the day." This was a jab, not at Spurgeon, but at the Lord Mayor. Spurgeon had titled his sermon, "Do You Know Him"; the Lord Mayor had titled his message, "The True Knowledge of Christ." But the Mayor used the same text as Charles. A cartoon of Lord Mayor appeared with the top of his head opening up and there was Charles Haddon Spurgeon preaching. Other cartoons were published. Many letters came to the editors of the papers, some defending the Mayor, others not. Every possible explanation was suggested. One paper published parallel columns of Spurgeon's and the Mayor's messages. Most of it was verbatim. No doubt he plagiarized. The Lord Mayor said he had some old notes from a sermon he read or heard, and had dug these out and used them, not realizing the real situation. It "amazed" him the notes were so like Spurgeon's sermon. It may have been just a lapse of the Mayor, but that is extremely doubtful. Charles did not make much of it, although he did give a word of warning to stealers of sermons in *The Sword and the Trowel.*

The work continued to go well, however, just as the work had gone well during those last few difficult years for Spurgeon. He loved his church, and his church loved him. He said:

> I have beheld in this church apostolical piety revived; I will say it to the glory of God that I have seen as earnest and as true piety as Paul or Peter ever witnessed. I have marked in some here present, such godly zeal, such holiness, such devotion to the Master's business, as Christ Himself must look upon with joy and satisfaction. . . . Though we are not free from ten thousand faults, yet I have often admired the goodness of God which has enabled us with a hearty grip to hold each other by the hand and say, 'We love each other for Christ's sake and for the truth's sake, and we hope to live in each other's love till we die, wishing, if it were possible, to be buried side by side.'[23]

The College, his "first born and best beloved," had also grown in strength. The institution emerged as a central and important part in ministerial training for the entire British Baptist Union. The Pastors' College Society of Evangelists had seen similar growth. Many were won to Christ and several churches were planted through their efforts. Commitment to evangelical theology and evangelistic fervor characterized the College. The students made a tremendous contribution throughout the British Isles, on the continent, the United States, and around the globe. Of course, London especially felt their influence. Spurgeon, himself committed to the principle that those God called should "do the work of an evangelist," led his students to that commitment. Spurgeon felt great joy to see God-called men come forward and offer themselves for service. Especially did Spurgeon rejoice over the

Society of Evangelists. Some quite well-known names of the nineteenth century had emerged in that context; for example, A. J. Clarke, J. Manton Smith, and W. Y. Fullerton. Fullerton and Smith's evangelistic work made them "familiar as household words in tens of thousands of homes in various parts of the United Kingdom."[24] Others in the Society of Evangelists were J. Burham, E. A. Carter, A. A. Harmar, J. S. Harrison, along with many other dedicated men.

The Pastors' College Missionary Association formed another useful branch of the College work. Spurgeon himself supported Mr. Patrick and Dr. Churchur in North Africa through this agency. He also contributed toward the maintenance of Mr. Blamire and Mr. Wigston in Spain. Mention has already been made of Spurgeon's close friendship with Hudson Taylor and the China Inland Mission, now known as the Overseas Missionary Fellowship. Taylor's life of faith enlisted Spurgeon's deep appreciation. Spurgeon, convinced that God called people to the mission field, rejoiced to see his students "go into all the world" and thus fulfill the Great Commission.

By the last year of Spurgeon's life, the Colporteurs Association had reached the number of 96 full-time workers. Their sales that year amounted to £11,255, a higher total than had ever been reached before. During 1891, they sold nearly 20,000 Bibles and Testaments and more than a quarter of a million Scripture texts and cards. The total sales from the beginning of the Association in Spurgeon's early days up to the close of his last year came to £153,784. During the quarter century of their existence, 11,822,637 visits had been made to families. It is impossible to calculate how many were won to Christ and the blessings that God had wrought through this significant work. In this too, Spurgeon rejoiced.

The Tabernacle itself had seen significant growth, even during the last difficult years. At the time of Spurgeon's home call, the number of members on the church roll came to 5,311. At the end of 1891, the Tabernacle supported 22 missions stations and 27 Sunday and Ragged Schools with 612 teachers, 8,034 scholars, and accommodations for 3,840 worshippers in the various halls that had been the outgrowth of the Tabernacle ministry. As Spurgeon himself would often say, "What hath God wrought!" It was true, God's mighty hand rested on the "Boy Preacher from the Fens," now known world wide as the "Prince of Preachers."

THE TIME DRAWS NEAR

But now the time drew near for Spurgeon's home-going. When that last year opened, it opened with an ominous note. Charles himself was rather depressed with the passing of so many of his dear friends, especially William Olney. He had a very tender heart. Someone said, "He was one of the kindest men that ever breathed."[25] That was true. Quickly following the death of Olney, another devoted deacon, B. Wildon Carr, passed away. Carr had been a pastor in Newcastle-on-Tyne for some years before coming to London. Through the years he worked with Spurgeon directly or indirectly. A man of culture, he had stood firmly with Spurgeon in all the theological battles that had fallen across their paths. He also wielded a very able pen. Many times he wrote reviews on theological works for *The Sword and the Trowel.* Just a short time before he died, he edited a new edition of Goussen's significant work on the inspiration of Scripture. Spurgeon had requested this and he ably filled the role.

Still, many good events were recorded that last year. On Sunday, February 8, Charles was back in London from Mentone and preached at the Tabernacle. His sermon that morning was "A Call to Prayer and Testimony" from Isaiah 62:6-7. On the Monday evening prayer meeting Spurgeon was in good spirits and showed the congregation that though he had been quite ill, he felt that he had regained much strength and was looking forward to a lengthened period of service to Christ.

Mr. William Stott of Abbey Road Chapel, St. John's Wood, had just recently been appointed as assistant minister at the Tabernacle. Spurgeon placed high value on Stott's service. He was a friend of Charles and a genuine man of God. Stott did not attend the Pastors' College, but they had known one another for many years.

One can imagine the delight at the College on Friday afternoon, the 13th, the very week of Spurgeon's return from Mentone, when the students heard again their beloved founder and president give one of his scintillating lectures. Spurgeon entitled the lecture for that particular day "Styles of Preaching." He pointed out that many preachers fail to consider the real life situation of their hearers. He said to hear such preachers is like hearing rote read from the Prayer Book. Their sermons miss pertinency to where people actually live their lives. Spurgeon always opposed generalizations and never getting to a sharp point; he called it "Prayer Book preaching." He said, "You must know who are in Christ and who are out of Christ. There are some duties to all, but the unconverted need to be told that it is not by these but by the blood of Christ that they must find acceptance."[26] He admonished young students that they should take special care not to shut out any part of Scripture. He then went on to declare that God's preachers have the greatest possible reason for sticking to the old truths. He said, "The truth reached me when a lad, and the same kind of preaching reaches the lad still."[27] As he walked from his office to the lecture hall on that particular Friday afternoon, everyone could sense his excellent spirits; he even had some snap in his step. But he was not really as well as he appeared. He almost immediately came down with a severe cold that forced him to stay away from the Tabernacle prayer meeting the next week. On the next Tuesday he had recovered sufficiently to attend and preside over the annual meeting of the church, but he had missed the regular Monday night prayer meeting he loved so much.

The work at the Metropolitan Tabernacle continued to prosper. In just a few weeks after Spurgeon's return from the continent, 84 persons were ready to be proposed for church membership. The Memorial Hall, mentioned earlier, was almost complete. Spurgeon still had much to say about the false doctrines that were afoot, although the Down Grade had died down to some extent. He also leveled a shot at churches providing their members with worldly amusements. In the same general time frame, Spurgeon again caused a bit of a sensation by his withdrawal from the Liberation Society, as mentioned earlier.

On Easter Tuesday, March 31, the Tabernacle again filled to overflowing. Charles Cook spoke describing his experiences as a visitor to the Russian prisons. Considerable distrust and distaste of Czarist rule in Russia permeated Britain; most Britishers saw it as an iniquitous system. In that same month he refused the use of the Metropolitan Tabernacle to the Liberation Society. As previously seen, he became disillusioned over the work because of its involvement in politics and questionable theology.

THE LAST CONFERENCE

The last College Conference that Spurgeon ever attended opened on Monday, April 20 at Upton Chapel, Lambeth Road. If only Charles had known how near his final call was, he surely would have rejoiced even more in the results that had been achieved during his lifetime. By 1891 the "new" Pastors' College Evangelistic Association reached 707 members. To that date, 845 men had been received into the College and 618 were still working in the Baptist Union. There were 414 churches served by Spurgeon's men supplied statistics for 1890, and reported that close to 8,000 persons had been received into the fellowship of those churches. Spurgeon, in his inevitable eloquent style, addressed the men and said, "The brethren present have come from the war, and they have brought their shields with them. They remind me of the Spartan woman who told her son either to bring his shield back or to come back on it." He went on to say concerning the Lord's second coming, "The wheels of Christ's chariot are already red hot. He went to heaven to prepare and to set all things right that Satan had ruined, and He is coming back quickly."[28]

On the second day of the Conference, Spurgeon woke with a very bad headache. Nevertheless, up by noon he gave his last great manifesto to the students he loved and to the College, his "best beloved." He preached on "The Greatest Fight in the World." On Friday of the Conference week, he preached before the College Association for the last time, his text being John 16:14, "He Shall Glorify Me." Biographer Pike, who heard him preach for the last time on that occasion, said that the sermon "was in all respects one of his greatest efforts."[29]

That spring an epidemic of influenza raged through London, but Spurgeon worked on, despite his own physical weaknesses. One would have thought he was in great health and in no danger. But the College Conference had considerably weakened and exhausted him. Still, he threw himself into the work with his old enthusiasm. In reality, it was a "reckless ardor, nevertheless—the last supreme effort of the great man, who was visibly breaking down." [30] He was unable to attend the Home Counties Baptist Association in May of '91 and James Archer Spurgeon preached. On Monday, May 4, he edited his Sunday sermon for publication and saw many inquirers at the Tabernacle. He presided at the prayer meeting in the evening. The following evening he preached a sermon to Sunday School teachers in Bloomsbury Chapel, and on Thursday evening he gave a special discourse to sailors, which always delighted the preacher. Charles preached to the men of the sea from Job 7:12, on the subject "Am I a Sea, or a Whale?"

On Friday of that week Spurgeon attended the Ministers' Fraternal Society at Hamdon; on the fifteenth of the month he spoke at Exeter Hall on behalf of Presbyterian missions. However, he was growing steadily weaker as he tried to keep up the hectic pace. It must be realized that these various engagements caused considerable travel. Although many of them were in the greater London area, he had to go by carriage, not a very pleasant way to travel in Victorian days. As usual, all the services at the Tabernacle continued and he gave himself to those as well.

THE LAST SERMON

Spurgeon had come down with influenza, a victim of the epidemic. But in two weeks' time he seemed well and he decided to preach on the morning of Sunday the 17th. He preached on 1 Samuel 30:21-25. It was to be his last sermon at the great Metropolitan Tabernacle. No one, not even the great preacher himself, realized that this would be the final time he would preach from the pulpit of the church he loved so dearly and to which he had given so much of himself. He was not quite 57 years of age, but he had now preached the Gospel for 40 years.

After the service, however, he found himself in such good spirits that he thought it might speed his recovery from the influenza to travel to his grandfather's country. Friends William Higgs and James Douglas had a foreboding about Charles attempting the trip to Stambourne. They tried to dissuade him from going. But he was completing a book, one of his best known works, *Memories of Stambourne*. He wanted some photos of the lovely countryside and little village to put in his *Memories*. He deeply wanted to go. On Monday he made his way to the beloved site of his early years as the guest of Mr. Gursteen at Haverhill. The pastor at Stambourne at that time was J. C. Hoachin. Charles thoroughly enjoyed the opportunity of seeing the old sites and scenes that had thrilled him as a boy.

A Serious Illness

On Thursday of that week another severe headache came on and the following day he was so much worse that he had to hasten home. He completely broke down. The next day, Friday, June 12, the symptoms became even more alarming. Charles said, "I suffered beyond measure, and was often between the jaws of *death*."[31] The opening of the Surrey Gardens Memorial Hall had been set for June 18, and Spurgeon had looked forward to being there, but it was impossible. Some say the new Hall was in sight of the old Surrey Gardens Music Hall. But the old Hall was in Kennington and the new Hall sat on Penrose Street in Walworth, so it probably would have been impossible to see the old site from the new. Spurgeon had preached to thousands at the old Hall. The foundation stone of the new Hall was laid October 20, 1890 by James Archer Spurgeon. Charles had grown so ill by this time that he could not even send a message. He worsened day by day. His personal physician, Dr. Miller, of Norwood, wanted the professional opinion of a medical colleague, Dr. Kidd. The Tabernacle friends held an all day prayer meeting on Monday, June 29, for their pastor. The meeting started at 7:00 in the morning and went on until 9:00 that night. It proved to be a remarkable prayer meeting. Clergymen of the Establishment and Nonconformists of all denominations attended.

The first public mention of kidney problems surfaced at this time. Charles even had "delirium" the first week in July. The media was full of the details of his illness. They began to say what the world would lose if he died. The papers wrote: "The worse was evidently feared"; "condition is extremely critical." He had to go on a virtual liquid diet, and at last was reduced to eating only oatmeal. The physicians were almost constantly at his bedside. Papers all over the world carried reports. On July 16th the reports read: "extreme danger." All began to say good things about Charles now. *The Brooklyn Daily Guide*, July 17, 1891 said: "Charles Spurgeon is dying . . . his life seems to be hanging by a thread." *The Speakers* July 18, 1891 reported a slight improvement. It seemed to be true, for on July 20 he took solid food for the first time in four weeks. *The Philadelphia National Baptist* July 23, '91 reported: "for the past two weeks the English-speaking world has been watching the sick-bed of the great preacher." *Joyful News* wrote on July 23, 1891: "Just as we go to press we learn that Mr. Spurgeon continues to improve, and that though not out of danger, there is now hope that he will yet live to do work for the Master he loves so much." "No recent illness has excited one tenth of the interest awakened over Mr. Spurgeon's sick-bed. The latest bulletins have been eagerly read in clubs, theatres, and where men of all classes assemble," reported *The Illustrated London House*. "Is Mr. Spurgeon going to die? has been the question on everybody's lips," said *The Penny Illustrated Paper* on July 25, 1891. Letters and cards came from everywhere. Poems were written; telegrams flooded in. The number of telegrams received at Westwood, where he was confined to bed, were so overwhelming that the telegraph office at Norwood literally broke down under the weight of incoming telegrams. Among those who sent words of consolation were the Prince of Wales, many of Britain's nobility, and high dignitaries of the Established Church. The chief Rabbi sent a very cordial letter. Mr. Gladstone wrote Mrs. Spurgeon on that occasion. It reads:

> Corton, Lowestoft, July 16, 1891
>
> MY DEAR MADAM,—In my own home, darkened at the present time, I have read with studied interest the daily accounts of Mr. Spurgeon's illness, and I cannot help conveying to you the earnest assurance of my sympathy with you and with him, and of my cordial admiration, not only of his splendid powers, but still more of his devoted and unfailing character. May I humbly commend you and him in all contingencies to the infinite stores of the Divine love and mercy, and subscribe myself, my dear Madam, faithfully yours,
> W. E. Gladstone. [32]

The first week in August saw real hope for a complete recovery. Charles wrote to the Metropolitan Tabernacle on August 9. Even on his sickbed he said—and it was recorded and read at the Wesleyan Conference: "The German critics are not to be trusted. This is my theology—Jesus Christ for me. I want nothing more. What else can I need? This is my only hope." [33]

Spurgeon's illness was very serious; it was not just another bout with his gout. Dr. Kidd said, "The case is a very difficult and dangerous one." His chronic Bright's disease was taking its final toll. As Spurgeon's condition varied from day to day, finally the official diagnosis came down; he had Bright's Disease, today called nephritis, and it was of the most severe type. In the 19th century, physicians considered it a terminal disease. Spurgeon was deathly ill, but he began to recover, at least to a degree. On August 9 he wrote a short letter to be read to his Metropolitan Tabernacle people on Sunday, August 9, at the morning service. The quite touching letter reads:

> DEAR BRETHREN,—The Lord's name be praised for first giving, and then hearing, the loving prayers of His people. Through those prayers my life is prolonged. I feel greatly humbled and very grateful at being the object of so great a love and so wonderful an outburst of prayer. I have not strength to say more. Let the name of the Lord be glorified.
> —Yours most heartily, C. H. SPURGEON. [34]

Prayer meetings continued to be held twice each day at the Tabernacle. During this prolonged illness Spurgeon had been in delirium at times. He thought he was away from home and would call on friends to take him home. But eventually the deliriums subsided and he seemed to be genuinely improving. He himself felt quite confident of being on the road to recovery. On September 12, his old friend, George Rogers, the first principal of the

Pastors' College, and the oldest congregational minister in England, passed away. That must have been something of a blow to Spurgeon in the light of his own illness. But he continued to improve and in the early days of September, which were unusually clear and warm, for the first time since his prolonged illness, he indulged himself in a drive. The next day, September 13, he penned the following letter to his beloved congregation:

September 13, 1891

DEAR FRIENDS,—I cannot write much, but I cannot withhold my heart and pen from saying, 'O bless the Lord with me, and let us exalt His name together.' This week has, by its fine weather, set me free from a three months' captivity. Those believers of all denominations who so lovingly prayed for me will now help me to praise the Lord. Verily, the loving Lord heareth prayer!

I fear my doctors would have a mournful tale to tell of my disease, and from inward consciousness I must agree with them; but I feel better, and I get into the open air, and therefore I hope my face is turned toward recovery. Reading, writing, thinking, etc., are not yet easy to me. I am forced to vegetate. I fear it will be long before I can be at my beloved work.

I send my hearty love to you all, and my humble gratitude to that great army of praying people who have been heard of the Lord in their cries for the prolongation of my life. May we believe more, pray more, and therefore receive more!—Yours, in bonds of true affection, C. H. Spurgeon. [35]

Charles continued to write to his people and on September 27th and 30th he wrote lengthy letters which seemed to indicate growing strength. But this illness put a "faraway tone" in his once magnificent voice. The multitudes would never hear that voice again.

Still, as cruel as it sounds, even Charles' illness and the many people praying for his recovery caused caustic comments. *The New Zealand Baptist* in September, 1891 reported a dispute in Sydney as to whether a telegram should be sent offering condolences. One man, against any communications, was reported to have said, "How could they pray for this man, one who was living in a state of apostasy from the faith and schism from the Church?" Other reports were positive. The *Review of Reviews* in October 1891 reported: "The Prince of Wales has been among the numerous distinguished persons who have made inquiries as to the condition of the rev. gentleman." Later, the same periodical said: "The Rev. C. H. Spurgeon is reported to be much weaker." Another interesting anecdote tells the story of regret expressed by the *Astrologer's Magazine* that they did not know Spurgeon's birth so they could make definite predictions about his future. One wonders why the editors did not make the effort to find out; it was no secret. By September the 18th he got out for some exercise; his health seemed to be returning.

The Last Trip to Mentone

In the first week in October, Charles traveled to Eastbourne on the south coast, staying at the Queen's Hotel. The short trip seemed to contribute to his improvement. Then, he returned to London on the 16th and left for Mentone on the 26th. It was then that the well known Dr. A. T. Pierson of Philadelphia began his ministry at the Tabernacle the last Sunday of the month.

Rev. and Mrs. James A. Spurgeon, Mr. Harrald, along with Charles and Susannah, left Herne Hill station on the boat train for Calais. Deacons Allison and Higgs accompanied them as far as Calais. They traveled through Marseilles, Paris, and Lyon. In France they rode on the saloon carriage of Baron Rothschild. The carriage was not free; Passmore, Alabaster, and John Cook paid for it. Nevertheless, it seemed a very good trip. What made this journey to Mentone so much more enjoyable than his many other trips, and perhaps contributed to his improving health, was that Susannah traveled with him. This was the first time that his beloved wife could accompany him to the south of France. What a delightful experience it must have been for Spurgeon, his Susie, and the others who journeyed with them. The first letter that Spurgeon sent back to London from his beloved "sunny south" seemed to indicate he was decidedly getting better. He wrote, "Not wearied but improved by the thousand miles journey. Almost miraculous. Hallelujah!" Spurgeon wrote a short time later, "My brother, whose care has made the journey less formidable, when he returns will have a cheering tale of me and of my dear wife, whose presence with me makes every single enjoyment into seven." [36]

James Archer returned to the Metropolitan Tabernacle in November and gave a good report. He said Charles "looked a new man." James said his brother had moved slowly toward a fair measure of health and strength. He had hoped to surprise his people and return in February, but his doctors said no. In a later letter written to the Tabernacle, however, Spurgeon revealed something of his physical weakness, even though he seemed to be on the mend. He wrote, "To go up a few steps, to take a short walk, to move a parcel, and all such trifles, becomes a difficulty; so that Solomon's words are true, 'The grasshopper is a burden.' I think I could preach, but when I have seen a friend for five minutes I begin to feel that I have had as much of speaking as I can well manage." A week later in a letter he wrote, "No striking progress to report. But I feel I must be better, whatever the signs may say. Still, feelings are doubtful evidences. One thing is forced upon my mind—namely, that I am weak as water, and that the building up is slower work than pulling down." [37] He wrote again saying, "I am tossed up and down upon the waves of my disease, and what is thought progress today is gone tomorrow." [38] Nevertheless, Spurgeon and his company genuinely believed he was gradually improving; he was able to give himself to some responsibilities in his work. Charles seemed able to get on quite well with various writing projects. For example, he must have intended to write a biography of his grandfather James Spurgeon. From Mentone he wrote his father on November 2, 1891: "Yes, do send me anything about grandfather. I have a good deal of materials toward a life of him, but know not where to look for more." [39] He also did articles for *The Sword and the Trowel*. He said himself that he felt "strangely better." He even schemed that he would surprise his congregation by suddenly appearing back in London. He got his book, *Memories of Stambourne*, produced and published. By all accounts, in December, he seemed reasonably improved. He felt so optimistic concerning his recovery that he said, "In comparison for these dumb Sabbaths the Lord will give me years of free utterance of His word." [40] A week later he went on to say in a letter to his friends back in London, "I feel better, and have no fear but in due season I shall be as strong as aforetime." [41] They were encouraged. The deacons planned to put a hydraulic lift in the Metropolitan Tabernacle for their pastor when he returned. Shortly before Christmas, Charles wrote, "I feel I have turned the corner." [42] The entire Mentone party must have felt that way. Even as late as the middle of January 23, Susannah wrote to Charles' father: "Gout has attacked his hand, and rendered him ill and depressed. The doctor says this morning that many symptoms are favourable, so we are hoping, that by God's mercy, the trial may not be very severe or long." [43]

Charles was feeling so well that on the 21st of December he wrote a lengthy letter to the Stockwell Orphanage. It unfolds as follows:

> DEAR BOYS AND GIRLS,—I send you all my love so far as the post can carry it at twopence-halfpenny for half-an-ounce. I wish you a real glorious Christmas. I might have said a *jolly Christmas* if we had all been boys; but as some of us are girls, I will be proper, and say, 'A merry Christmas!' Enjoy yourselves and feel grateful to the kind friends who find money to keep the Stockwell Orphanage supplied. Bless their loving hearts, they never let you want for anything; may they have pleasure in seeing you all grow up to be good men and women. Feel very grateful also to the trustees. These gentlemen are always at work arranging for your good. Give them three times three. Then there are Mr. Charlesworth, Mr. Ladds, and all the masters and the matrons. Each one of them deserves your love and gratitude and obedience. They try to do you good; try to cheer them all you can. I should like you to have a fine day—such a day as we have here; but if not, you will be warm and bright indoors. Three cheers for those who give us the good things for this festival. I want you for a moment in the day to be all still and spend the time in thanking our Heavenly Father and the Lord Jesus for great goodness shown to you and to me, and then pray for me that I may get quite well. Mrs. Spurgeon and I both send our love to all the Stockwell family.—Yours very heartily,
>
> C. H. Spurgeon. [44]

He wrote, quite touchingly, to his people on Christmas Eve, saying,

> I have nearly finished thirty-eight years of my ministry among you, and have completed XXXVII Volumes of published sermons, preached in your midst. Yet we are not wearied of each other. . . . Honestly, I do *not* think you are losers by my absence, so long as the Lord enables our dear friend Dr. Pierson to preach as he does. There is a cloud of blessing resting on you now. Turn the cloud into a shower by the heavenly electricity of believing prayer. To be denied activities which have become part of my nature seems so strange; but as I cannot alter it, and as I am sure that infinite wisdom rules it, I bow before the Divine will—my Father's will.[45]

Then he wrote to his church again on January 6, 1892:

> On looking back from the Valley of the Shadow of death through which I passed so short a time ago, I feel my mind grasping with firmer grip than ever that everlasting gospel which for so many years I have preached to you. We have not been deceived. Jesus does give rest to those who come to him, he does save those who trust him, he does photograph his image on those who learn of him. I hate the Christian infidelity of the modern school more than ever, as I see how it sends away from sinful man this last and only hope.[46]

Again on January 14, 1892, he wrote his beloved people:

> May the saturating showers of blessings for which I am looking, soon fall in tropical abundance, and may no part of the field be left dry.[47]

The first sermon published in 1892, number 2,237 in the Penny Pulpit, had been ironically entitled, "Gratitude for Deliverance from the Grave"; Psalm 118, verses 17-18: "I shall not die, but live, and declare the works of the Lord. The Lord hath chastened me sore: but he hath not given me over unto death." Luther had inscribed that text on his study wall. Little did Spurgeon know what the next few weeks had in store!

The amount of correspondence Charles produced during those difficult days is amazing. He wrote to many friends as well as to his beloved people at the Tabernacle. On the basis of the correspondence, one would have almost thought he was well on the road to recovery.

The press did seem to think Spurgeon was improving. On December 17, 1891, *The Christian World* wrote: "The gradual improvement in his general condition still continued." *The London Herald* said on December 31, '91: "Mr. S. has so far recovered health and strength that he is able this week to resume the revision of the published weekly sermons." A report in *The British Weekly* on January 14, 1892 of a man who had visited Charles in Mentone, and when asked how he was getting on, Charles had replied: "Splendidly."[48]

IMPROVEMENT?

There actually did seem some reason for the optimism; Charles began speaking again to those that would gather in the Beau Revage Hotel. On New Year's Eve of 1891, and on the New Year's Day morning of 1892, he spoke to the people and again shared the great truths of God's promises from the Bible. Susannah played the piano for the short services. The title of Charles' two messages was "Breaking the Long Silence." The last photo taken of Spurgeon was on January 9th. In the last days he also sent a letter and contribution to Archibald Brown of the East London Tabernacle on celebration of 25 years of ministry. He said, "You have long been dear to me, but in protest against deadly error, we have become more than ever one." On Sunday evenings, January 10 and 17, he conducted brief services in his room, reading some of his own writings. On the 17th they all sang the hymn, "The Sands of Time are Sinking, The Dawn of Heaven Breaks." Again, little did they know how true that was. That short service became the end of all worship services for Charles on earth. January 15th saw Mrs. Spurgeon's birthday, and the same day the Duke of Clarence died.

Spurgeon continued to be hopeful that in a short time he could return to his beloved people and pick up his London ministry. On January 10 he said, "The steady and solid progress which had begun is continued and will continue."[49] That became his last written communication by his own hand to the Tabernacle. It was read before the people on Sunday, January 24. It continued, "The sun shines at length, and now I hope to get on." That bright, hopeful message encouraged the people. Then suddenly and unexpectedly a telegram came telling of a serious relapse. On January 25, *The Daily News* reported the telegram from Mentone: "Pastor been very ill; cannot write; kept his bed three days . . . Pray earnestly." All the papers began a diligent watch on Charles' condition. *The Times* recorded on January 28, "Mr. Spurgeon's condition still continues critical." Charles himself had been able to write on January 22, '92, "Whether I live or die, I would say, in the words of Israel to Joseph 'God shall be with you.'" That was recorded in *The Ross-Shue Journal*. Then on the 29th *The Daily News* reported: "The critical condition of Mr. Spurgeon is again awakening anxious feelings." On January 28 a telegram came from Mentone stating Spurgeon had an attack of gout in the head and hands, and was in bed. At 3:43 p.m. on the 31st a telegram was sent, saying, "There is no hope." Yet, people held on to hope.

THE APPROACHING END

Spurgeon himself, however, seemed to realize that God was drawing the curtain on his work. He had once said in a sermon, "In a little while, there will be a concourse of persons in the streets. Methinks I hear some one enquiring:—

"What are all these people waiting for?
Do you not know? He is to be buried to-day.
And who is that?
It is Spurgeon.
What! the man that preached at the Tabernacle?
Yes; he is to be buried to-day.

"That will happen very soon. And when you see my coffin carried to the silent grave, I should like every one of you, whether converted or not, to be constrained to say, 'He did earnestly urge us, in plain and simple language, not to put off the consideration of eternal things; he did entreat us to look to Christ. Now he is gone, our blood is not at his door if we perish.'"[50] It was coming to pass, the great drama had reached its finale.

Charles sent a brief message to the Prince of Wales who had just lost a son. Then, just before he slipped into a coma on the last day of his life, he dictated his last, brief message to his beloved church. He sent them £100 for Tabernacle expenses. Spurgeon wrote, "Self and wife, £100, hearty thanks offering toward Tabernacle general expenses. Love to all friends." This was his last generous act and his last message.

Near the end, he said to his Susie, "Oh Wifey, I have had such a blessed time with my Lord."[51] As he sensed earth receding and heaven opening, he said in hushed tones, "My work is done." The last verse of Scripture he was heard to recite was, "I have fought a good fight. I have finished my course. I have kept the faith." He seemed to recognize Susannah once or twice, but shortly after that he slipped quietly into sleep and became totally unconscious. Beloved Susie and dear friends sat about his bedside praying, weeping, hoping.

Bulletins started being received in London through Reuter's News, all signed by Dr. Fitzhenry, the physician in Mentone. They read:

Mentone   January 31   11 a.m.
Rev. C.H.S. has had another restless night, and his condition this morning gives cause for the greatest anxiety . . .

                                     3:30 p.m.
The Rev. C. H. Spurgeon is now insensible, and much weaker than he was this morning.

                                     6:30 p.m.
Mr. Spurgeon's condition this evening is extremely critical . . .

                                     10:00 p.m.
Mr. Spurgeon is sinking fast, and all hope of his recovery has been abandoned. He is quite unconscious and suffers no pain.

Charles remained unconscious, breathing heavier and heavier. Friends shed a few tears. The hour had come. Then, at five minutes past eleven on the Sabbath night, January 31, 1892, "After this it was noised abroad that Mr. Valiant-for-truth was taken with a summons by the same post as the other, and had this for a token that the summons was true, that his pitcher was broken at the fountain. When he understood it, he called for his friends, and told them of it. Then said he—I am going to my Father's; and though with great difficulty I have got hither, yet now I do not repent me of all the trouble I have been at to arrive where I am. My sword I give to him that shall succeed me in my pilgrimage, and my courage and skill to him that can get it. My marks and scars I carry with me, to be a witness for me that I have fought His battles, who now will be my rewarder. When the day that he must go hence was come, many accompanied him to the river-side; into which as he went, he said—'Death where is thy sting?' and he said—'Grave where is thy victory?' So he passed over, and all the trumpets sounded for him on the other side." [52] The Pilgrim had arrived home.

The five who were standing by his bedside, who "accompanied him to the riverside," were Susannah, Miss Thorne, Mr. Harrald, his secretary, Mr. Allison, a deacon at the Metropolitan Tabernacle, and Mr. Samuel. When Charles passed over, Mr. Harrald offered prayer and Mrs. Spurgeon "thanked the Lord for the previous treasure so long left to her, and sought, at the throne of grace, strength and guidance for all the future." [53] She praised God for the "unspeakable joy" she had with her beloved. She must have found comfort in Charles' words when he said, "How blessed not to be afraid to die." [54] Susannah sent a short telegram to Thomas in Australia. It was simply, "Father in Heaven, Mother resigned." [55] Mr. Harrald wired a telegram to the Metropolitan Tabernacle. It reads as follows: "Mentone 11:50—Spurgeon's Tab. London—Our beloved pastor entered Heaven 11:05 Sunday night—Harrald." When Charles' father John received the news he said, "What a happy meeting there has been between Charles and his mother."

The news flashed all over the globe. Every part of the world heard the message and a veritable flood tide of sympathy and encouragement swept into Mentone. The telegraph wires in Mentone were blocked with the multitudes of messages to Mrs. Spurgeon. The Prince and Princess of Wales were among the first to "desire to express their deep sympathy with her in her great sorrow." [56] The whole world mourned for the loss of the pulpit giant and devout man of God. Papers everywhere recorded the "sad day." Typical was *The Freeman* which wrote: "A Prince has fallen in Israel." *The Baptist* recorded (February 5, '92): "At last the blow has fallen! . . . One of England's bravest, noblest, holiest hearts lies still in death." So many eulogies were written, they almost make a book. A host of personal words were also given. "The greatest preacher of his time," declared F. B. Meyer. John Clifford said, "The enthusiasm of the great evangelical revival reappeared in him; and the passion for 'saving souls,' characteristic of Whitefield, was supreme." The great American preacher and educator, B. H. Carroll said, "Last Sunday night at Mentone, France, there died the greatest man of modern times. If every crowned head in Europe had died that night, the event would not be so momentous as the death of this one man."[57]

The Beau Revage Hotel put a notice on its door reading, "Mr. Spurgeon fell asleep in Jesus at 11:05 p.m." Because of local French laws it was mandatory that the body be removed from the hotel within 24 hours. So it was embalmed and removed so as to send it to London. Friends covered with flowers the bed in which Spurgeon lay at the time of his death. The "precious body," as Susannah expressed it, rested sealed in a lead shell and in a beautiful olive wood casket. On the casket was the following inscription:

In ever-loving memory of
CHARLES HADDON SPURGEON,
Born at Kelvedon, June 19, 1834;
Fell asleep in Jesus at Mentone, January 31, 1892.
"I have fought a good fight, I have finished my course, I have kept the faith."

The Scottish Presbyterian Church of Mentone held a memorial service at 10:00 a.m. Pastor Delapierre spoke and prayed in French. Back in London, on the next Sunday, the entire front of the Tabernacle was draped in black. The people deeply mourned. The church was full as Dr. Murray Mitchel and Rev. Somerville, along with Mr. Harrald conducted the service.

In the meantime, Spurgeon's remains were removed and sent back to London by train. The body reached London's Victoria Station, Platform #3, on the morning of Monday, February 8. A large crowd, over a thousand, had gathered in the station. A procession of friends formed and bore his body directly to the Pastors' College. There, in the common room, the massive olive casket lay in state for the day. Two private services were held that Monday at the College. That same night the students lovingly carried the body into the Tabernacle and placed it on a platform just below the pulpit from which Charles had preached for so many years. On both sides of the coffin were palm branches that had been sent from the south of France by Mrs. Spurgeon. On the top of the casket lay Spurgeon's Bible that he had used at the Metropolitan Tabernacle. It was opened to the text Isaiah 14:22, "Look unto me, and be ye saved, all the ends of the earth," the verse that God had used to bring about Charles' conversion more than 40 years earlier.

THE FUNERAL CEREMONIES

On Tuesday, the next morning, the Tabernacle opened its doors to the public so that those who wished might pass in front of the beloved pastor's remains. The procession started before daybreak and continued after dark.

No less than 60,000 of all classes entered the Tabernacle to pay their last respects to the man who, in some sense, they all felt had been their preacher. Everyone who came to view the scene received a copy of Spurgeon's sermon published the previous week, entitled "God's Will About the Future."

On Wednesday, memorial services were held. One service would never suffice. In the morning at 11:00 the members of the church and Spurgeon's various organizations were invited. They filled the Tabernacle. Dr. Joseph Angus, principal of Regent's Park College, spoke as James Archer Spurgeon conducted the service. At 3:00 p.m., V. J. Charlesworth, headmaster of the Stockwell Orphanage and Deacon Thomas H. Olney, church treasurer, along with elder J. T. Dunn took part in an afternoon service held for ministers and students of all denominations; they too filled the church building. Dr. Alexander Maclaren spoke that afternoon as did Canon Flemny of the Church of England, along with J. Monro Gibson, Moderator of the English Presbyterian Synod, Herbert Evans, Chairman of the Congregational Union; A. T. Pierson, and T. B. Stephenson, President of the Wesleyan Conference, also took part. At 7:00 that evening, a service devoted to Christian workers and church members of various denominations was held. In that service George Williams of the YMCA presided and Ira Sankey sang the hymn, "Sleep On, Beloved, Sleep and Take Thy Rest." Every service proved to be tremendously moving and touching. At the night service George Williams spoke as did Sir Arthur Blackwood, President of the Meldmay Conference. Also Canon Palmer, Anglican Rector of Newington parish near the Metropolitan Tabernacle, and Colonel Griffin of the Baptist Union spoke. Some who attended the services were Dr. Barnardo of the orphanage work, Col. Griffin, President of the Baptist Union, and other notables. Rev. J. W. Harrald, Spurgeon's secretary prayed as did Rev. Newman Hall. In all, sixty different deputations attended.

So many wanted to take part in the funeral services that an additional service had to be held Wednesday night at 10:00 p.m. for the general public. They announced the service for 10:30 p.m., but by 10 the building filled to excess and the service started. W. Y. Fullerton spoke and Sankey, Moody's singer, sang, "Only Remembered By What I Have Done." A paper reported, "Men in (working) aprons, workgirls, who had run over from the factory—all were there."[58] That must have pleased Spurgeon. In all 20,000 people attended the services of the day.

Thursday, the day of Spurgeon's internment, Dr. A. T. Pierson, who had preached at the Tabernacle on Wednesday afternoon, spoke again at a service in the Metropolitan Tabernacle. In his message he emphasized the fact that Spurgeon's death had occurred almost exactly a century after that of John Wesley. He referred to the intertwining of the lives of John and Charles Wesley and then of Charles Spurgeon and his brother James. Pierson went on to say that the work of Wesley, after his death, became greater than the work that he did in life through the legacy of his ministry and writings. The same would surely be true of Spurgeon, Pierson prophetically stated. He said: "The posthumous work of Charles Haddon Spurgeon no man can at this time estimate or conjecture."[59] How right he was! In many senses, Spurgeon has a greater impact today, one hundred years after his death, than he did even in his lifetime.

> While we gathered around the grave, a little patch of blue sky appeared, just over our heads, as if to remind us of the glory-land above; and while Mr. Brown was speaking, a dove flew from the direction of the Tabernacle toward the tomb, and, wheeling in its flight over the crowd, almost seemed to pause. In ancient days, it would have been an augury: to us, it spoke only peace. As the service proceeded, a little robin poured forth its liquid note all the while from a neighbouring tombstone; the redbreast made appropriate music, fabled as it was to have had its crimson coat ever since it picked a thorn from the Saviour's bleeding brow. Well, we do not believe that; but we believe what we sang at the grave, the truth that Mr. Spurgeon lived to preach, and died to defend,—

> > Dear dying Lamb, Thy precious blood
> > Shall never lose its power,
> > Till all the ransomed Church of God
> > Be saved to sin no more.

> Many remarked that the whole of the memorial services, unique as they were, were characterized by a simplicity and heartiness completely in harmony with the entire life of the beloved Pastor; and it was most significant that, when the olive casket was lowered into the vault, not even the glorified preacher's name was visible;—it was just as *he* would have wished it;—there was nothing to be seen but the text at the foot of the coffin, and the open Bible. Of course, the Bible was not buried; it is not dead, it 'liveth and abideth for ever;' and who knows whether it may not prove, more than ever, the means of quickening the dead, now that he, who loved it dearer that his life, can no longer proclaim its blessed truths with the living voice? God grant it!'[60]

The Canon in Resident of St. Paul's Cathedral of London, Archdeacon Sinclair, paid his tribute:

> Our country has lost its greatest living preacher. I use the words deliberately, because I do not believe that there are any among us who remain, who, for thirty years, every Sunday during the twelve months, could gather together, morning and evening, more than 6,000 earnest patient hearers, eager to receive from one untiring tongue the word of life.[61]

The newspapers eulogized him:

> The death of Charles Haddon Spurgeon removed one of the most remarkable preachers of the time, and whose name has been familiar for more than a generation wherever Christianity has a foothold. *N.Y. Press*, 1/2/1892

Mr. Spurgeon's death will be mourned wherever the English language is spoken. *News of the World*, 2/3/92

Cardinal R. C. Manning died a fortnight earlier than Spurgeon. Many papers spoke of both, even paralleled them, calling Spurgeon the "poor-man's cardinal." This poem was in *Scotsman*, 2/15/92:

> Two pillars in God's House of Prayer
> Lie fallen side by side today;
> One rich and canoned and hoary gray,
> The other simple, rude, and bare.

Other papers reported:

Moral character beyond all range of impeachment. *Morning Advertiser*, 9/2/92

He was a real British heart of oak. *Pall Mall Gazette*, 6/2/92

French paper *Journal des Depots* — He was gifted in extraordinary measure.

Even the *Saturday Review* gave a positive word: "most famous and influential of Baptist ministers." 6/2/92

"He stood level with the best of the Puritans," said the *Inquirer* 6/2/92

"A religious influence . . . unparalleled in our day," wrote the *Daily Telegraph* 8/2/92.

Joseph Parker gave his eulogies to Spurgeon, despite the conflict they had over the "Open Letter." He said:

Spurgeon illustrated the divine election which chooses its own instruments, protects them in the face of all hostility, and brings obscurity to the point of world-wide renown. Mr. Spurgeon was ordained in a mountain apart.

Parker also said, "The English pulpit has lost its most conspicuous figure." And, "The Bible came straight from Heaven . . . this was his faith and it made him strong." Parker went on:

He has proved that evangelical preaching can draw around itself the greatest congregation in the world, and hold it for a lifetime . . . He has also proved that it is possible to draw and to hold the greatest congregation without organ, or band, or choir, or painted windows. . . .

After the beautiful tributes and services that preceded the internment, on Thursday morning, February 11, 1892, the cortege prepared itself for the journey to the Norwood Cemetery. A. T. Pierson presided and Archibald G. Brown spoke. Brown was very close to Spurgeon. He had grown a great church of 3,000 members in east London himself, much like his mentor C. H. Spurgeon. Secretary Harrald prayed. Newman Hall also prayed and some boys of the Orphanage sang "Thou Art Gone to the Grave" as the coffin was carried out.

In the early years of Charles' visits to Wooton, in Surrey, he had said that he would always like to be buried in the churchyard of that village. Later, after the building of the great Stockwell Orphanage, he expressed the wish to lie in the center of the grounds thinking that many would come to look at his grave and then help the orphans for whom he so deeply cared. Another time he said he would like to be buried in Mentone, but after he attended the funeral of a friend there, he gave up that notion. Last of all, he expressed the desire, as he pointed to a site in the Norwood Cemetery, to be buried there waiting for the Lord's return. He wanted to be at a spot where his church officers and members (many of whom were buried there) might be around him in death as they were in life. When the Tabernacle deacons heard of the death of their beloved pastor, they met on Monday morning and sent an urgent request to Mrs. Spurgeon, asking that this arrangement for burial might be made as they generously offered to defray all the expenses. Susannah had expressed a wish that he be buried in Mentone. But it seemed wise to fulfill Charles' desire, so the matter was settled.

Thus the procession made its way five miles south to the Norwood Cemetery. The cortege itself was two miles long. The procession, led by mounted police, was immediately followed by the empty brougham (carriage) of the pastor. Forty-one other carriages followed the first. As the cortege started, the College students held a worship service at the Chatsworth Road Baptist Church, then joined the mourners at the Norwood Cemetery. On both sides of the open hearse the passage, *"I have fought a good fight, I have finished my course, I have kept the faith,"* was to be seen. Eight hundred uniformed police stood at attention along the route. The procession made its way down Clapham Road, then on past the Stockwell Orphanage. There, on a black-draped platform, were all the boys and girls of the Orphanage. All along the entire route, the people lined the streets by the hundreds of thousands. As the cortege passed, men bared their heads and women could be seen and heard weeping and sobbing. All of the shops along the route, even the public houses, were closed. Houses had drawn their shades. Many buildings were draped with black, all the flags hung at half-mast, and the bells of the churches rang. As Ray expressed it, "Such a funeral had never been seen in south London before and was unlikely to be seen again. Scarcely an eye was dry . . . everyone present felt that indeed a great man and a master of Israel had been laid to rest."[62]

At the gate of the cemetery, the bishop of Rochester entered the carriage of James Spurgeon, deeply desiring to pay a parting tribute in behalf of the Anglican Church and himself to C. H. Spurgeon. As the cortege made its way up to the grave, many of the near relatives of the great preacher assembled. Then another 1,000 mourners stood within the barriers that had been erected, as outside a multitude of the general public waited in silence. Also attending were Dr. Barnardo, Col. Griffin, President of the Baptist Union, and George Williams. The total attendees came to 2,000.

Pastor Archibald Brown conducted the burial service. In touching words he said:

> Beloved President, Faithful Pastor, Prince of Preachers, Brother Beloved, Dear Spurgeon! we bid thee not 'Farewell,' but only for a little while, 'Goodnight.' Thou shalt rise soon at the first dawn of the Resurrection-day of the redeemed. Yet is not the good-night ours to bid, but thine; it is we who linger in the darkness; thou art in God's holy light. Our night shall soon be passed, and with it all our weeping. Then, with thine, our songs shall greet the morning of a day that knows neither cloud nor close; for there is no night there.
>
> Hard worker in the field! thy toil is ended. Straight has been the furrow thou hast ploughed. No looking back has marred thy course. Harvests have followed thy patient sowing, and Heaven is already rich with thine ingathered sheaves, and shall be still enriched through years yet lying in eternity.
>
> Champion of God! thy battle long and nobly fought is over; the sword which clave to thy hand has dropped at last; a palm branch takes its place. No longer does the helmet press thy brow, oft weary with its surging thoughts of battle, a victor's wreath from the great Commander's hand has already proved thy full reward.
>
> Here for a little while shall rest thy precious dust, Then shall thy Well-Beloved come; and at His voice thou shalt spring from thy couch of earth, fashioned like unto His body, unto glory. Then spirit, soul and body shall magnify thy Lord's redemption. Until then, beloved sleep. We praise God for thee, and by the blood of the everlasting covenant, hope and expect to praise God with thee. Amen. [63]

As Brown spoke, and as a dove hovered over the scene, it was as if the Holy Spirit smiled and said Charles was all right; he was resting in Jesus. The mourners sang, "There Is a Fountain Filled with Blood." Dr. A. T. Pierson of America led in prayer and the Bishop of Rochester, Dr. Randall Davidson, pronounced the benediction. Actually, the memorial services were quite simple, although thousands attended. Spurgeon himself would have well approved. It was a fitting closure for one whose whole life had been simple and plain and had been a quest to reach simple and plain people.

One of the paradoxes of this elaborate funeral centers in Spurgeon's words about funerals. He said:

> I would sooner be eaten by crows than have pride and pomp feeding on my little savings, which are meant for my bereaved wife and children. . . . It seems to me to be mighty fine nonsense, more for the pride of the living than the honor of the dead, more for the profit of the undertaker than anyone else.

But Spurgeon need not have worried. The Metropolitan Tabernacle bore all the expenses. Actually, Charles left only £20,000. He had given away for Christian causes practically all his money, but what Charles did leave was sufficient for Susannah.

An era had passed, an epoch was history. The great preacher was laid to his final rest. The "martyr" for truth had gone. Many saw him as that. A thousand or more churches, societies, colleges, corporations, school boards and other institutions sent deputations to the services or letters of condolence. Even the United States Congress was officially represented. On February 14, almost 10,000 children of the Metropolitan Tabernacle Sunday School and the Stockwell Orphanage and Mrs. Sharman's Homes assembled for a memorial service.

The deacons erected a simple monument over the vault that contained the remains of the great preacher. On the front of the monument a medallion of the preacher and a representative of the open Bible on a cushion was placed with a short inscription:

HERE LIES THE BODY

OF

CHARLES HADDON SPURGEON

WAITING FOR THE APPEARING OF HIS

LORD AND SAVIOUR

JESUS CHRIST. [64]

On the right side of the tomb were the two verses from C. H. Spurgeon's favorite hymn,

> E'er since by faith I saw the stream
> Thy flowing wounds supply,
> Redeeming love has been my theme,
> And shall be till I die;
>
> Then in a nobler, sweeter song,
> I'll sing Thy power to save,
> When this poor lisping, stammering tongue
> Lies silent in the grave. [65]

The tomb remains the same to the present hour. Although bombs fell on the Norwood Cemetery during the second World War and destroyed many of the graves of the deacons and church leaders who either proceeded or later followed Spurgeon in death, there was scarcely a scratch on Spurgeon's tomb. It seemed almost a token to the continuing witness of the pulpit giant.

God's pilgrim had reached God's Celestial City, and what a reception he must have had; for "they that be wise shall shine as the brightness of the firmament; and they that turn many to righteousness as the stars for ever and ever" (Daniel 12:3). So we say:

Farewell, O mighty 'Prince of God,'
   Defender of the faith once given;
By the 'old paths' the martyrs trod,
   Thou, too, hast gained the courts of heaven;
      Fought the good fight, the victory won,
      Crowned with the warrior's crown—Well done!

How the *London Illustrated News* of February 13, 1892, saw a portion of the crowd of 100,000 who filed past Spurgeon's casket in the Tabernacle as it lay there in state over three days.   —*courtesy of Dr. Craig Skinner*

Epilogue

SPURGEON'S CONTINUING INFLUENCE

Twelve thousand persons crowd the entrance to Upper Norwood Cemetery on February 11, 1892, to watch Spurgeon's funeral cortege enter. Many more thousands had lined the route, and shops and businesses closed while 800 traffic police controlled the procession.

—*courtesy of Dr. Craig Skinner*

Art thou for something rare and profitable?

—*John Bunyan*

Introduction

The Tabernacle Church's "In Memoriam" Resolution

Annual Church Meeting
held on Tuesday March 4th 1892
Pastor J. A. Spurgeon presiding

In Memoriam

That, with unutterable grief, we record the sad fact that our much-beloved Senior pastor, CHARLES HADDON SPURGEON, departed this life for the higher home, January 31st, at Mentone. He was a good man, full of faith and of the Holy Ghost; he feared God only; gave much alms, and prayed continually; he was greatly afflicted, but bore the divine will, as he did it also, with conspicuous grace, and to the glory of God.

He was buried by us, amidst tokens of national sorrow and universal esteem, at Norwood Cemetery, on February 11th, 1892. Devout men of all sections of the Church of Christ shared our mourning, and accompanied us to the grave. We put his sacred remains to rest in the sure and certain hope of a glorious resurrection to everlasting life.

We feel that the decease of our dear Pastor has deprived us of a father in Israel, the like of whom has never been given to any people. For the long period of thirty-eight years, we have been favoured by the Lord, through him, with such manifestations of the Spirit's presence and power, that we have been linked on to apostolic times in fulness of blessing attending the preaching of the Word, and in the richness of blessing attending the preaching of the Word, and in the richness of increase rewarding His servant's toil. As the result of his sowing of the good seed of the kingdom in our midst, no less than 14,691 souls have been added to our communion-roll during his pastorate; but these are only as the first-fruits of the far larger harvest which has reached, for the glory of God, to the ends of the earth.

With bleeding hearts, we thus record the loss we have sustained, as we feel we shall hear his melodious voice no more in the ministry of the truth; but we bless God that our dearly-loved one was given to us, and honoured amongst us so long. Endowed with talents of the highest order, alike in preaching and guiding, and enriched with an irresistible charm of character, he was a true leader for godly men in every good word and work. Instant in season and out of season, he counted not his life dear unto him in the service of the Church of Christ. He was to us a pattern to imitate, as well as a guide to follow. We cherish his memory beyond all that words can express.

Full of honours rather than of years, he has passed from us. Having faithfully served his day and generation by the will of God, he has fallen on sleep; and we hereby testify our undying love for him for his own sake, but more for that truth's sake which he so fully, so lovingly, and so eloquently preached throughout his whole career and life with us. We hereby pledge ourselves to the maintenance and defence of the same gospel and doctrines, and to the carrying on of his varied works for Christ, until our time shall come to join him in the rest and reward of heaven.[1]

When Spurgeon first came to London, a harsh critic, it will be remembered, said he would "go up like a rocket and come down ere long like a stick." He did go up, but more like a meteor producing a great light in the sky. And he did not come down like a stick. More correctly, he stayed in orbit and shone continually like a bright star. As one expressed it, "The meteor became for the time a fixed star."[2] When he passed over the river, the whole world felt the loss. The tremendous crowds, praise, and eulogies surrounding his funeral make all these words patent.

There had been talk of a burial for Spurgeon in Westminster Abbey, along with Britain's great. It would have been appropriate; yet, a few days before the end at Mentone, Spurgeon himself had said, "Remember—a plain slab, with CHS upon it: nothing more."[3] But that really could never be; a little more elaborate memorial was called for.

Of course, Spurgeon's departure left a vacancy in the lives of many. He was deeply missed by the Metropolitan Tabernacle. In his last years he became known as the *Senior* Pastor. At his death, the church passed the following resolution concerning their "Senior" Pastor:

Statement of Deacons and Elders read to the Church at
the Metropolitan Tabernacle Lord's Day Evening Feb. 7, 1892.

To the members of the church assembled at the first communion service after the decease of our beloved and revered pastor Charles Haddon Spurgeon held Lord's Day Evening Feb. 7, 1892

Under the great calamity which has fallen upon the Church, the Deacons and Elders have endeavored to give effect to the wise counsel, and to carry out the wishes of our late beloved pastor in every particular and they take the earliest opportunity of thanking their fellow members for their confidence and support and for their hearty co-operation by which under the blessing of God the unity and usefulness of the church have been maintained.

By the removal of the Senior Pastor upon whom the great Head of the Church bestowed such abundant honour, we have been called to suffer a loss and a grief impossible to express. In order that the trial may be sanctified to us as a church and that we may glorify our covenant God in His visitation we must bow in humble submission to the ruling of the Divine Will and prayerfully wait for the further leadings of the Holy Spirit.[4]

Especially did Susannah miss her "Tirshatha." Yet, the God of all comfort touched her and gave her "the peace which passeth all understanding" (Philippians 4:7). In a letter to Charles' father (March 11, 1892) she wrote, "This is a desolate house without the sunshine of his sweet presence, yet I can bear my loneliness when I think of *his* joy—my tears cease to flow when I remember that God has wiped away all his!" The world mourned, but he has not been forgotten, even one hundred years later. Upon the death of Spurgeon a host of biographies and writings emerged. They are still read—and being written.

Being loved in his own day, Charles Haddon Spurgeon is loved and appreciated to the present moment. He left footprints in the sands of history that shall not soon be erased, if ever. This is the considered opinion of many able scholars and historians. As *The Episcopal Recorder* (March 17, 1892) correctly said: "Charles Spurgeon's ministry on earth had ended, but its results continue. The streams of influence he set in motion move onward in their ceaseless flow. While time shall last, the echo of his voice will be heard."

Spurgeon will be remembered in many ways, but what stands out with singular significance is his virtually unparalleled preaching. The 19th century academician, principal Tullock, wrote:

> We have just been to hear Spurgeon, and have been both so much impressed that I wish to give you my impressions while they are fresh. . . . The sermon is about the most real thing I have come in contact with for a long time. Guthrie is as sounding brass and a tinkling cymbal to it; . . . In fact, the whole was a wonderful display of mental vigour and Christian sense, and gave me a good idea of what good such a man may do.[5]

Another well-known 19th century Roman Catholic writer who wrote under the previously cited name of "Sacerdos Hibernicus," declared:

> I willingly admit that Mr. Spurgeon in his day kept many a man morally good—kept him from substantial sin and therefore morally good. Again I willingly admit that men who entered the 'Tabernacle' to 'scoff' left it 'not scoffers,' left it in the belief of some moral laws, left it not the worse because of Mr. Spurgeon's teaching. This certainly was a gain. Better have a belief in some moral laws than believe all moral laws to be shams.[6]

Joseph Parker, famous London preacher, wrote:

> The only pulpit-name of the nineteenth century that will be remembered is no
> longer the name of a living man. Mr. Spurgeon was absolutely destitute of
> intellectual benevolence. . . . But who could compare with him in moral
> sympathy? In this view he was in very deed two men. The theologian and the
> philanthropist lived at opposite sides of the universe. Those who were damned
> by the theologian were saved by the philanthropist. Mr. Spurgeon's . . . (em-
> phasis) was emphatically religious or spiritual preaching. He had but one
> sermon, yet it was always new. . . . No good could come of my reasoning with
> him, because it was impossible for him to change. I had no apology to make.
> The greatest honour conferred upon my pulpit was Mr. Beecher's occupancy
> of it. So we parted; yet I trust to meet where we shall see all things in a clearer
> light. Mr. Spurgeon's career has proved that evangelical teaching can draw
> around itself the greatest congregation in the world, and hold it for a life-
> time. . . . The great voice has ceased. It was the mightiest voice I ever heard—
> a voice that could give orders in a tempest, and find its way across a torrent as
> through a silent aisle. Meanwhile, the stress is greater upon those who remain.
> Each must further tax his strength so as to lessen the loss which has come upon
> the whole Church. [7]

Principal Charles Edwards, of Bala Theological College, spoke these
words: "Spurgeon was the Gera liddon, the Jeremiah of our age. . . . He is
not rhetorical. If anything, he is sometimes too familiar. He does not pitch
his voice at all, anymore than a person pitches his voice in his own parlor.
He knows he is speaking to some thousands. But, without the slightest
apparent effort, he speaks so that the man that sits furthest from him can
hear, and not more than hear, every syllable. . . . He was so perfectly natural!
. . . He consecrated every other gift to the work of winning men to Christ." [8]

Archdeacon Sinclair of St. Paul's Cathedral said:

> We cannot hear untouched that our country has lost its greatest living preacher.
> I use the words deliberately, because I do not believe that there are any of us
> who remain who for thirty years, every Sunday during the twelvemonth, could
> gather together, morning and evening, more than six thousand earnest, patient
> hearers, eager to receive from one untiring tongue the Word of Life. Analyse
> the gifts of that powerful evangelist as accurately as you can; measure, as
> closely as may be possible, the secret of his influence; but I do not believe that
> you will find any other teacher whose printed sermons would be read week
> after week, year after year, by tens and hundreds of thousands, not only all
> over England, Scotland, and Wales, but in the backwoods of Canada, on the
> prairies of America, in the remotest settlements of Australia and New Zealand,
> wherever an English newspaper can reach, or the English tongue is spoken.
> The thing is absolutely unique. It has no parallel. . . . What was it that gave this
> plain, uncultured preacher a religious influence so unparalleled in our day, and

made his name a household word all over the wide world? No doubt he had rare gifts. He was courageous, resolute, and lively in these times of the faint heart, irresolution, and dulness. He had that genuine eloquence which is all the more effective because of its directness and simplicity. He had a matchless voice, powerful, and vibrating with every quality of earnestness and variety. He had abundant humour, tender pathos, and never failed to be interesting. He was utterly untrammelled by the questionings of criticism. But it was, above all, the splendid completeness, the unswerving strength, the exuberant vitality of his faith in God's revelation to man through His Son Jesus Christ, combined with the width and warmth of his zealous love for souls, that gave him that unbounded power which he exercised so loyally for Christian belief among the middle classes, who are the very backbone of England, and throughout the English-speaking race.[9]

The eulogies of Spurgeon's preaching are almost endless. That preaching legacy can never be forgotten; it may never be surpassed. He will stand, no doubt, for many years to come as the epitome of pulpit mastery. In an age when so often preaching seems weak—many writers say that the age of great preaching is past—Spurgeon stands as the model of what can be accomplished in the pulpit, even in an age of mass media.

What more could be said about Spurgeon's writings? True, he never produced a great theological tome or lingering poetry. His writings were far from "classical." Yet, every preacher, and many people in the pew, know about Spurgeon, and read him. It does seem unbelievable that a simple Baptist preacher who has been gone from the scene for a century, who never professed to be a professional writer, certainly not a Shakespeare or a great novelist or poet, could still be read so widely and avidly. But such is the continuing ministry of Spurgeon the author. His over 150 books and his millions of sermons are phenomenal. Few preachers have not at least read something of Spurgeon and innumerable are the lay people whose lives have been blessed from his writings. As he was a preacher to the masses, so was he a writer to the masses. What more needs to be said!

Then there is the continuing influence of Spurgeon's institutional and social ministry. The Stockwell Orphanage still ministers to homeless children. Thousands have come through that institution to live productive lives, many who may well have seen their lives devastated by the slums of London. Multitudes rise up to bless the man who loved them, saw their plight, and stepped in to meet their needs. Loving care for needy people was so central to the Spurgeon ministry that he is an inspiration to the present hour, much in the train of the great George Müller of Bristol. He was a man of faith, he raised up institutions of faith, and instilled faith in millions.

Then there is the Pastors' College, now, and rightly so, called Spurgeon's College; it was his college, his "firstborn and best beloved." Let it be repeated again, thousands have been touched and educated for the ministry through that superb institution. The Kingdom of God itself has been furthered in a significant and profound way. Anyone whom God has called to preach is welcomed through its doors to this day, regardless of ability to pay. The work of faith goes on. Never were fees charged and everyone's needs were met if they had been genuinely set apart by God and thus wanted a theological education to serve Christ more effectively. Spurgeon's College is now located in South Norwood and is as strong today as it was in Spurgeon's own day. The academic level is considerably higher, but still the basic philosophy persists. Students are admitted with no requirements for educational background if they are genuinely called of God and have a future in the ministry.

The legacy of Spurgeon's evangelistic commitment carries on in the College. Students still go out to conduct evangelistic missions, and invariably come back with glowing reports of people won to faith in Christ. The basic evangelical theology that characterized Spurgeon prevails. Morning prayers and the spiritual commitment of the students and faculty alike reflect the spirituality of "the Gov'nor" himself. The atmosphere of the entire College speaks of its founder. So the legacy carries on. Only Heaven itself will be able to recount all of the benefits that accrued from that day when the first student, Mr. D. W. Medhurst, came to Spurgeon to be trained to serve Christ.

Then there is Spurgeon's stand for, and preaching of, pure biblical truth, as he understood it. Granted, Spurgeon had at times a rather strange theological mix. In certain areas, he was hard to be pinned down on any single issue that was not balanced off by another. For example, his strong Calvinism found its counterpart in his Arminian style appeal for people to come to faith in Christ. But in that he echoed the Puritans. One biographer put it correctly: "His supreme significance lies in this: that he was the chief agent in renewing the strength of Puritanism and in bringing it into sympathetic touch with this wonderful nineteenth century."[10] And he remained opened to all evangelicals. Even his insistence on believer's baptism did not move him to a position of alienating himself from other believers of different persuasion nor bar them from the Lord's Table. There was something in that dynamic mix, if not paradoxical approach, that made his theological stance most attractive.

Above all, on the central issues of the faith, Spurgeon stood unswerving. The question earlier raised, did Spurgeon "win" in the Down Grade Controversy, is still often repeated. But the answer must always be, it was not a question of whether or not he "won," the question is, did he stand? That he did! "Mr. Valiant-for-Truth" stood firm on the great verities of the Christian faith, putting his life and ministry in the balance, defending the fundamental doctrines of Christian truth. He would never compromise on the person and work of the Lord Jesus Christ. For Spurgeon, Jesus was totally divine and totally human. He stood firm on the substitutionary atonement of our Lord upon the cross. He would be willing to go to the grave himself rather than say Jesus did not come out of the grave in a bodily resurrection. For Spurgeon, as for Luther, "the just shall live by faith." Salvation comes by grace through faith, not human works, no matter how ardent or fervent or sacrificial they may be. Upon these bedrock truths of Christianity, Spurgeon put everything on the line. He should always be seen, therefore, as the symbol of a true defender of the faith. Though criticized by many for his stand, he moved in the train of the great Reformers, the Puritans whom he loved and identified with, the early Church fathers and martyrs (many of whom literally died for their faith), and back to the Apostles and the Lord Jesus Christ Himself. If anything noble, right and just can be said of Spurgeon, it was that he loved the truth and willingly stood for it at any cost. As one put it:

> Through all the years of his ministry when a burden had to be carried, he lifted; when money had to be given, he gave; when battles had to be fought, he fought; when errors had to be assailed, he assailed; and would have regarded any man with amazement who should have expressed surprise at his so doing. [11]

Rather strangely, Spurgeon's combination of conservative orthodox theology and fresh pulpit style remained more of a legacy in America than in England. But then, a prophet is not without honor except in his own country. Still, England will never be quite the same either because of Spurgeon. His contribution is not only to his contemporary age, but to the history of God's dealings among people around the world. Of course, there are those who disagree with such an assessment. For example, Kruppa has said, "It was Spurgeon's tragedy that he lived to witness traditional Christianity disrupted by the twin challenges of science and higher criticisms. He saw his task as one of resistance rather than reconciliation, and he devoted his last years in a fruitless crusade against modern thought. That decision has impaired his reputation with posterity, for the future belonged to his opponents." [12] Such a criticism is highly questionable. The truth of God's Word will *always* ultimately triumph, and the great defenders of the evangelical faith are invariably remembered while the opponents soon fade into the twilight dusk of history, forgotten.

Spurgeon once said, "I am content to live and die as a mere repeater of scriptural teaching; as a person who has thought out nothing and invented nothing." [13] But that is too modest. His stand did have a most significant influence on the future of the Church, especially theologically and pragmatically, not to mention other significant aspects of ministry. His stand for conservative orthodoxy inspires Christians to this day. As Craig Skinner points out:

> But the most surprising influence arising from Spurgeonic sources today, recently documented, was the effect of his ministry on A. C. Dixon and its relation to the birth of original fundamentalism in Britain. English fundamen-

talism broke forth many years before the American aberrations of the 1920's developed with their belligerence and narrow extremism. A. C. Dixon and G. Campbell Morgan, along with many other progenitors of the original emphasis, withdrew from the official fundamentalist movement when it became obvious that it departed from its original mainstream stance, moving into areas of dispensationalism, interpretative inerrancy, and vitriolic separatism.

Spurgeon's original 'evangelical' perspective was not of the 'fighting' fundamentalist order. If he were alive today, he would possibly ally himself with the mainstream evangelicalism which is more characteristic of most Baptists and seek to support whatever endeavors exalt Christ rather than those which tend to divide his body.[14]

Furthermore, it is most significant that Spurgeon first and foremost geared his ministry as an evangelist. As so often seen, his heart literally beat for the conversion of the lost. All of his sermons and social ministry ultimately pointed to that end. For the Metropolitan Tabernacle preacher, anything that did not result in the winning of the lost to Christ was unworthy of a Christian minister. And God honored that commitment. The literal hundreds of thousands, ultimately the millions, that directly or indirectly entered the Kingdom of God through the influence of Spurgeon's preaching, writing, social, and personal ministry is virtually impossible to calculate. The Bible says, "they that turn many to righteousness shall shine as the stars forever" (Daniel 12:13). This being true, Spurgeon will shine as a stellar star through all eternity. Perhaps this is his greatest legacy. As one generation of "born again" people precipitate another generation of believers, so the legacy carries on. There are people who enter the Kingdom of God today because of Spurgeon who lived over a hundred years ago. What greater tribute to the lasting ministry of a man than that! It is certainly true, Spurgeon missed perfection. He had his weaknesses, which this biography has attempted graciously but honestly to point out. At times he appeared arrogant. At other times he seemed so dogmatic he could not see other points of view. Moreover, when he made up his mind, he determined to have his way. He prided himself a bit inordinately in some areas of his life and ministry. Further, some say he surrounded himself with lesser personalities in his last days, although that is open to question. But then, he was a human being with his frailties and sins like anyone else. Still, he loved God with all of his heart, and as one said, "His very limitations added a charm to his merits."[15] If ever there were a man who sought the honor and will of his Savior, Charles Haddon Spurgeon did. Therefore, he not only made a mark in his own day, he has a unique place in history. He loved to talk about the chain reaction of spiritual history. His previously quoted statement bears to be repeated here: "You may take a step from Paul to Augustine, then from Augustine to Calvin, and then —well you may keep your foot up a good while before you find such another." In some sense, he probably saw himself in something of that line, and in a very real sense, he was. It will be recalled that Prime Minister Gladstone was the one who called him the "Last of the Puritans." But that cannot be true. That he was a Puritan, in step with the giants of the seventeenth century, there is no doubt. That he drew his theology from the Reformers, especially Calvin, is incontestable. That his spirituality found its roots in many of the medieval personalities as did the Puritans, to this all agree. That Paul became his hero in theology and in practice is quite obvious. Above all, that Jesus Christ was his Lord and Savior, whom he loved unreservedly, is beyond doubt. Therefore, he does fit in that historical Puritan train. But let us trust God that Spurgeon is not "the last," but the beginning of a more modern lineage of the great Puritan giants. He may not have been the theologian that some of the Puritans were. His theology was a "Theology for the road," but perhaps that theology is best, at least the "common people" heard him gladly.

Simply put, history rests on Spurgeon's side. After all, his critics are gone and forgotten, long will he be remembered and revered as one of God's choice gifts to the Church. When he left us, he left a void that in some senses of the word has never really been filled to the present hour. But yet, his legacy so lingers on that it is a void which is not empty, paradoxical as that may sound. In a word, Spurgeon lives on and fills his own void. When as a Pilgrim he completed his journey and entered the Celestial City, he left behind a road to travel upon which many trod, inspired by his journey. As Charles Spurgeon crossed the river to the other side, the trumpets must have sounded a glad welcome as multitudes whose lives he had touched were there to greet him, while others still follow on. Above all, when he fell at the foot of the throne and looked face to face in the eyes of the Savior whom he loved and served so faithfully, he surely heard the words, "Well done, thou good and faithful servant, enter into the joy of thy Lord." That's what being a pilgrim is all about.

THE REST OF THE STORY

Spurgeon was gone. The pulpit giant had been silenced. But the work must go on, and even in small matters as well as the larger issues, he left his imprint. For example, in the Metropolitan Tabernacle archives is found a letter from a Mr. W. Brookman, dated 1892, rebuking a Mr. Hibbot for posting a notice on the church bulletin board that a Reverend William Williams would preach as a pulpit supply on September 19, 1892. Brookman wrote concerning the moniker "Reverend":

> a title which was treated with contempt by our late dear Pastor . . . let those who wish for Romish titles go to the Church of Rome and not disgrace a Christian Church. Such titles are not of God, therefore, whatever is not of God is Sin. Why do you wish to bring sin into the House of God, there is plenty of it outside. [16]

You do not soon forget a man and ministry like that of Charles Haddon Spurgeon.

But the Metropolitan Tabernacle immediately faced a number of serious questions at Spurgeon's demise. After the days of grief and mourning had somewhat subsided, issues immediately surfaced: Who would follow in the footsteps of the great pulpiteer? Could anyone even be found who might approach the preaching ability and power of Spurgeon's pulpit oratory? Who could possibly supervise all the social ministries that Spurgeon had founded? Could anyone begin to inspire the students at the Pastors' College, carry on the great orphanage work, and captivate the imagination of London as Spurgeon had so ably done for thirty-seven years? Was there anyone of stature and name who could attract the crowds that Charles did? Is it possible that anyone could even hold together the 5,000 member congregation? In the English-speaking world, could anyone possibly walk in Spurgeon's steps? The deacons, elders, and entire congregation asked these questions and earnestly sought God for an answer.

Any church faces a series of questions, often problems, when it loses its pastor. The Metropolitan Tabernacle had grown into the largest evangelical congregation of worshipers in the Western world. It had become something of the Citadel of evangelical thought and evangelistic fervency. Thus it had a corresponding problem of some proportion. Would anyone even aspire to fill that pulpit and that ministry?

As the congregation began to face seriously these issues, and seek whom God would send their way, four different names, unofficial suggestions to be sure, almost immediately came to the fore. Naturally, Dr. James Archer Spurgeon, the late pastor's brother and co-pastor at the Tabernacle, received immediate consideration by several in the congregation. He had superintended all the business and administrative affairs of the various organizations, including the Orphanage, the Pastors' College, and many missions and the almshouses. His administrative gifts were evident to all. It would seem that he would be a natural heir to his brother's pulpit. Not only that, he had been very well trained as a minister. He had also served for several years as the pastor of the so-called Spurgeon's Tabernacle in Croydon. Although he preached in the Croydon church on Sundays, hence known as their pastor, he had given himself during the week to the Metropolitan Tabernacle. Probably no one knew the Tabernacle and its ministry better than James Archer. But would he be the right man? Everyone realized the fact that he did not nearly measure up in preaching skill to his brother Charles. In March of 1892, *The Daily Graphic* reported that James Archer Spurgeon had become the new pastor of the Metropolitan Tabernacle. *The Sunday Telegraph* (March 13, 1892) reported the same thing. Of course, it was not true. *The Christian Commonwealth* had it correct when on March 17, 1892 they wrote, "At the unanimous desire of the late C. H. Spurgeon's church officers, (they) agreed to continue (James A. Spurgeon in) the discharge of the leadership vacated by (Charles') removal." But that did not constitute a call to James Archer to be pastor. When asked who the next pastor would be, James simply replied, "That's very uncertain at present."

Then Spurgeon's twin sons received considerable attention. Charles, Jr. had been pastor for some years in Greenwich, and had carried on a very effective ministry there. He had received his training at the Pastors' College and had won the respect of all. He was a quite acceptable preacher, although no one would have called him outstanding. Yet, he seemed a most likely candidate at the outset.

Then, "son Tom" began to be talked about as a possibility by certain members of the congregation. He was not as well known as his twin brother Charles, or certainly as his Uncle James. Most of his ministry had been spent in the South Pacific, pastoring in far-off Auckland, New Zealand. Back in England, he had gained some reputation as an excellent preacher, but that is all. Very few knew him well. His brief visit to London in 1885 could hardly establish a reputation like Charles, Jr. or James Archer. Yet, he had many things to commend him to the pulpit of his famous father. He was a very able preacher and had done an outstanding work in New Zealand. He commanded much respect in Auckland and in Australia as well. The reports that constantly came back to the Metropolitan Tabernacle were very strong and affirming of his ability as a pastor, preacher, and administrator. He too, as his brother Charles, received his education at the Pastors' College. He held much of the same theological position and evangelistic fervency of his renowned father.

The fourth person who gained considerable favor was Dr. Arthur T. Pierson. It will be recalled that he was filling the pulpit at the Metropolitan Tabernacle when Spurgeon left for Mentone and subsequently went to his reward. He had two things against him, however. First, he was an American, although that bothered very few. But secondly, his denominational affiliation was with the Presbyterian Church. Still, he proved to the Tabernacle congregation that he was a very able preacher. Moreover, his popularity extended to interdenominational circles. Speaking at mission and spiritual life conferences was his forté. Being very popular in America, he had also endeared himself to the Metropolitan Tabernacle during his months of ministry there.

Pierson had a strong evangelistic message. His magnetic and logical delivery fitted well in the general ethos of the London evangelical scene. His biblical exposition and God's obvious blessings on his ministry endeared him to many at the Tabernacle. In his personal diary, Pierson wrote the following comments concerning his relationship to the Metropolitan Tabernacle:

> Three months of uninterrupted health and happiness. Everybody cordial, sympathetic, and responsive. Fifty souls gathered in December, and many more enquiring. Immense after-meetings in the Tabernacle. Prayer meetings of the profoundest interest. [17]

Pierson was having a very effective London ministry.

At the request of the officers of the church, Pierson consented to carry on with his ministry through June of 1892. He preached very effectively in the months that followed the death of the pastor. Pierson greatly admired Spurgeon, and being very sympathetic and pastoral with the congregation, ably led them through much of the grief process. At Spurgeon's funeral he brought a beautiful message. A portion of it is as follows:

> We have come together to bury our dead. . . . The rich and noble and the affluent might have made a pilgrimage to his tomb, but we thank God we are met to lay his sacred ashes in our own Norwood, where the common people who heard him gladly may wend their way to his place of burial. You have no occasion to build him a monument, for his monument is in the hearts of millions of people, more enduring than brass. You have no need to hire a gardener to keep his grave green, for the tears of widows and orphans will water the sod. You have no occasion to see that flowers are planted around his sepulchre, for there will be flowers blooming in all parts of the earth that will be brought by pilgrim bands in remembrance of untold blessings that came from his lips, that will be brought from all quarters of the earth to be set alongside his place of rest. My brother we shall never see another like unto thee! Those eyes now closed in death . . . have lost their light for ever. The voice that spoke in tones so convincing and persuading is hushed in death, and the hand whose grasp uplifted many a fallen one, and gave new strength and encouragement to many a stricken one, will never again take ours within its grasp. . . . We are glad that heaven is richer although we may be made poorer; and by this bier we pledge ourselves that we will undertake by God's grace to follow thy blessed footsteps even as thou didst follow those of thy blessed Master.[18]

Pierson had taken his theological training at Union Seminary in New York, in those days a quite evangelically oriented institution. He assumed a leadership role in the Student Volunteer Missions Movement and was closely associated with D. L. Moody. He had preached for Spurgeon in December of 1890 prior to his longer time of supplying the pulpit following Charles' death. Years earlier, Pierson had come to know and appreciate Spurgeon through the reading of the sermons in America. He first heard Spurgeon on August 19, 1866 on a visit to London. When Spurgeon became very ill in July of 1891, Pierson gathered people together at the Niagara Bible Conference in the United States to pray for his recovery. A warm fellowship had thus developed through the years between the two men, and between Pierson and the Metropolitan Tabernacle. Many thought he should be the man to succeed Spurgeon, regardless of his denominational affiliation. But, despite all of the positive indicators that he might be the logical one to follow in the great preacher's footsteps, Pierson publicly declared his ambivalence to such a move. He had even expressed some concern as to whether or not he should even supply for a protracted period of time. Still, it seemed to be the thing to do. The congregation warmly affirmed him.

As the questions continued to be raised by the congregation, it appears that James A. Spurgeon began to assume a very prominent position in the church. That may seem natural; he did serve as associate or co-pastor with his late brother. He had not won the respect over the many years as had Charles however. Nor did he seem to have the sensitivity to people that his brother so obviously possessed. He took a quite authoritarian stance in the Tabernacle affairs. As a result, some resentment began to well up concerning his leadership style. In a letter dated August 20, 1892, W. Stubbs, upset by the style of James, wrote:

> Many of us think that in some respects Mr. James Spurgeon has mistaken his calling, as he appears to be more at home in commercial pursuits than in the pulpit, and as a private member, in common with many fellow-members, we scarcely know him except that we hear his voice for a few minutes at the Monday evening prayer meeting, occasionally at the baptismal service, and on the first Sunday evening in the month for a few minutes only. It is a long time since we heard a sermon from him, and I think, in common with other members, that he cannot be pastor of two churches, and that 500 pounds per annum for a few hours during the week is altogether out of place.[19]

It must be granted that the general situation thrust James Spurgeon into a difficult position. As stated, he obviously could not fill the shoes of his brother Charles from the standpoint of preaching; nor could he seemingly gain the congregational loyalty that his brother had earned. In *The Echo* an editorial came out under the title, "A Ticklish Position." It presented an interesting insight into James' position. It reads:

> Few men of mediocre talents have ever been placed in a more difficult and delicate position than Dr. James Spurgeon. Had he not been the brother of our most popular preacher of the day he would never have risen above the ordinary ruck of Baptist ministers. He is a good solid man, but has not a spark of his late brother's genius. This fact was fully recognised when he became his late brother's assistant. Accident has left him temporary master of the situation. And as he thus became a sort of Nonconformist pluralist, he has been criticised with no little asperity. . . . Such high-handed proceedings cannot but aggravate ill-feeling. Were I a Piersonite I should wish Dr. James Spurgeon on the other side of the Atlantic.[20]

It seems that even after the death of Spurgeon, the media spotlight continued to focus upon the Metropolitan Tabernacle ministry. And though it could not shed its beam upon Spurgeon himself, many comments were made about who should follow him. In *The Baptist*, October 21, 1892, the following report was given:

... Impossible to aquit either Dr. James Spurgeon or Dr. Pierson of serious blame, and even of inconsistent trifling. . . . the future pastor of the Tabernacle may or may not have appeared in sight, on that point we have no right to anticipate the ultimate judgment of the church; although Dr. James Spurgeon has hardly exhibited all the sweet sympathy and meekness, which, as the brother of the departed saint, was his rightful heritage. [21]

The writer of the article even went so far as to compare James' arrogant administrative style to the Roman Catholic tradition rather than the congregational style of the Baptists. It began to look as if James Spurgeon would not make it as the pastor of the Metropolitan Tabernacle.

The question then became, would A. T. Pierson be acceptable? He was not a Baptist, although he did later say that he and his wife intended to be baptized by immersion, but in light of the problems at the Metropolitan Tabernacle he felt he should not do so at that time. But more serious than the baptism issue, a relatively large number did not particularly care for Pierson's expository style, although it must be granted he was a very faithful delineator of the Word of God. They argued that his sermons tended to be, as one correspondent put it, "learned discourses." The writer went on to say the messages "felt like Ezekiel's dry bones." [22] Consequently, A. T. Pierson's likelihood of following Spurgeon as pastor began to diminish, although many were very favorably disposed towards him, as also was James Archer Spurgeon. James began almost to carry on a crusade for Pierson.

Pierson left the Tabernacle, his pulpit supply commitment completed, and took up his scheduled conference work. When he left, he did not indicate with any certainty that he would ever return. Later, in September, he wrote the church officers informing them that he still held the deep conviction that he should baptize infants. He went on further to say that he believed a Baptist Church should have a Baptist minister. That letter would come up again. After Pierson's departure from the Tabernacle, "son Tom" took to the pulpit. Thomas Spurgeon had come to London from Auckland at the death of his father. The church minutes relative to this invitation read:

April 22, 1892
Special Church Meeting
Pastor J. A. Spurgeon presided. Prayer was offered by the Pastor; and after Hymn 451 was sung Prayer was offered by Brethren W. Olney and Everette.

The Pastor then made a statement in reference to our present condition as a Church and suggested that no step having reference to the supply of the Pulpit should be taken without consulting the Church.

The Pastor also stated that Dr. Pierson would according to a previous arrangement be returning to America for three months and that the officers had agreed subject to the Church's decision to invite our late beloved Pastor's Son Mr. Thomas Spurgeon to occupy the Pulpit during his absence.

The following resolution was then proposed by the Treasurer Mr. T. H. Olney and seconded by Elder J. Cox—that an invitation be sent to Dr. Pierson asking him to supply the Pulpit for 12 months—and that the letter now read by the Pastor be sent to him thanking him on behalf of the entire Church for the noble and Self Sacrificing labours he had bestowed on behalf of the Church.

The Resolution was carried with one dissention.

So for three months, "son Tom" took to the pulpit. Thomas' preaching style stood in stark contrast to Pierson's more labored, heavy approach. It soon became evident to all that he possessed a very fine preaching gift. His bright analogies from the Scriptures caused some to want him as pastor after only two Sundays. Again, the papers, particularly *The Baptist*, got into the discussion about Thomas. But that was understandable. The entire evangelical world, in some senses, looked to the Metropolitan Tabernacle as the epitome of what a great ministering church should be. Furthermore, the influence of the Metropolitan Tabernacle upon London had not diminished one iota since Spurgeon died. The Sunday Schools were filled, the congregations packed out the large auditorium every service, and all of the social ministries carried on. And it seemed as though Thomas fit into the scene very amicably. One said about Thomas Spurgeon, "He is unlike his lamented father in appearance, being short, and rather spare, but he preaches with true Spurgeonic fire and faith." [23] The Tabernacle continued to overflow and the ministry went on apace. Thomas seemed at home. But all was not well.

Division began to develop in the great church. Considerable agitation ensued as people started dividing over the possible candidates, especially Pierson and Thomas. By this time, James Archer was seemingly fading out of the scene as a possible successor of his brother Charles. Moreover, very few had allegiance to Thomas' twin brother, Charles, Jr. He just never seemed to captivate the minds of the Metropolitan Tabernacle congregation. It began to come down to a choice between Pierson or Thomas. The media invaded the scenario by drawing contrasts between the two men. One interesting article reads:

> Those who have heard the eloquence of the latter [Thomas] will need no words of mine to remind them of the spiritual stirring his discourses have caused; those who know of the noble work of this somewhat young life will not require me to emphasise that his zeal is second to that of nobody working in the Christian Church, and those who would make capital for their side of the argument out of the fact that he does not enjoy the most robust health will surely stand ashamed when they are confronted with the fact that on that account alone, which is dispensation of God Himself, they would debar him from the pleasure and the honour of serving his great Master in the highest capacity which is open to him, and would thrust into his father's place other less fitted to bear our deceased leader's mantle, because, however unworthily, they might stumble along with it for a longer period. [24]

The agitation deepened until finally by August of 1892, a genuine rift had developed in the congregation. In the meantime, the church had asked A. T. Pierson for another extended period of preaching. On October 7, 1892 James Spurgeon wrote a letter urging the Tabernacle to affirm the invitation to A. T. Pierson to come as pulpit supply. All these dynamics deepened the problem. The church officers, who had issued the invitation, did not wish to draw back on their invitation to Pierson, but sentiment grew that Thomas should be his father's successor. Then, the time for Thomas to return to his work in New Zealand was at hand. So the quandary continued and a decision had to be made. As the situation developed, one described it as a "terrible unsettled state." It was said that "among the rank and file discontent reigns supreme." A large segment of the congregation found themselves very much committed to the idea that Thomas Spurgeon should at least be invited for an extended period of pulpit supply. But what about the commitment to Pierson? Then a crisis surfaced. James Archer had suppressed the aforementioned letter of Pierson to the church concerning infant baptism, and that a Baptist should be the pastor. The congregation did not know about this correspondence, but it leaked out. Clearly, this caused more hard feelings. Apparently James Archer wanted A. T. Pierson to become the new pastor, or perhaps even he himself still had a strong eye on the pulpit. At that stage, James Archer threatened to resign his position in the church if they approached Thomas to be pastor. As can be imagined, this went over very negatively to the congregation. Actually, a special church meeting was called in October about this Pierson letter and other matters, but James Archer still refused to let them see the letter. The uproar was of such a nature that the church leaders gave the assurance that they would issue no future invitations, even for pulpit supply, until such a decision had been brought before the congregation for their vote. This was somewhat out of the ordinary for Baptist churches in Britain at that time. The church officers normally selected pulpit supplies. But it seemed the prudent thing to do and to some extent it brought down some of the high temperatures the Pierson-James Archer Spurgeon affair had raised.

At that stage, James Spurgeon informed the congregation that according to the deed of trust of the Metropolitan Tabernacle, no other pastor than a Baptist could be chosen for the office. Yet, his opposition to Thomas becoming their minister remained adamant. This obviously raises the question: did James Archer want to be pastor? Or, had he in mind that Pierson would become a committed Baptist and could fill the pastoral role? Did he try to eliminate others so that he would be the only logical choice left? No one can really know. At any rate, James Archer seemed almost vehemently opposed to Thomas filling his father's shoes. Later, A. T. Pierson, who was a genuine man of God, confessed that he had been somewhat insensitive to the situation and being a Presbyterian probably did not understand Baptist methodologies very well. This was a noble admission on the part of Pierson. *The Baptist,* in an editorial, brought the entire situation before the evangelical world in a very succinct fashion. It stated that the Metropolitan Tabernacle seemed about ready to go on the rocks for several reasons:

> . . . a weakening of the confidence hitherto existing between the acting commander and the passengers. Meanwhile, indications have also not been wanting of a condition very near akin to mutiny on the part of the officers. It was not because the principal navigator was ignorant of the ship's proper course, but rather by reason of his idea of conceiving the idea of experimenting in the neighborhood of reefs. . . . his resolve on so new and serious a departure has, it is idle to deny, precipitated a crisis which, but for the over-ruling hand of the Master Mariner of his Church, might prove disastrous beyond parallel. . . . To perform any act or utter any words which might reasonably bear the interpretation of hauling down the Baptist flag, obviously endangered the ship. . . . it is impossible to aquit either Dr. James Spurgeon or Dr. Pierson of serious blame, and even of inconsistent trifling. [25]

Dr. Craig Skinner, in his excellent research on these dynamics, brought the scenario to a fine summary with these words:

> On October 9 a meeting was called on petition from a group of church members. Their announcement quoted a letter from Dr. Pierson to Mr. Brookman, in which the correspondent said '. . . the officers of the Tabernacle know that they are free to act in any manner pertaining to the Tabernacle without reference to me.' In it Pierson also affirmed cooperation in a potential call to anyone they desired. [Letter from Pierson, August 30, 1892, included a call petitioning officers for the special church meeting. Copy of the leaflet containing these materials from New Zealand Baptist Historical archives, Auckland.] Even this failed to resolve matters. Much ground was apparently gained, however, by the Thomas party circulating a quotation from C. H. Spurgeon's sermon number 1,164 in which he stated:
>
> > It may not be my honour to be succeeded in this pulpit by one of my own sons, greatly as I would rejoice it, it might be so; but, at least, I hope they will be here in this church to serve their father's God, and be regarded with affection by you for the sake of him who spent his life in your midst. (Report in *The Baptist,* October 14, 1892.)
>
> This many regarded as near to an endorsement of an approach to Thomas as C. H. Spurgeon could make in retrospect. The Baptist commented on the special meeting as dealing with 'grave issues involved at a crisis.' It is reported the tension created by James Spurgeon's dissent from the officers' desire to invite Thomas for a further period of supply after Dr. Pierson had fulfilled the coming return engagement. Further discussion elicited the fact that the officers were also seriously divided over the resolution put to the meeting that all

matters be left in their hands for the time being. Mr. Higgs affirmed that he strongly objected to Dr. James Spurgeon placing his veto on the proposal to approach Thomas over the desire of the officers. A final decision sustained the responsibility of the officers in future arrangements, but secured agreement for congregational approval for them. This also included a warm letter to Thomas in which the words that the church 'hopes to see him again in the Tabernacle pulpit at the expiration of Dr. Pierson's term of service' were added with enthusiastic approval. [26]

Things now moved along quite rapidly. Thomas fulfilled his obligation of supply work at the Metropolitan Tabernacle on October 9, 1892. He preached a farewell sermon as some 7,000 people crowded into the Tabernacle. He gave them a resounding word of admonition to go forward and see the Metropolitan Tabernacle become even greater than it had been in the past. He concluded his message with these words:

> I came at your call, and, as I thought, and I still think, at the Master's call. I have tried to serve you under circumstances which, I confess, have been most trying, for I had hardly recovered from what was to me the shock of returning to stand here when sorrow of another sort possessed my heart. I seem to have been unwillingly in the midst of strife. Well, dear friends, I have tried to serve you, or perhaps I might say tried rather to serve my Master, and I am glad to know that many of the Lord's people have been helped by my poor words. I thought when I went away last that I might never come here again, for my dear father said to me, 'Good-bye, son Tom, but you must not come back for I could not say "good-bye" to you again for I shall never see you in the flesh,' and so it was. The hope of seeing Jesus makes our hearts one. In my heart the flag flies half-mast high, but it is still the flag of the Master whom we all serve. [27]

The sermon greatly moved the people. Women were actually weeping and sobbing aloud. Even some men were literally carried out of the service overcome by the tremendous emotional impact of the service.

On Friday, October 14, Thomas made his way to the Old Swan Pier near London Bridge and some 400 people on a special chartered river boat traveled with him to Gravesend. There he and his family boarded the Kaikoura steamship for the journey home to New Zealand. So many had accompanied him to the steamship that he had difficulty actually boarding. Before Thomas left, he made a special trip to see his Uncle James. James could not make the farewell party because he was "indisposed." Thomas showed a graciousness much like his father. So off to New Zealand he went.

Back at the Tabernacle, in the months that followed, James Spurgeon continued his adamant negative attitude towards Thomas. He had become so vehement in his protestations that the officers of the church were apprehensive that the split would widen even more. They seriously feared for the

Tabernacle fellowship. On January 2, 1893, Thomas Olney wrote to James stating that he deeply regretted the differences that had existed between them. Matters finally reached the point that a special church business meeting had to be called to deal with the matter. Most important decisions were reached at that time. The church met on March 29, 1893, and James Spurgeon presented his resignation. The church minutes concerning James Archer's resignation read:

> Pastor James A. Spurgeon stated that 'he had been associated with his brother as Co-Pastor for the past 25 years and now in accordance with the terms of the agreement made at the first his office ceases. He therefore now renders his resignation leaving it in the hands of the Church.' He then retired to the Vestry and Deacon T. H. Olney was called to preside. [28]

In May of that year James Spurgeon was elected on the council of the Baptist Union and as a committee member of the Baptist Missionary Society.

But by far the most significant event of the March 29th business meeting entered in the fact that the congregation voted to invite Thomas Spurgeon to accept the pulpit supply of the Metropolitan Tabernacle for a period of twelve months from July 30, "with a view to the pastorate." As someone expressed it, "The church emerged like a ship that had been through a hurricane, battered and torn, but still seaworthy." [29]

A majority of 1,600 voted for the invitation to Thomas Spurgeon, another 569 did not vote but were not in opposition to the invitation. They simply wanted to express a preference that the matter be left in the hands of the church officers. Consequently, the message was cabled to Thomas, and after much prayer he cabled back his acceptance.

When Thomas left Auckland, a very affectionate crowd gathered in large numbers at the wharf to bid him farewell. They wished him God's blessings in his service in London. He traveled east and crossed the Pacific without his wife and child. He really did not know what his future would be. At a brief stopover in Honolulu, when the people discovered who he was, they insisted he conduct a service in one of the local churches. He obliged and preached admirably. He arrived in San Francisco on June 9, 1893. He had made it to the United States, as his father had never done. He then traveled through Salt Lake City, Denver, and Omaha, on his way to Chicago where D. L. Moody joined him. A great evangelistic service was held. The Chicago World's Fair Gospel Campaign was in progress at that time and Thomas had the opportunity of preaching in that setting. He also preached for Moody at the First Congregational Church of Chicago, and at Moody's own Chicago Avenue Church on the evening of Sunday, June 18.

Thomas then traveled on through Boston, Plymouth, and Martha's Vineyard in New England and took ship to London. Much to the surprise of the Metropolitan Tabernacle Congregation, he appeared unexpectedly at the Tabernacle prayer meeting on Friday, July 28, 1893. The next Sunday he spoke to the Metropolitan Tabernacle. He preached on the call of Peter and Andrew. The people were delighted with his ministry. He took the same basic approach as his father. He adhered tenaciously to the doctrines of grace, but he gave strong Gospel invitations, thus keeping that balance and tension intact as did his famous father. It looked like a fine ministry was beginning to unfold for another Spurgeon.

The work did go on in a very positive fashion. By January of 1894, two hundred persons had been baptized into the fellowship of the Metropolitan Tabernacle. Thus the congregation felt that Thomas should receive a final call to the permanent pastorate of the Tabernacle. The previous March (1893) showed that the church still had 5,179 members, 19 preaching stations, 25 branch Sunday Schools, with 491 teachers and almost 8,000 attending. The work progressed well under Thomas.

The church was called into order on March 21, 1894. Deacon Olney presented five reasons why "son Tom" should be invited to become their permanent pastor. He outlined his reasons:

1. He preached Christ crucified.
2. His sermons appealed, as they were so well illustrated.
3. His ministry had the seal of God upon it.
4. He had worked harmoniously with Dr. James Spurgeon in a difficult situation.
5. The various works such as the College and the Orphanage were as prosperous under his leadership as was the church itself. [30]

The church voted. Would Thomas be called? Craig Skinner again summed up the situation well:

> The counting of the ballots of the almost 3,000 members who were present, occupied almost an hour. While the church trust deed provided that only a simple majority was sufficient for election of a pastor, the 2,127 who supported the motion represented almost 80 percent approval, as only 649 felt they could not approve the motion. Of the latter, many accepted the consensus with good grace, while others felt led to withdraw from the fellowship. The agreement that, 'Thomas Spurgeon, having supplied the pulpit, with a view to the pastorate, for eight months, be elected pastor,' (Fullerton, 1919, p. 172) was viewed by the press as settling the matter completely. The prestigious *British Weekly* commented that 'if the minority was considerable, the majority was nevertheless decisive.' (Fullerton, 1919, p. 172.) [31]

Thomas had the pulpit. In grateful response, at the next week's business meeting, he responded with the following acceptance letter:

> To the Members of the Baptized Church of Jesus Christ
>
> Worshiping at the Metropolitan Tabernacle
> BELOVED BROTHERS AND SISTERS

I was in due course informed of the result of your meeting of last Wednesday week. I find that you did then confer on me, by a decided majority, the highest honour that could be afforded to a servant of Christ Jesus. You have, with no uncertain sound, proclaimed your desire that I shall become your permanent pastor. I can scarcely believe that this is really so—that I of all men am requested to follow such men as Keach, and Gill, and Rippon, and Angus, and (more wondrous still!) to succeed my own beloved and illustrious Father. Yet, with these figures, and your Chairman's letter before me, I must believe what seems incredible.

Since hearing of your choice, I have been wondering if your voice is indeed the voice of God, and I have seriously considered the whole question in all its bearings.

When I regard, gratefully, and with surprise, the steps which have led to this resolve of yours, and the way by which I myself have been conducted; when I find that I can conscientiously say that I have never sought the post, and that I do not now even personally desire it; when I think of the strength vouchsafed to me for the not altogether easy task of the past eight months, and of the measure of blessing graciously granted; above all, when I remember the right hand of the most High, and His exceeding great and precious promises, I feel constrained to say, 'I must not shrink from this evident duty, nor fail to enter this open door.'

In humble and absolute dependence upon Divine aid, and counting on the earnest and affectionate co-operation of officers, and members, and hoping for the prayers of not these only, but of Christians the world over, I do accept the position to which you have invited me, with its glorious privileges, its stupendous tasks, and its solemn responsibilities. It will be my joy to serve you for Christ's sake just so long as the Lord evidently would have me do so. . . .

My manner of life from my youth know all the members. My articles of faith and methods of work you are all aware of. The ever-new old Gospel is all I have to preach, and I propose to carry on the work in the same spirit which has obtained hitherto, and as far as possible, on the same lines, and with the helpers. O that we might have somewhat of the same success! [32]

At the dramatic meeting of Thomas Spurgeon's acceptance of the pastorate of the Metropolitan Tabernacle, he presented a letter that he had carried with him for almost nine years. It was from his father. Thomas had carried the letter in the inner pocket of his wallet all those years, but had never revealed it. The congregation sat in rapt attention. They did not know that C. H. Spurgeon, their beloved late pastor, had written to his son in such a way that Thomas would carry the letter nine years. What did it say? Thomas wanted the people to know that he had possessed the letter all those years, and that included all the time he was with them as a supply. But he would not reveal it until the right moment, should that moment ever come. Now that dramatic moment had arrived, so he read from his beloved father. The passage that simply gripped the heart of every church member read: "Get very strong, and when I am older, and feebler, be ready to take my place!"[33]

As can be imagined, the congregation was virtually stunned. Charles had chosen his "son Tom" to be his successor. Slowly the words settled in on them. Suddenly an outburst of absolute cheering erupted. Applause arose until it appeared that it would never stop. Then the new pastor stood up and said:

> You see, you called me, and from the Glory came the voice of my father's God, and there is the voice of my earthly father. What wonder that I have said I must enter in this open door! Let us sing 'Praise God, from Whom All Blessings Flow'! [34]

The Doxology was sung and many a tear shed. The congregation then gave a vote of thanks to Thomas Olney for his marvelous Christian Spirit in holding the fellowship together during the very difficult time and the meeting was then dismissed. The Metropolitan Tabernacle had a new pastor—and a Spurgeon at that.

After the call of Thomas, some of the members left the church. Other factors began to conspire to make the ministry not easy for the new pastor. The Victorian era was rapidly coming to an end and a new secular mind-set increasingly engulfed England. Still, the work prospered. One reporter described a worship service at the Tabernacle two years into the ministry of Thomas saying it was quite as equal to that which he had experienced under C. H. Spurgeon's ministry.

The third week of April, 1898, the year of James A. Spurgeon's death, became a day of tragedy for the entire Metropolitan Tabernacle. The annual Conference was in progress at the Pastors' College when suddenly someone burst in to tell them that the Tabernacle was engulfed in flames. The fire devastated the building. The major portion of the roof collapsed as Thomas stood and watched, his body literally shaking with sobs. It looked as if the beautiful sanctuary of worship was gone. Although there had been church conferences going on in the building at the time of the outbreak of the blaze, no panic ensued and everyone escaped without injury. But the building itself lay in ashes. Thomas seemed a broken man. But he soon rose to the occasion and the building was completely rebuilt. Fortunately, the facade and vestibule were able to be kept intact, so from the frontage view, it appeared the same as it did in C. H. Spurgeon's time. The new auditorium, however, was reduced in size, seating about 4,000 people as over against the original 5,000 to 6,000 capacity. But the ministry of Thomas went on unabated until his resignation. Thomas had the privilege of ministering through the Welsh Revival (1904-1906) and its general influence on Britain, as his father had done in the great Prayer Revival of 1860. God blessed the work in a marvelous way. In 1905, during Thomas' ministry, at the birth of the Baptist World Alliance in London, a large bronze statue of C. H. Spurgeon was unveiled.

For years it stood in the vestibule of the Baptist Church House. When the Baptist Union headquarters were moved from London to Didcot, the statue was placed at Spurgeon's College. Thomas resigned in 1911 and died in 1917. Rather strangely, he was succeeded by A. C. Dixon, who had been pastor of the Hanson Place Baptist Church in Brooklyn, New York. Dixon did not impress the Tabernacle congregation when he preached there years earlier while C. H. Spurgeon was still alive. Regardless, the church called him. Charles Spurgeon, Jr. died in 1926. Spurgeon's sermons, as mentioned previously, continued to be published weekly until 1917 when the shortage of metal and paper in World War I brought the publishing of his "Penny Pulpit" to a close. The last sermon was number 3,555.

In 1930, just before World War II broke out, Spurgeon's College applied for affiliation with the Baptist Union. Later the Metropolitan Tabernacle rejoined the Union. During World War II, the Metropolitan Tabernacle building was bombed heavily, but rebuilt again in 1959. Once more, the facade was kept intact and so its frontage view still appears as it did in Charles Haddon Spurgeon's day, as pointed out previously. But again the auditorium was reduced so that it seated approximately 1,600 in its rebuilding in 1959. Then, again, it was considerably shortened in 1980. It now seats some 600–700 worshipers. The congregation is rather small.

The Metropolitan Tabernacle remained in the Baptist Union for some years, but then left again. Two of the great institutions that Spurgeon commenced still carry on. The Stockwell Orphanage remains strong, although relocated outside London. Perhaps the most lasting tribute to the ministry of the great preacher is Spurgeon's Theological College. This author had the privilege to be a professor of evangelism there for a number of years and can give testimony that the spirit of Spurgeon's evangelism, evangelical commitment to biblical preaching, a solid orthodox theology rooted and grounded in the Word of God, and a commitment to the worldwide cause of Christ carries on. The College is the largest Baptist theological school in Europe.

So an epic has ended, but yet, it has not. Running the risk of sounding redundant, it must be said that a ministry like that of Charles Haddon Spurgeon never dies. One hundred years after Spurgeon's birth, in a Centenary Sermon given in the Royal Albert Hall, London on April 25, 1934, the American pulpiteer, George W. Truett, said, "From my earliest recollections, my sense of gratitude to Charles Haddon Spurgeon has been a living thing in my life." Down through the ages, men of the calibre of Spurgeon live on. The influence of the "Last of the Puritans," shall remain. Another pilgrim had progressed marvelously. As he himself said, "What scenery enchants the Christian pilgrim? The towering mountains of predestination, the great sea of providence, the rocks of sheer promise, the green fields of revelation, the river that makes glad the city of God—all these compose the scenery that surrounds the Christian, and at every step fresh sublimities meet his view."

Perhaps he would like to be remembered best by what Nicoll said of him, "Mr. Spurgeon always made salvation a wonderful, a supernatural thing—won through battle and agony and garments rattled in blood. That the blood of God should be one of the ordinary forces of the universe was to him a thing incredible."[35] So the pilgrimage ended but the sublimities of it all linger on.

Blessed are the dead who die in the Lord from now on.

"Yes," says the Spirit, "they will rest from their labors, for their deeds will follow them." Revelation 14:13b (NIV)

Crowds throng the rebuilt Tabernacle restored by Pastor Thomas Spurgeon (son of C. H. Spurgeon) in 1900.

—courtesy of Dr. Craig Skinner

Appendix A

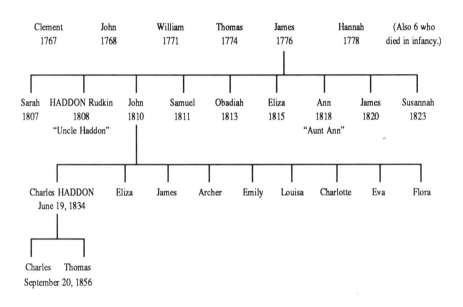

| Clement | John | William | Thomas | James | | Hannah | (Also 6 who |
| 1767 | 1768 | 1771 | 1774 | 1776 | | 1778 | died in infancy.) |

Sarah	HADDON Rudkin	John	Samuel	Obadiah	Eliza	Ann	James	Susannah
1807	1808	1810	1811	1813	1815	1818	1820	1823
	"Uncle Haddon"					"Aunt Ann"		

| Charles HADDON | Eliza | James | Archer | Emily | Louisa | Charlotte | Eva | Flora |
| June 19, 1834 | | | | | | | | |

| Charles | Thomas |
| September 20, 1856 | |

Appendix B

BAPTISMAL REGENERATION

A Sermon
Delivered on Sunday Morning, June 5th, 1864 by the
REV. C. H. SPURGEON
At the Metropolitan Tabernacle, Newington.

"And he said unto them, Go ye into all the world, and preach the gospel to every creature. He that believeth and is baptized shall be saved; but he that believeth not shall be damned."—Mark xvi. 15,16.

In the preceding verse our Lord Jesus Christ gives us some little insight into the natural character of the apostles whom he selected to be the first ministers of the Word. They were evidently men of like passions with us, and needed to be rebuked even as we do. On the occasion when our Lord sent forth the eleven to preach the

787

gospel to every creature, he "appeared unto them as they sat at meat, and upbraided them with their unbelief and hardness of heart, because they believed not them which had seen him after he was risen;" from which we may surely gather that to preach the Word, the Lord was pleased to choose imperfect men; men, too, who of themselves were very weak in the grace of faith in which it was most important that they should excel. Faith is the conquering grace, and is of all things the main requisite in the preacher of the Word; and yet the honoured men who were chosen to be the leaders of the divine crusade needed a rebuke concerning their unbelief. Why was this? Why, my brethren, because the Lord has ordained evermore that we should have this treasure in *earthen* vessels, that the excellency of the power may be of God and not of us. If you should find a perfect minister, then might the praise and honour of his usefulness accrue to man; but God is frequently pleased to select for eminent usefulness men evidently honest and sincere, but who have some manifest infirmity by which all the glory is cast off from them and laid upon Himself, and upon Himself alone. Let it never be supposed that we who are God's ministers either excuse our faults or pretend to perfection. We labour to walk in holiness, but we cannot claim to be all that we wish to be. We do not base the claims of God's truth upon the spotlessness of our characters, but upon the fact that it comes from him. You have believed in spite of our infirmities, and not because of our virtues; if, indeed, you had believed our word because of our supposed perfection, your faith would stand in the excellency of man and not in the power of God. We come unto you often with much trembling, sorrow over our follies and weaknesses, but we deliver to you God's Word as God's Word, and we beseech you to receive it not as coming from us poor, sinful mortals, but as proceeding from the Eternal and Thrice Holy God; and if you so receive it, and by its own vital force are moved and stirred up towards God and his ways, then is the work of the Word sure work, which it could not and would not be if it rested in any way upon man.

Our Lord having thus given us an insight into the character of the persons whom he has chosen to proclaim his truth, then goes on to deliver to the chosen champions their commission for the Holy War. I pray you mark the words with solemn care. He sums up in a few words the whole of their work, and at the same time foretells the result of it, telling them that some would doubtless believe and so be saved, and some on the other hand would not believe and would most certainly, therefore, be damned, that is, condemned for ever to the penalties of God's wrath. The lines containing the commission of our ascended Lord are certainly of the utmost importance, and demand devout attention and implicit obedience, not only from all who aspire to the work of the ministry, but also from all who hear the message of mercy. A clear understanding of these words is absolutely necessary to our success in our Master's work, for if we do not understand the commission it is not at all likely that we shall discharge it aright. To alter these words were more than impertinence, it would involve the crime of treason against the authority of Christ and the best interests of the souls of men. O for grace to be very jealous here.

Wherever the apostles went they met with obstacles to the preaching of the gospel, and the more open and effectual was the door of utterance the more numerous were the adversaries. These brave men so wielded the sword of the Spirit as to put to flight all their foes; and this they did not by craft and guile, but by making a direct cut at the error which impeded them. Never did they dream for a moment of adapting the gospel to the unhallowed tastes or prejudices of the people, but at once directly and boldly they brought down with both their hands the mighty sword of the Spirit upon the crown of the opposing error. This morning, in the name of the Lord of Hosts, my Helper and Defence, I shall attempt to do the same; and if I should provoke some hostility—if I should through speaking what I believe to be the truth lose the friendship of some and stir up the enmity of more, I cannot help it. The burden of the Lord is upon me, and I must deliver my soul. I have been loath enough to undertake the work, but I am forced to it by an awful and overwhelming sense of solemn duty. As I am soon to appear before my Master's bar, I will this day, if ever in my life, bear by testimony for truth, and run all risks. I am content to be cast out as evil if it must be so, but I cannot, I dare not, hold my peace. The Lord knoweth I have nothing in my heart but the purest love to the souls of those whom I feel imperatively called to rebuke sternly in the Lord's name. Among my hearers and readers, a considerable number will censure if not condemn me, but I cannot help it. If I forfeit your love for truth's sake I am grieved for you, but I cannot, I dare not, do otherwise. It is as much as my soul is worth to hold my peace any longer, and whether you approve or not I must speak out. Did I ever court your approbation? It is sweet to everyone to be applauded; but if for the sake of the comforts of respectability and the smiles of men any Christian minister shall keep back a part of his testimony, his Master at the last shall require it at his hands. This day, standing in the immediate presence of God, I shall speak honestly what I feel, as the Holy Spirit shall enable me; and I shall leave the matter with you to judge concerning it, as you will answer for that judgment at the last great day.

I find that the great error which we have to contend with throughout England (and it is growing more and more), is one in direct opposition to my text, well known to you as the doctrine of baptismal regeneration. We will confront this dogma with the assertion, that BAPTISM WITHOUT FAITH SAVES NO ONE. The text says, "He *that believeth* and is baptized shall be saved;" but whether a man be baptized or no, it asserts that "*he that believeth not* shall be damned:" so that baptism does not save the unbeliever, nay, it does not in any degree exempt him from the common doom of all the ungodly. He may have baptism, or he may not have baptism, but if he believeth not, he shall be in any case most surely damned. Let him be baptized by immersion or sprinkling, in his infancy, or in his adult age, if he be not led to put his trust in Jesus Christ—if he remaineth an unbeliever, then this terrible doom is pronounced upon him—"He that believeth not shall be damned." I am not aware that any Protestant Church in England teaches the doctrine of baptismal regeneration except one, and that happens to be the corporation which with none too much humility calls itself *the* Church of England. This very powerful sect does not teach this doctrine merely through a section of its ministers, who might charitably be considered as evil branches of the vine, but it openly, boldly, and plainly declares this doctrine in her own appointed standard, the Book of

Common Prayer, and that in words so express, that while language is the channel of conveying intelligible sense, no process short of violent wresting from their plain meaning can ever make them say anything else.

Here are the words: we quote them from the Catechism which is intended for the instruction of youth, and is naturally very plain and simple, since it would be foolish to trouble the young with metaphysical refinements. The child is asked its name, and then questioned, "Who gave you this name?" *"My godfathers and godmothers in my baptism: wherein I was made a member of Christ, the child of God, and an inheritor of the kingdom of heaven."* Is not this definite and plain enough? I prize the words for their candour; they could not speak more plainly. Three times over the thing is put, lest there should be any doubt in it. The word regeneration may, by some sort of juggling, be made to mean something else, but here there can be no misunderstanding. The child is not only made "a member of Christ"—union to Jesus is no mean spiritual gift—but he is made in baptism "the child of God" also; and, since the rule is, "if children then heirs," he is also made "an inheritor of the kingdom of heaven." Nothing can be more plain. I venture to say that while honesty remains on earth the meaning of these words will not admit of dispute. It is clear as noonday that, as Rubric hath it, "Fathers, mothers, masters, and dames, are to cause their children, servants, and apprentices," no matter how idle, giddy, or wicked they may be, to learn the Catechism, and to say that in baptism they were made members of Christ and children of God. The form for the administration of this baptism is scarcely less plain and outspoken, seeing that thanks are expressly returned unto Almighty God, because the person baptized is regenerate. *"Then shall the priest say, 'Seeing now, dearly beloved brethren, that this child is regenerate and grafted into the body of Christ's Church, let us give thanks unto Almighty God for these benefits; and with one accord make our prayers unto him, that this child may lead the rest of his life according to this beginning.'"* Nor is this all, for to leave no mistake, we have the words of the thanksgiving prescribed, *"Then shall the priest say, 'We yield thee hearty thanks, most merciful Father, that it hath pleased thee to regenerate this infant with thy Holy Spirit, to receive him for thine own child by adoption, and to incorporate him into thy holy Church.'"*

This, then, is the clear and unmistakable teaching of a Church calling itself Protestant. I am not now dealing at all with the question of infant baptism: I have nothing to do with that this morning. I am now considering the question of baptismal regeneration, whether in adults or infants, or ascribed to sprinkling, pouring, or immersion. Here is a Church which teaches every Lord's day in the Sunday-school, and should, according to the Rubric, teach openly in the Church, all children that they were made members of Christ, children of God, and inheritors of the kingdom of heaven when they were baptized! Here is a professedly Protestant Church, which, every time its minister goes to the font, declares that every person there receiving baptism is there and then "regenerated and grafted into the body of Christ's Church."

"But," I hear many good people exclaim, "there are many good clergymen in the Church who do not believe in baptismal regeneration." To this my answer is prompt. Why then do they belong to a Church which teaches that doctrine in the plainest terms? I am told that many in the Church of England preach against her own teaching. I know they do, and herein I rejoice in their enlightenment, but I question, gravely question their morality. To take oath that I sincerely assent and consent to a doctrine which I do not believe, would to my conscience appear little short of perjury, if not absolute downright perjury; but those who do so must be judged by their own Lord. For me to take money for defending what I do not believe—for me to take the money of a Church, and then to preach against what are most evidently its doctrines— I say for me to do this (I shall not judge the peculiar views of other men) for me, or for any other simple, honest man to do so, were an atrocity so great, that if I had perpetrated the deed, I should consider myself out of the pale of truthfulness, honesty, and common morality. Sirs, when I accepted the office of minister of this congregation, I looked to see what were your articles of faith; if I had not believed them I should not have accepted your call, and when I change my opinions, rest assured that as an honest man I shall resign the office, for how could I profess one thing in your declaration of faith, and quite another thing in my own preaching? Would I accept your pay, and then stand up every Sabbath-day and talk against the doctrines of your standards? For clergymen to swear or say that they give their solemn assent and consent to what they do not believe is one of the grossest pieces of immorality perpetrated in England, and is most pestilential in its influence, since it directly teaches men to lie whenever it seems necessary to do so in order to get a living or increase their supposed usefulness: it is in fact an open testimony from priestly lips that at least in ecclesiastical matters falsehood may express truth, and truth itself is a mere unimportant nonentity. I know of nothing more calculated to debauch the public mind than a want of straightforwardness in ministers; and when worldly men hear ministers denouncing the very things which their own Prayer Book teaches, they imagine that words have no meaning among ecclesiastics, and that vital differences in religion are merely a matter of tweedle-dee and tweedle-dum, and that it does not much matter what a man does believe so long as he is charitable towards other people. If baptism does regenerate people, let the fact be preached with a trumpet tongue, and let no man be ashamed of his belief in it. If this be really their creed, by all means let them have full liberty for its propagation. My brethren, those are honest Churchmen in this matter who, sub-scribing to the Prayer Book, believe in baptismal regeneration, and preach it plain-ly. God forbid that we should censure those who believe that baptism saves the soul, because they adhere to a Church which teaches the same doctrine. So far they are honest men; and in England, wherever else, let them never lack a full toleration. Let us oppose their teaching by all Scriptural and intelligent means, but let us respect their courage in plainly giving us their views. I hate their doctrine, but I love their honesty; and as they speak but what they believe to be true, let them speak it out, and the more clearly the better. Out with it, sirs, be it what it may, but do let us know what you mean. For my part, I love to stand foot to foot with an honest foeman. To open warfare, bold and true hearts raise no objection but the ground of quarrel; it is convert enmity which we have most cause to fear, and best reason to loathe. That crafty kindness which inveigles me to sacrifice principle is the serpent in the grass—deadly to the incautious wayfarer. Where union and friendship are not cemented by truth, they are an unhallowed confederacy. It is time that there should be an end put to the flirtations of honest men with those who believe one way and swear another. If men believe baptism works regeneration, let them say so; but if they do not believe it in their hearts, and yet subscribe, and yet more, get their livings by subscribing to words asserting it, let them find congenial associates among men who can equivocate and shuffle, for honest men will neither ask nor accept their friendship.

We ourselves are not dubious on this point, we protest that persons are not saved by being baptized. In such an audience as this, I am almost ashamed to go into the matter, because you surely know better than to be misled. Nevertheless, for the good of others we will drive at it. We hold that persons are not saved by baptism, for we think, first of all, that *it seems out of character with the spiritual religion which Christ came to teach,* that he should make salvation depend upon mere ceremony. Judaism might possibly absorb the ceremony by way of type into her ordinances essential to eternal life; for it was a religion of types and shadows. The false religions of the heathen might inculcate salvation by a physical process, but Jesus Christ claims for his faith that it is purely spiritual, and how could he connect regeneration with a peculiar application of aqueous fluid? I cannot see how it would be a spiritual gospel, but I can see how it would be mechanical, if I were sent forth to teach that the mere dropping of so many drops upon the brow, or even the plunging a person in water can save the soul. This seems to me to be the most mechanical religion now existing, and to be on a par with the praying windmills of Thibet, or the climbing up and down of Pilate's staircase to which Luther subjected himself in the days of his darkness. The operation of water-baptism does not appear even to my faith to touch the point involved in the regeneration of the soul. What is the necessary connection between water and the overcoming of sin? I cannot see any connection which can exist between sprinkling, or immersion, and regeneration, so that the one shall necessarily be tied to the other in the absence of faith. Used by faith, had God commanded it, miracles might be wrought; but without faith or even consciousness, as in the case of babes, how can spiritual benefits be connected necessarily with the sprinkling of water? If this be your teaching, that regeneration goes with baptism, I say it looks like the teaching of a spurious Church, which has craftily invented a mechanical salvation to deceive ignorant, sensual, and grovelling minds, rather than the teaching of the most profoundly spiritual of all teachers, who rebuked Scribes and Pharisees for regarding outward rights as more important than inward grace.

But it strikes me that a more forcible argument is that *the dogma is not supported by facts.* Are all persons who are baptized children of God? Well, let us look at the divine family. Let us mark their resemblance to their glorious Parent! Am I untruthful if I say that thousands of those who were baptized in their infancy are now in our gaols? You can ascertain the fact if you please, by application to prison authorities. Do you believe that these men, many of whom have been living by plunder, felony, burglary, or forgery, are regenerate? If so, the Lord deliver us from such regeneration. Are these villains members of Christ? If so, Christ has sadly altered since the day when he was holy, harmless, undefiled, separate from sinners. Has he really taken baptized drunkards and harlots to be members of his body? Do you not revolt at the supposition? It is a well-known fact that baptized persons have been hanged. Surely it can hardly be right to hang the inheritors of the kingdom of heaven! Our sheriffs have much to answer for when they officiate at the execution of the children of God, and suspend the members of Christ on the gallows! What a detestable farce is that which is transacted at the Old Bailey, when "a dear brother" has his neck broken to the music of "a sure and certain hope of the resurrection to eternal life," and the prayer that "when we shall depart this life we may rest in Christ, as our hope is that this our brother doth." Here is a regenerate brother, who is far too vile to live in this world and must be hanged by the neck until dead—but though he is not good enough for the society of sinners, and man rejects him, he is quite prepared to enter into the presence of God, and enters eternity with "a sure and certain hope of a resurrection unto eternal life." If old Rome in her worst days ever perpetrated a grosser piece of imposture than this, I do not read things aright; if it does not require a Luther to cry down this hypocrisy as much as Popery ever did, then I do not even know that twice two make four. Do we find—we who baptize on profession of faith, and baptize by immersion in a way which is confessed to be correct, though not allowed by some to be absolutely necessary to its validity—do we who baptize in the name of the sacred Trinity as others do, do we find that baptism regenerates? *We do not.* Neither in the righteous nor the wicked do we find regeneration by baptism. We have never met with one believer, however instructed in divine things, who could trace his regeneration to his baptism; and on the other hand, we confess it with sorrow, but still with no surprise, that we have seen those whom we have ourselves baptized, according to apostolic precedent, go back into the world and wander into the foulest sin, and their baptism had scarcely been so much as a restraint to them, because they have not believed in the Lord Jesus Christ. Facts all show that whatever good there may be in baptism, it certainly does not make man "a member of Christ, the child of God, and an inheritor of the kingdom of heaven," or else many thieves, whoremongers, drunkards, fornicators, and murderers, are members of Christ, the children of God, and inheritors of the kingdom of heaven. Facts, brethren, are dead against this Popish doctrine; and facts are subborn things.

Yet further, I am persuaded *that the performance styled baptism by the Prayer Book is not at all likely to regenerate and save.* How is the thing done? One is very curious to know when one hears of an operation which makes men members of Christ, children of God, and inheritors of the kingdom of heaven, how the thing is done. It must in itself be a holy thing, truthful in all its details, and edifying in every portion. Now, we will suppose them all to be *godly people.* The clergyman officiating is a profound believer in the Lord Jesus, and the father and mother are exemplary Christian, and the godfathers and godmothers are all gracious persons. We will suppose this—it is a supposition fraught with charity, but it may be correct. What are these godly people supposed to say? Let us look to the Prayer Book. The clergyman is supposed to tell these people, *"Ye have heard also that our Lord Jesus Christ hath promised in his gospel to grant all these things that ye have prayed for: which promise he, for his part, will most surely keep and perform. Wherefore, after this promise made by Christ, this infant must also faithfully, for his part, promise by you that are his sureties (until he come of age to take it upon himself) that he will renounce the devil and all his works, and constantly believe God's holy Word, and obediently keep his commandments."* This small child is to promise to do this, or more truly others are to take upon themselves to promise, and even vow that he shall do so. But we must not break the quotation, and therefore let us return to the Book. "I demand therefore, dost thou, in the name of this child, renounce the devil and all his works, the vain pomp and glory of the world, with all covetous desires of the same, and the carnal desires of the flesh, so that thou wilt not follow, nor be led by them?" Answer: "I renounce them all." That is to say, on the name and behalf of this tender infant about to be baptized, these godly people, these enlightened Christian people, these who know better, who are not dupes, who know all the while that they are promising impossibilities—renounce on behalf of this child what they find it very hard to renounce for themselves—"all covetous desires of the world and the carnal desires of the flesh, so that they will not follow nor be led by them." How can they harden their faces to utter such a false promise, such a mockery of renunciation before the presence of the Father Almighty? Might not angels weep as they hear the awful promise uttered? Then in the presence of high heaven they profess on behalf of this child that he stedfastly believes the creed, when they know, or might pretty shrewdly judge that the little creature is not yet a steadfast believer in anything, much less in Christ's going down into hell. Mark, they do not say merely that the babe *shall* believe the creed, but they affirm that he does, for they answer in the child's name, "All this I steadfastly believe." Not we stedfastly believe, but I, the little baby there, unconscious of all their professions and confessions of faith. In answer to the question, "Wilt thou be baptized in this faith?" they reply for the infant, "That is my desire." Surely the infant has no desire in the matter, or at the least, no one has been authorised to declare any desires on his behalf. But this is not all, for then these godly, intelligent people next promise on the behalf of the infant, that "he shall obediently keep all God's holy will and commandments, and walk in the same all the days of his life." Now, I ask you, dear friends, you who know what true religion means, can you walk in all God's holy commandments yourselves? Dare you make this day a vow on your own part that you would renounce the devil and all his works, the pomps and vanities of this wicked world, and all the sinful lusts of the flesh? Dare you, before God, make such a promise as that? You desire such holiness, you earnestly strive after it, but you look for it from God's promise, not from your own. If you dare make such vows I doubt your knowledge of your own hearts and of the spirituality of God's law. But even if you could do this for yourself, would you venture to make such a promise for any other person? For the best-born infant on earth? Come, brethren, what say you? Is not your reply ready and plain? There is not room for two opinions among men determined to observe truth in all their ways and words. I can understand a simple, ignorant rustic, who has never learned to read, doing all this at the command of a priest and under the eye of a squire. I can even understand persons doing this when the Reformation was in its dawn, and men had newly crept out of the darkness of Popery; but I cannot understand gracious, godly people, standing at the font to insult the all-gracious Father with vows and promises framed upon a fiction, and involving practical falsehood. How dare intelligent believers in Christ to utter words which they know in their conscience to be wickedly aside from truth? When I shall be able to understand the process by which gracious men so accommodate their consciences, even then I shall have a confirmed belief that the God of truth never did and never will confer a spiritual blessing of the highest order in connection with the utterance of such false promises and untruthful vows. My brethren, does it not strike you that declarations so fictitious are not likely to be connected with a new birth wrought by the Spirit of truth?

I have not done with this point, I must take another case, and suppose the sponsors and others to be *ungodly*, and that is no hard supposition, for in many cases we know that godfathers and parents have no more thought of religion than that idolatrous hollowed stone around which they gather. When these sinners have taken their places, what are they about to say? Why, they are about to make the solemn vows I have already recounted in your hearing! Totally irreligious they are, but yet they promise for the baby what they never did, and never thought of doing for themselves—they promise on behalf of this child, "that he will renounce the devil and all his works, and constantly believe God's holy Word, and obediently keep his commandments." My brethren, do not think I speak severely here. Really I think there is something here to make mockery for devils. Let every honest man lament, that ever God's Church should tolerate such a thing as this, and that there should be found gracious people who will feel grieved because I, in all kindness of heart, rebuke the atrocity. Unregenerate sinners promising for a poor babe that he shall keep all God's holy commandments which they themselves wantonly break every day! How can anything but the longsuffering of God endure this? What! not speak against it? The very stones in the street might cry out against the infamy of wicked men and women promising that another should renounce the devil and all his works, while they themselves serve the devil and do his works with greediness! As a climax to all this, I am asked to believe that God accepts that wicked promise, and as the result of it, regenerates that child. You cannot believe in regeneration by this operation, whether saints or sinners are the performers. Take them to be godly, then they are wrong for doing what their conscience must condemn; view them as ungodly, and they are wrong for promising what they know they cannot perform; and in neither case can God accept such worship, much less infallibly append regeneration to such a baptism as this.

But you will say "Why do you cry out against it?" I cry out against it because I believe that baptism does not save the soul, and that *the preaching of it has a wrong and evil influence upon men.* We meet with persons who, when we tell them that they must be born again, assure us that they were born again when they were baptized. The number of these persons is increasing, fearfully increasing, until all grades of society are misled by this belief. How can any man stand up in his pulpit and say "Ye must be born again" to his congregation, when he has already assured them, by his own "unfeigned assent and consent" to it, that they are themselves, every one of them, born again in baptism. What is he to do with them? Why, my dear friends, the gospel then has no voice; they have rammed this ceremony down its throat and it cannot speak to rebuke sin. The man who has been baptized or sprinkled says, "I am saved, I am a member of Christ, a child of God, and an inheritor of the kingdom of heaven. Who are you, that you should rebuke me? Call me to repentance? Call me to a new life? What better life can I have? for I am a member of Christ—a part of Christ's body. What! rebuke me? I am a child of God. Cannot you see it in my face? No matter what my walk and conversation is, I am a child of God. Moreover, I am an inheritor of the kingdom of heaven. It is true, I drink and swear, and all that, but you know I am an inheritor of the kingdom of heaven, for when I die, though I live in constant sin, you will put me in the grave, and tell everybody that I died "in sure and certain hope of a blessed resurrection."

Now, what can be the influence of such preaching as this upon our beloved England? Upon my dear and blessed country? What but the worst of ills? If I loved her not, but loved myself most, I might be silent here, but, loving England, I cannot and dare not; and having soon to render an account before my God, whose servant I hope I am, I must free myself from this evil as well as from every other, or else on my head may be the doom of souls.

Here let me bring in another point. It is a most fearful fact, that *in no age since the Reformation has Popery made such fearful strides in England as during the last few years*. I had comfortably believed that Popery was only feeding itself upon foreign subscriptions, upon a few titled perverts, and imported monks and nuns. I dreamed that its progress was not real. In fact, I have often smiled at the alarm of many of my brethren at the progress of Popery. But, my dear friends, we have been mistaken, grievously mistaken. If you will read a valuable paper in the magazine called "Christian Work," those of you who are not acquainted with it will be perfectly startled at its revelations. This great city is now covered with a network of monks, and priests, and sisters of mercy, and the conversions made are not by ones or twos, but by scores, till England is being regarded as the most hopeful spot for Romish missionary enterprise in the whole world; and at the present moment there is not a mission which is succeeding to anything like the extent which the English mission is. I covet not their money, I despise their sophistries, but I marvel at the way in which they gain their funds for the erection of their ecclesiastical buildings. It really is an alarming matter to see so many of our countrymen going off to that superstition which as a nation we once rejected, and which it was supposed we should never again receive. Popery is making advances such as you would never believe, though a spectator should tell it to you. Close to your very doors, perhaps even in your own houses, you may have evidence ere long of what a march Romanism is making. And to what is it to be ascribed? I say, with every ground of probability, that there is no marvel that Popery should increase when you have two things to make it grow: first of all, the falsehood of those who profess a faith which they do not believe, which is quite contrary to the honesty of the Romanist, who does through evil report and good report hold his faith; and then you have, second-ly, this form of error known as baptismal regeneration, and commonly called Puseyism, which is not only Puseyism, but Church-of-Englandism, because it is in the Prayer Book, as plainly as words can express it—you have this baptismal regeneration preparing stepping-stones to make it easy for men to go to Rome. I have but to open my eyes a little to foresee Romanism rampant everywhere in the future, since its germs are spreading everywhere in the present. In one of our courts of legislature but last Tuesday, the Lord Chief Justice showed his superstition, by speaking of "the risk of the calamity of children dying unbaptized!" Among Dis-senters you see a veneration for structures, a modified belief in the sacredness of places, which is all idolatry; for to believe in the sacredness of anything but of God and of his own Word, is to idolize, whether it is to believe in the sacredness of the men, the priests, or in the sacredness of the bricks and mortar, or of the fine linen, or what not, which you may use in the worship of God. I see this coming up everywhere—a belief in ceremony, a resting in ceremony, a veneration for altars, fonts, and Churches—a veneration so profound that we must not venture upon a remark, or straightway of sinners we are chief. Here is the essence and soul of Popery, peeping up under the garb of a decent respect for sacred things. It is impossible but that the Church of Rome must spread, when we who are the watch-dogs of the fold are silent, and others are gently and smoothly turfing the road, and making it as soft and smooth as possible, that converts may travel down to the nethermost hell of Popery. We want John Knox back again. Do not talk to me of mild and gentle men, of soft manners and squeamish words, we want the fiery Knox, and even though his vehemence should "ding our pulpits into blades," it were well if he did but rouse our hearts to action. We want Luther to tell men the truth unmistakably, in homely phrase. The velvet has got into our ministers' mouths of late, but we must unrobe ourselves of soft raiment, and truth must be spoken, and nothing but truth, for all lies which have dragged millions down to hell, I look upon this as being one of the most atrocious—that in a Protestant Church there should be found those who swear that baptism saves the soul. Call a man a Baptist, or a Presbyterian, or a Dissenter, or a Churchman, that is nothing to me—if he says that baptism saves the soul, out upon him, out upon him, he states what God never taught, what the Bible never laid down, and what ought never to be maintained by men who profess that the Bible, and the whole Bible, is the religion of Protestants.

I have spoken thus much, and there will be some who will say—spoken thus much bitterly. Very well, be it so. Physic is often bitter, but it shall work well, and the physician is not bitter because his medicine is so; or if he be accounted so, it will not matter, so long as the patient is cured; at all events, it is no business of the patient whether the physician is bitter or not, his business is with his own soul's health. There is the truth, and I have told it to you; and if there should be one among you, or if there should be one among the readers of this sermon when it is printed, who is resting on baptism, or resting upon ceremonies of any sort, I do beseech you, shake off this venomous faith into the fire as Paul did the viper which fastened on his hand. I pray you do not rest on baptism.

> "No outward forms can make you clean,
> The leprosy lies deep within."

I do beseech you to remember that you must have a new heart and a right spirit, and baptism cannot give you these. You must turn from your sins and follow after Christ; you must have such a faith as shall make your life holy and your speech devout, or else you have not the faith of God's elect, and into God's kingdom you shall never come. I pray you never rest upon this wretched and rotten foundation, this deceitful invention of antichrist. O, may God save you from it, and bring you to seek the true rock of refuge for weary souls.

I come with much brevity, and I hope with much earnestness, in the second place, to say that FAITH IS THE INDISPENSABLE REQUISITE TO SALVA-TION. "He that *believeth* and is baptized shall be saved; he that *believeth not* shall be damned." Faith is the one indispensable requisite for salvation. This faith is the gift of God. It is the work of the Holy Spirit. Some men believe not on Jesus; they believe not, because they are not of Christ's sheep, as he himself said unto them; but his sheep hear his voice: he knows them and they follow him: he gives to them eternal life, and they shall never perish, neither shall any pluck them out of his hand. What is this believing? Believing consists in two things; first there is *an accrediting of the testimony of God* concerning his Son. God tells you that his Son came into the world and was made flesh, that he lived upon earth for men's sake, that after having spent his life in holiness he was offered up a propitiation for sin, that upon the cross he there and then made expiation—so made expiation for the sins of the world that "Whosoever believeth in him shall not perish, but have everlasting life." If you would be saved, you must accredit this testimony which God gives concerning his own Son. Having received this testimony, the next thing is to *confide in it*—indeed here lies, I think, the essence of saving faith, to rest yourself for eternal salvation upon the atonement and the righteousness of Jesus Christ, to have done once for all with all reliance upon feelings or upon doings, and to trust in Jesus Christ and in what he did for your salvation.

This is faith, receiving of the truth of Christ: first knowing it to be true, and then acting upon that belief. Such a faith as this—such real faith as this makes the man henceforth hate sin. How can he love the thing which made the Saviour bleed? It makes him live in holiness. How can he but seek to honour that God who has loved him so much as to give his Son to die for him. This faith is spiritual in its nature and effects; it operates upon the entire man; it changes his heart, enlightens his judgment, and subdues his will; it subjects him to God's supremacy, and makes him receive God's Word as a little child, willing to receive the truth upon the *ipse dixit* of the divine One; it sanctifies his intellect, and makes him willing to be taught God's Word; it cleanses within; it makes clean the inside of the cup and platter, and it beautifies without; it makes clean the exterior conduct and the inner motive, so that the man, if his faith be true and real, becomes henceforth another man to what he ever was before.

Now that such a faith as this should save the soul, is, I believe, reasonable; yea, more, it is certain, for *we have seen men saved by it* in this very house of prayer. We have seen the harlot lifted out of the Stygian ditch of her sin, and made an honest woman; we have seen the thief reclaimed; we have known the drunkard in hundreds of instances to be sobered; we have observed faith to work such a change, that all the neighbours who have seen it have gazed and admired, even though they hated it; we have seen faith deliver men in the hour of temptation, and help them to consecrate themselves and their substance to God; we have seen, and hope still to see yet more widely, deeds of heroic consecration to God, and displays of witness-bearing against the common current of the times, which have proved to us that faith does affect the man, does save the soul. My hearers, if you would be saved, you must believe in the Lord Jesus Christ. Let me urge you with all my heart to look nowhere but to Christ crucified for your salvation. Oh! if you rest upon any ceremony, though it be not baptism—if you rest upon any other than Jesus Christ, you must perish, as surely as this Book is true. I pray you believe not every spirit, but though I, or an angel from heaven, preach any other doctrine than this, let him be accursed, for this, and this alone, is the soul-saving truth which shall regenerate the world—"He that believeth and is baptized shall be saved." Away from all the tag-rags, wax candles, and millinery of Puseyism! away from all the gorgeous pomp of Popery! away from the fonts of Church-of-Englandism! we bid you turn your eyes to that naked cross, where hangs as a bleeding man the Son of God.

> "None but Jesus, none but Jesus
> Can do helpless sinner good."

There is life in a look at the crucified; there is life at this moment for you. Whoever among you can believe in the great love of God towards man in Christ Jesus. You shall be saved. If you can believe that our great Father desireth us to come to him—that he panteth for us—that he calleth us every day with the loud voice of his Son's wounds; if you can believe now that in Christ there is pardon for transgressions past, and cleansing for years to come; if you can trust him to save you, you have already the marks of regeneration. The work of salvation is commenced in you, so far as the Spirit's work is concerned: it is finished in you so far as Christ's work is concerned. O, I would plead with you—lay hold on Jesus Christ. This is *the* foundation: build on it. This is *the* rock of refuge: fly to it. I pray you fly to it now. Life is short: time speeds with eagle's-wing. Swift as the dove pursued by the hawk, fly, fly poor sinner, to God's dear Son; now touch the hem of his garment; now look into that dear face, once marred with sorrows for you; look into those eyes, once shedding tears for you. Trust him, and if you find him false, then you must perish; but false you never will find him while this word standeth true, "He that believeth and is baptized shall be saved; but he that believeth not shall be damned." God give us this vital, essential faith, without which there is no salvation. Baptized, re-baptized, circumcised, confirmed, fed upon sacraments, and buried in consecrated ground—ye shall all perish except ye believe in him. The word is express and plain—he that believeth not may plead his baptism, may plead anything he likes, "But he that believeth not shall be damned;" for him there is nothing but the wrath of God, the flames of hell, eternal perdition. So Christ declares, and so must it be.

But now to close, there are some who say, "Ah! but baptism is in the text; where do you put that?" That shall be another point, and then we have done.

THE BAPTISM IN THE TEXT IS ONE EVIDENTLY CONNECTED WITH FAITH. "He that believeth and is baptized shall be saved." It strikes me, there is no supposition here, that anybody would be baptized who did not believe; or, if there be such a supposition, it is very clearly laid down that his baptism will be of no use to him, for he will be damned, baptized or not, unless he believes. The baptism of the text seems to me—my brethren, if you differ from me I am sorry for it, but I must hold my opinion and out with it—it seems to me that baptism is connected with, nay, directly follows belief. I would not insist too much upon the order of the words, but for other reasons, I think that baptism should follow believing. At any rate it effectually avoids the error we have been combating. A man who knows that he is saved by believing in Christ does not, when he is baptized, lift his baptism into a saving ordinance. In fact, he is the very best protester against that mistake, because he holds that he has no right to be baptized until he is saved. He bears a testimony against baptismal regeneration in his being baptized as professedly an already regenerate person. Brethren, the baptism here meant is a baptism connected with faith, and to this baptism I will admit there is very much ascribed in Scripture. Into that question I am not going; but I do find some very remarkable passages in which baptism is spoken of very strongly. I find this—"Arise, and be baptized, and wash away thy sins, calling on the name of the Lord." I find as much as this elsewhere; I know that believer's baptism itself does not wash away sin, yet it is so the outward sign and emblem of it to the believer, that the thing visible may be described as the thing signified. Just as our Saviour said—"This is my body," when it was not his body, but bread; yet, inasmuch as it represented his body, it was fair and right according to the usage of language to say, "Take, eat, this is my body." And so, inasmuch as baptism to the believer representeth the washing of sin—it may be called the washing of sin—not that it is so, but that it is to saved souls the outward Spirit, in the man who believes in Christ.

What connection has this baptism with faith? I think it has just this, *baptism is the avowal of faith*; the man was Christ's soldier, but now in baptism he puts on his regimentals. The man believed in Christ, but his faith remained between God and his own soul. In baptism he says to the baptizer, "I believe in Jesus Christ;" he says to the Church, "I unite with you as a believer in the common truths of Christianity;" he saith to the onlooker, "Whatever you may do, as for me, I will serve the Lord." It is the avowal of his faith.

Next, we think baptism is also to the believer a *testimony of his faith*; he does in baptism tell the world what he believes. "I am about," saith he, "to be buried in water. I believe that the Son of God was metaphorically baptized in suffering: I believe he was literally dead and buried." To rise again out of the water sets forth to all men that he believes in the resurrection of Christ. There is a showing forth in the

Lord's Supper of Christ's death, and there is a showing forth in baptism of Christ's burial and resurrection. It is a type, a sign, a symbol, a mirror to the world: a looking-glass in which religion is as it were reflected. We say to the onlooker, when he asks what is the meaning of this ordinance, "We mean to set forth our faith that Christ was buried, and that he rose again from the dead, and we avow this death and resurrection to be the ground of our trust."

Again, baptism is also *Faith's taking her proper place*. It is, or should be, one of her first acts of obedience. Reason looks at baptism, and says, "Perhaps there is nothing in it; it cannot do me any good." "True," says Faith, "and therefore will I observe it. If it did me some good my selfishness would make me do it, but inasmuch as to my sense there is no good in it, since I am bidden by my Lord thus to fulfil all righteousness, it is my first public declaration that a thing which looks to be unreasonable and seems to be unprofitable, being commanded by God, is law, is law to me. If my Master had told me to pick up six stones and lay them in a row I would do it, without demanding of him, 'What good will it do?' *Cui bono?* is no fit question for soldiers of Jesus. The very simplicity and apparent uselessness of the ordinance should make the believer say, 'Therefore I do it because it becomes the better test to me of my obedience to my Master.'" When you tell your servant to do something, and he cannot comprehend it, if he turns round and says, "Please, sir, what for?" you are quite clear that he hardly understands the relation between master and servant. So when God tells me to do a thing, if I say, "What for?" I cannot have taken the place which Faith ought to occupy, which is that of simple obedience to whatever the Lord hath said. Baptism is commanded, and Faith obeys because it is commanded, and thus takes her proper place.

Once more, *baptism is a refreshment to Faith*. While we are made up of body and soul as we are, we shall need some means by which the body shall sometimes be stirred up to co-work with the soul. In the Lord's Supper my faith is assisted by the outward and visible sign. In the bread and in the wine I see no superstitious mystery, I see nothing but bread and wine, but in that bread and wine I do see to my faith an assistant. Through the sign my faith sees the thing signified. So in baptism there is no mysterious efficacy in the baptistry or in the water. We attach no reverence to the one or to the other, but we do see in the water and in the baptism such an assistance as brings home to our faith most manifestly our being buried with Christ, and our rising again in newness of life with him. Explain baptism thus, dear friends, and there is no fear of Popery rising out of it—ah! my friends, how much of mischief that one falsehood has done and may do, eternity alone will disclose. Would to God another George Fox would spring up in all his quaint simplicity and rude honesty to rebuke the idol-worship of this age; to rail at their holy bricks and mortar, holy lecterns, holy altars, holy surplices, right reverend fathers, and I know not what. These things are not holy. God is holy; his truth is holy; holiness belongs not to the carnal and the material, but to the spiritual. O that a trumpet-tongue would cry out against the superstition of the age. I cannot, as George Fox did, give up baptism and the Lord's Supper, but I would infinitely sooner do it, counting it the smaller mistake of the two than perpetrate and assist in perpetrating the uplifting of baptism and the Lord's Supper out of their proper place. O my beloved friends, the comrades of my struggles and witnessings, cling to the salvation of faith, and abhor the salvation of priests. If I am not mistaken, the day will come when we shall have to fight for a simple spiritual religion far more than we do now. We have been cultivating friendship with those who are either unscriptural in creed or else dishonest, who either believe baptismal regeneration, or profess that they do, and swear before God that they do when they do not. The time is come when there shall be no more truce or parley between God's servants and time-servers. The time is come when those who follow God must follow God, and those who try to trim and dress themselves and find out a way which is pleasing to the flesh and gentle to carnal desires, must go their way. A great winnowing time is coming to God's saints, and we shall be clearer one of these days than we now are from union with those who are upholding Popery, under the pretence of teaching Protestantism. We shall be clear, I say, of those who teach salvation by baptism, instead of salvation by the blood of our blessed Master, Jesus Christ. O may the Lord gird up your loins. Believe me, it is no trifle. It may be that on this ground Armageddon shall be fought. Here shall come the great battle between Christ and his saints on the one hand, and the world, and forms, and ceremonies, on the other. If we are overcome here, there may be years of blood and persecution, and tossing to and fro between darkness and light; but if we are brave and bold, and flinch not here, but stand to God's truth, the future of England may be bright and glorious. O for a truly reformed Church in England, and a godly race to maintain it! The world's future depends on it under God, for in proportion as truth is marred at home, truth is maimed abroad. Out of any system which teaches salvation by baptism must spring infidelity, and infidelity which the false Church already seems willing to nourish and foster beneath her wing. God save this favoured land from the brood of her own established religion. Brethren, stand fast in the liberty wherewith Christ has made you free, and be not afraid of any sudden fear nor calamity when it cometh, for he who trusteth to the Lord, mercy shall compass him about, and he who is faithful to God and Christ shall hear it said at the last, "Well done, good and faithful servant, enter thou into the joy of the Lord." May the Lord bless the word for Christ's sake.

Appendix C

The Sword and the Trowel
March, 1887

THE DOWN GRADE

The Act of Uniformity, which came into effect in 1662, accomplished the purpose of its framers in expelling Puritanism from the Church established by law in England and Wales. Puritanism was obnoxious to King Charles II and his court, and a large majority of the men high in office in both Church and State, chiefly for the godliness of living which it enjoined, and for the Calvinism of its teaching.

With the ejectment of the two thousand ministers who preferred freedom and purity of conscience to the retention of their livings, Calvinism was banished from the Church of England, excepting so far as the Articles were concerned. Arminianism took its place. Then the State Church, which the great reformers had planted, and which some of them had watered with their blood, presented the spectacle which went far to justify the sarcasm of an eminent writer, that she possessed "A Popish Liturgy, a Calvinistic Creed, and an Arminian Clergy." The ejected were Calvinists almost to a man. Previous to this period, some few Free Churches had been founded, and were Independent or Baptist, the latter being mainly of the General section, and of Dutch origin.

The ejected, who were in one sense alone the first Nonconformists, were mainly Presbyterians; some, however, were Independents, and a few Baptists. The Churches they established were all Calvinistic in their faith, and such they remained for at least that generation. It is a matter of veritable history, however, that such they did not all continue for any great length of time. Some of them, in the course of two or three generations, or even less, became either Arian or Socinian. This was eventually the case with nearly all the Presbyterians, and later on, with some of the Independents, and with many of the General Baptist Communities. By some means or other, first the ministers, and then the Churches, got on "the down grade," and in some cases, the descent was rapid, and in all, very disastrous. In proportion as the ministers seceded from the old Puritan godliness of life, and the old Calvinistic form of doctrine, they commonly became less earnest and less simple in their preaching, more speculative and less spiritual in the matter of their discourses, and dwelt more on the moral teachings of the New Testament, than on the great central truths of revelation. Natural theology frequently took the place which the great truths of the gospel ought to have held, and the sermons became more and more Christless. Corresponding results in the character and life, first of the preachers and then of the people, were only too plainly apparent.

The race of preachers which followed the first Nonconformists, that is, the ejected ministers who became Nonconformists, retained the soundness of doctrine, and purity of life, for which they were everywhere remarkable. Their sermons were less lengthy, but still long, and less burdened with divisions and sub-divisions. The life, savour, and power of the gospel remained among them, and the churches, walking in the fear of God and the comfort of the Holy Ghost, were slowly increased.

The Presbyterians were the first to get on the down line. They paid more attention to classical attainments and other branches of learning in their ministry than the Independents, while the Baptists had no academical institution of any kind. It would be an easy step in the wrong direction to pay increased attention to academical attainments in their ministers, and less to spiritual qualifications; and to set a higher value on scholarship and oratory, than on evangelical zeal and ability to rightly divide the word of truth.

Some of the ministers retained their Calvinistic soundness and their purity of character and life, and these, as a rule, gave prominence to the doctrines of the

gospel, and were zealous in their ministry. But some embraced Arminian sentiments, while others professed to take a middle path, and called themselves Baxterians. These displayed, not only zeal for the salvation of sinners, and, in many cases,
less purity or strictness of life, but they adopted a different strain in preaching,
dwelt more on general principles of religion, and less on the vital truths of the
gospel. Ruin by sin, regeneration by the Holy Spirit, and redemption by the blood
of Christ—truths on the preaching of which God has always set the seal of his
approbation—were conspicuous chiefly by their absence. In fact, the "wine on the
lees well refined" was so mixed with the muddy water of human speculation, that it
was no longer wine at all.

There was another section among the Presbyterians who, like the former two,
retained a nominal orthodoxy, and professed to believe, though they seldom preached,
evangelical sentiments. Men of this stamp were chiefly remarkable for the extreme
coldness of their sermons, and the extreme dullness of their delivery.

Among those who called themselves Baxterians there was little likeness to
Baxter; and his zeal and earnestness, and his close, penetrating preaching, and
powerful appeals to the heart and conscience were wholly wanting, except in a very
few. This remark will apply also to those who called themselves Arminians.

It would appear that the Arian and other heresies did not spread at first so quickly
in London as in the country. The author of a manuscript written about 1730, professes
to give the sentiments of all the Nonconformist ministers in London at that time.
Among the Presbyterians there were, he says, nineteen Calvinists, thirteen Arminians,
and twelve Baxterians. All the Independents, he avows, were Calvinists: "twenty-
seven thoroughly, one somewhat dubious, three inclined to Antinomianism, and two
who were disorderly." There were sixteen Baptists, of the Particular order; of whom
seven were Calvinists, and "nine inclined to the Antinomian strain."

Antinomianism was the term applied to the teaching of Dr. Tobias Crisp. Crisp
had been an Arminian, but became an ardent Calvinist, going perhaps, a little
beyond Calvin in some things. He died in 1642, and his sermons were published by
his son forty-five years after his death. They were printed from short-hand notes
compared with Dr. Crisp's own notes, and therefore were lacking in that correctness and finish which the author's own hand would have given them. This will
account for the crudeness of some of his expressions. He was a man of strong faith,
ardent zeal, holy life, and great devotion and faithfulness in his ministerial work.
He was called an Antinomian, but the term was misapplied. Many of his statements, however, while they will readily admit of an orthodox sense, lie open to the
charge of going beyond the truth.

The publication of his sermons awoke a fierce controversy, which lasted some
years, and did much mischief. Dr. Williams exposed what he considered the errors
and erroneous tendency of some of his utterances; and even John Flavel was among
those who denounced his teaching as erroneous and Antinomian. There need not
have been such an outcry. The books written against Crisp, many of them good in
their way, had the effect of frightening the timid, the doubtful, and the hesitating,
who, to avoid *Crispianism*, as it was called, went as far as they could to the opposite

extreme. They verged upon Arminianism, and some actually became Arminians. The Arminianism of that day was a cold, dry, heartless thing, and many who took that name proved that they were already on "the down grade" towards Socinianism.

As is usual with people on an incline, some who got on "the down grade" went further than they intended, showing that it is easier to get on than to get off, and that where there is no brake it is very difficult to stop. Those who turned from Calvinism may not have dreamed of denying the proper deity of the Son of God, renouncing faith in his atoning death and justifying righteousness, and denouncing the doctrine of human depravity, the need of Divine renewal, and the necessity for the Holy Spirit's gracious work, in order that men might become new creatures; but, dreaming or not dreaming, this result became a reality.

It is exceedingly painful to have to state—and the conduct is no less censurable than pitiable—that among the two classes into which those who held Arian sentiments may be divided, the first were so mean and dishonest as to conceal their sentiments under ambiguous phrases. They so expressed themselves that their orthodox hearers might appropriate their statements in support of their own views, while their Arian adherents could turn them to support their scheme. It is stated on very good authority that "many wore this disguise all their days, and the most cautious carried the secret with them to the grave." This is terrible to think of; men going down to the grave with a whole life of the very worst kind of hypocrisy unconfessed, the basest deceit and dishonesty unacknowledged, the life-long practice of a lie unrepented of. Such a course is the very worst form of lying, for it is telling lies in the name of the Lord. Others were only a little less hardened in their career of falsehood; they prepared a sermon, or other composition, revealing their true sentiments, which was made public after their decease. Still more confided their real sentiments to a small circle of adherents, who told the tale of heresy to the world only when the grave had closed over the teacher.

Such were the crafty devices of the men of "broad views," and "free thought," and "advanced sentiments," in those days of "rebuke and blasphemy." The almost blasphemous utterances of Mr. Voysey, daring and frightful as they are,[1] have the one redeeming feature of honesty. He puts the mark of unbelief in large characters on his own brow, and does not seek in the least to hide it from any one, but rather to glory in it, that he has set himself to deny and denounce all that is sacred, and true, and holy in the gospel of our salvation. But these men deepened their own condemnation, and promoted the everlasting ruin of many of their followers by their hypocrisy and deceit; professing to be the ambassadors of Christ, and the heralds of his glorious gospel, their aim was to ignore his claims, deny him his rights, lower his character, rend the glorious vesture of his salvation, and trample his crown in the dust.

The second, and less numerous, class of Arian preachers were more honest. They boldly avowed their sentiments to their congregations, who as readily received them. In most cases, in both preachers and hearers, it was only a short step down from the Arianism which makes the eternal son of God a super-angelic being to the Socinianism (miscalled Unitarianism) which makes him a man only, denying alike original sin, human depravity, the mediation of Christ, the personality and work of the eternal Spirit, and that new birth without which divine truth has declared no one can see the kingdom of God.

The descent of some few was less gradual, but more commonly, when once on "the down grade" their progress was slow, though unhappily sure. The central truth of Calvinism, as of the Gospel, is the person and work and offices of the Lord Jesus Christ. We love to use this Pauline and inspired description of our divine Saviour and royal Master, and so to "give unto the Lord the glory due unto his name." When men begin to hesitate about, and hold back the truth in relation to him, it is a sign of an unhealthy state of soul; and when these truths are diluted, omitted, or otherwise tampered with, it is a sign which in plain words means "Beware."

The remark of a writer of reliable ability in reference to these times is worthy of quotation:—

"The deficiency of evangelical principles in some, and the coldness with which they came from the lips of others, seem to have prepared the way for the relinquishment of them, and for the introduction; first of Arminianism, and then of Arianism."

Those who were really orthodox in their sentiments were too often lax and unfaithful as to the introduction of heretical ministers into their pulpits, either as assistants or occasional preachers. In this way the Arian and Socinian heresies were introduced into the Presbyterian congregations in the city of Exeter. The Rev. Stephen Towgood and Mr. Walrond, the ministers, were both reputed as orthodox, but the Rev. Micaiah Towgood, an avowed Arian, was chosen their assistant. The old ministers preached evangelical doctrine, but they complied all too readily with the wishes of their new colleague, and ceased to require a declaration of faith in the divinity of Christ in those who sought admission to the Lord's table. Sad to say, they continued to labour on in peace, the older men dealing out the "wine of the kingdom," and the "Living Bread," while the younger minister intermixed his rationalistic concoctions and his Socinian leaven. A similar case occurred in London. Dr. William Harris, an avowed Calvinist, and whose preaching was in accordance with Calvinistic doctrine, had for his assistant, during the last twenty years of his life, an avowed though not strongly pronounced Socinian, Dr. Lardner, who took the afternoon lectureship. When Dr. Harris died, Dr. Lardner was elected to be his successor. For some reason he declined, when Dr. Benson, another Socinian, succeeded to the pastorate. Thus, the old, old proverb was again proved true, "The fathers have eaten a sour grape, and the children's teeth are set on edge."

This down-grade course was, we have said, more rapid, more general, and more fatal among the Presbyterians than among the Independents and General Baptists. We say *General* Baptists, for the deadening doctrines of Socinianism had made little inroad upon the *Particular* Baptists. We could not point to a single case of perversion to Socinianism during more than two centuries, though other and less vital errors have dealt much mischief among the churches of that order. Will our children and grandchildren be able to say as much of this and the next generation in fifty years time? Who can tell? But we pray and hope that they will be.

The principal cause of the quicker descent on "the down grade" among the Presbyterians than among the Nonconformists, may be traced, not so much to their more scholarly ministry, nor altogether to their renunciation of Puritan habits, but to their rule of admitting to the privileges of church membership. Of course their children received the rite of baptism, according to their views of baptism, in infancy. They were thereby received—so the ministers taught, and so the people believed—into covenant with God, and had a right to the Lord's table, without any other qualification than a moral life. Many such children grew up unregenerate, and strangers to the work of renewing grace; yet they claimed to be Christians, and to be admitted to all the privileges of the church, and their claim was not disallowed. To such the earnest appeals of faithful ministers of Christ would be irksome and unpalatable. The broader road and easier way of the "men of reason and culture," which admitted of laxity of discipline and pliancy of sentiments and habits, was far more agreeable to their tastes and ideas, while the homage paid to reason and understanding, at the expense of revelation, gratified their pride, and left them free to walk after their own hearts, men who could, and would and did, cry "Peace, peace," when the only way of peace was ignored or denied.

These facts furnish a lesson for the present time, when, as in some cases, it is all too plainly apparent men are willing to forego the old for the sake of the new. But commonly it is found in theology that that which is true is not new, and that which is new is not true.

In another paper we propose to trace "the down grade" course among other Protestants in this country—a sad piece of business, but one which must needs be done. Oh that it might act as a warning to the unsettled and unsettling spirits of our own day!

Appendix D

The Sword and the Trowel
April, 1887

THE DOWN GRADE [2]

Second Article.

The period from 1688, when William III. began his reign, to the time of the commencement of the long reign of George III., has been described as "a quiet time" among Nonconformists. It was so in more senses than one. There was a cessation of open and organized persecution. The Laudian spirit still lived, but it did not reign. The battle between Conformists and Nonconformists was no longer as it had been, one of the sword and of force, but rather of the pen, and by means of that quiet, subtle influence which abettors of State churches know so well how to wield. It was quiet, too, in the sense that there were few instances of lively faith, earnest zeal, and whole-souled devotedness in the cause of the gospel. To a large extent, and with some notable and happy exceptions, it was the quiet of corruption and death. The profligacy of Charles II., and the perfidy of James II., had told upon the Court, upon the nobility, upon pulpit and press, and upon society generally. True religion languished; and, but for a small remnant of earnest and faithful men, the decay and death would have been complete. It was a fitting time for the propagation of the Pelagian and Socinian heresies. Arminianism, which is only Pelagianism under another name, had, to a large extent, eaten out the life of the Church of England, and Arianism followed to further and complete the destruction.

As if to show how powerless in themselves are the best defined articles of faith, the first open advocates of Arianism were clergymen of the Established Church. Dr. William Whiston, Professor of Mathematics in the University of Cambridge, and Dr. Samuel Clarke, Rector, of St. James's, Westminster, were the captains in this unholy war with truth. Many of the clergy, and a few among the laity, embraced their sentiments. The majority of professed adherents to the State Church were too indifferent to religion to trouble themselves about the matter. But it was otherwise among Nonconformists. Many of the hearers were not much, if at all, behind their ministers in intelligence and interest in theological matters; and where this was the case, the bungling theories of Whiston and Clarke were readily embraced as agreeable to their taste and flattering to their reason. James Pierce, a Presbyterian minister, first at Cambridge, then at Newbury, and afterwards at Exeter, wrought incalculable mischief. He was a man who, for learning, eloquence, and other natural and acquired abilities, held a high place in the esteem of the congregations to which he ministered. So much the more subtle and powerful was the influence of his teaching, and so much the more disastrous were the results.

Among the Independents the leaven worked. In the colleges, or academies, as they were then called, the mischief first came to a head. Doctor Doddridge was as sound as he was amiable; but perhaps he was not always judicious; or more probably still, he was too judicious, and not sufficiently bold and decided. As the pastor of an influential church, and as the head of an academy which ranked higher than any other, his amiable disposition permitted him to do what men made of sterner stuff would not have done. He sometimes mingled in a fraternal manner, even exchanging pulpits, with men whose orthodoxy was called in question. It had its effect on many of the younger men, and served to lessen in the estimate of the people generally the growing divergence of sentiment. No one, however, could, and certainly the present writer will not, insinuate even the suspicion of heresy against the author of

"Jesus, I love thy charming name."

Dr. Doddridge was succeeded by Dr. Ashworth, of Daventry. He was recommended to the Independent church at Northampton as his successor in the pastorate, as well as in the academy, in Dr. Doddridge's will. But Dr. Ashworth elected to remain at Daventry, and the Academy was removed thither. Great abilities, much learning, consummate prudence, unaffected modesty, with great devotion and diligence in his tutorial duties, are the outlines of his character as drawn by the historian. He was a Calvinist of the moderate order, and we should be disposed to put a strong emphasis on the "moderate." So, at least, it is fair to infer from the testimony of one of his pupils, Dr. Joseph Priestley, the great champion of Socinianism among Nonconformists. He says:—"In my time the academy was in a state peculiarly favourable to the serious pursuit of truth, as the students were about equally divided upon every question of much importance, such as liberty, necessity, the sleep of the soul, and *all the articles of theological orthodoxy and heresy*; in consequence of which, all these topics were the subject of continual discussion. Our tutors, also, were of different opinions, Dr. Ashworth taking the orthodox side of every question, and Mr. Clark, the sub-tutor, that of heresy, though always with great modesty. Both of our tutors being young, at least as tutors, and some of the senior students excelling more than they could pretend to do in several branches of study, they indulged us in the greatest freedoms. The general plan of our studies, which may be seen in Dr. Doddridge's published lectures, was exceedingly favourable to free enquiry, as we were referred to authors on both sides of every question. In this situation I saw reason to embrace what is generally called the heterodox side of every question."

The subsequent history of the famous academy, founded and supported by Mr. Coward, and afterwards endowed by him, "with the express condition that the students shall be educated in the principles of the Assembly's Catechism," illustrates the folly and the virtual unfaithfulness of the course adopted by the professors. Mr. Robins was Dr. Ashworth's successor as pastor and tutor, and he was reputed as sound in the faith. His assistant tutor, however, was Thomas Belsham, who afterwards succeeded him in the theological chair. Belsham was a fellow-student of Priestley, and became an avowed opponent of Calvinism, and the open advocate of Socinianism. He had the honesty to resign his tutorship. But the mischief had been done. When the enemy had sowed tares among the wheat, "he went his way." The seed could not easily be dislodged. Mr. Horsey, his successor, could have been little better, for "most of the pupils were found to be Socinians." He had to resign, as not faithfully executing the will of the founder, and the Academy was dissolved.

This was the application to an institution thoroughly infected with theological leprosy of the wise law—wise in both a sanitary and spiritual sense—which God gave of old. The house had been scraped, and patched, and repaired, but the leprosy increased. "And, behold, if the plague be spread in the house it is a fretting leprosy in the house: it is unclean. And he shall break down the house, the stones of it, and the timber thereof, and all the mortar of the house; and he shall carry them forth out of the city into an unclean place."

As the fish decays first at the head, and as the old, old proverb is still commonly true, "Like priest like people," so little good can be expected of such ministers, and little hoped for of the hearers who approve their sentiments. Surely there was need enough of Whitefield and the other great preachers connected with the evangelical revival. That revival came not a day too soon, for the churches in general were indeed "low in a low place."

The Independent churches, though many of them were grievously tainted with heresy, did not remain corrupt. A race of earnest and faithful ministers were raised up who build again that which had been thrown down, leaving their mark on the age and their example to their successors. Do the present race of men prove themselves worthy successors of their fathers? Some do, no doubt. Would that the same could be said of all! But in too many cases sceptical daring seems to have taken the place of evangelical zeal, and the husks of theological speculations are preferred to the wholesome bread of gospel truth. With some the endeavour seems to be not how steadily and faithfully they can walk in the truth, but how far they can get from it. To them divine truth is like a lion or a tiger, and they give it "a wide berth." Our counsel is— Do not go too near the precipice; you may slip or fall over. Keep where the ground is firm; do not venture on the rotten ice. Take the advice of an old missionary, the late Thomas Morgan, of Howrah. The writer, and worthy brother who fell asleep twenty years ago, were all journeying in the direction of Maidstone, where the missionary was to meet the late Mr. Dobney. Said one of us to him, "How about Mr. D.'s theory concerning future punishment?" The old Welshman replied, "Well, if he brings up the subject to me, I shall say, 'Don't try it, that's all.'" So we venture to say to any venturesome spirit who want to follow the Will-with-a-wisp of modern thought, "Don't try it, there are dangerous bogs near, where you may soon lose yourself and all that is dear to you." If anyone wishes to know where the tadpole of Darwinism was hatched, we could point him to the pew of the old chapel in High Street, Shrewsbury, where Mr. Darwin, his father, and we believe his father's father, received their religious training. The chapel was built for Mr. Talents, an ejected minister; but for very many years full-blown Socinianism has been taught there, as also in the old chapel at Chester, where Matthew Henry used to minister, and where a copy of his Commentary, of the original edition, is kept for public use, the only witness, we fear, to the truths he taught there. It is of less importance, but still worthy of note, that the property with which the old High Street church at Shrewsbury was endowed, producing now from £300 to £400 per annum, has long been appropriated to uphold Socinian teaching.

The General Baptists have yet to be noticed. And here we must draw a line hard and sharp between the Old Connexion and the New Connexion. The latter was formed in 1770, and was the result of the heterodoxy of the former. The Old Connexion generally became Arianized, and, with hardly an exception, followed on "the down grade" to Socinianism. A writer of acknowledged repute, writing at the early part of the present century, makes this rather startling statement:—

"Arminianism among the dissenters has, in general, been a cold, dry and lifeless system, and its effects upon the heart have been commonly weak and spiritless. With the General Baptists, who avowed it to be their creed, this was remarkably the effect, and their congregations did not increase. Besides, from facts too stubborn to be bent, and too numerous to be contradicted, Arminianism has been among them the common road to Arianism and Socinianism. Their ministers and congregations were the first who openly professed these opinions; and their societies have felt the decay which these opinions have uniformly produced."

The writer can point to several places in the county of Kent where General Baptist congregations of the Old Connexion existed, and he can describe their present condition. That at Dover has been for many years Socinian, and perhaps, it is one of the most vigorous in the county, though the chapel is small and the attendance few. That at Deal is Socinian likewise, if we can describe it as being anything, when the place is open for one service only in three weeks. That at Wingham has been closed very many years. That in the large and wealthy parish of Yalding, has been closed for half a century. The writer often visited and preached in this old, stable-like building thirty years ago, the place being lent for the purpose; but of all dead places, that was the most dead. Spiritually, it was like the face of the country around Dowlais Top—not a vestige of herb, or grass, or any living thing to be seen.

The old church at Eythorne was nearly two hundred and fifty years General Baptist, belonging first to the Old Connexion, and then to the New. About a hundred years ago the pastor and congregation became Calvinistic, and joined the Particular Baptist Body. Strange to say, but the fact is so, that from that time it began to develop and increase in numbers, spiritual power, and social position. And now it can be said with truth, that there are very few churches in Great Britain whose career, during the past hundred years, has been equally remarkable. From the church in this village of less than six hundred inhabitants swarms have been sent out to Dover, Canterbury, and Deal, while its members or their descendants have been instruments in planting, or have helped to found, churches in Folkestone, in Ramsgate, Margate, and other places in the Isle of Thanet.

In the General Baptist Church at Bessels Green, near Sevenoaks, there was a long, and fierce, and painful struggle between Socinianism and evangelical orthodoxy, the latter at last prevailing.

These last two cases illustrate the "up grade," rather than the "down grade," and they will bring out the latter in bolder relief.

Narrowness of space and abundance of facts have burdened and hampered us in these sketches, and we can only add a few hints as to the cause or causes of the sad decay in piety and principle which it has been our painful duty to narrate.

In the case of every errant course there is always a first wrong step. If we can trace that wrong step, we may be able to avoid it and its results. Where, then, is the point of divergence from the "King's highway of truth"? What is the first step astray? Is it doubting this doctrine, or questioning that sentiment, or being sceptical as to the other article or orthodox belief? We think not. These doubts and this scepticism are the outcome of something going before.

If a mariner, having to traverse an unknown sea, does not put implicit confidence in his charts, and therefore does not consult them for guidance in steering the ship, he is, as anyone can see, every moment exposed to dangers of various kinds. Now, the Word of God—the Book written by holy men as they were moved by the Spirit of God—is the Christian's chart; and though, in a ship's company, some of the men may have little critical knowledge of navigation, the captain is supposed to be well instructed therein, and to be able, by consulting the charts, to steer the ship aright; so in reference to ministers of Christ's gospel, and pastors of Christ's church, which he hath purchased with his blood. The first step astray is a want of adequate faith in the divine inspiration of the sacred Scriptures. All the while a man bows to the authority of God's Word, he will not entertain any sentiment contrary to its teaching. "To the law and to the testimony," is his appeal concerning every doctrine. He esteems that holy Book, concerning all things, to be right, and therefore he hates every false way. But let a man question, or entertain low views of the inspiration and authority of the Bible, and he is without chart to guide him, and without anchor to hold him.

In looking carefully over the history of the times, and the movement of the times, of which we have written briefly, this fact is apparent: that where ministers and Christian churches have held fast to the truth that the Holy Scriptures have been given by God as an authoritative and infallible rule of faith and practice, they have never wandered very seriously out of the right way. But when, on the other hand, reason has been exalted above revelation, and made the exponent of revelation, all kinds of errors and mischiefs have been the result.

If this be a fact—and who can disprove it?—then we live in dangerous times, and there is great peril very near all those, whoever they may be, who call in question the inspiration—the divine inspiration—of the Word of God. "O earth, earth, earth! hear the word of the Lord."

The writer is of the opinion that the great majority of those who are sound in the doctrine of inspiration, and more or less Calvinistic in doctrine; and that the more the oracles of divine truth are humbly and prayerfully studied, the more closely the student's views will coincide with evangelical truth. That he is not alone in his opinion will be seen from the following:—"Veneration for the sacred Scriptures may certainly be considered as a test of the general purity of religious sentiments. Whether any will be found to equal Calvinists in this respect, shall be left to the judgment of those readers who have made extensive observations on the subject. Perhaps it cannot be contradicted that, in proportion as any sect recedes from Calvinism, their veneration for the Scriptures is diminished. The Bible is the Calvinist's creed. Whatever God has spoken, he feels himself bound to receive and believe, however mysterious the doctrine may be. Arminians, in general, will not be found to be equal to them in this respect, and many of that creed lay down their ideas of the moral perfections of the Deity as the foundation, and explain every part of Scripture in consonance with them, though, in order to accomplish this, no small degree of force must be employed. The Arian venerates the Scriptures still less than the Arminian; his ideas of inspiration are lower; his canons of criticism less honourable to the sacred writers; human reason is exalted to a higher office, and what is not comprehensible by its grasp, is not readily received. The mind of the Socinian feels still less veneration for the Word of God; for, according to his sentiments, some parts of it are not inspired; mistakes occur in the reasoning of the apostles; not a few passages are unauthentic, and what remains is interpreted with a latitude as to the expressions and language of Scripture, which would not be tolerated in expounding the sense of any other writer."[3]

The Rev. Job Orton, one of Dr. Doddridge's students, and for a short time an assistant tutor with him at Northampton, was the minister of the united congregation of Presbyterians and Independents, meeting at High Street, Shrewsbury, from 1741 to 1765. He was not considered fully orthodox, though many of his sentiments were sound and good. Many of his hearers suspected him of heresy concerning the Godhead of Christ, and when, in preaching, those expositions of the Bible, which were afterwards published in six volumes, he came to Isaiah ix. 6, "Unto us a son is born," & c., and they were listening with breathless attention as to what he would say on that part, "The mighty God," they were sadly disappointed when he passed the glorious declaration over by saying, "The mighty God. The meaning of this I cannot tell; and how should I, when his name is called Wonderful?" It need be no matter of surprise that his successor at High Street was a Socinian, and that the orthodox part of his congregation founded the Independent church at Swan Hill, which retains, in all essential things, its primitive soundness.

And yet Mr. Orton strongly recommended Philip Henry's statement of his religious belief, and has left on record, in his letters, remarks which are worthy to be pondered, as coming from a man whom Socinians regarded with favour.

"I have long since found," says he "(and every year that I live increases my conviction of it), that when ministers entertain their people with lively and pretty things, confine themselves to general harangues, insist principally on moral duties, without enforcing them warmly and affectionately by evangelical motives; while they neglect the peculiars of the gospel, never or seldom display the grace of God, and the love of Christ in our redemption; the necessity of regeneration and sanctification by a constant dependence on the Holy Spirit of God for assistance and strength in the duties of the Christian life, their congregations are in a wretched state; some are dwindling to nothing, as is the case with several in this neighbourhood, where there are now not as many scores as there were hundreds in their meeting-places, fifty years ago. But where, by trade and manufacturers, new persons come to the place, and fill up the vacant seats, there is a fatal deadness spread over the congregation. They run in 'the course of the world,' follow every fashionable folly, and family and personal godliness seems in general to be lost among them. There is scarcely any appearance of life and zeal in the cause of religion, which demands and deserves the greatest.

"Whereas, on the contrary, I never knew an instance where a minister was a pious, serious man, whose strain was evangelical and affectionate, but his congregation kept up, though death and removals had made many breaches in it.

"These letters were written when he had retired from the pastorate, residing at Kidderminster for the last eighteen years of his life."

It would seem that Orton had seen the folly of "the down grade" course, and was anxious to bear his testimony, to deter others.

But leaving men and their opinions, the Word of the Lord standeth fast for ever; and that Word to every one who undertakes to be God's messenger, and to speak the Lord's message to people, is "He that hath my word, let him speak my word faithfully. What is the chaff to the wheat? saith the Lord."

The Lord help us all to be "steadfast, immovable, always abounding in the work of the Lord, forasmuch as we know our labour shall not be in vain in the Lord."

Appendix E

The Sword and the Trowel

ANDOVER THEOLOGY

By the Writer of "The Down Grade."

The trial of the Professors of the Andover Theological Seminary, Andover, Massachusetts, has been attended by a great deal that is deeply interesting and immensely important, involving, as the matters under debate do, momentous issues.

It may be stated, in belief, that Andover Theological Seminary is an ancient institution—ancient, at least, for America—founded for the training of young men for the Congregational ministry. Its founders were sound Calvinists of the Cotton Mather type, and the College was instituted for the special purpose of training men in that faith. Accordingly, in connection with the institution and its endowments, there is a clear and definite statement of the doctrines which are to be taught, maintained, and propagated. To these doctrines the various professors are required to subscribe. It has come to pass, however, that the five gentlemen who now fill professorial chairs, articles of faith and subscription notwithstanding, have seriously departed from the faith of the founders. This has been manifest, not only in the tone and character of their divinity lectures and the too palpable heterodoxy of some of the students, but in the articles published in the *Andover Review* contributed by the professors. They do not, however, openly assail the creed of the founders to which they have subscribed, and for the teaching in which they have received their emoluments. They show unto us, as they suppose, "a more excellent way." The new theology is produced by some kind of evolution from the old; and hence it is called "Progressive Orthodoxy." This term may prove misleading. The unwary may conclude that its promoters are closely in sympathy with orthodox belief, and that their teaching in relation to the creed of the founders is really the same thing under another name. But a careful consideration of the points in dispute, and a candid comparison of the new with the old will lead to a far different conclusion. The *progressiveness* of the professors seems to be like that of the preacher whose two divisions of his subject were: "First, my brethren, I shall go right round the text; and, secondly, my friends, I shall go right away from it." Indeed the *progression* is so considerable that the "orthodoxy" is lost sight of. It may be remarked that there are two kinds of progression in nature—that of life, resulting in a thing of beauty and of joy; and that of death, of which a butcher's shop in very hot weather sometimes furnishes an example. There are similar processes in theology. Gold, we know, is the most malleable of metals. It may be beaten out into very thin plates, drawn into very fine wire, and even reduced to an impalpable dust; but it never becomes iron, or tin, or brass by the process. The plates, however thin, are gold plates; the wire, however fine, is gold wire; and the dust, however extreme the attenuation, is gold dust still. Some amount of beating, and drawing, and attenuation is needed in the inculcation of the great truths of the gospel, especially in the use of some congregations, and certain preachers and orators achieve wonderful success in this direction—like an amateur gardener whom I knew, who grew fine onions, so fine, he said, that he could hardly see them. But the men who hammer thin gold to the thinnest, and draw their wire to the finest, never come within sight of these Andover professors in their achievements, who, in the extreme progressiveness of their "orthodoxy," come near to fulfilling the Scripture in a novel sense: "Old things are passed away; behold all things have become new."

The trial took place at the United States Hotel, Boston, commencing 28th December, 1886, and extending over several days. It is testified by several witnesses—for the trial was a public one—that the proceedings were conducted themselves in such a manner, and that all parties concerned conducted themselves in such a becoming spirit, as reflected great credit on all engaged therein. First of all, after the proceedings had been opened by Professor Dwight, of New York, the several professors stated at length their whole case, which occupied the chief part of three days, when Judge Aea French opened the arguments for the prosecution. From his statement, and the statements of Dr. Wellman, who followed him, the whole question at issue may be seen. Judge French said:—

"The question is now, not what these gentlemen would have the creed to be, or how they would have drawn it, but what was the intent of the founders, and what did they mean when they declared that nothing should be taken from it? The question is simple: Do these men hold the doctrines laid down in that creed, or do they depart from them in ever so slight a degree?"

This is a shorter cut, and a truer aim, than lawyers in general take.

The question of the orthodoxy or otherwise of the professors was not the chief question; it was subordinate, for all practical purposes, to this other: Is their theology in harmony with, or opposed to, the articles of the creed laid down by the founders of the Seminary? or, in other words, is their teaching, denominated "progressive orthodoxy," what the founders of the Seminary willed to have taught, and what the professors engaged to teach? It needs but little penetration to see that the divergence is very general and very great, and that on the most vital points it is the most remote from the old theology, the creed of the founders.

Let us enumerate some of these points.

As is usual in all cases of departure from orthodox belief, the professors are at variance with the creed of the Seminary and the general belief of orthodox Christians, on the subject of inspiration. Their sentiments on this subject are boldly expressed, and with as much subtlety as daring. We have heard the same sentiments avowed from a Congregational pulpit in this country by a young man at his ordination. Sad as this was, and it went to the heart of the writer, it was even sadder that neither the venerable professor who gave the charge, nor any of the other ministers engaged—some of them venerable, too—uttered a single word of protest or regret, or asked for any explanation or qualification of the statements made.

It was alleged against the Andover professors that they held the Bible to be fallible, not only in matters of science and chronology, but in some of its religious teachings also. According to their notion the writers of the Bible were inspired, but only in the sense in which men are inspired now. The Scriptures are not, therefore, a true or infallible standard of faith. The Scriptures sprang out of the religious consciousness of the writers, and they must be interpreted by the religious consciousness of the readers. God's Word is not a revelation, but a *vehicle of revelation*. Thus we are taught by the professors that the words as uttered by the prophets do not necessarily carry with them the authority of infallible truth. It is written—and David wrote out of his inner consciousness as well as by divine inspiration—"Thy word is true from the beginning: and every one of thy righteous judgments endureth for ever." But for all that, it is not true, only as it is formulated, shaped, and fashioned by some advocate of "progressive orthodoxy."

The written Andover Creed states, in accordance with the terms of the Westminster Confession and the Assembly's Shorter Catechism, that the Word of God is infallible, and of paramount authority in all matters of faith and practice. This is very different from what the present professors would write.

Dr. Wellman stated concerning the professors that their views "dishonour and depreciate the Holy Scriptures." They violently antagonize the old Andover creed in various ways, but especially in that they erect a standard of truth and faith equal or superior to that of the Holy Scriptures, and render it impossible that the Bible should be, as the creed states, "the only perfect rule of faith and practice." They are repugnant to Article II. of the statutes of the Associate Foundation, which says that every professor shall be an orthodox and consistent Calvinist, and it is impossible for one to be a man of sound and orthodox principles in divinity within the meaning of the statutes who holds the views set forth in "Progressive Orthodoxy."

These views are by no means novel; they pervade a vast deal of German theology, and have been taught by men of the Maurice and Kingsley school in this country. They find favour in the columns of our contemporary, "The Christian World," where the Andover professors find sympathy, and are regarded rather as being sinned against than sinning. But this is by no means surprising. "Like loves its like," as the proverb says. We expect, however, that it will be found true after all, that God's commandments are sure; and that his words are "pure words: as silver tried in a furnace of earth, seven times purified."

Another departure from the orthodox faith, as alleged against the professors, is concerning the Person of Christ. They teach that the humanity of Christ so limited his faculties that he was fallible, or not omniscient, and hence not perfect God and man, as the creed of the founders teaches, and as evangelical Christians believe. This, to say the very least, is dangerous ground, and argues a mind already greatly warped and corrupted from "the simplicity that is in Christ." To hold and teach such fundamental errors is bad enough, but to make them the outcome of the teaching of Calvinism, and the proper expansion of the doctrine of the old creed, is even worse. But then it comes from the infallible "religious consciousness" which is to stamp every vagary of man's disordered fancy as true, and put its mint-mark on all the speculations of those who have never become fools that they may be wise.

As the professors have departed from the form of sound words is to the Person of Christ, so in relation to his work they have *progressed* beyond "the faith once for all delivered unto the saints." The atonement of Christ, according to these gentlemen, consists not in his vicarious sufferings and death, whereby he bought his redeemed ones with the price of his own blood, and presented an offering infinite in its efficacy, and boundless in its merit, but in his assumption of human nature and his holy life. By his assumption of human nature he takes the whole human family into union with himself, making all men salvable, and giving them power to repent. Thus, by this "progressive orthodoxy" the sufferings of Christ to satisfy the claims of divine justice are practically ignored, and such passages as, "We have redemption by his blood, the forgiveness of sin, according to the riches of his grace," lose their light and glory, or are lost in the depth of man's "religious consciousness."

Sound Calvinism, as taught in the creed of the Andover Seminary, makes provision for the application of the blessings of redemption in the sense of our Lord's words, "All that the Father giveth me shall come to me." Hence the Person, work, teaching, and influence of the Holy Spirit have a prominent place in orthodox belief. In the "progressive orthodoxy" of the Andover professors this is lost sight of, and the drawings of divine grace are left out of the question. According to this scheme, man has the power to repent, but his heart remains hard. He is united to Christ, in common with the whole of humanity; but there is no life, no attractive power, and he continues alienated. His crimes have been somehow atoned for by Christ's holy life; but he is still far off by wicked works, a lover of pleasure more than a lover of God, and the promise of Christ to his disciples. "Because I live, ye shall live also," is a dead letter. The gospel would be a poor gospel, or rather, no gospel at all, if these things were so. It may be well, therefore, to recall the words which the apostle Paul wrote to the church at Galatia—words which were not merely evolved from his inner consciousness, but which were dictated by the Holy Spirit. It may be well, too, for all who sympathize with the views of the said professors, or who may be disposed to look upon their aberrations from the doctrinal formula they have subscribed as harmless, or as matters of quite secondary importance, to ponder the apostle's words, which on account of their great pertinence, we quote in full:—

"I marvel that ye are so soon removed from him that called you into the grace of Christ unto another gospel: which is not another; but there be some that trouble you, and would pervert the gospel of Christ. But though we, or an angel from heaven, preach any other gospel unto you than that which we have preached unto you, let him be accursed. As we said before, so say I now again, If any man preach any other gospel unto you than that ye have received, let him be accursed." "A very uncharitable imprecation," some would say: and we should join them in saying so, if Paul had no higher authority than his inner consciousness; indeed he had the infallible authority of One who cannot err, and who is infinitely above all the passions which may actuate the human mind and guide the pen of even the most holy among the children of men. And it was under the authority and direct influence of God that he wrote, "I certify you, brethren, that the gospel which was preached of me is not after man. For I neither received it of man, neither was I taught it, but by the revelation of Jesus Christ." Thus spake the man of God, whom

God moved to write the Epistles to the Romans, Ephesians, &c., whence in part Calvinists draw their doctrinal statements.

Another very serious charge brought against the professors is, that they hold that men who have not heard of Christ are not sinners, or are not sinners so as to be exposed to perdition. One, at least, of them denies this conclusion; but this is the legitimate inference to be drawn from their statements. The natural depravity of man, his loss of original righteousness, and his consequent exposure to eternal misery, are all either denied or ignored; so that, according to these conclusions, there is no such thing as original sin, and Paul was seriously wrong and off the line when he said, "Wherefore, as by one man sin entered into the world, and death by sin; and so death passed upon all men, for that all have sinned." The simple-minded people, who are not philosophical in their tendencies, who are not advanced thinkers, and who have not been perverted from the truth to accept human speculations as veritable gospel, will, perhaps, be ready to respond to Paul's vehement words, which may well sum up the dispute, "Let God be true, but every man a liar."

Another heresy charged upon the professors—and it is a chief point of the departure from the lines of revealed truth, and the creed of the Seminary—is the notion of a second probation. "Men who have never had Christ offered to them in this life, will meet his gracious face in the mercury of a future state. Their choice then will fix their doom for ever." The defence the men set up for teaching this sentiment is, not that there is anything in the creed for it, but that there is nothing against it, and that the framers of the creed, were they now living in this day of greater light, advanced thought, and "progressive orthodoxy," might possibly include it. It must be a poor case that stands in need of such a sorry argument. What wrong might not be proved right, what evil might not be made to appear good, upon such a principle? The process of their reasoning seems to be widely different from the straightforward methods which Paul so highly commends. We "have renounced the hidden things of dishonesty, not walking in craftiness, nor handling the Word of God deceitfully; but by manifestation of the truth, commending ourselves to every man's conscience in the sight of God."

Thus we have given a brief statement of the case of the accused professors, and of their wide departure from the orthodox belief of the founders. To call their sentiments "advanced orthodoxy" is a misnomer. They have little, if any, relation to orthodoxy, except as they controvert its teachings. It is the same case again of the water being added to the wine, until the liquor is no longer wine at all, or only so in imagination.

It will be seen that the points of departure affect nearly all the vital truths of the gospel. Original sin is denied or ignored; the Person and offices of Christ are greatly shorn of their glory, though there is a strange setting forth of his worth and love. The three R's are nowhere. The Person and offices of the Holy Spirit are somehow dispensed with. The "blood of the eternal covenant"—the blood that redeems from death and hell into God, and imparts its constant cleansing to all who walk in fellowship with God through Christ—is a matter of very secondary importance. The grand old doctrine, so beautifully emblemized by Christ in his parting discourse to his disciples, "I am the vine, ye are the branches," is a mistake or a dream. All the grand and beautiful imagery by which the Holy Spirit, in guiding Paul's pen, set forth the actual living oneness of Christ and his church—the Head and the body, the Foundation and the house, the Shepherd and the sheep—are, practically, so many myths. In fact, so far as regards the Christ of the epistles, the whole family of the Saviour might weep and sigh with Mary, "They have taken away my Lord, and I know not where they have laid him." If such sentiments, such negations of the truth, are to be the gospel of the day, then we say, "Alas! alas! the glory is departed from Israel!" But this cannot well be. "The foundation of God standeth sure, having this seal, the Lord knoweth them that are his." This is not the first time that the truth of God has been assailed. Alas! many and many a time men have gone out as with the high authority of the church's sanction, "speaking perverse things, to draw away disciples after them." But the gospel of God is the gospel of power, while the gospel of heresy is the gospel of weakness.

The truth of man's fallen and lost condition underlies all aggressive theology and all Christian activity, Paul's teaching in his day was in keeping with the teaching of the prophets: "O Israel, thou hast destroyed thyself; but in me is thine help." Sin and utter misery and ruin in man's case, grace and sovereign mercy through Christ, on God's part, were the themes everywhere of Paul. Augustine, Calvin, and Luther taught the same. And it is this teaching which has done for the world what has thus far been achieved by Christianity. The living hymnody of the Church in all ages embodies the same facts: Greek, Latin, German, English, French, Swiss and American, all unite their voices. The theology of Paul was the theology of the Puritans, and the theology of the Puritans did much to build the American people into a great nation. The Pilgrim Fathers were all men of this right noble mould, and would as soon have thought of questioning their right to live and be free as to entertain for a single moment a doubt of the inspiration of the Word of God.

The roots of all evangelical preaching strike deep down into the truths of man's sin and ruin and of the grace of God in Christ to sinners deserving eternal wrath. The mighty men of old, the men of renown in all ages, the captains and leaders of the "Sacramental host of God's elect" in all lands, have ever been men who were strong and steadfast in all those truths which relate to the perfection of the Scriptures, the person and work of the Redeemer, and of salvation through faith in his name. Beyond the Word they would not stop. Christ in his mediation, his substitution, his redeeming death and his glorious resurrection, was ever the centre of their life, the foundation of their faith, the theme of their faithful testimony. To him they all bore witness. Search the history of religious revivals, and you will find that wherever real revivals have been experienced, they have been in connection with evangelical preaching, more or less sound and thorough. Look at the work of Luther and others in Germany, at the work of Zwingle in Switzerland, and the work of Calvin in France, and at the work of the Puritans in England. Mark the career of President Edwards, or George Whitefield, of the founders of Welsh Methodism of the Haldanes in Scotland, of Robert Haldane at Geneva, of the late Dr. Malan in Geneva, of the Erskines and Bostons and such like in Scotland, and the most successful soul-winners in England, and you will find them to a man sound on the inspiration of the Holy Scripture. The Wesleyan Methodists of all parties are sound on that question. And whatever "down grade" tendency there may be in their Arminian theology, faith in the inspiration of the Word of God and in the atoning work of the Lamb checks all downward progress. Shall we forsake the faith of our fathers? Shall we give place by subjection to fundamental error dressed in the guise of "Progressive Orthodoxy"? No, not for an hour. That were to put out the fire of evangelical zeal, to quench the altar flames of love to Christ, and to undermine the very foundation of all that is stable and strong and true in religion. "No man having tasted old wine straightway desireth new; for he saith, The old is better."

Appendix F

The Sword and the Trowel
August, 1887

ANOTHER WORD CONCERNING THE DOWN-GRADE

By C. H. Spurgeon

No lover of the gospel can conceal from himself the fact that the days are evil. We are willing to make a large discount from our apprehensions on the score of natural timidity, the caution of age, and the weakness produced by pain; but yet our solemn conviction is that things are much worse in many churches than they seem to be, and are rapidly tending downward. Read those newspapers which represent the Broad School of Dissent, and ask yourself, How much farther could they go? What doctrine remains to be abandoned? What other truth to be the object of contempt? A new religion has been initiated, which is no more Christianity than chalk is cheese; and this religion, being destitute of moral honesty, palms itself off as the old faith with slight improvements, and on this plea usurps pulpits which were erected for gospel preaching. The Atonement is scouted, the inspiration of Scripture is derided, the Holy Spirit is degraded into an influence, the punishment of sin is turned into fiction, and the resurrection into a myth, and yet these enemies of our faith expect us to call them brethren, and maintain a confederacy with them!

At the back of doctrinal falsehood comes a natural decline of spiritual life, evidenced by a taste for questionable amusements, and a weariness of devotional meetings. At a certain meeting of ministers and church-officers, one after another doubted the value of prayer-meetings; all confessed that they had a very small attendance, and several acknowledged without the slightest compunction that they had quite given them up. What means this? Are churches in a right condition when they have only one meeting for prayer in a week, and that a mere skeleton? Churches which have prayer-meetings several times on the Lord's day, and very frequently during the week, yet feel their need of more prayer; but what can be said of those who very seldom practise united supplication? Are there few conversions? Do the congregations dwindle? Who wonders that this is the case when the spirit of prayer has departed?

As for questionable amusements—time was when a Nonconformist minister who was known to attend the play-house would soon have found himself without a church. And justly so; for no man can long possess the confidence, even of the most worldly, who is known to be a haunter of theatres. Yet at the present time it is matter of notoriety that preachers of no mean repute defend the play-house, and do so because they have been seen there. Is it any wonder that church members forget their vows of consecration, and run with the unholy in the ways of frivolity, when they hear that persons are tolerated in the pastorate who do the same? We doubt not that, for writing these lines we shall incur the charge of prudery and bigotry, and this will but prove how low are the tone and spirit of the churches in many places. The fact is, that many would like to unite church and stage, cards and prayer, dancing and sacraments. If we are powerless to stem this torrent, we can at least warn men of its existence, and entreat them to keep out of it. When the old faith is gone, and enthusiasm for the gospel is extinct, it is no wonder that people seek something else in the way of delight. Lacking bread, they feed on ashes; rejecting the way of the Lord, they run greedily in the path of folly.

An eminent minister, who is well versed in the records of Nonconformity, remarked to us the other day that he feared history was about to repeat itself among Dissenters. In days gone by, they aimed at being thought respectable, judicious, moderate, and learned, and, in consequence, they abandoned the Puritanic teaching with which they started, and toned down their doctrines. The spiritual life which had been the impelling cause of their dissent declined almost to death's door, and the very existence of evangelical Nonconformity was threatened. Then came the outburst of living godliness under Whitefield and Wesley, and with it new life for Dissent, and increased influence in every direction.

Alas! many are returning to the poisoned cups which drugged that declining generation, when it surrendered itself to Unitarian lethargy. Too many ministers are toying with the deadly cobra of "another gospel," in the form of "modern thought." As a consequence, their congregations are thinning: the more spiritual of their members join the "Brethren," or some other company of "believers unattached"; while the more wealthy, and show-loving, with some of unquestionable devoutness, go off to the Church of England.

Let us not hide from ourselves the fact that the Episcopal Church is awake, and is full of zeal and force. Dissenting as we do most intensely from her Ritualism, and especially abhorring her establishment by the State, we cannot but perceive that she grows, and grows, among other reasons, because spiritual life is waning among certain Dissenters. Where the gospel is fully and powerfully preached, with the Holy Ghost sent down from heaven, our churches not only hold their own, but win converts; but when that which constitutes their strength is gone—we mean when the gospel is concealed, and the life of prayer is slighted—the whole thing becomes a mere form and fiction. For this thing our heart is sore grieved. Dissent for mere dissent's sake would be the bitter fruit of a wilful mind. Dissent as mere political partisanship is a degradation and travesty of religion. Dissent for truth's sake, carried out by force of the life within, is noble, praiseworthy, and fraught with the highest benefits to the race. Are we to have the genuine living thing, or are we to have that corruption of the best from which the worst is produced? Conformity, or nonconformity, *per se,* is nothing; but a new creature is everything, and the truth upon which alone that new creature can live is worth dying a thousand deaths to conserve. It is not the shell that is so precious, but the kernel which it contains; when the kernel is gone, what is there left that is worth a thought? Our nonconformity is beyond measure precious as a vital spiritual force, but only while it remains such will it justify its own existence.

The case is mournful. Certain ministers are making infidels. Avowed atheists are not a tenth as dangerous as those preachers who scatter doubt and stab at faith. A plain man told us the other day that two ministers had derided him because he thought we should pray for rain. A gracious woman bemoaned in my presence that a precious promise in Isaiah which had comforted her had been declared by her minister to be uninspired. It is a common thing to hear working-men excuse their wickedness by the statement that there is no hell, "the parson says so." But we need not prolong our mention of painful facts. Germany was made unbelieving by her preachers, and England is following in her track. Attendance at places of worship is declining, and reverence for holy things is vanishing; and we solemnly believe this to be largely attributable to the scepticism which has flashed from the pulpit and spread among the people. Possibly the men who uttered the doubt never intended it to go so far; but none the less they have done the ill, and cannot undo it. Their own observation ought to teach them better. Have these advanced thinkers filled their own chapels? Have they, after all, prospered through discarding the old methods? Possibly, in a few cases genius and tact have carried these gentry over the destructive results of their ministry; but in many cases their pretty new theology has scattered their congregations. In meeting-houses holding a thousand, or twelve hundred, or fifteen hundred, places once packed to the ceiling with ardent hearers, how small are the numbers now! We would mention instances, but we forbear. The places which the gospel filled the new nonsense has emptied, and will keep empty.

This fact will have little influence with "the cultured"; for, as a rule, they have cultivated a fine development of conceit. "Yes," said one, whose pews held only here and there a worshipper, "it will always be found that in proportion as the preacher's mind enlarges, his congregation diminishes." These destroyers of our churches appear to be as content with their work as monkeys with their mischief. That which their fathers would have lamented they rejoice in: the alienation of the poor and simple-minded from their ministry they accept as a compliment, and the grief of the spiritually-minded they regard as an evidence of their power. Truly, unless the Lord had kept his own we should long before this have seen our Zion ploughed as a field.

The other day we were asked to mention the name of some person who might be a suitable pastor for a vacant church, and the deacon who wrote said, "Let him be a converted man, and let him be one who believes what he preaches; for there are those around us who give us the idea that they have neither part nor lot in the matter." This remark is more commonly made than we like to remember, and there is, alas! too much need for it. A student from a certain college preached to a congregation we sometimes visit such a sermon that the deacon said to him in the vestry, "Sir, do you believe in the Holy Ghost?" The youth, "I suppose I do." To which the deacon answered, "I suppose you do *not*, or you would not have insulted us with such false doctrine." A little plain-speaking would do a world of good just now. These gentlemen desire to be let alone. They want no noise raised. Of course thieves hate watch-dogs, and love darkness. It is time that somebody should spring his rattle, and call attention to the way in which God is being robbed of his glory, and man of his hope.

It now becomes a serious question how far those who abide by the faith once delivered to the saints should fraternize with those who have turned aside to another gospel. Christian love has its claims, and divisions are to be shunned as grievous evils; but how far are we justified in being in confederacy with those who are departing from the truth? It is a difficult question to answer so as to keep the balance of the duties. For the present it behoves believers to be cautious, lest they lend their support and countenance to the betrayers of the Lord. It is one thing to overleap all boundaries of denominational restriction for the truth's sake: this we hope all godly men will do more and more. It is quite another policy which would urge us to subordinate the maintenance of truth to denominational prosperity and unity. Numbers of easy-minded people wink at error so long as it is committed by a clever man and a good-natured brother, who has so many fine points about him. Let each believer judge for himself; but, for our part, we have put on a few fresh bolts to our door, and we have given orders to keep the chain up; for, under colour of begging the friendship of the servant, there are those about who aim at robbing THE MASTER.

We fear it is hopeless ever to form a society which can keep out men base enough to profess one thing and believe another; but it might be possible to make an informal alliance among all who hold the Christianity of their fathers. Little as they might be able to do, they could at least protest, and as far as possible free themselves of that complicity which will be involved in a conspiracy of silence. If for a while the evangelicals are doomed to go down, let them die fighting, and in the full assurance that their gospel will have a resurrection when the inventions of "modern thought" shall be burned up with fire unquenchable.

Appendix G

The Sword and the Trowel
September, 1887

OUR REPLY TO SUNDRY CRITICS AND ENQUIRERS

By C. H. Spurgeon

According to the best of our ability we sounded an alarm in Zion concerning the growing evils of the times, and we have received abundant proof that it was none too soon. Letters from all quarters declare that the case of the church at this present is even worse than we thought it to be. It seems that, instead of being guilty of exaggeration, we should have been justified in the production of a far more terrible picture. This fact causes us real sorrow. Had we been convicted of mis-statement we would have recanted with sincerely penitent confessions, and we should have been glad to have had our fears removed. It is no joy to us to bring accusations; it is no pleasure to our heart to seem to be in antagonism with so many. We are never better pleased than when in fellowship with our brethren we can rejoice in the progress of the gospel.

But no one has set himself to disprove our allegations. One gentleman, of neutral tint, has dared to speak of them as vague, when he knows that nothing could be more definite. But no one has shown that prayer-meetings are valued, and are largely attended; no one has denied that certain ministers frequent the-atres; no one has claimed that the Broad School newspapers have respected a single truth of revelation; and no one has borne witness to the sound doctrine of our entire ministry. Now we submit that these are the main points at issue: at least, these are the only things we contend about. Differences of judgment upon minor matters, and varieties of mode in action, are not now under question; but matters vital to religion. Others may trifle about such things; we cannot, and dare not.

Instead of dealing with these weighty things, our opponents have set to work to make sneering allusions to our sickness. All the solemn things we have written are the suggestions of our pain, and we are advised to take a long rest. With pretended compassion, but with real insolence, they would detract from the truth by pointing to the lameness of its witness. Upon this trifling we have this much to say:—In the first place, our article was written when we were in vigorous health, and it was in print before any sign of an approaching attack was discoverable. In the second place, if we were in a debate with Christians we should feel that, however short they might run of arguments, they would not resort to personalities; least of all, to those personalities which make a painful malady their target. Incidentally, this breach of Christian courtesy goes to show that the new theology is introducing, not only a new code of morals, but a new tone and spirit. It would seem to be taken for granted, that if men are such fools as to adhere to an old-fashioned faith, of course they must be idiots, and they deserve to be treated with that contemptuous pity which is the quintessence of hate. If you can find out that they are sufferers, impute their faith to their disease, and pretend that their earnestness is nothing but petulance arising from their pain. But enough of this: we are so little embittered in spirit by our pangs that we can laugh at the arrows aimed at our weaker member. Do our critics think that, like Achilles, our vulnerable point lies, not in our head, but in our heel?

We are grateful to the editor of Word and Work for speaking out so plainly. He says:—

"In *The Sword and the Trowel* for the present month Mr. Spurgeon gives no uncertain sound concerning departures from the faith. His exposure of the dishonesty which, under the cover of orthodoxy, assails the very foundations of faith is opportune in the interests of truth. No doubt, like a faithful prophet in like evil times, he will be called a 'troubler of Israel,' and already we have noticed he has been spoken of as a pessimist; but any such attempts to lessen the weight of his testimony are only certain to make it more effective. When a strong sense of duty prompts public speech it will be no easy task to silence it.

"The preachers of false doctrine dislike nothing more than the premature detection of their doings. Only give them time enough to prepare men's minds for the reception of the 'new views,' and they are confident of success. They have had too much time already, and any who refuse to speak out now must be held to be 'partakers of their evil deeds.' As Mr. Spurgeon says, 'A little plain-speaking would do a world of good just now. These gentlemen desire to be let alone. They want no noise raised. Of course thieves hate watch-dogs, and love darkness. It is time that somebody should spring his rattle, and call attention to the way in which God is being robbed of his glory and man of his hope.'

"Only those who have given some attention to the progress of error during recent years can form any just idea of the rapid strides with which it is now advancing. Under the plea of liberalism, unscriptural doctrines are allowed to pass current in sermons and periodicals, which, only a few years ago, would have been faithfully resisted unto the death. When anyone even mildly protests, preachers and journalists are almost unanimous in drowning the feeble testimony either by sneers or shouts. Throughout the wide realm of literature there seems to be a conspiracy to hate and hunt down every Scriptural truth. Let any man, especially if he belongs to an evangelical church, denounce or deny any part of the creed he has solemnly vowed to defend, and at once his fortune is made. The press makes the world ring with his fame, and even defends the dishonesty which clings to a stipend forfeited by the violation of his vow. It is far otherwise with the defender of the faith. He is mocked, insulted, and laughed to scorn. The spirit of the age is against him. So in greater or lesser measure it has always been. But when he remembers who is the prince of this world and the ruler of the age, he may be well content to possess his soul in patience."

This witness is true.

Let no man dream that a sudden crotchet has entered our head, and that we have written in hot haste: we have waited long, perhaps too long, and have been slow to speak. Neither let any one suppose that we build up our statements upon a few isolated facts, and bring to the front certain regrettable incidents which might as well have been forgotten. He who knows all things can alone reveal the wretched facts which have come under our notice. Their memory will, we trust, die and be buried with the man who has borne their burden, and held his peace because he had no wish to create disunion. Resolved to respect the claims both of truth and love, we have pursued an anxious pathway. To protest when nothing could come of it but anger, has seemed senseless; to assail evil and crush a vast amount of good in the process, has appeared to be injurious. If all knew all, our reticence would be wondered at and we are not sure that it would be approved. Whether approved or not, we have had no motive but the general progress of the cause of truth, and the glory of God.

Had there been a right spirit in those who resent our warning, they would either have disproved our charge, or else they would have lamented its truthfulness, and have set to work to correct the evil which we lamented. Alas, the levity which plays ducks and drakes with doctrines, makes game of all earnestness, and finds sport in Christian decision! Yet, surely there is a remnant of faithful ones, and these will be stirred to action, and will cry mightily unto God that the plague may be stayed. The gospel is too precious for us to be indifferent to its adulteration. By the love we bear to the Lord Jesus we are bound to defend the treasure with which he has put us in trust.

That ugly word "pessimist" has been hurled at our devoted head. We are denounced as "gloomy." Well, well! The day was when we were censured for being wickedly humorous, and many were the floggings we received for our unseemly jests. Now we are morose and bitter. So the world's opinion changes. A half-a-farthing would be an extravagant price to pay for the verdict one way or another. In truth, we are quite able to take an *optimist* view of things. (Is that the correct word, Sir Critic?) We are glad to admit that there is much of Christian zeal, self-sacrifice, and holy perseverance in the world. Possibly there is more than ever. Did we ever say otherwise? We rejoice in the thousands of gracious, holy, large-hearted men around us. Who dares to say we do not? We see much that is hopeful and delightful in many quarters. Is this at all to the point? May there not be much that is beautiful and healthful in a countenance where yet there may be the symptoms of a foul disease? The church is large, and while one end of her field may rejoice us with golden grain, another part of it may be full of thorns and briers. It often happens that causes of sorrow may be increased at the very same moment when occasions of joy are most numerous. We judge that it is so just now. The cause of God goes on in spite of foes, and his truth is sure to conquer in the long run, however influential its opposers. No, no, we are by no means despondent for the Lord's kingdom. That would be a dishonour to his eternal power and Godhead. Our amiable critics may possibly be pleased to know that they will not find us bathing in vinegar, nor covering our swollen foot with wormwood, nor even drinking quinine with our vegetables; but they will find us rejoicing in the Lord, and buckling on our harness for the war with as firm a confidence as if all men were on our side. Bad as things are from one point of view, there is a bright side to affairs: the Lord has yet his men in reserve who have not bowed the knee to Baal.

We have said, with deep grief that we should have had to say it, that many ministers have departed from the faith; and this was no unkind suspicion on our part, but a matter of fact, ascertained in many ways, and made most sadly sure. We trust that the Baptists are by no means so far gone as the Independents: indeed, we feel sure that they are not. Still, we do not say this in order to throw stones at others. A well-known Congregational minister, who is preparing a book upon this painful subject, writes us—"I have not a large acquaintance with the state of opinion in your denomination. I groan over my own. There are many faithful to Christ, and to the souls of men; but, alas! it seems to me that many have no kind of gospel to preach, and the people are willing that it should be so. Some of our colleges are poisoning the churches at the fountains. I very much fear that an unconverted ministry is multiplying." To the same import is a letter from another brother of the same denomination, who says—"I cannot agree with *The British Weekly*, that you take an 'extremely pessimistic' view of the evil. On the contrary, I am disposed to think that your conviction is faint compared with what the reality would warrant. —College, for example, continues to pour forth men to take charge of our churches who do not believe, in any proper sense, in the inspiration of the Scriptures, who deny the vicarious sacrifice on the cross, and hold that, if sinners are not saved on this side the grave, they may, can, or must be on the other. And the worst of it is, the people love it." We could multiply this painful evidence, but there is no need, since the charge is not denied. It is ridiculed; it is treated as a matter of no consequence, but it is not seriously met. Is this what we have come to? Is there no doctrine left which is to be maintained? Is there no revelation? Or is that revelation a nose of wax to be shaped by the finger of fashion? Are the sceptics so much to the fore that no man will open his mouth against them? Are all the orthodox afraid of the ridicule of the "cultured"? We cannot believe it. The private knowledge which we possess will not allow of so unhappy a conclusion; yet Christian people are now so tame that they shrink from expressing themselves. The house is being robbed, its very walls are being digged down, but the good people who are in bed are too fond of the warmth, and too much afraid of getting broken heads, to go downstairs and meet the burglars; they are even half vexed that a certain noisy fellow will spring his rattle, or cry, "Thieves!"

That the evil leaven is working in the churches as well as among the ministers, is also sadly certain. A heterodox party exists in many congregations, and those who compose it are causing trouble to the faithful, and sadly influencing the more timid towards a vacillating policy. An earnest preacher, who is only one of a class, says: "The old truths are unpopular here. I am told that I have preached the doctrines of grace to my cost—that is, in a pecuniary aspect; and I know that it is so. I cannot find anything to rest upon in the modern theories, but this places me in antagonism to the supporters of the chapel. They find fault, not with the style of my preaching, but with the subjects of it." In another place the witness is—"Our minister is an able and gracious man, but there are those in the church who are determined that no one shall remain here unless he is in favour of advanced opinions." Yes, the divergence is every day becoming more manifest. A chasm is opening between the men who believe their Bibles and the men who are prepared for an advance upon Scripture. Inspiration and speculation cannot long abide in peace. Compromise there can be none. We cannot believe in the atonement and deny it; we cannot hold the doctrine of the fall and yet talk of the evolution of spiritual life from human nature; we cannot recognise the punishment of the impenitent and yet indulge the "larger hope." One way or the other we must go. Decision is the virtue of the hour.

Neither when we have chosen our way can we keep company with those who go the other way. There must come with decision for truth a corresponding protest against error. Let those who will keep the narrow way keep it, and suffer for their choice; but to hope to follow the broad road at the same time is absurdity. What communion hath Christ with Belial?

Thus far we come, and pause. Let us, as many as are of one mind, wait upon the Lord to know what Israel ought to do. With steadfast faith let us take our places;

not in anger, not in the spirit of suspicion or division, but in watchfulness and resolve. Let us not pretend to a fellowship which we do not feel, nor hide convictions which are burning in our hearts. The times are perilous, and the responsibility of every individual believer is a burden which he must bear, or prove a traitor. What each man's place and course should be the Lord will make clear unto him.

Appendix H

The Sword and the Trowel
October, 1887

THE CASE PROVED

By C. H. Spurgeon

The controversy which has arisen out of our previous articles is very wide in its range. Different minds will have their own opinions as to the manner in which the combatants have behaved themselves; for our own part we are content to let a thousand personal matters pass by unheeded. What does it matter what sarcasms or pleasantries may have been uttered at our expense? The dust of battle will blow away in due time; for the present the chief concern is to keep the standard in its place, and bear up against the rush of the foe.

Our warning was intended to call attention to an evil which we thought was apparent to all: we never dreamed that "the previous question" would be raised, and that a company of esteemed friends would rush in between the combatants, and declare that there was no cause for war, but that our motto might continue to be "Peace, peace!" Yet such has been the case, and in many quarters, the main question has been, not "How can we remove the evil?" but, "Is there any evil to remove?" No end of letters have been written with this as their theme—"Are the charges *made by Mr. Spurgeon at all true*?" Setting aside the question of our own veracity, we could have no objection to the most searching discussion of the matter. By all means let the truth be known.

The Baptist and *The British Weekly,* in the most friendly spirit, have opened their columns, and invited correspondence upon the point in hand. The result has been that varied opinions have been expressed; but among the letters there has been a considerable number which may be roughly summarized as declaring that it would be best to let well alone, and that the writers see little or nothing of departure from the faith among Baptist and Congregational ministers. This is reassuring as far as it goes, but how far does it go? It goes no farther than this—it proves that these worthy men view matters from a standpoint which makes them regard as mere changes of expression novelties which we judge to be fatal errors from the truth; or else they move in a peculiarly favoured circle; or else they are so supremely amiable that they see all things through spectacles of tinted glass. We cannot help it, but in reading these carefully-prepared epistles, there has passed before our mind the vision of the heroic Nelson, with the telescope at his blind eye, and we have heard him say again and again, "I cannot see it." With a brave blindness he refused to see that which might have silenced his guns. Brethren who have been officials of a denomination have a paternal partiality about them which is so natural, and so sacred, that we have not the heart to censure it. Above all things, these prudent brethren feel bound to preserve the prestige of "the body," and the peace of the committee. Our Unions, Boards, and Associations are so justly dear to the fathers, that quite unconsciously and innocently, they grow oblivious of evils which, to the unofficial mind, are as manifest as the sun in the heavens. This could not induce our honoured brethren to be untruthful; but it does influence them in their judgment, and still more in the expression of that judgment. With one or two exceptions in the letters now before us, there are evidences of a careful balancing of sentences, and a guardedness of statement, which enable us to read a good deal between the lines.

If we were not extremely anxious to avoid personalities, we could point to other utterances of some of these esteemed writers which, if they did not contradict what they have now written, would be such a supplement to it that their entire mind would be better known. To break the seal of confidential correspondence, or to reveal private conversations, would not occur to us; but we feel compelled to say that, in one or two cases, the writers have not put in print what we have personally gathered from them on other occasions. Their evident desire to allay the apprehensions of others may have helped them to forget their own fears. We say no more.

Had there been no other letters but those of this class, we should have hoped that perhaps the men of the new theology were few and feeble. Let it be noted that we have never made an estimate of their number or strength: we have said "many," and after reading the consoling letters of our optimistic brethren we try to hope that possibly they may not be so many as we feared. We should be rejoiced to believe that there were none at all, but our wish cannot create a fact. There is little in the letters which can affect our declarations, even if we read them in their most unqualified sense, and accept them as true. If twenty persons did *not* see a certain fact, their *not* seeing cannot alter the conviction of a man in his senses who has seen it, has seen it for years, and is seeing it now. The witness rubs his eyes to see whether he is awake; and then, bewildered as he may be for a moment that so many good people are contradicting him, he still believes the evidence of his own senses in the teeth of them all. I believe in the conscientiousness of the divines and doctors of divinity who tell us that all is well, and I cannot but congratulate them upon their ability to be so serenely thankful for small mercies.

But over against the bearers of cheering news we have to set the far more numerous testimonies of those to whom things wear no such roseate hue. What we have said already is true, but it is a meagre and feeble statement of the actual case, if we judge by the reports of our correspondents. We have been likened by one of our opponents to the boy in the fable who cried, "Wolf!" The parallel only fails in the all-important point that he cried "Wolf!" when there was none, and we are crying "Wolf!" when packs of them are howling so loudly that it would be superfluous for us to shout at all if a wretched indifferentism had not brought a deep slumber upon those who ought to guard the flocks. The evidence is to our mind so overwhelming that we thought that our statements only gave voice to a matter of common notoriety. Either we are dreaming, or our brethren are; let the godly judge who it is that is asleep. We consider that what we have written in former papers is quite sufficient to justify our earnest endeavour to arouse the churches; but as more proof is demanded we will give it. Our difficulty is to make a selection out of the mass of material before us, and we will not burden our readers with more than may suffice.

In the month of July last the secretaries of the Evangelical Alliance issued a circular, from which we quote a paragraph:—

"It is only too evident to all who are jealous for God and his truth, that on one side there is a perilous growth of superstition and sacerdotalism, and on the other, of unbelief and indifference to vital religion. The substitutionary sacrifice of our blessed Lord and Saviour is lightly esteemed, and even repudiated, by some prominent teachers; the future destiny of the sinner has become, in consequence, a vain speculation in the thoughts of many. The plenary inspiration of the Holy Scriptures, the personality of the Holy Ghost, and his presence and power in the church of God, with other verities of the faith of Christ, are qualified or explained away in many instances. The results of this erroneous teaching and perversion of the gospel are painfully apparent; worldliness, sensuality, and luxury, with the desecration of the Lord's day, abound, and Christian liberty has become license in the walk and conversation of many professed disciples of Christ."

This circular we had not seen or heard of when our first "Down-grade" article appeared in August. We had had no communication, directly or indirectly, with the Alliance. This Association has a Council, by no means fanatical or precipitate, and we are prepared to say, with no disrespect to the happy brethren who judge everything to be so eminently satisfactory, that we think as much of the judgment of this Council as we do of theirs. Possibly we now think far more of that opinion, since we have seen extracts from letters of brethren of all denominations, sent to the Alliance, in which they cry "Wolf!" in tones as earnest as our own.

There is no use in mincing matters: there are thousands of us in all denominations who believe that many ministers have seriously departed from the truths of the gospel, and that a sad decline of spiritual life is manifest in many churches. Many a time have others said the same things which we have now said, and small notice has been taken of their protests, only this day we have received by post the Report of the Gloucestershire and Herefordshire Association of Baptist Churches, issued in June last. It contains an admirable paper by its President, of which the keynote will be found in the following sentences:—

"We live in perilous times: we are passing through a most eventful period; the Christian world is convulsed; there is a mighty upheaval of the old foundations of faith; a great overhauling of old teaching. The Bible is made to speak to-day in a language which to our fathers would be an unknown tongue. Gospel teachings, the proclamation of which made men fear to sin, and dread the thought of eternity, are being shelved. Calvary is being robbed of its glory, sin of its horror, and we are said to be evolving into a reign of vigorous and blessed sentimentality, in which heaven and earth, God and man are to become a heap of sensational emotions; but in the process of evolution is not the power of the gospel weakened? Are not our chapels emptying? Is there not growing up among men a greater influence to the claims of Christ? Are not the theories of evolution retrogressive in their effect upon the age? Where is the fiery zeal for the salvation of men which marked the Nonconformity of the past? Where is the noble enthusiasm that made heroes and martyrs for the truth? Where is the force which carried Nonconformity forward like a mighty avalanche? Alas! where?"

Dr. David Brown, Principal of the Free Church College, Aberdeen, in a valuable paper upon Scepticism in Ministers, which will be found in *The Christian Age* of Sept. 14th, says:—

"This is a very covert form of scepticism, which is more to be feared than all other forms combined; I mean the scepticism of ministers of the gospel—of those who profess to hold, and are expected to preach, the faith of all orthodox Christendom, and, as the basis of this faith, the authority of Scripture; yet neither hold nor teach that faith, but do their best to undermine the sacred records of it. Now, what is the root of this kind of scepticism? I answer, just the same as of the more sweeping and naked forms of it, the desire to *naturalize*, as far as possible, everything in religion."

"The one thing common to them all is the studious avoidance of all those sharp features of the gospel which are repulsive to the natural man—which *'are hid from the wise and prudent, and are revealed only to babes.'* The divinity of Christ is recognized indeed; but it is the loftiness of his human character, the sublimity of his teaching, and the unparalleled example of self-sacrifice which his death exhibited that they dwell on. The *Atonement* is not in so many words denied; but his sufferings are not held forth in their vicarious and expiatory character. Christ, according to their teaching, was in no sense our Substitute, and in justification the righteousness of the glorious Surety is not imputed to the guilty believer. It is not often that this is nakedly expressed. But some are becoming bold enough to speak it out."

"I should not have said so much in this strain were it not that all our churches are honeycombed with this mischievous tendency to minimize all those features of the gospel which the natural man cannot receive. And no wonder, for their object seems to be to attract the natural mind. Wherever this is the case, the spirituality of the pulpit is done away, and the Spirit himself is not there. Conversion of souls is rarely heard of there, if even it is expected, and those who come for the children's bread get only a stone—beautiful it may be, and sparkling; but stones cannot be digested."

We have occupied no time in selecting these three testimonies, neither are they more remarkable than a host of others; but they suffice to show that it is not a solitary dyspeptic who alone judges that there is much evil occurrent.

The most conclusive evidence that we are correct in our statement, that "the new theology" is rampant among us, is supplied by *The Christian World*. To this paper is largely due the prevalence of the mischief; and it by no means hides its hand. Whoever else may hesitate, we have in this paper plain and bold avowals of its faith, or want of faith. Its articles and the letters which it has inserted prove our position up to the hilt; nay, more, they lead us into inner "chambers of imagery" into which little light has as yet been admitted. What is meant by the allusion to the doctrine of the Trinity in the extract which is now before us? We forbear further comment, the paragraph speaks very plainly for itself:—

"We are now at the parting of the ways, and the younger ministers especially must decide whether or not they will embrace and undisguisedly proclaim that 'modern thought' which in Mr. Spurgeon's eyes is a 'deadly cobra,' while in ours it is the glory of the century. It discards many of the doctrines dear to Mr. Spurgeon and his school, not only as untrue and unscriptural, but as in the strictest sense immoral; for it cannot recognize the moral possibility of imputing either guilt or goodness, or the justice of inflicting everlasting punishment for temporary sin. It is not so irrational as to pin its faith to verbal inspiration, or so idolatrous as to make its acceptance of a true Trinity of divine manifestation cover polytheism."

Nothing can be required more definite than this; and if there had been any such need, the letters which have been inserted in the same paper would have super-abundantly supplied it. As several of these are from Baptist ministers, and are an ingenuous avowal of the most thorough-going advance from the things which have been assuredly believed among us, we are led to ask the practical question: *Are brethren who remain orthodox prepared to endorse such sentiments by remaining in union with those who hold and teach them?* These gentlemen have full liberty to think as they like; but, on the other hand, those who love the old gospel have equally the liberty to dissociate themselves from them, and that liberty also involves a responsibility from which there is no escaping. If we do not believe in Universalism, or in Purgatory, and if we do believe in the inspiration of Scripture, the Fall, and the great sacrifice of Christ for sin, it behoves us to see that we do not become accomplices with those who teach another gospel, and as it would seem from one writer, have avowedly another God.

A friendly critic advised us at the first to mention the names of those who had quitted the old faith; but, if we had done so, he would have been among the first to lament the introduction of personalities. At the same time, there can be no objection to a gentleman's coming forward, and glorying in his "modern thought": it spares others the trouble of judging his position, and it is an exhibition of manliness which others might copy to advantage. Those who have read the statements of the advanced school, and still think that from the orthodox point of view there is no cause for alarm, must surely be a very sanguine temperament, or resolutely blind.

Our lament was not, however, confined to vital doctrines; we mentioned a decline of spiritual life, and the growth of worldliness, and gave as two outward signs thereof the falling-off in prayer-meetings, and ministers attending the theatre. The first has been pooh-poohed as a mere trifle. *The Nonconformist*, which is a fit companion for *The Christian World*, dismisses the subject in the following sentence: "If the conventional prayer-meetings are not largely attended, why should the Christian community be judged by its greater or less use of one particular religious expedient?" What would James and Jay have said of this dismissal of "conventional prayer-meetings," whatever that may mean? At any rate, we are not yet alone in the opinion that our meetings for prayer are very excellent thermometers of the spiritual condition of our people. God save us from the spirit which regards gathering together for prayer as "a religious expedient"! This one paragraph is sorrowfully sufficient to justify much more than we have written.

The same newspaper thus deals with our mention of theatre-going preachers. Let the reader note what a fine mouthful of words it is, and how unwittingly it admits, with a guarded commendation, that which we remarked upon with censure:—

"As for theatres, while we should be much surprised to learn that many ministers of the gospel take a view of life which would permit them to spend much time there, yet, remembering that men of unquestionable piety do find recreation for themselves and their families in the drama, we are not content to see a great branch of art placed under a ban, as if it were no more than an agency of evil."

Let it never be forgotten that even irreligious men, who themselves enjoy the amusements of the theatre, lose all respect for ministers when they see them in the play-house. Their common sense tells them that men of such an order are unfit to be their guides in spiritual things. But we will not debate the point: the fact that it is debated is to us sufficient evidence that spiritual religion is at a low ebb in such quarters.

Very unwillingly have we fulfilled our unhappy task of justifying a warning which we felt bound to utter; we deplore the necessity of doing so; but if we have not in this paper given overwhelming evidence, it is from want of space, and want of will, and not from want of power. Those who have made up their minds to ignore the gravity of the crisis, would not be aroused from their composure though we told our tale in miles of mournful detail.

It only remains to remark that brethren who are afraid that great discouragement will arise out of our statements have our hearty sympathy so far as there is cause for such discouragement. Our heart would rejoice indeed if we could describe our Nonconformity in a very different manner, and assure our friends that we were never in a sounder or more hopeful condition. But encouragement founded upon fiction would lead to false hopes, and to ultimate dismay. Confidence in our principles is what is most to be relied on, next to confidence in God. Brave men will hold to a right cause none the less tenaciously because for a season it is under a cloud. Increased difficulty only brings out increased faith, more fervent prayer, and greater zeal. The weakest of minds are those which go forward because they are borne along by the throng; the truly strong are accustomed to stand alone, and are not cast down if they find themselves in a minority. Let no man's heart fail him because of the Philistine. This new enemy is doomed to die like those who have gone before him; only let him not be mistaken for a friend.

Deeply do we agree with the call of the more devout among the letter-writers for a more determined effort to spread the gospel. Wherever more can be done, let it be done at once, in dependence upon the Spirit of God. But it is idle to go down to the battle with enemies in the camp. With what weapons are we to go forth? If those which we have proved "mighty through God to the pulling down of strong-holds" are taken from us, what are we to do? How can those evangelize who have no evangel? What fruit but evil can come of "the new theology"? Let us know where we are. In the meantime, those of us who raise these questions are not among the idlers, nor are we a whit behind the very chief of those who seek to win souls.

Some words have been used which call the writer a Pope, and speak of this enquiry as an Inquisition. Nothing can be more silly. Is it come to this, that if we use our freedom to speak our mind we must needs be charged with arrogance? Is decision the same thing as Popery? It is playing with edged tools when the advanced men introduce that word, for we would remind them that there is another phase of Popery of which a portion of them have furnished us grievous examples. To hide your beliefs, to bring out your opinions cautiously, to use expressions in other senses than those in which they are usually understood, to "show," as *The Christian World* so honestly puts it, "a good deal of trimming, and a balancing of opposite opinions in a way that is confusing and unsatisfactory to the hearer," is a meaner sort of Popery than even the arrogance which is so graciously imputed to *us*. It is, however, very suggestive that the letting in of light upon men should be to them a torment equal to an Inquisition, and that open discussion should so spoil their schemes that they regard it as a torture comparable to the rack and the stake. What other harm have we done them? We would not touch a hair of their heads, or deprive them of an inch of liberty. Let them speak, that we may know them; but let them not deny us the same freedom; neither let them denounce *us* for defending what they are so eager to assail.

What action is to be taken we leave to those who can more plainly than we do what Israel ought to do. One thing is clear to us: we cannot be expected to meet in any Union which comprehends those whose teaching is upon fundamental points exactly the reverse of that which we hold dear. Those who *can* do so will, no doubt, have weighty reasons with which to justify their action, and we will not sit in judgment upon those reasons: they may judge that a minority should not drive them out. To us it appears that there are many things upon which compromise is possible, but there are others in which it would be an act of treason to pretend to fellowship. With deep regret we abstain from assembling with those whom we dearly love and heartily respect, since it would involve us in a confederacy with those with whom we can have no communion in the Lord. Garibaldi complained that, by the cession of Nice to France, he had been made a foreigner in his native land; and our heart is burdened with a like sorrow; but those who banish us may yet be of another mind, and enable us to return.

Appendix I

CHRONOLOGICAL SUMMARY OF SPURGEON'S LIFE

Charles Haddon Spurgeon, born at Kelvedon, Essex, June 19, 1834, lived with his grandparents in Stambourne during his early years.

Parents moved to Colchester in 1835.

Moved back to parents' in Colchester in 1840.

Attends St. Augustine's College, Maidstone, 1848.

Became pupil - assistant usher at Newmarket, Cambridge, August 17, 1849.

Converted at Colchester, in a Primitive Methodist Church January, 1850.

Applied for Church membership at Newmarket, April 4, 1850.

Baptized in the river Lark at Isleham May 3, 1850, by Baptist minister, Reverend Catlow.

Moved from Newmarket to Cambridge, attends Mr. Leeding's school, August, 1850.

First sermon in Teversham, August, 1850.

Joined the St. Andrew's Street Baptist Church, October 3, 1850.

Became Minister of the Waterbeach Baptist Chapel, 1851.

First published work, No. 1 of *Waterbeach Tracts*, issued 1853.

Preached at New Park Street Chapel, London, for the first time, December, 1853.

Accepted Pastorate of New Park Street Chapel, April, 1854.

First sermon in the series: "New Park Street Pulpit," published by Passmore and Alabaster January, 1855.

Earliest attack in the Press appears in *The Earthen Vessel*, January, 1855. A continuous barrage of criticisms went on for years.

First preached at Exeter Hall on the Strand, a secular setting, February, 1855.

Mr. T. W. Medhurst became C. H. Spurgeon's first ministerial student, July, 1855. This ultimately gave birth to the Pastors' College.

Visited Scotland for the first of several times, July, 1855.

Married Miss Susannah Thompson, January 8, 1856.

Metropolitan Tabernacle Building Committee appointed to build the Tabernacle, June, 1856.

Twin sons Thomas and Charles born, September 20, 1856. Both became pastors.

Surrey Gardens Music Hall Disaster where seven were killed, October 19, 1856.

Sunday Services again started at the Music Hall, in the morning, November 23, 1856.

A second student enters the Pastors' College, actually founding the College in 1857.

Preached to 23,654 persons at the Crystal Palace on Fast Day, over the Indian Rebellion, October 7, 1857.

First visit to Ireland, August, 1858.

Foundation Stone of the Metropolitan Tabernacle laid, August 16, 1859.

Last service at the Surrey Gardens Music Hall, December 11, 1859.

Visited Paris and eulogized in the Roman Catholic Press of that city, February, 1860.

Preached in Calvin's gown and pulpit at Geneva, 1860, much to his delight.

Metropolitan Tabernacle opened with many services, March 18, 1861.

First communion service held at the Tabernacle, April 7, 1861.

Delivery of the famous "Gorilla" Lecture, against evolution, October, 1861.

The famous "Baptismal Regeneration" sermon that sparked the controversy preached, June 5, 1862.

Metropolitan Tabernacle Colportage Association founded, 1866.

Sunday services, each attended by over 20,000 persons, held at the Agricultural Hall, Islington, during the renovation of the Metropolitan Tabernacle, March 24 to April 21, 1867.

Stockwell Orphanage (Boys' side) founded, 1867.

The Rev. James Spurgeon appointed assistant Pastor and business administrator at the Tabernacle, January 6, 1868. He also pastored the Baptist Church in Croydon.

Foundation Stone of the Pastors' College Building laid, October 14, 1873.

Mrs. Spurgeon's Book Fund commenced, 1875.

Girls' section of the Stockwell Orphanage founded, 1879.

Presentation of the Pastoral "Silver Wedding" gift of 6,476 pounds 9 shillings, May 20, 1879.

The preacher removed from his home in Clapham to "Westwood," Norwood, 1880.

Jubilee Celebrations and presentation of testimonial (4,500 pounds), June 18 and 19, 1884.

First "Down Grade" paper published in *The Sword and the Trowel*, August, 1887. It ignited the largest of his controversies.

Withdrawal of pastor and church from the Baptist Union, October, 1887 over the "Down Grade."

Last sermon preached at the Metropolitan Tabernacle, June 7, 1891.

Traveled to Mentone with his wife for the last time, October 26, 1891.

Took to his sick bed, January 20, 1892.

Passed on to his reward, January 31, 1892.

Interred at Norwood Cemetery, February 11, 1892.

ENDNOTES

Chapter One

1. *C. H. Spurgeon's Autobiography: Compiled from His Diary, Letters, and Records*, by His Wife and His Private Secretary, Susannah Spurgeon and Joseph Harrald, 4 Volumes, (London: Passmore and Alabaster, Paternosta Bulldongs, E.C., 1897), Vol. I, p. 68.
2. Ibid., pp. 104-108.
3. The details and the historical controversy that surround Spurgeon's conversion will be discussed fully in Chapter Three.
4. Henry Davenport Northrop, *Life and Works of Rev. Charles H. Spurgeon* (Memorial Publishing Co., 1892), pp. iii, iv, 17.
5. Helmut Thielicke, ed., *Encounter With Spurgeon*, trans. John Doberstein (Philadelphia: Fortress Press, 1963), p. 45.
6. *Charles H. Spurgeon, Great Pulpit Masters*, Vol. 2 (New York: Fleming H. Revell Co., 1949), p. 10.
7. Clyde E. Fant, Jr., William M. Pinson, Jr., *20 Centuries of Great Preaching: An Encyclopedia of Preaching*, 13 Volumes, (Waco, Texas: Word Book Publishers, 1971), Vol. 6, p. 12.
8. A Spurgeon "Memorial Address" delivered at Nashville, Tennessee on the first Sunday in February, 1892.
9. Charles H. Spurgeon, *The Metropolitan Tabernacle Pulpit* (London: Passmore and Alabaster, 1864), Vol. 10, p. 614.
10. Ibid., p. 337.
11. Ibid., Vol. 26 (1880), p. 391.
12. Spurgeon's personal library is now housed in William Jewell College in Liberty, Missouri.
13. William Williams, *Personal Reminiscences of Charles Haddon Spurgeon* (London: Religious Tract Society, n.d.), p. 17.
14. Helmut Thielicke, ed., *Encounter with Spurgeon*, p. 24.
15. Ibid., p. 25.
16. The form is housed in the Archives at Spurgeon's College, London.
17. Archives, Spurgeon's College, London.
18. C. H. Spurgeon, *C. H. Spurgeon Anecdotes* (London: Passmore and Alabaster, 1900), p. 75.
19. *Mission to the World*, Ed. Paul Beasley-Murray (London, Baptist Historical Society, 1991) p. 20.

20. Ibid., p. 20.
21. Ibid., p. 20.
22. Ibid., p. 24.
23. Williams, *Personal Reminiscences of Charles Haddon Spurgeon*, p. 166.
24. Ibid., p. 166.
25. Ibid., p. 165.
26. Spurgeon, *The Metropolitan Tabernacle Pulpit*, Vol. 58, p. 521.

Chapter Two
  1. George C. Lorimer, *A Monograph: Charles Haddon Spurgeon, The Puritan Preacher in the Nineteenth Century* (Boston, J.H. Earle, 1892), p. 204.
  2. Horton Davies, "Expository Preaching: Charles Haddon Spurgeon," *Foundations*, 1963 (see pp. 14-25).
  3. Frederic H. Young, Jr., Henry L. Snyder, A. E. Rutan, *The English Heritage*, Second Edition (Arlington Heights, Illinois, Forum Press, Inc., 1978, 1988), p. 292.
  4. Ibid.
  5. Kenneth Scott Latourette, *Christianity in a Revolutionary Age: A History of Christianity in the Nineteenth and Twentieth Centuries. Vol. II* (New York: Harper and Brothers, Publisher, 1959).
  6. Ibid., p. 1164.
  7. Young, Snyder, and Rutan, *The English Heritage*, p. 311.
  8. H. C. G. Matthew, "The Liberal Age (1851-1914)," *The Oxford Illustrated History of Britain*, ed. Kenneth O. Morgan (Oxford: Oxford University Press, 1984), p. 496.
  9. Gordon A. Craig, *Europe, 1815-1914*, 3rd ed., (Hinsdale, Illinois: Dryden Press, 1972), p. 111.
 10. Winston S. Churchill, *The Great Democracies of a History of the English-Speaking Peoples*, Vol. 3 (New York: Dodd, Mead and Co. 1958), pp. 61-90.
 11. Charles H. Spurgeon, *All-Round Ministry: Addresses to Ministers and Students*. 1900. Reprint (Edinburgh: Banner of Truth, 1960), p. 132.
 12. "The Rev. Charles H. Spurgeon, at Waterlooville," *The Evening News*, 24 September 1885.
 13. R. K. A. Ensor, *England, 1870-1914* (London: Oxford University Press, 1936), p. 137.
 14. Owen Chadwick, *The Victorian Church*, 2 volumes, (New York: Oxford University Press, 1966), Vol. I, p. 5.
 15. D. C. Somervell, *English Thought in the Nineteenth Century* (New York: Longmans, Greer and Co., 1929), p. 101.
 16. William Gladstone from *No Greater Love* (Wheaton: Bibles for the World, 1967), see back cover.
 17. Albert R. Meredith, "The Social and Political Views of Charles Haddon Spurgeon, 1834-1892," (unpublished Ph.D. dissertation, Michigan State University, 1973).
 18. Rather strangely, at least from a spiritual perspective, the remains of Darwin are interred in Westminster Abbey in London.
 19. Chadwick, *The Victorian Church*, Vol I., p.1.
 20. E. T. Raymond, *Portraits of the Nineties* (London: Unwin, 1921), p. 262.
 21. Charles H. Spurgeon, *The Soul-Winner: How to Lead Sinners to the Saviour*

(New York: Fleming H. Revell, 1895; reprint, with Foreword by Helmut Thielicke, Grand Rapids: Eerdmans, 1963), p. 235.

22. M. A. Crowther, *Church Embattled: Religious Controversy in Mid-Victorian England* (Devon, England: David and Charles Ltd., 1970), p. 32.

23. Thomas Jerrell Sutton, "A Comparison Between the Downgrade Controversy and Tensions Over Biblical Inerrancy in the Southern Baptist Convention," (unpublished Ph.D. dissertation, Southwestern Baptist Theological Seminary, Fort Worth, Texas, 1982), p. 23.

24. Ernest F. Stoeffler, *The Rise of Evangelical Pietism* (Luden, Netherlands: E. J. Brill, 1971), p. 36.

25. Ibid., p. 51.

26. Ibid., p. 68.

27. Paulus Scharpff, *The History of Evangelism* (Grand Rapids, Michigan: William B. Eerdmans Publishing Company, 1966), p. 34.

28. Stoeffler, *The Rise of Evangelical Pietism*, p. 228.

29. Ibid., p. 228.

30. Barend Klaas Kuiper, *The Church in History* (Grand Rapids, Michigan: William B. Eerdmans Publishing Company, 1951), p. 345.

31. Scharpff, *The History of Evangelism*, p. 42.

32. Ibid., p. 44-54.

33. Mendell Taylor, *Exploring Evangelism* (Kansas City, Missouri: Beacon Hill Press, 1964), p. 252.

34. The famous statue of *Eros* in the center of Picadilly Circus in London was raised in honor of Lord Shaftesbury's social work.

35. This church was a "seed bed" to the Particular Baptist movement, as the first *full* Particular church did not develop until some years later.

36. Ernest A. Payne, *The Baptist Union, A Short History* (London: The Carey Kingsgate Press, Ltd., 1959), p. 2.

37. Ibid, p. 21.

38. Ibid, p. 3.

39. Robert Torbet, *Ecumenism . . . Free Church Dilemma* (Valley Forge: Judson Press, 1962), p. 39.

40. Gerald Borchert, "The Nature of the Church: A Baptist Perspective," unpublished paper given to the Baptist World Alliance, Montreal, Canada, July 1991.

Chapter Three

1. *Autobiography*, Vol. I, p. 8.

2. W. Y. Fullerton, *C. H. Spurgeon: A Biography* (London: Williams and Norgate, 1920) p. 2.

3. Ibid., p. 3. (Spergin was how the family name was spelled at that time.)

4. Ibid.

5. Ibid., p. 4.

6. G. Holden Pike, *The Life and Work of Charles Haddon Spurgeon*, 6 Volumes, (London, Paris & Melbourne: Cassell & Company, Limited, n.d.), Vol. I, p. 1.

7. Ibid., p. 3.

8. Ibid.

9. Fullerton, *C. H. Spurgeon: A Biography*, p. 4.

10. *Autobiography*, Vol. I, pp. 9-10.

11. Ibid., p. 10.
12. Rev. Richard Briscoe Cook, *The Wit and Wisdom of Rev. Charles H. Spurgeon* (Baltimore, R. H. Woodward and Co., 1892), p. 11.
13. *Autobiography*, Vol. I, *The Early Years: 1834-1859*, Revised edition published in two volumes (Edinburgh: Banner of Truth Trust, 1962). p. v.
14. *Autobiography*, Vol. I, *The Early Years*, p. 2.
15. *Autobiography*, Vol. I, p. 14.
16. Ibid.
17. Ibid.
18. Ibid., p. 15.
19. Northrop, Henry Davenport, *Life and Works of Rev. Charles H. Spurgeon* (Memorial Publishing Co., 1892), p. 19.
20. Richard Ellsworth Day, *The Shadow of the Broad Brim: The Life Story of Charles Haddon Spurgeon, Heir of the Puritans* (Philadelphia: The Judson Press, 1934), p. 21.
21. James J. Ellis, *Charles Haddon Spurgeon* (London: James Nisbet & Company, n.d.), p. 12.
22. Fullerton, *C. H. Spurgeon: A Biography*, p. 6.
23. Cook, *The Wit and Wisdom of Rev. Charles H. Spurgeon*, p. 23.
24. Day, *The Shadow of the Broad Brim*, p. 32.
25. C. H. Spurgeon, *Come Ye Children* (London: Passmore and Alabaster, 1897), p. 99.
26. Charles Ray, *The Life of Charles Haddon Spurgeon* (London: Passmore and Alabaster, 1903), p. 27.
27. Cook, *The Wit and Wisdom of Rev. Charles H. Spurgeon*, p. 27.
28. *Autobiography*, Vol. I, p. 16.
29. Ibid., p. 18.
30. Ibid., pp. 15, 16.
31. *Autobiography*, Vol. I, *The Early Years*, p. 8.
32. The entire story is found in the *Autobiography*, Vol. I, pp. 23-24.
33. Ibid., p. 27.
34. Ibid., p. 28.
35. Ibid., pp. 29-30.
36. Ibid., p. 30.
37. Ibid., p. 31.
38. Ibid.
39. Ibid.
40. Ibid., p. 28.
41. Fullerton, *C. H. Spurgeon: A Biography*, pp. 7-8.
42. Ibid., p. 11.
43. Some writers say it was only a Sunday and Monday that Knill stayed at the Stambourne parsonage—others say it was several days. Spurgeon's own account seems to substantiate a longer stay.
44. *Autobiography*, Vol. I, p. 33.
45. Pike, *The Life of Charles Haddon Spurgeon*, Vol. I, p. 26.
46. *Autobiography*, Vol. I, p. 34.
47. Ibid., p. 34. (Rowland Hill's Chapel was one of the largest Nonconformist churches in England.)
48. Ibid.

49. Ibid.
50. Ibid.
51. Ibid.
52. Ibid., p. 35.
53. Ibid., pp. 39-41.
54. Ibid., p. 45.
55. Russell H. Conwell, *Life of Charles H. Spurgeon: The World's Great Preacher* (Edgewood Publishing Co., 1892) p. 34. Fullerton contends that he was a precocious child. (See Fullerton, *C. H. Spurgeon: A Biography*, p. 10.)
56. Arnold Dallimore, *Spurgeon* (Chicago: Moody Press, 1984), pp. 9-10.
57. G. Holden Pike, *James Archer Spurgeon, D.D., LL.D., Preacher, Philanthropist, and Co-Pastor with C. H. Spurgeon at the Metropolitan Tabernacle* (London: Alexander & Shepheard, 1894), p. 23.
58. Pike, *James Archer Spurgeon*, pp. 20, 23.
59. Fullerton, *C. H. Spurgeon: A Biography*, pp. 13-14.
60. *Autobiography*, Vol. I, pp. 47-48.
61. Ibid., pp. 34-35.
62. Ibid., pp. 48-50.
63. Ibid., p. 53.
64. Fullerton, *C. H. Spurgeon: A Biography*, p. 13.
65. *Autobiography*, Vol. I, p. 53.
66. Ray, *The Life of Charles Haddon Spurgeon*, p. 41.
67. Fullerton, *C. H. Spurgeon: A Biography*, pp. 55-56.
68. *Autobiography*, Vol. I, p. 61.
69. Fullerton, *C. H. Spurgeon: A Biography*, p. 28.
70. Edward R. Norman, *Anti-Catholicism in Victorian England* (London: George Unwin, 1968), p. 52.
71. Patricia Stallings Kruppa, "Charles Haddon Spurgeon, A Preacher's Progress," (unpublished Ph.D. dissertation, Columbia University, 1968), p. 21.
72. *Autobiography*, Vol. I, p. 67.
73. Ibid., p. 68.
74. Ibid., p. 123.
75. Ibid., p. 68.
76. Ibid.
77. Ibid., p. 69.
78. Ibid.
79. Ibid.
80. Ibid., p. 70.
81. Ibid., p. 74.
82. Ibid., p. 73.
83. Ibid., p. 75.
84. Ibid.
85. Spurgeon, *C. H. Spurgeon Anecdotes*, p. 29.
86. *Autobiography*, Vol. I, p. 79.
87. Ibid., p. 77.
88. Day, *The Shadow of the Broad Brim*, p. 52.
89. *Autobiography*, Vol. I, p. 75.
90. Ibid., p. 80.

91. Ibid., p. 78.
92. Ibid., p. 83.
93. Fullerton, *C. H. Spurgeon: A Biography*, p. 22.
94. *Autobiography*, Vol. I, p. 98.
95. Ibid., p. 89-90.
96. Ibid., pp. 91-92.
97. Fullerton, *C. H. Spurgeon: A Biography*, p. 17.
98. Ibid., Vol. I, pp. 87-88.
99. Ibid., p. 97.
100. J. C. Carlile, *C. H. Spurgeon: An Interpretative Biography* (London: Religious Tract Society and Kingsgate Press, 1933), p. 51.

Chapter Four

1. C. H. Spurgeon, *The Saint and His Saviour* (London: Hodder and Stoughton, 1880), pp. 176-179.
2. *Autobiography*, Vol. 1, p. 129.
3. C. H. Spurgeon, *The New Park Street Pulpit, 1855-1860* (London: The Banner of Truth Trust), Vol. 2 (1850), p. 49, also see *Autobiography*, Vol. I, p. 108.
4. Spurgeon, *The Metropolitan Tabernacle Pulpit*, Vol. 50, p. 37.
5. Spurgeon, *The New Park Street Pulpit*, Vol. 1 (1855) p. 310.
6. *Autobiography*, Vol. I, p. 105.
7. Ibid., pp. 105-106.
8. Spurgeon, *The New Park Street Pulpit*, Vol. 1 (1855) p. 310.
9. *Autobiography*, Vol. I, p. 105.
10. Ibid.
11. George John Stevenson, *Sketch of the Life and Ministry of The Rev. C. H. Spurgeon. From Original Documents, . . . And An Outline Of Mr. Spurgeon's Articles Of Faith* (New York: Sheldon, Blakeman & Co., 1857), p. 39.
12. Danzy Sheen, *Pastor C. H. Spurgeon, His Conversion, Career, and Coronation* (London: J. B. Knapp, [1892]), p. 20.
13. Spurgeon, *The New Park Street Pulpit*, Vol. 1 (1855), p. 407.
14. *The Sword and the Trowel*, Vol. 5 (1869), p. 477.
15. Letter, Robert Eaglen to Danzy Sheen, n.d., Spurgeon's College, London.
16. Sheen, *Pastor C. H. Spurgeon*, p. 29.
17. Ibid.
18. Ibid., p. 34.
19. Letter, John Blomfield to Robert Eaglen, 3 November 1868, Archives, Spurgeon's College, London. The office mentioned in this letter, in which both Blomfield and John Spurgeon worked, was that of Charles Parker Jarvis, uncle of C. H. Spurgeon. At the time of Spurgeon's conversion, John Spurgeon was the manager and Blomfield was foreman of the coal yard.
20. Letter, John Blomfield to Danzy Sheen, 4 January 1869, Archives, Spurgeon's College, London. Obviously, the grammar and punctuation of Blomfield's letter are quite poor.
21. Pamphlet entitled "The Conversion of Charles Haddon Spurgeon: New Light on the Preacher of the Sermon."
22. Of course, it could be argued that Spurgeon was merely home for the holidays in December of 1850. Still, that throws all the dating of Spurgeon's life off.

23. Letter, Archives, Regent's Park College, Oxford.
24. Ibid.
25. Eva Hope, *Spurgeon: The People's Preacher* (London and Felling-on-Tyne: The Walter Scott Publishing Co., Ld.), p. 22.
26. *Autobiography*, Vol. I, p. 149.
27. G. Holden Pike, *Charles Haddon Spurgeon*, World's Workers Series (London: Cassell and Co., 1893), p. 20.
28. Timothy McCoy, "The Evangelistic Ministry of C. H. Spurgeon: Implications for a Contemporary Model for Pastoral Evangelism," (unpublished Ph.D. dissertation, Southern Baptist Theological Seminary, Louisville, Kentucky). Much of what is presented here is McCoy's excellent research.
29. Charles Spurgeon, *The Quotable Spurgeon* (Wheaton, Illinois: Harold Shaw Publishers, 1990), p. 12.
30. Ibid., p. 18.
31. Spurgeon, *Autobiography*, Vol. I, p. 158.
32. Ibid.
33. Ibid., pp. 159-160.
34. Ibid., p. 161.
35. Ibid.
36. Ray, *The Life of Charles Haddon Spurgeon*, p. 73.
37. Ibid., pp. 73-74.
38. Day, *The Shadow of the Broad Brim*, p. 65.
39. *Autobiography*, Vol. I, pp. 127-146.
40. Ibid., p. 120.
41. James Douglas, *The Prince of Preachers: A Sketch; A Portraiture; and a Tribute* (London: Morgan and Scott, n.d.), p. 84.
42. Ibid., p. 83.
43. *Autobiography*, Vol. I, p. 122.
44. Ibid.
45. Ibid., pp. 124-125.
46. Ray, *The Life of Charles Haddon Spurgeon*, p. 79.
47. *Autobiography*, Vol. I, pp. 118-119.
48. Ray, *The Life of Charles Haddon Spurgeon*, p. 76.
49. Fullerton, *C. H. Spurgeon: A Biography*, p. 39.
50. Ibid.
51. Archives, Spurgeon's College, London.
52. Fullerton, *C. H. Spurgeon: A Biography*, p. 40.
53. Ibid.
54. Ray, *The Life of Charles Haddon Spurgeon*, p. 72.
55. Church records of St. Andrew's Street Baptist Church, Cambridge.
56. G. Holden Pike says Robert Robinson turned to a liberal (Socinian) theology later in life. But his hymn remains a blessing to many, and Pike's contention is seriously questioned by historians.
57. Fullerton, *C. H. Spurgeon: A Biography*, pp. 44-45.
58. Pike, *The Life and Work of Charles Haddon Spurgeon*, Vol. I, p. 47.
59. Day, *The Shadow of the Broad Brim*, p. 70.
60. Fullerton, *C. H. Spurgeon: A Biography*, p. 45.

61. *The Travelling Companion*, p. 23, (publication information unknown).
62. *Autobiography*, Vol. I, p. 204.
63. Ibid.
64. Ray, *The Life of Charles Haddon Spurgeon*, pp. 95-96.
65. Pike, *The Life and Work of Charles Haddon Spurgeon*, Vol. I, p. 59.
66. Ellis, *Charles Haddon Spurgeon*, p. 38.
67. Spurgeon began preaching at New Park Street Baptist Church in London in January 1854. But he was still "officially" pastor in Waterbeach until May.
68. Archives, Spurgeon's College, London.
69. Day, *The Shadow of the Broad Brim*, p. 71.
70. *Autobiography*, Vol. I, pp. 227-228.
71. Day, *The Shadow of the Broad Brim*, p. 72.
72. Ibid., p. 73.
73. Ibid.
74. Ray, *The Life of Charles Haddon Spurgeon*, p. 92.
75. Fullerton, *C. H. Spurgeon: A Biography*, p. 49.
76. Archives, Spurgeon's College, London.
77. Fullerton, *C. H. Spurgeon: A Biography*, p. 50.
78. Pike, *James Archer Spurgeon*, p. 25.
79. Ellis, *Charles Haddon Spurgeon*, p. 38-39.
80. Fullerton, *C. H. Spurgeon: A Biography*, p. 53.
81. Ibid., pp. 53-54.
82. Day, *The Shadow of the Broad Brim*, p. 84.
83. Ibid., 80-81.
84. Fullerton, *C. H. Spurgeon: A Biography*, p. 55.
85. Day, *The Shadow of the Broad Brim*, p. 80.
86. Dallimore, *Spurgeon*, p. 39.
87. Conwell, *Life of Charles Haddon Spurgeon*, p. 115.

Chapter Five

1. *Autobiography*, Vol. I, p. 272.
2. Fullerton, *C. H. Spurgeon: A Biography*, pp. 77-78.
3. Ibid., p. 78.
4. Ibid., p. 57.
5. *Autobiography*, Vol. I., p. 315
6. Conwell, *Life of Charles H. Spurgeon*, p. 122.
7. Ibid.
8. Ibid., p. 125.
9. *Autobiography*, Vol. I, p. 308.
10. Conwell, *Life of Charles H. Spurgeon*, p. 130.
11. Ibid., p. 135.
12. *Autobiography*, Vol. I, p. 310.
13. Conwell, *Life of Charles H. Spurgeon*, p. 137.
14. *Autobiography*, Vol. I, p. 312-313.
15. Ibid., p. 313.
16. Ibid., p. 317.
17. Ibid.
18. Ibid., p. 318.

19. Ibid.
20. Ibid., p. 319.
21. Ibid., pp. 321-326.
22. Ibid., p. 289.
23. Ellis, *Charles Haddon Spurgeon*, p. 50.
24. Day, *The Shadow of the Broad Brim*, p. 222.
25. Ibid., p. 223
26. *Autobiography*, Vol. I, p. 319.
27. Fullerton, *C. H. Spurgeon: A Biography*, p. 62.
28. C. H. Spurgeon, *Commenting and Commentaries* (London: n.p., n.d.).
29. Archives Regent's Park College, Oxford University, Oxford, England.
30. *Autobiography*, Vol. I, p. 341.
31. Williams, *Personal Reminiscences of Charles Haddon Spurgeon*, p. 159.
32. *Autobiography*, Vol. I, p. 348.
33. Ibid., p. 349.
34. Ibid., pp. 340-341.
35. Ibid., p. 341.
36. Ibid., p. 348.
37. Ibid., p. 344.
38. Ibid.
39. Pike, *The Life and Work of Charles Haddon Spurgeon*, Vol. I, p. 103.
40. G. Holden Pike, *C. H. Spurgeon, Preacher, Author, Philanthropist* (London: Hodder and Stoughton, 1887), p. 60.
41. Fullerton, *C. H. Spurgeon: A Biography*, p. 66.
42. *Autobiography*, Vol. I, pp. 351-352.
43. Ibid., pp. 352-353.
44. Ibid., p. 351.
45. Ibid., p. 350.
46. C. H. Spurgeon, *John Ploughman's Talks* (London: Passmore and Alabaster, 1868), p. 27.
47. Fullerton, *C. H. Spurgeon: A Biography*, pp. 66-67.
48. J. H. Plumb, ed., *Studies in Social History* (London: Thomas Nelson, 1963), p. 223.
49. *Autobiography*, Vol. I., p. 354. Knowles lived until 1862 and saw his prophecy, akin to Knill's, fulfilled. His widow left a legacy to the College and Orphanage.
50. Fullerton, *C. H. Spurgeon: A Biography*, p. 73.
51. Archives, Spurgeon's College, London.
52. *Autobiography*, Vol. I, p. 342.
53. Pike, *The Life and Work of Charles Haddon Spurgeon*, Vol. II, p. 225.
54. *Autobiography*, Vol. I, p. 369.
55. Day, *The Shadow of the Broad Brim*, p. 213.
56. *Autobiography*, Vol. I, p. 355-356.
57. Ibid., pp. 356-357.
58. C. H. Spurgeon, *Only a Prayer Meeting* (London: Passmore and Alabaster, 1901), p. 351.
59. *Vanity Fair*, December 10, 1870.
60. *Autobiography*, Vol. I, p. 275.
61. Fullerton, *C. H. Spurgeon: A Biography*, p. 75.

62. *Autobiography*, Vol. I, p. 340.
63. Ibid., p. 369.
64. Williams, *Personal Reminiscences of Charles Haddon Spurgeon*, p. 204.
65. Ibid., p. 198.
66. Dallimore, *Spurgeon*, p. 49.
67. *The Echo*, February 16, 1889.
68. Pike, *The Life and Work of Charles Haddon Spurgeon*, Vol. I, p. 160.
69. Ibid., 160-161.
70. *The Times*, cited by Eva Hope, *Spurgeon: The People's Preacher* p. 69.
71. Archives, Spurgeon's College, London.
72. Ray, *The Life of Charles Haddon Spurgeon*, p. 160.
73. *Saturday Review*, II (October 25, 1856), pp. 563-564.
74. Kruppa, "Charles Haddon Spurgeon: A Preacher's Progress," p. 104.
75. Anonymous, *The Popularity of the Rev. C. H. Spurgeon* (London: Daniel Oakey, 1858), p. 3.
76. Archives, Spurgeon's College, London.
77. Ibid.
78. Archives, Regent's Park College, Oxford University, Oxford, England.
79. *Autobiography*, Vol. II, pp. 34-35.
80. Archives in Spurgeon's College, London.
81. Edmond Fry, *Life and Labors of the Reverend C. H. Spurgeon* (London: William Arthrop, 1855), p. 311.
82. *Autobiography*, Vol. II, p. 52.
83. Helmut Thielicke, ed., *Encounter with Spurgeon*.
84. Archives, Spurgeon's College, London.
85. *Autobiography*, Vol. II, p. 50.
86. Anonymous, *Mr. Spurgeon's Critics Criticised* (London: W. H. Collingridge, 1857), p. 6.
87. All in Archives at Spurgeon's College, London.
88. *Autobiography*, Vol. II, p. 35.
89. Fullerton, *C. H. Spurgeon: A Biography*, p. 77.
90. Ibid.
91. *Autobiography*, Vol. II, p. 61.
92. William Freeman, *Who Is Spurgeon*, a pamphlet, p. 1.
93. *Autobiography*, Vol. II, p. 44.
94. Ibid., p. 18.
95. Ray, *The Life of Charles Haddon Spurgeon*, p. 178.
96. Fullerton, *C. H. Spurgeon: A Biography*, p. 81.
97. Pike, *The Life and Work of Charles Haddon Spurgeon*, Vol. II, p. 217.
98. Fullerton, *C. H. Spurgeon: A Biography*, p. 82.
99. Pike, *The Life and Work of Charles Haddon Spurgeon*, Vol. II, p. 343.
100. Fullerton, *C. H. Spurgeon: A Biography*, p. 98.
101. *Autobiography*, Vol. II, p. 99.
102. Ibid., p. 52.
103. Fullerton, *C. H. Spurgeon: A Biography*, p. 78.
104. Archives, Spurgeon's College, London.
105. Source unknown. Can be located in Archives, Spurgeon's College, London.
106. Archives, Spurgeon's College, London.

107. *Autobiography*, Vol. II, p. 20.
108. Fullerton, *C. H. Spurgeon: A Biography*, pp. 83-84.
109. Source unknown. Can be located in Archives, Spurgeon's College, London.
110. Ibid.
111. Charles Ray, *Mrs. C. H. Spurgeon* (London: Passmore and Alabaster, 1903), p. 10.
112. Day, *The Shadow of the Broad Brim*, p. 107.
113. Charles Ray, *Mrs. C. H. Spurgeon*, p. 11.
114. Ibid., pp. 11-12.
115. Ibid., p. 16.
116. Ray, *The Life of Charles Haddon Spurgeon*, p. 147.
117. Ray, *Mrs. C. H. Spurgeon*, p. 19.
118. Ibid., pp. 20, 23.
119. Ibid., p. 28.
120. Ray, *Mrs. C. H. Spurgeon*, pp. 29-30.
121. Ibid., p. 32.
122. *Autobiography*, Vol. II, pp. 190-191.
123. Ray, *Mrs. C. H. Spurgeon*, pp. 36-37.
124. Ibid., pp. 36-39.
125. A brass plaque commemorating the Spurgeons' second home is affixed to the front of the house. It was completely renovated in the 1970s and remains a residence to this day.
126. *Autobiography*, Vol. II, pp. 286-287.
127. Ibid., p. 289.
128. Hope, *Spurgeon: The People's Preacher*, pp. 42-43.
129. Ibid., pp. 49-50.
130. Ray, *The Life of Charles Haddon Spurgeon*, p. 138.
131. Ray, p. 202.
132. Williams, *Personal Reminiscences of Charles Haddon Spurgeon*, p. 195.
133. Fullerton, *C. H. Spurgeon: A Biography*, pp. 90-91.
134. Ibid., p. 91.
135. Ray, *The Life of Charles Haddon Spurgeon*, pp. 203-204.
136. Pike, *The Life and Work of Charles Haddon Spurgeon*, Vol. II, p. 240.
137. Fullerton, *C. H. Spurgeon: A Biography*, p. 92.
138. Spurgeon, *The Saint and His Saviour*, pp. 371-373.
139. Pike, *The Life and Work of Charles Haddon Spurgeon*, Vol. II, p. 248.
140. *The British Banner*, October 21, 1856.
141. Ray, *The Life of Charles Haddon Spurgeon*, pp. 219-220.
142. C. H. Spurgeon, *The Saint And His Saviour*, pp. 373-375.
143. Pike, *The Life and Work of Charles Haddon Spurgeon*, Vol. II, p. 251.
144. Ray, *The Life of Charles Haddon Spurgeon*, p. 224.
145. Ellis, *Charles Haddon Spurgeon*, pp. 42-43.
146. Fullerton, *C. H. Spurgeon: A Biography*, p. 95.
147. Ibid., pp. 95-96.
148. Source unknown. Can be located in Archives, Spurgeon's College, London.
149. Fullerton, *C. H. Spurgeon: A Biography*, p. 98.
150. *The British Standard*, January 9, 1857.
151. Fullerton, *C. H. Spurgeon: A Biography*, p. 99.
152. *The Greville Memoirs* (Third Part), Vol. II., p. 83.

153. Pike, *The Life and Work of Charles Haddon Spurgeon*, Vol. II, p. 264.
154. The old area site of the Crystal Palace which burned in the 1930s is now called Crystal Place and is only a short distance from where the present day Spurgeon's College is located.
155. Douglas, *Prince of Preachers*, p. 64.
156. Fullerton, *C. H. Spurgeon: A Biography*, pp. 104-105.
157. Williams, *Personal Reminiscences of Charles Haddon Spurgeon*, p. 237.
158. *The Daily Bulletin*, July 16, 1865.
159. Fullerton, *C. H. Spurgeon: A Biography*, p. 125.
160. James Morgan, D.D., *Recollections of My Life*, p. 314. See Fullerton, *C. H. Spurgeon*, pp. 114-115.
161. Fullerton, *C. H. Spurgeon: A Biography*, p. 125.
162. Ibid., p. 116.
163. Ibid.
164. Ibid.
165. Ibid.
166. Ibid.
167. Ibid., p. 117.
168. *Pall Mall Gazette*, February 1, 1892.
169. Fullerton, *C. H. Spurgeon: A Biography*, p. 120.
170. Ibid., p. 117.
171. Ibid., p. 121.
172. Ibid., p. 122.
173. Ibid., p. 130.
174. On one occasion Finney actually saved the *New York Evangelist* by allowing a series of lectures he gave on revival to be published weekly. The lectures were later compiled in a volume entitled, *Lectures on Revivals of Religion*. That book remains in print and has spawned many true revivals.
175. Fullerton, *C. H. Spurgeon: A Biography*, p. 87.
176. *Autobiography*, Vol. I, *The Early Years*, p. 299.
177. Ernest A. Payne, *The Congregational Quarterly*, "The Evangelical Revival and the Beginnings of the Modern Missionary Movement," July 1943.
178. Ibid., p. 227.
179. Ibid.
180. Eric Hayden, *Spurgeon on Revival: A Biblical and Theological Approach* (Grand Rapids: Zondervan, 1962), p. 57.
181. James Burns, *Revivals: Their Laws and Leaders* (Grand Rapids: Baker Book Houses, 1960), p. 24.
182. Robert E. Coleman, *One Divine Movement* (Old Tappan, New Jersey: Fleming H. Revell Co. 1970), p. 27.
183. James Burns, *Revivals: Their Laws and Leaders*, p. 28.
184. Ibid.
185. Ibid., p. 58.
186. Ibid., p. 44.
187. Iain Murray, *The Forgotten Spurgeon*, 2nd ed. (Edinburgh: Banner of Truth Trust, 1973), p. 48.
188. *Autobiography*, Vol. I, *The Early Years*, p. 263.
189. *Autobiography*, Vol. I, p. 361.

190. C. H. Spurgeon, *The Bible and the Newspaper* (London: Passmore and Alabaster, 1880), pp. 109-110.
191. Eric Hayden, *Spurgeon on Revival*.
192. Spurgeon, *The New Park Street Pulpit*, p. V. Preface.

Chapter Six
1. Lorimer, *Charles Haddon Spurgeon*, p. 9.
2. Lewis O. Brastow, *Representative Modern Preachers* (New York: The MacMillan Co., 1904), p. 387.
3. *The Victorian Church*, 2 Volumes (London: Adam & Charles Black, 1966-70), Vol. 1, p. 418. cf. Horton Davies, "Expository Preaching: Charles Haddon Spurgeon," *Foundations*, Vol. 6 (1963), p. 15; and Helmut Thielicke, ed., *Encounter with Spurgeon*, pp. 1-45.
4. Fullerton, *C. H. Spurgeon: A Biography*, p. 72.
5. Archives, Spurgeon's College, London.
6. Fullerton, *C. H. Spurgeon: A Biography*, p. 73.
7. Ibid., 80.
8. Lorimer, *Charles Haddon Spurgeon*, pp. 74-75.
9. *The Morning Advertiser*, February 19, 1855.
10. Pike, *The Life and Work of Charles Haddon Spurgeon*, Vol. II, p. 223.
11. *British Standard*, Jan. 9, 1857.
12. Charles Ray, *The Life of Charles Haddon Spurgeon*, pp. 191-192.
13. Anonymous, *Charles Haddon Spurgeon: A Biographical Sketch and An Appreciation* (London: Andrew Melrose, 1903), p. 105. [Authorship of this volume is ascribed to "One who knew him well".]
14. Charles Ray, *The Life of Charles Haddon Spurgeon*, p. 192.
15. Ibid.
16. Ibid., p. 194.
17. Ibid., p. 194-195.
18. Archives, Spurgeon's College, London.
19. Thielicke, ed., *Encounter with Spurgeon*, p. 346.
20. Ray, *The Life of Charles Haddon Spurgeon*, p. 195.
21. Ibid., p. 196.
22. Ibid., pp. 196-197.
23. Anonymous, *An Apology for Spurgeon* (London, Pattie, n.d.), p. 6.
24. *Punch*, XXXI, (Dec. 6, 1856), p. 228.
25. Frank Faithful, *The Reverend C. H. Spurgeon, His Friends and Foes* (London: W. & H. S. Warr, 1856), p. 4.
26. *The Universe*, Aug. 19, 1882.
27. Spurgeon, *The Metropolitan Tabernacle Pulpit*, Vol. 7, 1861, p. 169.
28. Ibid., Vol. 37, 1891, pp. 323-324.
29. Williams, *Personal Reminiscences of Charles Haddon Spurgeon*, p. 175.
30. Douglas, *Prince of Preachers*, pp. 124-125.
31. Ibid., p. 125.
32. C. H. Spurgeon, *The Soul-Winner: How to Lead Sinners to the Saviour* (New York: Fleming H. Revell, 1895), p. 178.
33. C. H. Spurgeon, *An All-Round Ministry: Addresses to Ministers and Students* (1900; reprint, Edinburgh: Banner of Truth, 1960), p. 127.

34. Spurgeon, *The New Park Street Pulpit*, Vol. 1 (1855), Preface, n.p.
35. J. B. Weatherspoon, "Charles Haddon Spurgeon," *Review and Expositor*, Vol. 31, (Louisville, Ky., Southern Baptist Theological Seminary, 1934) p. 412.
36. McCoy, "The Evangelistic Ministry of Charles Haddon Spurgeon," p. 134.
37. Weatherspoon, "Charles Haddon Spurgeon," *The Review and Expositor*, Vol. 31, p. 411.
38. C. H. Spurgeon, *Lectures to My Students: A Selection from Addresses Delivered to the Students of the Pastors' College, Metropolitan Tabernacle* (London: Passmore and Alabaster, 1890), p. 79.
39. Ibid., (italics mine).
40. Spurgeon, *The Metropolitan Tabernacle Pulpit*, Vol. 7 (1861), pp. 174-175.
41. Hudson Baggett, "A Study of Spurgeon's Preaching Method," unpublished Th.M. thesis, Southern Baptist Theological Seminary, Louisville, Kentucky, 1951, p. 3.
42. On Isaiah 53, see *The Metropolitan Tabernacle Pulpit*, Vol. 8 (1862), pp. 378-379. On 2 Corinthians 5:21, see *The New Park Street Pulpit*, Vol. 6 (1860), pp. 193-194. On Galatians 3:13, see *The Metropolitan Tabernacle Pulpit*, Vol. 15 (1869), pp. 306-309. On 1 Peter 2:24 see *The Metropolitan Tabernacle Pulpit*, Vol. 19 (1873), pp. 651-652.
43. Spurgeon, *The Metropolitan Tabernacle Pulpit*, Vol. 8 (1862), pp. 378-379. Cf. *The Metropolitan Tabernacle Pulpit*, Vol. 12 (1866), p. 314; and *The Metropolitan Tabernacle Pulpit*, Vol. 49 (1903, [1877]), p. 348.
44. That is, Spurgeon held that Jesus "became legally amenable to the penalty due for our transgression." *The Metropolitan Tabernacle Pulpit*, Vol. 35 (1889), p. 650.
45. Spurgeon, *The Metropolitan Tabernacle Pulpit*, Vol. 13 (1866), p. 315. Cf. *The Metropolitan Tabernacle Pulpit*, Vol. 30 (1884), p. 130.
46. Spurgeon, *The New Park Street Pulpit*, Vol. 4, 1858, p. 69, (italics mine).
47. Ibid., Vol. 159, 1913, p. 605.
48. Ibid., Vol. 36, 1890, p. 40.
49. Ibid., Vol. 55, 1909 (1873), p. 67.
50. Spurgeon, *The Metropolitan Tabernacle Pulpit*, Vol. 34 (1888), p. 508.
51. Lorimer, *Charles Haddon Spurgeon*, p. 83.
52. *The Christian World*, Oct. 20, 1887.
53. *The Chicago Standard*, November 10, 1887.
54. *The Popular Preacher* (London: William Walker and Son), p. 4.
55. *The Sword and the Trowel*, XIX (1883), p. 421.
56. G. Holden Pike, ed., *Speeches by C. H. Spurgeon at Home and Abroad* (London, 1878), p. 73.
57. Spurgeon, *Lectures to My Students*, p. 179-180.
58. Brastow, *Representative Modern Preachers*, p. 402.
59. Ibid.
60. Lorimer, *Charles Haddon Spurgeon*, pp. 60, 62.
61. C. H. Spurgeon, *The Soul-Winner*, p. 58.
62. Ibid., p. 57.
63. "Pulpit Photography: C. H. Spurgeon," *The Study and the Pulpit*, Vol. 1 (October 1876), p. 577.
64. McCoy, "The Evangelistic Ministry of C. H. Spurgeon," p. 211.
65. Williams, *Personal Reminiscences of Charles Haddon Spurgeon*, p. 203.

66. J. Ewing Ritchie, *The London Pulpit*, 2nd ed., (London: William Tweedie, 1858), p. 162.
67. Spurgeon, *Lectures to My Students*, p. 184.
68. *The South London Press*, May 11, 1889.
69. E. F. Adcock, *Charles H. Spurgeon: Prince of Preachers*, Christian Hero Series, (Anderson, Indiana: Warner Press, 1925), p. 102.
70. Spurgeon, *The Metropolitan Tabernacle Pulpit*, Vol. 7 (1861), p. 221.
71. Spurgeon, *The New Park Street Pulpit*, Vol. 4 (1858), p. 160.
72. Spurgeon, *The Metropolitan Tabernacle Pulpit*, Vol. 35 (1889, [1888]), p. 240.
73. *Pall Mall Gazette* (June 19, 1884), p. 11.
74. Anonymous, *The Popular Preachers: The Reverend C. H. Spurgeon, His Extraordinary 'Sayings and Doings'* (London: C. Kerbey, 1856), p. 4.
75. Lorimer, *Charles Haddon Spurgeon*, p. 73.
76. Brastow, *Representative Modern Preachers*, p. 391.
77. Fullerton, *C. H. Spurgeon: A Biography*, p. 192.
78. *Western Morning News*, February 1, 1892.
79. Lorimer, *Charles Haddon Spurgeon*, p. 70.
80. Ellis, *Charles Haddon Spurgeon*, p. 238-239.
81. Kruppa, "Charles Haddon Spurgeon, A Preacher's Progress," p. 151.
82. Arthur Christopher Benson, *The Life of Edward White Benson, Sometime Archbishop of Canterbury* (London, 1899), Vol. I, p. 276.
83. *Good Words*, Vol. XXXIII (1892) p. 236.
84. Archives, Spurgeon's College, London.
85. Spurgeon, *Lectures to My Students*, p. 141.
86. Personal memorabilia of Lewis A. Drummond.
87. Baggett, "A Study of Spurgeon's Preaching Method," p. 8.
88. Ibid.
89. Fullerton, *C. H. Spurgeon: A Biography*, p. 217.
90. Ellis, *Charles Haddon Spurgeon*, pp. 178-179.
91. Thielicke, ed., *Encounter with Spurgeon*, p. 10.
92. Ibid.
93. Personal correspondence with the author.
94. *Autobiography*, Vol. II, p. 137.
95. A. Cunningham Burley, *Spurgeon and His Friendships* (London: Epworth Press, 1933) p. 33.
96. Spurgeon, *The Metropolitan Tabernacle Pulpit*, Vol. 13 (1867, [n.d.]), pp. 44-45.
97. McCoy, "The Evangelistic Ministry of C. H. Spurgeon," p. 217.
98. "Notes," *The Sword and the Trowel*, Vol. 10 (1874), p. 191
99. McCoy, "The Evangelistic Ministry of C. H. Spurgeon," p. 218.
100. *The Sword and the Trowel*, Vol. 11, 1875, p. 44.
101. "The Work of Our Evangelists," *The Sword and the Trowel*, Vol. 14 (1878), p. 428.
102. Spurgeon, *The Metropolitan Tabernacle Pulpit*, Vol. 30 (1884), p. 456.
103. Spurgeon, *All-Round Ministry*, pp. 372-373.
104. Pamphlet, *The Preacher's Personal Conditions*, p. 16, Archives, Spurgeon's College, London.
105. Baggett, "A Study of Spurgeon's Preaching Method," p. 9.
106. Kruppa, "Charles Haddon Spurgeon, A Preacher's Progress," p. 200.

107. *Autobiography*, Vol. II, pp. 154-155.
108. Ibid., p. 160.
109. Ray, *The Life of Charles Haddon Spurgeon*, p. 199.
110. C. H. Spurgeon, *The Best of C. H. Spurgeon* (Grand Rapids, Baker Books, 1986), p. 80.
111. C. H. Spurgeon, *Around the Wicket Gate; or, A Friendly Talk with Seekers Concerning Faith in the Lord Jesus Christ* (London: Passmore and Alabaster, 1899), p. 10-11.
112. Ibid., preface.
113. Author's personal memorabilia.
114. Kruppa, "Charles Haddon Spurgeon, A Preacher's Progress," p. 200.
115. *British and Foreign Evangelical Review*, April 1877, and *British Weekly*, Feb. 17, 1888.
116. *Christian World*, Feb. 4, 1892.
117. Fullerton, *C. H. Spurgeon: A Biography*, p. 209.
118. *Times*, June 19, 1884.
119. Fullerton, *C. H. Spurgeon: A Biography*, p. 211.
120. Ibid., pp. 211-212.
121. Ibid., p. 214.
122. Ibid., p. 213.
123. Source unknown. Can be located in Archives, Spurgeon's College, London.
124. McCoy, "The Evangelistic Ministry of C. H. Spurgeon."
125. Fullerton, *C. H. Spurgeon: A Biography*, p. 224.
126. Archives, Spurgeon's College, London.
127. Kruppa, "Charles Haddon Spurgeon, A Preacher's Progress," p. 204.
128. Williams, *Personal Reminiscences of C. H. Spurgeon*, p. 52.
129. *The Sword and the Trowel*, Vol. 20, 1884, p. 200.
130. *Autobiography*, Vol. 2, p. 154.
131. Ibid.
132. C. H. Spurgeon, *Eccentric Preachers* (London, 1879) p. 9.
133. Ian McClaren (Dr. John Watson), "Dinna Forget Spurgeon," in *His Majesty Baby and Some Common People* (London, 1902), pp. 158-163.
134. *The Sword and the Trowel*, Vol. 18, 1882, p. 502.
135. *Contemporary Review*, Vol. 61, March 1892, p. 305.
136. *The Christian Herald*, Jan. 1879.
137. *Richmond Herald*, Oct. 1879. North American Review, Vol. 86, 1858.
138. *Review of Reviews*, Vol. 5, Feb. 1892, p. 117.
139. Number 37, J. C. Pollack Moodium (New York, 1963), pp. 64 and 66.
140. Number 38, Manuscript letter from Lucretia Garfield, Aug. 29, 1882, Spurgeon's Papers, Archives, Spurgeon's College, London.
141. Fullerton, *C. H. Spurgeon: A Biography*, p. 219.
142. Thielicke, ed., *Encounter with Spurgeon*, pp. 1, 34,

Chapter Seven
1. Hope, *Spurgeon: The People's Preacher*, p. 91.
2. *The Times*, August 22, 1860.
3. Lorimer, *Charles Haddon Spurgeon*, p. 169.
4. Ibid., p. 89.

5. Day, *The Shadow of the Broad Brim*, p. 157.
6. Lorimer, *Charles Haddon Spurgeon*, p. 139.
7. Ibid., p. 172.
8. Ibid., p. 171.
9. Ibid., p. 200.
10. Ray, *The Life of Charles Haddon Spurgeon*, p. xiii.
11. Ibid., p. 1.
12. Archives, Spurgeon College, London.
13. Ray, *The Life of Charles Haddon Spurgeon*, p. 252.
14. Day, *The Shadow of the Broad Brim*, p. 154.
15. Ibid., p. 155.
16. Ray, *The Life of Charles Spurgeon*, pp. 250-251.
17. Day, *The Shadow of the Broad Brim*, p. 155.
18. Ibid., p. 156.
19. Charles Ray, *The Life of Charles Haddon Spurgeon*, p. 266.
20. Ibid., pp. 257-258.
21. Lorimer, *Charles Haddon Spurgeon*, p. 76.
22. Ray, *The Life of Charles Haddon Spurgeon*, p. 262.
23. Ibid., pp. 263-264.
24. Ibid., p. 264.
25. Fullerton, *C. H. Spurgeon: A Biography*, p. 134.
26. Ibid., pp. 134-135.
27. Ibid., pp. 135-136.
28. Lorimer, *Charles Haddon Spurgeon*, pp. 85-86.
29. Hope, *Spurgeon: The People's Preacher*, p. 93.
30. Ray, *The Life of Charles Haddon Spurgeon*, p. 266-267.
31. Ibid., p. 268.
32. Ibid., p. 269.
33. Ibid., pp. 270-272.
34. Fullerton, *C. H. Spurgeon: A Biography*, p. 139.
35. Day, *The Shadow of the Broad Brim*, pp. 159-160.
36. Ibid., p. 169.
37. Archives, Metropolitan Tabernacle.
38. *Autobiography*, Vol. III, pp. 73-74.
39. Ibid., pp. 75-76.
40. Ibid., pp. 79-80. This was sermon number 500 in Spurgeon's Penny Pulpit Series.
41. Ray, *The Life of Charles Haddon Spurgeon*, pp. 275-276.
42. Ellis, *Charles Haddon Spurgeon*, p. 240.
43. Archives, Metropolitan Tabernacle, London, England.
44. Ray, *The Life of Charles Haddon Spurgeon*, pp. 281-282.
45. Ibid., p. 284.
46. Ibid.
47. Archives, Metropolitan Tabernacle, London.
48. Ray, *The Life of Charles Haddon Spurgeon*, p. 286.
49. Ibid.
50. Ellis, *Charles Haddon Spurgeon*, p. 88.
51. Archives, Metropolitan Tabernacle, London.
52. Spurgeon, *C. H. Spurgeon Anecdotes*, pp. 12-13.

53. Archives, Metropolitan Tabernacle, London.
54. Ibid.
55. Ibid.
56. Fullerton, *C. H. Spurgeon: A Biography*, p. 142.
57. *Leeds Mercury*, November 15, 1879.
58. *The Hornet*, April 4, 1878.
59. *The Globe*, March, 1889.
60. *Irish Ecclesiastical Gazette*, July 25, 1886.
61. Fullerton, *C. H. Spurgeon: A Biography*, p. 157.
62. *Daily Chronicle*, February 1, 1892.
63. *The Christian World*, September 8, 1887.
64. *Irish Times*, February 16, 1892.
65. Fullerton, *C. H. Spurgeon: A Biography*, p. 158.
66. Ibid., p. 183.
67. Ibid., p. 184.
68. Ibid.
69. Lorimer, *Charles Haddon Spurgeon*, p. 16.
70. *The Christian World*, Feb. 11, 1892.
71. Fullerton, *C. H. Spurgeon: A Biography*, pp. 185-186.
72. Ibid., pp. 186-187.
73. Personal Memorabilia of Lewis A. Drummond.
74. E. Paxton Hood, *The Lamps of the Temple: Crayon Sketches of the Modern Pulpit* (London: John Snow, 1856), p. 545.
75. Fullerton, *C. H. Spurgeon: A Biography*, p. 187.
76. James Douglas, *The Prince of Preachers*, pp. 82-84, 86-87.
77. Ray, *The Life of Charles H. Spurgeon*.
78. Ibid., pp. 292-297.
79. Ibid., p. 299.
80. Archives, Metropolitan Tabernacle, London.
81. Archives, Spurgeon's College, London.
82. Ray, *The Life of Charles Haddon Spurgeon*, pp. 314-315.
83. Ibid., p. 316.
84. Ibid., p. 375.
85. Lorimer, *Charles Haddon Spurgeon*, p. 57.
86. Hope, *Spurgeon: The People's Preacher*, p. 104.
87. Lorimer, *Charles Haddon Spurgeon*, p. 91.

Chapter Eight
1. Henry Mayhew, *London Labour and the London Poor, A Cyclopedia of the Conditions and Earnings of Those that will Work, Those that Cannot Work, and Those that will not Work*, 4 Volumes, (New York: Dover Publications, Inc., 1968), Vol. 1, p. 159.
2. Ibid, pp. 40-41.
3. Ibid., p. 146.
4. E. Royston Pike, *Golden Times, Human Document of the Victorian Age* (New York: Shocken Books, 1972), p. 119.
5. Mayhew, *London Labour and the London Poor*, Vol. 3, p. 307.
6. Archives, Spurgeon's College, London.

7. Kathleen Heasman, *Evangelicals in Action, An Appraisal of their Social Work in the Victorian Era* (London: Geoffrey Bleo, 1962), pp. 48-49, from W. C. Preston, *The Bitter Cry and Outcast of London, and Enquiry of the Abject Poor*, p. 1.

8. G. M. Trevelyan, *English Social History, A Survey of Six Centuries: Chaucer to Queen Victoria* (London: Longmans, Green & Co., 1942), pp. 476-77.

9. *The Sword and the Trowel*, Vol. 16, pp. 17-18.

10. Spurgeon, *The New Park Street Pulpit*, Vol. 4, p. 254.

11. C. H. Spurgeon, "To the Readers of the 'Commonwealth,'" *The Christian Commonwealth*, October 20, 1881.

12. C. H. Spurgeon, *Poland* (London: Passmore & Alabaster, 1864), p. 23.

13. Spurgeon, *The New Park Street Pulpit*, Vol. 3, 1857, p. 302.

14. C. H. Spurgeon, *John Ploughman's Pictures, or More of His Plain Talk for Plain People*, (Philadelphia: J. D. Lippencott & Co. 1881), p. 52.

15. C. H. Spurgeon, *Barbed Arrows from the Quiver of C. H. Spurgeon* (London: Passmore & Alabaster, 1896), p. 24.

16. *The Sword and the Trowel*, Vol. 27, 1891, p. 34.

17. Ibid., Vol. 28, 1892, p. 87.

18. Ibid., Vol. 19, 1883, p. 148.

19. Pike, *Charles Haddon Spurgeon, Preacher, Author, Philanthropist*, p. 319.

20. Ellis, *Charles Haddon Spurgeon*, p. 113.

21. Fullerton, *C. H. Spurgeon: A Biography*, p. 227.

22. Lorimer, *Charles Haddon Spurgeon*, pp. 121-122.

23. Ray, *The Life of Charles Haddon Spurgeon*, p. 14

24. Ibid.

25. Ibid., p. 323.

26. Ibid.

27. Fullerton, *C. H. Spurgeon: A Biography*.

28. Ibid., p. 229.

29. Ibid., p. 230.

30. Pike, *The Life and Work of Charles Haddon Spurgeon*, Vol. V, p. 99.

31. Fullerton, *C. H. Spurgeon: A Biography*, p. 230.

32. Archives, Spurgeon's College, London.

33. Ray, *The Life of Charles Haddon Spurgeon*, pp. 325-328.

34. Ibid., p. 328.

35. Fullerton, *C. H. Spurgeon: A Biography*, p. 233.

36. Ibid.

37. Ray, *The Life of Charles Haddon Spurgeon*, p. 340.

38. Fullerton, *C. H. Spurgeon: A Biography*, pp. 237-238.

39. Ibid., p. 238.

40. Archives, Spurgeon's College, London.

41. Ray, *The Life of Charles Haddon Spurgeon*, p. 333.

42. Ibid., p. 334.

43. Ibid., pp. 334-336.

44. Ibid., p. 337.

45. Ibid., p. 338.

46. Conwell, *Life of Charles Haddon Spurgeon*, p. 374.

47. Ibid., p. 389.

48. Ibid., pp. 389-390.

49. Ibid., p. 392.
50. Ibid., 394.
51. Ibid., p. 396.
52. C. H. Spurgeon, "Outline of the Lord's Work by the Pastor's College and Its Kindred Organizations at the Metropolitan Tabernacle," (London: Passmore and Alabaster, 1867), pp. 36-37.
53. Day, *The Shadow of the Broad Brim*, p. 124.
54. Burley, *Spurgeon and His Friendships*, p. 106.
55. Fullerton, *C. H. Spurgeon: A Biography*, p. 242.
56. Ray, *The Life of Charles Haddon Spurgeon*, pp. 343-344.
57. Ibid., p. 347.
58. Ibid., p. 349.
59. Ibid., p. 355.
60. Ibid., pp. 340-350.
61. Conwell, *Life of Charles Haddon Spurgeon*, p. 415.
62. Ray, *The Life of Charles Haddon Spurgeon*, pp. 356-357.
63. Ibid., p. 357.
64. Spurgeon, *C. H. Spurgeon Anecdotes*, pp. 83-85.
65. Ellis, *Charles Haddon Spurgeon*, p. 90.
66. Ray, *The Life of Charles Haddon Spurgeon*, pp. 361-362.
67. Fullerton, *C. H. Spurgeon: A Biography*, p. 246.
68. Source unknown. Can be located in Archives, Spurgeon's College, London.
69. Ray, *The Life of Charles Haddon Spurgeon*, p. 365.
70. Ibid., p. 366.
71. Ibid.
72. Ibid., p. 370.
73. Ibid., p. 371.
74. Susannah Spurgeon, *Ten Years After* (London: Passmore and Alabaster, 1895), preface.
75. Susannah Spurgeon, *Ten Years of My Life in the Service of the Book Fund* (London: Passmore & Alabaster, 1886) preface.
76. M. Dorothy George, *London Life in the Eighteenth Century*, (New York: Capricorn Books, 1965), p. 38.
77. "Mr. Booth in London, A Daring Mission," *The Baptist*, August 26, 1887.
78. *The Sword and the Trowel*, Vol. 18, 1882, p. 201.
79. C. H. Spurgeon, *John Ploughman's Talks and Pictures*, p. 3.
80. Meredith, "The Social and Political Views of Charles Haddon Spurgeon, 1834-1892," p. 231.
81. Sir James Marchant, *Dr. John Clifford, C. H. Spurgeon; Life, Letters, and Reminiscences* (London: Cassel & Co. Ltd., 1924), p. XII.
82. Meredith, "The Social and Political Views of Charles Haddon Spurgeon, 1834-1892," p. 178.
83. "Mr. Spurgeon on Sunday and Ragged Schools," *Sunday School Chronicle*, October 20, 1882.

Chapter Nine
1. Kruppa, "Charles Haddon Spurgeon, A Preacher's Progress," p. 182.
2. *The Baptist Messenger*, 1865, pp. 67-68.

3. *Autobiography*, Vol. III, p. 179.
4. *The Freeman*, March 15, 1865.
5. Archives, Spurgeon's College, London.
6. *The Freeman*, March 22, 1865.
7. *The Saturday Review*, March 18, 1865.
8. *Autobiography*, Vol. III, p. 90.
9. Ibid., pp. 91-92.
10. Ibid., pp. 93-94.
11. Williams, *Personal Reminiscences of Charles Haddon Spurgeon*, p. 201.
12. *Autobiography*, Vol. III, pp. 98-98.
13. Ibid., pp. 100-101.
14. Ibid., p. 100.
15. Archives, Spurgeon's College, London.
16. Ibid.
17. Ibid.
18. *Autobiography*, Vol. III, p. 113.
19. Ibid., pp. 114-115.
20. Ibid., p. 115.
21. Ibid., pp. 116-117.
22. Ibid., pp. 121-122.
23. Ibid., p. 122.
24. Ibid., p. 203.
25. Ibid., pp. 237-238.
26. Archives, Spurgeon's College, London.
27. Ibid.
28. *Autobiography*, Vol. IV, p. 4.
29. Ibid.
30. Ibid.
31. Ibid., p. 6. This occurred on one of their trips together in Europe.
32. *Autobiography*, Vol. IV, p. 13.
33. Ibid., Vol. III, p. 192.
34. Ibid., pp. 196-197.
35. Ibid., p. 197.
36. Ibid.
37. Ibid., pp. 200-201.
38. Ibid., pp. 201-202.
39. Pike, *The Life and Work of Charles Haddon Spurgeon*, Vol. III, p. 132.
40. Ibid.
41. Ibid., p. 137.
42. Ibid., pp. 157-158.
43. Williams, *Personal Reminiscences of Charles Haddon Spurgeon*, p. 176.
44. Pike, *The Life and Work of Charles Haddon Spurgeon*, Vol. III, pp. 177-178.
44. *The Christian Advocate*, May 24, 1890.
45. Williams, *Personal Reminiscences of Charles Haddon Spurgeon*, p. 138.
46. Pike, *The Life and Work of Charles Haddon Spurgeon*, Vol. III, p. 160.
47. Ibid., pp. 177-178.
48. Ibid., p. 180.
49. Ibid., p. 137.

50. Ibid., p. 137-138.
51. Ibid., p. 138.
52. Ibid., p. 139.
53. Ibid.
54. Ibid., p. 140.
55. Ibid.
56. Ibid., pp. 141-142.
57. *The Christian World*, March 16, 1866.
58. Pike, *The Life and Work of Charles Haddon Spurgeon*, Vol. III, p. 157.
59. Ibid., Vol. IV, p. 241.
60. Anonymous, *Mr. Spurgeon's Critics Criticised*, p. 5.
61. *Spurgeon Pamphlets*, Vol. I, number 20.
62. *Autobiography*, Vol. I, p. 173.
63. Williams, *Personal Reminiscences of Charles Haddon Spurgeon*, p. 180.
64. *The Morning Advertiser*, February 7, 1856.
65. Pike, *The Life and Work of Charles Haddon Spurgeon*, Vol. II, p. 213.
66. Ibid.
67. Ray, *The Life of Charles Haddon Spurgeon*, p. 240.
68. "The Baptist Magazine," March and April issues, 1860.
69. *Autobiography*, Vol. I, p. 484.
70. Ray, *The Life of Charles Haddon Spurgeon*, p. 248.
71. Carlile, *C. H. Spurgeon: An Interpretive Biography*, p. 159.
72. *The Christian Cabinet*, Dec. 14, 1859.
73. Pike, *The Life and Work of Charles Haddon Spurgeon*, Vol. II, p. 324.
74. Ibid., p. 331.
75. Ibid.
76. *The Freeman*, March 28, 1860.
77. *Baptist Quarterly*, Vol. 22, July 1982, Number 7, p. 319.
78. Ibid. p. 322.
79. Ibid.
80. Ibid.
81. Pike, *The Life and Work of Charles Haddon Spurgeon*, Vol. III, p. 83.
82. Ibid., p. 85.
83. *Baptist Quarterly*, Vol. 22, July 1990, Number 7, p. 324.
84. Ibid, p. 326.
85. Preface to Spurgeon's pamphlet cited in the *Autobiography*, Vol. II, "The Full Harvest" (Banner of Truth Trust: Carlisle, Pennsylvania, 1973), p. 56.
86. Chadwick, *The Victorian Church*, Vol. I, p. 261.
87. Murray, *The Forgotten Spurgeon*, p. 131.
88. *The Sword and the Trowel*, Vol. 2, 1866, p. 4.
89. Kruppa, "Charles Haddon Spurgeon, A Preacher's Progress," p. 223.
90. Spurgeon, *The Metropolitan Tabernacle Pulpit*, Vol. 10, 1871, p. 323.
91. Archives, Spurgeon's College, London.
92. Spurgeon, *The Metropolitan Tabernacle Pulpit*, Vol. 10, 1871, p. 314.
93. Ibid., p. 315.
94. Ibid., p. 321.
95. Ibid., p. 316.
96. Ibid., p. 317.

97. Ibid.
98. Ibid., p. 323.
99. Ibid., p. 327-328.
100. Ibid., p. 328.
101. Pike, *The Life and Work of Charles Haddon Spurgeon*, Vol. IV, p. 146.
102. *Autobiography*, Vol. II, p. 55.
103. *Spurgeon Pamphlets*, vol. 3, no. 31.
104. Rev. Charles Willis, *Baptismal Regeneration—a Letter to the Rev. C.H. Spurgeon* (London, 1864), p. 15.
105. Published by William Macintosh (24 Paternaster Row, London).
106. Spurgeon, *The New Park Street Pulpit*, Vol. 1, 1855, p. 105. Preached on March 18, 1855.
107. Wilbur M. Smith, ed., *The Best of C.H. Spurgeon, a Treasury of Extracts from His Writings* (Grand Rapids, Michigan: Baker Book House, 1983), p. 186.
108. J. S. Jenkinson, *The Popish Era of Baptismal Regeneration -Not the Doctrine of the Church of England* (London: William MacIntosh, 1864), p. 5.
109. *The Dean of Rippon's Letter to Mr. Spurgeon's Sermons* (London: J. Paul, 1864), p. 6.
110. Murray, *The Forgotten Spurgeon*, p. 130.
111. Spurgeon, *The Metropolitan Tabernacle Pulpit*, Vol. 10, p. 321.
112. J. T. Titcomb, *The Washing of Regeneration* (London, 1864), p. 19.
113. A Baptist Missionary Society Address, Exeter Hall, April 28, 1864.
114. Carlile, *C. H. Spurgeon: An Interpretive Biography*, p. 145.
115. Fullerton, *C. H. Spurgeon: A Biography*, p. 251.
116. Pike, *The Life and Work of Charles Haddon Spurgeon*, Vol. III, p. 108.
117. L. E. Elliott-Binns, *Religion in the Victorian Era* (London, Luterworth Press, 1953), p. 206.
118. Pike, *The Life and Work of Charles Haddon Spurgeon*, Vol. III, p. 103.
119. Ibid.
120. Spurgeon's pamphlets, Vol. 2, Number 7.
121. *Autobiography*, Vol. II, p. 57.
122. Spurgeon's pamphlets, Vol. 2. pp. 2-4.
123. Ibid., p. 9.
124. Ibid., p. 12.
125. Ibid. p. 5.
126. Spurgeon's College, London.
127. Pike, *The Life and Work of Charles Haddon Spurgeon*, Vol. IV, p. 265.
128. Lorimer, *Charles Haddon Spurgeon*, p. 173.
129. Fullerton, *C. H. Spurgeon, A Biography*, p. 251.
130. Pike, *The Life and Work of Charles Haddon Spurgeon*, Vol. IV, p. 372.
131. Ibid., p. 283.
132. Ibid., p. 311.
133. *The Freeman*, July 2, 1869.
134. Burley, *Spurgeon and His Friendships*, p. 3.
135. *The Saturday Review*, July 12, 1869.
136. Ray, *The Life of Charles Haddon Spurgeon*, pp. 490-491.
137. Archives, Spurgeon's College, London.
138. Ibid.

139. Ibid.
140. Ibid.
141. Pike, *The Life and Work of Charles Haddon Spurgeon*, Vol. IV, p. 350.

Chapter Ten
 1. Philip Magnus, *Gladstone, A Biography* (New York: E. P. Dutton and Company, Inc., 1954), p. XI.
 2. Ibid.
 3. Archives, Spurgeon's College, London.
 4. Pike, *The Life and Work of Charles Haddon Spurgeon*, Vol. VI, p. 259.
 5. Ibid., pp. 260-61.
 6. Ibid., p. 259.
 7. *The Acrostic*, Vol. V, p. 134, scrapbook clipping. Cited in Kruppa, "A Preacher's Progress," p. 303.
 8. Spurgeon, *The New Park Street Pulpit*, Vol. 6, 1860, p. 456.
 9. Ibid., Vol. 1, 1855, p. 61.
10. *The Sword and the Trowel*, XV (1879), p. 245.
11. Ibid., Vol. 15, p. 279.
12. Ibid., Vol. 3, 1867, p. 158.
13. Burley, *Spurgeon and His Friendships*, p. 128.
14. Leaflet, "Mr. Spurgeon and the Election," 1880.
15. Ray, *The Life of Charles Haddon Spurgeon*, p. 386.
16. Spurgeon, *Metropolitan Tabernacle Pulpit*, Vol. 28, 1881, p. 225.
17. *The Sword and the Trowel*, VI, 1870, pp. 330-31.
18. Archives, Spurgeon's College, London.
19. *The Sword and the Trowel*, Vol. 16, 1880, p. 191.
20. W. T. Stead, "Topics of the Day by Heroes of the Hour," *Pall Mall Gazette*, June 19, 1884.
21. From a leaflet dated March 19, 1880.
22. "Eminent Radicals out of Parliament," *Weekly Dispatch*, Number 5, November 9, 1879.
23. Ibid.
24. "Mr. Spurgeon on Home Rule," *The Times* (London), June 3, 1886.
25. "Monday's London Pollings," *The Daily News*, July 3, 1886.
26. Henry Pelling, *Social British of British Election, 1885-1910* (New York: St. Martin's Press, 1967) pp. 55-56.
27. Meredith, "The Social and Political Views of Charles Haddon Spurgeon, 1834-1892," p. 71.
28. *The Sword and the Trowel*, Vol. 25, 1889, p. 381.
29. MS. letter, April 16, 1869, Gladstone Papers, British Museum, CCCXXXV, 44420, f. 133.
30. Spurgeon, *Metropolitan Tabernacle Pulpit*, Vol. 19, 1873, pp.
31. W. T. Stead, *Topics of the Day*, pp. 50-51.
32. *The Sword and the Trowel*, Vol. 12, 1876, pp. 285-286.
33. Ibid., Vol. 17, 1891, p. 199.
34. Meredith, "The Social and Political Views of Charles Haddon Spurgeon, 1834-1892," p. 77.
35. Ibid., p. 78.

36. Douglas, *Prince of Preachers*, p. 156.
37. *The Sword and the Trowel*, Vol. 16, 1880, p. 38.
38. Ibid, Vol. 12, 1876, p. 433.
39. Spurgeon, *The New Park Street Pulpit*, Vol. 4, 1858, p. 179.
40. Spurgeon, *The Metropolitan Tabernacle Pulpit*, Vol. 35, 1889, p. 252.
41. C. H. Spurgeon, *Only a Prayer Meeting*, p. 55.
42. Spurgeon, *The Sword and the Trowel*, Vol 21, 1885, p. 147.
43. Spurgeon, *The New Park Street Pulpit*, Vol. 6, 1860, p. 485.
44. Ibid., Vol. 3, 1857, pp. 334-335.
45. *The Sword and the Trowel*, Vol. 15, 1870. p. 338.
46. Ibid., Vol. 6, 1887, p. 433.
47. Ibid., Vol. 6, 1870, p. 107.
48. R. T. Shannon, *Gladstone and the Bulgarian Agitation 1876* (London: Thomas Nelson, 1963), pp. 167-168.
49. *Autobiography*, Vol. III, p. 44.
50. Pike, *The Life and Work of Charles Haddon Spurgeon*, Vol. II, p. 276.
51. Spurgeon, *The New Park Street Pulpit*, Vol. 1, 1855, p. 293.
52. *The Sword and the Trowel*, Vol. 6, 1870, pp. 352-353.
53. Ibid., Vol. 20, 1884, p. 508.
54. Ibid., Vol. 4, 1858, pp. 204-205.
55. Ibid., Vol. 14, 1878, pp. 145-149.
56. C. H. Spurgeon, *Feathers for Arrows; or, Illustrations for Preachers and Teachers. From my Note Book* (London: Passmore and Alabaster, 1884), p. 209.
57. Geoffrey Shaw, "Navigating Educational Storms," *Christian Teacher*, Vol. 9, No. 2 (March/April 1972), p. 14.
58. Kruppa, "Charles Haddon Spurgeon, A Preacher's Progress," p. 22.
59. Mayhew, *London Labour and the London Poor*, Vol. 1, p. 370.
60. Meredith, "The Social and Political Views of Charles Haddon Spurgeon, 1834-1892," pp. 110-111.
61. C. H. Spurgeon, ed., "Can Nothing More be Done for the Young?" *The Sword and the Trowel*, April, 1868, pp. 147-149.
62. "Memoranda," June, 1870, p. 285.
63. Archives, Spurgeon's College, London.
64. *The Claims of the Free Church*, p. 155.
65. *The Sword and the Trowel*, Vol. 4, March 1868, p. 100.
66. C. H. Spurgeon, *A Good Start, A Book for Young Men and Women*, with a Prefatory Note by Sir George Williams (London: Passmore and Alabaster, 1898), pp. 21-22.
67. Spurgeon, *The New Park Street Pulpit*, Vol. 3, 1857, p. 302.
68. Spurgeon, *Poland*, p. 23.
69. *The Sword and the Trowel*, Vol. 28, 1892, p. 87.

Chapter Eleven
1. Pike, *The Life and Work of Charles Haddon Spurgeon*, Vol. IV, p. 253.
2. Ibid., p.254.
3. Ibid, p. 254.
4. Ibid., p. 259.
5. Ibid., p. 260-261.

6. Ibid., Vol. VI, p. 199.
7. Ibid, p. 354.
8. *The Baptist*, March 8, 1889.
9. *The Musical Herald*, July 1889.
10. Pike, *The Life and Work of Charles Haddon Spurgeon*, Vol. IV, p. 356.
11. Ibid, p. 358.
12. Ibid., Vol. V, p. 178.
13. Ibid., Vol. VI, p. 198.
14. Ibid., Vol. V, p. 33.
15. Ibid., Vol. V, pp. 34-35.
16. *The Unitarian Herald* (Manchester) in Pike, Vol. VI, pp. 245-246.
17. J. G. Greenhough, M.A., and James Thew in *The Baptist*, November 9, 1883.
18. *Autobiography*, Vol. IV, p. 178.
19. Ibid., p. 179.
20. Ibid., p. 170.
21. Ibid., p. 184.
22. Ibid., p. 186.
23. Ibid., p. 188-190.
24. Ibid., p. 82.
25. Ibid., Vol. V, p. 40.
26. Ibid., p. 49.
27. Ibid., p. 57.
28. John De Kewer Williams, "My Memories and Estimate of My Friend Spurgeon." See also Pike, Vol. 5, pp. 82-83.
29. Pike, *The Life and Work of Charles Haddon Spurgeon*, Vol. V, p. 83.
30. Ibid., p. 96.
31. Lecture given by Raymond Brown at the Celebration of Spurgeon's 150th anniversary of his birth at William Jewell College, Liberty, Missouri.
32. Ibid.
33. Ibid.
34. Ibid.
35. Ibid.
36. Ibid.
37. Ibid.
38. Ibid.
39. *The Birmingham Daily Mail*, September 6, 1990.
40. Williams, *Personal Reminiscences of Charles Haddon Spurgeon*, p. 177.
41. Douglas, *Prince of Preachers*, p. 56.
42. *The Baptist*, January 9, 1874.
43. Lorimer, *Charles Haddon Spurgeon*, p. 53.
44. *The Freeman*, July 10, 1874.
45. Pike, *The Life and Work of Charles Haddon Spurgeon*, Vol. V, p. 132.
46. Fullerton, *C. H. Spurgeon: A Biography*, p. 254.
47. Ibid., p. 255.
48. Archives, Spurgeon's College, London.
49. Ibid.
50. Day, *The Shadow of the Broad Brim*, p. 172.
51. Archives, Spurgeon's College, London.

52. Day, *The Shadow of the Broad Brim*, p. 174.
53. *Autobiography*, Vol. IV, pp. 204-205.
54. Ibid., p. 211.
56. Ibid., pp. 216-217.
57. Ibid, pp. 228-229.
57. Day, *The Shadow of the Broad Brim*, p. 174-175.
58. Pike, *The Life and Work of Charles Haddon Spurgeon*, Vol. VI, p. 213.
59. Ibid., p. 238.
60. Day, *The Shadow of the Broad Brim*, p. 175.
61. Ibid.
62. Ibid., p. 175-176.
63. Ibid., p. 176.
64. Ibid., p. 177.
65. Ibid.
66. Ibid., p. 178.
67. Ibid., p. 179.
68. Ibid., p. 178.
69. Pike, *The Life and Work of Charles Haddon Spurgeon*, Vol. VI, p. 225.
70. *The Manchester Examiner and Times*, March 3, 1879.
71. Ibid.
72. Pike, *The Life and Work of Charles Haddon Spurgeon*, Vol. V, p. 48.
73. Ibid., Vol. IV, p. 361-362.
74. Ibid, p. 362.
75. Ibid., p. 360.
76. Ibid., Vol. V, p. 47.
77. Ibid., p. 173-174.
78. Ibid., Vol. IV, p. 366.
79. Ibid., p. 377.
80. Ibid.
81. Ibid., p. 378-379.
82. Ibid., p. 379-380.
83. Ibid., p. 381.
84. Spurgeon, *C. H. Spurgeon Anecdotes*, p. 89.
85. Day, *The Shadow of the Broad Brim*, p. 166.
86. Ibid.
87. Ibid., p. 167.
88. Ibid., p. 168-169.
89. Ibid., p. 169.
90. Ibid., p. 170.
91. Archives, Spurgeon's College, London.
92. Ray, *The Life of Charles Haddon Spurgeon*, p. 392-394.
93. Ibid., p. 394.
94. Ibid., p. 379.
95. Ibid., p. 397-399.
96. Ibid., p. 401.
97. Ibid., pp. 404-405.
98. Archives, Spurgeon's College, London.
99. Lorimer, *Charles Haddon Spurgeon*, p. 45.

100. Dallimore, *Spurgeon*, p. 164.
101. Archives, Spurgeon's College, London.
102. Dallimore, *Spurgeon*, p. 163.
103. *Autobiography*, Vol. IV, p. 169.
104. Pike, *The Life and Work of Charles Haddon Spurgeon*, Vol. 5, p. 155.
105. Ibid., Vol. IV, p. 214.
106. Ibid., Vol VI, p. 275.
107. Ibid., Vol. 5, p. 7.
108. Ibid., p. 10.
109. *The Pall Mall Gazette*, June 18, 1884.
110. Pike, *The Life and Work of Charles Haddon Spurgeon*, Vol. V, p. 17.
111. Archives, Spurgeon's College, London.

Chapter Twelve
  1. Day, *The Shadow of the Broad Brim*, p. 124.
  2. Williams, *Personal Reminiscences of Charles Haddon Spurgeon*, p. 34.
  3. *Autobiography*, Vol. I, *The Early Years*, p. 162.
  4. Archives, Spurgeon's Library, William Jewell College, Liberty, Mo.
  5. Ibid.
  6. *The Baptist*, April 24, 1891.
  7. Spurgeon, *An All-Round Ministry*, pp. 9-10.
  8. Archives, Spurgeon's Library, William Jewell College, Liberty, Missouri.
  9. Ibid.
 10. Ibid.
 11. Ibid.
 12. Ibid.
 13. Lewis Drummond, *Leading Your Church in Evangelism* (Nashville: Broadman Press, 1975), p. 35.
 14. C. E. Autrey, *Basic Evangelism* (Grand Rapids: Zondervan, 1959), pp. 13-16.
 15. Billy Graham, "Why Lausanne?" in *Let the Earth Hear His Voice*, ed. J. D. Douglas (Minneapolis: Worldwide Publications, 1975), p. 28.
 16. Spurgeon, *An All-Round Ministry*, pp. 35-36.
 17. Spurgeon, *Lectures to My Students*, p. 341.
 18. Spurgeon, *The Soul-Winner*, p. 22.
 19. Spurgeon, *An All-Round Ministry*, pp. 39-40.
 20. Douglas, *Prince of Preachers*, p. 113.
 21. Spurgeon, *The New Park Street Pulpit*, Vol. 1, 1855, p. 313.
 22. Spurgeon, *The Metropolitan Tabernacle Pulpit*, Vol. 33, 1887, p. 430.
 23. Spurgeon, *An All-Round Ministry*, pp. 25-26.
 24. Spurgeon, *The Metropolitan Tabernacle Pulpit*, Vol. 10, 1864, p. 534.
 25. Ibid., Vol. 29, 1883, p. 605.
 26. Ibid., Vol. 26, 1880, p. 50.
 27. Ibid., Vol. 18, 1872, p. 450.
 28. Spurgeon, *Lectures to My Students*, p. 341.
 29. Ibid.
 30. Spurgeon, *The Metropolitan Tabernacle Pulpit*, Vol. 29, 1883, p. 605.
 31. Ibid., Vol. 10, 1864, p. 535.

32. C. H. Spurgeon, *The Treasury of the New Testament*, 4 Volumes, (London and Edinburgh: Marshall, Morgan & Scott, n.d.), Vol. II, p. 388.
33. Spurgeon, *The Metropolitan Tabernacle Pulpit*, Vol. 35, 1889, p. 256.
34. C. H. Spurgeon, *The Treasury of the Old Testament*, 4 Volumes, (London and Edinburgh: Marshall, Morgan & Scott, n.d.), Vol. II, p. 387.
35. Charles H. Spurgeon, *The Greatest Fight in the World. Conference Address* (London: Passmore and Alabaster, 1895), p. 27.
36. Ernest W. Bacon, *Spurgeon: Heir of the Puritans* (London: George Allen & Unwin Ltd., 1967), p. 110.
37. Spurgeon, *The New Park Street Pulpit*, Vol. 1 (1855), p. 110.
38. Spurgeon, *The Treasury of the New Testament*, Vol. I, p. 28.
39. Spurgeon, *The Treasury of the Old Testament*, Vol. III, p. 427.
40. Spurgeon, *The New Park Street Pulpit*, Vol. 1 (1855), p. 110.
41. Spurgeon, *The Metropolitan Tabernacle Pulpit*, Vol. 29, 1883, p. 602.
42. *The Newcastle Daily Chronicle*, June 24, 1891.
43. Spurgeon, *The Metropolitan Tabernacle Pulpit*, Vol. 35, 1889, p. 257.
44. C. H. Spurgeon, "The Human Side of Inspiration," *The Sword and the Trowel*, Vol. 25 (1889), p. 551.
45. Spurgeon, *The Metropolitan Tabernacle Pulpit*, Vol. 35 (1889), p. 257.
46. Spurgeon, *The Treasury of David*, 7 Volumes, (New York: Funk & Wagnalls, 1882), Vol. II, p. 697.
47. Ibid., Vol. IV, p. 38-44.
48. Spurgeon, *The Treasury of the New Testament*, Vol. III, p. 863.
49. Spurgeon, *Memorial Library*, 20 Volumes, (New York & London: Funk & Wagnalls Co., 1857), p. 291.
50. Spurgeon, *The New Park Street Pulpit*, Vol. I, 1855, p. 26.
51. Ibid., p. 27.
52. Spurgeon, *The Treasury of the New Testament*, Vol. III, p. 428.
53. Spurgeon, *Memorial Library*, Vol. 1, p. 58.
54. Ibid., p. 374.
55. Charles Haddon Spurgeon, *All of Grace: An Earnest Word with Those Who Are Seeking Salvation by the Lord Jesus Christ* (London: Passmore and Alabaster, 1892), p. 88.
56. Bacon, *Spurgeon: Heir of the Puritans*, p. 115.
57. Spurgeon, *An All-Round Ministry*, p. 320-321.
58. Charles Haddon Spurgeon, *The Soul-Winner*, p. 21.
59. Spurgeon, *The Treasury of the New Testament*, Vol. 2, p. 282.
60. Spurgeon, *Memorial Library*, p. 291.
61. Ibid., Vol. 1, p. 58.
62. Eric W. Hayden, *Spurgeon on Revival*, p. 75.
63. Spurgeon, *The New Park Street Pulpit*, Vol. 1 (1855) Preface.
64. Spurgeon, *Lectures to My Students*, p. 79.
65. Spurgeon, *The New Park Street Pulpit*, Vol. 7, 1861 (pp. 173-174).
66. Ibid., Vol. 5 (1859), p. 417.
67. Spurgeon, *The Metropolitan Tabernacle Pulpit*, Vol. 48, 1902, and 1879, p. 25.
68. Ibid., Vol. 20, 1874, p. 444.
69. Spurgeon, *The New Park Street Pulpit*, Vol. 2 (1856), p. 121.
70. Ibid., p. 122.

71. Ibid.
72. Ibid.
73. Spurgeon, *Memorial Library*, p. 291.
74. Spurgeon, *The Treasury of the New Testament*, Vol. 2, p. 526.
75. Hayden, *Spurgeon on Revival*, p. 75.
76. Bacon, *Spurgeon: Heir of the Puritans*, p. 115.
77. Spurgeon, *Lectures to my Students*, p. 195.
78. Spurgeon, *Memorial Library*, Vol. 2, p. 192.
79. Spurgeon, *The Treasury of the Old Testament* Vol. 3, p. 421.
80. Spurgeon, *Memorial Library*, Vol. 2, p. 192.
81. Ibid., Vol. 10, pp. 192-193.
82. Spurgeon, *The Treasury of the Old Testament*, Vol. 1, p. 6.
83. Spurgeon, *The Treasury of the New Testament*, Vol. 4, p. 760.
84. Ibid., p. 530.
85. Spurgeon, *The New Park Street Pulpit*, Vol. 2 (1856), p. 370.
86. Spurgeon, *The Metropolitan Tabernacle Pulpit*, Vol. 7 (1861), p. 297.
87. Ibid., p. 298.
88. *Autobiography*, Vol. II, p. 271.
89. Spurgeon, *The New Park Street Pulpit*, Vol. 11 (1865), p. 29.
90. Ibid., (1855) p. 262.
91. Spurgeon, *The Sword and the Trowel*, (1887), p. 642.
92. Spurgeon, *The New Park Street Pulpit*, (1855), pp. 529-554.
93. Ibid., Vol. I, p. 50, (italics mine).
94. *Autobiography*, Vol. I, *The Early Years*, p. 551.
95. Spurgeon, *The Treasury of the New Testament*, Vol. 3, p. 29.
96. Williams, *Personal Reminiscences of Charles Haddon Spurgeon*, p. 136.
97. C. H. Spurgeon, *A Catechism with Proofs* (London: Evangelical Press, 1967), p. 12.
98. Spurgeon, *The New Park Street Pulpit*, Vol. 6, p. 104.
99. Spurgeon, *The Treasury of the New Testament*, Vol. 2, p. 900.
100. Spurgeon, *The Metropolitan Tabernacle Pulpit*, Vol. 11 (1865), p. 106.
101. Ibid.
102. Ibid., Vol. 16 (1870), p. 209.
103. Ibid., Vol. 27 (1881), p. 99.
104. Ibid., Vol. 31 (1885), p. 391.
105. Ibid., Vol. 8 (1862), p. 183.
106. Ibid., Vol. 61 (1871), p. 595.
107. Spurgeon, *The New Park Street Pulpit* , Vol. 4 (1858), p. 140.
108. Ibid., Vol. 5 (1859), p. 86.
109. Murray, *The Forgotten Spurgeon*, p. 100.
110. Letter to Heath Street Church, Hampstead, March 1, 1855, Archives, Spurgeon's College, London.
111. Spurgeon, *Memorial Library*, Vol. 13, p. 108.
112. Spurgeon, *The Metropolitan Tabernacle Pulpit*, Vol. 51 (1862), p. 51.
113. Spurgeon, *The New Park Street Pulpit*, Vol. 6 (1860), p. 134.
114. Spurgeon, *The Metropolitan Tabernacle Pulpit*, Vol. 29 (1883), p. 490.
115. Spurgeon, *The New Park Street Pulpit*, Vol. 3 (1857), p. 131.
116. Spurgeon, *The Metropolitan Tabernacle Pulpit*, Vol. 8 (1862), p. 201.

117. Ibid., Vol. 7 (1861), pp. 301-302.
118. Spurgeon, *The New Park Street Pulpit*, Vol. 3 (1857), p. 200.
119. Ibid., Vol. 4 (1858), p. 337.
120. Spurgeon, *The Metropolitan Tabernacle Pulpit*, Vol. 30 (1884), p. 50.
121. Spurgeon, *A Good Start*, p. 101.
122. Kruppa, "Charles Haddon Spurgeon, A Preacher's Progress," p. 96.
123. Spurgeon, *The New Park Street Pulpit*, Vol. 1 (1855), p. 322.
124. Spurgeon, *The Metropolitan Tabernacle Pulpit*, Vol. 48 (1878), p. 164.
125. *Autobiography*, Vol. I, pp. 246-247.
126. Spurgeon, *The Metropolitan Tabernacle Pulpit*, Vol. 31 (1885), p. 495.
127. Ibid., Vol. 34 (1888), p. 514.
128. Spurgeon, *The New Park Street Pulpit*, Vol. 3 (1857), p. 275.
129. Ibid., p. 277.
130. Hayden, *Spurgeon on Revival*, p. 90.
131. Spurgeon, *The Metropolitan Tabernacle Pulpit*, Vol. 10 (1864), p. 170.
132. McCoy, "The Evangelistic Ministry of C. H. Spurgeon.", pp. 162, 163.
133. Spurgeon, *The Metropolitan Tabernacle Pulpit*, Vol 21 (1875, n.d.), p. 174.
134. Ibid., Vol. 45 (1899), p. 152.
135. Ibid., Vol. 8 (1862), pp. 378-379.
136. Spurgeon, *The Treasury of the New Testament*, Vol. 3, p. 23.
137. Spurgeon, *The New Park Street Pulpit*, Vol. 6, p. 129.
138. *Word and Work*, June 23, 1881.
139. Letter dated February 11, 1889, Archives, Spurgeon's College, London.
140. Spurgeon, *The Metropolitan Tabernacle Pulpit*, Vol. 29 (1883), p. 149.
141. Ibid., Vol. 34, 1888, p. 508.
142. Ibid., Vol. 17, 1871, p. 389.
143. Spurgeon, *The New Park Street Pulpit*, Vol. 5, 1859, p. 130.
144. Ibid., Vol 3 (1857), p. 130.
145. Ibid., Vol. 5 (1859), p.130.
146. Ibid., p. 131.
147. C. Irving Shaw, *Spurgeonism Examined: or, Modern Calvinism Analysed. A Pamphlet for the Times* (London: Thickbroom Brothers, 1859), p. 28,
148. Spurgeon, *The New Park Street Pulpit*, Vol. 5 (1859), p. 136.
149. Ibid., Vol. 6 (1860, [1859]), p. 12.
150. W. L. Mills, *The Baptist Confession of Faith* (London: Billing and Sons, Ltd., 1966), p. 19.
151. Spurgeon, *The Metropolitan Tabernacle Pulpit*, Vol. 35, 1889, p. 691.
152. Ibid., (1877), p. 362.
153. Ibid., Vol. 15 (1869), p. 299.
154. Archives, Spurgeon's College, London.
155. Douglas, *Prince of Preachers*, p. 119.
156. Pike, *The Life and Work of Charles Haddon Spurgeon*, Vol. V, p. 133.
157. Spurgeon, *Memorial Library*, Vol. 7, p. 361-362.
158. Spurgeon, *The New Park Street Pulpit*, Vol. 2, p. 98.
159. Bacon, *Spurgeon: Heir of the Puritans*, p. 119.
160. Spurgeon, *The Treasury of the New Testament*, Vol. 3, p. 125.
161. Ibid., Vol. 4, p. 832.
162. Williams, *Personal Reminiscences of Charles Haddon Spurgeon*, p. 27.

163. Spurgeon, *The Treasury of the New Testament*, Vol. 3, p. 408.
164. Ibid., p. 826.
165. Mills, *The Baptist Confession of Faith*, pp. 45-46.
166. Spurgeon, *Memorial Library*, Vol. 10, p. 55-56.
167. Spurgeon, *Lectures to My Students*, p. 22.
168. *The Baptist*, April 24, 1891.
169. Douglas, *Prince of Preachers*, p. 32.
170. Kruppa, "Charles Haddon Spurgeon, A Preacher's Progress," p. 317.
171. *The Sword and Trowel*, 1887, pp. 195-196.
172. Spurgeon, *The Metropolitan Tabernacle Pulpit*, 1867, p. 706.
173. Eric Hayden, *Searchlight on Spurgeon* (Pasadena, Texas: Pilgrim Publications, 1973).
174. Spurgeon, *The Metropolitan Tabernacle Pulpit*, Vol. 34, 1888, p. 364.
175. Ibid., Vol. 52 (1906 [n.d.]), p. 101.
176. Jeremy F. Thornton, "The Soteriology of C. H. Spurgeon: Its Biblical and Historical Roots and Its Place in His Preaching," (unpublished Ph.D. dissertation, University of Cambridge University, 1974), p. 296.
177. Spurgeon, *An All-Round Ministry*, p. 285.
178. Alfred North Whitehead, *Science and the Modern World* (New York, 1959), p. 96.
179. Sutton, "A Comparison Between the Down Grade Controversy and Tensions Over Biblical Inerrancy in the Southern Baptist Convention," p. 24.
180. Ibid., p. 28
181. Spurgeon, *The Greatest Fight in the World*, p. 33.
182. Ibid.
183. *The Sword and the Trowel* XIII (1887), p. 399.
184. Ibid.
185. Sutton, "A Comparison Between the Down Grade Controversy and Tensions Over Biblical Inerrancy in the Southern Baptist Convention," p. 30.
186. Hugh McLeod, *Class and Religion in the Late Victorian City* (Hamden, Connecticut: Archon Books, 1974), p. 233.
187. *Autobiography*, Vol. II, p. 141.
188. Spurgeon, *The Greatest Fight in the World*.
189. *The Sword and the Trowel* IV (1868), p. 227.
190. Ray, *The Life of Charles Haddon Spurgeon*, p. 248.
191. *The Sword and the Trowel*, II (1866), p. 4.
192. *The Baptist*, November 4, 1881.
193. Ibid., May 27, 1881.
194. *The Sword and the Trowel*, Vol. 13, 1877, p. 294.
195. Ernest Payne, "The Down Grade Controversy: A Postscript," *Baptist Quarterly*, Vol. 28, 1979, p. 198.
196. Ernest Payne, *The Baptist Union, A Short History* (London: The Kingsgate Press, 1959) p. 130 and 124.
197. Kruppa, "Charles Haddon Spurgeon, A Preacher's Progress," p. 333.
198. October 11, 1883, Archives, Spurgeon's College, London.
199. Payne, "The Down Grade Controversy: A Postscript," p. 148.
200. Letter, October 16, 1883.
201. Letter written from Archibald Brown to Spurgeon which quoted Glover's speech.
202. Archives, Spurgeon's College, London.

203. *The Southern Baptist Educator*, August, 1891, p. 5.
204. *The Sword and the Trowel*, June.
205. *Word and Work*, March 9, 1886.
206. Payne, "The Down Grade Controversy: A Postscript," p. 149.
207. Ibid.
208. Leonard Phillips and Robert Gardiner, *A Solid Building—An Open Fellowship*, A History of Beckenham Baptist Church (Elm Road Chapel), 1883-1983, pp. 9-16.
209. Larry J. Michael, "The Effects of Controversy on the Evangelistic Ministry of C. H. Spurgeon," (unpublished Ph.D. dissertation, The Southern Baptist Theological Seminary, 1989), pp. 222-223.
210. Payne, "The Down Grade Controversy: A Postscript," p. 150.
211. Letter from Pearce Carey to Seymour Price, 1887.
212. George Howells, "Christian Problems, Settled; and awaiting further exploration," *The Baptist Quarterly*, Vol. 7 (1934-35), pp. 107-108.
213. A. C. Underwood, *A History of the English Baptists* (London: Kingsgate Press, 1947), p. 243.
214. Payne, *The Baptist Union, A Short History*, pp. 130-131.
215. Payne, "The Down Grade Controversy: A Postscript," p. 151.
216. Ibid.
217. Ibid.
219. Ibid., p. 152.
220. James Marchant, *Dr. John Clifford* (London: Cassell and Co. Ltd., 1924), p. 111.
220. Payne, *The Baptist Union, A Short History*, p. 129.
221. *The Baptist*, March 18, 1892.
222. *Review of Reviews* V (March, 1892) p. 249.
223. Robert Shindler, "The Down Grade," *The Sword and the Trowel*, Vol. 23 (March 1887), p. 122.
224. Ibid.
225. Ibid., p. 124.
226. Ibid., p. 126.
227. Ibid.
228. Robert Shindler, "The Down Grade: Second Article," *The Sword and the Trowel*, April 1887, p. 170.
229. Ibid.
230. Ibid.
231. Ibid.
232. Spurgeon, "Notes," *The Sword and the Trowel*, Vol. 23 (April 1887), pp. 195-196.
233. Ibid., p. 169.
234. Sydney Ahlstrom, *A Religious History of the American People* (New Haven: Yale University Press, 1972), pp. 393-394, 778.
235. Robert Shindler, "Andover Theology," *The Sword and the Trowel*, Vol. 23 (June 1887), p. 274.
236. Ibid., pp. 279-280.
237. Payne, *The Baptist Union, A Short History*, p. 131.
238. Spurgeon, "Another Word Concerning the Down-Grade," *The Sword and the Trowel*, Vol. 23 (August 1887), p. 397.
239. Ibid., pp. 397, 400.
240. Ibid., p. 400.

241. Ibid., p. 398.
242. Ibid., p. 399.
243. *The Sword and the Trowel* XIX (1883), p. 83.
244. Spurgeon, "Another Word Concerning the Down-Grade," pp. 399-400.
245. Spurgeon, "Our Reply to Sundry Critics and Enquirers," *The Sword and the Trowel*, Vol. 23 (September 1887), p. 462.
246. Ibid., p. 463.
247. *The South London Press*, May 11, 1889.
248. *The News*, May 29, 1891.
249. *The Baptist*, May 24, 1889.
250. Spurgeon, "The Case Proved," *The Sword and the Trowel*, Vol. 23 (October, 1887), pp. 509-510.
251. Ibid., p. 510.
252. Ibid.
253. Craig Skinner, "The Preaching of Charles Haddon Spurgeon," *Baptist History and Heritage*, Vol. 19, October 1984, No. 4 (Nashville, Tennessee: Southern Baptist Convention, 1984), p. 20.
254. Ibid., p. 513.
255. Sutton, "A Comparison Between the Down Grade Controversy and Tensions Over Biblical Inerrancy in the Southern Baptist Convention," p.73.
256. Douglas, *Prince of Preachers*, p. 165.
257. Kruppa, "Charles Haddon Spurgeon, A Preacher's Progress," p. 375.
258. C. H. Spurgeon, "The Case Proved," *The Sword and Trowel*, Vol. 23, October 1887, p. 515.
259. Letter to Rev. Lockhart, Nov. 19, 1887, Archives, Spurgeon's College.
260. Pike, *The Life and Work of Charles Haddon Spurgeon*, Vol. VI, p. 287.
261. Ibid.
262. *The Christian World*, Sep. 13, 1888.
263. Archives, Southern Baptist Theological Seminary, Louisville, Kentucky.
264. Archives, Spurgeon's College, London, England.
265. C. H. Spurgeon, "A Fragment Upon the Down Grade Controversy," *The Sword and the Trowel*, Vol. 23 (November 1887), p. 558.
266. Ray, *The Life of Charles Haddon Spurgeon*, p. 420.
267. *The Christian Commonwealth*, March 20, 1890.
268. Archives, Spurgeon's College, London.
269. *The Christian Commonwealth*, Feb. 10, 1887.
270. Ibid.
271. R. F. Weymouth, "The 'Down-Grade' Joke," *The Sword and the Trowel*, Vol. 23 (November 1887), pp. 561-563.
272. Ibid.
273. Letter dated May 26, 1888 in Archives, Spurgeon's College, London.
274. *The Baptist Magazine*.
275. Pike, *The Life and Work of Charles Haddon Spurgeon*, Vol. VI, p. 290.
276. Ibid., pp. 290-291.
277. Ibid., p. 291.
279. Ibid.
279. *Autobiography*, Vol. IV, pp. 262-263.
280. Ibid., p. 263.

281. Ibid.
282. Ibid.
283. Minutes, Archives, Regent's Park College, Oxford B. U.
284. Ibid.
285. Ibid.
286. Ibid.
287. Carlile, *C. H. Spurgeon: An Interpretive Biography*, p. 247.
288. Archives, Spurgeon's College, London.
289. Carlile, *C. H. Spurgeon: An Interpretive Biography*, p. 247.
290. Pike, *The Life and Work of Charles Haddon Spurgeon*, Vol. 6, p. 292.
291. Ibid., p. 293.
292. *The Sword and the Trowel*, XXIV (1888), 82.
293. Archives, Regent's Park College, Oxford (italics mine).
294. Payne, *The Baptist Union, A Short History*, p. 136.
295. "Mr. Spurgeon's Appeal to Christendom," *Pall Mall Gazette*, XCVII February 13, 1888), p. 5.
296. Payne, *The Baptist Union, A Short History*, p. 136.
297. Recorded in James Marchant, *The Life of Dr. John Clifford* (London: Cassell & Co., 1924), p. 160.
298. Ibid.
299. Glover, *Evangelical Nonconformists*, pp. 1172-173.
300. Payne, *The Baptist Union, A Short History*, p. 137.
301. *The Baptist Magazine*, Vol. 80, February 1888, p. 86.
302. Ibid.
303. C. H. Spurgeon, "The Baptist Union Censure," *The Sword and the Trowel*, 26 (February 1881) p. 81.
304. Ibid.
305. Underwood, *A History of the English Baptists*, p. 230.
306. Carlile, *C. H. Spurgeon: An Interpretive Biography*, pp. 248-249.
307. Payne, *The Baptist Union, A Short History*, p. 138.
308. Ibid., p. 140.
309. Fullerton, *C. H. Spurgeon: A Biography*, p. 256.
310. Ibid.
311. *The Christian World*, May 2, 1889.
312. Copy of a letter to Mr. Near, February 21, 1888, Archives, Spurgeon's College, London.
313. Archives, Spurgeon's College, London.
314. Ibid.
315. C. H. Spurgeon, *The Sword and the Trowel*, Vol. 23 (September 1887), p. 464.
316. E. J. Poole-Conner, *Evangelicalism in England* (London: Henry Walter Ltd., 1966), p. 247.
317. Correspondence of C. H. Spurgeon found in Spurgeon's College Archives, London, England.
318. Archives, Spurgeon's College, London.
319. Ibid.
320. Letter Sept. 6, 1890, Archives, Spurgeon's College, London.
321. Ibid.
322. Ibid., Nov. 4, 1888.

323. Archives, Metropolitan Tabernacle, London.
324. Ibid.
325. Ibid.
326. Original correspondence of C. H. Spurgeon, no. 112, Spurgeon's College, London.
327. *The Scarborough Evening News*, June 24, 1891.
328. Lorimer, *Charles Haddon Spurgeon*, p. 152.
329. George Carter Needham, compiler and editor, *The Life and Labors of Charles H. Spurgeon, The Faithful Preacher, The Devoted Pastor, The Noble Philanthropist, The Beloved College President, and The Voluminous Writer, Author, etc., etc.* (Boston: D. L. Guernsey, 1883), p. 76.
330. *The Baptist Magazine*, Vol. 4, April, 1892, p. 191.

Chapter Thirteen
1. Quoted by Kruppa, "Charles Haddon Spurgeon, A Preacher's Progress," p. 388.
2. *The National Baptist*, Philadelphia, July 31, 1889.
3. Pike, *The Life and Work of Charles Haddon Spurgeon*, Vol. VI, p. 303.
4. Ibid., p. 304.
5. Ibid.
6. Ibid., p. 305.
7. Ibid., pp. 306-307.
8. Ibid., p. 309.
9. Ibid., p. 310-11.
10. Ibid., p. 312.
11. *The Baptist*, November 22, 1889.
12. Pike, *The Life and Work of Charles Haddon Spurgeon*, Vol. VI, p. 313.
13. Ibid., p. 317.
14. Archives, Spurgeon's College, London.
15. *Autobiography*, Vol. IV, pp. 325-330.
16. Archives, Spurgeon's College, London.
17. Ibid.
18. Pike, *The Life and Work of Charles Haddon Spurgeon*, Vol. VI, p. 314.
19. From his "Own Funeral Sermon" on Acts 13:36 originally preached at funeral of deacon William Olney.
20. Pike, *The Life and Work of Charles Haddon Spurgeon*, Vol. VI, p. 315.
21. Ibid.
22. Archives, Metropolitan Tabernacle, London.
23. Letter to *Pall Mall Gazette*, February 20, 1891.
24. Ray, *The Life of Charles Haddon Spurgeon*, p. 379.
25. *Autobiography*, Vol. IV, p. 335.
26. Archives, Spurgeon's College, London.
27. Pike, *The Life and Work of Charles Haddon Spurgeon*, Vol. VI, pp. 317-318.
28. Ibid., p. 318.
29. Ibid., p. 319.
30. Ibid., p. 320.
31. Ibid.
32. Fullerton, *C. H. Spurgeon: A Biography*, p. 338.

33. Pike, *The Life and Work of Charles Haddon Spurgeon*, Vol. VI, p. 322.
34. *The Baptist*, August 7, 1991.
35. Pike, *The Life and Work of Charles Haddon Spurgeon*, Vol. VI, p. 323.
36. Ibid., p. 323-324.
37. Ibid., p. 325.
38. Ibid.
39. Archives, Spurgeon's College, London.
40. Ibid.
41. Pike, *The Life and Work of Charles Haddon Spurgeon*, Vol. VI, p. 326.
42. Ibid.
43. Ibid.
44. Archives, Spurgeon's College, London.
45. Pike, *The Life and Work of Charles Haddon Spurgeon*, Vol. VI, p. 326-327.
46. Ibid., p. 327.
47. Archives, Spurgeon's College, London.
48. Ibid.
49. Ibid.
50. Pike, *The Life and Work of Charles Haddon Spurgeon*, Vol. VI, p. 329.
51. Fullerton, *C. H. Spurgeon: A Biography*, p. 338.
52. Day, *The Shadow of the Broad Brim*, p. 227.
53. John Bunyan, *The Pilgrim's Progress and Other Works*, The prefaces, indices, and the text revised by George Offor, esq., with copious notes, original and selected; and "An Original Memoir of the Author," by The Rev. George B. Cheever, D.D., (Glasgow: William Mackenzie, n.d.), p. 438.
54. *Autobiography*, Vol. IV, p. 371.
55. Hope, *Spurgeon: The People's Preacher*, p. 174.
56. *Autobiography*, Vol. IV, p. 371.
57. Ibid.
58. "A Spurgeon Memorial Address" delivered at Nashville, Tenn. on first Sunday, Feb. 1892.
59. Archives, Spurgeon's College, London.
60. Ray, *The Life of Charles Haddon Spurgeon*, p. 482.
61. *Autobiography*, Vol. IV, p. 376.
62. Ibid.
63. Ray, *The Life of Charles Haddon Spurgeon*, p. 483-484.
64. Ibid., pp. 484-485.
65. Ibid., p. 486.
66. Ibid.

Epilogue

1. Archives, Metropolitan Tabernacle, London.
2. Anonymous, *Charles Haddon Spurgeon: A Biographical Sketch and An Appreciation*, p. 13.
3. Fullerton, *C. H. Spurgeon: A Biography*, p. 339.
4. Archives, Metropolitan Tabernacle, London.
5. Mrs. Oliphant, *The Life of Principal Tulloch*, pp. 132-133. See Fullerton, *C. H. Spurgeon: A Biography*, p. 101.
6. *The Speaker*, February 13, 1892.

7. Pike, *The Life and Work of Charles Haddon Spurgeon*, Vol. VI, p. 337.

8. Ibid., p. 338.

9. Ibid., pp. 338-340.

10. Lorimer, *Charles Haddon Spurgeon*, p. 214.

11. Source unknown.

12. Kruppa, "Charles Haddon Spurgeon, A Preacher's Progress," p. 417.

13. C. H. Spurgeon, *Messages to the Multitudes* (London: Sampson, Low, Marston, and Co, 1892), p. 269.

14. Craig Skinner, "The Preaching of Charles Haddon Spurgeon," *Baptist History and Heritage*, Vol. 19, October 1984, No. 4, p. 25.

15. Anonymous, *Charles Haddon Spurgeon: A Biographical Sketch and An Appreciation*, p. 18.

16. Archives, Metropolitan Tabernacle, London.

17. Craig Skinner, *Lamplighter and Son* (Nashville, Tennessee: Broadman Press, 1984), p. 100.

18. *Daily Chronicle*, February 12, 1892.

19. Letter to the editor of *The Baptist* from Lambeth, dated August 20, 1892.

20. *The Echo*, October 21, 1892.

21. *The Baptist*, October 21, 1892.

22. W. Y. Fullerton, *Thomas Spurgeon* (London: Hodder and Stoughton, 1919), pp. 150-151.

23. Archives, Metropolitan Tabernacle, London.

24. Archives, Spurgeon's College, London.

25. Letter by S. Chandler, written August 30, published in *The Baptist* the next week.

26. *The Baptist*, editorial, October 21, 1892.

27. Skinner, *Lamplighter and Son*, pp. 108-109.

28. *The Sword and the Trowel*, (1892), pp. 668-669.

29. Archives, Metropolitan Tabernacle, London.

30. *The Sword and the Trowel*, (1893), p. 244.

31. Skinner, *Lamplighter and Son*, p. 113. Church Minutes of the Metropolitan Tabernacle Archives.

32. Ibid., p. 114.

33. From the printed letter distributed to Tabernacle members, copy in the Archives of the New Zealand Baptist Historical Society, Auckland.

34. Craig Skinner, *Lamplighter and Son*, p. 117.

35. Ibid.

36. Spurgeon, *The Quotable Spurgeon*, p. 134.

37. W. Robertson Nicoll, *Princes in the Church* (London: Hodder and Stoughton, 1921), p. 50.

Appendices

1. See "Fortnightly Review" for Jan., 1887.

2. Again we call special attention to this most important theme. The growing evil demands the attention of all who desire the prosperity of the church of God.

3. "History of Dissenters," by Bogue and Bennet.

BIBLIOGRAPHY

A. WORKS BY C. H. SPURGEON

Spurgeon, Charles Haddon. *Able to the Uttermost: Twenty Gospel Sermons by C. H. Spurgeon Selected from His hitherto Unpublished Manuscripts*. London and Edinburgh: Marshall Brothers, Limited, n.d. 240 pp.

_____. *According to Promise; or, The Lord's Method of Dealing with His Chosen People*. A Companion Volume to *All of Grace*. London: Passmore and Alabaster, 1887. 128 pp.

_____. *All of Grace: An Earnest Word with Those Who Are Seeking Salvation by the Lord Jesus Christ*. London: Passmore and Alabaster, 1892. 128 pp.

_____. *An All-Round Ministry: Addresses to Ministers and Students*. London: Passmore and Alabaster, 1900. 404 pp.

_____. *Around the Wicket Gate; or, A Friendly Talk with Seekers Concerning Faith in the Lord Jesus Christ*. London: Passmore and Alabaster, 1899. 104 pp.

_____. *Barbed Arrows from the Quiver of C. H. Spurgeon*. London: Passmore and Alabaster, 1896. 295 pp. [Companion volume to *Feathers for Arrows*; a collection of illustrations, anecdotes, similes, etc. by Charles Spurgeon from the sermons of CHS in the Met. Tab. Pulpit.]

_____. *"Behold The Throne of Grace:" C. H. Spurgeon's Prayers and Hymns*, selected and arranged by Chas. T. Cook. London and Edinburgh: Marshall, Morgan & Scott, n.d. 160 pp.

_____. *The Bible and The Newspaper*. London: Passmore and Alabaster, 1890. 224 pp. [One of *Spurgeon's Shilling Series*]. Samuel Manning and G. Holden Pike. *Booksellers and Bookbuyers in Byeways and Highways*. With a Preface by The Right Hon. the Earl of Shaftesbury. London: Passmore and Alabaster, 1882. 135 pp. *C. H. Spurgeon Anecdotes*. London: Passmore and Alabaster, 1900. 102 pp.

_____. *C. H. Spurgeon Autobiography: Volume 1, The Early Years, 1834-59*. Rev. ed. Edinburgh: Banner of Truth Trust, 1962.

_____. *C. H. Spurgeon Autobiography: Volume 2, The Full Harvest, 1860-1892*. Rev. ed. Edinburgh: Banner of Truth Trust, 1973.

_____. *C. H. Spurgeon's Autobiography: Compiled from His Diary, Letters, and Records, by His Wife and His Private Secretary*. 4 vols. London: Passmore and Alabaster, 1897-1900.

_____. *C. H. Spurgeon's Facsimile Pulpit Notes, with the Sermons Preached from them in the Metropolitan Tabernacle*. London: Passmore and Alabaster, 1894. 516 pp.

_____. *C. H. Spurgeon's Fifty Most Remarkable Sermons*. London: Passmore & Alabaster, 1908. [All are also found in the *Metropolitan Tabernacle Pulpit*].

_____. *The Rev. C. H. Spurgeon's Illustrated Almanack and Christian's Companion for 1864 [- 1898].* 2 vols. Vol. I, 1864-80; Vol. II, 1881-98. London: Passmore and Alabaster, n.d. [Titles vary with the year.]

_____. *C. H. Spurgeon's Prayers.* With an Introduction by Dinsdale T. Young. London: Passmore and Alabaster, 1905. 177 pp.

_____. *C. H. Spurgeon's Prayers: Prayers from Metropolitan Pulpit* 2nd ed. New York: Fleming H. Revell Co., 1906.

_____. *A Catechism with Proofs, compiled by the Rev. C. H. Spurgeon from the Assembly's Shorter Catechism, and the Baptist Catechism.* London & Edinburgh: Marshall Brothers, Ltd., n.d. 32 pp. [In pamphlet form.]

_____. *The Cheque Book of The Bank of Faith.* London: Passmore and Alabaster, 1888. 370 pp.

_____. *Christ in the Old Testament: Sermons on the Foreshadowings of our Lord in Old Testament History, Ceremony & Prophecy.* (A companion volume to "The Messiah: Sermons on Our Lord's Names, Titles and Attributes"; uniform with "Sermons on Our Lord's Parables," "Sermons on Our Lord's Miracles," and "The Most Holy Place.") London: Passmore and Alabaster, 1899. 714 pp.

_____. *Christ's Relation to His People: Sermons by C. H. Spurgeon.* With Preface by Andrew Murray. London: Passmore and Alabaster, n.d. 702 pp.

_____. *Christ's Glorious Achievements. Set Forth in Seven Sermons.* London: Passmore & Alabaster, n.d. 224 pp.

_____. "Closing Words to Lay Preachers," Chapter XXII in *The Lay Preacher's Guide.* London: Passmore and Alabaster, n.d. 239 pp. [Must date from sometime after death of CHS; the above chapter is contributed by the Publishers from various addresses of CHS to Lay Preaching Associations.]

_____. *The Clue of the Maze: A Voice Lifted Up on Behalf of Honest Faith.* London: Passmore & Alabaster, 1899. 92 pp.

_____. *Commenting and Commentaries: Two Lectures Addressed to the Students of The Pastors' College, Metropolitan Tabernacle, together with A Catalogue of Biblical Commentaries and Expositions.* London: Passmore and Alabaster, 1876. 200 pp.

_____. [No title page.] Probable title is *A Curiosity in Religious Literature.* On the front fly-leaf is written: "A Curiosity in Religious Literature. Specimen of a collection of sermons given to all the crowned heads of Europe, & the students of Oxford, Cambridge, Trin Coll, Dublin, &c. &c. Given by Mr. Noble, who kept himself out of sight, but at his own expense distributed a vast number of sermons."

_____. "De Propaganda Fide. A Lecture by the Rev. C. H. Spurgeon." Found on pages 151-88 of *Lectures Delivered Before The Young Men's Christian Association, in Exeter Hall, From November, 1858, to February, 1859.* London: James Nisbet and Co., 1859. 442 pp.

_____. *The Despised Friend.* Extracted from "The Saint and His Saviour." London: Hodder and Stoughton, 1883. 96 pp. [One of the *Ninepenny Pocket Series*].

_____. *Eccentric Preachers.* London: Passmore and Alabaster, 1888. 224 pp. [One of *Spurgeon's Shilling Series*].

_____. *Evening by Evening: or, Readings at Eventide for The Family or the Closet.* London: Passmore and Alabaster, n.d. 400 pp. [Preface dated May, 1868]

_____. *"The Everlasting Gospel" of the Old and New Testaments.* Sermons preached by C. H. Spurgeon. selected by General Sir Robert Phayre, K.C.B. London: Passmore & Alabaster, n.d. 424 pp.

_____. *Faith; What It Is, and What It Leads To.* London: Passmore and Alabaster, 1903. 77 pp.

_____. *Farm Sermons*. London: Passmore and Alabaster, 1882. 328 pp.

_____. *Feathers for Arrows; or, Illustrations for Preachers and Teachers. From My Note Book*. London: Passmore and Alabaster, 1884. 280 pp.

_____. *Flashes of Thought; Being One Thousand Choice Extracts from the Works of C. H. Spurgeon*. London: Passmore & Alabaster, 1875. 521 pp.

_____. *Gleanings Among the Sheaves*. London: Passmore and Alabaster, n.d. 188 pp.

_____. *Glorious Themes for Saints and Sinners*. London: Passmore and Alabaster, n.d. 310 pp.

_____. *The Golden Alphabet of the Praises of Holy Scripture, Setting Forth the Believer's Delight in the Word of the Lord: Being a Devotional Commentary Upon the One Hundred and Nineteenth Psalm*. Mainly excerpted from "The Treasury of David." London: Passmore and Alabaster, 1887. 301 pp.

_____. *A Good Start. A Book for Young Men and Women*. With a Prefatory Note by Sir George Williams. London: Passmore and Alabaster, 1898. 329 pp.

_____. *"Good Tidings of Great Joy." Christ's Incarnation the Foundation of Christianity*. Central Truths Series, Vol. I. London: Passmore and Alabaster, 1901. 152 pp.

_____. *The Gospel of the Kingdom: A Popular Exposition of the Gospel According to Matthew*. With Introductory Note by Mrs. C. H. Spurgeon. London: Passmore and Alabaster, 1893. 263 pp.

_____. *The Gospel for the People. Sixty Short Sermons by C. H. Spurgeon, with a Sketch of His Life and Fourteen Portraits and Engravings*. With a Preface by Pastor Thomas Spurgeon. London: Passmore and Alabaster, 1895.

_____. *Grace Triumphant: A Series of Sermons by Charles Haddon Spurgeon*. London: The Religious Tract Society, 1904. 320 pp.

_____. *The Greatest Fight in the World. Conference Address*. London: Passmore and Alabaster, 1891. 64 pp.

_____. *Illustrations and Meditations: or, Flowers from a Puritan Garden*. London: Passmore & Alabaster, 1883. 280 pp.

_____. *The Interpreter, or, Scriptures for Family Worship: Being Selected Passages of the Word of God for every Morning and Evening throughout the Year Accompanied by a Running Comment and Suitable Hymns*. London: Passmore and Alabaster, n.d. 784 pp.

_____. *John Ploughman's Pictures; or More of His Plain Talk for Plain People*. London: Passmore & Alabaster, 1880. 160 pp.

_____. *John Ploughman's Talk; or, Plain Advice for Plain People*. London: Passmore & Alabaster, n.d. 170 pp.

_____. *Lectures to my Students: A Selection from Addresses Delivered to the Students of the Pastors' College, Metropolitan Tabernacle*. London: Passmore and Alabaster, 1890. 200 pp.

_____. *The Letters of Charles Haddon Spurgeon*, comp. by Charles Spurgeon. London: Marshall Brothers, Limited, n.d. 224 pp. [Introduction dated 1923]

_____. [No Title Page.] Probable title is *Memorable Sermons, Etc*. A bound collection of sermons and addresses by CHS, all appearing to be from the Metropolitan Tabernacle Pulpit. No theme is discernible.

_____. *Memories of Stambourne*. Authored jointly with Benjamin Beddow. London: Passmore & Alabaster, 1891. 144 pp.

_____. *Messages to the Multitude: Being Ten Representative Sermons Selected at Mentone, and Two Unpublished Addresses Delivered on Memorable Occasions*. London: Sampson Low, Marston & Co., 1899. 125 pp.

_____. *Messages to the Multitude: Christ Put On, ... Let Us Pray, ... The Talking Book, ... And ... Other Remarkable Addresses*. London: Passmore & Alabaster, n.d. 125 pp.

_____. *The Messiah: Sermons on Our Lord's Names, Titles and Attributes.* (Uniform with "Sermons on Our Lord's Parables," "Sermons on Our Lord's Miracles," and "The Most Holy Place.") London: Passmore and Alabaster, 1898. 710 pp. [A collection of sermons form the Met. Tab. Pulpit].

_____. *The Metropolitan Tabernacle: Its History and Work.* London: Passmore & Alabaster, 1876. 119 pp. [RB]

_____. *The Metropolitan Tabernacle Pulpit.* 57 volumes. London: Passmore & Alabaster, 1861-1917.

_____. *"The Modern Whitefield." Sermons of the Rev. C. H. Spurgeon, of London; with an Introduction and Sketch of His Life, by E. L. Magoon.* New York: Sheldon, Blakeman and Co., 1857. 320 pp.

_____. *Morning by Morning: or, Daily Readings for the Family or the Closet.* London: Passmore and Alabaster, n.d. 408 pp. [Preface dated December, 1865]

_____. *Morning by Morning.* Reprint. Grand Rapids: Baker Book House, 1975. 368 pp. [TAM]

_____. *"The Most Holy Place." Sermons on The Song of Solomon.* (Uniform with "Sermons on Our Lord's Parables," and "Sermons on Our Lord's Miracles.") Delivered at the Metropolitan Tabernacle and New Park Street Chapel. London: Passmore and Alabaster, 1896. 570 pp.

_____. *The Mourner's Comforter: Being Seven Discourses Upon Isaiah 1-3.* London: Passmore and Alabaster, n.d. 224 pp. [One of *Spurgeon's Shilling Series*]

_____. *My Sermon-Notes: A Selection from Outlines of Discourses Delivered at The Metropolitan Tabernacle by C. H. Spurgeon.* From Genesis to Proverbs. I. to LXIV. London: Passmore and Alabaster, 1887. 200 pp.

_____. *My Sermon-Notes: A Selection from Outlines of Discourses Delivered at The Metropolitan Tabernacle by C. H. Spurgeon.* From Ecclesiastes to Malachi. LXV. to CXXIX. London: Passmore and Alabaster, 1885. Paginated 201-392.

_____. *My Sermon-Notes: A Selection from Outlines of Discourses Delivered at The Metropolitan Tabernacle by C. H. Spurgeon.* From Matthew to Acts. CXXX. to CXCV. London: Passmore and Alabaster, 1886. 200 pp.

_____. *My Sermon-Notes: A Selection from Outlines of Discourses Delivered at The Metropolitan Tabernacle by C. H. Spurgeon.* From Romans to Revelation. CXCVI. to CCLXIV. London: Passmore and Alabaster, 1895. Paginated 201 to 400.

_____. *My Sermon-Notes: A Selection from Outlines of Discourses Delivered at the Metropolitan Tabernacle by C. H. Spurgeon.* Old Testament Series, I. to CXXIX. London: Passmore and Alabaster, 1885. 392 pp.

_____. *My Sermon-Notes: A Selection from Outlines of Discourses Delivered at the Metropolitan Tabernacle by C. H. Spurgeon.* New Testament Series, CXXX. to CCLXIV. London: Passmore and Alabaster, 1887. 408 pp.

_____. ed. *The New Park Street Almanack for 1857; etc.* London: Passmore and Alabaster, n.d. 2 vols.: Vol. I, 1857-80; Vol. II, 1881-98. [Titles vary with the year; see also entry under "The Rev. C. H. Spurgeon's Illustrated Almanack."]

_____. *The New Park Street Pulpit.* 6 volumes. London: Passmore and Alabaster, 1855-60.

_____. *"Only a Prayer-Meeting!" Forty Addresses at Metropolitan Tabernacle and Other Prayer-Meetings.* London: Passmore and Alabaster, 1901. 366 pp.

_____. *Our Own Hymn-Book: A Collection of Psalms and Hymns for Public, Social, and Private Worship.* London: Passmore and Alabaster, 1866.

_____. *The Pastor in Prayer: Being a Choice Selection of C. H. Spurgeon's Sunday Morning Prayers.* London: Elliot Stock, 1893. 164 pp.

_____. *The People's Christ and Other Sermons*. The Crown Imperial Series. London: Hodder and Stoughton, 1903. 416 pp.

_____. *Poland: A Lecture by the Rev. C. H. Spurgeon in Aid of the Funds of the "Band of Hope Union," delivered at the Metropolitan Tabernacle, Newington, on Tuesday Evening, February 16th, 1864*. London: Passmore and Alabaster, 1864. 23 pp.

_____. *The Present Truth: A Collection of Sermons Preached at the Metropolitan Tabernacle, by C. H. Spurgeon*. London: Passmore and Alabaster, 1883. 376 pp.

_____. "Proving God." The Spurgeon Centenary Booklets, No. 5. London: Marshall, Morgan & Scott, Ltd., n.d. 32 pp.

_____. *The Pulpit Library. Sermons, etc., by The Rev. C. H. Spurgeon, Minister of the Metropolitan Tabernacle, Newington*. London: James Paul, 1856. 184 pp.

_____. *The Pulpit Library, Vol. II. Sermons by the Rev. C. H. Spurgeon, Minister of New Park Street Chapel Southwark*. London: Alabaster & Passmore, 1858. 235 pp.

_____. *The Report of the Spies*. n.p., n.d. 16 pp. [In booklet form. Back cover says: "To commemorate the Centenary of C. H. Spurgeon's Conversion, six of the great Preacher's Sermons have been produced in this series, representing The Best of Spurgeon." The six sermons listed include: Supposing Him to Be the Gardener; There Go the Ships; Robinson Crusoe's Text; The Lord Is My Shepherd; The Report of the Spies; Life for a Look. The series title is *The C. H. Spurgeon Booklets*.]

_____. *The Royal Wedding, The Banquet and the Guests*. London: Passmore and Alabaster, 1887. 80 pp.

_____. *The Saint and His Saviour: The Progress of the Soul in the Knowledge of Jesus*. London: Hodder and Stoughton, 1881. 471 pp.

_____. *The Salt-Cellars: Being a Collection of Proverbs, together with Homely Notes Thereon*. Vol. I, A to L; Vol. II, M to Z. London: Passmore and Alabaster, 1889. Vol. I, 334 pp.; Vol. II, 367 pp.

_____. *The Second Coming of Christ. Twelve Sermons by C. H. Spurgeon*. London: Passmore and Alabaster, n.d.

_____. [No title page.] *Selected Sermons on Election*. Sixteen sermons preached by C. H. Spurgeon on the themes of election. All are found in the NPSP or the MTP.

_____. *Second Series of Lectures to My Students: Being Addresses Delivered to the Students of The Pastors' College, Metropolitan Tabernacle*. London: Passmore and Alabaster, 1890. 192 pp.

_____. *Sermons Delivered in Exeter Hall, Strand; by the Rev. C. H. Spurgeon during the Enlargement of New Park Street Chapel, Southwark*. London: Alabaster & Passmore, 1855.

_____. *Sermons in Candles: Being Two Lectures upon the Illustrations Which May Be Found in Common Candles*. London: Passmore and Alabaster, 1890. 170 pp.

_____. *Sermons by the Rev. C. H. Spurgeon. One of The Contemporary Pulpit Library series*. London: Swan Sonnenschein & Co., 1892. 184 pp.

_____. *Sermons of the Rev. C. H. Spurgeon, of London*. First Series, Fiftieth Edition. With Additional Discourses: and an Introduction and Biographical Sketch by E. L. Magoon. New York: Sheldon & Company, 1866. 383 pp.

_____. *Sermons of the Rev. C. H. Spurgeon, of London*. Second Series. New York: Sheldon & Company, 1865. 441 pp.

_____. *Sermons of the Rev. C. H. Spurgeon, of London*. Third Series. New York: Sheldon & Company, 1867. 448 pp.

_____. *Sermons of the Rev. C. H. Spurgeon, of London*. Fourth Series. New York: Sheldon and Company, 1867. 445 pp..

_____. *Sermons of the Rev. C. H. Spurgeon. Preached at the Metropolitan Tabernacle, London.* Eighth Series. New York: Sheldon and Company, 1865. 372 pp.

_____. *Sermons on Our Lord's Miracles. (Uniform with "Sermons on Our Lord's Parables." Delivered at the Metropolitan Tabernacle and New Park Street Chapel.* Vol. I. London: Passmore and Alabaster, 1895.)

_____. *Sermons on Our Lord's Miracles. (Uniform with "Sermons on Our Lord's Parables.") Delivered at the Metropolitan Tabernacle and New Park Street Chapel.* Vol. II. London: Passmore and Alabaster, 1895.

_____. *Sermons on Our Lord's Parables. Delivered at the Metropolitan Tabernacle and New Park Street Chapel.* London: Passmore and Alabaster, 1894.

_____. *Sermons Preached and Revised by the Rev. C. H. Spurgeon.* Fifth Series. New York: Sheldon and Company, 1859. 454 pp.

_____. *Sermons Preached and Revised by the Rev. C. H. Spurgeon.* Sixth Series. New York: Sheldon and Company, 1864. 450 pp.

_____. *Sermons Preached and Revised by the Rev. C. H. Spurgeon.* Seventh Series. New York: Sheldon & Company, 1866. 378 pp.

_____. *Seven Wonders of Grace.* London: Passmore and Alabaster, n.d. 224 pp. [One of *Spurgeon's Shilling Series*]

_____. *Smooth Stones Taken from Ancient Brooks.* London: Passmore and Alabaster, 1903. 189 pp.

_____. *The Soul-Winner; or, How To Lead Sinners to the Saviour.* London: Passmore & Alabaster, 1895. 343 pp.

_____. *Southwark. A Lecture Delivered in the Metropolitan Tabernacle Lecture Hall, on December 26th, 1860.* London: Passmore & Alabaster, 1894. 55 pp.

_____. *The Space Half Hour.* London: Passmore and Alabaster, n.d. 224 pp. One of *Spurgeon's Shilling Series.* [The Preface indicates that the contents of this work are "occasional papers" which first appeared in the *Sword and Trowel.*]

_____. *Speeches by C. H. Spurgeon at Home and Abroad.* London: Passmore & Alabaster, 1878. 190 pp.

_____. *The Spurgeon Birthday Book and Autographic Register, Containing a Metaphor, Simile, Allegory, or Illustration for Every Day in the Year.* London: Passmore and Alabaster, 1879.

_____. [Title page missing.] Probable title is *Spurgeon's Gems.* 352 pp.

_____. [No title page.] Probable title is *Spurgeon's Sermons.* Consists of five sermons, all also in the Met. Tab. Pulpit, preached in the Agricultural Hall, Islington Sunday mornings March 24 and 31, 1867 and Sunday mornings April 7, 14, and 21, 1867. Each sermon is preceded by a printed sheet entitled "Hymns to be Sung."

_____. *Storm Signals: Being a Collection of Sermons Preached on Sunday and Thursday Evenings, at the Metropolitan Tabernacle, by C. H. Spurgeon.* London: Passmore and Alabaster, 1885. 368 pp.

_____. *"Supposing Him to be the Gardener."* London, Edinburgh & New York: Marshall Brothers, Ltd., n.d. 16 pp. [Sermon in pamphlet form.]

_____. *There Go the Ships.* London and Edinburgh: Marshall Brothers, Ltd., n.d. 32 pp. [Sermon in booklet form.]

_____. *Third Series of Lectures to My Students. The Art of Illustration: Being Addresses Delivered to the Students of the Pastors' College, Metropolitan Tabernacle.* London: Passmore & Alabaster, 1894. 200 pp.

_____. *"Till He Come." Communion Meditations and Addresses by C. H. Spurgeon.* (Not published in *The Metropolitan Tabernacle Pulpit*) London: Passmore & Alabaster, 1896. 358 pp.

_____. *The Treasury of David: Containing An Original Exposition of the Book of Psalms; A Collection of Illustrative Extracts from the Whole Range of Literature; A Series of Homiletical Hints Upon Almost Every Verse; and Lists of Writers upon Each Psalm.* 7 volumes. London: Passmore and Alabaster, n.d.

_____. *The Treasury of the New Testament.* 4 Volumes. London and Edinburgh: Marshall, Morgan & Scott, n.d.

_____. *The Treasury of the Old Testament.* 4 Volumes. London and Edinburgh: Marshall, Morgan & Scott, n.d.

_____. *The True Gospel and Other Sermons.* London and Edinburgh: Marshall Brothers, Ltd., n.d.

_____. *Trumpet Calls to Christian Energy: Being a Collection of Sermons preached on Sunday and Thursday Evenings at the Metropolitan Tabernacle, by C. H. Spurgeon.* London: Passmore and Alabaster, 1875. 348 pp.

_____. *Twelve Christmas Sermons.* n.p., n.d.

_____. *Twelve Missionary Sermons.* London: Passmore & Alabaster, n.d.

_____. *Twelve New Year's Sermons.* London: Passmore & Alabaster, n.d.

_____. *Twelve Selected Sermons, by C. H. Spurgeon, with Portrait.* London: Passmore & Alabaster, nd.

_____. *Twelve Selected Soul-Winning Sermons.* London: Passmore& Alabaster, n.d.

_____. *Twelve Sermons on Death.* n.p., n.d.

_____. *Twelve Sermons on Faith.* London: Passmore & Alabaster, n.d.

_____. *Twelve Sermons on Forgiveness.* n.p., n.d.

_____. *Twelve Sermons on the Gospel for Sinners.* n.p., n.d.

_____. *Twelve Sermons on Grace Abounding.* London: Passmore & Alabaster, n.d.

_____. *Twelve Sermons on Holiness.* London: Passmore & Alabaster, n.d.

_____. *Twelve Sermons on Humility.* London: Passmore & Alabaster, n.d.

_____. *Twelve Sermons on Joy.* London: Passmore & Alabaster, n.d.

_____. *Twelve Sermons on Obedience.* London: Passmore & Alabaster, n.d.

_____. *Twelve Sermons on the Plan of Salvation.* n.p., n.d.

_____. *Twelve Sermons on Prayer, Etc.* n.p., n.d.

_____. *Twelve Sermons on Repentance.* n.p., n.d.

_____. *Twelve Sermons on the Resurrection.* 1937 edition. London: Marshall, Morgan & Scott, 1937. 152 pp.

_____. *Twelve Sermons on Sanctification.* London: Passmore & Alabaster, n.d.

_____. *Twelve Sermons for Seekers.* London: Passmore & Alabaster, n.d.

_____. *Twelve Sermons on Temptation.* n.p., n.d.

_____. *Twelve Sermons on Unbelief.* n.p., n.d.

_____. *Twelve Sermons to Young Men.* London: Passmore and Alabaster, n.d.

_____. *Twelve Striking Sermons.* n.p., n.d.

_____. *Types and Emblems: Being a Collection of Sermons Preached on Sunday and Thursday Evenings at the Metropolitan Tabernacle.* London: Passmore and Alabaster. 1888. 280 pp.

_____. *"We Endeavor." Helpful Words for Members of the Young People's Society of Christian Endeavour.* London: Passmore and Alabaster, 1897. 160 pp.

_____. *What the Stones Say: or, Sermons in Stone.* With notes by J. L. Keys and Introduction by Thomas Spurgeon. London: Christian Herald Publishing Co., n.d. 126 pp.

_____. *Words of Advice for Seekers.* London: Passmore and Alabaster, 1896. 159 pp.

_____. *Words of Cheer for Daily Life.* London: Passmore and Alabaster, 1895. 155 pp.

_____. *Word of Counsel for Christian Workers.* London: Passmore and Alabaster, 1896. 156 pp.

_____. *Words of Warning for Daily Life.* London: Passmore and Alabaster, 1895. 153 pp.

_____. *Words of Wisdom for Daily Life*. London: Passmore and Alabaster, 1893. 156 pp.

B. BIOGRAPHIES OF C. H. SPURGEON

Adcock, E. F. *Charles H. Spurgeon: Prince of Preachers*. Christian Hero Series. Anderson, Indiana: Warner Press, 1925.

Allen, James T. *Charles H. Spurgeon*. London: Pickering and Inglis, 1931.

Anonymous. *Charles Haddon Spurgeon: A Biographical Sketch and an Appreciation*. London: Andrew Melrose, 1903. 208 pp. [Authorship of this volume is ascribed to "One who knew him well".]

Bacon, Ernest W. *Spurgeon: Heir of the Puritans*. London: George Allen & Unwin Ltd., 1967. 184 pp.

Barnes, R. H. and C. E. Brown. *Spurgeon, the People's Preacher*. London: Epworth Press, 1933.

Burley, A. Cunningham. *Spurgeon and His Friendships*. London: Epworth Press, 1933.

Carlile, John Charles. *C. H. Spurgeon: An Interpretive Biography*. London: The Religious Tract Society, 1933. 312 pp.

Conwell, Russell. *Life of Charles Haddon Spurgeon, the World's Greatest Preacher*. New York: Edgewood Publ. Co., 1892.

Dallimore, Arnold. *Spurgeon*. Chicago: Moody Press, 1984.

Day, Richard Ellsworth. *The Shadow of the Broad Brim: The Life Story of Charles Haddon Spurgeon, Heir of the Puritans*. Philadelphia: The Judson Press, 1934. 236 pp.

Douglas, James. *The Prince of Preachers: A Sketch; A Portraiture; and a Tribute*. London: Morgan and Scott, n.d. 189 pp.

Ellis, James J. *Charles Haddon Spurgeon*. One of the *Lives That Speak* series. London: James Nisbet & Co., n.d. 240 pp. [Appendix records that bulk of the work was prepared in spring, 1891; Appendix was written after Spurgeon's death.]

Fullerton, William Young. *C. H. Spurgeon: A Biography*. London: Williams and Norgate, 1920. 358 pp.

Hope, Eva. *Spurgeon: The People's Preacher*. London and Felling-on-Tyne: The Walter Scott Publishing Co., Ld., n.d. 330 pp.

Lorimer, George Claude. *Charles Haddon Spurgeon: The Puritan Preacher in the Nineteenth Century*. Boston: James H. Earle, 1892. 230 pp.

Needham, George Carter, compiler and editor. *The Life and Labors of Charles H. Spurgeon, The Faithful Preacher, The Devoted Pastor, The Noble Philanthropist, The Beloved College President, and The Voluminous Writer, Author, etc., etc.* Boston: D. L. Guernsey, 1883. 603 pp.

Page, Jesse. *C. H. Spurgeon: His Life and Ministry*, 2nd ed. London: S. W. Partridge & Co., n.d. 160 pp.

Perry, Charles F. *Spurgeon's Boyhood and Wonderful Life; For Young People*. London: Arthur H. Stockwell, Ltd., n.d. 48 pp.

Pike, Godfrey Holden. *Charles Haddon Spurgeon: Preacher, Author, and Philanthropist*. London: Hodder and Stoughton, 1887. 312 pp.

_____. *Charles Haddon Spurgeon*. London, Paris, & Melbourne: Cassell and Company Limited, 1893. 128 pp. [One of *The World's Workers* series.]

_____. *The Life and Work of Charles Haddon Spurgeon*. London, Paris & Melbourne: Cassell & Company, Limited, n.d. 6 vols.

_____. *The Life and Work of Charles Haddon Spurgeon*. London, Paris, & Melbourne: Cassell & Co., Limited, n.d. 3 vols.

Ray, Charles. *The Life of Charles Haddon Spurgeon*. London: Passmore and Alabaster, 1903. 506 pp.

Reeve, B. *The Prince of Preachers: C. H. Spurgeon.* London: The Protestant Truth Society, 1934. 64 pp.

Sheen, Danzy. *Pastor C. H. Spurgeon: His Conversion, Career, and Coronation.* London: J. B. Knapp, n.d. (Preface, 1892).

Shindler, Robert. *From the Usher's Desk to the Tabernacle Pulpit: The Life and Labours of Pastor C. H. Spurgeon.* Authorized edition. London: Passmore and Alabaster, 1892. 316 pp.

Smith, J. Manton. *The Essex Lad Who Became England's Greatest Preacher. The Life Story of Charles Haddon Spurgeon for Young People.* London: Passmore and Alabaster, n.d. 169 pp. [The preface written by CHS' father is dated May 9, 1892.]

Stevenson, George John. *Pastor C. H. Spurgeon: His Life and Work to His Forty-Third Birthday.* London: Passmore and Alabaster, 1877. 112 pp. [Copy in Spurpamp.7]

_____. *Pastor C. H. Spurgeon: His Life and Work to His Fiftieth Birthday.* London: Passmore and Alabaster, 1885. 136 pp.

_____. *The Prince of Preachers, Charles H. Spurgeon.* Second edition. London: George John Stevenson, 1867. 24 pp. [Copy in Spurpamp.5]

_____. *Sketch of the Life and Ministry of the Rev. C. H. Spurgeon.* Second edition. London: George John Stevenson, n.d. 56 pp. [Copy in Spurpamp.5]

Triggs, Kathy. *Charles H. Spurgeon: The Boy Preacher of the Fens.* Basingstoke, England: Pickering & Inglis, 1984; Pickering Paperbacks, 1984.

Wayland, H. L. *Charles H. Spurgeon: His Faith and Works.* Philadelphia: American Baptist Publication Society, 1892.

Williams, William. *Charles Haddon Spurgeon: Personal Reminiscences.* Rev. and ed. Marguerite Williams. London: Religious Tract Society, n.d.

Yarrow, William H. *The Life and Work of Charles H. Spurgeon.* New York: I. K. Funk & Co., 1880. 100 pp.

C. NEWSPAPERS AND PERIODICALS

The Baptist.
The Baptist Magazine.
The Baptist Quarterly.
The British Weekly.
The Christian.
The Christian Age.
The Christian Commonwealth.
The Christian World.
The Daily News.
The Daily Telegraph.
The Evening News.
The Freeman.
The Hornet.
The Pall Mall Gazette.
The Postman.
The Referee.
The Saturday Review.
South London Press.
Sunday School Chronicle.
The Sword and the Trowel.
Westminster Review.

D. DISSERTATIONS AND THESES

Adams, Jay Edward. "Sense Appeal in the sermons of Charles Haddon Spurgeon." S.T.M. thesis, Temple University, 1958.

Baggett, Hudson. "A Study of Spurgeon's Preaching Method." Th.M. thesis, The Southern Baptist Theological Seminary, 1951.

Colquitt, Henry Franklin. "The Soteriology of Charles Haddon Spurgeon Revealed in His Sermons and Controversial Writings." Ph.D. dissertation, University of Edinburgh, 1951.

Crook, William Herbert. "The Contributive Factors in the Life and Preaching of Charles Haddon Spurgeon." Th.D. dissertation, Southwestern Baptist Theological Seminary, 1956.

Duncan, Robert L. "An Investigation of the Preaching of Charles Haddon Spurgeon and Its Relevance to Contemporary Preaching." Th.D. dissertation, Southwestern Baptist Theological Seminary, 1979.

Kruppa, Patricia Stallings. "Charles Haddon Spurgeon, A Preacher's Progress." Ph.D. dissertation, Columbia University, 1968.

Mason Jr., Melton. "The Theology of Charles Haddon Spurgeon." Ph.D. dissertation, Luther Rice Seminary, 1963.

Meredith, Albert R. "The Social and Political Views of Charles Haddon Spurgeon, 1834-1892." Ph.D. dissertation, Michigan State University, 1973.

Michael, Larry J. "The Effects of Controversy on the Evangelistic Ministry of C. H. Spurgeon." Ph.D. dissertation, The Southern Baptist Theological Seminary, 1989.

Strong, Robert. "A Study of the Factors of Persuasion in the Sermons of Charles Haddon Spurgeon." M.A. thesis, University of Southern California, 1933.

Sutton, Thomas Jerell. "A Comparison Between the Down Grade Controversy and Tensions Over Biblical Inerrancy in the Southern Baptist Convention." Ph.D. dissertation, Southwestern Baptist Theological Seminary, 1982.

Talpos, Vasile F. "The Importance of Evangelism in Ministerial Training: A Critical Analysis of the Contribution of Selected Nineteenth Century Christian Educators." Ph.D. dissertation, The Southern Baptist Theological Seminary, 1983.

Thornton, Jeremy F. "The Soteriology of C. H. Spurgeon: Its Biblical and Historical Roots and Its Place in His Preaching." Ph.D. dissertation, University of Cambridge, 1974.

Zeluff, Daniel. "A Critique of English Speaking Preaching 1864-1964, (As demonstrated by the theory and practice of C. H. Spurgeon, H. E. Fosdick, and J. E. Stewart)." Ph.D. dissertation, University of Aberdeen, 1964.

E. JOURNAL AND PERIODICAL ARTICLES

"Annual Paper Descriptive of the Lord's Work connected with the Pastors' College." *The Sword and the Trowel*, (1878, 1881-1885, 1887-1892, 1902).

"Annual Reports of the Metropolitan Tabernacle Colportage Association." *The Sword and the Trowel*, (1869, 1875, 1880, 1888, 1890, 1892).

"The Awakening in the North." *The Sword and the Trowel*, 10 (1874): 153-160.

Ashmall, Donald H. "Spiritual Development and the Free Church Tradition: The Inner Pilgrimage." *Andover Newton Quarterly*. 20 (1980), 141-152.

Bailey, Ivor. "The Challenge of Change: A Study of Relevance versus Authority in the Victorian Pulpit." *Expository Times*, 86 (1974), 18-22.

Brown, Donald C. "Spurgeon's Hymnals." Hymn, 30 (1979), 39-48.

"Colportage." *The Sword and the Trowel*, 2 (1866): 463.

"Colportage." *The Sword and the Trowel*, 2 (1866): 559-561.

"Colportage." *The Sword and the Trowel*, 3 (1867): 321.

"The Colportage Association." *The Sword and the Trowel*, 4 (1868): 465-468.

Cox, James W. "'Eloquent . . . , Mighty in the Scriptures': Biblical Preachers from Chryston to Thielicke." *Review and Expositor*, 72 (1975), 189-201.
Curr, H. S. "Spurgeon and Gladstone." Baptist Quarterly, 11 (1942-45), 46-54.
"Daily Prayer Meetings." *The Sword and the Trowel*, 3 (1867): 321.
Davies, Horton. "Expository Preaching: Charles Haddon Spurgeon." *Foundations*, 6 (1963), 14-25.
"A Day's Entries in a Colporteur's Diary." *The Sword and the Trowel*, 12 (1876): 373-374.
Estep, William R. "The Making of a Prophet: An Introduction to Charles Haddon Spurgeon." *Baptist History and Heritage*, 19 (1984), 3-15.
Ferguson, Duncan S. "The Bible and Protestant Orthodoxy: The Hermeneutics of Charles Spurgeon." *Journal of the Evangelical Theological Society*, 25 (1982), 455-466.
Glasson, T. Francis. "Spurgeon's Conversion." *Expository Times*, 79 (1968), 342.
Glover, Willis B. "English Baptists at the Time of the Down Grade Controversy." *Foundations*, 1 (1958), 41-51.
Hughes, Graham W. "Spurgeon's Homes." *Baptist Quarterly*, 15 (1954), 297-310.
James, C. D. T. "Spurgeon and Simpson." *Baptist Quarterly*, 20 (1964), 365-368.
Kingdon, D. P. "Spurgeon and Gladstone." *Baptist Quarterly*, 20 (1963)m 62-64.
Lamkin, Adrian. "The Spurgeon Library of William Jewell College: A Hidden Treasure Among Baptists in America." *Baptist History and Heritage*, 19 (1984), 39-44.
Manley, K. R. "Ordination Among Australian Baptists." *Baptist Quarterly*, 28 (1979), 159-183.
May, Lynn E., Jr. "The Impact of One Life: Charles Haddon Spurgeon." *Baptist History and Heritage*, 19 (1984), 2.
"Meetings at the Metropolitan Tabernacle." *The Sword and the Trowel*, 2 (1866): 184-186.
Music, David. "C. H. Spurgeon and Hymnody." *Foundations*, 22 (1979), 174-181.
Paul, Philip. "Spurgeon and Social Reform." *Expository Times*, 86 (1975), 246-247.
Payne, Ernest A. "The Down Grade Controversy: A Postscript." *Baptist Quarterly*, 28 (1979), 146-158.
Pitts, John. "The Genius of Charles Haddon Spurgeon." *Christianity Today*, 14 (1970), 608.
_____. "The Genius of Charles Haddon Spurgeon." *Theology Today*, 6 (1950), 524-530.
Rushbrooke, J. H. "John Clifford." *Baptist Quarterly*, 11 (1942-45), 288-294.
Skinner, Craig. "The Preaching of Charles Haddon Spurgeon." *Baptist History and Heritage*, 19 (1984), 16-26.
Stanley, Brian. "C. H. Spurgeon and the Baptist Missionary Society: 1863-1866." *Baptist Quarterly*, 29 (1982), 319-328.
Weatherspoon, J. B. "Charles Haddon Spurgeon." *Review and Expositor*, 31 (1934), 411-420.

F. OTHER WORKS

Byrt, G. W. John Clifford: *A Fighting Free Churchman*. London: Kingsgate Press, 1947.

Cater, Philip. *Punch in the Pulpit*. Second edition. London: William Freeman, 1862. 240 pp.
Chadwick, Owen. *The Victorian Church, Part I*. Part of An Ecclesiastical History of England series, gen. ed. J. C. Dickinson. London: Adam & Charles Black, 1966. 606 pp.
Channon, W. G. *C. H. Spurgeon's Conversion and Its Message for Today*. London: Spurgeon's Colportage Association Ltd., 1949. 45 pp.
Chapple, Stewart. *The Story of Our Church: The Origin of Nonconformity in Streatham*. Streatham Baptist Church. No publication data. 68 pp.
Evans, David V. *More Light, More Power*. Unpublished history of Shoreditch Tabernacle Baptist Church, London, England. October, 1985.

Hayden, Eric W. *Searchlight on Spurgeon:* "Spurgeon Speaks for Himself." Pasadena, Texas: Pilgrim Publications, 1973. 250 pp. [RB]

———. *Spurgeon on Revival:* A Biblical and Theological Approach. Grand Rapids: Zondervan, 1962. 144 pp.

Hemmens, H. L. and Albert E. Oakeley. C. H. Spurgeon: A Cantata with illustrative Recitals and appropriate Music. London: The Carey Press, n.d.

Henn, Silas. *Spurgeon's Calvinism Examined and Refuted.* London: J. B. Cooke, 1858. 81 pp.

Higgs, W. Miller. *The Spurgeon Family.* London: Elliot Stock, 1906. 54 pp.

Marchant, James. Dr. John Clifford, C.H.: *Life, Letters, and Reminiscences.* London: Cassell and Co., 1924.

Murray, Iain H. *The Forgotten Spurgeon.* 2nd ed. Edinburgh: Banner of Truth Trust, 1973.

Nicoll, W. Robertson. *Princies of the Church.* Second edition. London: Hodder and Stoughton, n.d. [Preface is dated September 1921]

No author. [Title page missing.] Probable title is *Bigotry and Sectarianism.* A collection of various sermons by CHS and his contemporaries primarily concerning the Baptismal Regeneration controversy. Note on front fly-leaf indicates that the volume comes from CHS's personal library and that the annotations are his.

No author. *From the Pulpit to the Palm-Branch: A Memorial of C. H. Spurgeon.* London: Passmore and Alabaster, 1892. 281 pp.

No author. *Fundamental Truths Re-Affirmed. Being Addresses Delivered at the Conference Held in the Jubilee Year of the Pastors' College, April 15th - 19th, 1907, And Published by Request of the Pastors' College Evangelical Association.* London: Passmore and Alabaster, n.d. 84 pp. [Preface dated May 1907]

No author. *Memorial Volume. Mr. Spurgeon's Jubilee. Report of the Proceedings at the Metropolitan Tabernacle, on Wednesday and Thursday Evenings, June 18th and 19th, 1884.* London: Passmore and Alabaster, 1884. 51 pp.

No author. *Memorial Volume. Sermons and Addresses delivered in the Metropolitan Tabernacle, Newington, in connection with the Presentation of a Testimonial to Pastor C. H. Spurgeon, to commemorate the completion of The Twenty-Fifth Year of His Pastorate, with Selection of Music Sung on the Occasion.* London: Passmore & Alabaster, 1879. 88 pp.

No author. *Missionary Sermons: A Selection from the Discourses delivered on behalf of The Baptist Missionary Society on various occasions.* London: The Carey Press, n.d. 326 pp. [Preface dated October, 1924]

No author. [Title page missing.] Probable title is *Reminiscences of Spurgeon: Memorial Sermons, Articles, Etc.* A bound collection of sermons, articles, newspaper clippings, pamphlets, etc. Most have to do with the life of CHS or his death and funeral.

No author. [Title page missing.] Probable title is *Spurgeon's Baptismal Controversy.* A bound collection of 29 articles, sermons, pamphlets, etc. primarily concerning the Baptismal Regeneration controversy. Index provided at the end of the volume.

No author. [Title page missing.] Probable title is *Spurgeon's Sermons, Etc.: 1864, Baptismal Controversy.* A bound collection of sermons and pamphlets all related to the Baptismal Regeneration controversy.

No author. *Thirty-Two Articles of Christian Faith and Practice; Baptist Confession of Faith, with Scripture Proofs, adopted by The Ministers and Messengers of the General Assembly, which met in London, in 1689. With a Preface by The Rev. C. H. Spurgeon.* London: Passmore and Alabaster, 1855. 35 pp. [Preface dated October, 1855].

Norcott, John. *Baptism Discovered Plainly & Faithfully, According to the Word of God, etc.* A New Edition Corrected and Somewhat Altered by Charles Haddon Spurgeon. London: Passmore & Alabaster, 1878. 79 pp.

Nuttall, Geoffrey F. and Owen Chadwick. *From Uniformity to Unity: 1662-1962*. London: S.P.C.K., 1962.

Olney, William. *Public Prayer*. Dublin: Alex. Thom & Co., n.d. 14 pp. [Reprinted from the *Baptist Quarterly*]

Orr, J. Edwin. *The Second Evangelical Awakening in Britain*. London: Marshall, Morgan & Scott, 1949.

Payne, Ernest A. *The Free Church Tradition in the Life of England*. 3rd ed. London: SCM Press, 1951.

Pickering, Ernest D. *The Theology of Evangelism*. Clarks Summit, Pennsylvania: Baptist Bible College Press, 1974.

Pike, G. Holden. *James Archer Spurgeon, D.D., LL.D., Preacher, Philanthropist, and Co-Pastor with C. H. Spurgeon at the Metropolitan Tabernacle*. London: Alexander & Shepheard, 1894. 216 pp.

_____. *The Metropolitan Tabernacle; or An Historical Account of the Society, From Its First Planting in the Puritan Era to the Present Time, with Other Sketches Relating to the Rise, Growth, and Customs of Nonconformity in Southwark, The Stockwell Orphanage, and The Pastors' College*. London: Passmore & Alabaster, 1870. 179 pp.

_____. *Seven Portraits of the Rev. C. H. Spurgeon, with Reminiscences of His Life at Waterbeach and London*. London: Passmore and Alabaster, 1879. 48 pp.

Ray, Charles. *A Marvellous Ministry: The Story of C. H. Spurgeon's Sermons 1855 to 1905*. London: Passmore and Alabaster, 1905. 100 pp.

Ritchie, J. Ewing. *The London Pulpit*. Second edition. London: William Tweedie, 1863. 236 pp.

Rushbrooke, J. H., General Editor. *Baptist World Alliance. First European Baptist Congress, Held in Berlin, 1908 (Agust29th to September 3). Authorised Record of Proceedings*. London: Baptist Union Publication Department, 1908. 261 pp.

Sheehan, R. J. *C. H. Spurgeon and the Modern Church: Lessons for Today from the 'Downgrade' Controversy*. London: Grace Publications Trust, 1985.

Skinner, Craig. "The Preaching of Charles Haddon Spurgeon." *Baptist History and Heritage*, October (1984), pp. 16-26.

_____. *Lamplighter and Son*. Nashville: Broadman Press, 1984. 269 pp. Spurgeon, Susannah. A Carillon of Bells, To Ring Out the Old Truths of "Free Grace and Dying Love." London: Passmore and Alabaster, n.d. 132 pp.

_____. *Ten Years of My Life in the Service of the Book Fund: Being A Grateful Record of My Experience of the Lord's Ways, and Work, and Wages*. Second edition. London: Passmore & Alabaster, 1886. 432 pp.

Thielicke, Helmut. *Encounter with Spurgeon*. Trans. by John W. Doberstein. London: James Clarke & Co., Ltd., 1964. 283 pp.

Williams, William. *Personal Reminiscences of Charles Haddon Spurgeon*. Second edition. London: The Religious Tract Society, 1895. 288 pp.

_____. *Charles Haddon Spurgeon: Personal Reminiscences*. Rev. and ed. by Marguerite Williams. London: The Religious Tract Society, n.d. 128 pp.

INDEX

Quotes

26, 27, 29, 30
221,

668

(765)

22 his conversion 74, 124
26 Revival
his character
132 his depression

212, 213
244 health & depression
258 Def of humility
(298)
310
313 his social ministry
(414) His faith faced trials
(449) CHS sent petitions to Parliament
484 Baptismal Regeneration
497 original Bad text
511 politics 514 > 518-519 (5-6)
523 > 540 (547)

573
575
his depression
dangers of the middle years
God's attributes

629 Covenants of works & grace
636 > T.U.L.I.P.
(659)
663 As today
665

Coruscations
extant
costermongers
colporteur

CHS' creedal statement after
"Down-Grade"

Alexander MacLaren, Joseph Parker